Game Theory

Second Edition

Covering both noncooperative and cooperative games, this comprehensive introduction to game theory also includes some advanced chapters on auctions, games with incomplete information, games with vector payoffs, stable matchings, and the bargaining set. Mathematically oriented, the book presents every theorem alongside a proof. The material is presented clearly and every concept is illustrated with concrete examples from a broad range of disciplines. With numerous exercises the book is a thorough and extensive guide to game theory from undergraduate through graduate courses in economics, mathematics, computer science, engineering, and life sciences to being an authoritative reference for researchers.

MICHAEL MASCHLER was a professor in the Einstein Institute of Mathematics and the Center for the Study of Rationality at the Hebrew University of Jerusalem in Israel. He greatly contributed to cooperative game theory and to repeated games with incomplete information.

EILON SOLAN is a professor in the School of Mathematical Sciences at Tel Aviv University in Israel. The main topic of his research is repeated games. He serves on the editorial board of several academic journals.

SHMUEL ZAMIR is a professor emeritus in the Department of Statistics and the Center for the Study of Rationality at the Hebrew University of Jerusalem in Israel. The main topics of his research are games with incomplete information and auction theory. He is the editor-in-chief of the *International Journal of Game Theory*.

Game Theory

Second Edition

MICHAEL MASCHLER

EILON SOLAN

SHMUEL ZAMIR

Translated from Hebrew by Ziv Hellman

English Editor Mike Borns

CAMBRIDGE
UNIVERSITY PRESS

CAMBRIDGE
UNIVERSITY PRESS

University Printing House, Cambridge CB2 8BS, United Kingdom

One Liberty Plaza, 20th Floor, New York, NY 10006, USA

477 Williamstown Road, Port Melbourne, VIC 3207, Australia

314–321, 3rd Floor, Plot 3, Splendor Forum, Jasola District Centre, New Delhi – 110025, India

79 Anson Road, #06–04/06, Singapore 079906

Cambridge University Press is part of the University of Cambridge.

It furthers the University's mission by disseminating knowledge in the pursuit of
education, learning, and research at the highest international levels of excellence.

www.cambridge.org
Information on this title: www.cambridge.org/9781108493451

First published 2013
Second Edition 2020

Printed in the United Kingdom by TJ International Ltd. Padstow, Cornwall

A catalogue record for this publication is available from the British Library.

Library of Congress Cataloging-in-Publication Data
Names: Zamir, Shmuel, author. | Maschler, Michael, 1927–2008, author. |
    Solan, Eilon, author.
Title: Game theory / Michael Maschler, Eilon Solan, Shmuel Zamir ;
    translated from Hebrew by Ziv Hellman ; English editor, Mike Borns.
Other titles: Torat ha-miśḥaḳim. English
Description: Second edition. | New York : Cambridge University Press, 2020. |
    Includes bibliographical references and index.
Identifiers: LCCN 2019056230 | ISBN 9781108493451 (hardback) | ISBN
    9781108636049 (paperback)
Subjects: LCSH: Game theory.
Classification: LCC QA269 .Z3613 2020 | DDC 519.3–dc23
LC record available at https://lccn.loc.gov/2019056230

ISBN 978-1-108-49345-1 Hardback
ISBN 978-1-108-82514-6 Paperback

Cambridge University Press has no responsibility for the persistence or accuracy of
URLs for external or third-party internet websites referred to in this publication,
and does not guarantee that any content on such websites is, or will remain,
accurate or appropriate.

To Michael Maschler

CONTENTS

ACKNOWLEDGMENTS

A great many people helped in the composition of the book and we are grateful to all of them. We thank Ziv Hellman, the devoted translator of the book. When he undertook this project he did not know that it would take up so much of his time. Nevertheless, he implemented all our requests with patience. We also thank Mike Borns, the English editor, who efficiently read through the text and brought it to its present state. We thank Ehud Lehrer who contributed exercises and answered questions that we had while writing the book, Uzi Motro who commented on the section on evolutionarily stable strategies, Dov Samet who commented on several chapters and contributed exercises, Tzachi Gilboa, Sergiu Hart, Aviad Heifetz, Bo'az Klartag, Vijay Krishna, Rida Laraki, Nimrod Megiddo, Abraham Neyman, Guni Orshan, Bezalel Peleg, David Schmeidler, Rann Smorodinsky, Peter Sudhölter, Yair Tauman, Rakesh Vohra, and Peter Wakker who answered our questions, and the many friends and students who read portions of the text, suggested improvements and exercises and spotted mistakes, including Alon Amit, Itai Arieli, Galit Ashkenazi-Golan, Yaron Azrieli, Shani Bar-Gera, Asaf Cohen, Ronen Eldan, Gadi Fibich, Tal Galili, Yuval Heller, John Levy, Maya Liran, C Maor, Ayala Mashiach-Yaakovi, Noa Nitzan, Gilad Pagi, Dori Reuveni, Erez Sheiner, Eran Shmaya, Omri Solan, Ron Solan, Roee Teper, Zorit Varmaz, and Saar Zilberman. Samson Alva, Krzysztof Apt and his students, Dolev Bracha, Clemens Buchen, Yonatan Elhanani, Kousha Etessami, Piotr Frackiewicz, Yotam Gafni, Ronald Harstad, Guy Holdengreber, Johannes Hörner, Vincent Lin, Ismael Martínez-Martínez, Shiva Navabi, Todd Neller, Oriel Nofekh, Bezalel Peleg, Ron Peretz and his students, Justin Sun, Yair Tauman, Son Trung To, Yevgeny Tsodikovich, Avishay Weinbaum, Amir Weiss, Lin Zhang, and Chang Zhao. Finally, we thank the Center for the Study of Rationality at the Hebrew University of Jerusalem and Hana Shemesh for the assistance they provided from the beginning of this project.

We thank Dr. Ron Peretz and his students, Prof. Krzysztof Apt and his students, Prof. Ehud Lehrer, Prof. Bezalel Peleg, Yotam Gafni, and Yonatan Elhanani for spotting typos in the first print of the book. These typos are corrected in this print.

NOTATIONS

The book makes use of a large number of notations; we have striven to stick to accepted notations and to be consistent throughout the book. The coordinates of a vector are always denoted by a subscript index, $x = (x_i)_{i=1}^n$, while the indices of the elements of sequences are always denoted by a superscript index, $x^1, x^2, \ldots$ The index of a player in a set of players is always denoted by a subscript index, while a time index (in repeated games) is always denoted by a superscript index. The end of the proof of a theorem is indicated by $\square$, the end of an example is indicated by $\blacktriangleleft$, and the end of a remark is indicated by $\blacklozenge$.

For convenience we provide a list of the mathematical notations used throughout the book, accompanied by a short explanation and the pages on which they are formally defined. The notations that appear below are those that are used more than once.

0	chance move in an extensive-form game	50
$\vec{0}$	origin of a Euclidean space	579
$\emptyset$	strategy used by a player who has no decision vertices in an extensive-form game	5
$\mathbf{1}_A$	function that is equal to 1 on event A and to 0 otherwise	595
2^Y	collection of all subsets of Y	336
$|X|$	number of elements in finite set X	603
$\|x\|_\infty$	L_∞ norm, $\|x\|_\infty := \max_{i=1,2,\ldots,n} |x_i|$	539
$\|x\|$	norm of a vector, $\|x\| := \sqrt{\sum_{l=1}^d (x_l)^2}$	579
$A \vee B$	maximum matching (for men) in a matching problem	942
$A \wedge B$	maximum matching (for women) in a matching problem	943
$A \subseteq B$	set A contains set B or is equal to it	
$A \subset B$	set A strictly contains set B	
$\langle x, y \rangle$	inner product	579
$\langle\langle x^0, \ldots, x^k \rangle\rangle$	k-dimensional simplex	965
$\succsim_i$	preference relation of player i	13
$\succ_i$	strict preference relation of player i	10
$\approx_i$	indifference relation of player i	10, 944
$\succsim_P$	preference relation of an individual	905
$\succ_Q$	strict preference relation of society	905
$\approx_Q$	indifference relation of society	905
$x \geq y$	$x_k \geq y_k$ for each coordinate k, where x, y are vectors in a Euclidean space	676
$x > y$	$x \geq y$ and $x \neq y$	676

P	set of all weakly balancing weights for collection $\mathcal{D}^*$ of all coalitions	749
$\mathbf{P}$	common prior in an Aumann model of incomplete information	345
$\mathbf{P}_\sigma(x)$	probability that the play reaches vertex x when the players implement strategy vector σ in an extensive-form game	265
$\mathbf{P}_\sigma(U)$	probability that the play reaches a vertex in information set U when the players implement strategy vector σ in an extensive-form game	284
P^N	vector of preference relations	905
$PO(S)$	set of efficient (Pareto optimal) points in S	678
$PO^W(S)$	set of weakly efficient points in S	678
$\mathcal{P}(A)$	set of all strict preference relations over a set of alternatives A	905
$\mathcal{P}(N)$	collection of nonempty subsets of N, $\mathcal{P}(N) := \{S \subseteq N, S \neq \emptyset\}$	720, 749
$\mathcal{P}^*(A)$	set of all preference relations over a set of alternatives A	905
$\mathcal{PN}(N;v)$	prenucleolus of a coalitional game	853
$\mathcal{PN}(N;v;\mathcal{B})$	prenucleolus of a coalitional game for coalitional structure $\mathcal{B}$	853
q	quota in a weighted majority game	714
$q(w)$	minimal weight of a winning coalition in a weighted majority game, $q(w) := \min_{S \in \mathcal{W}^m} w(S)$	876
$\mathbb{Q}_{++}$	set of positive rational numbers	
r_k	total probability that the result of a compound lottery is A_k	18
$R_1(p)$	set of possible payoffs when Player 1 plays mixed action p, $R_1(p) := \{puq^\top : q \in \Delta(\mathcal{J})\}$	585
$R_2(p)$	set of possible payoffs when Player 2 plays mixed action q, $R_2(p) := \{puq^\top : q \in \Delta(\mathcal{I})\}$	585
$\mathbb{R}$	real line	
$\mathbb{R}_+$	set of nonnegative numbers	
$\mathbb{R}_{++}$	set of positive numbers	
$\mathbb{R}^n$	n-dimensional Euclidean space	
$\mathbb{R}^n_+$	nonnegative orthant in an n-dimensional Euclidean space, $\mathbb{R}^n_+ := \{x \in \mathbb{R}^n : x_i \geq 0, \quad \forall i = 1, 2, \ldots, n\}$	
$\mathbb{R}^S$	$|S|$-dimensional Euclidean space, where each coordinate corresponds to a player in S	719
range(G)	range of a social choice function	918
s	strategy vector	45
$\mathfrak{s}$	function that assigns a state of nature to each state of the world	334
s^t	action vector played at stage t of a repeated game	532
s_i	strategy of player i	45, 56

INTRODUCTION

What is game theory?

Game theory is the name given to the methodology of using mathematical tools to model and analyze situations of interactive decision making. These are situations involving several decision makers (called *players*) with different goals, in which the decision of each affects the outcome for all the decision makers. This interactivity distinguishes game theory from standard decision theory, which involves a single decision maker, and it is its main focus. Game theory tries to predict the behavior of the players and sometimes also provides decision makers with suggestions regarding ways in which they can achieve their goals.

The foundations of game theory were laid down in the book *The Theory of Games and Economic Behavior*, published in 1944 by the mathematician John von Neumann and the economist Oskar Morgenstern. The theory has been developed extensively since then and today it has applications in a wide range of fields. The applicability of game theory is due to the fact that it is a context-free mathematical toolbox that can be used in any situation of interactive decision making. A partial list of fields where the theory is applied, along with examples of some questions that are studied within each field using game theory, includes:

- **Theoretical economics.** A market in which vendors sell items to buyers is an example of a game. Each vendor sets the price of the items that he or she wishes to sell, and each buyer decides from which vendor he or she will buy items and in what quantities. In models of markets, game theory attempts to predict the prices that will be set for the items along with the demand for each item, and to study the relationships between prices and demand. Another example of a game is an auction. Each participant in an auction determines the price that he or she will bid, with the item being sold to the highest bidder. In models of auctions, game theory is used to predict the bids submitted by the participants, the expected revenue of the seller, and how the expected revenue will change if a different auction method is used.

- **Networks.** The contemporary world is full of networks; the Internet and mobile telephone networks are two prominent examples. Each network user wishes to obtain the best possible service (for example, to send and receive the maximal amount of information in the shortest span of time over the Internet, or to conduct the highest-quality calls using a mobile telephone) at the lowest possible cost. A user has to choose an Internet service provider or a mobile telephone provider, where those providers are also players in the game, since they set the prices of the service they provide. Game theory tries to predict the behavior of all the participants in these markets. This game is more complicated from the perspective of the service providers than from the perspective of the buyers, because the service providers can cooperate with each other (for example, mobile telephone providers can use each other's network infrastructure to carry communications in order to reduce costs), and game theory is used to predict which cooperative coalitions will be formed and suggest ways to determine a "fair" division of the profit of such cooperation among the participants.

- **Political science.** Political parties forming a governing coalition after parliamentary elections are playing a game whose outcome is the formation of a coalition that includes some of the parties. This coalition then divides government ministries and other elected offices, such as parliamentary speaker and committee chairmanships, among the members of the coalition. Game theory has developed indices measuring the power of each political party. These indices can predict or explain the division of government ministries and other elected offices given the results of the elections. Another branch of game theory suggests various voting methods and studies their properties.

- **Military applications.** A classical military application of game theory models a missile pursuing a fighter plane. What is the best missile pursuit strategy? What is the best strategy that the pilot of the plane can use to avoid being struck by the missile? Game theory has contributed to the field of defense the insight that the study of such situations requires strategic thinking: when coming to decide what you should do, put yourself in the place of your rival and think about what he/she would do and why, while taking into account that he/she is doing the same and knows that you are thinking strategically and that you are putting yourself in his/her place.

- **Inspection.** A broad family of problems from different fields can be described as two-player games in which one player is an entity that can profit by breaking the law and the other player is an "inspector" who monitors the behavior of the first player. One example of such a game is the activities of the International Atomic Energy Agency, in its role of enforcing the Treaty on the Non-Proliferation of Nuclear Weapons by inspecting the nuclear facilities of signatory countries. Additional examples include the enforcement of laws prohibiting drug smuggling, auditing of tax declarations by the tax authorities, and ticket inspections on public trains and buses.

- **Biology.** Plants and animals also play games. Evolution "determines" strategies that flowers use to attract insects for pollination and it "determines" strategies that the insects use to choose which flowers they will visit. Darwin's principle of the "survival of the fittest" states that only those organisms with the inherited properties that are best adapted to the environmental conditions in which they are located will survive. This principle can be explained by the notion of *Evolutionarily Stable Strategy*, which is a variant of the notion of *Nash equilibrium*, the most prominent game-theoretic concept. The introduction of game theory to biology in general and to evolutionary biology in particular explains, sometimes surprisingly well, various biological phenomena.

Game theory has applications to other fields as well. For example, to philosophy it contributes some insights into concepts related to morality and social justice, and it raises questions regarding human behavior in various situations that are of interest to psychology. Methodologically, game theory is intimately tied to mathematics: the study of game-theoretic models makes use of a variety of mathematical tools, from probability and combinatorics to differential equations and algebraic topology. Analyzing game-theoretic models sometimes requires developing new mathematical tools.

Traditionally, game theory is divided into two major subfields: strategic games, also called noncooperative games, and coalitional games, also called cooperative games. Broadly speaking, in strategic games the players act independently of each other, with each player trying to obtain the most desirable outcome given his or her preferences, while in coalitional games the same holds true with the stipulation that the players can agree on and sign binding contracts that enforce coordinated actions. Mechanisms enforcing such contracts include law courts and behavioral norms. Game theory does not deal with the quality or justification of these enforcement mechanisms; the cooperative game model simply assumes that such mechanisms exist and studies their consequences for the outcomes of the game.

The categories of strategic games and coalitional games are not well defined. In many cases interactive decision problems include aspects of both coalitional games and strategic games, and a complete theory of games should contain an amalgam of the elements of both types of models. Nevertheless, in a clear and focused introductory presentation of the main ideas of game theory it is convenient to stick to the traditional categorization. We will therefore present each of the two models, strategic games and coalitional games, separately. Chapters 1–15 are devoted to strategic games, and Chapters 16–21 are devoted to coalitional games. Chapters 22 and 23 are devoted to social choice and stable matching, which include aspects of both noncooperative and cooperative games.

How to use this book

The main objective of this book is to serve as an introductory textbook for the study of game theory at both the undergraduate and the graduate levels. A secondary goal is to serve as a reference book for students and scholars who are interested in an acquaintance with some basic or advanced topics of game theory. The number of introductory topics is large and different teachers may choose to teach different topics in introductory courses. We have therefore composed the book as a collection of chapters that are, to a large extent, independent of each other, enabling teachers to use any combination of the chapters as the basis for a course tailored to their individual taste. To help teachers plan a course, we have included an abstract at the beginning of each chapter that presents its content in a short and concise manner.

Each chapter begins with the basic concepts and eventually goes farther than what may be termed the "necessary minimum" in the subject that it covers. Most chapters include, in addition to introductory concepts, material that is appropriate for advanced courses. This gives teachers the option of teaching only the necessary minimum, presenting deeper material, or asking students to complement classroom lectures with independent readings or guided seminar presentations. We could not, of course, include all known results of game theory in one textbook, and therefore the end of each chapter contains references to other books and journal articles in which the interested reader can find more material for a deeper understanding of the subject. Each chapter also contains exercises, many of which are relatively easy, while some are more advanced and challenging.

This book was composed by mathematicians; the writing is therefore mathematically oriented, and every theorem in the book is presented with a proof. Nevertheless, an effort has been made to make the material clear and transparent, and every concept is illustrated with examples intended to impart as much intuition and motivation as possible. The book is appropriate for teaching undergraduate and graduate students in mathematics, computer science and exact sciences, economics and social sciences, engineering, and life sciences. It can be used as a textbook for teaching different courses in game theory, depending on the level of the students, the time available to the teacher, and the specific subject of the course. For example, it could be used in introductory level or advanced level semester courses on coalitional games, strategic games, a general course in game theory, or a course on applications of game theory. It could also be used for advanced mini-courses on, e.g., incomplete information (Chapters 9, 10, and 11), auctions (Chapter 12), or repeated games (Chapters 13 and 14). As mentioned previously, the material in the chapters of the book will in many cases encompass more than a teacher would choose to teach in a single course. This requires teachers to choose carefully which chapters to teach and which parts to cover in each chapter. For example, the material on strategic games (Chapters 4 and 5) can be taught without covering extensive-form games (Chapter 3) or utility theory (Chapter 2). Similarly, the material on games with incomplete information (Chapter 9) can be taught without teaching the other two chapters on models of incomplete information (Chapters 10 and 11).

For the sake of completeness, we have included an appendix containing the proofs of some theorems used throughout the book, including Brouwer's Fixed Point Theorem, Kakutani's Fixed Point Theorem, the Knaster–Kuratowski–Mazurkiewicz (KKM) Theorem, and the Separating Hyperplane Theorem. The appendix also contains a brief survey of linear programming. A teacher can choose to prove each of these theorems in class, assign the proofs of the theorems as independent reading to the students, or state any of the theorems without proof based on the assumption that students will see the proofs in other courses.

1 The game of chess

Chapter summary

In the opening chapter of this book, we use the well-known game of chess to illustrate the notions of *strategy* and *winning strategy*. We then prove one of the first results in game theory, due to John von Neumann: in the game of chess either White (the first mover) has a winning strategy, or Black (the second mover) has a winning strategy, or each player has a strategy guaranteeing at least a draw. This is an important and nontrivial result, especially in view of the fact that to date, it is not known which of the above three alternatives holds, let alone what the winning strategy is, if one exists.

In later chapters of the book, this result takes a more general form and is applied to a large class of games.

We begin with an exposition of the elementary ideas in noncooperative game theory, by analyzing the game of chess. Although the theory that we will develop in this chapter relates to that specific game, in later chapters it will be developed to apply to much more general situations.

1.1 Schematic description of the game

The game of chess is played by two players, traditionally referred to as White and Black. At the start of a match, each player has sixteen pieces arranged on the chessboard. White is granted the opening move, following which each player in turn moves pieces on the board, according to a set of fixed rules. A match has three possible outcomes:

- Victory for White, if White captures the Black King.
- Victory for Black, if Black captures the White King.
- A draw, if:

    1. it is Black's turn, but he has no possible legal moves available, and his King is not in check;
    2. it is White's turn, but he has no possible legal moves available, and his King is not in check;
    3. both players agree to declare a draw;
    4. a board position precludes victory for both sides;
    5. 50 consecutive turns have been played without a pawn having been moved and without the capture of any piece on the board, and the player whose turn it is requests that a draw be declared;

6. or if the same board position appears three times, and the player whose turn it is requests that a draw be declared.

Analysis and results

· ·

For the purposes of our analysis all we need to assume is that the game is finite, i.e., the number of possible turns is bounded (even if that bound is an astronomically large number). This does not apply, strictly speaking, to the game of chess, but since our lifetimes are finite, we can safely assume that every chess match is finite.

We will denote the set of all possible board positions in chess by X. A board position by definition includes the identity of each piece on the board, and the board square on which it is located.

A board position, however, does not provide full details on the sequence of moves that led to it: there may well be two or more sequences of moves leading to the same board position. We therefore need to distinguish between a "board position" and a "game situation," which is defined as follows.

Definition 1.1 *A* game situation *(in the game of chess) is a finite sequence* $(x_0, x_1, x_2, \ldots, x_K)$ *of board positions in X satisfying*

1. *x_0 is the opening board position.*
2. *For each even integer k, $0 \le k < K$, going from board position x_k to x_{k+1} can be accomplished by a single legal move on the part of White.*
3. *For each odd integer k, $0 \le k < K$, going from board position x_k to x_{k+1} can be accomplished by a single legal move on the part of Black.*

We will denote the set of game situations by H.

Suppose that a player wishes to program a computer to play chess. The computer would need a plan of action that would tell it what to do in any given game situation that could arise. A full plan of action for behavior in a game is called a *strategy*.

Definition 1.2 *A* strategy *for White is a function s_W that associates every game situation* $(x_0, x_1, x_2, \ldots, x_K) \in H$, *where K is even, with a board position x_{K+1}, such that going from board position x_K to x_{K+1} can be accomplished by a single legal move on the part of White.*

Analogously, a strategy *for Black is a function s_B that associates every game situation* $(x_0, x_1, x_2, \ldots, x_K) \in H$, *where K is odd, with a board position x_{K+1} such that going from board position x_K to x_{K+1} can be accomplished by a single legal move on the part of Black.*

Any pair of strategies (s_W, s_B) determines an entire course of moves, as follows. In the opening move, White plays the move that leads to board position $x_1 = s_W(x_0)$. Black then plays the move leading to board position $x_2 = s_B(x_0, x_1)$, and so on. The succeeding board positions are determined by $x_{2K+1} = s_W(x_0, x_1, \ldots, x_{2K})$ and $x_{2K+2} = s_B(x_0, x_1, \ldots, x_{2K+1})$ for all $K = 0, 1, 2, \ldots$.

An entire course of moves (from the opening move to the closing one) is termed a *play* of the game.

Every play of the game of chess ends in either a victory for White, a victory for Black, or a draw. A strategy for White is termed a *winning strategy* if it guarantees that White will win, no matter what strategy Black chooses.

Definition 1.3 *A strategy s_W is a* winning strategy *for White if for every strategy s_B of Black, the play of the game determined by the pair (s_W, s_B) ends in victory for White. A strategy s_W is a* strategy guaranteeing at least a draw *for White if for every strategy s_B of Black, the play of the game determined by the pair (s_W, s_B) ends in either a victory for White or a draw.*

If s_W is a winning strategy for White, then any White player (or even computer program) adopting that strategy is guaranteed to win, even if he faces the world's chess champion.

The concepts of "winning strategy" and "strategy guaranteeing at least a draw" for Black are defined analogously, in an obvious manner.

The next theorem follows from one of the earliest theorems ever published in game theory (see Theorem 3.13 on page 46).

Theorem 1.4 *In chess, one and only one of the following must be true:*

 (i) White has a winning strategy.
 (ii) Black has a winning strategy.
(iii) Each of the two players has a strategy guaranteeing at least a draw.

We emphasize that the theorem does not relate to a particular chess match, but to all chess matches. That is, suppose that alternative (i) is the true case, i.e., White has a winning strategy s_W. Then any person who is the White player and follows the prescriptions of that strategy will always win every chess match he ever plays, no matter who the opponent is. If, however, alternative (ii) is the true case, then Black has a winning strategy s_B, and any person who is the Black player and follows the prescriptions of that strategy will always win every chess match he ever plays, no matter who the opponent is. Finally, if alternative (iii) is the true case, then White has a strategy s_W guaranteeing at least a draw, and Black has a strategy s_B guaranteeing at least a draw. Any person who is the White player (or the Black player) and follows the prescriptions of s_W (or s_B, respectively) will always get at least a draw in every chess match he ever plays, no matter who the opponent is. Note that if alternative (i) holds, there may be more than one winning strategy, and similar statements can be made with regard to the other two alternatives.

So, given that one of the three alternatives *must* be true, which one is it? We do not know. If the day ever dawns in which a winning strategy for one of the players is discovered, or strategies guaranteeing at least a draw for each player are discovered, the game of chess will cease to be of interest. In the meantime, we can continue to enjoy the challenge of playing (or watching) a good chess match.

Despite the fact that we do not know which alternative is the true one, the theorem is significant, because a priori it might have been the case that none of the alternatives

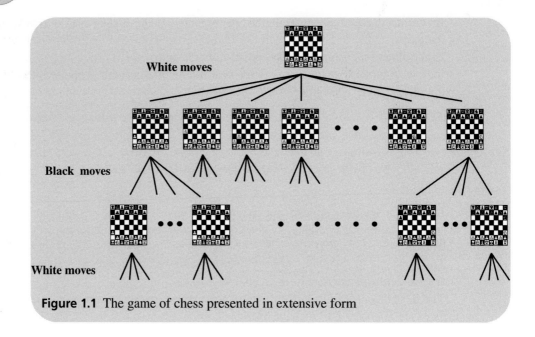

White moves

Black moves

White moves

Figure 1.1 The game of chess presented in extensive form

was possible; one could have postulated that no player could ever have a strategy *always* guaranteeing a victory, or at least a draw.

We present two proofs of the theorem. The first proof is the "classic" proof, which in principle shows how to find a winning strategy for one of the players (if such a strategy exists) or a strategy guaranteeing at least a draw (if such a strategy exists). The second proof is shorter, but it cannot be used to find a winning strategy for one of the players (if such a strategy exists) or a strategy guaranteeing at least a draw (if such a strategy exists).

We start with several definitions that are needed for the first proof of the theorem. The set of game situations can be depicted by a tree[1] (see Figure 1.1). Such a tree is called a *game tree*. Each vertex of the game tree represents a possible game situation. Denote the set of vertices of the game tree by H.

The *root vertex* is the opening game situation x_0, and for each vertex x, the set of *children vertices* of x is the set of game situations that can be reached from x in one legal move. For example, in his opening move, White can move one of his pawns one or two squares forward, or one of his two knights. So White has 20 possible opening moves, which means that the root vertex of the tree has 20 children vertices. Every vertex that can be reached from x by a sequence of moves is called a *descendant* of x. Every *leaf* of the tree corresponds to a terminal game situation, in which either White has won, Black has won, or a draw has been declared.

Given a vertex $x \in H$, we may consider the subtree beginning at x, which is by definition the tree whose root is x that is obtained by removing all vertices that are not descendants of x. This subtree of the game tree, which we will denote by $\Gamma(x)$,

---

1 The mathematical definition of a *tree* appears in the sequel (see Definition 3.5 on page 42).

corresponds to a game that is called the *subgame beginning at x*. We will denote by n_x the number of vertices in $\Gamma(x)$. The game $\Gamma(x_0)$ is by definition the game that starts with the opening situation of the game, and is therefore the standard chess game.

If y is a child vertex of x, then $\Gamma(y)$ is a subtree of $\Gamma(x)$ that does not contain x. In particular, $n_x > n_y$. Moreover, $n_x = 1$ if and only if x is a terminal situation of the game, i.e., the players cannot implement any moves at this subgame. In such a case, the strategy of a player is denoted by $\emptyset$.

Denote by

$$\mathcal{F} = \{\Gamma(x) : x \in H\} \tag{1.1}$$

the collection of all subgames that are defined by subtrees of the game of chess.

Theorem 1.4 can be proved using the result of Theorem 1.5.

Theorem 1.5 *Every game in $\mathcal{F}$ satisfies one and only one of the following alternatives:*

(i) White has a winning strategy.
(ii) Black has a winning strategy.
(iii) Each of the players has a strategy guaranteeing at least a draw.

Proof: The proof proceeds by induction on n_x, the number of vertices in the subgame $\Gamma(x)$.

Suppose x is a vertex such that $n_x = 1$. As noted above, that means that x is a terminal vertex. If the White King has been removed from the board, Black has won, in which case $\emptyset$ is a winning strategy for Black. If the Black King has been removed from the board, White has won, in which case $\emptyset$ is a winning strategy for White. Alternatively, if both Kings are on the board at the end of play, the game has ended in a draw, in which case $\emptyset$ is a strategy guaranteeing a draw for both Black and White.

Next, suppose that x is a vertex such that $n_x > 1$. Assume by induction that at all vertices y satisfying $n_y < n_x$, one and only one of the alternatives (i), (ii), or (iii) is true in the subgame $\Gamma(y)$.

Suppose, without loss of generality, that White has the first move in $\Gamma(x)$. Any board position y that can be reached from x satisfies $n_y < n_x$, and so the inductive assumption is true in the corresponding subgame $\Gamma(y)$. Denote by $C(x)$ the collection of vertices that can be reached from x in one of White's moves.

1. If there is a vertex $y_0 \in C(x)$ such that White has a winning strategy in $\Gamma(y_0)$, then alternative (i) is true in $\Gamma(x)$: the winning strategy for White in $\Gamma(x)$ is to choose as his first move the move leading to vertex y_0, and to follow the winning strategy in $\Gamma(y_0)$ at all subsequent moves.
2. If Black has a winning strategy in $\Gamma(y)$ for every vertex $y \in C(x)$, then alternative (ii) is true in $\Gamma(x)$: Black can win by ascertaining what the vertex y is after White's first move, and following his winning strategy in $\Gamma(y)$ at all subsequent moves.
3. Otherwise:

   • (1) does not hold, i.e., White has no winning strategy in $\Gamma(y)$ for any $y \in C(x)$. Because the induction hypothesis holds for every vertex $y \in C(x)$, either Black has a winning strategy in $\Gamma(y)$, or both players have a strategy guaranteeing at least a draw in $\Gamma(y)$.

- (2) does not hold, i.e., there is a vertex $y_0 \in C(x)$ such that Black does not have a winning strategy in $\Gamma(y_0)$. But because (1) does not hold, White also does not have a winning strategy in $\Gamma(y_0)$. Therefore, by the induction hypothesis applied to $\Gamma(y_0)$, both players have a strategy guaranteeing at least a draw in $\Gamma(y_0)$.

As we now show, in this case, in $\Gamma(x)$ both players have a strategy guaranteeing at least a draw. White can guarantee at least a draw by choosing a move leading to vertex y_0, and from there by following the strategy that guarantees at least a draw in $\Gamma(y_0)$. Black can guarantee at least a draw by ascertaining what the board position y is after White's first move, and at all subsequent moves in $\Gamma(y)$ either by following a winning strategy or following a strategy that guarantees at least a draw in that subgame. $\qquad\square$

The proof just presented is a standard inductive proof over a tree: one assumes that the theorem is true for every subtree starting from the root vertex, and then shows that it is true for the entire tree. The proof can also be accomplished in the following way: select any vertex x that is neither a terminal vertex nor the root vertex. The subgame starting from this vertex, $\Gamma(x)$, contains at least two vertices, but fewer vertices than the original game (because it does not include the root vertex), and the induction hypothesis can therefore be applied to $\Gamma(x)$. Now "fold up" the subgame and replace it with a terminal vertex whose outcome is the outcome that is guaranteed by the induction hypothesis to be obtained in $\Gamma(x)$. This leads to a new game $\widehat{\Gamma}$. Since $\Gamma(x)$ has at least two vertices, $\widehat{\Gamma}$ has fewer vertices than the original game, and therefore by the induction hypothesis the theorem is true for $\widehat{\Gamma}$. It is straightforward to ascertain that a player has a winning strategy in $\widehat{\Gamma}$ if and only if he has a winning strategy in the original game.

In the proof of Theorem 1.5 we used the following properties of the game of chess:

(C1) The game is finite.

(C2) The strategies of the players determine the play of the game. In other words, there is no element of chance in the game; neither dice nor card draws are involved.

(C3) Each player, at each turn, knows the moves that were made at all previous stages of the game.

We will later see examples of games in which at least one of the above properties fails to hold, for which the statement of Theorem 1.5 also fails to hold (see for example the game "Matching Pennies," Example 3.20 on page 52).

We next present a second proof of Theorem 1.4. We will need the following two facts from formal logic for the proof. Let X be a finite set and let $A(x)$ be an arbitrary logical formula.[2] Then:

- If it is not the case that "for every $x \in X$ the formula $A(x)$ holds," then there exists an $x \in X$ where the formula $A(x)$ does not hold:

$$\neg\,(\forall x(A)) = \exists x(\neg A). \tag{1.2}$$

---

2 Recall that the logical statement "for every $x \in X$ event A obtains" is written formally as $\forall x(A)$, and the statement "there exists an $x \in X$ for which event A obtains" is written as $\exists x(A)$, while "event A does not obtain" is written as $\neg A$. For ease of exposition, we will omit the set X from each of the formal statements in the proof.

• If it is not the case that "there exists an $x \in X$ where the formula $A(x)$ holds," then for every $x \in X$ the formula $A(x)$ does not hold:

$$\neg\left(\exists x(A)\right) = \forall x(\neg A). \tag{1.3}$$

Second Proof of Theorem 1.4: As stated above, we assume that the game of chess is a finite game, i.e., there is a natural number K such that every play of the game concludes after at most $2K$ turns (K turns on the part of White and K turns on the part of Black). Assume that there are exactly $2K$ turns in every play of the game: every play that ends in fewer turns can be continued by adding more turns, up to $2K$, at which each player alternately implements the move "do nothing," which has no effect on the board position.

For every k, $1 \leq k \leq K$, denote by a_k the move implemented by White at his k-th turn, and by b_k the move implemented by Black at his k-th turn. Denote by W the sentence that White wins (after $2K$ turns). Then $\neg W$ is the sentence that the play ends in either a draw or a victory for Black. Using these symbols, the statement "White has a winning strategy" can be written formally as

$$\exists a_1 \forall b_1 \exists a_2 \forall b_2 \exists a_3 \cdots \exists a_K \forall b_K(W). \tag{1.4}$$

It follows that the statement "White does not have a winning strategy" can be written formally as

$$\neg(\exists a_1 \forall b_1 \exists a_2 \forall b_2 \exists a_3 \cdots \exists a_K \forall b_K(W)). \tag{1.5}$$

By repeated application of Equations (1.2) and (1.3) we deduce that this is equivalent to

$$\forall a_1 \exists b_1 \forall a_2 \exists b_2 \forall a_3 \cdots \forall a_K \exists b_K(\neg W). \tag{1.6}$$

This, however, says that Black has a strategy guaranteeing at least a draw. In other words, we have proved that if White has no winning strategy, then Black has a strategy that guarantees at least a draw. We can similarly prove that if Black has no winning strategy, then White has a strategy that guarantees at least a draw. This leads to the conclusion that one of the three alternatives of Theorem 1.4 must hold. □

1.3 Remarks

The second proof of Theorem 1.4 was brought to the attention of the authors by Abraham Neyman, to whom thanks are due.

1.4 Exercises

1.1 "The outcome of every play of the game of chess is either a victory for White, a victory for Black, or a draw." Is that statement equivalent to the result of Theorem 1.4? Justify your answer.

1.2 Find three more games that satisfy Properties (C1)–(C3) on page 6 that are needed for proving Theorem 1.4.

1.3 Theorem 1.4 was proved in this chapter under the assumption that the length of a game of chess is bounded. In this exercise we will prove the theorem without that assumption, that is, we will allow an infinite number of moves. We will agree that the outcome of an infinitely long game of chess is a draw.

When one allows infinite plays, the set of game situations is an infinite set. However, to know how to continue playing, the players need not know all the sequence of past moves. In fact, only a bounded amount of information needs to be told to the players, e.g.,

- What is the current game position?
- Have the players played an even or an odd number of moves up to now (for knowing whose turn it is)?
- For every board position, has it appeared in the play up to now 0 times, once, or more than once (for knowing whether the player whose turn it is may ask for a draw)?
- Did the king and the rooks of each player move in the past (for knowing whether castling is allowed)?

Below we will refer to this bounded amount of information as *game position*. We will therefore make use of the fact that one may suppose that there are only a finite number of game positions in chess.

Consider the following version of chess. The rules of the game are identical to the rules on page 1, with the one difference that if a game position is repeated during a play, the play ends in a draw. Since the number of game positions is finite, this version of chess is a finite game. We will call it "finite chess."

(a) Prove that in finite chess exactly one of the following holds:

  (i) White has a winning strategy.
  (ii) Black has a winning strategy.
  (iii) Each of the two players has a strategy guaranteeing at least a draw.

(b) Prove that if one of the players has a winning strategy in finite chess, then that player also has a winning strategy in chess.

  We now prove that if each player has a strategy guaranteeing at least a draw in finite chess, then each player has a strategy guaranteeing at least a draw in chess. We will prove this claim for White. Suppose, therefore, that White has a strategy σ_W in finite chess that guarantees at least a draw. Consider the following strategy $\hat{\sigma}_W$ for White in chess:

  - Implement strategy σ_W until either the play of chess terminates or a game position repeats itself (at which point the play of finite chess terminates).
  - If the play of chess arrives at a game position x that has previously appeared, implement the strategy σ_W restricted to the subgame beginning at x until the play arrives at a game position y that has previously appeared, and so on.

(c) Prove that the strategy $\hat{\sigma}_W$ guarantees at least a draw for White in chess.

2 Utility theory

Chapter summary

The objective of this chapter is to provide a quantitative representation of players' preference relations over the possible outcomes of the game, by what is called a *utility function*. This is a fundamental element of game theory, economic theory, and decision theory in general, since it facilitates the application of mathematical tools in analyzing game situations whose outcomes may vary in their nature, and often be uncertain.

The utility function representation of preference relations over uncertain outcomes was developed and named after John von Neumann and Oskar Morgenstern. The main feature of the von Neumann–Morgenstern utility is that it is linear in the probabilities of the outcomes. This implies that a player evaluates an uncertain outcome by its *expected utility*.

We present some properties (also known as axioms) that players' preference relations can satisfy. We then prove that any preference relation having these properties can be represented by a von Neumann–Morgenstern utility and that this representation is determined up to a positive affine transformation. Finally we note how a player's attitude towards risk is expressed in his von Neumann–Morgenstern utility function.

2.1 Preference relations and their representation

A game is a mathematical model of a situation of interactive decision making, in which every decision maker (or *player*) strives to attain his "best possible" outcome, knowing that each of the other players is striving to do the same thing.

But what does a player's "best possible" outcome mean? The outcomes of a game need not be restricted to "Win," "Loss," or "Draw." They may well be monetary payoffs or non-monetary payoffs, such as "your team has won the competition," "congratulations, you're a father," "you have a headache," or "you have granted much-needed assistance to a friend in distress."

To analyze the behavior of players in a game, we first need to ascertain the set of outcomes of a game and then we need to know the preferences of each player with respect to the set of outcomes. This means that for every pair of outcomes x and y, we need to know for each player whether he prefers x to y, whether he prefers y to x, or whether he is indifferent between them. We denote by O the set of outcomes of the game. The preferences of each player over the set O are captured by the mathematical concept that is termed *preference relation*.

Definition 2.1 *A* preference relation *of player i over a set of outcomes O is a binary relation denoted by* $\gtrsim_i$.

A binary relation is formally a subset of $O \times O$, but instead of writing $(x, y) \in \gtrsim_i$ we write $x \gtrsim_i y$, and read that as saying "player i either prefers x to y or is indifferent between the two outcomes"; sometimes we will also say in this case that the player "weakly prefers" x to y. Given the preference relation $\gtrsim_i$ we can define the corresponding *strict preference relation* $\succ_i$, which describes when player i strictly prefers one outcome to another:

$$x \succ_i y \iff x \gtrsim_i y \text{ and } y \not\gtrsim_i x. \tag{2.1}$$

We can similarly define the *indifference* relation $\approx_i$, which expresses the fact that a player is indifferent between two possible outcomes:

$$x \approx_i y \iff x \gtrsim_i y \text{ and } y \gtrsim_i x. \tag{2.2}$$

We will assume that every player's preference relation satisfies the following three properties.

Assumption 2.2 *The preference relation* $\gtrsim_i$ *over O is* complete; *that is, for any pair of outcomes x and y in O either* $x \gtrsim_i y$, *or* $y \gtrsim_i x$, *or both.*

Assumption 2.3 *The preference relation* $\gtrsim_i$ *over O is* reflexive; *that is,* $x \gtrsim_i x$ *for every* $x \in O$.

Assumption 2.4 *The preference relation* $\gtrsim_i$ *over O is* transitive; *that is, for any triple of outcomes x, y, and z in O, if* $x \gtrsim_i y$ *and* $y \gtrsim_i z$ *then* $x \gtrsim_i z$.

The assumption of completeness says that a player should be able to compare any two possible outcomes and state whether he is indifferent between the two, or has a definite preference for one of them, in which case he should be able to state which is the preferred outcome. One can imagine real-life situations in which this assumption does not obtain, where a player is unable to rank his preferences between two or more outcomes (or is uninterested in doing so). The assumption of completeness is necessary for the mathematical analysis conducted in this chapter.

The assumption of reflexivity is quite natural: every outcome is weakly preferred to itself.

The assumption of transitivity is needed under any reasonable interpretation of what a preference relation means. If this assumption does not obtain, then there exist three outcomes x, y, z such that $x \gtrsim_i y$ and $y \gtrsim_i z$, but $z \succ_i x$. That would mean that if a player were asked to choose directly between x and z he would choose z, but if he were first asked to choose between z and y and then between the outcome he just preferred (y) and x, he would choose x, so that his choices would depend on the order in which alternatives are offered to him. Without the assumption of transitivity, it is unclear what a player means when he says that he prefers z to x.

The greater than or equal to relation over the real numbers $\geq$ is a familiar preference relation. It is complete and transitive. If a game's outcomes for player i are sums of dollars, it is reasonable to suppose that the player will compare different outcomes using this preference relation. Since using real numbers and the $\geq$ ordering relation is very convenient for the purposes of conducting analysis, it would be an advantage to be able in general to represent game outcomes by real numbers, and player preferences by the familiar $\geq$ relation. Such a representation of a preference relation is called a *utility function*, and is defined as follows.

Definition 2.5 *Let O be a set of outcomes and $\succsim$ be a complete, reflexive, and transitive preference relation over O. A function $u : O \to \mathbb{R}$ is called a* utility function representing $\succsim$ *if for all $x, y \in O$,*

$$x \succsim y \iff u(x) \geq u(y). \tag{2.3}$$

In other words, a utility function u is a function associating each outcome x with a real number $u(x)$ in such a way that the more an outcome is preferred, the larger is the real number associated with it.

If the set of outcomes is finite, any complete, reflexive, and transitive preference relation can easily be represented by a utility function.

Example 2.6 Suppose that $O = \{a, b, c, d\}$ and the preference relation $\succsim$ is given by

$$a > b \approx c > d. \tag{2.4}$$

Note that although the relation is defined only on part of the set of all pairs of outcomes, the assumptions of reflexivity and transitivity enable us to extend the relation to every pair of outcomes. For example, from the above we can immediately conclude that $a > c$.

The utility function u defined by

$$u(a) = 22, \ u(b) = 13, \ u(c) = 13, \ u(d) = 0, \tag{2.5}$$

represents $\succsim$. There are, in fact, a continuum of utility functions that represent this relation, because the only condition that a utility function needs to meet in order to represent $\succsim$ is

$$u(a) > u(b) = u(c) > u(d). \tag{2.6}$$

◀

The following theorem, whose proof is left to the reader (Exercise 2.2), generalizes the conclusion of the example.

Theorem 2.7 *Let O be a set of outcomes and let $\succsim$ be a complete, reflexive, and transitive preference relation over O. Suppose that u is a utility function representing $\succsim$. Then for every monotonically strictly increasing function $v : \mathbb{R} \to \mathbb{R}$, the composition $v \circ u$ defined by*

$$(v \circ u)(x) = v(u(x)) \tag{2.7}$$

is also a utility function representing $\succsim$.

Given the result of this theorem, a utility function is often called an *ordinal* function, because it represents only the order of preferences between outcomes. The numerical values that a utility function associates with outcomes have no significance, and do not in any way represent the "intensity" of a player's preferences.

Once we have represented a player's preferences by a utility function, we need to deal with another problem: the outcome of a game may well be uncertain and determined by a lottery. This can occur for two reasons:

- The game may include moves of chance. Examples of such games include backgammon and Monopoly (where dice are tossed) and bridge and poker (where the shuffling of the deck introduces chance into the game). In many economic situations, an outcome may depend on uncertain factors such as changes in currency conversion rates or the valuation of stocks in the stock market, and the outcome itself may therefore be uncertain. The most convenient way to model such situations is to describe some of the determining factors as lottery outcomes.
- One or more of the players may play in a non-deterministic manner, choosing moves by lottery. For example, in a chess match, a player may choose his opening move by tossing a coin. The formal analysis of strategies that depend on lotteries will be presented in Chapter 5.

Example 2.8 Consider the following situation involving one player who has two possible moves, T and B. The outcome is the amount of dollars that the player receives. If she chooses B, she receives $7,000. If she chooses T, she receives the result of a lottery that grants a payoff of $0 or $20,000 with equal probability. The lottery is denoted by $[\frac{1}{2}(\$20,000), \frac{1}{2}(\$0)]$. What move can we expect the player to prefer? The answer depends on the player's attitude to risk. There are many people who would rather receive $7,000 with certainty than take their chances with a toss of a coin determining whether they receive $20,000 or $0, while others would take a chance on the large sum of $20,000. Risk attitude is a personal characteristic that varies from one individual to another, and therefore affects a player's preference relation. ◄

To analyze situations in which the outcome of a game may depend on a lottery over several possible outcomes, the preference relations of players need to be extended to cover preferences over lotteries involving the outcomes.

Given an extended preference relation of a player, which includes preferences over both individual outcomes and lotteries, we can again ask whether such a relation can be represented by a utility function. In other words, can we assign a real number to each lottery in such a way that one lottery is preferred by the player to another lottery if and only if the number assigned to the more-preferred lottery is greater than the number assigned to the less-preferred lottery?

A convenient property that such a utility function can satisfy is linearity, meaning that the number assigned to a lottery is equal to the expected value of the numbers assigned to the individual outcomes over which the lottery is being conducted. For example, if $L = [px, (1-p)y]$ is a lottery assigning probability p to outcome x, and probability $1-p$ to outcome y, then the linearity requirement would imply that

$$u(L) = pu(x) + (1-p)u(y). \tag{2.8}$$

Such a utility function is linear in the probabilities p and $1-p$; hence the name. The use of linear utility functions is very convenient for analyzing games in which the outcomes are uncertain (a topic studied in depth in Section 5.5 on page 171). But we still need to

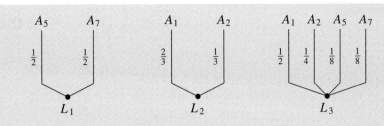

Figure 2.1 Lotteries over outcomes

answer the question: which preference relation of a player (over lotteries of outcomes) can be represented by a linear utility function, as expressed in Equation (2.8)?

The subject of linear utility functions was first explored by the mathematician John von Neumann and the economist Oskar Morgenstern [1944], and it is the subject matter of this chapter.

Suppose that a decision maker is faced with a decision determining which of a finite number of possible outcomes, sometimes designated "prizes," he will receive. (The terms "outcome" and "prize" will be used interchangeably in this section.) Denote the set of possible outcomes by $O = \{A_1, A_2, \ldots, A_K\}$.

In Example 2.8 there are three outcomes $O = \{A_1, A_2, A_3\}$, where $A_1 = \$0$, $A_2 = \$7,000$, and $A_3 = \$20,000$.

Given the set of outcomes O, the relevant space for conducting analysis is the set of lotteries over the outcomes in O. Figure 2.1 depicts three possible lotteries over outcomes.

The three lotteries in Figure 2.1 are: L_1, a lottery granting A_5 and A_7 with equal probability; L_2, a lottery granting A_1 with probability $\frac{2}{3}$ and A_2 with probability $\frac{1}{3}$; and L_3 granting A_1, A_2, A_5, and A_7 with respective probabilities $\frac{1}{2}, \frac{1}{4}, \frac{1}{8}$, and $\frac{1}{8}$.

A lottery L in which outcome A_k has probability p_k (where $p_1, \ldots, p_K$ are nonnegative real numbers summing to 1) is denoted by

$$L = [p_1(A_1), p_2(A_2), \ldots, p_K(A_K)], \tag{2.9}$$

and the set of all lotteries over O is denoted by $\mathcal{L}$.

The three lotteries in Figure 2.1 can thus be written as

$$L_1 = \left[\tfrac{1}{2}(A_5), \tfrac{1}{2}(A_7)\right], \quad L_2 = \left[\tfrac{2}{3}(A_1), \tfrac{1}{3}(A_2)\right],$$
$$L_3 = \left[\tfrac{1}{2}(A_1), \tfrac{1}{4}(A_2), \tfrac{1}{8}(A_5), \tfrac{1}{8}(A_7)\right].$$

The set of outcomes O may be regarded as a subset of the set of lotteries $\mathcal{L}$ by identifying each outcome A_k with the lottery yielding A_k with probability 1. In other words, receiving outcome A_k with certainty is equivalent to conducting a lottery that yields A_k with probability 1 and yields all the other outcomes with probability 0,

$$[0(A_1), 0(A_2), \ldots, 0(A_{k-1}), 1(A_k), 0(A_{k+1}), \ldots, 0(A_K)]. \tag{2.10}$$

We will denote a preference relation for player i over the set of all lotteries by $\succsim_i$, so that $L_1 \succsim_i L_2$ indicates that player i either prefers lottery L_1 to lottery L_2 or is indifferent between the two lotteries.

Definition 2.9 *Let $\succsim_i$ be a preference relation for player i over the set of lotteries $\mathcal{L}$. A utility function u_i representing the preferences of player i is a real-valued function defined over $\mathcal{L}$ satisfying*

$$u_i(L_1) \geq u_i(L_2) \iff L_1 \succsim_i L_2 \quad \forall L_1, L_2 \in \mathcal{L}. \tag{2.11}$$

In words, a utility function is a function whose values reflect the preferences of a player over lotteries.

Definition 2.10 *A utility function u_i is called* linear *if for every lottery $L = [p_1(A_1), p_2(A_2), \ldots, p_K(A_K)]$, it satisfies*[1]

$$u_i(L) = p_1 u_i(A_1) + p_2 u_i(A_2) + \cdots + p_K u_i(A_K). \tag{2.12}$$

As noted above, the term "linear" expresses the fact that the function u_i is a linear function in the probabilities $(p_k)_{k=1}^{K}$. If the utility function is linear, the utility of a lottery is the expected value of the utilities of the outcomes. A linear utility function is also called a *von Neumann–Morgenstern utility function*.

Which preference relation of a player can be represented by a linear utility function? First of all, since $\geq$ is a transitive relation, it cannot possibly represent a preference relation $\succsim_i$ that is not transitive. The transitivity assumption that we imposed on the preferences over the outcomes O must therefore be extended to preference relations over lotteries. This alone, however, is still insufficient for the existence of a linear utility function over lotteries: there are complete, reflexive, and transitive preference relations over the set of simple lotteries that cannot be represented by linear utility functions (see Exercise 2.18).

The next section presents four requirements on preference relations that ensure that a preference relation $\succsim_i$ over O can be represented by a linear utility function. These requirements are also termed the *von Neumann–Morgenstern axioms*.

2.3   The axioms of utility theory

Given the observations of the previous section, we would like to identify which preference relations $\succsim_i$ over lotteries can be represented by linear utility functions u_i. The first requirement that must be imposed is that the preference relation be extended beyond the set of simple lotteries to a larger set: the set of compound lotteries.

Definition 2.11 *A compound lottery is a lottery of lotteries.*

A compound lottery is therefore given by

$$\hat{L} = [q_1(L_1), q_2(L_1), \ldots, q_J(L_J)], \tag{2.13}$$

where $q_1, \ldots, q_J$ are nonnegative numbers summing to 1, and $L_1, \ldots, L_J$ are lotteries in $\mathcal{L}$. This means that for each $1 \leq j \leq J$ there are nonnegative numbers $(p_k^j)_{k=1}^{K}$ summing to 1 such that

---

1   Given the identification of outcomes with lotteries, we use the notation $u_i(A_k)$ to denote the utility of the lottery in Equation (2.10), in which the probability of receiving outcome A_k is one.

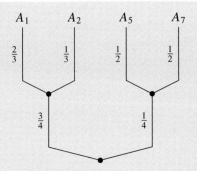

Figure 2.2 An example of a compound lottery

$$L_j = \left[p_1^j(A_1), p_2^j(A_1), \ldots, p_K^j(A_K) \right]. \tag{2.14}$$

Compound lotteries naturally arise in many situations. Consider, for example, an individual who chooses his route to work based on the weather: on rainy days he travels by Route 1, and on sunny days he travels by Route 2. Travel time along each route is inconstant, because it depends on many factors (beyond the weather). We are therefore dealing with a "travel time to work" random variable, whose value depends on a lottery of a lottery: there is some probability that tomorrow morning will be rainy, in which case travel time will be determined by a probability distribution depending on the factors affecting travel along Route 1, and there is a complementary probability that tomorrow will be sunny, so that travel time will be determined by a probability distribution depending on the factors affecting travel along Route 2.

We will show in the sequel that under proper assumptions there is no need to consider lotteries that are more compound than compound lotteries, namely, lotteries of compound lotteries. All our analysis can be conducted by limiting consideration to only one level of compounding.

To distinguish between the two types of lotteries with which we will be working, we will call the lotteries in $L \in \mathcal{L}$ *simple lotteries*. The set of compound lotteries is denoted by $\widehat{\mathcal{L}}$.

A graphic depiction of a compound lottery appears in Figure 2.2. Denoting $L_1 = \left[\frac{2}{3}(A_1), \frac{1}{3}(A_2) \right]$ and $L_2 = \left[\frac{1}{2}(A_5), \frac{1}{2}(A_7) \right]$, the compound lottery in Figure 2.2 is

$$\widehat{L} = \left[\tfrac{3}{4}(L_1), \tfrac{1}{4}(L_2) \right]. \tag{2.15}$$

Every simple lottery L can be identified with the compound lottery $\widehat{L}$ that yields the simple lottery L with probability 1:

$$\widehat{L} = [1(L)]. \tag{2.16}$$

As every outcome A_k is identified with the simple lottery

$$L = [0(A_1), \ldots, 0(A_{k-1}), 1(A_k), 0(A_{k+1}), \ldots, 0(A_K)], \tag{2.17}$$

it follows that an outcome A_k is also identified with the compound lottery $[1(L)]$, in which L is the simple lottery defined in Equation (2.17).

Given these identifications, the space we will work with will be the set of compound lotteries,[2] which includes within it the set of simple lotteries $\mathcal{L}$, and the set of outcomes O.

We will assume from now on that the preference relation $\succsim_i$ is defined over the set of compound lotteries. Player i's utility function, representing his preference relation $\succsim_i$, is therefore a function $u_i : \widehat{\mathcal{L}} \to \mathbb{R}$ satisfying

$$u_i(\widehat{L}_1) \geq u_i(\widehat{L}_2) \iff \widehat{L}_1 \succsim_i \widehat{L}_2, \quad \forall \widehat{L}_1, \widehat{L}_2 \in \widehat{\mathcal{L}}. \tag{2.18}$$

Given the identification of outcomes with simple lotteries, $u_i(A_k)$ and $u_i(L)$ denote the utility of compound lotteries corresponding to the outcome A_k and the simple lottery L, respectively.

Because the preference relation is complete, it determines the preference between any two outcomes A_i and A_j. Since it is transitive, the outcomes can be ordered, from most preferred to least preferred. We will number the outcomes (recall that the set of outcomes is finite) in such a way that

$$A_K \succsim_i \cdots \succsim_i A_2 \succsim_i A_1. \tag{2.19}$$

2.3.1 Continuity

Every reasonable decision maker will prefer receiving $300 to $100, and prefer receiving $100 to $0, that is,

$$\$300 >_i \$100 >_i \$0. \tag{2.20}$$

It is also a reasonable assumption that a decision maker will prefer receiving $300 with probability 0.9999 (and $0 with probability 0.0001) to receiving $100 with probability 1. It is reasonable to assume he would prefer receiving $100 with probability 1 to receiving $300 with probability 0.0001 (and $0 with probability 0.9999). Formally,

$$[0.9999(\$300), 0.0001(\$0)] >_i \$100 >_i [0.0001(\$300), 0.9999(\$0)].$$

The higher the probability of receiving $300 (and correspondingly, the lower the probability of receiving $0), the more the lottery will be preferred. By continuity, it is reasonable to suppose that there will be a particular probability p at which the decision maker will be indifferent between receiving $100 and a lottery granting $300 with probability p and $0 with probability $1 - p$:

$$\$100 \approx_i [p(\$300), (1-p)(\$0)]. \tag{2.21}$$

The exact value of p will vary depending on the decision maker: a pension fund making many investments is interested in maximizing expected profits, and its p will likely be close to $\frac{1}{3}$. The p of a risk-averse individual will be higher than $\frac{1}{3}$, whereas for the risk

---

2 The set of lotteries, as well as the set of compound lotteries, depends on the set of outcomes O, so that in fact we should denote the set of lotteries by $L(O)$, and the set of compound lotteries by $\widehat{\mathcal{L}}(O)$. For the sake of readability, we take the underlying set of outcomes O to be fixed, and we will not specify this dependence in our formal presentation.

lovers among us p will be less than $\frac{1}{3}$. Furthermore, the size of p, even for one individual, may be situation-dependent: for example, a person may generally be risk averse, and have p higher than $\frac{1}{3}$. However, if this person has a pressing need to return a debt of \$200, then \$100 will not help him, and his p may be temporarily lower than $\frac{1}{3}$, despite his risk aversion.

The next axiom encapsulates the idea behind this example.

Axiom 2.12 (Continuity) *For every triplet of outcomes $A \succsim_i B \succsim_i C$, there exists a number $\theta_i \in [0,1]$ such that*

$$B \approx_i [\theta_i(A), (1 - \theta_i)(C)]. \tag{2.22}$$

2.3.2   Monotonicity

Every reasonable decision maker will prefer to increase his probability of receiving a more-preferred outcome and lower the probability of receiving a less-preferred outcome. This natural property is captured in the next axiom.

Axiom 2.13 (Monotonicity) *Let α, β be numbers in $[0,1]$, and suppose that $A \succ_i B$. Then*

$$[\alpha(A), (1 - \alpha)(B)] \succsim_i [\beta(A), (1 - \beta)(B)] \tag{2.23}$$

if and only if $\alpha \geq \beta$.

Assuming the Axioms of Continuity and Monotonicity yields the next theorem, whose proof is left to the reader (Exercise 2.4).

Theorem 2.14 *If the preference relation $\succsim_i$ is transitive and satisfies the Axioms of Continuity and Monotonicity, and if $A \succsim_i B \succsim_i C$, and $A \succ_i C$, then the value of θ_i defined in the Axiom of Continuity is unique.*

Recall that A_K is the most preferred outcome and A_1 is the least preferred outcome.

Corollary 2.15 *If a preference relation $\succsim_i$ over $\widehat{\mathcal{L}}$ satisfies the Axioms of Continuity and Monotonicity, and if $A_K \succ_i A_1$, then for each $k = 1, 2, \ldots, K$ there exists a unique $\theta_i^k \in [0,1]$ such that*

$$A_k \approx_i \left[\theta_i^k(A_K), \left(1 - \theta_i^k\right)(A_1)\right]. \tag{2.24}$$

The corollary and the fact that $A_1 \approx_i [0(A_K), 1(A_1)]$ and $A_K \approx_i [1(A_K), 0(A_1)]$ imply that

$$\theta_i^1 = 0, \quad \theta_i^K = 1. \tag{2.25}$$

2.3.3   Simplification of lotteries

The next axiom states that the only considerations that determine the preference between lotteries are the probabilities attached to each outcome, and not the way that the lottery is conducted. For example, if we consider the lottery in Figure 2.2, with respect to the probabilities attached to each outcome that lottery is equivalent to lottery L_3 in Figure 2.1: in both lotteries the probability of receiving outcome A_1 is $\frac{1}{2}$, the probability of receiving outcome A_2 is $\frac{1}{4}$, the probability of receiving outcome A_5 is $\frac{1}{8}$, and the probability of receiving outcome A_7 is $\frac{1}{8}$. The next axiom captures the intuition that it is reasonable to suppose that a player will be indifferent between these two lotteries.

Axiom 2.16 (Simplification) *For each* $j = 1, \ldots, J$, *let* L_j *be the following simple lottery:*

$$L_j = \left[p_1^j(A_1), p_2^j(A_2), \ldots, p_K^j(A_K) \right], \tag{2.26}$$

and let $\widehat{L}$ *be the following compound lottery:*

$$\widehat{L} = \left[q_1(L_1), q_2(L_2), \ldots, q_J(L_J) \right]. \tag{2.27}$$

For each $k = 1, \ldots, K$ *define*

$$r_k = q_1 p_k^1 + q_2 p_k^2 + \cdots + q_J p_k^J; \tag{2.28}$$

this is the overall probability that the outcome of the compound lottery $\widehat{L}$ *will be* A_k. *Consider the simple lottery*

$$L = \left[r_1(A_1), r_2(A_2), \ldots, r_K(A_K) \right]. \tag{2.29}$$

Then

$$\widehat{L} \approx_i L. \tag{2.30}$$

As noted above, the motivation for the axiom is that it should not matter whether a lottery is conducted in a single stage or in several stages, provided the probability of receiving the various outcomes is identical in the two lotteries. The axiom ignores all aspects of the lottery except for the overall probability attached to each outcome, so that, for example, it takes no account of the possibility that conducting a lottery in several stages might make participants feel tense, which could alter their preferences, or their readiness to accept risk.

2.3.4   Independence

Our last requirement regarding the preference relation $\succsim_i$ relates to the following scenario. Suppose that we create a new compound lottery out of a given compound lottery by replacing one of the simple lotteries involved in the compound lottery with a different simple lottery. The axiom then requires a player who is indifferent between the original simple lottery and its replacement to be indifferent between the two corresponding compound lotteries.

Axiom 2.17 (Independence) *Let* $\widehat{L} = \left[q_1(L_1), \ldots, q_J(L_J) \right]$ *be a compound lottery, and let* M *be a simple lottery. If* $L_j \approx_i M$ *then*

$$\widehat{L} \approx_i \left[q_1(L_1), \ldots, q_{j-1}(L_{j-1}), q_j(M), q_{j+1}(L_{j+1}), \ldots, q_J(L_J) \right]. \tag{2.31}$$

One can extend the Axioms of Simplification and Independence to compound lotteries of any order (i.e., lotteries over lotteries over lotteries ... over lotteries over outcomes) in a natural way. By induction over the levels of compounding, it follows that the player's preference relation over all compound lotteries (of any order) is determined by the player's preference relation over simple lotteries (why?).

2.4 The characterization theorem for utility functions

. . . .

The next theorem characterizes when a player has a linear utility function.

Theorem 2.18 *If player i's preference relation $\succeq_i$ over $\widehat{\mathcal{L}}$ is complete, reflexive, and transitive, and satisfies the four von Neumann–Morgenstern axioms (Axioms 2.12, 2.13, 2.16, and 2.17), then this preference relation can be represented by a linear utility function.*

The next example shows how a player whose preference relation satisfies the von Neumann–Morgenstern axioms compares two lotteries based on his utility from the outcomes of the lottery.

Example 2.19 Suppose that Joshua is choosing which of the following two lotteries he prefers:

- $[\frac{1}{2}(\text{New car}), \frac{1}{2}(\text{New computer})]$ – a lottery in which his probability of receiving a new car is $\frac{1}{2}$, and his probability of receiving a new computer is $\frac{1}{2}$.
- $[\frac{1}{3}(\text{New motorcycle}), \frac{2}{3}(\text{Trip around the world})]$ – a lottery in which his probability of receiving a new motorcycle is $\frac{1}{3}$, and his probability of receiving a trip around the world is $\frac{2}{3}$.

Suppose that Joshua's preference relation over the set of lotteries satisfies the von Neumann–Morgenstern axioms. Then Theorem 2.18 implies that there is a linear utility function u representing his preference relation. Suppose that according to this function u:

$$u(\text{New car}) = 25,$$
$$u(\text{Trip around the world}) = 14,$$
$$u(\text{New motorcycle}) = 3,$$
$$u(\text{New computer}) = 1.$$

Then Joshua's utility from the first lottery is

$$u\left(\left[\tfrac{1}{2}(\text{New car}), \tfrac{1}{2}(\text{New computer})\right]\right) = \tfrac{1}{2} \times 25 + \tfrac{1}{2} \times 1 = 13, \tag{2.32}$$

and his utility from the second lottery is

$$u\left(\left[\tfrac{1}{3}(\text{New motorcycle}), \tfrac{2}{3}(\text{Trip around the world})\right]\right) = \tfrac{1}{3} \times 3 + \tfrac{2}{3} \times 14 = \tfrac{31}{3} = 10\tfrac{1}{3}. \tag{2.33}$$

It follows that he prefers the first lottery (whose outcomes are a new car and a new computer) to the second lottery (whose outcomes are a new motorcycle and a trip around the world). ◄

Proof of Theorem 2.18: We first assume that $A_K \succ_i A_1$, i.e., the most-desired outcome A_K is strictly preferred to the least-desired outcome A_1. If $A_1 \approx_i A_K$, then by transitivity, the player is indifferent between all the outcomes. That case is simple to handle, and we will deal with it at the end of the proof.

Step 1: Definition of a function u_i over the set of lotteries.

By Corollary 2.15, for each $1 \leq k \leq K$ there exists a unique real number $0 \leq \theta_i^k \leq 1$ satisfying

$$A_k \approx_i \left[\theta_i^k (A_K), (1 - \theta_i^k)(A_1) \right]. \tag{2.34}$$

We now define a function u_i over the set of compound lotteries $\widehat{\mathcal{L}}$. Suppose $\widehat{L} = [q_1(L_1), \ldots, q_J(L_J)]$ is a compound lottery, in which $q_1, \ldots, q_J$ are nonnegative numbers summing to 1, and $L_1, \ldots, L_J$ are simple lotteries given by $L_j = [p_1^j(A_1), \ldots, p_K^j(A_K)]$.

For each $1 \leq k \leq K$ define

$$r_k = q_1 p_k^1 + q_2 p_k^2 + \cdots + q_J p_k^J. \tag{2.35}$$

This is the probability that the outcome of the lottery is A_k. Define a function u_i on the set of compound lotteries $\widehat{\mathcal{L}}$:

$$u_i(\widehat{L}) = r_1 \theta_i^1 + r_2 \theta_i^2 + \cdots + r_K \theta_i^k. \tag{2.36}$$

It follows from (2.36) that, in particular, every simple lottery $L = [p_1(A_1), \ldots, p_K(A_K)]$ satisfies

$$u_i(L) = \sum_{k=1}^{K} p_k \theta_i^k. \tag{2.37}$$

Step 2: $u_i(A_k) = \theta_i^k$ for all $1 \leq k \leq K$.

Outcome A_k is equivalent to the lottery $L = [1(A_k)]$, which in turn is equivalent to the compound lottery $\widehat{L} = [1(L)]$. The outcome of this lottery $\widehat{L}$ is A_k with probability 1, so that in this case

$$r_l = \begin{cases} 1 & \text{if } l = k, \\ 0 & \text{if } l \neq k. \end{cases} \tag{2.38}$$

We deduce that

$$u_i(A_k) = \theta_i^k, \quad \forall k \in \{1, 2, \ldots, K\}. \tag{2.39}$$

Since $\theta_i^1 = 0$ and $\theta_i^K = 1$, we deduce that in particular $u_i(A_1) = 0$ and $u_i(A_K) = 1$.

Step 3: The function u_i is linear.

To show that u_i is linear, it suffices to show that for each simple lottery $L = [p_1(A_1), \ldots, p_K(A_K)]$,

$$u_i(L) = \sum_{k=1}^{K} p_k u_i(A_k). \tag{2.40}$$

This equation holds, because Equation (2.37) implies that the left-hand side of this equation equals $\sum_{i=1}^{K} p_k \theta_i^k$, and Equation (2.39) implies that the right-hand side also equals $\sum_{i=1}^{K} p_k \theta_i^k$.

Step 4: $\widehat{L} \approx_i [u_i(\widehat{L})(A_K), (1 - u_i(\widehat{L}))(A_1)]$ for every compound lottery $\widehat{L}$.

Let $\widehat{L} = [q_1(L_1), \ldots, q_J(L_J)]$ be a compound lottery, where

$$L_j = [p_1^j(A_1), \ldots, p_K^j(A_K)], \quad \forall j = 1, 2, \ldots, J. \tag{2.41}$$

Denote, as before,

$$r_k = \sum_{j=1}^J q_j p_k^j, \quad \forall k = 1, 2, \ldots, K. \tag{2.42}$$

By the Simplification Axiom,

$$\widehat{L} \approx_i [r_1(A_1), r_2(A_2), \ldots, r_K(A_K)]. \tag{2.43}$$

Denote $M_k = [\theta_i^k(A_K), (1 - \theta_i^k)(A_1)]$ for every $1 \le k \le K$. By definition, $A_k \approx_i M_k$ for every $1 \le k \le K$. Therefore, K applications of the Independence Axiom yield.

$$\widehat{L} \approx_i [r_1(M_1), r_2(M_2), \ldots, r_K(M_K)]. \tag{2.44}$$

Since all the lotteries $(M_k)_{k=1}^K$ are lotteries over outcomes A_1 and A_K, the lottery on the right-hand side of Equation (2.44) is also a lottery over these two outcomes. Therefore, if we denote by r_* the total probability of A_K in the lottery on the right-hand side of Equation (2.44), then

$$r_* = \sum_{k=1}^K r_k \theta_i^k = u_i(\widehat{L}), \tag{2.45}$$

and the Simplification Axiom implies that

$$\widehat{L} \approx_i [r_*(A_K), (1 - r_*)(A_1)] = [u_i(\widehat{L})(A_K), (1 - u_i(\widehat{L}))(A_1)]. \tag{2.46}$$

Step 5: The function u_i is a utility function.

To prove that u_i is a utility function, we need to show that for any pair of compound lotteries $\widehat{L}$ and $\widehat{L}'$,

$$\widehat{L} \succsim_i \widehat{L}' \quad \Longleftrightarrow \quad u_i(\widehat{L}) \ge u_i(\widehat{L}') \quad \forall \widehat{L}_1, \widehat{L}_2 \in \widehat{\mathcal{L}}, \tag{2.47}$$

and this follows from Step 4 and the Monotonicity Axiom. This concludes the proof, under the assumption that $A_K \succ_i A_1$.

We next turn to deal with the degenerate case in which the player is indifferent between all the outcomes:

$$A_1 \approx_i A_2 \approx_i \cdots \approx_i A_K. \tag{2.48}$$

By the Axioms of Independence and Simplification, the player is indifferent between *any* two simple lotteries. To see why, consider the simple lottery $L = [p_1(A_1), \ldots, p_K(A_K)]$. By repeated use of the Axiom of Independence,

$$L \approx_i [p_1(A_1), p_2(A_1), \ldots, p_K(A_1)]. \tag{2.49}$$

The Axiom of Simplification implies that $L \approx_i [1(A_1)]$, so every compound lottery $\widehat{L}$ satisfies $\widehat{L} \approx_i [1(A_1)]$. It follows that the player is indifferent between any two compound lotteries, so that any constant function u_i represents his preference relation. $\qquad\qquad\square$

Theorem 2.18 implies that if a player's preference relation satisfies the von Neumann–Morgenstern axioms, then in order to know the player's preferences over lotteries it suffices to know the utility he attaches to each individual outcome, because the utility of any lottery can then be calculated from these utilities (see Equation (2.37) and Example 2.19).

Note that the linearity of utility functions in the probabilities of the individual outcomes, together with the Axiom of Simplification, implies the linearity of utility functions in the probabilities of simple lotteries. In words, if L_1 and L_2 are simple lotteries and $\widehat{L} = [q(L_1), (1-q)(L_2)]$, then $u_i(\widehat{L}) = qu_i(L_1) + (1-q)u_i(L_2)$ (see Exercise 2.11).

2.5   Utility functions and affine transformations

Definition 2.20 *Let $u : X \rightarrow \mathbb{R}$ be a function. A function $v : X \rightarrow \mathbb{R}$ is a positive affine transformation of u if there exists a positive real number $\alpha > 0$ and a real number β such that*

$$v(x) = \alpha u(x) + \beta, \quad \forall x \in X. \tag{2.50}$$

The definition implies that if v is a positive affine transformation of u, then u is a positive affine transformation of v (Exercise 2.19).

The next theorem states that every affine transformation of a utility function is also a utility function.

Theorem 2.21 *If u_i is a linear utility function representing player i's preference relation $\succsim_i$, then every positive affine transformation of u_i is also a linear utility function representing $\succsim_i$.*

Proof: Let $\succsim_i$ be player i's preference relation, and let $v_i = \alpha u_i + \beta$ be a positive affine transformation of u_i. In particular, $\alpha > 0$. The first step is to show that v_i is a utility function representing $\succsim_i$. Let $\widehat{L}_1$ and $\widehat{L}_2$ be compound lotteries. We will show that $\widehat{L}_1 \succsim_i \widehat{L}_2$ if and only if $v_i(\widehat{L}_1) \geq v_i(\widehat{L}_2)$.

Note that since u_i is a utility function representing $\succsim_i$,

$$\widehat{L}_1 \succsim_i \widehat{L}_2 \iff u_i(\widehat{L}_1) \geq u_i(\widehat{L}_2) \tag{2.51}$$

$$\iff \alpha u_i(\widehat{L}_1) + \beta \geq \alpha u_i(\widehat{L}_2) + \beta \tag{2.52}$$

$$\iff v_i(\widehat{L}_1) \geq v_i(\widehat{L}_2), \tag{2.53}$$

which is what we needed to show.

Next, we need to show that v_i is linear. Let $L = [p_1(A_1), p_2(A_2), \ldots, p_K(A_K)]$ be a simple lottery. Since $p_1 + p_2 + \cdots + p_K = 1$, and u_i is linear, we get

$$v_i(L) = \alpha u_i(L) + \beta \tag{2.54}$$

$$= \alpha(p_1 u_i(A_1) + p_2 u_i(A_2) + \cdots + p_K u_i(A_K)) + (p_1 + p_2 + \cdots + p_K)\beta \tag{2.55}$$

$$= p_1 v_i(A_1) + p_2 v_i(A_2) + \cdots + p_K v_i(A_K), \tag{2.56}$$

which shows that v_i is linear. □

The next theorem states the opposite direction of the previous theorem. Its proof is left to the reader (Exercise 2.21).

Theorem 2.22 *If u_i and v_i are two linear utility functions representing player i's preference relation, where that preference relation satisfies the von Neumann–Morgenstern axioms, then v_i is a positive affine transformation of u_i.*

Corollary 2.23 *A preference relation of a player that satisfies the von Neumann–Morgenstern axioms is representable by a linear utility function that is uniquely determined up to a positive affine transformation.*

2.6 Infinite outcome set

We have so far assumed that the set of outcomes O is finite. A careful review of the proofs reveals that all the results above continue to hold if the following conditions are satisfied:

- The set of outcomes O is any set, finite or infinite.
- The set of simple lotteries $\mathcal{L}$ contains every lottery over a finite number of outcomes.
- The set of compound lotteries $\widehat{\mathcal{L}}$ contains every lottery over a finite number of simple lotteries.
- The player has a complete, reflexive, and transitive preference relation over the set of compound lotteries $\widehat{\mathcal{L}}$.
- There exists a (weakly) most-preferred outcome $A_K \in O$: the player (weakly) prefers A_K to any other outcome in O.
- There exists a (weakly) least-preferred outcome $A_1 \in O$: the player (weakly) prefers any other outcome in O to A_1.

In Exercise 2.22, the reader is asked to check that Theorems 2.18 and 2.22, and Corollary 2.23, hold in this general model.

2.7 Attitude towards risk

There are people who are risk averse, people who are risk neutral, and people who are risk seeking. The risk attitude of an individual can change over time; it may depend, for example, on the individual's family status or financial holdings. How does risk attitude affect a player's utility function?

In this section, we will assume that the set of outcomes is given by the interval $O = [-R, R]$: the real number $x \in [-R, R]$ represents the monetary outcome that the player receives. We will assume that every player prefers receiving more, in dollars, to receiving less, so that $x \succ_i y$ if and only if $x > y$. We will similarly assume that the player has a complete, reflexive, and transitive preference relation over the set of compound lotteries that satisfies the von Neumann–Morgenstern axioms.

Denote by u_i player i's utility function. As previously noted, the function u_i is determined by player i's utility from every outcome of a lottery. These utilities are given by a real-valued function $U_i : \mathbb{R} \to \mathbb{R}$. In words, for every $x \in O$,

$$U_i(x) := u_i([1(x)]). \tag{2.57}$$

Since players are assumed to prefer getting as large a monetary amount as possible, U_i is a monotonically increasing function.

By the assumption that each player's preference relation satisfies the von Neumann–Morgenstern axioms, it follows that for every simple lottery $L = [p_1(x_1), p_2(x_2), \dots, p_K(x_k)]$,

$$u_i(L) = \sum_{k=1}^{K} p_k U_i(x_k) = \sum_{k=1}^{K} p_k u_i([1(x_k)]). \tag{2.58}$$

The significance of this equation is that the utility $u_i(L)$ of a lottery L is the expected utility of the resulting payoff.

Given a lottery $L = [p_1(x_1), p_2(x_2), \dots, p_K(x_k)]$ with a finite number of possible outcomes, we will denote by μ_L the expected value of L, given by

$$\mu_L = \sum_{i=1}^{K} p_k x_k. \tag{2.59}$$

Definition 2.24 *A player i is termed* risk neutral *if for every lottery L with a finite number of possible outcomes,*

$$u_i(L) = u_i([1(\mu_L)]). \tag{2.60}$$

A player i is termed risk averse *if for every lottery L with a finite number of possible outcomes,*

$$u_i(L) \leq u_i([1(\mu_L)]). \tag{2.61}$$

A player i is termed risk seeking *(or risk loving) if for every lottery L with a finite number of possible outcomes,*

$$u_i(L) \geq u_i([1(\mu_L)]). \tag{2.62}$$

Using Definition 2.24, to establish a player's risk attitude, we need to compare the utility he ascribes to every lottery with the utility he ascribes to the expected value of that lottery. Conducting such a comparison can be exhausting, because it involves checking the condition with respect to every possible lottery. The next theorem, whose proof is left to the reader (Exercise 2.23), shows that it suffices to conduct the comparisons only between lotteries involving pairs of outcomes.

Theorem 2.25 *A player i is risk neutral if and only if for each $p \in [0,1]$ and every pair of outcomes $x, y \in \mathbb{R}$,*

$$u_i([p(x), (1-p)(y)]) = u_i([1(px + (1-p)y)]). \tag{2.63}$$

A player i is risk averse if and only if for each $p \in [0,1]$ and every pair of outcomes $x, y \in \mathbb{R}$,

$$u_i([p(x), (1-p)(y)]) \leq u_i([1(px + (1-p)y)]). \tag{2.64}$$

A player i is risk seeking if and only if for each $p \in [0,1]$ and every pair of outcomes $x, y \in \mathbb{R}$,

$$u_i([p(x), (1-p)(y)]) \geq u_i([1(px + (1-p)y)]). \tag{2.65}$$

Example 2.26 Consider a player whose preference relation is represented by the utility function $U_i(x)$ that is depicted in Figure 2.3, which is concave.

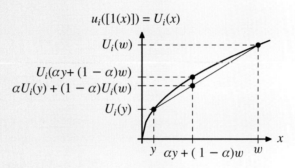

Figure 2.3 The utility function of a risk-averse player

The figure depicts the graph of the function U_i, which associates each x with the utility of the player from definitely receiving outcome x (see Equation (2.57)). We will show that the concavity of the function U_i is an expression of the fact that player i is risk averse. Since the function U_i is concave, the chord connecting the two points on the graph of the function passes underneath the graph. Hence for every $y, w \in \mathbb{R}$ and every $\alpha \in (0, 1)$,

$$u_i([1(\alpha y + (1-\alpha)w))]) = U_i(\alpha y + (1-\alpha)w) \tag{2.66}$$

$$> \alpha U_i(y) + (1-\alpha)U_i(w) \tag{2.67}$$

$$= \alpha u_i([1(y)]) + (1-\alpha)u_i([1(w)]) \tag{2.68}$$

$$= u_i([\alpha(y), (1-\alpha)(w)]). \tag{2.69}$$

In words, player i prefers receiving with certainty the expectation $\alpha y + (1-\alpha)w$ to receiving y with probability α and w with probability $1 - \alpha$, which is precisely what risk aversion means. ◄

As Example 2.26 suggests, one's attitude to risk can be described in simple geometrical terms, using the utility function.

Theorem 2.27 *A player i, whose preference relation satisfies the von Neumann–Morgenstern axioms, is risk neutral if and only if U_i is a linear function, he is risk averse if and only if U_i is a concave function, and he is risk seeking if and only if U_i is a convex function.*

Proof: Since by assumption the player's preference relation satisfies the von Neumann–Morgenstern axioms, the utility of every simple lottery $L = [p_1(x_1), p_2(x_2), \ldots, p_K(x_K)]$ is given by

$$u_i(L) = \sum_{k=1}^{K} p_k u_i([1(x_k)]) = \sum_{k=1}^{K} p_k U_i(x_k). \tag{2.70}$$

A player is risk averse if and only if $u_i(L) \leq u_i([1(\mu_L)]) = U_i(\mu_L)$, or, in other words, if and only if

$$\sum_{k=1}^{K} p_k U_i(x_k) = u_i(L) \leq U_i(\mu_L) = U_i\left(\sum_{k=1}^{K} p_k x_k\right). \tag{2.71}$$

In summary, a player is risk averse if and only if

$$\sum_{k=1}^{K} p_k U_i(x_k) \leq U_i\left(\sum_{k=1}^{K} p_k x_k\right). \tag{2.72}$$

This inequality holds for every $(x_1, x_2, \ldots, x_K)$ and for every vector of nonnegative numbers $(p_1, p_2, \ldots, p_K)$ summing to 1, if and only if U_i is concave. Similarly, player i is risk seeking if and only if

$$\sum_{k=1}^{K} p_k U_i(x_k) \geq U_i\left(\sum_{k=1}^{K} p_k x_k\right). \tag{2.73}$$

This inequality holds for every $(x_1, x_2, \ldots, x_K)$ and for every vector of nonnegative numbers $(p_1, p_2, \ldots, p_K)$ summing to 1, if and only if U_i is convex.

A player is risk neutral if and only if he is both risk seeking and risk averse. Since a function is both concave and convex if and only if it is linear, player i is risk neutral if and only if U_i is linear. □

2.8　Subjective probability

A major milestone in the study of utility theory was attained in 1954, with Leonard Savage's publication of *The Foundations of Statistics*. Savage generalized von Neumann and Morgenstern's model, in which the probability of each outcome in every lottery is "objective" and known to the participants. That model is reasonable when the outcome is determined by a flip of a coin or a toss of dice, but in most of the lotteries we face in real life, probabilities are often unknown. Consider, for example, the probability of a major earthquake occurring over the next year in the San Fernando Valley, or the probability that a particular candidate will win the next presidential election. The exact probabilities of these occurrences are unknown. Different people will differ in their assessments of these probabilities, which are subjective. In addition, as noted above, people often fail to perceive probability correctly, so that their perceptions contradict the laws of probability.

Savage supposed that there is an infinite set of states of the world, Ω; each state of the world is a complete description of all the variables characterizing the players, including the information they have. Players are asked to choose between "gambles," which formally are functions $f : \Omega \to O$. What this means is that if a player chooses gamble f, and the state of the world (i.e., the true reality) is ω, then the outcome the player receives is $f(\omega)$. Players are assumed to have complete, reflexive, and transitive preference relations over the set of all gambles. For example, if $E, F \subset \Omega$ are two events, and A_1, A_2, A_3, and A_4 are outcomes, a player can compare a gamble in which he receives A_1 if the true state is in E and A_2 if the true state is not in E, with a gamble in which he receives A_3 if the true state is in F and A_4 if the true state is not in F.

Savage proved that if the preference relation of player i satisfies certain axioms, then there exists a probability distribution q_i over Ω and a function $u_i : O \to \mathbb{R}$ representing player i's preference relation. In other words, the player, by preferring one gamble to another, behaves as if he is maximizing expected utility, where the expected utility is calculated using the probability distribution q_i:

$$u_i(f) = \int_\Omega u_i(f(\omega)) dq_i(\omega). \tag{2.74}$$

Similarly to von Neumann–Morgenstern utility, the utility of f is the expected value of the utility of the outcomes, with q_i representing player i's subjective probability, and utility u_i representing the player's preferences (whether or not he is conscious of using a probability distribution and a utility function at all).

A further development in subjective probability theory, slightly different from Savage's, was published by Anscombe and Aumann [1963].

2.9   Discussion

Theoretically, a simple interview is all that is needed to ascertain a player's utility function, assuming his preference relation satisfies the von Neumann–Morgenstern axioms. One can set the utility of A_1, the least-preferred outcome, to be 0, the utility of A_k, the most-preferred outcome, to be 1, and then find, for every $k \in \{2, 3, \ldots, K-1\}$, the values of θ_i^k such that the player is indifferent between A_K and the lottery $[\theta_i^k(A_K), (1-\theta_i^k)(A_1)]$.

Experimental evidence shows that in interviews, people often give responses that indicate their preferences do not always satisfy the von Neumann–Morgenstern axioms. Here are some examples.

2.9.1   The assumption of completeness

The assumption of completeness appears to be very reasonable, but it should not be regarded as self-evident. There are cases in which people find it difficult to express clear preferences between outcomes. For example, imagine a child whose parents are divorced, who is asked whether he prefers a day with his mother or his father. Many children find the choice too difficult, and refuse to answer the question.

2.9.2   The assumption of transitivity

Give a person a sufficiently large set of choices between outcomes, and you are likely to discover that his declared preferences contradict the assumption of transitivity. Some of these "errors" can be corrected by presenting the player with evidence of inconsistencies, careful analysis of the answers, and attempts to correct the player's valuations.

Violations of transitivity are not always due to inconsistencies on the part of an individual player. If a "player" is actually composed of a group of individuals, each of whom has a transitive preference relation, it is possible for the group's collective preferences to be non-transitive. The next example illustrates this phenomenon.

Example 2.28   The Condorcet Paradox   Three alternative political policies, A, B, and C, are being debated. It is suggested that a referendum be conducted to choose between them. The voters, however, have divided opinions on the relative preferences between the policies, as follows:

$$
\begin{array}{ll}
\text{Democrats:} & A >_D B >_D C \\
\text{Republicans:} & B >_R C >_R A \\
\text{Independents:} & C >_I A >_I B
\end{array}
$$

Suppose that the population is roughly equally divided between Democrats, Republicans, and Independents. It is possible to fashion a referendum that will result in a nearly two-thirds majority approving any one of the alternative policies. For example, if the referendum asks the electorate to choose between A and B, a majority will vote $A > B$. If, instead, the referendum presents a choice between B and C, a majority will vote $B > C$; and a similar result can be fashioned for $C > A$. Which of these three policies, then, can we say the electorate prefers?

The lack of transitivity in preferences resulting from the use of the majority rule is an important subject in "social choice theory" (see Chapter 22). This was first studied by Condorcet[3] (see Example 22.1 on page 902). ◀

2.9.3   Perceptions of probability

If a person's preference relation over three possible outcomes A, B, and C satisfies $A > B > C$, we may by trial and error present him with various different probability values p, until we eventually identify a value p_0 such that

$$ B \approx [p_0(A), (1 - p_0)(C)]. \tag{2.75} $$

Let's say, for example, that the player reports that he is indifferent between the following:

$$ \$7,000 \approx \left[\tfrac{2}{3}(\$20,000), \tfrac{1}{3}(\$0)\right]. \tag{2.76} $$

Empirically, however, if the same person is asked how large x must be in order for him to be indifferent between the following:

$$ \$7,000 \approx \left[\tfrac{2}{3}(\$x), \tfrac{1}{3}(\$0)\right], \tag{2.77} $$

the answer often[4] differs from $20,000.

---

3 Marie Jean Antoine Nicolas Caritat, Marquis de Condorcet, 1743–94, was a French philosopher and mathematician who wrote about political science.

4 The authors wish to thank Reinhard Selten for providing them with this example.

This shows that the perceptions of probability that often occur naturally to decision makers may diverge from the mathematical formulations. People are not born with internal calculators, and we must accept the fact that what people perceive may not always follow the laws of probability.

2.9.4 The Axiom of Simplification

The Axiom of Simplification states that the utility of a compound lottery depends solely on the probability it eventually assigns to each outcome. We have already noted that this ignores other aspects of compound lotteries; for example, it ignores the pleasure (or lack of pleasure) a participant gains from the very act of participating in a lottery. It is therefore entirely possible that a person may prefer a compound lottery to a simple lottery with exactly the same outcome probabilities, or vice versa.

2.9.5 Other aspects that can influence preferences

People's preferences change over time and with changing circumstances. A person may prefer steak to roast beef today, and roast beef to steak tomorrow.

One also needs to guard against drawing conclusions regarding preferences to quickly given answers to interview questions, because the answers are liable to depend on the information available to the player. Take, for example, the following story, based on a similar story appearing in Luce and Raiffa [1957]. A man at a restaurant asks a waiter to list the available items on the menu. The waiter replies "steak and roast beef." The man orders the roast beef. A few minutes later, the waiter returns and informs him that he forgot to note an additional item on the menu, filet mignon. "In that case," says the restaurant guest, "I'll have the steak, please."

Does this behavior reveal inconsistency in preferences? Not necessarily. The man may love steak, but may also be concerned that in most restaurants, the steak is not served sufficiently tender to his taste. He therefore orders the roast beef, confident that most chefs know how to cook a decent roast. When he is informed that the restaurant serves filet mignon, he concludes that there is a high-quality chef in the kitchen, and feels more confident in the chef's ability to prepare a tender steak.

In other words, the fact that given a choice between steak and roast beef, a player chooses roast beef, does not necessarily mean that he prefers roast beef to steak. It may only indicate that the quality of the steak is unknown, in which case choosing "steak" may translate into a lottery between quality steak and intolerable steak. Before receiving additional information, the player ascribes low probability to receiving quality steak. After the additional information has been given, the probability of quality steak increases in the player's estimation, thus affecting his choice. The player's preference of steak to roast beef has not changed at all over time, but rather his perception of the lottery with which he is presented.

This story illustrates how additional information can bring about changes in choices without contradicting the assumptions of utility theory.

Another story, this one a true event that occurred during the Second World War on the Pacific front,[5] seems to contradict utility theory. A United States bomber squadron, charged with bombing Tokyo, was based on the island of Saipan, 3000 kilometers from the bombers' targets. Given the vast distance the bombers had to cover, they flew without fighter-plane accompaniment and carried few bombs, in order to cut down on fuel consumption. Each pilot was scheduled to rotate back to the United States after 30 successful bombing runs, but Japanese air defenses were so efficient that only half the pilots sent on the missions managed to survive 30 bombing runs.

Experts in operations research calculated a way to raise the odds of overall pilot survival by increasing the bomb load carried by each plane – at the cost of placing only enough fuel in each plane to travel in one direction. The calculations indicated that increasing the number of bombs per plane would significantly reduce the number of required bombing runs, enabling three-quarters of the pilots to be rotated back to the United States immediately, without requiring them to undertake any more missions. The remaining pilots, however, would face certain death, since they would have no way of returning to base after dropping their bombs over Tokyo.

If the pilots who are sent home are chosen randomly, then the pilots were, in fact, being offered the lottery

$$\left[\tfrac{3}{4}(\text{Life}), \tfrac{1}{4}(\text{Death}) \right],$$

in place of their existing situation, which was equivalent to the lottery

$$\left[\tfrac{1}{2}(\text{Life}), \tfrac{1}{2}(\text{Death}) \right].$$

Every single pilot rejected the suggested lottery outright. They all preferred their existing situation.

Were the pilots lacking a basic understanding of probability? Were they contradicting the von Neumann–Morgenstern axioms? One possible explanation for why they failed to act in accordance with the axioms is that they were optimists by nature, believing that "it will not happen to me." But there are other explanations, that do not necessarily lead to a rejection of standard utility theory. The choice between life and death may not have been the only factor that the pilots took into account. There may also have been moral issues, such as taboos against sending some comrades on certain suicide missions while others got to return home safely. In addition, survival rates are not fixed in war situations. There was always the chance that the war would take a dramatic turn, rendering the suicide missions unnecessary, or that another ingenious solution would be found. And indeed, a short time after the suicide mission suggestion was raised, American forces captured the island of Iwo Jima. The air base in Iwo Jima was sufficiently close to Tokyo, only 600 kilometers away, to enable fighter planes to accompany the bombers, significantly raising the survival rates of American bombers, and the suicide mission suggestion was rapidly consigned to oblivion.[6]

---

5 The story was related to the authors by Kenneth Arrow, who heard of it from Merrill F. Flood.
6 Bombing missions emanating from Iwo Jima also proved to be largely inefficient – only ten such missions were attempted – but American military advances in the Spring of 1945 rapidly made those unnecessary as well.

2.10 Remarks

The authors wish to thank Tzachi Gilboa and Peter Wakker for answering several questions that arose during the composition of this chapter.

The Sure-Thing Principle, which appears in Exercise 2.12, first appeared in Savage [1954]. The property described in Exercise 2.13 is a strong version of the independence property introduced in Marschak [1950] and Nash [1950a]. The property described in Exercise 2.14 is called "Betweenness." Exercise 2.15 is based on a column written by John Branch in *The New York Times* on August 30, 2010. Exercise 2.25 is based on Rothschild and Stiglitz [1970], which also contains an example of the phenomenon appearing in Exercise 2.27. The Arrow–Pratt measure of absolute risk aversion, which appears in Exercise 2.28, was first defined by Arrow [1965] and Pratt [1964].

2.11 Exercises

2.1 Prove the following claims:

(a) A strict preference relation $>$ is anti-symmetric and transitive.[7]
(b) An indifference relation $\approx$ is symmetric and transitive.[8]

2.2 Prove Theorem 2.7 (page 11): let O be a set of outcomes, and let $\succsim$ be a complete, reflexive, and transitive relation over O. Suppose that u is a utility function representing $\succsim$. Prove that for every monotonically increasing function $v : \mathbb{R} \to \mathbb{R}$, the composition $v \circ u$ defined by

$$(v \circ u)(x) = v(u(x)) \tag{2.78}$$

is also a utility function representing $\succsim$.

2.3 Give an example of a countable set of outcomes O and a preference relation $\succsim$ over O, such that every utility function representing $\succsim$ must include values that are not integers.

2.4 Prove Theorem 2.14 (page 17): if a transitive preference relation $\succsim_i$ satisfies the axioms of continuity and monotonicity, and if $A \succsim_i B \succsim_i C$ and $A >_i C$, then there exists a unique number $\theta_i \in [0, 1]$ that satisfies

$$B \approx_i [\theta_i(A), (1 - \theta_i)(C)]. \tag{2.79}$$

2.5 Prove that the von Neumann–Morgenstern axioms are independent. In other words, for every axiom there exists a set of outcomes and a preference relation that does not satisfy that axiom but does satisfy the other three axioms.

---

7 A relation $>$ is *anti-symmetric* if for each x, y, if $x > y$, then it is not the case that $y > x$.
8 A relation $\approx$ is *symmetric* if for each x, y, if $x \approx y$, then $y \approx x$.

2.6 Prove the converse of Theorem 2.18 (page 19): if there exists a linear utility function representing a preference relation $\succsim_i$ of player i, then $\succsim_i$ satisfies the von Neumann–Morgenstern axioms.

2.7 Suppose that a person whose preferences satisfy the von Neumann–Morgenstern axioms, and who always prefers more money to less money, says that:

- he is indifferent between receiving \$500 and participating in a lottery in which he receives \$1,000 with probability $\frac{2}{3}$ and receives \$0 with probability $\frac{1}{3}$;
- he is indifferent between receiving \$100 and participating in a lottery in which he receives \$500 with probability $\frac{3}{8}$ and receives \$0 with probability $\frac{5}{8}$.

   (a) Find a linear utility function representing this person's preferences, and in addition satisfying $u(\$1,000) = 1$ and $u(\$0) = 0$.

   (b) Determine which of the following two lotteries will be preferred by this person:

- A lottery in which he receives \$1,000 with probability $\frac{3}{10}$, \$500 with probability $\frac{1}{10}$, \$100 with probability $\frac{1}{2}$, and \$0 with probability $\frac{1}{10}$.
- A lottery in which he receives \$1,000 with probability $\frac{2}{10}$, \$500 with probability $\frac{3}{10}$, \$100 with probability $\frac{2}{10}$, and \$0 with probability $\frac{3}{10}$.

   (c) Is it possible to ascertain which of the following two lotteries he will prefer? Justify your answer.

- A lottery in which he receives \$1,000 with probability $\frac{3}{10}$, \$500 with probability $\frac{1}{10}$, \$100 with probability $\frac{1}{2}$, and \$0 with probability $\frac{1}{10}$.
- Receiving \$400 with probability 1.

   (d) Is it possible to ascertain which of the following two lotteries he will prefer? Justify your answer.

- A lottery in which he receives \$1,000 with probability $\frac{3}{10}$, \$500 with probability $\frac{1}{10}$, \$100 with probability $\frac{1}{2}$, and \$0 with probability $\frac{1}{10}$.
- Receiving \$600 with probability 1.

2.8 How would the preferences between the two lotteries in Exercise 2.7(b) change if $u(\$1,000) = 8$ and $u(\$0) = 3$? Justify your answer.

2.9 Suppose that a person whose preferences satisfy the von Neumann–Morgenstern axioms says that his preferences regarding outcomes A, B, C, and D satisfy

$$C \approx_i \left[\tfrac{3}{5}(A), \tfrac{2}{5}(D)\right], \quad B \approx_i \left[\tfrac{3}{4}(A), \tfrac{1}{4}(C)\right], \quad A >_i D. \qquad (2.80)$$

Determine which of the following two lotteries will be preferred by this person:

$$L_1 = \left[\tfrac{2}{5}(A), \tfrac{1}{5}(B), \tfrac{1}{5}(C), \tfrac{1}{5}(D)\right] \text{ or } L_2 = \left[\tfrac{2}{5}(B), \tfrac{3}{5}(C)\right]. \qquad (2.81)$$

2.10 What would be your answer to Exercise 2.9 if $D >_i A$ instead of $A >_i D$? Relate your answer to this exercise with your answer to Exercise 2.9.

2.11 Prove that if u_i is a linear utility function, then

$$u_i(\widehat{L}) = \sum_{j=1}^{J} q_j u_i(L_j) \tag{2.82}$$

is satisfied for every compound lottery $\widehat{L} = [q_1(L_1), q_2(L_2), \ldots, q_J(L_J)]$.

2.12 **The Sure-Thing Principle** Prove that a preference relation that satisfies the von Neumann–Morgenstern axioms also satisfies

$$[\alpha(L_1), (1 - \alpha)(L_3)] \succ [\alpha(L_2), (1 - \alpha)(L_3)] \tag{2.83}$$

if and only if

$$[\alpha(L_1), (1 - \alpha)(L_4)] \succ [\alpha(L_2), (1 - \alpha)(L_4)] \tag{2.84}$$

for any four lotteries L_1, L_2, L_3, L_4, and any $\alpha \in [0, 1]$.

2.13 Suppose a person whose preferences satisfy the von Neumann–Morgenstern axioms says that with respect to lotteries L_1, L_2, L_3, L_4, his preferences are $L_1 \succ L_2$ and $L_3 \succ L_4$. Prove that for all $0 \leq \alpha \leq 1$,

$$[\alpha(L_1), (1 - \alpha)(L_3)] \succ [\alpha(L_2), (1 - \alpha)(L_4)]. \tag{2.85}$$

2.14 Suppose a person whose preferences satisfy the von Neumann–Morgenstern axioms says that with respect to lotteries L_1 and L_2, his preference is $L_1 \succ L_2$. Prove that for all $0 < \alpha \leq 1$,

$$[\alpha(L_1), (1 - \alpha)(L_2)] \succ L_2. \tag{2.86}$$

2.15 A tennis player who is serving at the beginning of a point has two attempts to serve; if the ball does not land within the white lines of the opponent's court on his first attempt, he receives a second attempt. If the second attempt also fails to land in the opponent's court, the serving player loses the point. If the ball lands in the opponent's court during either attempt, the players volley the ball over the net until one or the other player wins the point.

While serving, a player has two alternatives. He may strike the ball with great force, or with medium force. Statistics gathered from a large number of tennis matches indicate that if the server strikes the ball with great force, the ball lands in the opponent's court with probability 0.65, with the server subsequently winning the point with probability 0.75. If, however, the server strikes the ball with medium force, the ball lands in the opponent's court with probability 0.9, with the server subsequently winning the point with probability 0.5.

In most cases, servers strike the ball with great force on their first-serve attempts, and with medium force on their second attempts.

(a) Assume that there are two possible outcomes: winning a point or losing a point, and that the server's preference relation over compound lotteries satisfies the von Neumann–Morgenstern axioms. Find a linear utility function representing the server's preference relation.

(b) Write down the compound lottery that takes place when the server strikes the ball with great force, and when he strikes the ball with medium force.

(c) The server has four alternatives: two alternatives in his first serve attempt (striking the ball with great force or with medium force), and similarly two alternatives in his second serve attempt if the first attempt failed. Write down the compound lotteries corresponding to each of these four alternatives. Note that in this case the compound lotteries are of order 3: lotteries over lotteries over lotteries.

(d) Which compound lottery is most preferred by the server, out of the four compound lotteries you identified in item (c) above? Is this alternative the one chosen by most tennis players?

2.16 Ron eats yogurt every morning. Ron especially loves yogurt that comes with a small attached container containing white and dark chocolate balls, which he mixes into his yogurt prior to eating it. Because Ron prefers white chocolate to dark chocolate, he counts the number of white chocolate balls in the container, his excitement climbing higher the greater the number of white chocolate balls. One day, Ron's brother Tom has an idea for increasing his brother's happiness: he will write to the company producing the yogurt and ask them to place only white chocolate balls in the containers attached to the yogurt! To Tom's surprise, Ron opposes this idea: he prefers the current situation, in which he does not know how many white chocolate balls are in the container, to the situation his brother is proposing, in which he knows that each container has only white chocolate balls. Answer the following questions.

(a) Write down the set of outcomes in this situation, and Ron's preference relation over those outcomes.

(b) Does Ron's preference relation over lotteries satisfy the von Neumann–Morgenstern axioms? Justify your answer.

2.17 A farmer wishes to dig a well in a square field whose coordinates are $(0,0)$, $(0, 1000)$, $(1000, 0)$, and $(1000, 1000)$. The well must be located at a point whose coordinates (x, y) are integers. The farmer's preferences are lexicographic: if $x_1 > x_2$, he prefers that the well be dug at the point (x_1, y_1) to the point (x_2, y_2), for all y_1, y_2. If $x_1 = x_2$, he prefers the first point only if $y_1 > y_2$.

Does there exist a preference relation over compound lotteries over pairs of integers (x, y), $0 \leq x, y \leq 1000$, that satisfies the von Neumann–Morgenstern axioms and extends the lexicographic preference relation? If so, give an example of a linear utility function representing such a preference relation, and if not, explain why such a preference relation does not exist.

2.18 In this exercise, we will show that in the situation described in Exercise 2.17, when the coordinates (x, y) can be any real numbers in the square $[0, 1000]^2$, there does not exist a utility function that represents the lexicographic preference relation. Suppose, by contradiction, that there does exist a preference relation over $[0, 1000]^2$ that represents the lexicographic preference relation.

(a) Prove that for each $(x, y) \in [0, 1000]^2$ there exists a unique $\theta_{x,y} \in [0, 1]$ such that the farmer is indifferent between locating the well at point (x, y) and a lottery in which the well is located at point $(0,0)$ with probability $1 - \theta_{x,y}$ and located at point $(1000, 1000)$ with probability $\theta_{x,y}$.

(b) Prove that the function $(x, y) \mapsto \theta_{x,y}$ is injective, that is, $\theta_{x',y'} \neq \theta_{x,y}$ whenever $(x', y') \neq (x, y)$.

(c) For each x, define $A_x := \{\theta_{x,y} : y \in [0, 1000]\}$. Prove that for each x the set A_x contains at least two elements, and that the sets $\{A_x, x \in [0, 1]\}$ are pairwise disjoint.

(d) Prove that if $x_1 < x_2$ then $\theta_1 < \theta_2$ for all $\theta_1 \in A_{x_1}$ and for all $\theta_2 \in A_{x_2}$.

(e) Prove that there does not exist a set $\{A_x : x \in [0; 1]\}$ satisfying (c) and (d).

(f) Deduce that there does not exist a utility function over $[0, 1000]^2$ that represents the lexicographic preference relation.

(g) Which of the von Neumann–Morgenstern axioms is not satisfied by the preference relation in this exercise?

2.19 Prove that if v is a positive affine transformation of u, then u is a positive affine transformation of v.

2.20 Prove that if v is a positive affine transformation of u, and if w is a positive affine transformation of v, then w is a positive affine transformation of u.

2.21 Prove Theorem 2.22 (page 23): suppose a person's preferences, which satisfy the von Neumann–Morgenstern axioms, are representable by two linear utility functions u and v. Prove that v is a positive affine transformation of u.

2.22 Let O be an infinite set of outcomes. Let $\mathcal{L}$ be the set of all lotteries over a finite number of outcomes in O, and let $\hat{\mathcal{L}}$ be the set of all compound lotteries over a finite number of simple lotteries in $\mathcal{L}$. Suppose that a player has a complete, reflexive, and transitive preference relation $\succeq$ over the set of compound lotteries $\hat{\mathcal{L}}$ that satisfies the von Neumann–Morgenstern axioms, and also satisfies the property that O contains a most-preferred outcome A_K, and a least-preferred outcome A_1, that is, $A_K \succeq A \succeq A_1$ holds for every outcome A in O. Answer the following questions:

(a) Prove Theorem 2.18 (page 19): there exists a linear utility function that represents the player's preference relation.

(b) Prove Theorem 2.22 (page 23): if u and v are two linear utility functions of the player that represent $\succsim$, then v is a positive affine transformation of u.

(c) Prove Corollary 2.23 (page 23): there exists a unique linear utility function (up to a positive affine transformation) representing the player's preference relation.

2.23 Prove Theorem 2.25 on page 25.

2.24 Recall that a linear utility function u_i over lotteries with outcomes in the interval $[-R, R]$ defines a utility function U_i over payoffs in the interval $[-R, R]$ by setting $U_i(x) := u_i([1(x)])$. In the other direction, every function $U_i : [-R, R] \to \mathbb{R}$ defines a linear utility function u_i over lotteries with outcomes in the interval $[-R, R]$ by $u_i([p_1(x_1), p_2(x_2), \ldots, p_K(x_K)]) := \sum_{k=1}^{K} p_k U_i(x_k)$.

For each of the following functions U_i defined on $[-R, R]$, determine whether it defines a linear utility function of a risk-neutral, risk-averse, or risk-seeking player, or none of the above: (a) $2x + 5$, (b) $-7x + 5$, (c) $7x - 5$, (d) x^2, (e) x^3, (f) e^x, (g) $\ln(x)$, (h) x for $x \geq 0$, and $6x$ for $x < 0$, (i) $6x$ for $x \geq 0$, and x for $x < 0$, (j) $x^{3/2}$ for $x \geq 0$, and x for $x < 0$, (k) $x/\ln(2 + x)$ for $x \geq 0$, and x for $x < 0$. Justify your answers.

2.25 In this exercise, we show that a risk-averse player dislikes the addition of noise to a lottery.

Let $U : \mathbb{R} \to \mathbb{R}$ be a concave function, let X be a random variable with a finite expected value, and let Y be a random variable that is independent of X and has an expected value 0. Define $Z = X + Y$. Prove that $\mathbf{E}[U(X)] \geq \mathbf{E}[U(Z)]$.

2.26 In this exercise, we show that in choosing between two random variables with the same expected value, each with a normal distribution, a risk-averse player will prefer the random variable that has a smaller variance.

Let $U : \mathbb{R} \to \mathbb{R}$ be a concave function, and let X be a random variable with a normal distribution, expected value μ, and standard deviation σ. Let $\lambda > 1$, and let Y be a random variable with a normal distribution, expected value μ, and standard deviation $\lambda\sigma$.

(a) Prove that $U(\mu + c) + U(\mu - c) \geq U(\mu + c\lambda) + U(\mu - c\lambda)$ for all $c > 0$.

(b) By a proper change of variable, and using item (a) above, prove that

$$\int_{-\infty}^{\infty} u(x) \frac{1}{\sqrt{2\pi}\sigma} e^{-\frac{(x-\mu)^2}{2\sigma}} dx \geq \int_{-\infty}^{\infty} u(y) \frac{1}{\sqrt{2\pi}\lambda\sigma} e^{-\frac{(y-\mu)^2}{2\lambda\sigma}} dy. \quad (2.87)$$

(c) Conclude that $\mathbf{E}[U(X)] \geq \mathbf{E}[U(Y)]$.

2.27 In Exercises 2.25 and 2.26, a risk-averse player, in choosing between two random variables with the same expected value, prefers the random variable with smaller variance. This exercise shows that this does not always hold: sometimes a risk-averse player called upon to choose between two random variables with the same expected value will actually prefer the random variable with greater variance.

Let $U(x) = 1 - e^{-x}$ be a player's utility function.

(a) Is the player risk averse, risk neutral, or risk seeking? Justify your answer.

For each $a \in (0, 1)$ and each $p \in (0, 1)$, let $X_{a,p}$ be a random variable whose distribution is

$$\mathbf{P}(X_{a,p} = 1 - a) = \frac{1-p}{2}, \quad \mathbf{P}(X_{a,p} = 1) = p, \quad \mathbf{P}(X_{a,p} = 1 + a) = \frac{1-p}{2}.$$

(b) Calculate the expected value $\mathbf{E}[X_{a,p}]$ and the variance $\mathrm{Var}(X_{a,p})$ for each $a \in (0, 1)$ and each $p \in (0, 1)$.

(c) Let $c^2 = a^2(1 - p)$. Show that the expected value of the lottery $X_{a,p}$ is given by

$$\mathbf{E}[U(X_{a,p})] = 1 - \frac{1}{2e}\left((e^a + e^{-a} + 2)\frac{c^2}{a^2} - 2\right), \quad (2.88)$$

which is not a constant function in a and p.

(d) Show that there exist $a_1, a_2, p_1, p_2 \in (0, 1)$ such that

$$\mathbf{E}[X_{a_1,p_1}] = \mathbf{E}[X_{a_2,p_2}], \text{ and } \mathrm{Var}(X_{a_1,p_1}) = \mathrm{Var}(X_{a_2,p_2}), \tag{2.89}$$

but $\mathbf{E}[U(X_{a_1,p_1})] < \mathbf{E}[U(X_{a_2,p_2})]$.

(e) Conclude that there exist $a_1, a_2, p_1, p_2 \in (0, 1)$ such that

$$\mathbf{E}[X_{a_1,p_1}] = \mathbf{E}[X_{a_2,p_2}], \quad \mathrm{Var}(X_{a_1,p_1}) < \mathrm{Var}(X_{a_2,p_2}),$$
$$\text{and} \quad \mathbf{E}[U(X_{a_1,p_1})] < \mathbf{E}[U(X_{a_2,p_2})]. \tag{2.90}$$

2.28 The Arrow–Pratt measure of absolute risk aversion Let U_i be a monotonically increasing, strictly concave, and twice continuously differentiable function over $\mathbb{R}$, and let i be a player for which U_i is his utility function for money. The Arrow–Pratt measure of absolute risk aversion for player i is

$$r_{U_i}(x) := -\frac{U_i''(x)}{U_i'(x)}. \tag{2.91}$$

The purpose of this exercise is to understand the meaning of this measure.

(a) Suppose the player has $\$x$, and is required to participate in a lottery in which he stands to gain or lose a small amount $\$h$, with equal probability. Denote by Y the amount of money the player will have after the lottery is conducted. Calculate the expected value of Y, $\mathbf{E}[Y]$, and the variance of Y, $\mathrm{Var}(Y)$.

(b) What is the utility of the lottery, $u_i(Y)$, for this player? What is the player's utility loss due to the fact that he is required to participate in the lottery; in other words, what is $\Delta u_h := U_i(x) - u_i(Y)$?

(c) Prove that $\lim_{h \to 0} \frac{\Delta u_h}{h^2} = -\frac{U_i''(x)}{2}$.

(d) Denote by $y_{x,h}$ the amount of money that satisfies $u_i(y_{x,h}) = u_i(Y)$, and by Δx_h the difference $\Delta x_h := x - y_{x,h}$. Explain why $\Delta x_h \geq 0$. Make use of the following figure in order to understand the significance of the various sizes.

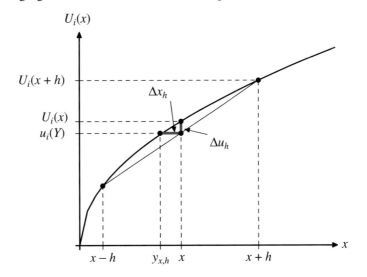

(e) Using the fact that $\lim_{h \to 0} \frac{\Delta u_h}{\Delta x_h} = U_i'(x)$, and your answers to the items (b) and (d) above, prove that

$$\lim_{h \to 0} \frac{\Delta x_h}{\text{Var}(Y)} = -\frac{U_i''(x)}{2U_i'(x)} = \tfrac{1}{2} r_{U_i}(x). \tag{2.92}$$

We can now understand the meaning of the Arrow–Pratt measure of absolute risk aversion $r_{U_i}(x)$: it is the sum of money, multiplied by the constant $\frac{1}{2}$, that a player starting out with $\$x$ is willing to pay in order to avoid participating in a fair lottery over an infinitesimal amount $\$h$ with expected value 0, measured in units of lottery variance.

(f) Calculate the Arrow–Pratt measure of absolute risk aversion for the following utility functions: (a) $U_i(x) = x^\alpha$ for $0 < \alpha < 1$, (b) $U_i(x) = 1 - e^{-\alpha x}$ for $\alpha > 0$.

(g) A function U_i exhibits *constant absolute risk aversion* if r_{U_i} is a constant function (i.e., does not depend on x). It exhibits *increasing absolute risk aversion* if r_{U_i} is an increasing function in x, and exhibits *decreasing absolute risk aversion* if r_{U_i} is a decreasing function in x. Check which functions in part (f) exhibit constant, increasing, or decreasing absolute risk aversion.

2.29 Which of the von Neumann–Morgenstern axioms were violated by the preferences expressed by the Second World War pilots in the story described on page 30?

3 Extensive-form games

Chapter summary

In this chapter we introduce a graphic way of describing a game, the description in *extensive form*, which depicts the rules of the game, the order in which the players make their moves, the information available to players when they are called to take an action, the termination rules, and the outcome at any terminal point. A game in extensive form is given by a *game tree*, which consists of a directed graph in which the set of vertices represents positions in the game, and a distinguished vertex, called the *root*, represents the starting position of the game. A vertex with no outgoing edges represents a terminal position in which play ends. To each terminal vertex corresponds an outcome that is realized when the play terminates at that vertex. Any nonterminal vertex represents either a chance move (e.g., a toss of a die or a shuffle of a deck of cards) or a move of one of the players. To any chance-move vertex corresponds a probability distribution over the edges emanating from that vertex, which correspond to the possible outcomes of the chance move.

To describe games with imperfect information, in which players do not necessarily know the full board position (like poker), we introduce the notion of *information sets*. An information set of a player is a set of decision vertices of the player that are indistinguishable by him given his information at that stage of the game. A game of *perfect information* is a game in which all information sets consist of a single vertex. In such a game, whenever a player is called to take an action, he knows the exact history of actions and chance moves that led to that position.

A *strategy* of a player is a function that assigns to each of his information sets an action available to him at that information set. A path from the root to a terminal vertex is called a *play* of the game. When the game has no chance moves, any vector of strategies (one for each player) determines the play of the game, and hence the outcome. In a game with chance moves, any vector of strategies determines a probability distribution over the possible outcomes of the game.

This chapter presents the theory of games in extensive form. It will be shown that many familiar games, including the game of chess studied in Chapter 1, can be described formally as extensive-form games, and that Theorem 1.4 can be generalized to every finite extensive-form game.

3.1 An example

How does one describe a game? Every description of a game must include the following elements:

- A set of players (decision makers).
- The possible actions available to each player.
- Rules determining the order in which players make their moves.
- A rule determining when the game ends.
- A rule determining the outcome of every possible game ending.

A natural way to depict a game is graphically, where every player's action is depicted as a transition from one vertex to another vertex in a graph (as we saw in Figure 1.1 for the game of chess).

Example 3.1 Consider the simple game shown in Figure 3.1. We start with a table with four squares, labeled 1, 2, 3, and 4.

2	4
1	3

Figure 3.1 The game board in Example 3.1

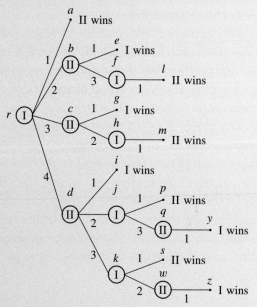

Figure 3.2 The game tree in Example 3.1

Two players, labeled Players I and II, participate in the game. Player I has the opening move, in which he "captures" one of the squares. By alternate turns, each player captures one of the squares, subject to the following conditions:

1. A square may be captured by a player only if it has not been previously captured by either player.
2. Square 4 may not be captured if Square 2 or Square 3 has been previously captured.
3. The game ends when Square 1 is captured. The player who captures Square 1 is the losing player.

A graphic depiction of this game appears in Figure 3.2.

Every circled vertex in Figure 3.2 represents a decision by a player, and is labeled with the number of that player. The terminal vertices of the game are indicated by dark dots. The edges of the graph depict game actions. The number that appears next to each edge corresponds to the square that is captured. Next to every terminal vertex, the corresponding game outcome is indicated. A game depicted by such a graph is called a **game in extensive form**, or **extensive-form game**. ◄

As the example illustrates, a graph that describes a game has a special structure, and is sometimes called a **game tree**. To provide a formal definition of a game tree, we first define a tree.

3.2   Graphs and trees

Definition 3.2 *A (finite) directed graph is a pair $G = (V, E)$, where:*

- *V is a finite set, whose elements are called vertices.*
- *$E \subseteq V \times V$ is a finite set of pairs of vertices, whose elements are called edges. Each directed edge is composed of two vertices: the two ends of the edge (it is possible for both ends of a single edge to be the same vertex).*

A convenient way of depicting a graph geometrically is by representing each vertex by a dot and each edge by an arrow (a straight line, an arc, or a circle) connecting two vertices. Illustrative examples of geometric depictions of graphs are presented in Figure 3.3.

Remark 3.3 *Most of the games that are described in this book are finite games, and can therefore be represented by finite graphs. But there are infinite games, whose representation requires infinite graphs.* ◆

Definition 3.4 *Let x^1 and x^{K+1} be two vertices in a graph G. A path from x^1 to x^{K+1} is a finite sequence of vertices and edges of the form*

$$x^1, e^1, x^2, e^2, \ldots, e^K, x^{K+1} \tag{3.1}$$

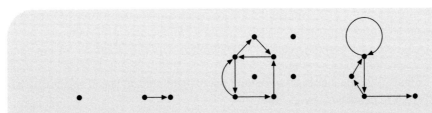

Figure 3.3 Examples of graphs

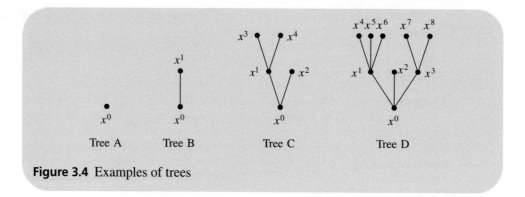

Figure 3.4 Examples of trees

in which the vertices are distinct: $e^k \neq e^l$ for every $k \neq l$ and for $1 \leq k \leq K$, the edge e^k connects vertex x^k with vertex x^{k+1}. The number K is called the path length. *A path is called* cyclic *if $K \geq 1$ and $x^1 = x^{K+1}$.*

Definition 3.5 *A* tree *is a triple $G = (V, E, x^0)$, where (V, E) is a directed graph, $x^0 \in V$ is a vertex called the* root *of the tree, and for every vertex $x \in V$ there is a unique path in the graph from x^0 to x.*

The definition of a tree implies that a graph containing only one vertex is a tree: the triple $(\{x^0\}, \emptyset, x^0)$ is a tree. The requirement that for each vertex $x \in V$ there exists a unique path from the root to x guarantees that if there is an edge from a vertex $\hat{x}$ to a vertex x then $\hat{x}$ is "closer" to the root than x: the path leading from the root to x passes through $\hat{x}$ (while the path from the root to $\hat{x}$ does not pass through x). It follows that there is no need to state explicitly the directions of the edges in the tree. Figure 3.4 shows several trees. Tree A contains only one vertex, the root x^0. Tree B contains two vertices and one edge, from x^0 to x^1. Tree C contains four edges, from x^0 to x^1, from x^0 to x^2, from x^1 to x^3, and from x^1 to x^4.

A vertex x is called a *child* of a vertex $\hat{x}$ if there is a directed edge from $\hat{x}$ to x. For example, in the tree in Figure 3.2, g and h are children of c, and s and w are children of k. A vertex x is a *leaf* (or a *terminal point*) if it has no children, meaning that there are no directed edges emanating from x.

3.3) Game trees

Various games can be represented by trees. When a tree represents a game, the root of the tree corresponds to the *initial position* of the game, and every *game position* is represented by a vertex of the tree. The children of each vertex v are the vertices corresponding to the game positions that can be arrived at from v via one action. In other words, the number of children of a vertex is equal to the number of possible actions in the game position corresponding to that vertex.

Figure 3.2 indicates that in addition to the game tree, we need two further components in order to describe a game fully:

- For every vertex that is not a leaf, we need to specify the player who is to take an action at that vertex.
- At each leaf, we need to describe the outcome of the game.

Definition 3.6 *Let B be a nonempty set. A* partition *of B is a collection* $B_1, B_2, \ldots, B_K$ *of pairwise disjoint subsets of B whose union is B.*

We are now ready for the first definition of a game in extensive form. We will later add more elements to this definition.

Definition 3.7 *A game in* extensive form *(or* extensive-form game) *is an ordered vector*[1]

$$\Gamma = (N, V, E, x^0, (V_i)_{i \in N}, O, u), \tag{3.2}$$

where:

- *N is a finite set of players.*
- (V, E, x^0) *is a tree called the* game tree.
- $(V_i)_{i \in N}$ *is a partition of the set of vertices that are not leaves.*
- *O is the set of possible game outcomes.*
- *u is a function associating every leaf of the tree with a game outcome in the set O.*

By "possible outcome" we mean a detailed description of what happens as a result of the actions undertaken by the players. Some examples of outcomes include:

1. Player I is declared the winner of the game, and Player II the loser.
2. Player I receives $2, Player II receives $3, and Player III receives $5.
3. Player I gets to go out to the cinema with Player II, while Player III is left at home.
4. If the game describes bargaining between two parties, the outcome is the detailed description of the points agreed upon in the bargaining.
5. In most of the following chapters, an outcome $u(x)$ at a leaf x will be a vector of real numbers representing the utility[2] of each player when a play reaches leaf x.

For each player $i \in N$, the set V_i is player i's set of decision vertices, and for each leaf x, the outcome at that leaf is $u(x)$.

Note that the partition $(V_i)_{i \in N}$ may contain empty sets. We accept the possibility of empty sets in $(V_i)_{i \in N}$ in order to be able to treat games in which a player may not be required to make any moves, but is still a game participant who is affected by the outcome of the game.

In the example in Figure 3.2,

$$N = \{\text{I}, \text{II}\},$$

$$V = \{r, a, b, c, d, e, f, g, h, i, j, k, l, m, p, q, s, w, y, z\},$$

$$x^0 = r,$$

$$V_{\text{I}} = \{r, f, h, j, k\},$$

$$V_{\text{II}} = \{b, c, d, q, w\}.$$

The set of possible outcomes is

$$O = \{\text{I wins}, \text{II wins}\}, \tag{3.3}$$

---

1 The word "ordered" indicates the convention that the elements of the game in extensive form appear in a specific order: the first element is the set of players, the second is the set of vertices, etc.

2 The subject of utility theory is discussed in Chapter 2.

and the function u is given by

$$u(a) = u(l) = u(m) = u(p) = u(s) = \text{II wins},$$
$$u(e) = u(g) = u(i) = u(y) = u(z) = \text{I wins}.$$

The requirement that $(V_i)_{i \in N}$ be a partition of the set of vertices that are not leaves stems from the fact that at each game situation there is one and only one player who is called upon to take an action. For each vertex x that is not a leaf, there is a single player $i \in N$ for whom $x \in V_i$. That player is called the *decision maker at vertex x*, and denoted by $J(x)$. In the example in Figure 3.2,

$$J(r) = J(f) = J(h) = J(j) = J(k) = \text{I},$$
$$J(b) = J(c) = J(d) = J(q) = J(w) = \text{II}.$$

Denote by $C(x)$ the set of all children of a non-leaf vertex x. Every edge that leads from x to one of its children is called a possible *action* at x. We will associate every action with the child to which it is connected, and denote by $A(x)$ the set of all actions that are possible at the vertex x. Later, we will define more complicated games, in which such a mapping between the possible actions at x and the children of x does not exist.

An extensive-form game proceeds in the following manner:

- Player $J(x^0)$ initiates the game by choosing a possible action in $A(x^0)$. Equivalently, he chooses an element x^1 in the set $C(x^0)$.
- If x^1 is not a leaf, player $J(x^1)$ chooses a possible action in $A(x^1)$ (equivalently, an element $x^2 \in C(x^1)$).
- The game continues in this manner, until a leaf vertex x is reached, and then the game ends with outcome $u(x)$.

By definition, the collection of the vertices of the graph is a finite set, so that the game necessarily ends at a leaf, yielding a sequence of vertices $(x^0, x^1, \ldots, x^k)$, where x^0 is the root of the tree, x^k is a leaf, and $x^{l+1} \in C(x^l)$ for $l = 0, 1, \ldots, k - 1$. This sequence is called a *play*.[3] Every play ends at a particular leaf x^k with outcome $u(x^k)$. Similarly, every leaf x^k determines a unique play, which corresponds to the unique path connecting the root x^0 with x^k.

It follows from the above description that every player who is to take an action knows the current state of the game, meaning that he knows all the actions in the game that led to the current point in the play. This implicit assumption is called *perfect information*, an important concept to be studied in detail when we discuss the broader family of games with imperfect information. Definition 3.7 therefore defines extensive-form games with perfect information.

Remark 3.8 *An extensive-form game, as defined here, is a finite game: the number of vertices V is finite. It is possible to define extensive-form games in which the game tree (V, E, x^0) is infinite. When the game tree is infinite, there are two possibilities to be*

---

3 Note carefully the words that are used here: a *game* is a general description of rules, whereas a *play* is a sequence of actions conducted in a particular instance of playing the game. For example, chess is a game; the sequence of actions in a particular chess match between two players is a play.

considered. It is possible that the depth of the tree is bounded, i.e., that there exists a natural number L such that the length of every path in the tree is less than or equal to L. This corresponds to a game that ends after at most L actions have been played, and there is at least one player who has an infinite number of actions available at an information set. The other possibility is that the depth of the vertices of the tree is not bounded; that is, there exists an infinite path in the game tree. This corresponds to a game that might never end. The definition of extensive-form game can be generalized to the case in which the game tree is infinite. Accomplishing this requires implementing mathematical tools from measure theory that go beyond the scope of this book. With the exception of a few examples in this chapter, we will assume here that extensive-form games are finite. ◆

We are now ready to present one of the central concepts of game theory: the concept of strategy. A strategy is a prescription for how to play a game. The definition is as follows.

Definition 3.9 *A strategy for player i is a function s_i mapping each vertex $x \in V_i$ to an element in $A(x)$ (equivalently, to an element in $C(x)$).*

According to this definition, a strategy includes instructions on how to behave at each vertex in the game tree, including vertices that previous actions by the player preclude from being reached. For example, in the game of chess, even if White's strategy calls for opening by moving a pawn from c2 to c3, the strategy must include instructions on how White should play in his second move if in his first move he instead moved a pawn from c2 to c4, and Black then took his action.

The main reason this definition is used is its simplicity: it does not require us to provide details regarding which vertices need to be dealt with in the strategy and which can be ignored. We will later see that this definition is also needed for further developments of the theory, which take into account the possibility of errors on the part of players, leading to situations that were unintended.

Definition 3.10 *A strategy vector is a list of strategies $s = (s_i)_{i \in N}$, one for each player.*

Player i's set of strategies is denoted by S_i, and the set of all strategy vectors is denoted by $S = S_1 \times S_2 \times \ldots \times S_n$. Every strategy vector $s = (s_i)_{i \in N}$ determines a unique play (path from the root to a leaf). The play that is determined by a strategy vector $s = (s_i)_{i \in N}$ is $(x^0, x^1, x^2, \ldots, x^k)$, where x^1 is the choice of player $J(x^0)$, based on his strategy, x^2 is the choice of player $J(x^1)$, based on his strategy, and so on, and x^k is a leaf. The play corresponds to the terminal point x^k (with outcome $u(x^k)$), which we also denote by $u(s)$.

We next proceed to define the concept of subgame:

Definition 3.11 *Let $\Gamma = (N, V, E, x^0, (V_i)_{i \in N}, O, u)$ be an extensive-form game (with perfect information), and let $x \in V$ be a vertex in the game tree. The subgame starting at x, denoted by $\Gamma(x)$, is the extensive-form game $\Gamma(x) = (N, V(x), E(x), x, (V_i(x))_{i \in N}, O, u)$, where:*

- *The set of players N is as in the game Γ.*
- *The set of vertices $V(x)$ includes x, and all the vertices that are descendants of x in the game tree (V, E, x^0), that is, the children of x, their children, the children of these children, and so on.*

- *The set of edges $E(x)$ includes all the edges in E that connect the vertices in $V(x)$.*
- *The set of vertices at which player i is a decision maker is $V_i(x) = V_i \cap V(x)$.*
- *The set of possible outcomes is the set of possible outcomes in the game Γ.*
- *The function mapping leaves to outcomes is the function u, restricted to the set of leaves in the game tree $(V(x), E(x), x)$.*

The original game Γ is itself a subgame: $\Gamma(x^0) = \Gamma$. In addition, every leaf x defines a subgame in which no player can make a choice. We next focus on games with two players, I and II, whose set of outcomes is $O = \{\text{I wins}, \text{II wins}, \text{Draw}\}$. We will define the concepts of a winning strategy and a strategy guaranteeing at least a draw for such games.

Definition 3.12 *Let Γ be an extensive-form game with Players I and II, whose set of outcomes is $O = \{I\ wins, II\ wins, Draw\}$. A strategy s_I of Player I is called a* winning strategy *if*

$$u(s_I, s_{II}) = I\ wins, \quad \forall s_{II} \in S_{II}. \tag{3.4}$$

A strategy s_I of Player I is called a strategy guaranteeing at least a draw *if*

$$u(s_I, s_{II}) \in \{I\ wins, Draw\}, \quad \forall s_{II} \in S_{II}. \tag{3.5}$$

A winning strategy for Player II, and a strategy guaranteeing at least a draw for Player II, are defined similarly.

Theorem 3.13 (von Neumann [1928]) *In every two-player game (with perfect information) in which the set of outcomes is $O = \{I\ wins, II\ wins, Draw\}$, one and only one of the following three alternatives holds:*

1. *Player I has a winning strategy.*
2. *Player II has a winning strategy.*
3. *Each of the two players has a strategy guaranteeing at least a draw.*

The proof of Theorem 3.13 is similar to the proof of Theorem 1.4 for the game of chess (page 3), and it is left to the reader as an exercise (Exercise 3.7). As we saw above, in proving Theorem 1.4 we did not, in fact, make use of any of the rules specific to the game of chess; the proof is valid for any game that satisfies the three properties (C1)–(C3) specified on page 6.

Examples of additional games to which Theorem 3.13 applies include, for example, checkers, the game Nim (see Exercise 3.14), and the game Hex (see Exercise 3.19).

Remark 3.14 *In our definition of a game in extensive form, we assumed that the game tree is finite. The proof of Theorem 3.13 shows that the theorem also holds when the game tree is infinite, but the depth of the vertices of the tree is bounded: there exists a natural number L such that the depth of each vertex in the tree is less than or equal to L. It turns out that the theorem is not true when the depth of the vertices of the tree is unbounded. See Mycielski [1992], Claim 3.1.* ♦

We now consider another game that satisfies the conditions of Theorem 3.13. This game is interesting because we can prove which of the three possibilities of the theorem holds in this game, but we do not know how to calculate the appropriate strategy, in contrast to the game of chess, in which we do not even know which of the three alternatives holds.

3.4 Chomp: David Gale's game

The game described in this section is known by the name of Chomp, and was invented by David Gale (see Gale [1974]). It is played on an $n \times m$ board of squares. Each square is denoted by a pair of coordinates (i, j), $1 \leq i \leq n$ and $1 \leq j \leq m$: i is the horizontal coordinate, and j is the vertical coordinate. Figure 3.5 depicts the game board for $n = m = 8$.

Every player in turn captures a square, subject to the following rules: if at a certain stage the square (i_0, j_0) has been captured, no square that is located north-east of (i_0, j_0) can be captured in subsequent moves. This means that after (i_0, j_0) has been captured, all the squares (i, j) satisfying $i \geq i_0$ and $j \geq j_0$ can be regarded as if they have been removed from the board. In Figure 3.5, for example, square $(4, 7)$ has been captured, so that all the darkened squares in the figure are regarded as having been removed.

Player I has the opening move. The player who captures square $(1, 1)$ (which is marked in Figure 3.5 with a black inner square) is declared the loser. We note that the game in Example 3.1 is David Gale's game for $n = m = 2$.

Theorem 3.15 *In David Gale's game on an $n \times n$ board, the following strategy is a winning strategy for Player I: in the opening move capture square $(2, 2)$, thus leaving only the squares in row $j = 1$ and column $i = 1$ (see Figure 3.6). From that point on, play symmetrically to Player II's actions. That is, if Player II captures square (i, j), Player I captures square (j, i) in the following move.*

The above strategy is well defined. That is, if Player II captures square (i, j) (and $(i, j) \neq (1, 1)$), square (j, i) has not yet been removed from the board (verify this!). This strategy is also a winning strategy when the board is infinite, $\infty \times \infty$.

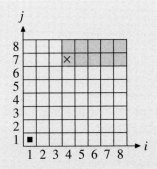

Figure 3.5 Gale's game for $n = m = 8$

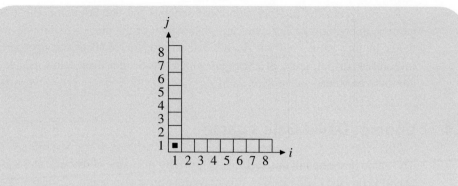

Figure 3.6 The game board after Player I has captured square $(2, 2)$

What happens if the board is rectangular but not square? Which player then has a winning strategy? As the next theorem states, the opening player always has a winning strategy.

Theorem 3.16 *For every finite $n \times m$ board (with $n > 1$ or $m > 1$), Player I, who has the opening move, has a winning strategy.*

Proof: The game satisfies the conditions of von Neumann's Theorem (Theorem 3.13), and therefore one of the three possibilities of the theorem must hold. Since the game cannot end in a draw, there are only two remaining possibilities:

1. Player I has a winning strategy.
2. Player II has a winning strategy.

Theorem 3.16 will be proved once the following claim is proved:

Claim 3.17 *For every finite $n \times m$ board (with $n > 1$ or $m > 1$), if Player II has a winning strategy, then Player I also has a winning strategy.*

Since it is impossible for both players to have winning strategies, it follows that Player II cannot have a winning strategy, and therefore the only remaining possibility is that Player I has a winning strategy.

Proof of Claim 3.17: Suppose that Player II has a winning strategy s_{II}. This strategy guarantees Player II victory over any strategy used by Player I. In particular, the strategy grants Player II victory even if Player I captures square (n, m) (the top-rightmost square) in the opening move. Suppose that Player II's next action, as called for by strategy s_{II}, is to capture square (i_0, j_0) (see Figure 3.7(a)).

From this point on, a new game is effectively being played, as depicted in Figure 3.7(b). In this game Player I has the opening move, and Player II, using strategy s_{II}, guarantees himself victory. In other words, the player who implements the opening move in this game is the losing player. But Player I can guarantee himself the situation depicted in Figure 3.7(b) when Player II opens, by choosing the square (i_0, j_0) on his first move. In conclusion, a winning strategy in the original game for Player I is to open with (i_0, j_0) and then continue according to strategy s_{II}, thus completing the proof of the claim. $\square$

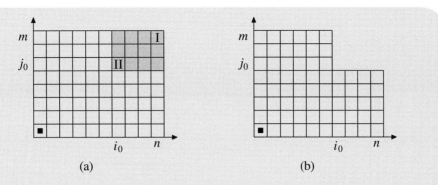

Figure 3.7 The board after the first action (a) and the board after the second action (b)

It follows from Claim 3.17 that Player II has no winning strategy, so that Player I must have a winning strategy.   □

The conclusion of the theorem is particularly striking, given the fact that for $n \neq m$ we do not know how to find the winning strategy for Player I, even with the aid of computers, on relatively small boards of n and m between 30 to 40.

3.5 Games with chance moves

In the games we have seen so far, the transition from one state to another is always accomplished by actions undertaken by the players. Such a model is appropriate for games such as chess and checkers, but not for card games or dice games (such as poker or backgammon) in which the transition from one state to another may depend on a chance process: in card games the shuffle of the deck, and in backgammon the toss of the dice. It is possible to come up with situations in which transitions from state to state depend on other chance factors, such as the weather, earthquakes, or the stock market. These sorts of state transitions are called *chance moves*. To accommodate this feature, our model is expanded by labeling some of the vertices in the game tree (V, E, x^0) as chance moves. The edges emanating from vertices corresponding to chance moves represent the possible outcomes of a lottery, and next to each such edge is listed the probability that the outcome it represents will be the result of the lottery.

Example 3.18 **A game with chance moves** Consider the two-player game depicted in Figure 3.8. The outcomes of the game are denoted by pairs of numbers (z_I, z_{II}), where z_I is the monetary payoff to Player I, and z_{II} is the monetary payoff to Player II.

The verbal description of this game is as follows. At the root of the game (vertex R) Player I has the choice of selecting between action a, which leads to the termination of the game with payoff $(0, 0)$, and action b, which leads to a chance move at vertex A. The chance move is a lottery (or a flip of a coin) leading with probability $\frac{1}{2}$ to state B, which is a decision vertex of Player II, and with probability $\frac{1}{2}$ to state C, which is a decision vertex of Player I. At state B, Player II chooses

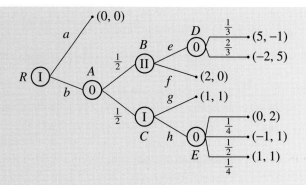

Figure 3.8 An example of a game with chance moves

between action f, leading to a termination of the game with payoff $(2,0)$, and action e, leading to state D which is a chance move; at this chance move, with probability $\frac{1}{3}$ the game ends with payoff $(5,-1)$, and with probability $\frac{2}{3}$ the game ends with payoff $(-2,5)$. At state C, Player I chooses between action g, leading to the termination of the game with payoff $(1,1)$, and action h, leading to a chance move at vertex E. At this chance move the game ends, with payoff $(0,2)$, or $(-1,1)$, or $(1,1)$, with respective probabilities $\frac{1}{4}$, $\frac{1}{2}$, and $\frac{1}{4}$. ◀

Formally, the addition of chance moves to the model proceeds as follows. We add a new player, who is called "Nature," and denoted by 0. The set of players is thus expanded to $N \cup \{0\}$. For every vertex x at which a chance move is implemented, we denote by p_x the probability vector over the possible outcomes of a lottery that is implemented at vertex x. This leads to the following definition of a game in extensive form:

Definition 3.19 *A game in extensive form (with perfect information and chance moves) is a vector*

$$\Gamma = (N, V, E, x^0, (V_i)_{i\in N\cup\{0\}}, (p_x)_{x\in V_0}, O, u), \tag{3.6}$$

where:

- *N is a finite set of players.*
- *(V, E, x^0) is the game tree.*
- *$(V_i)_{i\in N\cup\{0\}}$ is a partition of the set of vertices that are not leaves.*
- *For every vertex $x \in V_0$, p_x is a probability distribution over the edges emanating from x.*
- *O is the set of possible outcomes.*
- *u is a function mapping each leaf of the game tree to an outcome in O.*

The notation used in the extension of the model is the same as the previous notation, with the following changes:

- The partition of the set of vertices is now $(V_i)_{i\in N\cup\{0\}}$. We have, therefore, added the set V_0 to the partition, where V_0 is the set of vertices at which a chance move is implemented.

- For each vertex $x \in V_0$, a vector p_x, which is a probability distribution over the edges emanating from x, has been added to the model.

Games with chance moves are played similarly to games without chance moves, the only difference being that at vertices with chance moves a lottery is implemented, to determine the action to be undertaken at that vertex. We can regard a vertex x with a chance move as a roulette wheel, with the area of the pockets of the roulette wheel proportional to the values p_x. When the game is at a chance vertex, the wheel is spun, and the pocket at which the wheel settles specifies the new state of the game.

Note that in this description we have included a hidden assumption, namely, that the probabilities of the chance moves are known to all the players, even when the game includes moves that involve the probability of rain, or an earthquake, or a stock market crash, and so forth. In such situations, we presume that the probability assessments of these occurrences are known by all the players. More advanced models take into account the possibility that the players do not all necessarily share the same assessments of the probabilities of chance moves. Such models are considered in Chapters 9, 10, and 11.

In a game without chance moves, a strategy vector determines a unique play of the game (and therefore also a unique game outcome). When a game includes chance moves, a strategy vector determines a probability distribution over the possible game outcomes.

Example 3.18 (*Continued*) (See Figure 3.8.) Suppose that Player I uses strategy s_I, defined as

$$s_I(R) = b, s_I(C) = h, \tag{3.7}$$

and that Player II uses strategy s_{II}, defined as

$$s_{II}(B) = f. \tag{3.8}$$

Then:
- the play $R \rightarrow A \rightarrow B \rightarrow (2,0)$ occurs with probability $1/2$, leading to outcome $(2,0)$;
- the play $R \rightarrow A \rightarrow C \rightarrow E \rightarrow (0,2)$ occurs with probability $1/8$, leading to outcome $(0,2)$;
- the play $R \rightarrow A \rightarrow C \rightarrow E \rightarrow (-1,1)$ occurs with probability $1/4$, leading to outcome $(-1,1)$;
- the play $R \rightarrow A \rightarrow C \rightarrow E \rightarrow (1,1)$ occurs with probability $1/8$, leading to outcome $(1,1)$.

◀

Using this model of games with chance moves, we can represent games such as backgammon, Monopoly, Chutes and Ladders, and dice games (but not card games such as poker and bridge, which are not games with perfect information, because players do not know what cards the other players are holding). Note that von Neumann's Theorem (Theorem 3.13) does not hold in games with chance moves. In dice games, such as backgammon, a player who benefits from favorable rolls of the dice can win regardless of whether or not he has the first move, and regardless of the strategy adopted by his opponent.

3.6 Games with imperfect information

One of the distinguishing properties of the games we have seen so far is that at every stage of the game each of the players has perfect knowledge of all the developments in the game prior to that stage: he knows exactly which actions were taken by all the other players, and if there were chance moves, he knows what the results of the chance moves were. In other words, every player, when it is his turn to take an action, knows precisely at which vertex in the game tree the game is currently at. A game satisfying this condition is called a *game with perfect information*.

The assumption of perfect information is clearly a very restrictive assumption, limiting the potential scope of analysis. Players often do not know all the actions taken by the other players and/or the results of chance moves (for example, in many card games the hand of cards each player holds is not known to the other players). The following game is perhaps the simplest example of a game with imperfect information.

Example 3.20 **Matching Pennies** The game Matching Pennies is a two-player game in which each player chooses one of the sides of a coin, H (for heads) or T (for tails) in the following way: each player inserts into an envelope a slip of paper on which his choice is written. The envelopes are sealed and submitted to a referee. If both players have selected the same side of the coin, Player II pays one dollar to Player I. If they have selected opposite sides of the coin, Player I pays one dollar to Player II. The depiction of Matching Pennies as an extensive-form game appears in Figure 3.9. In Figure 3.9, Player I's actions are denoted by uppercase letters, and Player II's actions are depicted by lowercase letters.

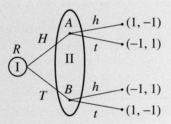

Figure 3.9 Matching Pennies as a game in extensive form

Figure 3.9 introduces a new element to the depictions of extensive-form games: the two vertices A and B of Player II are surrounded by an ellipse. This visual element represents the fact that when Player II is in the position of selecting between h and t, he does not know whether the game state is currently at vertex A or vertex B, because he does not know whether Player I has selected H or T. These two vertices together form an *information set* of Player II. ◀

Remark 3.21 *The verbal description of Matching Pennies is symmetric between the two players, but in Figure 3.9 the players are not symmetric. The figure depicts Player I making his choice before Player II's choice, with Player II not knowing which choice Player I made; this is done in order to depict the game conveniently as a tree. We could alternatively have drawn the tree with Player II making his choice before Player I, with Player I not knowing which choice Player II made. Both trees are equivalent, and they are equivalent to the verbal description of the game in which the two players make their choices simultaneously.* ♦

In general, a player's information set consists of a set of vertices that satisfy the property that when play reaches one of these vertices, the player knows that play has reached one of these vertices, but he does not know which vertex has been reached. The next example illustrates this concept.

Example 3.22   Consider the following situation. David Beckham, star mid-fielder for Manchester United, is interested in leaving the team and signing up instead with either Real Madrid, Bayern Munich, or AC Milan. Both Bayern Munich and AC Milan have told Beckham they want to hire him, and even announced their interest in the star to the media.

Beckham has yet to hear anything on the matter from Real Madrid. With the season fast approaching, Beckham has only a week to determine which club he will be playing for. Real Madrid announces that it will entertain proposals of interest from players only up to midnight tonight, because its Board of Directors will be meeting tomorrow to discuss to which players the club will be making offers (Real Madrid's Board of Directors does not rule out making offers to players who have not approached it with proposals of interest). Only after the meeting will Real Madrid make offers to the players it wishes to add to its roster for the next season.

Beckham needs to decide whether to approach Real Madrid today with an expression of interest, or wait until tomorrow, hoping that the club will make him an offer on its own initiative. Real Madrid's Board of Directors will be called upon to consider two alternatives: hiring an outside expert to assess Beckham's potential contribution to the team, or dropping all considerations of hiring Beckham, without even asking for an expert's opinion. If Real Madrid hires an outside expert, the club will make an offer to Beckham if the outside expert's assessment is positive, and decline to make an offer to Beckham if the assessment is negative. The outside expert, if hired by Real Madrid, will not be informed whether or not Beckham has approached Real Madrid. If Beckham fails to receive an offer from Real Madrid, he will not know whether that is because the expert determined his contribution to the team unworthy of a contract, or because the team did not even ask for an expert's opinion. After a week, whether or not he receives an offer from Real Madrid, Beckham must decide which club he will be playing for next season, Bayern Munich, AC Milan, or Real Madrid, assuming the latter has sent him an offer. This situation can be described as a three-player game (see Figure 3.10) (verify this).

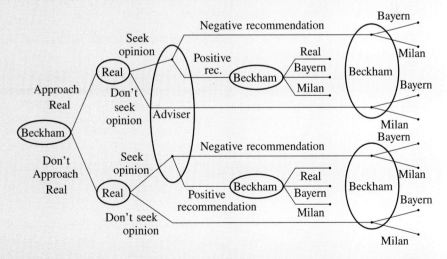

Figure 3.10 The game in Example 3.22 in extensive form

There are three information sets in this game that contain more than one vertex. The expert does not know whether or not Beckham has approached Real Madrid with an expression of interest. If Beckham has not received an offer from Real Madrid, he does not know whether that is because the expert determined his contribution to the team unworthy of a contract, or because the team did not even ask for an expert's opinion. ◀

The addition of information sets to our model leads to the following definition:

Definition 3.23 *Let* $\Gamma = (N, V, E, x^0, (V_i)_{i \in N \cup \{0\}}, (p_x)_{x \in V_0}, O, u)$ *be a game in extensive form. An* information set *of player* i *is a pair* $(U_i, A(U_i))$ *such that*

- $U_i = \{x_i^1, x_i^2, \ldots, x_i^m\}$ *is a subset of* V_i *that satisfies the property that at each vertex in* U_i *player* i *has the same number of actions* $l_i = l_i(U_i)$, *i.e.,*

$$|A(x_i^j)| = l_i, \quad \forall j = 1, 2, \ldots, m. \tag{3.9}$$

- $A(U_i)$ *is a partition of the* ml_i *edges* $\bigcup_{j=1}^m A(x_i^j)$ *to* l_i *disjoint sets, each of which contains one element from the sets* $(A(x_i^j))_{j=1}^m$. *We denote the elements of the partition by* $a_i^1, a_i^2, \ldots, a_i^{l_i}$. *The partition* $A(U_i)$ *is called the* action set *of player* i *in the information set* U_i.

We now explain the significance of the definition. When the play of the game arrives at vertex x in information set U_i, all that player i knows is that the play has arrived at one of the vertices in this information set. The player therefore cannot choose a particular edge emanating from x. Each element of the partition a_i^l contains m edges, one edge for each vertex in the information set. The partition elements $a_i^1, a_i^2, \ldots, a_i^{l_i}$ are the "actions" from which the player can choose; if player i chooses one of the elements from the partition a_i^l, the play continues along the unique edge in the intersection $a_i^l \cap A(x)$. For this reason, when we depict games with information sets, we denote edges located in the same partition elements by the same letter.

Definition 3.24 *A game in extensive form* (with chance moves and with imperfect information) *is a vector*

$$\Gamma = (N, V, E, x^0, (V_i)_{i \in N \cup \{0\}}, (p_x)_{x \in V_0}, (U_i^j)_{i \in N}^{j=1,\ldots,k_i}, O, u), \tag{3.10}$$

where:

- *N is a finite set of players.*
- *(V, E, x^0) is a game tree.*
- *$(V_i)_{i \in N \cup \{0\}}$ is a partition of the set of vertices that are not leaves.*
- *For each vertex $x \in V_0$, p_x is a probability distribution over the set of edges emanating from x.*
- *For each player $i \in N$, $(U_i^j)^{j=1,\ldots,k_i}$ is a partition of V_i.*
- *For each player $i \in N$ and every $j \in \{1, 2, \ldots, k_i\}$, the pair $(U_i^j, A(U_i^j))$ is an information set of player i.*
- *O is a set of possible outcomes.*
- *u is a function mapping each leaf of the game tree to a possible outcome in O.*

We have added information sets to the previous definition of a game in extensive form (Definition 3.19): $(U_i^j)^{j=1,\ldots,k_i}$ is a partition of V_i. Every element U_i^j in this partition is an information set of player i. Note that the information sets are defined only for players $i \in N$, because, as noted above, Nature has no information sets.

In a game with imperfect information, each player i, when choosing an action, does not know at which vertex x the play is located. He only knows the information set U_i^j that contains x. The player then chooses one of the equivalence classes of actions available to him in U_i^j, i.e., an element in $A(U_i^j)$.

The game proceeds as described on pages 44 and 51, with one difference: when the play is x, the decision maker at that state, player $J(x)$, knows only the information set $U_{J(x)}^j$ that contains x, and he chooses an element a in $A(U_{J(x)}^j)$.

We can now describe many more games as games in extensive form: various card games such as poker and bridge, games of strategy such as Stratego, and many real-life situations such as bargaining between two parties.

Definition 3.25 *An extensive-form game is called a* game with perfect information for player i *if each information set of player i contains only one vertex. An extensive-form game is called a* game with perfect information *if it is a game with perfect information for all of the players.*

In Definition 3.11 (page 45), we defined a subgame starting at vertex x to be the game defined by restriction to the subtree starting at x. A natural question arises as to how this definition can be adapted to games in which players have information sets that contain several vertices, because player i may have an information set $(U_i, A(U_i))$ where U_i contains both vertices that are in the subtree starting at x, and vertices that are outside this subtree. We will say that $\Gamma(x)$ is a *subgame* only if for every player i and each of the information sets $(U_i, A(U_i))$, the set U_i is either contained entirely inside the subtree starting at x, or disjoint from this subtree. For simplicity we will often refer to U_i as an information set, and omit the set partition $A(U_i)$.

Example 3.26 Consider the two-player game with chance moves and with imperfect information that is described in Figure 3.11. The outcomes of the game are not specified as they are not needed for our discussion.

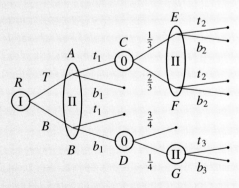

Figure 3.11 The game in Example 3.26 in extensive form

The game in Figure 3.11 has four subgames: $\Gamma(R)$, $\Gamma(C)$, $\Gamma(D)$, and $\Gamma(G)$. The subtree starting at A (or at B) cannot represent a subgame, because the information set $\{A, B\}$ of Player II is neither contained in, nor disjoint from, the subtree. It would therefore be incorrect to write $\Gamma(A)$ (or $\Gamma(B)$). Similarly, the subtrees that start at E and F cannot represent subgames, because the information set $\{E, F\}$ of Player II is neither contained in, nor disjoint from, each of these subtrees. ◄

3.6.1 Strategies in games with imperfect information

Recall that a player's strategy is a set of instructions telling the player which action to choose, every time he is called upon to play. When we dealt with games with perfect information, in which each player, when coming to make a decision, knows the current vertex x, a strategy was defined as a function $s_i : V_i \rightarrow V$, where $s_i(x) \in C(x)$ for every $x \in V_i$. In a game with imperfect information, when choosing an action, the player knows the information set that contains the current vertex. Therefore a strategy is a function that assigns an action to each information set.

Definition 3.27 *A strategy of player i is a function from each of his information sets to the set of actions available at that information set, i.e.,*

$$s_i : \mathcal{U}_i \rightarrow \bigcup_{j=1}^{k_i} A(U_i^j), \tag{3.11}$$

where $\mathcal{U}_i = \{U_i^1, \ldots, U_i^{k_i}\}$ is the collection of player i's information sets, and for each information set $U_i^j \in \mathcal{U}_i$,

$$s_i(U_i^j) \in A(U_i^j). \tag{3.12}$$

Just as in games with chance moves and perfect information, a strategy vector determines a distribution over the outcomes of a game. For example, in Example 3.22, suppose that the players implement the following strategies:

- David Beckham approaches Real Madrid, and then chooses to play for Real Madrid if Real Madrid makes him an offer; otherwise, he chooses to play for Bayern Munich.
- Real Madrid hires an outside expert if Beckham approaches it, and does not hire an outside expert if Beckham does not approach the club. Real Madrid makes an offer to Beckham only if Beckham first approaches the club, and if the outside expert gives a positive recommendation.
- The outside expert recommends that Real Madrid not make an offer to Beckham.

There are no chance moves in this game, so that the strategy vector determines a unique play of the game, and therefore also a unique outcome: Beckham ends up playing for Bayern Munich, after he approaches Real Madrid, Real Madrid in turn hires an outside expert to provide a recommendation, the expert returns with a negative recommendation, Real Madrid does not make an offer to Beckham, and Beckham then decides to play for Bayern Munich.

3.7 Exercises

. . . .

3.1 Describe the following situation as an extensive-form game. Three piles of matches are on a table. One pile contains a single match, a second pile contains two matches, and the third pile contains three matches. Two players alternately remove matches from the table. In each move, the player whose turn it is to act at that move may remove matches from one and only one pile, and must remove at least one match. The player who removes the last match loses the game.

By drawing arrows on the game tree, identify a way that one of the players can guarantee victory.

3.2 Candidate choice Depict the following situation as a game in extensive form. Eric, Larry, and Sergey are senior partners in a law firm. The three are considering candidates for joining their firm. Three candidates are under consideration: Lee, Rebecca, and John. The choice procedure, which reflects the seniority relations between the three law firm partners, is as follows:

- Eric makes the initial proposal of one of the candidates.
- Larry follows by proposing a candidate of his own (who may be the same candidate that Eric proposed).
- Sergey then proposes a candidate (who may be one of the previously proposed candidates).
- A candidate who receives the support of two of the partners is accepted into the firm. If no candidate has the support of two partners, all three candidates are rejected.

3.3 Does aggressiveness pay off? Depict the following situation as a game in extensive form. A bird is defending its territory. When another bird attempts to invade this territory, the first bird is faced with two alternatives: to stand and fight for its territory, or to flee and seek another place for its home. The payoff to each bird is defined to be the expected number of descendants it will leave for posterity, and these are calculated as follows:

- If the invading bird yields to the defending bird and instead flies to another territory, the payoff is: 6 descendants for the defending bird, 4 descendants for the invading bird.
- If the invading bird presses an attack and the defending bird flies to another territory, the payoff is: 4 descendants for the defending bird, 6 descendants for the invading bird.
- If the invading bird presses an attack and the defending bird stands its ground and fights, the payoff is: 2 descendants for the defending bird, 2 descendants for the invading bird.

3.4 Depict the following situation as a game in extensive form. Peter and his three children, Andrew, James, and John, manage a communications corporation. Andrew is the eldest child, James the second-born, and John the youngest of the children. Two candidates have submitted offers for the position of corporate accountant at the communications corporation. The choice of a new accountant is conducted as follows: Peter first chooses two of his three children. The two selected children conduct a meeting to discuss the strengths and weaknesses of each of the two candidates. The elder of the two children then proposes a candidate. The younger of the two children expresses either agreement or disagreement to the proposed candidate. A candidate is accepted to the position only if two children support his candidacy. If neither candidate enjoys the support of two children, both candidates are rejected.

3.5 (a) How many strategies has each player got in each of the following three games (the outcomes of the games are not specified in the figures).

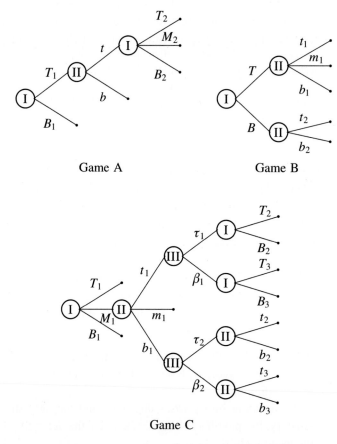

Game A   Game B

Game C

(b) Write out in full all the strategies of each player in each of the three games.

(c) How many different plays are possible in each of the games?

3.6 In a single-player game in which at each vertex x that is not the root the player has m_x actions, how many strategies has the player got?

3.7 Prove von Neumann's Theorem (Theorem 3.13 on page 46): in every two-player finite game with perfect information in which the set of outcomes is $O = \{$I wins, II wins, Draw$\}$, one and only one of the following three alternatives holds:

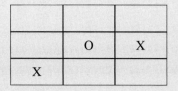

Figure 3.12 The board of the game Tic-Tac-Toe, after three moves

(a) Player I has a winning strategy.

(b) Player II has a winning strategy.

(c) Each of the two players has a strategy guaranteeing at least a draw.

Where does your proof make use of the assumption that the game is finite?

3.8 Tic-Tac-Toe How many strategies has Player I got in Tic-Tac-Toe, in which two players play on a 3×3 board, as depicted in Figure 3.12? Player I makes the first move, and each player in turn chooses a square that has not previously been selected. Player I places an X in every square that he chooses, and Player II places an O in every square that he chooses. The game ends when every square has been selected. The first player who has managed to place his mark in three adjoining squares, where those three squares form either a column, a row, or a diagonal, is the winner.[4] (Do not attempt to draw a full game tree. Despite the fact that the rules of the game are quite simple, the game tree is exceedingly large. Despite the size of the game tree, with a little experience players quickly learn how to ensure at least a draw in every play of the game.)

3.9 By definition, a player's strategy prescribes his selected action at each vertex in the game tree. Consider the following game:

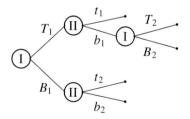

Player I has four strategies, $T_1 T_2, T_1 B_2, B_1 T_2,$ and $B_1 B_2$. Two of these strategies, $B_1 T_2$ and $B_1 B_2$, regardless of the strategy used by Player II, yield the same play of the game, because if Player I has selected action B_1 at the root vertex, he will never get to his second decision vertex. We can therefore eliminate one of

---

4 The game, of course, can effectively be ended when one of the players has clearly ensured victory for himself, but calculating the number of strategies in that case is more complicated.

these two strategies and define a *reduced strategy* B_1, which only stipulates that Player I chooses B_1 at the root of the game. In the game appearing in the above figure, the reduced strategies of Player I are T_1T_2, T_1B_2, and B_1. The reduced strategies of Player II are the same as his regular strategies, t_1t_2, t_1b_2, b_1t_2, and b_1b_2, because Player II does not know to which vertex Player I's choice will lead. Formally, a *reduced strategy* τ_i of player i is a function from a subcollection $\widehat{\mathcal{U}}_i$ of player i's collection of information sets to actions, satisfying the following two conditions:

(i) For any strategy vector of the remaining players σ_{-i}, given the vector (τ_i, σ_{-i}), the game will definitely not get to an information set of player i that is not in the collection $\widehat{\mathcal{U}}_i$.

(ii) There is no strict subcollection of $\widehat{\mathcal{U}}_i$ satisfying condition (i).

    (a) List the reduced strategies of each of the players in the game depicted in the following figure:

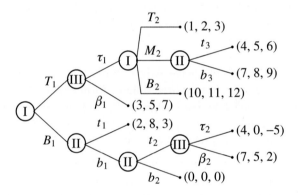

    (b) What outcome of the game will obtain if the three players make use of the reduced strategies $\{(B_1), (t_1, t_3), (\beta_1, \tau_2)\}$?

    (c) Can any player increase his payoff by unilaterally making use of a different strategy (assuming that the other two players continue to play according to the strategies of part (b))?

3.10 Consider the game in the following figure:

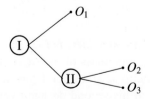

The outcomes O_1, O_2, and O_3 are distinct and taken from the set {I wins, II wins, Draw}.

(a) Is there a choice of O_1, O_2, and O_3 such that Player I can guarantee victory for himself? Justify your answer.

(b) Is there a choice of O_1, O_2, and O_3 such that Player II can guarantee victory for himself? Justify your answer.

(c) Is there a choice of O_1, O_2, and O_3 such that both players can guarantee for themselves at least a draw? Justify your answer.

3.11 The Battle of the Sexes The game in this exercise, called Battle of the Sexes, is an oft-quoted example in game theory (see also Example 4.21 on page 98). The name given to the game comes from the story often attached to it: a couple is trying to determine how to spend their time next Friday night. The available activities in their town are attending a concert (C), or watching a football match (F). The man prefers football, while the woman prefers the concert, but both of them prefer being together to spending time apart.

The pleasure each member of the couple receives from the available alternatives is quantified as follows:

- From watching the football match together: 2 for the man, 1 for the woman.
- From attending the concert together: 1 for the man, 2 for the woman.
- From spending time apart: 0 for the man, 0 for the woman.

The couple do not communicate well with each other, so each one chooses where he or she will go on Friday night before discovering what the other selected, and refuses to change his or her mind (alternatively, we can imagine each one going directly to his or her choice directly from work, without informing the other). Depict this situation as a game in extensive form.

3.12 The Centipede game[5] The game tree appearing in Figure 3.13 depicts a two-player game in extensive form (note that the tree is shortened; there are another 94 choice vertices and another 94 leaves that do not appear in the figure). The payoffs appear as pairs (x, y), where x is the payoff to Player I (in thousands of dollars) and y is the payoff to Player II (in thousands of dollars). The players make moves in alternating turns, with Player I making the first move.

Every player has a till into which money is added throughout the play of the game. At the root of the game, Player I's till contains $1,000, and Player II's till is empty. Every player in turn, at her move, can elect either to stop the game (S), in which case every player receives as payoff the amount of money in her till, or to continue to play. Each time a player elects to continue the game, she removes $1,000 from her till and places them in the other player's till, while simultaneously the game-master adds another $2,000 to the other player's till. If no player has stopped the game after 100 turns have passed, the game ends, and each player receives the amount of money in her till at that point.

How would you play this game in the role of Player I? Justify your answer!

---

5 The Centipede game was invented by Robert Rosenthal (see Rosenthal [1981]).

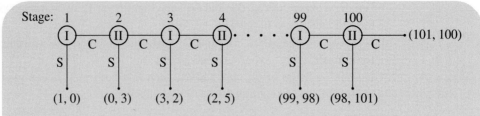

Figure 3.13 The Centipede game (outcomes are in payoffs of thousands of dollars)

3.13 Consider the following game. Two players, each in turn, place a quarter on a round table, in such a way that the coins are never stacked one over another (although the coins may touch each other); every quarter must be placed fully on the table. The first player who cannot place an additional quarter on the table at his turn, without stacking it on an already placed quarter, loses the game (and the other player is the winner). Prove that the opening player has a winning strategy.

3.14 Nim[6] Nim is a two-player game, in which piles of matches are placed before the players (the number of piles in the game is finite, and each pile contains a finite number of matches). Each player in turn chooses a pile, and removes any number of matches from the pile he has selected (he must remove at least one match). The player who removes the last match wins the game.

(a) Does von Neumann's Theorem (Theorem 3.13 on page 46) imply that one of the players must have a winning strategy? Justify your answer!

We present here a series of guided exercises for constructing a winning strategy in the game of Nim.

At the beginning of play, list, in a column, the number of matches in each pile, expressed in base 2. For example, if there are four piles containing, respectively, $2, 12, 13,$ and 21 matches, list:

$$10$$
$$1100$$
$$1101$$
$$10101$$

Next, check whether the number of 1s in each column is odd or even. In the above example, counting from the right, in the first and fourth columns the number of 1s is even, while in the second, third, and fifth columns the number of 1s is odd.

A position in the game will be called a "winning position" if the number of 1s in each column is even. The game state depicted above is not a winning position.

(b) Prove that, starting from any position that is not a winning position, it is possible to get to a winning position in one move (that is, by removing matches from a single pile). In our example, if 18 matches are removed from the largest

6 Nim is an ancient game, probably originating in China. There are accounts of the game being played in Europe as early as the fifteenth century. The proof presented in this exercise is due to Bouton [1901].

pile, the remaining four piles will have 2, 12, 13, and 3 matches, respectively, which in base 2 are represented as

$$10$$
$$1100$$
$$1101$$
$$11$$

which is a winning position, as every column has an even number of 1s.

(c) Prove that at a winning position, every legal action leads to a non-winning position.

(d) Explain why at the end of every play of the game, the position of the game will be a winning position.

(e) Explain how we can identify which player can guarantee victory for himself (given the initial number of piles of matches and the number of matches in each pile), and describe that player's winning strategy.

3.15 The game considered in this exercise is exactly like the game of Nim of the previous exercise, except that here the player who removes the last match loses the game. (The game described in Exercise 3.1 is an example of such a game.)

(a) Is it possible for one of the players in this game to guarantee victory? Justify your answer.

(b) Explain how we can identify which player can guarantee victory for himself in this game (given the initial number of piles of matches and the number of matches in each pile), and describe that player's winning strategy.

3.16 Answer the following questions relating to David Gale's game of Chomp (see Section 3.4 on page 47):

(a) Which of the two players has a winning strategy in a game of Chomp played on a $2 \times \infty$ board? Justify your answer. Describe the winning strategy.

(b) Which of the two players has a winning strategy in a game of Chomp played on an $m \times \infty$ board, where m is any finite integer? Justify your answer. Describe the winning strategy.

(c) Find two winning strategies for Player I in a game of Chomp played on an $\infty \times \infty$ board.

3.17 Show that the conclusion of von Neumann's Theorem (Theorem 3.13, page 46) does not hold for the Matching Pennies game (Example 3.20, page 52), where we interpret the payoff $(1, -1)$ as victory for Player I and the payoff $(-1, 1)$ as victory for Player II.

Which condition in the statement of the theorem fails to obtain in Matching Pennies?

3.18 Prove that von Neumann's Theorem (Theorem 3.13, page 46) holds in games in extensive form with perfect information and without chance moves, in which the game tree has a countable number of vertices, but the depth of every vertex is bounded; i.e., there exists a positive integer K that is greater than the length of every path in the game tree.

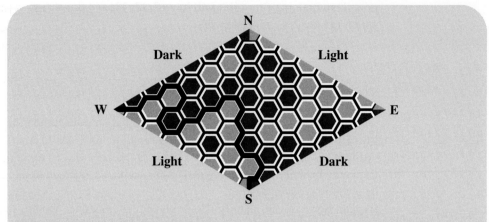

Figure 3.14 The Hex game board for $n = 6$ (in the play depicted here, dark is the winner)

3.19 Hex Hex[7] is a two-player game conducted on a rhombus containing n^2 hexagonal cells, as depicted in Figure 3.14 for $n = 6$.

The players control opposite sides of the rhombus (in Figure 3.14, the names of the players are "Light" and "Dark"). Light controls the south-west (*SW*) and north-east (*NE*) sides, while Dark controls the north-west (*NW*) and south-east (*SE*) sides. The game proceeds as follows. Dark has the opening move. Every player in turn chooses an unoccupied hexagon, and occupies it with a colored game piece. A player who manages to connect the two sides he controls with a continuous path[8] of hexagons occupied by his pieces is declared a winner. If neither player can do so, a draw is called. We will show that a play of the game can never end in a draw. In Figure 3.14, we depict a play of the game won by Dark. Note that, by the rules, the players can keep placing game pieces until the entire board has been filled, so that a priori it might seem as if it might be possible for both players to win, but it turns out to be impossible, as we will prove. There is, in fact, an intuitive argument for why a draw cannot occur: imagine that one player's game pieces are bodies of water, and the other player's game pieces are dry land. If the water player is a winner, it means that he has managed to create a water channel connecting his sides, through which no land-bridge constructed by the opposing player can cross. We will see that turning this intuitive argument into a formal proof is not at all easy.[9]

---

7 Hex was invented in 1942 by a student named Piet Hein, who called it Polygon. It was reinvented, independently, by John Nash in 1948. The name Hex was given to the game by Parker Bros., who sold a commercial version of it. The proof that the game cannot end in a draw, and that there cannot be two winners, is due to David Gale [1979]. The presentation in this exercise is due to Jack van Rijswijck (see http://www.cs.ualberta.ca/~javhar/). The authors thank Taco Hoekwater for assisting them in preparing the figure of the game board.

8 A *continuous path* is a chain of adjacent hexagons, where two hexagons are called "adjacent" if they share a common edge.

9 This argument is equivalent to Jordan's Theorem, which states that a closed, continuous curve divides a plane into two parts, in such a way that every continuous curve that connects a point in one of the two disconnected parts with a point in the other part must necessarily pass through the original curve.

For simplicity, assume that the edges of the board, as in Figure 3.14, are also composed of (half) hexagons. The hexagons composing each edge will be assumed to be colored with the color of the player who controls that respective edge of the board. Given a fully covered board, we construct a broken line (which begins at the corner labeled W). Every leg of the broken line separates a game piece of one color from a game piece of the other color (see Figure 3.14).

(a) Prove that within the board, with the exception of the corners, the line can always be continued in a unique manner.
(b) Prove that the broken line will never return to a vertex through which it previously passed (hint: use induction).
(c) From the first two claims, and the fact that the board is finite, conclude that the broken line must end at a corner of the board (not the corner from which it starts). Keep in mind that one side of the broken line always touches hexagons of one color (including the hexagons comprising the edges of the rhombus), and the other side of the line always touches hexagons of the other color.
(d) Prove that if the broken line ends at corner S, the sides controlled by Dark are connected by dark-colored hexagons, so that Dark has won (as in Figure 3.14). Similarly, if the broken line ends at corner N, Light has won.
(e) Prove that it is impossible for the broken line to end at corner E.
(f) Conclude that a draw is impossible.
(g) Conclude that it is impossible for both players to win.
(h) Prove that the player with the opening move has a winning strategy.

Guidance for the last part: Based on von Neumann's Theorem (Theorem 3.13, page 46), and previous claims, one (and only one) of the players has a winning strategy. Call the player with the opening move Player I, and the other player Player II. Suppose that Player II has a winning strategy. We will prove then that Player I has a winning strategy too, contradicting von Neumann's Theorem. The winning strategy for Player I is as follows: in the opening move, place a game piece on any hexagon on the board. Call that game piece the "special piece." In subsequent moves, play as if (i) you are Player II (and use his winning strategy), (ii) the special piece has not been placed, and (iii) your opponent is Player I. If the strategy requires placing a game piece where the special game piece has already been placed, put a piece on any empty hexagon, and from there on call that game piece the "special piece."

3.20 *And-Or* is a two-player game played on a full binary tree with a root, of depth n (see Figure 3.15). Every player in turn chooses a leaf of the tree that has not previously been selected, and assigns it the value 1 or 0. After all the leaves have been assigned a value, a value for the entire tree is calculated as in the figure. The first step involves calculating the value of the vertices at one level above the level of the leaves: the value of each such vertex is calculated using the logic "or" function, operating on the values assigned to its children. Next, a value is calculated for each vertex one level up, with that value calculated using the logic

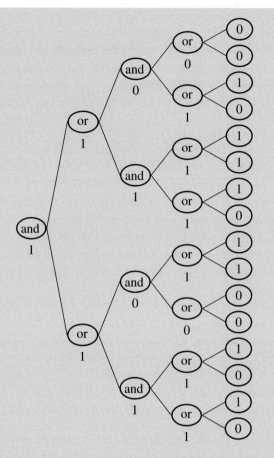

Figure 3.15 A depiction of the game And-Or of depth $n = 4$ as an extensive-form game

"and" function, operating on the values previously calculated for their respective children. The truth tables of the "and" and "or" functions are:[10]

x	y	x and y	x or y
0	0	0	0
0	1	0	1
1	0	0	1
1	1	1	1

Equivalently, x and $y = \min\{x, y\}$ and x or $y = \max\{x, y\}$. The values of all the vertices of the tree are alternately calculated in this manner recursively, with the value of each vertex calculated using either the "and" or "or" functions, operating

---

10 Equivalently, "x or y" $= x \vee y = \max\{x, y\}$, and "$x$ and y" $= x \wedge y = \min\{x, y\}$.

on values calculated for their respective children. Player I wins if the value of the root vertex is 1, and loses if the value of the root vertex is 0. Figure 3.15 shows the end of a play of this game, and the calculations of vertex values by use of the "and" and "or" functions. In this figure, Player I is the winner.

Answer the following questions:

(a) Which player has a winning strategy in a game played on a tree of depth two?
(b) Which player has a winning strategy in a game played on a tree of depth $2k$, where k is any positive integer?

Guidance: To find the winning strategy in a game played on a tree of depth $2k$, keep in mind that you can first calculate inductively the winning strategy for a game played on a tree of depth $2k - 2$.

3.21 Each one of the following figures cannot depict a game in extensive form. For each one, explain why.

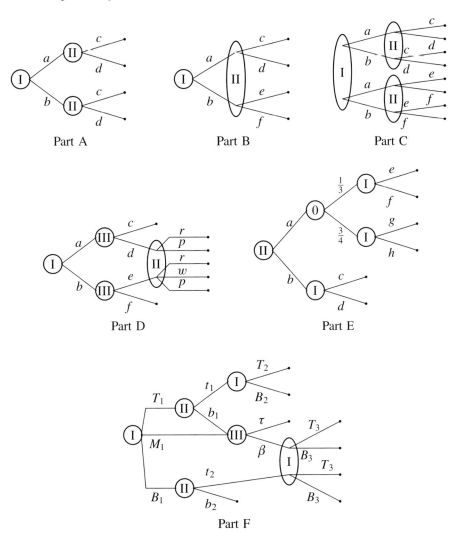

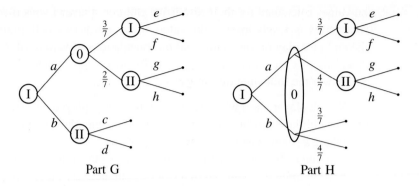

Part G   Part H

3.22 In each of the following games, Player I has an information set containing more than one vertex. What exactly has Player I "forgotten" (or could "forget") during the play of each game?

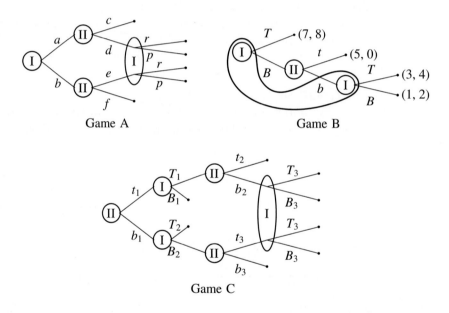

Game A   Game B

Game C

3.23 In which information sets for the following game does Player II know the action taken by Player I?

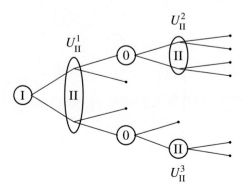

3.24 Sketch the information sets in the following game tree in each of the situations described in this exercise.

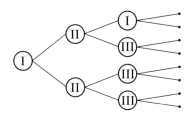

(a) Player II does not know what Player I selected, while Player III knows what Player I selected, but if Player I moved down, Player III does not know what Player II selected.

(b) Player II does not know what Player I selected, and Player III does not know the selections of either Player I or Player II.

(c) At every one of his decision points, Player I cannot remember whether or not he has previously made any moves.

3.25 For each of the following games:

(a) List all of the subgames.

(b) For each information set, note what the player to whom the information set belongs knows, and what he does not know, at that information set.

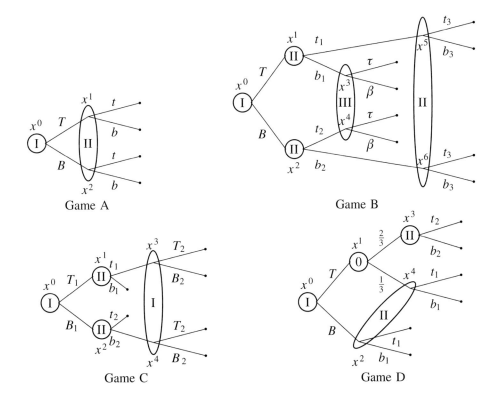

Game A

Game B

Game C

Game D

3.26 Only a partial depiction of a game in extensive form is presented in the accompanying figure to this exercise. Sketch the information sets describing each of the following situations.

(a) Player II, at his decision points, knows what Player I selected, but does not know the result of the chance move.

(b) Player II, at his decision points, knows the result of the chance move (where relevant). If Player I has selected T, Player II knows that this is the case, but if Player I selected either B or M, Player II does not know which of these two actions was selected.

(c) Player II, at his decision points, knows both the result of the chance move and any choice made by Player I.

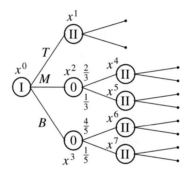

3.27 (a) What does Player I know, and what does he not know, at each information set in the following game:

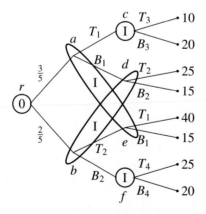

(b) How many strategies has Player I got?

(c) The outcome of the game is the payment to Player I. What do you recommend Player I should play in this game?

3.28 How many strategies has Player II got in the game in the figure in this exercise, in each of the described situations? Justify your answers.

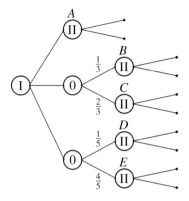

(a) The information sets of Player II are: $\{A\}, \{B, C\}, \{D, E\}$.
(b) The information sets of Player II are: $\{A, B\}, \{C\}, \{D, E\}$.
(c) The information sets of Player II are: $\{A, B, C\}, \{D, E\}$.
(d) The information sets of Player II are: $\{A, B, D\}, \{C\}, \{E\}$.

3.29 Consider the following two-player game:

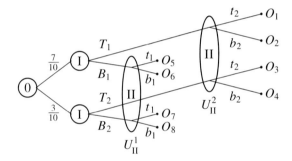

(a) What does Player II know, and what does he not know, at each of his information sets?
(b) Depict the same game as a game in extensive form in which Player II makes his move prior to the chance move, and Player I makes his move after the chance move.
(c) Depict the same game as a game in extensive form in which Player I makes his move prior to the chance move, and Player II makes his move after the chance move.

3.30 Depict the following situation as a game in extensive form. Two corporations manufacturing nearly identical chocolate bars are independently considering whether or not to increase their advertising budgets by $500,000. The sales experts of both corporations are of the opinion that if both corporations increase their advertising budgets, they will each get an equal share of the market, and the same result will ensue if neither corporation increases its advertising budget. In contrast, if one corporation increases its advertising budget while the other maintains the same level of advertising, the corporation that increases its advertising budget will grab an 80% market share, and the other will be left with a 20% market share.

The decisions of the chief executives of the two corporations are made simultaneously; neither one of the chief executives knows what the decision of the other chief executive is at the time he makes his decision.

3.31 Investments Depict the following situation as a game in extensive form. Jack has $100,000 at his disposal, which he would like to invest. His options include investing in gold for one year; if he does so, the expectation is that there is a probability of 30% that the price of gold will rise, yielding Jack a profit of $20,000, and a probability of 70% that the price of gold will drop, causing Jack to lose $10,000. Jack can alternatively invest his money in shares of the Future Energies corporation; if he does so, the expectation is that there is a probability of 60% that the price of the shares will rise, yielding Jack a profit of $50,000, and a probability of 40% that the price of the shares will drop to such an extent that Jack will lose his entire investment. Another option open to Jack is placing the money in a safe index-linked money market account yielding a 5% return.

3.32 In the game depicted in Figure 3.16, if Player I chooses T, there is an ensuing chance move, after which Player II has a turn, but if Player I chooses B, there is no chance move, and Player II has an immediately ensuing turn (without a chance move). The outcome of the game is a pair of numbers (x, y) in which x is the payoff for Player I and y is the payoff for Player II.

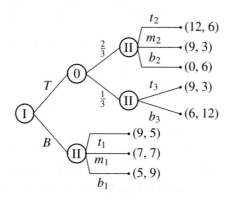

(a) What are all the strategies available to Player I?

(b) How many strategies has Player II got? List all of them.

(c) What is the expected payoff to each player if Player I plays B and Player II plays (t_1, b_2, t_3)?

(d) What is the expected payoff to each player if Player I plays T and Player II plays (t_1, b_2, t_3)?

3.33 The following questions relate to Figure 3.16. The outcome of the game is a triple (x, y, z) representing the payoff to each player, with x denoting the payoff to Player I, y the payoff to Player II, and z the payoff to Player III.

The outcome of the game is a pair of numbers, representing a payment to each player.

(a) Depict, by drawing arrows, strategies (a, c, e), (h, j, l), and (m, p, q) of the three players.

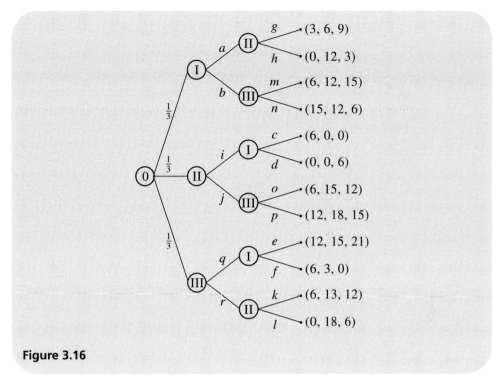

Figure 3.16

(b) Calculate the expected payoff if the players make use of the strategies in part (a).

(c) How would you play this game, if you were Player I? Assume that each player is striving to maximize his expected payoff.

3.34 Bill asks Al to choose heads or tails. After Al has made his choice (without disclosing it to Bill), Bill flips a coin. If the coin falls on Al's choice, Al wins. Otherwise, Bill wins. Depict this situation as a game in extensive form.

3.35 A pack of three cards, labeled 1, 2, and 3, is shuffled. William, Mary, and Anne each take a card from the pack. Each of the two players holding a card with low values (1 or 2) pays the amount of money appearing on the card he or she is holding to the player holding the high-valued card (namely, 3). Depict this situation as a game in extensive form.

3.36 Depict the game trees of the following variants of the candidate game appearing in Exercise 3.2:

(a) Eric does not announce which candidate he prefers until the end of the game. He instead writes down the name of his candidate on a slip of paper, and shows that slip of paper to the others only after Larry and Sergey have announced their preferred candidate.

(b) A secret ballot is conducted: no player announces his preferred candidate until the end of the game.

(c) Eric and Sergey keep their candidate preference a secret until the end of the game, but Larry announces his candidate preference as soon as he has made his choice.

3.37 Describe the game Rock, Paper, Scissors as an extensive-form game (if you are unfamiliar with this game, see page 77 for a description).

3.38 Consider the following game. Player I has the opening move, in which he chooses an action in the set $\{L, R\}$. A lottery is then conducted, with either λ or ρ selected, both with probability $\frac{1}{2}$. Finally, Player II chooses either l or r. The outcomes of the game are not specified. Depict the game tree associated with the extensive-form game in each of the following situations:

    (a) Player II, at his turn, knows Player I's choice, but does not know the outcome of the lottery.

    (b) Player II, at his turn, knows the outcome of the lottery, but does not know Player I's choice.

    (c) Player II, at his turn, knows the outcome of the lottery only if Player I has selected L.

    (d) Player II, at his turn, knows Player I's choice if the outcome of the lottery is λ, but does not know Player I's choice if the outcome of the lottery is ρ.

    (e) Player II, at his turn, does not know Player I's choice, and also does not know the outcome of the lottery.

3.39 In the following game, the root is a chance move, Player I has three information sets, and the outcome is the amount of money that Player I receives.

    (a) What does Player I know in each of his information sets, and what does he not know?

    (b) What would you recommend Player I to play, assuming that he wants to maximize his expected payoff? Justify your answer.

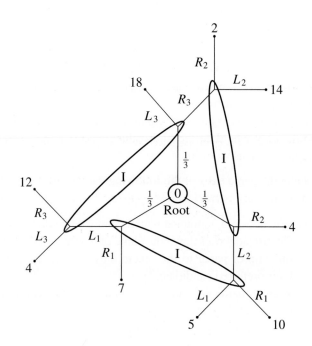

4 Strategic-form games

Chapter summary

In this chapter we present the model of *strategic-form games*. A game in strategic form consists of a set of players, a strategy set for each player, and an outcome to each vector of strategies, which is usually given by the vector of utilities the players enjoy from the outcome. The strategic-form description ignores dynamic aspects of the game, such as the order of the moves by the players, chance moves, and the informational structure of the game.

The goal of the theory is to suggest which strategies are more likely to be played by the players, or to recommend to players which strategy to implement (or not to implement). We present several concepts that allow one to achieve these goals. The first concept introduced is *domination* (strict or weak), which provides a partial ordering of strategies of the same player; it tells when one strategy is "better" than another strategy. Under the hypothesis that it is commonly known that "rational" players do not implement a dominated strategy we can then introduce the process of *iterated elimination of dominated strategies*. In this process, dominated strategies are successively eliminated from the game, thereby simplifying it. We go on to introduce the notion of *stability*, captured by the concept of *Nash equilibrium*, and the notion of *security*, captured by the concept of the maxmin value and maxmin strategies. The important class of *two-player zero-sum* games is introduced along with its solution called the *value* (or the *minmax value*). This solution concept shares both properties of security and stability. When the game is not zero-sum, security and stability lead typically to different predictions.

We prove that every extensive-form game with perfect information has a Nash equilibrium. This is actually a generalization of the theorem on the game of chess proved in Chapter 1.

To better understand the relationships between the various concepts, we study the effects of elimination of dominated strategies on the maxmin value and on equilibrium payoffs. Finally, as a precursor to mixed strategies introduced in the next chapter, we look at an example of a two-player game on the unit square and compute its Nash equilibrium.

As we saw in Chapter 3, a player's strategy in an extensive-form game is a decision rule that determines that player's action in each and every one of his information sets. When there are no chance moves in the game, each vector of strategies – one strategy per player – determines the play of the game and therefore also the outcome. If there are chance moves, a vector of strategies determines a probability distribution over possible plays of the game, and therefore also over the outcomes of the game. The strategy chosen by a player therefore influences the outcome (or the probability distribution of outcomes, if there are chance moves).

If all we are interested in is the outcomes of the game and not the specific actions that brought about those outcomes, then it suffices to describe the game as the set of strategies available to each player, along with the distribution over the outcomes that each vector of strategies brings about.

4.1　Examples and definition of strategic-form games

For the analysis of games, every player must have preferences with respect to the set of outcomes. This subject was covered in detail in Chapter 2 on utility theory, where we saw that if player i's preference relation $\succeq_i$ satisfies the von Neumann–Morgenstern axioms, then it can be represented by a linear utility function u_i. In other words, to every possible outcome o, we can associate a real number $u_i(o)$ representing the utility that player i ascribes to o, with the player preferring one outcome to another if and only if the utility of the first outcome is higher than the utility of the second outcome. The player prefers one lottery to another lottery if and only if the expected utility of the outcomes according to the first lottery is greater than the expected utility of the outcomes according to the second lottery.

In most games we analyze in this book, we assume that the preference relations of the players satisfy the von Neumann–Morgenstern axioms. We will also assume that the outcomes of plays of games are given in utility terms. This means that the outcome of a play of a game is an n-dimensional vector, where the i-th coordinate is player i's utility from that play of the game.[1]

Example 4.1　Consider the following two-player game (Figure 4.1) presented in extensive form with six possible outcomes.

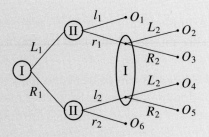

Figure 4.1 A two-player game in extensive form

---

1 This is equivalent to the situation where the outcomes are monetary payoffs and the players are risk neutral, in which case every lottery over payoffs is equivalent to the expected monetary payoff in the lottery drawing.

Player I has four strategies: L_1L_2, L_1R_2, R_1L_2, R_1R_2, and Player II has four strategies: l_1l_2, l_1r_2, r_1l_2, r_1r_2. The extensive-form description presents in detail what each player knows at each of his decision points. But we can ignore all that information, and present the players' strategies, along with the outcomes they lead to, in the table in Figure 4.2:

		Player II			
		l_1l_2	l_1r_2	r_1l_2	r_1r_2
	L_1L_2	O_1	O_1	O_2	O_2
	L_1R_2	O_1	O_1	O_3	O_3
Player I	R_1L_2	O_4	O_6	O_4	O_6
	R_1R_2	O_5	O_6	O_5	O_6

Figure 4.2 The game in Figure 4.1 in strategic form

In this description of the game, the rows represent the strategies of Player I and the columns those of Player II. In each cell of the table appears the outcome that arises if the two players choose the pair of strategies associated with that cell. For example, if Player I chooses strategy L_1L_2 and Player II chooses strategy l_1l_2, we will be in the upper-leftmost cell of the table, leading to outcome O_1. ◀

A game presented in this way is called a game in *strategic form* or a game in *normal form*.

Definition 4.2 *A game in* strategic form *(or in* normal form*) is an ordered triple* $G = (N, (S_i)_{i \in N}, (u_i)_{i \in N})$*, in which:*

- $N = \{1, 2, \ldots, n\}$ *is a finite set of players.*
- S_i *is the set of strategies of player i, for every player* $i \in N$.

We denote the set of all vectors of strategies by $S = S_1 \times S_2 \times \cdots \times S_n$.

- $u_i : S \to \mathbb{R}$ *is a function associating each vector of strategies* $s = (s_i)_{i \in N}$ *with the payoff (= utility)* $u_i(s)$ *to player i, for every player* $i \in N$.

In this definition, the sets of strategies available to the players are not required to be finite, and in fact we will see games with infinite strategy sets in this book. A game in which the strategy set of each player is finite is termed a *finite game*. The fact that u_i is a function of the vector of strategies s, and not solely of player i's strategy s_i, is what makes this a *game*, i.e., a situation of interactive decisions in which the outcome for each player depends not on his strategy alone, but on the strategies chosen by all the players.

Example 4.3 Rock, Paper, Scissors In the game Rock, Paper, Scissors, each one of two players chooses an action from three alternatives: Rock, Paper, or Scissors. The actions are selected by the players simultaneously, with a circular dominance relationship obtaining between the three alternatives: rock smashes scissors, which cut paper, which in turn covers rock. The game in extensive form is described in Figure 4.3, in which the terminal vertices are labeled by the outcomes "I wins," "II wins," or Draw.

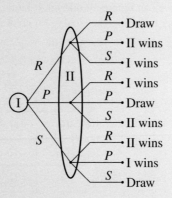

Figure 4.3 Rock, Paper, Scissors as a game in extensive form

Setting the payoff to a player to be 1 for a win, -1 for a loss, and 0 for a draw, we obtain the game in strategic form appearing in Figure 4.4. In each cell in Figure 4.4 the left number denotes the payoff to Player I and the right number denotes the payoff to Player II.

		Player II		
		Rock	Paper	Scissors
	Rock	0, 0	−1, 1	1, −1
Player I	Paper	1, −1	0, 0	− 1, 1
	Scissors	−1, 1	1, −1	0, 0

Figure 4.4 Rock, Paper, Scissors as a strategic-form game

Games in strategic form are sometimes called *matrix games* because they are described by matrices.[2] When the number of players n is greater than 2, the corresponding matrix is n-dimensional, and each cell of the matrix contains a vector with n coordinates, representing the payoffs to the n players.

When there are no chance moves, a game in strategic form is derived from a game in extensive form in the following way:

- List the set of all strategies S_i available to each player i in the extensive-form game.
- For each vector of strategies $s = (s_i)_{i \in N}$, find the play determined by this vector of strategies, and then derive the payoffs induced by this play:

$$u(s) := (u_1(s), u_2(s), \ldots, u_n(s)).$$

2 When $n = 2$ it is customary to call these games *bimatrix games*, as they are given by two matrices, one for the payoff of each player.

- Draw the appropriate n-dimensional matrix. When there are two players, the number of rows in the matrix equals the number of strategies of Player I, the number of columns equals the number of strategies of Player II, and the pair of numbers appearing in each cell is the pair of payoffs defined by the pair of strategies associated with that cell. When there are more than two players, the matrix is multi-dimensional (see Exercises 4.17 and 4.18 for examples of games with three players).

How is a strategic-form game derived from an extensive-form game when there are chance moves? In that case, every strategy vector $s = (s_i)_{i \in N}$ determines a probability distribution μ_s over the set O of the game's possible outcomes, where for each $o \in O$ the value of $\mu_s(o)$ is the probability that if the players play according to strategy vector s, the outcome will be o. The cell corresponding to strategy vector s contains the average of the payoffs corresponding to the possible outcomes according to this probability distribution, i.e., the vector $u(s) = (u_i(s))_{i \in N} \in \mathbb{R}^N$ defined by

$$u_i(s) := \sum_{o \in O} \mu_s(o) \times u_i(o). \tag{4.1}$$

Since we are assuming that the preference relations of all players satisfy the von Neumann–Morgenstern axioms, $u_i(s)$ is the utility that player i receives from the lottery over the outcomes of the game that is induced when the players play according to strategy vector s.

Example 4.4 Consider the game in extensive form presented in Figure 4.5.

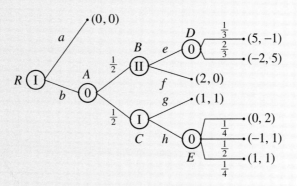

Figure 4.5 An extensive-form game with chance moves

In this game the outcome is a payoff to each of the players. This is a game of perfect information. Player I has two decision nodes, in each of which he has two possible actions. Player I's strategy set is therefore

$$S_I = \{(a, g), (a, h), (b, g), (b, h)\}. \tag{4.2}$$

Player II has one decision node with two possible actions, so that Player II's strategy set is

$$S_{II} = \{e, f\}. \tag{4.3}$$

To see how the payoffs are calculated, look, for example, at Player I's strategy (b, g) and at Player II's strategy e. If the players choose these strategies, three possible plays can occur with positive probability:

- The play $R \to A \to B \to D \to (5, -1)$, with probability $\frac{1}{6}$.
- The play $R \to A \to B \to D \to (-2, 5)$, with probability $\frac{1}{3}$.
- The play $R \to A \to C \to (1, 1)$, with probability $\frac{1}{2}$.

It follows that the expected payoff is

$$\tfrac{1}{6}(5, -1) + \tfrac{1}{3}(-2, 5) + \tfrac{1}{2}(1, 1) = \left(\tfrac{2}{3}, 2\right). \tag{4.4}$$

We can similarly calculate the payoffs to each pair of strategies. The resulting strategic-form game appears in Figure 4.6 (verify!).

Player II

	f	e
(a, g)	$0, 0$	$0, 0$
(a, h)	$0, 0$	$0, 0$
(b, g)	$\frac{3}{2}, \frac{1}{2}$	$\frac{2}{3}, 2$
(b, h)	$\frac{7}{8}, \frac{5}{8}$	$\frac{1}{24}, \frac{17}{8}$

Player I

Figure 4.6 The strategic form of the game in Figure 4.5

◄

In the game in Figure 4.6, Player I's two strategies (a, g) and (a, h) correspond to the same row of payoffs. This means that, independently of Player II's strategy, the strategy (a, g) leads to the same payoffs as does the strategy (a, h). We say that these two strategies are *equivalent*. This equivalence can be understood by considering the corresponding game in extensive form (Figure 4.5): when Player I chooses a (at vertex R), the choice between g and h has no effect on the outcome of the game, because the play never arrives at vertex C. We can therefore represent the two strategies (a, g) and (a, h) by one strategy, (a), and derive the strategic-form game described in Figure 4.7.

Player II

	f	e
(a)	$0, 0$	$0, 0$
(b, g)	$\frac{3}{2}, \frac{1}{2}$	$\frac{2}{3}, 2$
(b, h)	$\frac{7}{8}, \frac{5}{8}$	$\frac{1}{24}, \frac{17}{8}$

Player I

Figure 4.7 The reduced strategic form of the game in Figure 4.5

A strategic-form game in which every set of equivalent strategies is represented by a single strategy ("the equivalence set") is called a *game in reduced strategic form*. This is essentially the form of the game that is arrived at when we take into account the fact that a particular action by a player excludes reaching some information sets of that player. In that case, there is no need to specify his strategies at those information sets.

Example 4.5   **The game of chess in strategic form**   The number of strategies in the game of chess is immense even if we impose a maximal (large) number of moves, after which the outcome is declared as a draw. There is no practical way to write down its game matrix (just as there is no practical way to present the game in extensive form). But it is significant that in principle the game can be represented by a finite matrix (even if its size is astronomic) (see Figure 4.8). The only possible outcomes of the game appearing in the cells of the matrix are W (victory for White), B (victory for Black), and D (draw).

$$
\begin{array}{c}
 & \text{Black} \\
 & \begin{array}{c|ccccccc}
 & 1 & 2 & 3 & \cdot & \cdot & \cdot \\
\hline
1 & W & D & W & \cdot & \cdot & \cdot \\
2 & D & D & B & \cdot & \cdot & \cdot \\
3 & B & B & D & \cdot & \cdot & \cdot \\
\cdot & & \cdot & & \cdot & & \\
\cdot & & \cdot & & & & \\
\cdot & & \cdot & & & & \\
\end{array}
\end{array}
$$

Figure 4.8 The game of chess in strategic form

A winning strategy for the White player (if one exists) would be represented by a row, all of whose elements are W. A winning strategy for the Black player (if one exists) would be represented in this matrix by a column, all of whose elements are B. A strategy ensuring at least a draw for White (or Black) is a row (or a column), all of whose elements are D or W (or B or D).

It follows from Theorem 1.4 (page 3) that in the matrix representing the game of chess, one and only one of the following alternatives holds:

1. There is a row all of whose elements are W.
2. There is a column all of whose elements are B.
3. There is a row all of whose elements are W or D, and a column all of whose elements are B or D.

If the third possibility obtains, then the cell at the intersection of the row ensuring at least a draw for White and the column guaranteeing at least a draw for Black must contain D: if both players are playing a strategy guaranteeing at least a draw, then the outcome of the play must necessarily be a draw.   ◄

4.2   The relationship between the extensive form and the strategic form

We have shown that every extensive-form game can be associated with a unique reduced strategic-form game (meaning that every set of equivalent strategies in the extensive-form game is represented by one strategy in the strategic-form game). We have also

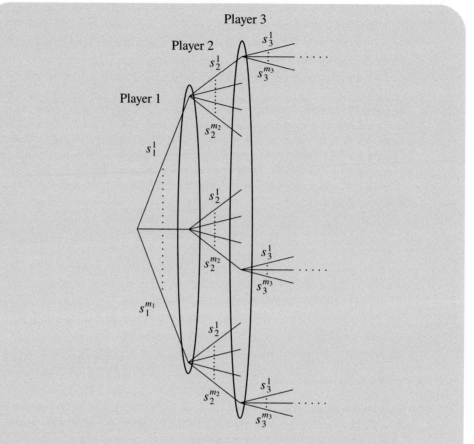

Figure 4.9 A canonical representation of a strategic-form game as an extensive-form game

exhibited a way of deriving a strategic-form game from an extensive-form game. There are two natural questions that arise with respect to the inverse operation: Does every strategic-form game have an extensive-form game from which it is derived? Is there a unique extensive-form game associated with a strategic-form game? The answer to the first question is affirmative, while the answer to the second question is negative. To show that the first question has an affirmative answer, we will now describe how to associate an extensive-form game with a given strategic-form game.

Let $G = (N, (S_i)_{i \in N}, (u_i)_{i \in N})$ be a game in strategic form, and denote the strategies of each player i by $S_i = \{s_i^1, \ldots, s_i^{m_i}\}$. The reader can verify that G is the strategic-form game associated with the extensive-form game that appears in Figure 4.9.

This is a natural description that is also called the "canonical representation" of the game. It captures the main characteristic of a strategic-form game: in essence, the players choose their strategies simultaneously. This property is expressed in Figure 4.9 by the fact that each player has a single information set. For example, despite the fact that in the

Player II

		$r\tilde{r}$	$r\tilde{l}$	$l\tilde{r}$	$l\tilde{l}$
Player I	L	2, −1	2, −1	2, 0	2, 0
	R	3, 1	1, 0	3, 1	1, 0

Figure 4.10 The strategic-form game derived from each of the three games in Figure 4.11

extensive-form game Player 1 chooses his strategy first, none of the other players, when coming to choose their strategies, know which strategy Player 1 has chosen. Clearly, the order of the players that appear in Figure 4.9 can be selected arbitrarily. Since there are $n!$ permutations over the set of n players, and each permutation defines a different ordering of the players, there are $n!$ such extensive-form canonical descriptions of the same strategic-form game.

Are there other, significantly different, ways of describing the same strategic-form game? The answer is positive. For example, each one of the three games in Figure 4.11 yields the two-player strategic-form game of Figure 4.10.

Representation A in Figure 4.11 is the canonical representation of the game. In representation C we have changed the order of the players: instead of Player I playing first followed by Player II, we have divided the choice made by Player II into two parts: one choice is made before Player I makes his selection, and one afterwards. As neither player knows which strategy was selected by the other player, the difference is immaterial to the game. Representation B is more interesting, because in that game Player II knows Player I's selection before he makes his selection (verify that the strategic form of each of the extensive-form games in Figure 4.11 is identical to the strategic-form game in Figure 4.10).

The fact that a single strategic-form game can be derived from several different extensive-form games is not surprising, because the strategic-form description of a game is a condensed description of the extensive-form game. It ignores many of the dynamic aspects of the extensive-form description. An interesting mathematical question that arises here is "what is the extent of the difference" between two extensive-form games associated with the same strategic-form game? Given two extensive-form games, is it possible to identify whether or not they yield the same strategic-form game, without explicitly calculating their strategic-form representation? This subject was studied by Thompson [1952], who defined three elementary operations that do not change the "essence" of a game. He then proved that if two games in extensive form with the same set of players can be transformed into each other by a finite number of these three elementary operations, then those two extensive-form games correspond to the same strategic-form game. He also showed that the other direction obtains: if two games in extensive form yield the same strategic-form game, then they can be transformed into each other by a finite number of these three elementary operations.

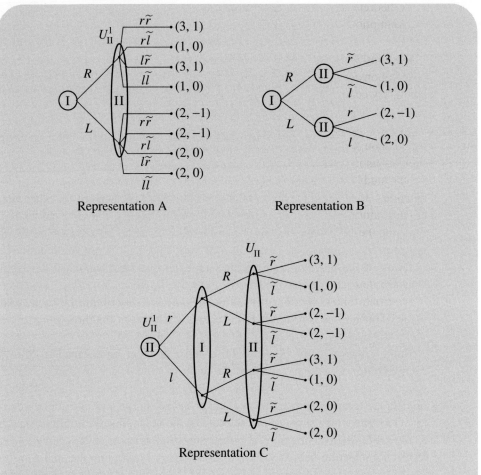

Representation A

Representation B

Representation C

Figure 4.11 Three extensive-form games corresponding to the same strategic-form game in Figure 4.10

4.3   Strategic-form games: solution concepts

We have dealt so far only with the different ways of describing games in extensive and strategic form. We discussed von Neumann's theorem in the special case of two players and three possible outcomes: victory for White, a draw, or victory for Black. Now we will look at more general games, and consider the central question of game theory: What can we say about what "will happen" in a given game? First of all, note that this question has at least three different possible interpretations:

1. An empirical, descriptive interpretation: How do players, in fact, play in a given game?
2. A normative interpretation: How "should" the players play in a given game?

3. A theoretical interpretation: What can we predict will happen in a game given certain assumptions regarding "reasonable" or "rational" behavior on the part of the players?

Descriptive game theory deals with the first interpretation. This field of study involves observations of the actual behavior of players, both in real-life situations and in artificial laboratory conditions where they are asked to play games and their behavior is recorded. This book will not address that area of game theory.

The second interpretation would be appropriate for a judge, legislator, or arbitrator called upon to determine the outcome of a game based on several agreed-upon principles, such as justice, efficiency, nondiscrimination, and fairness. This approach is best suited for the study of cooperative games, in which binding agreements are possible, enabling outcomes to be derived from "norms" or agreed-upon principles, or determined by an arbitrator who bases his decision on those principles. This is indeed the approach used for the study of bargaining games (see Chapter 16) and the Shapley value (see Chapter 19).

In this chapter we will address the third interpretation, the theoretical approach. After we have described a game, in either extensive or strategic form, what can we expect to happen? What outcomes, or set of outcomes, will reasonably ensue, given certain assumptions regarding the behavior of the players?

4.4   Notation

Let $N = \{1, \ldots, n\}$ be a finite set, and for each $i \in N$ let X_i be any set. Denote $X := \times_{i \in N} X_i$, and for each $i \in N$ define $X_{-i} := \times_{j \neq i} X_j$ the Cartesian product of all the sets X_j except for the set X_i. In other words,

$$X_{-i} = \{(x_1, \ldots, x_{i-1}, x_{i+1}, \ldots, x_n) : x_j \in X_j, \quad \forall j \neq i\}. \tag{4.5}$$

An element in X_{-i} will be denoted $x_{-i} = (x_1, \ldots, x_{i-1}, x_{i+1}, \ldots, x_n)$, which is the $(n-1)$-dimensional vector derived from $(x_1, \ldots, x_n) \in X$ by suppressing the i-th coordinate.

4.5   Domination

Consider the two-player game that appears in Figure 4.12, in which Player I chooses a row and Player II chooses a column.

Comparing Player II's strategies M and R, we find that:

- If Player I plays T, the payoff to Player II under strategy M is 2, compared to only 1 under strategy R.
- If Player I plays B, the payoff to Player II under strategy M is 1, compared to only 0 under strategy R.

		Player II		
		L	M	R
Player I	T	1, 0	1, 2	0, 1
	B	0, 3	0, 1	2, 0

Figure 4.12 Strategy *M* dominates strategy *R*

We see that independently of whichever strategy is played by Player I, strategy *M* always yields a higher payoff to Player II than strategy *R*. This motivates the following definition:

Definition 4.6 *A strategy s_i of player i is* strictly dominated *if there exists another strategy t_i of player i such that for each strategy vector $s_{-i} \in S_{-i}$ of the other players,*

$$u_i(s_i, s_{-i}) < u_i(t_i, s_{-i}). \tag{4.6}$$

If this is the case, we say that s_i is strictly dominated by t_i, *or that t_i* strictly dominates s_i.

In the example in Figure 4.12, strategy *R* is strictly dominated by strategy *M*. It is therefore reasonable to assume that if Player II is "rational," he will not choose *R*, because under any scenario in which he might consider selecting *R*, the strategy *M* would be a better choice. This is the first rationality property that we assume.

Assumption 4.7 *A rational player will not choose a strictly dominated strategy.*

We will assume that all the players are rational.

Assumption 4.8 *All the players in a game are rational.*

Can a strictly dominated strategy (such as strategy *R* in Figure 4.12) be eliminated, under these two assumptions? The answer is: not necessarily. It is true that if Player II is rational he will not choose strategy *R*, but if Player I does not know that Player II is rational, he is liable to believe that Player II may choose strategy *R*, in which case it would be in Player I's interest to play strategy *B*. So, in order to eliminate the strictly dominated strategies one needs to postulate that:

- Player II is rational, and
- Player I knows that Player II is rational.

On further reflection, it becomes clear that this, too, is insufficient, and we also need to assume that:

- Player II knows that Player I knows that Player II is rational.

Otherwise, Player II would need to consider the possibility that Player I may play *B*, considering *R* to be a strategy contemplated by Player II, in which case Player II may be

Player II

L   M

	L	M
T	1, 0	1, 2
B	0, 3	0, 1

Player I

Figure 4.13 The game in Figure 4.12 after the elimination of strategy R

tempted to play L. Once again, further scrutiny reveals that this is still insufficient, and we need to assume that:

- Player I knows that Player II knows that Player I knows that Player II is rational.
- Player II knows that Player I knows that Player II knows that Player I knows that Player II is rational.
- And so forth.

If all the infinite conditions implied by the above are satisfied, we say that the fact that Player II is rational is *common knowledge* among the players. This is an important concept underlying most of our presentation. Here we will give only an informal presentation of the concept of common knowledge. A formal definition appears in Chapter 9, where we extensively study common knowledge.

Definition 4.9 *A fact is* common knowledge *among the players of a game if for any finite chain of players* $i_1, i_2, \ldots, i_k$ *the following holds: player* i_1 *knows that player* i_2 *knows that player* i_3 *knows ... that player* i_k *knows the fact.*

The chain in Definition 4.9 may contain several instances of the same player (as indeed happens in the above example). Definition 4.9 is an informal definition since we have not formally defined what the term "fact" means, nor have we defined the significance of knowing a fact. We will now add a further assumption to the two assumptions listed above:

Assumption 4.10 *The fact that all players are rational (Assumption 4.8) is common knowledge among the players.*

Strictly dominated strategies can be eliminated under Assumptions 4.7, 4.8, and 4.10 (we will not provide a formal proof of this claim). In the example in Figure 4.12, this means that, given the assumptions, we should focus on the game obtained by the elimination of strategy R, which appears in Figure 4.13.

In this game, strategy B of Player I is strictly dominated by strategy T. Because the rationality of Player I is common knowledge, as is the fact that B is a strictly dominated strategy, after the elimination of strategy R, strategy B can also be eliminated. The players therefore need to consider a game with even fewer strategies, which is given in Figure 4.14.

Because in this game strategy L is strictly dominated (for Player II) by strategy M, after its elimination only one result remains, $(1, 2)$, which obtains when Player I plays T and Player II plays M.

Player II

$L \qquad M$

Player I T | 1, 0 | 1, 2 |

Figure 4.14 The game in Figure 4.12 following the elimination of strategies *R* and *B*

The process we have just described is called *iterated elimination of strictly dominated strategies*. When this process yields a single strategy vector (one strategy per player), as in the example above, then, under Assumptions 4.7, 4.8, and 4.10, that is the strategy vector that will obtain, and it may be regarded as the *solution* of the game.

A special case in which such a solution is guaranteed to exist is the family of games in which every player has a strategy that strictly dominates all of his other strategies, that is, a *strictly dominant strategy*. Clearly, in that case, the elimination of all strictly dominated strategies leaves each player with only one strategy: his strictly dominant strategy. When this occurs we say that the game has a solution in *strictly dominant strategies*.

Example 4.11 **The Prisoner's Dilemma** The Prisoner's Dilemma is a very simple game that is interesting in several respects. It appears in the literature in the form of the following story.

Two individuals who have committed a serious crime are apprehended. Lacking incriminating evidence, the prosecution can obtain an indictment only by persuading one (or both) of the prisoners to confess to the crime. Interrogators give each of the prisoners – both of whom are isolated in separate cells and unable to communicate with each other – the following choices:

1. If you confess and your friend refuses to confess, you will be released from custody and receive immunity as a state's witness.
2. If you refuse to confess and your friend confesses, you will receive the maximum penalty for your crime (ten years of incarceration).
3. If both of you sit tight and refuse to confess, we will make use of evidence that you have committed tax evasion to ensure that both of you are sentenced to a year in prison.
4. If both of you confess, it will count in your favor and we will reduce each of your prison terms to six years.

This situation defines a two-player strategic-form game in which each player has two strategies: *D*, which stands for Defection, betraying your fellow criminal by confessing, and *C*, which stands for Cooperation, cooperating with your fellow criminal and not confessing to the crime. In this notation, the outcome of the game (in prison years) is shown in Figure 4.15.

Player II

$D \qquad C$

Player I

D | 6, 6 | 0, 10 |
C | 10, 0 | 1, 1 |

Figure 4.15 The Prisoner's Dilemma in prison years

As usual, the left-hand number in each cell of the matrix represents the outcome (in prison years) for Player I, and the right-hand number represents the outcome for Player II.

We now present the game in utility units. For example, suppose the utility of both players is given by the following function u:

$$u(\text{release}) = 5, \qquad u(1 \text{ year in prison}) = 4,$$
$$u(6 \text{ years in prison}) = 1, \qquad u(10 \text{ years in prison}) = 0.$$

The game, in utility terms, appears in Figure 4.16.

Player II

	D	C
D	1, 1	5, 0
C	0, 5	4, 4

Player I

Figure 4.16 The Prisoner's Dilemma in utility units

For both players, strategy D (Defect) strictly dominates strategy C (Cooperate). Elimination of strictly dominated strategies leads to the single solution (D, D) in which both prisoners confess, resulting in the payoff $(1, 1)$.   ◄

What makes the Prisoner's Dilemma interesting is the fact that if both players choose strategy C, the payoff they receive is $(4, 4)$, which is preferable for both of them. The solution derived from Assumptions 4.7, 4.8, and 4.10, which appear to be quite reasonable assumptions, is "inefficient": The pair of strategies (C, C) is unstable, because each individual player can deviate (by defecting) and gain an even better payoff of 5 (instead of 4) for himself (at the expense of the other player, who would receive 0).

In the last example, two strictly dominated strategies were eliminated (one per player), but there was no specification regarding the order in which these strategies were eliminated: was Player I's strategy C eliminated first, or Player II's, or were they both eliminated simultaneously? In this case, a direct verification reveals that the order of elimination makes no difference. It turns out that this is a general result: whenever iterated elimination of strictly dominated strategies leads to a single strategy vector, that outcome is independent of the order of elimination. In fact, we can make an even stronger statement: even if iterated elimination of strictly dominated strategies yields a set of strategies (not necessarily a single strategy), that set does not depend on the order of elimination (see Exercise 4.10).

There are games in which iterated elimination of strictly dominated strategies does not yield a single strategy vector. For example, in a game that has no strictly dominated strategies, the process fails to eliminate any strategy. The game in Figure 4.17 provides an example of such a game.

Although there are no strictly dominated strategies in this game, strategy B does have a special attribute: although it does not always guarantee a higher payoff to Player I relative to strategy T, in all cases it does grant him a payoff at least as high, and in the special case in which Player II chooses strategy L, B is a strictly better choice than T. In this case we say that strategy B *weakly dominates* strategy T (and strategy T is *weakly dominated by* strategy B).

Player II

		L	R
Player I	T	1, 2	2, 3
	B	2, 2	2, 0

Figure 4.17 A game with no strictly dominated strategies

Definition 4.12 *Strategy s_i of player i is termed* weakly dominated *if there exists another strategy t_i of player i satisfying the following two conditions:*

(a) For every strategy vector $s_{-i} \in S_{-i}$ of the other players,

$$u_i(s_i, s_{-i}) \leq u_i(t_i, s_{-i}). \tag{4.7}$$

(b) There exists a strategy vector $t_{-i} \in S_{-i}$ of the other players such that

$$u_i(s_i, t_{-i}) < u_i(t_i, t_{-i}). \tag{4.8}$$

In this case we say that strategy s_i is weakly dominated by *strategy t_i, and that strategy t_i* weakly dominates *strategy s_i.*

If strategy t_i dominates (weakly or strictly) strategy s_i, then s_i does not (weakly or strictly) dominate t_i. Clearly, strict domination implies weak domination. Because we will refer henceforth almost exclusively to weak domination, we use the term "domination" to mean "weak domination," unless the term "strict domination" is explicitly used. The following rationality assumption is stronger than Assumption 4.7.

Assumption 4.13 *A rational player does not use a dominated strategy.*

Under Assumptions 4.8, 4.10, and 4.13 we may eliminate strategy T in the game in Figure 4.17 (as it is weakly dominated), and then proceed to eliminate strategy R (which is strictly dominated after the elimination of T). The only remaining strategy vector is (B, L), with a payoff of $(2, 2)$. Such a strategy vector is called *rational*.

Definition 4.14 *A strategy vector $s \in S$ is termed* rational *if it is the unique result of a process of iterative elimination of weakly dominated strategies.*

Whereas Assumption 4.7 looks reasonable, Assumption 4.13 is quite strong. Reinhard Selten, in trying to justify Assumption 4.13, suggested a concept he termed the *trembling hand principle*. The basic postulate of this principle is that every single strategy available to a player may be used with positive probability, which may well be extremely small. This may happen simply by mistake (the player's hand might tremble as he reaches to press the button setting in motion his chosen strategy, so that by mistake the button associated with a different strategy is activated instead), by irrationality on the part of the player, or because the player chose a wrong strategy due to miscalculations. This topic will be explored in greater depth in Section 7.3 (page 273).

To illustrate the trembling hand principle, suppose that Player II in the example of Figure 4.17 chooses strategies L and R with respective probabilities x and $1 - x$, where $0 < x < 1$. The expected payoff to Player I in that case is $x + 2(1 - x) = 2 - x$ if he chooses strategy T, as opposed to a payoff of 2 if he chooses strategy B. It follows that strategy B grants him a strictly higher expected payoff than T, so that a rational Player I facing Player II who has a trembling hand will choose B and not T; i.e., he will not choose the weakly dominated strategy.

The fact that strategy s_i of player i (weakly or strictly) dominates his strategy t_i depends only on player i's payoff function, and is independent of the payoff functions of the other players. Therefore, a player can eliminate his dominated strategies even when he does not know the payoff functions of the other players. This property will be useful in Section 4.6. Eliminating strategy s_i of player i after strategy s_j of player j means that we assume that player i believes that player j will not implement s_j. This assumption is reasonable only if player i knows player j's payoff function. Therefore, the process of iterative elimination of dominated strategies can be justified only if the payoff functions of the players are common knowledge among them; if this condition does not hold, this process is harder to justify.

The process of iterated elimination of dominated strategies is an efficient tool that leads, sometimes surprisingly, to significant results. The following example, taken from the theory of auctions, provides an illustration.

4.6   Second-price auctions

A detailed study of auction theory is presented in Chapter 12. In this section we will concentrate on the relevance of the concept of dominance to auctions known as *sealed-bid second-price auctions*, which are conducted as follows:

- An indivisible object is offered for sale.
- The set of buyers in the auction is denoted by N. Each buyer i attaches a value v_i to the object; that is, he is willing to pay at most v_i for the object (and is indifferent between walking away without the object and obtaining it at price v_i). The value v_i is buyer i's *private value*, which may arise from entirely subjective considerations, such as his preference for certain types of artistic objects or styles, or from potential profits (for example, the auctioned object might be a license to operate a television channel). This state of affairs motivates our additional assumption that each buyer i knows his own private value v_i but not the values that the other buyers attach to the object. This does not, however, prevent him from assessing the private values of the other buyers, or from believing that he knows their private values with some level of certainty.
- Each buyer i bids a price b_i (presented to the auctioneer in a sealed envelope).
- The winner of the object is the buyer who makes the highest bid. That may not be surprising, but in contrast to the auctions most of us usually see, the winner does not proceed to pay the bid he submitted. Instead he pays the *second-highest* price offered (hence the name second-price auction). If several buyers bid the same maximal price,

a fair lottery is conducted between them to determine who will receive the object in exchange for paying that amount (which in this case is also the second-highest price offered).

Let us take a concrete example. Suppose there are four buyers respectively bidding 5, 15, 2, and 21. The buyer bidding 21 is the winner, paying 15 in exchange for the object. In general, the winner of the auction is a buyer i for which

$$b_i = \max_{j \in N} b_j. \qquad (4.9)$$

If buyer i is the winner, the amount he pays is $\max_{j \neq i} b_j$. We now proceed to describe a sealed-bid second-price auction as a strategic-form game:[3]

1. The set of players is the set N of buyers in the auction.
2. The set of strategies available to buyer i is the set of possible bids $S_i = [0, \infty)$.
3. The payoff to buyer i, when the strategy vector is $b = (b_1, \ldots, b_n)$, is

$$u_i(b) = \begin{cases} 0 & \text{if } b_i < \max_{j \in N} b_j, \\ \dfrac{v_i - \max_{j \neq i} b_j}{|\{k : b_k = \max_{j \in N} b_j\}|} & \text{if } b_i = \max_{j \in N} b_j. \end{cases} \qquad (4.10)$$

How should we expect a rational buyer to act in this auction? At first glance, this appears to be a very difficult problem to solve, because no buyer knows the private values of his competitors, let alone the prices they will bid. He may not even know how many other buyers are participating in the auction. So what price b_i will buyer i bid? Will he bid a price lower than v_i, in order to ensure that he does not lose money in the auction, or higher than v_i, in order to increase his probability of winning, all the while hoping that the second-highest bid will be lower than v_i? The process of rationalizability leads to the following result:

Theorem 4.15 *In a second-price sealed-bid auction, the strategy $b_i = v_i$ weakly dominates all other strategies.*

In other words, under Assumptions 4.8, 4.10, and 4.13, the auction will proceed as follows:

- Every buyer will bid $b_i = v_i$.
- The winner will be the buyer whose private valuation of the object is the highest.[4] The price paid by the winning buyer (i.e., the object's sale price) is the second-highest private value. If several buyers share the same maximal bid, one of them, selected randomly by a fair lottery, will get the object, and will pay his private value (which in this special case is also the second-highest bid, and his profit will therefore be 0).

Each buyer knows his private value v_i and therefore he also knows his payoff function. Since buyers do not necessarily know each other's private value, they do not necessarily

---

3 The relation between this auction method and other, more familiar, auction methods is discussed in Chapter 12.
4 This property is termed *efficiency* in the game theory and economics literature.

know each other's payoff functions. Nevertheless, as we mentioned on page 91, the concept of domination is defined also when a player does not know the other players' payoff functions.

Proof: Consider a buyer i whose private value is v_i. Divide the set of strategies available to him, $S_i = [0, \infty)$, into three subsets:

- The strategies in which his bid is less than v_i: $[0, v_i)$.
- The strategy in which his bid is equal to v_i: $\{v_i\}$.
- The strategies in which his bid is higher than v_i: (v_i, ∞).

We now show that strategy $b_i = v_i$ dominates all the strategies in the other two subsets.

Given the procedure of the auction, the payment eventually made by buyer i depends on the strategies selected by the other buyers, through their highest bid, and the number of buyers bidding that highest bid. Denote the maximal bid put forward by the other buyers by

$$B_{-i} = \max_{j \neq i} b_j, \tag{4.11}$$

and the number of buyers who offered this bid by

$$N_{-i} = \left| \left\{ k \neq i : b_k = \max_{j \neq i} b_j \right\} \right|. \tag{4.12}$$

The payoff function of buyer i, as a function of the strategy vector b (i.e., the vector of all the bids made by the buyers) is

$$u_i(b) = \begin{cases} 0 & \text{if } b_i < B_{-i}, \\ \frac{v_i - B_{-i}}{N_{-i}+1} & \text{if } b_i = B_{-i}, \\ v_i - B_{-i} & \text{if } b_i > B_{-i}. \end{cases} \tag{4.13}$$

Since the only dependence that the payoff function $u_i(b)$ has on the bids b_{-i} of the other buyers is via the highest bid, B_{-i}, we sometimes denote this function by $u_i(b_i, B_{-i})$. If buyer i chooses strategy $b_i = v_i$, his payoff as a function of B_{-i} is given in Figure 4.18.

If buyer i chooses strategy b_i satisfying $b_i < v_i$, his payoff function is given by Figure 4.19.

The height of the dot in Figure 4.19, when $b_i = B_{-i}$, depends on the number of buyers who bid B_{-i}.

The payoff function in Figure 4.18 (which corresponds to the strategy $b_i = v_i$) is (weakly) greater than the one in Figure 4.19 (corresponding to a strategy b_i with $b_i < v_i$). The former is strictly greater than the latter when $b_i \leq B_{-i} < v_i$. It follows that strategy $b_i = v_i$ dominates all strategies in which the bid is lower than buyer i's private value.

The payoff function for a strategy b_i satisfying $b_i > v_i$ is displayed in Figure 4.20.

Again, we see that the payoff function in Figure 4.18 is (weakly) greater than the payoff function in Figure 4.20. The former is strictly greater than the latter when $v_i < B_{-i} \leq b_i$. It follows that the strategy in which the bid is equal to the private value weakly dominates all other strategies, as claimed. □

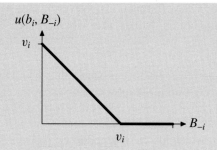

Figure 4.18 The payoff function for strategy $b_i = v_i$

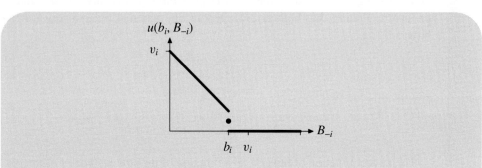

Figure 4.19 The payoff function for strategy $b_i < v_i$

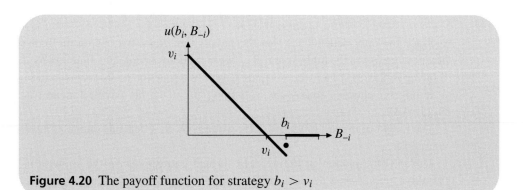

Figure 4.20 The payoff function for strategy $b_i > v_i$

Theorem 4.15 holds also when some buyers do not know the number of buyers participating in the auction, their private values, their beliefs (about the number of buyers and the private values of the other buyers), and their utility functions (for example, information on whether the other players are risk seekers, risk averse, or risk neutral; see Section 2.7). The only condition needed for Theorem 4.15 to hold is that each buyer knows the rules of the auction.

4.7 ▸ The order of elimination of dominated strategies

As we have argued, when only strictly dominated strategies are involved in a process of iterated elimination, the result is independent of the order in which strategies are eliminated (Exercise 4.10). In iterated elimination of weakly dominated strategies, the result may be sensitive to the order of elimination. This phenomenon occurs for example in the following game.

Example 4.16 Consider the strategic-form game that appears in Figure 4.21.

Player II

		L	C	R
	T	1, 2	2, 3	0, 3
Player I	M	2, 2	2, 1	3, 2
	B	2, 1	0, 0	1, 0

Figure 4.21 A game in which the order of the elimination of dominated strategies influences the yielded result

In the table below, we present three strategy-elimination procedures, each leading to a different result (verify!).

	Order of elimination from left to right	Result	Payoff
(1)	T, R, B, C	ML	2, 2
(2)	B, L, C, T	MR	3, 2
(3)	T, C, R	ML or BL	2, 2 or 2, 1

The last line shows that eliminating strategies in the order T, C, R leaves two results ML and BL, with no possibility for further elimination because Player I is indifferent between the two results. This means that the order of elimination may determine not only the yielded strategy vector, but also whether or not the process yields a single strategy vector.   ◀

4.8 ▸ Stability: Nash equilibrium

Dominance is a very important concept in game theory. As we saw in the previous section, it has several limitations, and it is insufficient for predicting a rational result in every game. In this section we present another important principle, *stability*.

Consider the two-player game in strategic form shown in Figure 4.22. There is no dominance relationship between the strategies in this game. For example, if we compare the strategies T and M of Player I, it turns out that neither of them is always preferable to the other: M is better than T if Player II chooses L, and T is better than M if Player II chooses C. In fact, M is the best reply of Player I to L, while T is his best reply to C, and B is his best reply to R. Similarly, for Player II, L is the best reply to T and C is the best reply to M, while strategy R is the best reply to B.

Figure 4.22 A two-player game with no dominated strategies

A player who knows the strategies used by the other players is in effect playing a game in which only he is called upon to choose a strategy. If that player is rational, he will choose the best reply to those strategies used by the other players. For example, in the game in Figure 4.22:

- If Player II knows that Player I will choose T, he will choose L (his best reply to T).
- If Player I knows that Player II will choose L, he will choose M (his best reply to L).
- If Player II knows that Player I will choose M, he will choose C (his best reply to M).
- If Player I knows that Player II will choose C, he will choose T (his best reply to C).
- If Player II knows that Player I will choose B, he will choose R (his best reply to B).
- If Player I knows that Player II will choose R, he will choose B (his best reply to R).

The pair of strategies (B, R) satisfies a stability property: each strategy in this pair is the best reply to the other strategy. Alternatively, we can state this property in the following way: assuming the players choose (B, R), neither player has a *profitable deviation*; that is, under the assumption that the other player indeed chooses his strategy according to (B, R), neither player has a strategy that grants a higher payoff than sticking to (B, R). This stability property was defined by John Nash, who invented the equilibrium concept that bears his name.

Definition 4.17 *A strategy vector* $s^* = (s_1^*, \ldots, s_n^*)$ *is a* Nash equilibrium *if for each player* $i \in N$ *and each strategy* $s_i \in S_i$, *the following is satisfied:*

$$u_i(s^*) \geq u_i(s_i, s_{-i}^*). \tag{4.14}$$

The payoff vector $u(s^*)$ *is the* equilibrium payoff *corresponding to the Nash equilibrium* s^*.

The strategy $\widehat{s}_i \in S_i$ is *a profitable deviation* of player i at a strategy vector $s \in S$ if $u_i(\widehat{s}_i, s_{-i}) > u_i(s)$. A Nash equilibrium is a strategy vector at which no player has a profitable deviation.

The Nash equilibrium is often simply referred to as an *equilibrium*, and sometimes as an *equilibrium point*. As defined above, it says that no player i has a profitable unilateral deviation from s^*. The Nash equilibrium can equivalently be expressed in terms of the best-reply concept, which we first define.

Definition 4.18 *Let* s_{-i} *be a strategy vector of all the players not including player i. Player i's strategy* s_i *is termed a* best reply *to* s_{-i} *if*

$$u_i(s_i, s_{-i}) = \max_{t_i \in S_i} u_i(t_i, s_{-i}). \tag{4.15}$$

The next definition, based on the best-reply concept, is equivalent to the definition of Nash equilibrium in Definition 4.17 (Exercise 4.15).

Definition 4.19 *The strategy vector* $s^* = (s_1^*, \ldots, s_n^*)$ *is a* Nash equilibrium *if* s_i^* *is a best reply to* s_{-i}^* *for every player* $i \in N$.

In the example in Figure 4.22, the pair of strategies (B, R) is the unique Nash equilibrium (verify!). For example, the pair (T, L) is not an equilibrium, because T is not a best reply to L; Player I has a profitable deviation from T to M or to B. Out of all the nine strategy pairs, (B, R) is the only equilibrium (verify!).

Social behavioral norms may be viewed as Nash equilibria. If a norm were not an equilibrium, some individuals in society would find some deviation from that behavioral norm to be profitable, and it would cease to be a norm.

A great deal of research in game theory is devoted to identifying equilibria and studying the properties of equilibria in various games. One important research direction that has been emerging in recent years studies processes (such as learning, imitation, or regret) leading to equilibrium behavior, along with the development of algorithms for calculating equilibria.

Example 4.11   The Prisoner's Dilemma (*continued*)   The Prisoner's Dilemma is presented in the matrix in Figure 4.23.

Player II

		D	C
Player I	D	1, 1	5, 0
	C	0, 5	4, 4

Figure 4.23 The Prisoner's Dilemma

The unique equilibrium is (D, D), in which both prisoners confess to the crime, resulting in payoff $(1, 1)$. Recall that this is the same result that is obtained by elimination of strictly dominated strategies.   ◀

Example 4.20   Coordination game   The game presented in Figure 4.24 is an example of a broad class of games called "coordination games." In a coordination game, it is in the interests of both players to coordinate their strategies. In this example both (A, a) and (B, b) are equilibrium points. The equilibrium payoff associated with (A, a) is $(1, 1)$, and the equilibrium payoff of (B, b) is $(3, 3)$. In both cases, and for both players, the payoff is better than $(0, 0)$, which is the payoff for "miscoordinated" strategies (A, b) or (B, a).

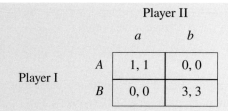

Figure 4.24 A coordination game

Example 4.21   Battle of the Sexes   The game in Figure 4.25 is called the "Battle of the Sexes."

		Woman	
		F	C
	F	2, 1	0, 0
Man	C	0, 0	1, 2

Figure 4.25 Battle of the Sexes

The name of the game is derived from the following description. A couple is trying to plan what they will be doing at the weekend. The alternatives are going to a concert (C) or watching a football match (F). The man prefers football and the woman prefers the concert, but both prefer being together to being alone, even if that means agreeing to the less-preferred recreational pastime.

There are two equilibrium points: (F, F) with a payoff of $(2, 1)$ and (C, C) with a payoff of $(1, 2)$. The woman would prefer the strategy pair (C, C) while the man would rather see (F, F) chosen. However, either one is an equilibrium. ◄

Example 4.22   The Security Dilemma   The game illustrated in Figure 4.26 is also a coordination game called the "Security Dilemma." The game describes the situation involving the Union of Soviet Socialist Republics (USSR, Player 1) and the United States (US, Player 2) after the Second World War. Each of these countries had the capacity to produce nuclear weapons. The best outcome for each country (4 utility units in the figure) was the one in which neither country had nuclear weapons, because producing nuclear weapons is expensive and possession of such weapons is liable to lead to war, with severe consequences. A less desirable outcome for each country (3 utility units in the figure) is for it to have nuclear weapons while the other country lacks nuclear weapons. Even less desirable for each country (2 utility units in the figure) is for both countries to have nuclear weapons. The worst outcome for a country (1 utility unit in the figure) is for it to lack nuclear weapons while the other country has nuclear weapons.

There are two Nash equilibria in this game: in one equilibrium neither country produces nuclear weapons and in the other equilibrium both countries produce nuclear weapons. If the US believes that the USSR is not going to produce nuclear weapons then it has no reason to produce nuclear weapons, while if the US believes that the USSR is going to produce nuclear weapons then it would be better off producing nuclear weapons. In the first equilibrium each country runs the risk that the other country will produce nuclear weapons, but in the second equilibrium there is no such

US

	Don't produce nuclear weapons	Produce nuclear weapons
Produce nuclear weapons	3, 1	2, 2
Don't produce nuclear weapons	4, 4	1, 3

USSR

Figure 4.26 The Security Dilemma

risk: if the US does produce nuclear weapons then if the USSR also produces nuclear weapons then the US has implemented the best strategy under the circumstances, while if the USSR does not produce nuclear weapons then the outcome for the US has improved from 2 to 3. In other words, the more desirable equilibrium for both players is also the more risky one. This is why this game got the name the Security Dilemma. Some have claimed that the equilibrium under which both countries produce nuclear weapons is the more reasonable equilibrium (and that is in fact the equilibrium that has obtained historically).   ◀

Example 4.23   **Cournot[5] duopoly competition** Two manufacturers, labeled 1 and 2, produce the same product and compete for the same market of potential customers. The manufacturers simultaneously select their production quantities, with demand determining the market price of the product, which is identical for both manufacturers. Denote by q_1 and q_2 the quantities respectively produced by Manufacturers 1 and 2. The total quantity of products in the market is therefore $q_1 + q_2$. Assume that when the supply is $q_1 + q_2$, the price of each item is $2 - q_1 - q_2$. Assume also that the per-item production cost for the first manufacturer is $c_1 > 0$ and that for the second manufacturer it is $c_2 > 0$. Does there exist an equilibrium in this game? If so, what is it?

This is a two-player game (Manufacturers 1 and 2 are the players), and the strategy set of each player is $[0, \infty)$. If Player 1 chooses strategy q_1 and Player 2 chooses strategy q_2, the payoff for Player 1 is

$$u_1(q_1, q_2) = q_1(2 - q_1 - q_2) - q_1 c_1 = q_1(2 - c_1 - q_1 - q_2), \qquad (4.16)$$

and the payoff for Player 2 is

$$u_2(q_1, q_2) = q_2(2 - q_1 - q_2) - q_2 c_2 = q_2(2 - c_2 - q_1 - q_2). \qquad (4.17)$$

Player 1's best reply to Player 2's strategy q_2 is the value q_1 maximizing $u_1(q_1, q_2)$. The function $q_1 \mapsto u_1(q_1, q_2)$ is a quadratic function that attains its maximum at the point where the derivative of the function is zero:

$$\frac{\partial u_1}{\partial q_1}(q_1, q_2) = 0. \qquad (4.18)$$

5 Antoine Augustin Cournot, August 28, 1801–March 31, 1877, was a French philosopher and mathematician. In his book *Researches on the Mathematical Principles of the Theory of Wealth*, published in 1838, he presented the first systematic application of mathematical tools for studying economic theory. The book marks the beginning of modern economic analysis.

Differentiating the right-hand side of Equation (4.16) yields the first-order condition $2 - c_1 - 2q_1 - q_2 = 0$, or

$$q_1 = \frac{2 - c_1 - q_2}{2}. \tag{4.19}$$

Similarly, Player 2's best reply to Player 1's strategy q_1 is given by the point where the derivative of $u_2(q_1, q_2)$ with respect to q_2 is zero. Taking the derivative, we get

$$q_2 = \frac{2 - c_2 - q_1}{2}. \tag{4.20}$$

Solving Equations (4.19) and (4.20) yields

$$q_1^* = \frac{2 - 2c_1 + c_2}{3}, \quad q_2^* = \frac{2 - 2c_2 + c_1}{3}. \tag{4.21}$$

A careful check indicates that this is an equilibrium (Exercise 4.24) and this is the only equilibrium of the game. The payoffs to the players at equilibrium are

$$u_1(q_1^*, q_2^*) = \left(\frac{2 - 2c_1 + c_2}{3}\right)^2 = (q_1^*)^2, \tag{4.22}$$

$$u_2(q_1^*, q_2^*) = \left(\frac{2 - 2c_2 + c_1}{3}\right)^2 = (q_2^*)^2. \tag{4.23}$$

For example, if the two players have identical production costs $c_1 = c_2 = 1$, then the equilibrium production quantities will be $q_1^* = q_2^* = \frac{1}{3}$, and the payoff to each player is $\left(\frac{1}{3}\right)^2 = \frac{1}{9}$.   ◄

4.9   Properties of the Nash equilibrium

The Nash equilibrium is the most central and important solution concept for games in strategic form or extensive form. To understand why, it is worthwhile to consider both the advantages and limitations of Nash's seminal concept.

4.9.1   Stability

The most important property expressed by the Nash equilibrium is stability: under the Nash equilibrium, each player acts to his best possible advantage with respect to the behavior of the other players. Indeed, this would appear to be a requirement for any solution concept: if there is to be any "expected" result (by any conceivable theory predicting the result of a game), that result must be in equilibrium, because otherwise there will be at least one player with a profitable deviation and the "expected" result will not materialize. From this perspective, the Nash equilibrium is not a solution concept but rather a meta-solution: the stability property is one that we would like every "expected" or "reasonable" solution to exhibit.

4.9.2   A self-fulfilling agreement

Another way to express the property of stability is to require that if there is "agreement" to play a particular equilibrium, then, even if the agreement is not binding, it will not

Player II

		L	R
Player I	T	0, 0	4, 2
	B	3, 5	0, 0

Figure 4.27 A coordination game

be breached: no player will deviate from the equilibrium point, because there is no way to profit from any unilateral violation of the agreement. This appears to be particularly convincing in games of coordination, as in the example in Figure 4.27.

This game has two Nash equilibria, (T, R) and (B, L), and it is reasonable to suppose that if the players were to communicate they would "agree" (probably after a certain amount of debate) to play one of them. The properties of the equilibrium concept imply that whether they choose (T, R) or (B, L) they will both fulfill the agreement and not deviate from it, because any unilateral deviation will bring about a loss to the deviator (and to the other player).

4.9.3 Equilibrium and evolution

The principle of the *survival of the fittest* is one of the fundamental principles of Darwin's Theory of Evolution. The principle postulates that our world is populated by a multitude of species of plants and animals, including many mutations, but only those whose inherited traits are fitter than those of others to withstand the test of survival will pass on their genes to posterity. For example, if an animal that has been endowed with certain inherited characteristics has on average four offspring who manage to live to adulthood, while a mutation of the animal with a different set of traits has on average only three offspring living to adulthood, then, over several generations, the descendants of the first animal will overwhelm the descendants of the mutation in absolute numbers.

A picturesque way of expressing Darwin's principle depicts an animal (or plant) being granted the capacity of rational intelligence prior to birth and selecting the genetic traits with which it will enter the world. Under that imaginary scenario we would expect the animal (or plant) to choose those traits that grant the greatest possible advantages in the struggle for survival. Animals, of course, are not typically endowed with rational thought and no animal can choose its own genetic inheritance. What actually happens is that those individuals born with traits that are a poor fit relative to the conditions for survival will pass those same characteristics on to their progeny, and over time their numbers will dwindle.

In other words, the surviving and prevailing traits are a kind of "best reply" to the environment – from which the relationship to the concept of Nash equilibrium follows. Section 5.9 (page 190) presents in greater detail how evolutionary processes can be modeled in game-theoretic terms and the role played by the Nash equilibrium in the theory of evolution.

4.9.4 Equilibrium from the normative perspective

Consider the concept of equilibrium from the normative perspective of an arbitrator or judge recommending a certain course of action (hopefully based on reasonable and acceptable principles). In that case we should expect the arbitrator's recommendation to be an equilibrium point. Otherwise (since it is a recommendation and not a binding agreement) there will be at least one agent who will be tempted to benefit from not following his end of the recommendation. Seeking equilibrium alone, however, is not enough for the arbitrator to arrive at a decision. If, for example, there is more than one equilibrium point, as in the coordination game in Figure 4.27, choosing between them requires more considerations and principles. A rich literature, in fact, deals with "refinements" of the concept of equilibrium, which seek to choose (or "invalidate") certain equilibria within the set of all possible equilibria. This subject will be discussed in Chapter 7.

Despite all its advantages, the Nash equilibrium is not the final be-all and end-all in the study of strategic- or extensive-form games. Beyond the fact that in some games there is no equilibrium and in others there may be a multiplicity of equilibria, even when there is a single Nash equilibrium it is not always entirely clear that the equilibrium will be the strategy vector that is "recommended" or "predicted" by a specific theory. There are many who believe, for example, that the unique equilibrium of the Prisoner's Dilemma does not constitute a "good recommendation" or a "good prediction" of the outcome of the game. We will later see additional examples in which it is unclear that an equilibrium will necessarily be the outcome of a game (cf. the first example in Section 4.10, the repeated Prisoner's Dilemma in Example 7.15 (page 270), the Centipede game (Example 7.16, page 270), and Example 7.17 on page 272).

4.10 Security: the maxmin concept

As we have already pointed out, the concept of equilibrium, despite its advantages, does not always describe the expected behavior of rational players, even in those cases where an equilibrium exists and is unique. Consider, for example, the game described in Figure 4.28.

		Player II	
		L	*R*
	T	2, 1	2, −20
Player I	*M*	3, 0	−10, 1
	B	−100, 2	3, 3

Figure 4.28 A game with a unique but "dangerous" equilibrium

The unique equilibrium in this game is (B, R), with a payoff of $(3, 3)$. But thinking this over carefully, can we really expect this result to obtain with high probability? One can imagine Player I hesitating to choose B: what if Player II were to choose L (whether by accident, due to irrationality, or for any other reason)? Given that the result (B, L) is catastrophic for Player I, he may prefer strategy T, guaranteeing a payoff of only 2 (compared to the equilibrium payoff of 3), but also guaranteeing that he will avoid getting -100 instead. If Player II is aware of this hesitation, and believes that there is a reasonable chance that Player I will flee to the safety of T, he will also be wary of choosing the equilibrium strategy R (and risking the -20 payoff), and will likely choose strategy L instead. This, in turn, increases Player I's motivation to choose T.

This underscores an additional aspect of rational behavior that exists to some extent in the behavior of every player: guaranteeing the best possible result without "relying" on the rationality of the other players, and even making the most pessimistic assessment of their potential behavior.

So what can player i, in a general game, guarantee for himself? If he chooses strategy s_i, the worst possible payoff he can get is

$$\min_{t_{-i} \in S_{-i}} u_i(s_i, t_{-i}). \tag{4.24}$$

Player i can choose the strategy s_i that maximizes this value. In other words, disregarding the possible rationality (or irrationality) of the other players, he can guarantee for himself a payoff of

$$\underline{v}_i := \max_{s_i \in S_i} \min_{t_{-i} \in S_{-i}} u_i(s_i, t_{-i}). \tag{4.25}$$

The quantity $\underline{v}_i$ is called the *maxmin value* of player i, which is sometimes also called the player's *security level*. A strategy s_i^* that guarantees this value is called a *maxmin strategy*. Such a strategy satisfies

$$\min_{t_{-i} \in S_{-i}} u_i(s_i^*, t_{-i}) \geq \min_{t_{-i} \in S_{-i}} u_i(s_i, t_{-i}), \quad \forall s_i \in S_i, \tag{4.26}$$

which is equivalent to

$$u_i(s_i^*, t_{-i}) \geq \underline{v}_i, \quad \forall t_{-i} \in S_{-i}. \tag{4.27}$$

Remark 4.24 *The definition of a game in strategic form does not include a requirement that the set of strategies available to any of the players be finite. When the strategy set is infinite, the minimum in Equation (4.24) may not exist for certain strategies $s_i \in S_i$. Even if the minimum in Equation (4.24) is attained for every strategy $s_i \in S_i$, the maximum in Equation (4.25) may not exist. It follows that when the strategy set of one or more players is infinite, we need to replace the minimum and maximum in the definition of the maxmin value by infimum and supremum, respectively:*

$$\underline{v}_i := \sup_{s_i \in S_i} \inf_{t_{-i} \in S_{-i}} u_i(s_i, t_{-i}). \tag{4.28}$$

If the supremum is never attained there is no maxmin strategy: for each $\varepsilon > 0$ the player can guarantee for himself at least $\underline{v}_i - \varepsilon$, but not at least $\underline{v}_i$.

Player II

		L	R	$\min_{s_{II} \in S_{II}} u_I(s_I, s_{II})$
	T	2, 1	2, −20	2
Player I	M	3, 0	−10, 1	−10
	B	−100, 2	3, 3	−100
$\min_{s_I \in S_I} u_{II}(s_I, s_{II})$		0	−20	(2, 0)

Figure 4.29 The game in Figure 4.28 with the security value of each player

A continuous function defined over a compact domain always attains a maximum and a minimum. Moreover, when X and Y are compact sets in $\mathbb{R}^m$ and $f : X \times Y \to \mathbb{R}$ is a continuous function, the function $x \mapsto \min_{y \in Y} f(x, y)$ is also continuous (Exercise 4.22). It follows that when the strategy sets of the players are compact and the payoff functions are continuous, the maxmin strategies of the players are well defined. ◆

We will now proceed to calculate the value guaranteed by each strategy in the example in Figure 4.28. In Figure 4.29, the numbers in the right-most column (outside the payoff matrix) indicate the worst payoff to Player I if he chooses the strategy of the corresponding row. Similarly, the numbers in the bottom-most row (outside the payoff matrix) indicate the worst payoff to Player II if he chooses the strategy of the corresponding column. Finally, the oval contains the maxmin value of both players.

The maxmin value of Player I is 2 and the strategy that guarantees this value is T. The maxmin value of Player II is 0 with maxmin strategy L. If the two players choose their maxmin strategies, the result is (T, L) with payoff $(2, 1)$, in which Player II's payoff of 1 is greater than his maxmin value.

As the next example illustrates, a player may have several maxmin strategies. In such a case, when the players use maxmin strategies the payoff depends on which strategies they have chosen.

Example 4.25   Consider the two-player game appearing in Figure 4.30.

Player II

		L	R	$\min_{s_{II} \in S_{II}} u_I(s_I, s_{II})$
	T	3, 1	0, 4	0
Player I	B	2, 3	1, 1	1
$\min_{s_I \in S_I} u_{II}(s_I, s_{II})$		1	1	(1, 1)

Figure 4.30 A game with the maxmin values of the players

The maxmin value of Player I is 1 and his unique maxmin strategy is B. The maxmin value of Player II is 1, and both L and R are his maxmin strategies. It follows that when the two players implement maxmin strategies the payoff might be $(2,3)$, or $(1,1)$, depending on which maxmin strategy is implemented by Player II.   ◀

We next explore the connection between the maxmin strategy and dominant strategies.

Theorem 4.26 *A strategy of player i that dominates all his other strategies is a maxmin strategy for that player. Such a strategy, furthermore, is a best reply of player i to any strategy vector of the other players.*

The proof of this theorem is left to the reader (Exercise 4.25). The theorem implies the following conclusion:

Corollary 4.27 *In a game in which every player has a strategy that dominates all of his other strategies, the vector of dominant strategies is an equilibrium point and a vector of maxmin strategies.*

An example of this kind of game is a sealed-bid second-price auction, as we saw in Section 4.6. The next theorem constitutes a strengthening of Corollary 4.27 in the case of strict domination (for the proof see Exercise 4.26).

Theorem 4.28 *In a game in which every player i has a strategy s_i^* that strictly dominates all of his other strategies, the strategy vector $(s_1^*, \ldots, s_n^*)$ is the unique equilibrium point of the game as well as the unique vector of maxmin strategies.*

Is there a relation between the maxmin value of a player and his payoff in a Nash equilibrium? As the next theorem states, the payoff of each player in a Nash equilibrium is at least his maxmin value.

Theorem 4.29 *Every Nash equilibrium σ^* of a strategic-form game satisfies $u_i(\sigma^*) \geq \underline{v}_i$ for every player i.*

Proof: For every strategy $s_i \in S_i$ we have

$$u_i(s_i, s_{-i}^*) \geq \min_{s_{-i} \in S_{-i}} u_i(s_i, s_{-i}). \tag{4.29}$$

Since the definition of an equilibrium implies that $u_i(s^*) = \max_{s_i \in S_i} u_i(s_i, s_{-i}^*)$, we deduce that

$$u_i(s^*) = \max_{s_i \in S_i} u_i(s_i, s_{-i}^*) \geq \max_{s_i \in S_i} \min_{s_{-i} \in S_{-i}} u_i(s_i, s_{-i}) = \underline{v}_i, \tag{4.30}$$

as required.   □

4.11 The effect of elimination of dominated strategies

Elimination of dominated strategies was discussed in Section 4.5 (page 85). A natural question that arises is how does the process of iterative elimination of dominated strategies change the maxmin values and the set of equilibria of the game? We will show here that the elimination of strictly dominated strategies has no effect on a game's set of equilibria. The iterated elimination of weakly dominated strategies can reduce the set of equilibria, but it cannot create new equilibria. On the other hand, the maxmin value of any particular player is unaffected by the elimination of his dominated strategies, whether those strategies are weakly or strictly dominated.

Theorem 4.30 *Let $G = (N, (S_i)_{i \in N}, (u_i)_{i \in N})$ be a strategic-form game, and let $\widehat{s}_j \in S_j$ be a dominated strategy of player j. Let $\widehat{G}$ be the game derived from G by the elimination of strategy $\widehat{s}_j$. Then the maxmin value of player j in $\widehat{G}$ is equal to his maxmin value in G.*

Proof: The maxmin value of player j in G is

$$\underline{v}_j = \max_{s_j \in S_j} \min_{s_{-j} \in S_{-j}} u_j(s_j, s_{-j}), \tag{4.31}$$

and his maxmin value in $\widehat{G}$ is

$$\widehat{\underline{v}}_j = \max_{\{s_j \in S_j, s_j \neq \widehat{s}_j\}} \min_{s_{-j} \in S_{-j}} u_j(s_j, s_{-j}). \tag{4.32}$$

Let t_j be a strategy of player j that dominates $\widehat{s}_j$ in G. Then the following is satisfied:

$$u_j(\widehat{s}_j, s_{-j}) \leq u_j(t_j, s_{-j}), \quad \forall s_{-j} \in S_{-j}, \tag{4.33}$$

and therefore

$$\min_{s_{-j} \in S_{-j}} u_j(\widehat{s}_j, s_{-j}) \leq \min_{s_{-j} \in S_{-j}} u_j(t_j, s_{-j}) \leq \max_{\{s_j \in S_j, s_j \neq \widehat{s}_j\}} \min_{s_{-j} \in S_{-j}} u_j(s_j, s_{-j}). \tag{4.34}$$

This leads to the conclusion that

$$\underline{v}_j = \max_{s_j \in S_j} \min_{s_{-j} \in S_{-j}} u_j(s_j, s_{-j}) \tag{4.35}$$

$$= \max\left\{ \max_{\{s_j \in S_j, s_j \neq \widehat{s}_j\}} \min_{s_{-j} \in S_{-j}} u_j(s_j, s_{-j}), \min_{s_{-j} \in S_{-j}} u_j(\widehat{s}_j, s_{-j}) \right\} \tag{4.36}$$

$$= \max_{\{s_j \in S_j, s_j \neq \widehat{s}_j\}} \min_{s_{-j} \in S_{-j}} u_j(s_j, s_{-j}) = \widehat{\underline{v}}_j, \tag{4.37}$$

which is what we wanted to prove. $\qquad \square$

Note that the elimination of a (strictly or weakly) dominated strategy of one player may increase the maxmin values of other players (but not decrease them; see Exercise 4.27).

It follows that when calculating the maxmin value of player i we can eliminate his dominated strategies, but we must not eliminate the dominated strategies of other players, since this may result in increasing player i's maxmin value. Therefore, iterated elimination of (weakly or strictly) dominated strategies may increase the maxmin value of some players.

The next theorem states that if we eliminate some of the strategies of each player (whether or not they are dominated), then every equilibrium of the original game (the game prior to the elimination of strategies) is also an equilibrium of the game resulting from the elimination process, provided that none of the strategies of that equilibrium were eliminated.

Theorem 4.31 *Let* $G = (N, (S_i)_{i \in N}, (u_i)_{i \in N})$ *be a game in strategic form, and let* $\widehat{G} = (N, (\widehat{S}_i)_{i \in N}, (u_i)_{i \in N})$ *be the game derived from G through the elimination of some of the strategies, namely,* $\widehat{S}_i \subseteq S_i$ *for each player* $i \in N$. *If* s^* *is an equilibrium in game G, and if* $s_i^* \in \widehat{S}_i$ *for each player i, then* s^* *is an equilibrium in the game* $\widehat{G}$.

Proof: Because s^* is an equilibrium of the game G, it follows that for each player i,

$$u_i(s_i, s_{-i}^*) \leq u_i(s^*), \quad \forall s_i \in S_i. \tag{4.38}$$

Because $\widehat{S}_i \subseteq S_i$ for each player $i \in N$, it is the case that

$$u_i(s_i, s_{-i}^*) \leq u_i(s^*), \quad \forall s_i \in \widehat{S}_i. \tag{4.39}$$

Because s^* is a vector of strategies in the game $\widehat{G}$, we conclude that it is an equilibrium of $\widehat{G}$. □

It should be noted that in general the post-elimination game $\widehat{G}$ may contain *new* equilibria that were not equilibria in the original game (Exercise 4.28). The next theorem shows that this cannot happen if the eliminated strategies are weakly dominated – that is, no new equilibria are created if a weakly dominated strategy of a particular player is eliminated. Repeated application of the theorem then yields the fact that the process of iterated elimination of weakly dominated strategies does not lead to the creation of new equilibria (Corollary 4.33).

Theorem 4.32 *Let* $G = (N, (S_i)_{i \in N}, (u_i)_{i \in N})$ *be a game in strategic form, let* $j \in N$, *and let* $\widehat{s}_j \in S_j$ *be a weakly dominated strategy of player j in this game. Denote by* $\widehat{G}$ *the game derived from G by the elimination of the strategy* $\widehat{s}_j$. *Then every equilibrium of* $\widehat{G}$ *is also an equilibrium of G.*

Proof: The strategy sets of the game $\widehat{G}$ are

$$\widehat{S}_i = \begin{cases} S_i & \text{if } i \neq j, \\ S_j \setminus \{\widehat{s}_j\} & \text{if } i = j. \end{cases} \tag{4.40}$$

Let $s^* = (s_i^*)_{i \in N}$ be an equilibrium strategy vector of the game $\widehat{G}$. Then

$$u_i(s_i, s_{-i}^*) \leq u_i(s^*), \quad \forall i \neq j, \ \forall s_i \in \widehat{S}_i = S_i, \tag{4.41}$$

$$u_j(s_j, s_{-j}^*) \leq u_j(s^*), \quad \forall s_j \in \widehat{S}_j. \tag{4.42}$$

To show that s^* is an equilibrium of the game G we must show that no player i can profit in G by deviating to a strategy that differs from s_i^*. First we will show that this is true of every player i, $i \neq j$. Let i be a player who is not player j. Since $\widehat{S}_i = S_i$, by Equation (4.41) player i has no deviation from s_i^* that is profitable for him. As for player j, Equation (4.42) implies that he cannot profit from deviating to any strategy in $\widehat{S}_j = S_j \setminus \{\widehat{s}_j\}$. It only remains, then, to check that player j sees no gain from switching from strategy s_j^* to strategy $\widehat{s}_j$.

Because $\widehat{s}_j$ is a dominated strategy, there exists a strategy $t_j \in S_j$ that dominates it. It follows that $t_j \neq \widehat{s}_j$, and in particular that $t_j \in \widehat{S}_j$, so that

$$u_j(\widehat{s}_j, s_{-j}) \leq u_j(t_j, s_{-j}), \quad \forall s_{-j} \in S_{-j}. \tag{4.43}$$

Inserting $s_{-j} = s^*_{-j}$ in Equation (4.43) and $s_j = t_j$ in Equation (4.42), we get

$$u_j(\widehat{s}_j, s^*_{-j}) \le u_j(t_j, s^*_{-j}) \le u_j(s^*_j, s^*_{-j}), \tag{4.44}$$

which shows that deviating to strategy $\widehat{s}_j$ is indeed not profitable for player j. □

The following corollary (whose proof is left to the reader in Exercise 4.29) is implied by Theorem 4.32.

Corollary 4.33 *Let $G = (N, (S_i)_{i \in N}, (u_i)_{i \in N})$ be a game in strategic form, and let $\widehat{G}$ be the game derived from the game G by iterative elimination of dominated strategies. Then every equilibrium s^* of $\widehat{G}$ is also an equilibrium of G. In particular, if the iterative elimination results in a single vector s^*, then s^* is an equilibrium of the game G.*

Iterated elimination of dominated strategies, therefore, cannot create new equilibria. However, as the next example shows, it can result in the loss of some of the equilibria of the original game. This can happen even when there is only one elimination process possible.

Example 4.34 Consider the two-player game given by the matrix in Figure 4.31.

Player II

		L	R
Player I	T	0, 0	2, 1
	B	3, 2	1, 2

Figure 4.31 Elimination of dominated strategies may eliminate an equilibrium point

The game has two equilibria: (T, R) and (B, L). The only dominated strategy in the game is L (dominated by R). The elimination of strategy L results in a game in which B is dominated, and its elimination in turn yields the result (T, R). Thus, the elimination of L also eliminates the strategy vector (B, L) – an equilibrium point in the original game. The payoff corresponding to the eliminated equilibrium is $(3, 2)$, which for both players is preferable to $(2, 1)$, the payoff corresponding to (T, R), the equilibrium of the post-elimination game. ◀

In fact, the iterative elimination of weakly dominated strategies can result in the elimination of all the equilibria of the original game (Exercise 4.12). But this cannot happen under iterative elimination of strictly dominated strategies, which preserves the set of equilibrium points. That is the content of the following theorem.

Theorem 4.35 *Let $G = (N, (S_i)_{i \in N}, (u_i)_{i \in N})$ be a game in strategic form, let $j \in N$, and let $\widehat{s}_j \in S_j$ be a strictly dominated strategy of player j. Let $\widehat{G}$ be the game derived from G by the elimination of strategy $\widehat{s}_j$. Then the set of equilibria in the game $\widehat{G}$ is identical to the set of equilibria of the game G.*

Theorem 4.35 leads to the next corollary.

Corollary 4.36 *A strictly dominated strategy cannot be an element of a game's equilibrium.*

The conclusion of the last corollary is not true for weakly dominated strategies. As can be seen in Example 4.34, a weakly dominated strategy can be an element of an equilibrium. Indeed, there are cases in which an equilibrium strategy vector s^* is comprised of a weakly dominated strategy s_i^* for each player $i \in N$ (Exercise 4.30).

Proof of Theorem 4.35: Denote by E the set of equilibria of the game G, and by $\widehat{E}$ the set of equilibria of the game $\widehat{G}$. Theorem 4.32 implies that $\widehat{E} \subseteq E$, because every strictly dominated strategy is also a weakly dominated strategy. It remains to show that $E \subseteq \widehat{E}$.

Let $s^* \in E$ be an equilibrium of the game G. To show that $s^* \in \widehat{E}$, we will show that s^* is a strategy vector in the game $\widehat{G}$, which by Theorem 4.31 then implies that $s^* \in \widehat{E}$. As the game $\widehat{G}$ was derived from the game G by elimination of player j's strategy $\widehat{s}_j$, it suffices to show that $s_j^* \neq \widehat{s}_j$. Strategy $\widehat{s}_j$ is strictly dominated in the game G, so that there exists a strategy $t_j \in S_j$ that strictly dominates it:

$$u_j(\widehat{s}_j, s_{-j}) < u_j(t_j, s_{-j}), \quad \forall s_{-j} \in S_{-j}. \tag{4.45}$$

Because s^* is an equilibrium point, by setting $s_{-j} = s_{-j}^*$ in Equation (4.45) we get

$$u_j(\widehat{s}_j, s_{-j}^*) < u_j(t_j, s_{-j}^*) \leq u_i(s_j^*, s_{-j}^*), \tag{4.46}$$

thus yielding the conclusion that $\widehat{s}_j \neq s_j^*$, which is what we needed to show.   □

When we put together Corollary 4.33 and Theorem 4.35, the following picture emerges: in implementing a process of iterated elimination of dominated strategies we may lose equilibria, but no new equilibria are created. If the elimination is of only strictly dominated strategies, the set of equilibria remains unchanged throughout the process. In particular, if the process of eliminating strictly dominated strategies results in a single strategy vector, this strategy vector is the unique equilibrium point of the original game (because it is the equilibrium of the game at the end of the process in which each player has only one strategy remaining). The uniqueness of the equilibrium constitutes a strengthening of Corollary 4.33 in the case in which only strictly dominated strategies are eliminated.

Corollary 4.37 *If iterative elimination of strictly dominated strategies yields a unique strategy vector s^*, then s^* is the unique Nash equilibrium of the game.*

In summary, to find a player's maxmin values we can first eliminate his (strictly or weakly) dominated strategies. In implementing this elimination process we may eliminate some of his maxmin strategies and also change the maxmin values of some other players. For finding equilibria we can also eliminate strictly dominated strategies without changing the set of equilibria of the game. Elimination of weakly dominated strategies may eliminate some equilibria of the game. The process of iterated elimination of weakly dominated strategies is useful for cases in which finding all equilibrium points is a difficult problem and we can be content with finding at least one equilibrium.

4.12 Two-player zero-sum games

As we have seen, the Nash equilibrium and the maxmin are two different concepts that reflect different behavioral aspects: the first is an expression of stability, while the second captures the notion of security. Despite the different roots of the two concepts, there are cases in which both lead to the same results. A special case where this occurs is in the class of two-player zero-sum games, which is the subject of this section.

In a given two-player game, denote, as we have done so far, the set of players by $N = \{I, II\}$ and the set of strategies respectively by S_I and S_{II}.

Example 4.38 Consider the two-player game appearing in Figure 4.32.

Player II

		L	C	R	$\min_{s_{II} \in S_{II}} u_I(s_I, s_{II})$
	T	3, −3	−5, 5	−2, 2	−5
Player I	M	1, −1	4, −4	1, −1	1
	B	6, −6	−3, 3	−5, 5	−5
$\min_{s_I \in S_I} u_{II}(s_I, s_{II})$		−6	−4	−1	1, −1

Figure 4.32 A two-player zero-sum game

In this example, $\underline{v}_I = 1$ and $\underline{v}_{II} = -1$. The maxmin strategy of Player I is M and that of Player II is R. The strategy pair (M, R) is also the equilibrium of this game (check!). In other words, here we have a case where the vector of maxmin strategies is also an equilibrium point: the two concepts lead to the same result.   ◀

In the game in Example 4.38, for each pair of strategies the sum of the payoffs that the two players receive is zero. In other words, in any possible outcome of the game the payoff one player receives is exactly equal to the payoff the other player has to pay.

Definition 4.39 *A two-player game is a* zero-sum game *if for each pair of strategies* (s_I, s_{II}) *one has*

$$u_I(s_I, s_{II}) + u_{II}(s_I, s_{II}) = 0. \tag{4.47}$$

In other words, a two-player game is a zero-sum game if it is a closed system from the perspective of the payoffs: each player gains what the other player loses. It is clear that in such a game the two players have diametrically opposed interests.

Remark 4.40 *As we saw in Chapter 2, assuming that the players have von Neumann–Morgenstern linear utilities, any player's utility function is determined only up to a positive affine transformation. Therefore, if the payoffs represent the players' utilities from the various outcomes of the game, then they are determined up to a positive affine transformation. Changing the representation of the utility function of the players can then transform a zero-sum game into a non-zero-sum game. We will return to this issue* *in Section 5.5 (page 171); it will be proved there that the results of this chapter are independent of the particular representation of utility functions, and they hold true in two-player non-zero-sum games that are obtained from two-player zero-sum games by applying positive affine transformations to the players' payoffs.*   ◆

Most real-life situations analyzed using game theory are not two-player zero-sum games, because even though the interests of the players diverge in many cases, they are often not completely diametrically opposed. Despite this, two-player zero-sum games have a special importance that justifies studying them carefully, as we do in this section. Here are some of the reasons:

1. Many classical games, such as chess, backgammon, checkers, and a plethora of dice games, are two-player zero-sum games. These were the first games to be studied mathematically and the first to yield formal results, results that spawned and shaped game theory as a young field of study in the early part of the twentieth century.
2. Given their special and highly restrictive properties, these games are generally simpler and easier to analyze mathematically than many other games. As is usually the case in mathematics, this makes them convenient objects for the initial exploration of ideas and possible directions for research in game theory.
3. Because of the fact that two-player zero-sum games leave no room for cooperation between the players, they are useful for isolating certain aspects of games and checking which results stem from cooperative considerations and which stem from other aspects of the game (information flows, repetitions, and so on).
4. In every situation, no matter how complicated, a natural benchmark for each player is his "security level": what he can guarantee for himself based solely on his own efforts, without relying on the behavior of other players. In practice, calculating the security level means assuming a worst-case scenario in which all other players are acting as an adversary. This means that the player is considering an auxiliary zero-sum game, in which all the other players act as if they were one opponent whose payoff is the opposite of his own payoff. In other words, even when analyzing a game that is non-zero-sum, the analysis of auxiliary zero-sum games can prove useful.
5. Two-player zero-sum games emerge naturally in other models. One example is games involving only a single player, which are often termed *decision problems*. They involve a decision maker choosing an action from among a set of alternatives, with the resultant payoff dependent both on his choice of action and on certain, often unknown, parameters over which he has no control. To calculate what the decision maker can guarantee for himself, we model the player's environment as if it were a second player who controls the unknown parameters and whose intent is to minimize the decision maker's payoff. This in effect yields a two-player zero-sum game. This approach is used in statistics, and we will return to it in Section 14.8 (page 608).

Let us now turn to the study of two-player zero-sum games. Since the payoffs u_I and u_{II} satisfy $u_I + u_{II} = 0$, we can confine our attention to one function, $u_I = u$, with $u_{II} = -u$. The function u will be termed the *payoff function* of the game, and it represents the payment that Player II makes to Player I. Note that this creates an artificial asymmetry (albeit only with respect to the symbols being used) between the two players: Player I,

Player II

		L	C	R
	T	3	−5	−2
Player I	M	1	4	1
	B	6	−3	−5

Figure 4.33 The payoff function u of the zero-sum game in Example 4.38

Player II

		H	T
	H	1	−1
Player I	T	−1	1

Figure 4.34 The payoff function u of the game of Matching Pennies

who is usually the row player, seeks to maximize $u(s)$ (his payoff) and Player II, who is usually the column player, is trying to minimize $u(s)$, which is what he is paying (since his payoff is $-u(s)$).

The game in Example 4.38 (page 110) can therefore be represented as shown in Figure 4.33.

The game of Matching Pennies (Example 3.20, page 52) can also be represented as a zero-sum game (see Figure 4.34).

Consider now the maxmin values of the players in a two-player zero-sum game. Player I's maxmin value is given by

$$\underline{v}_{\mathrm{I}} = \max_{s_{\mathrm{I}} \in S_{\mathrm{I}}} \min_{s_{\mathrm{II}} \in S_{\mathrm{II}}} u(s_{\mathrm{I}}, s_{\mathrm{II}}), \tag{4.48}$$

and Player II's maxmin value is

$$\underline{v}_{\mathrm{II}} = \max_{s_{\mathrm{II}} \in S_{\mathrm{II}}} \min_{s_{\mathrm{I}} \in S_{\mathrm{I}}} (-u(s_{\mathrm{I}}, s_{\mathrm{II}})) = - \min_{s_{\mathrm{II}} \in S_{\mathrm{II}}} \max_{s_{\mathrm{I}} \in S_{\mathrm{I}}} u(s_{\mathrm{I}}, s_{\mathrm{II}}). \tag{4.49}$$

Denote

$$\underline{v} := \max_{s_{\mathrm{I}} \in S_{\mathrm{I}}} \min_{s_{\mathrm{II}} \in S_{\mathrm{II}}} u(s_{\mathrm{I}}, s_{\mathrm{II}}), \tag{4.50}$$

$$\overline{v} := \min_{s_{\mathrm{II}} \in S_{\mathrm{II}}} \max_{s_{\mathrm{I}} \in S_{\mathrm{I}}} u(s_{\mathrm{I}}, s_{\mathrm{II}}). \tag{4.51}$$

The value $\underline{v}$ is called the *maxmin value* of the game, and $\overline{v}$ is called the *minmax value*. Player I can guarantee that he will get at least $\underline{v}$, and Player II can guarantee that he will

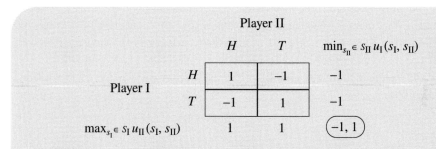

Figure 4.35 A game in strategic form with the maxmin and minmax values

Player II

		H	T	$\min_{s_{II} \in S_{II}} u_I(s_I, s_{II})$
Player I	H	1	−1	−1
	T	−1	1	−1
$\max_{s_I \in S_I} u_{II}(s_I, s_{II})$		1	1	−1, 1

Figure 4.36 Matching Pennies with the maxmin and minmax values

pay no more than $\overline{v}$. A strategy of Player I that guarantees $\underline{v}$ is termed a *maxmin strategy*. A strategy of Player II that guarantees $\overline{v}$ is called a *minmax strategy*.

We next calculate the maxmin value and minmax value in various examples of games. In Example 4.38, $\underline{v} = 1$ and $\overline{v} = 1$. In other words, Player I can guarantee that he will get a payoff of at least 1 (using the maxmin strategy M), while Player II can guarantee that he will pay at most 1 (by way of the minmax strategy R).

Consider the game shown in Figure 4.35. In this figure we have indicated on the right of each row the minimal payoff that the corresponding strategy of Player I guarantees him. Beneath each column we have indicated the maximal amount that Player II will pay if he implements the corresponding strategy.

In this game $\underline{v} = 0$ but $\overline{v} = 3$. Player I cannot guarantee that he will get a payoff higher than 0 (which he can guarantee using his maxmin strategy B) and Player II cannot guarantee that he will pay less than 3 (which he can guarantee using his minmax strategy L).

Finally, look again at the game of Matching Pennies (Figure 4.36). In this game $\underline{v} = -1$ and $\overline{v} = 1$. Neither of the two players can guarantee a result that is better than the loss of one dollar (the strategies H and T of Player I are both maxmin strategies, and the strategies H and T of Player II are both minmax strategies).

As these examples indicate, the maxmin value $\underline{v}$ and the minmax value $\overline{v}$ may be unequal, but it is always the case that $\underline{v} \leq \overline{v}$. The inequality is clear from the definitions of the maxmin and minmax: Player I can guarantee that he will get at least $\underline{v}$, while

Player II can guarantee that he will not pay more than $\bar{v}$. As the game is a zero-sum game, the inequality $\underline{v} \leq \bar{v}$ must hold. A formal proof of this fact can of course also be given (Exercise 4.34).

Definition 4.41 *A two-player game has a* value *if $\underline{v} = \bar{v}$. The quantity $v := \underline{v} = \bar{v}$ is then called the* value *of the game.*[6] *Any maxmin and minmax strategies of Player I and Player II respectively are then called* optimal strategies.

Consider again the game shown in Figure 4.33. This game has a value equal to 1. Player I can guarantee that he will get at least 1 for himself by selecting the optimal strategy M, and Player II can guarantee that he will not pay more than 1 by choosing the optimal strategy R. Note that the strategy pair (M, R) is also a Nash equilibrium.

Another example of a game that has a value is the game of chess, assuming that if the play does not end after a predetermined number of moves, it terminates in a draw. We do not know what that value is, but the existence of a value follows from Theorem 1.4 (page 3). Since it is manifestly a two-player game in which the interests of the players are diametrically opposed, we describe chess as a zero-sum game where White is the maximizer and Black is the minimizer by use of the following payoff function:

$$u(\text{White wins}) = 1,$$
$$u(\text{Black wins}) = -1, \qquad (4.52)$$
$$u(\text{Draw}) = 0.$$

Theorem 1.4 (page 3) implies that one and only one of the following must occur:

(i) White has a strategy guaranteeing a payoff of 1.
(ii) Black has a strategy guaranteeing a payoff of -1.
(iii) Each of the two players has a strategy guaranteeing a payoff of 0; that is, White can guarantee a payoff in the set $\{0, 1\}$, and Black can guarantee a payoff in the set $\{0, -1\}$.

If case (i) holds, then $\underline{v} \geq 1$. As the maximal payoff is 1, it must be true that $\bar{v} \leq 1$. Since we always have $\underline{v} \leq \bar{v}$, we deduce that $1 \leq \underline{v} \leq \bar{v} \leq 1$, which means that $\underline{v} = \bar{v} = 1$. Thus, the game has a value and $\underline{v} = \bar{v} = 1$ is its value.

If case (ii) holds, then $\bar{v} \leq -1$. Since the minimal payoff is -1, it follows that $\underline{v} \geq -1$. Hence $-1 \leq \underline{v} \leq \bar{v} \leq -1$, leading to $\underline{v} = \bar{v} = -1$, and the game has a value of -1.

Finally, suppose case (iii) holds. Then $\underline{v} \geq 0$ and $\bar{v} \leq 0$. So $0 \leq \underline{v} \leq \bar{v} \leq 0$, leading to $\underline{v} = \bar{v} = 0$, and the game has a value of 0.

Note that in chess each pair of optimal strategies is again a Nash equilibrium. For example, if case (i) above holds, then White's strategy is optimal if and only if it is a winning strategy. On the other hand, any strategy of Black guarantees him a payoff of at least -1 and therefore all his strategies are optimal. Every pair consisting of a winning strategy for White and any strategy for Black is an equilibrium. Since White can guarantee victory for himself, he certainly has no profitable deviation; since Black will lose no

---

6 The value of a game is sometimes also called the *minmax value of the game*.

matter what, no deviation is strictly profitable for him either. The following conclusion has therefore been proved.

Corollary 4.42 *The game of chess has a value that is either* 1 *(if case (i) holds), or* −1 *(if case (ii) holds), or* 0 *(if case (iii) holds).*

The following theorem can be proven in the same way that Theorem 3.13 (page 46) was proved. Later in this book, a more general result is shown to be true, for games that are not zero-sum (see Theorem 4.49 on page 118).

Theorem 4.43 *Every finite two-player zero-sum extensive-form game with perfect information has a value.*

In every example we have considered so far, every zero-sum game with a value also has an equilibrium. The following two theorems establish a close relationship between the concepts of the value and of Nash equilibrium in two-player zero-sum games.

Theorem 4.44 *If a two-player zero-sum game has a value v, and if s_I^* and s_{II}^* are optimal strategies of the two players, then $s^* = (s_I^*, s_{II}^*)$ is an equilibrium with payoff $(v, -v)$.*

Theorem 4.45 *If $s^* = (s_I^*, s_{II}^*)$ is an equilibrium of a two-player zero-sum game, then the game has a value $v = u(s_I^*, s_{II}^*)$, and the strategies s_I^* and s_{II}^* are optimal strategies.*

Before we prove Theorems 4.44 and 4.45, we wish to stress that these theorems show that in two-player zero-sum games the concept of equilibrium, which is based on stability, and the concept of minmax, which is based on security levels, coincide. If security-level considerations are important factors in determining players' behavior, one may expect that the concept of equilibrium will have greater predictive power in two-player zero-sum games (where equilibrium strategies are also minmax strategies) than in more general games in which the two concepts lead to different predictions regarding players' behavior.

Note that despite the fact that the strategic form of the game is implicitly a simultaneously played game in which each player, in selecting his strategy, does not know the strategy selected by the other player, if the game has a value then each player can reveal the optimal strategy that he intends to play to the other player and still guarantees his maxmin value. Suppose that s_I^* is an optimal strategy for Player I in a game with value v. Then

$$\min_{s_{II} \in S_{II}} u(s_I^*, s_{II}) = v, \tag{4.53}$$

and therefore for each $s_{II} \in S_{II}$ the following inequality is satisfied:

$$u(s_I^*, s_{II}) \geq v. \tag{4.54}$$

In other words, even if Player I were to "announce" to Player II that he intends to play s_I^*, Player II cannot bring about a situation in which the payoff (to Player I) will be less than the value. This simple observation has technical implications for the search for optimal strategies: in order to check whether or not a particular strategy, say of Player I, is optimal, we check what it can guarantee, that is, what the payoff will be when Player II knows that this is the strategy chosen by Player I and does his best to counter it.

Proof of Theorem 4.44: From the fact that both s_I^* and s_{II}^* are optimal strategies, we deduce that

$$u(s_I^*, s_{II}) \geq v, \quad \forall s_{II} \in S_{II}, \tag{4.55}$$

$$u(s_I, s_{II}^*) \leq v, \quad \forall s_I \in S_I. \tag{4.56}$$

Inserting $s_{II} = s_{II}^*$ into Equation (4.55) we deduce $u(s_I^*, s_{II}^*) \geq v$, and inserting $s_I = s_I^*$ into Equation (4.56) we get $u(s_I^*, s_{II}^*) \leq v$. The equation $v = u(s_I^*, s_{II}^*)$ follows. Equations (4.55) and (4.56) can now be written as

$$u(s_I^*, s_{II}) \geq u(s_I^*, s_{II}^*), \quad \forall s_{II} \in S_{II}, \tag{4.57}$$

$$u(s_I, s_{II}^*) \leq u(s_I^*, s_{II}^*), \quad \forall s_I \in S_I, \tag{4.58}$$

and therefore (s_I^*, s_{II}^*) is an equilibrium with payoff $(v, -v)$.   □

Proof of Theorem 4.45: Since (s_I^*, s_{II}^*) is an equilibrium, no player can benefit by a unilateral deviation:

$$u(s_I, s_{II}^*) \leq u(s_I^*, s_{II}^*), \quad \forall s_I \in S_I, \tag{4.59}$$

$$u(s_I^*, s_{II}) \geq u(s_I^*, s_{II}^*), \quad \forall s_{II} \in S_{II}. \tag{4.60}$$

Let $v = u(s_I^*, s_{II}^*)$. We will prove that v is indeed the value of the game. From Equation (4.60) we get

$$u(s_I^*, s_{II}) \geq v, \quad \forall s_{II} \in S_{II}, \tag{4.61}$$

and therefore $\underline{v} \geq v$. From Equation (4.59) we deduce that

$$u(s_I, s_{II}^*) \leq v, \quad \forall s_I \in S_I, \tag{4.62}$$

and therefore $\overline{v} \leq v$. Because it is always the case that $\underline{v} \leq \overline{v}$, we get

$$v \leq \underline{v} \leq \overline{v} \leq v, \tag{4.63}$$

which implies that the value exists and is equal to v. Furthermore, from Equation (4.61) we deduce that s_I^* is an optimal strategy for Player I, and from Equation (4.62) we deduce that s_{II}^* is an optimal strategy for Player II.   □

Corollary 4.46 *In a two-player zero-sum game, if (s_I^*, s_{II}^*) and (s_I^{**}, s_{II}^{**}) are two equilibria, then it follows that*

1. *Both equilibria yield the same payoff: $u(s_I^*, s_{II}^*) = u(s_I^{**}, s_{II}^{**})$.*
2. *Both (s_I^*, s_{II}^{**}) and (s_I^{**}, s_{II}^*) are also equilibria (and, given the above, they also yield the same payoff).*

Proof: The first part follows from Theorem 4.45, because the payoff of each one of the equilibria is necessarily equal to the value of the game. For the second part, note that Theorem 4.45 implies that all the strategies $s_I^*, s_I^{**}, s_{II}^*, s_{II}^{**}$ are optimal strategies. By Theorem 4.44 we conclude that (s_I^*, s_{II}^{**}) and (s_I^{**}, s_{II}^*) are equilibria.   □

Neither of the two conclusions of Corollary 4.46 is necessarily true in a two-player game that is not zero-sum. Consider, for example, the coordination game in Example 4.20, shown in Figure 4.37.

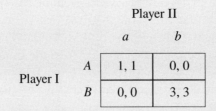

Figure 4.37 Coordination game

(A, a) and (B, b) are two equilibria with different payoffs (thus, the first part of Corollary 4.46 does not hold in this example) and (A, b) and (B, a) are not equilibria (thus the second part of the corollary does not hold).

The most important conclusion to take away from this section is that in two-player zero-sum games the value and Nash equilibrium, two different solution concepts, actually coincide and lead to the same results. Put another way, in two-player zero-sum games, the goals of security and stability are unified. John Nash regarded his concept of equilibrium to be a generalization of the value. But while the concept of the value expresses both the aspects of security and stability, the Nash equilibrium expresses only the aspect of stability. In games that are not zero-sum games, security and stability are different concepts, as we saw in the game depicted in Figure 4.28.

There is a geometric interpretation to the value of a two-player zero-sum game, which finds expression in the concept of the saddle point.

Definition 4.47 *A pair of strategies (s_I^*, s_{II}^*) is a* saddle point *of the function $u : S_I \times S_{II} \to \mathbb{R}$ if*

$$u(s_I^*, s_{II}^*) \geq u(s_I, s_{II}^*), \quad \forall s_I \in S_I, \tag{4.64}$$

$$u(s_I^*, s_{II}^*) \leq u(s_I^*, s_{II}), \quad \forall s_{II} \in S_{II}. \tag{4.65}$$

In other words, $u(s_I^*, s_{II}^*)$ is the highest value in column s_{II}^*, and the smallest in row s_I^*.

The name "saddle point" stems from the shape of a horse's saddle, whose center is perceived to be the minimal point of the saddle from one direction and the maximal point from the other direction.

The proof of the next theorem is left to the reader (Exercise 4.36).

Theorem 4.48 *In a two-player zero-sum game, (s_I^*, s_{II}^*) is a saddle point of the payoff function u if and only if s_I^* is an optimal strategy for Player I and s_{II}^* is an optimal strategy for Player II. In that case, $u(s_I^*, s_{II}^*)$ is the value of the game.*

4.13 Games with perfect information

As we have shown, there are games in which there exists no Nash equilibrium. These games will be treated in Chapter 5. In this section we focus instead on a large class of widely applicable games that all have Nash equilibria. These games are best characterized in extensive form. We will show that if an extensive-form game satisfies a particular characteristic, then it always has a Nash equilibrium. Furthermore, there are even equilibria that can be calculated directly from the game tree, without requiring that the game first be transformed into strategic form. Because it is often more convenient to work directly with the extensive form of a game, this way of calculating equilibria has a significant advantage.

In this section we study extensive-form games with perfect information. Recall that an extensive-form game is of perfect information if every information set of every player consists of only one vertex.

Theorem 4.49 (Kuhn) *Every finite game with perfect information has at least one Nash equilibrium.*

Kuhn's Theorem constitutes a generalization of Theorem 4.43, which states that every two-player zero-sum game with perfect information has a value. The proof of the theorem is similar to the proof of The payoff function Theorem 1.4 (page 3), and involves induction on the number of vertices in the game tree. Every child of the root of a game tree defines a subgame containing fewer vertices than the original game (a fact that follows from the assumption that the game has perfect recall) and the induction hypothesis then implies that the subgame has an equilibrium. Choose one equilibrium for each such subgame. If the root of the original game involves a chance move, then the union of the equilibria of all the subgames defines an equilibrium for the entire game. If the root involves a decision taken by player i, then that player will survey the subgames that will be played (one for each child that he may choose), calculate the payoff he will receive under the chosen equilibrium in each of those subgames, and choose the vertex leading to the subgame that grants him the maximal payoff. These intuitive ideas will now be turned into a formal proof.

Proof of Theorem 4.49: It is convenient to assume that if a player in any particular game has no action available in any vertex in the game tree, then his strategy set consists of a single strategy denoted by $\emptyset$.

The proof of the theorem is by induction on the number of vertices in the game tree. If the game tree is comprised of a single vertex, then the unique strategy vector is $(\emptyset, \ldots, \emptyset)$ (so a fortiori there are no available deviations), and it is therefore the unique Nash equilibrium.

Assume by induction that the claim is true for each game in extensive form containing fewer than K vertices, and consider a game Γ with K vertices. Denote by $x^1, \ldots, x^L$ the children of the root v^0, and by $\Gamma(x^l)$ the subgame whose root is x^l and whose vertices are those following x^l in the tree (see Figure 4.38). Because the game is one with perfect information, $\Gamma(x^l)$ is indeed a subgame. If we had not assumed this, then $\Gamma(x^l)$ would not necessarily be a subgame, because there could be an information set containing vertices that are descendants of both x^{l_1} and x^{l_2} (where $l_1 \neq l_2$) and we would be unable to make use of the induction hypothesis.

The payoff functions of the game Γ are, as usual, $u_i : \times_{i \in N} S_i \to \mathbb{R}$. For each $l \in 1, 2, \ldots, L$, the payoff functions in the subgame $\Gamma(x^l)$ are $u_i^l : \times_{i \in N} S_i^l \to \mathbb{R}$, where S_i^l is player i's set of strategies in the subgame $\Gamma(x^l)$.

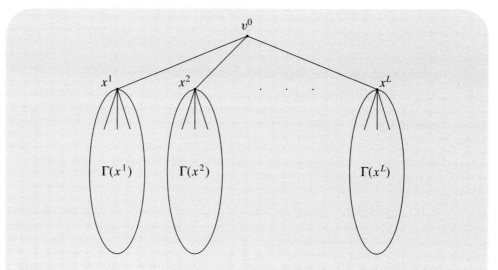

Figure 4.38 The game tree and subgames starting at the children of the root

For any $l \in \{1, \ldots, L\}$, the root v^0 of the original game Γ is not a vertex of $\Gamma(x^l)$, and therefore the number of vertices in $\Gamma(x^l)$ is less than K. By the induction hypothesis, for each $l \in \{1, 2, \ldots, L\}$ the game $\Gamma(x^l)$ has an equilibrium $s^{*l} = (s_i^{*l})_{i \in N}$ (if there are several such equilibria we arbitrarily choose one of them).

Case 1: The root v^0 is a chance move.
For each $l \in \{1, 2, \ldots, L\}$ denote by p^l the probability that child x^l is chosen. For each player i consider the strategy s_i^* in the game Γ defined as follows. If vertex x^l is chosen in the first move of the play of the game, implement strategy s_i^{*l} in the subgame $\Gamma(x^l)$. By definition it follows that $u_i(s^*) = \sum_{l=1}^{L} p^l u_i^l(s^{*l})$.

We will show that the strategy vector $s^* = (s_i^*)_{i \in N}$ is a Nash equilibrium. Suppose that player j deviates to a different strategy s_j. Let s_j^l be the restriction of s_j to the subgame $\Gamma(x^l)$. The expected payoff to player j under the strategy vector (s_j^l, s_{-j}^{*l}) is $\sum_{l=1}^{L} p^l u_j^l(s_j^l, s_{-j}^{*l})$.

Since s^{*l} is an equilibrium of $\Gamma(x^l)$, $u_j^l(s_j^l, s_{-j}^{*l}) \leq u_j^l(s^{*l})$ for all $l = 1, \ldots, L$, and therefore

$$u_j(s_j, s_{-j}^*) = \sum_{l=1}^{L} p^l u_j^l\left(s_j^l, s_{-j}^{*l}\right) \leq \sum_{l=1}^{L} p^l u_j^l(s^{*l}) = u_j(s^*). \qquad (4.66)$$

In other words, player j does not profit by deviating from s_j^* to s_j. Since this holds true for every player $j \in N$, the strategy vector s^* is indeed a Nash equilibrium.

Case 2: The root is a decision vertex for player i_0.
We first define a strategy vector $s^* = (s_i^*)_{i \in N}$ and then show that it is a Nash equilibrium. For each player i, $i \neq i_0$, consider the strategy s_i^* defined as follows. If vertex x^l is chosen in the first move of the play of the game, in the subgame $\Gamma(x^l)$ implement strategy s_i^{*l}. For player i_0 define the following strategy $s_{i_0}^*$: at the root choose a child x^{l_0} at which

the maximum $\max_{1 \leq l \leq L} u^l_{i_0}(s^{*l})$ is attained. For each $l \in \{1, 2, \ldots, L\}$, in the subgame $\Gamma(x^l)$ implement[7] the strategy $s^{*l}_{i_0}$. The payoff under the strategy vector $s^* = (s^*_i)_{i \in N}$ is $u^{l_0}(s^{*l_0})$.

The proof that each player i, except for player i_0, cannot profit from a deviation from s^*_i is similar to the proof in Case 1 above. We will show that player i_0 also cannot profit by deviating from $s^*_{i_0}$, thus completing the proof that the strategy vector s^* is a Nash equilibrium.

Suppose that player i_0 deviates by selecting strategy s_{i_0}. Let $x^{\widehat{l}}$ be the child of the root selected by this strategy, and for each child x^l of the root let $s^l_{i_0}$ be the strategy s_{i_0} restricted to the subgame $\Gamma(x^l)$.

- If $\widehat{l} = l_0$, since s^{*l_0} is an equilibrium of the subgame $\Gamma(x^{l_0})$, the payoff to player i_0 is

$$u_{i_0}(s_{i_0}, s^*_{-i_0}) = u^{l_0}_{i_0}\left(s^{l_0}_{i_0}, s^{*l_0}_{-i_0}\right) \leq u^{l_0}_{i_0}(s^{*l_0}) = u_{i_0}(s^*). \qquad (4.67)$$

In other words, the deviation is not a profitable one.

- If $\widehat{l} \neq l_0$, since $s^{*\widehat{l}}$ is an equilibrium of the subgame $\Gamma(x^{\widehat{l}})$ and using the definition of l_0, we obtain

$$u_{i_0}(s_{i_0}, s^*_{-i_0}) = u^{\widehat{l}}_{i_0}\left(s^{\widehat{l}}_{i_0}, s^{*\widehat{l}}_{-i_0}\right) \leq u^{\widehat{l}}_{i_0}(s^{*\widehat{l}}) \leq u^{l_0}_{i_0}(s^{*l_0}) = u_{i_0}(s^*). \qquad (4.68)$$

This too is not a profitable deviation, which completes the proof. $\qquad \square$

Remark 4.50 *In the course of the last proof, we proceeded by induction from the root to its children and beyond. This is called* forward induction. *We can prove the theorem by backward induction, as follows. Let x be a vertex all of whose children are leaves. Since the game has perfect recall, the player choosing an action at vertex x knows that the play of the game has arrived at that vertex (and not at a larger information set containing x) and he therefore chooses the leaf l giving him the maximal payoff. We can imagine erasing the leaves following x and thus turning x into a leaf with a payoff equal to the payoff of l. The resulting game tree has fewer vertices than the original tree, so we can apply the induction hypothesis to it. The reader is asked to complete this proof in Exercise 4.39. This process is called* backward induction. *It yields a practical algorithm for finding an equilibrium in finite games with perfect information: start at vertices leading immediately to leaves. Assuming the play of the game gets to such a vertex, the player at that vertex will presumably choose the leaf granting him the maximal payoff (if there are two or more such vertices, the player may arbitrarily choose any one of them). We then attach that payoff to such a vertex. If one of these vertices is the vertex of a chance move, the payoff at that vertex is the expectation of the payoff at the leaf reached by the chance move. From here we proceed in stages: at each stage, we attach payoffs to vertices leading immediately to vertices that had payoffs attached to them in previous stages. At each such vertex, the player controlling that vertex will make a selection leading to the maximal possible payoff to him, and that is the payoff associated with the vertex. We continue by*

---

7 Since defining a strategy requires defining how a player plays at each node at which he chooses an action, we also need to define $s^*_{i_0}$ in the subgames $\Gamma(x^l)$ which the first move of the play of the game does not lead to ($l \neq l_0$).

this process to climb the tree until we reach the root. In some cases this process leads to multiple equilibria. As shown in Exercise 4.40, some equilibria cannot be obtained by this process.   ♦

4.14 Games on the unit square

In this section we analyze two examples of two-player games in which the set of strategies is infinite, namely, the unit interval $[0, 1]$. These examples will be referred to in Chapter 5, where we introduce mixed strategies.

4.14.1 A two-player zero-sum game on the unit square

Consider the two-player zero-sum strategic-form game in which:[8]

- the strategy set of Player I is $X = [0, 1]$;
- the strategy set of Player II is $Y = [0, 1]$;
- the payoff function (which is what Player II pays Player I) is

$$u(x, y) = 4xy - 2x - y + 3, \quad \forall x \in [0, 1], \forall y \in [0, 1]. \tag{4.69}$$

This game is called a *game on the unit square*, because the set of strategy vectors is the unit square in $\mathbb{R}^2$. We can check whether or not this game has a value, and if it does, we can identify optimal strategies for the two players, as follows. First we calculate

$$\underline{v} = \max_{x \in [0,1]} \min_{y \in [0,1]} u(x, y), \tag{4.70}$$

and

$$\overline{v} = \min_{y \in [0,1]} \max_{x \in [0,1]} u(x, y), \tag{4.71}$$

and check whether or not they are equal. For each $x \in [0, 1]$,

$$\min_{y \in [0,1]} u(x, y) = \min_{y \in [0,1]} (4xy - 2x - y + 3) = \min_{y \in [0,1]} (y(4x - 1) - 2x + 3). \tag{4.72}$$

For each fixed x, this is a linear function in y, and therefore the point at which the minimum is attained is determined by the slope $4x - 1$: if the slope is positive, the function is increasing and the minimum is attained at $y = 0$; if the slope is negative, this is a decreasing function and the minimum is attained at $y = 1$; if the slope is 0, the function is constant in y and every point is a minimum point. This leads to the following (see Figure 4.39):

$$\min_{y \in [0,1]} u(x, y) = \begin{cases} 2x + 2 & \text{if } x \leq \frac{1}{4}, \\ -2x + 3 & \text{if } x \geq \frac{1}{4}. \end{cases} \tag{4.73}$$

---

8 In games on the unit square it is convenient to represent a strategy as a continuous variable, and we therefore denote player strategies by x and y (rather than s_I and s_{II}), and the sets of strategies are denoted by X and Y respectively (rather than S_I and S_{II}).

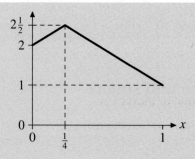

Figure 4.39 The function $x \mapsto \min_{y \in [0,1]} u(x,y)$

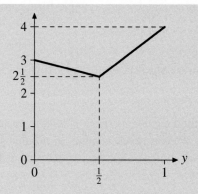

Figure 4.40 The function $y \mapsto \max_{x \in [0,1]} u(x,y)$

This function of x attains a unique maximum at $x = \frac{1}{4}$, and its value there is $2\frac{1}{2}$. Therefore,

$$\underline{v} = \max_{x \in [0,1]} \min_{y \in [0,1]} u(x,y) = 2\tfrac{1}{2}. \tag{4.74}$$

We similarly calculate the following (see Figure 4.40):

$$\max_{x \in [0,1]} u(x,y) = \max_{x \in [0,1]} (4xy - 2x - y + 3) = \max_{x \in [0,1]} (x(4y - 2) - y + 3) \tag{4.75}$$

$$= \begin{cases} -y + 3 & \text{if } y \leq \frac{1}{2}, \\ 3y + 1 & \text{if } y \geq \frac{1}{2}. \end{cases} \tag{4.76}$$

This function of y attains a unique minimum at $y = \frac{1}{2}$, and its value there is $2\frac{1}{2}$.

$$\overline{v} = \min_{y \in [0,1]} \max_{x \in [0,1]} u(x,y) = 2\tfrac{1}{2}. \tag{4.77}$$

In other words, the game has a value $v = 2\frac{1}{2}$, and $x^* = \frac{1}{4}$ and $y^* = \frac{1}{2}$ are optimal strategies (in fact the only optimal strategies in this game).

Since x^* and y^* are the only optimal strategies of the players, we deduce from Theorems 4.44 and 4.45 that (x^*, y^*) is the only equilibrium of the game.

4.14.2 A two-player non-zero-sum game on the unit square

Consider the following two-player non-zero-sum game in strategic form:

- the strategy set of Player I is $X = [0, 1]$;
- the strategy set of Player II is $Y = [0, 1]$;
- the payoff function of Player I is

$$u_I(x, y) = 3xy - 2x - 2y + 2, \quad \forall x \in [0, 1], \forall y \in [0, 1]; \quad (4.78)$$

- the payoff function of Player II is

$$u_{II}(x, y) = -4xy + 2x + y, \quad \forall x \in [0, 1], \forall y \in [0, 1]. \quad (4.79)$$

Even though this is not a zero-sum game, the maxmin concept, reflecting the security level of a player, is still well defined (see Equation (4.25)). Player I can guarantee

$$\underline{v}_I = \max_{x \in [0,1]} \min_{y \in [0,1]} u_I(x, y), \quad (4.80)$$

and Player II can guarantee

$$\underline{v}_{II} = \max_{y \in [0,1]} \min_{x \in [0,1]} u_{II}(x, y). \quad (4.81)$$

Similar to the calculations carried out in Section 4.14.1, we derive the following (see Figure 4.41):

$$\min_{y \in [0,1]} u_I(x, y) = \min_{y \in [0,1]} (3xy - 2x - 2y + 2) = \min_{y \in [0,1]} (y(3x - 2) - 2x + 2) \quad (4.82)$$

$$= \begin{cases} x & \text{for } x \leq \frac{2}{3}, \\ -2x + 2 & \text{for } x \geq \frac{2}{3}. \end{cases} \quad (4.83)$$

This function of x has a single maximum, attained at $x = \frac{2}{3}$, with the value $\frac{2}{3}$. We therefore have

$$\underline{v}_I = \max_{x \in [0,1]} \min_{y \in [0,1]} u_I(x, y) = \frac{2}{3}. \quad (4.84)$$

The sole maxmin strategy available to Player I is $\hat{x} = \frac{2}{3}$. We similarly calculate for Player II (see Figure 4.42):

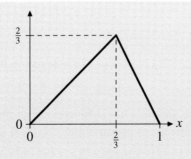

Figure 4.41 The function $x \mapsto \min_{y \in [0,1]} u_I(x, y)$

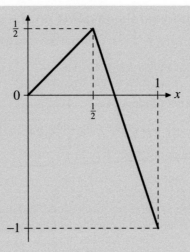

Figure 4.42 The function $y \mapsto \min_{x \in [0,1]} u_{II}(x, y)$

$$\min_{x \in [0,1]} u_{II}(x, y) = \min_{x \in [0,1]} (-4xy + 2x + y) = \min_{x \in [0,1]} (x(2 - 4y) + y) \qquad (4.85)$$

$$= \begin{cases} y & \text{for } y \leq \frac{1}{2}, \\ 2 - 3y & \text{for } y \geq \frac{1}{2}. \end{cases} \qquad (4.86)$$

This function of y has a single maximum, attained at $y = \frac{1}{2}$, with value $\frac{1}{2}$. We therefore have

$$\underline{v}_{II} = \max_{y \in [0,1]} \min_{x \in [0,1]} u_{II}(x, y) = \frac{1}{2}, \qquad (4.87)$$

and the sole maxmin strategy of Player II is $\widehat{y} = \frac{1}{2}$.

The next step is to calculate a Nash equilibrium of this game, assuming that there is one. The most convenient way to do so is to use the definition of the Nash equilibrium based on the "best reply" concept (Definition 4.18 on page 97): a pair of strategies (x^*, y^*) is a Nash equilibrium if x^* is Player I's best reply to y^*, and y^* is Player II's best reply to x^*.

For each $x \in [0, 1]$, denote by $\mathrm{br}_{II}(x)$ the collection of best replies[9] of Player II to the strategy x:

$$\mathrm{br}_{II}(x) := \mathrm{argmax}_{y \in [0,1]} u_{II}(x, y) = \{y \in [0, 1] : u_{II}(x, y) \geq u_{II}(x, z) \quad \forall z \in [0, 1]\}. \qquad (4.88)$$

In other words, $\mathrm{br}_{II}(x)$ is the collection of values y at which the maximum of $u_{II}(x, y)$ is attained. To calculate $\mathrm{br}_{II}(x)$ in this example, we will write $u_{II}(x, y)$ as

$$u_{II}(x, y) = y(1 - 4x) + 2x. \qquad (4.89)$$

For each fixed x, this is a linear function of y: if it has a positive slope, the function is increasing and attains its maximum at $y = 1$. If the slope is negative, the function is

---

9 br stands for best reply.

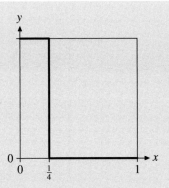

Figure 4.43 The graph of $\mathrm{br}_{\mathrm{II}}(x)$

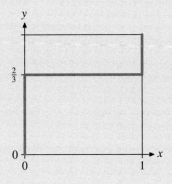

Figure 4.44 The graph of $\mathrm{br}_{\mathrm{I}}(y)$

decreasing and the maximum point is $y = 0$. If the slope of the function is 0, then the function is constant and every point $y \in [0, 1]$ is a maximum point. The slope turns from positive to negative at $x = \frac{1}{4}$, and the graph of $\mathrm{br}_{\mathrm{II}}(x)$ is given in Figure 4.43.

Note that $\mathrm{br}_{\mathrm{II}}$ is not a function, because $\mathrm{br}_{\mathrm{II}}(\frac{1}{4})$ is not a single point but the interval $[0, 1]$.

The calculation of $\mathrm{br}_{\mathrm{I}}(y)$ is carried out similarly. The best reply of Player I to each $y \in [0, 1]$ is

$$\mathrm{br}_{\mathrm{I}}(y) := \mathrm{argmax}_{x \in [0,1]} u_{\mathrm{I}}(x, y) = \{x \in [0, 1]: u_{\mathrm{I}}(x, y) \geq u_{\mathrm{I}}(z, y) \ \forall z \in [0, 1]\}. \tag{4.90}$$

Writing $u_{\mathrm{I}}(x, y)$ as

$$u_{\mathrm{I}}(x, y) = x(3y - 2) - 2y + 2 \tag{4.91}$$

shows that, for each fixed y, this is a linear function in x: if it has a positive slope, the function is increasing and attains its maximum at $x = 1$. A negative slope implies that the function is decreasing and its maximum point is $x = 0$, and a slope of 0 indicates a constant function where every point $x \in [0, 1]$ is a maximum point. The slope turns from negative to positive at $y = \frac{2}{3}$, and the graph of $\mathrm{br}_{\mathrm{I}}(y)$ is given in Figure 4.44.

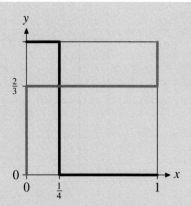

Figure 4.45 The graphs of $x \mapsto \mathrm{br}_{\mathrm{II}}(x)$ (darker line) and $y \mapsto \mathrm{br}_{\mathrm{I}}(y)$ (lighter line)

Note that the variable y is represented by the vertical axis, even though it is the variable of the function $\mathrm{br}_{\mathrm{I}}(y)$. This is done so that both graphs, $\mathrm{br}_{\mathrm{I}}(y)$ and $\mathrm{br}_{\mathrm{II}}(x)$, can be conveniently depicted within the same system of axes, as shown in Figure 4.45.

In terms of the best-reply concept, the pair of strategies (x^*, y^*) is an equilibrium point if and only if $x^* \in \mathrm{br}_{\mathrm{I}}(y^*)$ and $y^* \in \mathrm{br}_{\mathrm{II}}(x^*)$. In other words, we require (x^*, y^*) to be on *both* graphs $\mathrm{br}_{\mathrm{II}}(x)$ and $\mathrm{br}_{\mathrm{I}}(y)$. As is clear from Figure 4.40, the only point satisfying this condition is $(x^* = \frac{1}{4}, y^* = \frac{2}{3})$.

We conclude that the game has a single Nash equilibrium (x^*, y^*) where $x^* = \frac{1}{4}$ and $y^* = \frac{2}{3}$, with the equilibrium payoff of $u_{\mathrm{I}}(x^*, y^*) = \frac{2}{3}$ to Player I and $u_{\mathrm{II}}(x^*, y^*) = \frac{1}{2}$ to Player II.

This example shows, again, that in games that are not zero-sum the concepts of Nash equilibrium and optimal strategies differ; despite the fact that for both players the equilibrium payoff is equal to the security level ($\frac{2}{3}$ for Player I and $\frac{1}{2}$ for Player II), the maxmin strategies are not the equilibrium strategies. The maxmin strategies are $\hat{x} = \frac{2}{3}$ and $\hat{y} = \frac{1}{2}$, while the equilibrium strategies are $x^* = \frac{1}{4}$ and $y^* = \frac{2}{3}$.

- The pair of maxmin strategies, $\hat{x} = \frac{2}{3}$ and $\hat{y} = \frac{1}{2}$, is not an equilibrium. The payoff to Player I is $\frac{2}{3}$, but he can increase his payoff by deviating to $x = 0$ because

$$u_{\mathrm{I}}(0, \hat{y}) = u_{\mathrm{I}}\left(0, \tfrac{1}{2}\right) = 1 > \tfrac{2}{3} = u_{\mathrm{I}}(\hat{x}, \hat{y}). \tag{4.92}$$

The payoff to Player II is $\frac{1}{2}$, and he can also increase his payoff by deviating to $y = 0$ because

$$u_{\mathrm{II}}(\hat{x}, 0) = u_{\mathrm{II}}\left(\tfrac{2}{3}, 0\right) = \tfrac{4}{3} > \tfrac{1}{2} = u_{\mathrm{II}}(\hat{x}, \hat{y}). \tag{4.93}$$

- The equilibrium strategies $x^* = \frac{1}{4}$ and $y^* = \frac{2}{3}$ are not optimal strategies. If Player I chooses strategy $x^* = \frac{1}{4}$ and Player II plays $y = 1$, the payoff to Player I is less than his security level $\frac{2}{3}$:

$$u_{\mathrm{I}}\left(\tfrac{1}{4}, 1\right) = \tfrac{1}{4} < \tfrac{2}{3} = \underline{v}_{\mathrm{I}}. \tag{4.94}$$

Similarly, when Player II plays $y^* = \frac{2}{3}$, if Player I plays $x = 1$ then the payoff to Player II is less than his security level $\frac{1}{2}$:

$$u_{\text{II}}\left(1, \tfrac{2}{3}\right) = 0 < \tfrac{1}{2} = \underline{v}_{\text{II}}. \tag{4.95}$$

Note that $u_{\text{I}}(x, \tfrac{2}{3}) = \tfrac{2}{3}$ for all $x \in [0, 1]$. It follows that when Player II implements the strategy $y^* = \tfrac{2}{3}$, Player I is "indifferent" between all of his strategies. Similarly, $u_{\text{II}}(\tfrac{1}{4}, y) = \tfrac{1}{2}$ for all $y \in [0, 1]$. It follows that when Player I implements the strategy $x^* = \tfrac{1}{4}$, Player II is "indifferent" between all of his strategies. This outcome occurs in every two-player game on the unit square when the payoff functions are bilinear functions with a unique equilibrium (x^*, y^*) satisfying $0 < x^*, y^* < 1$. This is not a coincidence: it is the result of a general game-theoretic principle called the indifference principle, which is studied in Chapter 5 (Section 5.2.3).

4.15 Remarks

Mathematician John Nash received the Nobel Memorial Prize in Economics in 1994 for the equilibrium concept that is named after him. The Nash equilibrium is a central concept in mathematical economics.

The Prisoner's Dilemma game was first defined and studied by Merrill Flood and Melvin Dresher in 1950. The name commonly given to that game, as well as the accompanying story, was first suggested by Albert Tucker. The version of the Prisoner's Dilemma appearing in Exercise 4.1 was suggested by Reinhard Selten.

The name "Security Dilemma" (see Example 4.22 on page 98) was coined by Herz [1950]. The dilemma was extensively studied in the political science literature (see, for example, Jervis [1978]). Alain Ledoux [1985] was the first to present the Guessing Game appearing in Exercise 4.43. Many experiments have been based on this game, including experiments conducted by Rosmarie Nagel. Exercise 4.46 describes the Braess Paradox, which first appeared in Braess [1968]. Exercise 4.47 is a variation of the Braess Paradox, due to Kameda and Hosokawa [2000]. The authors wish to thank Hisao Kameda for bringing this example to their attention. Exercise 4.48 is adapted from Pigou (1920). Exercise 4.49 is an example of a location game, a concept that was first introduced and studied in Hotelling [1929].

4.16 Exercises

4.1 William and Henry are participants in a televised game show, seated in separate booths with no possibility of communicating with each other. Each one of them is asked to submit, in a sealed envelope, one of the following two requests (requests that are guaranteed to be honored):

- Give me $1,000.
- Give the other participant $4,000.

  Describe this situation as a strategic-form game. What is the resulting game? What will the players do, and why?

4.2 Describe the following games in strategic form.

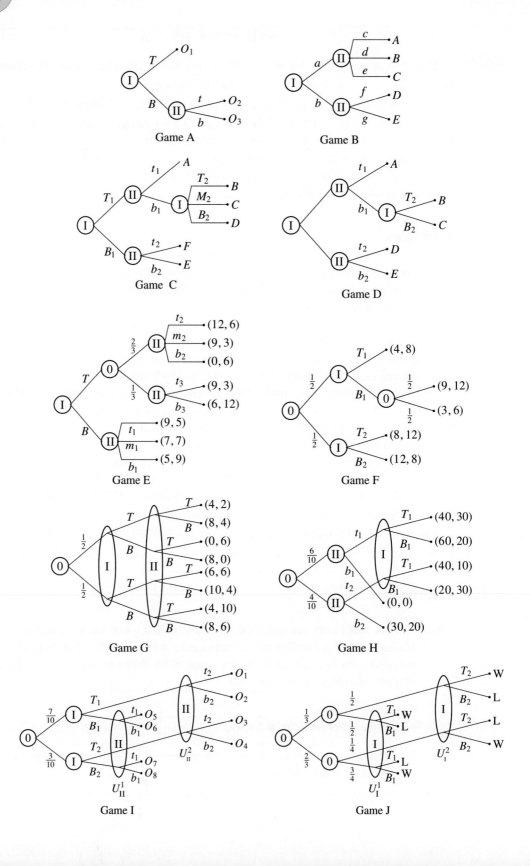

Game A

Game B

Game C

Game D

Game E

Game F

Game G

Game H

Game I

Game J

4.3 Consider the following two-player game.

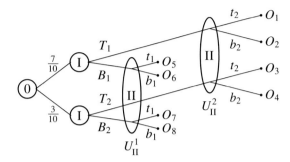

(a) What does Player II know in each one of his information sets? What does he not know?
(b) Describe as a game in extensive form the version of this game in which Player II knows the result of the chance move but does not know the action chosen by Player I.
(c) Describe as a game in extensive form the version of this game in which Player II knows both the result of the chance move and the action chosen by Player I.
(d) Convert all three games into strategic-form games. Are all the matrices you derived in this way identical?

4.4 In the game of Hex (Exercise 3.19 on page 64) the two players eliminate (weakly) dominated strategies. What remains of the game once the elimination process ends?

4.5 Establish whether there exists a two-player game in extensive form with perfect information, and possible outcomes I (Player I wins), II (Player II wins), and D (a draw), whose strategic-form description is

Player II

		s_{II}^1	s_{II}^2	s_{II}^3	s_{II}^4
	s_I^1	D	I	II	I
Player I	s_I^2	I	II	I	D
	s_I^3	I	I	II	II

If the answer is yes, describe the game. If not, explain why not.

4.6 Repeat Exercise 4.5, with respect to the following strategic-form game:

Player II

	s_{II}^1	s_{II}^2	s_{II}^3	s_{II}^4
s_I^1	D	D	D	D
s_I^2	I	I	II	II
s_I^3	II	II	D	D

Player I is the row label (s_I^1, s_I^2, s_I^3).

4.7 In each of the following games, where Player I is the row player and Player II is the column player, determine whether the process of iterated elimination of strictly dominated strategies yields a single strategy vector when it is completed. If so, what is that vector? Verify that it is the only Nash equilibrium of the game.

	L	R
H	4, 2	0, 1
T	1, 1	3, 3

Game A

	L	R
H	1, 3	2, 3
T	0, 4	0, 2

Game B

	a	b	c
γ	1, 0	3, 0	2, 1
β	3, 1	0, 1	1, 2
α	2, 1	1, 6	0, 2

Game C

4.8 What advice would you give to the players in each of the following four games? Provide a detailed justification for all advice given.

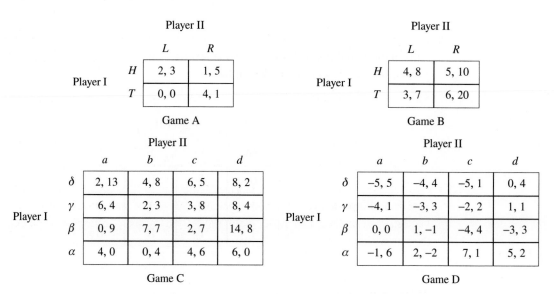

Player II

	L	R
H	2, 3	1, 5
T	0, 0	4, 1

Game A

Player II

	L	R
H	4, 8	5, 10
T	3, 7	6, 20

Game B

Player II

	a	b	c	d
δ	2, 13	4, 8	6, 5	8, 2
γ	6, 4	2, 3	3, 8	8, 4
β	0, 9	7, 7	2, 7	14, 8
α	4, 0	0, 4	4, 6	6, 0

Game C

Player II

	a	b	c	d
δ	−5, 5	−4, 4	−5, 1	0, 4
γ	−4, 1	−3, 3	−2, 2	1, 1
β	0, 0	1, −1	−4, 4	−3, 3
α	−1, 6	2, −2	7, 1	5, 2

Game D

4.9 A Nash equilibrium s^* is termed *strict* if every deviation undertaken by a player yields a definite loss for that player, i.e., $u_i(s^*) > u_i(s_i, s^*_{-i})$ for each player $i \in N$ and each strategy $s_i \in S_i \setminus \{s^*_i\}$.

   (a) Prove that if the process of iterative elimination of strictly dominated strategies results in a unique strategy vector s^*, then s^* is a strict Nash equilibrium and it is the only Nash equilibrium of the game.

   (b) Prove that if $s^* = (s^*_i)^n_{i=1}$ is a strict Nash equilibrium, then none of the strategies s^*_i can be eliminated by iterative elimination of dominated strategies (under either strict or weak domination).[10]

4.10 Prove that the result of iterated elimination of strictly dominated strategies (that is, the set of strategies remaining after the elimination process has been completed) is independent of the order of elimination. Deduce that if the result of the elimination process is a single vector s^*, then that same vector will be obtained under every possible order of the elimination of strictly dominated strategies.

4.11 Find all rational strategy vectors in the following games:

Player II

	a	b	c	d
α	6, 2	6, 3	7, 6	2, 8
β	8, 5	6, 9	4, 6	4, 7

(Player I on left)

Game A

Player II

	a	b
α	9, 5	5, 3
β	8, 6	8, 4

(Player I on left)

Game B

Player II

	a	b	c	d
α	−1, 20	−7, −7	−1, 2	−5, 8
β	27, 20	13, −1	21, 2	13, −1
γ	−5, 20	−3, 5	7, −1	3, −4

(Player I on left)

Game C

Player II

	a	b	c	d
α	3, 7	0, 13	4, 5	5, 3
β	5, 3	4, 5	4, 5	3, 7
γ	4, 5	3, 7	4, 5	5, 3
δ	4, 5	4, 5	4, 5	4, 5

(Player I on left)

Game D

4.12 Find a game that has at least one equilibrium, but in which iterative elimination of dominated strategies yields a game with no equilibria.

4.13 Prove directly that a strictly dominated strategy cannot be an element of a game's equilibrium (Corollary 4.36, page 109). In other words, show that in every strategy vector in which there is a player using a strictly dominated strategy, that player can deviate and increase his payoff.

....

10 This is not true of equilibria that are not strict. See Example 4.16, where there are four non-strict Nash equilibria (T, C), (M, L), (M, R), and (B, L).

4.14 In a first-price auction, each buyer submits his bid in a sealed envelope. The winner of the auction is the buyer who submits the highest bid, and the amount he pays is equal to what he bid. If several buyers have submitted bids equal to the highest bid, a fair lottery is conducted among them to choose one winner, who then pays his bid.

(a) In this situation, does the strategy β_i^* of buyer i, in which he bids his private value for the item, weakly dominate all his other strategies?

(b) Find a strategy of buyer i that weakly dominates strategy β_i^*.

Does the strategy under which each buyer bids his private value weakly dominate all the other strategies? Justify your answer.

4.15 Prove that the two definitions of the Nash equilibrium, presented in Definitions 4.17 and 4.19, are equivalent to each other.

4.16 Find all the equilibria in the following games:

Player II

		a	b	c	d
	γ	7, 3	6, 3	5, 5	4, 7
Player I	β	4, 2	5, 8	8, 6	5, 8
	α	6, 1	3, 8	2, 4	6, 9

Game A

Player II

		a	b	c	d
	δ	5, 2	3, 1	2, 2	4, 5
Player I	γ	0, 3	2, 2	0, 1	−1, 3
	β	8, 4	7, 0	6, −1	5, 2
	α	0, 5	1, −2	2, 2	3, 4

Game B

Player II

		a	b	c	d
	ϵ	0, 0	−1, 1	1, 1	0, −1
	δ	1, −1	1, 0	0, 1	0, 0
Player I	γ	0, 1	−1, −1	1, 0	1, −1
	β	−1, 1	0, −1	−1, 1	0, 0
	α	1, 1	0, 0	−1, −1	0, 0

Game C

4.17 In the following three-player game, Player I chooses a row (A or B), Player II chooses a column (a or b), and Player III chooses a matrix (α, β, or γ). Find all the equilibria of this game.

	a	b
A	0, 0, 5	0, 0, 0
B	2, 0, 0	0, 0, 0

α

	a	b
A	1, 2, 3	0, 0, 0
B	0, 0, 0	1, 2, 3

β

	a	b
A	0, 0, 0	0, 0, 0
B	0, 5, 0	0, 0, 4

γ

4.18 Find the equilibria of the following three-player game (Player I chooses row T, C, or B, Player II a column L, M, or R, and Player III chooses matrix P or Q).

	L	M	R
T	3, 10, 8	8, 14, 6	4, 12, 7
C	4, 7, 2	5, 5, 2	2, 2, 8
B	3, −5, 0	0, 3, 4	−3, 5, 0

P

	L	M	R
T	4, 9, 3	7, 8, 10	5, 7, −1
C	3, 4, 5	17, 3, 12	3, 5, 2
B	9, 7, 2	20, 0, 13	0, 15, 0

Q

4.19 Prove that in the Centipede game (see Exercise 3.12 on page 61), at every Nash equilibrium, Player I chooses S at the first move in the game.

4.20 A two-player game is *symmetric* if the two players have the same strategy set $S_1 = S_2$ and the payoff functions satisfy $u_1(s_1, s_2) = u_2(s_2, s_1)$ for each $s_1, s_2 \in S_1$. Prove that the set of equilibria of a two-player symmetric game is a symmetric set: if (s_1, s_2) is an equilibrium, then (s_2, s_1) is also an equilibrium.

4.21 Describe the following games in strategic form (in three-player games, let Player I choose the row, Player II choose the column, and Player III choose the matrix). In each game, find all the equilibria, if any exist.

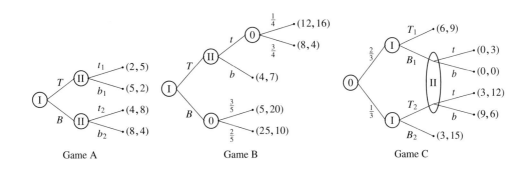

Game A   Game B   Game C

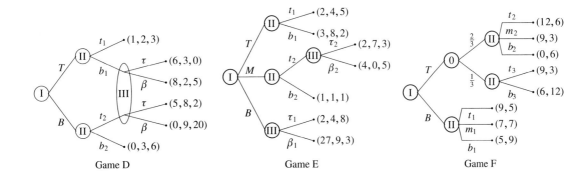

Game D   Game E   Game F

4.22 Let X and Y be two compact sets in $\mathbb{R}^m$, and let $f : X \times Y \to \mathbb{R}$ be a continuous function. Prove that the function $x \mapsto \min_{y \in Y} f(x, y)$ is also a continuous function.

4.23 In each of the following two-player zero-sum games, implement a process of iterative elimination of dominated strategies. For each game list the strategies you have eliminated and find the maxmin strategy of Player I and the minmax strategy of Player II.

Player II

		a	b	c	d
	γ	8	4	8	4
Player I	β	2	5	3	8
	α	6	1	4	5

Game A

Player II

		a	b	c	d
	δ	6	4	2	1
	γ	5	3	3	0
Player I	β	1	0	5	4
	α	2	−3	2	3

Game B

Player II

		a	b	c	d
	δ	3	6	5	5
	γ	5	5	5	5
Player I	β	5	3	5	6
	α	6	5	5	3

Game C

4.24 Prove that in Example 4.23 on page 99 (duopoly competition), the pair of strategies (q_1^*, q_2^*) defined by

$$q_1^* = \frac{2 - 2c_1 + c_2}{3}, \quad q_2^* = \frac{2 - 2c_2 + c_1}{3} \tag{4.96}$$

is an equilibrium.

4.25 Prove Theorem 4.26 (page 105): if player i has a (weakly) dominant strategy, then it is his (not necessarily unique) maxmin strategy. Moreover, this strategy is his best reply to every strategy vector of the other players.

4.26 Prove Theorem 4.28 (page 105): in a game in which every player i has a strategy s_i^* that strictly dominates all of his other strategies, the strategy vector $(s_1^*, \ldots, s_n^*)$ is the unique equilibrium point of the game as well as the unique vector of maxmin strategies.

4.27 Let $G = (N, (S_i)_{i \in N}, (u_i)_{i \in N})$ be a game in strategic form, and let $\hat{s}_i \in S_i$ be an arbitrary strategy of player i in this game. Let $\widehat{G}$ be the game derived from G by the elimination of strategy $\widehat{s}_i$. Prove that for each player $j, j \neq i$, the maxmin value of player j in the game $\widehat{G}$ is greater than or equal to his maxmin value in G. Is the maxmin value of player i in game $\widehat{G}$ necessarily less than his maxmin value in G? Prove this last statement, or find a counterexample.

4.28 Find an example of a game $G = (N, (S_i)_{i \in N}, (u_i)_{i \in N})$ in strategic form such that the game $\widehat{G}$ derived from G by elimination of one strategy in one player's strategy set has an equilibrium that is not an equilibrium in the game G.

4.29 Prove Corollary 4.33 on page 108: let $G = (N, (S_i)_{i \in N}, (u_i)_{i \in N})$ be a strategic form game and let $\widehat{G}$ be the game derived from G by iterative elimination of dominated strategies. Then every equilibrium s^* in the game $\widehat{G}$ is also an equilibrium in the game G.

4.30 Find an example of a strategic-form game G and of an equilibrium s^* of that game such that for each player $i \in N$ the strategy s_i^* is dominated.

4.31 The following questions relate to the following two-player zero-sum game:

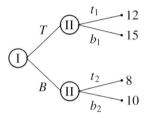

(a) Find an optimal strategy for each player by applying backward induction.
(b) Describe this game in strategic form.
(c) Find all the optimal strategies of the two players.
(d) Explain why there are optimal strategies in addition to the one you identified by backward induction.

4.32 (a) Let $A = (a_{ij})$ be an $n \times m$ matrix representing a two-player zero-sum game, where the row player is Ann and the column player is Bill. Let $B = (b_{ji})$ be a new $m \times n$ matrix in which the row player is Bill and the column player is Ann. What is the relation between the matrices A and B?

(b) Conduct a similar transformation of the names of the players in the following matrix and write down the new matrix.

<table>
<tr><td></td><td></td><td colspan="3">Player II</td></tr>
<tr><td></td><td></td><td>L</td><td>M</td><td>R</td></tr>
<tr><td></td><td>T</td><td>3</td><td>−5</td><td>7</td></tr>
<tr><td>Player I</td><td></td><td></td><td></td><td></td></tr>
<tr><td></td><td>B</td><td>−2</td><td>8</td><td>4</td></tr>
</table>

4.33 The value of the two-player zero-sum game given by the matrix A is 0. Is it necessarily true that the value of the two-player zero-sum game given by the matrix $-A$ is also 0? If your answer is yes, prove this. If your answer is no, provide a counterexample.

4.34 Let A and B be two finite sets, and let $u : A \times B \to \mathbb{R}$ be an arbitrary function.[11] Prove that

$$\max_{a \in A} \min_{b \in B} u(a, b) \leq \min_{b \in B} \max_{a \in A} u(a, b). \qquad (4.97)$$

4.35 Show whether or not the value exists in each of the following games. If the value exists, find it and find all the optimal strategies for each player. As usual, Player I is the row player and Player II is the column player.

	a	b
A	2	2
B	1	3

Game A

	a	b	c
A	1	2	3
B	4	3	0

Game B

	a	b	c	d
A	$3\frac{1}{2}$	3	4	12
B	7	5	6	13
C	4	2	3	0

Game C

	a	b
A	3	0
B	2	2
C	0	3

Game D

4.36 Prove Theorem 4.48 (page 117): in a two-player zero-sum game, (s_I^*, s_{II}^*) is a saddle point if and only if s_I^* is an optimal strategy for Player I and s_{II}^* is an optimal strategy for Player II.

4.37 Let A and B be two finite-dimensional matrices with positive payoffs. Show that the game

A	0
0	B

has no value. (Each 0 here represents a matrix of the proper dimensions, such that all of its entries are 0.)

---

11 The finiteness of A and B is needed to ensure the existence of a minimum and maximum in Equation (4.97). The claim holds (using the same proof) for each pair of sets A and B and function u for which the min and the max of the function in Equation (4.97) exist (for example, if A and B are compact sets and u is a continuous function; see Exercise 4.22). Alternatively, we may remove all restrictions on A, B, and u and replace min by inf and max by sup.

4.38 Answer the following questions with reference to Game A and Game B that appear in the diagram below.

(a) Find all equilibria obtained by backward induction.
(b) Describe the games in strategic form.
(c) Check whether there are other Nash equilibria in addition to those found by backward induction.

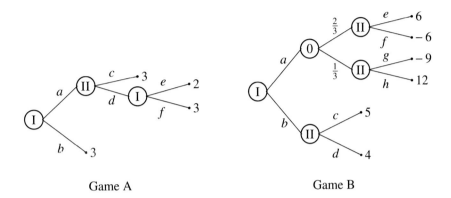

Game A   Game B

4.39 Prove Theorem 4.49 (on page 118) using backward induction (a general outline for the proof can be found in Remark 4.50 on page 120).

4.40 Find a Nash equilibrium in the following game using backward induction:

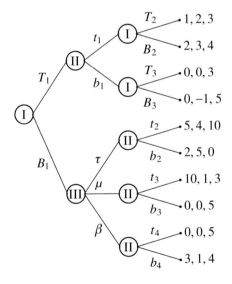

Find an additional Nash equilibrium of this game.

4.41 In a two-player zero-sum game on the unit square where Player I's strategy set is $X = [0, 1]$ and Player II's strategy set is $Y = [0, 1]$, check whether or not the game associated with each of the following payoff functions has a value, and if so, find the value and optimal strategies for the two players:

(a) $u(x, y) = 1 + 4x + y - 5xy$.

(b) $u(x, y) = 4 + 2y - 4xy$.

4.42 Consider a two-player non-zero-sum game on the unit square in which Player I's strategy set is $X = [0, 1]$, and Player II's strategy set is $Y = [0, 1]$, which has a unique equilibrium (x^*, y^*), where $x^*, y^* \in (0, 1)$. Prove that the equilibrium payoff to each player equals his maxmin value.

4.43 Fifty people are playing the following game. Each player writes down, on a separate slip of paper, one integer in the set $\{0, 1, \ldots, 100\}$, alongside his name. The game-master then reads the numbers on each slip of paper, and calculates the average x of all the numbers written by the players. The winner of the game is the player (or players) who wrote down the number that is closest to $\frac{2}{3}x$. The winners equally divide the prize of \$1,000 between them.

Describe this as a strategic-form game, and find all the Nash equilibria of the game. What would be your strategy in this game? Why?

4.44 Peter, Andrew, and James are playing the following game in which the winner is awarded M dollars. Each of the three players receives a coupon and is to decide whether or not to bet on it. If a player chooses to bet, he or she loses the coupon with probability $\frac{1}{2}$ and wins an additional coupon with probability $\frac{1}{2}$ (thus resulting in two coupons in total). The success of each player in the bet is independent of the results of the bets of the other players. The winner of the prize is the player with the greatest number of coupons. If there is more than one such player, the winner is selected from among them in a lottery where each has an equal chance of winning. The goal of each player is to maximize the probability of winning the award.

(a) Describe this game as a game in strategic form and find all its Nash equilibria.

(b) Now assume that the wins and losses of the players are perfectly correlated: a single coin flip determines whether all the players who decided to bid either all win an additional coupon or all lose their coupons. Describe this new situation as a game in strategic form and find all its Nash equilibria.

4.45 Partnership Game   Lee (Player 1) and Julie (Player 2) are business partners. Each of the partners has to determine the amount of effort he or she will put into the business, which is denoted by e_i, $i = 1, 2$, and may be any nonnegative real number. The cost of effort e_i for Player i is ce_i, where $c > 0$ is equal for both players. The success of the business depends on the amount of effort put in by the players; the business's profit is denoted by $r(e_1, e_2) = e_1^{\alpha_1} e_2^{\alpha_2}$, where $\alpha_1, \alpha_2 \in (0, 1)$ are fixed constants known by Lee and Julie, and the profit is shared equally between the two partners. Each player's utility is given by the difference between the share of the profit received by that player and the cost of the effort he or she put into the business. Answer the following questions:

(a) Describe this situation as a strategic-form game. Note that the set of strategies of each player is the continuum.

(b) Find all the Nash equilibria of the game.

4.46 Braess Paradox   There are two main roads connecting San Francisco and San Jose, a northern road via Mountain View and a southern road via Cupertino. Travel time on each of the roads depends on the number x of cars using the road per minute, as indicated in the following diagram.

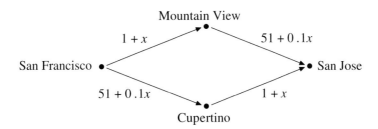

For example, the travel time between San Francisco and Mountain View is $1 + x$, where x is the number of cars per minute using the road connecting these cities, and the travel time between Mountain View and San Jose is $51 + 0.1x$, where x is the number of cars per minute using the road connecting those two cities. Each driver chooses which road to take in going from San Francisco to San Jose, with the goal of reducing to a minimum the amount of travel time. Early in the morning, 60 cars per minute get on the road from San Francisco to San Jose (where we assume the travellers leave early enough in the morning so that they are the only ones on the road at that hour).

(a) Describe this situation as a strategic-form game, in which each driver chooses the route he will take.
(b) What are all the Nash equilibria of this game? At these equilibria, how much time does the trip take at an early morning hour?
(c) The California Department of Transportation constructs a new road between Mountain View and Cupertino, with travel time between these cities $10 + 0.1x$ (see the diagram below). This road is one-way, enabling travel solely from Mountain View to Cupertino.

   Find a Nash equilibrium in the new game. Under this equilibrium, how much time does it take to get to San Jose from San Francisco at an early morning hour?
(d) Does the construction of the additional road improve travel time?

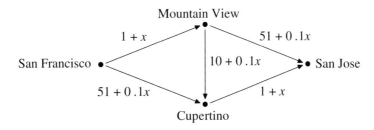

This phenomenon is "paradoxical" because, as you discovered in the answers to (b) and (c), the construction of a new road increases the travel time for all travellers. This is because when the new road is opened, travel along the San Francisco–Mountain View–Cupertino–San Jose route takes less time than along the San Francisco–Mountain View–San Jose route and the San Francisco–Cupertino–San Jose route, causing drivers to take the new route. But that causes the total number of cars along the two routes San Francisco–Mountain View–San Jose and San Francisco–Cupertino–San Jose to increase: travel time along each stretch of road increases.

Such a phenomenon was in fact noted in New York (where the closure of a road for construction work had the effect of decreasing travel time) and in Stuttgart (where the opening of a new road increased travel time).

4.47 The Davis Removal Company and its main rival, Roland Ltd, have fleets of ten trucks each, which leave the companies' headquarters for Chicago each morning at 5 am for their daily assignments. At that early hour, these trucks are the only vehicles on the roads. Travel time along the road between the Davis Removal Company and Chicago is $20 + 2\sqrt{x}$, where x is the number of cars on the road, and it is similarly $20 + 2\sqrt{x}$ on the road connecting the headquarters of Roland Ltd with Chicago, where x is the number of cars on the road.

The Illinois Department of Transportation paves a new two-way road between the companies' headquarters, where travel time on this new road is 0.2, independent of the number of cars on the road. This situation is described in the following diagram:

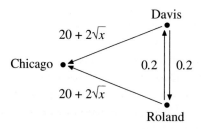

Answer the following questions:

(a) Before the new road is constructed, what is the travel time of each truck between its headquarters and Chicago?

(b) Describe the situation after the construction of the new road as a two-player strategic-form game, in which the players are the managers of the removal companies and each player must determine the number of trucks to send on the road connecting his company with Chicago (with the rest traveling on the newly opened road and the road connecting the other company's headquarters and Chicago), with the goal of keeping to a minimum the total travel time to Chicago of all the trucks in its fleet. Note that if Davis, for example, instructs all its drivers to go on the road between company headquarters and Chicago, and Roland sends seven of its trucks directly to Chicago and three first to the

Davis headquarters and then to Chicago, the total time racked up by the fleet of Roland Ltd is

$$7 \times (20 + 2\sqrt{7}) + 3 \times (0.2 + 20 + 2\sqrt{13}). \tag{4.98}$$

(c) Is the strategy vector in which both Davis and Roland send their entire fleets directly to Chicago, ignoring the new road, a Nash equilibrium?

(d) Show that the strategy vector in which both Davis and Roland send six drivers directly to Chicago and four via the new road is an equilibrium. What is the total travel time of the trucks of the two companies in this equilibrium? Did the construction of a new road decrease or increase total travel time?

(e) Construct the payoff matrix of this game, with the aid of a spreadsheet program. Are there any additional equilibria in this game?

4.48 Two roads connect Liverpool to Manchester, a northern road and a southern road. The travel time on the northern road is one hour, regardless of the number of vehicles using it, while the travel time on the southern road depends on the number of vehicles using it, and is given by the function $c(x) = x$, where x is the number of vehicles (in thousands) using the road. Answer the following questions, assuming the number of cars that go from Liverpool to Manchester is $a \geq 0$.

(a) Describe this situation as a strategic-form game, in which each driver chooses the road he will take.

(b) Calculate the Nash equilibrium of this game and show that it is unique. At this equilibrium, what is the average time of the trip from Liverpool to Manchester?

(c) Suppose that the police can order each driver to use a specific road. If the goal is to minimize the average travel time from Liverpool to Manchester, what is the number of cars that will use the northern road, and what is the number of cars that will use the southern road? What is the average time of the trip from Liverpool to Manchester in this case?

(d) The ratio between the most efficient average time that was calculated in part (c) and the average time in equilibrium calculated in part (b) is called the *price of anarchy*[12]. Calculate the price of anarchy in this game as a function of a.

4.49 Location games Two competing coffee house chains, Pete's Coffee and Caribou Coffee, are seeking locations for new branch stores in Cambridge. The town is comprised of only one street, along which all the residents live. Each of the two chains therefore needs to choose a single point within the interval $[0, 1]$, which represents the exact location of the branch store along the road. It is assumed that each resident will go to the coffee house that is nearest to his place of residence. If the two chains choose the exact same location, they will each attract an equal number of customers. Each chain, of course, seeks to maximize its number of customers.

----

12 In case of multiplicity of equilibria, the price of anarchy is the ratio between the most efficient average time and the worst average time in equilibrium.

To simplify the analysis required here, suppose that each point along the interval $[0, 1]$ represents a town resident, and that the fraction of residents who frequent each coffee house is the fraction of points closer to one store than to the other.

(a) Describe this situation as a two-player strategic-form game.
(b) Prove that the only equilibrium in this game is that given by both chains selecting the location $x = \frac{1}{2}$.
(c) Prove that if three chains were to compete for a location in Cambridge, the resulting game would have no equilibrium. (Under this scenario, if two or three of the chains choose the same location, they will split the points closest to them equally between them.)

4.50 For each of the following two games, determine whether or not it can represent a strategic-form game corresponding to an extensive-form game with perfect information. If so, describe a corresponding extensive-form game; if not, justify your answer.

Player II

		a	b
	A	1, 1	5, 3
Player I	B	3, 0	5, 3
	C	1, 1	0, 4
	D	3, 0	5, 3

Game A

Player II

		a	b
	A	3, 0	0, 4
Player I	B	3, 0	0, 4
	C	3, 0	1, 1
	D	3, 0	5, 3

Game B

4.51 Let Γ be a game in extensive form. The *agent-form game* derived from Γ is a strategic-form game where each player i in Γ is split into several players: for each information set $U_i \in \mathcal{U}_i$ of player i we define a player (i, U_i) in the agent-form game. Thus, if each player i has k_i information sets in Γ, then there are $\sum_{i \in N} k_i$ players in the agent-form game. The set of strategies of player (i, U_i) is $A(U_i)$. There is a bijection between the set of strategy vectors in the game Γ and the set of strategy vectors in the corresponding agent-form game: the strategy vector $\sigma = (\sigma_i)_{i \in N}$ in Γ corresponds to the strategy vector $(\sigma_i(U_i))_{\{i \in N, U_i \in \mathcal{U}_i\}}$ in the agent-form game. The payoff function of player (i, U_i) in the agent-form game is the payoff function of player i in the game Γ.

Prove that if $\sigma = (\sigma_i)_{i \in N}$ is a Nash equilibrium in the game Γ, then the strategy vector $(\sigma_i(U_i))_{\{i \in N, U_i \in \mathcal{U}_i\}}$ is a Nash equilibrium in the agent-form game derived from Γ.

5 Mixed strategies

Chapter summary

Given a game in strategic form we extend the strategy set of a player to the set of all probability distributions over his strategies. The elements of the new set are called *mixed strategies*, while the elements of the original strategy set are called *pure strategies*. Thus, a mixed strategy is a probability distribution over pure strategies. For a strategic-form game with finitely many pure strategies for each player we define the *mixed extension* of the game, which is a game in strategic form in which the set of strategies of each player is his set of mixed strategies, and his payoff function is the multilinear extension of his payoff function in the original game.

The main result of the chapter is the Nash Theorem, which is one of the milestones of game theory. It states that the mixed extension always has a Nash equilibrium; that is, a Nash equilibrium in mixed strategies exists in every strategic-form game in which all players have finitely many pure strategies. We prove the theorem and provide ways to compute equilibria in special classes of games, although the problem of computing Nash equilibrium in general games is computationally hard.

We generalize the Nash Theorem to mixed extensions in which the set of strategies of each player is not the whole set of mixed strategies, but rather a polytope subset of this set.

We investigate the relation between utility theory discussed in Chapter 2 and mixed strategies, and define the *maxmin value* and the *minmax value* of a player (in mixed strategies), which measure respectively the amount that the player can guarantee to himself, and the lowest possible payoff that the other players can force on the player.

The concept of *evolutionary stable strategy*, which is the Nash equilibrium adapted to Darwin's Theory of Evolution, is presented in Section 5.9.

There are many examples of interactive situations (games) in which it is to a decision maker's advantage to be "unpredictable":

- If a baseball pitcher throws a waist-high fastball on every pitch, the other team's batters will have an easy time hitting the ball.
- If a tennis player always serves the ball to the same side of the court, his opponent will have an advantage in returning the serve.
- If a candidate for political office predictably issues announcements on particular dates, his opponents can adjust their campaign messages ahead of time to pre-empt him and gain valuable points at the polls.

• If a traffic police car is placed at the same junction at the same time every day, its effectiveness is reduced.

It is easy to add many more such examples, in a wide range of situations. How can we integrate this very natural consideration into our mathematical model?

Example 5.1　Consider the two-player zero-sum game depicted in Figure 5.1.

Player II

		L	R	$\min_{s_{II}} u(s_I, s_{II})$
Player I	T	4	1	1
	B	2	3	2
$\max_{s_I} u(s_I, s_{II})$		4	3	(2, 3)

Figure 5.1 A two-player zero-sum game; the security values of the players are circled

Player I's security level is 2; if he plays B he guarantees himself a payoff of at least 2. Player II's security level is 3; if he plays R he guarantees himself a payoff of at most 3.

This is written as

$$\underline{v} = \max_{s_I \in \{T,B\}} \min_{s_{II} \in \{L,R\}} u(s_I, s_{II}) = 2, \tag{5.1}$$

$$\bar{v} = \min_{s_{II} \in \{L,R\}} \max_{s_I \in \{T,B\}} u(s_I, s_{II}) = 3. \tag{5.2}$$

Since

$$\bar{v} = 3 > 2 = \underline{v}, \tag{5.3}$$

the game has no value.

Can one of the players, say Player I, guarantee a "better outcome" by playing "unpredictably"? Suppose that Player I tosses a coin with parameter $\frac{1}{4}$, that is, a coin that comes up heads with probability $\frac{1}{4}$ and tails with probability $\frac{3}{4}$. Suppose furthermore that Player I plays T if the result of the coin toss is heads and B if the result of the coin toss is tails. Such a strategy is called a mixed strategy.

What would that lead to? First of all, the payoffs would no longer be definite, but instead would be probabilistic payoffs. If Player II plays L the result is a lottery $[\frac{1}{4}(4), \frac{3}{4}(2)]$; that is, with probability $\frac{1}{4}$ Player II pays 4, and with probability $\frac{3}{4}$ pays 2. If these payoffs are the utilities of a player whose preference relation satisfies the von Neumann–Morgenstern axioms (see Chapter 2), then Player I's utility from this lottery is $\frac{1}{4} \times 4 + \frac{3}{4} \times 2 = 2\frac{1}{2}$. If, however, Player II plays R the result is the lottery $[\frac{1}{4}(1), \frac{3}{4}(3)]$. In this case, if the payoffs are utilities, Player I's utility from this lottery is $\frac{1}{4} \times 1 + \frac{3}{4} \times 3 = 2\frac{1}{2}$. ◀

5.1　The mixed extension of a strategic-form game

In the rest of this section, we will assume that the utilities of the players satisfy the von Neumann–Morgenstern axioms; hence their utility functions are linear (in probabilities). In other words, the payoff (= utility) to a player from a lottery is the expected payoff of that lottery. With this definition of what a payoff is, Player I can guarantee that no matter what happens his expected payoff will be at least $2\frac{1}{3}$, in contrast to a security level of 2 if he does not base his strategy on the coin toss.

Definition 5.2 *Let $G = (N, (S_i)_{i \in N}, (u_i)_{i \in N})$ be a strategic-form game in which the set of strategies of each player is finite. A* mixed strategy *of player i is a probability distribution over his set of strategies S_i. Denote by*

$$\Sigma_i := \left\{ \sigma_i : S_i \to [0, 1] : \sum_{s_i \in S_i} \sigma_i(s_i) = 1 \right\} \tag{5.4}$$

the set of mixed strategies of player i.

A mixed strategy of player i is, therefore, a probability distribution over S_i: $\sigma_i = (\sigma_i(s_i))_{s_i \in S_i}$. The number $\sigma_i(s_i)$ is the probability of playing the strategy s_i. To distinguish between the mixed strategies Σ_i and the strategies S_i, the latter are called *pure strategies*. Because all the results proved in previous chapters involved only pure strategies, the claims in them should be qualified accordingly. For example, Kuhn's Theorem (Theorem 4.49 on page 118) should be read as saying: In every finite game with perfect information, there is at least one equilibrium point in pure strategies.

We usually denote a mixed strategy using the notations for lotteries (see Chapter 2). For example, if Player I's set of pure strategies is $S_I = \{A, B, C\}$, we denote the mixed strategy σ_I under which he chooses each pure strategy with probability $\frac{1}{3}$ by $\sigma_I = [\frac{1}{3}(A), \frac{1}{3}(B), \frac{1}{3}(C)]$.

If $S_I = \{H, T\}$, Player I's set of mixed strategies is

$$\Sigma_I = \{[p_1(H), p_2(T)] : p_1 \geq 0, \quad p_2 \geq 0, \quad p_1 + p_2 = 1\}. \tag{5.5}$$

In this case, the set Σ_I is equivalent to the interval in $\mathbb{R}^2$ connecting $(1, 0)$ to $(0, 1)$. We can identify Σ_I with the interval $[0, 1]$ by identifying every real number $x \in [0, 1]$ with the probability distribution over $\{H, T\}$ that satisfies $p(H) = x$ and $p(T) = 1 - x$. If $S_{II} = \{L, M, R\}$, Player II's set of mixed strategies is

$$\Sigma_{II} = \{[p_1(L), p_2(M), p_2(R)] : p_1 \geq 0, \quad p_2 \geq 0, \quad p_3 \geq 0, \quad p_1 + p_2 + p_3 = 1\}. \tag{5.6}$$

In this case, the set Σ_{II} is equivalent to the triangle in $\mathbb{R}^3$ whose vertices are $(1, 0, 0)$, $(0, 1, 0)$, and $(0, 0, 1)$.

For any finite set A, denote by $\Delta(A)$ the set of all probability distributions over A. That is,

$$\Delta(A) := \left\{ p : A \to [0, 1] : \sum_{a \in A} p(a) = 1 \right\}. \tag{5.7}$$

The set $\Delta(A)$ is termed a *simplex* in $\mathbb{R}^{|A|}$. The dimension of the simplex $\Delta(A)$ is $|A| - 1$ (this follows from the constraint that $\sum_{a \in A} p(a) = 1$). We denote the number of pure strategies of player i by m_i, and we assume that his pure strategies have a particular ordering, with the denotation $S_i = \{s_i^1, s_i^2, \ldots, s_i^{m_i}\}$. It follows that the set of mixed strategies $\Sigma_i = \Delta(S_i)$ is a subset of $\mathbb{R}^{m_i}$ of dimension $m_i - 1$.

We identify a mixed strategy s_i with the pure strategy $\sigma_i = [1(s_i)]$, in which the pure strategy s_i is chosen with probability 1. This implies that every pure strategy can also be considered a mixed strategy.

We now define the mixed extension of a game.

Definition 5.3 *Let $G = (N, (S_i)_{i \in N}, (u_i)_{i \in N})$ be a strategic-form game in which for every player $i \in N$, the set of pure strategies S_i is nonempty and finite. Denote by $S := S_1 \times S_2 \times \cdots \times S_n$ the set of pure strategy vectors. The* mixed extension *of G is the game*

$$\Gamma = (N, (\Sigma_i)_{i \in N}, (U_i)_{i \in N}), \tag{5.8}$$

in which, for each $i \in N$, player i's set of strategies is $\Sigma_i = \Delta(S_i)$, and his payoff function is the function $U_i : \Sigma \to \mathbb{R}$, which associates each strategy vector $\sigma = (\sigma_1, \ldots, \sigma_n) \in \Sigma = \Sigma_1 \times \cdots \times \Sigma_n$ with the payoff

$$U_i(\sigma) = \mathbf{E}_\sigma[u_i(\sigma)] = \sum_{(s_1, \ldots, s_n) \in S} u_i(s_1, \ldots, s_n)\sigma_1(s_1)\sigma_2(s_2) \cdots \sigma_n(s_n). \tag{5.9}$$

Remark 5.4 *Mixed strategies were defined above only for the case in which the sets of pure strategies are finite. It follows that the mixed extension of a game is only defined when the set of pure strategies of each player is finite. However, the concept of mixed strategy, and hence the mixed extension of a game, can be defined when the set of pure strategies of a player is a countable set (see Example 5.12 and Exercise 5.55). In that case the set $\Sigma_i = \Delta(S_i)$ is an infinite-dimensional set. It is possible to extend the definition of mixed strategy further to the case in which the set of strategies is any set in a measurable space, but that requires making use of concepts from measure theory that go beyond the background in mathematics assumed for this book.* ◆

Note that the fact that the mixed strategies of the players are statistically independent of each other plays a role in Equation (5.9), because the probability of drawing a particular vector of pure strategies $(s_1, s_2, \ldots, s_n)$ is the product $\sigma_1(s_1)\sigma_2(s_2) \cdots \sigma_n(s_n)$. In other words, each player i conducts the lottery σ_i that chooses s_i independently of the lotteries conducted by the other players.

The mixed extension Γ of a strategic-form game G is itself a strategic-form game, in which the set of strategies of each player is of the cardinality of the continuum. It follows that all the concepts we defined in Chapter 4, such as dominant strategy, security level, and equilibrium, are also defined for Γ, and all the results we proved in Chapter 4 apply to mixed extensions of games.

Definition 5.5 *Let G be a game in strategic form, and Γ be its mixed extensions. Every equilibrium of Γ is called an* equilibrium in mixed strategies *of G. If G is a two-player zero-sum game, and if Γ has value v, then v is called the* value *of G in mixed strategies.*

Example 5.1 (*Continued*) Consider the two-player zero-sum game in Figure 5.2.

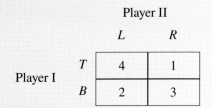

Figure 5.2 The game in strategic form

When Player I's strategy set contains two actions, T and B, we identify the mixed strategy $[x(T), (1-x)(B)]$ with the probability x of selecting the pure strategy T. Similarly, when Player II's strategy set contains two actions, L and R, we identify the mixed strategy $[y(L), (1-y)(R)]$ with the probability y of selecting the pure strategy L. For each pair of mixed strategies $x, y \in [0, 1]$ (with the identifications $x \approx [x(T), (1-x)(B)]$ and $y \approx [y(L), (1-y)(R)]$) the payoff is

$$U(x,y) = 4xy + 1x(1-y) + 2(1-x)y + 3(1-x)(1-y) \tag{5.10}$$

$$= 3 - 2x - y + 4xy. \tag{5.11}$$

This mixed extension is identical to the game over the unit square presented in Section 4.14.1. As we showed there, the game has the value $2\frac{1}{2}$, and its optimal strategies are $x = \frac{1}{4}$ and $y = \frac{1}{2}$. It follows that the value in mixed strategies of the game in Figure 5.2 is $2\frac{1}{2}$, and the optimal strategies of the players are $x^* = [\frac{1}{4}(T), \frac{3}{4}(B)]$ and $y^* = [\frac{1}{2}(L), \frac{1}{2}(R)]$. We conclude that this game has no value in pure strategies, but it does have a value in mixed strategies. ◀

The payoff function defined in Equation (5.10) is a linear function over x for each fixed y and, similarly, a linear function over y for each fixed x. Such a function is called a *bilinear function*. The analysis we conducted in Example 5.1 can be generalized to all two-player games where each player has two pure strategies. The extension to mixed strategies of such a game is a game on the unit square with bilinear payoff functions. In the converse direction, every zero-sum two-player game over the unit square with bilinear payoff functions is the extension to mixed strategies of a two-player zero-sum game in which each player has two pure strategies (Exercise 5.6).

The next theorem states that this property can be generalized to any number of players and any number of actions, as long as we properly generalize the concept of bilinearity to multilinearity.

Theorem 5.6 *Let $G = (N, (S_i)_{i \in N}, (u_i)_{i \in N})$ be a game in strategic form in which the set of strategies S_i of every player is finite, and let $\Gamma = (N, (\Sigma_i)_{i \in N}, (U_i)_{i \in N})$ be its mixed extension. Then for each player $i \in N$, the function U_i is a multilinear function in the n variables $(\sigma_i)_{i \in N}$, i.e., for every player i, for every $\sigma_i, \sigma_i' \in \Sigma_i$, and for every $\lambda \in [0, 1]$,*

$$U_i(\lambda \sigma_i + (1-\lambda)\sigma_i', \sigma_{-i}) = \lambda U_i(\sigma_i, \sigma_{-i}) + (1-\lambda)U_i(\sigma_i', \sigma_{-i}), \quad \forall \sigma_{-i} \in \Sigma_{-i}.$$

Proof: Recall that

$$U_i(\sigma) = \sum_{(s_1,\ldots,s_n) \in S} u_i(s_1,\ldots,s_n)\sigma_1(s_1)\sigma_2(s_2)\cdots\sigma_n(s_n). \tag{5.12}$$

The function U_i is a function of $\sum_{i=1}^{n} m_i$ variables:

$$\sigma_1\left(s_1^1\right), \sigma_1\left(s_1^2\right), \ldots, \sigma_1\left(s_1^{m_1}\right), \sigma_2\left(s_2^1\right), \ldots, \sigma_2\left(s_2^{m_2}\right), \ldots, \sigma_n(s_n^1), \ldots, \sigma_n(s_n^{m_n}). \tag{5.13}$$

For each $i \in N$, for all j, $1 \leq j \leq m_i$ and for each $s = (s_1, \ldots, s_n) \in S$, the function

$$\sigma_i\left(s_i^j\right) \mapsto u_i(s_1, \ldots, s_n)\sigma_1(s_1)\sigma_2(s_2) \cdots \sigma_n(s_n) \tag{5.14}$$

is a constant function if $s_i \neq s_i^j$ and a linear function of $\sigma_i(s_i^j)$ with slope

$$u_i(s_1, \ldots, s_n)\sigma_1(s_1)\sigma_2(s_2) \cdots \sigma_{i-1}(s_{i-1})\sigma_{i+1}(s_{i+1}) \cdots \sigma_n(s_n). \tag{5.15}$$

if $s_i = s_i^j$. Thus, the function U_i, as the sum of linear functions in $\sigma_i(s_i^j)$, is also linear in $\sigma_i(s_i^j)$. It follows that for every $i \in N$, the function $U_i(\cdot, \sigma_{-i})$ is linear in each of the coordinates $\sigma_i(s_i^j)$ of σ_i, for all $\sigma_{-i} \in \Sigma_{-i}$:

$$U_i(\lambda\sigma_i + (1-\lambda)\sigma_i', \sigma_{-i}) = \lambda U_i(\sigma_i, \sigma_{-i}) + (1-\lambda)U_i(\sigma_i', \sigma_{-i}), \tag{5.16}$$

for every $\lambda \in [0, 1]$, and every $\sigma_i, \sigma_i' \in \Sigma_i$.　　　　□

Since a multilinear function over Σ is a continuous function (see Exercise 5.4), we have the following corollary of Theorem 5.6.

Corollary 5.7 *The payoff function U_i of player i is a continuous function in the extension to mixed strategies of every finite strategic-form game $G = (N, (S_i)_{i \in N}, (u_i)_{i \in N})$.*

We can also derive a second corollary from Theorem 5.6, which can be used to determine whether a particular mixed-strategy vector is an equilibrium.

Corollary 5.8 *Let $G = (N, (S_i)_{i \in N}, (u_i)_{i \in N})$ be a strategic-form game, and let Γ be its mixed extension. A mixed-strategy vector σ^* is an equilibrium in mixed strategies of Γ if and only if for every player $i \in N$ and every pure strategy $s^i \in S^i$,*

$$U_i(\sigma^*) \geq U_i(s_i, \sigma_{-i}^*). \tag{5.17}$$

Proof: If σ^* is an equilibrium in mixed strategies of Γ, then $U_i(\sigma^*) \geq U_i(\sigma_i, \sigma_{-i}^*)$ for every player $i \in N$ and every mixed strategy $\sigma_i \in \Sigma_i$. Since every pure strategy is in particular a mixed strategy, $U_i(\sigma^*) \geq U_i(s_i, \sigma_{-i}^*)$ for every player $i \in N$ and every pure strategy $s^i \in S^i$, and Equation (5.17) holds.

To show the converse implication, suppose that the mixed-strategy vector σ^* satisfies Equation (5.17) for every player $i \in N$ and every pure strategy $s^i \in S^i$. Then for each mixed strategy σ_i of player i,

$$U_i(\sigma_i, \sigma_{-i}^*) = \sum_{s_i \in S_i} \sigma_i(s_i)U_i(s_i, \sigma_{-i}^*) \tag{5.18}$$

$$\leq \sum_{s_i \in S_i} \sigma_i(s_i)U_i(\sigma^*) \tag{5.19}$$

$$= U_i(\sigma^*)\sum_{s_i \in S_i} \sigma_i(s_i) = U_i(\sigma^*), \tag{5.20}$$

where Equation (5.18) follows from the fact that U_i is a multilinear function, and Equation (5.19) follows from Equation (5.17). In particular, σ^* is an equilibrium in mixed strategies of Γ. □

Example 5.9 A mixed extension of a two-player game that is not zero-sum Consider the two-player non-zero-sum game given by the payoff matrix shown in Figure 5.3.

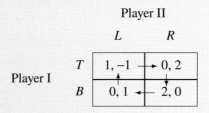

Figure 5.3 A two-player, non-zero-sum game without an equilibrium

As we now show, this game has no equilibrium in pure strategies (you can follow the arrows in Figure 5.3 to see why this is so).

- (T, L) is not an equilibrium, since Player II can gain by deviating to R.
- (T, R) is not an equilibrium, since Player I can gain by deviating to B.
- (B, L) is not an equilibrium, since Player I can gain by deviating to T.
- (B, R) is not an equilibrium, since Player II can gain by deviating to L.

Does this game have an equilibrium in mixed strategies? To answer this question, we first write out the mixed extension of the game:

- The set of players is the same as the set of players in the original game: $N = \{\mathrm{I}, \mathrm{II}\}$.
- Player I's set of strategies is $\Sigma_{\mathrm{I}} = \{[x(T), (1-x)(B)] : x \in [0, 1]\}$, which can be identified with the interval $[0, 1]$.
- Player II's set of strategies is $\Sigma_{\mathrm{II}} = \{[y(L), (1-y)(R)] : y \in [0, 1]\}$, which can be identified with the interval $[0, 1]$.
- Player I's payoff function is

$$U_{\mathrm{I}}(x, y) = xy + 2(1-x)(1-y) = 3xy - 2x - 2y + 2. \tag{5.21}$$

- Player II's payoff function is

$$U_{\mathrm{II}}(x, y) = -xy + 2x(1-y) + y(1-x) = -4xy + 2x + y. \tag{5.22}$$

This is the game on the unit square that we studied in Section 4.14.2 (page 123). We found a unique equilibrium for this game: $x^* = \frac{1}{4}$ and $y^* = \frac{2}{3}$. The unique equilibrium in mixed strategies of the given game is therefore

$$\left(\left[\tfrac{1}{4}(T), \tfrac{3}{4}(B) \right], \left[\tfrac{2}{3}(L), \tfrac{1}{3}(R) \right] \right). \tag{5.23}$$

◀

We have seen in this section two examples of two-player games, one a zero-sum game and the other a non-zero-sum game. Neither of them has an equilibrium in pure strategies, but they both have equilibria in mixed strategies. Do all games have equilibria in mixed strategies? John Nash, who defined the concept of equilibrium, answered this question affirmatively.

Theorem 5.10 (Nash [1950b, 1951]) *Every game in strategic form G, with a finite number of players and in which every player has a finite number of pure strategies, has an equilibrium in mixed strategies.*

The proof of Nash's Theorem will be presented later in this chapter. As a corollary, along with Theorem 4.45 on page 115, we have an analogous theorem for two-player zero-sum games. This special case was proven by von Neumann 22 years before Nash proved his theorem on the existence of the equilibrium that bears his name.

Theorem 5.11 (von Neumann's Minmax Theorem [1928]) *Every two-player zero-sum game in which every player has a finite number of pure strategies has a value in mixed strategies.*

In other words, in every two-player zero-sum game the minmax value in mixed strategies is equal to the maxmin value in mixed strategies. Nash regarded his result as a generalization of the Minmax Theorem to n players. This is, in fact, a generalization of the Minmax Theorem here to two-player games that may not be zero-sum, and to games with any finite number of players. On the other hand, as we noted on page 117, this is a generalization of only one aspect of the notion of the "value" of a game, namely, the aspect of stability. The other aspect of the value of a game – the security level – which characterizes the value in two-player zero-sum games, is not generalized by the Nash equilibrium.

Recall that the value in mixed strategies of a two-player zero-sum game, if it exists, is given by

$$v := \max_{\sigma_I \in \Sigma_I} \min_{\sigma_{II} \in \Sigma_{II}} U(\sigma_I, \sigma_{II}) = \min_{\sigma_{II} \in \Sigma_{II}} \max_{\sigma_I \in \Sigma_I} U(\sigma_I, \sigma_{II}). \qquad (5.24)$$

Since the payoff function is multilinear, for every strategy σ_I of Player I, the function $\sigma_{II} \mapsto U(\sigma_I, \sigma_{II})$ is linear.

A point x in a set $X \subseteq \mathbb{R}^n$ is called an *extreme point* if it is not the linear combination of two other points in the set (see Definition 24.2 on page 963). Every linear function defined over a compact set attains its maximum and minimum at extreme points. The set of extreme points of a collection of mixed strategies is the set of pure strategies (Exercise 5.5). It follows that for every strategy σ_I of Player I, it suffices to calculate the internal minimum in the middle term in Equation (5.24) over pure strategies. Similarly, for every strategy σ_{II} of Player II, it suffices to compute the internal maximum in the right-hand term in Equation (5.24) over pure strategies. That is, if v is the value in mixed strategies of the game, then

$$v = \max_{\sigma_I \in \Sigma_I} \min_{s_{II} \in S_{II}} U(\sigma_I, s_{II}) = \min_{\sigma_{II} \in \Sigma_{II}} \max_{s_I \in S_I} U(s_I, \sigma_{II}). \qquad (5.25)$$

As the next example shows, when the number of pure strategies is infinite, Nash's Theorem and the Minmax Theorem do not hold.

Example 5.12 **Choosing the largest number** Consider the following two-player zero-sum game. Two players simultaneously and independently choose a positive integer. The player who chooses the smaller number pays a dollar to the player who chooses the largest number. If the two players choose the same integer, no exchange of money occurs. We will model this as a game in strategic form, and then show that it has no value in mixed strategies.

Both players have the same set of pure strategies:

$$S_I = S_{II} = \mathbb{N} = \{1, 2, 3, \ldots\}. \tag{5.26}$$

This set is not finite; it is a countably infinite set. The payoff function is

$$u(s_I, s_{II}) = \begin{cases} 1 & \text{when } s_I > s_{II}, \\ 0 & \text{when } s_I = s_{II}, \\ -1 & \text{when } s_I < s_{II}. \end{cases} \tag{5.27}$$

A mixed strategy in this game is a probability distribution over the set of nonnegative integers:

$$\Sigma_I = \Sigma_{II} = \left\{ (x_1, x_2, \ldots) : \sum_{k=1}^{\infty} x_k = 1, \quad x_k \geq 0 \;\; \forall k \in \mathbb{N} \right\}. \tag{5.28}$$

We will show that

$$\sup_{\sigma_I \in \Sigma_I} \inf_{\sigma_{II} \in \Sigma_{II}} U(\sigma_I, \sigma_{II}) = -1 \tag{5.29}$$

and

$$\inf_{\sigma_{II} \in \Sigma_{II}} \sup_{\sigma_I \in \Sigma_I} U(\sigma_I, \sigma_{II}) = 1. \tag{5.30}$$

It will then follow from Equations (5.29) and (5.30) that the game has no value in mixed strategies. Let σ_I be the strategy of Player I, and let $\varepsilon \in (0, 1)$. Since σ_I is a distribution over $\mathbb{N}$, there exists a sufficiently large $k \in \mathbb{N}$ satisfying

$$\sigma_I(\{1, 2, \ldots, k\}) > 1 - \varepsilon. \tag{5.31}$$

In words, the probability that Player I will choose a number that is less than or equal to k is greater than $1 - \varepsilon$. But then, if Player II chooses the pure strategy $k + 1$ we will have

$$U(\sigma_I, k + 1) < (1 - \varepsilon) \times (-1) + \varepsilon \times 1 = -1 + 2\varepsilon, \tag{5.32}$$

because with probability greater than $1 - \varepsilon$, Player I loses and the payoff is -1, and with probability less than ε, he wins and the payoff is 1. Since this is true for any $\varepsilon \in (0, 1)$, Equation (5.29) holds. Equation (5.30) is proved in a similar manner. ◀

We defined extensive-form games with the use of finite games; in particular, in every extensive-form game every player has a finite number of pure strategies. We therefore have the following corollary of Theorem 5.10:

Theorem 5.13 *Every extensive-form game has an equilibrium in mixed strategies.*

5.2 Computing equilibria in mixed strategies

Before we proceed to the proof of Nash's Theorem, we will consider the subject of computing equilibria in mixed strategies. When the number of players is large, and similarly when the number of strategies is large, finding an equilibrium, to say nothing of finding all the equilibria, is a very difficult problem, both theoretically and computationally. We will present only a few examples of computing equilibria in simple games.

5.2.1 The direct approach

The direct approach to finding equilibria is to write down the mixed extension of the strategic-form game and then to compute the equilibria in the mixed extension (assuming we can do that). In the case of a two-player game where each player has two pure strategies, the mixed extension is a game over the unit square with bilinear payoff functions, which can be solved as we did in Section 4.14 (page 121). Although this approach works well in two-player games where each player has two pure strategies, when there are more strategies, or more players, it becomes quite complicated.

We present here a few examples of this sort of computation. We start with two-player zero-sum games, where finding equilibria is equivalent to finding the value of the game, and equilibrium strategies are optimal strategies. Using Equation (5.25) we can find the value of the game by computing $\max_{\sigma_I \in \Sigma_I} \min_{s_{II} \in S_{II}} U(\sigma_I, s_{II})$ or $\min_{\sigma_{II} \in \Sigma_{II}} \max_{s_I \in S_I} U(s_I, \sigma_{II})$, which also enables us to find the optimal strategies of the players: every strategy σ_I at which the maximum in the expression $\max_{\sigma_I \in \Sigma_I} \min_{s_{II} \in S_{II}} U(\sigma_I, s_{II})$ is obtained is an optimal strategy of Player I, and every strategy σ_{II} at which the minimum in the expression $\min_{\sigma_{II} \in \Sigma_{II}} \max_{s_I \in S_I} U(s_I, \sigma_{II})$ is obtained is an optimal strategy of Player II.

The first game we consider is a game over the unit square. The computation presented here differs slightly from the computation in Section 4.14 (page 121).

Example 5.14 **A two-player zero-sum game, in which each player has two pure strategies** Consider the two-player zero-sum game in Figure 5.4.

Player II

		L	R
Player I	T	5	0
	B	3	4

Figure 5.4 A two-player zero-sum game

We begin by computing $\max_{\sigma_I \in \Sigma_I} \min_{s_{II} \in S_{II}} U(\sigma_I, s_{II})$ in this example. If Player I plays the mixed strategy $[x(T), (1-x)(B)]$, his payoff, as a function of x, depends on the strategy of Player II:

- If Player II plays L: $U(x, L) = 5x + 3(1-x) = 2x + 3$.
- If Player II plays R: $U(x, R) = 4(1-x) = -4x + 4$.

The graph in Figure 5.5 shows these two functions. The thick line plots the function representing the minimum payoff that Player I can receive if he plays x: $\min_{s_{II} \in S_{II}} U(x, s_{II})$. This minimum is called the *lower envelope* of the payoffs of Player I.

The value of the game in mixed strategies equals $\max_{\sigma_I \in \Sigma_I} \min_{s_{II} \in S_{II}} U(\sigma_I, s_{II})$, which is the maximum of the lower envelope. This maximum is attained at the intersection point of the two corresponding lines appearing in Figure 5.5, i.e., at the point at which

$$2x + 3 = -4x + 4, \tag{5.33}$$

whose solution is $x = \frac{1}{6}$. It follows that Player I's optimal strategy is $x^* = [\frac{1}{6}(T), \frac{5}{6}(B)]$. The value of the game is the height of the intersection point, $v = 2 \times \frac{1}{6} + 3 = 3\frac{1}{3}$.

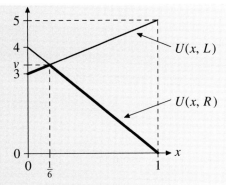

Figure 5.5 The payoff function of Player I and the lower envelope of those payoffs, in the game in Figure 5.4

We conduct a similar calculation for finding Player II's optimal strategy, aimed at finding the strategy σ_{II} at which the minimum of $\min_{\sigma_{II} \in \Sigma_{II}} \max_{s_I \in S_I} U(s_I, \sigma_{II})$ is attained. For each one of the pure strategies T and B of Player I, we compute the payoff as a function of the mixed strategy y of Player II, and look at the upper envelope of these two lines (see Figure 5.6).

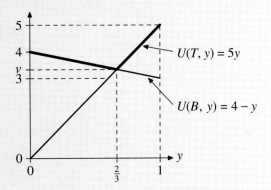

Figure 5.6 The payoff function of Player II and the upper envelope of those payoffs, in the game in Figure 5.4

The minimum of the upper envelope is attained at the point of intersection of these two lines. It is the solution of the equation $5y = 4 - y$, which is $y = \frac{2}{3}$. It follows that the optimal strategy of Player II is $y^* = [\frac{2}{3}(L), \frac{1}{3}(R)]$. The value of the game is the height of the intersection point,

$$U(B, y^*) = 4 - \tfrac{2}{3} = 3\tfrac{1}{3}. \tag{5.34}$$

This procedure can be used for finding the optimal strategies of every game in which the players each have two pure strategies. Note that the value v, as computed in Figure 5.6 (the minmax value), is identical to the value v computed in Figure 5.5 (the maxmin value): both are equal to $3\frac{1}{3}$. This equality follows from Theorem 5.11, which states that the game has a value in mixed strategies. ◀

The graphical procedure presented in Example 5.14 is very convenient. It can be extended to games in which one of the players has two pure strategies and the other player has any finite number of strategies. Suppose that Player I has two pure strategies. We can plot (as a straight line) the payoffs for each pure strategy of Player II as a function of x, the mixed strategy chosen by Player I. We can find the minimum of these lines (the lower envelope), and then find the maximum of the lower envelope. This maximum is the value of the game in mixed strategies.

Example 5.15   Consider the two-player zero-sum game in Figure 5.7.

Player II

		L	M	R
Player I	T	2	5	−1
	B	1	−2	5

Figure 5.7 The two-player zero-sum game in Example 5.15

If Player I plays the mixed strategy $[x(T),(1-x)(B)]$, his payoff, as a function of x, depends on the strategy chosen by Player II:

- If Player II plays L: $U(x,L) = 2x + (1-x) = 1 + x$.
- If Player II plays M: $U(x,M) = 5x - 2(1-x) = 7x - 2$.
- If Player II plays R: $U(x,R) = -x + 5(1-x) = -6x + 5$.

Figure 5.8 shows these three functions. As before, the thick line represents the function $\min_{y \in [0,1]} U(x,y)$. The maximum of the lower envelope is attained at the point x in the intersection of the lines $U(x,L)$ and $U(x,R)$, and it is therefore the solution of the equation $1 + x = -6x + 5$, which is $x = \frac{4}{7}$. It follows that the optimal strategy of Player I is $x^* = [\frac{4}{7}(T), \frac{3}{7}(B)]$. The maximum of the lower envelope is $U(\frac{4}{7},L) = U(\frac{4}{7},R) = 1\frac{4}{7}$; hence the value of the game in mixed strategies is $1\frac{4}{7}$.

How can we find optimal strategies for Player II? For each mixed strategy σ_{II} of Player II, the payoff $U(x,\sigma_{II})$, as a function of x, is a linear function. In fact, it is the average of the functions $U(x,L)$, $U(x,M)$, and $U(x,R)$. If σ_{II}^* is an optimal strategy of Player II, then it guarantees that the payoff will be at most the value of the game, regardless of the mixed strategy x chosen by Player I. In other words, we must have

$$U(x,\sigma_{II}^*) \leq 1\tfrac{4}{7}, \quad \forall x \in [0,1]. \tag{5.35}$$

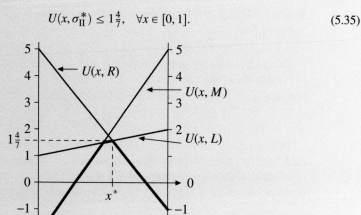

Figure 5.8 The graphs of the payoff functions of Player 1

Consider the graph in Figure 5.8. Since $U(\frac{4}{7}, \sigma_{II}^*)$ is at most $1\frac{4}{7}$, but $U(\frac{4}{7}, L) = U(\frac{4}{7}, R) = 1\frac{4}{7}$ and $U(\frac{4}{7}, M) > 1\frac{4}{7}$, the only mixed strategies for which $U(\frac{4}{7}, \sigma_{II}) \leq 1\frac{4}{7}$ are mixed strategies in which the probability of choosing the pure strategy M is 0, and in those mixed strategies $U(\frac{4}{7}, \sigma_I) = 1\frac{4}{7}$.

Our task, therefore, is to find the appropriate weights for the pure strategies L and R that guarantee that the weighted average of $U(x, L)$ and $U(x, R)$ is the constant function $1\frac{4}{7}$. Since every weighted average of these functions equals $1\frac{4}{7}$ at the point $x = \frac{4}{7}$, it suffices to find weights that guarantee that the weighted average will be $1\frac{4}{7}$ at one additional point x, for example, at $x = 0$ (because a linear function that attains the same value at two distinct points is a constant function). This means we need to consider the equation

$$1\frac{4}{7} = qU(0, L) + (1 - q)U(0, R) = q + 5(1 - q) = 5 - 4q. \tag{5.36}$$

The solution to this equation is $q = \frac{6}{7}$, and therefore the unique optimal strategy of Player II is $\sigma_{II}^* = [\frac{6}{7}(L), \frac{1}{7}(R)]$.   ◄

The procedure used in the last example for finding an optimal strategy for Player II is a general one: after finding the value of the game and the optimal strategy of Player I, we need only look for pure strategies of Player II for which the intersection of the lines corresponding to their payoffs comprises the maximum of the lower envelope. In the above example, there were only two such pure strategies. In other cases, there may be more than two pure strategies comprising the maximum of the lower envelope. In such cases, we need only choose two such strategies: one for which the corresponding line is nonincreasing, and one for which the corresponding line is nondecreasing (see, for example, Figure 5.9(F)). After we have identified two such strategies, it remains to solve one linear equation and find a weighted average of the lines that yields a horizontal line.

Remark 5.16 *The above discussion shows that in every two-player zero-sum game in which Player I has two pure strategies and Player II has m_{II} pure strategies, Player II has an optimal mixed strategy that chooses, with positive probability, at most two pure strategies. This is a special case of a more general result: in every two-player zero-sum game where Player I has m_I pure strategies and Player II has m_{II} pure strategies, if $m_I < m_{II}$ then Player II has an optimal mixed strategy that chooses, with positive probability, at most m_I pure strategies.*   ◆

To compute the value, we found the maximum of the lower envelope. In the example above, there was a unique maximum, which was attained in the line segment $[0, 1]$. In general there may not be a unique maximum, and the maximal value may be attained at one of the extreme points, $x = 0$ or $x = 1$. Figure 5.9 depicts six distinct possible graphs of payoff functions of $(U(x, s_{II}))_{s_{II} \in S_{II}}$.

In cases A and F, the optimal strategy of Player I is attained at an internal point x^*. In case B, the maximum of the lower envelope is attained at $x^* = 1$, and in case C the maximum is attained at $x^* = 0$. In case D, the maximum is attained in the interval $[x_0, 1]$; hence every point in this interval is an optimal strategy of Player I. In case E, the maximum is attained in the interval $[x_0, x_1]$; hence every point in this interval is an optimal strategy of Player I.

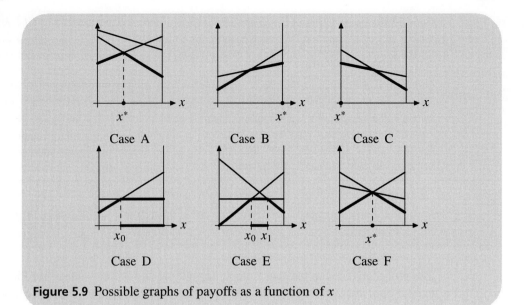

Figure 5.9 Possible graphs of payoffs as a function of x

As for Player II, his unique optimal strategy is at an internal point in case A (and therefore is not a pure strategy). His unique optimal strategy is a pure strategy in cases B, C, D, and E. In case F, Player II has a continuum of optimal strategies (see Exercise 5.11).

5.2.2 Computing equilibrium points

When dealing with a game that is not zero-sum, the Nash equilibrium solution concept is not equivalent to the maxmin value. The computational procedure above will therefore not lead to Nash equilibrium points in that case, and we need other procedures.

The most straightforward and natural way to develop such a procedure is to build on the definition of the Nash equilibrium in terms of the "best reply." We have already seen such a procedure in Section 4.14.2 (page 123), when we looked at non-zero-sum games on the unit square. We present another example here, in which there is more than one equilibrium point.

Example 5.17 **Battle of the Sexes** The Battle of the Sexes game, which we saw in Example 4.21 (page 98), appears in Figure 5.10.

Player II

		F	C
Player I	F	2, 1	0, 0
	C	0, 0	1, 2

Figure 5.10 Battle of the Sexes

---

1 A *set-valued function*, or a *correspondence*, is a multivalued function that associates every point in the domain with a set of values (as opposed to a single value, as is the case with an ordinary function).

Recall that for each mixed strategy $[x(F), (1-x)(C)]$ of Player I (which we will refer to as x for short), we denoted the collection of best replies of Player II by:

$$br_{II}(x) = \text{argmax}_{y\in[0,1]} u_{II}(x, y) \tag{5.37}$$

$$= \{y \in [0, 1] : u_{II}(x, y) \geq u_{II}(x, z) \quad \forall z \in [0, 1]\}. \tag{5.38}$$

Similarly, for each mixed strategy $[y(F), (1-y)(C)]$ of Player II (which we will refer to as y for short), we denoted the collection of best replies of Player I by:

$$br_I(y) = \text{argmax}_{x\in[0,1]} u_I(x, y) \tag{5.39}$$

$$= \{x \in [0, 1] : u_I(x, y) \geq u_I(z, y) \quad \forall z \in [0, 1]\}. \tag{5.40}$$

In the Battle of the Sexes, these correspondences[1] are given by

$$br_{II}(x) = \begin{cases} 0 & \text{if } x < \frac{2}{3}, \\ [0, 1] & \text{if } x = \frac{2}{3}, \\ 1 & \text{if } x > \frac{2}{3}. \end{cases} \quad br_I(y) = \begin{cases} 0 & \text{if } y < \frac{1}{3}, \\ [0, 1] & \text{if } y = \frac{1}{3}, \\ 1 & \text{if } y > \frac{1}{3}. \end{cases}$$

Figure 5.11 depicts the graphs of these two set-valued functions, br_I and br_{II}. The graph of br_{II} is the lighter line, and the graph of br_I is the darker line. The two graphs are shown on the same set of axes, where the x-axis is the horizontal line and the y-axis is the vertical line. For each $x \in [0, 1]$, $br_{II}(x)$ is a point or a line located above x. For each $y \in [0, 1]$, $br_I(y)$ is a point or a line located to the right of y.

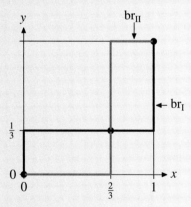

Figure 5.11 The graphs of br_I (black line) and of br_{II} (gray line)

A point (x^*, y^*) is an equilibrium point if and only if $x^* \in br_I(y^*)$ and $y^* \in br_{II}(x^*)$. This is equivalent to (x^*, y^*) being a point at which the two graphs br_I and br_{II} intersect (verify this for yourself). As Figure 5.11 shows, these graphs intersect in three points:

- $(x^*, y^*) = (0, 0)$: corresponding to the pure strategy equilibrium (C, C).
- $(x^*, y^*) = (1, 1)$: corresponding to the pure strategy equilibrium (F, F).
- $(x^*, y^*) = (\frac{2}{3}, \frac{1}{3})$: corresponding to the equilibrium in mixed strategies

$$x^* = \left[\tfrac{2}{3}(F), \tfrac{1}{3}(C)\right], \quad y^* = \left[\tfrac{1}{3}(F), \tfrac{2}{3}(C)\right]. \tag{5.41}$$

Note two interesting points:

- The payoff at the mixed strategy equilibrium is $(\frac{2}{3}, \frac{2}{3})$. For each player, this payoff is worse than the worst payoff he would receive if either of the pure strategy equilibria were chosen instead.

- The payoff $\frac{2}{3}$ is also the security level (maxmin value) of each of the two players (verify this), but the maxmin strategies guaranteeing this level are not equilibrium strategies; the maxmin strategy of Player I is $[\frac{1}{3}(F), \frac{2}{3}(C)]$, and the maxmin strategy of Player II is $[\frac{2}{3}(F), \frac{1}{3}(C)]$.

◀

This geometric procedure for computing equilibrium points, as intersection points of the graphs of the best replies of the players, is not applicable if there are more than two players or if each player has more than two pure strategies. But there are cases in which this procedure can be mimicked by finding solutions of algebraic equations corresponding to the intersections of best-response graphs.

5.2.3 The indifference principle

One effective tool for finding equilibria is the *indifference principle*. The indifference principle says that if a mixed equilibrium calls for a player to use two distinct pure strategies with positive probability, then the expected payoff to that player for using one of those pure strategies equals the expected payoff to him for using the other pure strategy, assuming that the other players are playing according to the equilibrium.

Theorem 5.18 *Let σ^* be an equilibrium in mixed strategies of a strategic-form game, and let s_i and $\widehat{s}_i$ be two pure strategies of player i. If $\sigma_i^*(s_i) > 0$ and $\sigma_i^*(\widehat{s}_i) > 0$, then*

$$U_i(s_i, \sigma_{-i}^*) = U_i(\widehat{s}_i, \sigma_{-i}^*). \tag{5.42}$$

The reason this theorem holds is simple: if the expected payoff to player i when he plays pure strategy s_i is higher than when he plays $\widehat{s}_i$, then he can improve his expected payoff by increasing the probability of playing s_i and decreasing the probability of playing $\widehat{s}_i$.

Proof: Suppose by contradiction that Equation (5.42) does not hold. Without loss of generality, suppose that

$$U_i(s_i, \sigma_{-i}^*) > U_i(\widehat{s}_i, \sigma_{-i}^*). \tag{5.43}$$

Let σ_i be the strategy of player i defined by

$$\sigma_i(t_i) := \begin{cases} \sigma_i^*(t_i) & \text{if } t_i \notin \{s_i, \widehat{s}_i\}, \\ 0 & \text{if } t_i = \widehat{s}_i, \\ \sigma_i^*(s_i) + \sigma_i^*(\widehat{s}_i) & \text{if } t_i = s_i. \end{cases}$$

Then

$$U_i(\sigma_i, \sigma_{-i}^*) = \sum_{t_i \in S_i} \sigma(t_i) U_i(t_i, \sigma_{-i}^*) \tag{5.44}$$

$$= \sum_{t_i \notin \{s_i, \widehat{s}_i\}} \sigma^*(t_i) U_i(t_i, \sigma_{-i}^*) + (\sigma_i^*(s_i) + \sigma_i^*(\widehat{s}_i)) U_i(s_i, \sigma_{-i}^*) \tag{5.45}$$

$$> \sum_{t_i \notin \{s_i, \widehat{s}_i\}} \sigma^*(t_i) U_i(t_i, \sigma_{-i}^*) + \sigma_i^*(s_i) U_i(s_i, \sigma_{-i}^*) + \sigma_i^*(\widehat{s}_i) U_i(\widehat{s}_i, \sigma_{-i}^*) \tag{5.46}$$

5.2 Computing equilibria in mixed strategies

$$= \sum_{t_i \in s_i} \sigma_i^*(t_i) U_i(t_i, \sigma_{-i}^*) \tag{5.47}$$

$$= U_i(\sigma^*). \tag{5.48}$$

The equalities in Equation (5.45) and Equation (5.47) follow from the definition of σ, and Equation (5.46) follows from Equation (5.43). But this contradicts the assumption that σ^* is an equilibrium, because player i can increase his payoff by deviating to strategy σ_i'. This contradiction shows that the assumption that Equation (5.42) does not hold was wrong, and the theorem therefore holds. $\qquad\square$

The Indifference Principle implies the following result, which simplifies the computation of equilibrium points in strategic-form games. Its proof is left to the reader (Exercise 5.19).

Corollary 5.19 *Let σ^* be an equilibrium in a strategic-form game and let s_i and $\widehat{s}_i$ be two pure strategies of Player i.*

(a) *If $U_i(s_i, \sigma_{-i}^*) < U_i(\sigma^*)$ then $\sigma_i^*(s_i) = 0$.*
(b) *If $U_i(s_i, \sigma_{-i}^*) < U_i(\widehat{s}_i, \sigma_{-i}^*)$ then $\sigma_i^*(s_i) = 0$.*
(c) *If $\sigma_i^*(s_i) > 0$ and $\sigma_i^*(\widehat{s}_i) > 0$ then $U_i(s_i, \sigma_{-i}^*) = U_i(\widehat{s}_i, \sigma_{-i}^*)$.*
(d) *If s_i is strictly dominated by $\widehat{s}_i$ then $\sigma_i^*(s_i) = 0$.*

We will show how the indifference principle can be used to find equilibria, by reconsidering the game in Example 5.9.

Example 5.9 (*Continued*) The payoff matrix in this game appears in Figure 5.12.

Player II

		L	R
	T	1, −1	0, 2
Player I	B	0, 1	2, 0

Figure 5.12 The payoff matrix in Example 5.9

As we have already seen, the only equilibrium point in this game is

$$\left(\left[\tfrac{1}{4}(T), \tfrac{3}{4}(B) \right], \left[\tfrac{2}{3}(L), \tfrac{1}{3}(R) \right] \right). \tag{5.49}$$

Definition 5.19 *A mixed strategy σ_i of player i is called a* completely mixed strategy *if $\sigma_i(s_i) > 0$ for every pure strategy $s_i \in S_i$. An equilibrium $\sigma^* = (\sigma_i^*)_{i \in N}$ is called a* completely mixed *equilibrium if for every player $i \in N$ the strategy σ_i^* is a completely mixed strategy.*

In words, a player's completely mixed strategy chooses each pure strategy with positive probability. It follows that at every completely mixed equilibrium, every pure strategy vector is chosen with positive probability.

A consequence of the Indifference Principle is the following.

Corollary 5.20 *Let σ^* be an equilibrium in a strategic-form game and let $i \in N$ be a player. If σ_i^* is a completely mixed strategy then $U_i(s_i, \sigma_{-i}^*) = U_i(\hat{s}_i, \sigma_{-i}^*)$ for every two pure strategies $s_i, \hat{s}_i \in S_i$.*

We will now compute the equilibrium using the indifference principle. The first step is to ascertain, by direct inspection, that the game has no pure strategy equilibria. We can also ascertain that there is no Nash equilibrium of this game in which one of the two players plays a pure strategy. By Nash's Theorem (Theorem 5.10), the game has at least one equilibrium in mixed strategies, and it follows that at every equilibrium of the game both players play completely mixed strategies. For every pair of mixed strategies (x, y), we have that $U_{II}(x, L) = 1 - 2x$, $U_{II}(x, R) - 2x$, $U_I(T, y) = y$, and $U_I(B, y) = 2(1 - y)$. By the indifference principle, at equilibrium Player I is indifferent between playing T and playing B, and Player II is indifferent between L and R. In other words, if the equilibrium is (x^*, y^*), then:

- Player I is indifferent between T and B:

$$U_I(T, y^*) = U_I(B, y^*) \implies y^* = 2(1 - y^*) \implies y^* = \tfrac{2}{3}. \tag{5.50}$$

- Player II is indifferent between L and R:

$$U_{II}(x^*, L) = U_{II}(x^*, R) \implies 1 - 2x^* = 2x^* \implies x^* = \tfrac{1}{4}. \tag{5.51}$$

We have, indeed, found the same equilibrium that we found above, using a different procedure. Interestingly, in computing the mixed strategy equilibrium, each player's strategy is determined by the payoffs of the other player; each player plays in such a way that the other player is indifferent between his two pure strategies (and therefore the other player has no incentive to deviate). This is in marked contrast to the maxmin strategy of a player, which is determined solely by the player's own payoffs. This is yet another expression of the significant difference between the solution concepts of Nash equilibrium and maxmin strategy, in games that are not two-player zero-sum games. ◀

5.2.4 Dominance and equilibrium

The concept of strict dominance (Definition 4.6 on page 86) is a useful tool for computing equilibrium points. As we saw in Corollary 4.36 (page 109), in strategic-form games a strictly dominated strategy is chosen with probability 0 in each equilibrium. The following result, which is a generalization of that corollary, is useful for finding equilibria in mixed strategies.

Theorem 5.21 *Let $G = (N, (S_i)_{i \in N}, (u_i)_{i \in N})$ be a game in strategic form in which the sets $(S_i)_{i \in N}$ are all finite sets. If a pure strategy $s_i \in S_i$ of player i is strictly dominated by a mixed strategy $\sigma_i \in \Sigma_i$, then in every equilibrium of the game, the pure strategy s_i is chosen by player i with probability 0.*

Proof: Let s_i be a pure strategy of player i that is strictly dominated by a mixed strategy σ_i, and let $\hat{\sigma} = (\hat{\sigma}_i)_{i \in N}$ be a strategy vector in which player i chooses strategy s_i with positive probability: $\hat{\sigma}_i(s_i) > 0$. We will show that $\hat{\sigma}$ is not an equilibrium by showing that $\hat{\sigma}_i$ is not a best reply of player i to $\hat{\sigma}_{-i}$.

Define a mixed strategy $\sigma'_i \in \Sigma_i$ as follows:

$$\sigma'_i(t_i) = \begin{cases} \widehat{\sigma}_i(s_i) \cdot \sigma_i(s_i) & t_i = s_i, \\ \widehat{\sigma}_i(t_i) + \widehat{\sigma}_i(s_i) \cdot \sigma_i(t_i) & t_i \neq s_i. \end{cases} \tag{5.52}$$

In words, player i, using strategy σ'_i, chooses his pure strategy in two stages: first he chooses a pure strategy using the probability distribution $\widehat{\sigma}_i$. If this choice leads to a pure strategy that differs from s_i, he plays that strategy. But if s_i is chosen, player i chooses another pure strategy using the distribution σ_i, and plays whichever pure strategy that leads to.

Finally, we show that σ'_i yields player i a payoff that is higher than $\widehat{\sigma}_i$, when played against $\widehat{\sigma}_{-i}$, and hence $\widehat{\sigma}$ cannot be an equilibrium. Since σ_i strictly dominates s_i, it follows that, in particular,

$$U_i(s_i, \widehat{\sigma}_{-i}) < U_i(\sigma_i, \widehat{\sigma}_{-i}), \tag{5.53}$$

and we have

$$U_i(\widehat{\sigma}_i, \widehat{\sigma}_{-i}) = \sum_{t_i \in S_i} \widehat{\sigma}_i(t_i) U_i(t_i, \widehat{\sigma}_{-i}) \tag{5.54}$$

$$= \sum_{t_i \neq s_i} \widehat{\sigma}_i(t_i) U_i(t_i, \widehat{\sigma}_{-i}) + \widehat{\sigma}_i(s_i) U_i(s_i, \widehat{\sigma}_{-i}) \tag{5.55}$$

$$< \sum_{t_i \neq s_i} \widehat{\sigma}_i(t_i) U_i(t_i, \widehat{\sigma}_{-i}) + \widehat{\sigma}_i(s_i) U_i(\sigma_i, \widehat{\sigma}_{-i}) \tag{5.56}$$

$$= \sum_{t_i \neq s_i} \sigma'_i(t_i) U_i(t_i, \widehat{\sigma}_{-i}) + \widehat{\sigma}_i(s_i) \sum_{t_i \in S_i} \sigma'_i(t_i) U_i(t_i, \widehat{\sigma}_{-i}) \tag{5.57}$$

$$= \sum_{t_i \in S_i} \sigma'_i(t_i) U_i(t_i, \widehat{\sigma}_{-i}) \tag{5.58}$$

$$= U_i(\sigma'_i, \widehat{\sigma}_{-i}). \tag{5.59}$$

□

The next example shows how to use Theorem 5.21 to find equilibrium points in a game.

Example 5.21 Consider the two-player game of Figure 5.13 in which $N = \{\mathrm{I}, \mathrm{II}\}$.

Player II

		L	C	R
	T	6, 2	0, 6	4, 4
Player I	M	2, 12	4, 3	2, 5
	B	0, 6	10, 0	2, 2

Figure 5.13 The strategic-form game in Example 5.21

In this game, no pure strategy is dominated by another pure strategy (verify this). However, strategy M of Player I is strictly dominated by the mixed strategy $[\frac{1}{2}(T), \frac{1}{2}(B)]$ (verify this). It follows from Theorem 5.21 that the deletion of strategy M has no effect on the set of equilibria in the game. Following the deletion of strategy M, we are left with the game shown in Figure 5.14.

Player II

		L	C	R
	T	6, 2	0, 6	4, 4
Player I	B	0, 6	10, 0	2, 2

Figure 5.14 The game after eliminating strategy M

In this game, strategy R of Player II is strictly dominated by the mixed strategy $[\frac{5}{12}(L), \frac{7}{12}(C)]$. We then delete R, which leaves us with the game shown in Figure 5.15.

Player II

		L	C
	T	6, 2	0, 6
Player I	B	0, 6	10, 0

Figure 5.15 The game after eliminating strategies M and R

The game shown in Figure 5.15 has no pure-strategy equilibria (verify this). The only mixed equilibrium of this game, which can be computed using the indifference principle, is $([\frac{3}{5}(T), \frac{2}{5}(B)], [\frac{5}{8}(L), \frac{3}{8}(R)])$, which yields payoff $(\frac{15}{4}, \frac{18}{5})$ (verify this, too).

Since the strategies that were deleted were all strictly dominated strategies, the above equilibrium is also the only equilibrium of the original game. ◀

5.2.5   Two-player zero-sum games and linear programming

Computing the value of two-player zero-sum games, where each player has a finite number of strategies, and finding optimal strategies in such games, can be presented as a linear programming problem. It follows that these computations can be accomplished using known linear programming algorithms. In this section, we present linear programs that correspond to finding the value and optimal strategies of a two-player game. A brief survey of linear programming appears in Section 24.3 (page 991).

Let $(N, (S_i)_{i \in N}, u)$ be a two-player zero-sum game, in which the set of players is $N = \{I, II\}$. As usual, U denotes the multilinear extension of u.

Theorem 5.22 *Denote by Z_P the value of the following linear program in the variables* $(x_{s_I})_{s_I \in S_I}$.

5.2 Computing equilibria in mixed strategies

$$\textit{Compute:} \quad Z_P := \max z$$
$$\textit{subject to:} \quad \sum_{s_I \in S_I} x(s_I) u(s_I, s_{II}) \geq z, \quad \forall s_{II} \in S_{II};$$
$$\sum_{s_I \in S_I} x(s_I) = 1;$$
$$x(s_I) \geq 0, \quad \forall s_I \in S_I.$$

Then Z_P is the value in mixed strategies of the game.

Proof: Denote by v the value of the game $(N, (S_i)_{i \in N}, u)$ in mixed strategies. We will show that $Z_P = v$ by showing that $Z_P \geq v$ and $Z_P \leq v$.

Step 1: $Z_P \geq v$.
If v is the value of the game, then Player I has an optimal strategy σ_I^* that guarantees a payoff of at least v, for every mixed strategy of Player II:

$$U(\sigma_I^*, \sigma_{II}) \geq v, \quad \forall \sigma_{II} \in \Sigma_{II}. \tag{5.60}$$

Since this inequality holds, in particular, for each pure strategy $s_{II} \in S_{II}$, the vector $(x, z) = (\sigma_I^*, v)$ satisfies the constraints. Since Z_P is the largest real number z for which there exists a mixed strategy for Player I at which the constraints are satisfied, we have $Z_P \geq v$.

Step 2: $Z_P \leq v$.
We first show that $Z_P < \infty$. Suppose that (x, z) is a vector satisfying the constraints. Then $\sum_{s_I \in S_I} x(s_I) u(s_I, s_{II}) \geq z$ and $\sum_{s_I \in S_I} x(s_I) = 1$. This leads to

$$z \leq \sum_{s_I \in S_I} x(s_I) u(s_I, s_{II}) \leq \max_{s_I \in S_I} \max_{s_{II} \in S_{II}} |u(s_I, s_{II})| \times \sum_{s_I \in S_I} x(s_I) \tag{5.61}$$

$$= \max_{s_I \in S_I} \max_{s_{II} \in S_{II}} |u(s_I, s_{II})| < \infty. \tag{5.62}$$

The finiteness of the expression in (5.62) is due to the fact that each of the players has a finite number of pure strategies. Since Z_P is the value of the linear program, there exists a vector x such that (x, Z_P) satisfies the constraints. These constraints require x to be a mixed strategy of Player I. Similarly, the constraints imply that $u(x, s_{II}) \geq Z_P$ for every pure strategy $s_{II} \in S_{II}$. The multilinearity of U implies that

$$U(x, \sigma_{II}) \geq Z_P, \quad \forall \sigma_{II} \in \Sigma_{II}. \tag{5.63}$$

It follows that Player I has a mixed strategy guaranteeing a payoff of at least Z_P, and hence $v \geq Z_P$. $\qquad\square$

The fact that the value of a game in mixed strategies can be found using linear programming is an expression of the strong connection that exists between the Minmax Theorem and the Duality Theorem. These two theorems are actually equivalent to each other. Exercise 5.70 presents a guided proof of the Minmax Theorem using the Duality Theorem. For the proof of the Duality Theorem using the Minmax Theorem, see Luce and Raiffa [1957], Section A5.2.

5.2.6   Two-player games that are not zero-sum

Computing the value of a two-player zero-sum game can be accomplished by solving a linear program. Similarly, computing equilibria in a two-player game that is not zero-sum can be accomplished by solving a quadratic program. However, while there are efficient algorithms for solving linear programs, there are no known efficient algorithms for solving generic quadratic programs.

A straightforward method for finding equilibria in two-player games that are not zero-sum is based on the following idea. Let $(\sigma_I^*, \sigma_{II}^*)$ be a Nash equilibrium in mixed strategies. Denote

$$\text{supp}(\sigma_I^*) := \{s_I \in S_I : \sigma_I^*(s_I) > 0\}, \tag{5.64}$$

$$\text{supp}(\sigma_{II}^*) := \{s_{II} \in S_{II} : \sigma_{II}^*(s_{II}) > 0\}. \tag{5.65}$$

The sets $\text{supp}(\sigma_I^*)$ and $\text{supp}(\sigma_{II}^*)$ are called the *support* of the mixed strategies σ_I^* and σ_{II}^* respectively, and they contain all the pure strategies that are chosen with positive probability under σ_I^* and σ_{II}^* respectively. By the indifference principle (see Theorem 5.18 on page 158), at equilibrium any two pure strategies that are played by a particular player with positive probability yield the same payoff to that player. Choose $s_I^0 \in \text{supp}(\sigma_I)$ and $s_{II}^0 \in \text{supp}(\sigma_{II}^*)$. Then $(\sigma_I^*, \sigma_{II}^*)$ satisfies the following constraints:

$$U_I(s_I^0, \sigma_{II}^*) = U_I(s_I, \sigma_{II}^*), \quad \forall s_I \in \text{supp}(\sigma_I^*), \tag{5.66}$$

$$U_{II}(\sigma_I^*, s_{II}^0) = U_{II}(\sigma_I^*, s_{II}), \quad \forall s_{II} \in \text{supp}(\sigma_{II}^*). \tag{5.67}$$

At equilibrium, neither player can profit from unilateral deviation; in particular,

$$U_I(s_I^0, \sigma_{II}^*) \geq U_I(s_I, \sigma_{II}^*), \quad \forall s_I \in S_I \backslash \text{supp}(\sigma_I), \tag{5.68}$$

$$U_{II}(\sigma_I^*, s_{II}^0) \geq U_{II}(\sigma_I^*, s_{II}), \quad \forall s_{II} \in S_{II} \backslash \text{supp}(\sigma_{II}). \tag{5.69}$$

Since U_I and U_{II} are multilinear functions, this is a system of equations that are linear in σ_I^* and σ_{II}^*. By taking into account the constraint that σ_I^* and σ_{II}^* are probability distributions, we conclude that $(\sigma_I^*, \sigma_{II}^*)$ is the solution of a system of linear equations. In addition, every pair of mixed strategies $(\sigma_I^*, \sigma_{II}^*)$ that solves Equations (5.66)–(5.69) is a Nash equilibrium.

This leads to the following direct algorithm for finding equilibria in a two-player game that is not zero-sum: For every nonempty subset Y_I of S_I and every nonempty subset Y_{II} of S_{II}, determine whether there exists an equilibrium $(\sigma_I^*, \sigma_{II}^*)$ satisfying $Y_I = \text{supp}(\sigma_I^*)$ and $Y_{II} = \text{supp}(\sigma_{II}^*)$. The set of equilibria whose support is Y_I and Y_{II} is the set of solutions of the system of equations comprised of Equations (5.70)–(5.79), in which s_I^0 and s_{II}^0 are any two pure strategies in Y_I and Y_{II}, respectively (Exercise 5.59):

$$\sum_{s_{II} \in S_{II}} \sigma_{II}(s_{II}) u_I\left(s_I^0, s_{II}\right) = \sum_{s_{II} \in S_{II}} \sigma_{II}(s_{II}) u_I(s_I, s_{II}), \quad \forall s_I \in Y_I, \tag{5.70}$$

$$\sum_{s_I \in S_I} \sigma_I(s_I) u_I\left(s_I, s_{II}^0\right) = \sum_{s_I \in S_I} \sigma_I(s_I) u_I(s_I, s_{II}), \quad \forall s_{II} \in Y_{II}, \tag{5.71}$$

$$\sum_{s_{\mathrm{II}} \in S_{\mathrm{II}}} \sigma_{\mathrm{II}}(s_{\mathrm{II}}) u_{\mathrm{I}}\left(s_{\mathrm{I}}^0, s_{\mathrm{II}}\right) \geq \sum_{s_{\mathrm{II}} \in S_{\mathrm{II}}} \sigma_{\mathrm{II}}(s_{\mathrm{II}}) u_{\mathrm{I}}(s_{\mathrm{I}}, s_{\mathrm{II}}), \quad \forall s_{\mathrm{I}} \in S_{\mathrm{I}} \backslash Y_{\mathrm{I}}, \tag{5.72}$$

$$\sum_{s_{\mathrm{I}} \in S_{\mathrm{I}}} \sigma_{\mathrm{I}}(s_{\mathrm{I}}) u_{\mathrm{I}}\left(s_{\mathrm{I}}, s_{\mathrm{II}}^0\right) \geq \sum_{s_{\mathrm{I}} \in S_{\mathrm{I}}} \sigma_{\mathrm{I}}(s_{\mathrm{I}}) u_{\mathrm{I}}(s_{\mathrm{I}}, s_{\mathrm{II}}), \quad \forall s_{\mathrm{II}} \in S_{\mathrm{II}} \backslash Y_{\mathrm{II}}, \tag{5.73}$$

$$\sum_{s_{\mathrm{I}} \in S_{\mathrm{I}}} \sigma_{\mathrm{I}}(s_{\mathrm{I}}) = 1, \tag{5.74}$$

$$\sum_{s_{\mathrm{II}} \in S_{\mathrm{II}}} \sigma_{\mathrm{II}}(s_{\mathrm{II}}) = 1, \tag{5.75}$$

$$\sigma_{\mathrm{I}}(s_{\mathrm{I}}) > 0, \quad \forall s_{\mathrm{I}} \in Y_{\mathrm{I}}, \tag{5.76}$$

$$\sigma_{\mathrm{II}}(s_{\mathrm{II}}) > 0, \quad \forall s_{\mathrm{II}} \in Y_{\mathrm{II}}, \tag{5.77}$$

$$\sigma_{\mathrm{I}}(s_{\mathrm{I}}) = 0, \quad \forall s_{\mathrm{I}} \in S_{\mathrm{I}} \backslash Y_{\mathrm{I}}, \tag{5.78}$$

$$\sigma_{\mathrm{II}}(s_{\mathrm{II}}) = 0, \quad \forall s_{\mathrm{II}} \in S_{\mathrm{II}} \backslash Y_{\mathrm{II}}. \tag{5.79}$$

Determining whether this system of equations has a solution can be accomplished by solving a linear program. Because the number of nonempty subsets of S_{I} is $2^{m_{\mathrm{I}}} - 1$ and the number of empty subsets of S_{II} is $2^{m_{\mathrm{II}}} - 1$, the complexity of this algorithm is exponential in m_{I} and m_{II}, and hence this algorithm is computationally inefficient.

5.3 The proof of Nash's Theorem

This section is devoted to proving Nash's Theorem (Theorem 5.10), which states that every finite game has an equilibrium in mixed strategies. The proof of the theorem makes use of the following result.

Theorem 5.23 (Brouwer's Fixed Point Theorem) *Let X be a convex and compact set in a d-dimensional Euclidean space, and let $f : X \to X$ be a continuous function. Then there exists a point $x \in X$ such that $f(x) = x$. Such a point x is called a* fixed point *of f.*

Brouwer's Fixed Point Theorem states that every continuous function from a convex and compact set to itself has a fixed point, that is, a point that the function maps to itself.

In one dimension, Brouwer's Theorem takes an especially simple form. In one dimension, a convex and compact space is a closed line segment $[a, b]$. When $f : [a, b] \to [a, b]$ is a continuous function, one of the following three alternatives must obtain:

1. $f(a) = a$, hence a is a fixed point of f.
2. $f(b) = b$, hence b is a fixed point of f.
3. $f(a) > a$ and $f(b) < b$. Consider the function $g(x) = f(x) - x$, which is continuous, where $g(a) > 0$ and $g(b) < 0$. The Intermediate Value Theorem implies that there exists $x \in [a, b]$ satisfying $g(x) = 0$, that is to say, $f(x) = x$. Every such x is a fixed point of f.

The graphical expression of the proof of Brouwer's Fixed Point Theorem in one dimension is as follows: every continuous function on the segment $[a, b]$ must intersect the main diagonal in at least one point (see Figure 5.16).

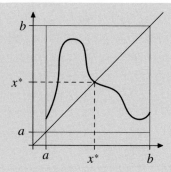

Figure 5.16 Brouwer's Theorem: a fixed point in the one-dimensional case

If the dimension is two or greater, the proof of Brouwer's Fixed Point Theorem is not simple. It can be proved in several different ways, with a variety of mathematical tools. A proof of the theorem using Sperner's Lemma appears in Section 24.1.2 (page 981).

We will now prove Nash's Theorem using Brouwer's Fixed Point Theorem. The proofs of the following two claims are left to the reader (Exercises 5.1 and 5.2).

Theorem 5.24 *If player i's set of pure strategies S_i is finite, then his set of mixed strategies Σ_i is convex and compact.*

Theorem 5.25 *If $A \subset \mathbb{R}^n$ and $B \subset \mathbb{R}^m$ are compact sets, then the set $A \times B$ is a compact subset of $\mathbb{R}^{n+m}$. If A and B are convex sets, then $A \times B$ is a convex subset of $\mathbb{R}^{n+m}$.*

Theorems 5.24 and 5.25 imply that the set $\Sigma = \Sigma_1 \times \Sigma_2 \times \cdots \times \Sigma_n$ is a convex and compact subset of the Euclidean space $\mathbb{R}^{m_1+m_2+\cdots+m_n}$. The proof of Nash's Theorem then proceeds as follows. We will define a function $f : \Sigma \to \Sigma$, and prove that it satisfies the following two properties:

- f is a continuous function.
- Every fixed point of f is an equilibrium of the game.

Since Σ is convex and compact, and f is continuous, it follows from Brouwer's Fixed Point Theorem that f has at least one fixed point. The second property above then implies that the game has at least one equilibrium point.

The idea behind the definition of f is as follows. For each strategy vector σ, we define $f(\sigma) = (f_i(\sigma))_{i \in N}$ to be a vector of strategies, where $f_i(\sigma)$ is a strategy of player i. $f_i(\sigma)$ is defined in such a way that if σ_i is not a best reply to σ_{-i}, then $f_i(\sigma)$ is given by shifting σ_i in the direction of a "better reply" to σ_{-i}. It then follows that $f_i(\sigma) = \sigma_i$ if and only if σ_i is a best reply to σ_{-i}.

To define f, we first define an auxiliary function $g_i^j : \Sigma \to [0, \infty)$ for each player i and each index j, where $1 \leq j \leq m_i$. That is, for each vector of mixed strategies σ we define a nonnegative number $g_i^j(\sigma)$.

The payoff that player i receives under the vector of mixed strategies σ is $U_i(\sigma)$. The payoff he receives when he plays the pure strategy s_i^j, but all the other players play σ, is $U_i(s_i^j, \sigma_{-i})$. We define the function g_i^j as follows:

$$g_i^j(\sigma) := \max \left\{ 0, U_i\big(s_i^j, \sigma_{-i}\big) - U_i(\sigma) \right\}. \tag{5.80}$$

In words, $g_i^j(\sigma)$ equals 0 if player i cannot profit from deviating from σ_i to s_i^j. When $g_i^j(\sigma) > 0$, player i gains a higher payoff if he increases the probability of playing the pure strategy s_i^j. Because a player has a profitable deviation if and only if he has a profitable deviation to a pure strategy, we have the following result:

Claim 5.26 *The strategy vector σ is an equilibrium if and only if $g_i^j(\sigma) = 0$, for each player $i \in N$ and for all $j = 1, 2, \ldots, m_i$.*

To proceed with the proof, we need the following claim:

Claim 5.27 *For every player $i \in N$, and every $j = 1, 2, \ldots, m_i$, the function g_i^j is continuous.*

Proof: Let $i \in N$ be a player, and let $j \in \{1, 2, \ldots, m_i\}$. From Corollary 5.7 (page 148) the function U_i is continuous. The function $\sigma_{-i} \mapsto U_i(s_i^j, \sigma_{-i})$, as a function of σ_{-1}, is therefore also continuous. In particular, the difference $U_i(s_i^j, \sigma_{-i}) - U_i(\sigma)$ is a continuous function. Since 0 is a continuous function, and since the maximum of continuous functions is a continuous function, we have that the function g_i^j is continuous. $\square$

We can now define the function f. The function f has to satisfy the property that every one of its fixed points is an equilibrium of the game. It then follows that if σ is not an equilibrium, it must be the case that $\sigma \neq f(\sigma)$. How can we guarantee that? The main idea is to consider, for every player i, the indices j such that $g_i^j(\sigma) > 0$; these indices correspond to pure strategies at which $g_i^j(\sigma) > 0$, i.e., the strategies that will increase player i's payoff if he increases the probability that they will be played (and decreases the probability of playing pure strategies that do not satisfy this inequality). This idea leads to the following definition.

Because $f(\sigma)$ is an element in Σ, i.e., it is a vector of mixed strategies, $f_i^j(\sigma)$ is the probability that player i will play the pure strategy s_i^j. Define:

$$f_i^j(\sigma) := \frac{\sigma_i\big(s_i^j\big) + g_i^j(\sigma)}{1 + \sum_{k=1}^{m_i} g_i^k(\sigma)}. \tag{5.81}$$

In words, if s_i^j is a better reply than σ_i to σ_{-i}, we increase its probability by $g_i^j(\sigma)$, and then normalize the resulting numbers so that we obtain a probability distribution. We now turn our attention to the proof that f satisfies all its required properties.

Claim 5.28 *The range of f is Σ, i.e., $f(\Sigma) \subseteq \Sigma$.*

Proof: We need to show that $f(\sigma)$ is a vector of mixed strategies, for every $\sigma \in \Sigma$, i.e.,

1. $f_i^j(\sigma) \geq 0$ for all i, and for all $j \in \{1, 2, \ldots, m_i\}$.
2. $\sum_{j=1}^{m_i} f_i^j(\sigma) = 1$ for all players $i \in \mathbb{N}$.

The first condition holds because $g_i^j(\sigma)$ is nonnegative by definition, and hence the denominator in Equation (5.81) is at least 1, and the numerator is nonnegative.

As for the second condition, because $\sum_{j=1}^{m_i} \sigma_i(s_i^j) = 1$, it follows that

$$\sum_{j=1}^{m_i} f_i^j(\sigma) = \sum_{j=1}^{m_i} \frac{\sigma_i(s_i^j) + g_i^j(\sigma)}{1 + \sum_{k=1}^{m_i} g_i^k(\sigma)} \tag{5.82}$$

$$= \frac{\sum_{j=1}^{m_i}(\sigma_i(s_i^j) + g_i^j(\sigma))}{1 + \sum_{k=1}^{m_i} g_i^k(\sigma)} \tag{5.83}$$

$$= \frac{\sum_{j=1}^{m_i} \sigma_i(s_i^j) + \sum_{j=1}^{m_i} g_i^j(\sigma)}{1 + \sum_{j=1}^{m_i} g_i^j(\sigma)} = 1. \tag{5.84}$$

$\square$

Claim 5.29 f *is a continuous function.*

Proof: Claim 5.27 implies that both the numerator and the denominator in the definition of f_i^j are continuous functions. As mentioned in the proof of Claim 5.28, the denominator in the definition of f_i^j is at least 1. Thus, f is the ratio of two continuous functions, where the denominator is always positive, and therefore it is a continuous function. $\square$

To complete the proof of the theorem, we need to show that every fixed point of f is an equilibrium of the game. This is accomplished in several steps.

Claim 5.30 *Let σ be a fixed point of f. Then*

$$g_i^j(\sigma) = \sigma_i(s_i^j) \sum_{k=1}^{m_i} g_i^k(\sigma), \quad \forall i \in N, j \in \{1, 2, \ldots, m_i\}. \tag{5.85}$$

Proof: The strategy vector σ is a fixed point of f, and therefore $f(\sigma) = \sigma$. This is an equality between vectors; hence every coordinate in the vector on the left-hand side of the equation equals the corresponding coordinate in the vector on the right-hand side, i.e.,

$$f_i^j(\sigma) = \sigma_i(s_i^j), \quad \forall i \in N, j \in \{1, 2, \ldots, m_i\}. \tag{5.86}$$

From the definition of f,

$$\frac{\sigma_i(s_i^j) + g_i^j(\sigma)}{1 + \sum_{k=1}^{m_i} g_i^k(\sigma)} = \sigma_i(s_i^j), \quad \forall i \in N, j \in \{1, 2, \ldots, m_i\}. \tag{5.87}$$

The denominator on the left-hand side is positive; multiplying both sides of the equations by the denominator yields

$$\sigma_i(s_i^j) + g_i^j(\sigma) = \sigma_i(s_i^j) + \sigma_i(s_i^j) \sum_{k=1}^{m_i} g_i^k(\sigma), \forall i \in N, j \in \{1, 2, \ldots, m_i\}. \tag{5.88}$$

Canceling the term $\sigma_i(s_i^j)$ from both sides of Equation (5.88) leads to Equation (5.85). $\square$

We now turn to the proof of the last step.

Claim 5.31 *Let σ be a fixed point of f. Then σ is a Nash equilibrium.*

Proof: Suppose by contradiction that σ is not an equilibrium. Claim 5.26 implies that there exists a player i, and $l \in \{1, 2, \ldots, m_i\}$, such that $g_i^l(\sigma) > 0$. In particular, $\sum_{k=1}^{m_i} g_i^k(\sigma) > 0$; hence from Equation (5.85) we have

$$\sigma_i(s_i^j) > 0 \iff g_i^j(\sigma) > 0, \quad \forall j \in \{1, 2, \ldots, m_i\}. \tag{5.89}$$

Because $g_i^l(\sigma) > 0$, one has in particular that $\sigma_i(s_i^l) > 0$. Since the function U_i is multilinear, $U_i(\sigma) = \sum_{j=1}^{m_i} \sigma_i(s_i^j) U_i(s_i^j, \sigma_{-i})$. This yields

$$0 = \sum_{j=1}^{m_i} \sigma_i(s_i^j)(U_i(s_i^j, \sigma_{-i}) - U_i(\sigma)) \tag{5.90}$$

$$= \sum_{\{j:\, \sigma_i(s_i^j) > 0\}} \sigma_i(s_i^j)(U_i(s_i^j, \sigma_{-i}) - U_i(\sigma)) \tag{5.91}$$

$$= \sum_{\{j:\, \sigma_i(s_i^j) > 0\}} \sigma_i(s_i^j) g_i^j(\sigma), \tag{5.92}$$

where the last equality holds because from Equation (5.89), if $\sigma_i(s_i^j) > 0$, then $g_i^j(\sigma) > 0$, and in this case $g_i^j(\sigma) = U_i(s_i^j, \sigma_{-i}) - U_i(\sigma)$. But the sum (Equation (5.92)) is positive: it contains at least one element ($j = l$), and by Equation (5.89) every summand in the sum is positive. This contradiction leads to the conclusion that σ must be a Nash equilibrium. □

5.4 Generalizing Nash's Theorem

There are situations in which, due to various constraints, a player cannot make use of some mixed strategies. For example, there may be situations in which player i cannot choose two pure strategies s_i and $\hat{s}_i$ with different probability, and he is then forced to limit himself to mixed strategies σ_i in which $\sigma_i(s_i) = \sigma_i(\hat{s}_i)$. A player may find himself in a situation in which he must choose a particular pure strategy s_i with probability greater than or equal to some given number $p_i(s_i)$, and he is then forced to limit himself to mixed strategies σ_i in which $\sigma_i(s_i) \geq p_i(s_i)$. In both of these examples, the constraints can be translated into linear inequalities. A bounded set that is defined by the intersection of a finite number of half-spaces is called a *polytope*. The number of extreme points of every polytope S is finite, and every polytope is the convex hull of its extreme points: if $x^1, x^2, \ldots, x^K$ are the extreme points of S, then S is the smallest convex set containing $x^1, x^2, \ldots, x^K$ (see Definition 24.1 on page 963). In other words, for each $s \in S$ there exist nonnegative numbers $(\alpha^l)_{l=1}^K$ whose sum is 1, such that $s = \sum_{l=1}^K \alpha^l x^l$; conversely, for each vector of nonnegative numbers $(\alpha^l)_{l=1}^K$ whose sum is 1, the vector $\sum_{l=1}^K \alpha^l x^l$ is in S.

The space of mixed strategies Σ_i is a simplex, which is a polytope whose extreme points are unit vectors $e^1, e^2, \ldots, e^{m_i}$, where $e^k = (0, \ldots, 0, 1, 0, \ldots, 0)$ is an m_i-dimensional vector whose k-th coordinate is 1, and all the other coordinates of e^k are 0. We will now show that Nash's Theorem still holds when the space of strategies of a player is a polytope, and not necessarily a simplex. We note that Nash's Theorem holds under even more generalized conditions, but we will not present those generalizations in this book.

Theorem 5.32 *Let $G = (N, (X_i)_{i \in N}, (U_i)_{i \in N})$ be a strategic-form game in which, for each player i,*

- *The set X_i is a polytope in $\mathbb{R}^{d_i}$.*
- *The function U_i is a multilinear function over the variables $(s_i)_{i \in N}$.*

Then G has an equilibrium.

Nash's Theorem (Theorem 5.10 on page 150) is a special case of Theorem 5.32, where $X_i = \Sigma_i$ for every player $i \in N$.

Proof: The set of strategies X_i of player i in the game G is a polytope. Denote the extreme points of this set by $\{x_i^1, x_i^2, \ldots, x_i^{K_i}\}$. Define an auxiliary strategic-form game $\widehat{G}$ in which:

- The set of players is N.
- The set of pure strategies of player $i \in N$ is $L_i := \{1, 2, \ldots, K_i\}$. Denote $L := \times_{i \in N} L_i$.
- For each vector of pure strategies $l = (l_1, l_2, \ldots, l_n) \in L$, the payoff to player i is

$$v_i(l) := U_i\left(x_1^{l_1}, x_2^{l_2}, \ldots, x_n^{l_n}\right). \tag{5.93}$$

It follows that in the auxiliary game every player i chooses an extreme point in his set of strategies X_i, and his payoff in the auxiliary game is given by U_i. For each $i \in N$, denote by V_i the multilinear extension of v_i. Since U_i is a multilinear function, player i's payoff function in the extension of $\widehat{G}$ to mixed strategies is

$$V_i(\alpha) = \sum_{l_1=1}^{k_1} \sum_{l_2=1}^{k_2} \cdots \sum_{l_n=1}^{k_n} \alpha_1^{l_1} \alpha_2^{l_2} \cdots \alpha_n^{l_n} v_i(l_1, l_2, \ldots, l_n) \tag{5.94}$$

$$= \sum_{l_1=1}^{k_1} \sum_{l_2=1}^{k_2} \cdots \sum_{l_n=1}^{k_n} \alpha_1^{l_1} \alpha_2^{l_2} \cdots \alpha_n^{l_n} U_i\left(x_1^{l_1}, x_2^{l_2}, \ldots, x_n^{l_n}\right) \tag{5.95}$$

$$= U_i\left(\sum_{l_1=1}^{k_1} \alpha_1^{l_1} x_1^{l_1}, \ldots, \sum_{l_n=1}^{k_n} \alpha_n^{l_n} x_n^{l_n}\right). \tag{5.96}$$

The auxiliary game $\widehat{G}$ satisfies the conditions of Nash's Theorem (Theorem 5.10 on page 150), and it therefore has a Nash equilibrium in mixed strategies α^*. It follows that for every player i,

$$V_i(\alpha^*) \geq V_i(\alpha_i, \alpha_{-i}^*), \quad \forall i \in N, \forall \alpha_i \in \Delta(L_i). \tag{5.97}$$

Denote by $\alpha_i^* = (\alpha_i^{*, l_i})_{l_i=1}^{K_i}$ player i's strategy in the equilibrium α^*. Since X_i is a convex set, the weighted average

$$s_i^* := \sum_{l_i=1}^{K_i} \alpha_i^{*, l_i} x_i^{l_i} \tag{5.98}$$

is a point in X_i. We will now show that $s^* = (s_i^*)_{i \in N}$ is an equilibrium of the game G. Let $i \in N$ be a player, and let s_i be any strategy of player i. Since $\{x_i^1, x_i^2, \ldots, x_i^{K_i}\}$ are extreme points of S_i there exists a distribution $\alpha_i = (\alpha_i^{l_i})_{l_i=1}^{K_i}$ over L_i such that $s_i = \sum_{l_i=1}^{K_i} \alpha_i x_i^{l_i}$. Equations (5.98), (5.94), and (5.97) imply that, for each player $i \in N$,

$$U_i(s^*) = V_i(^*\alpha) \geq V_i(\alpha_i, \alpha_{-i}) = U_i(s_i, s_{-i}^*). \tag{5.99}$$

That is, if player i deviates to s_i, he cannot profit. Since this is true for every player $i \in N$ and every strategy $s_i \in S_i$, the strategy vector s^* is an equilibrium of the game G. $\square$

5.5 Utility theory and mixed strategies

In defining the mixed extension of a game, we defined the payoff that a vector of mixed strategies yields as the expected payoff when every player chooses a pure strategy according to the probability given by his mixed strategy. But how is this definition justified? In this section we will show that if the preferences of the players satisfy the von Neumann–Morgenstern axioms of utility theory (see Chapter 2), we can interpret the numerical values in each cell of the payoff matrix as the utility the players receive when the outcome of the game is that cell (see Figure 5.17).

Suppose that we are considering a two-player game, such as the game in Figure 5.17. In this game there are six possible outcomes, $O = \{A_1, A_2, \ldots, A_6\}$. Each player has a preference relation over the set of lotteries over O. Suppose that the two players have linear utility functions, u_1 and u_2 respectively, over the set of lotteries. Every pair of mixed strategies $x = (x_1, x_2)$ and $y = (y_1, y_2, y_3)$ induces a lottery over the possible outcomes. The probability of reaching each one of the possible outcomes is indicated in Figure 5.18.

In other words, every pair of mixed strategies (x, y) induces the following lottery $L_{x,y}$ over the outcomes:

$$L = L_{x,y} = \left[x_1 y_1(A_1), x_1 y_2(A_2), x_1 y_3(A_3), x_2 y_1(A_4), x_2 y_2(A_5), x_2 y_3(A_6) \right].$$

Player II

		y_1	y_2	y_3
Player I	x_1	A_1	A_2	A_3
	x_2	A_4	A_5	A_6

Figure 5.17 A two-player game in terms of outcomes

Outcome	A_1	A_2	A_3	A_4	A_5	A_6
Probability	$x_1 y_1$	$x_1 y_2$	$x_1 y_3$	$x_2 y_1$	$x_2 y_2$	$x_2 y_3$

Figure 5.18 The probability of reaching each of the outcomes

		Player II		
		y_1	y_2	y_3
Player I	x_1	$u_1(A_1), u_2(A_1)$	$u_1(A_2), u_2(A_2)$	$u_1(A_3), u_2(A_3)$
	x_2	$u_1(A_4), u_2(A_4)$	$u_1(A_5), u_2(A_5)$	$u_1(A_6), u_2(A_6)$

Figure 5.19 The game in Figure 5.17 in terms of utilities

Since the utility function of the two players is linear, player i's utility from this lottery is

$$u_i(L_{x,y}) = x_1y_1u_i(A_1) + x_1y_2u_i(A_2) + x_1y_3u_i(A_3) + x_2y_1u_i(A_4) + x_2y_2u_i(A_5) + x_2y_3u_i(A_6). \quad (5.100)$$

Player i's utility from this lottery is therefore equal to his expected payoff in the strategic-form game in which, in each cell of the payoff matrix, we write the utilities of the players from the outcome obtained at that cell (Figure 5.19).

If, therefore, we assume that each player's goal is to maximize his utility, what we are seeking is the equilibria of the game in Figure 5.19. If (x, y) is an equilibrium of this game, then any player who unilaterally deviates from his equilibrium strategy cannot increase his utility.

Note that because, in general, the utility functions of the players differ from each other, the game in terms of utilities (Figure 5.19) is not a zero-sum game, even if the original game is a zero-sum game in which the outcome is a sum of money that Player II pays to Player I.

Recall that a player's utility function is determined up to a positive affine transformation (Corollary 2.23, on page 23). How does the presentation of a game change if a different choice of players' utility functions is made? Let v_1 and v_2 be two positive affine transformations of u_1 and u_2 respectively; i.e., u_i and v_i are equivalent representations of the utilities of player i that satisfy $v_i(L) = \alpha_i u_i(L) + \beta_i$ for every lottery L where $\alpha_i > 0$ and $\beta_i \in \mathbb{R}$ for $i = 1, 2$. The game in Figure 5.17 in terms of the utility functions v_1 and v_2 will be analogous to the matrix that appears in Figure 5.19, with u_1 and u_2 replaced by v_1 and v_2 respectively.

Example 5.33 Consider the two games depicted in Figure 5.20. Game B is derived from Game A by adding a constant value of 6 to the payoff of Player II in every cell, whereby we have implemented a positive affine transformation (where $\alpha = 1$, $\beta = 6$) on the payoffs of Player II.

While Game A is a zero-sum game, Game B is not a zero-sum game, because the sum of the utilities in each cell of the matrix is 6. Such a game is called a *constant-sum game*. Every constant-sum game can be transformed to a zero-sum game by adding a constant value to the payoffs of one of the players, whereby the concepts constant-sum game and zero-sum game are equivalent. As we will argue in Theorem 5.35 below, the equilibria of a game are unchanged by adding constant values to the payoffs. For example, in the two games in Figure 5.20, strategy B strictly dominates T for Player I, and strategy M strictly dominates L for Player II. It follows that in both of these games, the only equilibrium point is (B, M).

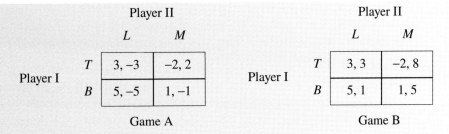

Figure 5.20 Adding a constant value to the payoffs of one of the players

If we implement a positive affine transformation in which $\alpha \neq 1$ on the payoffs of the players, we will still end up with a game in which the only thing that has changed is the units in which we are measuring the utilities of the players. For example, the game in Figure 5.21 is derived from Game A in Figure 5.20 by implementing the affine transformation $x \mapsto 5x + 7$ on the payoffs of Player I.

Player II

		L	M
Player I	T	22, −3	−3, 2
	B	32, −5	12, −1

Figure 5.21 The utilities in Game A in Figure 5.20 after implementing the affine transformation $x \mapsto 5x + 7$ on the payoffs to Player I

◀

Games that differ only in the utility representations of the players are considered to be equivalent games.

Definition 5.34 *Two games in strategic form* $(N, (S_i)_{i \in N}, (u_i)_{i \in N})$ *and* $(N, (S_i)_{i \in N}, (v_i)_{i \in N})$ *with the same set of players and the same sets of pure strategies are strategically equivalent if for each player $i \in N$ the function v_i is a positive affine transformation of the function u_i. In other words, there exist $\alpha_i > 0$ and $\beta_i \in \mathbb{R}$ such that*

$$v_i(s) = \alpha_i u_i(s) + \beta_i, \quad \forall s \in S. \tag{5.101}$$

The name "strategic equivalence" comes from the next theorem, whose proof we leave as an exercise (Exercise 5.63).

Theorem 5.35 *Let G and $\widehat{G}$ be two strategically equivalent strategic-form games. Every equilibrium $\sigma = (\sigma_1, \ldots, \sigma_n)$ in mixed strategies of the game G is an equilibrium in mixed strategies of the game $\widehat{G}$.*

In other words, each equilibrium in the original game remains an equilibrium after changing the utility functions of the players by positive affine transformations. Note, however, that the equilibrium payoffs do change from one strategically equivalent game to another, in accordance with the positive affine transformation that has been implemented.

Corollary 5.36 *If the preferences of every player over lotteries over the outcomes of the game satisfy the von Neumann–Morgenstern axioms, then the set of equilibria of the game is independent of the particular utility functions used to represent the preferences.*

Given the payoff matrix in Figure 5.21 and asked whether or not this game is strategically equivalent to a zero-sum game, what should we do? If the game is strategically equivalent to a zero-sum game, then there exist two positive affine transformations f_1 and f_2 such that $f_2(u_2(s)) = -f_1(u_1(s))$ for every strategy vector $s \in S$. Since the inverse of a positive affine transformation is also a positive affine transformation (Exercise 2.19 on page 35), and the concatenation of two positive affine transformations is also a positive affine transformation (Exercise 2.20 on page 35), in this case the positive affine transformation $f_3 = -((f_1)^{-1} \circ (-f_2))$ satisfies the property that $f_3(u_2(s)) = -u_1(s)$ for every strategy vector $s \in S$. In other words, if the game is strategically equivalent to a zero-sum game, there exists a positive affine transformation that, when applied to the utilities of Player II, yields the negative of the utilities of Player I. Denote such a transformation, assuming it exists, by $\alpha u + \beta$. Then we need to check whether there exist $\alpha > 0$ and $\beta \in \mathbb{R}$ such that

$$-5\alpha + \beta = -32, \tag{5.102}$$

$$-3\alpha + \beta = -22, \tag{5.103}$$

$$-1\alpha + \beta = -12, \tag{5.104}$$

$$2\alpha + \beta = 3. \tag{5.105}$$

In order to ascertain whether this system of equations has a solution, we can find α and β that solve two of the above equations, and check whether they satisfy the rest of the equations. For example, if we solve Equations (5.102) and (5.103), we get $\alpha = 5$ and $\beta = -7$, and we can then check that these values do indeed also solve Equations (5.104) and (5.105). Since we have found α and β solving the system of equations, we deduce that this game is strategically equivalent to a zero-sum game.

Remark 5.37 *Given the above, some people define a zero-sum game to be a game strategically equivalent to a game $(N, (S_i)_{i \in N}, (v_i)_{i \in N})$ in which $v_1 + v_2 = 0$.* ◆

The connection presented in this section between utility theory and game theory underscores the significance of utility theory. Representing the utilities of players by linear functions enables us to compute Nash equilibria with relative ease. Had we represented the players' preferences/indifferences by nonlinear utility functions, calculating equilibria would be far more complicated. This is similar to the way we select measurement scales in various fields. Many physical laws are expressed using the Celsius scale, because they can be given a simple expression. For example, consider the physical law which states that the change in the length of a metal rod is proportional to the change in its temperature. If temperature is measured in Fahrenheit, that law remains unchanged, since the Fahrenheit scale is a positive affine transformation of the Celsius scale. In contrast, if we were to measure temperature using, say, the log of the Celsius scale, many physical laws would have much more complicated formulations. Using linear utilities enables us to compute the utilities of simple lotteries using expected-value calculations, which simplifies the analysis of strategic-form games. This, of course, depends on the assumption that the preferences of the players can be represented by linear utility functions, i.e., that their preferences satisfy the von Neumann–Morgenstern axioms.

Another important point that has emerged from this discussion is that most daily situations do not correspond to two-player zero-sum games, even if the outcomes are in fact sums of money one person pays to another. This is because the utility of one player from receiving an amount of money x is usually not diametrically opposite to the utility of the other from paying this amount. That is, there are amounts $x \in \mathbb{R}$ for which $u_1(x) + u_2(-x) \neq 0$. On the other hand, as far as equilibria are concerned, the particular representation of the utilities of the players does not affect the set of equilibria of a game. If there exists a representation that leads to a zero-sum game, we are free to choose that representation, and if we do so, we can find equilibria by solving a linear program (see Section 5.2.5 on page 162).

One family of games that is always amenable to such a representation, which can be found easily, is the family of two-person games with two outcomes, where the preferences of the two players for the two alternative outcomes are diametrically opposed in these games. In such games we can always define the utilities of one of the players over the outcomes to be 1 or 0, and define the utilities of the other player over the outcomes to be -1 or 0. In contrast, zero-sum games are rare in the general family of two-player games. Nevertheless, two-player zero-sum games are very important in the study of game theory, as explained on pages 110–117.

5.6 The maxmin and the minmax in *n*-player games

In Section 4.10 (page 102), we defined the maxmin to be the best outcome that a player can guarantee for himself under his most pessimistic assumption regarding the behavior of the other players.

Definition 5.38 *The* maxmin in mixed strategies *of player i is defined as follows:*

$$\underline{v_i} := \max_{\sigma_i \in \Sigma_i} \min_{\sigma_{-i} \in \Sigma_{-i}} U_i(\sigma_i, \sigma_{-i}). \tag{5.106}$$

In two-player zero-sum games we also defined the concept of the minmax value, which is interpreted as the least payoff that the other players can guarantee that a player will get. In two-player zero-sum games, minimizing the payoff of one player is equivalent to maximizing the payoff of his opponent, and hence in two-player zero-sum games the maxmin of Player I is equal to the minmax of Player II. This is not true, however, in two-player games that are not zero-sum games, and in games with more than two players.

Analogous to the definition of the maxmin in Equation (5.106), the minmax value of a player is defined as follows:

Definition 5.39 *Let* $G = (N, (S_i)_{i \in N}, (u_i)_{i \in N})$ *be a strategic-form game. The* minmax value in mixed strategies *of player i is*

$$\bar{v_i} := \min_{\sigma_{-i} \in \Sigma_{-i}} \max_{\sigma_i \in \Sigma_i} U_i(\sigma_i, \sigma_{-i}). \tag{5.107}$$

$\bar{v_i}$ is the lowest possible payoff that the other players can force on player i.

A player's maxmin and minmax values depend solely on his payoff function, which is why different players in the same game may well have different maxmin and minmax values. One of the basic characteristics of these values is that a player's minmax value in mixed strategies is greater than or equal to his maxmin value in mixed strategies.

Theorem 5.40 *In every strategic-form game* $G = (N, (S_i)_{i\in N}, (u_i)_{i\in N})$, *for each player* $i \in N$,

$$\overline{v}_i \geq \underline{v}_i. \tag{5.108}$$

Equation (5.108) is expected: if the other players can guarantee that player i will not receive more than $\overline{v}_i$, and player i can guarantee himself at least $\underline{v}_i$, then $\overline{v}_i \geq \underline{v}_i$.

Proof: Let $\hat{\sigma}_{-i} \in \Sigma_{-i}$ be a strategy vector in which the minimum in Equation (5.107) is attained; i.e.,

$$\overline{v}_i = \max_{\sigma_i \in \Sigma_i} U_i(\sigma_i, \hat{\sigma}_{-i}) \leq \max_{\sigma_i \in \Sigma_i} U_i(\sigma_i, \sigma_{-i}), \quad \forall \sigma_{-i} \in \Sigma_{-i}. \tag{5.109}$$

On the other hand,

$$U_i(\sigma_i, \hat{\sigma}_{-i}) \geq \min_{\sigma_{-i} \in \Sigma_{-i}} U_i(\sigma_i, \sigma_{-i}), \quad \forall \sigma_i \in \Sigma_i. \tag{5.110}$$

Taking the maximum over all mixed strategies $\sigma_i \in \Sigma_i$ on both sides of the inequality sign in (5.110) yields

$$\overline{v}_i = \max_{\sigma_i \in \Sigma_i} U_i(\sigma_i, \hat{\sigma}_{-i}) \geq \max_{\sigma_i \in \Sigma_i} \min_{\sigma_{-i} \in \Sigma_{-i}} U_i(\sigma_i, \sigma_{-i}) = \underline{v}_i. \tag{5.111}$$

We conclude that $\overline{v}_i \geq \underline{v}_i$, which is what we needed to show. □

In a two-player game $G = (N, (S_i)_{i\in N}, (u_i)_{i\in N})$ where $N = \{I, II\}$, the maxmin value in mixed strategies of each player is always equal to his minmax value in mixed strategies. For Player I, for example, these two values equal the value of the second two-player zero-sum game $G = (N, (S_i)_{i\in N}, (v_i)_{i\in N})$, in which $v_I = u_I$ and $v_{II} = -u_I$ (Exercise 5.69). As the next example shows, in a game with more than two players, the maxmin value may be less than the minmax value.

Example 5.41 Consider the three-player game in which the set of players is $N = \{I, II, III\}$, and every player has two pure strategies; Player I chooses a row (T or B), Player II chooses a column (L or R), and Player III chooses a matrix (W or E). The payoff function u_1 of Player I is shown in Figure 5.22.

	L	R
T	0	1
B	1	1

W

	L	R
T	1	1
B	1	0

E

Figure 5.22 Player I's payoff function in the game in Example 5.41

We compute the maxmin value in mixed strategies of Player I. If Player I uses the mixed strategy $[x(T), (1-x)(B)]$, Player II uses the mixed strategy $[y(L), (1-y)(R)]$, and Player III uses the mixed strategy $[z(W), (1-z)(E)]$, then Player I's payoff is

$$U_I(x, y, z) = 1 - xyz - (1-x)(1-y)(1-z). \tag{5.112}$$

We first find

$$\underline{v_I} = \max_x \min_{y,z} U_I(x, y, z) = \tfrac{1}{2}. \tag{5.113}$$

To see this, note that $U_I(x, 0, 0) = x \le \tfrac{1}{2}$ for every $x \le \tfrac{1}{2}$, and $U_I(x, 1, 1) = 1 - x \le \tfrac{1}{2}$ for every $x \ge \tfrac{1}{2}$, and hence $\min_{y,z} U_I(x, y, z) \le \tfrac{1}{2}$ for every x. On the other hand, $U_I(\tfrac{1}{2}, y, z) \ge \tfrac{1}{2}$ for each y and z and hence $\max_x \min_{y,z} U_I(x, y, z) = \tfrac{1}{2}$, which is what we claimed.

We next turn to calculating the minmax value of Player I:

$$\bar{v_I} = \min_{y,z} \max_x U_I(x, y, z) \tag{5.114}$$

$$= \min_{y,z} \max_x (1 - xyz - (1-x)(1-y)(1-z)) \tag{5.115}$$

$$= \min_{y,z} \max_x (1 - (1-y)(1-z) + x(1 - y - z)). \tag{5.116}$$

For every fixed y and z the function $x \mapsto (1 - (1-y)(1-z) + x(1 - y - z))$ is linear; hence the maximum of Equation (5.116) is attained at the extreme point $x = 1$ if $1 - y - z \ge 0$, and at the extreme point $x = 0$ if $1 - y - z \le 0$. This yields

$$\max_x(1 - (1-y)(1-z) + x(1 - y - z)) = \begin{cases} 1 - (1-y)(1-z) & \text{if } y + z \ge 1, \\ 1 - yz & \text{if } y + z \le 1. \end{cases}$$

The minimum of the function $1 - (1-y)(1-z)$ over the domain $y + z \ge 1$ is $\tfrac{3}{4}$, and is attained at $y = z = \tfrac{1}{2}$. The minimum of the function $1 - yz$ over the domain $y + z \le 1$ is also $\tfrac{3}{4}$, and is attained at $y = z = \tfrac{1}{2}$. We therefore deduce that

$$\bar{v_I} = \tfrac{3}{4}. \tag{5.117}$$

In other words, in this example

$$\underline{v_I} = \tfrac{1}{2} < \tfrac{3}{4} = \bar{v_I}. \tag{5.118}$$

◄

Why can the minmax value in mixed strategies of player i in a game with more than two players be greater than his maxmin value in mixed strategies? Note that since U_i is a function that is linear in σ_{-i}, the minimum in Equation (5.106) is attained at an extreme point of Σ_{-i}, i.e., at a point in S_{-i}. It follows that

$$\underline{v_i} = \max_{\sigma_i \in \Sigma_i} \min_{s_{-i} \in S_{-i}} U_i(\sigma_i, s_{-i}). \tag{5.119}$$

Consider the following two-player zero-sum auxiliary game $\widehat{G}$:

- The set of players is $\{I, II\}$.
- Player I's set of pure strategies is S_i.
- Player II's set of pure strategies is $S_{-i} = \times_{j \ne i} S_j$: Player II chooses a pure strategy for every player who is not player i.
- The payoff function is u_i, the payoff function of player i in the original game.

Player I's set of mixed strategies in the auxiliary game $\widehat{G}$ is $\Delta(S_i) = \Sigma_i$, which is player i's set of mixed strategies in the original game. Player II's set of mixed strategies in the auxiliary game $\widehat{G}$ is $\Delta(S_{-i})$; i.e., a mixed strategy of Player II in $\widehat{G}$ is a probability distribution over the set of pure strategy vectors of the players who are not player i. The Minmax Theorem (Theorem 5.11 on page 150) then implies that the game $\widehat{G}$ has a value in mixed strategies, which is equal to

$$\widehat{v} = \max_{\sigma_i \in \Sigma_i} \min_{\sigma_{-i} \in \Delta(S_{-i})} U_i(\sigma_i, \sigma_{-i}) = \min_{\sigma_{-i} \in \Delta(S_{-i})} \max_{\sigma_i \in \Sigma_i} U_i(\sigma_i, \sigma_{-i}). \tag{5.120}$$

Since for every mixed strategy σ_i of player i the function $\sigma_{-i} \mapsto U_i(\sigma_i, \sigma_{-i})$ is linear in the variables σ_{-i}, the minimum in the expression in the middle term of Equation (5.120) equals the minimum over the extreme points of $\Delta(S_{-i})$, which is the set S_{-i}. Therefore,

$$\widehat{v} = \max_{\sigma_i \in \Sigma_i} \min_{\sigma_{-i} \in \Delta(S_{-i})} U_i(\sigma_i, \sigma_{-i}) = \max_{\sigma_i \in \Sigma_i} \min_{s_{-i} \in S_{-i}} U_i(\sigma_i, s_{-i}) = \underline{v}_i, \tag{5.121}$$

where the last equality follows from Equation (5.119). Combining Equations (5.120) and (5.121) and substituting $S_{-i} = \times_{j \neq i} S_j$ yields

$$\underline{v}_i = \min_{\sigma_{-i} \in \Delta(\times_{j \neq i} S_j)} \max_{\sigma_i \in \Sigma_i} U_i(\sigma_i, \sigma_{-i}), \tag{5.122}$$

and using Equation (5.107) and substituting $\Sigma_{-i} = \times_{j \neq i} \Delta(S_j)$ yields

$$\overline{v}_i = \min_{\sigma_{-i} \in \times_{j \neq i} \Delta(S_j)} \max_{\sigma_i \in \Sigma_i} U_i(\sigma_i, \sigma_{-i}). \tag{5.123}$$

With the help of the last two equations, we can see that the difference between $\underline{v}_i$ (the value of the auxiliary game) and $\overline{v}_i$ is in the set over which the minimization is implemented, or more precisely, the order in which the Δ operator (the set of distributions over ...) and $\times_{j \neq i}$ (the Cartesian product over ...) are implemented. $\times_{j \neq i} \Delta(S_j)$ appears in the calculation of the minmax value $\overline{v}_i$, and $\Delta(\times_{j \neq i} S_j)$ appears in the calculation of the maxmin value $\underline{v}_i$. The relationship between these two sets is given by

$$\Delta(\times_{j \neq i} S_j) \supseteq \times_{j \neq i} \Delta(S_j). \tag{5.124}$$

The two sets in Equation (5.124) have the same extreme points, namely, the elements of the set S_{-i}. This fact was used in the derivation of Equation (5.122). Despite this, the inclusion in Equation (5.124) is a proper inclusion when the number of players is greater than 2. In this case $\underline{v}_i$ may be less than $\overline{v}_i$, since the minimization in Equation (5.122) is over a set larger than the set over which the minimization in Equation (5.123) is conducted.

In summary, in the auxiliary game, Player II represents all the players who are not player i, and his mixed strategy is not necessarily the product distribution over the set $\times_{j \neq i} S_j$: for instance, in Example 5.41, for $i = 1$, the mixed strategy $[\frac{1}{2}(L, W), \frac{1}{2}(R, E)]$ is a possible strategy for Player II in the auxiliary game; i.e., it is in the set $\Delta(S_2 \times S_3)$, but it is not an element in $\Delta(S_2) \times \Delta(S_3)$. It follows that in the auxiliary game Player II can choose the vector of pure strategies for the players who are not player i in a correlated manner, while in the original game, in which the players choose mixed strategies independently of each other, such correlation is impossible.

Theorem 4.29 (page 105) states that player i's payoff in any equilibrium is at least his maxmin value. As we now show, this payoff is also at least the player's minmax value.

Theorem 5.42 *For every Nash equilibrium σ^* in a strategic-form game and every player i we have $u_i(\sigma^*) \geq \overline{v}_i$.*

Proof: The result holds since

$$u_i(s^*) = \max_{s_i \in S_i} u_i(s_i, s^*_{-i}) \geq \min_{s_{-i} \in S_{-i}} \max_{s_i \in S_i} u_i(s_i, s_{-i}) = \overline{v}_i. \tag{5.125}$$

$\square$

5.7 Imperfect information: the value of information

Recall that every extensive-form game is also a strategic-form game. In this section we study extensive-form games with information sets, and look into how their maxmin and minmax values in mixed strategies change when we add information for one of the players. Adding information to a player is expressed by splitting one or more of his information sets into subsets. Note that this gives the player pure strategies that were previously unavailable to him, while he does not lose any strategies that were available to him before he received the new information. The intuitive reason for this is that the player can always ignore the additional information he has received, and play the way he would have played before.

In this section only we denote the multilinear extension of player i's payoff function by u_i rather than U_i, which will denote an information set of player i.

Example 5.43 Consider Game A in Figure 5.23. In this game, every player has one information set. The set of pure strategies of Player I is $\{L, M, R\}$, and that of Player II is $\{l, r\}$. This game is equivalent to a strategic-form game, in which Player II, in choosing his action, does not know what action was chosen by Player I (Game A in Figure 5.24, where Player I is the row player and Player II is the column player).

Game B in Figure 5.23 is similar to Game A, except that we have split the information set of Player II into two information sets. In other words, Player II, in choosing his action, knows whether or not Player I has chosen L, and hence we have increased Player II's information.

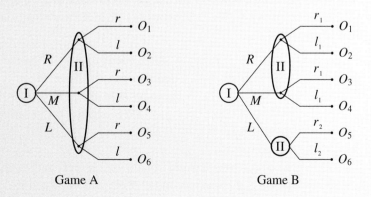

Game A   Game B

Figure 5.23 Adding information to Player II

With this additional information, the set of pure strategies of Player II is $\{l_1l_2, l_1r_2, r_1l_2, r_1r_2\}$, and the strategic description of this game is Game B in Figure 5.24.

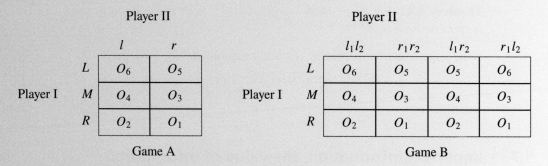

Figure 5.24 Splitting an information set: the games in strategic form

Note that Game B in Figure 5.24, restricted only to the strategies l_1l_2 and r_1r_2, is equivalent, from the perspective of its outcomes, to Game A. In other words, the strategies l_1l_2 and r_1r_2 are identical to the strategies l and r, respectively, in Game A. In summary, adding information to a player enlarges his set of pure strategies. ◀

The phenomenon that we just saw in Example 5.43 can be generalized to every game in extensive form: if we split an information set of player i into two information sets, then every strategy in the original game is equivalent to a strategy in the new game, in which the player takes the same action in each of the two information sets split from the original information set. If we identify these two strategies, in the original game and the new game, we see that as a result of splitting an information set of player i, his set of pure strategies in the new game includes his set of strategies in the original game. Since every addition of information to a player is equivalent to splitting one of his information sets into a finite number of subsets, we can conclude that adding information to a player leads to a game with "more" pure strategies available to that player.

What effect does adding information to a player have on the outcome of a game? Does the additional information lead to a better or worse outcome for him? As we will now show, in a two-player zero-sum game, adding information to a player can never be to his detriment, and may well be to his advantage. In contrast, in a game that is not zero-sum, adding information to a player may sometimes be to his advantage, and sometimes to his detriment.

Theorem 5.44 *Let* Γ *be an extensive-form game, and let* Γ' *be the game derived from* Γ *by splitting several of player i's information sets. Then the maxmin value in mixed strategies of player i in the game* Γ' *is greater than or equal to his maxmin value in mixed strategies in* Γ, *and his minmax value in mixed strategies in* Γ' *is greater than or equal to his minmax value in mixed strategies in* Γ.

Proof: We will first prove the theorem's claim with respect to the maxmin value in mixed strategies. Denote by $\underline{v}_i$ the maxmin value of player i in Γ, and by $\underline{v}'_i$ the maxmin value of Γ'. For every player j, let S_j be the set of j's pure strategies in Γ, and S'_j be his set of pure strategies in Γ'. Denote by Σ_j player j's set of mixed strategies in Γ, and by Σ'_j his set of mixed strategies in Γ'. In going from Γ to Γ', the set of information sets of player j, for $j \neq i$, remains unchanged, and the set of pure strategies of each of these players also remains unchanged: $S_j = S'_j$, and therefore $\Sigma_j = \Sigma'_j$. In contrast, in going from Γ to Γ', some of player i's information sets have been split. In particular, every information set U'_i of player i in Γ' is contained in a single information set U_i of player i in Γ. It follows that every pure strategy in S_i can be regarded as a pure strategy in S'_i. Indeed, let $s_i \in S_i$ be a strategy of player i in Γ. Define a strategy $s'_i \in S'_i$ of player i in Γ' as follows: in each information set U'_i, the strategy s'_i chooses the action that s_i chooses in the unique information set U_i in Γ that contains U'_i. The strategies s_i and s'_i are effectively identical.

Consequently, every mixed strategy σ_i of player i in Γ can be regarded as a mixed strategy of player i in Γ': for every mixed strategy σ_i of player i in Γ there exists a mixed strategy σ'_i of player i in Γ' satisfying

$$u_i(\sigma_i, \sigma_{-i}) = u_i(\sigma'_i, \sigma_{-i}), \quad \forall \sigma_{-i} \in \Sigma_{-i}. \tag{5.126}$$

Therefore,

$$\underline{v}_i = \max_{\sigma_i \in \Sigma_i} \min_{\sigma_{-i} \in \Sigma_{-i}} u_i(\sigma_i, \sigma_{-i}) \leq \max_{\sigma_i \in \Sigma'_i} \min_{\sigma_{-i} \in \Sigma_{-i}} u_i(\sigma_i, \sigma_{-i}) = \underline{v}'_i. \tag{5.127}$$

In words, player i's maxmin value in mixed strategies, as a result of having additional information, is no less than his maxmin value in mixed strategies without this information. The proof for the analogous claim for the minmax value follows similarly by the same argument. Denote by $\overline{v}_i$ player i's minmax value in Γ, and by $\overline{v}'_i$ his minmax value in Γ'. Since we can regard every mixed strategy of player i in Γ as a mixed strategy in Γ', then, for all $\sigma_{-i} \in \Sigma_{-i}$,

$$\max_{\sigma_i \in \Sigma_i} U_i(\sigma_i, \sigma_{-i}) \leq \max_{\sigma_i \in \Sigma'_i} U_i(\sigma_i, \sigma_{-i}). \tag{5.128}$$

Therefore, when we take the minimum over all mixed-strategy vectors of the players in $N \setminus \{i\}$ we get

$$\overline{v}_i = \min_{\sigma_{-i} \in \Sigma_{-i}} \max_{\sigma_i \in \Sigma_i} U_i(\sigma_i, \sigma_{-i}) \leq \min_{\sigma_{-i} \in \Sigma_{-i}} \max_{\sigma_i \in \Sigma'_i} U_i(\sigma_i, \sigma_{-i}) = \overline{v}'_i. \tag{5.129}$$

Thus, the minmax value in mixed strategies of player i does not decrease when additional information is received. □

For two-player zero-sum games for which a value in mixed strategies always exists, we have the following corollary (see Exercise 5.66):

Theorem 5.45 *Let Γ be a two-player zero-sum game in extensive form and let Γ' be the game derived from Γ by splitting several information sets of Player I. Then the value of the game Γ' in mixed strategies is greater than or equal to the value of Γ in mixed strategies.*

The theorem is depicted in the following example.

Example 5.46 Consider the two-player zero-sum game comprised of the following two stages. In the first stage, one of the two matrices in Figure 5.25 is chosen by a coin toss (each of the matrices is chosen with probability $\frac{1}{2}$). The players are not informed which matrix has been chosen. In stage two, the two players play the game whose payoffs are given by the chosen matrix (the payoffs represent payments made by Player II to Player I).

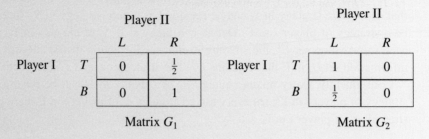

Figure 5.25 The matrices in Example 5.46

Figure 5.26 shows the game in extensive form and in strategic form.

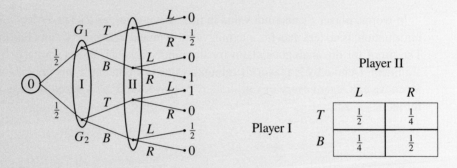

Figure 5.26 The game in Example 5.46, shown in extensive form and in strategic form

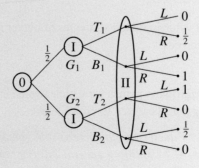

Figure 5.27 The game derived from the game in Figure 5.26 if Player I knows which matrix is chosen

Since the two players do not know which matrix has been chosen, each player has two pure strategies. Since the probability that each of the payoff matrices G_1 and G_2 will be chosen is $\frac{1}{2}$, the payoff matrix in this figure is the average of the payoff matrices G_1 and G_2: the payoff corresponding to each pure strategy vector is the average of the payoffs in the entries corresponding to that strategy vector in the two payoff matrices G_1 and G_2 (see page 79).

The value in mixed strategies of the game in Figure 5.26 is $\frac{3}{8}$. Player I's optimal strategy is $[\frac{1}{2}(T), \frac{1}{2}(B)]$, and Player II's optimal strategy is $[\frac{1}{2}(L), \frac{1}{2}(R)]$.

Consider now what happens if Player I is informed which matrix was chosen, but Player II remains ignorant of the choice. In that case, in the extensive form of the game, Player I's information set in Figure 5.26 splits into two information sets, yielding the extensive-form game shown in Figure 5.27.

In this game, Player I has four pure strategies $(T_1 T_2, T_1 B_2, B_1 T_2, B_1 B_2)$, while Player II has two strategies (L and R). The corresponding strategic-form game appears in Figure 5.28.

Player II

	L	R
$T_1 T_2$	$\frac{1}{2}$	$\frac{1}{4}$
$T_1 B_2$	$\frac{1}{4}$	$\frac{1}{4}$
$B_1 T_2$	$\frac{1}{2}$	$\frac{1}{2}$
$B_1 B_2$	$\frac{1}{4}$	$\frac{1}{2}$

Player I (label at left of table)

Figure 5.28 The game in Figure 5.27 in strategic form

The value in mixed strategies of this game is $\frac{1}{2}$, and $B_1 T_2$ is Player I's optimal strategy. Since $\frac{1}{2} > \frac{3}{8}$, the added information is advantageous to Player I, in accordance with Theorem 5.45. ◄

In games that are not zero-sum, however, the situation is completely different. In the following example, Player I receives additional information, but this leads him to lose at the equilibrium point.

Example 5.47 Detrimental addition of information Consider Game A in Figure 5.29.

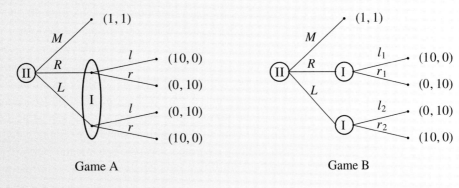

Game A   Game B

Figure 5.29 The games in Example 5.47

The only equilibrium point of this game is the following pair of mixed strategies:

- Player I plays $[\frac{1}{2}(l), \frac{1}{2}(r)]$.
- Player II plays $[\frac{1}{2}(L), \frac{1}{2}(R), 0(M)]$.

To see this, note that strategy M is strictly dominated by strategy $[\frac{1}{2}(L), \frac{1}{2}(R), 0(M)]$, and it follows from Theorem 4.35 (page 108) that it may be eliminated. After the elimination of this strategy, the resulting game is equivalent to Matching Pennies (Example 3.20 on page 52), whose sole equilibrium point is the mixed strategy under which both players choose each of their pure strategies with probability $\frac{1}{2}$ (verify that this is true). The equilibrium payoff is therefore $(5, 5)$. When Player I receives additional information and can distinguish between the two vertices (see Game B in Figure 5.29), an equilibrium in the game is:

- Player I plays the pure strategy (l_1, r_2).
- Player II plays $[0(L), 0(R), 1(M)]$.

To see this, note that the pure strategy (l_1, r_2) of Player I is his best reply to Player II's strategy, and strategy $[0(L), 0(R), 1(M)]$ is Player II's best reply to (l_1, r_2). The equilibrium payoff is therefore $(1, 1)$. This is not the only equilibrium of this game; there are more equilibria, but they all yield an equilibrium payoff of $(1, 1)$ (Exercise 5.72). Adding information in this game is to Player I's detriment, because his payoff drops from 5 to 1. In this particular example, the additional information has also impacted Player II's payoff negatively, but this is not always the case (see Exercise 5.67).

The reason that additional information is to Player I's detriment is that he cannot ignore the new information: if the play of the game reaches one of the vertices that Player I controls, it is to his advantage to exploit the information he has, since ignoring it lowers his expected payoff. As a rational player, he must make use of the information. Player II knows this, and adapts his strategy to this new situation. It would be to Player I's advantage to commit to not using his additional information, but without such a binding commitment, Player II may not believe any "promise" that Player I makes to disregard his information. Careful consideration of this example brings out the source of this phenomenon: it is not the addition of information, *per se*, that is the cause of Player I's loss, but the fact that Player II knows that Player I has additional information, which leads Player II to change his behavior. ◀

A question naturally arises from the material in this section: why does the addition of information always (weakly) help a player in two-player zero-sum games, while in games that are not zero-sum, it may be advantageous or detrimental? The answer lies in the fact that there is a distinction between the concepts of the maxmin value and the equilibrium in games that are not zero sum, while in two-player zero-sum games the two concepts coincide. Additional information to a player (weakly) increases his maxmin value in every game, whether or not it is a two-player zero-sum game (Theorem 5.44). In a two-player zero-sum game, the unique equilibrium payoff is the value of the game (which is also the maxmin value), which is why adding information to a player always (weakly) increases his payoff. If the game is not a two-player zero-sum game, equilibrium payoffs, which can rise or fall with the addition of information, need not equal a player's maxmin value. The statement "adding information can be detrimental" specifically relates to situations in which a player's equilibrium payoff, after he gains information, can fall.

But this is only relevant if we are expecting the outcome of a game to be an equilibrium, both before and after the addition of new information (we may perhaps expect this if the game has a unique equilibrium, or strictly dominant strategies, as in Exercise 5.68). In contrast, in situations in which we expect the players to play their maxmin strategies, adding information cannot be detrimental.

5.8   Rationalizability

In Section 4.4 we used two assumptions to develop the process of iterative elimination of dominated strategies: (a) a rational player will not choose a strictly dominated strategy, and (b) it is common knowledge that all players are rational, that is, all players are rational, all players know that all players are rational, all players know that all players know that all players are rational, and so on ad infinitum. In this section we use these assumptions to study more generally the predictions on the players' behavior that can be drawn from them. The resulting solution concept, which was introduced by Bernheim [1984] and Pearce [1984], is called *rationalizability*. We will restrict attention to strategic-form games $\Gamma = (N, (S_i)_{i \in N}, (u_i)_{i \in N})$, where for each player i the set S_i of pure strategies is finite.

Usually, a player in a strategic-form game faces uncertainty about the pure strategies that the other players will play. In this section we assume that the uncertainty of player i about the behavior of player j, $j \neq i$, can be presented as a probability distribution $\sigma_j \in \Delta(S_j)$; for each pure strategy $s_j \in S_j$, player i assigns probability $\sigma_j(s_j)$ that player j will choose the pure strategy s_j.

Definition 5.48 *Let* $i \in N$. *A belief of player i about the pure strategies of the other players is a vector* $\sigma_{-i} = (\sigma_j)_{j \neq i} \in \Sigma_{-i}$.

Though mathematically beliefs and mixed strategies are both probability distributions over the set of pure strategies, conceptually these two concepts differ: a mixed strategy of player j captures the way player j selects the pure strategy that he plays, while a belief of player i about player j captures the way player i perceives that player j will play.

Remark 5.49 *The belief of player i about the pure strategies of the other players is given by* $|N| - 1$ *probability distributions, one for each player. One could alternatively describe such a belief by a probability distribution on the product set* S_{-i}. *Such a belief indicates the probability that player i assigns to the event that the other players choose each vector of pure strategies* $s_{-i} \in S_{-i}$. *For example, in the three-player game presented in Example 5.41 (page 176), Player I may believe that with probability* $\frac{1}{3}$ *Players II and III will play the pure strategies* (L, W) *and with probability* $\frac{2}{3}$ *they will play the pure strategies* (R, E). *Such a distribution cannot be obtained by independent mixed strategies of Players II and III; the players must correlate their pure strategies to generate it. The fact that the belief is given by* $|N| - 1$ *probability distributions captures the assumption that the game is a noncooperative game: each player believes that the other players* *play independently and do not coordinate their play. In Exercise 5.79 we elaborate on the case where players believe that the other players may coordinate their pure strategies.*

If the belief of player i is given by the vector σ_{-i}, then his *subjective payoff* when playing the pure strategy s_i is $U_i(s_i, \sigma_{-i})$. We denote by $\mathrm{br}_i(\sigma_{-i})$ the set of pure strategies that are best replies to the belief σ_{-i}:

$$\mathrm{br}_i(\sigma_{-i}) := \mathrm{argmax}_{s_i \in S_i} U_i(s_i, \sigma_{-i}).$$

Suppose now that it is known that player i reached the conclusion that some pure strategies of the other players will not be played; that is, for each $j \neq i$ player i believes that the pure strategy chosen by player j will lie in some subset $D_j \subseteq S_j$. Based on this information and the fact that player i is rational, and without knowing the explicit belief of player i, we can conclude that any pure strategy chosen by player i will be a best reply to some belief in $\times_{j\neq i}\Delta(D_j)$. We denote this set by $\mathrm{br}_i(D_{-i})$, where $D_{-i} = \times_{j\neq i}D_j$:

$$\mathrm{br}_i(D_{-i}) := \cup_{\sigma_{-i} \in \times_{j\neq i}\Delta(D_j)}\mathrm{br}_i(\sigma_{-i}) \subseteq S_i. \tag{5.130}$$

Though the set $\mathrm{br}_i(D_{-i})$ is a union of infinitely many sets, it consists of only pure strategies, and hence it is finite.

Thus, if player i is rational, he will not play pure strategies that are outside the set $\mathrm{br}_i(D_{-i})$. If some solution concept predicts that each player i will select one of the pure strategies in the set D_i, and will not choose pure strategies in the complement of D_i, and if this fact is common knowledge among the players, then, because the players are rational, every player i will play only pure strategies in $\mathrm{br}_i(D_{-i})$. Consequently, we must have

$$D_i \subseteq \mathrm{br}_i(D_{-i}), \quad \forall i \in N. \tag{5.131}$$

Indeed, if there were a pure strategy $s_i \in D_i$ that is not in $\mathrm{br}_i(D_{-i})$, then player i would not play it, and therefore it would not be in the set D_i, which is the set of pure strategies predicted as possible outcomes by the solution concept.

Example 5.50 Let $\Gamma = (N, (S_i)_{i\in N}, (u_i)_{i\in N})$ be a strategic-form game with a pure-strategy Nash equilibrium s^*. For each player i, denote $D_i = \{s_i^*\}$. For each $i \in N$ the set $\times_{j\neq i}\Delta(D_j)$ consists of a single element, s_{-i}^*. Since s_i^* is a best reply to s_{-i}^* for each player i, Equation (5.131) is satisfied.   ◀

Theorem 5.51 *Let* $\Gamma = (N, (S_i)_{i\in N}, (u_i)_{i\in N})$ *be a strategic-form game where the sets of pure strategies of the players are finite. For every player $i \in N$ there exists a nonempty set of pure strategies $R_i \subseteq S_i$ such that $R_i = \mathrm{br}_i(R_{-i})$, where $R_{-i} = (R_j)_{j\neq i}$. Moreover, every collection of nonempty sets $(D_i)_{i\in N}$ that satisfies Equation (5.131) also satisfies $D_i \subseteq R_i$ for every $i \in N$.*

Proof: Define

$$D_i^0 := S_i, \quad \forall i \in N,$$

and iteratively define, for every $k \geq 0$,

$$D_i^{k+1} := \mathrm{br}_i(D_{-i}^k), \quad \forall i \in N,$$

where $D_{-i}^k := (D_j^k)_{j \neq i}$. We prove by induction that $(D_i^k)_{k \geq 0}$ is a weakly decreasing sequence of sets, that is, $D_i^{k+1} \subseteq D_i^k$ for every $k \geq 0$ and every $i \in N$. Indeed, for $k = 0$ we have by definition

$$D_i^1 \subseteq S_i = D_i^0, \quad \forall i \in N.$$

Assume now by induction that $D_j^{k+1} \subseteq D_j^k$ for every $j \in N$. Then the set $\times_{j \neq i} \Delta(D_j^{k+1})$ is a subset of $\times_{j \neq i} \Delta(D_j^k)$. By Equation (5.130), the set $\mathrm{br}_i(D_{-i}^{k+1})$ is a union of fewer sets than the set $\mathrm{br}_i(D_{-i}^k)$, and hence $D_i^{k+1} \subseteq D_i^k$.

Since the sequence $(D_i^k)_{k \geq 0}$ is weakly decreasing for every $i \in N$, and since the sets $(S_i)_{i \in N}$ are finite, it follows that there exists $k^* \in \mathbb{N}$ such that $D_i^{k^*+1} = D_i^{k^*}$ for every $i \in N$. Set $R_i := D_i^{k^*}$ for every $i \in N$ and $R_{-i} = (R_j)_{j \neq i}$. Then $R_i = \mathrm{br}_i(R_{-i})$, as we wanted to show.

Let now $(D_i)_{i \in N}$ be a collection of sets that satisfy Equation (5.131), and fix $i \in N$. To prove that $D_i \subseteq R_i$, we will prove by induction that $D_i \subseteq D_i^k$ for every $k \geq 0$. For $k = 0$ we have $D_i \subseteq S_i = D_i^0$. Assume by induction that for some $k \geq 0$ we have $D_j \subseteq D_j^k$ for every $j \in N$. As in the first part of the proof, this implies that $\mathrm{br}_i(D_{-i}) \subseteq \mathrm{br}_i(D_{-i}^k)$. From Equation (5.131) we obtain

$$D_i \subseteq \mathrm{br}_i(D_{-i}) \subseteq \mathrm{br}_i(D_{-i}^k) = D_i^{k+1},$$

as claimed. $\qquad\qquad\qquad\qquad\qquad\qquad\qquad\qquad\qquad\qquad\qquad\qquad\qquad\quad\square$

Definition 5.52 *In the notation of Theorem 5.51, every strategy profile $s \in \times_{i \in N} R_i$ is called a* rationalizable *pure-strategy profile, and the set R_i is called the set of* rationalizable *pure-strategies of player i, for every $i \in N$.*

The solution concept of rationalizability assigns to every strategic-form game Γ and every player i the set of pure strategies $R_i(\Gamma) \subseteq S_i$ of rationalizable pure strategies. A pure strategy that is not in $R_i(\Gamma)$ will not be played by a rational player i. Since it is common knowledge that all players are rational, the strategies not in $R_i(\Gamma)$ are not relevant in the analysis of the game. The last statement in Theorem 5.51 states that if there exists some other solution concept, say $D_i(\Gamma)$, that is derived from the assumption that it is common knowledge that all players are rational and possibly from additional assumptions, then all outcomes of the game predicted by this solution concept are rationalizable. In this sense, rationalizability is the weakest solution concept that is based on common knowledge of rationality.

As a corollary, we deduce that every pure-strategy profile that lies in the support of a mixed-strategy Nash equilibrium is rationalizable.

Corollary 5.53 *Let $\sigma^* = (\sigma_i^*)_{i \in N}$ be a mixed-strategy Nash equilibrium. Let $s = (s_i)_{i \in I}$ be a pure-strategy profile that is played under σ^* with positive probability: $\sigma_i^*(s_i) > 0$ for every $i \in N$. Then s is a rationalizable pure-strategy profile.*

The proof of the corollary is left for the reader (Exercise 5.76).

Given a collection of nonempty subsets of pure strategies $(D_i)_{i \in I}$ such that $D_i \subseteq S_i$ for every $i \in N$, we say that a pure strategy $s_i \in S_i$ is a *never-best reply for D_{-i}* if it is not in $\mathrm{br}_i(D_{-i})$.

The notion of a never-best reply and the constructive proof of Theorem 5.51 yield the following equivalent definition of rationalizable strategies:

Definition 5.54 *The set of rationalizable strategy profiles is the set of strategy profiles that survive the iterated elimination of never-best-reply strategies.*

This presentation of the concept of rationalizability calls for a comparison between rationalizability and the other process of iterated elimination that we encountered before (Section 4.5 on page 85), namely, the process of iterated elimination of strictly dominated strategies.

We first extend the notion of strict domination by pure strategies, defined in Section 4.5, to strict domination by mixed strategies.

Definition 5.55 *In a strategic-form game* $\Gamma = (N, (S_i)_{i \in N}, (u_i)_{i \in N})$, *a strategy* $s_i \in S_i$ *is strictly dominated if there exists a mixed strategy* $\sigma_i \in \Delta(S_i)$ *such that*

$$U_i(\sigma_i, s_{-i}) > U_i(s_i, s_{-i}), \quad \forall s_{-i} \in S_{-i}.$$

The following example shows that a pure strategy may be strictly dominated by a mixed strategy even though it is not dominated by any pure strategy.

Example 5.56   Consider the two-player game in Figure 5.30, where only the payoffs of Player II are provided.

Player II

		L	C	R
	T	0	4	1
Player I	B	4	0	1

Figure 5.30 Strict domination by a mixed strategy

The pure strategy R is not dominated by either L or C. The reader can verify that it is strictly dominated by the mixed strategy $[\frac{1}{2}(L), \frac{1}{2}(C)]$.   ◄

We first observe that a strictly dominated pure strategy is a never-best-reply strategy.

Lemma 5.57 *If* s_i *is a strictly dominated pure strategy, then* $s_i \notin \mathrm{br}_i(D_{-i})$, *for every collection of nonempty sets of pure strategies* $D_{-i} = (D_j)_{j \neq i}$.

The proof is left for the reader (Exercise 5.73). As a corollary of Lemma 5.57 we deduce the following result, whose proof is left for the reader (Exercise 5.74).

Lemma 5.58 *If the pure-strategy profile* $s \in S$ *is rationalizable, then it survives the process of iterated elimination of strictly dominated strategies.*

For two-player games, the converse of Lemma 5.57 also holds.

Theorem 5.59 *Let* $\Gamma = (\{I, II\}, S_I, S_{II}, u_I, u_{II})$ *be a two-player strategic-form game where the sets of pure strategies of the players are finite. If the strategy* $s_I \in S_I$ *is a never-best reply for* S_{II}, *then it is strictly dominated by a mixed strategy.*

Proof: Let $\hat{s}_I \in S_I$ be a never-best-reply pure strategy of Player I. Then for every mixed strategy $\sigma_{II} \in \Sigma_{II}$ there is a pure strategy $b(\sigma_{II}) \in S_I$ such that

$$U_I(b(\sigma_{II}), \sigma_{II}) > U_I(\hat{s}_I, \sigma_{II}). \tag{5.132}$$

Consider an auxiliary two-player zero-sum strategic-form game $\hat{\Gamma}$ in which the set of players is $\{I, II\}$, the sets of pure strategies are S_I and S_{II}, and the payoff function $\hat{U}$ is given by

$$\hat{u}(s_I, s_{II}) := u_I(s_I, s_{II}) - u_I(\hat{s}_I, s_{II}).$$

Let $\hat{\sigma}_I$ and $\hat{\sigma}_{II}$ be optimal strategies of the two players in the game $\hat{\Gamma}$. Then for every pure strategy s_{II} of Player II,

$$U_I(\hat{\sigma}_I, s_{II}) - U_I(\hat{s}_I, s_{II}) = \hat{U}(\hat{\sigma}_I, s_{II}), \tag{5.133}$$

$$\geq \hat{U}(\hat{\sigma}_I, \hat{\sigma}_{II}), \tag{5.134}$$

$$\geq \hat{U}(b(\hat{\sigma}_I), \hat{\sigma}_{II}), \tag{5.135}$$

$$= U_I(b(\hat{\sigma}_I), \hat{\sigma}_{II}) - U_I(\hat{s}_I, \hat{\sigma}_{II}), \tag{5.136}$$

$$> 0, \tag{5.137}$$

where Equations (5.133) and (5.136) hold by the definition of $\hat{u}$, Equation (5.134) holds since $\hat{\sigma}_{II}$ is an optimal strategy of Player II, Equation (5.135) holds since $\hat{\sigma}_I$ is an optimal strategy of Player I, and Equation (5.137) holds by Equation (5.132). We deduce that $U_I(\hat{\sigma}_I, s_{II}) > U_I(\hat{s}_I, s_{II})$. Since this holds for every $s_{II} \in S_{II}$, the pure strategy $\hat{s}_I$ is strictly dominated by the mixed strategy $\hat{\sigma}_I$. $\qquad \square$

The previous discussion yields the following result:

Corollary 5.60 *For two-player strategic-form games, the set of rationalizable strategies coincides with the set of pure-strategy profiles that survive iterated elimination of strictly dominated strategies.*

The conclusion of Corollary 5.60 is not valid for games with more than two players; see Exercise 5.78.

To summarize this section, we introduced the solution concept of rationalizable pure-strategy profiles. These are pure-strategy profiles that can be played in the game, under the assumption that it is common knowledge among the players that they are all rational. Unlike the concept of Nash equilibrium in pure strategies, which does not exist in all games, rationalizable pure-strategy profiles always exist. This concept is a generalization of the Nash equilibrium: every pure-strategy profile that is realized with positive probability when the players play a mixed-strategy Nash equilibrium is rationalizable (Corollary 5.53). We have also seen that this concept is a refinement of iterated elimination of strictly dominated strategies: every rationalizable pure-strategy profile survives the process of iterated elimination of strictly dominated strategies (Lemma 5.58). Which rationalizable pure-strategy profile will be the outcome of the game? The theory presented in this section does not enable us to answer the question. All we can say is that pure-strategy profiles that are *not* rationalizable are unlikely to be the outcome of the game.

5.9 Evolutionarily stable strategies

Darwin's Theory of Evolution is based on the principle of the survival of the fittest, according to which new generations of the world's flora and fauna bear mutations.[2] An individual who has undergone a mutation will pass it on to his descendants. Only those individuals most adapted to their environment succeed in the struggle for survival.

It follows from this principle that, in the context of the process of evolution, every organism acts as if it were a rational creature, by which we mean a creature whose behavior is directed towards one goal: to maximize the expected number of its reproducing descendants. We say that it acts "as if" it were rational in order to stress that the individual organism is not a strategically planning creature. If an organism's inherited properties are not adapted to the struggle for survival, however, it will simply not have descendants.

For example, suppose that the expected number of surviving offspring per individual in a given population is three in every generation. If a mutation raising the number of expected offspring to four occurs in only one individual, eventually there will be essentially no individuals in the population carrying genes yielding the expected number of three offspring, because the ratio of individuals carrying the gene for an expected number of four descendants to individuals carrying the gene for an expected number of three descendants will grow exponentially over the generations.

If we relate to an organism's number of offspring as a payoff, we have described a process that is propelled by the maximization of payoffs. Since the concept of equilibrium in a game is also predicated on the idea that only strategies that maximize expected payoffs (against the strategies used by the other players) will be chosen, we have a motivation for using ideas from game theory in order to explain evolutionary phenomena. Maynard Smith and Price [1973] showed that, in fact, it is possible to use the Nash equilibrium concept to shed new light on Darwin's theory. This section presents the basic ideas behind the application of game theory to the study of evolutionary biology. The interested reader can find descriptions of many phenomena in biology that are explicable using the theory developed in this section in Richard Dawkins's popular book, *The Selfish Gene* (Dawkins [1976]).

The next example, taken from Maynard Smith and Price [1973], introduces the main idea, and the general approach, used in this theory.

Example 5.61 Suppose that a particular animal can exhibit one of two possible behaviors: aggressive behavior or peaceful behavior. We will describe this by saying that there are two types of animals: hawks (who are aggressive), and doves (who are peaceful). The different types of behavior are expressed when an animal invades the territory of another animal of the same species. A hawk will aggressively repel the invader. A dove, in contrast, will yield to the aggressor and be driven out of its territory. If one of the two animals is a hawk and the other a dove, the outcome of this struggle is that the hawk ends up in the territory, while the dove is driven out, exposed to predators and other dangers.

---

2 A mutation is a change in a characteristic that an individual has that is brought on by a change in genetic material. In this section, we will use the term mutation to mean an individual in a population whose behavior has changed, and who passes on that change in behavior to his descendants.

If both animals are doves, one of them will end up leaving the territory. Suppose that each of them leaves the territory in that situation with a probability of $\frac{1}{2}$. If both animals are hawks, a fight ensues, during which both of them are injured, perhaps fatally, and at most one of them will remain in the territory and produce offspring. Figure 5.31 presents an example of a matrix describing the expected number of offspring of each type of animal in this situation.

Note that the game in Figure 5.31 is symmetric; that is, both players have the same set of strategies $S_1 = S_2$, and their payoff functions satisfy $u_1(s_1, s_2) = u_2(s_2, s_1)$ for each $s_1, s_2 \in S$. This is an example of a "single-species" population, i.e., a population comprised of only one species of animal, where each individual can exhibit one of several possible behaviors.

Player II

		L	C	R
Player I	T	0	4	1
	B	4	0	1

Figure 5.31 The expected number of offspring following an encounter between two individuals in the population

Our focus here is on the dynamic process that develops under conditions of many random encounters between individuals in the population, along with the appearance of random mutations. A mutation is an individual in the population characterized by a particular behavior: it may be of type dove, or type hawk. More generally, a mutation can be of type x ($0 \le x \le 1$); that is, the individual[3] will behave as a dove with probability x, and as a hawk with probability $1 - x$.

The expected number of offspring of an individual who randomly encounters another individual in the population depends on both its type and the type of the individual it has encountered; to be more precise, the expected number depends on the probability y that the encountered individual is a dove (or the probability $1 - y$ that the encountered individual is a hawk). This probability depends on the composition of the population, that is, on how many individuals there are of a given type in the population, and whether those types are "pure" doves or hawks, or mixed types x. Every population composition determines a unique real number y ($0 \le y \le 1$), which is the probability that a randomly chosen individual in the population will behave as a dove (in its next encounter).

Population

		Dove y	Hawk $1 - y$
Mutation	Dove	4, 4	2, 8
	Hawk	8, 2	1, 1

Figure 5.32 The Mutation–Population game

3 For convenience, we will use the same symbol x to stand both for the real number between 0 and 1 specifying the probability of being of type "dove," and for the lottery $[x(\text{dove}), (1 - x)(\text{hawk})]$.

Suppose now that a mutation, before it is born, can "decide" what type it will be (dove, hawk, or x between 0 and 1). This "decision" and the subsequent interactions the mutation will have with the population can be described by the matrix in Figure 5.32.

In this matrix, the columns and the rows represent behavioral types. If we treat the matrix as a game, the column player is the "population," which is implementing a fixed mixed strategy $[y(\text{Dove}), (1 - y)(\text{Hawk})]$; i.e., with probability y the column player will behave as a dove and with probability $1 - y$ he will behave as a hawk. The row player, who is the mutation, in contrast chooses its type.

The expected payoff of a mutation from a random encounter is $4y + 2(1 - y)$ if it is a dove, $8y + (1 - y)$ if it is a hawk, and $x(4y + 2(1 - y)) + (1 - x)(8y + (1 - y))$ if it is of type x. For example, if the population is comprised of 80% doves ($y = 0.8$) and 20% hawks, and a new mutation is called upon to choose its type when it is born, what "should" the mutation choose? If the mutation chooses to be born a dove ($x = 1$), its expected number of offspring is $0.8 \times 4 + 0.2 \times 2 = 3.6$, while if it chooses to be born a hawk ($x = 0$), its expected number of offspring is $0.8 \times 8 + 0.2 \times 1 = 6.6$. It is therefore to the mutation's advantage to be born a hawk. No mutation, of course, has the capacity to decide whether it will be a hawk or a dove, because these characteristics are either inherited, or the result of a random change in genetic composition. What happens in practice is that individuals who have the characteristics of a hawk will reproduce more than individuals who have the characteristics of a dove. Over the generations, the number of hawks will rise, and the ratio of doves to hawks will not be 80% : 20% (because the percentage of hawks will be increasing). A population in which the ratio of doves to hawks is 80% : 20% is therefore evolutionarily unstable. Similarly, if the population is comprised of 10% doves ($y = 0.1$) and 90% hawks, we have an evolutionarily unstable situation (because the percentage of doves will increase). It can be shown that only if the population is comprised of 20% doves and 80% hawks will the expected number of offspring of each type be equal. When $y^* = 0.2$

$$0.2 \times 4 + 0.8 \times 2 = 2.4 = 0.2 \times 8 + 0.8 \times 1. \tag{5.138}$$

We therefore have $u_1(x, y^*) = 2.4$ for all $x \in [0, 1]$. Note that $y^* = 0.2$ is the symmetric equilibrium of the game in Figure 5.32, even when the player represented by the "population" can choose any mixed strategy. In other words, $u_1(x, y^*) \leq u_1(y^*, y^*)$ for each x, and $u_2(y^*, x) \leq u_2(y^*, y^*)$ for each x (in fact, the expressions on both sides of the inequality sign in all these cases is 2.4). Can we conclude that when the distribution of the population corresponds to the symmetric Nash equilibrium of the associated game, the population will be evolutionarily stable? The following example shows that to attain evolutionary stability, we need to impose a stronger condition that takes into account encounters between two mutations.   ◀

Example 5.62   Consider the situation shown in Figure 5.33, in which the payoffs in each encounter are different from the ones above.

Population

		Dove y	Hawk $1 - y$
Mutation	Dove	4, 4	2, 2
	Hawk	2, 2	2, 2

Figure 5.33 The payoff matrix in a symmetric game

This game has two Nash equilibria, (Dove, Dove) and (Hawk, Hawk). The former corresponds to a population comprised solely of doves, and the latter to a population comprised solely of hawks. When the population is entirely doves ($y = 1$), the expected number of offspring of type dove is 4, and the expected number of offspring of type hawk is 2, and therefore hawk mutations disappear over the generations, and the dove population remains stable. When the population is entirely hawks ($y = 0$), the expected number of offspring, of either type, is 2. But in this case, as long as the percentage of doves born is greater than 0, it is to a mutation's advantage to be born a dove. This is because the expected number of offspring of a mutation that is born a hawk is 2, but the expected number of offspring of a mutation that is born a dove is $2(1 - \varepsilon) + 4\varepsilon = 2 + 2\varepsilon$, where ε is the percentage of doves in the population (including mutations). In other words, when there are random changes in the composition of the population, it is to a mutation's advantage to be born a dove, because its expected number of offspring will be slightly higher than the expected number of offspring of a hawk. After a large number of generations have passed, the doves will form a majority of the population. This shows that a population comprised solely of hawks is not evolutionarily stable.

What happens if the population is comprised of doves, but many mutations occur, and the percentage of hawks in the population becomes ε? By a calculation similar to the one above, the expected number of offspring of a hawk is 2, while the expected number of offspring of a dove is $4 - 2\varepsilon$. As long as $\varepsilon < 1$, the expected number of offspring of a dove will be greater than that of a hawk, and hence the percentage of hawks in the population will decrease. This shows that a population comprised entirely of doves is evolutionarily stable.

If the population is comprised solely of hawks, where can a dove mutation come from? Such a mutation can arise randomly, as the result of a genetic change that occurs in an individual in the population. In general, even when a particular type is entirely absent from a population, in order to check whether the population is evolutionarily stable it is necessary to check what would happen if the absent type were to appear "ab initio." ◀

We will limit our focus in this section to two-player symmetric games. We will also assume that payoffs are nonnegative, since the payoffs in these games represent the expected number of offspring, which cannot be a negative number. Examples 5.61 and 5.62 lead to the following definition of evolutionarily stable strategy.

Definition 5.63 *A mixed strategy x^* in a two-player symmetric game is an* evolutionarily stable strategy (ESS) *if for every mixed strategy x that differs from x^* there exists $\varepsilon_0 = \varepsilon_0(x) > 0$ such that, for all $\varepsilon \in (0, \varepsilon_0)$,*

$$(1 - \varepsilon)u_1(x, x^*) + \varepsilon u_1(x, x) < (1 - \varepsilon)u_1(x^*, x^*) + \varepsilon u_1(x^*, x). \tag{5.139}$$

The biological interpretation of this definition is as follows. Since mutations occur in nature on a regular basis, we are dealing with populations mostly composed of "normal" individuals, with a minority of mutations. We will interpret x^* as the distribution of types among the normal individuals. Consider a mutation making use of strategy x, and assume that the proportion of this mutation in the population is ε. Every individual of type x will encounter a normal individual of type x^* with probability $1 - \varepsilon$, receiving in that case the payoff $u_1(x, x^*)$, and will encounter a mutation of type x with probability ε, receiving in that case the payoff $u_1(x, x)$. Equation (5.139) therefore says that in a population in which the proportion of mutations is ε, the expected payoff of a mutation (the left-hand side of the equal sign in Equation (5.139)) is smaller than the expected payoff of a normal individual (the right-hand side of the equal sign in Equation (5.139)), and hence the proportion of mutations will decrease and eventually disappear over time, with the composition of the population returning to being mostly x^*. An "evolutionarily stable equilibrium" is therefore a mixed strategy of the column player that corresponds to a population that is immune to being overtaken by mutations.

In Example 5.62, Equation (5.139) holds for the dove strategy ($x^* = 1$) for every $\varepsilon < 1$ and it is therefore an evolutionarily stable strategy. In contrast, Equation (5.139) does not hold for the hawk strategy ($x^* = 0$), and the hawk strategy is therefore not evolutionarily stable. As we saw in that example, for each $x \neq 0$ (where x denotes the proportion of doves in the population),

$$(1 - \varepsilon)u_1(x, x^*) + \varepsilon u_1(x, x) = 2 + 2\varepsilon x^2 > 2 = (1 - \varepsilon)u_1(x^*, x^*) + \varepsilon u_1(x^*, x).$$

By continuity, Equation (5.139) holds as a weak inequality for $\varepsilon = 0$. From this we deduce that every evolutionarily stable strategy defines a symmetric Nash equilibrium in the game. In particular, the concept of an evolutionarily stable equilibrium constitutes a refinement of the concept of Nash equilibrium.

Theorem 5.64 *If x^* is an evolutionarily stable strategy in a two-player symmetric game, then (x^*, x^*) is a symmetric Nash equilibrium in the game.*

As Example 5.62 shows, the opposite direction does not hold: if (x^*, x^*) is a symmetric Nash equilibrium, x^* is not necessarily an evolutionarily stable strategy. In this example, the strategy vector (Hawk, Hawk) is a symmetric Nash equilibrium, but the Hawk strategy is not an evolutionarily stable strategy.

The next theorem characterizes evolutionarily stable strategies.

Theorem 5.65 *A strategy x^* is evolutionarily stable if and only if for each $x \neq x^*$ only one of the following two conditions obtains:*

$$u_1(x, x^*) < u_1(x^*, x^*), \tag{5.140}$$

or

$$u_1(x, x^*) = u_1(x^*, x^*) \quad and \quad u_1(x, x) < u_1(x^*, x). \tag{5.141}$$

The first condition states that if a mutation deviates from x^*, it will lose in its encounters with the normal population. The second condition says that if the payoff a mutation receives from encountering a normal individual is equal to that received by a normal individual encountering a normal individual, that mutation will receive a smaller payoff when it encounters the same mutation that a normal individual would in encountering the mutation. In both cases the population of normal individuals will increase faster than the population of mutations.

Proof: We will first prove that if x^* is an evolutionarily stable strategy then for each $x \neq x^*$ one of the conditions (5.140) or (5.141) holds. From Theorem 5.64, (x^*, x^*) is a Nash equilibrium, and therefore $u_1(x, x^*) \leq u_1(x^*, x^*)$ for each $x \neq x^*$. If for a particular x neither of the conditions (5.140) or (5.141) holds, then $u_1(x, x^*) = u_1(x^*, x^*)$ and $u_1(x, x) \geq u_1(x^*, x)$, but then Equation (5.139) does not hold for this x for any $\varepsilon > 0$, contradicting the fact that x^* is an evolutionarily stable strategy. It follows that for each x at least one of the two conditions (5.140) or (5.141) obtains.

Suppose next that for any mixed strategy $x \neq x^*$, at least one of the two conditions (5.140) or (5.141) obtains. We will prove that x^* is an evolutionarily stable strategy. If condition (5.140) obtains, then Equation (5.139) obtains for all $\varepsilon < \frac{u_1(x^*,x^*)-u_1(x,x^*)}{4M}$, where M is the upper bound of the payoffs: $M = \max_{s_1 \in S_1} \max_{s_2 \in S_2} u_1(s_1, s_2)$ (verify!). If condition (5.141) obtains, then Equation (5.139) obtains for all $\varepsilon \in (0, 1]$. It follows that Equation (5.139) obtains in both cases, and therefore x^* is an evolutionarily stable strategy. □

If condition (5.140) obtains, then for each $x \neq x^*$, the equilibrium (x^*, x^*) is called a *strict equilibrium*. The next corollary follows from Theorem 5.65.

Corollary 5.66 *In a symmetric game, if (x^*, x^*) is a strict symmetric equilibrium then x^* is an evolutionarily stable equilibrium.*

Indeed, if (x^*, x^*) is a strict symmetric equilibrium, then condition (5.140) holds for every $x \neq x^*$. Theorem 5.65 and Corollary 5.66 yield a method for finding evolutionarily stable strategies: find all symmetric equilibria in the game, and for each one of them, determine whether or not it is a strict equilibrium. Every strict symmetric equilibrium defines an evolutionarily stable strategy. For every Nash equilibrium that is not strict, check whether condition (5.141) obtains for each x different from x^* for which condition (5.140) does not obtain (hence necessarily $u_1(x, x^*) = u_1(x^*, x^*)$).

Example 5.67 (*Continued*) Recall that the payoff function in this example is as shown in Figure 5.34.

Population

		Dove	Hawk
	Dove	4, 4	2, 8
Mutation	Hawk	8, 2	1, 1

Figure 5.34 The expected number of offspring from encounters between two individuals in Example 5.61

The symmetric mixed equilibrium is $([\frac{1}{5}(\text{Dove}), \frac{4}{5}(\text{Hawk})], [\frac{1}{5}(\text{Dove}), \frac{4}{5}(\text{Hawk})])$. The proportion of doves at equilibrium is $x^* = \frac{1}{5}$. Denote by x the proportion of doves in a mutation. Since the equilibrium is completely mixed, each of the two pure strategies yields the same expected payoff, and therefore $u_1(x, x^*) = u_1(x^*, x^*)$ for all $x \neq x^*$. To check whether $[\frac{1}{5}(\text{Dove}), \frac{4}{5}(\text{Hawk})]$ is an evolutionarily stable strategy, we need to check whether condition (5.141) obtains; that is, we need to check whether $u_1(x, x) < u_1(x^*, x)$ for every $x \neq x^*$.

This inequality can be written as

$$4x^2 + 2x(1-x) + 8(1-x)x + (1-x)^2 < \tfrac{1}{5}4x + \tfrac{1}{5}2(1-x) + \tfrac{4}{5}8x + \tfrac{4}{5}(1-x),$$

which can be simplified to

$$(5x-1)^2 > 0, \tag{5.142}$$

and this inequality obtains for each x different from $\frac{1}{5}$. We have thus proved that $[\frac{1}{5}(\text{Dove}), \frac{4}{5}(\text{Hawk})]$ is an evolutionarily stable strategy.

This game has two additional asymmetric Nash equilibria: (Dove, Hawk) and (Hawk, Dove). These equilibria do not contribute to the search for evolutionarily stable equilibria, since Theorem 5.64 relates evolutionarily stable equilibria solely to symmetric equilibria. ◀

Example 5.68 Consider another version of the Hawk–Dove game, in which the payoffs are as shown in Figure 5.35. This game has three symmetric equilibria: two pure equilibria, (Dove, Dove), (Hawk, Hawk), and one mixed, $([\frac{1}{2}(\text{Dove}), \frac{1}{2}(\text{Hawk})], [\frac{1}{2}(\text{Dove}), \frac{1}{2}(\text{Hawk})])$.

The pure equilibria (Dove, Dove) and (Hawk, Hawk) are strict equilibria, and hence the two pure strategies Dove and Hawk are evolutionarily stable strategies (Corollary 5.66) (see Figure 5.35).

		Population	
		Dove	Hawk
Mutation	Dove	4, 4	1, 3
	Hawk	3, 1	2, 2

Figure 5.35 The expected number of offspring in encounters between two individuals in Example 5.68

The strategy $x^* = [\frac{1}{2}(\text{Dove}), \frac{1}{2}(\text{Hawk})]$ is not evolutionarily stable. To see this, denote $x = [1(\text{Dove}), 0(\text{Hawk})]$. Then $u_1(x^*, x^*) = 2\frac{1}{2} = u_1(x, x^*)$, and $u_1(x, x) = 4 > 2\frac{1}{2} = u_1(x^*, x)$. From Theorem 5.65 it follows that the strategy $[\frac{1}{2}(\text{Dove}), \frac{1}{2}(\text{Hawk})]$ is not evolutionarily stable.

We can conclude from this that the population would be stable against mutations if the population were comprised entirely of doves or entirely of hawks. Any other composition of the population would not be stable against mutations. In addition, if the percentage of doves is greater than 50%, doves will reproduce faster than hawks and take over the population. On the other hand, if the percentage of doves is less than 50%, doves will reproduce more slowly than hawks, and eventually disappear from the population. If the percentage of doves is exactly 50%, as a result of mutations or random changes in the population stemming from variability in the number of offspring, the percentage of doves will differ from 50% in one of the subsequent generations, and then one of the two types will take over the population.

Although in this example a population composed entirely of doves reproduces at twice the rate of a population composed entirely of hawks, both populations are evolutionarily stable. ◀

Since Nash's Theorem (Theorem 5.10, page 150) guarantees the existence of a Nash equilibrium, an interesting question arises: does an evolutionarily stable strategy always exist? The answer is negative. It may well happen that an evolutionary process has no evolutionarily stable strategies. The next example, which is similar to Rock, Paper, Scissors, is taken from Maynard Smith [1982].

Example 5.69 Consider the symmetric game in which each player has the three pure strategies appearing in Figure 5.36.

This game has only one Nash equilibrium (Exercise 5.82), which is symmetric, in which the players play the mixed strategy:

$$x^* = \left[\frac{1}{3}(\text{Rock}), \frac{1}{3}(\text{Paper}), \frac{1}{3}(\text{Scissors})\right]. \tag{5.143}$$

Player II

		Rock	Paper	Scissors
	Rock	$\frac{2}{3}, \frac{2}{3}$	0, 1	1, 0
Player I	Paper	1, 0	$\frac{2}{3}, \frac{2}{3}$	0, 1
	Scissors	0, 1	1, 0	$\frac{2}{3}, \frac{2}{3}$

Figure 5.36 A game without an evolutionarily stable strategy

The corresponding equilibrium payoff is $u_1(x^*, x^*) = \frac{5}{9}$. We want to show that there is no evolutionarily stable strategy in this game. Since every evolutionarily stable strategy defines a symmetric Nash equilibrium, to ascertain that there is no evolutionarily stable strategy it suffices to check that the strategy x^* is not an evolutionarily stable strategy. The strategy x^* is completely mixed, and hence it leads to an identical payoff against any pure strategy: $u_1(x, x^*) = u_1(x^*, x^*)$ for all $x \neq x^*$.

Consider a mutation $x = [1(\text{Rock}), 0(\text{Paper}), 0(\text{Scissors})]$; condition (5.141) does not obtain for this mutation. To see this, note that $u_1(x, x) = \frac{2}{3}$, while $u_1(x^*, x) = \frac{2}{9} + \frac{1}{3} = \frac{5}{9}$, and hence $u_1(x, x) > u_1(x^*, x)$.

It is interesting to note that a biological system in which the number of offspring is given by the table in Figure 5.36 and the initial distribution of the population is $\left[\frac{1}{3}(\text{Rock}), \frac{1}{3}(\text{Paper}), \frac{1}{3}(\text{Scissors})\right]$ will never attain population stability, and instead will endlessly cycle through population configurations (see Hofbauer and Sigmund [2003] or Zeeman [1980]). If, for example, through mutation the proportion of rocks in the population were to increase slightly, their relative numbers would keep rising, up to a certain point. At that point, the proportion of papers would rise, until that process too stopped, with the proportion of scissors then rising. But at a certain point the rise in the relative numbers of scissors would stop, with rocks then increasing, and the cycle would repeat endlessly. Analyzing the evolution of such systems is accomplished using tools from the theory of dynamic processes. The interested reader is directed to Hofbauer and Sigmund [2003]. ◀

5.10 The dependence of Nash equilibria on the payoffs of the game

So far we have studied Nash equilibria and their properties in a specific game. In this section we address the question of how a change in the payoffs of the game affects the set of its equilibria. Why is this issue important? One answer is that the payoffs of a game are typically not precisely known and the numbers that we plug in as payoffs are often an estimate or a guess or an approximation of the real payoffs. Therefore a natural question is how robust are our results to these uncertainties or inaccuracies.

The way we shall study this problem is by looking at a family of games, all with the same set of players and the same set of pure strategies, that differ in their payoff functions. The main concept in this study is the *equilibrium manifold*, which is the graph of the correspondence assigning to each vector of payoff functions the set of Nash equilibria of the game with these payoff functions.

Let $N = \{1, 2, \ldots, n\}$ be a set of players and for each player $i \in N$, and let S_i be the set of player i's pure strategies. In this section we assume that all the sets $(S_i)_{i \in N}$ are finite. The set $S = S_1 \times S_2 \times \cdots \times S_n$ is the set of (pure) strategy vectors. The pair (N, S), which we will refer to as the *game form*, will be fixed in our discussion, and we shall only change the payoff functions of the players.

The payoff function of player i is a function $u_i : S \to \mathbb{R}$, which can be viewed as a vector $u_i \in \mathbb{R}^S$. Denote by $\mathcal{G}_i(N, S) := \mathbb{R}^S$ the set of all possible payoff functions of player i. To define a game we have to add to the game form the payoff functions $u = (u_i)_{i \in N}$, one for each player. Therefore, a game is given by n vectors in $\mathbb{R}^S$, or, equivalently, by a vector in $\mathbb{R}^{N \times S}$.

Definition 5.69 *The space of games over the game form* (N, S) *is the set* $\mathcal{G}(N, S) :=$ $\times_{i \in N} \mathcal{G}_i(N, S) = \mathbb{R}^{N \times S}$.

Denote by $m_i := |S_i|$ the number of pure strategies of player i, by $S_{-i} := \times_{j \neq i} S_j$ the set of strategy vectors of all players except player i, by $m_{-i} := |S_{-i}| = \prod_{j \neq i} m_j$ the number of vectors of pure strategies of all players except player i, and by $m := \sum_{i \in N} m_i$ the number of pure strategies of all players in the game. Recall that $\Sigma_i = \Delta(S_i) \subseteq \mathbb{R}^{m_i}$ is the set of mixed strategies of player i, and $\Sigma = \times_{i \in N} \Sigma_i \subseteq \mathbb{R}^m$ is the set of all vectors of mixed strategies.

Definition 5.70 *The* equilibrium manifold *over the game form* (N, S) *is the set*

$$E := \{(u, \sigma) \in \mathcal{G}(N, S) \times \Sigma : \sigma \text{ is a Nash equilibrium of the game } (N, (S_i)_{i \in N}, u)\}.$$

The equilibrium manifold is a subset of a Euclidian space of dimension $n \prod_{i \in N} m_i + \sum_{i \in N} m_i$. By Exercise 5.86, the set E is a closed set.

Let X and Y be two sets in a Euclidian space. A function $\varphi : X \to Y$ is called a *homeomorphism* if it is one-to-one, onto, continuous, and its inverse $\varphi^{-1} : Y \to X$ is also continuous. It follows from this definition that if φ is a homeomorphism from X to Y, then its inverse φ^{-1} is a homeomorphism from Y to X. Two sets X and Y are said to be *homeomorphic* if there is a homeomorphism from X to Y.

Homeomorphisms preserve many topological properties, and two sets that are homeomorphic are viewed as "topologically similar." Roughly, two sets are homeomorphic if we can obtain one by "bending" and "stretching" the other. Thus, a d-dimensional open ball is homeomorphic to a d-dimensional open cube and to $\mathbb{R}^d$, but not to a d-dimensional closed ball or to $\mathbb{R}^d \backslash \{\vec{0}\}$.

The following theorem is the main result of this section, and it states that the equilibrium manifold is homeomorphic to the space of games, which is of dimension $n \prod_{i \in N} m_i$. In other words, the equilibrium manifold "looks like" the Euclidian space $\mathbb{R}^{n \prod_{i \in N} m_i}$.

Theorem 5.71 *(Kohlberg and Mertens [1986]) Fix a game form* (N, S). *The equilibrium manifold* E *and the space of games* $\mathcal{G}(N, S)$ *are homeomorphic.*

Proof: Step 1: A convenient representation of the space of games.

Since the game form (N, S) is fixed, the game is given by the players' payoff functions. We now introduce an alternative representation of a game over the game form (N, S). First, for each player $i \in N$ we define two sets, $\widetilde{\mathcal{G}}_i(N, S)$ and $\overline{\mathcal{G}}_i(S_i)$. Then we define

$$\tilde{\mathcal{G}}_i(N, S) := \left\{ \tilde{u}_i \in \mathbb{R}^S : \sum_{s_{-i} \in S_{-i}} \tilde{u}_i(s_i, s_{-i}) = 0 \right\}. \tag{5.144}$$

This is the set of payoff functions in which, for each pure strategy s_i of player i, the sum of his payoff in all cells in the payoff matrix corresponding to the pure strategy s_i is 0 (and therefore the average of the payoff in these cells is also 0). Then we define $\overline{\mathcal{G}}_i(S_i) := \mathbb{R}^{S_i}$.

The following claim states that the space of payoff functions of player i is homeomorphic to $\tilde{\mathcal{G}}_i(N, S) \times \overline{\mathcal{G}}_i(S_i)$.

Claim 5.72 *Fix a game form (N, S) and a player $i \in N$. The sets $\mathcal{G}_i(N, S)$ and $\tilde{\mathcal{G}}_i(N, S) \times \overline{\mathcal{G}}_i(S_i)$ are homeomorphic.*

The intuition for this result is the following: every vector $x \in \mathbb{R}^m$ is uniquely characterized by its average $\overline{x}$ and the vector $\tilde{x}$ that is given by the vector x after subtracting the average from all its entries. The homeomorphism we construct between $\mathcal{G}_i(N, S)$ and $\tilde{\mathcal{G}}_i(N, S) \times \overline{\mathcal{G}}_i(S_i)$ is the application of this operation "row by row"; that is, we apply this operation to each vector $(u_i(s_i, s_{-i}))_{s_{-i} \in S_{-i}}$ separately.

Proof of claim 5.72: Let $u_i \in \mathcal{G}_i(N, S)$ be a payoff function of player i. For every strategy $s_i \in S_i$ denote

$$\overline{u}_i(s_i) := \frac{1}{m_{-i}} \sum_{s_{-i} \in S_{-i}} u_i(s_i, s_{-i}). \tag{5.145}$$

This is the payoff to player i when player i plays s_i and every other player $j \neq i$ plays his uniform mixed strategy, i.e., the strategy assigning equal probability to all his pure strategies. The vector $\overline{u}_i = (\overline{u}_i(s_i))_{s_i \in S_i}$ is in $\overline{\mathcal{G}}_i(S_i)$. For every $i \in N$ define a payoff function $\tilde{u}_i \in \mathcal{G}_i(N, S)$ as follows:

$$\tilde{u}_i(s_i, s_{-i}) := u_i(s_i, s_{-i}) - \overline{u}_i(s_i), \quad \forall s_i \in S_i, \forall s_{-i} \in S_{-i}. \tag{5.146}$$

We note that for every $s_i \in S_i$ we have

$$\sum_{s_{-i} \in S_{-i}} \tilde{u}_i(s_i, s_{-i}) = \sum_{s_{-i} \in S_{-i}} u_i(s_i, s_{-i}) - m_{-i}\overline{u}_i(s_i) = 0, \tag{5.147}$$

and therefore $\tilde{u}_i = (\tilde{u}_i(s_i, s_{-i}))_{(s_i, s_{-i}) \in S} \in \tilde{\mathcal{G}}_i(N, S)$. Equations (5.145) and (5.146) define a continuous function $\eta : \mathcal{G}_i(N, S) \to \tilde{\mathcal{G}}_i(N, S) \times \overline{\mathcal{G}}_i(S_i)$. It is left to the reader to verify that this function is one-to-one, onto, and its inverse η^{-1} is continuous (Exercise 5.87). □

Step 2: The function z and its properties.
For each player $i \in N$ and every pure strategy $s_i \in S_i$, define a function $z_{i,s_i} : E \to \mathbb{R}$ by

$$z_{i,s_i}(u, \sigma) := \sigma_i(s_i) + U_i(s_i, \sigma_{-i}), \quad \forall (u, \sigma) \in E. \tag{5.148}$$

The number $z_{i,s_i}(u, \sigma)$ is the sum of two terms that have different units: a probability and a payoff. Therefore it has no clear interpretation.

The following claim shows how $(z_{i,s_i}(u, \sigma))_{s_i \in S_i}$ can be used to compute the equilibrium payoffs of the players. For every real number c we denote $c_+ := \max\{c, 0\}$.

Claim 5.73 *For every* $(u, \sigma) \in E$ *we have*

$$U_i(\sigma) = \min \left\{ \alpha \in \mathbb{R} : \sum_{s_i \in S_i} (z_{i,s_i}(u, \sigma) - \alpha)_+ \leq 1 \right\}, \quad \forall i \in N. \tag{5.149}$$

Proof of claim 5.73: Let $\alpha_{\min}$ be the real number that attains the minimum in Equation (5.149). To show that $\alpha_{\min} = U_i(\sigma)$, we first show that $\alpha_{\min} \leq U_i(\sigma)$, and then we show that $\alpha_{\min} \geq U_i(\sigma)$.

Since σ is an equilibrium in the game in which the payoff functions are u, the following inequality must hold for every $s_i \in S_i$:

$$U_i(s_i, \sigma_{-i}) \leq U_i(\sigma). \tag{5.150}$$

Moreover, if Equation (5.150) holds with strict inequality, then $\sigma_i(s_i) = 0$, since in equilibrium a pure strategy yielding a payoff strictly less than the equilibrium payoff is played with probability 0. In particular, using the definition of z_{i,s_i} (Equation (5.148)), the following two properties hold:

$$\text{If } \sigma_i(s_i) = 0, \text{ then } z_{i,s_i}(u, \sigma) - U_i(\sigma) \leq 0. \tag{5.151}$$

$$\text{If } \sigma_i(s_i) > 0, \text{ then } z_{i,s_i}(u, \sigma) - U_i(\sigma) = \sigma_i(s_i). \tag{5.152}$$

From this we get that $\sum_{s_i \in S_i} (z_{i,s_i}(u, \sigma) - U_i(\sigma))_+ = 1$. Setting $\alpha = U_i(\sigma)$, we conclude that this real number α is in the set on the right-hand side of Equation (5.149), and therefore $\alpha_{\min} \leq U_i(\sigma)$.

Take now $\alpha < U_i(\sigma)$. Then

$$\sum_{s_i \in S_i} (z_{i,s_i}(u, \sigma) - \alpha)_+ \geq \sum_{s_i \in S_i} (z_{i,s_i}(u, \sigma) - U_i(\sigma))_+ = 1. \tag{5.153}$$

Since the sum of the summands $z_{i,s_i}(u, \sigma) - U_i(\sigma)$ over $s_i \in S_i$ is 1, at least one of them is positive, and for that summand we have

$$(z_{i,s_i}(u, \sigma) - \alpha)_+ = z_{i,s_i}(u, \sigma) - \alpha > z_{i,s_i}(u, \sigma) - U_i(\sigma) = (z_{i,s_i}(u, \sigma) - U_i(\sigma))_+.$$

It follows that the first inequality in Equation (5.153) is strict, and therefore α is not in the set on the right-hand side of Equation (5.149). Since this is true for every $\alpha < U_i(\sigma)$, we deduce that $\alpha_{\min} \leq U_i(\sigma)$, and the claim follows. $\square$

Denote by $z_i(u, \sigma) \in \mathbb{R}^{S_i}$ the vector of real numbers $(z_{i,s_i}(u, \sigma))_{s_i \in S_i}$ and define the function $z : E \to \mathbb{R}^{\sum_{i \in N} m_i}$ by $z(u, \sigma) = (z_{i,s_i}(u, \sigma))_{i \in N, s_i \in S_i}$.

By Claim 5.72, the payoff function u_i of player i can be represented as a pair $(\tilde{u}_i, \bar{u}_i)$, in which $\tilde{u}_i$ is defined as in Equation (5.146) and $\bar{u}_i$ is defined as in Equation (5.145).

Lemma 5.74 *Let* (u, σ) *and* (u', σ') *be two points in E satisfying:*

- $z_i(u, \sigma) = z_i(u', \sigma')$ *for every player $i \in N$,*
- $\tilde{u}_i = \tilde{u}'_i$ *for every player $i \in N$.*

Then $\bar{u}_i = \bar{u}'_i$ *and* $\sigma_i = \sigma'_i$ *for every player $i \in N$.*

Proof of Lemma 5.74: To prove the lemma we show that σ_i and $\bar{u}_i$ can be computed from $\tilde{u}_i$ and $z(u, \sigma)$.

Let $(u, \sigma) \in E$. By Claim 5.73 and Equations (5.151) and (5.152),

$$\sigma_i(s_i) = (z_{i,s_i}(u, \sigma) - U_i(\sigma))_+. \tag{5.154}$$

Thus, the equilibrium strategy σ_i of player i can be computed from the vector $z_i(u, \sigma)$ and $U_i(\sigma)$ (note that $U_i(\sigma)$ can be computed from u and σ). Now,

$$z_{i,s_i}(u, \sigma) = \sigma_i(s_i) + U_i(s_i, \sigma_{-i}), \tag{5.155}$$

$$= \sigma_i(s_i) + \sum_{s_{-i} \in S_{-i}} \left(u_i(s_i, s_{-i}) \prod_{j \neq i} \sigma_j(s_j) \right), \tag{5.156}$$

$$= \sigma_i(s_i) + \sum_{s_{-i} \in S_{-i}} \left(\tilde{u}_i(s_i, s_{-i}) \prod_{j \neq i} \sigma_j(s_j) \right), \tag{5.157}$$

$$+ \sum_{s_{-i} \in S_{-i}} \left(\bar{u}_i(s_i) \prod_{j \neq i} \sigma_j(s_j) \right), \tag{5.158}$$

$$= \sigma_i(s_i) + \sum_{s_{-i} \in S_{-i}} \left(\tilde{u}_i(s_i, s_{-i}) \prod_{j \neq i} \sigma_j(s_j) \right) + \bar{u}_i(s_i). \tag{5.159}$$

Therefore,

$$\bar{u}_i(s_i) = z_{i,s_i}(u, \sigma) - \sigma_i(s_i) - \sum_{s_{-i} \in S_{-i}} \left(\tilde{u}_i(s_i, s_{-i}) \prod_{j \neq i} \sigma_j(s_j) \right), \tag{5.160}$$

and hence the vector $\bar{u}_i$ can also be computed from $z_i(u, \sigma)$ and $\tilde{u}_i$.   □

Step 3: The function φ and its properties.
We are now ready to prove Theorem 5.71. We have to define a function $\varphi : E \to \mathcal{G}(N, S)$. To this end, for every player i we define a function $\varphi_i(u, \sigma) : E \to \mathcal{G}_i(N, S)$, that is, a payoff function for player i. For every player $i \in N$ define

$$\varphi_i(u, \sigma) := (\tilde{u}_i, z_i(u, \sigma)) \in \tilde{\mathcal{G}}_i(N, S) \times \overline{\mathcal{G}}_i(S_i). \tag{5.161}$$

Recall that the range of φ_i, which is $\tilde{\mathcal{G}}_i(N, S) \times \overline{\mathcal{G}}_i(S_i)$, is homeomorphic to the space of games $\mathcal{G}(N, S)$. We now prove that the function φ is continuous. Indeed, from Equations (5.145), (5.146), and (5.148) it follows that the functions $u_i \mapsto \tilde{u}_i$ and $(u, \sigma) \mapsto z_i(u, \sigma)$ are continuous functions, and therefore φ_i is continuous.

By Lemma 5.74, the function φ is one-to-one. We now show that it is also onto $\mathcal{G}(S, N)$. From the proof of Lemma 5.74 it follows that for every player $i \in N$ and every pair $(\tilde{u}_i, z_i)$ we can construct a vector $\bar{u}_i \in \mathbb{R}^{S_i}$ and a mixed strategy $\sigma_i \in \Delta(S_i)$ such that the vector of strategies $\sigma := (\sigma_i)_{i \in N}$ is an equilibrium of the game $(\tilde{u}_i, \bar{u}_i)_{i \in N}$, which means that $\varphi((\tilde{u}_i, \bar{u}_i)_{i \in N}, \sigma) = (\tilde{u}_i, z_i)$, proving that φ is indeed onto $\mathcal{G}(N, S)$.

Finally we observe that, by construction, the inverse function φ^{-1} is also continuous, concluding the proof of the theorem.   □

Theorem 5.71 provides the geometry of the equilibrium manifold: this set is homeomorphic to a Euclidean space. As mentioned earlier, once we fix the game form (N, S), a

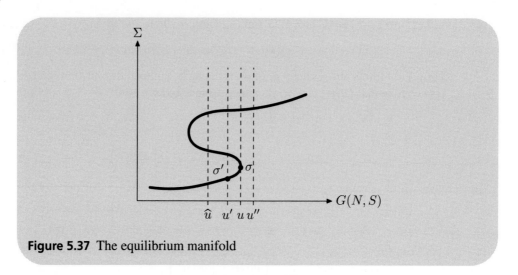

Figure 5.37 The equilibrium manifold

game is characterized by the vector of n payoff functions $u = (u_i)_{i \in N}$. When drawing the equilibrium manifold in the product space $\mathcal{G}(N, S) \times \Sigma$, above each game $u \in \mathcal{G}(N, S)$ we find the set of its Nash equilibria, which can be finite or infinite (see Figure 5.37). When we change the game to a nearby game u' (nearby in the maximum norm), the set of equilibria typically changes as well. For some games, like the game $\hat{u}$ in Figure 5.37, for every equilibrium $\hat{\sigma}$ and every small perturbation $\hat{u}'$ of $\hat{u}$ there is an equilibrium $\hat{\sigma}'$ that is close to $\hat{\sigma}$. Sometimes when we perturb the payoffs of the players to u', we find that in the game u' there is an equilibrium σ' close to σ, as is the case in Figure 5.37. Sometimes this does not happen: there are small perturbations u'' of u such that the game u'' has no equilibrium that is close to σ, as is the case in Figure 5.37.

The fact that the equilibrium manifold is homeomorphic to a Euclidean space implies the following observations:

- If σ is the unique equilibrium of the game u, then *every* small enough perturbation u' of u has an equilibrium σ' that is close to σ.
- More generally, every game u has a stable equilibrium σ, in the sense that every small enough perturbation u' of u has an equilibrium σ' that is close to σ.

5.11) Remarks

Theorem 5.64 was proven by Bernheim [1984] and Pearce [1984]. Corollary 5.60 was proven by Pearce [1984]. Exercise 5.13 is based on Alon et al. [2006]. Exercises 5.1 and 5.2 are taken from Myerson and Weibull [2013]. Exercise 5.31 is based on a discovery due to Lloyd Shapley, which indicates that the equilibrium concept has disadvantages (in addition to its advantages). A generalization of this result appears in Shapley [1994]. The Inspector Game in Exercise 5.32 is a special case of an example in Maschler [1966b], in which r on-site inspection teams may be sent, and there are n possible dates on which the Partial Test Ban Treaty can be abrogated. For a generalization of this model to the case in which there are several detectors, with varying probabilities of detecting what they are looking for, see Maschler [1967]. The interested reader can find a survey of several alternative models for the Inspector Game in Avenhaus et al. [2002]. Exercise

5.33 is based on Biran and Tauman [2007]. Exercise 5.37 is based on an example in Diekmann [1985]. Exercise 5.38 is a variation of a popular lottery game conducted in Sweden by the Talpa Corporation. Exercise 5.49 is taken from Lehrer and Solan [2007]. Exercise 5.56 is from Peleg [1969]. Exercise 5.57 is taken from Foster and Hart [2016]. Parts of Exercise 5.65 are taken from Altman and Solan [2006].

The authors thank Uzi Motro for reading and commenting on Section 5.9 and for suggesting Exercise 5.83. We also thank Avi Shmida, who provided us with the presentation of Exercise 5.84.

5.12 Exercises

5.1 Prove that if S is a finite set then $\Delta(S)$ is a convex and compact set.

5.2 Let $A \subseteq \mathbb{R}^n$ and $B \subseteq \mathbb{R}^m$ be two compact sets. Prove that the product set $A \times B \subseteq \mathbb{R}^{n+m}$ is a compact set.

5.3 Let $A \subseteq \mathbb{R}^n$ and $B \subseteq \mathbb{R}^m$ be two convex sets. Prove that the product set $A \times B \subseteq \mathbb{R}^{n+m}$ is a convex set.

5.4 Show that every multilinear function $f : \Sigma \to \mathbb{R}$ is continuous.

5.5 Prove that for every player i the set of extreme points of player i's collection of mixed strategies is his set of pure strategies.

5.6 Prove that every two-player zero-sum game over the unit square with bilinear payoff functions is the extension to mixed strategies of a two-player game in which each player has two pure strategies.

5.7 Show that for every vector σ_{-i} of mixed strategies of the other players, player i has a best reply that is a pure strategy.

5.8 Answer the following questions for each of the following games, which are all two-player zero-sum games. As is usually the case in this book, Player I is the row player and Player II is the column player.

(a) Write out the mixed extension of each game.
(b) Find the value in mixed strategies, and all the optimal mixed strategies of each of the two players.

	L	R
T	-1	-4
B	-3	3

Game A

	L	R
T	5	8
B	5	1

Game B

	L	R
T	5	4
B	2	3

Game C

	L	R
T	4	2
B	2	9

Game D

	L	R
T	5	4
B	5	6

Game E

	L	R
T	7	7
B	3	10

Game F

5.9 Find the value of the game in mixed strategies and all the optimal strategies of both players in each of the following two-player zero-sum games, where Player I is the row player and Player II is the column player.

	L	R
T	2	6
M	5	5
B	7	4

Game A

	L	R
d	15	-8
c	10	-4
b	5	-2
a	-3	8

Game B

	a	b	c	d
T	5	3	4	0
B	-3	2	-5	6

Game C

	L	M	R
T	6	4	3
B	3	7	9

Game D

	L	M	R
T	18	11	4
B	6	11	16

Game E

5.10 In each of the following items, find a two-player game in strategic form in which each player has two pure strategies, such that in the mixed extension of the game the payoff functions of the players are the specified functions. (Note that the games in parts (a) and (b) are zero-sum, but that the games in parts (c) and (d) are not zero-sum.)

(a) $U(x, y) = 5xy - 2x + 6y - 2$.
(b) $U(x, y) = -2xy + 4x - 7y$.
(c) $U_1(x, y) = 3xy - 4x + 5$, $U_2(x, y) = 7xy + 7x - 8y + 12$.
(d) $U_1(x, y) = 3xy - 3x + 3y - 5$, $U_2(x, y) = 7x - 8y + 12$.

5.11 For each of the graphs appearing in Figure 5.9 (page 155) find a two-player zero-sum game such that the graph of the functions $(U(x, s_{II}))_{s_{II} \in S_{II}}$ is the same as the graph in the figure. For each of these games, compute the value in mixed strategies, and all the optimal strategies of Player I.

5.12 A (finite) square matrix $A = (a_{i,j})_{i,j}$ is called *anti-symmetric* if $a_{i,j} = -a_{j,i}$ for all i and j. Prove that if the payoff matrix of a two-player zero-sum game is anti-symmetric, then the value of the game in mixed strategies is 0. In addition, Player I's set of optimal strategies is identical to that of Player II, when we identify Player I's pure strategy given by row k with Player II's pure strategy given by column k.

5.13 Let $G = (V, E)$ be a directed graph, where V is a set of vertices, and E is a set of edges. A directed edge from vertex x to vertex y is denoted by (x, y). Suppose that the graph is complete, i.e., for every pair of edges $x, y \in V$, either $(x, y) \in E$ or $(y, x) \in E$, but not both. In particular, $(x, x) \in E$ for all $x \in E$. In this exercise, we will prove that there exists a distribution $q \in \Delta(V)$ satisfying

$$\sum_{\{y\in V:\ (y,x)\in E\}} q(y) \geq \tfrac{1}{2}, \quad \forall x \in V. \tag{5.162}$$

(a) Define a two-player zero-sum game in which the set of pure strategies of the two players is V, and the payoff function is defined as follows:

$$u(x, y) = \begin{cases} 0 & x = y, \\ 1 & x \neq y, (x, y) \in E, \\ -1 & x \neq y, (x, y) \notin E. \end{cases} \tag{5.163}$$

Prove that the payoff matrix of this game is an anti-symmetric matrix, and, using Exercise 5.12, deduce that its value in mixed strategies is 0.

(b) Show that every optimal strategy q of Player II in this game satisfies Equation (5.162).

5.14 A mixed strategy σ_i of player i is called *weakly dominated (by a mixed strategy)* if it is weakly dominated in the mixed extension of the game: there exists a mixed strategy $\widehat{\sigma}_i$ of player i satisfying

(a) For each strategy $s_{-i} \in S_{-i}$ of the other players:

$$U_i(\sigma_i, s_{-i}) \leq U_i(\widehat{\sigma}_i, s_{-i}). \tag{5.164}$$

(b) There exists a strategy $t_{-i} \in S_{-i}$ of the other players for which

$$U_i(\sigma_i, t_{-i}) < U_i(\widehat{\sigma}_i, t_{-i}). \tag{5.165}$$

Prove that the set of weakly dominated mixed strategies is a convex set.

5.15 Suppose that a mixed strategy σ_i of player i strictly dominates another of his mixed strategies, $\widehat{\sigma}_i$. Prove or disprove each of the following claims:

(a) Player i has a pure strategy $s_i \in S_i$ satisfying: (i) $\widehat{\sigma}_i(s_i) > 0$ and (ii) strategy s_i is not chosen by player i in any equilibrium.

(b) For each equilibrium $\sigma^* = (\sigma_i^*)_{i\in N}$ player i has a pure strategy $s_i \in S_i$ satisfying (a) $\widehat{\sigma}_i(s_i) > 0$ and (b) $\sigma_i^*(s_i) = 0$.

5.16 Suppose player i has a pure strategy s_i that is chosen with positive probability in each of his maxmin strategies. Prove that s_i is not weakly dominated by any other strategy (pure or mixed).

5.17 Suppose player i has a pure strategy s_i that is chosen with positive probability in one of his maxmin strategies. Is s_i chosen with positive probability in each of player i's maxmin strategies? Prove this claim, or provide a counterexample.

5.18 Suppose player i has a pure strategy s_i that is not weakly dominated by any of his other pure strategies. Is s_i chosen with positive probability in one of player i's maxmin strategies? Prove this claim, or provide a counterexample.

5.19 Prove Corollary 5.19: Let σ^* be an equilibrium in a strategic-form game and let s_i and $\widehat{s}_i$ be two pure strategies of Player i.

(a) If $U_i(s_i, \sigma_{-i}^*) < U_i(\sigma^*)$ then $\sigma_i^*(s_i) = 0$.

(b) If $U_i(s_i, \sigma^*_{-i}) < U_i(\hat{s}_i, \sigma^*_{-i})$ then $\sigma^*_i(s_i) = 0$.

(c) If $\sigma^*_i(s_i) > 0 - \sigma^*_i(\hat{s}_i) > 0$ then $U_i(s_i, \sigma^*_{-i}) = U_i(\hat{s}_i, \sigma^*_{-i})$.

(d) If s_i is strictly dominated by $\hat{s}_i$ then $\sigma^*_i(s_i) = 0$.

5.20 Let $(a_{i,j})_{1 \le i,j \le n}$ be nonnegative numbers satisfying $\sum_{j \ne i} a_{i,j} = a_{i,i}$ for all i. Julie and Sam are playing the following game. Julie writes down a natural number i, $1 \le i \le n$, on a slip of paper. Sam does not see the number that Julie has written. Sam then guesses what number Julie has chosen, and writes his guess, which is a natural number j, $1 \le j \le n$, on a slip of paper. The two players simultaneously show each other the numbers they have written down. If Sam has guessed correctly, Julie pays him $a_{i,i}$ dollars, where i is the number that Julie chose (and that Sam correctly guesses). If Sam was wrong in his guess $(i \ne j)$, Sam pays Julie $a_{i,j}$ dollars.

Depict this game as a two-player zero-sum game in strategic form, and prove that the value in mixed strategies of the game is 0.

5.21 Consider the following two-player zero-sum game.

Player II

		L	C	R
	T	3	−3	0
Player I	M	2	6	4
	B	2	5	6

(a) Find a mixed strategy of Player I that guarantees him the same payoff against any pure strategy of Player II.

(b) Find a mixed strategy of Player II that guarantees him the same payoff against any pure strategy of Player I.

(c) Prove that the two strategies you found in (a) and (b) are the optimal strategies of the two players.

(d) Generalize this result: Suppose a two-player zero-sum game is represented by an $n \times m$ matrix.[4] Suppose each player has an *equalizing strategy*, meaning a strategy guaranteeing him the same payoff against any pure strategy his opponent may play. Prove that any equalizing strategy is an optimal strategy.

(e) Give an example of a two-player zero-sum game in which one of the players has an equalizing strategy that is not optimal. Why is this not a contradiction to (d)?

5.22 In the following payoff matrix of a two-person zero-sum game, no player has an optimal pure strategy.

---

4 This means that the matrix has n rows (pure strategies of Player I) and m columns (pure strategies of Player II).

Player II

		L	R
	T	a	b
Player I	B	c	d

What inequalities must the numbers a, b, c, d satisfy? Find the value in mixed strategies of this game.

5.23 Prove that in any n-person game, at Nash equilibrium, each player's payoff is greater than or equal to his maxmin value.

5.24 The goal of this exercise is to prove that in a two-player zero-sum game, each player's set of optimal strategies is a convex set. Let $G = (N, (S_i)_{i \in N}, (u_i)_{i \in N})$ be a two-player zero-sum game in which $N = \{I, II\}$. For each pair of mixed strategies $\sigma_I = [p_I^1(s_I^1), \ldots, p_I^{m_I}(s_I^{m_I})]$ and $\widehat{\sigma}_I = [\widehat{p}_I^1(s_I^1), \ldots, \widehat{p}_I^{m_I}(s_I^{m_I})]$, and each real number in the unit line interval $\alpha \in [0, 1]$, define a vector $q_I = (q_I^j)_{j=1}^{m_I}$ as follows:

$$q_I^j = \alpha p_I^j + (1 - \alpha)\widehat{p}_I^j. \tag{5.166}$$

(a) Prove that $q = (q_I^j)_{j=1}^{m_I}$ is a probability distribution.
(b) Define a mixed strategy τ_I of Player I as follows:

$$\tau_I = \left[q_I^1\left(s_I^1\right), \ldots, q_I^{m_I}\left(s_I^{m_I}\right)\right]. \tag{5.167}$$

Prove that for every mixed strategy σ_{II} of Player II:

$$U(\tau_I, \sigma_{II}) = \alpha U(\sigma_I, \sigma_{II}) + (1 - \alpha)U(\widehat{\sigma}_I, \sigma_{II}). \tag{5.168}$$

(c) We say that a strategy σ_I of Player I *guarantees* payoff v if $U(\sigma_I, \sigma_{II}) \geq v$ for every strategy σ_{II} of Player II. Prove that if σ_I and $\widehat{\sigma}_I$ guarantee Player I payoff v, then τ_I also guarantees Player I payoff v.
(d) Deduce that if σ_I and $\widehat{\sigma}_I$ are optimal strategies of Player I, then τ_I is also an optimal strategy of Player I.
(e) Deduce that Player I's set of optimal strategies is a convex set in $\Delta(S_I)$.

5.25 The goal of this exercise is to prove that in a two-player zero-sum game, each player's set of optimal strategies, which we proved is a convex set in Exercise 5.24, is also a compact set. Let $(\sigma_I^k)_{k \in \mathbb{N}}$ be a sequence of optimal strategies of Player I, and for each $k \in \mathbb{N}$ denote $\sigma_I^k = [p_I^{k,1}(s_I^1), \ldots, p_I^{k,m_I}(s_I^{m_I})]$. Suppose that for each $j = 1, 2, \ldots, m_I$, the limit $p_I^{*,j} = \lim_{k \to \infty} p_I^{k,j}$ exists. Prove the following claims:

(a) The vector $(p_I^{*,j})_{j=1}^{m_I}$ is a probability distribution over S_I.
(b) Define a mixed strategy σ_I^* as follows:

$$\sigma_I^* = \left[p_I^{*,1}\left(s_I^1\right), \ldots, p_I^{*,m_I}\left(s_I^{m_I}\right)\right]. \tag{5.169}$$

Prove that σ_I^* is also an optimal strategy of Player I.
(c) Deduce from this that Player I's set of optimal strategies is a compact subset of the set of mixed strategies $\Delta(S_I)$.

5.26 For each of the following games, where Player I is the row player and Player II is the column player:

    (a) Write out the mixed extension of the game.

    (b) Compute all the equilibria in mixed strategies.

	L	R
T	1, 1	4, 0
B	2, 10	3, 5

Game A

	L	R
T	1, 2	2, 2
B	0, 3	1, 1

Game B

	L	M	R
T	1, 1	0, 2	2, 0
B	0, 0	1, 0	−1, 3

Game C

5.27 Calculate all equilibria in the following two-player game:

	A	B	C	D
a	0, 5	1, 4	0, 3	1, 0
b	1, 0	0, 3	1, 4	0, 5

5.28 Calculate all equilibria in the following two-player game:

	L	R
T	4, −4	−4, 4
M	−4, 4	4, −4
B	2, 3	2, 3

5.29 For each of the following games, where Player I is the row player and Player II is the column player:

    (a) Find all the equilibria in mixed strategies, and all the equilibrium payoffs.

    (b) Find each player's maxmin strategy.

    (c) What strategy would you advise each player to use in the game?

	L	R
T	5, 5	0, 8
B	8, 0	1, 1

Game A

	L	R
T	9, 5	10, 4
B	8, 4	15, 6

Game B

	L	R
T	5, 16	15, 8
B	16, 7	8, 15

Game C

	L	R
T	8, 3	10, 1
B	6, −6	3, 5

Game D

	L	R
T	4, 12	5, 10
B	3, 16	6, 22

Game E

	L	R
T	2, 2	3, 3
B	4, 0	2, −2

Game F

	L	R
T	15, 3	15, 10
B	15, 4	15, 7

Game G

5.30 In this exercise we will see that increasing the payoff function of a player may lead to a decrease in his equilibrium payoff. Consider the following two-player game in which the payoff function of Player 1 depends on a parameter x:

	L	R
T	$3+x, 0$	$0, 1$
B	$2, 1$	$1, 0$

Show that for every $x \in (-1, \infty)$ the game has a unique equilibrium, calculate the corresponding equilibrium payoff, and show that the equilibrium payoff is monotonic decreasing in x.

5.31 Consider the two-player game in the figure below, in which each player has three pure strategies.

Player II

		L	C	R
	T	$0, 0$	$7, 6$	$6, 7$
Player I	M	$6, 7$	$0, 0$	$7, 6$
	B	$7, 6$	$6, 7$	$0, 0$

(a) Prove that $([\frac{1}{3}(T), \frac{1}{3}(M), \frac{1}{3}(B)]; [\frac{1}{3}(L), \frac{1}{3}(C), \frac{1}{3}(R)])$ is the game's unique equilibrium.
(b) Check that if Player I deviates to T, then Player II has a reply that leads both players to a higher payoff, relative to the equilibrium payoff. Why, then, will Player II not play that strategy?

5.32 The Inspector Game During the 1960s, within the framework of negotiations between the United States (US) and the Union of Soviet Socialist Republics (USSR) over nuclear arms limitations, a suggestion was raised that both countries commit to a moratorium on nuclear testing. One of the objections to this suggestion was the difficulty of supervising compliance with such a commitment. Detecting above-ground nuclear tests posed no problem, because it was easy to detect the radioactive fallout from a nuclear explosion conducted in the open. This was not true, however, with respect to underground tests, because it was difficult at the time to distinguish seismographically between an underground nuclear explosion and an earthquake. The US therefore suggested that in every case of suspicion that a nuclear test had been conducted, an inspection team be sent to perform on-site inspection. The USSR initially objected, regarding any inspection team sent by the US as a potential spy operation. At later stages in the negotiations, Soviet negotiators expressed readiness to accept three on-site inspections annually, while American negotiators demanded at least eight on-site inspections. The expected number of seismic events per year considered sufficiently strong to arouse suspicion was 300.

The model presented in this exercise assumes the following:

- The USSR can potentially conduct underground nuclear tests on one of two possible distinct dates, labeled A and B, where B is the later date.
- The USSR gains nothing from choosing one of these dates over the other for conducting an underground nuclear test, and the US loses nothing if one date is chosen over another.
- The USSR gains nothing from conducting nuclear tests on both of these dates over its utility from conducting a test on only one date, and the US loses nothing if tests are conducted on both dates over its utility from conducting a test on only one date.
- The US may send an inspection team on only one of the two dates, A or B, but not on both.
- The utilities of the two countries from the possible outcomes are:
  - If the Partial Test Ban Treaty (PTBT) is violated by the USSR and the US does not send an inspection team: the US receives 0 and the USSR receives 0.
  - If the PTBT is violated by the USSR and the US sends an inspection team: the US receives 1 and the USSR receives 1.
  - If the PTBT is not violated, the US receives α and the USSR receives β, where $\alpha > 1$ and $0 < \beta < 1$ (whether or not the US sends an inspection team).

Answer the following questions:

(a) Explain why the above conditions are imposed on the values of α and β.
(b) Plot, in the space of the utilities of the players, the convex hull of the points $(0, 1)$, $(1, 0)$, and (α, β). The convex hull includes all the results of all possible lotteries conducted on pairs of actions undertaken by the players.
(c) List the pure strategies available to each of the two countries.
(d) Write down the matrix of the game in which the pure strategies permitted to the US (the row player) are:

- A: Send an inspection team on date A
- B: Send an inspection team on date B

and the pure strategies permitted to the USSR (the column player) are:

- L: Conduct a nuclear test on date A
- R: Do not conduct a nuclear test on date A. Conduct a nuclear test on date B, only if the US sent an inspection team on date A.

(e) Explain why the other pure strategies you wrote down in part (c) are either dominated by the strategies in part (d), or equivalent to them.
(f) Show that the game you wrote down in part (d) has only one equilibrium. Compute that equilibrium. Denote by (v_I^*, v_{II}^*) the equilibrium payoff, and by $[x^*(A), (1 - x^*)(B)]$ the equilibrium strategy of the US.
(g) Add to the graph you sketched in part (b) the equilibrium payoff, and the payoff $U([x^*(A), (1 - x^*)(B)], R)$ (where $U = (U_I, U_{II})$ is the vector of the utilities

of the two players). Show that the point $U([x^*(A), (1 - x^*)(B)], R)$ is located on the line segment connecting $(0, 1)$ with (α, β).

(h) Consider the following possible strategy of the US: play $[(x^* + \varepsilon)(A), (1 - x^* - \varepsilon)(B)]$, where $\varepsilon > 0$ is small, and commit to playing this mixed strategy.[5] Show that the best reply of the USSR to this mixed strategy is to play strategy R. What is the payoff to the two players from the strategy vector $([(x^* + \varepsilon)(A), (1 - x^* - \varepsilon)(B)], R)$? Which of the two countries gains from this, relative to the equilibrium payoff?

(i) Prove that the USSR can guarantee itself a payoff of v_{II}^*, regardless of the mixed strategy used by the US, when it plays its maxmin strategy.

(j) Deduce from the last two paragraphs that, up to an order of ε, the US cannot expect to receive a payoff higher than the payoff it would receive from committing to play the strategy $[(x^* + \varepsilon)(A), (1 - x^* - \varepsilon)(B)]$, assuming that the USSR makes no errors in choosing its strategy.

5.33 Suppose Country A constructs facilities for the development of nuclear weapons. Country B sends a spy ring to Country A to ascertain whether it is developing nuclear weapons, and is considering bombing the new facilities. The spy ring sent by Country B is of quality α: if Country A is developing nuclear weapons, Country B's spy ring will correctly report this with probability α, and with probability $1 - \alpha$ it will report a false negative. If Country A is not developing nuclear weapons, Country B's spy ring will correctly report this with probability α, and with probability $1 - \alpha$ it will report a false positive. Country A must decide whether or not to develop nuclear weapons, and Country B, after receiving its spy reports, must decide whether or not to bomb Country A's new facilities. The payoffs to the two countries appear in the following table.

		Country B	
		Bomb	Don't Bomb
Country A	Don't Develop	$\frac{1}{2}, \frac{1}{2}$	$\frac{3}{4}, 1$
	Develop	$0, \frac{3}{4}$	$1, 0$

(a) Depict this situation as a strategic-form game. Are there any dominating strategies in the game?

(b) Verbally describe what it means to say that the quality of Country B's spy ring is $\alpha = \frac{1}{2}$. What if $\alpha = 1$?

(c) For each $\alpha \in [\frac{1}{2}, 1]$, find the game's set of equilibria.

---

5 This model in effect extends the model of a strategic game by assuming that one of the players has the option to commit to implementing a particular strategy. One way of implementing this would be to conduct a public spin of a roulette wheel in the United Nations building, and to commit to letting the result of the roulette spin determine whether an inspection team will be sent: if the result indicates that the US should send an inspection team on date A, the USSR will be free to deny entry to a US inspection team on date B, without penalty.

(d) What is the set of equilibrium payoffs as a function of α? What is the α at which Country A's maximal equilibrium payoff is obtained? What is the α at which Country B's maximal equilibrium payoff is obtained?

(e) Assuming both countries play their equilibrium strategy, what is the probability that Country A will manage to develop nuclear weapons without being bombed?

5.34 Prove that in any two-player game,

$$\max_{\sigma_I \in \Sigma_I} \min_{\sigma_{II} \in \Sigma_{II}} u_I(\sigma_I, \sigma_{II}) = \max_{\sigma_I \in \Sigma_I} \min_{s_{II} \in S_{II}} u_I(\sigma_I, s_{II}). \tag{5.170}$$

That is, given a mixed strategy of Player I, Player II can guarantee that Player I will receive the minimal possible payoff by playing a pure strategy, without needing to resort to a mixed strategy.

5.35 Let σ_{-i} be a vector of mixed strategies of all players except for player i, in a strategic-form game. Let σ_i be a best reply of player i to σ_{-i}. The *support* of σ_i is the set of all pure strategies given positive probability in σ_i (see Equation (5.64) on page 164). Answer the following questions:

(a) Prove that for any pure strategy s_i of player i in the support of σ_i,

$$U_i(s_i, \sigma_{-i}) = U_i(\sigma_i, \sigma_{-i}). \tag{5.171}$$

(b) Prove that for any mixed strategy $\widehat{\sigma}_i$ of player i whose support is contained in the support of σ_i,

$$U_i(\widehat{\sigma}_i, \sigma_{-i}) = U_i(\sigma_i, \sigma_{-i}). \tag{5.172}$$

(c) Deduce that player i's set of best replies to every mixed strategy of the other players σ_{-i} is the convex hull of the pure strategies that give him a maximal payoff against σ_{-i}.

Recall that the *convex hull* of a set of points in a Euclidean space is the smallest convex set containing all of those points.

5.36 A game $G = (N, (S_i)_{i \in N}, (u_i)_{i \in N})$ is called *symmetric* if (a) each player has the same set of strategies: $S_i = S_j$ for each $i, j \in N$, and (b) the payoff functions satisfy

$$u_i(s_1, s_2, \ldots, s_n) = u_j(s_1, \ldots, s_{i-1}, s_j, s_{i+1}, \ldots, s_{j-1}, s_i, s_{j+1}, \ldots, s_n) \tag{5.173}$$

for any vector of pure strategies $s = (s_1, s_2, \ldots, s_n) \in S$ and for each pair of players i, j satisfying $i < j$.

Prove that in every symmetric game there exists a symmetric equilibrium in mixed strategies: an equilibrium $\sigma = (\sigma_i)_{i \in N}$ satisfying $\sigma_i = \sigma_j$ for each $i, j \in N$.

5.37 **The Volunteer's Dilemma**   Ten people are arrested after committing a crime. The police lack sufficient resources to investigate the crime thoroughly. The chief investigator therefore presents the suspects with the following proposal: if at least one of them confesses, every suspect who has confessed will serve a one-year jail sentence, and all the rest will be released. If no one confesses to the crime, the police will continue their investigation, at the end of which each one of them will receive a ten-year jail sentence.

(a) Write down this situation as a strategic-form game, where the set of players is the set of people arrested, and the utility of each player (suspect) is 10 minus the number of years he spends in jail.

(b) Find all the equilibrium points in pure strategies. What is the intuitive meaning of such an equilibrium, and under what conditions is it reasonable for such an equilibrium to be attained?

(c) Find a symmetric equilibrium in mixed strategies. What is the probability that at this equilibrium no one volunteers to confess?

(d) Suppose the number of suspects is not 10, but n. Find a symmetric equilibrium in mixed strategies. What is the limit, as n goes to infinity, of the probability that in a symmetric equilibrium no one volunteers? What can we conclude from this analysis for the topic of volunteering in large groups?

5.38 Consider the following lottery game, with n participants competing for a prize worth M ($M > 1$). Every player may purchase as many numbers as he wishes in the range $\{1, 2, \ldots, K\}$, at a cost of \$1 per number. The set of all the numbers that have been purchased by only one of the players is then identified, and the winning number is the smallest number in that set. The (necessarily only) player who purchased that number is the lottery winner, receiving the full prize. If no number is purchased by only one player, no player receives a prize.

(a) Write down every player's set of pure strategies and payoff function.

(b) Show that a symmetric equilibrium exists, i.e., there exists an equilibrium in which every player uses the same mixed strategy.

(c) For $p_1 \in (0, 1)$, consider the following mixed strategy $\sigma_i(p_1)$ of player i: with probability p_1 purchase only the number 1, and with probability $1 - p_1$ do not purchase any number. What conditions must M, n, and p_1 satisfy for the strategy vector in which player i plays strategy $\sigma_i(p_1)$ to be a symmetric equilibrium?

(d) Show that if at equilibrium there is a positive probability that player i will not purchase any number, then his expected payoff is 0.

(e) Show that if $M < n$, meaning that the number of participants is greater than the value of the prize at equilibrium, there is a positive probability that no player purchases a number. Conclude from this that at every symmetric equilibrium the expected payoff of every player is 0. (Hint: Show that if with probability 1 every player purchases at least one number, the expected number of natural numbers purchased by all the players together is greater than the value of the prize M, and hence there is a player whose expected payoff is negative.)

5.39 The set of equilibria is a subset of the product space $\Delta(S_1) \times \Delta(S_2) \times \cdots \times \Delta(S_n)$. Prove that it is a compact set. Is it also a convex set? If you answer yes, provide a proof; if you answer no, provide a counterexample.

5.40 Let $M_{n,m}$ be the space of matrices of order $n \times m$ representing two-player zero-sum games in which Player I has n pure strategies and Player II has m pure strategies. Prove that the function that associates with every matrix $A = (a_{ij}) \in M_{n,m}$ the value in mixed strategies of the game that it represents is continuous in (a_{ij}).

Remark: The sequence of matrices $(A^k)_{k \in \mathbb{N}}$ in $M_{n,m}$, where $A^k = (a_{ij}^k)$, converges to $A = (a_{ij})$, if

$$a_{ij} = \lim_{k \to \infty} a_{ij}^k, \quad \forall i, j. \tag{5.174}$$

5.41 Let $A = (a_{ij})$ and $B = (b_{ij})$ be two $n \times m$ matrices representing two-player zero-sum games in strategic form. Prove that the difference between the value of A and the value of B is less than or equal to

$$\max_{i=1}^{n} \max_{j=1}^{m} |a_{ij} - b_{ij}|. \tag{5.175}$$

5.42 Find matrices A and B of order $n \times m$ representing two-player zero-sum games, such that the value of the matrix $C := \frac{1}{2}A + \frac{1}{2}B$ is less than the value of A and less than the value of B.

5.43 Let $\Gamma = (N, (S_i)_{i \in N}, (u_i)_{i \in N})$ and $\widehat{\Gamma} = (N, (S_i)_{i \in N}, (\widehat{u}_i)_{i \in N})$ be two strategic-form games with the same sets of pure strategies. Denote the maximal difference between the payoff functions of the two games by

$$c = \max_{s \in S_1 \times \cdots \times S_n} \max_{i \in N} |u_i(s) - \widehat{u}_i(s)|. \tag{5.176}$$

We say that the set of equilibria of G is *close to* the set of equilibria of $\widehat{G}$ if for every equilibrium x^* of G there is an equilibrium $\widehat{x}^*$ of $\widehat{G}$ such that

$$|u_i(x^*) - \widehat{u}_i(\widehat{x}^*)| \leq c, \quad \forall i \in N. \tag{5.177}$$

Find two games $\Gamma = (N, (S_i)_{i \in N}, (u_i)_{i \in N})$ and $\widehat{\Gamma} = (N, (S_i)_{i \in N}, (\widehat{u}_i)_{i \in N})$ such that the set of equilibria of G is not close to the set of equilibria of $\widehat{G}$. Can such a phenomenon exist in two-player zero-sum games? (See Exercise 5.41.)

5.44 Let $\Gamma = (N, (S_i)_{i \in N}, (u_i)_{i \in N})$ and $\widehat{\Gamma} = (N, (S_i)_{i \in N}, (\widehat{u}_i)_{i \in N})$ be two strategic-form games with the same sets of players, and the same sets of pure strategies such that $u_i(s) \geq \widehat{u}_i(s)$ for each strategy vector $s \in S$. Denote the multilinear extension of $\widehat{u}_i$ by $\widehat{U}_i$. Is it necessarily true that for each equilibrium σ of Γ there exists an equilibrium $\widehat{\sigma}$ of $\widehat{\Gamma}$ such that $U_i(\sigma) \geq \widehat{U}_i(\widehat{\sigma})$ for each player $i \in N$? In other words, when the payoffs increase, do the equilibrium payoffs also increase? Prove this claim, or find a counterexample.

5.45 Prove that in a two-player strategic-form game, the minmax value in mixed strategies of a player equals his maxmin value in mixed strategies.

5.46 Suppose that the following game has a unique equilibrium, given by a completely mixed strategy, and that the maxmin strategies of both players are also completely mixed:

Player II

$$
\begin{array}{c c}
 & \begin{array}{c c} L & R \end{array} \\
\begin{array}{c} \\ \text{Player I} \end{array}
\begin{array}{c} T \\ B \end{array}
&
\begin{array}{|c|c|}
\hline
a, b & e, f \\
\hline
c, d & g, h \\
\hline
\end{array}
\end{array}
$$

Answer the following questions with regards to the mixed extension of the game:

(a) Prove that the payoff of each player at this equilibrium equals his maxmin value in mixed strategies.

(b) Compute the equilibrium and the maxmin strategies of the two players. Did you find the same strategies in both cases?

5.47 Prove that the only equilibrium in the following three-player game, where Player I chooses a row (T or B), Player II chooses a column (L or R), and Player III chooses a matrix (W or E), is (T, L, W).

$$
\begin{array}{cc}
\begin{array}{cc} L & R \end{array} & \begin{array}{cc} L & R \end{array} \\
\begin{array}{c} T \\ B \end{array}
\begin{array}{|c|c|}
\hline
1,1,1 & 0,1,3 \\
\hline
1,3,0 & 1,0,1 \\
\hline
\end{array}
&
\begin{array}{c} T \\ B \end{array}
\begin{array}{|c|c|}
\hline
3,0,1 & 1,1,0 \\
\hline
0,1,1 & 0,0,0 \\
\hline
\end{array} \\
W & E
\end{array}
$$

Guidance: First check whether there are equilibria in pure strategies. Then check whether there are equilibria in which two players play pure strategies, while the third plays a completely mixed strategy (meaning a strategy in which each one of his two pure strategies is chosen with positive probability). After that, check whether there are equilibria in which one player plays a pure strategy, and the other two play completely mixed strategies. Finally, check whether there are equilibria in which all the players play completely mixed strategies. Note the symmetry between the players; making use of the symmetry will reduce the amount of work you need to do.

5.48 In two-player games where each player has two actions and all payoffs are different, the number of equilibria is finite. In this exercise we will see that this property does not hold in three-player games.

(a) Consider a three-player game in which each player has two pure strategies: $S_1 = S_2 = S_3 = \{a, b\}$. Denote $S = S_1 \times S_2 \times S_3$ and let the payoff function $u_1 : S \to \mathbb{R}$ of Player 1 be defined as follows: $u_1(s_1, s_2, s_3) = 1$ if the number of indices i such that $s_i = a$ is odd, and $u_1(s_1, s_2, s_3) = 0$ if it is even. Prove that when Player 2 plays the mixed strategy $[\frac{1}{2}(a), \frac{1}{2}(b)]$, Player 1 is indifferent between his two pure strategies, regardless of the mixed strategy played by Player 3.

(b) Show that in the three-player game in which the payoff function of each player coincides with u_1 there are continuum of equilibria in mixed strategies.

(c) Design a three-player game in which each player has two pure strategies, no payoff appears twice in the payoff matrix, and there are continua of equilibria in mixed strategies.

5.49 In this exercise we will prove the following theorem:

Theorem 5.56 *A set $E \subseteq \mathbb{R}^2$ is the set of Nash equilibrium payoffs in a two-player game in strategic form if and only if E is the union of a finite number of rectangles of the form $[a, b] \times [c, d]$ (the rectangles are not necessarily disjoint from each other, and we do not rule out the possibility that in some of them $a = b$ and/or $c = d$).*

For every distribution x over a finite set S, the *support* of x, which is denoted $\text{supp}(x)$, is the set of all elements of S that have positive probability under x:

$$\text{supp}(x) := \{s \in S \colon x(s) > 0\}. \tag{5.178}$$

(a) Let (x_1, y_1) and (x_2, y_2) be two equilibria of a two-player strategic-form game with payoffs (a, c) and (b, d) satisfying $\text{supp}(x_1) = \text{supp}(x_2)$ and $\text{supp}(y_1) = \text{supp}(y_2)$. Prove that for every $0 \leq \alpha, \beta \leq 1$ the strategy vector $(\alpha x_1 + (1 - \alpha)x_2, \beta y_1 + (1 - \beta)y_2)$ is a Nash equilibrium with the same support, and with payoff $(\beta a + (1 - \beta)c, \alpha b + (1 - \alpha)d)$.

(b) Deduce that for any subset S'_{I} of Player I's pure strategies, and any subset S'_{II} of Player II's pure strategies, the set of Nash equilibria payoffs yielded by strategy vectors (x, y) satisfying $\text{supp}(x) = S'_{\text{I}}$ and $\text{supp}(y) = S'_{\text{II}}$ is a rectangle.

(c) Since the number of possible supports is finite, deduce that the set of equilibrium payoffs of every two-player game in strategic form is a union of a finite number of rectangles of the form $[a, b] \times [c, d]$.

(d) In this part, we will prove the converse of Theorem 5.56. Let K be a positive integer, and let $(a_k, b_k, c_k, d_k)_{k=1}^K$ be positive numbers satisfying $a_k \leq b_k$ and $c_k \leq d_k$ for all k. Define the set $A = \bigcup_{k=1}^K ([a_k, b_k] \times [c_k, d_k])$, which is the union of a finite number of rectangles (if $a_k = b_k$ and/or $c_k = d_k$, the rectangle is degenerate). Prove that the set of equilibrium payoffs in the following game in strategic form in which each player has $2K$ actions is A.

a_1, b_1	c_1, b_1	$0, 0$	$0, 0$	$\cdots$	$0, b_1$	$0, b_1$
a_1, d_1	c_1, d_1	$0, 0$	$0, 0$	$\cdots$	$0, d_1$	$0, d_1$
$0, 0$	$0, 0$	a_2, b_2	c_2, b_2	$\cdots$	$0, b_2$	$0, b_2$
$0, 0$	$0, 0$	a_2, d_2	c_2, d_2	$\cdots$	$0, d_2$	$0, d_2$
$\cdots$	$\cdots$	$\cdots$	$\cdots$	$\cdots$	$\cdots$	$\cdots$
$a_1, 0$	$c_1, 0$	$a_2, 0$	$c_2, 0$	$\cdots$	a_K, b_K	c_K, b_K
$a_1, 0$	$c_1, 0$	$a_2, 0$	$c_2, 0$	$\cdots$	a_K, d_K	c_K, d_K

5.50 In this exercise, we will show that Theorem 5.56 (page 216) only holds true in two-player games: when there are more than two players, the set of equilibrium payoffs is not necessarily a union of polytopes. Consider the following three-player game, in which Player I chooses a row (T or B), Player II chooses a column (L or R), and Player III chooses a matrix (W or E).

	L	R
T	$1,0,3$	$0,0,1$
B	$1,1,1$	$0,1,1$

W

	L	R
T	$0,1,4$	$0,0,0$
B	$1,1,0$	$1,0,0$

E

Show that the set of equilibria is

$$\left\{ ([x(T), (1-x)(B)], [y(L), (1-y)(R)], W) : 0 \leq x, y \leq 1, \ xy \leq \tfrac{1}{2} \right\}. \tag{5.179}$$

Deduce that the set of equilibrium payoffs is

$$\left\{ (y, 1-x, 1+2xy) : 0 \leq x, y \leq 1, xy \leq \frac{1}{2} \right\}, \tag{5.180}$$

and hence it is not the union of polytopes in $\mathbb{R}^3$.

Guidance: First show that at every equilibrium, Player III plays his pure strategy W with probability 1, by ascertaining what the best replies of Players I and II are if he does not do so, and what Player III's best reply is to these best replies.

5.51 Find all the equilibria in the following three-player game, in which Player I chooses a row (T or B), Player II chooses a column (L or R), and Player III chooses a matrix (W or E).

	L	R
T	$0,0,0$	$1,0,0$
B	$0,0,1$	$0,1,0$

W

	L	R
T	$0,1,0$	$0,0,1$
B	$1,0,0$	$0,0,0$

E

5.52 Tom, Dick, and Harry play the following game. At the first stage, Dick or Harry is chosen, each with probability $\frac{1}{2}$. If Dick has been chosen, he plays the Game A in Figure 5.38, with Tom as his opponent. If Harry has been chosen, he plays the Game B in Figure 5.38, with Tom as his opponent. Tom, however, does not know who his opponent is (and which of the two games is being played). The payoff to the player who is not chosen is 0.

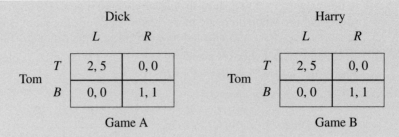

Figure 5.38 The payoff matrices of the game in Exercise 5.52

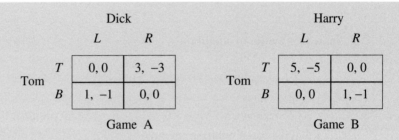

Figure 5.39 The payoff matrices of the game in Exercise 5.53

Do the following:

(a) Draw the extensive form of the game.
(b) Write down the strategic form of the game.
(c) Find two equilibria in pure strategies.
(d) Find an additional equilibrium in mixed strategies.

5.53 In this exercise, Tom, Dick, and Harry are in a situation similar to the one described in Exercise 5.52, but this time the payoff matrices are those shown in Figure 5.39.

(a) Depict the game in extensive form.
(b) Depict the game in strategic form.
(c) Find all the equilibria of this game.

5.54 Prove that in every two-player game on the unit square that is not zero-sum, and in which the payoff functions of the two players are bilinear (see Section 4.14.2 on page 123), there exists an equilibrium in pure strategies.

5.55 In this exercise, we generalize Theorem 5.11 (page 150) to the case in which the set of pure strategies of one of the players is countable. Let Γ be a two-player zero-sum game in which Player I's set of pure strategies S_I, is finite, Player II's set of pure strategies $S_{II} = \{1, 2, 3, \ldots\}$ is a countable set, and the payoff function u is bounded.

Let Γ^n be a two-player zero-sum game in which Player I's set of pure strategies is S_I, Player II's set of pure strategies is $S_{II}^n = \{1, 2, \ldots, n\}$, and the payoff functions are identical to those of Γ. Let v^n be the value of the game Γ^n, and let $\sigma_I^n \in$

$\Delta(S_{\mathrm{I}})$ and $\sigma_{\mathrm{II}}^n \in \Delta(S_{\mathrm{II}}^n)$ be the optimal strategies of the two players in this game, respectively.

(a) Prove that $(v^n)_{n\in\mathbb{N}}$ is a sequence of nonincreasing real numbers. Deduce that $v := \lim_{n\to\infty} v^n$ exists.

(b) Prove that each accumulation point σ_{I} of the sequence $(\sigma_{\mathrm{I}}^n)_{n\in\mathbb{N}}$ satisfies[6]

$$\inf_{\sigma_{\mathrm{II}}\in\Delta(S_{\mathrm{II}})} U(\sigma_{\mathrm{I}}, \sigma_{\mathrm{II}}) \geq v. \tag{5.181}$$

(c) Prove that for each $n \in \mathbb{N}$, the mixed strategy σ_{II}^n satisfies

$$\sup_{\sigma_{\mathrm{I}}\in\Delta(S_{\mathrm{I}})} U(\sigma_1, \sigma_{\mathrm{II}}^n) \leq v^n. \tag{5.182}$$

(d) Deduce that

$$\sup_{\sigma_{\mathrm{I}}\in\Delta(S_{\mathrm{I}})} \inf_{\sigma_{\mathrm{II}}\in\Delta(S_{\mathrm{II}})} U(\sigma_{\mathrm{I}}, \sigma_{\mathrm{II}}) = \inf_{\sigma_{\mathrm{II}}\in\Delta(S_{\mathrm{II}})} \sup_{\sigma_{\mathrm{I}}\in\Delta(S_{\mathrm{I}})} U(\sigma_{\mathrm{I}}, \sigma_{\mathrm{II}}) = v.$$

(e) Find an example of a game Γ in which the sequence $(\sigma_{\mathrm{II}}^n)_{n\in\mathbb{N}}$ has no accumulation point.

(f) Show by a counterexample that (d) above does not necessarily hold when S_{I} is also countably infinite.

5.56 In this exercise we will present an example of a game with an infinite set of players that has no equilibrium in mixed strategies. Let $(N, (S_i)_{i\in N}, (u_i)_{i\in N})$ be a game in strategic form in which the set of players is the set of natural numbers $N = \{1, 2, 3, \ldots\}$, each player $i \in N$ has two pure strategies $S_i = \{0, 1\}$, and player i's payoff function is

$$u_i(s_1, s_2, \ldots) = \begin{cases} s_i & \text{if } \sum_{j\in N} s_j < \infty, \\ -s_i & \text{if } \sum_{j\in N} s_j = \infty. \end{cases} \tag{5.183}$$

(a) Prove that this game has no equilibrium in pure strategies.

(b) Using Kolmogorov's 0–1 Law,[7] prove that the game has no equilibrium in mixed strategies.

5.57 In this exercise we provide an alternative proof for Nash's Theorem (Theorem 5.10 on page 150).

(a) Let $X \subseteq \mathbb{R}^n$ be a nonempty convex and compact set, and let $f : X \to \mathbb{R}^n$ be a continuous function. Prove that there is a point $x^* \in X$ such that $\langle x - x^*, f(x^*) \rangle \leq 0$ for every $x \in X$, where $\langle x, y \rangle := \sum_{i=1}^n x_i y_i$ is the scalar product in $\mathbb{R}^n$.

---

6 Recall that σ_{I} is an *accumulation point* of a sequence $(\sigma_{\mathrm{I}}^n)_{n\in\mathbb{N}}$ if there exists a subsequence $(\sigma_{\mathrm{I}}^{n_k})_{k\in\mathbb{N}}$ converging to σ^{I}.

7 Let $(X_i)_{i\in\mathbb{N}}$ be a sequence of independent random numbers defined over a probability space $(\Omega, \mathcal{F}, p)$. An event A is called a *tail event* if it depends only on $(X_i)_{i\geq n}$, for each $n \in \mathbb{N}$. In other words, for any $n \in \mathbb{N}$, to ascertain whether $\omega \in A$ it suffices to know the values $(X_i(\omega))_{i\geq n}$, which means that we can ignore a finite number of the initial variables $X_1, X_2, \ldots, X_n$ (for any n). *Kolmogorov's 0–1 law* says that the probability of a tail event is either 0 or 1.

Hint: Consider the function $g : X \to X$ defined by $g(x) := \pi_X(x + f(x))$ for every $x \in X$, where π_X is the projection on X, and use Brouwer's Fixed Point Theorem.

(b) Let $G = (N, (S_i)_{i \in N}, (u_i)_{i \in N})$ be a strategic-form game and let $\Gamma = (N, (\Sigma_i)_{i \in N}, (U_i)_{i \in N})$ be its mixed extension. Recall that $\Sigma := \times_{i \in N} \Sigma_i$ is the set of all mixed action profiles. Let $f : \Sigma \to \mathbb{R}^{\sum_{i \in I} |S_i|}$ be the function defined by

$$f_{i,s_i}(\sigma) := U_i(s_i, \sigma_{-i}), \quad \forall i \in N, s_i \in S_i.$$

Using part (a) prove that the point x^* established there is a Nash equilibrium in mixed strategies of the game Γ.

5.58 Show that every two-player constant-sum game is strategically equivalent to a zero-sum game. For the definition of strategic equivalence, see Definition 5.34 (page 173).

5.59 Prove that if (σ_I, σ_{II}) is the solution of the system of linear equations (5.70)–(5.79) (page 164), then (σ_I, σ_{II}) is a Nash equilibrium.

5.60 Suppose that the preferences of two players satisfy the von Neumann–Morgenstern axioms. Player I is indifferent between receiving $600 with certainty and participating in a lottery in which he receives $300 with probability $\frac{1}{4}$ and $1,500 with probability $\frac{3}{4}$. He is also indifferent between receiving $800 with certainty and participating in a lottery in which he receives $600 with probability $\frac{1}{2}$ and $1,500 with probability $\frac{1}{2}$.

Player II is indifferent between losing $600 with certainty and participating in a lottery in which he loses $300 with probability $\frac{1}{7}$ and $800 with probability $\frac{6}{7}$. He is also indifferent between losing $800 with certainty and participating in a lottery in which he loses $300 with probability $\frac{1}{8}$ and $1,500 with probability $\frac{7}{8}$. The players play the game whose payoff matrix is as follows, where the payoffs are dollars that Player II pays to Player I:

Player II

		L	M	R
Player I	T	$300	$800	$1,500
	B	$1,500	$600	$300

(a) Find linear utility functions for the two players representing the preference relations of the players over the possible outcomes.
(b) Determine whether the game is zero-sum.
(c) If you answered yes to the last question, find optimal strategies for each of the players. If not, find an equilibrium.

5.61 Which of the following games, where Player I is the row player and Player II is the column player, are strategically equivalent to two-player zero-sum games? For each game that is equivalent to a two-player zero-sum game, write explicitly the positive affine transformation that proves your answer.

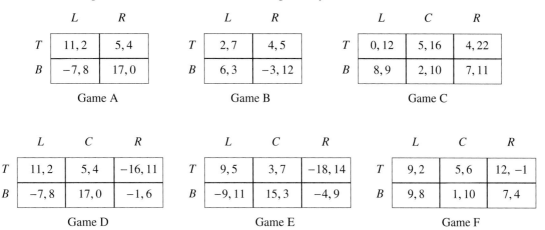

	L	R
T	11, 2	5, 4
B	−7, 8	17, 0

Game A

	L	R
T	2, 7	4, 5
B	6, 3	−3, 12

Game B

	L	C	R
T	0, 12	5, 16	4, 22
B	8, 9	2, 10	7, 11

Game C

	L	C	R
T	11, 2	5, 4	−16, 11
B	−7, 8	17, 0	−1, 6

Game D

	L	C	R
T	9, 5	3, 7	−18, 14
B	−9, 11	15, 3	−4, 9

Game E

	L	C	R
T	9, 2	5, 6	12, −1
B	9, 8	1, 10	7, 4

Game F

5.62 (a) Find the value in mixed strategies and all the optimal strategies of each of the two players in the following two-player zero-sum game:

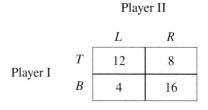

Player II

	L	R
T	12	8
B	4	16

Player I

(b) Increase the utility of Player II by 18, to get

Player II

	L	R
T	12, 6	8, 10
B	4, 14	16, 2

Player I

What are all the equilibria of this game? Justify your answer.

(c) Multiply the utility of the first player in the original game by 2, and add 3, to get the following game:

Player II

	L	R
T	27, −12	19, −8
B	11, −4	35, −16

Player I

What are the equilibrium strategies and equilibrium payoffs in this game?

5.63 Prove Theorem 5.35 on page 173: let G and $\widehat{G}$ be two strategically equivalent strategic-form games. Every equilibrium in mixed strategies σ of G is an equilibrium in mixed strategies of $\widehat{G}$.

5.64 (a) Consider the following two-player game:

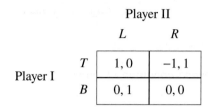

Player II

		L	R
Player I	T	1, 0	−1, 1
	B	0, 1	0, 0

Show that the only equilibrium in the game is $\left[\frac{1}{2}(T), \frac{1}{2}(B)\right], \left[\frac{1}{2}(L), \frac{1}{2}(R)\right]$.

(b) Consider next the two-player zero-sum game derived from the above game in which these payoffs are Player I's payoffs. Compute the value in mixed strategies of this game and all the optimal strategies of Player I.

(c) Suppose that Player I knows that Player II is implementing strategy $\left[\frac{1}{2}(L), \frac{1}{2}(R)\right]$, and he needs to decide whether to implement the mixed strategy $\left[\frac{1}{2}(T), \frac{1}{2}(B)\right]$, which is his part in the equilibrium, or whether to implement instead the pure strategy B, which guarantees him a payoff of 0. Explain in what sense the mixed strategy $\left[\frac{1}{2}(T), \frac{1}{2}(B)\right]$ is equivalent to the pure strategy B, from Player I's perspective.

5.65 A *strategic-form game with constraints* is a quintuple $(N, (S_i, u_i)_{i \in N}, c, \gamma)$ where N is the set of players, S_i is player i's set of pure strategies, $u_i : S \to \mathbb{R}$ is player i's payoff function, where $S = \times_{i \in N} S_i$, $c : S \to \mathbb{R}$ is a constraint function, and $\gamma \in \mathbb{R}$ is a bound. Extend c to mixed strategies in the following way:

$$C(\sigma) = \sum_{s \in S} \sigma_1(s_1)\sigma_2(s_2) \cdots \sigma_n(s_n)c(s). \tag{5.184}$$

In a game with constraints, the vectors of mixed strategies that the players can play are limited to those vectors of mixed strategies satisfying the constraints. Formally, a vector of mixed strategies $\sigma = (\sigma_i)_{i \in N}$ is called *permissible* if $C(\sigma) \leq \gamma$. Games with constraints occur naturally when there is a resource whose use is limited.

(a) Consider the following two-player zero-sum game, with the payoffs and constraints given. The bound is $\gamma = 1$.

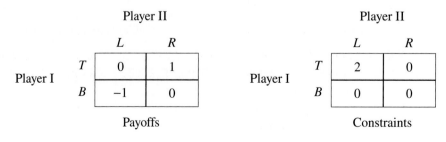

Player II		L	R		Player II		L	R
Player I	T	0	1		Player I	T	2	0
	B	−1	0			B	0	0

Payoffs   Constraints

Compute

$$\max_{\sigma_{\mathrm{I}}\in\Sigma_{\mathrm{I}}} \quad \min_{\{\sigma_{\mathrm{II}}\in\Sigma_{\mathrm{II}}\,:\,C(\sigma_{\mathrm{I}},\sigma_{\mathrm{II}})\leq\gamma\}} \quad U(\sigma_{\mathrm{I}},\sigma_{\mathrm{II}})$$

and

$$\min_{\sigma_{\mathrm{II}}\in\Sigma_{\mathrm{II}}} \quad \max_{\{\sigma_{\mathrm{I}}\in\Sigma_{\mathrm{I}}\,:\,C(\sigma_{\mathrm{I}},\sigma_{\mathrm{II}})\leq\gamma\}} \quad U(\sigma_{\mathrm{I}},\sigma_{\mathrm{II}}).$$

(b) How many equilibria can you find in this game?

The following condition in games with constraints is called the Slater condition. For each player i and every vector of mixed strategies of the other players σ_{-i} there exists a mixed strategy σ_i of player i such that $C(\sigma_i, \sigma_{-i}) < \gamma$ (note the strict inequality). The following items refer to games with constraints satisfying the Slater condition.

(c) Prove that in a two-player zero-sum game with constraints

$$\max_{\sigma_{\mathrm{I}}\in\Sigma_{\mathrm{I}}}\,\min_{\{\sigma_{\mathrm{II}}\in\Sigma_{\mathrm{II}}\,:\,C(\sigma_{\mathrm{I}},\sigma_{\mathrm{II}})\leq\gamma\}} U(\sigma_{\mathrm{I}},\sigma_{\mathrm{II}}) \geq \min_{\sigma_{\mathrm{II}}\in\Sigma_{\mathrm{II}}}\,\max_{\{\sigma_{\mathrm{I}}\in\Sigma_{\mathrm{I}}\,:\,C(\sigma_{\mathrm{I}},\sigma_{\mathrm{II}})\leq\gamma\}} U(\sigma_{\mathrm{I}},\sigma_{\mathrm{II}}).$$

Does this result contradict Theorem 5.40 on page 176? Explain.

(d) Go back to the n-player case. Using the compactness of Σ_i and Σ_{-i}, prove that for every player i,

$$\sup_{\sigma_{-i}\in\Sigma_{-i}} \quad \inf_{\{\sigma_i\in\Sigma_i\,:\,C(\sigma_i,\sigma_{-i})\leq\gamma\}} \quad C(\sigma_i, \sigma_{-i}) < \gamma. \tag{5.185}$$

(e) Prove that for each strategy vector σ satisfying the constraints (i.e., $C(\sigma) \leq \gamma$), for each player i, and each sequence of strategy vectors $(\sigma_{-i}^k)_{k=1}^{\infty}$ converging to σ_{-i}, there exists a sequence $(\sigma_i^k)_{k=1}^{\infty}$ converging to σ_i such that $C(\sigma_i^k, \sigma_{-i}^k) \leq \gamma$ for every k.

(f) Using Kakutani's Fixed Point Theorem (Theorem 24.32 on page 985), show that in every strategic-form game with constraints there exists an equilibrium. In other words, show that there exists a permissible vector σ^* satisfying the condition that for each player $i \in N$ and each strategy σ_i^* of player i, if $(\sigma_i, \sigma_{-i}^*)$ is a permissible strategy vector, then $U_i(\sigma_i, \sigma_{-i}^*) \leq U_i(\sigma^*)$.

Hint: To prove part (c), denote by v the value of the game without constraints, and prove that the left-hand side of the inequality is greater than or equal to v, and the right-hand side of the inequality is less than or equal to v.

5.66 Prove Theorem 5.45 on page 181: If information is added to Player I in a two-player zero-sum game, the value of the game in mixed strategies does not decrease.

5.67 Compute the (unique) equilibrium payoff in each of the following two-player extensive-form games. Which player gains, and which player loses, from the addition of information to Player I, i.e., when moving from Game A to Game B? Is the result of adding information here identical to the result of adding information in Example 5.47 (page 183)? Why?

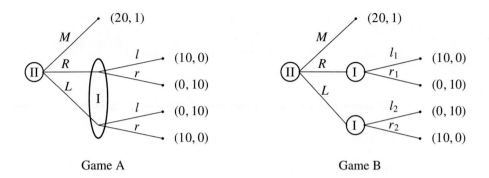

Game A   Game B

5.68 Consider the following two-player game composed of two stages. In the first stage, one of the two following matrices is chosen by a coin toss (with each matrix chosen with probability $\frac{1}{2}$). In the second stage, the two players play the strategic-form game whose payoff matrix is given by the matrix that has been chosen.

Player II

	L	C	R
T	0, 0	1, −1	−1, 10
B	−2, −2	−2, −2	−3, −12

Player I

Player II

	L	C	R
T	−1, 1	−2, −1	−2, −11
B	0, $\frac{1}{2}$	−1, 0	−1, 10

Player I

For each of the following cases, depict the game as an extensive-form game, and find the unique equilibrium:

(a) No player knows which matrix was chosen.
(b) Player I knows which matrix was chosen, but Player II does not know which matrix was chosen.

What effect does adding information to Player I have on the payoffs to the players at equilibrium?

5.69 Prove that in a two-player game, the maxmin value in mixed strategies of a player equals his minmax value in mixed strategies.

5.70 In this exercise we will prove von Neumann's Minmax Theorem (Exercise 5.11 on page 150), using the Duality Theorem from the theory of linear programming (see Section 24.3 on page 991 for a brief review of linear programming).

Let G be a two-player zero-sum game in which Player I has n pure strategies, Player II has m pure strategies, and the payoff matrix is A. Consider the following linear program, in the variables $y = (y_j)_{j=1}^m$, in which c is a real number and $\vec{c}$ is an n-dimensional vector, all of whose coordinates equal c:

$$
\begin{aligned}
\text{Compute:} \quad & Z_P := \min c, \\
\text{subject to:} \quad & Ay^\top \le \vec{c}, \\
& \textstyle\sum_{j=1}^m y_j = 1, \\
& y \ge \vec{0}.
\end{aligned}
$$

(a) Write down the dual program.

(b) Show that the set of all y satisfying the constraints of the primal program is a compact set, and conclude that Z_P is finite.

(c) Show that the optimal solution to the primal program defines a mixed strategy for Player II that guarantees him an expected payoff of at most Z_P.

(d) Show that the optimal solution to the dual program defines a mixed strategy for Player I that guarantees an expected payoff of at least Z_D.

(e) Explain why the Duality Theorem is applicable here. Since the Duality Theorem implies that $Z_P = Z_D$, deduce that Z_P is the value of the game.

5.71 Prove the following claims for n-player extensive-form games:

(a) Adding information to one of the players does not increase the maxmin or the minmax value of the other players.

(b) Adding information to one of the players does not increase the minmax value of the other players.

(c) Adding information to one of the players may have no effect on his maxmin value.

(d) Adding information to one of the players may decrease the maxmin value of the other players.

5.72 Find all the equilibria of Game B in Figure 5.29 (page 183). What are the equilibria payoffs corresponding to these equilibria?

5.73 Prove Lemma 5.57 (page 188): If s_i is a strictly dominated pure strategy, then $s_i \notin \mathrm{br}_i(D_{-i})$, for every collection of nonempty sets of pure strategies $(D_j)_{j \neq i}$.

5.74 Prove Lemma 5.58 (page 188): If the pure-strategy profile $s \in S$ is rationalizable, then it survives the process of iterated elimination of strictly dominated strategies.

5.75 Find the set of rationalizable strategy profiles in the following games:

Player II

		L	M
Player I	T	3, 3	0, 0
	B	0, 0	1, 1

Game A

Player II

		L	M
Player I	T	4, 4	1, 4
	B	4, 1	3, 3

Game B

Player II

		L	C	R
Player I	T	4, 2	1, 1	4, 3
	M	1, 3	0, 4	1, 2
	B	0, 1	1, 1	0, 1

Game C

Player II

		L	C	R
Player I	T	2, 5	2, 2	0, 4
	M	1, 2	0, 4	3, 2
	B	0, 0	1, 5	4, 1

Game D

5.76 Prove Corollary 5.53 (page 187): Let $\sigma^* = (\sigma_i^*)_{i \in N}$ be a mixed-strategy Nash equilibrium. Let $s = (s_i)_{i \in I}$ be a pure-strategy profile that is played under σ^* with positive probability: $\sigma_i^*(s_i) > 0$ for every $i \in N$. Then s is a rationalizable pure-strategy profile.

5.77 A game is called *solvable by dominance* if the process of iterated elimination of strictly dominated strategies (by mixed strategies) results in a single strategy profile. Answer the following questions:

(a) Prove that if a strategic-form game is solvable by dominance, then it has a unique rationalizable strategy profile.

(b) Show that if a strategic-form game is solvable by dominance, then its unique outcome is a Nash equilibrium, and it is the only Nash equilibrium in mixed strategies of the game.

5.78 Construct a three-player strategic-form game in which one player has a never-best-reply strategy that is not strictly dominated. For this game, find the set of rationalizable strategy profiles and the set of strategies obtained by iterated elimination of strictly dominated strategies. Verify that the set of rationalizable strategy profiles is strictly included in the set of strategy profiles obtained by iterated elimination of strictly dominated strategies.

5.79 In this exercise we study a variation of the concept of rationalizability, where players believe that the other players may coordinate their pure strategies. For every player $i \in N$, every pure strategy $s_i \in S_i$, and every probability distribution $\sigma_{-i} \in \Delta(S_{-i})$, define

$$U_i(s_i, \sigma_{-i}) := \sum_{s_{-i} \in S_{-i}} \sigma_{-i}(s_{-i}) u_i(s_i, s_{-i}).$$

For every collection of nonempty sets of pure strategies $(D_j)_{j \in N}$, define

$$\mathrm{br}_i^*(D_{-i}) := \cup_{\sigma_{-i} \in \Delta(\times_{j \neq i} D_j)} \mathrm{argmax}_{s_i \in S_i} U_i(s_i, \sigma_{-i}) \subseteq S_i. \tag{5.186}$$

Answer the following questions:

(a) Prove the analogue of Theorem 5.51: For every player $i \in N$ there exists a nonempty set of pure strategies $T_i \subseteq S_i$ such that $T_i = \mathrm{br}_i^*(T_{-i})$, where $T_{-i} = (T_j)_{j \neq i}$. Moreover, every collection of nonempty sets $(D_i)_{i \in N}$ that satisfies $D_i \subseteq \mathrm{br}_i^*(D_{-i})$ for each $i \in N$ also satisfies $D_i \subseteq T_i$ for each $i \in N$.

(b) Prove the analogue of Theorem 5.59: Let $\Gamma = (N, (S_i)_{i \in N}, (u_i)_{i \in N})$ be a strategic-form game where the sets of pure strategies of the players are finite. Let $i \in N$ be a player and let $s_i \notin \mathrm{br}_i^*(S_{-i})$. Prove that the strategy s_i is strictly dominated by a mixed strategy.

(c) Prove the analogue of Corollary 5.60: For any number of players, the set $\times_{i \in N} T_i$ is the set of pure-strategy profiles that survive iterated elimination of strictly dominated strategies.

5.80 Find all the equilibrium points of the following games, and ascertain which of them defines an evolutionarily stable strategy.

	Population	
	Dove	Hawk
Dove	2, 2	8, 3
Hawk	3, 8	7, 7

Mutation

Game A

	Population	
	Dove	Hawk
Dove	2, 2	1, 3
Hawk	3, 1	7, 7

Mutation

Game B

	Population	
	Dove	Hawk
Dove	2, 2	0, 1
Hawk	1, 0	7, 7

Mutation

Game C

	Population	
	Dove	Hawk
Dove	1, 1	1, 1
Hawk	1, 1	1, 1

Mutation

Game D

	Population	
	Dove	Hawk
Dove	2, 2	8, 8
Hawk	8, 8	7, 7

Mutation

Game E

	Population	
	Dove	Hawk
Dove	1, 1	1, 1
Hawk	1, 1	2, 2

Mutation

Game F

5.81 Suppose that a symmetric two-player game, in which each player has two pure strategies and all payoffs are nonnegative, is given by the following figure:

Player II

	L	R
T	a, a	d, c
B	c, d	b, b

Player I

What conditions on a, b, c, d guarantee the existence of an ESS?

5.82 Prove that the unique Nash equilibrium of Rock, Paper, Scissors (Example 4.3, on page 77) is

$$\left(\left[\tfrac{1}{3}(\text{Rock}), \tfrac{1}{3}(\text{Paper}), \tfrac{1}{3}(\text{Scissors})\right]; \left[\tfrac{1}{3}(\text{Rock}), \tfrac{1}{3}(\text{Paper}), \tfrac{1}{3}(\text{Scissors})\right]\right).$$

5.83 Suppose that the males and females of a particular animal species have two types of behavior: care for offspring, or abandonment of offspring. The expected number of offspring are presented in the following matrix.

	Mother	
	Care	Abandon
Father Care	$V-c, V-c$	$\alpha V - c, \alpha V$
Abandon	$\alpha V, \alpha V - c$	$0, 0$

Explanation: V is the expected number of surviving offspring if they are cared for by both parents. If only one parent cares for the offspring, the expected number of surviving offspring is reduced to αV, $0 < \alpha < 1$. In addition, a parent who cares for his or her offspring invests energy and time into that care, which reduces the number of surviving offspring he or she has by c (because he or she has fewer mating encounters with other animals).

Prove the following claims:

(a) If $V - c > \alpha V$ and $\alpha V - c > 0$ (which results in a relatively smaller investment, since $c < \alpha V$ and $c < (1 - \alpha)V$), then the only evolutionarily stable strategy is Care, meaning that both parents care for their offspring.

(b) If $V - c < \alpha V$ and $\alpha V - c < 0$ (which results in a high cost for caring for offspring), the only evolutionarily stable strategy is Abandon, and hence both parents abandon their offspring.

(c) If $\alpha < \frac{1}{2}$ (in this case $(1 - \alpha)V > \alpha V$, and investment in caring for offspring satisfies $(1 - \alpha)V > c > \alpha V$), there are two evolutionarily stable equilibria, Care and Abandon, showing that both Care and Abandon are evolutionarily stable strategies. Which equilibrium emerges in practice in the population depends on the initial conditions.

(d) If $\alpha > \frac{1}{2}$ (in this case $\alpha V > (1 - \alpha)V$, and investment in caring for offspring satisfies $\alpha V > c > (1 - \alpha)V$), the only evolutionarily stable equilibrium is the mixed strategy in which Care is chosen with probability $\frac{\alpha V - c}{(2\alpha - 1)V}$.

Remark: The significance of $\alpha < \frac{1}{2}$ is that "two together are better than two separately." The significance of $\alpha > \frac{1}{2}$ is that "two together are worse than two separately."

5.84 A single male leopard can mate with all the female leopards on the savanna. Why, then, is every generation of leopards composed of 50% males and 50% females? Does this not constitute a waste of resources? Explain, using ideas presented in Section 5.9 (page 190), why the evolutionarily stable strategy is that at which the number of male leopards born equals the number of female leopards born.[8]

5.85 In the following two-player game, the payoffs in the cell (T, L) are parameters. For every $x, y \in \mathbb{R}$, find all the equilibria of the game.

---

8 In actual fact, the ratio of the males to females in most species is close to 50%, but not exactly 50%. We will not present here various explanations that have been suggested for this phenomenon.

Player II

		L	R
		L	R
Player I	T	x, y	$0, 0$
	B	$0, 0$	$1, 1$

5.86 Let N be a finite set of players and for every player $i \in N$ let S_i be a finite set of pure strategies of that player. Let $(u^k)_{k=1}^{\infty}$ be an infinite sequence of payoff functions; that is, $u^k = (u_i^k)_{i \in N}$ is a vector of payoff functions for every $k \in \mathbb{N}$, so that $u^k : \times_{i \in N} S_i \to \mathbb{R}^N$. For every $k \in \mathbb{N}$ let σ^k be an equilibrium of the strategic form game $(N, (S_i)_{i \in N}, (u_i^k)_{i \in N})$. Suppose that for every player $i \in N$ and every $s \in \times_{i \in N} S_i$ we have:

- $\lim_{k \to \infty} u_i^k(s)$ exists and is equal to $u_i^*(s)$.
- $\lim_{k \to \infty} \sigma_i^k(s_i)$ exists and is equal to $\sigma_i^*(s_i)$.

Prove that $\sigma^* = (\sigma_i^*)_{i \in N}$ is an equilibrium of the game $(N, (S_i)_{i \in N}, (u_i^*)_{i \in N})$. Explain why this result does not contradict Exercise 5.42.

5.87 Let $\eta : \mathcal{G}_i \to \widetilde{\mathcal{G}}_i(N, S) \times \overline{\mathcal{G}}_i(S_i)$ be the function defined by $\eta(u_i) := (\widetilde{u}_i, \overline{u}_i)$, where $\widetilde{u}_i$ is defined as in Equation (5.146) and $\overline{u}_i$ is defined as in Equation (5.145).

(a) Prove that the function η is one-to-one and onto.
(b) Prove that the inverse function η^{-1} is continuous.

5.88 Prove that the function φ defined in Equation (5.161) has the following property: If $(u^k, \sigma^k)_{k \in \mathbb{N}}$ is a sequence of points in E satisfying $\lim_{k \to \infty} \|u^k\|_{\infty} = \infty$, then $\lim_{k \to \infty} \|\varphi(u^k, \sigma^k)\|_{\infty} = \infty$.

Behavior strategies and Kuhn's Theorem

Chapter summary

In strategic-form games, a mixed strategy extends the player's possibilities by allowing him to choose a pure strategy randomly. In extensive-form games, random choices can be executed in two ways. The player can randomly choose a pure strategy for the whole play at the outset of the game; this type of randomization yields in fact the concept of mixed strategy in an extensive-form game. Alternatively, at every one of his information sets, the player can randomly choose one of his available actions; this type of randomization yields the concept of *behavior strategy*, which is the subject of this chapter.

We study the relationship between behavior strategies and mixed strategies in extensive-form games. To this end we define an *equivalence* relation between strategies and we show by examples that there are games in which some mixed strategies do not have equivalent behavior strategies, and there are games in which some behavior strategies do not have equivalent mixed strategies. We then introduce the concept of *perfect recall*: a player has perfect recall in an extensive-form game if along the play of the game he does not forget any information that he knew in the past (regarding his moves, the other players' moves, or chance moves). We prove Kuhn's Theorem, which states that if a player has perfect recall, then any one of his behavior strategies is equivalent to a mixed strategy, and vice versa. It follows that a game in which all players have perfect recall possesses an equilibrium in behavior strategies.

As noted in previous chapters, extensive-form games and strategic-form games are not related in a one-to-one manner. In general, the extensive form is richer in detail, and incorporates "dynamic aspects" of the game that are not expressed in strategic form. Strategic-form games focus exclusively on strategies and outcomes. Given this, it is worthwhile to take a closer look at the concepts developed for the two forms of games and detect differences between them, if there are any, due to the different representations of the game. We have already seen that the concept of pure strategy, which is a fundamental element of strategic-form games, is also well defined in extensive-form games, where a pure strategy of a player is a function that maps each of his information sets to an action that is feasible at that information set.

In this chapter (only), we will denote the multilinear extension (expectation) of player i's payoff function by u_i, rather than U_i, because U_i will denote an information set of player i.

Example 6.1   Consider the two-player extensive-form game given in Figure 6.1.

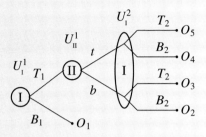

Figure 6.1 The game in Example 6.1

In this game, Player I has two information sets, U_I^1 and U_I^2, and four pure strategies:

$$S_I = \{T_1 T_2, T_1 B_2, B_1 T_2, B_1 B_2\}. \tag{6.1}$$

Player II has one information set, U_{II}^1, and two pure strategies:

$$S_{II} = \{t, b\}. \tag{6.2}$$

Mixed strategies are defined as probability distributions over sets of pure strategies. The concept of mixed strategy is therefore well defined in every game in which the set of pure strategies is a finite or countable set, whether the game is an extensive-form game or a strategic-form game. The sets of mixed strategies are[1]

$$\Sigma_I = \Delta(S_I), \quad \Sigma_{II} = \Delta(S_{II}). \tag{6.3}$$

One of the interpretations of the concept of mixed strategy is that it is a random choice of how to play the game. But there may be different ways of attaining such randomness. Clearly, if a player has only one move (only one information set), such as Player II in the game in Figure 6.1, there is only one way to implement a random choice of an action: to pick t with probability α, and b with probability $1 - \alpha$. That does indeed define a mixed strategy.

What about Player I, who has two information sets in the game in Figure 6.1? Suppose that he implements a mixed strategy, such as, for example, $\sigma_I = [\frac{1}{3}(T_1 T_2), 0(T_1 B_2), \frac{1}{3}(B_1 T_2), \frac{1}{3}(B_1 B_2)]$. Then he is essentially conducting a lottery at the start of the game, and then implementing the pure strategy that has been chosen by the lottery.

However, Player I has another, equally natural, alternative way to attain randomness: he can choose randomly between T_1 and B_1 when the play of the game arrives at his information set U_I^1, and then choose randomly between T_2 and B_2 when the play of the game arrives at his information set U_I^2. Such a strategy is described by two lotteries: $[\alpha(T_1), (1 - \alpha)(B_1)]$ at U_I^1, and $[\beta(T_2), (1 - \beta)(B_2)]$ at U_I^2. In other words, instead of randomly choosing a grand plan (a pure strategy) that determines his actions at each of his information sets, the player randomly chooses his action every time he is at a particular information set. Such a strategy is called a *behavior strategy*.   ◀

Is there an essential difference between these two strategies? Can a player attain a higher payoff by using a behavior strategy instead of a mixed strategy? Alternatively, can he attain a higher payoff by using a mixed strategy instead of a behavior strategy? We will answer these questions in this chapter, and find conditions under which it makes no difference which of these alternative strategy concepts is used.

----

1 Recall that for every finite set S, $\Delta(S)$ is the set of all probability distributions over S (Definition 5.2, page 145).

Behavior strategies

Definition 6.2 *A* behavior strategy *of a player in an extensive-form game is a function mapping each of his information sets to a probability distribution over the set of possible actions at that information set.*

Recall that we denote by $\mathcal{U}_i$ the collection of information sets of player i, and for every information set $U_i \in \mathcal{U}_i$, we denote by $A(U_i)$ the set of possible actions at U_i. A behavior strategy of player i in an extensive-form game is a function $b_i : \mathcal{U}_i \to \cup_{U_i \in \mathcal{U}_i} \Delta(A(U_i))$ such that $b_i(U_i) \in \Delta(A(U_i))$ for all $U_i \in \mathcal{U}_i$. Equivalently, a behavior strategy is a vector of probability distributions (lotteries), one per information set. This is in contrast with the single probability distribution (single lottery) defining a mixed strategy. The probability that a behavior strategy b_i will choose an action $a_i \in A(U_i)$ at an information set U_i is denoted by $b_i(a_i; U_i)$.

Recall that Σ_i is player i's set of mixed strategies; player i's set of behavior strategies is denoted by $\mathcal{B}_i$. What is the relationship between $\mathcal{B}_i$ and Σ_i? Note first that in every case in which player i has at least two information sets at which he has at least two possible actions, the sets $\mathcal{B}_i$ and Σ_i are different mathematical structures – two sets in different spaces. This is illustrated in Example 6.1.

Example 6.1 (*Continued*) As noted above, in the example Player I's behavior strategy is described by two lotteries: $b_{\mathrm{I}} = ([\alpha(T_1), (1 - \alpha)(B_1)], [\beta(T_2), (1 - \beta)(B_2)])$. Equivalently, we can describe this behavior strategy by a pair of real numbers α, β in the unit interval. The set $\mathcal{B}_{\mathrm{I}}$ is thus equivalent to the set

$$\{(\alpha, \beta) : 0 \le \alpha \le 1, 0 \le \beta \le 1\}, \tag{6.4}$$

while Σ_{I} is equivalent to the set

$$\left\{ (x_1, x_2, x_3, x_4) : x_j \ge 0, \sum_{j=1}^{4} x_j = 1 \right\}. \tag{6.5}$$

In other words, Σ_{I} is equivalent to a subset of $\mathbb{R}^4$ (which is three-dimensional, due to the constraint $\sum_{j=1}^{4} x_j = 1$). By contrast, $\mathcal{B}_{\mathrm{I}}$ is equivalent to a subset of $\mathbb{R}^2$: the unit square $[0, 1]^2$. The fact that Σ_{I} is of higher dimension than $\mathcal{B}_{\mathrm{I}}$ (three dimensions versus two dimensions) suggests that Σ_{I} may be a "richer," or a "larger," set.

In fact, in the example, for every behavior strategy one can define an "equivalent" mixed strategy: the behavior strategy

$$([\alpha(T_1), (1 - \alpha)(B_1)], [\beta(T_2), (1 - \beta)(B_2)]) \tag{6.6}$$

is equivalent to the mixed strategy

$$[\alpha\beta(T_1T_2), \alpha(1 - \beta)T_1B_2, (1 - \alpha)\beta B_1T_2, (1 - \alpha)(1 - \beta)B_1B_2]. \tag{6.7}$$

The sense in which these two strategies are equivalent is as follows: for each one of Player II's mixed strategies, the probability of reaching a particular vertex of the tree when Player I uses the behavior strategy (α, β) of Equation (6.6) equals the probability of reaching that vertex when Player I uses the mixed strategy of Equation (6.7).　◀

To define formally the equivalence between a mixed strategy and a behavior strategy, we consider strategy vectors that consist of both mixed strategies and behavior strategies.

Definition 6.3 *A mixed/behavior strategy vector is a vector of strategies* $\sigma = (\sigma_i)_i$ *in which* σ_i *can be either a mixed strategy or a behavior strategy of player i, for each i.*

For every mixed/behavior strategy vector $\sigma = (\sigma_i)_{i \in N}$ and every vertex x in the game tree, denote by $\rho(x; \sigma)$ the probability that vertex x will be visited during the course of the play of the game when the players implement strategies $(\sigma_i)_{i \in N}$.

Example 6.4 Consider the two-player game depicted in Figure 6.2. In this figure, the vertices of the tree are denoted by $x_1, x_2, \ldots, x_{17}$.

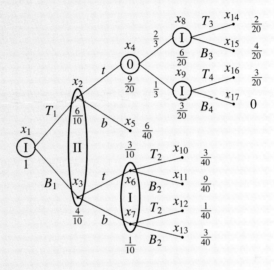

Figure 6.2 A two-player game, including the probabilities of arriving at each vertex

Suppose that the players implement the following mixed strategies:

$$\sigma_{\mathrm{I}} = \left[\frac{3}{10}(B_1 B_1 B_3 B_4), \frac{1}{10}(B_1 T_2 B_3 B_4), \frac{4}{10}(T_1 B_2 B_3 T_4), \frac{2}{10}(T_1 B_2 T_3 T_4) \right], \tag{6.8}$$

$$\sigma_{\mathrm{II}} = \left[\frac{3}{4}(t), \frac{1}{4}(b) \right]. \tag{6.9}$$

Given these mixed strategies, we have computed the probabilities that the play of the game will reach the various vertices of the game tree, and these probabilities are listed alongside the vertices in Figure 6.2. We began at the leaves of the tree; for example, the probability of arriving at leaf x_{13} is the probability that Player I will play B_1 at vertex x_1, and B_2 at information set $\{x_6, x_7\}$, and that Player II will play b at information set $\{x_2, x_3\}$. From among the four pure strategies of Player I for which σ_{I} assigns positive probability, Player I will play B_1 at vertex x_1 and B_2 at information set $\{x_6, x_7\}$ only at the pure strategy $(B_1 B_2 B_3 B_4)$, with this pure strategy chosen by σ_{I} with probability $\frac{3}{10}$. Since the mixed strategies of the two players (which are probability distributions over their pure strategy sets) are independent, the probability that the play of the game will reach the leaf x_{13} is $\frac{3}{10} \times \frac{1}{4} = \frac{3}{40}$. We compute the probability of getting to a vertex that is not a leaf by recursion from the leaves to the root: the probability of getting to a vertex x is the sum of the probabilities of getting to one of the children of x. ◄

Definition 6.5 *A mixed strategy σ_i and a behavior strategy b_i of player i in an extensive-form game are equivalent to each other if for every mixed/behavior strategy vector σ_{-i} of the players $N \setminus \{i\}$ and every vertex x in the game tree*

$$\rho(x; \sigma_i, \sigma_{-i}) = \rho(x; b_i, \sigma_{-i}). \tag{6.10}$$

In other words, the mixed strategy σ_i and the behavior strategy b_i are equivalent if for every mixed/behavior strategy vector σ_{-i}, the two strategy vectors (σ_i, σ_{-i}) and (b_i, σ_{-i}) induce the same probability of arriving at each vertex in the game tree. In particular, $\rho(x; \sigma_i, \sigma_{-i}) = \rho(x; b_i, \sigma_{-i})$ for every leaf x. The probability $\rho(x; \sigma)$ that the vertex x will be visited during a play of the game equals the sum of the probabilities that the leaves that are descendants of x will be visited. It follows that to check that Equation (6.10) holds for every vertex x it suffices to check that it holds for every leaf of the game tree. It further follows from the definition that when the behavior strategy b_i is equivalent to the mixed strategy σ_i, then for every mixed/behavior strategy vector σ_{-i} of the other players the two strategy vectors (σ_i, σ_{-i}) and (b_i, σ_{-i}) lead to the same expected payoff (Exercise 6.6).

Theorem 6.6 *If a mixed strategy σ_i of player i is equivalent to a behavior strategy b_i, then for every mixed/behavior strategy vector σ_{-i} of the other players and every player $j \in N$,*

$$u_j(\sigma_i, \sigma_{-i}) = u_j(b_i, \sigma_{-i}). \tag{6.11}$$

Repeated application of Theorem 6.6 leads to the following corollary:

Corollary 6.7 *Let $\sigma = (\sigma_i)_{i \in N}$ be a vector of mixed strategies. For each player i, let b_i be a behavior strategy that is equivalent to σ_i, and denote $b = (b_i)_{i \in N}$. Then, for each player i,*

$$u_i(\sigma) = u_i(b). \tag{6.12}$$

Example 6.4   (*Continued*) Given the probabilities calculated in Figure 6.2, the behavior strategy b_{I} defined by

$$b_{\mathrm{I}} = \left(\left[\tfrac{3}{5}(T_1), \tfrac{2}{5}(B_1) \right], \left[\tfrac{1}{4}(T_2), \tfrac{3}{4}(B_2) \right], \left[\tfrac{1}{3}(T_3), \tfrac{2}{3}(B_3) \right], \left[1(T_4), 0(B_4) \right] \right) \tag{6.13}$$

is equivalent to the mixed strategy σ_{I} defined in Equation (6.8),

$$\sigma_{\mathrm{I}} = \left[\tfrac{3}{10}(B_1 B_2 B_3 B_4), \tfrac{1}{10}(B_1 T_2 B_3 B_4), \tfrac{4}{10}(T_1 B_2 B_3 T_4), \tfrac{2}{10}(T_1 B_2 T_3 T_4) \right]. \tag{6.14}$$

To see how behavior strategy b_{I} was computed from the mixed strategy σ_{I}, suppose that Player II implements strategy $\sigma_{\mathrm{I}} = [\tfrac{3}{4}(t), \tfrac{1}{4}(b)]$. The probability that the play of the game will arrive at each vertex x appears in the game tree in Figure 6.2. If behavior strategy b_{I} is equivalent to the mixed strategy σ_{I}, then the probability that an action in a particular information set is chosen is the ratio between the probability of arriving at the vertex that leads to that action and the probability of arriving at the vertex at which the action is chosen. For example, in order to compute the probability at which the action B_2 is chosen in the information set $\{x_6, x_7\}$, we divide the probability $\tfrac{3}{40}$ of reaching vertex x_{13} by the probability $\tfrac{1}{10}$ of reaching vertex x_7, to obtain $\tfrac{3/40}{1/10} = \tfrac{3}{4}$, corresponding to $[\tfrac{1}{4}(T_2), \tfrac{3}{4}(B_2)]$ in strategy b_{I} (we obtain a similar result, of course, if we divide the probability

$\frac{9}{40}$ of reaching vertex x_{11} by the probability $\frac{3}{10}$ of reaching vertex x_6). To complete the construction of b_I from the mixed strategy σ_I, similar computations need to be conducted at Player I's other information sets, and it must be shown that these computations lead to the same outcome for all strategies $[\alpha(t), (1-\alpha)(b)]$ of Player II (Exercise 6.7).   ◄

Using a behavior strategy, instead of a mixed strategy, may be advantageous for two reasons. Firstly, the set $\mathcal{B}_i$ is "smaller," and defined by fewer parameters, than the set Σ_i. For example, if the player has four information sets, with two actions at each information set (as happens in Example 6.4), the total number of pure strategies available is $2^4 = 16$, so that a mixed strategy involves 15 variables, as opposed to a behavior strategy, which involves only four variables (namely, the probability of selecting the first action in each one of the information sets). Secondly, in large extensive-form games, behavior strategies appear to be "more natural," because in behavior strategies, players choose randomly between their actions at each information set at which they find themselves, rather than making one grand random choice of a "master plan" (i.e., a pure strategy) for the entire game, all at once. This motivates the questions of whether each mixed strategy has an equivalent behavior strategy, and whether each behavior strategy has an equivalent mixed strategy. As the next two examples show, the answers to both questions may, in general, be negative.

Example 6.8 **A mixed strategy that has no equivalent behavior strategy** Consider the game in Figure 6.3, involving only one player.

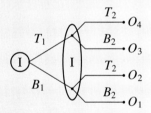

Figure 6.3 A game with a mixed strategy that has no equivalent behavior strategy

There are four pure strategies, $\{T_1T_2, T_1B_2, B_1T_2, B_1B_2\}$. We will show that there is no behavior strategy that is equivalent to the mixed strategy $\sigma_I = [\frac{1}{2}(T_1T_2), 0(T_1B_2), 0(T_2B_1), \frac{1}{2}(B_1B_2)]$. This mixed strategy induces the following probability distribution over the outcomes of the game:

$$\left[\tfrac{1}{2}(O_1), 0(O_2), 0(O_3), \tfrac{1}{2}(O_4)\right]. \tag{6.15}$$

A behavior strategy $([\alpha(T_1), (1-\alpha)(B_1)], [\beta(T_2), (1-\beta)(B_2)])$ induces the following probability distribution over the outcomes of the game:

$$[(1-\alpha)(1-\beta)(O_1), (1-\alpha)\beta(O_2), \alpha(1-\beta)(O_3), \alpha\beta(O_4)]. \tag{6.16}$$

If this behavior strategy were equivalent to the mixed strategy σ_I, they would both induce the same probability distributions over the outcomes of the game, so that the following equalities would have to obtain:

$$\alpha\beta = \tfrac{1}{2}, \tag{6.17}$$

$$\alpha(1-\beta) = 0, \tag{6.18}$$

$$(1 - \alpha)\beta = 0, \tag{6.19}$$

$$(1 - \alpha)(1 - \beta) = \tfrac{1}{2}. \tag{6.20}$$

But this system of equations has no solution: Equation (6.18) implies that either $\alpha = 0$ or $\beta = 1$. If $\alpha = 0$, Equation (6.17) does not hold, and if $\beta = 1$, Equation (6.20) does not hold. ◀

Example 6.9   **The Absent-Minded Driver: a game with a behavior strategy that has no equivalent mixed strategy** Consider the game in Figure 6.4, involving only one player, Player I. In this game, the player, when he comes to choosing an action, cannot recall whether or not he has chosen an action in the past. An illustrative story that often accompanies this example is that of an absent-minded driver, motoring down a road with two exits. When the driver arrives at an exit, he cannot recall whether it is the first exit on the road, or the second exit.

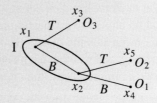

Figure 6.4 The Absent-Minded Driver game

There are two pure strategies: T and B. The pure strategy T yields the outcome O_3, while the pure strategy B yields the outcome O_1. Since a mixed strategy is a probability distribution over the set of pure strategies, no mixed strategy can yield the outcome O_2 with positive probability.

In contrast, the behavior strategy $[\tfrac{1}{2}(T), \tfrac{1}{2}(B)]$, where the player chooses one of the two actions with equal probability at each of the two vertices in his information set, leads to the following probability distribution over outcomes:

$$\left[\tfrac{1}{4}(O_1), \tfrac{1}{4}(O_2), \tfrac{1}{2}(O_3)\right]. \tag{6.21}$$

Since this probability distribution can never be the result of implementing a mixed strategy, we conclude that there is no mixed strategy equivalent to this behavior strategy. ◀

6.2   Kuhn's Theorem

Let us note that the player suffers from forgetfulness of a different kind in each of the above examples. In Example 6.8, when the player is about to take an action the second time, he cannot recall what action he chose the first time; he knows that he has made a previous move, but cannot recall what action he took. In Example 6.9, the player does not even recall whether or not he has made a move in the past (although he does know that if he did make a prior move, he necessarily must have chosen action B). What happens when the player is not forgetful? Will this ensure that every behavior strategy has an equivalent mixed strategy, and that every mixed strategy has an equivalent behavior strategy? As we will show in this section, the answer to these questions is affirmative.

6.2.1 Conditions for the existence of an equivalent mixed strategy to any behavior strategy

Let x be a vertex in the game tree that is not the root, and let x_1 be a vertex on the path from the root to x. The (unique) edge emanating from x_1 on the path from the root to x is called the *action at x_1 leading to x*.

A pure strategy selects the same action at every vertex in each one of the corresponding player's information sets. It follows that if the path from the root to x passes through two vertices x_1 and $\widehat{x}_1$ that are in the same information set of player i, and if the action at x_1 leading to x differs from the action at $\widehat{x}_1$ leading to x, then when player i implements a pure strategy the play of the game cannot arrive at x. For this reason, in Example 6.9 there is no pure strategy leading to the vertex x_5. Since a mixed strategy is a probability distribution over pure strategies, the probability that a play of the game will arrive at such a vertex x is 0 when player i implements any mixed strategy. In contrast, if all the players implement behavior strategies in which at every information set every possible action is played with positive probability, then for each vertex in the game tree there is a positive probability that the play of the game will reach that vertex. This leads to the following conclusion (Exercise 6.8).

Corollary 6.10 *If there exists a path from the root to some vertex x that passes at least twice through the same information set U_i of player i, and if the action leading in the direction of x is not the same action at each of these information sets, then player i has a behavior strategy that has no equivalent mixed strategy.*

The last corollary will be used to prove the next theorem, which gives a necessary and sufficient condition for the existence of a mixed strategy equivalent to every behavior strategy. If every path emanating from the root passes through each information set at most once, then every behavior strategy has an equivalent mixed strategy.

Theorem 6.11 *Let $\Gamma = (N, V, E, v_0, (V_i)_{i \in N \cup \{0\}}, (p_x)_{x \in V_0}, (\mathcal{U}_i)_{i \in N}, O, u)$ be an extensive-form game that satisfies the condition that at every vertex there are at least two actions. Every behavior strategy of player i has an equivalent mixed strategy if and only if each information set of player i intersects every path emanating from the root at most once.*

In the game in Example 6.9, there is a path that twice intersects the same information set, and we indeed identified a behavior strategy of that game that has no equivalent mixed strategy. The theorem does not hold without the condition that there are at least two actions at each vertex (Exercise 6.9). We first prove that the condition in the statement of the theorem is necessary.

Proof of Theorem 6.11 – the condition is necessary: Suppose that there exists a path from the root to a vertex x that intersects the same information set U_i of player i at least twice. We will prove that there is a behavior strategy of player i that has no mixed strategy equivalent to it. Let x_1 and $\widehat{x}_1$ be two distinct vertices in the above-mentioned information set that are located along the path (see Figure 6.5). Denote by a the action at x_1 leading to x, and by b an action at x_1 that differs from a. Let x_2 be the vertex that the play of the game reaches if at vertex $\widehat{x}_1$ player i chooses action b.

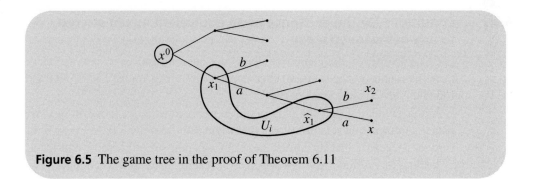

Figure 6.5 The game tree in the proof of Theorem 6.11

The path from the root to x_2 passes through the vertices x_1 and $\hat{x}_1$, the action at x_1 leading to x_2 is a, and the action at $\hat{x}_1$ leading to x_2 is b. By Corollary 6.10 it follows that there is a behavior strategy of player i that has no mixed strategy equivalent to it, which is what we needed to show. $\qquad\square$

We now explain the idea underlying the proof of the second direction. The proof itself will be presented in Section 6.2.3 after we introduce several definitions. Let b_i be a behavior strategy of player i. When the play of the game arrives at information set U_i, player i conducts a lottery based on the probability distribution $b_i(U_i)$ to choose one of the actions available at information set U_i. Player i could just as easily conduct this lottery at the start of the game, instead of waiting until he gets to the information set U_i. In other words, at the start of the game, the player can conduct a lottery for each one of his information sets U_i, using in each case the probability distribution $b_i(U_i)$, and then play the action thus chosen at each information set, respectively, if and when the play of the game reaches it. Since all the lotteries are conducted at the start of the game, we have essentially defined a mixed strategy that is equivalent to b_i.

This construction would not be possible without the condition that any path from the root intersects every information set at most once. Indeed, if there were a path intersecting the same information set of player i several times, then the mechanism described in the previous paragraph would require player i to choose the same action every time he gets to that information set. In contrast, a behavior strategy enables the player to choose his actions at the information sets independently every time the play of the game arrives at the information set. It follows that in this case the mixed strategy that the process defines is not equivalent to the behavior strategies b_i. Before we prove the other direction of Theorem 6.11 (sufficiency), we present $\rho(x; \sigma)$, the probability that the play of the game reaches vertex x, as the product of probabilities, each of which depends solely on one player.

This representation will serve us in several proofs in this section, as will the notation that we now introduce.

6.2.2 Representing $\rho(x;\sigma)$ as a product of probabilities

For each decision vertex x of player i, denote by $U_i(x) \in \mathcal{U}_i$ the information set of player i containing x. For each descendant $\hat{x}$ of x denote by $a_i(x \rightarrow \hat{x}) \in A(U_i(x))$ the equivalence class containing the action leading from x to $\hat{x}$. This is the action that player i must choose at vertex x for the play of the game to continue in the direction of vertex $\hat{x}$.

For each vertex x (not necessarily a decision vertex of player i) denote the number of vertices along the path from the root to x (not including x) at which player i is the decision maker by L_i^x, and denote these nodes by $x_{10,i}^1, x_{10,i}^2, \ldots, x_i^{L_i^x}$. In Example 6.4, $L_1^{x_{10}} = 2$, $x_i^1 = x_1, x_i^2 = x_6$, and

$$U_1(x_1) = \{x_1\}, \qquad U_1(x_{10}) = \{x_6, x_7\}. \tag{6.22}$$

Since an information set can contain several vertices on the path from the root to x, as happens in the Absent-Minded Driver game (Example 6.9), it is possible that $U_i(x_i^{l_1}) = U_i(x_i^{l_2})$ even when $l_1 \neq l_2$. In Example 6.9, $L_1^{x_4} = 2$ and

$$U_1(x_{4,i}^1) = U_1(x_{4,i}^2) = \{x_1, x_2\}. \tag{6.23}$$

What is the probability that under the strategy implemented by player i, he will choose the action leading to x at each one of the information sets preceding x? If player i implements behavior strategy b_i, this probability equals

$$\rho_i(x; b_i) := \begin{cases} \prod_{l=1}^{L_i^x} b_i\big(a_i(x_i^l \to x); U_i(x_i^l)\big) & \text{if } L_i^x > 0, \\ 1 & \text{if } L_i^x = 0. \end{cases} \tag{6.24}$$

If player i implements the mixed strategy σ_i, then $\sigma_i(s_i)$ is the probability that he chooses pure strategy s_i. Denote by $S_i^*(x) \subseteq S_i$ all of player i's pure strategies under which at each information set $U_i(x_i^l)$, $1 \leq l \leq L_i^x$, he chooses the action $a(U_i(x_i^l) \to x)$. The set $S_i^*(x)$ may be empty; since a pure strategy cannot choose two different actions at the same information set, this happens when the path from the root to x passes at least twice through the same information set of player i, and the action leading to x is not the same action in every case.

When $S_i^*(x) \neq \emptyset$, the probability that player i chooses the actions leading to vertex x is

$$\rho_i(x; \sigma_i) := \sum_{s_i \in S_i^*(x)} \sigma_i(s_i). \tag{6.25}$$

When $S_i^*(x) = \emptyset$, this probability is defined by $\rho_i(x; \sigma_i) := 0$. Because the lotteries conducted by the players are independent, we get that for each mixed/behavior strategy vector σ and every vertex x,

$$\rho(x; \sigma) = \prod_{i \in N} \rho_i(x; \sigma_i). \tag{6.26}$$

We turn now to the proof of the second direction of Theorem 6.11.

6.2.3   Proof of the second direction of Theorem 6.11: sufficiency

We want to prove that if every path intersects each information set of player i at most once, then every behavior strategy of player i has an equivalent mixed strategy.

A pure strategy of player i is a choice of an action from his action set at each of his information sets. Hence the set of pure strategies of player i is

$$S_i = \bigtimes_{U_i \in \mathcal{U}_i} A(U_i). \tag{6.27}$$

For every pure strategy s_i of player i, and every information set U_i, the action that the player chooses at U_i is $s_i(U_i)$. It follows that for every behavior strategy b_i and every pure strategy s_i of player i, $b_i(s_i(U_i); U_i)$ is the probability that under behavior strategy b_i, at each time that the play of the game reaches a vertex in information set U_i, player i chooses the same action that s_i chooses at this information set.

Given a behavior strategy b_i of player i, we will now define a mixed strategy σ_i that is equivalent to b_i. For every pure strategy s_i of player i define the "probability that this strategy is chosen according to b_i" as

$$\sigma_i(s_i) := \prod_{U_i \in \mathcal{U}_i} b_i(s_i(U_i); U_i). \tag{6.28}$$

First, we will show that $\sigma_i := (\sigma_i(s_i))_{s_i \in S_i}$ is a probability distribution over S_i, and hence it defines a mixed strategy for player i. Since $\sigma_i(s_i)$ is a product of nonnegative numbers, $\sigma_i(s_i) \geq 0$ for every pure strategy $s_i \in S_i$. We now verify that $\sum_{s_i \in S_i} \sigma_i(s_i) = 1$. Indeed,

$$\sum_{s_i \in S_i} \sigma_i(s_i) = \sum_{s_i \in S_i} \left(\prod_{U_i \in \mathcal{U}_i} b_i(s_i(U_i); U_i) \right) \tag{6.29}$$

$$= \prod_{U_i \in \mathcal{U}_i} \sum_{a_i \in A(U_i)} b_i(a_i; U_i) \tag{6.30}$$

$$= \prod_{U_i \in \mathcal{U}_i} 1 = 1. \tag{6.31}$$

Equation (6.30) follows from changing the order of the product and the summation and from the assumption that every path intersects every information set at most once.

Finally, we need to check that the mixed strategy σ_i is equivalent to b_i. Let x be a vertex. We will show that for each mixed/behavior strategy vector σ_{-i} of players $N \setminus \{i\}$,

$$\rho(x; b_i, \sigma_{-i}) = \rho(x; \sigma_i, \sigma_{-i}). \tag{6.32}$$

From Equation (6.26), we deduce that

$$\rho(x; b_i, \sigma_{-i}) = \rho_i(x; b_i) \times \prod_{j \neq i} \rho_j(x; \sigma_j), \tag{6.33}$$

and

$$\rho(x; \sigma_i, \sigma_{-i}) = \rho_i(x; \sigma_i) \times \prod_{j \neq i} \rho_j(x; \sigma_j). \tag{6.34}$$

It follows that in order to show that Equation (6.32) is satisfied, it suffices to show that

$$\rho_i(x; b_i) = \rho_i(x; \sigma_i). \tag{6.35}$$

Divide player i's collection of information sets into two: $\mathcal{U}_i^1$, containing all the information sets intersected by the path from the root to x, and $\mathcal{U}_i^2$, containing all the information sets that are not intersected by this path. Since $S_i^*(x)$ is the set of pure strategies of player i in which he implements the action leading to vertex x in all information sets intersected by the path from the root to x,

$$\rho_i(x; \sigma_i) = \sum_{s_i \in S_i^*(x)} \sigma_i(s_i) \tag{6.36}$$

$$= \sum_{s_i \in S_i^*(x)} \prod_{U_i \in \mathcal{U}_i} b_i(s_i(U_i); U_i) \tag{6.37}$$

$$= \sum_{s_i \in S_i^*(x)} \left(\prod_{U_i \in \mathcal{U}_i^1} b_i(s_i(U_i); U_i) \times \prod_{U_i \in \mathcal{U}_i^2} b_i(s_i(U_i); U_i) \right). \tag{6.38}$$

Since $\mathcal{U}_i^1$ contains only the information sets $U_i(x_i^1), U_i(x_i^2), \ldots, U_i(x_i^{L_i^x})$, and since for every $l \in \{1, 2, \ldots, L_i^x\}$ the pure strategy $s_i \in S_i^*(x)$ instructs player i to play action $a(U_i(x_i^l) \to x)$ at information set $U_i(x_i^l)$, we deduce, using Equation (6.24), that

$$\prod_{U_i \in \mathcal{U}_i^1} b_i(s_i(U_i); U_i) = \prod_{l=1}^{L_i^x} b_i(a_i(x_i^l \to x); U_i(x_i^l)) = \rho_i(x; b_i). \tag{6.39}$$

In particular, this product is independent of $s_i \in S_i^*(s)$. We can therefore move the product outside of the sum in Equation (6.38), yielding

$$\rho_i(x; \sigma_i) = \rho_i(x; b_i) \times \left(\sum_{s_i \in S_i^*(x)} \prod_{U_i \in \mathcal{U}_i^2} b_i(s_i(U_i); U_i) \right). \tag{6.40}$$

We will now show that the second element on the right-hand side of Equation (6.40) equals 1. The fact that s_i is contained in $S_i^*(x)$ does not impose any constraints on the actions implemented by player i at the information sets in $\mathcal{U}_i^2$. For every sequence $(a_{U_i})_{U_i \in \mathcal{U}_i^2}$ at which $a_{U_i} \in A(U_i)$ is a possible action for player i at information set U_i for all $U_i \in \mathcal{U}_i^2$, there is a pure strategy $s_i \in S_i^*(x)$ such that $a_{U_i} = s_i(U_i)$ for all $U_i \in \mathcal{U}_i^2$. Moreover, there is an injective mapping between the set of pure strategies $S_i^*(x)$ and the set of the sequences $(a_{U_i})_{U_i \in \mathcal{U}_i^2} \in \times_{U_i \in \mathcal{U}_i^2} A(U_i)$. Therefore,

$$\sum_{s_i \in S_i^*(x)} \prod_{U_i \in \mathcal{U}_i^2} b_i(s_i(U_i); U_i) = \sum_{\left\{ (a_{U_i})_{U_i \in \mathcal{U}_i^2} \in \times_{U_i \in \mathcal{U}_i^2} A(U_i) \right\}} \prod_{U_i \in \mathcal{U}_i^2} b_i(a_{U_i}; U_i)$$

$$= \prod_{U_i \in \mathcal{U}_i^2} \sum_{a_{U_i} \in A(U_i)} b_i(a_{U_i}; U_i) = \prod_{U_i \in \mathcal{U}_i^2} 1 = 1. \tag{6.41}$$

Equation (6.40) therefore implies that

$$\rho_i(x; \sigma_i) = \rho_i(x; b_i) \tag{6.42}$$

which is what we wanted to prove.

6.2.4   Conditions guaranteeing the existence of a behavior strategy equivalent to a mixed strategy

In this section, we present a condition guaranteeing that every mixed strategy has an equivalent behavior strategy. This requires formalizing when a player never forgets anything. During the play of a game, a player can forget many things:

- He can forget what moves he made in the past (as in Example 6.8).
- He can forget whether or not he made a move at all in the past (as in Example 6.9).
- He can forget things he knew at earlier stages of the games, such as the result of a chance move, what actions another player has played, which players acted in the past, or how many times a particular player played in the past.

The next definition guarantees that a player never forgets any of the items in the above list (Exercises 6.11–6.15). Recall that all the vertices in the same information set must have the same associated action set (Definition 3.23 on page 54).

Definition 6.12 *Let* $\mathcal{X} = (x^0 \to x^1 \to \ldots \to x^K)$ *and* $\widehat{\mathcal{X}} = (x^0 \to \widehat{x}^1 \to \ldots \to \widehat{x}^L)$ *be two paths[2] in the game tree. Let* U_i *be an information set of player* i, *which intersects each of these two paths at only one vertex:* $\mathcal{X}$ *at* x^k, *and* $\widehat{\mathcal{X}}$ *at* $\widehat{x}^l$. *We say that these two paths choose the same action at information set* U_i *if* $k < K$, $l < L$, *and the action at* x^k *leading to* x^{k+1} *is identical to the action at* $\widehat{x}^l$ *leading to* $\widehat{x}^{l+1}$, *i.e.,* $a_i(x^k \to x^{k+1}) = a_i(\widehat{x}^l \to \widehat{x}^{l+1})$.

Definition 6.13 *Player* i *has* perfect recall *if the following conditions are satisfied:*

(a) *Every information set of player* i *intersects every path from the root to a leaf at most once.*

(b) *Every two paths from the root that end in the same information set of player* i *pass through the same information sets of player* i, *and in the same order, and in every such information set the two paths choose the same action. In other words, for every information set* U_i *of player* i *and every pair of vertices* $x, \widehat{x}$ *in* U_i, *if the decision vertices of player* i *on the path from the root to* x *are* $x_i^1, x_i^2, \ldots, x_i^L = x$ *and his decision vertices on the path from the root to* $\widehat{x}$ *are* $\widehat{x}_i^1, \widehat{x}_i^2, \ldots, \widehat{x}_i^{\widehat{L}} = \widehat{x}$, *then* $L = \widehat{L}$, *and* $U_i(x_i^l) = U_i(\widehat{x}_i^l)$, *and* $a_i(x_i^l \to x) = a_i(\widehat{x}_i^l \to \widehat{x})$ *for all* $l \in \{1, 2, \ldots, L\}$.

A game is called a game with perfect recall *if all the players have perfect recall.*

Two games are shown in Figure 6.6. In Game A, every player has a single information set, and all the players have perfect recall. In Game B, in contrast, Player I has imperfect recall, because the two paths connecting the root to the vertices in information set $\{x_3, x_4\}$ do not choose the same action in information set $\{x_1\}$. Player II, however, has perfect recall in this game.

---

2 In the description of a path in a game tree we list only the vertices, because the edges along the path are uniquely determined by those vertices.

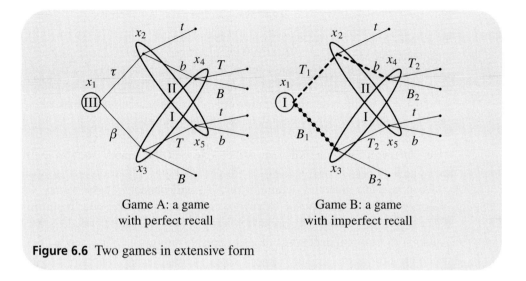

Game A: a game
with perfect recall

Game B: a game
with imperfect recall

Figure 6.6 Two games in extensive form

Recall that $S_i^*(x)$ is the set of pure strategies of player i at which he chooses the actions leading to vertex x (see page 239). The definition of perfect recall implies the following corollary (Exercise 6.16).

Theorem 6.14 *Let i be a player with perfect recall in an extensive-form game, and let x and x' be two vertices in the same information set of player i. Then $S_i^*(x) = S_i^*(x')$.*

Theorem 6.15 (Kuhn [1957]) *In every game in extensive form, if player i has perfect recall, then for every mixed strategy of player i there exists an equivalent behavior strategy.*

Proof: We make use of the following notation: for each vertex x of player i, and each possible action a in $A(U_i(x))$, we denote by x^a the vertex in the game tree that the play of the game reaches if player i chooses action a at vertex x.

Let σ_i be a mixed strategy of player i. Our goal is to define a behavior strategy b_i equivalent to σ_i.

Step 1: Defining a behavior strategy b_i.
To define a behavior strategy b_i we have to define, for each information set U_i of player i, a probability distribution over the set of possible actions at U_i.

So suppose U_i is an information set of player i, and let x be a vertex in U_i. For each action $a_i \in A(U_i)$, the collection $S_i^*(x^{a_i})$ contains all the pure strategies s_i in $S_i^*(x)$ satisfying $s_i(U_i) = a_i$.
If $\sum_{s_i \in S_i^*(x')} \sigma_i(s_i) = 0$ define

$$b_i(a_i; U_i) := \frac{\sum_{s_i \in S_i^*(x^{a_i})} \sigma_i(s_i)}{\sum_{s_i \in S_i^*(x)} \sigma_i(s_i)}, \qquad \forall a_i \in A(x). \tag{6.43}$$

The numerator on the right-hand side of Equation (6.43) is the probability that player i will play the actions leading to x^a, and the denominator is the probability that player i will play the actions leading to x. It follows that the ratio between the two values equals the conditional probability that player i plays action a if the play reaches vertex x.

If $\sum_{s_i \in S_i^*(x)} \sigma_i(s_i) = 0$, by Theorem 6.14 it follows that $\sum_{s_i \in S_i^*(x')} \sigma_i(s_i) = 0$ for each vertex x' in the information set of x. Therefore, when player i implements σ_i the probability that the play of the game will visit the information set containing x is 0, i.e., $\rho_i(x; \sigma_i) = 0$. In this case, the definition of b_i, for information set U_i, makes no difference. For the definition of b_i to be complete, we define in this case

$$b_i(a_i; U_i) = \frac{1}{|A(U_i)|}, \quad \forall a_i \in A(x). \tag{6.44}$$

We now show that the definition of b_i is independent of the vertex x chosen in information set U_i, so that the behavior strategy b_i is well defined. It suffices to check the case $\sum_{s_i \in S_i^*(x)} \sigma_i(s_i) > 0$, because when $\sum_{s_i \in S_i^*(x)} \sigma_i(s_i) = 0$, the definition of b_i (see Equation (6.44)) is independent of x; it depends only on U_i. Let then x_1 and x_2 be two different vertices in U_i. Since player i has perfect recall, Theorem 6.14 implies that $S_i^*(x_1) = S_i^*(x_2)$. Since x_1 and x_2 are in the same information set, the set of possible actions at x_1 equals the set of possible actions at x_2: $A(x_1) = A(x_2)$. If a is a possible action at these vertices, x_1^a and x_2^a are the vertices reached by the play of the game from x_1 and from x_2 respectively, if player i implements action a at these vertices. Using Theorem 6.14 we deduce that $S_i^*(x_1^a) = S_i^*(x_2^a)$. In particular, it follows that the numerator and denominator of Equation (6.43) are independent of the choice of vertex x in U_i.

Step 2: Showing that b_i is a behavior strategy.

We need to prove that for every information set U_i of player i, $b_i(U_i)$ is a probability distribution over $A(U_i)$, i.e., that $b_i(U_i)$ is a vector of nonnegative numbers summing to one. Equation (6.44) defines a probability distribution over $A(U_i)$ for the case $\sum_{s_i \in S_i^*(x)} \sigma_i(s_i) = 0$. We show now that when $\sum_{s_i \in S_i^*(x)} \sigma_i(s_i) > 0$, Equation (6.43) defines a probability distribution over $A(U_i)$. Since $\sigma_i(s_i) \geq 0$ for every pure strategy s_i, the numerator in Equation (6.43) is nonnegative, and hence $b_i(a_i; U_i) \geq 0$ for every action $a_i \in A(U_i)$. The sets $\{S_i^*(x^a): a \in A(U_i)\}$ are disjoint, and their union is $S_i^*(x)$. It follows that

$$\sum_{a \in A(U_i)} \sum_{s_i \in S_i^*(x^a)} \sigma_i(s_i) = \sum_{s_i \in S_i^*(x)} \sigma_i(s_i). \tag{6.45}$$

We deduce from Equations (6.43) and (6.45) that in this case $\sum_{a_i \in A(U_i)} b_i(a_i; U_i) = 1$.

Step 3: Showing that b_i is equivalent to σ_i.

Let σ_{-i} be a mixed/behavior strategy vector of the other players, and let x be a vertex in the game tree (not necessarily a decision vertex of player i). We need to show that

$$\rho(x; b_i, \sigma_{-i}) = \rho(x; \sigma_i, \sigma_{-i}). \tag{6.46}$$

As we saw previously, Equation (6.26) implies that

$$\rho(x; b_i, \sigma_{-i}) = \rho_i(x; b_i) \times \prod_{j \neq i} \rho_j(x; \sigma_j), \tag{6.47}$$

and

$$\rho(x; \sigma_i, \sigma_{-i}) = \rho_i(x; \sigma_i) \times \prod_{j \neq i} \rho_j(x; \sigma_j). \tag{6.48}$$

To show that Equation (6.46) is satisfied, it therefore suffices to show that

$$\rho_i(x; b_i) = \rho_i(x; \sigma_i). \tag{6.49}$$

In words, we need to show that the probability that player i will play actions leading to x under σ_i equals the probability that player i will do the same under b_i. Recall that $x_i^1, x_i^2, \ldots, x_i^{L_i^x}$ is the sequence of decision vertices of player i along the path from the root to x (not including the vertex x if player i is the decision maker there). If $L_i^x = 0$, then player i has no information set intersected by the path from the root to x, so $S_i^*(x) = S_i$. In this case, we have defined $\rho_i(x; b_i) = 1$ (see Equation (6.24)), and also

$$\rho_i(x; \sigma_i) = \sum_{s_i \in S_i^*(x)} \sigma_i(s_i) = \sum_{s_i \in S_i} \sigma_i(s_i) = 1. \tag{6.50}$$

Hence Equation (6.49) is satisfied.

Suppose, then, that $L_i^x > 0$. Every strategy of player i that chooses, at each information set $U_i(x_i^1), U_i(x_i^2), \ldots, U_i(x_i^l)$, the action leading to x is a strategy that does so at each information set $U_i(x_i^1), U_i(x_i^2), \ldots, U_i(x_i^{l-1})$ and at information set $U_i(x_i^l)$ chooses the action $a_l := a_i(x_i^l \to x)$. In other words,

$$S_i^*\left(x_i^{l+1}\right) = S_i^*\left(x_i^{l,a_l}\right). \tag{6.51}$$

Since b_i is a behavior strategy, Equation (6.24) implies that

$$\rho_i(x; b_i) = \prod_{l=1}^{L_i^x} b_i\left(a_l; U_i\left(x_i^l\right)\right). \tag{6.52}$$

If $\rho_i(x; b_i) \neq 0$, then the definition of b_i (Equation (6.43)) implies that

$$\rho_i(x; b_i) = \prod_{l=1}^{L_i^x} \frac{\sum_{s_i \in S_i^*\left(x_i^{l,a_l}\right)} \sigma_i(s_i)}{\sum_{s_i \in S_i^*\left(x_i^l\right)} \sigma_i(s_i)}. \tag{6.53}$$

From Equation (6.51) we deduce that

$$\sum_{s_i \in S_i^*\left(x_i^{l,a_l}\right)} \sigma_i(s_i) = \sum_{s_i \in S_i^*\left(x_i^{l+1}\right)} \sigma_i(s_i). \tag{6.54}$$

It follows that the product on the right-hand side of Equation (6.53) is a telescopic product: the numerator in the l-th element of the product equals the denominator in the $(l+1)$-th element of the product. This means that adjacent product elements cancel each other out. Note that $S_i^*(x_l^{a_l}) = S_i^*(x)$ is satisfied for $l = L_i^x$, so that canceling adjacent product elements in Equation (6.53) yields

$$\rho_i(x; b_i) = \frac{\sum_{s_i \in S_i^*(x)} \sigma_i(s_i)}{\sum_{s_i \in S_i^*\left(x_i^1\right)} \sigma_i(s_i)}. \tag{6.55}$$

Recall that x_i^1 is player i's first decision vertex on the path from the root to x. Since player i has no information set prior to x_i^1, every strategy of player i is in $S_i^*(x_i^1)$, i.e., $S_i^*(x_i^1) = S_i$. The denominator in Equation (6.55) therefore equals 1, so that

$$\rho_i(x; b_i) = \sum_{s_i \in S_i^*(x)} \sigma_i(s_i) = \rho_i(x; \sigma_i), \tag{6.56}$$

which is what we claimed.

To wrap up, we turn our attention to the case $\rho_i(x; b_i) = 0$. From Equation (6.24), we deduce that $\rho_i(x; b_i)$ is given by a product of elements and therefore one of those elements vanishes: there exists l, $1 \leq l \leq L_i^x$, such that $b_i(a_l; U_i(x_i^l)) = 0$. From the definition of b_i (Equation (6.43)) we deduce that $\sum_{s_i \in S_i^*(x_i^{l,a_l})} \sigma_i(s_i) = 0$. On the other hand, $S_i^*(x_i^{l,a_l}) \supseteq S_i^*(x)$ and therefore by Equation (6.25)

$$\rho_i(x; \sigma_i) = \sum_{s_i \in S_i^*(x)} \sigma_i(s_i) \leq \sum_{s_i \in S_i^*(x_i^{l,a_l})} \sigma_i(s_i) = 0. \tag{6.57}$$

Hence Equation (6.49) is satisfied in this case. □

6.3　Equilibria in behavior strategies

By Nash's Theorem (Theorem 5.10 on page 150) every finite extensive-form game has a Nash equilibrium in mixed strategies. In other words, there exists a vector of mixed strategies under which no player has a profitable deviation to another mixed strategy. An equilibrium in behavior strategies is a vector of behavior strategies under which no player has a profitable deviation to another behavior strategy.

The next theorem states that to ensure the existence of a Nash equilibrium in behavior strategies, it suffices that all the players have perfect recall.

Theorem 6.16 *If all the players in an extensive-form game have perfect recall then the game has a Nash equilibrium in behavior strategies.*

Proof: Since an extensive-form game is by definition a finite game, Nash's Theorem (Theorem 5.10 on page 150) implies that the game has a Nash equilibrium in mixed strategies $\sigma^* = (\sigma_i^*)_{i \in N}$. Since all the players in the game have perfect recall, we know from Kuhn's Theorem (Theorem 6.15) that for each player i there exists a behavior strategy b_i^* equivalent to σ_i^*. Corollary 6.7 then implies that

$$u_i(\sigma^*) = u_i(b^*), \quad \forall i \in N, \tag{6.58}$$

where $b^* = (b_i^*)_{i \in N}$. We show now that no player can increase his expected payoff by deviating to another behavior strategy. Let b_i be a behavior strategy of player i. From Theorem 6.11, there exists a mixed strategy σ_i equivalent to b_i. Since σ^* is an equilibrium in mixed strategies,

$$u_i(\sigma^*) \geq u_i(\sigma_i, \sigma_{-i}^*). \tag{6.59}$$

Since σ_i is equivalent to b_i, and for each $j \neq i$ the strategy σ_j^* is equivalent to b_j^*, Corollary 6.7 implies that

$$u_i(\sigma_i, \sigma_{-i}^*) = u_i(b_i, b_{-i}^*). \tag{6.60}$$

From Equations (6.58)–(6.60) we then have

$$u_i(b^*) = u_i(\sigma^*) \geq u_i(\sigma_i, \sigma_{-i}^*) = u_i(b_i, b_{-i}^*). \tag{6.61}$$

In other words, player i cannot profit by deviating from b_i^* to b_i, so that the strategy vector b^* is an equilibrium in behavior strategies.   □

As the proof of the theorem shows, when a game has perfect recall, at each equilibrium in mixed strategies no player has a profitable deviation to a behavior strategy, and at each equilibrium in behavior strategies no player has a profitable deviation to a mixed strategy. Moreover, there exist equilibria at which some players implement mixed strategies and some players implement behavior strategies, and at each such equilibrium no player has a profitable deviation to either a mixed strategy or a behavior strategy.

The next example shows that when it is not the case that all players have perfect recall, the game may not have a pure strategy equilibrium.

Example 6.17   Figure 6.7 depicts a two-player zero-sum game.

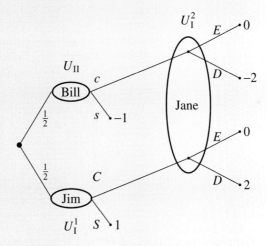

Figure 6.7 The game in Example 6.17, in extensive form

This game may be interpreted as follows: Player I represents a couple, Jim and Jane. Player II is named Bill. At the first stage of the game, a winning card is handed either to Jim or to Bill, with equal probability. The player who receives the card may choose to show ("S" or "s") his card, and receive a payoff of 1 from the other player (thus ending the play of the game), or to continue ("C" or "c"). If the player holding the winning card chooses to continue, Jane (who does not know who has the card) is called upon to choose between declaring end ("E"), and thus putting an end to the play of the game without any player receiving a payoff, or declaring double ("D"), which results in the player holding the winning card receiving a payoff of 2 from the other player.

In this game, Player I has imperfect recall, because the paths from the root to the two vertices in information set U_I^2 do not intersect the same information set of Player I: one path intersects U_I^1, while the other does not intersect it.

Player I's set of pure strategies is $\{SD, SE, CD, CE\}$, and Player II's set of pure strategies is $\{S, C\}$. The strategic form of this game is given in the matrix in Figure 6.8 (in terms of payments from Player II to I):

Player II

		c	s
	CE	0	$-\frac{1}{2}$
	CD	0	$\frac{1}{2}$
Player I	SE	$\frac{1}{2}$	0
	SD	$-\frac{1}{2}$	0

Figure 6.8 The game in Example 6.17 in strategic form

The value of the game in mixed strategies is $v = \frac{1}{4}$, and an optimal mixed strategy guaranteeing this payoff to Player I is $\sigma_I = [0(CE), \frac{1}{2}(CD), \frac{1}{2}(SE), 0(SD)]$. Player II's only optimal (mixed) strategy is $\sigma_{II} = [\frac{1}{2}(c), \frac{1}{2}(s)]$.

To check whether the game has a value in behavior strategies we compute the minmax value $\bar{v}_b$ and the maxmin value $\underline{v}_b$ in behavior strategies. The maxmin value in behavior strategies equals the maxmin value in mixed strategies, since Player II has one information set. It follows that his set of behavior strategies $\mathcal{B}_{II}$ equals his set of mixed strategies Σ_{II} (Exercise 6.4). Since he can guarantee $\frac{1}{4}$ in mixed strategies he can guarantee $\frac{1}{4}$ in behavior strategies. Formally,

$$\bar{v}_b = \min_{b_{II} \in \mathcal{B}_{II}} \max_{b_I \in \mathcal{B}_I} U(b_I, b_{II}) \tag{6.62}$$

$$= \min_{\sigma_{II} \in \mathcal{B}_{II}} \max_{b_I \in \mathcal{B}_I} U(b_I, b_{II}) \tag{6.63}$$

$$= \min_{\sigma_{II} \in \mathcal{B}_{II}} \max_{s_I \in S_I} U(b_I, b_{II}) \tag{6.64}$$

$$= \min_{\sigma_{II} \in \mathcal{B}_{II}} \max_{\sigma_I \in \Sigma_I} U(b_I, b_{II}) = v = \frac{1}{4}. \tag{6.65}$$

Equation (6.64) holds because, as explained on page 178, it suffices to conduct maximization on the right-hand side of Equation (6.63) over the pure strategies of Player I, and Equation (6.65) holds because the function U is bilinear.

We now compute the maxmin value in behavior strategies $\underline{v}_b$. In other words, we will calculate Player I's maxmin value when he is restricted to using only behavior strategies. A behavior strategy of Player I can be written as $b_I = ([\alpha(S), (1-\alpha)(C)], [\beta(D), (1-\beta)(E)])$. His expected payoff, when he plays b_I, depends on Player II's strategy:

- If Player II plays s, Player I's expected payoff is

$$\tfrac{1}{2}(\alpha + (1-\alpha)(2\beta + 0(1-\beta))) + \tfrac{1}{2}(-1) = (1-\alpha)\left(\beta - \tfrac{1}{2}\right). \tag{6.66}$$

- If Player II plays c, Player I's expected payoff is

$$\tfrac{1}{2}(\alpha + (1-\alpha)(2\beta + 0(1-\beta))) + \tfrac{1}{2}(\beta(-2) + 0(1-\beta)) = \alpha\left(\tfrac{1}{2} - \beta\right). \tag{6.67}$$

Player I's maxmin value in behavior strategies is therefore[3]

$$v_b = \max_{\alpha,\beta} \min \left\{ (1-\alpha)\left(\beta - \tfrac{1}{2}\right), \alpha\left(\tfrac{1}{2} - \beta\right) \right\} = 0. \tag{6.68}$$

To see that indeed $v_b = 0$, note that if $\beta \leq \tfrac{1}{2}$, then the first element in the minimization in Equation (6.68) is nonpositive; if $\beta \geq \tfrac{1}{2}$, then the second element is nonpositive; and if $\beta = \tfrac{1}{2}$, both elements are zero. We conclude that $\bar{v}_b = \tfrac{1}{4} \neq 0 = v_b$, and therefore the game has no value in behavior strategies.

Since the strategy $\sigma_I = [0(CE), \tfrac{1}{2}(CD), \tfrac{1}{2}(SE), 0(SD)]$ guarantees Player I an expected payoff of $\tfrac{1}{4}$, while any behavior strategy guarantees him at most 0, we confirm that there does not exist a behavior strategy equivalent to σ_I, which can also be proved directly (prove it!).

The source of the difference between the two types of strategies in this case lies in the fact that Player I wants to coordinate his actions at his two information sets: ideally, Jane should play E if Jim plays S, and should play D if Jim plays C. This coordination is possible using a mixed strategy, but cannot be achieved with a behavior strategy, because in any behavior strategy the lotteries $[\alpha(S), (1-\alpha)(C)]$ and $[\beta(D), (1-\beta)(E)]$ are independent lotteries.   ◀

6.4 Kuhn's Theorem for infinite games

In Section 6.2 we proved Kuhn's Theorem when the game tree is finite. There are extensive-form games with infinite game trees. This can happen in two ways: when there is a vertex with an infinite number of children, and when there are infinitely long paths in the game tree. In this section we generalize the theorem to the case in which each vertex has a finite number of children and the game tree has infinitely long paths. Infinitely long paths exist in games that may never end, such as backgammon and Monopoly. In Chapters 13 and 14 we present models of games that may not end. Generalizing Kuhn's Theorem to infinite games involves several technical challenges:

- The set of pure strategies has the cardinality of the continuum. Indeed, if for example player i has a countable number of information sets and in each of his information sets there are only two possible actions, a pure strategy of player i is equivalent to an infinite sequence of zeros and ones. The collection of all such sequences is equivalent to the interval $[0,1]$ of real numbers, which has the cardinality of the continuum. Since a mixed strategy is a probability distribution over pure strategies, we need to define a σ-algebra over the collection of all pure strategies in order to be able to define probability distributions over this set.
- In finite games, the equivalence of mixed strategies and behavior strategies was defined using the equivalence between the probabilities that they induce over the vertices of the game tree, and in particular over the set of leaves, which determines the outcome of the game. In infinite games, the outcome of the game may be determined by an infinitely long path in the game tree that corresponds to an infinitely long play of the game. It follows that instead of probability distributions induced over a finite set of leaves, in the case of an infinite game we need to deal with probability distributions induced over

---

3 Again, it suffices to conduct maximization over the pure strategies of Player II, which are c and s.

the set of paths in the game tree, which as we showed above has the cardinality of the continuum. This requires defining a measurable space over the set of plays of the game, that is, over the set of paths (finite and infinite) starting at the root of the tree.

We first introduce several definitions that will be used in this section.

Definition 6.18 *Let X be a set. A collection $\mathcal{Y}$ of subsets of X is a σ-algebra over X if (a) $\emptyset \in \mathcal{Y}$, (b) $X \backslash Y \in \mathcal{Y}$ for all $Y \in \mathcal{Y}$, and (c) $\cup_{i \in \mathbb{N}} Y_i \in \mathcal{Y}$ for every sequence $(Y_i)_{i \in \mathbb{N}}$ of elements in $\mathcal{Y}$.*

De Morgan's Laws imply that a σ-algebra is also closed under countable intersections: if $(Y_i)_{i \in \mathbb{N}}$ is a sequence of elements of $\mathcal{Y}$, then $\cap_{i \in \mathbb{N}} Y_i \in \mathcal{Y}$. For each family $\widehat{\mathcal{Y}}$ of subsets of X, the *σ-algebra generated by $\widehat{\mathcal{Y}}$* is the smallest σ-algebra of $\mathcal{Y}$ (with respect to set inclusion) satisfying $\widehat{\mathcal{Y}} \subseteq \mathcal{Y}$. The σ-algebra that we will use in the rest of this section is the σ-algebra of cylinder sets.

Definition 6.19 *Let $(X_n)_{n \in \mathbb{N}}$ be a sequence of finite sets, and let $X^\infty := \times_{n \in \mathbb{N}} X_n$. A set $B \in X^\infty$ is called a* cylinder set *if there exist $N \in \mathbb{N}$ and $(A_n)_{n=1}^N$, $A_n \subseteq X_n$ for all $n \in \{1, 2, \ldots, N\}$, such that $B = (\times_{n=1}^N A_n) \times (\times_{n=N+1}^\infty X_n)$. The σ-algebra of cylinder sets is the σ-algebra $\mathcal{Y}$ generated by the cylinder sets in X^∞.*

Definition 6.20 *A* measurable space *is a pair $(X, \mathcal{Y})$ such that X is a set and $\mathcal{Y}$ is a σ-algebra over X. A* probability distribution *over a measurable space $(X, \mathcal{Y})$ is a function $p : \mathcal{Y} \to [0, 1]$ satisfying:*

- $p(\emptyset) = 0$.
- $p(X \backslash Y) = 1 - p(Y)$ *for every $Y \in \mathcal{Y}$.*
- $p(\cup_{n \in \mathbb{N}} Y_n) = \sum_{n \in \mathbb{N}} p(Y_n)$ *for any sequence $(Y_n)_{n \in \mathbb{N}}$ of pairwise disjoint sets in $\mathcal{Y}$.*

The third property in the definition of a probability distribution is called σ-*additivity*.

The next theorem follows from the Kolmogorov Extension Theorem (see, for example, Theorem A.3.1 in Durrett [2004]) and the Carathéodory Extension Theorem (see, for example, Theorem 13.A in Halmos [1994]). Given an infinite product of spaces $X^\infty = \times_{n \in \mathbb{N}} X_n$ and a sequence $(p^N)_{N \in \mathbb{N}}$ of probability distributions, where each p^N is a probability distribution over the finite product $X^N := \times_{n=1}^N X_n$, the theorem presents a condition guaranteeing the existence of an extension of the probability distributions $(p^N)_{N \in \mathbb{N}}$ to X^∞, i.e., a probability distribution p over X^∞ whose marginal distribution over X^N is p^N, for each $N \in \mathbb{N}$.

Theorem 6.21 *Let $(X_n)_{n \in \mathbb{N}}$ be a sequence of finite sets. Suppose that for each $N \in \mathbb{N}$ there exists a probability distribution p^N over $X^N := \times_{n=1}^N X_n$ that satisfies*

$$p^N(A) = p^{N+1}(A \times X_{N+1}), \quad \forall N \in \mathbb{N}, \forall A \subseteq X^N. \tag{6.69}$$

Let $X^\infty := \times_{n \in \mathbb{N}} X_n$ and let $\mathcal{Y}$ be the σ-algebra of cylinder sets over X^∞. Then there exists a unique probability distribution p over $(X^\infty, \mathcal{Y})$ extending $(p^N)_{N \in \mathbb{N}}$, i.e.,

$$p^N(A) = p(A \times X_{N+1} \times X_{N+2} \times \cdots), \quad \forall N \in \mathbb{N}, \forall A \subseteq X^N. \tag{6.70}$$

When (V, E, x^0) is a (finite or infinite) game tree, denote by H the set of *maximal paths* in the tree, meaning paths from the root to a leaf, and infinite paths from the root. For each vertex x denote by $H(x)$ the set of paths in H passing through x. Let $\mathcal{H}$ be the σ-algebra generated by the sets $H(x)$ for all $x \in V$. Recall that for each vertex x that is not a leaf the set of children of x is denoted by $C(x)$.

In this section we also make use of the following version of Theorem 6.21, which states that if there is an infinite tree such that each vertex x in the tree has an associated probability distribution $p(x)$, and if these probability distributions are consistent in the sense that the probability associated with a vertex equals the sum of the probabilities associated with its children, then there is a unique probability distribution $\hat{p}$ over the set of maximal paths satisfying the property that the probability that the set of paths passing through vertex x equals $p(x)$. The proof of the theorem is left to the reader (Exercise 6.24).

Theorem 6.22 *Let (V, E, x^0) be a (finite or infinite) game tree such that $|C(x)| < \infty$ for each vertex x. Denote by H the set of maximal paths. Let $p : V \to [0, 1]$ be a function satisfying $p(x^0) = 1$ and $p(x) = \sum_{x' \in C(x)} p(x')$ for each vertex $x \in V$ that is not a leaf. Then there exists a unique probability distribution $\hat{p}$ over $(H, \mathcal{H})$ satisfying $\hat{p}(H(x)) = p(x)$ for all $x \in V$.*

6.4.1   Definitions of pure strategy, mixed strategy, and behavior strategy

Let G be an extensive-form game with an infinite game tree such that each vertex has a finite number of children. In such a game, as in the finite case, a pure strategy of player i is a function that associates each information set of player i with a possible action at that information set. A behavior strategy of player i is a function associating each one of his information sets with a probability distribution over the set of possible actions at that information set. Denote by $S_i = \times_{U_i \in \mathcal{U}_i} A(U_i)$ player i's set of pure strategies and by $\mathcal{B}_i = \times_{U_i \in \mathcal{U}_i} \Delta(A(U_i))$ his set of behavior strategies.

A mixed strategy is a probability distribution over the collection of pure strategies. When the game has finite depth,[4] the set of pure strategies is a finite set and the set of player i's mixed strategies Σ_i is a simplex. When player i has an infinite number of information sets at which he has at least two possible actions the set of pure strategies S_i has the cardinality of the continuum. To define a probability distribution over this set we need to define a σ-algebra over it. Let $\mathcal{S}_i$ be the σ-algebra of cylinder sets of S_i. The pair $(S_i, \mathcal{S}_i)$ is a measurable space and the set of probability distributions over it is the set of mixed strategies Σ_i of player i.

6.4.2   Equivalence between mixed strategies and behavior strategies

In a finite game of depth T, a mixed strategy σ_i^T is equivalent to a behavior strategy b_i^T if $\rho(x; \sigma_i^T, \sigma_{-i}^T) = \rho(x; b_i^T, \sigma_{-i}^T)$ for every mixed/behavior strategy vector σ_{-i}^T of the other players and every vertex x in the game tree. In this section we extend the definition of equivalence between mixed and behavior strategies to infinite games.

We begin by defining $\rho_i(x; \sigma_i)$ and $\rho_i(x; b_i)$, the probability that player i implementing either mixed strategy σ_i or behavior strategy b_i will choose actions leading to the vertex x at each vertex along the path from the root to x that is in his information sets.

---

4 The *depth* of a vertex is the number of edges in the path from the root to the vertex. The *depth of a game* is the maximum (or supremum) of the depth of all vertices in the game tree.

For each behavior strategy b_i of player i, and each vertex x in the game tree,

$$\rho_i(x; b_i) := \Pi_{l=1}^{L_i^x} b_i\left(a_i; U_i^l\right), \tag{6.71}$$

where L_i^x is the number of vertices along the path from the root to x that are in player i's information sets (not including the vertex x, if at vertex x player i chooses an action), and $U_i^1, U_i^2, \ldots, U_1^{L_i^x}$ are the information sets containing these vertices (if there are several vertices along the path to x in the same information set U_i of player i, then this information set will appear more than once in the list $U_i^1, U_i^2, \ldots, U_1^{L_i^x}$).

We now define the probability $\rho_i(x; \sigma_i)$ for a mixed strategy σ_i. For any $T \in \mathbb{N}$ let G^T be the game that includes the first T stages of the game G.

- The set of vertices V^T of G^T contains all vertices of G with depth at most T.
- The information sets of each player i in G^T are all nonempty subsets of V^T that are obtained as the intersection of an information set in $\mathcal{U}_i^T$ with V^{T-1}; that is, an information set in G^T contains only vertices whose depth is strictly less than T. This is because the vertices whose depth is T are leaves of G^T. Denote by $\mathcal{U}_i^T$ the collection of player i's information sets in the game G that have a nonempty intersection with V^{T-1}. With this notation, player i's collection of information sets in the game G^T is all the nonempty intersections of V^{T-1} with a set in $\mathcal{U}_i^T$. Below, for any $T \in \mathbb{N}$, we identify each information set U_i^T of player i in the game G^T with the information set $U_i \in \mathcal{U}_i^T$ for which $U_i^T = V^{T-1} \cap U_i$.

Since each vertex has a finite number of children, the set V^T contains a finite number of vertices. To simplify the notation, an information set of player i in the game G^T, which is the intersection of V^T and an information set U_i of player i in the game G, will also be denoted by U_i. Since Kuhn's Theorem does not involve the payoffs of a game, we will not specify the payoffs in the game G^T.

Player i's set of pure strategies in the game G^T is $S_i^T := \times_{U_i \in \mathcal{U}_i^T} A(U_i)$. For each mixed strategy σ_i in the game G, let σ_i^T be its marginal distribution over S_i^T. Then σ_i^T is a mixed strategy in the game G^T. The sequence of probability distributions $(\sigma_i^T)_{T \in \mathbb{N}}$ satisfies the following property: the marginal distribution of σ_i^T over S_i^{T-1} is σ_i^{T-1}. It follows that for each vertex x whose depth is less than or equal to T we have $\rho_i(x; \sigma_i^{T_1}) = \rho_i(x; \sigma_i^{T_2})$ for all $T_1, T_2 \geq T$. Define for each vertex x

$$\rho_i(x; \sigma_i) := \rho_i\left(x; \sigma_i^T\right), \tag{6.72}$$

where T is greater than or equal to the depth of x. Finally, define, for each mixed/behavior strategy vector σ,

$$\rho(x; \sigma) := \Pi_{i \in N} \rho_i(x; \sigma_i). \tag{6.73}$$

This is the probability that the play of the game reaches vertex x when the players implement the strategy vector σ.

The following theorem, which states that every vector of strategies uniquely defines a probability distribution over the set of infinite plays, follows from Theorem 6.22 and the definition of ρ (Exercise 6.25).

Theorem 6.23 *Let σ be a mixed/behavior strategy vector in a (finite or infinite) extensive-form game. Then there exists a unique probability distribution μ_σ over $(H, \mathcal{H})$ satisfying $\mu_\sigma(H(x)) = \rho(x; \sigma)$ for every vertex x.*

Definition 6.24 *A mixed strategy σ_i of player i is* equivalent *to a behavior strategy b_i of player i if, for every mixed/behavior strategy vector σ_{-i} of the other players, $\mu_{(\sigma_i, \sigma_{-i})} = \mu_{(b_i, \sigma_{-i})}$.*

Theorems 6.22 and 6.23 imply the following theorem.

Theorem 6.25 *A mixed strategy σ_i of player i is* equivalent *to his behavior strategy b_i if for every mixed/behavior strategy vector σ_{-i} of the other players and every vertex x we have $\rho(x; \sigma_i, \sigma_{-i}) = \rho(x; b_i, \sigma_{-i})$.*

6.4.3   Statement of Kuhn's Theorem for infinite games and its proof

The definition of a player with perfect recall in an infinite extensive-form game is identical to the definition for finite games (Definition 6.13 on page 242). If player i has perfect recall in a game G, then he also has perfect recall in the game G^T for all $T \in \mathbb{N}$ (verify!).

Theorem 6.26 *Let G be an extensive-form game with an infinite game tree such that each vertex in the game tree has a finite number of children. If player i has perfect recall, then for each mixed strategy of player i there is an equivalent behavior strategy and for each behavior strategy of player i there is an equivalent mixed strategy.*

Proof: Let G be an extensive-form game with an infinite game tree such that each vertex in the game tree has a finite number of children. Let i be a player with perfect recall. We begin by proving one direction of the statement of the theorem: for each mixed strategy of player i there is an equivalent behavior strategy. Let σ_i be a mixed strategy of player i in the game G. For each $T \in \mathbb{N}$, let σ_i^T be the restriction of σ_i to the game G^T; in other words, σ_i^T is the marginal distribution of σ_i over S_i^T. In the proof of Kuhn's Theorem (Theorem 6.15 on page 243), we constructed an equivalent behavior strategy for any given mixed strategy in a finite extensive-form game. Let b_i^T be the behavior strategy equivalent to the mixed strategy σ_i^T in the game G^T, constructed according to that theorem. Since σ_i^{T+1} is equivalent to b_i^{T+1} in the game G_i^{T+1}, since the marginal distribution of σ_i^{T+1} over S_i^T is σ_i^T, and since σ_i^T is equivalent to b_i^T in the game G_i^T, it follows that for each vertex x whose depth is less than or equal to T,

$$\rho_i\left(x; b_i^{T+1}\right) = \rho_i\left(x; \sigma_i^{T+1}\right) = \rho_i\left(x; \sigma_i^T\right) = \rho_i\left(x; b_i^T\right). \tag{6.74}$$

It follows that

$$b_i^{T+1}(U_i) = b_i^T(U_i), \quad \forall U_i \in \mathcal{U}_i^T. \tag{6.75}$$

In other words, the behavior strategies $(b_i^T)_{T \in \mathbb{N}}$ are consistent, in the sense that every two of them coincide on information sets that are in the domain of both. Define a behavior strategy b_i of player i by

$$b_i(U_i) := b_i^T(U_i), \quad \forall U_i \in \mathcal{U}_i, \tag{6.76}$$

where T satisfies $U_i \in \mathcal{U}_i^T$. By Equation (6.75) it follows that $b_i(U_i)$ is well defined. We will prove that σ_i and b_i are equivalent in the game G. Let $\sigma_{-i} = (\sigma_j)_{j \neq i}$ be a mixed/behavior strategy vector of the other players. For each $T \in \mathbb{N}$, let σ_j^T be the strategy σ_j restricted to the game G^T. Denote $\sigma_{-i}^T = (\sigma_j^T)_{j \neq i}$. Since the strategies σ_i^T and b_i^T are equivalent in the game G^T,

$$\rho\left(x; \sigma_i^T, \sigma_{-i}^T\right) = \rho\left(x; b_i^T, \sigma_{-i}^T\right) \tag{6.77}$$

for each vertex whose depth is less than or equal to T. By definition, it follows that for each vertex x

$$\rho(x; \sigma_i, \sigma_{-i}) = \rho(x; b_i, \sigma_{-i}). \tag{6.78}$$

Theorem 6.25 implies that σ_i and b_i are equivalent strategies.

We now prove the other direction of the statement of the theorem. Let b_i be a behavior strategy of player i. For each $T \in \mathbb{N}$ let b_i^T be the restriction of b_i to the collection of information sets $\mathcal{U}_i^T$. It follows that b_i^T is a behavior strategy of player i in the game G^T. Since player i has perfect recall in the game G^T, and since the game G^T is a finite game, there exists a mixed strategy σ_i^T equivalent to b_i^T in the game G^T.

Since σ_i^{T+1} is equivalent to b_i^{T+1} in the game G_i^{T+1}, since the restriction of b_i^{T+1} to $\mathcal{U}_i^T$ is b_i^T, and since σ_i^T is equivalent to b_i^T in the game G_i^T, it follows that σ_i^T is the marginal distribution of σ_i^{T+1} on S_i^T. By Theorem 6.21 (with respect to the product space $S_i = \times_{U_i \in \mathcal{U}_i} A(U_i)$) we deduce that there exists a mixed strategy σ_i whose projection over S_i^T is σ_i^T for all $T \in \mathbb{N}$. Reasoning similar to that used in the first part of this proof shows that σ_i and b_i are equivalent strategies in the game G (Exercise 6.26). $\square$

Using methods similar to those presented in this section one can prove Kuhn's Theorem for extensive-form games with game trees of finite depth in which every vertex has a finite or countable number of children. Combining that result with the proof of Theorem 6.26 shows that Kuhn's Theorem holds in extensive-form games with game trees of infinite depth in which every vertex has a finite or countable number of children.

6.5   Remarks

The Absent-Minded Driver game appearing in Example 6.9 (page 236) was first introduced in Piccione and Rubinstein [1997], and an entire issue of the journal *Games and Economic Behavior* (1997, issue 1) was devoted to analyzing it. Item (b) of Exercise 6.17 is taken from von Stengel and Forges [2008].

6.6 · Exercises

6.1 In each of the games in the following diagrams, identify which players have perfect recall. In each case in which there is a player with imperfect recall, indicate what the player may forget during a play of the game, and in what way the condition in Definition 6.13 (page 242) fails to obtain.

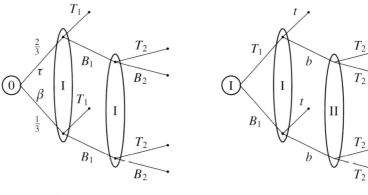

Game A   Game B

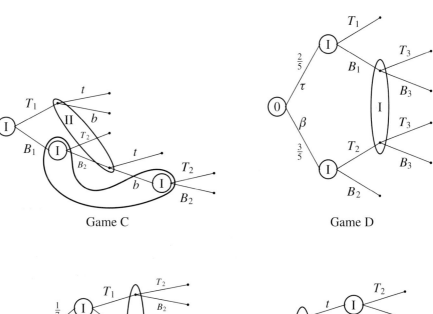

Game C   Game D

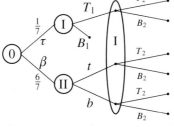

Game E

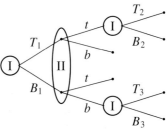

Game F

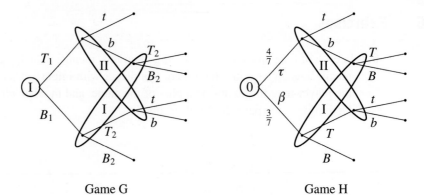

Game G   Game H

6.2 In each of the following games, find a mixed strategy equivalent to the noted behavior strategy.

(a) $b_{\mathrm{I}} = \left[\frac{1}{3}(T), \frac{2}{3}(B)\right]$, in the game

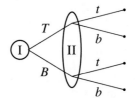

(b) $b_{\mathrm{II}} = \left(\left[\frac{4}{9}(t_1), \frac{5}{9}(b_1)\right], \left[\frac{3}{5}(t_2), \frac{2}{5}(b_2)\right], \left[\frac{2}{3}(t_3), \frac{1}{3}(b_3)\right]\right)$, in the game

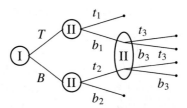

(c) $b_{\mathrm{II}} = \left(\left[\frac{4}{9}(t_1), \frac{5}{9}(b_1)\right], \left[\frac{1}{4}(t_2), \frac{3}{4}(b_2)\right]\right)$, in the game

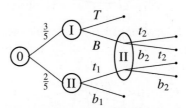

6.3 Identify the payoff that each player can guarantee for himself in each of the following two-player zero-sum games using mixed strategies and using behavior strategies.

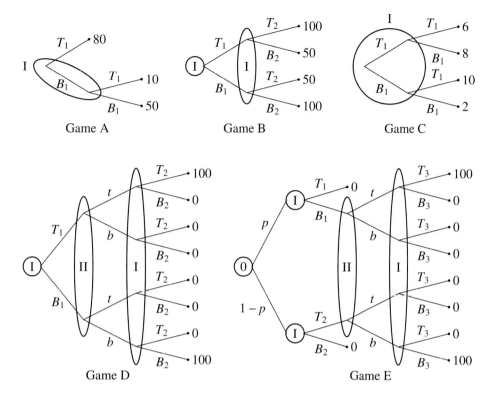

Game A   Game B   Game C

Game D   Game E

6.4 Consider an extensive-form game (not necessarily with perfect information) in which Player I has a single information set, denoted U_I.

(a) Show that there is a natural identification between the set of mixed strategies of Player I and the set $\Delta(A(U_I))$.

(b) Show that there is a natural identification between the set of behavior strategies of Player I and the set $\Delta(A(U_I))$.

(c) Conclude from parts (a) and (b) that there is a natural identification between the set of mixed strategies of Player I and the set of his behavior strategies. Explain why two strategies that are identified with each other are not necessarily equivalent when the game does not have perfect recall.

Hint: To answer part (c) determine the behavior strategy that is identified with the mixed strategy $[\frac{1}{2}(T), \frac{1}{2}(B)]$ in Example 6.9 (page 236) and explain why the two are not equivalent.

6.5 Does there exist a two-player zero-sum extensive-form game that has a value in mixed strategies and a value in behavior strategies, but these two values are not equal to each other? Either prove that such a game exists or provide a counterexample.

6.6 Prove Theorem 6.6 (page 234): if b_i is a behavior strategy equivalent to the mixed strategy σ_i, then for every strategy vector σ_{-i},

$$u_j(\sigma_i, \sigma_{-i}) = u_j(b_i, \sigma_{-i}), \quad \forall j \in N. \tag{6.79}$$

6.7 Prove that in Example 6.4 (page 233) for every mixed strategy $\hat{\sigma}_{II}$ of Player II the probability distribution induced by $(\sigma_I, \hat{\sigma}_{II})$ over the leaves of the game tree is identical with the probability distribution induced by $(b_I, \hat{\sigma}_{II})$ over the leaves of the game tree. The mixed strategy σ_I defined in Equation (6.14) and the behavior strategy b_I defined in Equation (6.13) (page 234).

6.8 Prove Corollary 6.10 (page 237): if there exists a path from the root to the vertex x that passes at least twice through the same information set U_i of player i, and if the action leading to x is not the same action in each of these passes through the information set, then player i has a behavior strategy that has no equivalent mixed strategy.

6.9 Show that Theorem 6.11 does not hold without the condition that there are at least two possible actions at each vertex.

6.10 Explain why Equation (6.37) in the proof of Theorem 6.11 (page 241) does not necessarily hold when a game does not have perfect recall.

6.11 Prove that if a player does not know whether or not he has previously made a move during the play of a game, then he does not have perfect recall (according to Definition 6.13 on page 242).

6.12 Prove that if a player knows during the play of a game how many moves he has previously made, but later forgets this, then he does not have perfect recall (according to Definition 6.13 on page 242).

6.13 Prove that if a player knows during the play of a game which action another player has chosen at a particular information set, but later forgets this, then he does not have perfect recall (according to Definition 6.13 on page 242).

6.14 Prove that if a player does not know what action he chose at a previous information set in a game, then he has imperfect recall in that game (according to Definition 6.13 on page 242).

6.15 Prove that if at a particular information set in a game a player knows which player made the move leading to that information set, but later forgets this, then he does not have perfect recall (according to Definition 6.13 on page 242).

6.16 Prove that if x_1 and x_2 are two vertices in the same information set of player i, and if player i has perfect recall in the game, then $S_i^*(x_1) = S_i^*(x_2)$. (See page 239 for the definition of the set $S_i^*(x)$.)

6.17 Let U and $\hat{U}$ be two information sets (they may both be the information sets of the same player, or of two different players). U will be said to *precede* $\hat{U}$ if there exist a vertex $x \in U$ and a vertex $\hat{x} \in \hat{U}$ such that the path from the root to $\hat{x}$ passes through x.

(a) Prove that if U is an information set of a player with perfect recall, then U does not precede U.

(b) Prove that in a two-player game without chance moves, where both players have perfect recall, if U precedes $\hat{U}$, then $\hat{U}$ does not precede U.

(c) Find a two-player game with chance moves, where both players have perfect recall and there exist two information sets U and $\hat{U}$ such that U precedes $\hat{U}$, and $\hat{U}$ precedes U.

(d) Find a three-player game without chance moves, where all the players have perfect recall and there exist two information sets U and $\hat{U}$ such that U precedes $\hat{U}$, and $\hat{U}$ precedes U.

6.18 Find a behavior strategy equivalent to the given mixed strategies in each of the following games.

(a) $s_{\mathrm{I}} = \left[\frac{1}{2}(B_1, B_2), \frac{1}{2}(T_1, T_2)\right]$, in the game

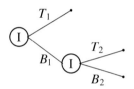

(b) $s_{\mathrm{I}} = \left[\frac{3}{7}(B_1 B_2 M_3), \frac{1}{7}(B_1 T_2 B_3), \frac{2}{7}(T_1 B_2 M_3), \frac{1}{7}(T_3 T_2 T_3)\right]$ and
$s_{\mathrm{II}} = \left[\frac{3}{7}(b_1 b_2), \frac{1}{7}(b_1 t_2), \frac{1}{7}(t_1 b_2), \frac{2}{7}(t_1 t_2)\right]$, in the game

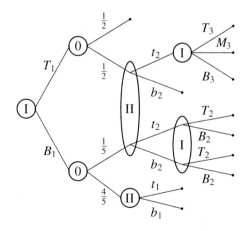

6.19 (a) Let i be a player with perfect recall in an extensive-form game and let σ_i be a mixed strategy of player i. Suppose that there is a strategy vector σ_{-i} of the other players such that $\rho(x; \sigma_i, \sigma_{-i}) > 0$ for each leaf x in the game tree. Prove that there exists a unique behavior strategy b_i equivalent to σ_i.

(b) Give an example of an extensive-form game in which player i has perfect recall and there is a mixed strategy σ_i with more than one behavior strategy equivalent to it.

6.20 Let i be a player with perfect recall in an extensive-form game and let b_i be a behavior strategy of player i. Suppose that there is a strategy vector σ_{-i} of the other players such that $\rho(x; b_i, \sigma_{-i}) > 0$ for each leaf in the game tree. Give an example that shows that there need not exist a unique mixed strategy σ_i equivalent to b_i.

6.21 In the following two-player zero-sum game, find the optimal behavior strategies of the two players. (Why must such strategies exist?)

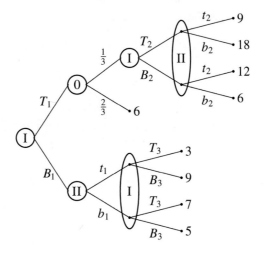

6.22 Compute the value of the following game, in mixed strategies, and in behavior strategies, if these values exist.

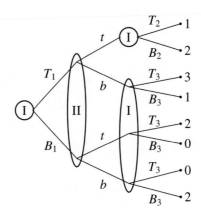

6.23 (a) Compute the value in mixed strategies of the game below.

(b) Compute what each player can guarantee using behavior strategies (in other words, compute each player's security value in behavior strategies).

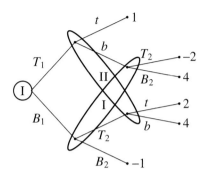

6.24 Prove Theorem 6.22 (page 251).

6.25 Prove Theorem 6.23 (page 253): let σ be a mixed/behavior strategy vector in a (finite or infinite) extensive-form game. Then there exists a unique probability distribution μ_σ over $(H, \mathcal{H})$ satisfying $\mu_\sigma(H(x)) = \rho(x; \sigma)$ for each vertex x.

6.26 Complete the proof of the second direction of Kuhn's Theorem for infinite games (Theorem 6.26, page 253): prove that the mixed strategy σ_i constructed in the proof is equivalent to the given behavior strategy b_i.

7 Equilibrium refinements

Chapter summary

The most important solution concept in noncooperative game theory is the Nash equilibrium. When games possess many Nash equilibria, we sometimes want to know which equilibria are more reasonable than others. In this chapter we present and study some refinements of the concept of Nash equilibrium.

In Section 7.1 we study *subgame perfect equilibrium*, which is a solution concept for extensive-form games. The idea behind this refinement is to rule out noncredible threats, that is, "irrational" behavior off the equilibrium path whose goal is to deter deviations. In games with perfect information, a subgame perfect equilibrium always exists, and it can be found using the process of *backward induction*.

The second refinement, presented in Section 7.3, is the *perfect equilibrium*, which is based on the idea that players might make mistakes when choosing their strategies. In extensive-form games there are two types of perfect equilibria corresponding to the two types of mistakes that players may make: one, called *strategic-form perfect equilibrium*, assumes that players may make a mistake at the outset of the game, when they choose the pure strategy they will implement throughout the game. The other, called *extensive-form perfect equilibrium*, assumes that players may make mistakes in choosing an action in each information set. We show by examples that these two concepts are different and prove that every extensive-form game possesses perfect equilibria of both types, and that every extensive-form perfect equilibrium is a subgame perfect equilibrium.

The last concept in this chapter, presented in Section 7.4, is the *sequential equilibrium* in extensive-form games. It is proved that every finite extensive-form game with perfect recall has a sequential equilibrium. Finally, we study the relationship between the sequential equilibrium and the extensive-form perfect equilibrium.

When a game has more than one equilibrium, we may wish to choose some equilibria over others based on "reasonable" criteria. Such a choice is termed a "refinement" of the equilibrium concept. Refinements can be derived in both extensive-form games and strategic-form games. We will consider several equilibrium refinements in this chapter, namely, perfect equilibrium, subgame perfect equilibrium, and sequential equilibrium.

Throughout this chapter, when we analyze extensive-form games, we will assume that if the game has chance vertices, every possible move at every chance vertex is chosen with positive probability. If there is a move at a chance vertex that is chosen with probability 0, it, and all the vertices following it in the tree, may be omitted, and we may consider instead the resulting smaller tree.

7.1 Subgame perfect equilibrium

The concept of subgame perfect equilibrium, which is a refinement of equilibrium in extensive-form games, is presented in this section. In an extensive-form game, each strategy vector σ defines a path from the root to one of the leaves of the game tree, namely, the path that is obtained when each player implements the strategy vector σ. When the strategy vector σ is a Nash equilibrium, the path that is thus obtained is called the *equilibrium path*. If x is a vertex along the equilibrium path, and if $\Gamma(x)$ is a subgame, then the strategy vector σ restricted to the subgame $\Gamma(x)$ is also a Nash equilibrium because each profitable deviation for a player in the subgame $\Gamma(x)$ is also a profitable deviation in the original game (explain why). In contrast, if the vertex x is not located along the equilibrium path (in which case it is said to be *off the equilibrium path*) then the strategy vector σ restricted to the subgame $\Gamma(x)$ is not necessarily a Nash equilibrium of the subgame. The following example illustrates this point.

Example 7.1 Consider the two-player extensive-form game shown in Figure 7.1.

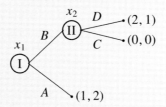

Figure 7.1 The extensive-form game in Example 7.1

Figure 7.2 shows the corresponding strategic form of this game.

Player II

		C	D
Player I	A	1, 2	1, 2
	B	0, 0	2, 1

Figure 7.2 The strategic-form game, and two pure-strategy equilibria of the game

This game has two pure-strategy equilibria, (B, D) and (A, C). Player I clearly prefers (B, D), while Player II prefers (A, C). In addition, the game has a continuum of mixed-strategy equilibria: $(A, [y(C), (1 - y)(D)])$ for $y \geq \frac{1}{2}$, with payoff $(1, 2)$, which is identical to the payoff of (A, C). Which equilibrium is more likely to be played?

The extensive form of the game is depicted again twice in Figure 7.3, with the thick lines corresponding to the two pure-strategy equilibria.

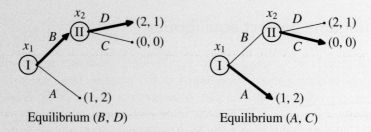

Equilibrium (B, D) Equilibrium (A, C)

Figure 7.3 The pure-strategy equilibria of the game in extensive form

This game has one proper subgame, $\Gamma(x_2)$, in which only Player II is active. The two equilibria (A, C) and (B, D) induce different plays in this subgame. While the restriction of the equilibrium (B, D) to $\Gamma(x_2)$, namely D, is an equilibrium of the subgame $\Gamma(x_2)$, the restriction of the equilibrium (A, C) to $\Gamma(x_2)$, namely C, is not an equilibrium in this subgame, since a deviation to D is profitable for Player II. The vertex x_2 is on the equilibrium path of (B, D), which is $x_1 \to x_2 \to (2, 1)$, and it is not on the equilibrium path of (A, C), which is $x_1 \to (1, 2)$. This is necessarily so, since if x_2 were on the equilibrium path of (A, C) and Player II did not play an equilibrium in the subgame $\Gamma(x_2)$, then (A, C) could not be an equilibrium (why?).

Player II's strategy at vertex x_2 seems irrational: the equilibrium strategy calls on him to choose C, which yields him a payoff of 0, instead of D, which yields him a payoff of 1. This choice, in fact, is never actually made when this equilibrium is played, because Player I chooses A at vertex x_1, but the equilibrium, as constructed, says that "if Player I were to choose B, then Player II would choose C." This may be regarded as a threat directed by Player II to Player I: if you "dare" choose B, I will choose C, and then you will get 0 instead of 1, which you would get by choosing A. This threat is intended by Player II to persuade Player I to choose the action that leads to payoff $(1, 2)$, which Player II prefers to $(2, 1)$. Is this a *credible* threat?

Whether or not a threat is credible depends on many factors, which are not expressed in our model of the game: previous interaction between the players, reputation, behavioral norms, and so on. Consideration of these factors, which may be important and interesting, is beyond the scope of this book. We will, however, consider what happens if we invalidate such threats, on the grounds that they are not "rational."

Another way of saying the same thing is: the restriction of the equilibrium (A, C) to the subgame $\Gamma(x_2)$, which begins at vertex x_2 (the subgame in which only Player II has a move), yields the strategy C, which is not an equilibrium of that subgame. This observation led to the concept of subgame perfect equilibrium that we develop in this section. ◀

Reinhard Selten [1965, 1973] suggested that the equilibria that should be chosen in extensive-form games are those equilibria that are also equilibria when restricted to each subgame. In other words, Selten suggested choosing those equilibria at which the actions of the players are still in equilibrium even when they are off the equilibrium path.

By definition, a strategy σ_i tells player i which action to choose at each of his information sets, even at information sets that will not be arrived at during the play of the game that results from implementing σ_i (whether due to moves chosen by player i, or moves chosen by the other players). It follows that, for every strategy vector σ, it is possible to compute the payoff of each player if the play of the game is at vertex x (even if the play has not arrived at x when the players implement σ). Denote by $u_i(\sigma \mid x)$ player i's payoff in the subgame $\Gamma(x)$ when the players implement the strategy vector σ, if the play of the game is at vertex x. For example, in the game in Example 7.1, $u_1((A, C) \mid x_1) = 1$ and $u_1((A, C) \mid x_2) = 0$ (note that x_2 is not reached when (A, C) is played).

The payoff $u_i(\sigma \mid x)$ depends only on the restriction of the strategy vector σ to the subgame $\Gamma(x)$. We will therefore use the same notation to denote the payoff when σ is a strategy vector in $\Gamma(x)$ and when in the strategy vector σ some of the strategies are in Γ and some in $\Gamma(x)$.

Definition 7.2 *A strategy vector σ^* (in mixed strategies or behavior strategies) in an extensive-form game Γ is called a* subgame perfect equilibrium *if for every subgame, the restriction of the strategy vector σ^* to the subgame is a Nash equilibrium of that subgame: for every player $i \in N$, every strategy σ_i, and every subgame $\Gamma(x)$,*

$$u_i(\sigma^* \mid x) \geq u_i(\sigma_i, \sigma^*_{-i} \mid x). \tag{7.1}$$

As we saw in Example 7.1, the equilibrium (A, C) is not a subgame perfect equilibrium. In contrast, the equilibrium (B, D) is a subgame perfect equilibrium: the choice D is an equilibrium of the subgame starting at x_2. For each $y \in [\frac{1}{2}, 1)$, the equilibrium in mixed strategies $(A, [y(C), (1-y)(D)])$ is not a subgame perfect equilibrium, because the choice of C with positive probability is not an equilibrium of the subgame starting at x_2.

Note that in the strategic form of the game, Player II's strategy C is (weakly) dominated by the strategy D, and hence the elimination of dominated strategies in this game eliminates the equilibrium (A, C) (and the mixed-strategy equilibria for $y \in [\frac{1}{2}, 1)$), leaving only the subgame perfect equilibrium (B, D). A solution concept based on the elimination of weakly dominated strategies, and its relation to the concept of subgame perfect equilibrium, will be studied in Section 7.3.

Remark 7.3 *Since every game is a subgame of itself, by definition, every subgame perfect equilibrium is a Nash equilibrium. The concept of subgame perfect equilibrium is therefore a refinement of the concept of Nash equilibrium.* ◆

As previously stated, each leaf x in a game tree defines a subtree $\Gamma(x)$ in which effectively no player participates. An extensive-form game that does not include any subgame other than itself and the subgames defined by the leaves is called a *game without nontrivial subgames*. For such games, the condition appearing in Definition 7.2 holds vacuously, and we therefore deduce the following corollary.

Theorem 7.4 *In an extensive-form game without nontrivial subgames, every Nash equilibrium (in mixed strategies or behavior strategies) is a subgame perfect equilibrium.*

For each strategy vector σ, and each vertex x in the game tree, denote by $\mathbf{P}_\sigma(x)$ the probability that the play of the game will visit vertex x when the players implement the strategy vector σ.

Theorem 7.5 *Let σ^* be a Nash equilibrium (in mixed strategies or behavior strategies) of an extensive-form game Γ, and let $\Gamma(x)$ be a subgame of Γ. If $\mathbf{P}_{\sigma^*}(x) > 0$, then the strategy vector σ^* restricted to the subgame $\Gamma(x)$ is a Nash equilibrium (in mixed strategies or behavior strategies) of $\Gamma(x)$.*

This theorem underscores the fact that the extra conditions that make a Nash equilibrium a subgame perfect equilibrium apply to subgames $\Gamma(x)$ for which $\mathbf{P}_\sigma(x) = 0$, such as for example the subgame $\Gamma(x_2)$ in Example 7.1, under the equilibrium (A, C).

Proof: The idea behind the proof is as follows. If in the subgame $\Gamma(x)$ the strategy vector σ^* restricted to the subgame were not a Nash equilibrium, then there would exist a player i who could profit in that subgame by deviating from σ_i^* to a different strategy, say σ_i^x, in the subgame. Since the play of the game visits the subgame $\Gamma(x)$ with positive probability, the player can profit in Γ by deviating from σ_i^*, by implementing σ_i^x if the game gets to x.

We now proceed to the formal proof. Let $\Gamma(x)$ be the subgame of Γ starting at vertex x and let σ^* be a Nash equilibrium of Γ satisfying $\mathbf{P}_{\sigma^*}(x) > 0$. Let σ_i^x be a strategy of player i in the subgame $\Gamma(x)$. Denote by σ_i the strategy[1] of player i that coincides with σ^* except in the subgame $\Gamma(x)$, where it coincides with σ_i^x.

Since σ^* and $(\sigma_i, \sigma_{-i}^*)$ coincide at all vertices that are not in $\Gamma(x)$,

$$\mathbf{P}_{\sigma^*}(x) = \mathbf{P}_{(\sigma_i, \sigma_{-i}^*)}(x). \tag{7.2}$$

Denote by $\hat{u}_i$ the expected payoff of player i, conditional on the play of the game not arriving at the subgame $\Gamma(x)$ when the players implement the strategy vector σ^*. Then

$$u_i(\sigma^*) = \mathbf{P}_{\sigma^*}(x)u_i(\sigma^* \mid x) + (1 - \mathbf{P}_{\sigma^*}(x))\hat{u}_i. \tag{7.3}$$

Writing out the analogous equation for the strategy vector $(\sigma_i, \sigma_{-i}^*)$ and using Equation (7.2) yields

$$u_i(\sigma_i, \sigma_{-i}^*) = \mathbf{P}_{(\sigma_i, \sigma_{-i}^*)}(x)u_i((\sigma_i^x, \sigma_{-i}^*) \mid x) + (1 - \mathbf{P}_{(\sigma_i, \sigma_{-i}^*)}(x))\hat{u}_i \tag{7.4}$$

$$= \mathbf{P}_{\sigma^*}(x)u_i((\sigma_i^x, \sigma_{-i}^*) \mid x) + (1 - \mathbf{P}_{\sigma^*}(x))\hat{u}_i. \tag{7.5}$$

Since σ^* is an equilibrium,

$$\mathbf{P}_{\sigma^*}(x)u_i(\sigma^* \mid x) + (1 - \mathbf{P}_{\sigma^*}(x))\hat{u}_i = u_i(\sigma^*) \tag{7.6}$$

$$\geq u_i(\sigma_i, \sigma_{-i}^*) \tag{7.7}$$

$$= \mathbf{P}_{\sigma^*}(x)u_i((\sigma_i^x, \sigma_{-i}^*) \mid x) + (1 - \mathbf{P}_{\sigma^*}(x))\hat{u}_i. \tag{7.8}$$

Since $\mathbf{P}_{\sigma^*}(x) > 0$, one has

$$u_i(\sigma^* \mid x) \geq u_i((\sigma_i^x, \sigma_{-i}^*) \mid x). \tag{7.9}$$

Since this inequality is satisfied for each player i, and each strategy σ_i, in the subgame $\Gamma(x)$, the strategy vector σ^* restricted to the subgame $\Gamma(x)$ is a Nash equilibrium of $\Gamma(x)$. □

---

1 When σ_i^* and σ_i' are behavior strategies, the strategy σ_i coincides with σ_i^* in player i's information sets that are not in $\Gamma(x)$, and with σ_i' in player i's information sets that are in the subgame of $\Gamma(x)$.

When σ_i^* and σ_i' are mixed strategies, the strategy σ_i is defined as follows: every pure strategy s_i of player i is composed of the pair (s_i^1, s_i^2), in which s_i^1 associates a move with each of player i's information sets in the subgame $\Gamma(x)$, and s_i^2 associates a move with each of player i's information sets that are not in the subgame $\Gamma(x)$. Then $\sigma_i(s_i^1, s_i^2) := \sigma_i'(s_i^1)\sum_{\{\tilde{s}_i : \tilde{s}_i^2 = s_i^2\}} \sigma^*(\tilde{s}_i)$.

Since $\Gamma(x)$ is a subgame, every information set that is in $\Gamma(x)$ does not contain vertices that are not in that subgame; hence the strategy σ_i is well defined in both cases.

Recall that, given a mixed strategy σ_i of player i, we denote by $\sigma_i(s_i)$ the probability that the pure strategy s_i will be chosen, and given a behavior strategy σ_i, we denote by $\sigma_i(U_i; a_i)$ the probability that the action a_i will be chosen in the information set U_i of player i.

Definition 7.6 *A mixed strategy σ_i of player i is called* completely mixed *if $\sigma_i(s_i) > 0$ for each $s_i \in S_i$. A behavior strategy σ_i of player i is called* completely mixed *if $\sigma_i(U_i; a_i) > 0$ for each information set U_i of player i, and each action $a_i \in A(U_i)$.*

A mixed strategy is completely mixed if under the strategy a player chooses each of his pure strategies with positive probability, and a behavior strategy is completely mixed if at each of his information sets, the player chooses with positive probability each of his possible actions at that information set.

Since at each chance vertex every action is chosen with positive probability, if each player i uses a completely mixed strategy σ_i, then $\mathbf{P}_\sigma(x) > 0$ for each vertex x in the game tree. This leads to the following corollary of Theorem 7.5.

Corollary 7.7 *Let Γ be an extensive-form game. Then every Nash equilibrium in completely mixed strategies (behavior strategies or mixed strategies) is a subgame perfect equilibrium.*

As Theorem 7.4 states, in games whose only subgames are the game itself, every Nash equilibrium is a subgame perfect equilibrium; in such cases, subgame perfection imposes no further conditions beyond the conditions defining the Nash equilibrium. In contrast, when a game has a large number of subgames, the concept of subgame perfection becomes significant, because a Nash equilibrium must meet a large number of conditions to be a subgame perfect equilibrium. The most extreme case of such a game is a game with perfect information. Recall that a game with perfect information is a game in which every information set is composed of only one vertex. In such a game, every vertex is the root of a subgame.

Example 7.8   Figure 7.4 depicts a two-player game with perfect information.

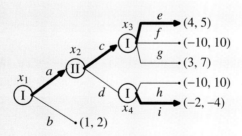

Figure 7.4 A subgame perfect equilibrium in a game with perfect information

To find a subgame perfect equilibrium, start with the smallest subgames: those whose roots are vertices adjacent to the leaf vertices, in this case the subgames $\Gamma(x_3)$ and $\Gamma(x_4)$. The only equilibrium in the subgame $\Gamma(x_3)$ is the one in which Player I chooses e, because this action leads to the result $(4, 5)$, which includes the best payoff Player I can receive in the subgame. Similar reasoning shows that the only equilibrium in the subgame $\Gamma(x_4)$ is the one in which Player I chooses i, leading to the result $(-2, -4)$. We can now replace the subgame $\Gamma(x_3)$ with the result of its equilibrium, $(4, 5)$, and the subgame $\Gamma(x_4)$ with the result of its equilibrium, $(-2, -4)$. This yields the game depicted in Figure 7.5 (this procedure is called "folding" the game).

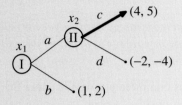

Figure 7.5 The folded game

Now, in the subgame starting at x_2, at equilibrium, Player II chooses c, leading to the result $(4, 5)$. Folding this subgame leads to the game depicted in Figure 7.6.

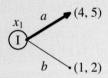

Figure 7.6 The game after further folding

In this game, at equilibrium, Player I chooses a, leading to the result $(4, 5)$. Recapitulating all the stages just described gives us the subgame perfect equilibrium shown in Figure 7.4.   ◄

This process is called *backward induction* (see Remark 4.50 on page 120). The process leads to the equilibrium $((a, e, i), c)$, which by construction is a subgame perfect equilibrium. Backward induction leads, in a similar way, to a subgame perfect equilibrium in pure strategies in every (finite) game with perfect information. We thus have the following theorem.

Theorem 7.9 *Every finite extensive-form game with perfect information has a subgame perfect equilibrium in pure strategies.*

The proof of the theorem is accomplished by backward induction on the subgames, from the smallest (starting from the vertices adjacent to the leaves) to the largest (starting from the root of the tree). The formal proof is left to the reader (Exercise 7.8). We will later show (Theorem 7.37 on page 282) that every extensive-form game with perfect recall has a subgame perfect equilibrium in behavior strategies.

With regard to games with incomplete information, we can reuse the idea of "folding" a game to prove the following theorem.

Theorem 7.10 *Every extensive-form game with perfect recall has a subgame perfect equilibrium in mixed strategies.*

The proof of the theorem is left to the reader as an exercise (Exercise 7.16).

Remark 7.11 *In the last two theorems we used the fact that an extensive-form game is finite by definition: the number of decision vertices is finite, and the number of actions at* *every decision vertex is finite. To prove Theorem 7.9, it is not necessary to assume that the game tree is finite; it suffices to assume that there exists a natural number L such that the length of each path emanating from the root is no greater than L. Without this assumption, the process of backward induction cannot begin, and these two theorems are not valid. These theorems do not hold in games that are not finite. There are examples of infinite two-player games that have no equilibria (see, for example, Mycielski [1992], Claim 3.1). Such examples are beyond the scope of this book. Exercise 7.17 presents an example of a game with imperfect information in which one of the players has a continuum of pure strategies, but the game has no subgame perfect equilibria.*   ♦

Remark 7.12 *In games with perfect information, when the backward induction process reaches a vertex at which a player has more than one action that maximizes his payoff, any one of them can be chosen in order to continue the process. Each choice leads to a different equilibrium, and therefore the backward induction process can identify several equilibria (all of which are subgame perfect equilibria).*   ♦

Remark 7.13 *The process of backward induction is in effect the game-theory version of the dynamic programming principle widely used in operations research. This is a very natural and useful approach to multistage optimization: start with optimizing the action chosen at the last stage, stage n, for every state of the system at stage n − 1. Continue by optimizing the action chosen at stage n − 1 for every state of the system at stage n − 2, and so on.*   ♦

Backward induction is a very convincing logical method. However, its use in game theory sometimes raises questions stemming from the fact that unlike dynamic optimization problems with a single decision maker, games involve several interacting decision makers. We will consider several examples illustrating the limits of backward induction in games. We first construct an example of a game that has an equilibrium that is not subgame perfect, but is preferred by both players to all the subgame perfect equilibria of the game.

Example 7.14   A two-player extensive-form game with two equilibria is depicted in Figure 7.7.

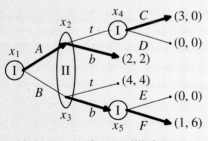

Subgame perfect equilibrium

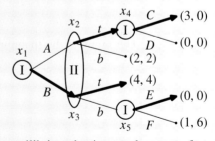

An equilibrium that is not subgame perfect

Figure 7.7 A game with two equilibria

Using backward induction, we find that the only subgame perfect equilibrium in the game is $((A, C, F,), b)$, leading to the payoff $(2, 2)$. The equilibrium $((B, C, E), t)$ leads to the payoff $(4, 4)$ (verify that this is indeed an equilibrium). This equilibrium is not a subgame perfect equilibrium, since it calls on Player I to choose E in the subgame $\Gamma(x_4)$, which is not an equilibrium. This choice by Player I may be regarded as a threat to Player II: "if you choose b (in an attempt to get 6) instead of t, I will choose E and you will get 0." What is interesting in this example is that both players have an "interest" in maintaining this threat, because it serves both of them: it enables them to receive the payoff $(4, 4)$, which is preferred by both of them to the payoff $(2, 2)$ that they would receive under the game's only subgame perfect equilibrium.   ◀

Example 7.15   **The repeated Prisoner's Dilemma** Consider the Prisoner's Dilemma game with the payoff shown in Figure 7.8.

Player II

		D	C
Player I	D	1, 1	4, 0
	C	0, 4	3, 3

Figure 7.8 Prisoner's Dilemma

Suppose two players play the Prisoner's Dilemma game 100 times, with each player at each stage informed of the action chosen by the other player (and therefore also the payoff at each stage).

We can analyze this game using backward induction: at equilibrium, at the 100th (i.e., the last) repetition, each of the players chooses D (which strictly dominates C), independently of the actions undertaken in the previous stages: for every other choice, a player choosing C can profit by deviating to D. This means that in the game played at the 99th stage, what the players choose has no effect on what will happen at the 100th stage, so that at equilibrium each player chooses D at stage 99, and so forth. Backward induction leads to the result that the only subgame perfect equilibrium is the strategy vector under which both players choose D at every stage.[2] In Exercise 7.9, the reader is asked to turn this proof idea into a formal proof.

In fact, it can be shown that in every equilibrium (not necessarily subgame perfect equilibrium) in this 100-stage game the players play (D, D) in every stage (see Chapter 13). This does not seem reasonable: one would most likely expect rational players to find a way to obtain the payoff $(3, 3)$, at least in the initial stages of the game, and not play (D, D), which yields only $(1, 1)$, in every stage. A large number of empirical studies confirm that in fact players do usually cooperate during many stages when playing the repeated Prisoner's Dilemma, in order to obtain a higher payoff than that indicated by the equilibrium strategy.   ◀

Example 7.16   **The Centipede game** The Centipede game that we saw in Exercise 3.12 on page 61 is also a two-player game with 100 stages, but unlike the repeated Prisoner's Dilemma, in the Centipede game the actions of the players are implemented sequentially, rather than simultaneously: in the odd stages, $t = 1, 3, \ldots, 99$, Player I has a turn, and he decides whether to stop the game (S) or to continue (C). If he stops the game at stage t, the payoff is $(t, t - 1)$ (hence Player I receives t, and Player II receives $t - 1$), and if he instead chooses C, the game continues on to the next stage. In the even stages, $t = 2, 4, \ldots, 100$, Player II has a turn, and he also chooses between stopping the game (S) and continuing (C). If he stops the game at stage t, the payoff is $(t - 2, t + 1)$. If neither

---

2 This is a verbal description of the process of backward induction in a game tree with 100 stages. Writing out the formal backward induction process in full when the game tree is this large is, of course, not practical.

player chooses to stop in the first 99 stages, the game ends after 100 stages, with the payoff of 101 to Player I and 100 to Player II. The visual depiction of the game in extensive form explains why it is called the Centipede game (see Figure 7.9).

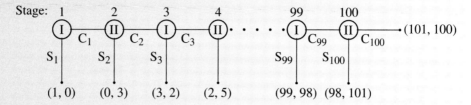

Figure 7.9 The Centipede game

What does backward induction lead to in this game? At stage 100, Player II should choose to stop the game: if he stops the game, he leaves the table with $101, while if the game continues he will only get $100. Since that is the case, at stage 99, Player I should stop the game: he knows that if he chooses to continue the game, Player II will stop the game at the next stage, and Player I will end up with $98, while if he stops, he walks away with $99. Subgame perfection requires him to stop at stage 99. A similar analysis obtains at every stage; hence the only subgame perfect equilibrium in the game is the strategy at which each player stops the game at every one of his turns. In particular, at this equilibrium, Player I stops the game at the first stage, and the payoff is $(1, 0)$. This result is unreasonable: shrewd players will not stop the game and be satisfied with the payoff $(1, 0)$ when they can both do much better by continuing for several stages. Empirical studies reveal that many people do indeed "climb the centipede" up to a certain level, and then one of them stops the game.

It can be shown that at every Nash equilibrium of the game (not necessarily subgame perfect equilibrium), Player I chooses S at the first stage (Exercise 4.19 on page 133).　◀

7.2　Rationality, backward induction, and forward induction

. . . .

The last two examples indicate that backward induction alone is insufficient to describe rational behavior. Kohlberg and Mertens [1986] argued that backward induction requires that at each stage every player looks only at the continuation of the game from that stage forwards, and ignores the fact that the game has reached that stage. But if the game has reached a particular vertex in the game tree, that fact itself gives information about the behavior of the other players, and this should be taken into account. For example, if I am playing the repeated Prisoner's Dilemma, and at the third stage it transpires that the other player played C in the previous two stages, then I need to take this into account, beyond regarding it as "irrational." Perhaps the other player is signaling that we should both play (C, C)? Similarly, if the Centipede game reaches the second stage, then Player I must have deviated from equilibrium, and not have stopped the game at the first stage. It seems reasonable to conjecture that if Player II chooses not to stop the game at that point, then Player I will not stop at stage 3. Backward induction implies that Player I should stop at stage 3, but it also implies that he should stop at stage 1. If he did not stop then, why should he stop now? The approach that grants significance to the history of the game is called *forward induction*. We will not present a formal description of the forward induction concept, and instead only give an example of it.

Example 7.17   Consider the two-player extensive-form game depicted in Figure 7.10.

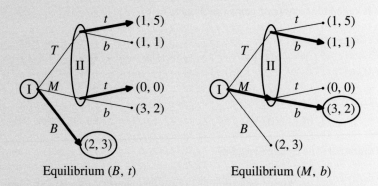

Equilibrium (B, t) Equilibrium (M, b)

Figure 7.10 An extensive-form game with two subgame perfect equilibria

This game has two equilibria in pure strategies:

- (B, t), with payoff $(2, 3)$.
- (M, b), with payoff $(3, 2)$.

Since the game has no nontrivial subgames, both equilibria are subgame perfect equilibria (Theorem 7.4). Is (B, t) a reasonable equilibrium? Is it reasonable for Player II to choose t? If he is called on to choose an action, that means that Player I has not chosen B, which would guarantee him a payment of 2. It is unreasonable for him to have chosen T, which guarantees him only 1, and he therefore must have chosen M, which gives him the chance to obtain 3. In other words, although Player II cannot distinguish between the two vertices in his information set, from the very fact that the game has arrived at the information set and that he is being called upon to choose an action, he can deduce, assuming that Player I is rational, that Player I has played M and not T. This analysis leads to the conclusion that Player II should prefer to play b, if called upon to choose an action, and (M, b) is therefore a more reasonable equilibrium. This convincing choice between the two equilibria was arrived at through forward induction.   ◄

Inductive reasoning, and the inductive use of the concept of rationality, has the potential of raising questions regarding the consistency of rationality itself. Consider the game depicted in Figure 7.11.

The only subgame perfect equilibrium of this game is $((r, c), a)$, which yields the payoff $(2, 1)$. Why does Player II choose a at x_2? Because if Player I is rational, he will

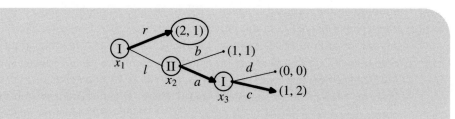

Figure 7.11 A game with only one subgame perfect equilibrium

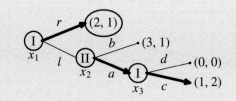

Figure 7.12 A game with only one subgame perfect equilibrium

then choose c, leading to the payoff $(1, 2)$, which Player II prefers to the payoff $(1, 1)$ that would result if he were to choose b. But is Player I really rational? Consider the fact that if the game has arrived at x_2, and Player II is called upon to play, then Player I must be irrational: Player I must have chosen l, which yields him at most 1, instead of choosing r, which guarantees him 2. Then why should Player II assume that Player I will be rational at x_3? Perhaps it would be more rational for Player II to choose b, and guarantee himself a payoff of 1, instead of running the risk that Player I may again be irrational and choose d, which will yield the payoff $(0, 0)$.

The game depicted in Figure 7.12, which is just like the previous game except that the payoff $(1, 1)$ is replaced by $(3, 1)$, is even more problematic.

This game also has only one subgame perfect equilibrium, $((r, c), a)$, yielding payoff $(2, 1)$. Again, by backward induction, Player I will not choose l, which leads to the payoff $(1, 2)$. Player II, at x_2, must therefore conclude that Player I is irrational (because Player I must have chosen l at x_1, which by backward induction leads to him getting 1, instead of r, which guarantees him a payoff of 2). And if Player I is irrational, then Player II may need to fear that if he chooses a, Player I will then choose d and the end result will be $(0, 0)$. It is therefore possible that at x_2, Player II will choose b, in order to guarantee himself a payoff of 1. But, if that is the case, Player I is better off choosing l at x_1, because then he will receive 3, instead of 2, which is what choosing r gets him. So is Player I really irrational if he chooses l? Perhaps Player I's choice of l is a calculated choice, aimed at making Player II think that he is irrational, and therefore leading Player II to choose b? Then which one of Player I's choices at vertex x_1 is rational, and which is irrational?

7.3   Perfect equilibrium

This section presents the concept of perfect equilibrium. While subgame perfect equilibrium is a refinement of the concept of Nash equilibrium applicable only to extensive-form games, perfect equilibrium is a refinement of the concept of Nash equilibrium that is applicable to extensive-form games and strategic-form games.

After introducing the concept of subgame perfect equilibrium in 1965, Selten revisited it in 1975, using the following example.

Example 7.18   Consider the three-player game depicted in Figure 7.13.

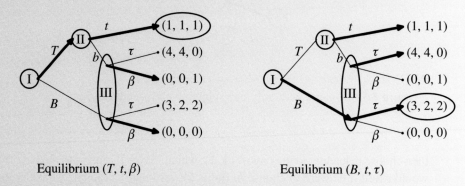

Equilibrium (T, t, β) Equilibrium (B, t, τ)

Figure 7.13   A game in extensive form, along with two equilibria

Since this game has no nontrivial subgames, every equilibrium of the game is a subgame perfect equilibrium. There are two equilibria in pure strategies:

- (T, t, β), with payoff $(1, 1, 1)$.
- (B, t, τ), with payoff $(3, 2, 2)$.

(Check that each of these two strategy vectors does indeed form a Nash equilibrium.)

Selten argued that Player II's behavior in the equilibrium (B, t, τ) is irrational. The reasoning is as follows: if Player II is called upon to play, that means that Player I misplayed, playing T instead of B, because at equilibrium he is supposed to play B. Since Player III is supposed to play τ at that equilibrium, if Player II deviates and plays b, he will get 4 instead of 1.   ◀

Selten introduced the concept of the "trembling hand," which requires rational players to take into account the possibility that mistakes may occur, even if they occur with small probability. The equilibrium concept corresponding to this type of rationality is called "perfect equilibrium." In an extensive-form game, a mistake can occur in two ways. A player may, at the beginning of the play of a game, with small probability mistakenly choose a pure strategy that differs from the one he intends to choose; such a mistake can cause deviations at every information set that is arrived at in the ensuing play. A second possibility is that the mistakes in different information sets are independent of each other; at each information set there is a small probability that a mistake will be made in choosing the action. As we will see later in this chapter, these two ways in which mistakes can occur lead to alternative perfect equilibrium concepts.

The analysis of this solution concept therefore requires careful attention to these details. We will first present the concept of perfect equilibrium for strategic-form games, in Section 7.3.1, and present its extensive-form game version in Section 7.3.2.

7.3.1   Perfect equilibrium in strategic-form games

Definition 7.19   *Let $\Gamma = (N, (S_i)_{i \in N}, (u_i)_{i \in N})$ be a game in strategic form in which the set of pure strategies of each player is finite. A perturbation vector of player i is a vector $\varepsilon_i = (\varepsilon_i(s_i))_{s_i \in S_i}$ satisfying $\varepsilon_i(s_i) > 0$ for each $s_i \in S_i$, and*

$$\sum_{s_i \in S_i} \varepsilon_i(s_i) \leq 1, \quad \forall i \in N. \tag{7.10}$$

A perturbation vector *is a vector* $\varepsilon = (\varepsilon_i)_{i \in N}$, *where* ε_i *is a perturbation vector of player i for each* $i \in N$.

For every perturbation vector ε, *the* ε-*perturbed game is the game* $\Gamma(\varepsilon) = (N, (\Sigma_i(\varepsilon))_{i \in N}, (u_i)_{i \in N})$ *where player i's strategy set is*

$$\Sigma_i(\varepsilon_i) := \{\sigma_i \in \Sigma_i : \sigma_i(s_i) \geq \varepsilon_i(s_i), \quad \forall s_i \in S_i\}. \tag{7.11}$$

In words, in the ε-perturbed game $\Gamma(\varepsilon)$, every pure strategy s_i is chosen with probability greater than or equal to $\varepsilon_i(s_i)$. The condition in Equation (7.10) guarantees that the strategy set $\Sigma_i(\varepsilon_i)$ is not empty. Furthermore, $\Sigma_i(\varepsilon_i)$ is a compact and convex set (Exercise 7.18). The following theorem therefore follows from Theorem 5.32 (page 170).

Theorem 7.20 *Every (finite)* ε-*perturbed game has an equilibrium; i.e., there exists a mixed-strategy vector* $\sigma^* = (\sigma_i^*)_{i \in N}$ *satisfying* $\sigma_i^* \in \Sigma_i(\varepsilon_i)$ *for each player* $i \in N$, *and*

$$U_i(\sigma^*) \geq U_i(\sigma_i, \sigma_{-i}^*), \quad \forall i \in N, \forall \sigma_i \in \Sigma_i(\varepsilon_i). \tag{7.12}$$

Given a perturbation vector ε, denote by

$$M(\varepsilon) := \max_{i \in N, s_i \in S_i} \varepsilon_i(s_i) \tag{7.13}$$

the maximal perturbation in $\Gamma(\varepsilon)$, and by

$$m(\varepsilon) := \min_{i \in N, s_i \in S_i} \varepsilon_i(s_i) \tag{7.14}$$

the minimal perturbation. Note that $m(\varepsilon) > 0$.

Example 7.21 Consider the two-player game depicted in Figure 7.14.

Player II

		L	R
	T	1, 1	0, 0
Player I	B	0, 0	0, 0

Figure 7.14 The strategic-form game of Example 7.21

This game has two pure strategy equilibria, (T, L) and (B, R). Consider now the ε-perturbed game, where the perturbation vector $\varepsilon = (\varepsilon_1, \varepsilon_2)$ is as follows:

$$\varepsilon_1(T) = \eta, \qquad \varepsilon_2(L) = \eta,$$
$$\varepsilon_1(B) = \eta^2, \qquad \varepsilon_2(R) = 2\eta,$$

where $\eta \in (0, \frac{1}{3}]$. Then

$$M(\varepsilon) = 2\eta, \quad m(\varepsilon) = \eta^2. \tag{7.15}$$

Since $m(\varepsilon) > 0$, all the strategies in $\Sigma_1(\varepsilon_1)$ and $\Sigma_2(\varepsilon_2)$ are completely mixed strategies. In particular, in the perturbed game, Player I's payoff under T is always greater than his payoff under B: if Player I plays B, he receives 0, while if he plays T his expected payoff is positive. It follows that Player I's best reply to every strategy in $\Sigma_2(\varepsilon_2)$ is to play T with the maximally allowed probability; this means that the best reply is $[(1 - \eta^2)(T), \eta^2(B)]$.

Similarly, we can calculate that Player II's expected payoff is greatest when he plays L, and his best reply to every strategy in $\Sigma_1(\varepsilon_1)$ is $[(1 - 2\eta)(L), 2\eta(R)]$. It follows that the only equilibrium in this ε-perturbed game is

$$([(1 - \eta^2)(T), \eta^2(B)], [(1 - 2\eta)(L), 2\eta(R)]). \tag{7.16}$$

◀

In Example 7.21 Player I's pure strategy T weakly dominates his pure strategy B. In this case, when Player II is restricted to playing mixed strategies, the strategy T always leads to a higher payoff than the strategy B, and therefore at equilibrium Player I plays the pure strategy B with the minimal possible probability. This line of reasoning is generalized to the following theorem, whose proof is left to the reader.

Theorem 7.22 *If s_i is a weakly dominated strategy, then at every equilibrium σ of the ε-perturbed game,*

$$\sigma_i(s_i) = \varepsilon_i(s_i). \tag{7.17}$$

Let $(\varepsilon^k)_{k \in \mathbb{N}}$ be a sequence of perturbation vectors satisfying $\lim_{k \to \infty} M(\varepsilon^k) = 0$: the maximal constraint converges to 0. Then for every completely mixed strategy σ_i of player i, there exists $k_0 \in \mathbb{N}$ such that $\sigma_i \in \Sigma_i(\varepsilon_i^k)$ for every $k_0 \geq k$. Indeed, denote $c := \min_{s_i \in S_i} \sigma_i(s_i) > 0$ and choose $k_0 \in \mathbb{N}$, where $M(\varepsilon_i^k) \leq c$ for all $k \geq k_0$. Then $\sigma_i \in \Sigma_i(\varepsilon_i^k)$ for every $k \geq k_0$. Since every mixed strategy in Σ_i can be approximated by a completely mixed strategy (Exercise 7.19), we deduce the following theorem:

Theorem 7.23 *Let $(\varepsilon^k)_{k \in \mathbb{N}}$ be a sequence of perturbation vectors satisfying $\lim_{k \to \infty} M(\varepsilon^k) = 0$. For every mixed strategy $\sigma_i \in \Sigma_i$ of player i, there exists a sequence $(\sigma_i^k)_{k \in \mathbb{N}}$ of mixed strategies of player i satisfying the following two properties:*

- $\sigma_i^k \in \Sigma_i(\varepsilon_i^k)$ *for each $k \in \mathbb{N}$.*
- $\lim_{k \to \infty} \sigma_i^k$ *exists and equals σ_i.*

The following theorem, which is a corollary of Theorem 7.23, states that the limit of equilibria in an ε-perturbed game, where the perturbation vectors $(\varepsilon^k)_{k \in \mathbb{N}}$ are positive and converge to zero, is necessarily a Nash equilibrium of the original unperturbed game.

Theorem 7.24 *Let $\Gamma = (N, (S_i)_{i \in N}, (u_i)_{i \in N})$ be a strategic-form game. For each $k \in \mathbb{N}$, let ε^k be a perturbation vector, and let σ^k be an equilibrium of the ε^k-perturbed game $\Gamma(\varepsilon^k)$. If*

1. $\lim_{k \to \infty} M(\varepsilon^k) = 0$,
2. $\lim_{k \to \infty} \sigma^k$ *exists and equals the mixed strategy vector σ,*

then σ is a Nash equilibrium of the original game Γ.

Proof: To show that σ is a Nash equilibrium, we need to show that no player can profit from a unilateral deviation. Let σ_i' be a strategy of player i. By Theorem 7.23, there exists a sequence of strategies $(\sigma_i'^k)_{k\in\mathbb{N}}$ converging to σ_i', and satisfying $\sigma_i'^k \in \Sigma_i(\varepsilon_i^k)$ for each $k \in \mathbb{N}$.

Since σ^k is an equilibrium in the ε^k-perturbed game $\Gamma(\varepsilon^k)$,

$$u_i(\sigma^k) \geq u_i\left(\sigma_i'^k, \sigma_{-i}^k\right). \tag{7.18}$$

By the continuity of the payoff function u_i,

$$u_i(\sigma) = \lim_{k\to\infty} u_i(\sigma^k) \geq \lim_{k\to\infty} u_i\left(\sigma_i'^k, \sigma_{-i}^k\right) = u_i(\sigma_i', \sigma_{-i}). \tag{7.19}$$

Since this inequality obtains for every player $i \in N$ and every mixed strategy $\sigma_i' \in \Sigma_i$, it follows that σ is a Nash equilibrium. $\qquad\square$

A mixed strategy vector that is the limit of equilibria in perturbed games, where the perturbation vectors are all positive, and converge to zero, is called a *perfect equilibrium*.

Definition 7.25 *A mixed strategy vector σ in a strategy-form game $(N, (S_i)_{i\in N}, (u_i)_{i\in N})$ is a perfect equilibrium if there exists a sequence of perturbation vectors $(\varepsilon^k)_{k\in\mathbb{N}}$ satisfying $\lim_{k\to\infty} M(\varepsilon^k) = 0$, and for each $k \in \mathbb{N}$ there exists an equilibrium σ^k of $\Gamma(\varepsilon^k)$ such that*

$$\lim_{k\to\infty} \sigma^k = \sigma. \tag{7.20}$$

The following corollary of Theorem 7.24 states that the concept of perfect equilibrium is a refinement of the concept of Nash equilibrium.

Corollary 7.26 *Every perfect equilibrium of a finite strategic-form game is a Nash equilibrium.*

The game in Example 7.21 (page 275) has two equilibria, (T, L) and (B, R). The equilibrium (T, L) is a perfect equilibrium: (T, L) is the limit of the equilibria given by Equation (7.16), as η converges to 0. We will later show that (B, R) is not a perfect equilibrium. In Example 7.18 (page 274), the equilibrium (T, t, β) is a perfect equilibrium, but the equilibrium (B, t, τ) is not a perfect equilibrium (Exercise 7.31). The next theorem states that every finite game has at least one perfect equilibrium.

Theorem 7.27 *Every finite strategic-form game has at least one perfect equilibrium.*

Proof: Let Γ be a finite strategic form game, and let $(\varepsilon^k)_{k\in\mathbb{N}}$ be a sequence of perturbation vectors satisfying $\lim_{k\to\infty} M(\varepsilon^k) = 0$. For example, $\varepsilon_i^k(s_i) = \frac{1}{k|S_i|}$ for each player $i \in N$ and for each $s_i \in S_i$. Theorem 7.20 implies that for each $k \in \mathbb{N}$ the game $\Gamma(\varepsilon^k)$ has an equilibrium in mixed strategies σ^k. Since the space of mixed strategy vectors Σ is compact (see Exercise 5.1 on page 203), the sequence $(\sigma^k)_{k\in\mathbb{N}}$ has a convergent subsequence $(\sigma^{k_j})_{j\in\mathbb{N}}$. Denote the limit of this subsequence by σ. Applying Theorem 7.24 to the sequence of perturbation vectors $(\varepsilon^{k_j})_{j\in\mathbb{N}}$, and to the sequence of equilibria $(\sigma^{k_j})_{j\in\mathbb{N}}$, leads to the conclusion that σ is a perfect equilibrium of the original game. $\qquad\square$

As a corollary of Theorem 7.22, and from the definition of perfect equilibrium, we can deduce the following theorem (Exercise 7.23).

Theorem 7.28 *In every perfect equilibrium, every (weakly) dominated strategy is chosen with probability zero.*

In other words, no weakly dominated strategy can be a part of a perfect equilibrium. This means that, for example, in Example 7.21, the strategy vector (B, R) is not a perfect equilibrium, since B is a dominated strategy of Player I (and R is a dominated strategy of Player II).

As Exercise 7.29 shows, it is possible for a Nash equilibrium to choose every dominated strategy with probability zero, but not to be a perfect equilibrium. The following theorem states that a completely mixed equilibrium must be a perfect equilibrium.

Theorem 7.29 *Every equilibrium in completely mixed strategies in a strategic-form game is a perfect equilibrium.*

Proof: Let σ^* be a completely mixed equilibrium of a strategic-form game Γ. Then $c :=$ $\min_{i \in N} \min_{s_i \in S_i} \sigma_i^*(s_i) > 0$.

Let $(\varepsilon^k)_{k \in \mathbb{N}}$ be a sequence of perturbation vectors satisfying $\lim_{k \to \infty} M(\varepsilon^k) = 0$. Since $\lim_{k \to \infty} M(\varepsilon^k) = 0$, it must be the case that $M(\varepsilon^k) < c$ for sufficiently large k. Hence for each such k, we may conclude that $\sigma_i^* \in \Sigma_i(\varepsilon_i^k)$ for every player i; i.e., σ^* is a possible strategy vector in the game $\Gamma(\varepsilon^k)$. Let $K_0 \in \mathbb{N}$ be sufficiently large so that for each $k \geq K_0$, one has $\sigma_i^* \in \Sigma_i(\varepsilon_i^k)$ for every player i. Since $\Gamma(\varepsilon^k)$ has fewer strategies than Γ, Theorem 4.31 (page 107) implies that σ^* is an equilibrium of $\Gamma(\varepsilon^k)$.

We may therefore apply Theorem 7.24 to the sequences $(\varepsilon^k)_{k \geq K_0}$ and the constant sequence $(\sigma^*)_{n=K_0}^{\infty}$, to conclude that σ^* is a perfect equilibrium, which is what we needed to show. □

7.3.2   Perfect equilibrium in extensive-form games

Since every extensive-form game can be presented as a strategic-form game, the concept of perfect equilibrium, as defined in Definition 7.25, also applies to extensive-form games. This definition of perfect equilibrium for extensive-form games is called *strategic-form perfect equilibrium*.

Theorem 7.27 implies the following corollary (Exercise 7.33).

Theorem 7.30 *Every extensive-form game has a strategic-form perfect equilibrium.*

In this section, we will study the concept of extensive-form perfect equilibrium, where the mistakes that each player makes in different information sets are independent of each other. We will limit our focus to extensive-form games with perfect recall. By Kuhn's Theorem, in such games each behavior strategy has an equivalent mixed strategy, and the converse also holds. Let Γ be an extensive-form game with perfect recall. Denote by $\mathcal{U}_i$ player i's set of information sets. Recall that we denote player i's set of possible actions at information set U_i by $A(U_i)$.

When we are dealing with behavior strategies, a perturbation vector δ_i of player i is a vector associating a positive real number with each action $a_i \in \bigcup_{U_i \in \mathcal{U}_i} A(U_i)$ of player i, such that $\sum_{a_i \in A(U_i)} \delta_i(a_i) \leq 1$ for each information set $U_i \in \mathcal{U}_i$. Let $\delta = (\delta_i)_{i \in N}$

be a set of perturbation vectors, one for each player. Denote the maximal perturbation in $\Gamma(\varepsilon)$ by

$$M(\delta) := \max_{\{i \in N, a_i \subset \bigcup_{U_i \in \mathcal{U}_i} A(U_i)\}} \delta_i(a_i), \tag{7.21}$$

and the minimal perturbation by

$$m(\delta) := \min_{\{i \in N, a_i \in \bigcup_{U_i \in \mathcal{U}_i} A(U_i)\}} \delta_i(a_i) > 0. \tag{7.22}$$

The game $\Gamma(\delta)$ is the extensive-form game such that player i's set of strategies, denoted by $\mathcal{B}_i(\delta_i)$, is the set of behavior strategies in which every action a_i is chosen with probability greater than or equal to $\delta_i(a_i)$, that is,

$$\mathcal{B}_i(\delta_i) := \left\{ \sigma_i \in \underset{U_i \in \mathcal{U}_i}{\times} \Delta(A(U_i)) : \sigma_i(U_i; a_i) \geq \delta_i(a_i), \quad \forall i \in N, \forall U_i \in \mathcal{U}_i, \forall a_i \in A(U_i) \right\}.$$

$$\tag{7.23}$$

Since every possible action at every chance vertex is chosen with positive probability, and since $m(\delta) > 0$, it follows that $\mathbf{P}_\sigma(x) > 0$ for every vertex x, and every behavior strategy vector $\sigma = (\sigma_i)_{i \in N}$ in $\Gamma(\delta)$: the play of the game arrives at every vertex x with positive probability. For each vertex x such that $\Gamma(x)$ is a subgame, denote by $\Gamma(x; \delta)$ the subgame of $\Gamma(\delta)$ starting at the vertex x. Similarly to Theorem 7.5, we have the following result, whose proof is left to the reader (Exercise 7.34).

Theorem 7.31 *Let Γ be an extensive-form game, and let $\Gamma(x)$ be a subgame of Γ. Let δ be a perturbation vector, and let σ^* be a Nash equilibrium (in behavior strategies) of the game $\Gamma(\delta)$. Then the strategy vector σ^*, restricted to the subgame $\Gamma(x)$, is a Nash equilibrium of $\Gamma(x; \delta)$.*

Similar to Definition 7.25, which is based on mixed strategies, the next definition bases the concept of perfect equilibrium on behavior strategies.

Definition 7.32 *A behavior strategy vector σ in an extensive-form game Γ is called an extensive-form perfect equilibrium if there exists a sequence of perturbation vectors $(\delta^k)_{k \in \mathbb{N}}$ satisfying $\lim_{k \to \infty} M(\delta^k) = 0$, and for each $k \in \mathbb{N}$ there exists an equilibrium σ^k of $\Gamma(\delta^k)$, such that $\lim_{k \to \infty} \sigma^k = \sigma$ is satisfied.*

These concepts, strategic-form perfect equilibrium and extensive-form perfect equilibrium, differ from each other: a strategic-form perfect equilibrium is a vector of mixed strategies, while an extensive-form perfect equilibrium is a vector of behavior strategies. Despite the fact that in games with perfect recall there is an equivalence between mixed strategies and behavior strategies (see Chapter 6), an extensive-form perfect equilibrium may fail to be a strategic-form perfect equilibrium. In other words, a vector of mixed strategies, each equivalent to a behavior strategy in an extensive-form perfect equilibrium, may fail to be a strategic-form perfect equilibrium (Exercise 7.36). Conversely, a strategic-form perfect equilibrium may not necessarily be an extensive-form equilibrium (Exercise 7.37). The conceptual difference between these two concepts is similar to the difference between mixed strategies and behavior strategies: in a mixed strategy, a player randomly chooses a pure strategy at the start of a game, while in a behavior strategy he randomly chooses an action at each of his information sets. Underlying the concept of strategic-form perfect equilibrium is the assumption that a player may mistakenly choose, at the start of the game, a pure strategy different from the one he intended to choose. In contrast, underlying the concept of extensive-form perfect equilibrium is the assumption that a player may mistakenly choose an action different from the one he intended at any of his information sets. In extensive-form games where each player has a single information set, these two concepts are identical, because in that case the set of mixed strategies of each player is identical with his set of behavior strategies.

As stated above, Selten defined the concept of perfect equilibrium in order to further "refine" the concept of subgame perfect equilibrium in extensive-form games. We will now show that this is indeed a refinement: every extensive-form perfect equilibrium is a subgame perfect equilibrium in behavior strategies. (This result can also be proved directly.) Since every subgame perfect equilibrium is a Nash equilibrium (Remark 7.3 on page 265), we will then conclude that every extensive-form perfect equilibrium is a Nash equilibrium in behavior strategies. This result can also be proved directly; see Exercise 7.32.

Theorem 7.33 *Let Γ be an extensive-form game. Every extensive-form perfect equilibrium of Γ is a subgame perfect equilibrium.*

The analogous theorem for strategic-form perfect equilibrium does not obtain (see Exercise 7.37). Before we proceed to the proof of the theorem, we present a technical result analogous to Theorem 7.23, which states that every behavior strategy may be approximated by a sequence of behavior strategies in perturbed games, where the perturbations converge to zero. The proof of this theorem is left to the reader (Exercise 7.35).

Theorem 7.34 *Let $(\delta^k)_{k \in \mathbb{N}}$ be a sequence of perturbation vectors satisfying $\lim_{k \to \infty} M(\delta^k) = 0$. For each behavior strategy $\sigma_i \in \mathcal{B}_i$ of player i, there exists a sequence $(\sigma_i^k)_{k \in \mathbb{N}}$ of behavior strategies satisfying the following two properties:*

- $\sigma_i^k \in \mathcal{B}_i(\delta_i^k)$ *for each $k \in \mathbb{N}$.*
- $\lim_{k \to \infty} \sigma_i^k$ *exists and equals σ_i.*

Proof of Theorem 7.33: Let $\sigma^* = (\sigma_i^*)_{i \in N}$ be an extensive-form perfect equilibrium, and let $\Gamma(x)$ be a subgame (starting at vertex x). We will show that the restriction of σ^* to this subgame is a subgame perfect equilibrium.

By the definition of extensive-form perfect equilibrium, for each $k \in \mathbb{N}$ there exists a perturbation vector δ^k, and an equilibrium σ^k in the δ^k-perturbed game satisfying $\lim_{k \to \infty} M(\delta^k) = 0$, and $\lim_{k \to \infty} \sigma^k = \sigma^*$. Theorem 7.31 implies that the strategy vector σ^k is a Nash equilibrium in behavior strategies of the game $\Gamma(x; \delta^k)$. Let σ_i' be a behavior strategy of player i. We will show that

$$u_i(\sigma^* \mid x) \geq u_i((\sigma_i', \sigma_{-i}^*) \mid x). \tag{7.24}$$

Theorem 7.34 implies that there exists a sequence $(\sigma_i'^k)_{k\in\mathbb{N}}$ of behavior strategies converging to σ_i' and satisfying $\sigma_i'^k \in \mathcal{B}_i(\delta_i^k)$ for each $k \in \mathbb{N}$. Since σ^k is an equilibrium of the subgame $\Gamma(x;\delta^k)$,

$$u_i(\sigma^k \mid x) \geq u_i\big((\sigma_i'^k,\sigma_{-i}^k) \mid x\big). \qquad (7.25)$$

Equation (7.24) is now derived from Equation (7.25) by using the continuity of the payoff function u_i and passing to the limit as $k \to \infty$. $\qquad\qquad\qquad\square$

The next example shows that the converse of Theorem 7.33 does not obtain; a subgame perfect equilibrium need not be an extensive-form perfect equilibrium.

Example 7.35 Consider the two-player extensive-form game depicted in Figure 7.15. This game has two pure-strategy equilibria, (A, L) and (B, R). Each of these equilibria is a subgame perfect equilibrium, since the game has no nontrivial subgames (see Theorem 7.4).

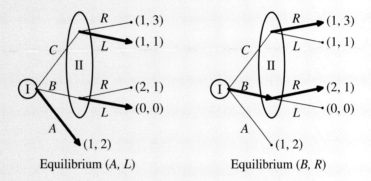

Equilibrium (A, L) Equilibrium (B, R)

Figure 7.15 The game in Example 7.35, along with two of its equilibria

The equilibrium (A, L) is not an extensive-form perfect equilibrium. Indeed, since each player has a single information set, if (A, L) were an extensive-form perfect equilibrium it would also be a strategic-form perfect equilibrium (Exercise 7.39). But the strategy L is a weakly dominated strategy, and therefore Theorem 7.28 implies that it cannot form part of a strategic-form perfect equilibrium.

Showing that (B, R) is an extensive-form perfect equilibrium is left to the reader (Exercise 7.47).

◀

Together with Theorem 7.33, the last example proves that the concept of extensive-form perfect equilibrium is a refinement of the concept of subgame perfect equilibrium. Note that in this example, a subgame perfect equilibrium that is not an extensive-form perfect equilibrium is given in pure strategies, and therefore the inclusion of the set of extensive-form perfect equilibria in the set of subgame perfect equilibria is a proper inclusion, even when only pure strategy equilibria are involved.

Theorem 7.33 states that every extensive-form perfect equilibrium is a subgame perfect equilibrium, and therefore also a Nash equilibrium. It follows that if a game has no Nash equilibria in behavior strategies, then it has no extensive-form perfect equilibria. By Theorem 6.16 (page 246) this can happen only if the game does not have perfect recall. Example 6.17 (page 247) describes such a game.

As we now show, a finite extensive-form game with perfect recall always has an extensive-form perfect equilibrium.

Theorem 7.36 *Every finite extensive-form game with perfect recall has an extensive-form perfect equilibrium.*

Proof: Let Γ be a finite extensive-form game with perfect recall, and let $(\delta^k)_{k \in \mathbb{N}}$ be a sequence of perturbation vectors satisfying $\lim_{k \to \infty} M(\delta^k) = 0$. Since all the players have perfect recall, Theorem 6.16 (page 246) shows that $\Gamma(\delta^k)$ has an equilibrium σ^k in behavior strategies. Since the space of behavior strategy vectors $\times_{i \in N} \mathcal{B}_i$ is compact, the sequence $(\sigma^k)_{k \in \mathbb{N}}$ has a convergent subsequence $(\sigma^{k_j})_{j \in \mathbb{N}}$, converging to a limit σ^*. Then σ^* is an extensive-form perfect equilibrium. $\square$

Theorems 7.36 and 7.33 lead to the following result.

Theorem 7.37 *Every finite extensive-form game with perfect recall has a subgame perfect equilibrium in behavior strategies.*

7.4 Sequential equilibrium

This section presents another equilibrium concept for extensive-form games, which differs from the three concepts we have studied so far in this chapter, subgame perfect equilibrium, strategic-form perfect equilibrium, and extensive-form perfect equilibrium. The subgame perfect equilibrium concept assumes that players analyze each game from the leaves to the root, with every player, at each of his information sets, choosing an action under the assumption that in each future subgame, all the players will implement equilibrium strategies. The two perfect equilibrium concepts assume that each player has a positive, albeit small, probability of making a mistake, and that the other players take this into account when they choose their actions. The sequential equilibrium concept is based on the principle that at each stage of a game, the player whose turn it is to choose an action has a belief, i.e., a probability distribution, about which vertex in his information set is the true vertex at which the game is currently located, and a belief about how the play of the game will proceed given any action that he may choose. These beliefs are based on the information structure of the game (the information sets) and the strategies of the players. Given these beliefs, at each of his information sets, each player chooses the action that gives him the highest expected payoff.

In this section we will deal only with games with perfect recall. We will later, in Example 7.60 (on page 293), remark on why it is unclear how the concept of sequential equilibrium can be generalized to games without perfect recall. Recall that a player's behavior strategy in an extensive-form game is a function associating each of that player's information sets with a probability distribution over the set of possible actions at that information set. Such a probability distribution is called a *mixed action*.

Before we begin the formal presentation, we will look at an example that illustrates the concept of sequential equilibrium and the ideas behind it.

Example 7.38   Consider the two-player extensive-form game depicted in Figure 7.16.

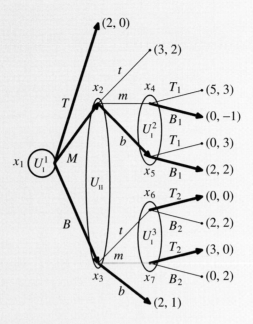

Figure 7.16 The game in Example 7.38 and a strategy vector

The following pair of behavior strategies $\sigma = (\sigma_I, \sigma_{II})$ is a Nash equilibrium of the game (see Figure 7.16, where the actions taken in this equilibrium appear as bold lines):

- Player I's strategy σ_I:
  - At information set U_I^1, choose the mixed action $[\frac{3}{12}(T), \frac{4}{12}(M), \frac{5}{12}(B)]$.
  - At information set U_I^2, choose B_1.
  - At information set U_I^3, choose T_2.
- Player II's strategy σ_{II}: Choose b.

(Check that this is indeed an equilibrium.) The strategy vector σ determines, for each vertex x, the probability $\mathbf{P}_\sigma(x)$ that a play of the game will visit this vertex:

$$\mathbf{P}_\sigma(x_2) = \tfrac{4}{12}, \qquad \mathbf{P}_\sigma(x_3) = \tfrac{5}{12}, \qquad \mathbf{P}_\sigma(x_4) = 0,$$
$$\mathbf{P}_\sigma(x_5) = \tfrac{4}{12}, \qquad \mathbf{P}_\sigma(x_6) = 0, \qquad \mathbf{P}_\sigma(x_7) = 0.$$

When Player II is called upon to play, he knows that the play of the game is located at information set $U_{II} = \{x_2, x_3\}$. Knowing Player I's strategy, he can calculate the conditional probability of each one of the vertices in this information set to be the actual position of the play,

$$\mathbf{P}_\sigma(x_2 \mid U_{II}) = \frac{\mathbf{P}_\sigma(x_2)}{\mathbf{P}_\sigma(x_2) + \mathbf{P}_\sigma(x_3)} = \frac{\frac{4}{12}}{\frac{4}{12} + \frac{5}{12}} = \frac{4}{9}, \tag{7.26}$$

and similarly, $\mathbf{P}_\sigma(x_3 \mid U_{II}) = \frac{5}{9}$. The conditional probability $\mathbf{P}_\sigma(\cdot \mid U_{II})$ is Player II's belief at information set U_{II}.

Similarly, when Player I is called to play at information set U_I^2, he cannot distinguish between x_4 and x_5, but knowing Player II's strategy σ_{II}, Player I can ascribe probability 1 to the play of the game being at vertex x_5. Formally, this is the following conditional distribution:

$$\mathbf{P}_\sigma\left(x_5 \mid U_1^2\right) = \frac{\mathbf{P}_\sigma(x_5)}{\mathbf{P}_\sigma(x_4) + \mathbf{P}_\sigma(x_5)} = \frac{\frac{4}{12}}{0 + \frac{4}{12}} = 1, \tag{7.27}$$

with a similar calculation yielding $\mathbf{P}_\sigma(x_4 \mid U_1^2) = 0$. The conditional distribution $\mathbf{P}_\sigma(\cdot \mid U_1^2)$ is Player I's belief at information set U_1^2. Does Player I also have a belief at information set U_1^3? The answer to this question is negative, because if the players implement the strategy vector σ, the play of the game will not visit this information set. Formally, the conditional distribution $\mathbf{P}_\sigma(\cdot \mid U_1^3)$ is undefined, because the probability $\mathbf{P}_\sigma(U_1^3) = \mathbf{P}_\sigma(x_6) + \mathbf{P}_\sigma(x_7)$, which represents the probability that the play of the game will arrive at information set U_1^3, equals 0. ◀

For each strategy vector σ, and for each player i and each of his information sets U_i, denote $\mathbf{P}_\sigma(U_i) := \sum_{x \in U_i} \mathbf{P}_\sigma(x)$. Since the game has perfect recall, every path from the root passes through every information set at most once, and hence $\mathbf{P}_\sigma(U_i)$ is the probability that a play of the game will visit information set U_i when the players implement the strategy vector σ. As we saw, the strategy vector σ determines a belief $\mathbf{P}_\sigma(\cdot \mid U_i)$ over the vertices of information set U_i, for each information set satisfying $\mathbf{P}_\sigma(U_i) > 0$: when player i is called upon to play in information set U_i, his belief about the vertex at which the play of the game is located is given by the conditional distribution $\mathbf{P}_\sigma(\cdot \mid U_i)$.

Beliefs, calculated this way from the strategy vector σ, satisfy the property of *consistency*. In other words, the beliefs are consistent with the distribution $\mathbf{P}_\sigma$ over the vertices of the game tree, and with Bayes' formula for calculating conditional probability. We say that the strategy vector σ determines a *partial belief system*. The word partial denotes the fact that the beliefs are defined only for some of the information sets; they are not defined for information sets that the strategy vector σ leads to with probability 0.

Example 7.38 (*Continued*) We will now explore the connection between an action chosen by a player at a given information set, and his belief at that information set. Player I, at information set U_1^1, ascribes probability 1 to the play of the game being located at vertex x_5. He therefore regards action B_1 as being the optimal action for him: B_1 leads to a payoff 2, while T_1 leads to a payoff 0. Given his belief at U_1^1, Player I is rational in choosing B_1. If, in contrast, according to his belief at U_1^1 he had ascribed high probability to the play of the game being located at vertex x_4 (a probability greater than or equal to $\frac{2}{7}$) it would have been rational for him to choose T_1. This property, in which a player's strategy calls on him to choose an action maximizing his expected payoff at each information set, given his belief at that information set, is termed *sequential rationality*.

We will now check whether sequential rationality obtains at Player II's information set U_{II} in the equilibrium we previously presented in this example. As we computed above, Player II's belief about the vertex at which the play of the game is located, given that it has arrived at information set U_{II}, is

$$\mathbf{P}_\sigma(x_2 \mid U_{II}) = \tfrac{4}{9}, \quad \mathbf{P}_\sigma(x_3 \mid U_{II}) = \tfrac{5}{9}. \tag{7.28}$$

Given this belief, and the strategy vector σ, if Player II chooses action b, he receives a payoff of 2 with probability $\frac{4}{9}$ (if the play of the game is at vertex x_2) and a payoff of 1 with probability $\frac{5}{9}$ (if the play of the game is at vertex x_3). His expected payoff is therefore

$$\tfrac{4}{9} \times 2 + \tfrac{5}{9} \times 1 = \tfrac{13}{9}. \tag{7.29}$$

A similar calculation shows that if he chooses action m, his expected payoff is

$$\tfrac{4}{9} \times (-1) + \tfrac{5}{9} \times 0 = -\tfrac{4}{9}, \qquad (7.30)$$

and if he chooses action t his expected payoff is

$$\tfrac{4}{9} \times 2 + \tfrac{5}{9} \times 0 = \tfrac{8}{9}. \qquad (7.31)$$

The strategy σ_{II} calls on Player II to choose action b at information set U_{II}, which does indeed maximize his expected payoff, relative to his belief. In other words, Player II's strategy is sequentially rational.

We next ascertain that Player I's strategy is sequentially rational at information set U_{I}^1, containing a single vertex, x_1. When the play of the game arrives at information set U_{I}^1, Player I knows that x_1 must be the vertex at which the play of the game is located, because the information set contains only one vertex. The mixed strategy $[\tfrac{3}{12}(T), \tfrac{4}{12}(M), \tfrac{5}{12}(B)]$ maximizes Player I's expected payoff if and only if all three actions yield him the same expected payoff. This is due to the fact that the payoff is a linear function of the probabilities in which the various actions are implemented by Player I at information set U_{I}^1. We encountered a similar argument at the indifference principle (Theorem 5.18, page 158). The reader is asked to verify that each of these three actions yield the payoff 2, and therefore any mixed action implemented by Player I at information set U_{I}^1 satisfies sequential rationality, in particular the mixed action $[\tfrac{3}{12}(T), \tfrac{4}{12}(M), \tfrac{5}{12}(B)]$ implemented in σ_{I}. ◀

In Example 7.38, we saw that the strategy vector σ induces a partial belief system over the players' information sets, and that each player i's strategy is sequentially rational at each information set U_i for which the belief $\mathbf{P}_\sigma(\cdot \mid U_i)$ is defined, i.e., at each information set at which the play of the game arrives with positive probability under the strategy vector σ.

The main idea behind the concept of sequential equilibrium is that the property of sequential rationality should be satisfied at every information set, including those information sets that are visited with probability 0 under the strategy vector σ. This requirement is similar to the requirement that the subgame perfect equilibrium be an equilibrium both on the equilibrium path, and off the equilibrium path. A sequential equilibrium therefore requires specifying players' beliefs at all information sets. A sequential equilibrium is thus a pair (σ, μ), where $\sigma = (\sigma_i)_{i \in N}$ is a vector of behavior strategies, and μ is a complete belief system; i.e., with every player and every information set of that player, μ associates a belief: a distribution over the vertices of that information set. The pair (σ, μ) must satisfy two properties: the beliefs μ must be consistent with Bayes' formula and with the strategy vector σ, and σ must be sequentially rational given the beliefs μ.

The main stage in the development of the concept of sequential equilibrium is defining the concept of consistency of beliefs μ with respect to a given strategy vector σ. Doing this requires extending the partial belief system $\mathbf{P}_\sigma$ to every information set U_i for which $\mathbf{P}_\sigma(U_i) = 0$. This extension is based on Selten's trembling hand principle, which was discussed in the section defining perfect equilibrium. Denote by $\mathcal{U}$ the set of the information sets of all the players.

Definition 7.39 *A complete belief system μ is a vector $\mu = (\mu_U)_{U \in \mathcal{U}}$ associating each information set $U \in \mathcal{U}$ with a distribution over the vertices in U.*

Definition 7.40 *Let $\mathcal{U}' \subseteq \mathcal{U}$ be a partial collection of information sets. A partial belief system μ (with respect to $\mathcal{U}'$) is a vector $\mu = (\mu_U)_{U \in \mathcal{U}'}$ associating each information set $U \in \mathcal{U}'$ with a distribution over the vertices in U.*

If μ is a partial belief system, denote by $\mathcal{U}_\mu$ the collection of information sets at which μ is defined.

Although the definition of a belief system is independent of the strategy vector implemented by the players, we are interested in belief systems that are closely related to the strategy vector σ. The partial belief system that is induced by σ plays a central role in the definition of sequential equilibrium.

Definition 7.41 *Let σ be a strategy vector. Let $\mathcal{U}_\sigma = \{U \in \mathcal{U} : \mathbf{P}_\sigma(U) > 0\}$ be the collection of all information sets that the play of the game visits with positive probability when the players implement the strategy vector σ. The partial belief system induced by the strategy vector σ is the collection of distributions $\mu_\sigma = (\mu_{\sigma,U})_{U \in \mathcal{U}_\sigma}$, satisfying, for each $U \in \mathcal{U}_\sigma$,*

$$\mu_{\sigma,U}(x) := \mathbf{P}_\sigma(x \mid U) = \frac{\mathbf{P}_\sigma(x)}{\mathbf{P}_\sigma(U)}, \quad \forall x \in U. \tag{7.32}$$

Note that $\mathcal{U}_\sigma = \mathcal{U}_{\mu_\sigma}$. To avoid using both denotations, we will henceforth use only the denotation $\mathcal{U}_{\mu_\sigma}$.

Remark 7.42 *Since we have assumed that at each chance vertex, every action is chosen with positive probability, it follows that if all the strategies in the strategy vector σ are completely mixed, i.e., at each information set every action is chosen with positive probability, then $\mathbf{P}_\sigma(U_i) > 0$ for each player i and each of his information sets U_i; hence in this case the belief system μ_σ is a complete belief system: it defines a belief at each information set in the game ($\mathcal{U}_{\mu_\sigma} = \mathcal{U}$).* ◆

Recall that $u_i(\sigma \mid x)$ is the expected payoff of player i when the players implement the strategy σ, given that the play of the game is at vertex x. It follows that player i's expected payoff when the players implement the strategy vector σ, given that the game arrives at information set U_i and given his belief, is

$$u_i(\sigma \mid U_i, \mu) := \sum_{x \in U_i} \mu_{\sigma,U_i}(x) u_i(\sigma \mid x). \tag{7.33}$$

Definition 7.43 *Let σ be a vector of behavior strategies, μ be a partial belief system, and $U_i \in \mathcal{U}_\mu$ be an information set of player i. The strategy vector σ is called* rational *at information set U_i, relative to μ, if for each behavior strategy σ_i' of player i*

$$u_i(\sigma \mid U_i, \mu) \geq u_i((\sigma_i', \sigma_{-i}) \mid U_i, \mu). \tag{7.34}$$

The pair (σ, μ) is called sequentially rational *if for each player i and each information set $U_i \in \mathcal{U}_\mu$, the strategy vector σ is rational at U_i relative to μ.*

As the following theorems show, there exists a close connection between the concepts of sequential rationality and those of Nash equilibrium and subgame perfect equilibrium.

Theorem 7.44 *In an extensive-form game with perfect recall, if the pair (σ, μ_σ) is sequentially rational, then the strategy vector σ is a Nash equilibrium in behavior strategies.*

Proof: Let $i \in N$ be a player, and let σ'_i be any behavior strategy of player i. We will prove that $u_i(\sigma) \geq u_i(\sigma'_i, \sigma_{-i})$.

We say that an information set U_i of player i is *highest* if every path from the root to a vertex in U_i does not pass through any other information set of player i. Denote by $\widehat{\mathcal{U}}_i$ the set of player i's highest information sets: any path from the root to a leaf that passes through an information set of player i necessarily passes through an information set in $\widehat{\mathcal{U}}_i$. Denote by $p^*_{\sigma,i}$ the probability that, when the strategy vector σ is played, a play of the game will not pass through any of player i's information sets, and denote by $u^*_{\sigma,i}$ player i's expected payoff, given that the play of the game according to the strategy vector does not pass through any of player i's information sets.

Note that $p^*_{\sigma,i}$ and $u^*_{\sigma,i}$ are independent of player i's strategy, since these values depend on plays of the game in which player i does not participate. Similarly, for every information set $U_i \in \widehat{\mathcal{U}}_i$, the probability $\mathbf{P}_\sigma(U_i)$ is independent of player i's strategy, since these probabilities depend on actions chosen at vertices that are not under player i's control.

Using this notation, we have that

$$\mathbf{P}_\sigma(U_i) = \mathbf{P}_{(\sigma'_i, \sigma_{-i})}(U_i), \quad \forall U_i \in \widehat{\mathcal{U}}_i, \tag{7.35}$$

$$u_i(\sigma) = \sum_{U_i \in \widehat{\mathcal{U}}_i} \mathbf{P}_\sigma(U_i) u_i(\sigma \mid U_i, \mu_\sigma) + p^*_{\sigma,i} u^*_{\sigma,i}, \tag{7.36}$$

$$u_i(\sigma'_i, \sigma_{-i}) = \sum_{U_i \in \widehat{\mathcal{U}}_i} \mathbf{P}_{(\sigma'_i, \sigma_{-i})}(U_i) u_i((\sigma'_i, \sigma_{-i}) \mid U_i, \mu_\sigma) + p^*_{\sigma,i} u^*_{\sigma,i} \tag{7.37}$$

$$= \sum_{U_i \in \widehat{\mathcal{U}}_i} \mathbf{P}_\sigma(U_i) u_i((\sigma'_i, \sigma_{-i}) \mid U_i, \mu_\sigma) + p^*_{\sigma,i} u^*_{\sigma,i}, \tag{7.38}$$

where Equation (7.38) follows from Equation (7.35). Since for every $U_i \in \mathcal{U}_{\mu_\sigma}$, the pair (σ, μ_σ) is sequentially rational at U_i,

$$u_i(\sigma \mid U_i, \mu_\sigma) \geq u_i((\sigma'_i, \sigma_{-i}) \mid U_i, \mu_\sigma). \tag{7.39}$$

Equations (7.36)–(7.39) imply that

$$u_i(\sigma) \geq u_i(\sigma'_i, \sigma_{-i}), \tag{7.40}$$

which is what we wanted to prove. $\qquad\qquad\Box$

The following theorem, whose proof is left to the reader (Exercise 7.41), is the converse of Theorem 7.44.

Theorem 7.45 *If σ^* is a Nash equilibrium in behavior strategies, then the pair $(\sigma^*, \mu_{\sigma^*})$ is sequentially rational at every information set in $\mathcal{U}_{\mu_{\sigma^*}}$.*

In a game with perfect information, every information set contains only one vertex, and therefore when called on to make a move, a player knows at which vertex the play of the game is located. In this case, we denote by $\hat{\mu}$ the complete belief system in which $\hat{\mu}_U = [1(x)]$, for every information set $U = \{x\}$. The next theorem, whose proof is left to the reader (Exercise 7.42), characterizes subgame perfect equilibria using sequential rationality.

Theorem 7.46 *In a game with perfect information, a behavior strategy vector σ is a subgame perfect equilibrium if and only if the pair $(\sigma, \hat{\mu})$ is sequentially rational at each vertex in the game.*

As previously stated, the main idea behind the sequential equilibrium refinement is to expand the definition of rationality to information sets U_i at which $\mathbf{P}_\sigma(U_i) = 0$. This is accomplished by the trembling hand principle: player i may find himself in an information set U_i for which $\mathbf{P}_\sigma(U_i) = 0$, due to a mistake (tremble) on the part of one of the players, and we require that even if this should happen, the player ought to behave rationally relative to beliefs that are "consistent" with such mistakes. In other words, we extend the partial belief system μ_σ to a complete belief system μ that is consistent with the trembling hand principle, and we require that σ be sequentially rational not only with respect to μ_σ, but also with respect to μ.

Remark 7.47 *A belief at an information set U_i is a probability distribution over the vertices in U_i, i.e., an element of the compact set $\Delta(U_i)$. A complete belief system is a vector of beliefs, one belief per information set, and therefore a vector in the compact set $\times_{U \in \mathcal{U}} \Delta(U)$. Since this set is compact, every sequence of complete belief systems has a convergent subsequence.* ◆

Definition 7.48 *An* assessment *is a pair (σ, μ) in which $\sigma = (\sigma_i)_{i \in N}$ is a vector of behavior strategies, and $\mu = (\mu_U)_{U \in \mathcal{U}}$ is a complete belief system.*

Definition 7.49 *An assessment (σ, μ) is called* consistent *if there exists a sequence of completely mixed behavior strategy vectors $(\sigma^k)_{k \in \mathbb{N}}$ satisfying the following conditions:*

1. *The strategies $(\sigma^k)_{k \in \mathbb{N}}$ converge to σ, i.e., $\lim_{k \to \infty} \sigma^k = \sigma$.*
2. *The sequence of beliefs $(\mu_{\sigma^k})_{k \in \mathbb{N}}$ induced by $(\sigma^k)_{k \in \mathbb{N}}$ converges to the belief system μ,*

$$\mu_\sigma(U) = \lim_{k \to \infty} \mu_{\sigma^k}(U), \quad \forall U \in \mathcal{U}. \tag{7.41}$$

Remark 7.50 *If σ is a completely mixed behavior strategy vector, then μ_σ is a complete belief system (Remark 7.42). In this case, (σ, μ_σ) is a consistent system. This follows directly from Definition 7.49, using the sequence $(\sigma^k)_{k \in \mathbb{N}}$ defined by $\sigma^k = \sigma$ for all $k \in \mathbb{N}$.* ◆

Remark 7.51 *Since the strategies σ^k in Definition 7.49 are completely mixed strategies, for every $k \in \mathbb{N}$ the belief system μ_{σ^k} is a complete belief system (Remark 7.42), and hence the limit μ is also a complete belief system (Remark 7.47).* ◆

Definition 7.52 *An assessment (σ, μ) is called a* sequential equilibrium *if it is consistent and sequentially rational.*

Remark 7.53 *By definition, if an assessment (σ, μ) is sequentially rational then it is rational at each information set at which the belief μ is defined. Since the belief system* *of an assessment is a complete belief system, it follows that a sequentially rational assessment (σ, μ) is rational at each information set.*   ♦

The following result, which is a corollary of Theorem 7.44, shows that the concept of sequential equilibrium is a refinement of the concept of Nash equilibrium.

Theorem 7.54 *In an extensive-form game with perfect recall, if the assessment (σ, μ) is a sequential equilibrium, then the strategy vector σ is a Nash equilibrium in behavior strategies.*

All of the above leads to:

Theorem 7.55 *In an extensive-form game with perfect recall, if σ is a Nash equilibrium in completely mixed behavior strategies, then (σ, μ_σ) is a sequential equilibrium.*

Proof: Remark 7.50 implies that the pair (σ, μ_σ) is a consistent assessment. Theorem 7.45 implies that this assessment is sequentially rational.   □

Example 7.56 Consider the two-player extensive-form game depicted in Figure 7.17.

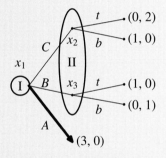

Figure 7.17 The game in Example 7.56, and a strictly dominant strategy of Player I

The strategy A strictly dominates Player I's two other strategies, and hence at every Nash equilibrium, Player I chooses A. This means that at any Nash equilibrium Player II's strategy has no effect at all on the play of the game, and hence in this game there is a continuum of equilibria in mixed strategies, $(A, [y(t), (1 - y)(b)])$, for $0 \leq y \leq 1$.

We now compute all the sequential equilibria of the game. Since every sequential equilibrium is a Nash equilibrium (Theorem 7.54), every sequential equilibrium (σ, μ) satisfies $\sigma_{\mathrm{I}} = A$.

Player II's belief at her sole information set is therefore $\mu_{U_{\mathrm{II}}} = (\mu_{U_{\mathrm{II}}}(x_2), \mu_{U_{\mathrm{II}}}(x_3))$. Is every belief $\mu_{U_{\mathrm{II}}}$ part of a consistent complete belief system? The answer is positive: the only condition that the assessment (σ, μ) needs to satisfy in order to be a consistent assessment is $\sigma_{\mathrm{I}} = A$. This follows directly from Definition 7.49, using the sequence

$$\sigma_{\mathrm{I}}^k = \left[\frac{k-1}{k}(A), \frac{\mu_{U_{\mathrm{II}}}(x_2)}{k}(B), \frac{\mu_{U_{\mathrm{II}}}(x_3)}{k}(C) \right]$$

for each $k \in \mathbb{N}$.

We next check which beliefs of Player II at information set U_{II} are rational at U_{II}. If the play of the game is at information set U_{II}, action t yields Player II the expected payoff $2\mu_{U_{\mathrm{II}}}(x_2)$, and action b yields the expected payoff $\mu_{U_{\mathrm{II}}}(x_3)$. Since $\mu_{U_{\mathrm{II}}}(x_2) + \mu_{U_{\mathrm{II}}}(x_3) = 1$, we deduce the following:

- If $\mu_{U_{\text{II}}}(x_2) > \frac{1}{3}$, then the only action that is rational for Player II at information set U_{II} is t.
- If $\mu_{U_{\text{II}}}(x_2) < \frac{1}{3}$, then the only action that is rational for Player II at information set U_{II} is b.
- If $\mu_{U_{\text{II}}}(x_2) = \frac{1}{3}$, then every mixed action of Player II is rational at information set U_{II}.

In other words, the set of sequentially rational equilibria consists of the following assessments:

- $\sigma_{\text{I}} = A$, $\sigma_{\text{II}} = t$, $\mu_{U_{\text{II}}} = [y(x_2), (1-y)(x_3)]$ for $y > \frac{1}{3}$.
- $\sigma_{\text{I}} = A$, $\sigma_{\text{II}} = b$, $\mu_{U_{\text{II}}} = [y(x_2), (1-y)(x_3)]$ for $y < \frac{1}{3}$.
- $\sigma_{\text{I}} = A$, $\sigma_{\text{II}} = [z(t), (1-z)(b)]$ for $z \in [0,1]$, $\mu_{U_{\text{II}}} = [\frac{1}{3}(x_2), \frac{2}{3}(x_3)]$.

◄

Example 7.38 (*Continued*) We have seen that the following pair (σ, μ_σ) satisfies the properties of partial consistency, and sequential rationality, at every information set U for which $\mathbf{P}_\sigma(U) > 0$:

- Player I:
  - plays the mixed action $[\frac{3}{12}(T), \frac{4}{12}(M), \frac{5}{12}(B)]$ at U_{I}^1.
  - chooses B_1 at information set U_{I}^1.
  - chooses T_2 at information set U_{I}^2.
- Player II chooses b.
- Player II's belief at information set U_{II} is $[\frac{4}{9}(x_2), \frac{5}{9}(x_3)]$.
- Player I's belief at information set U_{I}^2 is $[1(x_5)]$.

We now show that (σ, μ_σ) can be extended to a sequential equilibrium. To do so, we need to specify what Player I's belief is at information set U_{I}^3. Denote this belief by $\mu_{U_{\text{I}}^3} = (\mu_{U_{\text{I}}^3}(x_6), \mu_{U_{\text{I}}^3}(x_7))$. Note that for each $\mu_{U_{\text{I}}^3}$, the assessment $(\sigma, \mu_\sigma, \mu_{U_{\text{I}}^3})$ is consistent. This is achieved by defining

$$\sigma_{\text{I}}^k = \sigma_{\text{I}}, \quad \sigma_{\text{II}}^k = \left[\frac{\mu_{U_{\text{I}}^3}(x_6)}{k}(t), \frac{\mu_{U_{\text{I}}^3}(x_7)}{k}(m), \frac{k-1}{k}(b) \right], \quad (7.42)$$

and using Definition 7.49. Finally, the action T_2 yields Player I the expected payoff $3\mu_{U_{\text{I}}^3}(x_7)$, and action B_1 yields him the expected payoff $2\mu_{U_{\text{I}}^3}(x_6)$. It follows that action T_2 is rational if $\mu_{U_{\text{I}}^3}(x_6) \leq \frac{3}{5}$. We deduce that the assessment (σ, μ_σ) can be expanded to a sequential equilibrium (σ, μ) if we add:

- the belief of Player I at information set U_{I}^3 is $[p(x_6), (1-p)(x_7)]$, where $p \in [0, \frac{3}{5}]$.

◄

Sequential equilibrium, and extensive-form perfect equilibrium, are similar but not identical concepts. The following theorem states that every extensive-form perfect equilibrium can be completed to a sequential equilibrium. Example 7.59, which is presented after the proof of the theorem, shows that the converse does not obtain, and therefore the concept of extensive-form perfect equilibrium is a refinement of the concept of sequential equilibrium.

Theorem 7.57 *Let σ be an extensive-form perfect equilibrium in an extensive-form game with perfect recall Γ. Then σ can be completed to a sequential equilibrium: there exists* *a complete belief system* $\mu = (\mu_U)_{U \in \mathcal{U}}$ *satisfying the condition that the pair* (σ, μ) *is a sequential equilibrium.*

Since by Theorem 7.30 (page 278) every finite extensive-form game with perfect recall has an extensive-form perfect equilibrium, we immediately deduce the following corollary of Theorem 7.57.

Corollary 7.58 *Every finite extensive-form game with perfect recall has a sequential equilibrium.*

Proof of Theorem 7.57: Since σ is an extensive-form perfect equilibrium, there exists a sequence $(\delta^k)_{k \in \mathbb{N}}$ of perturbation vectors satisfying $\lim_{k \to \infty} M(\delta_k) = 0$, and for each $k \in \mathbb{N}$, there exists an equilibrium σ^k of the δ^k-perturbed game $\Gamma(\delta^k)$, satisfying $\lim_{k \to \infty} \sigma^k = \sigma$. Theorem 7.55 implies that for each $k \in \mathbb{N}$, the assessment $(\sigma^k, \mu_{\sigma^k})$ is a sequential equilibrium in the game $\Gamma(\delta^k)$.

By Remark 7.47, there exists an increasing sequence $(k_j)_{j \in \mathbb{N}}$ of natural numbers satisfying the condition that the sequence $(\mu_{\sigma^{k_j}})_{j \in \mathbb{N}}$ converges to a complete belief system μ. We deduce from this that (σ, μ) is a consistent assessment.

We now prove that (σ, μ) is a sequentially rational assessment. Let $i \in N$ be a player, U_i be an information set of player i, and σ'_i be a behavior strategy of player i. By Theorem 7.34, there exists a sequence $(\sigma_i'^k)_{k \in \mathbb{N}}$ of behavior strategies of player i converging to σ'_i and satisfying the condition that for each $k \in \mathbb{N}$, the strategy $\sigma_i'^k$ is a possible strategy for player i in the game $\Gamma(\delta^k)$. Since the assessment $(\sigma^k, \mu_{\sigma^k})$ is a sequential equilibrium in the game $\Gamma(\delta^k)$, one has

$$u_i(\sigma^k \mid U_i, \mu_{\sigma^k}) \geq u_i \left((\sigma_i'^k, \sigma_{-i}) \mid U_i, \mu_{\sigma^k} \right). \tag{7.43}$$

From the continuity of the payoff function, and consideration of the subsequence $(k_j)_{j \in \mathbb{N}}$, we conclude that

$$u_i(\sigma \mid U_i, \mu) \geq u_i((\sigma'_i, \sigma_{-i}) \mid U_i, \mu). \tag{7.44}$$

This completes the proof that the pair (σ, μ) is sequentially rational, and hence a sequential equilibrium. $\qquad\square$

We will now show that the converse of Theorem 7.57 does not hold: there exist games that have a sequential equilibrium of the form (σ, μ), where the strategy vector σ is not an extensive-form perfect equilibrium.

Example 7.59 Consider the two-player extensive-form game depicted in Figure 7.18. In this game there are two Nash equilibria in pure strategies: (T, t) and (B, b). Since every player has a single information set, the set of strategic-form perfect equilibria equals the set of extensive-form perfect equilibria. Since strategy T dominates strategy B (and strategy t dominates strategy b), only (T, t) is a strategic-form perfect equilibrium (see Theorem 7.28 on page 278). However, as we will now show, both (T, t) and (B, b) form elements of sequential equilibrium.

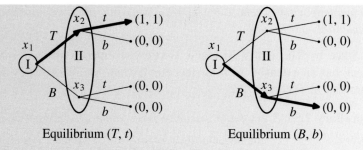

Figure 7.18 The game in Example 7.59, along with two sequential equilibria

Under both equilibria, the play of the game visits every information set, and therefore the beliefs of the players in these equilibria are as follows:

- At the equilibrium (T, t), the beliefs of the players are $[1(x_1)]$ and $[1(x_2)]$ respectively.
- At the equilibrium (B, b), the beliefs of the players are $[1(x_1)]$ and $[1(x_3)]$ respectively.

We first show that the pair $((T, t), [1(x_1)], [1(x_2)])$ is a sequential equilibrium. To show that this pair is consistent, define

$$\sigma^k = \left(\left[\frac{k-1}{k}(T), \frac{1}{k}(B) \right], \left[\frac{k-1}{k}(t), \frac{1}{k}(b) \right] \right), \quad \forall k \in \mathbb{N}. \tag{7.45}$$

Then $\mu_{\sigma^k}(U_{II}) = \left[\frac{k-1}{k}(x_2), \frac{1}{k}(x_3) \right]$ for all $k \in \mathbb{N}$, $\lim_{k \to \infty} \sigma^k = (T, t)$, and $\lim_{k \to \infty} \mu_{\sigma^k}(U_{II}) = [1(x_2)]$. This pair is sequentially rational because the payoff to each of the players is 1, which is the maximal payoff in the game.

We next show that the pair $((B, b), [1(x_1)], [1(x_3)])$ is also a sequential equilibrium. To show that this pair is consistent, define

$$\sigma^k = \left(\left[\frac{1}{k}(T), \frac{k-1}{k}(B) \right], \left[\frac{1}{k}(t), \frac{k-1}{k}(b) \right] \right), \quad \forall k \in \mathbb{N}. \tag{7.46}$$

Then $\mu_{\sigma^k}(U_{II}) = \left[\frac{1}{k}(x_2), \frac{k-1}{k}(x_3) \right]$ for all $k \in \mathbb{N}$, $\lim_{k \to \infty} \sigma^k = (B, b)$, and $\lim_{k \to \infty} \mu_{\sigma^k}(U_{II}) = [1(x_3)]$. This pair is sequentially rational because Player I receives 0 whether he plays T or B, and given his belief at information set $\{x_2, x_3\}$, Player II receives 0 whether he plays t or plays b.   ◄

In summary, the main differences between the three refinements of Nash equilibrium in extensive-form games are as follows:

- A mixed strategy vector σ is a strategic-form perfect equilibrium if it is the limit of equilibria in completely mixed strategies $(\sigma^k)_{k \in \mathbb{N}}$ of a sequence of perturbed games, where the perturbations converge to zero.
- A mixed strategy vector σ is an extensive-form perfect equilibrium if it is the limit of equilibria in completely mixed behavior strategies $(\sigma^k)_{k \in \mathbb{N}}$ of a sequence of perturbed games, where the perturbations converge to zero.
- An assessment (σ, μ) is a sequential equilibrium if μ is the limit of a sequence of beliefs $(\mu_{\sigma^k})_{k \in \mathbb{N}}$ induced by a sequence of strategies $(\sigma^k)_{k \in \mathbb{N}}$ converging to σ in a sequence of games with perturbations converging to zero (the consistency property), and for each

player i, at each of his information sets, σ_i is the best reply to σ_{-i} according to μ (the sequential rationality property).

As we saw in Example 7.59, if (σ, μ) is a sequential equilibrium then the strategy vector σ is not necessarily an extensive-form perfect equilibrium. This is due to the fact that the definition of extensive-form perfect equilibrium contains a condition that is not contained in the definition of sequential equilibrium: for σ to be an extensive-form perfect equilibrium, σ^k must be an equilibrium of the corresponding perturbed game for every $k \in \mathbb{N}$; i.e., the sequential rationality property must obtain for every element of the sequence $(\sigma^k)_{k\in\mathbb{N}}$, while for (σ, μ) to be a sequential equilibrium, the sequential rationality property must hold only in the limit, σ.

The next example illustrates why it is not clear how to extend the definition of sequential equilibrium to games with imperfect recall.

Example 7.60 **The Absent-Minded Driver** Consider the Absent-Minded Driver game depicted in Figure 7.19, which we previously encountered in Example 6.9 (page 236). The game contains a single player, who cannot distinguish between the two vertices in the game tree, and hence, at any vertex cannot recall whether or not he has played in the past.

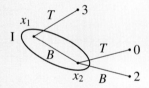

Figure 7.19 The Absent-Minded Driver game

The only Nash equilibrium in this game is T, because this strategy yields a payoff of 3, which is the game's highest payoff.

We now check whether the concept of sequential equilibrium can be adapted to this example. We first need to contend with the fact that because there are paths that visit the same information set several times, we need to reconsider what a belief at a vertex means. Suppose that the player implements strategy $\sigma = [1(B)]$, in which he plays action B. The play of the game will visit the vertex x_1, and the vertex x_2, hence $\mathbf{P}_\sigma(x_1) = \mathbf{P}_\sigma(x_2) = 1$, and $\mathbf{P}_\sigma(U) = 1$ holds for the information set $U = \{x_1, x_2\}$. It follows that Equation (7.32) does not define a belief system, because $\mathbf{P}_\sigma(U) \neq \mathbf{P}_\sigma(x_1) + \mathbf{P}_\sigma(x_2)$. We therefore need to define the player's belief system as follows:

$$\mu_U(x_1) = \frac{\mathbf{P}_\sigma(x_1)}{\mathbf{P}_\sigma(x_1) + \mathbf{P}_\sigma(x_2)} = \frac{1}{2}, \quad \mu_U(x_2) = \frac{\mathbf{P}_\sigma(x_2)}{\mathbf{P}_\sigma(x_1) + \mathbf{P}_\sigma(x_2)} = \frac{1}{2}. \tag{7.47}$$

In words, if the player implements strategy B, at his information set he ascribes equal probability to the play of the game being at either of the vertices x_1 and x_2.

Is the concept of sequential equilibrium applicable in this game? We will show that the assessment $(B, [\frac{1}{2}(x_1), \frac{1}{2}(x_2)])$ is sequentially rational, and therefore is a sequential equilibrium according to Definition 7.52, despite the fact that the strategy B is not a Nash equilibrium. If Player I implements strategy B at his information set, his expected payoff is 2, because he believes the play of the game is located at either x_1, or x_2, with equal probability, and in either case, if he implements strategy B, his expected payoff is 2. If, however, Player I implements strategy T at this information set, his expected payoff is $\frac{3}{2}$: the player ascribes probability $\frac{1}{2}$ to the play of the game being located at vertex x_1, which yields a payoff of 3 if he implements strategy T, and he ascribes probability $\frac{1}{2}$ to the play of the game being located at vertex x_2, in which case he receives a payoff of 0 if he implements strategy T. It follows that $(B, [\frac{1}{2}(x_1), \frac{1}{2}(x_2)])$ is a sequentially rational assessment, despite the fact that B is not an equilibrium.

The reason that Theorem 7.54 does not hold in games with imperfect recall is due to the fact that if there exists a path from the root that passes through two different vertices in the same information set U of a player, then when the player changes the action that he implements at U, he may also change his belief at U. This possibility is not taken into account in the definition of sequential equilibrium. ◀

7.5 Remarks

Sections 7.1 and 7.3 are based on the research conducted by Reinhardt Selten, who was awarded the Nobel Memorial Prize in Economics in 1994 for his contributions to refinements of the Nash equilibrium. The concept of sequential equilibrium first appeared in Kreps and Wilson [1982]. The interested reader may find a wealth of material on the concepts of subgame perfect equilibrium, and perfect equilibrium, in van Damme [1987]. Exercises 7.6 and 7.7 are based on Glazer and Ma [1989]. Exercise 7.14 is based on Selten [1978]. Exercise 7.15 is a variation of an example appearing in Rubinstein [1982]. Exercise 7.17 is based on an example appearing in Harris, Reny, and Robson [1995]. Exercise 7.27 is based on an example appearing in van Damme [1987, page 28]. Exercise 7.37 is based on an example appearing in Selten [1975]. The game in Exercise 7.46 is taken from Selten [1975]. The game in Exercise 7.48 is based on a game appearing in Kreps and Ramey [1987]. Exercise 7.49 is taken from Kohlberg and Mertens [1986]. Exercise 7.52 is based on an example appearing in Banks and Sobel [1987]. Exercise 7.53 is based on an example appearing in Cho and Kreps [1987]. Exercise 7.54 is based on an example appearing in Camerer and Weigelt [1988].

7.6 Exercises

7.1 (a) What is the number of subgames in a game with perfect information whose game tree has eight vertices?

(b) What is the number of subgames in a game whose game tree has eight vertices and one information set, which contains two vertices (with all other information sets containing only one vertex)?

(c) What is the number of subgames in a game whose game tree has eight vertices, three of which are chance vertices?

7.2 Answer the following questions, for each of the following two-player zero-sum extensive-form games:

(a) Find all the equilibria obtained by backward induction.

(b) Describe the corresponding strategic-form game.

(c) Check whether there exist additional equilibria.

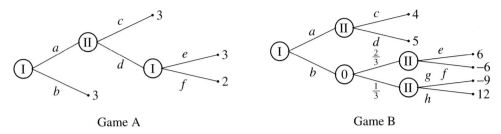

Game A   Game B

7.3 Find all the equilibria of the following two-player zero-sum game.

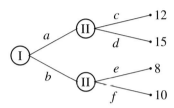

Explain why one cannot obtain all the equilibria of the game by implementing backward induction.

7.4 Find all the subgame perfect equilibria of the following games.

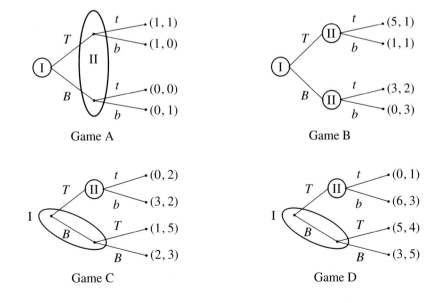

Game A   Game B

Game C   Game D

7.5 **The Ultimatum game** Allen and Rick need to divide $100 between them as follows: first Allen suggests an integer x between 0 and 100 (which is the amount of money he wants for himself). Rick, on hearing the suggested amount, decides whether to accept or reject. If Rick accepts, the payoff of the game is $(x, 1 - x)$:

Allen receives x dollars, and Rick receives $100-x$ dollars. If Rick chooses to reject, neither player receives any money.

(a) Describe this situation as an extensive-form game.

(b) What is the set of pure strategies each player has?

(c) Show that any result $(a, 100 - a)$, $a \in \{0, 1, \ldots, 100\}$, is a Nash equilibrium payoff. What are the corresponding equilibrium strategies?

(d) Find all the subgame perfect equilibria of this game.

7.6 The Judgment of Solomon Elizabeth and Mary appear before King Solomon at his palace, along with an infant. Each woman claims that the infant is her child. The child is "worth" 100 dinars to his true mother, but he is only "worth" 50 dinars to the woman who is not his mother. The king knows that one of these two women is the true mother of the child, and he knows the "value" that the true mother ascribes to the child, and the "value" that the impostor ascribes to the child, but he does not know which woman is the true mother, and which the impostor.

To determine which of the two women is the true mother, the king explains to Elizabeth and Mary that he will implement the following steps:

(i) He will ask Elizabeth whether the child is hers. If she answers negatively, the child will be given to Mary. If she answers affirmatively, the king will continue to the next step.

(ii) He will ask Mary if the child is hers. If she answers negatively, the child will be given to Elizabeth. If she answers affirmatively, Mary will pay the king 75 dinars, and receive the child, and Elizabeth will pay the king 10 dinars.

Answer the following questions:

(a) Describe the mechanism implemented by the king using two extensive-form games: in one extensive-form game Elizabeth is the true mother of the child, and in the second extensive-form game Mary is the true mother of the child.

(b) Prove that the mechanism implemented by the king guarantees that despite the fact that he does not know which of the above extensive-form games is being played, in each game the only subgame perfect equilibrium is the one under which the true mother gets her child and neither woman pays anything at all.

(c) Find another equilibrium of each game, which is not the subgame perfect equilibrium.

7.7 The following is a generalization of the "Judgment of Solomon," discussed in Exercise 7.6.

Emperor Caligula wishes to grant a prize-winning horse as a gift to one of his friends, Claudius or Marcus. The value that Claudius ascribes to the horse is in the set $\{u_1, u_2, \ldots, u_n\}$, and the value that Marcus ascribes to the horse is in the set $\{v_1, v_2, \ldots, v_m\}$. Each one of the emperor's friends knows the precise value that he ascribes to the horse, and he also knows the precise value that the other friend ascribes to the horse, but the only thing that the emperor knows is that the value that each of his friends ascribes to the horse is taken from the appropriate set of possible values. The emperor wishes to give the horse to the friend who values the horse most highly, but does not want to take money from his friends.

The emperor implements the following steps:

(i) Let $\varepsilon > 0$ be a positive number satisfying the condition that for each i and j, if $u_i \neq v_j$ then $|u_i - v_j| > \varepsilon$.

(ii) The emperor will ask Claudius if he values the horse at least as much as Marcus does. If Claudius answers negatively, the horse will be given to Marcus. If Claudius answers affirmatively, the emperor will continue to the next stage.

(iii) The emperor will ask Marcus if he values the horse more than Claudius does. If Marcus answers negatively, the horse will be given to Claudius. If Marcus answers affirmatively, the two friends will each pay the emperor $\varepsilon/4$, and the emperor will continue to the next step.

(iv) Claudius will be called upon to suggest a value $u \in \{u_1, u_2, \ldots, u_n\}$.

(v) Knowing Claudius' suggested value, Marcus will be called upon to suggest a value $v \in \{v_1, v_2, \ldots, v_m\}$.

(vi) The individual who suggested the higher value receives the horse, with the emperor keeping the horse in case of a draw. The winner pays $\max\{u, v\} - \frac{\varepsilon}{2}$ for the horse. The loser pays nothing.

Answer the following questions:

(a) Describe the sequence of steps implemented by the emperor as an extensive-form game. Assume that at the start of the game the following move of chance is implemented, which determines the private value of the horse for each of the two friends: the private value of the horse for Claudius is chosen from the set $\{u_1, u_2, \ldots, u_n\}$ using the uniform distribution, and the private value of the horse for Marcus is chosen from the set $\{v_1, v_2, \ldots, v_m\}$ using the uniform distribution.

(b) Prove that the only subgame perfect equilibrium of the game leads to the friend who values the horse the most receiving the horse (in case both friends equally value the horse, Claudius receives the horse).

7.8 Prove Theorem 7.9 on page 268: every (finite) extensive-form game with perfect information has a subgame perfect equilibrium in pure strategies.

7.9 Prove that in the 100-times-repeated Prisoner's Dilemma game (see Example 7.15 on page 270), the only subgame perfect equilibrium is the one where both players choose D in all stages of the game (after every history of previous actions).

7.10 (a) Find all the equilibria of the following two-player game.

Player II

		L	R
	T	3, 0	1, 2
Player I	B	2, 0	1, 5

(b) Suppose the players play the game twice; after the first time they have played the game, they know the actions chosen by both of them, and hence each player may condition his action in the second stage on the actions that were chosen in the first stage.

Describe this two-stage game as an extensive-form game.

(c) What are all the subgames of the two-stage game?

(d) Find all the subgame perfect equilibria of the two-stage game.

7.11 **The one-stage deviation principle for subgame perfect equilibria** Recall that $u_i(\sigma \mid x)$ is the payoff to player i when the players implement the strategy vector σ, given that the play of the game has arrived at the vertex x.

Prove that a strategy vector $\sigma^* = (\sigma_i^*)_{i\in N}$ in an extensive-form game with perfect information is a subgame perfect equilibrium if and only if for each player $i \in N$, every decision vertex x, and every strategy $\widehat{\sigma}_i$ of player i that is identical to σ_i^* at every one of his decision vertices except for x,

$$u_i(\sigma^* \mid x) \geq u_i((\widehat{\sigma}_i, \sigma_{-i}^*) \mid x). \tag{7.48}$$

Guidance: To prove that σ^* is a subgame perfect equilibrium if the condition above obtains, one needs to prove that the condition $u_i(\sigma^* \mid x) \geq u_i((\sigma_i, \sigma_{-i}^*) \mid x)$ holds for every vertex x, every player i, and every strategy σ_i. This can be accomplished by induction on the number of vertices in the game tree as follows. Suppose that this condition does not hold. Among all the triples (x, i, σ_i) for which it does not hold, choose a triple such that the number of vertices where σ_i differs from σ_i^* is minimal. Denote by $\mathcal{X}$ the set of all vertices such that σ_i differs from σ_i^*. By assumption, $|\mathcal{X}| \geq 1$. From the vertices in $\mathcal{X}$, choose a "highest" vertex, i.e., a vertex such that every path from the root to it does not pass through any other vertex in $\mathcal{X}$. Apply the inductive hypothesis to all the subgames beginning at the other vertices in $\mathcal{X}$.

7.12 Let Γ be a game in extensive form. The *agent-form game* derived from Γ is a strategic-form game where each player i in Γ is split into several players: for each information set $U_i \in \mathcal{U}_i$ of player i we define a player (i, U_i) in the agent-form game. Thus, if each player i has k_i information sets in Γ, then there are $\sum_{i\in N} k_i$ players in the agent-form game. The set of strategies of player (i, U_i) is $A(U_i)$. There is a bijection between the set of strategy vectors in the game Γ and the set of strategy vectors in the corresponding agent-form game: the strategy vector $\sigma = (\sigma_i)_{i\in N}$ in Γ corresponds to the strategy vector $(\sigma_i(U_i))_{\{i\in N, U_i\in\mathcal{U}_i\}}$ in the agent-form game. The payoff function of player (i, U_i) in the agent-form game is the payoff function of player i in the game Γ.

Prove that $\sigma = (\sigma_i)_{i\in N}$ is a subgame-perfect equilibrium in the game Γ, if and only if the strategy vector $(\sigma_i(U_i))_{\{i\in N, U_i\in\mathcal{U}_i\}}$ is a subgame-perfect equilibrium in the agent-form game derived from Γ. Is the result true when σ is a Nash equilibrium of the game Γ (not necessarily subgame perfect)? Prove or provide a counterexample.

7.13 Principal–Agent game Hillary manages a technology development company. A company customer asks Hillary to implement a particular project. Because it is unclear whether or not the project is feasible, the customer offers to pay Hillary $2 million at the start of work on the project, and an additional $4 million upon its completion (if the project is never completed, the customer pays nothing beyond the initial $2 million payment). Hillary seeks to hire Bill to implement the project. The success of the project depends on the amount of effort Bill invests in his work: if he fails to invest effort, the project will fail; if he does invest effort, the project will succeed with probability p, and will fail with probability $1 - p$. Bill assesses the cost of investing effort in the project (i.e., the amount of time he will need to devote to work at the expense of the time he would otherwise give to his family, friends, and hobbies) as equivalent to $1 million. Bill has received another job offer that will pay him $1 million without requiring him to invest a great deal of time and effort. In order to incentivize Bill to take the job she is offering, Hillary offers him a bonus, to be paid upon the successful completion of the project, beyond the salary of $1 million.

Answer the following questions:

(a) Depict this situation as an extensive-form game, where Hillary first determines the salary and bonus that she will offer Bill, and Bill afterwards decides whether or not to take the job offered by Hillary. If Bill takes the job offered by Hillary, Bill then needs to decide whether or not to invest effort in working on the project. Finally, if Bill decides to invest effort on the project, a chance move determines whether the project is a success or a failure. Note that the salary and bonus that Hillary can offer Bill need not be expressed in integers.

(b) Find all the subgame perfect equilibria of this game, assuming that both Hillary and Bill are risk-neutral, i.e., each of them seeks to maximize the expected payoff he or she receives.

(c) What does Hillary need to persuade Bill of during their job interview, in order to increase her expected payoff at equilibrium?

7.14 The Chainstore game A national chain of electronics stores has franchises in shopping centers in ten different cities. In each shopping center, the chainstore's franchise is the only electronics store. Ten local competitors, one in each city, are each contemplating opening a rival electronics store in the local shopping center, in the following sequence. The first competitor decides whether or not to open a rival electronics store in his city. The second competitor checks whether or not the first competitor has opened an electronics store, and takes into account the national chainstore's response to this development, before deciding whether or not he will open a rival electronics store in his city. The third competitor checks whether or not the first and second competitors have opened electronics stores, and takes into account the national chainstore's response to these developments, before deciding whether or not he will open a rival electronics store in his city, and so on. If a competitor decides not to open a rival electronics store, the competitor's payoff is 0, and the national chain store's payoff is 5. If a competitor does decide to open a rival electronics store, his payoff depends on the response of the national chainstore. If the national chainstore responds by undercutting prices in that city, the competitor and the chainstore lose 1 each. If the national chainstore does not respond by undercutting prices in that city, the competitor and the national chainstore each receive a payoff of 3.

(a) Describe this situation as an extensive-form game.
(b) Find all the subgame perfect equilibria.
(c) Find a Nash equilibrium that is not a subgame perfect equilibrium, and explain why it fails to be a subgame perfect equilibrium.

7.15 Alternating Offers game Debby and Barack are jointly conducting a project that will pay them a total payoff of $100. Every delay in implementing the project reduces payment for completing the project. How should they divide this money between them? The two decide to implement the following procedure: Debby starts by offering a division $(x_D, 100 - x_D)$, where x_D is a number in $[0, 100]$ representing the amount of money that Debby receives under the terms of this offer, while Barack receives $100 - x_D$. Barack may accept or reject Debby's offer. If he rejects the offer, he may propose a counteroffer $(y_D, 99 - y_D)$ where y_D is a number in $[0, 99]$ representing the amount of money that Debby receives under the terms of this offer, while Barack receives $99 - y_D$. Barack's offer can only divide $99 between the two players, because the delay caused by his rejection of Debby's offer has reduced the payment for completing the project by $1. Debby may accept or reject Barack's offer. If she rejects the offer, she may then propose yet another counteroffer, and so on. Each additional round of offers, however, reduces the amount of money available by $1: if the two players come to an agreement on a division after the k-th offer has been passed between them, then they can divide only $(101 - k)$ dollars between them. If the two players cannot come to any agreement, after 100 rounds of alternating offers, they drop plans to conduct the project jointly, and each receives 0.

Describe this situation as an extensive-form game, and find all of its subgame perfect equilibria.

7.16 Prove Theorem 7.10: every extensive-form game with perfect recall has a subgame perfect equilibrium in mixed strategies.

7.17 A game without a subgame perfect equilibrium Consider the four-player extensive-form game in Figure 7.20. In this game, Player I's set of pure strategies is the interval $[-1, 1]$; i.e., Player I chooses a number a in this interval. The other players, Players II, III, and IV, each have two available actions, at each of their information sets. Figure 7.20 depicts only one subgame tree, after Player I has chosen an action. All the other possible subtrees are identical to the one shown here.

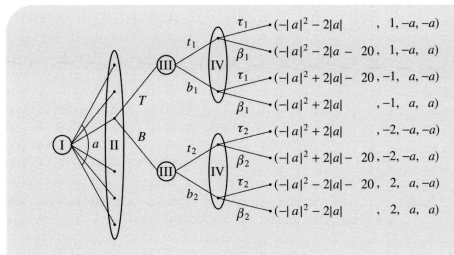

Figure 7.20 A game without subgame perfect equilibria

This game may be regarded as a two-stage game: in the first stage, Players I and II choose their actions simultaneously (where Player I chooses $a \in [-1, 1]$, and Player II chooses T or B), and in the second stage, Players III and IV, after learning which actions were chosen by Players I and II, choose their actions simultaneously.

Suppose that the game has a subgame perfect equilibrium, denoted by $\sigma = (\sigma_I, \sigma_{II}, \sigma_{III}, \sigma_{IV})$. Answer the following questions:

(a) What are all the subgames of this game?
(b) What will Players III and IV play under σ, when $a \neq 0$?
(c) What are the payoffs of Players III and IV, when $a = 0$?
(d) Denote by β the probability that Player II plays the pure strategy B, under strategy σ_{II}. Explain why there does not exist a subgame perfect equilibrium such that Player I plays $a = 0$, Player II plays $\beta = \frac{1}{2}$, and if $a = 0$, Player III chooses t_1 with probability $\frac{1}{4}$, and chooses t_2 with probability $\frac{1}{8}$, while Player IV chooses τ_1 and τ_2 with probability 1.
(e) Depict the expected payoff of Player I as a function of a and β, in the case where $a \neq 0$.
(f) Find the upper bound of the possible payoffs Player I can receive, in the case where $a = 0$.
(g) What is Player I's best reply when $\beta < \frac{1}{2}$? What are the best replies of Players III and IV, given Player I's strategy? What is Player II's best reply to these strategies of Players I, III, and IV?
(h) What is Player I's best reply when $\beta > \frac{1}{2}$? What are the best replies of Players III and IV, given Player I's strategy? What is Player II's best reply to these strategies of Players I, III, and IV?

(i) Suppose that $\beta = \frac{1}{2}$. What is the optimal payoff that Player I can receive? Deduce that under σ, Player I necessarily plays $a = 0$, and his payoff is then 0. What does this say about the strategies of Players III and IV? What is Player II's best reply to these strategies of Players I, III, and IV?

(j) Conclude that this game has no subgame perfect equilibrium.

(k) Find a Nash equilibrium of this game.

This exercise does not contradict Theorem 7.37, which states that every finite extensive-form game with perfect recall has a subgame perfect equilibrium in behavior strategies, because this game is infinite: Player I has a continuum of pure strategies.

7.18 Prove that for each player i, and every vector of perturbations ε_i, the set of strategies $\Sigma_i(\varepsilon_i)$ (see Equation (7.11)) is compact and convex.

7.19 Prove that every mixed strategy $\sigma_i \in \Sigma_i$ can be approximated by a completely mixed strategy; that is, for every $\delta > 0$ there is a completely mixed strategy σ'_i of player i that satisfies $\max_{s_i \in S_i} |\sigma_i(s_i) - \sigma'_i(s_i)| < \delta$.

7.20 Prove that the set of perfect equilibria of a strategic-form game is a closed subset of $\times_{i \in N} \Sigma_i$.

7.21 Find all the perfect equilibria in each of the following games, in which Player I is the row player and Player II is the column player.

	L	M
T	1, 1	1, 0
B	1, 0	0, 1

Game A

	L	C	R
T	1, 1	0, 0	−1, −2
M	0, 0	0, 0	0, −2
B	−2, 1	−2, 0	−2, −2

Game B

7.22 Consider the following two-player strategic-form game:

	L	C	R
T	1, 2	3, 0	0, 3
M	1, 1	2, 2	2, 0
B	1, 2	0, 3	3, 0

(a) Prove that $([x_1(T), x_2(M), (1 - x_1 - x_2)(B)], L)$ is a Nash equilibrium of this game if and only if $\frac{1}{3} \leq x_1 \leq \frac{2}{3}$, $0 \leq x_2 \leq 2 - 3x_1$, and $x_1 + x_2 \leq 1$.

(b) Prove that the equilibria identified in part (a) are all the Nash equilibria of the game.

(c) Prove that if $([x_1(T), x_2(M), (1-x_1-x_2)(B)], L)$ is a perfect equilibrium, then $1 - x_1 - x_2 = 0$.

(d) Prove that for every $x_1 \in \left(\frac{1}{3}, \frac{1}{2}\right)$ the strategy vector $\left([x_1(T), (1 - x_1)(M)], L\right)$ is a perfect equilibrium.

(e) Using Exercise 7.20, determine the set of perfect equilibria of this game.

7.23 Prove Theorem 7.28 (page 278): in a perfect equilibrium, every weakly dominated strategy is chosen with probability 0.

7.24 Let σ_I and σ_{II} be optimal strategies (in pure or mixed strategies) of two players in a two-player zero-sum game. Is (σ_I, σ_{II}) necessarily a perfect equilibrium? If so, prove it. If not, provide a counterexample.

7.25 A pure strategy s_i of player i is said to be *weakly dominated by a mixed strategy* if player i has a mixed strategy σ_i satisfying:

(a) For each strategy $s_{-i} \in S_{-i}$ of the other players,

$$u_i(s_i, s_{-i}) \leq U_i(\sigma_i, s_{-i}). \tag{7.49}$$

(b) There exists a strategy $t_{-i} \in S_{-i}$ of the other players satisfying

$$u_i(s_i, t_{-i}) < U_i(\sigma_i, t_{-i}). \tag{7.50}$$

Prove that in a perfect equilibrium, every pure strategy that is weakly dominated by a mixed strategy is chosen with probability 0.

7.26 (a) Prove that (T, L) is the only perfect equilibrium of the following game.

Player II

		L	M
Player I	T	6, 6	0, 0
	B	0, 4	4, 4

(b) Prove that in the following game, which is obtained from the game in part (a) by adding a dominated pure strategy to each player, (B, M) is a perfect equilibrium.

Player II

		L	M	R
	T	6, 6	0, 0	2, 0
Player I	B	0, 4	4, 4	2, 0
	I	0, 0	0, 2	2, 2

7.27 In this exercise, we will show that in a three-player game a vector of strategies that makes use solely of strategies that are not dominated is not necessarily a perfect equilibrium. To do so, consider the following three-player game, where Player I chooses a row (T or B), Player II chooses a column (L or R), and Player III chooses a matrix (W or E).

	L	R
T	1, 1, 1	1, 0, 1
B	1, 1, 1	0, 0, 1

W

	L	R
T	1, 1, 0	0, 0, 0
B	0, 1, 0	1, 0, 0

E

(a) Find all the dominated strategies.
(b) Find all the Nash equilibria of this game.
(c) Find all the perfect equilibria of this game.

7.28 Prove that the following definition of perfect equilibrium is equivalent to Definition 7.25 (page 277).

Definition 7.61 *A strategy vector σ is called a* perfect equilibrium *if there exists a sequence $(\sigma^k)_{k \in \mathbb{N}}$ of vectors of completely mixed strategies satisfying:*

- *For each player $i \in N$, the limit $\lim_{k \to \infty} \sigma_i^k$ exists and equals σ_i.*
- *σ is a best reply to σ_{-i}^k, for each $k \in \mathbb{N}$, and each player $i \in N$.*

7.29 Prove that, in the following game, (B, L) is a Nash equilibrium, but not a perfect equilibrium.

Player II

		L	M	R
	T	1, 1	3, 3	0, 0
Player I	C	1, 1	0, 0	3, 3
	B	1, 1	1, 1	1, 1

7.30 Show that in the game in Example 7.35 (page 281) the equilibrium (B, R) is an extensive-form perfect equilibrium. Does this game have additional Nash equilibria? If so, which of them is also an extensive-form perfect equilibrium? Justify your answer.

7.31 Prove that, in the game in Example 7.18 (page 274), the equilibrium (T, t, β) is an extensive-form perfect equilibrium, but the equilibrium (B, t, τ) is not an extensive-form perfect equilibrium.

7.32 Prove directly the following theorem which is analogous to Corollary 7.26 (page 277) for extensive-form perfect equilibria: every extensive-form perfect equilibrium is a Nash equilibrium in behavior strategies. To prove this, first prove the analogue result to Theorem 7.24 for a sequence of equilibria in perturbed games $(\Gamma(\delta^k))_{k \in \mathbb{N}}$.

7.33 Prove Theorem 7.30 (page 278): every finite extensive-form game has a strategic-form perfect equilibrium.

7.34 Prove Theorem 7.31 (page 279): let δ be a perturbation vector, let σ^* be a Nash equilibrium (in behavior strategies) in the game $\Gamma(\delta)$, and let $\Gamma(x)$ be a subgame of Γ. Then the strategy vector σ^*, restricted to the subgame $\Gamma(x)$, is a Nash equilibrium (in behavior strategies) of $\Gamma(x; \delta)$.

7.35 Prove Theorem 7.34 (page 280): let $(\delta^k)_{k\in\mathbb{N}}$ be a sequence of perturbation vectors satisfying $\lim_{k\to\infty} M(\delta^k) = 0$. Then for every behavior strategy $\sigma_i \in \mathcal{B}_i$ of player i there exists a sequence $(\sigma_i^k)_{k\in\mathbb{N}}$ of behavior strategies satisfying the following two properties:

- $\sigma_i^k \in \mathcal{B}_i(\delta_i^k)$ for each $k \in \mathbb{N}$.
- $\lim_{k\to\infty} \sigma_i^k$ exists and equals σ_i.

7.36 This exercise shows that an extensive-form perfect equilibrium is not necessarily a strategic-form perfect equilibrium.

In the following game, find an extensive-form perfect equilibrium that is not a strategic-form perfect equilibrium.

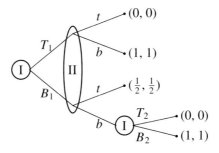

Does the game have another Nash equilibrium? Does it have another subgame perfect equilibrium?

7.37 This exercise proves the converse to what we showed in Exercise 7.36: a strategic-form perfect equilibrium is not necessarily an extensive-form perfect equilibrium.

(a) Prove that the following game has a unique extensive-form perfect equilibrium.

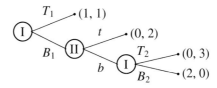

(b) Show that this game has another equilibrium, which is a strategic-form perfect equilibrium. To do so, construct the corresponding strategic-form game, and show that it has more than one perfect equilibrium.

(c) Does this game have a strategic-form perfect equilibrium that is not a subgame perfect equilibrium?

7.38 Show that the following game has a unique Nash equilibrium, and in particular a unique extensive-form perfect equilibrium and a unique strategic-form perfect equilibrium.

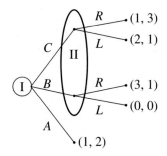

7.39 Prove that in an extensive-form game in which every player has a single information set, every strategic-form perfect equilibrium is equivalent to an extensive-form perfect equilibrium, and that the converse also holds.

7.40 Consider the extensive-form game shown in Figure 7.21.

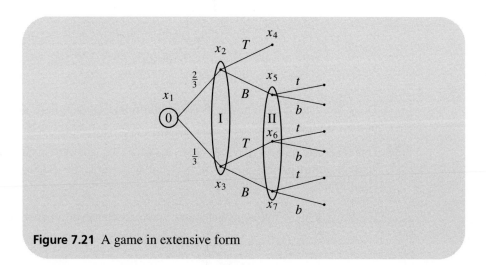

Figure 7.21 A game in extensive form

For each of the following pairs, explain why it is not a consistent assessment of the game:

(a) $([\frac{1}{2}(T), \frac{1}{2}(B)], t, [\frac{1}{2}(x_2), \frac{1}{2}(x_3)], [\frac{1}{4}(x_4), \frac{1}{4}(x_5), \frac{1}{2}(x_6)])$.

(b) $([\frac{1}{2}(T), \frac{1}{2}(B)], b, [\frac{2}{3}(x_2), \frac{1}{3}(x_3)], [\frac{1}{3}(x_4), \frac{1}{3}(x_5), \frac{1}{3}(x_6)])$.

(c) $(T, t, [\frac{2}{3}(x_2), \frac{1}{3}(x_3)], [\frac{2}{3}(x_4), \frac{1}{3}(x_6)])$.

(d) $(T, t, [\frac{2}{3}(x_2), \frac{1}{3}(x_3)], [\frac{1}{2}(x_5), \frac{1}{2}(x_6)])$.

7.41 Prove Theorem 7.45 (page 287): if σ^* is a Nash equilibrium in behavior strategies, then the pair $(\sigma^*, \mu_{\sigma^*})$ is sequentially rational in every information set U satisfying $\mathbf{P}_{\sigma^*}(U) > 0$.

7.42 Prove Theorem 7.46 (page 288): in a game with perfect information, a vector of behavior strategies σ is a subgame perfect equilibrium if and only if the pair $(\sigma, \hat{\mu})$ is sequentially rational at every information set of the game, where $\hat{\mu}$ is a complete belief system such that $\hat{\mu}_U = [1(x)]$ for every information set $U = \{x\}$.

7.43 List all the consistent assessments of the extensive-form game in Exercise 7.40 (Figure 7.21).

7.44 List all the consistent assessments of the extensive-form game in Example 7.17 (page 272).

7.45 List all the consistent assessments of the following extensive-form game.

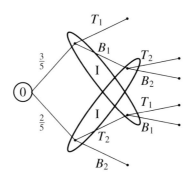

7.46 List all the consistent assessments, and all the sequentially rational assessments of the following game.

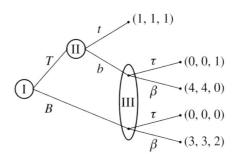

7.47 Find all the sequential equilibria of the game in Example 7.35 (page 281).

7.48 Consider the following extensive-form game:

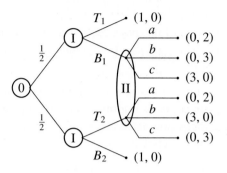

(a) Prove that in this game at every Nash equilibrium Player I plays (T_1, B_2).

(b) List all the Nash equilibria of the game.

(c) Which of these Nash equilibria can be completed to a sequential equilibrium, and for each such sequential equilibrium, what is the corresponding belief of Player II at his information sets? Justify your answer.

7.49 Find all the sequential equilibria of the following game.

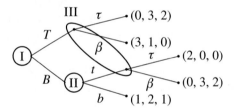

7.50 The following example shows that the set of sequential equilibria is sensitive to the way in which a player makes decisions: it makes a difference whether the player, when called upon to choose an action from among a set of three possible actions, eliminates the actions he will not choose one by one, or simultaneously.

Consider the two extensive-form games below. Show that $(2, 2)$ is a sequential equilibrium payoff in Game A, but not a sequential equilibrium payoff in Game B.

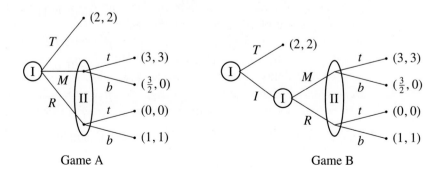

Game A   Game B

7.51 In an extensive-form game with perfect recall, is every Nash equilibrium part of a sequential equilibrium? That is, for every Nash equilibrium σ^* does there exist a belief system μ that satisfies the property that (σ^*, μ) is a sequential equilibrium? If yes, prove it. If not, construct a counterexample.

7.52 Pre-trial settlement A contractor is being sued for damages by a municipality that hired him to construct a bridge, because the bridge has collapsed. The contractor knows whether or not the collapse of the bridge is due to negligence on his part, or due to an act of nature beyond his control, but the municipality does not know which of these two alternatives is the true one. Both sides know that if the matter is settled by a court trial, the truth will eventually be uncovered.

   The contractor can try to arrive at a pre-trial settlement with the municipality. He has two alternatives: to make a low settlement offer, under which he pays the municipality $300,000, or a high offer, under which he pays the municipality $500,000. After the contractor has submitted a settlement offer, the municipality must decide whether or not to accept it. Both parties know that if the suit goes to trial, the contractor will pay lawyer fees of $600,000, and that, in addition to this expense, if the court finds him guilty of negligence, he will be required to pay the municipality $500,000 in damages. Assume that the municipality has no lawyer fees to pay.

   Answer the following questions:

   (a) Describe this situation as an extensive-form game, where the root of the game is a chance move that determines with equal probability whether the contractor was negligent or not.
   (b) Explain the significance of the above assumption, that a chance move determines with equal probability whether the contractor was negligent or not.
   (c) Find all the Nash equilibria of this game.
   (d) Find all the sequential equilibria of this game.
   (e) Repeat items (c) and (d) when the chance move selects whether the contractor was negligent or not with probabilities p and $1 - p$ respectively.

7.53 Signaling game Caesar is at a cafe, trying to choose what to drink with breakfast: beer or orange juice. Brutus, sitting at a nearby table, is pondering whether or not to challenge Caesar to a duel after breakfast. Brutus does not know whether Caesar is brave or cowardly, and he will only dare to challenge Caesar if Caesar is cowardly. If he fights a cowardly opponent, he receives one unit of utility, and he receives the same single unit of utility if he avoids fighting a brave opponent. In contrast, he loses one unit of utility if he fights a brave opponent, and similarly loses one unit of utility if he dishonors himself by failing to fight a cowardly opponent. Brutus ascribes probability 0.9 to Caesar being brave, and probability 0.1 to Caesar being a coward. Caesar has no interest in fighting Brutus: he loses 2 units of utility if he fights Brutus, but loses nothing if there is no fight. Caesar knows whether he is brave or cowardly. He can use the drink he orders for breakfast to signal his type, because it is commonly known that brave types receive one unit of utility if they drink beer (and receive nothing if they drink orange juice), while cowards receive one unit of utility if they drink orange juice (and receive nothing if they drink beer). Assume that Caesar's utility is additive; for example, he receives three units of utility if he is brave, drinks beer, and avoids fighting Brutus. Answer the following questions:

(a) Describe this situation as an extensive-form game, where the root of the game tree is a chance move that determines whether Caesar is brave (with probability 0.9) or cowardly (with probability 0.1).

(b) Find all the Nash equilibria of the game.

(c) Find all the sequential equilibria of the game.

7.54 Henry seeks a loan to form a new company, and submits a request for a loan to Rockefeller. Rockefeller knows that p percent of people asking him for loans are conscientious, who feel guilty if they default on their loans, and $1 - p$ percent of people asking him for loans have no compunction about defaulting on their loans, but he does not know whether or not Henry is a conscientious borrower. Rockefeller is free to grant Henry a loan, or to refuse to give him a loan. If Henry receives the loan, he can decide to repay the loan, or to default. If Rockefeller refuses to loan money to Henry, both sides receive 10 units. If Rockefeller loans Henry the money he needs to form a company, and Henry repays the loan, Rockefeller receives 40 units, while Henry receives 60 units. If Rockefeller loans Henry the money he needs to form a company, but Henry defaults on the loan, Rockefeller loses x units, and Henry's payoff depends on his type: if he is a conscientious borrower, he receives 0, but if he has no compunction about defaulting, he gains 150 units. Answer the following questions:

(a) Describe this situation as an extensive-form game, where the root of the game tree is a chance move that determines Henry's type.

(b) Find all the Nash equilibria, and the sequential equilibria, of this game, in the following three cases:

(i) $p = \frac{1}{3}$, and $x = 100$.
(ii) $p = 0.1$, and $x = 50$.
(iii) $p = 0$, and $x = 75$.

7.55 The one-stage deviation principle for sequential equilibria Let (σ, μ) be a consistent assessment in an extensive-form game Γ with perfect recall. Prove that the assessment (σ, μ) is a sequential equilibrium if and only if for each player $i \in N$, and every information set U_i

$$u_i(\sigma \mid U_i, \mu) \geq u_i(\widehat{\sigma}_i, \sigma_{-i} \mid U_i, \mu), \qquad (7.51)$$

under every strategy $\widehat{\sigma}_i$ that differs from σ_i only at the information set U_i.

Guidance: To prove that if the condition holds then (σ, μ) is a sequential equilibrium, consider a player i and any information set U_i of his, along with any strategy σ_i'. Show that $u_i(\sigma \mid U_i, \mu) \geq u_i((\sigma_i', \sigma_{-i}) \mid U_i, \mu)$. The proof of this inequality can be accomplished by induction on the number of information sets of player i over which σ_i' differs from σ_i.

8 Correlated equilibria

Chapter summary

This chapter introduces the concept of *correlated equilibrium* in strategic-form games. The motivation for this concept is that players' choices of pure strategies may be correlated due to the fact that they use the same random events in deciding which pure strategy to play. Consider an extended game that includes an observer who recommends to each player a pure strategy that he should play. The vector of recommended strategies is chosen by the observer according to a probability distribution over the set of pure strategy vectors, which is commonly known among the players. This probability distribution is called a correlated equilibrium if the strategy vector in which all players follow the observer's recommendations is a Nash equilibrium of the extended game.

The probability distribution over the set of strategy vectors induced by any Nash equilibrium is a correlated equilibrium. The set of correlated equilibria is a polytope that can be calculated as a solution of a set of linear equations.

In Chapters 4, 5, and 7 we considered strategic-form games and studied the concept of equilibrium. One of the underlying assumptions of those chapters was that the choices made by the players were independent. In practice, however, the choices of players may well depend on factors outside the game, and therefore these choices may be correlated. Players can even coordinate their actions among themselves.

A good example of such correlation is the invention of the traffic light: when a motorist arrives at an intersection, he needs to decide whether to cross it, or alternatively to give right of way to motorists approaching the intersection from different directions. If the motorist were to use a mixed strategy in this situation, that would be tantamount to tossing a coin and entering the intersection based on the outcome of the coin toss. If two motorists approaching an intersection simultaneously use this mixed strategy, there is a positive probability that both of them will try to cross the intersection at the same time – which means that there is a positive probability that a traffic accident will ensue. In some states in the United States, there is an equilibrium rule that requires motorists to stop before entering an intersection, and to give right of way to whoever arrived at the intersection earlier. The invention of the traffic light provided a different solution: the traffic light informs each motorist which pure strategy to play, at any given time. The traffic light thus correlates the pure strategies of the players. Note that the traffic light does not, strictly speaking, choose a pure strategy for the motorist; it recommends a pure strategy. It is in the interest of each motorist to follow that recommendation, even if we suppose there are no traffic police watching, no cameras, and no possible court summons awaiting a motorist who disregards the traffic light's recommendation.

The concept of correlated equilibrium, which is an equilibrium in a game where players' strategies may be correlated, is the subject of this chapter. As we will show, correlation can be beneficial to the players.

8.1 Examples

Example 8.1 **Battle of the Sexes** Consider the Battle of the Sexes game, as depicted in Figure 8.1 (see also Example 4.21 on page 98). The game has three equilibria (verify that this is true):

1. (F, F): the payoff is $(2, 1)$.
2. (C, C): the payoff is $(1, 2)$.
3. $([\frac{2}{3}(F), \frac{1}{3}(C)], [\frac{1}{3}(F), \frac{2}{3}(C)])$: in this equilibrium, every player uses mixed strategies. The row player plays $[\frac{2}{3}(F), \frac{1}{3}(C)]$ – he chooses F with probability two-thirds, and C with probability one-third. The column player plays $[\frac{1}{3}(F), \frac{2}{3}(C)]$. The expected payoff in this case is $(\frac{2}{3}, \frac{2}{3})$.

Player II

	F	C
F	2, 1	0, 0
C	0, 0	1, 2

Player I

Figure 8.1 The Battle of the Sexes

The first two equilibria are not symmetric; in each one, one of the players yields to the preference of the other player. The third equilibrium, in contrast, is symmetric and gives the same payoff to both players, but that payoff is less than 1, the lower payoff in each of the two pure equilibria.

The players can correlate their actions in the following way. They can toss a fair coin. If the coin comes up heads, they play (F, F), and if it comes up tails, they play (C, C). The expected payoff is then $(1\frac{1}{2}, 1\frac{1}{2})$. Since (F, F) and (C, C) are equilibria, the process we have just described is an equilibrium in an extended game, in which the players can toss a coin and choose their strategies in accordance with the result of the coin toss: after the coin toss, neither player can profit by unilaterally deviating from the strategy recommended by the result of the coin toss. ◄

The reasoning behind this example is as follows: if we enable the players to conduct a joint (public) lottery, prior to playing the game, they can receive as an equilibrium payoff every convex combination of the equilibrium payoffs of the original game. That is, if we denote by V the set of equilibrium payoffs in the original game, every payoff in the convex hull of V is an equilibrium payoff in the extended game in which the players can conduct a joint lottery prior to playing the game.

The question naturally arises whether it is possible to create a correlation mechanism, such that the set of equilibrium payoffs in the game that corresponds to this mechanism includes payoffs that are not in the convex hull of V. The following examples show that the answer to this question is affirmative.

Example 8.2 Consider the three-player game depicted in Figure 8.2, in which Player I chooses the row (T or B), Player II chooses the column (L or R), and Player III chooses the matrix (l, c, or r).

	L	R
T	0, 1, 3	0, 0, 0
B	1, 1, 1	1, 0, 0

l

	L	R
T	2, 2, 2	0, 0, 0
B	2, 2, 0	2, 2, 2

c

	L	R
T	0, 1, 0	0, 0, 0
B	1, 1, 1	1, 0, 3

r

Figure 8.2 The payoff matrix of Example 8.2

We will show that the only equilibrium payoff of this game is $(1, 1, 1)$, but there exists a correlation mechanism that induces an equilibrium payoff of $(2, 2, 2)$. In other words, every player gains by using the correlation mechanism. Since $(1, 1, 1)$ is the only equilibrium payoff of the original game, the vector $(2, 2, 2)$ is clearly outside the convex hull of the original game's set of equilibrium payoffs.

Step 1: The only equilibrium payoff is $(1, 1, 1)$.
We will show that every equilibrium is of the form $(B, L, [\alpha(l), (1 - \alpha)(r)])$, for some $0 \leq \alpha \leq 1$. (Check that the payoff given by any strategy vector of this form is $(1, 1, 1)$, and that each of these strategy vectors is indeed an equilibrium.) To this end we eliminate strictly dominated strategies (see Definition 4.6 on page 86). We first establish that at every equilibrium there is a positive probability that the pair of pure strategies chosen by Players II and III will not be (L, c). To see this, when Player II plays L, strategy l strictly dominates strategy c for Player III, so it cannot be the case that at equilibrium Player II plays L with probability 1 and Player III plays c with probability 1.

We next show that at every equilibrium, Player I plays strategy B. To see this, note that the pure strategy B weakly dominates T (for Player I). In addition, if the probability of (L, c) is not 1, strategy B yields a strictly higher payoff to Player I than strategy T. It follows that the pure strategy T cannot be played at equilibrium.

Finally, we show that at every equilibrium Player II plays strategy L and Player III plays either l or r. To see this, note that after eliminating strategy T, strategy r strictly dominates c for Player III, hence Player III does not play c at equilibrium, and after eliminating strategy c, strategy L strictly dominates R for Player II. We are left with only two entries in the matrix: (B, L, l) and (B, L, r), both of which yield the same payoff, $(1, 1, 1)$. Thus any convex combination of these two matrix entries is an equilibrium, and there are no other equilibria.

Step 2: The construction of a correlation mechanism leading to the payoff $(2, 2, 2)$.
Consider the following mechanism that the players can implement:

• Players I and II toss a fair coin, but do not reveal the result of the coin toss to Player III.
• Players I and II play either (T, L) or (B, R), depending on the result of the coin toss.
• Player III chooses strategy c.

Under the implementation of this mechanism, the action vectors that are chosen (with equal probability) are (T, L, c) and (B, R, c), hence the payoff is $(2, 2, 2)$.

Finally, we check that no player has a unilateral deviation that improves his payoff. Recall that because the payoff function is multilinear, it suffices to check whether or not this is true for a deviation to a pure strategy. If Player III deviates and chooses l or r, his expected payoff is $\frac{1}{2} \times 3 + \frac{1}{2} \times 0 = 1\frac{1}{2}$, and hence he cannot gain from deviating. Players I and II cannot profit from deviating, because whatever the outcome of the coin toss is, the payoff to each of them is 2, the maximal payoff in the game. ◀

For the mechanism described in Figure 8.2 to be an equilibrium, it is necessary that Players I and II know that Player III does not know the result of the coin toss. In other words, while every payoff in the convex hull of the set of equilibrium payoffs can be attained by a *public* lottery, to attain a payoff outside the convex hull of V it is necessary to conduct a lottery that is not public, in which case different players receive different partial information regarding the result of the lottery.

Example 8.3　**The game of "Chicken"** Consider the two-player non-zero-sum game depicted in Figure 8.3.

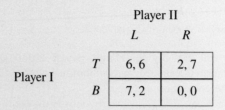

Player II

		L	R
Player I	T	6, 6	2, 7
	B	7, 2	0, 0

Figure 8.3 The game of "Chicken"

The following background story usually accompanies this game. Two drivers are racing directly towards each other down a single-lane road. The first to lose his nerve and swerve off the road before the cars collide is the loser of the game, the "chicken." In this case, the utility of the loser is 2, and the utility of the winner is 7. If neither player drives off the road, the cars collide, both players are injured, and they each have a utility of 0. If they both swerve off the road simultaneously, the utility of each of them is 6.

The game has three equilibria (check that this is true):

1. The players play (T, R). The payoff is $(2, 7)$.
2. The players play (B, L). The payoff is $(7, 2)$.
3. The players play $\left(\left[\frac{2}{3}(T), \frac{1}{3}(B)\right], \left[\frac{2}{3}(L), \frac{1}{3}(R)\right]\right)$. The payoff is $(4\frac{2}{3}, 4\frac{2}{3})$.

Consider the following mechanism, in which an outside observer gives each player a recommendation regarding which action to take, but the observer does not reveal to either player what recommendation the other player has received. The observer chooses between three action vectors, (T, L), (T, R), and (B, L), with equal probability (see Figure 8.4).

	L	R
T	$\frac{1}{3}$	$\frac{1}{3}$
B	$\frac{1}{3}$	0

Figure 8.4 The distribution that the observer uses to choose the action vector

After conducting a lottery to choose one of the three action vectors, the observer provides Player I with a recommendation to play the first coordinate of the vector that was chosen, and he provides Player II with a recommendation to play the second coordinate of that vector. For example, if the action vector (T, L) has been chosen, the observer recommends T to Player I and L to Player II. If Player I receives a recommendation to play T, the conditional probability that Player II has received a recommendation to play L is $\frac{\frac{1}{3}}{\frac{1}{3}+\frac{1}{3}} = \frac{1}{2}$, which is also the conditional probability that he has received a recommendation to play R. In contrast, if Player I receives a recommendation to play B, he knows that Player II has received L as his recommended action.

We now show that neither player can profit by a unilateral deviation from the recommendation received from the observer. As we stated above, if the recommendation to Player I is to play T, Player II has received a recommendation to play L with probability $\frac{1}{2}$, and a recommendation to play R with probability $\frac{1}{2}$. Player I's expected payoff if he follows the recommended strategy of T is therefore $\frac{1}{2} \times 6 + \frac{1}{2} \times 2 = 4$, while his expected payoff if he deviates and plays B is $\frac{1}{2} \times 7 + \frac{1}{2} \times 0 = 3\frac{1}{2}$. In this case, Player I cannot profit by unilaterally deviating from the recommended strategy. If the recommendation to Player I is to play B, then with certainty Player II has received a recommendation to play L. The payoff to Player I in this case is then 7 if he plays the recommended strategy B, and only 6 if he deviates to T. Again, in this case, Player I cannot profit by deviating from the recommended strategy. By symmetry, Player II similarly cannot profit by not following his recommended strategy. It follows that this mechanism induces an equilibrium in the extended game with an outside observer. The expected equilibrium payoff is

$$\tfrac{1}{3}(6,6) + \tfrac{1}{3}(7,2) + \tfrac{1}{3}(2,7) = (5,5), \tag{8.1}$$

which lies outside the convex hull of the three equilibrium payoffs of the original game, $(2,7)$, $(7,2)$, and $(4\frac{2}{3}, 4\frac{2}{3})$. (A quick way to become convinced of this is to notice that the sum of the payoffs in the vector $(5,5)$ is 10, while the sum of the payoffs in the three equilbrium payoffs is either 9 or $9\frac{1}{3}$, both of which are less than 10.)   ◀

Examples 8.1 and 8.3 show that the way to attain high payoffs for both players is to avoid the "worst" payoff $(0,0)$. This cannot be accomplished if the players implement independent mixed strategies; it requires correlating the players' actions. We have made the following assumptions regarding the extended game:

- The game includes an observer, who recommends strategies to the players.
- The observer chooses his recommendations probabilistically, based on a probability distribution that is commonly known to the players.
- The recommendations are private, with each player knowing only the recommendation addressed to him or her.
- The mechanism is common knowledge[1] among the players: each player knows that this mechanism is being used, each player knows that the other players know that this mechanism is being used, each player knows that the other players know that the other players know that this mechanism is being used, and so forth.

As we will see in the formal definition of correlated equilibria in the next section, the fact that the recommendations are privately provided to each player does not exclude the possibility that the recommendations may be public (in which case the recommendations to each player are identical), or that a player can deduce which recommendations the other players have received given the recommendation he has received, as we saw in Example 8.3: in the correlated equilibrium of the game of "Chicken," if Player I receives the recommendation to play B, he can deduce that Player II's recommended strategy is L.

---

1 See Definition 4.9 (page 87). The formal definition of common knowledge is Definition 9.2 on page 332.

8.2 Definition and properties of correlated equilibrium

The concept of correlated equilibrium formally captures the sort of correlation that we saw in Example 8.3. In that example, we added an outside observer to the strategic game G who chooses a pure strategy vector, and recommends that each player play his part in this vector. We will now present the formal definition of this concept. To distinguish between the strategies in the strategic-form game G and the strategies in the game that includes the observer we will call pure strategies in G *actions*.

Let $G = (N, (S_i)_{i \in N}, (u_i)_{i \in N})$ be a strategic-form game, where N is the set of players, S_i is the set of actions of player $i \in N$, and $u_i : S \to \mathbb{R}$ is player i's payoff function, where $S = \times_{i \in N} S_i$ is the set of strategy vectors. For every probability distribution p over the set S, define a game $\Gamma^*(p)$ as follows:

- An outside observer probabilistically chooses an action vector from S, according to the probability distribution p.
- To each player $i \in N$ the observer reveals s_i, but not s_{-i}. In other words, the observer reveals to player i his coordinate in the action vector that was chosen; to be interpreted as the recommended action to play.
- Each player i chooses an action $s_i' \in S_i$ (s_i' may be different from the action revealed by the observer).
- The payoff of each player i is $u_i(s_1', \ldots, s_n')$.

This describes an extensive-form game with information sets.

A presentation of the extensive-form game corresponding to the game of "Chicken," with the addition of the correlation mechanism described above, is shown in Figure 8.5. Near every chance move in the figure, we have noted the respective recommendation of the observer for that choice. The actions T_1 and T_2 in the figure correspond to the action T in the strategic-form game: T_1 represents the possible action T when the observer's recommendation is T; T_2 represents the possible action T when the observer's recommendation is B. Actions B_1 and B_2 similarly correspond to action B, and so forth.

The information revealed by the observer to player i will be termed a *recommendation*: the observer recommends that player i play the action s_i in the original game. The player is not obligated to follow the recommendation he receives, and is free to play a different action (or to use a mixed action, i.e., to conduct a lottery in order to choose between several actions). A player's pure strategy in an extensive-form game with information sets is a function that maps each of that player's information sets to a possible action. Since every information set in the game $\Gamma^*(p)$ is associated with a recommendation of the observer, and the set of possible actions at each information set of player i is S_i, we obtain the following definition of a pure strategy in $\Gamma^*(p)$.

Definition 8.4 *A (pure) strategy of player i in the game $\Gamma^*(p)$ is a function $\tau_i : S_i \to S_i$ mapping every recommendation s_i of the observer to an action $\tau_i(s_i) \in S_i$.*

Suppose the observer has recommended that player i play the action s_i. This fact enables player i to deduce the following regarding the recommendations that the other players have received: since the probability that player i receives recommendation s_i is

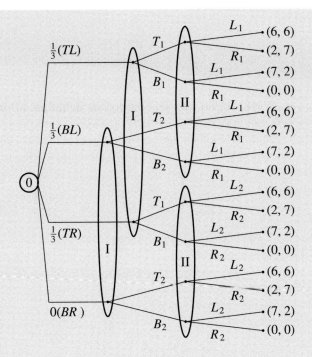

Figure 8.5 The game of "Chicken," for the probability distribution p given in Figure 8.4, in extensive form

$$\sum_{t_{-i} \in S_{-i}} p(s_i, t_{-i}), \tag{8.2}$$

the conditional probability that the observer has chosen the action vector $s = (s_i, s_{-i})$ is

$$p(s_{-i} \mid s_i) = \frac{p(s_i, s_{-i})}{\sum_{t_{-i} \in S_{-i}} p(s_i, t_{-i})}. \tag{8.3}$$

The conditional probability in Equation (8.3) is defined when the denominator is positive, i.e., when the probability that player i receives recommendation s_i is positive. When $\sum_{t_{-i} \in S_{-i}} p(s_i, t_{-i}) = 0$, the probability that player i receives recommendation s_i is zero, and in this case the conditional probability $p(s_{-i} \mid s_i)$ is undefined.

One strategy available to player i is to follow the observer's recommendation. For each player $i \in N$, define a strategy τ_i^* by

$$\tau_i^*(s_i) = s_i, \quad \forall s_i \in S_i. \tag{8.4}$$

Is the pure strategy vector $\tau^* = (\tau_1^*, \ldots, \tau_n^*)$, in which each player i follows the observer's recommendation, an equilibrium? As might be expected, the answer to that question depends on the probability distribution p, as specified in the following theorem.

Theorem 8.5 *The strategy vector τ^* is an equilibrium of the game $\Gamma^*(p)$ if and only if*

$$\sum_{s_{-i}\in S_{-i}} p(s_i, s_{-i})u_i(s_i, s_{-i}) \geq \sum_{s_{-i}\in S_{-i}} p(s_i, s_{-i})u_i(s_i', s_{-i}), \quad \forall i, \forall s_i, s_i' \in S_i. \tag{8.5}$$

Proof: The strategy vector τ^*, in which each player follows the recommendation he receives, is an equilibrium if and only if no player i can profit by deviating to a strategy that differs from his recommendation. Equation (8.3) implies that the payoff that player i has under the action vector τ^*, when his recommended action is s_i, is

$$\sum_{s_{-i}\in S_{-i}} \left(\frac{p(s_i, s_{-i})}{\sum_{t_{-i}\in S_{-i}} p(s_i, t_{-i})} \times u_i(s_i, s_{-i}) \right). \tag{8.6}$$

Suppose player i decides to deviate and play action s_i' instead of s_i, while the other players follow the recommendations (i.e., play τ_{-i}^*). The distribution of the actions of the other players is given by the conditional probability in Equation (8.3), and therefore player i's expected payoff if he deviates to action s_i' is

$$\sum_{s_{-i}\in S_{-i}} \left(\frac{p(s_i, s_{-i})}{\sum_{t_{-i}\in S_{-i}} p(s_i, t_{-i})} \times u_i(s_i', s_{-i}) \right). \tag{8.7}$$

This means that the strategy vector τ^* is an equilibrium if and only if for each player $i \in N$, for each action $s_i \in S_i$ for which $\sum_{s_{-i}\in S_{-i}} p(s_i, s_{-i}) > 0$, and for each action $s_i' \in S_i$:

$$\sum_{s_{-i}\in S_{-i}} \left(\frac{p(s_i, s_{-i})}{\sum_{t_{-i}\in S_{-i}} p(s_i, t_{-i})} \times u_i(s_i, s_{-i}) \right)$$

$$\geq \sum_{s_{-i}\in S_{-i}} \left(\frac{p(s_i, s_{-i})}{\sum_{t_{-i}\in S_{-i}} p(s_i, t_{-i})} \times u_i(s_i', s_{-i}) \right). \tag{8.8}$$

When the denominator of this equation is positive, we can reduce both sides of the inequality to obtain Equation (8.5). When $\sum_{t_{-i}\in S_{-i}} p(s_i, t_{-i}) = 0$, Equation (8.5) holds true with equality: since $(p(s_i, t_{-i}))_{t_{-i}\in S_{-i}}$ are nonnegative numbers, it is necessarily the case that $p(s_i, t_{-i}) = 0$ for each $t_{-i} \in S_{-i}$, and hence both sides of the inequality in Equation (8.5) are identically zero. $\qquad \square$

We can now define the concept of correlated equilibrium.

Definition 8.6 *A probability distribution p over the set of action vectors S is called a correlated equilibrium if the strategy vector τ^* is a Nash equilibrium of the game $\Gamma^*(p)$. In other words, for every player $i \in N$:*

$$\sum_{s_{-i}\in S_{-i}} p(s_i, s_{-i})u_i(s_i, s_{-i}) \geq \sum_{s_{-i}\in S_{-i}} p(s_i, s_{-i})u_i(s_i', s_{-i}), \quad \forall s_i, s_i' \in S_i. \tag{8.9}$$

Every strategy vector σ induces a probability distribution p_σ over the set of action vectors S,

$$p_\sigma(s_1, \ldots, s_n) := \sigma_1(s_1) \times \sigma_2(s_2) \times \cdots \times \sigma_n(s_n). \tag{8.10}$$

Under a Nash equilibrium σ^* the actions that each player chooses with positive probability are only those that give him maximal payoffs given that the other players implement the strategy vector σ^*_{-i},

$$u_i(s_i, \sigma^*_{-i}) \geq u_i(s'_i, \sigma^*_{-i}), \quad \forall s_i \in \mathrm{supp}(\sigma^*_i), \forall s'_i \in S_i. \tag{8.11}$$

This leads to the following theorem (whose proof is left to the reader in Exercise 8.2).

Theorem 8.7 *For every Nash equilibrium σ^*, the probability distribution p_{σ^*} is a correlated equilibrium.*

As Theorem 8.7 indicates, correlated equilibrium is in a sense an extension of the Nash equilibrium concept. When we relate to a Nash equilibrium σ^* as a correlated equilibrium we mean the probability distribution p_{σ^*} given by Equation (8.10). For example, the convex hull of the set of Nash equilibria is the set

$$\mathrm{conv}\{p_{\sigma^*} : \sigma^* \text{ is a Nash equilibrium}\} \subseteq \Delta(S). \tag{8.12}$$

Since every finite normal-form game has a Nash equilibrium, we deduce the following corollary.

Corollary 8.8 *Every finite strategic-form game has a correlated equilibrium.*

Theorem 8.9 *The set of correlated equilibria of a finite game is convex and compact.*

Proof: Recall that a half-space in $\mathbb{R}^m$ is defined by a vector $\alpha \in \mathbb{R}^m$ and a real number $\beta \in \mathbb{R}$, by the following equation:

$$H^+(\alpha, \beta) := \left\{ x \in \mathbb{R}^m : \sum_{i=1}^m \alpha_i x_i \geq \beta \right\}. \tag{8.13}$$

A half-space is a convex and closed set. Equation (8.9) implies that the set of correlated equilibria of a game is given by the intersection of a finite number of half-spaces. Since an intersection of convex and closed spaces is convex and closed, the set of correlated equilibria is convex and closed. Since the set of correlated equilibria is a subset of the set of probability distributions S, it is a bounded set, and so we conclude that it is a convex and compact set. $\square$

Remark 8.10 *A polytope in $\mathbb{R}^d$ is the convex hull of a finite number of points in $\mathbb{R}^d$. The minimal set of points satisfying the condition that the polytope is its convex hull is called the set of extreme points of the polytope. (For the definition of the extreme points of a general set see Definition 24.2 on page 963.) Every bounded set defined by the intersection of a finite number of half-spaces is a polytope, from which it follows that the set of correlated equilibria of a game is a polytope. Since there exist efficient algorithms for finding the extreme points of a polytope (such as the simplex algorithm), it is relatively easy to compute correlated equilibria, in contrast to computing Nash equilibria, which is computationally hard. (See, for example, Gilboa and Zemel [1989].)* ◆

Example 8.1 (*Continued*) Consider again the Battle of the Sexes, which is the two-player game shown in Figure 8.6.

Player II

		F	C
Player I	F	1, 2	0, 0
	C	0, 0	2, 1

Figure 8.6 Battle of the Sexes

We will compute the correlated equilibria of this game. Denote a probability distribution over the action vectors by $p = [\alpha(F,F), \beta(F,C), \gamma(C,F), \delta(C,C)]$. Figure 8.7 depicts this distribution graphically.

Player II

		F	C
Player I	F	α	β
	C	γ	δ

Figure 8.7 Graphic representation of the probability distribution p

For a probability distribution $p = [\alpha(F,F), \beta(F,C), \gamma(C,F), \delta(C,C)]$ to be a correlated equilibrium, the following inequalities must be satisfied (see Equation (8.9)):

$$\alpha u_1(F,F) + \beta u_1(F,C) \geq \alpha u_1(C,F) + \beta u_1(C,C), \tag{8.14}$$

$$\gamma u_1(C,F) + \delta u_1(C,C) \geq \gamma u_1(F,F) + \delta u_1(F,C), \tag{8.15}$$

$$\alpha u_2(F,F) + \gamma u_2(C,F) \geq \alpha u_2(F,C) + \gamma u_2(C,C), \tag{8.16}$$

$$\beta u_2(F,C) + \delta u_2(C,C) \geq \beta u_2(F,F) + \delta u_2(C,F), \tag{8.17}$$

$$\alpha + \beta + \gamma + \delta = 1, \tag{8.18}$$

$$\alpha, \beta, \gamma, \delta \geq 0. \tag{8.19}$$

Entering the values of the game matrix into these equations, we get

$$\alpha \geq 2\beta, 2\delta \geq \gamma, \delta \geq 2\beta, 2\alpha \geq \gamma. \tag{8.20}$$

In other words, both α and δ must be greater than 2γ and $\frac{\beta}{2}$. The set of possible payoffs of the game (the triangle formed by the coordinates $(0,0)$, $(1,2)$, and $(2,1)$) is shown in Figure 8.8, with the game's three Nash equilibrium payoffs $((1,2), (2,1), (\frac{2}{3}, \frac{2}{3}))$ along with the set of correlated equilibrium payoffs (the dark triangle formed by $(1,2)$, $(2,1)$, and $(\frac{2}{3}, \frac{2}{3})$). In this case, the set of correlated equilibrium payoffs is the convex hull of the Nash equilibrium payoffs.

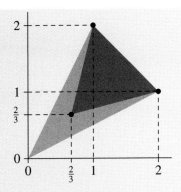

Figure 8.8 The set of possible payoffs, the set of correlated equilibrium payoffs, and the Nash equilibrium payoffs of the game in Figure 8.1

Example 8.3 (*Continued*) The payoff matrix of the game in this example is shown in Figure 8.9.

Player II

		L	R
	T	6, 6	2, 7
Player I	B	7, 2	0, 0

Figure 8.9 The game of "Chicken"

A probability distribution over the set of action vectors is again denoted by $p = [\alpha(T, L), \beta(T, R), \gamma(B, L), \delta(B, R)]$ (see Figure 8.10).

Player II

		L	R
	T	α	β
Player I	B	γ	δ

Figure 8.10 Graphic depiction of the probability distribution p

For the probability distribution p to be a correlated equilibrium (see Equation (8.9)), the following inequalities must be satisfied:

$$6\alpha + 2\beta \geq 7\alpha, \quad 7\gamma \geq 6\gamma + 2\delta, \quad 6\alpha + 2\gamma \geq 7\alpha, \quad 7\beta \geq 6\beta + 2\delta. \qquad (8.21)$$

The equations imply that both β and γ must be greater than 2δ and $\frac{\alpha}{2}$. The set of possible payoffs of the game (the rhombus formed by the coordinates $(0, 0)$, $(7, 2)$, $(2, 7)$, and $(6, 6)$) is shown in Figure 8.11, along with the game's three Nash equilibrium payoffs $((7, 2), (2, 7),$ and $(4\frac{2}{3}, 4\frac{2}{3}))$, with their convex hull (the dark triangle) and the set of correlated equilibrium payoffs (the dark-gray rhombus formed by $(3\frac{3}{5}, 3\frac{3}{5})$, $(7, 2)$, $(2, 7)$, and $(5\frac{1}{4}, 5\frac{1}{4})$).

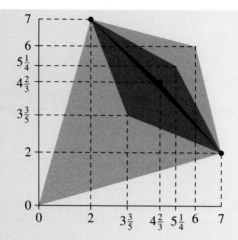

Figure 8.11 The set of possible payoffs (light rhombus), the Nash equilibrium payoffs, the convex hull of the Nash equilibrium payoffs (dark triangle), and the correlated equilibrium payoffs (dark rhombus) of the game in Figure 8.3

Example 8.11 Consider the two-player coordination game depicted in Figure 8.12, which resembles the Battle of the Sexes, but is not symmetric between the players. The game has three equilibria: (T, L), (B, R), and $[\frac{3}{5}(T), \frac{2}{5}(B)], [\frac{2}{3}(L), \frac{1}{3}(R)]$.

Player II

	L	R
T	1, 2	0, 0
B	0, 0	2, 3

Player I, with rows T and B.

Figure 8.12 The payoff matrix of the game in Example 8.11

We will compute the correlated equilibria of the game. For a probability distribution over the set of action vectors $p = [\alpha(T, L), \beta(T, R), \gamma(B, L), \delta(B, R)]$ to be a correlated equilibrium, the following inequalities must be satisfied (see Equation (8.9)):

$$\alpha \geq 2\beta, \tag{8.22}$$

$$2\delta \geq \gamma, \tag{8.23}$$

$$2\alpha \geq 3\gamma, \tag{8.24}$$

$$3\delta \geq 2\beta, \tag{8.25}$$

$$\alpha + \beta + \gamma + \delta = 1, \tag{8.26}$$

$$\alpha, \beta, \gamma, \delta \geq 0. \tag{8.27}$$

Note that the constraint $\alpha + \beta + \gamma + \delta = 1$ implies

$$2\delta \geq \gamma \iff \alpha + \beta + \tfrac{3}{2}\gamma \leq 1, \tag{8.28}$$

$$3\delta \geq 2\beta \iff \alpha + \tfrac{5}{3}\beta + \gamma \leq 1. \tag{8.29}$$

Figure 8.13 shows the sets defined by each of the four inequalities in Equations (8.22)–(8.25), along with the constraints that α, β, and γ be nonnegative, and that $\delta = 1 - \alpha - \beta - \gamma \geq 0$. The intersection of these four sets is the set of correlated equilibria. To find this set, we will seek out its extreme points. The set of all the correlated equilibria is the subset of $\mathbb{R}^3$ defined by the intersection of eight half-spaces (Equations (8.22)–(8.25), along with the constraints that $\alpha \geq 0$, $\beta \geq 0$, $\gamma \geq 0$, and $\alpha + \beta + \gamma \leq 1$). Note that in this case, if $\alpha + \tfrac{5}{3}\beta + \gamma \leq 1$ then $\alpha + \beta + \gamma \leq 1$, and hence there is no need explicitly to require that $\alpha + \beta + \gamma \leq 1$. In addition, if we look at the hyperplanes defining these half-spaces, we notice that three of them intersect at one point (there are $\binom{7}{3} = 35$ such intersection points, some of them identical to each other). Each such intersection point satisfying all the constraints is an extreme point.

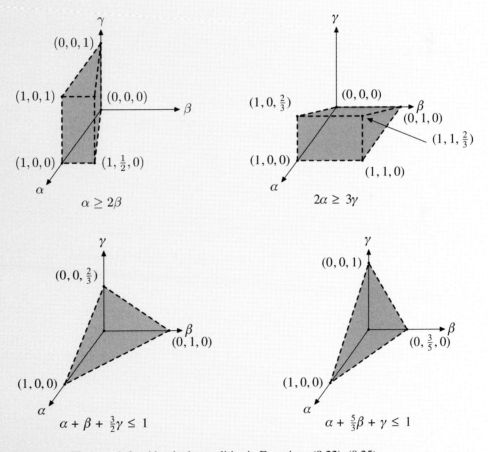

Figure 8.13 The sets defined by the inequalities in Equations (8.22)–(8.25)

A simple, yet tedious, calculation reveals that the set of all the correlated equilibria has five extreme points (recall that $\delta = 1 - \alpha - \beta - \gamma$):

$$(\alpha, \beta, \gamma) = (0, 0, 0), \tag{8.30}$$

$$(\alpha, \beta, \gamma) = (1, 0, 0), \tag{8.31}$$

$$(\alpha, \beta, \gamma) = \left(\tfrac{6}{11}, \tfrac{3}{11}, 0\right), \tag{8.32}$$

$$(\alpha, \beta, \gamma) = \left(\tfrac{1}{2}, 0, \tfrac{1}{3}\right), \tag{8.33}$$

$$(\alpha, \beta, \gamma) = \left(\tfrac{2}{5}, \tfrac{1}{5}, \tfrac{4}{15}\right). \tag{8.34}$$

It follows that the set of all the correlated equilibria is the smallest convex set containing these five points (see Figure 8.14). The three equilibrium points are: (T, L) corresponding to the point $(1, 0, 0)$, (B, R) corresponding to the point $(0, 0, 0)$, and $([\tfrac{3}{5}(T), \tfrac{2}{5}(B)], [\tfrac{2}{3}(L), \tfrac{1}{3}(R)])$ corresponding to the point $(\tfrac{2}{5}, \tfrac{1}{5}, \tfrac{4}{15})$. In general, the Nash equilibria need not correspond to extreme points of the set of correlated equilibria.

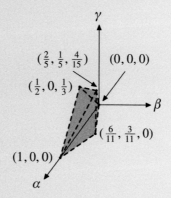

Figure 8.14 The set of correlated equilibria of the game in Example 8.11

8.3 Remarks

This chapter is based on Aumann [1974], a major work in which the concept of correlated equilibrium was developed. The game in Exercise 8.21 was suggested by Yannick Viossat, in response to a question posed by Ehud Lehrer.

8.4 Exercises

8.1 What is the set of possible payoffs of the following game (the Battle of the Sexes game; see Example 8.1 on page 312) if:

(a) the players are permitted to decide, and commit to, the mixed strategies that each player will use;

(b) the players are permitted to make use of a public lottery that chooses a strategy vector and instructs each player which pure strategy to choose.

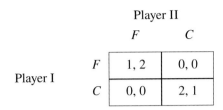

Player II

		F	C
Player I	F	1, 2	0, 0
	C	0, 0	2, 1

8.2 Prove Theorem 8.7 on page 319: for every Nash equilibrium σ^* in a strategic-form game, the probability distribution p_{σ^*} that σ^* induces on the set of action vectors S is a correlated equilibrium.

8.3 The set of all probability distributions p_σ over the set of action vectors S that are induced by Nash equilibria σ is

$$W := \{p_\sigma : \sigma \text{ is a Nash equilibrium}\} \subseteq \Delta(S). \qquad (8.35)$$

Prove that any point in the convex hull of W is a correlated equilibrium.

8.4 Prove that in every correlated equilibrium, the payoff to each player i is at least his maxmin value in mixed strategies:

$$\underline{v}_i = \max_{\sigma_i \in \Sigma_i} \min_{\sigma_{-i} \in \Sigma_{-i}} U_i(\sigma_i, \sigma_{-i}). \qquad (8.36)$$

8.5 Given a strategic-form game $G = (N, (S_i)_{i \in N}, (u_i)_{i \in N})$, write out a linear program whose set of solution vectors is the set of correlated equilibria of the game.

8.6 Let $G = (N, (S_i)_{i \in N}, (u_i)_{i \in N})$ and $\widehat{G} = (N, (S_i)_{i \in N}, (\widehat{u}_i)_{i \in N})$ be strategically equivalent games (see Definition 5.34 on page 173). What is the relation between the set of correlated equilibria of G and the set of correlated equilibria of $\widehat{G}$? What is the relation between the set of correlated equilibrium payoffs of G and the set of correlated equilibrium payoffs of $\widehat{G}$? Justify your answers.

8.7 Let $G = (N, (S_i)_{i \in N}, (u_i)_{i \in N})$ be a game in strategic form, and let $\widehat{G}$ be the game derived from G by a process of iterated elimination of strictly dominated strategies. What is the relation between the set of correlated equilibria of G and the set of correlated equilibria of $\widehat{G}$? Justify your answer.

8.8 Find the correlated equilibrium that maximizes the sum of the players' payoffs in Example 8.1 (page 312), and in Example 8.3 (page 314).

8.9 Find a correlated equilibrium whose expected payoff is $(\frac{40}{9}, \frac{36}{9})$ in the game of "Chicken" (Example 8.3 on page 314).

8.10 In the following game, compute all the Nash equilibria, and find a correlated equilibrium that is not in the convex hull of the Nash equilibria.

Player II

	L	C	R
T	0, 0	2, 4	4, 2
M	4, 2	0, 0	2, 4
B	2, 4	4, 2	0, 0

Player I (rows), with rows T, M, B.

8.11 Repeat Exercise 8.10 for the following game.

Player II

	L	R
T	8, 8	4, 9
B	9, 4	1, 1

Player I (rows T, B).

8.12 In this exercise, we present an extension of the correlated equilibrium concept. Let $G = (N, (S_i)_{i \in N}, (u_i)_{i \in N})$ be a strategic-form game, and $(M_i)_{i \in N}$ be finite sets of messages. For each probability distribution q over the product set $M := \times_{i \in N} M_i$ define a game $\Gamma_M^*(q)$ as follows:

- An outside observer chooses a vector of messages $m = (m_i)_{i \in N} \in M$ probabilistically, using the probability distribution q.
- The observer reveals m_i to player $i \in N$, but not m_{-i}. In other words, the observer reveals to player i his coordinate in the vector of messages that has been chosen.
- Each player i chooses an action $s_i \in S_i$.
- Each player i has payoff $u_i(s_1, \ldots, s_n)$.

This is a generalization of the game $\Gamma^*(p)$, which is $\Gamma_M^*(q)$ for the case $M_i = S_i$ for every player i and $q = p$. Answer the following questions:

(a) What is the set of behavior strategies of player i in the game $\Gamma_M^*(q)$?
(b) Show that every vector of behavior strategies induces a probability distribution over the set of action vectors $S = \times_{i \in N} S_i$.
(c) Prove that at every Nash equilibrium of $\Gamma_M^*(q)$, the probability distribution induced on the set of pure strategy vectors S is a correlated equilibrium.

8.13 Show that there exists a unique correlated equilibrium in the following game, in which $a, b, c, d \in (-\frac{1}{4}, \frac{1}{4})$. Find this correlated equilibrium. What is the limit of the correlated equilibrium payoff as a, b, c, and d approach 0?

Player II

	L	R
T	1, 0	$c, 1 + d$
B	0, 1	$1 + a, b$

Player I

8.14 Let s_i be a strictly dominated action of player i. Is there a correlated equilibrium under which s_i is chosen with positive probability, i.e., $\sum_{s_{-i} \in S_{-i}} p(s_i, s_{-i}) > 0$? Justify your answer.

8.15 Prove that in a two-player zero-sum game, every correlated equilibrium payoff to Player I is the value of the game in mixed strategies.

8.16 In this and the following exercise, we will show that the result of Exercise 8.15 partially obtains for equilibrium strategies. Prove that if p is a correlated equilibrium of a two-player zero-sum game, then for every recommendation s_I that Player I receives with positive probability, the conditional probability $(p(s_{II} \mid s_I))_{s_{II} \in S_{II}}$ is an optimal strategy for Player II. Deduce from this that the marginal distribution of p over the set of actions of each of the players is an optimal strategy for that player.

8.17 In the following two-player zero-sum game, find the value of the game, the optimal strategies of the two players, and the set of correlated equilibria. Does every correlated equilibrium lie in the convex hull of the product distributions that correspond to pairs of optimal strategies?

Player II

	L	C	R
T	0	0	1
M	1	1	0
B	1	1	0

Player I

8.18 Prove that the set-valued function that assigns to every game its set of correlated equilibria is an upper semi-continuous mapping.[2] In other words, let $(G^k)_{k \in \mathbb{N}}$ be a sequence of games $(G^k) = (N, (S_i)_{i \in N}, (u_i^k)_{k \in \mathbb{N}})$, all of which share the same set of players N and the same sets of actions $(S_i)_{i \in N}$. Further suppose that for each player i, the sequence of payoff functions $(u_i^k)_{k \in \mathbb{N}}$ converges to a limit u_i,

$$\lim_{k \to \infty} u_i^k(s) = u_i(s), \quad \forall s \in S. \tag{8.37}$$

....

2 A set-valued function $F : X \to Y$ between two topological spaces is called *upper semi-continuous* if its graph Graph$(F) = \{(x, y) : y \in F(x)\}$ is a closed set in the product space $X \times Y$.

Suppose that for each $k \in \mathbb{N}$ the probability distribution p^k is a correlated equilibrium of G^k, and the sequence $(p^k)_{k \in \mathbb{N}}$ converges to a limit p,

$$\lim_{k \to \infty} p^k(s) = p(s), \quad \forall s \in S. \tag{8.38}$$

Prove that p is a correlated equilibrium of the game $(N, (S_i)_{i \in N}, (u_i)_{i \in N})$.

8.19 A Nash equilibrium $\sigma^* = (\sigma_i^*)_{i \in N}$ is called a *strict equilibrium* if for every player i and every action $s_i \in S_i$ satisfying $\sigma_i^*(s_i) = 0$,

$$u_i(\sigma^*) > u_i(s_i, \sigma_{-i}^*). \tag{8.39}$$

In words, if player i deviates by playing an action that is not in the support of σ_i^* then he loses. A correlated equilibrium p is called a *strict correlated equilibrium* if the strategy vector τ^* is a strict equilibrium in the game $\Gamma^*(p)$.
  Answer the following questions:

(a) Does every game in strategic form have a strict correlated equilibrium? If your answer is yes, provide a proof. If your answer is no, provide a counterexample.
(b) Find all the strict correlated equilibria of the following two-player game.

Player II

		L	R
	T	4, 2	3, 4
Player I	B	5, 1	0, 0

8.20 Harry (Player I) is to choose between the payoff vector $(2, 1)$ and playing the following game, as a row player, against Harriet (Player II), the column player.

Player II

		L	R
	T	0, 0	1, 3
Player I	B	4, 2	0, 0

(a) What are Harry's pure strategies in this game? What are Harriet's?
(b) What are the Nash equilibria of the game?
(c) What is the set of correlated equilibria of the game?

8.21 Let $x_1, x_2, \ldots, x_n$ and $y_1, y_2, \ldots, y_n$ be positive numbers. Consider the two-player strategic game with the following payoff matrix.

Player II

x_1, y_1	$0, 0$	$0, 0$	$\cdots$	$0, y_1$
$0, 0$	x_2, y_2	$0, 0$	$\cdots$	$0, y_2$
$0, 0$	$0, 0$	x_3, y_3	$\cdots$	$0, y_3$
$\cdots$	$\cdots$	$\cdots$	$\cdots$	$\cdots$
$x_1, 0$	$x_2, 0$	$x_3, 0$	$\cdots$	x_n, y_n

Player I (label to the left of the table, on the row of x_3, y_3)

(a) Find the set of Nash equilibria of this game.
(b) Prove that the set of correlated equilibria of this game is the convex hull of the set of Nash equilibria.

8.22 Let A and B be two sets in $\mathbb{R}^2$ satisfying:

- $A \subseteq B$;
- A is a union of a finite number of rectangles;
- B is the convex hull of a finite number of points.

Prove that there is a two-player strategic-form game satisfying the property that its set of Nash equilibrium payoffs is A, and its set of correlated equilibrium payoffs is B.

Hint: Make use of the game in Exercise 8.21, along with Exercise 5.49 in Chapter 5.

8.23 Let x, y, a, b be positive numbers. Consider the two-player strategic-form game with the following payoff matrix, in which Player I chooses a row, and Player II chooses a column.

$x - 1, y + 1$	$0, 0$	$0, 0$	$x + 1, y - 1$	$0, y$
$x + 1, y - 1$	$x - 1, y + 1$	$0, 0$	$0, 0$	$0, y$
$0, 0$	$x + 1, y - 1$	$x - 1, y + 1$	$0, 0$	$0, y$
$0, 0$	$0, 0$	$x + 1, y - 1$	$x - 1, y + 1$	$0, y$
$x, 0$	$x, 0$	$x, 0$	$x, 0$	a, b

(a) Find the set of Nash equilibria of this game.
(b) Find the set of correlated equilibria of this game.

Games with incomplete information and common priors

Chapter summary

In this chapter we study situations in which players do not have complete information on the environment they face. Due to the interactive nature of the game, modeling such situations involves not only the *knowledge* and *beliefs* of the players, but also the whole *hierarchy of knowledge* of each player, that is, knowledge of the knowledge of the other players, knowledge of the knowledge of the other players of the knowledge of other players, and so on. When the players have beliefs (i.e., probability distributions) on the unknown parameters that define the game, we similarly run into the need to consider *infinitel hierarchies of beliefs*. The challenge of the theory was to incorporate these infinite hierarchies of knowledge and beliefs in a workable model.

We start by presenting the Aumann model of incomplete information, which models the knowledge of the players regarding the payoff-relevant parameters in the situation that they face. We define the *knowledge operator*, the concept of *common knowledge*, and characterize the collection of events that are common knowledge among the players.

We then add to the model the notion of belief and prove Aumann's agreement theorem: it cannot be common knowledge among the players that they disagree about the probability of a certain event.

An equivalent model to the Aumann model of incomplete information is a *Harsanyi game with incomplete information*. After presenting the game, we define two notions of equilibrium: the Nash equilibrium corresponding to the *ex ante* stage, before players receive information on the game they face, and the Bayesian equilibrium corresponding to the *interim* stage, after the players have received information. We prove that in a Harsanyi game these two concepts are equivalent.

Finally, using games with incomplete information, we present Harsanyi's interpretation of mixed strategies.

As we have seen, a very large number of real-life situations can be modeled and analyzed using extensive-form and strategic-form games. Yet, as Example 9.1 shows, there are situations that cannot be modeled using those tools alone.

Example 9.1 Consider the Matching Pennies game, which is depicted in Figure 9.1 in both extensive form and strategic form.

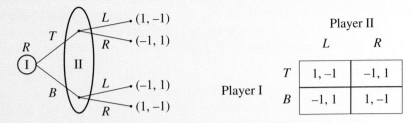

Figure 9.1 The game of Matching Pennies, in extensive form and strategic form

Suppose that Player I knows that he is playing Matching Pennies, but believes that Player II does not know that the pure strategy R is available to her. In other words, Player I believes that Player II is convinced that she has only one pure strategy, L. Suppose further that Player II does in fact know that she (Player II) is playing Matching Pennies, with both pure strategies available. How can we model this game? Neither the extensive-form nor the strategic-form descriptions of the game enable us to model such a state of players' knowledge and beliefs. If we try to analyze this situation using only the depictions of the game appearing in Figure 9.1, we will not be able to predict how the players will play, or recommend an optimal course of action.

For example, as we showed on page 52, the optimal strategy of Player I playing Matching Pennies is the mixed strategy $[\frac{1}{2}(T), \frac{1}{2}(B)]$. But in the situation we have just described, Player I believes that Player II will play L, so that his best reply is the pure strategy T.

Note that Player I's optimal strategy depends only on how he perceives the game: what he knows about the game and what he believes Player II knows about the game. The way that Player II really perceives the game (which is not necessarily known to Player I) has no effect on the strategy chosen by Player I.

Consider next a slightly more complicated situation, in which Player I knows that he is playing Matching Pennies, he believes that Player II knows that she is playing Matching Pennies, and he believes that Player II believes that Player I does not know that the pure strategy B is available to him. Then Player I will believe that Player II believes that Player I will play strategy T, and he will therefore conclude that Player II will select strategy R, and Player I's best strategy will therefore be B.

A similar situation obtains if there is incomplete information regarding some of the payoffs. For example, suppose that Player I knows that his payoff under the strategy profile (T, L) is 5 rather than 1, but believes that Player II does not know this, and that she thinks the payoff is 1. How should Player I play in this situation? Or consider an even more complicated situation, in which both Player I and Player II know that Player I's payoff under (T, L) is 5, but Player II believes Player I does not know that she (Player II) knows this; Player II believes Player I believes Player II thinks the payoff is 1. ◀

Situations like those described in Example 9.1, in which players do not necessarily know which game is being played, or are uncertain about whether the other players know which game is being played, or are uncertain whether the other players know whether the other players know which game is being played, and so on, are called situations of "incomplete information." In this chapter we study such situations, and see how they can be modeled and analyzed as games.

Notice that neither of the situations described in Example 9.1 is well defined, as we have not precisely defined what the players know. For example, in the second case we did not specify what Player I knows about what Player II knows about what Player I knows about what Player II knows, and we did not touch upon what Player II knows. Consideration of hierarchies of levels of knowledge leads to the concept of common knowledge, which we touched upon in Section 4.5 (page 87). An informal definition of common knowledge is:

Definition 9.2 *A fact F is* common knowledge *among the players of a game if all the players know F, all the players know that all the players know F, all the players know that all the players know that all the players know F, and so on (for every finite number of levels).*[1]

Definition 9.2 is incomplete, because we have not yet defined what we mean by a "fact," nor have we defined the significance of the expression "knowing a fact." These concepts will be modeled formally later in this chapter, but for now we will continue with an informal exposition.

So far we have seen that in situations involving several players, incomplete knowledge of the game that is being played leads us to consider infinite hierarchies of knowledge. In decision-making situations with incomplete information, describing the information that decision makers have usually cannot be captured by labeling a given fact as "known" or "unknown." Decision makers often have assessments or beliefs about the truthfulness of various facts. For example, when a person takes out a variable-rate loan he never has precise knowledge of the future fluctuations of the interest rate (which can significantly affect the total amount of loan repayment), but he may have certain beliefs about future rates, such as "I assign probability 0.7 to the event that there will be lower interest rates over the term of the loan." To take another example, a company bidding for oil exploration rights in a certain geographical location has beliefs about the amount of oil likely to be found there and the depth of drilling required (which affects costs and therefore expected profits). A trial jury passing judgment on a defendant expresses certain collective beliefs about the question: is the defendant guilty as charged? For our purposes in this chapter, the source of such probabilistic assessments is of no importance. The assessments may be based on "objective" measurements such as geological surveys (as in the oil exploration example), on impressions (as in the case of a jury deliberating the judgment it will render in a trial), or on personal hunches and information published in the media (as in the example of the variable-rate loan). Thus, probability assessments may be objective or subjective.[2] In our models, a decision maker's beliefs will be expressed by a probability distribution function over the possible values of parameters unknown to him.

---

1 A simple example of a fact that is common knowledge is a *public* event: when a teacher is standing before a class, that fact is common knowledge among the students, because every student knows that every student knows ... that the teacher is standing before the class.

2 A formal model for deriving an individual's subjective probability from his preferences was first put forward by Savage [1954], and later by Anscombe and Aumann [1963] (see also Section 2.8 on page 26).

The most widely accepted statistical approach for dealing with decision problems in situations of incomplete information is the *Bayesian approach*.[3] In the Bayesian approach, every decision maker has a probability distribution over parameters that are unknown to him, and he chooses his actions based on his beliefs as expressed by that distribution. When several decision makers (or players) interact, knowing the probability distribution (beliefs) of each individual decision maker is insufficient: we also need to know what each one's beliefs are about the beliefs of the other decision makers, what they believe about his beliefs about the others' beliefs, and so on. This point is illustrated by the following example.

Example 9.1 (*Continued*) Returning to the Matching Pennies example, suppose that Player I attributes probability p_1 to the event: "Player II knows that R is a possible action." The action that Player I will choose clearly depends on p_1, because the entire situation hinges on the value of p_1: if $p_1 = 1$, Player I believes that Player II knows that R is an action available to her, and if $p_1 = 0$, he believes that Player II does not know that R is possible at all. If $0 < p_1 < 1$, Player I believes that it is possible that Player II knows that R is an available strategy. But the action chosen by Player I also depends on his beliefs about the beliefs of Player II: because Player I's action depends on p_1, it follows that Player II's action depends on her beliefs about p_1, namely, on her beliefs about Player I's beliefs. By the same reasoning, Player I's action depends on his beliefs about Player II's beliefs about his own beliefs, p_1. As in the case of hierarchy of knowledge, we see that determining the best course of action of a Player requires considering an infinite hierarchy of beliefs.   ◄

Adding beliefs to our model is a natural step, but it leads us to an infinite hierarchy of beliefs. The concepts of knowledge and of beliefs are closely intertwined in games of incomplete information. For didactic reasons, however, we will treat the two notions separately, considering first hierarchies of knowledge and then hierarchies of beliefs.

9.1 The Aumann model of incomplete information and the concept of knowledge

In this section we will provide a formal definition of the concept of "knowledge," and then construct hierarchies of knowledge: what each player knows about what the other players know. We will start with an example to illustrate the basic elements of the model.

Example 9.3 Assume that racing cars are produced in three possible colors: gold, red, and purple. Color-blind individuals cannot distinguish between red and gold. Everyone knows that John is color-blind, but no one except Paul knows whether or not Paul is color-blind too. John and Paul are standing side by side viewing a photograph of the racing car that has just won first prize in the Grand Prix, and asking themselves what color it is. The parameter that is of interest in this example is the color of the car, which will later be called the *state of nature*, and we wish to describe the knowledge that the players possess regarding this parameter.

If the color of the car is purple, then both color-blind and non-color-blind individuals know that fact, so that both John and Paul know that the car is purple, and each of them knows that the other knows that the car is purple. If, however, the car is red or gold, then John knows that it is either

---

3 The Bayesian approach is named after Thomas Bayes, 1702–1761, a British clergyman and mathematician who formulated a special case of the rule now known as Bayes' rule.

red or gold. As he does not know whether or not Paul is color-blind, he does not know whether Paul knows the exact color of the car. Because Paul knows that John is color-blind, if the car is red or gold he knows that John does not know what the precise color is, and John knows that Paul knows this.

We therefore need to consider six distinct possibilities (three possibilities per car color times two possibilities regarding whether or not Paul is color-blind):

- The car is purple and Paul is not color-blind. John and Paul both know that the car is purple, they each know that the other knows that the car is purple, and so on.
- The car is purple and Paul is color-blind. Here, too, John and Paul both know that the car is purple, they each know that the other knows that the car is purple, and so on.
- The car is red and Paul is not color-blind. Paul knows the car is red; John knows that the car is red or gold; John does not know whether or not Paul knows the color of the car.
- The car is gold and Paul is not color-blind. Paul knows the car is gold; John knows that the car is red or gold; John does not know whether or not Paul knows the color of the car.
- The car is red and Paul is color-blind. Paul and John know that the car is red or gold; John does not know whether or not Paul knows the color of the car.
- The car is gold and Paul is color-blind. Paul and John know that the car is red or gold; John does not know whether or not Paul knows the color of the car.

In each of these possibilities, both John and Paul clearly know more than we have explicitly written above. For example, in the latter four situations, Paul knows that John does not know whether Paul knows the color of the car. Each of the six cases is associated with what will be defined below as a *state of the world*, which is a description of a state of nature (in this case, the color of the car) and the state of knowledge of the players. Note that the first two cases describe the same state of the world, because the difference between them (Paul's color-blindness) affects neither the color of the car, which is the parameter that is of interest to us, nor the knowledge of the players regarding the color of the car.　◀

The definition of the set of states of nature depends on the situation that we are analyzing. In Example 9.3 the color of the car was the focus of our interest – perhaps, for example, because a bet has been made regarding the color. Since the most relevant parameters in a game are the payoffs, in general we will want the states of nature to describe all the parameters that affect the payoffs of the players (these are therefore also called "payoff-relevant parameters"). For instance, if in Example 9.3 we were in a situation in which Paul's color-blindness (or lack thereof) were to affect his utility, then color-blindness would be a payoff-relevant parameter and would comprise a part of the description of the state of nature. In such a model there would be six distinct states of nature, rather than three.

Definition 9.4 *Let S be a finite set of states of nature. An* Aumann model of incomplete information *(over the set S of states of nature) consists of four components* $(N, Y, (\mathcal{F}_i)_{i \in N}, \mathfrak{s})$, *where:*

- *N is a finite set of players;*
- *Y is a finite set of elements called* states of the world;[4]

---

4 We will later examine the case where Y is infinite, and show that some of the results obtained in this chapter also hold in that case.

- $\mathcal{F}_i$ is a partition of Y, for each $i \in N$ (i.e., a collection of disjoint nonempty subsets of Y whose union is Y);
- $\mathfrak{s} : Y \to S$ is a function associating each state of the world with a state of nature.

The interpretation is that if the "true" state of the world is ω_*, then each player $i \in N$ knows only the element of his partition $\mathcal{F}_i$ that contains ω_*. For example, if $Y = \{\omega_1, \omega_2, \omega_3\}$ and $\mathcal{F}_i = \{\{\omega_1, \omega_2\}, \{\omega_3\}\}$, then player i cannot distinguish between ω_1 and ω_2. In other words, if the state of the world is ω_1, player i knows that the state of the world is either ω_1 or ω_2, and therefore knows that the state of the world is not ω_3. For this reason, the partition $\mathcal{F}_i$ is also called the *information* of player i. The element of the partition $\mathcal{F}_i$ that contains the state of the world ω is denoted $F_i(\omega)$. For convenience, we will use the expression "the information of player i" to refer both to the partition $\mathcal{F}_i$ and to the partition element $F_i(\omega_*)$ containing the true state of the world.

Definition 9.5 *An* Aumann situation of incomplete information *over a set of states of nature S is a quintuple $(N, Y, (\mathcal{F}_i)_{i \in N}, \mathfrak{s}, \omega_*)$, where $(N, Y, (\mathcal{F}_i)_{i \in N}, \mathfrak{s})$ is an Aumann model of incomplete information and $\omega_* \in Y$.*

The state ω_* is the "true state of the world" and each player knows the partition element $F_i(\omega_*)$ in his information partition that contains the true state. A situation of incomplete information describes a knowledge structure at a particular state of the world, i.e., in a particular reality. Models of incomplete information, in contrast, enable us to analyze all possible situations.

Example 9.3 (*Continued*) An Aumann model of incomplete information for this example is as follows:

- $N = \{\text{John}, \text{Paul}\}$.
- $S = \{\text{Purple Car}, \text{Red Car}, \text{Gold Car}\}$.
- $Y = \{\omega_{g,1}, \omega_{r,1}, \omega_{g,2}, \omega_{r,2}, \omega_p\}$.
- John's partition is $\mathcal{F}_J = \{\{\omega_{g,1}, \omega_{g,2}, \omega_{r,1}, \omega_{r,2}\}, \{\omega_p\}\}$.
- Paul's partition is $\mathcal{F}_P = \{\{\omega_{g,1}, \omega_{r,1}\}, \{\omega_{g,2}\}, \{\omega_{r,2}\}, \{\omega_p\}\}$.
- The function $\mathfrak{s}$ is defined by

$$\mathfrak{s}(\omega_{g,1}) = \mathfrak{s}(\omega_{g,2}) = \text{Gold Car}, \qquad \mathfrak{s}(\omega_{r,1}) = \mathfrak{s}(\omega_{r,2}) = \text{Red Car}, \qquad \mathfrak{s}(\omega_p) = \text{Purple Car}.$$

The state of the world ω_p is associated with the situation in which the car is purple, in which case both John and Paul know that it is purple, and each of them knows that the other knows that the car is purple. It represents the two situations in the two first bullets on page 334, which differ only in whether Paul is color-blind or not. As we said before, these two situations are equivalent, and can be represented by the same state of the world, as long as Paul's color-blindness is not payoff relevant, and hence is not part of the description of the state of nature. The state of the world $\omega_{g,1}$ is associated with the situation in which the car is gold and Paul is color-blind, while the state of the world $\omega_{r,1}$ is associated with the situation in which the car is red and Paul is color-blind; in both these situations, Paul cannot distinguish which state of the world holds, because he is color-blind and cannot tell red from gold. The state of the world $\omega_{g,2}$ is associated with the situation in which the car is gold and Paul is not color-blind, while the state of the world $\omega_{r,2}$ is associated with the situation in which the car is red and Paul is not color-blind; in both these cases Paul knows the true color of the car. Therefore, $F_P(\omega_{g,2}) = \{\omega_{g,2}\}$, and $F_P(\omega_{g,1}) = \{\omega_{g,1}, \omega_{r,1}\}$.

As for John, he is both color-blind and does not know whether Paul is color-blind. He therefore cannot distinguish between the four states of the world $\{\omega_{g,1}, \omega_{r,1}, \omega_{g,2}, \omega_{r,2}\}$, so that $F_J(\omega_{g,1}) = F_J(\omega_{g,2}) = F_J(\omega_{r,1}) = F_J(\omega_{r,2}) = \{\omega_{g,1}, \omega_{r,1}, \omega_{g,2}, \omega_{r,2}\}$.

The true state of the world is one of the possible states in the set Y. The Aumann model along with the true state of the world describes the actual situation faced by John and Paul.   ◀

Definition 9.6 *An* event *is a subset of Y.*

In Example 9.3 the event $\{\omega_{g,1}, \omega_{g,2}\}$ is the formal expression of the sentence "the car is gold," while the event $\{\omega_{g,1}, \omega_{g,2}, \omega_p\}$ is the formal expression of the sentence "the car is either gold or purple."

We say that an event A *obtains* in a state of the world ω if $\omega \in A$. It follows that if event A obtains in a state of the world ω and if $A \subseteq B$, then event B obtains in ω.

Definition 9.7 *Let $(N, Y, (\mathcal{F}_i)_{i \in N}, \mathfrak{s})$ be an Aumann model of incomplete information, let i be a player, let $\omega \in Y$ be a state of the world, and let $A \subseteq Y$ be an event. Player i knows A in ω if*

$$F_i(\omega) \subseteq A. \tag{9.1}$$

If $F_i(\omega) \subseteq A$, then in state of the world ω player i knows that event A obtains (even though he may not know that the state of the world is ω), because according to his information, all the possible states of the world, $F_i(\omega)$, are included in the event A.

Definition 9.8 *Let $(N, Y, (\mathcal{F}_i)_{i \in N}, \mathfrak{s})$ be an Aumann model of incomplete information, let i be a player, and let $A \subseteq Y$ be an event. Define an operator $K_i : 2^Y \to 2^Y$ by*[5]

$$K_i(A) := \{\omega \in Y : F_i(\omega) \subseteq A\}. \tag{9.2}$$

We will often denote $K_i(A)$, the set of all states of the world in which player i knows event A, by K_iA. Thus, player i knows event A in state of the world ω_* if and only if $\omega_* \in K_iA$. The definition implies that the set K_iA equals the union of all the elements in the partition $\mathcal{F}_i$ contained in A. The event $K_j(K_iA)$ (which we will write as K_jK_iA for short) is the event that player j knows that player i knows A:

$$K_jK_iA = \{\omega \in Y : F_j(\omega) \subseteq K_iA\}. \tag{9.3}$$

Example 9.3 *(Continued)* Denote $A = \{\omega_p\}$, $B = \{\omega_{r,2}\}$, and $C = \{\omega_{r,1}, \omega_{r,2}\}$. Then

$$K_JA = \{\omega_p\} = A, \qquad K_JB = \emptyset, \qquad K_JC = \emptyset,$$
$$K_PA = \{\omega_p\} = A, \qquad K_PB = \{\omega_{r,2}\}, \qquad K_PC = \{\omega_{r,2}\}.$$

The content of the expression $K_PB = \{\omega_{r,2}\}$ is that only in state of the world $\omega_{r,2}$ does Paul know that event B obtains (meaning that only in that state of the world does he know that the car is red). The content of $K_JB = \emptyset$ is that there is no state of the world in which John knows that B obtains; i.e., he never knows that the car is red and that Paul is not color-blind. From this we conclude that

$$K_JK_PC = K_JB = \emptyset. \tag{9.4}$$

---

5 The collection of all subsets of Y is denoted by 2^Y.

This means that there is no state of the world in which John knows that Paul knows that the car is red. In contrast, $\omega_p \in K_P K_J A$, which means that in state of the world ω_p Paul knows that John knows that the state of the world is ω_p (and in particular, that the car is purple). ◀

We can now present some simple results that follow from the above definition of knowledge. The first result states that if a player knows event A in state of the world ω, then it is necessarily true that $\omega \in A$. In other words, if a player knows the event A, then A necessarily obtains (because the true state of the world is contained within it).[6]

Theorem 9.9 $K_i A \subseteq A$ for every event $A \subseteq Y$ and every player $i \in N$.

Proof: Let $\omega \in K_i A$. From the definition of knowledge it follows that $F_i(\omega) \subseteq A$. Since $\omega \in F_i(\omega)$ it follows that $\omega \in A$, which is what we needed to prove. □

Our second result states that if event A is contained in event B, then the states of the world in which player i knows event A form a subset of the states of the world in which the player knows event B. In other words, in every state of the world in which a player knows event A, he also knows event B.

Theorem 9.10 For every pair of events $A, B \subseteq Y$, and every player $i \in N$,

$$A \subseteq B \implies K_i A \subseteq K_i B. \tag{9.5}$$

Proof: We will show that $\omega \in K_i A$ implies that $\omega \in K_i B$. Suppose that $\omega \in K_i A$. By definition, $F_i(\omega) \subseteq A$, and because $A \subseteq B$, one has $F_i(\omega) \subseteq B$. Therefore, $\omega \in K_i B$, which is what we need to show. □

Our third result[7] says that if a player knows event A, then he knows that he knows event A, and conversely, if he knows that he knows event A, then he knows event A.

Theorem 9.11 For every event $A \subseteq Y$ and every player $i \in N$, we have $K_i K_i A = K_i A$.

Proof: Theorems 9.9 and 9.10 imply that $K_i K_i A \subseteq K_i A$. We will show that the opposite inclusion holds, namely, if $\omega \in K_i A$ then $\omega \in K_i K_i A$. If $\omega \in K_i A$ then $F_i(\omega) \subseteq A$. Therefore, for every $\omega' \in F_i(\omega)$, we have $\omega' \in F_i(\omega') = F_i(\omega) \subseteq A$. It follows that $\omega' \in K_i A$. As this is true for every $\omega' \in F_i(\omega)$, we deduce that $F_i(\omega) \subseteq K_i A$, which implies that $\omega \in K_i K_i A$. Thus, $K_i A \subseteq K_i K_i A$, which is what we wanted to prove. □

More generally, the knowledge operator K_i of player i satisfies the following five properties, which collectively are called *Kripke's S5 system*:

1. $K_i Y = Y$: the player knows that Y is the set of all states of the world.
2. $K_i A \cap K_i B = K_i(A \cap B)$: if the player knows event A and knows event B then he knows event $A \cap B$.
3. $K_i A \subseteq A$: if the player knows event A then event A obtains.

....

6 In the literature, this is known as the "axiom of knowledge."
7 One part of this theorem, namely, the fact that if a player knows an event, then he knows that he knows the event, is known in the literature as the "axiom of positive introspection."

4. $K_i K_i A = K_i A$: if the player knows event A then he knows that he knows event A, and vice versa.

5. $(K_i A)^c = K_i((K_i A)^c)$: if the player does not know event A, then he knows that he does not know event A, and vice versa.[8,9]

Property 3 was proved in Theorem 9.9. Property 4 was proved in Theorem 9.11. The proof that the knowledge operator satisfies the other three properties is left to the reader (Exercise 9.1). In fact, Properties 1–5 characterize knowledge operators: for every operator $K : 2^Y \to 2^Y$ satisfying these properties there exists a partition $\mathcal{F}$ of Y that induces K via Equation (9.2) (Exercise 9.2).

Example 9.12 Anthony, Betty, and Carol are each wearing a hat. Hats may be red (r) or blue (b). Each one of the three sees the hats worn by the other two, but cannot see his or her own hat, and therefore does not know its color. This situation can be described by an Aumann model of incomplete information as follows:

- The set of players is $N = \{\text{Anthony}, \text{Betty}, \text{Carol}\}$.
- The set of states of nature is
  $S = \{(r,r,r), (r,r,b), (r,b,r), (r,b,b), (b,r,r), (b,r,b), (b,b,r), (b,b,b)\}$. A state of nature is described by three hat colors: that of Anthony's hat (the left letter), of Betty's hat (the middle letter), and of Carol's hat (the right letter).
- The set of states of the world is
  $Y = \{\omega_{rrr}, \omega_{rrb}, \omega_{rbr}, \omega_{rbb}, \omega_{brr}, \omega_{brb}, \omega_{bbr}, \omega_{bbb}\}$.
- The function $\mathfrak{s} : Y \to S$ that maps every state of the world to a state of nature is defined by

$$\mathfrak{s}(\omega_{rrr}) = (r,r,r), \quad \mathfrak{s}(\omega_{rrb}) = (r,r,b), \quad \mathfrak{s}(\omega_{rbr}) = (r,b,r), \quad \mathfrak{s}(\omega_{rbb}) = (r,b,b),$$
$$\mathfrak{s}(\omega_{brr}) = (b,r,r), \quad \mathfrak{s}(\omega_{brb}) = (b,r,b), \quad \mathfrak{s}(\omega_{bbr}) = (b,b,r), \quad \mathfrak{s}(\omega_{bbb}) = (b,b,b).$$

The information partitions of Anthony, Betty, and Carol are as follows:

$$\mathcal{F}_A = \{\{\omega_{rrr}, \omega_{brr}\}, \{\omega_{rrb}, \omega_{brb}\}, \{\omega_{rbr}, \omega_{bbr}\}, \{\omega_{rbb}, \omega_{bbb}\}\}, \tag{9.6}$$

$$\mathcal{F}_B = \{\{\omega_{rrr}, \omega_{rbr}\}, \{\omega_{rrb}, \omega_{rbb}\}, \{\omega_{brr}, \omega_{bbr}\}, \{\omega_{brb}, \omega_{bbb}\}\}, \tag{9.7}$$

$$\mathcal{F}_C = \{\{\omega_{rrr}, \omega_{rrb}\}, \{\omega_{rbr}, \omega_{rbb}\}, \{\omega_{brr}, \omega_{brb}\}, \{\omega_{bbr}, \omega_{bbb}\}\}. \tag{9.8}$$

For example, when the state of the world is ω_{brb}, Anthony sees that Betty is wearing a red hat and that Carol is wearing a blue hat, but does not know whether his hat is red or blue, so that he knows that the state of the world is in the set $\{\omega_{rrb}, \omega_{brb}\}$, which is one of the elements of his partition $\mathcal{F}_A$. Similarly, if the state of the world is ω_{brb}, Betty knows that the state of the world is in her partition element $\{\omega_{brb}, \omega_{bbb}\}$, and Carol knows that the state of the world is in her partition element $\{\omega_{brr}, \omega_{brb}\}$.

Let R be the event "there is at least one red hat," that is,

$$R = \{\omega_{rrr}, \omega_{rrb}, \omega_{rbr}, \omega_{rbb}, \omega_{brr}, \omega_{brb}, \omega_{bbr}\}. \tag{9.9}$$

In which states of the world does Anthony know R? In which states does Betty know that Anthony knows R? In which states does Carol know that Betty knows that Anthony knows R? To begin answering the first question, note that in state of the world ω_{rrr}, Anthony knows R, because

$$F_A(\omega_{rrr}) = \{\omega_{rrr}, \omega_{brr}\} \subseteq R. \tag{9.10}$$

---

8 The first part of this property, i.e., the fact that if a player does not know an event, then he knows that he does not know it, is known in the literature as the "axiom of negative introspection."

9 For any event A, the complement of A is denoted by $A^c := Y \backslash A$.

Anthony also knows R in each of the states of the world ω_{rrb}, ω_{rbr}, ω_{brb}, ω_{brr}, and ω_{bbr}. In contrast, in the states ω_{rbb} and ω_{bbb} he does not know R, because

$$F_A(\omega_{rbb}) = F_A(\omega_{bbb}) = \{\omega_{rbb}, \omega_{bbb}\} \nsubseteq R. \tag{9.11}$$

In summary,

$$K_A R = \{\omega \in Y : F_A(\omega) \subseteq R\} = \{\omega_{rrr}, \omega_{rbr}, \omega_{rrb}, \omega_{brb}, \omega_{brr}, \omega_{bbr}\}.$$

The analysis here is quite intuitive: Anthony knows R if either Betty or Carol (or both) is wearing a red hat, which occurs in the states of the world in the set $\{\omega_{rrr}, \omega_{rbr}, \omega_{rrb}, \omega_{brb}, \omega_{brr}, \omega_{bbr}\}$. When does Betty know that Anthony knows R? This requires calculating $K_B K_A R$:

$$K_B K_A R = \{\omega \in Y : F_B(\omega) \subseteq K_A R\}$$

$$= \{\omega \in Y : F_B(\omega) \subseteq \{\omega_{rrr}, \omega_{rbr}, \omega_{rrb}, \omega_{brb}, \omega_{brr}, \omega_{bbr}\}\}$$

$$= \{\omega_{rrr}, \omega_{brr}, \omega_{rbr}, \omega_{bbr}\}. \tag{9.12}$$

For example, since $F_B(\omega_{rbr}) = \{\omega_{rbr}, \omega_{rrr}\} \subseteq K_A R$ we conclude that $\omega_{rbr} \in K_B K_A R$. On the other hand, since $F_B(\omega_{brb}) = \{\omega_{brb}, \omega_{bbb}\} \nsubseteq K_A R$, it follows that $\omega_{brb} \notin K_B K_A R$. The analysis here is once again intuitively clear: Betty knows that Anthony knows R only if Carol is wearing a red hat, which only occurs in the states of the world $\{\omega_{rrr}, \omega_{brr}, \omega_{rbr}, \omega_{bbr}\}$.

Finally, we answer the third question: when does Carol know that Betty knows that Anthony knows R? This requires calculating $K_C K_B K_A R$:

$$K_C K_B K_A R = \{\omega \in Y : F_C(\omega) \subseteq K_B K_A R\}$$

$$= \{\omega \in Y : F_C(\omega) \subseteq \{\omega_{rrr}, \omega_{brr}, \omega_{rbr}, \omega_{bbr}\}\} = \emptyset. \tag{9.13}$$

For example, since $F_C(\omega_{rbr}) = \{\omega_{rbr}, \omega_{rbb}\} \nsubseteq K_B K_A R$, we conclude that $\omega_{rbr} \notin K_C K_B K_A R$. In other words, there is no state of the world in which Carol knows that Betty knows that Anthony knows R. This is true intuitively, because as we saw previously, Betty knows that Anthony knows R only if Carol is wearing a red hat, but Carol does not know the color of her own hat.

This analysis enables us to conclude, for example, that in state of the world ω_{rrr} Anthony knows R, Betty knows that Anthony knows R, but Carol does not know that Betty knows that Anthony knows R. ◄

Note the distinction in Example 9.12 between states of nature and states of the world. The state of nature is the parameter with respect to which there is incomplete information: the colors of the hats worn by the three players. The state of the world includes in addition the mutual knowledge structure of the players regarding the state of nature. For example, the state of the world ω_{rrr} says a lot more than the fact that all three players are wearing red hats; for example, in this state of the world Carol knows there is at least one red hat, Carol knows that Anthony knows that there is at least one red hat, and Carol does not know that Betty knows that Anthony knows that there is at least one red hat. In Example 9.12 there is a one-to-one correspondence between the set of states of nature S and the set of states of the world Y. This is so since the mutual knowledge structure is uniquely determined by the configuration of the colors of the hats.

Example 9.13 Arthur, Harry, and Tom are in a room with two windows, one facing north and the other facing south. Two hats, one yellow and one brown, are placed on a table in the center of the room. After Harry and Tom leave the room, Arthur selects one of the hats and places it on his head. Tom and Harry peek in, each through a different window, watching Arthur (so that they both know the color of the hat Arthur is wearing). Neither Tom nor Harry knows whether or not the other player who has left the room is peeking through a window, and Arthur has no idea whether or not Tom or Harry is spying on him as he places one of the hats on his head. An Aumann model of incomplete information describing this situation is as follows:

- $N = \{\text{Arthur, Harry, Tom}\}$.
- $S = \{\text{Arthur wears the brown hat, Arthur wears the yellow hat}\}$.
- There are eight states of the world, each of which is designated by two indices:
  $Y = \{\omega_{b,\emptyset}, \omega_{b,T}, \omega_{b,H}, \omega_{b,TH}, \omega_{y,\emptyset}, \omega_{y,T}, \omega_{y,H}, \omega_{y,TH}\}$. The left index of ω indicates the color of the hat that Arthur is wearing (which is either brown or yellow), and the right index indicates which of the other players has been peeking into the room (Tom (T), Harry (H), both (TH), or neither ($\emptyset$)).
- Arthur's partition contains two elements, because he knows the color of the hat on his head, but does not know who is peeking into the room: $\mathcal{F}_A = \{\{\omega_{b,\emptyset}, \omega_{b,H}, \omega_{b,T}, \omega_{b,TH}\}, \{\omega_{y,\emptyset}, \omega_{y,H}, \omega_{y,I}, \omega_{y,TH}\}\}$.
- Tom's partition contains three elements, one for each of his possible situations of information: Tom has not peeked into the room; Tom has peeked into the room and seen Arthur wearing the brown hat; Tom has peeked into the room and seen Arthur wearing the yellow hat. His partition is thus $\mathcal{F}_T = \{\{\omega_{b,\emptyset}, \omega_{b,H}, \omega_{y,\emptyset}, \omega_{y,H}\}, \{\omega_{b,T}, \omega_{b,TH}\}, \{\omega_{y,T}, \omega_{y,TH}\}\}$.

  For example, if Tom has peeked and seen the brown hat on Arthur's head, he knows that Arthur has selected the brown hat, but he does not know whether he is the only player who peeked (corresponding to the state of the world $\omega_{b,T}$) or whether Harry has also peeked (state of the world $\omega_{b,TH}$).
- Similarly, Harry's partition is
  $\mathcal{F}_H = \{\{\omega_{b,\emptyset}, \omega_{b,T}, \omega_{y,\emptyset}, \omega_{y,T}\}, \{\omega_{b,H}, \omega_{b,TH}\}, \{\omega_{y,H}, \omega_{y,TH}\}\}$.
- The function $\mathfrak{s}$ is defined by

$$\mathfrak{s}(\omega_{b,\emptyset}) = \mathfrak{s}(\omega_{b,T}) = \mathfrak{s}(\omega_{b,H}) = \mathfrak{s}(\omega_{b,TH}) = \text{Arthur wears the brown hat};$$

$$\mathfrak{s}(\omega_{y,\emptyset}) = \mathfrak{s}(\omega_{y,T}) = \mathfrak{s}(\omega_{y,H}) = \mathfrak{s}(\omega_{y,TH}) = \text{Arthur wears the yellow hat}.$$

In this model, for example, if the true state of the world is $\omega_* = \omega_{b,TH}$, then Arthur is wearing the brown hat, and both Tom and Harry have peeked into the room. The event "Arthur is wearing the brown hat" is $B = \{\omega_{b,\emptyset}, \omega_{b,T}, \omega_{b,H}, \omega_{b,TH}\}$. Tom and Harry know that Arthur's hat is brown only if they have peeked into the room. Therefore,

$$K_T B = \{\omega_{b,T}, \omega_{b,TH}\}, \qquad K_H B = \{\omega_{b,H}, \omega_{b,TH}\}. \tag{9.14}$$

Given Equation (9.14), since the set $K_H B$ is not included in any of the elements in Tom's partition, we conclude that $K_T K_H B = \emptyset$. In other words, in any state of the world, Tom does not know whether or not Harry knows that Arthur is wearing the brown hat, and therefore, in particular, this is the case at the given state of the world, $\omega_{b,TH}$. We similarly conclude that $K_H K_T B = \emptyset$: in any state of the world, Harry does not know that Tom knows that Arthur is wearing the brown hat (and in particular this is the case at the true state of the world, $\omega_{b,TH}$). This is all quite intuitive; Tom knows that Arthur is wearing the brown hat only if he has peeked into the room, but Harry does not know whether or not Tom has peeked into the room.

Note again the distinction between a state of nature and a state of the world. The objective fact about which the players have incomplete information is the color of the hat atop Arthur's head. Each one of the four states of the world $\{\omega_{y,\emptyset}, \omega_{y,H}, \omega_{y,T}, \omega_{y,TH}\}$ corresponds to the state of nature "Arthur wears the yellow hat," yet they differ in the knowledge that the players have regarding the state of nature. In the state of the world $\omega_{y,\emptyset}$, Arthur wears the yellow hat, but Tom and Harry do not know that, while in state of the world $\omega_{y,H}$, Arthur wears the yellow hat and Harry knows that, but Tom does not know that. Note that in both of these states of the world Tom and Arthur do not know that Harry knows the color of Arthur's hat, Harry and Arthur do not know whether or not Tom knows the color of the hat, and in each state of the world there are additional statements that can be made regarding the players' mutual knowledge of Arthur's hat.   ◀

The insights gleaned from these examples can be formulated and proven rigorously.

Definition 9.14 *A knowledge hierarchy* among players in state of the world ω over the *set of states of the world Y is a system of "yes" or "no" answers to each question of the form "in a state of the world ω, does player i_1 know that player i_2 knows that player i_3 knows ... that player i_l knows event A?" for any event $A \subseteq Y$ and any finite sequence $i_1, i_2, \ldots, i_l$ of players[10] in N.*

The answer to the question "does player i_1 know that player i_2 knows that player i_3 knows ... that player i_l knows event A?" in a state of the world ω is affirmative if $\omega \in K_{i_1} K_{i_2} \cdots K_{i_l} A$, and negative if $\omega \notin K_{i_1} K_{i_2} \cdots K_{i_l} A$. Since for every event A and every sequence of players $i_1, i_2, \ldots, i_l$ the event $K_{i_1} K_{i_2} \cdots K_{i_l} A$ is well defined and calculable in an Aumann model of incomplete information, every state of the world defines a knowledge hierarchy. We have therefore derived the following theorem:

Theorem 9.15 *Every situation of incomplete information $(N, Y, (\mathcal{F}_i)_{i \in N}, \mathfrak{s}, \omega_*)$ uniquely determines a knowledge hierarchy over the set of states of the world Y in state of the world ω_*.*

For every subset $C \subseteq S$ of the set of states of nature, we can consider the event that contains all states of the world whose state of nature is an element of C:

$$\mathfrak{s}^{-1}(C) := \{\omega \in Y \colon \mathfrak{s}(\omega) \in C\}. \tag{9.15}$$

For example, in Example 9.13 the set of states of nature $\{\text{yellow}\}$ corresponds to the event $\{\omega_{y,\emptyset}, \omega_{y,H}, \omega_{y,G}, \omega_{y,TH}\}$ in Y. Every subset of S is called an *event in S*. We define knowledge of events in S as follows: in state of the world ω player i knows event C in S if and only if he knows the event $\mathfrak{s}^{-1}(C)$, i.e., if and only if $\omega \in K_i(\mathfrak{s}^{-1}(C))$. In the same manner, in state of the world ω player i_1 knows that player i_2 knows that player i_3 knows ... that player i_l knows event C in S if and only if in state of the world ω player i_1 knows that player i_2 knows that player i_3 knows ... that player i_l knows $\mathfrak{s}^{-1}(C)$.

Corollary 9.16 is a consequence of Theorem 9.15 (Exercise 9.10).

Corollary 9.16 *Every situation of incomplete information $(N, Y, (\mathcal{F}_i)_{i \in N}, \mathfrak{s}, \omega_*)$ uniquely determines a knowledge hierarchy over the set of states of nature S in state of the world ω_*.*

Having defined the knowledge operators of the players, we next turn to the definition of the concept of common knowledge, which was previously defined informally (see Definition 9.2).

---

10 A player may appear several times in the chain $i_1, i_2, \ldots, i_l$. For example, the chain player 2 knows that player 1 knows that player 3 knows that player 2 knows event A is a legitimate chain.

Definition 9.17 *Let $(N, Y, (\mathcal{F}_i)_{i \in N}, \mathfrak{s})$ be an Aumann model of incomplete information, let $A \subseteq Y$ be an event, and let $\omega \in Y$ be a state of the world. The event A is* common knowledge *in ω if for every finite sequence of players $i_1, i_2, \ldots, i_l$,*

$$\omega \in K_{i_1} K_{i_2} \ldots K_{i_{l-1}} K_{i_l} A. \tag{9.16}$$

That is, event A is common knowledge at state of the world ω if in ω every player knows event A, every player knows that every player knows event A, etc. In Examples 9.12 and 9.13 the only event that is common knowledge in any state of the world is Y (Exercise 9.12). In Example 9.3 (page 333) the event $\{\omega_p\}$ (and every event containing it) is common knowledge in state of the world ω_p, and the event $\{\omega_{g,1}, \omega_{g,2}, \omega_{r,1}, \omega_{r,2}\}$ (and the event Y containing it) is common knowledge in every state of the world contained in this event.

Example 9.18 Abraham selects an integer from the set $\{5, 6, 7, 8, 9, 10, 11, 12, 13, 14\}$. He tells Jefferson whether the number he has selected is even or odd, and tells Ulysses the remainder left over from dividing that number by 4. The corresponding Aumann model of incomplete information depicting the induced situation of Jefferson and Ulysses is:

- $N = \{\text{Jefferson}, \text{Ulysses}\}$.
- $S = \{5, 6, 7, 8, 9, 10, 11, 12, 13, 14\}$: the state of nature is the number selected by Abraham.
- $Y = \{\omega_5, \omega_6, \omega_7, \omega_8, \omega_9, \omega_{10}, \omega_{11}, \omega_{12}, \omega_{13}, \omega_{14}\}$.
- The function $\mathfrak{s} : Y \to S$ is given by $\mathfrak{s}(\omega_k) = k$ for every $k \in S$.
- Since Jefferson knows whether the number is even or odd, his partition contains two elements, corresponding to the subset of even numbers and the subset of odd numbers in the set Y:

$$\mathcal{F}_J = \{\{\omega_5, \omega_7, \omega_9, \omega_{11}, \omega_{13}\}, \{\omega_6, \omega_8, \omega_{10}, \omega_{12}, \omega_{14}\}\}. \tag{9.17}$$

- As Ulysses knows the remainder left over from dividing the number by 4, his partition contains four elements, one for each possible remainder:

$$\mathcal{F}_U = \{\{\omega_8, \omega_{12}\}, \{\omega_5, \omega_9, \omega_{13}\}, \{\omega_6, \omega_{10}, \omega_{14}\}, \{\omega_7, \omega_{11}\}\}. \tag{9.18}$$

In the state of the world ω_6, the event that the selected number is even, i.e., $A = \{\omega_6, \omega_8, \omega_{10}, \omega_{12}, \omega_{14}\}$, is common knowledge. Indeed, $K_J A = K_U A = A$, and therefore it follows that $K_{i_1} K_{i_2} \ldots K_{i_{l-1}} K_{i_l} A = A$ for every finite sequence of players $i_1, i_2, \ldots, i_l$. Since $\omega_6 \in A$, it follows from Definition 9.17 that in state of the world ω_6 the event A is common knowledge among Jefferson and Ulysses. Similarly, in state of the world ω_9, the event that the selected number is odd, $B = \{\omega_5, \omega_7, \omega_9, \omega_{11}, \omega_{13}\}$, is common knowledge among Jefferson and Ulysses (verify!). ◀

Remark 9.19 *From Definition 9.17 and Theorem 9.10 we conclude that if event A is common knowledge in state of the world ω, then every event containing A is also common knowledge in ω.* ♦

Remark 9.20 *The definition of common knowledge can be expanded to events in S: an event C in S is common knowledge in state of the world ω if the event $\mathfrak{s}^{-1}(C)$ is common knowledge in ω. For example, in Example 9.13 in state of the world $\omega_{b,TH}$ the event (in the set of states of nature) "Arthur selects the brown hat" is not common knowledge among the players (verify!).* ♦

Remark 9.21 *If event A is common knowledge in state of the world ω, then in particular $\omega \in K_i A$ and so $F_i(\omega) \subseteq A$ for each $i \in N$. In other words, all players know A in ω.* ◆

Remark 9.22 *We can also speak of common knowledge among a subset of the players $M \subseteq N$: in a state of the world ω, event A is common knowledge among the players in M if Equation (9.16) is satisfied for any finite sequence $i_1, i_2, \ldots, i_l$ of players in M.* ◆

Theorem 9.23 states that if there is a player who cannot distinguish between ω and ω', then every event that is common knowledge in ω is also common knowledge in ω'.

Theorem 9.23 *If event A is common knowledge in state of the world ω, and if $\omega' \in F_i(\omega)$ for some player $i \in N$, then the event A is also common knowledge in state of the world ω'.*

Proof: Suppose that $\omega' \in F_i(\omega)$ for some player $i \in N$. As the event A is common knowledge in ω, for any sequence $i_1, i_2, \ldots, i_l$ of players we have

$$\omega \in K_i K_{i_1} K_{i_2} \ldots K_{i_{l-1}} K_{i_l} A. \tag{9.19}$$

Remark 9.21 implies that

$$F_i(\omega) \subseteq K_{i_1} K_{i_2} \ldots K_{i_{l-1}} K_{i_l} A. \tag{9.20}$$

Since $\omega' \in F_i(\omega') = F_i(\omega)$ it follows that $\omega' \in K_{i_1} K_{i_2} \ldots K_{i_{l-1}} K_{i_l} A$. As this is true for any sequence $i_1, i_2, \ldots, i_l$ of players, the event A is common knowledge in ω'. □

We next turn to characterizing sets that are common knowledge. Given an Aumann model of incomplete information $(N, Y, (\mathcal{F}_i)_{i \in N}, \mathfrak{s})$, define the graph $G = (Y, V)$ in which the set of vertices is the set of states of the world Y, and there is an edge between vertices ω and ω' if and only if there is a player i such that $\omega' \in F_i(\omega)$. Note that the condition defining the edges of the graph is symmetric: $\omega' \in F_i(\omega)$ if and only if $F_i(\omega) = F_i(\omega')$, if and only if $\omega \in F_i(\omega')$; hence $G = (Y, V)$ is an undirected graph.

A set of vertices C in a graph is a *connected component* if the following two conditions are satisfied:

- For every $\omega, \omega' \in C$, there exists a path connecting ω with ω', i.e., there exist $\omega = \omega_1, \omega_2, \ldots, \omega_K = \omega'$ such that for each $k = 1, 2, \ldots, K - 1$ the graph contains an edge connecting ω_k and ω_{k+1}.
- There is no edge connecting a vertex in C with a vertex that is not in C.

The *connected component of ω* in the graph, denoted by $C(\omega)$, is the (unique) connected component containing ω.

Theorem 9.24 *Let $(N, Y, (\mathcal{F}_i)_{i \in N}, \mathfrak{s})$ be an Aumann model of incomplete information and let G be the graph corresponding to this model. Let $\omega \in Y$ be a state of the world and let $A \subseteq Y$ be an event. Then event A is common knowledge in state of the world ω if and only if $A \supseteq C(\omega)$.*

Proof: First we prove that if A is common knowledge in ω, then $C(\omega) \subseteq A$. Suppose then that $\omega' \in C(\omega)$. We want to show that $\omega' \in A$. From the definition of a connected component, there is a path connecting ω with ω'; we denote that path by

$\omega = \omega_1, \omega_2, \ldots, \omega_K = \omega'$. We prove by induction on k that $\omega_k \in A$, and that A is common knowledge in ω_k, for every $1 \leq k \leq K$. For $k = 1$, because the event A is common knowledge in ω, we deduce that $\omega_1 = \omega \in A$. Suppose now that $\omega_k \in A$ and A is common knowledge in ω_k. We will show that $\omega_{k+1} \in A$ and that A is common knowledge in ω_{k+1}. Because there is an edge connecting ω_k and ω_{k+1}, there is a player i such that $\omega_{k+1} \in F_i(\omega_k)$. It follows from Theorem 9.23 that the event A is common knowledge in ω_{k+1}. From Remark 9.21 we conclude that $\omega_{k+1} \in A$. This completes the inductive step, so that in particular $\omega' = \omega_K \in A$.

Consider now the other direction: if $C(\omega) \subseteq A$, then event A is common knowledge in state of the world ω. To prove this, it suffices to show that $C(\omega)$ is common knowledge in ω, because from Remark 9.19 it will then follow that any event containing $C(\omega)$, and in particular A, is also common knowledge in ω. Let i be a player in N. Because $C(\omega)$ is a connected component of G, for each $\omega' \in C(\omega)$, we have $F_i(\omega') \subseteq C(\omega)$. It follows that

$$C(\omega) \supseteq \bigcup_{\omega' \in C(\omega)} F_i(\omega') \supseteq \bigcup_{\omega' \in C(\omega)} \{\omega'\} = C(\omega). \tag{9.21}$$

In other words, for each player i the set $C(\omega)$ is the union of all the elements of $\mathcal{F}_i$ contained in it. This implies that $K_i(C(\omega)) = C(\omega)$. As this is true for every player $i \in N$, it follows that for every sequence of players $i_1, i_2, \ldots, i_l$,

$$\omega \in C(\omega) = K_{i_1} K_{i_2} \cdots K_{i_l} C(\omega), \tag{9.22}$$

and therefore $C(\omega)$ is common knowledge in ω. □

The following corollary follows from Theorem 9.24 and Remark 9.19.

Corollary 9.25 *In every state of the world $\omega \in Y$, the event $C(\omega)$ is common knowledge among the players, and it is the smallest event that is common knowledge in ω.*

For this reason, $C(\omega)$ is sometimes called the *common knowledge component* among the players in state of the world ω.

Remark 9.26 *The proof of Theorem 9.24 shows that for each player $i \in N$, the set $C(\omega)$ is the union of the elements of $\mathcal{F}_i$ contained in it, and it is the smallest event containing ω that satisfies this property. The set of all the connected components of the graph G defines a partition of Y, which is called the* meet *of $\mathcal{F}_1, \mathcal{F}_2, \ldots, \mathcal{F}_n$. This is the finest partition that satisfies the property that each partition $\mathcal{F}_i$ is a refinement of it. We can therefore formulate Theorem 9.24 equivalently as follows. Let $(N, Y, (\mathcal{F}_i)_{i \in N}, s)$ be an Aumann model of incomplete information. Event A is common knowledge in state of the world $\omega \in Y$ if and only if A contains the element of the meet containing ω.* ◆

9.2 The Aumann model of incomplete information with beliefs

The following model extends the Aumann model of incomplete information presented in the previous section.

Definition 9.27 *An* Aumann model of incomplete information with beliefs *(over a set of states of nature S) consists of five elements* $(N, Y, (\mathcal{F}_i)_{i \in N}, \mathfrak{s}, \mathbf{P})$, *where:*

- *N is a finite set of players;*
- *Y is a finite set of states of the world;*
- $\mathcal{F}_i$ *is a partition of Y, for each $i \in N$;*
- $\mathfrak{s} : Y \to S$ *is a function associating a state of nature to every state of the world;*
- $\mathbf{P}$ *is a probability distribution over Y such that $\mathbf{P}(\omega) > 0$ for each $\omega \in Y$.*

Comparing this definition to that of the Aumann model of incomplete information (Definition 9.4), we have added one new element, namely, the probability distribution $\mathbf{P}$ over Y, which is called the *common prior*. In this model, a state of the world ω_* is selected by a random process in accordance with the common prior probability distribution $\mathbf{P}$. After the true state of the world has been selected by this random process, each player i learns his partition element $F_i(\omega_*)$ that contains ω_*. Prior to the stage at which private information is revealed, the players share a common prior distribution, which is interpreted as their belief about the probability that any specific state of the world in Y is the true one. After each player i has acquired his private information $F_i(\omega_*)$, he updates his beliefs. This process of belief updating is the main topic of this section.

The assumption that all the players share a common prior is a strong assumption, and in many cases there are good reasons to doubt that it obtains. We will return to this point later in the chapter. In contrast, the assumption that $\mathbf{P}(\omega) > 0$ for all $\omega \in Y$ is not a strong assumption. As we will show, a state of the world ω for which $\mathbf{P}(\omega) = 0$ is one to which all the players assign probability 0, and it can be removed from consideration in Y.

In the following examples and in the rest of this chapter, whenever the states of nature are irrelevant we will specify neither the set S nor the function $\mathfrak{s}$.

Example 9.28   Consider the following Aumann model:

- The set of players is $N = \{\mathrm{I}, \mathrm{II}\}$.
- The set of states of the world is $Y = \{\omega_1, \omega_2, \omega_3, \omega_4\}$.
- The information partitions of the players are

$$\mathcal{F}_{\mathrm{I}} = \{\{\omega_1, \omega_2\}, \{\omega_3, \omega_4\}\}, \qquad \mathcal{F}_{\mathrm{II}} = \{\{\omega_1, \omega_3\}, \{\omega_2, \omega_4\}\}. \tag{9.23}$$

- The common prior $\mathbf{P}$ is

$$\mathbf{P}(\omega_1) = \tfrac{1}{4}, \qquad \mathbf{P}(\omega_2) = \tfrac{1}{4}, \qquad \mathbf{P}(\omega_3) = \tfrac{1}{3}, \qquad \mathbf{P}(\omega_4) = \tfrac{1}{6}. \tag{9.24}$$

A graphic representation of the players' partitions and the prior probability distribution is provided in Figure 9.2. Player I's partition elements are marked by a solid line, while Player II's partition elements are denoted by a dotted line. What are the beliefs of each player about the state of the world? Prior to the chance move that selects the state of the world, the players have a common prior distribution over the states of the world. When a player receives information that indicates that the true state of the world is in the partition element $F_i(\omega_*)$, he updates his beliefs about the states of the world by calculating the conditional probability given his information. For example, if the state of the world is ω_1, Player I knows that the state of the world is either ω_1 or ω_2. Player I's beliefs are therefore

$$\mathbf{P}(\omega_1 \mid \{\omega_1, \omega_2\}) = \frac{p(\omega_1)}{p(\omega_1) + p(\omega_2)} = \frac{\tfrac{1}{4}}{\tfrac{1}{4} + \tfrac{1}{4}} = \tfrac{1}{2}, \tag{9.25}$$

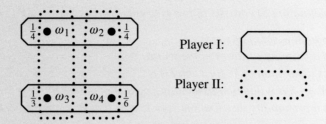

Figure 9.2 The information partitions and the prior distribution in Example 9.28

and similarly

$$\mathbf{P}(\omega_2 \mid \{\omega_1, \omega_2\}) = \frac{p(\omega_2)}{p(\omega_1) + p(\omega_2)} = \frac{\frac{1}{4}}{\frac{1}{4} + \frac{1}{4}} = \frac{1}{2}. \qquad (9.26)$$

In words, if Player I's information is that the state of the world is in $\{\omega_1, \omega_2\}$, he attributes probability $\frac{1}{2}$ to the state of the world ω_1 and probability $\frac{1}{2}$ to the state of the world ω_2. The tables appearing in Figure 9.3 are arrived at through a similar calculation. The upper table describes Player I's beliefs, as a function of his information partition, and the lower table represents Player II's beliefs, as a function of his information partition.

Player I's Information	ω_1	ω_2	ω_3	ω_4
$\{\omega_1, \omega_2\}$	$\frac{1}{2}$	$\frac{1}{2}$	0	0
$\{\omega_3, \omega_4\}$	0	0	$\frac{2}{3}$	$\frac{1}{3}$

Player I's beliefs:

Player II's Information	ω_1	ω_2	ω_3	ω_4
$\{\omega_1, \omega_3\}$	$\frac{3}{7}$	0	$\frac{4}{7}$	0
$\{\omega_2, \omega_4\}$	0	$\frac{3}{5}$	0	$\frac{2}{5}$

Player II's beliefs:

Figure 9.3 The beliefs of the players in Example 9.28

For example, if Player II's information is $\{\omega_2, \omega_4\}$ (i.e., the state of the world is either ω_2 or ω_4), he attributes probability $\frac{3}{5}$ to the state of the world ω_2 and probability $\frac{2}{5}$ to the state of the world ω_4.

A player's beliefs will be denoted by square brackets in which states of the world appear alongside the probabilities that are ascribed to them. For example, $[\frac{3}{5}(\omega_2), \frac{2}{5}(\omega_4)]$ represents beliefs in which probability $\frac{3}{5}$ is ascribed to state of the world ω_2, and probability $\frac{2}{5}$ is ascribed to state of the world ω_4. The calculations performed above yield the first-order beliefs of the players at all possible states of the world. These beliefs can be summarized as follows:

- In state of the world ω_1 the first-order belief of Player I is $[\frac{1}{2}(\omega_1), \frac{1}{2}(\omega_2)]$ and that of Player II is $[\frac{3}{7}(\omega_1), \frac{4}{7}(\omega_3)]$.
- In state of the world ω_2 the first-order belief of Player I is $[\frac{1}{2}(\omega_1), \frac{1}{2}(\omega_2)]$ and that of Player II is $[\frac{3}{5}(\omega_2), \frac{2}{5}(\omega_4)]$.
- In state of the world ω_3 the first-order belief of Player I is $[\frac{2}{3}(\omega_3), \frac{1}{3}(\omega_4)]$ and that of Player II is $[\frac{3}{7}(\omega_1), \frac{4}{7}(\omega_3)]$.

- In state of the world ω_4 the first-order belief of Player I is $[\frac{2}{3}(\omega_3), \frac{1}{3}(\omega_4)]$ and that of Player II is $[\frac{3}{5}(\omega_2), \frac{2}{5}(\omega_4)]$.

Given the first-order beliefs of the players over Y, we can construct the second-order beliefs, by which we mean the beliefs each player has about the state of the world and the first-order beliefs of the other player. In state of the world ω_1 (or ω_2) Player I attributes probability $\frac{1}{2}$ to the state of the world being ω_1 and probability $\frac{1}{2}$ to the state of the world being ω_2. As we noted above, when the state of the world is ω_1, the first-order belief of Player II is $[\frac{3}{7}(\omega_1), \frac{4}{7}(\omega_3)]$, and when the state of the world is ω_2, Player II's first-order belief is $[\frac{3}{5}(\omega_2), \frac{2}{5}(\omega_4)]$. Therefore:

- In state of the world ω_1 (or ω_2) Player I attributes probability $\frac{1}{2}$ to the state of the world being ω_1 and the first-order belief of Player II being $[\frac{3}{7}(\omega_1), \frac{4}{7}(\omega_3)]$, and probability $\frac{1}{2}$ to the state of the world being ω_2 and Player II's first-order belief being $[\frac{3}{5}(\omega_2), \frac{2}{5}(\omega_4)]$.

We can similarly calculate the second-order beliefs of each of the players in each state of the world:

- In state of the world ω_3 (or ω_4) Player I attributes probability $\frac{2}{3}$ to the state of the world being ω_3 and the first-order belief of Player II being $[\frac{3}{7}(\omega_1), \frac{4}{7}(\omega_3)]$, and probability $\frac{1}{3}$ to the state of the world being ω_4 and Player II's first-order belief being $[\frac{3}{5}(\omega_2), \frac{2}{5}(\omega_4)]$.
- In state of the world ω_1 (or ω_3) Player II attributes probability $\frac{3}{7}$ to the state of the world being ω_1 and the first-order belief of Player I being $[\frac{1}{2}(\omega_1), \frac{1}{2}(\omega_2)]$, and probability $\frac{4}{7}$ to the state of the world being ω_3 and Player I's first-order belief being $[\frac{2}{3}(\omega_3), \frac{1}{3}(\omega_4)]$.
- In state of the world ω_2 (or ω_4) Player II attributes probability $\frac{3}{5}$ to the state of the world being ω_2 and the first-order belief of Player I being $[\frac{1}{2}(\omega_1), \frac{1}{2}(\omega_2)]$, and probability $\frac{2}{5}$ to the state of the world being ω_4 and Player I's first-order belief being $[\frac{2}{3}(\omega_3), \frac{1}{3}(\omega_4)]$.

These calculations can be continued to arbitrarily high orders in a similar manner to yield belief hierarchies of the two players. ◀

Theorem 9.29 says that in an Aumann model, knowledge is equivalent to belief with probability 1. The theorem, however, requires assuming that $\mathbf{P}(\omega) > 0$ for each $\omega \in Y$; without that assumption the theorem's conclusion does not obtain (Exercise 9.21). In Example 9.36 we will see that the conclusion of the theorem also fails to hold when the set of states of the world is infinite.

Theorem 9.29 *Let* $(N, Y, (\mathcal{F}_i)_{i \in N}, \mathfrak{s}, \mathbf{P})$ *be an Aumann model of incomplete information with beliefs. Then for each* $\omega \in Y$, *for each player* $i \in N$, *and for every event* $A \subseteq Y$, *player* i *knows event* A *in state of the world* ω *if and only if he attributes probability 1 to that event:*

$$\mathbf{P}(A \mid F_i(\omega)) = 1 \quad \Longleftrightarrow \quad F_i(\omega) \subseteq A. \tag{9.27}$$

Notice that the assumption that $\mathbf{P}(\omega) > 0$ for every $\omega \in Y$, together with $\omega \in F_i(\omega)$ for every $\omega \in Y$, yields $\mathbf{P}(F_i(\omega)) > 0$ for each player $i \in N$ and every state of the world $\omega \in Y$, so that the conditional probability in Equation (9.27) is well defined.

Proof: Suppose first that $F_i(\omega) \subseteq A$. Then

$$\mathbf{P}(A \mid F_i(\omega)) \geq \mathbf{P}(F_i(\omega) \mid F_i(\omega)) = 1, \tag{9.28}$$

so that $\mathbf{P}(A \mid F_i(\omega)) = 1$. To prove the reverse implication, if $\mathbf{P}(A \mid F_i(\omega)) = 1$ then

$$\mathbf{P}(A \mid F_i(\omega)) = \frac{\mathbf{P}(A \cap F_i(\omega))}{\mathbf{P}(F_i(\omega))} = 1, \tag{9.29}$$

which yields $\mathbf{P}(A \cap F_i(\omega)) = \mathbf{P}(F_i(\omega))$. From the assumption that $\mathbf{P}(\omega') > 0$ for each $\omega' \in Y$ we conclude that $A \cap F_i(\omega) = F_i(\omega)$, that is, $F_i(\omega) \subseteq A$. □

A *situation of incomplete information with beliefs* is a vector $(N, Y, (\mathcal{F}_i)_{i \in N}, \mathfrak{s}, \mathbf{P}, \omega_*)$ composed of an Aumann model of incomplete information with beliefs $(N, Y, (\mathcal{F}_i)_{i \in N}, \mathfrak{s}, \mathbf{P})$ together with a state of the world $\omega_* \in Y$. The next theorem follows naturally from the analysis we performed in Example 9.28, and it generalizes Theorem 9.15 and Corollary 9.16 to situations of belief.

Theorem 9.30 *Every situation of incomplete information with beliefs* $(N, Y, (\mathcal{F}_i)_{i \in N}, \mathfrak{s}, \mathbf{P}, \omega_*)$ *uniquely determines a mutual belief hierarchy among the players over the states of the world Y, and therefore also a mutual belief hierarchy over the states of nature S.*

The above formulation is not precise, as we have not formally defined what the term "mutual belief hierarchy" means. The formal definition is presented in Chapter 11, where we will show that each state of the world is in fact a pair, consisting of a state of nature and a mutual belief hierarchy among the players over the states of nature S. The inductive description of belief hierarchies, as presented in the examples above and the examples below, will suffice for this chapter.

In Example 9.28 we calculated the belief hierarchy of the players in each state of the world. A similar calculation can be performed with respect to events.

Example 9.28 (*Continued*) Consider the situation in which $\omega_* = \omega_1$ and the event $A = \{\omega_2, \omega_3\}$. As Player I's information in state of the world ω_1 is $\{\omega_1, \omega_2\}$, the conditional probability that he ascribes to event A in state of the world ω_1 (or ω_2) is

$$\mathbf{P}(A \mid \{\omega_1, \omega_2\}) = \frac{\mathbf{P}(A \cap \{\omega_1, \omega_2\})}{\mathbf{P}(\{\omega_1, \omega_2\})} = \frac{\mathbf{P}(\{\omega_1\})}{\mathbf{P}(\{\omega_1, \omega_2\})} = \frac{\frac{1}{4}}{\frac{1}{4} + \frac{1}{4}} = \frac{1}{2}. \tag{9.30}$$

Because Player II's information in state of the world ω_1 is $\{\omega_1, \omega_3\}$, the conditional probability that he ascribes to event A in state of the world ω_1 (or ω_3) is

$$\mathbf{P}(A \mid \{\omega_1, \omega_3\}) = \frac{\mathbf{P}(A \cap \{\omega_1, \omega_3\})}{\mathbf{P}(\{\omega_1, \omega_3\})} = \frac{\mathbf{P}(\{\omega_3\})}{\mathbf{P}(\{\omega_1, \omega_3\})} = \frac{\frac{1}{3}}{\frac{1}{4} + \frac{1}{3}} = \frac{4}{7}. \tag{9.31}$$

Second-order beliefs can also be calculated readily. In state of the world ω_1, Player I ascribes probability $\frac{1}{2}$ to the true state being ω_1, in which case the probability that Player II ascribes to event A is $\frac{4}{7}$; he ascribes probability $\frac{1}{2}$ to the true state being ω_2, in which case the probability that Player II ascribes to event A is $(\frac{1}{4})/(\frac{1}{4} + \frac{1}{6}) = \frac{2}{5}$. These are Player I's second-order beliefs about event A in state of the world ω_1. We can similarly calculate the second-order beliefs of Player II, as well as all the higher-order beliefs of the two players. ◀

Example 9.31 Consider again the Aumann model of incomplete information with beliefs presented in Example 9.28, but now with the common prior given by

$$\mathbf{P}(\omega_1) = \mathbf{P}(\omega_4) = \tfrac{1}{6}, \quad \mathbf{P}(\omega_2) = \mathbf{P}(\omega_3) = \tfrac{1}{3}. \tag{9.32}$$

The partitions $\mathcal{F}_\mathrm{I}$ and $\mathcal{F}_\mathrm{II}$ are graphically depicted in Figure 9.4.

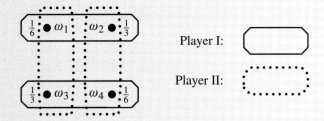

Figure 9.4 The information partitions and the prior distribution in Example 9.31

Since $\omega_1 \in F_\mathrm{I}(\omega_2)$, $\omega_2 \in F_\mathrm{II}(\omega_4)$, and $\omega_4 \in F_\mathrm{I}(\omega_3)$ in the graph corresponding to this Aumann model, all states in Y are connected. Hence the only connected component in the graph is Y (verify!), and therefore the only event that is common knowledge in any state of the world ω is Y (Theorem 9.24). Consider now the event $A = \{\omega_2, \omega_3\}$ and the situation in which $\omega_* = \omega_1$. What is the conditional probability that the players ascribe to A? Similarly to the calculation performed in Example 9.28,

$$\mathbf{P}(A \mid \{\omega_1, \omega_2\}) = \frac{\mathbf{P}(A \cap \{\omega_1, \omega_2\})}{\mathbf{P}(\{\omega_1, \omega_2\})} = \frac{\mathbf{P}(\{\omega_2\})}{\mathbf{P}(\{\omega_1, \omega_2\})} = \frac{\tfrac{1}{3}}{\tfrac{1}{6} + \tfrac{1}{3}} = \tfrac{2}{3}, \tag{9.33}$$

and we can also readily calculate that both players ascribe probability $\tfrac{2}{3}$ to event A in each state of the world. Formally:

$$\left\{ \omega : q_\mathrm{I} := \mathbf{P}(A \mid F_\mathrm{I}(\omega)) = \tfrac{2}{3} \right\} = Y, \quad \left\{ \omega : q_\mathrm{II} := \mathbf{P}(A \mid F_\mathrm{II}(\omega)) = \tfrac{2}{3} \right\} = Y. \tag{9.34}$$

It follows from the definition of the knowledge operator that the event "Player I ascribes probability $\tfrac{2}{3}$ to A" is common knowledge in each state of the world, and the event "Player II ascribes probability $\tfrac{2}{3}$ to A" is also common knowledge in each state of the world. In other words, in this situation the probabilities that the two players ascribe to event A are both common knowledge and equal to each other. ◄

Is it a coincidence that the probabilities q_I and q_II that the two players assign to the event A in Example 9.31 are equal (both being $\tfrac{2}{3}$)? Can there be a situation in which it is common knowledge that to the event A, Player I ascribes probability q_I and Player II ascribes probability q_II, where $q_\mathrm{I} \neq q_\mathrm{II}$? Theorem 9.32 asserts that this state of affairs is impossible.

Theorem 9.32 Aumann's Agreement Theorem (Aumann [1976]) *Let* $(N, Y, (\mathcal{F}_i)_{i \in N},$ $s, \mathbf{P})$ *be an Aumann model of incomplete information with beliefs, and suppose that* $n = 2$ *(i.e., there are two players). Let* $A \subseteq Y$ *be an event and let* $\omega \in Y$ *be a state of the world. If the event "Player* I *ascribes probability* q_I *to* A*" is common knowledge in* ω*, and the event "Player* II *ascribes probability* q_II *to* A*" is also common knowledge in* ω*, then* $q_\mathrm{I} = q_\mathrm{II}$*.*

Let us take a moment to consider the significance of this theorem before proceeding to its proof. The theorem states that if two players begin with "identical beliefs about the world" (represented by the common prior **P**) but receive disparate information (represented by their respective partition elements containing ω), then "they cannot agree to disagree": if they agree that the probability that Player I ascribes to a particular event is q_I, then they cannot also agree that Player II ascribes a probability q_{II} to the same event, unless $q_I = q_{II}$. If they disagree regarding a particular fact (for example, Player I ascribes probability q_I to event A and Player II ascribes probability q_{II} to the same event), then the fact that they disagree cannot be common knowledge. Since we know that people often agree to disagree, we must conclude that either (a) different people begin with different prior distributions over the states of the world, or (b) people incorrectly calculate conditional probabilities when they receive information regarding the true state of the world.

Proof of Theorem 9.32: Let C be the connected component of ω in the graph corresponding to the given Aumann model. It follows from Theorem 9.24 that event C is common knowledge in state of the world ω. The event C can be represented as a union of partition elements in $\mathcal{F}_I$; that is, $C = \bigcup_j F_I^j$, where $F_I^j \in \mathcal{F}_I$ for each j. Since $\mathbf{P}(\omega') > 0$ for every $\omega' \in Y$, it follows that $\mathbf{P}(F_I^j) > 0$ for every j, and therefore $\mathbf{P}(C) > 0$.

The fact that Player I ascribes probability q_I to the event A is common knowledge in ω. It follows that the event $\{\omega' \in \Omega : \mathbf{P}(A \mid F_I(\omega')) = q_I\}$ contains the event C (Corollary 9.25), and therefore each one of the events $(F_I^j)_j$. This implies that for each of the sets F_I^j the conditional probability of A, given that Player I's information is F_I^j, equals q_I. In other words, for each j,

$$\mathbf{P}\left(A \mid F_I^j\right) = \frac{\mathbf{P}\left(A \cap F_I^j\right)}{\mathbf{P}\left(F_I^j\right)} = q_I. \tag{9.35}$$

As this equality holds for every j, and $C = \bigcup_j F_I^j$, it follows from Equation (9.35) that

$$\mathbf{P}(A \cap C) = \sum_j \mathbf{P}\left(A \cap F_I^j\right) = q_I \sum_j \mathbf{P}\left(F_I^j\right) = q_I \mathbf{P}(C). \tag{9.36}$$

We similarly derive that

$$\mathbf{P}(A \cap C) = q_{II}\mathbf{P}(C). \tag{9.37}$$

Finally, since $\mathbf{P}(C) > 0$, Equations (9.36) and (9.37) imply that $q_I = q_{II}$, which is what we wanted to show. $\qquad\square$

How do players arrive at a situation in which the probabilities q_I and q_{II} that they ascribe to a particular event A are common knowledge? In Example 9.31, each player calculates the conditional probability of A given a partition element of the other player, and comes to the conclusion that no matter which partition element of the other player is used for the conditioning, the conditional probability turns out to be the same. That is why q_i is common knowledge among the players for $i = I, II$.

In most cases the conditional probability of an event is not common knowledge, because it varies from one partition element to another. We can, however, describe a process of information transmission between the players that guarantees that these conditional probabilities will become common knowledge when the process is complete (see Exercises 9.25 and 9.26). Suppose that each player publicly announces the conditional probability he ascribes to event A given the information (i.e., the partition element) at his disposal. After each player has heard the other player's announcement, he can rule out some states of the world, because they are impossible: possible states of the world are only those in which the conditional probability that the other player ascribes to event A is the conditional probability that he publicly announced. Each player can then update the conditional probability that he ascribes to event A following the elimination of impossible states of the world, and again publicly announce the new conditional probability he has calculated. Following this announcement, the players can again rule out the states of the world in which the updated conditional probability of the other player differs from that which he announced, update their conditional probabilities, and announce them publicly. This can be repeated again and again. Using Aumann's Agreement Theorem (Theorem 9.32), it can be shown that at the end of this process the players will converge to the same conditional probability, which will be common knowledge among them (Exercise 9.28).

Example 9.33 We provide now an example of the dynamic process just described. More examples can be found in Exercises 9.25 and 9.26. Consider the following Aumann model of incomplete information:

- $N = \{\mathrm{I}, \mathrm{II}\}$.
- $Y = \{\omega_1, \omega_2, \omega_3, \omega_4\}$.
- The information partitions of the players are

$$\mathcal{F}_{\mathrm{I}} = \{\{\omega_1, \omega_2\}, \{\omega_3, \omega_4\}\}, \qquad \mathcal{F}_{\mathrm{II}} = \{\{\omega_1, \omega_2, \omega_3\}, \{\omega_4\}\}. \tag{9.38}$$

- The prior distribution is

$$\mathbf{P}_{\mathrm{II}}(\omega_1) = \mathbf{P}_{\mathrm{II}}(\omega_4) = \tfrac{1}{3}, \qquad \mathbf{P}_{\mathrm{II}}(\omega_2) = \mathbf{P}_{\mathrm{II}}(\omega_3) = \tfrac{1}{6}. \tag{9.39}$$

The partition elements $\mathcal{F}_{\mathrm{I}}$ and $\mathcal{F}_{\mathrm{II}}$ are as depicted graphically in Figure 9.5.

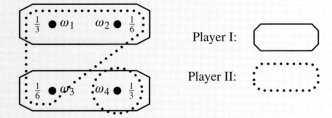

Figure 9.5 The information partitions and the prior distribution in Example 9.33

Let $A = \{\omega_2, \omega_3\}$, and suppose that the true state of the world is ω_3. We will now trace the dynamic process described above. Player I announces the conditional probability $\mathbf{P}(A \mid \{\omega_3, \omega_4\}) = \tfrac{1}{3}$ that he ascribes to event A, given his information. Notice that in every state of the world Player I ascribes probability $\tfrac{1}{3}$ to event A, so that this announcement does not add any new information to Player II.

Next, Player II announces the conditional probability $\mathbf{P}(A \mid \{\omega_3, \omega_4\}) = \tfrac{1}{2}$ that he ascribes to A, given his information. This enables Player I to learn that the true state of the world is not ω_4, because if it were ω_4, Player II would have ascribed conditional probability 0 to the event A.

Player I therefore knows, after Player II's announcement, that the true state of the world is ω_3, and then announces that the conditional probability he ascribes to the event A is 1. This informs Player II that the true state of the world is ω_3, because if the true state of the world were ω_1 or ω_2 (the two other possible states, given Player II's information), Player I would have announced that he ascribed conditional probability $\frac{1}{3}$ to the event A. Player II therefore announces that the conditional probability he ascribes to the event A is 1, and this probability is now common knowledge among the two players.

It is left to the reader to verify that if the true state of the world is ω_1 or ω_2, the dynamic process described above will lead the two players to common knowledge that the conditional probability of the event A is $\frac{1}{3}$. ◀

Aumann's Agreement Theorem has important implications regarding the rationality of betting between two risk-neutral players (or two players who share the same level of risk aversion). To simplify the analysis, suppose that the two players bet that if a certain event A occurs, Player II pays Player I one dollar, and if event A fails to occur, Player I pays Player II one dollar instead. Labeling the probabilities that the players ascribe to event A as q_I and q_{II} respectively, Player I should be willing to take this bet if and only if $q_I \geq \frac{1}{2}$, with Player II agreeing to the bet if and only if $q_{II} \leq \frac{1}{2}$. Suppose that Player I accepts the bet. Then the fact that he has accepted the bet is common knowledge, which means that the fact that $q_I \geq \frac{1}{2}$ is common knowledge. By the same reasoning, if Player II agrees to the bet, that fact is common knowledge, and therefore the fact that $q_{II} \leq \frac{1}{2}$ is common knowledge. Using a proof very similar to that of Aumann's Agreement Theorem, we conclude that it is impossible for both facts to be common knowledge unless $q_I = q_{II} = \frac{1}{2}$, in which case the expected payoff for each player is 0, and there is no point in betting (see Exercises 9.29 and 9.30).

Note that the agreement theorem rests on two main assumptions:

- Both players share a common prior over Y.
- The probability that each of the players ascribes to event A is common knowledge among them.

Regarding the first assumption, the common prior distribution $\mathbf{P}$ is part of the Aumann model of incomplete information with beliefs and it is used to compute the players' beliefs given their partitions. As the following example shows, if each player's belief is computed from a different probability distribution, we obtain a more general model in which the agreement theorem does not hold. We will return to Aumann models with incomplete information and different prior distributions in Chapter 10.

Example 9.34   In this example we will show that if the two players have different priors, Theorem 9.32 does not hold. Consider the following Aumann model of incomplete information:

- $N = \{\text{I}, \text{II}\}$.
- $Y = \{\omega_1, \omega_2, \omega_3, \omega_4\}$.
- The information that the two players have is given by

$$\mathcal{F}_{\text{I}} = \{\{\omega_1, \omega_2\}, \{\omega_3, \omega_4\}\}, \qquad \mathcal{F}_{\text{II}} = \{\{\omega_1, \omega_4\}, \{\omega_2, \omega_3\}\}. \tag{9.40}$$

- Player I calculates his beliefs based on the following prior distribution:

$$\mathbf{P}_I(\omega_1) = \mathbf{P}_I(\omega_2) = \mathbf{P}_I(\omega_3) = \mathbf{P}_I(\omega_4) = \tfrac{1}{4}. \tag{9.41}$$

- Player II calculates his beliefs based on the following prior distribution:

$$\mathbf{P}_{II}(\omega_1) = \mathbf{P}_{II}(\omega_3) = \tfrac{2}{10}, \quad \mathbf{P}_{II}(\omega_2) = \mathbf{P}_{II}(\omega_4) = \tfrac{3}{10}. \tag{9.42}$$

The only connected component in the graph corresponding to this Aumann model is Y (verify!), so that the only event that is common knowledge in any state of the world ω is Y. Let $A = \{\omega_1, \omega_3\}$. A quick calculation reveals that in each state $\omega \in Y$

$$\mathbf{P}_I(A \mid F_I(\omega)) = \tfrac{1}{2}, \quad \mathbf{P}_{II}(A \mid F_{II}(\omega)) = \tfrac{2}{5}. \tag{9.43}$$

That is,

$$\left\{\omega : q_I := \mathbf{P}(A \mid F_I(\omega)) = \tfrac{1}{2}\right\} = Y, \quad \left\{\omega : q_{II} := \mathbf{P}(A \mid F_{II}(\omega)) = \tfrac{2}{5}\right\} = Y. \tag{9.44}$$

From the definition of the knowledge operator it follows that the facts that $q_I = \tfrac{1}{2}$ and $q_{II} = \tfrac{2}{5}$ are common knowledge in every state of the world. In other words, it is common knowledge in every state of the world that the players ascribe different probabilities to the event A. This does not contradict Theorem 9.32 because the players do not share a common prior. In fact, this result is not surprising; because the players start off by "agreeing" that their initial probability distributions diverge (and that fact is common knowledge), it is no wonder that it is common knowledge among them that they ascribe different probabilities to event A (after learning which partition element they are in). ◀

Example 9.35 In this example we will show that even if the players share a common prior, if the fact that "Player II ascribes probability q_{II} to event A" is not common knowledge, Theorem 9.32 does not hold; that is, it is possible that $q_I \neq q_{II}$. Consider the following Aumann model of incomplete information:

- $N = \{I, II\}$.
- $Y = \{\omega_1, \omega_2, \omega_3, \omega_4\}$.
- The players' information partitions are

$$\mathcal{F}_I = \{\{\omega_1, \omega_2\}, \{\omega_3, \omega_4\}\}, \quad \mathcal{F}_{II} = \{\{\omega_1, \omega_2, \omega_3\}, \{\omega_4\}\}. \tag{9.45}$$

- The common prior distribution is

$$\mathbf{P}(\omega_1) = \mathbf{P}(\omega_2) = \mathbf{P}(\omega_3) = \mathbf{P}(\omega_4) = \tfrac{1}{4}. \tag{9.46}$$

The partitions $\mathcal{F}_I$ and $\mathcal{F}_{II}$ are depicted graphically in Figure 9.6.

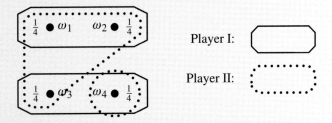

Figure 9.6 The partitions of the players in Example 9.35 and the common prior

The only connected component in the graph corresponding to this Aumann model is Y (verify!). Let $A = \{\omega_1, \omega_3\}$. In each state of the world, the probability that Player I ascribes to event A is $q_I = \tfrac{1}{2}$:

$$\left\{ w \in Y : q_{\mathrm{I}} = \mathbf{P}\left(A \mid F_{\mathrm{I}}(\omega)\right) = \tfrac{1}{2} \right\} = Y, \tag{9.47}$$

and therefore the fact that $q_{\mathrm{I}} = \tfrac{1}{2}$ is common knowledge in every state of the world.

In states of the world ω_1, ω_2, and ω_3, Player II ascribes probability $\tfrac{2}{3}$ to event A:

$$\left\{ w \in Y : q_{\mathrm{II}} = \mathbf{P}\left(A \mid F_{\mathrm{II}}(\omega) = \tfrac{2}{3}\right) \right\} = \{\omega_1, \omega_2, \omega_3\} \subset Y, \tag{9.48}$$

and in state of the world ω_4 he ascribes probability 0 to A. Since the only event that is common knowledge in any state of the world is Y, the event "Player II ascribes probability $\tfrac{2}{3}$ to A" is not common knowledge in any state of the world. For that reason, the fact that $q_{\mathrm{I}} \neq q_{\mathrm{II}}$ does not contradict Theorem 9.32.

Note that in state of the world ω_1, Player I knows that the state of the world is in $\{\omega_1, \omega_2\}$, and therefore he knows that Player II's information is $\{\omega_1, \omega_2, \omega_3\}$, and thus he (Player I) knows that Player II ascribes probability $q_{\mathrm{II}} = \tfrac{2}{3}$ to the event A. However, the fact that Player II ascribes probability $q_{\mathrm{II}} = \tfrac{2}{3}$ to event A is not common knowledge among the players in the state of the world ω_1. This is so because in that state of the world Player II cannot exclude the possibility that the state of the world is ω_3 (he ascribes to this probability $\tfrac{1}{3}$). If the state of the world is ω_3, Player I knows that the state of the world is in $\{\omega_3, \omega_4\}$, and therefore he (Player I) cannot exclude the possibility that the state of the world is ω_4 (he ascribes to this probability $\tfrac{1}{2}$), in which case Player II knows that the state of the world is ω_4, and then the probability that Player II ascribes to event A is 0 ($q_{\mathrm{II}} = 0$). Therefore, in state of the world ω_1 Player II ascribes probability $\tfrac{1}{3}$ to the fact that Player I ascribes probability $\tfrac{1}{2}$ to Player II ascribing probability 0 to event A. Thus, in state of the world ω_1 Player I knows that $q_{\mathrm{II}} = \tfrac{2}{3}$, yet this event is not common knowledge among the players. ◀

Before we proceed, let us recall that an Aumann model consists of two elements:

- The partitions of the players, which determine the information (knowledge) they possess.
- The common prior $\mathbf{P}$ that, together with the partitions, determines the beliefs of the players.

The knowledge structure in an Aumann model is independent of the common prior $\mathbf{P}$. Furthermore, as we saw in Example 9.34, even when there is no common prior, and instead every player has a different subjective prior distribution, the underlying knowledge structure and the set of common knowledge events are unchanged. Not surprisingly, the Agreement Theorem (Theorem 9.32), which deals with beliefs, depends on the assumption of a common prior, while the common knowledge characterization theorem (Theorem 9.24, page 343) is independent of the assumption of a common prior.

9.3 An infinite set of states of the world

Thus far in the chapter, we have assumed that the set of states of the world is finite. What if this set is infinite? With regard to set-theoretic operations, in the case of an infinite set of states of the world we can make use of the same operations that we implemented in the finite case. On the other hand, dealing with the beliefs of the players requires using tools from probability theory, which in the case of an infinite set of states of the world means that we need to ensure that this set is a measurable space.

A *measurable space* is a pair $(Y, \mathcal{F})$, with Y denoting a set, and $\mathcal{F}$ a σ-algebra over Y. This means that $\mathcal{F}$ is a family of subsets of Y that includes the empty set, is closed under complementation (i.e., if $A \in \mathcal{F}$ then $A^c = Y \backslash A \in \mathcal{F}$), and is closed under countable unions (i.e., if $(A_n)_{n=1}^{\infty}$ is a family of sets in $\mathcal{F}$ then $\bigcup_{n=1}^{\infty} A_n \in \mathcal{F}$). An event is any element of $\mathcal{F}$. In particular, the partitions of the players, $\mathcal{F}_i$, are composed solely of elements of $\mathcal{F}$.

The collection of all the subsets of Y, 2^Y, is a σ-algebra over Y, and therefore $(Y, 2^Y)$ is a measurable space. This is in fact the measurable space we used, without specifically mentioning it, in all the examples we have seen so far in which Y was a finite set. All the infinite sets of states of the world Y that we will consider in the rest of the section will be a subset of a Euclidean space, and the σ-algebra $\mathcal{F}$ will be the σ-algebra of Borel sets, that is, the smallest σ-algebra that contains all the relatively open sets[11] in Y.

The next example shows that when the set of states of the world is infinite, knowledge is not equivalent to belief with probability 1 (in contrast to the finite case; see Theorem 9.29 on page 347).

Example 9.36 Consider an Aumann model of incomplete information in which the set of players $N = \{I\}$ contains only one player, the set of states of the world is $Y = [0, 1]$, the σ-algebra $\mathcal{F}$ is the σ-algebra of Borel sets,[12] and the player has no information, which means that $\mathcal{F}_I = \{Y\}$. The common prior $\mathbf{P}$ is the uniform distribution over the interval $[0, 1]$.

Since there is only one player and his partition contains only one element, the only event that the player knows (in any state of the world ω) is Y. Let A be the set of irrational numbers in the interval $[0, 1]$, which is in $\mathcal{F}$. As the set A does not contain Y, the player does not know A. But $\mathbf{P}(A \mid \mathcal{F}_I(\omega)) = \mathbf{P}(A \mid Y) = \mathbf{P}(A) = 1$ for all $\omega \in Y$.   ◄

Next we show that when the set of states of the world is infinite, the very notion of knowledge hierarchy can be problematic. To make use of the knowledge structure, for every event $A \in \mathcal{F}$ the event $K_i A$ must also be an element of $\mathcal{F}$: if we can talk about the event A, we should also be able to talk about the event that "player i knows A."

Is it true that for every σ-algebra, every partition $(\mathcal{F}_i)_{i \in N}$ representing the information of the players, and every event $A \in \mathcal{F}$, it is necessarily true that $K_i A \in \mathcal{F}$? When the set of states of the world is infinite, the answer to that question is no. This is illustrated in the next example, which uses the fact that there is a Borel set in the unit square whose projection onto the first coordinate is not a Borel set in the interval $[0, 1]$ (see Suslin [1917]).

Example 9.37 Consider the following Aumann model of incomplete information:

- There are two players: $N = \{I, II\}$.
- The space of states of the world is the unit square: $Y = [0, 1] \times [0, 1]$, and $\mathcal{F}$ is the σ-algebra of Borel sets in the unit square.
- For $i = I, II$, the information of player i is the i-th coordinate of ω; that is, for each $x, y \in [0, 1]$ denote

---

11 When $Y \subseteq \mathbb{R}^d$, a set $A \subseteq Y$ is *relatively open in Y* if it is equal to the intersection of Y with an open set in $\mathbb{R}^d$.

12 In this case the σ-algebra of Borel sets is the smallest σ-algebra that contains all the open intervals in $[0, 1]$, and the intervals of the form $[0, \alpha)$ and $(\alpha, 1]$ for $\alpha \in (0, 1)$.

$$A_x = \{(x, y) \in Y : 0 \leq y \leq 1\}, \qquad B_y = \{(x, y) \in Y : 0 \leq x \leq 1\}. \qquad (9.49)$$

A_x is the set of all points in Y whose first coordinate is x, and B_y is the set of all points in Y whose second coordinate is y. We then have

$$\mathcal{F}_I = \{A_x : 0 \leq x \leq 1\}, \qquad \mathcal{F}_{II} = \{B_y : 0 \leq y \leq 1\}. \qquad (9.50)$$

In words, Player I's partition is the set of vertical sections of Y, and the partition of Player II is the set of horizontal sections of Y. Thus, for any $(x, y) \in Y$ Player I knows the x-coordinate and Player II knows the y-coordinate.

Let $E \subseteq Y$ be a Borel set whose projection onto the x-axis is not a Borel set, i.e., the set

$$F = \{x \in [0, 1] : \text{there exists } y \in [0, 1] \text{ such that } (x, y) \in E\} \qquad (9.51)$$

is not a Borel set, and hence $F^c = Y \setminus F$ is also not a Borel set in $[0, 1]$. Player I knows that the event E does not obtain when the x-coordinate is not in F:

$$K_I(E^c) = F^c \times [0, 1]. \qquad (9.52)$$

This implies that despite the fact that the set E^c is a Borel set, the set of states of the world in which Player I knows the event E^c is not a Borel set.   ◀

In spite of the technical difficulties indicated by Examples 9.36 and 9.37, in Chapter 10 we develop a general model of incomplete information that allows infinite sets of states of the world.

9.4 The Harsanyi model of games with incomplete information

In our treatment of the Aumann model of incomplete information, we concentrated on concepts such as mutual knowledge and mutual beliefs among players regarding the true state of the world. Now we will analyze games with incomplete information, which are models in which the incomplete information is about the game that the players play. In this case, a state of nature consists of all the parameters that have a bearing on the payoffs, that is, the set of actions of each player and his payoff function. This is why the state of nature in this case is also called the *payoff-relevant parameter* of the game. This model was first introduced by John Harsanyi [1967], nine years prior to the introduction of the Aumann model of incomplete information, and was the first model of incomplete information used in game theory.

The Harsanyi model consists of two elements. The first is the games in which the players may participate, which will be called "state games," and are the analogue of states of nature in Aumann's model of incomplete information. The second is the beliefs that the players have about both the state games and the beliefs of the other players.

Since the information the player has of the game is incomplete, a player is characterized by his beliefs about the state of nature (namely, the state game) and the beliefs of the other players. This characterization was called by Harsanyi the *type* of the player. In fact, as we shall see, a player's type in a Harsanyi model is equivalent to his belief hierarchy in an Aumann model. Just as we did when studying the Aumann model of incomplete information, we will also assume here that the space of states of the world is finite, so that the number of types of each player is finite. We will further assume that every player knows his own type, and that the set of types is common knowledge among the players.

Example 9.38 Harry (Player I, the row player) and William (Player II, the column player) are playing a game in which the payoff functions are determined by one of the two matrices appearing in Figure 9.7. William has two possible actions (t and b), while Harry has two or three possible actions (either T and B, or T, C, and B), depending on the payoff function.

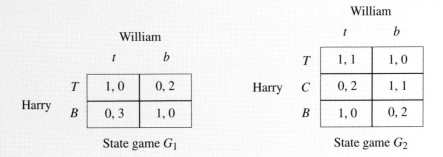

William

	t	b
T	1, 0	0, 2
B	0, 3	1, 0

State game G_1

William

	t	b
T	1, 1	1, 0
C	0, 2	1, 1
B	1, 0	0, 2

State game G_2

Figure 9.7 The state games in the game in Example 9.38

Harry knows the payoff function (and therefore in particular knows whether he has two or three actions available). William only knows that the payoff functions are given by either G_1 or G_2. He ascribes probability p to the payoff function being given by G_1 and probability $1 - p$ to the payoff function being given by G_2. This description is common knowledge among Harry and William.[13]

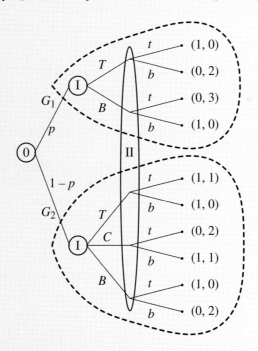

Figure 9.8 The game in Example 9.38 in extensive form

---

[13] In other words, both Harry and William know that this is the description of the game, each one knows that the other knows that this is the description of the game, and so on.

This situation can be captured by the extensive-form game appearing in Figure 9.8. In this game, Nature chooses G_1 or G_2 with probability p or $1 - p$, respectively, with the choice known to Harry but not to William. In Figure 9.8 the state games are delineated by broken lines. Neither of the two state games is a subgame (Definition 3.11, page 45), because there are information sets that contain vertices from two state games.

◄

The game appearing in Figure 9.8 is the game that Harsanyi suggested as the model for the situation described in Example 9.8. Such a game is called a *Harsanyi game with incomplete information* and defined as follows.

Definition 9.39 *A* Harasanyi *game* with *incomplete* information *is a vector* $(N, (T_i)_{i \in N}, p, S, (s_t)_{t \in \times_{i \in N} T_i})$ *where:*

- N *is a finite set of players.*
- T_i *is a finite set of* types *for player i, for each $i \in N$. The set of type vectors is denoted by $T = \times_{i \in N} T_i$.*
- $p \in \Delta(T)$ *is a probability distribution over the set of type vectors*[14] *that satisfies* $p(t_i) := \sum_{t_{-i} \in T_{-i}} p(t_i, t_{-i}) > 0$ *for every player $i \in N$ and every type $t_i \in T_i$.*
- S *is a set of states of nature, which will be called* state games.[15] *Every state of nature* $s \in S$ *is a vector* $s = (N, (A_i)_{i \in N}, (u_i)_{i \in N})$, *where A_i is a nonempty set of actions of player i and $u_i : \times_{i \in N} A_i \to \mathbb{R}$ is the payoff function of player i.*
- $s_t = (N, (A_i(t_i))_{i \in N}, (u_i(t))_{i \in N}) \in S$ *is the state game for the type vector t, for every $t \in T$. Thus, player i's action set in the state game s_t depends on his type t_i only, and is independent of the types of the other players.*

A game with incomplete information proceeds as follows:

- A chance move selects a type vector $t = (t_1, t_2, \ldots, t_n) \in T$ according to the probability distribution p.
- Every player i knows the type t_i that has been selected for him (i.e., his own type), but does not know the types $t_{-i} = (t_j)_{j \neq i}$ of the other players.
- The players select their actions simultaneously: each player i, knowing his type t_i, selects an action $a_i \in A_i(t_i)$.
- Every player i receives the payoff $u_i(t; a)$, where $a = (a_1, a_2, \ldots, a_n)$ is the vector of actions that have been selected by the players.

Player i, of type t_i, does not know the types of the other players; he has a belief about their types. This belief is the conditional probability distribution $p(\cdot \mid t_i)$ over the set $T_{-i} = \times_{j \neq i} T_j$ of the vectors of the types of the other players. The set of actions that player i believes that he has at his disposal is part of his type, and therefore the set $A_i(t_i)$ of actions available to player i in the state game s_t is determined by t_i only, and not by the types of other players. It is possible for a player, though, not to know the sets of

---

14 Recall that $T_{-i} = \times_{j \neq i} T_j$ and $t_{-i} = (t_j)_{j \neq i}$.

15 For the sake of notational convenience, every state game will be represented by a game in strategic form. Everything stated in this section also holds true in the case in which every state game is represented by a game in extensive form.

actions that the other players have at their disposal, as we saw in Example 9.38. He does have beliefs about the action sets of the other players, which are derived from his beliefs about their types. The payoff of player i depends on the state game s_t and on the vector of actions a selected by the players, so that it depends on the vector of types t in two ways:

- The set of action vectors $A(t) := \times_{i \in N} A_i(t_i)$ in the state game s_t depends on t.
- The payoff function $u_i(t)$ in the state game s_t depends on t; even when the sets of action $A_j(t_j)$ do not depend on the player j's type, player i's payoff depends on the types of all players.

Because a player may not know for certain the types of the other players, he may not know for certain the state of nature, which in turn implies that he may not know for certain his own payoff function. In summary, a Harsanyi game is an extensive-form game consisting of several state games related to each other through information sets, as depicted in Figure 9.8.

Remark 9.40 *The Harsanyi model, defined in Definition 9.39, provides a tool to describe the incomplete information a player may have regarding the possible action sets of the other players, their utility functions, and even the set of other players active in the game: a player j who is not active in state game s_t has type t_j such that $A_j(t_j)$ contains only one action. This interpretation makes sense because the set of equilibria in the game is independent of the payoffs to such a type t_j of player j (see Exercise 9.45).* ◆

Remark 9.41 *We note that in reality there is no chance move that selects one of the state games: the players play one, and only one, of the possible state games. The Harsanyi game is a construction we use to present the situation of interest to us, by describing the beliefs of the players about the game that they are playing. For instance, suppose that in Example 9.38 the players play the game G_1. Since William does not know whether the game he is playing is G_1 or G_2, from his standpoint he plays a state game that can be either one of these games. Therefore, he constructs the extensive-form game that is described in Figure 9.8, and the situation that he faces is a Harsanyi game with incomplete information.* ◆

In the economic literature the Harsanyi model is often referred to as the *ex ante stage*[16] model as it captures the situation of the players before knowing their types. The situation obtained after the chance move has selected the types of the players is referred to as the *interim stage* model. This model corresponds to an Aumann situation of incomplete information that captures the situation in a specific state of the world (Definition 9.5, page 335).

The next theorem generalizes Example 9.38, and states that any Harsanyi game with incomplete information can be described as an extensive-form game. Its proof is left to the reader (Exercise 9.35).

Theorem 9.42 *Every (Harsanyi) game with incomplete information can be described as an extensive-form game (with moves of chance and information sets).*

....

16 The Latin expression *ex ante* means "before."

9.4.1 Belief hierarchies

In any Aumann model of incomplete information we can attach a belief hierarchy to every state of the world (Theorem 9.30, page 348). Similarly, in any Harsanyi game with incomplete information we can attach a belief hierarchy to every type vector. We illustrate this point by the following example.

Example 9.43 The residents of the town of Smallville live in a closed and supportive tight-knit community. The personality characteristic that they regard as most important revolves around the question of whether a person puts his family life ahead of his career, or his career ahead of his family. Kevin, the local matchmaker, approaches two of the residents, Abe and Sarah, informing them that in his opinion they would be well suited as a couple. It is well known in the community from past experience that Kevin tends to match a man who stresses his career with a woman who emphasizes family life, and a man who puts family first with a woman who is career-oriented, but there were several instances in the past when Kevin did not stick to that rule. The distribution of past matches initiated by Kevin is presented in Figure 9.9.

	Family Woman	Career Woman
Family Man	$\frac{1}{10}$	$\frac{3}{10}$
Career Man	$\frac{4}{10}$	$\frac{2}{10}$

Figure 9.9 Player types with prior distribution

The above verbal description can be presented as a Harsanyi model (without specifying the state games) in the following way:

- The set of players is $N = \{\text{Abe}, \text{Sarah}\}$.
- Abe's set of types is $T_A = \{\text{Careerist}, \text{Family}\}$.
- Sarah's set of types is $T_S = \{\text{Careerist}, \text{Family}\}$.
- Because this match is one of Kevin's matches, the probability distribution p over $T = T_A \times T_S$ is calculated from past matches of Kevin; namely, it is the probability distribution given in Figure 9.9.
- Since the state game corresponding to each pair of types is not specified, we denote the set of states of nature by $S = \{s_{CC}, s_{CF}, s_{FC}, s_{FF}\}$, without specifying the details of each state game. For each state game, the left index indicates the type of Abe ("C" for Career man, "F" for Family man) and the right index indicates the type of Sarah ("C" for Career woman, "F" for Family woman).

As each player knows his own type, armed with knowledge of the past performance of the matchmaker (the prior distribution in Figure 9.9), each player can calculate the conditional probability of the type of the other player. For example, if Abe is a careerist, he can conclude that the conditional probability that Sarah is also a careerist is

$$p(\text{Sarah is a careerist} \mid \text{Abe is a careerist}) = \frac{\frac{2}{10}}{\frac{2}{10} + \frac{4}{10}} = \frac{1}{3},$$

while if Abe is a family man he can conclude that the conditional probability that Sarah is a careerist is

$$p(\text{Sarah is a careerist} \mid \text{Abe is a family man}) = \frac{\frac{3}{10}}{\frac{1}{10} + \frac{3}{10}} = \frac{3}{4}.$$

◄

Given his type, every player can calculate the infinite belief hierarchy. The continuation of our example illustrates this.

Example 9.43 (*Continued*) Suppose that Abe's type is careerist. As shown above, in that case his first-order beliefs about the state of nature is $[\frac{2}{3}(s_{CF}), \frac{1}{3}(s_{CC})]$. His second-order beliefs are as follows: he ascribes probability $\frac{2}{3}$ to the state of nature being s_{CF}, in which case Sarah's beliefs are $[\frac{1}{5}(s_{FF}), \frac{4}{5}(s_{CF})]$ (this follows from a similar calculation to the one performed above; verify!), and he ascribes probability $\frac{1}{3}$ to the state of nature being s_{CC}, in which case Sarah's beliefs are $[\frac{3}{5}(s_{FC}), \frac{2}{5}(s_{CC})]$. Abe's higher-order beliefs can similarly be calculated.   ◄

When we analyze a Harsanyi game without specifying the state game corresponding to each state of nature, we will refer to it as a *Harsanyi model of incomplete information*. Such a model is equivalent to an Aumann model of incomplete information in the sense that every situation of incomplete information that can be analyzed using one model can be analyzed using the other one: a partition element $F_i(\omega)$ of player i in an Aumann model is his type in a Harsanyi model. Let $(N, (T_i)_{i \in N}, p, S, (s_t)_{t \in \times_{i \in N} T_i})$ be a Harsanyi model of incomplete information. An Aumann model of incomplete information describing the same structure of mutual information is the model in which the set of states of the world is the set of type vectors that have positive probability

$$Y = \{t \in T : p(t) > 0\}. \tag{9.53}$$

The partition of each player i is given by his type: for every type $t_i \in T_i$, there is a partition element $F_i(t_i) \in \mathcal{F}_i$, given as follows:

$$F_i(t_i) = \{(t_i, t_{-i}) : t_{-i} \in T_{-i}, p(t_i, t_{-i}) > 0\}. \tag{9.54}$$

The common prior is $\mathbf{P} = p$.

In the other direction, let $(N, Y, (\mathcal{F}_i)_{i \in N}, \mathfrak{s})$ be an Aumann model of incomplete information over a set S of states of nature. A corresponding Harsanyi model of incomplete information is given by the model in which the set of types of each player i is the set of his partition elements $\mathcal{F}_i$:

$$T_i = \{F_i \in \mathcal{F}_i\}, \tag{9.55}$$

and the probability distribution p is given by

$$p(F_1, F_2, \ldots, F_n) = \mathbf{P}\left(\bigcap_{i \in N} F_i\right). \tag{9.56}$$

Note that the intersection in this equation may be empty, or it may contain only one state of the world, or it may contain several states of the world. If the intersection is empty, the corresponding type vector is ascribed a probability of 0. If the intersection contains more than one state of the world, then in the Aumann model of incomplete information no player can distinguish between these states. The Harsanyi model identifies all these states as one state, and ascribes to the corresponding type vector the sum of their probabilities.

This correspondence shows that a state of the world in an Aumann model of incomplete information is a vector containing the state of nature and the type of each player. The state of nature describes the payoff-relevant parameters, and the player's type describes his beliefs. This is why we sometimes write a state of the world ω in the following form (we will expand on this in Chapter 11):

$$\omega = (\mathfrak{s}(\omega); t_1(\omega), t_2(\omega), \ldots, t_n(\omega)), \tag{9.57}$$

where $\mathfrak{s}(\omega)$ is the state of nature and $t_i(\omega)$ is player i's type in the state of the world ω.

The following conclusion is a consequence of Theorem 9.30 (page 348) and the equivalence between the Aumann model and the Harsanyi model.

Theorem 9.44 *In a Harsanyi model of incomplete information, every state of the world $\omega = (\mathfrak{s}(\omega); t_1(\omega), t_2(\omega), \ldots, t_n(\omega))$ uniquely determines the belief hierarchy of each player over the state of nature and the beliefs of the other players.*

9.4.2 Strategies and payoffs

In the presentation of a game with incomplete information as an extensive-form game, each type $t_i \in T_i$ corresponds to an information set of player i. It follows that a *pure strategy*[17] of player i is a function $s_i : T_i \to \bigcup_{t_i \in T_i} A_i(t_i)$ that satisfies

$$s_i(t_i) \in A_i(t_i), \quad \forall t_i \in T_i. \tag{9.58}$$

In words, $s_i(t_i)$ is the action specified by the strategy s_i for player i of type t_i (which is an action available to him as a player of type t_i). A *mixed strategy* of player i is, as usual, a probability distribution over his pure strategies. A *behavior strategy* σ_i of player i is a function mapping each type $t_i \in T_i$ to a probability distribution over the actions available to that type. Notationally, $\sigma_i : T_i \to \bigcup_{t_i \in T_i} \Delta(A_i(t_i))$ that satisfies

$$\sigma_i(t_i) = (\sigma_i(t_i; a_i))_{a_i \in A_i(t_i)} \in \Delta(A_i(t_i)). \tag{9.59}$$

In words, $\sigma_i(t_i; a_i)$ is the probability that player i of type t_i chooses the action a_i. A Harsanyi game is an extensive-form game with perfect recall (Definition 9.39, page 358), and therefore by Kuhn's Theorem (Theorem 4.49, page 118) every mixed strategy is equivalent to a behavior strategy. For this reason, there is no loss of generality in using only behavior strategies, which is indeed what we do in this section.

Remark 9.45 *Behavior strategy, as defined here, is a behavior strategy in a Harsanyi game in which the state game corresponding to t is a strategic-form game. If the state game is an extensive-form game, then $A_i(t_i)$ is the set of pure strategies in that game, so that $\Delta(A_i(t_i))$ is the set of mixed strategies of this state game. In this case, a strategy $\sigma_i : T_i \to \bigcup_{t_i \in T_i} \Delta(A_i(t_i))$ in which $\sigma_i(t_i) \in \Delta(A_i(t_i))$ is not a behavior strategy of the Harsanyi game. Rather, a behavior strategy is a function $\sigma_i : T_i \to \bigcup_{t_i \in T_i} \mathcal{B}_i(t_i)$ with $\sigma_i(t_i) \in \mathcal{B}_i(t_i)$ for every $t_i \in T_i$, where $\mathcal{B}_i(t_i)$ is the set of behavior strategies of player i in*

---

17 We use the notation s_i for a pure strategy of player i, and s_t for the state game that corresponds to the type vector t.

the state game $s_{(t_i,t_{-i})}$, *which is the same for all* $t_{-i} \in T_{-i}$. *The distinction between these definitions is immaterial to the presentation in this section, and the results obtained here apply whether the state game is given in strategic form or in extensive form.*   ◆

If the vector of the players' behavior strategies is $\sigma = (\sigma_1, \sigma_2, \ldots, \sigma_n)$, and the vector of types that is selected by the chance move is $t = (t_1, \ldots, t_n)$, then each vector of actions $(a_1, \ldots, a_n)$ is selected with probability

$$\sigma_1(t_1; a_1) \times \sigma_2(t_2; a_2) \times \cdots \times \sigma_n(t_n; a_n). \tag{9.60}$$

Player i's expected payoff, which we denote by $U_i(t; \sigma)$, is therefore

$$U_i(t; \sigma) := \mathbf{E}_\sigma[u_i(t)] = \sum_{a \in A(t)} \sigma_1(t_1; a_1) \times \cdots \times \sigma_n(t_n; a_n) \times u_i(t; a). \tag{9.61}$$

It follows that when the players implement strategy vector σ, the expected payoff in the game for player i is

$$U_i(\sigma) := \sum_{t \in T} p(t) U_i(t; \sigma). \tag{9.62}$$

This is the expected payoff for player i at the ex ante stage, that is, before he has learned what type he is. After the chance move, the vector of types has been selected, and the conditional expected payoff to player i of type t_i is

$$U_i(\sigma \mid t_i) := \sum_{t_{-i} \in T_{-i}} p(t_{-i} \mid t_i) U_i((t_i, t_{-i}); \sigma), \tag{9.63}$$

where

$$p(t_{-i} \mid t_i) = \frac{p(t_i, t_{-i})}{\sum_{t'_{-i} \in T_{-i}} p(t_i, t'_{-i})} = \frac{p(t_i, t_{-i})}{p(t_i)}. \tag{9.64}$$

This is the expected payoff of player i at the interim stage. The connection between the ex ante (unconditional expected) payoff $U_i(\sigma)$ and the interim (conditional) payoff $(U_i(\sigma \mid t_i))_{t_i \in T_i}$ is given by the equation

$$U_i(\sigma) = \sum_{t_i \in T_i} p(t_i) U_i(\sigma \mid t_i). \tag{9.65}$$

Indeed,

$$\sum_{t_i \in T_i} p(t_i) U_i(\sigma \mid t_i) = \sum_{t_i \in T_i} p(t_i) \sum_{t_{-i} \in T_{-i}} p(t_{-i} \mid t_i) U_i((t_i, t_{-i}); \sigma) \tag{9.66}$$

$$= \sum_{t_{-i} \in T_{-i}} \sum_{t_i \in T_i} p(t_i) p(t_{-i} \mid t_i) U_i((t_i, t_{-i}); \sigma) \tag{9.67}$$

$$= \sum_{t \in T} p(t) U_i(t; \sigma) \tag{9.68}$$

$$= U_i(\sigma). \tag{9.69}$$

Equation (9.66) follows from Equation (9.63), Equation (9.67) is a rearrangement of sums, Equation (9.68) is a consequence of the definition of conditional probability, and Equation (9.69) follows from Equation (9.62).

9.4.3   Equilibrium in games with incomplete information

As we pointed out, Harsanyi games with incomplete information may be analyzed at two separate points in time: at the ex ante stage, before the players know their types, and at the interim stage, after they have learned what types they are. Accordingly, two different types of equilibria can be defined. The first equilibrium concept, which is Nash equilibrium in Harsanyi games, poses the requirement that no player can profit by a unilateral deviation before knowing his type. The second equilibrium concept, called Bayesian equilibrium, poses the requirement that no player i can profit by deviating at the interim stage, after learning his type t_i.

Definition 9.46 *A strategy vector σ^* is a* Nash equilibrium *if*[18] *for each player i and each strategy σ_i of player i,*

$$U_i(\sigma^*) \geq U_i(\sigma_i, \sigma_{-i}^*). \tag{9.70}$$

As every game with incomplete information can be described as an extensive-form game (Theorem 9.42), every finite extensive-form game has a Nash equilibrium in mixed strategies (Theorem 5.13, page 151), and every mixed strategy is equivalent to a behavior strategy, we arrive at the following conclusion:

Theorem 9.47 *Every game with incomplete information in which the set of types is finite and the set of actions of each type is finite has a Nash equilibrium in behavior strategies.*

Remark 9.48 *When the set of player types is countable, a Nash equilibrium is still guaranteed to exist (see Exercise 9.43). In contrast, when the set of player types is uncountable, it may be the case that all the equilibria involve strategies that are not measurable (see Simon [2003]).*   ♦

Definition 9.49 *A strategy vector $\sigma^* = (\sigma_1^*, \sigma_2^*, \ldots, \sigma_n^*)$ is a* Bayesian equilibrium *if for each player $i \in N$, each type $t_i \in T_i$, and each possible*[19] *action $a_i \in A_i(t_i)$,*

$$U_i(\sigma^* \mid t_i) \geq U_i((a_i, \sigma_{-i}^*) \mid t_i). \tag{9.71}$$

An equivalent way to define Bayesian equilibrium is by way of an auxiliary game, called the *agent-form game*.

Definition 9.50 *Let $\Gamma = (N, (T_i)_{i \in N}, p, S, (s_t)_{t \in T})$ be a game with incomplete information. The* agent-form game *$\widehat{\Gamma}$ corresponding to Γ is the following game in strategic form:*

- *The set of players is $\cup_{i \in N} T_i$: every type of each player in Γ is a player in $\widehat{\Gamma}$.*
- *The set of pure strategies of player t_i in $\widehat{\Gamma}$ is $A_i(t_i)$, the set of available actions of that type in the game Γ.*

---

[18] Recall that $\sigma_{-i}^* = (\sigma_j^*)_{j \neq i}$.

[19] In Equation (9.71), $U_i((a_i, \sigma_{-i}^*) \mid t_i)$ is the payoff of player i of type t_i, when all other players use σ^*, and he plays action a_i.

- *The payoff function $\widehat{u}_{t_i}$ of player t_i in $\widehat{\Gamma}$ is given by*

$$\widehat{u}_{t_i}(a) := \sum_{t_{-i} \in T_{-i}} p(t_{-i} \mid t_i) u_i(t_i, t_{-i}; (a_j(t_j))_{j \in N}), \tag{9.72}$$

where $a = (a_j(t_j))_{j \in N, t_j \in T_j}$ denotes a vector of actions of all the players in $\widehat{\Gamma}$.

The payoff $\widehat{u}_{t_i}(a)$ of player t_i in $\widehat{\Gamma}$ equals the expected payoff of player i of type t_i in the game Γ when he chooses action $a_i(t_i)$, and for any $j \neq i$, player j of type t_j chooses action $a_j(t_j)$. The conditional probability in Equation (9.72) is well defined because we have assumed that $p(t_i) > 0$ for each player i and each type t_i.

Note that every behavior strategy $\sigma_i = (\sigma_i(t_i))_{t_i \in T_i}$ of player i in the game Γ naturally defines a mixed strategy for the players in T_i in the agent-form game $\widehat{\Gamma}$. Conversely, every vector of mixed strategies of the players in T_i in the agent-form game $\widehat{\Gamma}$ naturally defines a behavior strategy $\sigma_i = (\sigma_i(t_i))_{t_i \in T_i}$ of player i in the game Γ.

Theorem 9.51 relates Bayesian equilibria in a game Γ to the Nash equilibria in the corresponding agent-form game $\widehat{\Gamma}$. The proof of the theorem is left to the reader (Exercise 9.44).

Theorem 9.51 *A strategy vector $\sigma^* = (\sigma_i^*)_{i \in N}$ is a Bayesian equilibrium in a game Γ with incomplete information if and only if the strategy vector $(\sigma_i^*(t_i))_{i \in N, t_i \in T_i}$ is a Nash equilibrium in the corresponding agent-form game $\widehat{\Gamma}$.*

As every game in strategic form in which the set of pure strategies available to each player is finite has a Nash equilibrium (Theorem 5.13, page 151), we derive the next theorem:

Theorem 9.52 *Every game with incomplete information in which the set of types is finite and the set of actions of each type is finite has a Bayesian equilibrium (in behavior strategies).*

As already noted, the two definitions of equilibrium presented in this section (Nash equilibrium and Bayesian equilibrium) express two different perspectives on the game: does each player regard the game prior to knowing his type or after knowing it? Theorem 9.53 states that these two definitions are in fact equivalent.

Theorem 9.53 (Harsanyi [1967]) *In a game with incomplete information in which the number of types of each player is finite, every Bayesian equilibrium is also a Nash equilibrium, and conversely every Nash equilibrium is also a Bayesian equilibrium.*

In other words, no player has a profitable deviation *after* he knows which type he is if and only if he has no profitable deviation *before* knowing his type. Recall that in the definition of a game with incomplete information we required that $p(t_i) > 0$ for each player i and each type $t_i \in T_i$. This is essential for the validity of Theorem 9.53, because if there is a type that is chosen with probability 0 in a Harsanyi game, the action selected by a player of that type has no effect on the payoff. In particular, in a Nash equilibrium a player of this type can take any action. In contrast, because the conditional probabilities $p(t_{-i} \mid t_i)$ in Equation (9.64) are not defined for such a type, the payoff function of this type is undefined, and in that case we cannot define a Bayesian equilibrium.

Proof of Theorem 9.53: The idea of the proof runs as follows. Because the expected payoff of player i in a game with incomplete information is the expectation of the conditional expected payoff of all of his types t_i, and because the probability of each type is positive, it follows that every deviation that increases the expected payoff of any single type of player i also increases the overall payoff for player i in the game. In the other direction, if there is a deviation that increases the total expected payoff of player i in the game, it must necessarily increase the conditional expected payoff of at least one type t_i.

Step 1: Every Bayesian equilibrium is a Nash equilibrium.
Let σ^* be a Bayesian equilibrium. Then for each player $i \in N$, each type $t_i \in T_i$, and each action $a_i \in A_i(t_i)$,

$$U_i(\sigma^* \mid t_i) \geq U_i(a_i, \sigma^*_{-i} \mid t_i). \tag{9.73}$$

Combined with Equation (9.65) this implies that for each pure strategy s_i of player i we have

$$U_i(s_i, \sigma^*_{-i}) = \sum_{t_i \in T_i} p(t_i) U_i(s_i(t_i), \sigma^*_{-i} \mid t_i) \leq \sum_{t_i \in T_i} p(t_i) U_i(\sigma^* \mid t_i) = U_i(\sigma^*). \tag{9.74}$$

As this inequality holds for any pure strategy s_i of player i, it also holds for any of his mixed strategies. This implies that σ^*_i is a best reply to σ^*_{-i}. Since this is true for each player $i \in N$, we conclude that σ^* is a Nash equilibrium.

Step 2: Every Nash equilibrium is a Bayesian equilibrium.
We will prove that if σ^* is not a Bayesian equilibrium, then it is also not a Nash equilibrium. As σ^* is not a Bayesian equilibrium, there is at least one player $i \in N$, type $t_i \in T_i$, and action $a_i \in A_i(t_i)$ satisfying

$$U_i(\sigma^* \mid t_i) < U_i((a_i, \sigma^*_{-i}) \mid t_i). \tag{9.75}$$

Consider a strategy $\widehat{\sigma}_i$ of player i defined by

$$\widehat{\sigma}_i(t'_i) = \begin{cases} \sigma^*_i(t'_i) & \text{when } t'_i \neq t_i, \\ a_i & \text{when } t'_i = t_i. \end{cases} \tag{9.76}$$

In words: strategy $\widehat{\sigma}_i$ is identical to strategy σ^*_i except in the case of type t_i, who plays a_i instead of $\sigma^*_i(t_i)$. Equations (9.65) and (9.75) then imply that

$$U_i(\widehat{\sigma}_i, \sigma^*_{-i}) = \sum_{t'_i \in T_i} p(t'_i) U_i(\widehat{\sigma}_i, \sigma^*_{-i} \mid t'_i) \tag{9.77}$$

$$= \sum_{t'_i \neq t_i} p(t'_i) U_i(\widehat{\sigma}_i, \sigma^*_{-i} \mid t'_i) + p(t_i) U_i(\widehat{\sigma}_i, \sigma^*_{-i} \mid t_i) \tag{9.78}$$

$$= \sum_{t'_i \neq t_i} p(t'_i) U_i(\sigma^*_i, \sigma^*_{-i} \mid t'_i) + p(t_i) U_i(a_i, \sigma^*_{-i} \mid t_i) \tag{9.79}$$

$$> \sum_{t_i' \neq t_i} p(t_i') U_i(\sigma_i^*, \sigma_{-i}^* \mid t_i') + p(t_i) U_i(\sigma_i^*, \sigma_{-i}^* \mid t_i) \tag{9.80}$$

$$= \sum_{t_i' \in T_i} p(t_i') U_i(\sigma^* \mid t_i') = U_i(\sigma^*). \tag{9.81}$$

Inequality (9.80) follows from (9.75) and the assumption that $p(t_i) > 0$ for each player i and every type $t_i \in T_i$. From the chain of Equations (9.77)–(9.81) we get

$$U_i(\widehat{\sigma}_i, \sigma_{-i}^*) > U_i(\sigma^*), \tag{9.82}$$

which implies that σ^* is not a Nash equilibrium. $\square$

We next present two examples of games with incomplete information and calculate their Bayesian equilibria.

Example 9.54   Consider the following game with incomplete information:

- $N = \{I, II\}$.
- $T_I = \{I_1, I_2\}$ and $T_{II} = \{II\}$: Player I has two types and Player II has one type.
- $p(I_1, II) = p(I_2, II) = \frac{1}{2}$: the two types of Player I have equal probabilities.
- There are two states of nature corresponding to two state games in which each player has two possible actions, and the payoff functions are given by the matrices shown in Figure 9.10.

Player II

	L	R
T_1	1, 0	0, 2
B_1	0, 3	1, 0

Player I

The state game for $t = (I_1, II)$

Player II

	L	R
T_2	0, 2	1, 1
B_2	1, 0	0, 2

Player I

The state game for $t = (I_2, II)$

Figure 9.10 The state games in Example 9.54

Because the information each player has is his own type, Player I knows the payoff matrix, while Player II does not know it (see Figure 9.11).

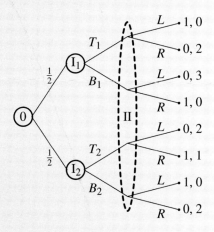

Figure 9.11 The game of Example 9.54 in extensive form

Turning to the calculation of Bayesian equilibria in this game, given such an equilibrium, denote by $[q(L), (1-q)(R)]$ the equilibrium strategy of Player II, by $[x(T_1), (1-x)(B_1)]$ the equilibrium strategy of Player I of type I_1, and by $[y(T_2), (1-y)(B_2)]$ the equilibrium strategy of Player I of type I_2 (see Figure 9.12).

Strategies in state game $t = (I_1, II)$ Strategies in state game $t = (I_2, II)$

Figure 9.12 The strategies of the players in the game of Example 9.54

We first show that $0 < q < 1$.

- If $q = 1$, then type I_1's best reply is T ($x = 1$) and I_2's best reply is B ($y = 0$). But Player II's best reply to this strategy is R ($q = 0$). It follows that $q = 1$ is not part of a Bayesian equilibrium.
- If $q = 0$, then type I_1's best reply is B ($x = 0$) and I_2's best reply is T ($y = 1$). But Player II's best reply to this strategy is L ($q = 1$). It follows that $q = 0$ is not part of a Bayesian equilibrium.

The conclusion is therefore that in a Bayesian equilibrium Player II's strategy must be completely mixed, so that he is necessarily indifferent between L and R. This implies that

$$\tfrac{1}{2} \cdot 3(1-x) + \tfrac{1}{2} \cdot 2y = \tfrac{1}{2} \cdot 2x + \tfrac{1}{2}(y + 2(1-y)), \tag{9.83}$$

giving us

$$x = \frac{1+3y}{5}. \tag{9.84}$$

Is every pair (x, y) satisfying Equation (9.84) part of a Bayesian equilibrium? For (x, y) to be part of a Bayesian equilibrium, it must be a best reply to q.

- If $q < \tfrac{1}{2}$, Player I's best reply is $x = 0, y = 1$, which does not satisfy Equation (9.84).
- If $q = \tfrac{1}{2}$, Player I's payoff is $\tfrac{1}{2}$ irrespective of what he plays, so that every pair (x, y) is a best reply to $q = \tfrac{1}{2}$.
- If $q > \tfrac{1}{2}$, Player I's best reply is $x = 1, y = 0$, which does not satisfy Equation (9.84).

This leads to the conclusion that a pair of strategies $(x, y; q)$ is a Bayesian equilibrium if and only if $q = \tfrac{1}{2}$ and Equation (9.84) is satisfied. Since x and y are both in the interval $[0, 1]$ we obtain

$$\tfrac{1}{5} \le x \le \tfrac{4}{5}, \quad 0 \le y \le 1, \quad x = \tfrac{1+3y}{5}. \tag{9.85}$$

We have thus obtained a continuum of Bayesian equilibria $(x, y; q)$, in all of which Player I's payoff (of either type) is $\tfrac{1}{2}$, and Player II's payoff is

$$\tfrac{1}{2} \cdot 3(1-x) + \tfrac{1}{2} \cdot 2y = \tfrac{12+y}{10}. \tag{9.86}$$

◀

Example 9.55 **Cournot duopoly competition with incomplete information** Consider the duopoly competition described in Example 4.23 (page 99) when there is incomplete information regarding production costs. Two manufacturers, labeled 1 and 2, produce the same product and compete for the same market of potential customers. The manufacturers simultaneously select their production quantities, with demand determining the market price of the product, which is identical for both manufacturers. Denote by q_1 and q_2 the quantities respectively produced by manufacturers 1 and 2. The total quantity of products in the market is therefore $q_1 + q_2$. Assume that when the supply is $q_1 + q_2$ the price of each item is $2 - q_1 - q_2$. The per-item production cost for Manufacturer 1 is $c_1 = 1$, and it is common knowledge among the two manufacturers. The per-item production cost for Manufacturer 2 is known only to him, not to Manufacturer 1. All that Manufacturer 1 knows about it is that it is either $c_2^L = \frac{3}{4}$ (low cost) or $c_2^H = \frac{5}{4}$ (high cost), with equal probability. Note that the average production cost of Manufacturer 2 is 1, which is equal to Manufacturer 1's cost.

Let us find a Bayesian equilibrium of this game. This is a game with incomplete information in which the types of each manufacturer correspond to their production costs:[20]

- $N = \{1, 2\}$.
- $T_1 = \{1\}, T_2 = \left\{ \frac{3}{4}, \frac{5}{4} \right\}$.
- $p(1, \frac{3}{4}) = p(1, \frac{5}{4}) = \frac{1}{2}$.
- There are two states of nature, corresponding respectively to the type vectors $(1, \frac{3}{4})$ and $(1, \frac{5}{4})$. Each one of these states of nature corresponds to a state game in which the action set of each player is $[0, \infty)$ (each player can produce any nonnegative quantity of items), and the payoff functions which we provide now.

Denote by $u_i(q_1, q_2^H, q_2^L)$ the net profit of Manufacturer i as a function of the quantities of items produced by each type, where q_1 is the quantity produced by Manufacturer 1, q_2^H is the quantity produced by Manufacturer 2 if his production costs are high, and q_2^L is the quantity produced by Manufacturer 2 if his production costs are low. As Manufacturer 1 does not know the type of Manufacturer 2, his expected profit is

$$u_1\left(q_1, q_2^H, q_2^L\right) = \tfrac{1}{2}q_1\left(2 - q_1 - q_2^H\right) + \tfrac{1}{2}q_1\left(2 - q_1 - q_2^L\right) - c_1 q_1$$

$$= q_1\left(2 - c_1 - q_1 - \tfrac{1}{2}q_2^H - \tfrac{1}{2}q_2^L\right). \tag{9.87}$$

The net profit of Manufacturer 2's two possible types is

$$u_2^H\left(q_1, q_2^H, q_2^L\right) = q_2^H\left(2 - q_1 - q_2^H\right) - c_2^H q_2^H = q_2^H\left(2 - c_2^H - q_1 - q_2^H\right), \tag{9.88}$$

$$u_2^L\left(q_1, q_2^H, q_2^L\right) = q_2^L\left(2 - q_1 - q_2^L\right) - c_2^L q_2^L = q_2^L\left(2 - c_2^L - q_1 - q_2^L\right). \tag{9.89}$$

Since each manufacturer has a continuum of actions, the existence of an equilibrium is not guaranteed. Nevertheless, we will assume that an equilibrium exists, and try to calculate it. Denote by q_1^* the quantity of items produced by Manufacturer 1 at equilibrium, by q_2^{*H} the quantity produced by Manufacturer 2 at equilibrium if his production costs are high, and by q_2^{*L} the quantity he produces at equilibrium under low production costs. At equilibrium, every

---

20 Similar to remarks we made with respect to the Aumann model regarding the distinction between states of nature and states of the world, the type $t_2 = \frac{3}{4}$ in this Harsanyi model contains far more information than the simple fact that the per-unit production cost of Manufacturer 2 is $\frac{3}{4}$; it contains the entire belief hierarchy of Manufacturer 2 with respect to the production costs of both manufacturers. Production costs are states of nature, with respect to which there is incomplete information.

manufacturer maximizes his expected payoff given the strategy of the other manufacturer: q_1^* maximizes $u_1(q_1, q_2^{*H}, q_2^{*L})$, q_2^{*H} maximizes $u_2^H(q_1^*, q_2^H, q_2^{*L})$, and q_2^{*L} maximizes $u_2^L(q_1^*, q_2^{*H}, q_2^L)$. Since u_2^H is a quadratic function of q_2^H, and the coefficient of $(q_2^H)^2$ is negative, it has a maximum at the point where its derivative with respect to q_2^H vanishes. This results in

$$q_2^H = \frac{\frac{3}{4} - q_1}{2}. \tag{9.90}$$

Similarly, we differentiate u_2^L with respect to q_2^L, set the derivative to zero, and get

$$q_2^L = \frac{\frac{5}{4} - q_1}{2}. \tag{9.91}$$

Finally, differentiate u_1 with respect to q_1 and set the derivative to zero, obtaining

$$q_1 = \frac{1 - \frac{1}{2}q_2^H - \frac{1}{2}q_2^L}{2}. \tag{9.92}$$

Insert Equations (9.90) and (9.91) in Equation (9.92) to obtain

$$q_1 = \frac{1 - \frac{1 - q_1}{2}}{2}, \tag{9.93}$$

or, in other words,

$$q_1^* = \frac{1}{3}. \tag{9.94}$$

This leads to

$$q_2^{*H} = \frac{\frac{3}{4} - \frac{1}{3}}{2} = \frac{5}{24}, \tag{9.95}$$

$$q_2^{*L} = \frac{\frac{5}{4} - \frac{1}{3}}{2} = \frac{11}{24}. \tag{9.96}$$

The conclusion is that $(q_1^*, q_2^{*H}, q_2^{*L}) = (\frac{1}{3}, \frac{5}{24}, \frac{11}{24})$ is the unique Bayesian equilibrium of the game. Note that $q_2^{*H} < q_1^* < q_2^{*L}$: the high (inefficient) type produces less than Manufacturer 1, and the low (more efficient) type produces more than Manufacturer 1, whose production costs are the average of the production costs of the two types of Manufacturer 2.

The profits gained by the manufacturers are

$$u_1\left(\frac{1}{3}, \frac{5}{24}, \frac{11}{24}\right) = \frac{1}{3}\left(2 - 1 - \frac{1}{3} - \frac{8}{24}\right) = \frac{1}{9}, \tag{9.97}$$

$$u_2^H\left(\frac{1}{3}, \frac{5}{24}, \frac{11}{24}\right) = \frac{5}{24}\left(\frac{3}{4} - \frac{1}{3} - \frac{5}{24}\right) = \left(\frac{5}{24}\right)^2, \tag{9.98}$$

$$u_2^L\left(\frac{1}{3}, \frac{5}{24}, \frac{11}{24}\right) = \frac{11}{24}\left(\frac{5}{4} - \frac{1}{3} - \frac{11}{24}\right) = \left(\frac{11}{24}\right)^2. \tag{9.99}$$

Therefore Manufacturer 2's expected profit is

$$\frac{1}{2}\left(\frac{5}{24}\right)^2 + \frac{1}{2}\left(\frac{11}{24}\right)^2 \approx 0.127. \tag{9.100}$$

The case in which Manufacturer 2 also does not know his exact production cost (but knows that the cost is either $\frac{3}{4}$ or $\frac{5}{4}$ with equal probability, and thus knows that his average production cost is 1) is equivalent to the case we looked at in Example 4.23 (page 99). In that case we derived the equilibrium $q_1^* = q_2^* = \frac{1}{3}$, with the profit of each manufacturer being $\frac{1}{9}$.

Comparing that figure with Equation (9.97), we see that relative to the incomplete information case, Manufacturer 1's profit is the same. Using Equations (9.98) and (9.99) and the fact that $0.127 > \frac{1}{9}$, we see that Manufacturer 2's profit when he does not know his own type is smaller than his expected profit when he knows his type; the added information is advantageous to Manufacturer 2.

We also gain insight by comparing this situation to one in which the production cost of Manufacturer 2 is common knowledge among the two manufacturers. In that case, after the selection of Manufacturer 2's type by the chance move, we arrive at a game similar to a Cournot competition with complete information, which we solved in Example 4.23 (page 99). With probability $\frac{1}{2}$ the manufacturers face a Cournot competition in which $c_1 = 1$ and $c_2 = c_2^H = \frac{5}{4}$, and with probability $\frac{1}{2}$ they face a Cournot competition in which $c_1 = 1$ and $c_2 = c_2^L = \frac{3}{4}$. In the first case, equilibrium is attained at $q_1^* = \frac{5}{12}$ and $q_2^* = \frac{1}{6}$, with profits of $u_1 = \left(\frac{5}{12}\right)^2$ and $u_2 = \left(\frac{1}{6}\right)^2$ (verify!). In the second case, equilibrium is attained at $q_1^* = \frac{1}{4}$ and $q_2^* = \frac{1}{2}$, corresponding to profits of $u_1 = \left(\frac{1}{4}\right)^2$ and $u_2 = \left(\frac{1}{2}\right)^2$ (verify!). The expected profits prior to the selection of the types is

$$\bar{u}_1 = \tfrac{1}{2}(\tfrac{5}{12})^2 + \tfrac{1}{2}(\tfrac{1}{4})^2 = \tfrac{1}{8} \tag{9.101}$$

$$\bar{u}_2 = \tfrac{1}{2}\left(\tfrac{1}{6}\right)^2 + \tfrac{1}{2}\left(\tfrac{1}{2}\right)^2 = \tfrac{5}{36}. \tag{9.102}$$

For comparison, we present in table form the profits attained by the manufacturers in each of the three cases dealt with in this example (with respect to the production costs of Manufacturer 2):

Knowledge regarding Manufacturer 2's type	Manufacturer 1's profit	Manufacturer 2's profit
Unknown to both manufacturers	$\frac{1}{9}$	$\frac{1}{9}$
Known only to Manufacturer 2	$\frac{1}{9}$	≈ 0.127
Known to both manufacturers	$\frac{1}{8}$	$\frac{5}{36}$

Note the following:

- Both manufacturers have an interest in Manufacturer 2's type being common knowledge, as opposed to the situation in which that type is unknown to both manufacturers, because $\frac{1}{8} > \frac{1}{9}$ and $\frac{5}{36} > \frac{1}{9}$.
- Both manufacturers have an interest in Manufacturer 2's type being common knowledge, as opposed to the situation in which that type is known solely to Manufacturer 2, because $\frac{1}{8} > \frac{1}{9}$ and $\frac{5}{36} > 0.127$.

This last conclusion may look surprising, because it says that Manufacturer 2 prefers that his private information regarding his production cost be exposed and made public knowledge.   ◄

9.5   Incomplete information as a possible interpretation of mixed strategies

There are cases in which it is difficult to interpret or justify the use of mixed strategies in equilibria. Consider for example the following two-player game in which the payoff functions are given by the matrix in Figure 9.13.

		Player II	
		L	R
Player I	T	0, 0	0, −1
	B	1, 0	−1, 3

Figure 9.13 The payoff matrix of a strategic-form game

		Player II	
		L	R
Player I	T	$\varepsilon\alpha, \varepsilon\beta$	$\varepsilon\alpha, -1$
	B	$1, \varepsilon\beta$	$-1, 3$

Figure 9.14 The payoff matrix of Figure 9.13 with "noise"

This game has only one Nash equilibrium, with Player I playing the mixed strategy $[\frac{3}{4}(T), \frac{1}{4}(B)]$ and Player II playing the mixed strategy $[\frac{1}{2}(L), \frac{1}{2}(R)]$. The payoff at equilibrium is 0 for both players. When Player II plays strategy $[\frac{1}{2}(L), \frac{1}{2}(R)]$ Player I is indifferent between T and B. If that is the case, why should he stick to playing a mixed strategy? And even if he does play a mixed strategy, why the mixed strategy $[\frac{3}{4}(T), \frac{1}{4}(B)]$? If he plays, for example, the pure strategy T, he guarantees himself a payoff of 0 without going to the bother of randomizing strategy selection.

As we now show, this equilibrium can be interpreted as the limit of a sequence of Bayesian equilibria of games in which the players play pure strategies. The idea is to add incomplete information by injecting "noise" into the game's payoffs; each player will know his own payoffs, but will be uncertain about the payoffs of the other player. To illustrate this idea, suppose the payoff function, rather than being known with certainty, is given by the matrix of Figure 9.14.

In Figure 9.14, ε (the amplitude of the noise) is small and α and β are independently and identically distributed random variables over the interval $[-1, 1]$, with uniform distribution. Note that for $\varepsilon = 0$ the resulting game is the original game appearing in Figure 9.13.

Suppose that Player I knows the value of α and Player II knows the value of β; i.e., each player has precise knowledge of his own payoff function. This game can be depicted as a game with incomplete information and a continuum of types, as follows:

- The set of players is $N = \{\text{I}, \text{II}\}$.
- The type space of Player I is $T_{\text{I}} = [-1, 1]$.
- The type space of Player II is $T_{\text{II}} = [-1, 1]$.
- The prior distribution over T is the uniform distribution over the square $[-1, 1]^2$.
- The state game corresponding to the pair of types $(\alpha, \beta) \in T := T_{\text{I}} \times T_{\text{II}}$ is given by the matrix in Figure 9.14.

The Harsanyi game that we constructed here has a continuum of types. The definition of a Harsanyi game is applicable also in this case, provided the set of type vectors is a measurable space, so that a common prior distribution can be defined. In the example presented here, the set of type vectors is $[-1, 1]^2$, which is a measurable space (with the σ-algebra of Borel sets), and the common prior distribution is the uniform distribution. The expected payoff and the conditional expected payoff are defined analogously to the definitions in Equations (9.62) and (9.63), by replacing the summation over T (in Equation (9.62)) or T_{-i} (in Equation (9.63)) with integration. To ensure that the expressions in these equations are meaningful, we need to require the strategies of the players to be measurable functions of their type, and the payoff functions have to be measurable as well (so that the expected payoffs are well defined). The definitions of Nash equilibrium and Bayesian equilibrium remain unchanged (Definitions 9.46 and 9.49).

Since each player has a continuum of types, the existence of a Bayesian equilibrium is not guaranteed. We will, nevertheless, assume that there exists a Bayesian equilibrium and try to identify it. In fact, we will prove that there exists an equilibrium in which the strategies are threshold strategies: the player plays one action if his type is less than or equal to a particular threshold, and he plays the other action if his type is greater than this threshold.

- Let $\alpha_0 \in [-1, 1]$, and let $s_I^{\alpha_0}$ be the following strategy:

$$s_I^{\alpha_0} = \begin{cases} T & \text{when } \alpha > \alpha_0, \\ B & \text{when } \alpha \leq \alpha_0. \end{cases} \tag{9.103}$$

  In words, if Player I's type is "high" ($\alpha > \alpha_0$) he plays T, and if his type is "low" ($\alpha \leq \alpha_0$) he plays B.
- Let $\beta_0 \in [-1, 1]$ and let $s_{II}^{\alpha_0}$ be the following strategy:

$$s_{II}^{\beta_0} = \begin{cases} L & \text{when } \beta > \beta_0, \\ R & \text{when } \beta \leq \beta_0. \end{cases} \tag{9.104}$$

  In words, if Player II's type is "high" ($\beta > \beta_0$) he plays L, and if his type is "low" ($\beta \leq \beta_0$) he plays R.

Next, we will identify two values, α_0 and β_0, for which the pair of strategies $(s_I^{\alpha_0}, s_{II}^{\beta_0})$ form a Bayesian equilibrium.

Since $\mathbf{P}(\beta > \beta_0) = \frac{1-\beta_0}{2}$ and $\mathbf{P}(\beta \leq \beta_0) = \frac{1+\beta_0}{2}$, the expected payoff of Player I of type α facing strategy $s_{II}^{\beta_0}$ of Player II is

$$U_I(T, s_{II}^{\beta_0} | \alpha) = \varepsilon \alpha, \tag{9.105}$$

if he plays T; and it is

$$U_I(B, s_{II}^{\beta_0} | \alpha) = 1 \frac{1 - \beta_0}{2} + (-1) \frac{1 + \beta_0}{2} = -\beta_0, \tag{9.106}$$

if he plays B. In order for $s_I^{\alpha_0}$ to be a best reply to $s_{II}^{\beta_0}$ the following conditions must hold:

$$\alpha > \alpha_0 \implies U_I(T, s_{II}^{\beta_0} | \alpha) \geq U_I(B, s_{II}^{\beta_0} | \alpha) \iff \varepsilon \alpha \geq -\beta_0, \tag{9.107}$$

$$\alpha \leq \alpha_0 \implies U_I(T, s_{II}^{\beta_0} | \alpha) \leq U_I(B, s_{II}^{\beta_0} | \alpha) \iff \varepsilon \alpha \leq -\beta_0. \tag{9.108}$$

From this we conclude that at equilibrium,

$$\varepsilon \alpha_0 = -\beta_0. \tag{9.109}$$

We can similarly calculate that the expected payoff of Player II of type β facing strategy $s_{\text{I}}^{\alpha_0}$ of Player I is

$$U_{\text{II}}\left(s_{\text{I}}^{\alpha_0}, L \mid \beta\right) = \varepsilon \beta, \tag{9.110}$$

$$U_{\text{II}}\left(s_{\text{I}}^{\alpha_0}, R \mid \beta\right) = (-1)\frac{1-\alpha_0}{2} + 3\frac{1+\alpha_0}{2} = 1 + 2\alpha_0. \tag{9.111}$$

In order for $s_{\text{II}}^{\beta_0}$ to be a best reply against $s_{\text{I}}^{\alpha_0}$, the following needs to hold:

$$\beta > \beta_0 \implies U_{\text{II}}\left(s_{\text{I}}^{\alpha_0}, L \mid \beta\right) \geq U_{\text{II}}\left(s_{\text{I}}^{\alpha_0}, R \mid \beta\right) \iff \varepsilon \beta \geq 1 + 2\alpha_0,$$

$$\beta \leq \beta_0 \implies U_{\text{II}}\left(s_{\text{I}}^{\alpha_0}, L \mid \beta\right) \leq U_{\text{II}}\left(s_{\text{I}}^{\alpha_0}, R \mid \beta\right) \iff \varepsilon \beta \leq 1 + 2\alpha_0.$$

From this we further deduce that at equilibrium

$$\varepsilon \beta_0 = 1 + 2\alpha_0 \tag{9.112}$$

must hold. The solution of Equations (9.109) and (9.112) is

$$\alpha_0 = -\frac{1}{2 + \varepsilon^2}, \qquad \beta_0 = \frac{\varepsilon}{2 + \varepsilon^2}. \tag{9.113}$$

The probability that Player I will play B is therefore

$$\mathbf{P}_\varepsilon(B) = \mathbf{P}\left(\alpha \leq -\frac{1}{2 + \varepsilon^2}\right) = \frac{1 - \frac{1}{2+\varepsilon^2}}{2} = \frac{1 + \varepsilon^2}{4 + 2\varepsilon^2}, \tag{9.114}$$

and the probability that Player II will play R is

$$\mathbf{P}_\varepsilon(R) = \mathbf{P}\left(\beta \leq \frac{\varepsilon}{2 + \varepsilon^2}\right) = \frac{1 + \frac{\varepsilon}{2+\varepsilon^2}}{2} = \frac{2 + \varepsilon + \varepsilon^2}{4 + 2\varepsilon^2}. \tag{9.115}$$

When ε approaches 0, that is, when we reduce the uncertainty regarding the payoffs down towards zero, we get

$$\lim_{\varepsilon \to 0} \mathbf{P}_\varepsilon(B) = \tfrac{1}{4}, \tag{9.116}$$

$$\lim_{\varepsilon \to 0} \mathbf{P}_\varepsilon(R) = \tfrac{1}{2}, \tag{9.117}$$

which is the mixed strategy equilibrium in the original game that began this discussion.

It follows that in the equilibrium $\left(s_{\text{I}}^{\alpha_0}, s_{\text{II}}^{\beta_0}\right)$ each player implements a pure strategy. Moreover, for $\alpha \neq \alpha_0$, the action chosen by Player I of type α yields a strictly higher payoff than the action not chosen by him. Similarly, when $\beta \neq \beta_0$, the action chosen by Player II of type β yields a strictly higher payoff than the action not chosen by him. Harsanyi [1973] proposed this sort of reasoning as a basis for a new interpretation of mixed strategies. According to Harsanyi, a mixed strategy can be viewed as a pure strategy of a player that can be of different types. Each type chooses a pure strategy, and different types may choose different pure strategies. From the perspective of other players, who do not know the player's type but rather have a belief (probability distribution) about the player's type, it is as if the player chooses his pure strategy randomly; that is, he is implementing a mixed strategy. It is proved in Harsanyi [1973] that this result can be applied to n-player strategic-form games in which the set of pure strategies is finite. That paper also identifies conditions guaranteeing that each equilibrium is the limit of equilibria in "games with added noise," similar to those presented in the above example, as the amplitude of the noise approaches zero.

We note that the same result obtains when the distribution of noise is not necessarily uniform over the interval $[-1, 1]$. Any probability distribution that is continuous over a compact, nonempty interval can be used (an example of such a probability distribution appears in Exercise 9.47).

9.6 The common prior assumption: inconsistent beliefs

As noted above, in both the Aumann and Harsanyi models, a situation of incomplete information can be assessed from two different perspectives: the *ex ante stage*, prior to the chance move selecting the state of the world (in the Aumann model) or the type vector (in the Harsanyi model), and the *interim stage*, after the chance move has selected the type vector and informed each player about his type, but before the players choose their actions. Prior to the selection of the state of the world, no player knows which information (the partition element in the Aumann model; the type in the Harsanyi model) he will receive; he only knows the prior distribution over the outcomes of the chance move. After the chance move, each player receives information, and updates his beliefs about the state of the world in the Aumann model (the distribution $\mathbf{P}$ conditioned on $\mathcal{F}_i(\omega)$) or about the types of the other players in the Harsanyi model (the distribution p conditioned on t_i).

The concept of interim beliefs is straightforward: a player's interim beliefs are his beliefs after they have been updated in light of new information he has privately received. In real-life situations, a player's beliefs may not be equal to his updated conditional probabilities for various reasons: errors in the calculation of conditional probability, lack of knowledge of the prior distribution, psychologically induced deviations from calculated probabilities, or in general any "subjective feeling" regarding the probability of any particular event, apart from any calculations. It therefore appears to be natural to demand that the interim beliefs be part of the fundamental data of the game, and not necessarily derived from prior distributions (whether or not those prior distributions are common). This is not the case in the Aumann and Harsanyi models: the fundamental data in these models includes a common prior distribution, with the interim beliefs derived from the common prior through the application of Bayes' rule. Assuming the existence of a common prior means adopting a very strong assumption. Can this assumption be justified? What is the exact role of the prior distribution p? Who, or what, makes that selection of the type vector (in the Harsanyi model) or the state of the world (in the Aumann model) at the beginning of the game? And how are the players supposed to "know" the prior distribution p that forms part of the game data?

When player beliefs in the interim stage are derived from one common prior by way of Bayes' rule, given the private information that the players receive, those beliefs are termed *consistent beliefs*. They are called consistent because they imply that the players' beliefs about the way the world works are identical; the only thing that distinguishes players from each other is the information each has received. In that case there is "no difference" between the Harsanyi depiction of the game and its depiction in the interim stage. Theorem 9.53 (page 365) states that the sets of equilibria in both depictions are identical (when the set of type vectors is finite). This means that the Aumann and Harsanyi models may be regarded as "convenient tools" for analyzing the interim stage, which is the stage in which we are really interested.

If we propose that the most relevant stage for analyzing the game is the interim stage, in which each player is equipped with his own (subjective) interim beliefs, the next question is: can every system of interim stage beliefs be described by a Harsanyi game? In other words, given a system of interim stage beliefs, can we find a prior distribution p such that the beliefs of each player's type is the conditional probability derived from p, given that the player is of that type? The next example shows that the answer to this question may be negative.

Example 9.56   Consider a model of incomplete information in which:

- there are two players: $N = \{I, II\}$, and
- each player has two types: $T_I = \{I_1, I_2\}$, $T_{II} = \{II_1, II_2\}$, and $T = T_I \times T_{II} = \{I_1 II_1, I_1 II_2, I_2 II_1, I_2 II_2\}$.

Suppose that in the interim stage, before actions are chosen by the players, the mutual beliefs of the players' types are given by the tables in Figure 9.15.

	II_1	II_2
I_1	3/7	4/7
I_2	2/3	1/3

	II_1	II_2
I_1	1/2	4/5
I_2	1/2	1/5

Player I's beliefs   Player II's beliefs

Figure 9.15 The mutual beliefs of the various types in the interim stage in Example 9.56

The tables in Figure 9.15 have the following interpretation. The table on the left describes the beliefs of the two possible types of Player I: Player I of type I_1 ascribes probability $\frac{3}{7}$ to the type of Player II being II_1 and probability $\frac{4}{7}$ to the type of Player II being II_2. Player I of type I_2 ascribes probability $\frac{2}{3}$ to the type of Player II being II_1 and probability $\frac{1}{3}$ to the type of Player II being II_2. The table on the right describes the beliefs of the two possible types of Player II. For example, Player II of type II_1 ascribes probability $\frac{1}{2}$ to the type of Player I being I_1 and probability $\frac{1}{2}$ to the type of Player I being I_2.

There is no common prior distribution p over $T = T_I \times T_{II}$ that leads to the beliefs described above. This can readily be seen with the assistance of Figure 9.16.

	II_1	II_2
I_1	$2x$	$4x$
I_2	$2x$	x

Figure 9.16 Conditions that must be satisfied in order for a common prior in Example 9.56 to exist

In Figure 9.16, we have denoted $x = p(I_2, II_2)$. In order for the beliefs of type I_2 to correspond with the data in Figure 9.15, it must be the case that $p(I_2, II_1) = 2x$ (because according to Figure 9.15 type I_2 believes that the probability that Player II's type II_1 is twice the probability that his type is II_2). In order for the beliefs of type II_1 to correspond with the data in Figure 9.15, it must be the case that $p(I_1, II_1) = 2x$, and in order for the beliefs of type II_2 to correspond with the data in Figure 9.15, it must be the case that $p(I_1, II_2) = 4x$. But then the beliefs of type I_1 are $[\frac{3}{7}(II_1), \frac{4}{7}(II_2)]$, while according to Figure 9.16, these beliefs are $[\frac{1}{3}(II_1), \frac{2}{3}(II_2)]$.   ◀

The incomplete information situation described in the last example is a situation of inconsistent beliefs. Such a situation cannot be described by a Harsanyi model, and it therefore cannot be described by an Aumann model. Analyzing such situations requires extending the Harsanyi model, which is what we will do in the next chapter, where we will construct a model of incomplete information in which the beliefs of the types are part of the data of the game. The question is what can be said about models of situations with inconsistent beliefs. For one thing, the concept of Bayesian equilibrium is still applicable, also when players' beliefs are inconsistent. In the definition of Bayesian equilibrium, the prior p has significance only in establishing the beliefs $p(t_{-i} \mid t_i)$ in Equation (9.63). That means that the definition is meaningful also when beliefs are not derived from a common prior. In the next chapter we will return to the topic of consistency, provide a formal definition of the concept, and define Bayesian equilibrium in general belief structures.

9.7   Remarks

Kripke's S5 system was defined in Kripke [1963] (see also Geanakoplos [1992]). The concept of common knowledge first appeared in Lewis [1969] and was independently defined in Aumann [1976]. Theorem 9.32 (page 349) is proved in Aumann [1976], in which he also proves the characterization theorem (Theorem 9.24, page 343) in a formulation that is equivalent to that appearing in Remark 9.26 (page 344). The same paper presents a dynamic process that leads to a posterior probability that is common knowledge. A formal description of that dynamic process is given by Geanakoplos and Polemarchakis [1982]. Further developments of this idea can be found in many papers, including Geanakoplos and Sebenius [1983], McKelvey and Page [1986], and Parikh and Krasucki [1990].

John Harsanyi proposed the Harsanyi model of incomplete information in a series of three papers titled "Games of incomplete information played by Bayesian players" (Harsanyi [1967, 1968a, 1968b]), for which he was awarded the Nobel Memorial Prize in Economics in 1994. Harsanyi also proposed the interpretation of the concept of mixed strategies and mixed equilibria as the limit of Bayesian equilibria (in Harsanyi [1973]), as explained in Section 9.5 (page 371).

For further discussions on the subject of the distinction between knowledge and probability-one belief, the reader is directed to Monderer and Samet [1989] and Vassilakis and Zamir [1993].

Exercise 9.14 is based on a question suggested by Ronen Eldan. Geanakoplos [1992] notes that the riddles on which Exercises 9.23 and 9.31 are based first appeared in

Bollobás [1953]. Exercise 9.25 is proved in Geanakoplos and Polemarchakis [1982], from which Exercise 9.28 is also taken. Exercise 9.26 was donated to the authors by Ayala Mashiah-Yaakovi. Exercises 9.29 and 9.30 are from Geanakoplos and Sebenius [1983]. Exercise 9.33 is taken from Geanakoplos [1992]. Exercise 9.34 is the famous "coordinated attack problem," studied in the field of distributed computing. The formulation of the exercise is from Halpern [1986]. Exercise 9.39 is from Harsanyi [1968a]. Exercise 9.40 is based on Spence [1974]. Exercise 9.41 is based on Akerlof [1970]. Exercise 9.46 is the "Electronic Mail game" of Rubinstein [1989]. Exercise 9.53 is based on Aumann [1987].

The authors thank Yaron Azrieli, Aviad Heifetz, Dov Samet, and Eran Shmaya for their comments on this chapter.

9.8 Exercises

In the exercises in this chapter, all announcements made by the players are considered common knowledge, and the game of each exercise is also considered common knowledge among the players.

9.1 Prove that the knowledge operator K_i (Definition 9.8, page 336) of each player i satisfies the following properties:

(a) $K_i Y = Y$: player i knows that Y is the set of all states.
(b) $K_i A \cap K_i B = K_i(A \cap B)$: player i knows event A and knows event B if and only if he knows event $A \cap B$.
(c) $(K_i A)^c = K_i((K_i A)^c)$: player i does not know event A if and only if he knows that he does not know event A.

9.2 This exercise shows that the Kripke S5 system characterizes the knowledge operator.

Let Y be a finite set, and let $K : 2^Y \to 2^Y$ be an operator that associates with each subset A of Y a subset $K(A)$ of Y. Suppose that the operator K satisfies the following properties:

(i) $K(Y) = Y$.
(ii) $K(A) \cap K(B) = K(A \cap B)$ for every pair of subsets $A, B \subseteq Y$.
(iii) $K(A) \subseteq A$ for every subset $A \subseteq Y$.
(iv) $K(K(A)) = K(A)$ for every subset $A \subseteq Y$.
(v) $(K(A))^c = K((K(A))^c)$ for every subset $A \subseteq Y$.

Associate with each $\omega \in Y$ a set $F(\omega)$ as follows:

$$F(\omega) := \bigcap \{A \subseteq Y, \omega \in K(A)\}. \tag{9.118}$$

(a) Prove that $\omega \in F(\omega)$ for each $\omega \in Y$.
(b) Prove that if $\omega' \in F(\omega)$, then $F(\omega) = F(\omega')$. Conclude from this that the family of sets $\mathcal{F} := \{F(\omega), \omega \in Y\}$ is a partition of Y.

(c) Let K' be the knowledge operator defined by the partition $\mathcal{F}$:

$$K'(A) = \{\omega \in Y : F(\omega) \subseteq A\}. \tag{9.119}$$

Prove that $K' = K$.

(d) Which of the five properties listed above did you use in order to prove that $K' = K$?

9.3 Prove that in Kripke's S5 system (see page 337), the fourth property, $K_i K_i A = K_i A$, is a consequence of the other four properties.

9.4 Consider an Aumann model of incomplete information in which

$N = \{1, 2\}$,
$Y = \{1, 2, 3, 4, 5, 6, 7\}$,
$\mathcal{F}_1 = \{\{1\}, \{2, 3\}, \{4, 5\}, \{6, 7\}\}$,
$\mathcal{F}_2 = \{\{1, 2\}, \{3, 4\}, \{5, 6\}, \{7\}\}$.

Let $A = \{1\}$ and $B = \{1, 2, 3, 4, 5, 6\}$. Identify the events $K_1 A$, $K_2 A$, $K_2 K_1 A$, $K_1 K_2 A$, $K_1 B$, $K_2 B$, $K_2 K_1 B$, $K_1 K_2 B$, $K_1 K_2 K_1 B$, $K_2 K_1 K_2 B$.

9.5 Emily, Marc, and Thomas meet at a party to which novelists and poets have been invited. Every attendee at the party is either a novelist or a poet (but not both). Every poet knows all the other poets, but every novelist does not know any of the other attendees, whether they are poets or novelists. What do Emily, Marc, and Thomas know about each other's professions? Provide an Aumann model of incomplete information that describes this situation (there are several ways to do so).

9.6 I love Juliet, and I know that Juliet loves me, but I do not know if Juliet knows that I love her. Provide an Aumann model of incomplete information that describes this situation, and specify a state of the world in that model that corresponds to this situation (there are several possible ways of including higher-order beliefs in this model).

9.7 Construct an Aumann model of incomplete information for each of the following situations, and specify a state of the world in that model which corresponds to the situation (there are several possible ways of including higher-order beliefs in each model):

(a) Mary gave birth to a baby, and Herod knows it.
(b) Mary gave birth to a baby, and Herod does not know it.
(c) Mary gave birth to a baby, Herod knows it, and Mary knows that Herod knows it.
(d) Mary gave birth to a baby, Herod knows it, but Mary does not know that Herod knows it.
(e) Mary gave birth to a baby, Herod does not know it, and Mary does not know whether Herod knows it or not.

9.8 Romeo composes a letter to Juliet, and gives it to Tybalt to deliver to Juliet. While on the way, Tybalt peeks at the letter's contents. Tybalt gives Juliet the letter, and Juliet reads it immediately, in Tybalt's presence. Neither Romeo nor Juliet knows that Tybalt has read the letter.

Answer the following questions relating to this story:

(a) Construct an Aumann model of incomplete information in which all the elements of the story above regarding the knowledge possessed by Romeo, Tybalt, and Juliet regarding the content of the letter hold true (there are several possible ways to do this). Specify a state of the world in the model that corresponds to the situation described above.

(b) In the state of the world you specified above, does Romeo know that Juliet has read the letter? Justify your answer.

(c) In the state of the world you specified above, does Tybalt know that Romeo knows that Juliet has read the letter? Justify your answer.

(d) Construct an Aumann model of incomplete information in which, in addition to the particulars of the story presented above, the following also holds: "Tybalt does not know that Juliet does not know that Tybalt read the letter," and specify a state of the world in your model that corresponds to this situation.

9.9 George, John, and Thomas are standing first, second, and third in a line, respectively. Each one sees the persons standing in front of him. James announces: "I have three red hats and two white hats. I will place a hat on the head of each one of you." After James places the hats, he asks Thomas (who can see the hats worn by John and George) if he knows the color of the hat on his own head. Thomas replies "no." He then asks John (who sees only George's hat) whether he knows the color of the hat on his own head, and he also replies "no." Finally, he asks George (who cannot see any of the hats) if he knows the color of the hat on his own head.

(a) Construct an Aumann model of incomplete information that contains 7 states of the world and describes this situation.

(b) What are the partitions of George, John, and Thomas after James's announcement and before he asked Thomas whether he knows the color of his hat?

(c) What are the partitions of George and John after Thomas's response and before John responded to James's question?

(d) What is George's partition after hearing John's response?

(e) What is George's answer to James's question? Does this answer depend on the the state of the world, that is, on the colors of the hats that the three wear?

9.10 Prove Corollary 9.16 (page 341): every situation of incomplete information $(N, Y, (\mathcal{F}_i)_{i \in N}, \mathfrak{s}, \omega_*)$ over a set of states of nature S uniquely determines a knowledge hierarchy among the players over the set of states of nature S in state of the world ω_*.

9.11 Consider an Aumann model of incomplete information in which $N = \{\mathrm{I}, \mathrm{II}\}$, $Y = \{1, 2, 3, 4, 5, 6, 7, 8, 9\}$, $\mathcal{F}_{\mathrm{I}} = \{\{1\}, \{2, 3\}, \{4, 5\}, \{6\}, \{7\}, \{8, 9\}\}$, and $\mathcal{F}_{\mathrm{II}} = \{\{1\}, \{2, 5\}, \{3\}, \{4, 7\}, \{6, 9\}, \{8\}\}$. What are the connected components in the graph corresponding to this Aumann model? Which events are common knowledge in state of the world $\omega = 1$? Which events are common knowledge in state of the world $\omega = 9$? Which events are common knowledge in state of the world $\omega = 5$?

9.12 Show that in Examples 9.12 (page 338) and 9.13 (page 339), in each state of the world, the only event that is common knowledge is Y.

9.13 Consider an Aumann model of incomplete information in which $N = \{I, II\}$, $Y = \{1, 2, 3, 4, 5, 6, 7, 8, 9\}$, $\mathcal{F}_I = \{\{1, 2, 3\}, \{4, 5, 6\}, \{7, 8, 9\}\}$, and $\mathcal{F}_{II} = \{\{1, 5\}, \{2, 6\}, \{3, 4\}, \{7\}, \{8, 9\}\}$. Answer the following questions:

(a) What are the connected components in the graph corresponding to the Aumann model?

(b) Which events are common knowledge in state of the world $\omega = 1$? In $\omega = 7$? In $\omega = 8$?

(c) Denote by A the event $\{1, 2, 3, 4, 5\}$. Find the shortest sequence of players $i_1, i_2, \ldots, i_k$ such that in the state of the world $\omega = 1$ it is not the case that i_1 knows that i_2 knows that $\ldots i_{k-1}$ knows that i_k knows event A.

9.14 A digital clock showing the hours between 00:00 and 23:59 hangs on a wall; the digits on the clock are displayed using straight lines, as depicted in the accompanying figure:

William and Dan are both looking at the clock. William sees only the top half of the clock (including the midline) while Dan sees only the bottom half of the clock (including the midline). Answer the following questions:

(a) At which times does William know the correct time?

(b) At which times does Dan know the correct time?

(c) At which times does William know that Dan knows the correct time?

(d) At which times does Dan know that William knows the correct time?

(e) At which times is the correct time common knowledge among William and Dan?

(f) Construct an Aumann model of incomplete information describing this situation. How many states of nature, and how many states of the world, are there in your model?

9.15 Prove that if in an Aumann model of incomplete information the events A and B are common knowledge among the players in state of the world ω, then the event $A \cap B$ is also common knowledge among the players in ω.

9.16 Given an Aumann model of incomplete information, prove that event A is common knowledge in every state of the world in A if and only if $K_1 K_2 \cdots K_n A = A$, where $N = \{1, 2, \ldots, n\}$ is the set of players.

9.17 Prove that in an Aumann model of incomplete information with n players, every event that is common knowledge among the players in state of the world ω is also common knowledge among any subset of the set of players (Remark 9.22, page 343).

9.18 Give an example of an Aumann model of incomplete information with a set of players $N = \{1, 2, 3\}$ and an event A that is not common knowledge among all the players N, but is common knowledge among players $\{2, 3\}$.

9.19 (a) In state of the world ω, Andrew knows that Sally knows the state of nature. Does this imply that Andrew knows the state of nature in ω? Is the fact that Sally knows the state of nature common knowledge among Andrew and Sally in ω?

(b) In every state of the world, Andrew knows that Sally knows the state of nature. Does this imply that Andrew knows the state of nature in every state of the world? Is the fact that Sally knows the state of nature common knowledge among Andrew and Sally in every state of the world?

(c) In state of the world ω, Andrew knows that Sally knows the state of the world. Does this imply that Andrew knows the state of the world in ω? Is the fact that Sally knows the state of the world common knowledge among Andrew and Sally in ω?

9.20 Let $(N, Y, (\mathcal{F}_i)_{i \in N}, \mathfrak{s}, \mathbf{P})$ be an Aumann model of incomplete information with beliefs, and let $W \subseteq Y$ be an event. Prove that $(N, W, (\mathcal{F}_i \cap W)_{i \in N}, \mathbf{P}(\cdot \mid W))$ is also an Aumann model of incomplete information with beliefs, where for each player $i \in N$

$$\mathcal{F}_i \cap W = \{F \cap W : F \in \mathcal{F}_i\} \tag{9.120}$$

is the partition $\mathcal{F}_i$ restricted to W, and $\mathbf{P}(\cdot \mid W)$ is the conditional distribution of $\mathbf{P}$ over W.

9.21 Prove that without the assumption that $\mathbf{P}(\omega) > 0$ for all $\omega \in Y$, Theorem 9.29 (page 347) does not obtain.

9.22 This exercise generalizes Aumann's Agreement Theorem to a set of players of arbitrary finite size. Given an Aumann model of incomplete information with beliefs $(N, Y, (\mathcal{F}_i)_{i \in N}, \mathfrak{s}, \mathbf{P})$ with n players, suppose that for each $i \in N$, the fact that player i ascribes probability q_i to an event A is common knowledge among the players. Prove that $q_1 = q_2 = \cdots = q_n$.
Hint: Use Theorem 9.32 on page 349 and Exercise 9.17.

9.23 Three individuals are seated in a room. Each one of them is wearing a hat, which may be either red or white. Each of them sees the hats worn by the others, but cannot see his own hat (and in particular does not know its color). The true situation is that every person in the room is wearing a red hat.

(a) Depict this situation as a Harsanyi model of incomplete information, where a player's type is the color of his hat, and specify the vector of types corresponding to the true situation.

(b) Depict this situation as an Aumann model of incomplete information, and specify the state of the world corresponding to the true situation.

(c) A stranger enters the room, holding a bell. Once a minute, he rings the bell while saying "If you know that the color of the hat on your head is red, leave this room immediately." Does anyone leave the room after a few rings? Why?

(d) At a certain point in time, the announcer says, "At least one of you is wearing a red hat." He continues to ring the bell once a minute and request that those who know their hat is red to leave. Use the Aumann model of incomplete information to prove that after the third ring, all three hat-wearers will leave the room.

(e) What information did the announcer add by saying that at least one person in the room was wearing a red hat, when this was known to everyone before the announcement was made?

Hint: See Example 9.12 on page 338.

(f) Generalize this result to n individuals (instead of 3).

9.24 Prove that in an Aumann model of incomplete information with a common prior $\mathbf{P}$, if in a state of the world ω Player 1 knows that Player 2 knows A, then $\mathbf{P}(A \mid F_1(\omega)) = 1$.

9.25 Consider an Aumann model of incomplete information with beliefs in which

$$N = \{\mathrm{I, II}\},$$
$$Y = \{1, 2, 3, 4, 5, 6, 7, 8, 9\},$$
$$\mathcal{F}_{\mathrm{I}} = \{\{1, 2, 3\}, \{4, 5, 6\}, \{7, 8, 9\}\},$$
$$\mathcal{F}_{\mathrm{II}} = \{\{1, 2, 3, 4\}, \{5, 6, 7, 8\}, \{9\}\},$$
$$\mathbf{P}(\omega) = \tfrac{1}{9}, \quad \forall \omega \in Y.$$

Let $A = \{1, 5, 9\}$, and suppose that the true state of the world is $\omega_* = 9$. Answer the following questions:

(a) What is the probability that Player I (given his information) ascribes to the event A?

(b) What is the probability that Player II ascribes to the event A?

(c) Suppose that Player I announces the probability you calculated in item (a) above. How will that affect the probability that Player II now ascribes to the event A?

(d) Suppose that Player II announces the probability you calculated in item (c). How will that affect the probability that Player I ascribes to the event A, after hearing Player II's announcement?

(e) Repeat the previous two questions, with each player updating his conditional probability following the announcement of the other player. What is the sequence of conditional probabilities the players calculate? Does the sequence converge, or oscillate periodically (or neither)?

(f) Repeat the above, with $\omega_* = 8$.

(g) Repeat the above, with $\omega_* = 6$.

(h) Repeat the above, with $\omega_* = 4$.

(i) Repeat the above, with $\omega_* = 1$.

9.26 Repeat Exercise 9.25, using the following Aumann model of incomplete information with beliefs:

$$N = \{I, II\},$$
$$Y = \{1, 2, 3, 4, 5\},$$
$$\mathcal{F}_I = \{\{1, 2\}, \{3, 4\}, \{5\}\},$$
$$\mathcal{F}_{II} = \{\{1, 3, 5\}, \{2\}, \{4\}\},$$
$$\mathbf{P}(\omega) = \tfrac{1}{5}, \quad \forall \omega \in Y.$$

$A = \{1, 4\}$ and $\omega_* = 3$.

9.27 Repeat Exercise 9.25 when the two players have different priors over Y:

$$\mathbf{P}_I(\omega) = \frac{\omega}{45}, \quad \forall \omega \in Y, \tag{9.121}$$

$$\mathbf{P}_{II}(\omega) = \frac{10 - \omega}{45}, \quad \forall \omega \in Y. \tag{9.122}$$

9.28 This exercise generalizes Exercise 9.25. Let $(N, Y, \mathcal{F}_I, \mathcal{F}_{II}, s, \mathbf{P})$ be an Aumann model of incomplete information with beliefs in which $N = \{I, II\}$ and let $A \subseteq Y$ be an event. Consider the following process:

- Player I informs Player II of the conditional probability $\mathbf{P}(A \mid F_I(\omega))$.
- Player II informs Player I of the conditional probability that he ascribes to event A given the partition element $F_{II}(\omega)$ and Player I's announcement.
- Player I informs Player II of the conditional probability that he ascribes to event A given the partition element $F_I(\omega)$ and all the announcements so far.
- Repeat indefinitely.

Answer the following questions:

(a) Prove that the sequence of conditional probabilities that Player I announces converges; that the sequence of conditional probabilities that Player II announces also converges; and that both sequences converge to the same limit.

(b) Prove that after at most $2|Y|$ announcements the sequence of announcements made by the players becomes constant.

9.29 The "No Trade Theorem" mentioned on page 352 is proved in this exercise. Let $(N, Y, \mathcal{F}_I, \mathcal{F}_{II}, s, \mathbf{P})$ be an Aumann model of incomplete information with beliefs where $N = \{I, II\}$, let $f : Y \to \mathbb{R}$ be a function, and let $\omega_* \in Y$ be a state of the world in Y. Suppose[21] that the fact that $\mathbf{E}[f \mid \mathcal{F}_I](\omega) \geq 0$ is common knowledge in ω_*, and that the fact that $\mathbf{E}[f \mid \mathcal{F}_{II}](\omega) \leq 0$ is also common knowledge in ω_*. In other words, the events $A_I := \{\omega \colon \mathbf{E}[f \mid \mathcal{F}_I](\omega) \geq 0\}$ and $A_{II} := \{\omega \colon \mathbf{E}[f \mid$

---

21 Recall that the conditional expectation $\mathbf{E}[f \mid \mathcal{F}_I]$ is the function on Y that is defined by $\mathbf{E}[f \mid \mathcal{F}_I](\omega) :=$ $\mathbf{E}[f \mid F_I(\omega)]$ for each $\omega \in Y$.

$\mathcal{F}_{\mathrm{II}}](\omega) \leq 0\}$ are common knowledge in ω_*. Prove that the event $D := \{\omega \in Y \colon \mathbf{E}[f \mid \mathcal{F}_{\mathrm{I}}](\omega) = \mathbf{E}[f \mid \mathcal{F}_{\mathrm{II}}](\omega) = 0\}$ is common knowledge in the state of the world ω_*.

9.30 This exercise is similar to Exercise 9.25, but instead of announcing the probability of a particular event given their private information, the players announce whether or not the expectation of a particular random variable is positive or not, given their private information. This is meant to model trade between two parties to an agreement, as follows. Suppose that Ralph (Player 2) owns an oil field. He expects the profit from the oil field to be negative, and therefore intends to sell it. Jack is of the opinion that the oil field can yield positive profits, and is therefore willing to purchase it (for the price of $0). Jack and Ralph arrive at different determinations regarding the oil field because they have different information. We will show that no trade can occur under these conditions, because of the following exchange between the parties:

- Jack: I am interested in purchasing the oil field; are you interested in selling?
- Ralph: Yes, I am interested in selling; are you interested in purchasing?
- Jack: Yes, I am interested in purchasing; are you still interested in selling?
- And so on, until one of the two parties announces that he has no interest in a deal.

The formal description of this process is as follows. Let $(N, Y, \mathcal{F}_1, \mathcal{F}_2, \mathfrak{s}, \mathbf{P})$ be an Aumann model of incomplete information with beliefs where $N = \{\mathrm{I}, \mathrm{II}\}$, let $f \colon Y \to \mathbb{R}$ be a function, and let $\omega \in Y$ be a state of the world. $f(\omega)$ represents the profit yielded by the oil field at the state of the world ω. At each stage, Jack will be interested in the deal only if the conditional expectation of f given his information is positive, and Ralph will be interested in the deal only if the conditional expectation of f given his information is negative. The process therefore looks like this:

- Player I states whether or not $\mathbf{E}[f \mid \mathcal{F}_{\mathrm{I}}](\omega) > 0$ (implicitly doing so by expressing or not expressing interest in purchasing the oil field). If he says "no" (i.e., his expectation is less than or equal to 0), the process ends here.
- If the process gets to the second stage, Player II states whether his expectation of f, given the information he has received so far, is negative or not. The information he has includes $F_{\mathrm{II}}(\omega)$ and the affirmative interest of Player I in the first stage. If Player II now says "no" (i.e., his expectation is greater than or equal to 0), the process ends here.
- If the process has not yet ended, Player I states whether his expectation of f, given the information he has received so far, is positive or not. The information he has includes $F_{\mathrm{I}}(\omega)$ and the affirmative interest of Player II in the second stage. If Player I now says "no" (i.e., his expectation is less than or equal to 0), the process ends here.
- And so on. The process ends the first time either Player I's expectation of f, given his information, is not positive, or Player II's expectation of f, given his information, is not negative.

Show that this process ends after a finite number of stages. In fact, show that the number of stages prior to the end of the process is at most $\max\{2|\mathcal{F}_I| - 1, 2|\mathcal{F}_{II}| - 1\}$.

9.31 Peter has two envelopes. He puts 10^k euros in one and 10^{k+1} euros in the other, where k is the outcome of the toss of a fair die. Peter gives one of the envelopes to Mark and one to Luke (neither Mark nor Luke knows the outcome of the toss). Mark and Luke both go to their respective rooms, open the envelopes they have received, and observe the amounts in them.

(a) Depict the situation as a model with incomplete information, where the state of nature is the amounts in Mark and Luke's envelopes.
(b) Mark finds 1,000 euros in his envelope, and Luke finds 10,000 euros in his envelope. What is the true state of the world in your model?
(c) According to the information Mark has, what is the expected amount of money in Luke's envelope?
(d) According to the information Luke has, what is the expected amount of money in Mark's envelope?
(e) Peter enters Mark's room and asks him whether he would like to switch envelopes with Luke. If the answer is positive, he goes to Luke's room and informs him: "Mark wants to switch envelopes with you. Would you like to switch envelopes with him?" If the answer is positive, he goes to Mark's room and tells him: "Luke wants to switch envelopes with you. Would you like to switch envelopes with him?" This process repeats itself as long as the answer received by Peter from Mark and Luke is positive.

Use your model of incomplete information to show that the answers of Mark and Luke will be positive at first, and then one of them will refuse to switch envelopes. Who will be the first to refuse? Assume that each of the two would like to change envelopes if the conditional expectation of the amount of money in the other's envelope is higher than the amount in his envelope.

9.32 The setup is just as in the previous exercise, but now Peter tells Mark and Luke that they can switch the envelopes if and only if both of them have an interest in switching envelopes: each one gives Peter a sealed envelope with "yes" or "no" written in it, and the switch is effected only if both envelopes read "yes." What will be Mark and Luke's answers after having properly analyzed the situation? Justify your answer.

9.33 The setup is again as in Exercise 9.31, but this time Peter chooses the integer k randomly according to a geometric distribution with parameter $\frac{1}{2}$, that is, $\mathbf{P}(k = n) = \frac{1}{2^n}$ for each $n \in \mathbb{N}$. How does this affect your answers to the questions in Exercise 9.31?

9.34 Two divisions of Napoleon's army are camped on opposite hillsides, both overlooking the valley in which enemy forces have massed. If both divisions attack their enemy simultaneously, victory is assured, but if only one division attacks alone, it will suffer a crushing defeat. The division commanders have not yet coordinated a joint attack time. The commander of Division A wishes to coordinate a joint attack time of 6 am the following day with the commander of Division B. Given the stakes involved, neither commander will give an order to his troops to attack until he is absolutely certain that the other commander is also attacking simultaneously. The only way the commanders can communicate with each other is by courier. The travel time between the two camps is an hour's trek through enemy-held territory, exposing the courier to possible capture by enemy patrols. It turns out that on that night no enemy patrols were scouting in the area. How much time will pass before the two commanders coordinate the attack? Justify your answer.

9.35 Prove Theorem 9.42 on page 359: every game with incomplete information can be described as an extensive-form game.

9.36 Describe the following game with incomplete information as an extensive-form game. There are two players $N = \{I, II\}$. Each player has three types, $T_I = \{I_1, I_2, I_3\}$ and $T_{II} = \{II_1, II_2, II_3\}$, with common prior:

$$p(I_k, II_l) = \frac{k(k+l)}{78}, \quad 1 \le k, l \le 3. \qquad (9.123)$$

The number of possible actions available to each type is given by the index of that type: the set of actions of Player I of type I_k contains k actions $\{1, 2, \ldots, k\}$; the set of actions of Player II of type II_l contains l actions $\{1, 2, \ldots, l\}$. When the type vector is (I_k, II_l), and the vector of actions chosen is (a_I, a_{II}), the payoffs to the players are given by

$$\begin{aligned} u_I(I_k, II_l; a_I, a_{II}) &= (k+l)(a_I - a_{II}), \\ u_{II}(I_k, II_l; a_I, a_{II}) &= (k-l)a_I a_{II}. \end{aligned} \qquad (9.124)$$

For each player, and each of his types, write down the conditional probability that the player ascribes to each of the types of the other player, given his own type.

9.37 Find a Bayesian equilibrium in the game described in Example 9.38 (page 357). *Hint:* To find a Bayesian equilibrium, you may remove weakly dominated strategies.

9.38 Find a Bayesian equilibrium in the following game with incomplete information:

- $N = \{I, II\}$.
- $T_I = \{I_1, I_2\}$ and $T_{II} = \{II_1\}$: Player I has two types, and Player II has one type.
- $p(I_1, II_1) = \frac{1}{3}$, $p(I_2, II_1) = \frac{2}{3}$.
- Every player has two possible actions, and state games are given by the following matrices:

		Player II	
		L	R
Player I	T	2, 0	0, 3
	B	0, 4	1, 0

The state game for $t = (I_1, II_1)$

		Player II	
		L	R
Player I	T	0, 3	3, 1
	B	2, 0	0, 1

The state game for $t = (I_2, II_1)$

9.39 Answer the following questions for the zero-sum game with incomplete information with two players I and II, in which each player has two types, $T_I = \{I_1, I_2\}$ and $T_{II} = \{II_1, II_2\}$, the common prior over the type vectors is

$$p(I_1, II_1) = 0.4, \ p(I_1, II_2) = 0.1, \ p(I_2, II_1) = 0.2, \ p(I_2, II_2) = 0.3,$$

and the state games are given by

Player II

		L	R
	T	2	5
Player I	B	−1	20

The state game for $t = (I_1, II_1)$

Player II

		L	R
	T	−24	−36
Player I	B	0	24

The state game for $t = (I_1, II_2)$

Player II

		L	R
	T	28	15
Player I	B	40	4

The state game for $t = (I_2, II_1)$

Player II

		L	R
	T	12	20
Player I	B	2	13

The state game for $t = (I_2, II_2)$

(a) List the set of pure strategies of each player.
(b) Depict the game in strategic form.
(c) Calculate the value of the game and find optimal strategies for the two players.

9.40 Signaling games This exercise illustrates that a college education serves as a form of signaling to potential employers, in addition to expanding the knowledge of students. A young person entering the job market may be talented or untalented. Suppose that one-quarter of high school graduates are talented, and the rest untalented. A recent high school graduate, who knows whether or not he is talented, has the option of spending a year traveling overseas or enrolling at college (we will assume that he or she cannot do both) before applying for a job. An employer seeking to fill a job opening cannot know whether or not a job applicant is talented; all he knows is that the applicant either went to college or traveled overseas. The payoff an employer gets from hiring a worker depends solely on the talents of the hired worker (and not on his educational level), while the payoff to the youth depends on what he chose to do after high school, on his talents (because talented students enjoy their studies at college more than untalented students), and on whether or not he gets a job. These payoffs are described in the following tables (where the employer is the row player and the youth is the column player, so that a payoff vector of (x, y) represents a payoff of x to the employer and y to the youth).

(a) Depict this situation as a Harsanyi game with incomplete information.
(b) List the pure strategies of the two players.
(c) Find two Bayesian equilibria in pure strategies.

	Youth Travel	Youth Study
Employer Hire	0, 6	0, 2
Employer Don't Hire	3, 3	3, –3

Payoff matrix
if youth is untalented

	Youth Travel	Youth Study
Employer Hire	8, 6	8, 4
Employer Don't Hire	3, 3	3, 1

Payoff matrix
if youth is talented

9.41 Lemon market This exercise illustrates that in situations in which a seller has more information than a buyer, transactions might not be possible. Consider a used car market in which a fraction q of the cars ($0 \le q \le 1$) are in good condition and $1 - q$ are in bad condition (lemons). The seller (Player 2) knows the quality of the car he is offering to sell while the buyer (Player 1) does not know the quality of the car that he is being offered to buy. Each used car is offered for sale at the price of $\$p$ (in units of thousands of dollars). The payoffs to the seller and the buyer, depending on whether or not the transaction is completed, are described in the following tables:

	Sell	Don't Sell
Buy	$6 - p, p$	0, 5
Don't Buy	0, 5	0, 5

State game
if car in good condition

	Sell	Don't Sell
Buy	$4 - p, p$	0, 0
Don't Buy	0, 0	0, 0

State game
if car in bad condition

Depict this situation as a Harsanyi game with incomplete information, and for each pair of parameters p and q, find all the Bayesian equilibria.

9.42 Nicolas would like to sell a company that he owns to Marc. The company's true value is an integer between 10 and 12 (including 10 and 12), in millions of dollars. Marc has to make a take-it-or-leave-it offer, and Nicolas has to decide whether to accept the offer or reject it. If Nicolas accepts the offer, the company is sold, Nicolas's payoff is the amount that he got, and Marc's payoff is the difference between the company's true value and the amount that he paid. If Nicolas rejects the offer, the company is not sold, Nicolas's payoff is the value of the company, and Marc's payoff is 0. For each one of the following three information structures, describe the situation as a game with incomplete information, and find all the Bayesian equilibria in the corresponding game. In each case, the description of the situation is common knowledge among the players. In determining Nicolas's action set, note that Nicolas knows what Marc's offer is when he decides whether or not to accept the offer.

(a) Neither Nicolas nor Marc knows the company's true value; both ascribe probability $\frac{1}{3}$ to each possible value.
(b) Nicolas knows the company's true value, whereas Marc does not know it, and ascribes probability $\frac{1}{3}$ to each possible value.

(c) Marc does not know the company's worth and ascribes probability $\frac{1}{3}$ to each possible value. Marc further ascribes probability p to the event that Nicolas knows the value of the company, and probability $1-p$ to the event that Nicolas does not know the value of the company, and instead ascribes probability $\frac{1}{3}$ to each possible value.

9.43 Prove that in each game with incomplete information with a finite set of players, where the set of types of each player is a countable set, and the set of possible actions of each type is finite, there exists a Bayesian equilibrium (in behavior strategies).

Guidance: Suppose that the set of types of player i, T_i, is the set of natural numbers $\mathbb{N}$. Denote $T_i^k := \{1, 2, \ldots, k\}$ and $T^k = \times_{i \in N} T_i^k$. Let p^k be the probability distribution p conditioned on the set T^k:

$$p^k(t) = \begin{cases} \frac{p(t)}{p(T^k)} & t \in T^k, \\ 0 & t \notin T^k. \end{cases} \tag{9.125}$$

Prove that for a sufficiently large k, the denominator $p(T^k)$ is positive and therefore the probability distribution p^k is well defined. Show that for each k, the game in which the probability distribution over the types is p^k has an equilibrium, and any accumulation point of such equilibria, as k goes to infinity, is an equilibrium of the original game.

9.44 Prove Theorem 9.51 on page 365: a strategy vector $\sigma^* = (\sigma_i^*)_{i \in N}$ is a Bayesian equilibrium in a game Γ with incomplete information if and only if the strategy vector $(\sigma_i^*(t_i))_{i \in N, t_i \in T_i}$ is a Nash equilibrium in the agent-form game $\widehat{\Gamma}$. (For the definition of an agent-form game, see Definition 9.50 on page 364.)

9.45 This exercise shows that in a game with incomplete information, the payoff function of an inactive type has no effect on the set of equilibria. Let $\Gamma = (N, (T_i)_{i \in N}, p, S, (s_t)_{t \in \times_{i \in N} T_i})$, where $s_t = (N, (A_i(t_i), u_i(t))_{i \in N})$ for each $t \in \times_{i \in N} T_i$, be a game with incomplete information in which there exists a player j and a type t_j^* of player j such that $|A_j(t_j^*)| = 1$. Let $\widehat{\Gamma}$ be a game with incomplete information that is identical to Γ, except that the payoff function $\widehat{u}_j(t_j^*)$ of player j of type t_j^* may be different from $u_j(t_j^*)$, that is, $\widehat{u}_i(t; a) = u_i(t; a)$ if $t_j \neq t_j^*$ or $i \neq j$. Show that the two games Γ and $\widehat{\Gamma}$ have the same set of Bayesian equilibria.

9.46 Electronic Mail game Let $L > M > 0$ be two positive real numbers. Two players play a game in which the payoff function is one of the following two, depending on the value of the state of nature s, which may be 1 or 2:

		Player II	
		A	B
Player I	A	M, M	$1, -L$
	B	$-L, 0$	$0, 0$

The state game for $s = 1$

		Player II	
		A	B
Player I	A	$0, 0$	$0, -L$
	B	$-L, 1$	M, M

The state game for $s = 2$

The probability that the state of nature is $s = 2$ is $p < \frac{1}{2}$. Player I knows the true state of nature, and Player II does not know it. The players would clearly prefer to coordinate their actions and play (A, A) if the state of nature is $s = 1$ and (B, B) if the state is $s = 2$, which requires that both of them know what the true state is. Suppose the players are on opposite sides of the globe, and the sole method of communication available to them is e-mail. Due to possible technical communication disruptions, there is a probability of $\varepsilon > 0$ that any e-mail message will fail to arrive at its destination. In order to transfer information regarding the state of nature from Player I to Player II, the two players have constructed an automated system that sends e-mail from Player I to Player II if the state of nature is $s = 2$, and does not send e-mail if the state is $s = 1$. To ensure that Player I knows that Player II received the message, the system also sends an automated confirmation of receipt of the message (by e-mail, of course) from Player II to Player I the instant Player I's message arrives at Player II's e-mail inbox. To ensure that Player II knows that Player I received the confirmation message, the system also sends an automated confirmation of receipt of the confirmation message from Player I to Player II the instant Player II's confirmation arrives at Player I's e-mail inbox. The system then proceeds to send an automated confirmation of the receipt of the confirmation of the receipt of the confirmation, and so forth. If any of these e-mail messages fail to arrive at their destination, the automated system stops sending new messages. After communication between the players is completed, each player is called upon to choose an action, A or B.

Answer the following questions:

(a) Depict the situation as a game with incomplete information, in which each type of each player is indexed by the number of e-mail messages he has received.

(b) Prove that the unique Bayesian equilibrium where Player I plays A when $s = 1$ is for both players to play A under all conditions.

(c) How would you play if you received 100 e-mail confirmation messages? Explain your answer.

9.47 In the example described in Section 9.5 (page 371), for each $\varepsilon \in [0, 1]$ find Bayesian equilibria in threshold strategies, where α has uniform distribution over the interval $\left[\frac{1}{4}, \frac{1}{2}\right]$ and β has uniform distribution over the interval $\left[-\frac{1}{3}, \frac{2}{3}\right]$.

9.48 In each of the two strategic-form games whose matrices appear below, find all the equilibria. For each equilibrium, describe a sequence of games with incomplete information in which the amplitude of the noise converges to 0, and find Bayesian equilibria in pure strategies in each of these games, such that when the amplitude of the noise converges to 0, the probability that each of the players will choose a particular action converges to the corresponding probability in the equilibrium of the original game (see Section 9.5 on page 371).

	Player II	
	L	R
T	1, 5	4, 1
B	2, 1	0, 3

Player I

Game A

	Player II	
	L	R
T	3, 4	2, 2
B	1, 1	2, 1

Player I

Game B

9.49 Consider a Harsanyi game with incomplete information in which $N = \{I, II\}$, $T_I = \{I_1, I_2\}$, and $T_{II} = \{II_1, II_2\}$. The mutual beliefs of the types in this game in the interim stage, before actions are chosen, are

	II_1	II_2
I_1	1/4	3/4
I_2	2/3	1/3

Player I's beliefs

	II_1	II_2
I_1	3/11	9/13
I_2	8/11	4/13

Player II's beliefs

and the state games are given by

Player II

	L	R
T	1	0
B	0	0

Player I

The state game for $t = (I_1, II_1)$

Player II

	L	R
T	0	1
B	0	0

Player I

The state game for $t = (I_1, II_2)$

Player II

	L	R
T	0	0
B	1	0

Player I

The state game for $t = (I_2, II_1)$

Player II

	L	R
T	0	0
B	0	1

Player I

The state game for $t = (I_2, II_2)$

Are the beliefs of the players consistent? In other words, can they be derived from common prior beliefs? If you answer no, justify your answer. If you answer yes, find the common prior, and find a Bayesian equilibrium in the game.

9.50 Repeat Exercise 9.49, with the following mutual beliefs:

	II_1	II_2
I_1	1/3	2/3
I_2	3/4	1/4

Player I's beliefs

	II_1	II_2
I_1	3/5	1/6
I_2	2/5	5/6

Player II's beliefs

9.51 Two or three players are about to play a game: with probability $\frac{1}{2}$ the game involves Players 1 and 2 and with probability $\frac{1}{2}$ the game involves Players 1, 2, and 3. Players 2 and 3 know which game is being played. In contrast, Player 1, who participates in the game under all conditions, does not know whether he is playing against Player 2 alone, or against both Players 2 and 3. If the game involves Players 1 and 2 the game is given by the following matrix, where Player 1 chooses the row, and Player 2 chooses the column:

	L	R
T	0, 0	2, 1
B	2, 1	0, 0

with Player 3 receiving no payoff. If the game involves all three players, the game is given by the following two matrices, where Player 1 chooses the row, Player 2 chooses the column, and Player 3 chooses the matrix:

	L	R
T	1, 2, 4	0, 0, 0
B	0, 0, 0	2, 1, 3

W

	L	R
T	2, 1, 3	0, 0, 0
B	0, 0, 0	1, 2, 4

E

(a) What are the states of nature in this game?
(b) How many pure strategies does each player have in this game?
(c) Depict this game as a game with incomplete information.
(d) Describe the game in extensive form.
(e) Find two Bayesian equilibria in pure strategies.
(f) Find an additional Bayesian equilibrium by identifying a strategy vector in which all the players of all types are indifferent between their two possible actions.

9.52 This exercise generalizes Theorems 9.47 (page 364) and 9.53 (page 365) to the case where the prior distributions of the players differ.

Let $(N, (T_i)_{i \in N}, (p_i)_{i \in N}, S, (s_t)_{t \in \times_{i \in N} T_i})$ be a game with incomplete information where each player has a different prior distribution: for each $i \in N$, player i's prior distribution is p_i. For each strategy vector σ, define the payoff function U_i as

$$U_i(\sigma) := \sum_{t \in T} p_i(t) U_i(t; \sigma),$$
(9.126)

and the payoff of player i of type t_i by

$$U_i(\sigma \mid t_i) := \sum_{t_{-i} \in T_{-i}} p_i(t_{-i} \mid t_i) U_i((t_i, t_{-i}); \sigma).$$
(9.127)

A strategy vector σ^* is a *Nash equilibrium* if for every player $i \in N$ and every strategy σ_i of player i,

$$U_i(\sigma^*) \geq U_i(\sigma_i, \sigma_{-i}^*), \tag{9.128}$$

and it is a *Bayesian equilibrium* if for every player $i \in N$, every type $t_i \in T_i$, and every strategy σ_i of player i,

$$U_i(\sigma^* \mid t_i) \geq U_i(\sigma_i, \sigma_{-i}^* \mid t_i). \tag{9.129}$$

(a) Prove that a Nash equilibrium exists when the number of players is finite and each player has finitely many types and actions.

(b) Prove that if each player assigns positive probability to every type of every player, i.e., if $p_i(t_j) := \sum_{t_{-j} \in T_{-j}} p_i(t_j, t_{-j}) > 0$ for every $i, j \in N$ and every $t_j \in T_j$, then every Nash equilibrium is a Bayesian equilibrium, and every Bayesian equilibrium is a Nash equilibrium.

9.53 In this exercise, we explore the connection between correlated equilibrium (see Chapter 8) and games with incomplete information.

(a) Let $\Gamma = (N, (T_i)_{i \in N}, p, S, (s_t)_{t \in \times_{i \in N} T_i})$ be a game with incomplete information, where the set of states of nature S contains only one state, which is a game in strategic form $G = (N, (A_i)_{i \in N}, (u_i)_{i \in N})$; that is, $s_t = G$ for every $t \in \times_{i \in N} T_i$. The game G is called "the base game" of Γ. Denote the set of action vectors by $A = \times_{i \in N} A_i$. Every strategy vector σ in Γ naturally induces a distribution μ_σ over the vectors in A:

$$\mu_\sigma(a) = \sum_{\omega \in \Omega} p(\omega) \times \sigma_1(t_1; a_1) \times \sigma_2(t_2; a_2) \times \cdots \times \sigma_n(t_n; a_n). \tag{9.130}$$

Prove that if a strategy vector σ^* is a Bayesian equilibrium of Γ, then the distribution μ_{σ^*} defined in Equation (9.130) is a correlated equilibrium in the base game G.

(b) Prove that for every strategic-form game $G = (N, (A_i)_{i \in N}, (u_i)_{i \in N})$, and every correlated equilibrium μ in this game there exists a game with incomplete information $\Gamma = (N, (T_i)_{i \in N}, p, S, (s_t)_{t \in \times_{i \in N} T_i})$ in which the set of states of nature S contains only one state, and that state corresponds to the base game, $s_t = G$ for every $t \in \times_{i \in N} T_i$, and there exists a Bayesian equilibrium σ^* in the game Γ, such that $\mu(a) = \sum_{\omega \in \Omega} p(\omega) \times \sigma_1^*(t_1; a_1) \times \sigma_2^*(t_2; a_2) \times \cdots \times \sigma_n^*(t_n; a_n)$ for every $a \in A$.

9.54 Carolyn and Maurice are playing the game "Chicken" (see Example 8.3 on page 314). Both Carolyn and Maurice know that Maurice knows who won the Wimbledon tennis tournament yesterday (out of three possible tennis players, Jim, John, and Arthur, who each had a probability of one-third of winning the tournament), but Carolyn does not know who won the tournament.

(a) Describe this situation as a game with incomplete information, and find the set of Bayesian equilibria of this game.

(b) Answer Part (a) of this exercise, under the assumption that both Carolyn and Maurice only know whether or not Jim has won the tournament.

(c) Answer Part (a) of this exercise, under the assumption that Maurice only knows whether or not Jim has won the tournament, while Carolyn only knows whether or not John has won the tournament.

10 Games with incomplete information: the general model

Chapter summary

In this chapter we extend Aumann's model of incomplete information with beliefs in two ways. First, we do not assume that the set of states of the world is finite, and allow it to be any measurable set. Second, we do not assume that the players share a common prior, but rather that the players' beliefs at the interim stage are part of the data of the game. These extensions lead to the concept of a *belief space*. We also define the concept of a *minimal belief subspace* of a player, which represents the model that the player "constructs in his mind" when facing the situation with incomplete information. The notion of games with incomplete information is extended to this setup, along with the concept of Bayesian equilibrium. We finally discuss in detail the concept of *consistent beliefs*, which are beliefs derived from a common prior and thus lead to an Aumann or Harsanyi model of incomplete information.

Chapter 9 focused on the Aumann model of incomplete information, and on Harsanyi games with incomplete information. In both of those models, players share a common prior distribution, either over the set of states of the world or over the set of type vectors. As noted in that chapter, there is no compelling reason to assume that such a common prior exists. In this chapter, we will expand the Aumann model of incomplete information to deal with the case where players may have heterogeneous priors, instead of a common prior.

The equilibrium concept we presented for analyzing Harsanyi games with incomplete information and a common prior was the Nash equilibrium. This is an equilibrium in a game that begins with a chance move that chooses the type vector. As shown in Chapter 9, every Nash equilibrium in a Harsanyi game is a Bayesian equilibrium, and conversely every Bayesian equilibrium is a Nash equilibrium. When there is no common prior, we cannot postulate a chance move choosing a type vector; hence the concept of Nash equilibrium is not applicable in this case. However, as we will show, the concept of Bayesian equilibrium is still applicable. We will study the properties of this concept in Section 10.5 (page 416).

10.1 Belief spaces

Recall that an Aumann model of incomplete information is given by a set of players N, a finite set Y of states of the world, a partition $\mathcal{F}_i$ of Y for each player $i \in N$, a set of states of nature S, a function $\mathfrak{s} : Y \to S$ mapping each state of the world to a state of nature, and a common prior $\mathbf{P}$ over Y. The next definition extends this model to the case in which there is no common prior.

Definition 10.1 *Let N be a finite set of players, and let $(S, \mathcal{S})$ be a measurable space of states of nature.*[1] *A belief space of the set of players N over the set of states of nature is an ordered vector* $\Pi = (Y, \mathcal{Y}, \mathfrak{s}, (\pi_i)_{i \in N})$, *where:*

- *$(Y, \mathcal{Y})$ is a measurable space of states of the world.*
- *$\mathfrak{s} : Y \to S$ is a measurable function,[2] mapping each state of the world to a state of nature.*
- *For each player $i \in N$, a function $\pi_i : Y \to \Delta(Y)$ maps each state of the world $\omega \in Y$ to a probability distribution over Y. We will denote the probability that player i ascribes to event E, according to the probability distribution $\pi_i(\omega)$, by $\pi_i(E \mid \omega)$. We require the function $(\pi_i)_{i \in N}$ to satisfy the following conditions:*

1. *Coherency: for each player $i \in N$ and each $\omega \in Y$, the set $\{\omega' \in Y : \pi_i(\omega') = \pi_i(\omega)\}$ is measurable in Y, and*

$$\pi_i(\{\omega' \in Y : \pi_i(\omega') = \pi_i(\omega)\} \mid \omega) = 1. \tag{10.1}$$

2. *Measurability: for each player $i \in N$ and each measurable set $E \in \mathcal{Y}$, the function $\pi_i(E \mid \cdot) : Y \to [0, 1]$ is a measurable function.*

As in the Aumann model of incomplete information, belief spaces describe situations in which there is a true state of the world ω_* but the players may not know which state is the true state. At the true state of the world ω_* each player $i \in N$ believes that the true state of the world is distributed according to the probability distribution $\pi_i(\omega^*)$. This probability distribution is called player i's belief at the state of the world ω_*. We assume that each player knows his own belief and therefore if at the state of the world ω_* player i believes that the state of the world might be ω, then his beliefs at ω_* and ω must coincide. Indeed, if his beliefs at ω differed from his beliefs at ω_*, then he would be able to distinguish between these states, and therefore at ω_* he could not ascribe a positive probability to the state of the world ω. It follows that at the state of the world ω_* player i ascribes probability 1 to the set of states of the world at which his beliefs equal his belief at ω_*. This is the reason we demand coherency in Definition 10.1. The measurability condition is a technical condition that is required for computing the expected payment in games in which incomplete information games are modeled using belief spaces.

The concept "belief space" generalizes the concept "Aumann model of incomplete information" that was presented in Definition 9.27 (page 345). Every Aumann model of incomplete information is a belief space. To see this, let $\Pi = (N, Y, (\mathcal{F}_i)_{i \in N}, \mathfrak{s}, \mathbf{P})$ be an

---

1 A *measurable space* is a pair $(X, \mathcal{X})$, where X is a set and $\mathcal{X}$ is a σ-algebra over X; i.e., $\mathcal{X}$ is a collection of subsets of X that includes the empty set, is closed under complementation, and is closed under countable intersections. A set in $\mathcal{X}$ is called a *measurable set*. This definition was mentioned on page 355.

2 A function $f : X \to Y$ is *measurable* if the inverse image under f of every measurable set in Y is a measurable set in X. In other words, for each measurable set C in Y, the set $f^{-1}(C) := \{x \in X : f(x) \in C\}$ is measurable in X.

Aumann model of incomplete information. Let $\mathcal{Y} = 2^Y$ be the collection of all subsets of Y. For each player $i \in N$ and every $\omega \in Y$, let $\pi_i(\omega) = \mathbf{P}(\cdot \mid F_i(\omega))$; i.e., player i's belief at state ω is the common prior $\mathbf{P}$, conditioned on his information. It follows that $(Y, \mathcal{Y}, \mathfrak{s}, (\pi_i)_{i \in N})$ is a belief space equivalent to the original Aumann model: for every event $A \subseteq Y$, the probability that player i ascribes at every state of the world ω to event A is equal in both models (verify!).

Since every Harsanyi model of incomplete information is equivalent to an Aumann model of incomplete information (see page 361), every Harsanyi model of incomplete information can be represented by a belief space.

Belief spaces generalize Aumann models of incomplete information with belief in the following ways:

1. The set of states of the world in an Aumann model of incomplete information is finite, while the set of states of the world in a belief space may be any measurable space.
2. The beliefs $(\pi_i)_{i \in N}$ in a belief space are not necessarily derived from a prior $\mathbf{P}$ common to all the players.

In most of the examples in this chapter, the set of states of the world Y is finite. In those examples, we assume that $\mathcal{Y} = 2^Y$: the σ-algebra over Y is the collection of all the subsets of Y.

Example 10.2 Let the set of players be $N = \{\text{I}, \text{II}\}$, and let the set of states of nature be $S = \{s_1, s_2\}$. Consider a belief space $Y = \{\omega_1, \omega_2, \omega_3\}$, where:

State of the world	$\mathfrak{s}(\cdot)$	$\pi_{\text{I}}(\cdot)$	$\pi_{\text{II}}(\cdot)$
ω_1	s_1	$\left[\frac{2}{3}(\omega_1), \frac{1}{3}(\omega_2)\right]$	$[1(\omega_1)]$
ω_2	s_1	$\left[\frac{2}{3}(\omega_1), \frac{1}{3}(\omega_2)\right]$	$\left[\frac{1}{2}(\omega_2), \frac{1}{2}(\omega_3)\right]$
ω_3	s_2	$[1(\omega_3)]$	$\left[\frac{1}{2}(\omega_2), \frac{1}{2}(\omega_3)\right]$

The states of the world appear in the left-hand column of the table, the next column displays the state of nature associated with each state of the world, and the two right-hand columns display the beliefs of the players at each state of the world.

At the state of the world ω_1, Player II ascribes probability 1 to the state of nature being s_1, while at the states ω_2 and ω_3 he ascribes probability $\frac{1}{2}$ to each of the two states of nature. At each state of the world, Player I ascribes probability 1 to the true state of nature. As for the beliefs of Player I about the beliefs of Player II about the state of nature, at the state of the world ω_3 he ascribes probability 1 to Player II ascribing equal probabilities to the two states of nature, while at the states of the world ω_1 and ω_2 he ascribes probability $\frac{2}{3}$ to Player II ascribing probability 1 to the true state of nature, and probability $\frac{1}{3}$ to Player II ascribing probability $\frac{1}{2}$ to the true state of nature.

The beliefs of the players can be calculated from the following common prior $\mathbf{P}$:

$$\mathbf{P}(\omega_1) = \tfrac{1}{2}, \quad \mathbf{P}(\omega_2) = \tfrac{1}{4}, \quad \mathbf{P}(\omega_3) = \tfrac{1}{4}, \tag{10.2}$$

and the following partitions of the two players (verify that this is true)

$$\mathcal{F}_{\text{I}} = \{\{\omega_1, \omega_2\}, \{\omega_3\}\}, \quad \mathcal{F}_{\text{II}} = \{\{\omega_1\}, \{\omega_2, \omega_3\}\}. \tag{10.3}$$

It follows that the belief space of this example is equivalent to an Aumann model of incomplete information.   ◀

As the next example shows, however, it is not true that every belief space is equivalent to an Aumann model of incomplete information; in other words, there are cases in which the beliefs of the players $(\pi_i)_{i \in N}$ cannot be calculated as conditional probabilities of a common prior.

Example 10.3 Let the set of players be $N = \{\text{I}, \text{II}\}$, and let the set of states of nature be $S = \{s_1, s_2\}$. Consider a belief space $Y = \{\omega_1, \omega_2\}$, where:

State of the world	$\mathfrak{s}(\cdot)$	$\pi_{\text{I}}(\cdot)$	$\pi_{\text{II}}(\cdot)$
ω_1	s_1	$\left[\frac{2}{3}(\omega_1), \frac{1}{3}(\omega_2)\right]$	$\left[\frac{1}{2}(\omega_1), \frac{1}{2}(\omega_2)\right]$
ω_2	s_2	$\left[\frac{2}{3}(\omega_1), \frac{1}{3}(\omega_2)\right]$	$\left[\frac{1}{2}(\omega_1), \frac{1}{2}(\omega_2)\right]$

In this space, at every state of the world Player I ascribes probability $\frac{2}{3}$ to the state of nature being s_1, while Player II ascribes probability $\frac{1}{2}$ to the state of nature being s_1. There is no common prior over Y that enables both of these statements to be true (verify that this is true).

Since each player has the same belief at both states of the world, if there is an Aumann model of incomplete information describing this situation, the partition of each player must be the trivial partition: $\mathcal{F}_i = \{Y\}$ for all $i \in N$.   ◄

Recall that the support of a probability distribution p defined on a finite set Y is the set of all elements of Y to which p assigns positive probability:

$$\text{supp}(p) := \{\omega \in Y : p(\omega) > 0\}. \tag{10.4}$$

In Example 10.3, in every state of the world, the support of the belief of each player is Y.

As the next example shows, it is possible for the support of $\pi_i(\omega)$ to be contained in the set $\{\omega' \in Y : \pi_i(\omega') = \pi_i(\omega)\}$, but not equal to it.

Example 10.4 Let the set of players be $N = \{\text{I}, \text{II}\}$, and let the set of states of nature be $S = \{s_1, s_2\}$. Consider a belief space $Y = \{\omega_1, \omega_2, \omega_3\}$, where:

State of the world	$\mathfrak{s}(\cdot)$	$\pi_{\text{I}}(\cdot)$	$\pi_{\text{II}}(\cdot)$
ω_1	s_1	$[1(\omega_1)]$	$\left[\frac{1}{2}(\omega_1), \frac{1}{2}(\omega_2)\right]$
ω_2	s_2	$[1(\omega_1)]$	$\left[\frac{1}{2}(\omega_1), \frac{1}{2}(\omega_2)\right]$
ω_3	s_2	$[1(\omega_3)]$	$\left[\frac{1}{2}(\omega_1), \frac{1}{2}(\omega_2)\right]$

At both states of the world ω_1 and ω_2, Player I believes that the true state is ω_1: the support of $\pi_{\text{I}}(\omega_1)$ is the set $\{\omega_1\}$, which is a proper subset of $\{\omega' \in Y : \pi_{\text{I}}(\omega') = \pi_{\text{I}}(\omega_1)\} = \{\omega_1, \omega_2\}$. Note that at the state of the world ω_2, the state of nature is s_2, but Player I believes that the state of nature is s_1.   ◄

The belief spaces described in Examples 10.3 and 10.4 are not equivalent to Aumann models of incomplete information, but they can be described as Aumann models in which every player has a prior distribution of his own. In Example 10.3, in both states of the world, Player I has a prior distribution $\left[\frac{2}{3}(\omega_1), \frac{1}{3}(\omega_2)\right]$, and Player II has a prior distribution $[\frac{1}{2}(\omega_1), \frac{1}{2}(\omega_2)]$. The beliefs of the players in the belief space of Example 10.4 can also be computed as being derived from prior distributions in the following way (verify!). The beliefs of Player II can be derived from the prior

$$\mathbf{P}_{\text{II}}(\omega_1) = \tfrac{1}{2}, \quad \mathbf{P}_{\text{II}}(\omega_2) = \tfrac{1}{2}, \quad \mathbf{P}_{\text{II}}(\omega_3) = 0 \tag{10.5}$$

and the partition

$$\mathcal{F}_{\text{II}} = \{Y\}. \tag{10.6}$$

The beliefs of Player I can be derived from any prior of the form

$$\mathbf{P}_{\text{I}}(\omega_1) = x, \quad \mathbf{P}_{\text{I}}(\omega_2) = 0, \quad \mathbf{P}_{\text{I}}(\omega_3) = 1 - x, \tag{10.7}$$

where $x \in (0, 1)$, and the partition

$$\mathcal{F}_{\text{I}} = \{\{\omega_1, \omega_2\}, \{\omega_3\}\}. \tag{10.8}$$

This is not coincidental: every belief space with a finite set of states of the world is an Aumann model of incomplete information in which every player has a prior distribution whose support is not necessarily all of Y, and the priors of the players may be heterogeneous.[3] To see this, for the case that Y is finite define, for each player i, a partition $\mathcal{F}_i$ of Y based on his beliefs:

$$F_i(\omega) = \{\omega' \in Y \colon \pi_i(\omega') = \pi_i(\omega)\}. \tag{10.9}$$

For each ω, the partition element $F_i(\omega)$ is the set of all states of the world at which the beliefs of player i equal his beliefs at ω: player i's beliefs do not distinguish between the states of the world in $F_i(\omega)$.

Define, for each player $i \in N$, a probability distribution $\mathbf{P}_i \in \Delta(Y)$ as follows (verify that this is indeed a probability distribution):

$$\mathbf{P}_i(A) = \sum_{\omega \in Y} \frac{1}{|Y|} \pi_i(A \mid \omega). \tag{10.10}$$

Then the belief $\pi_i(\omega)$ of player i at the state of the world ω is the probability distribution $\mathbf{P}_i$, conditioned on $F_i(\omega)$, which is his information at that state of the world (see Exercise 10.3):

$$\pi_i(A \mid \omega) = \mathbf{P}_i(A \mid F_i(\omega)), \quad \forall \omega \in Y, \forall A \in \mathcal{Y}. \tag{10.11}$$

It follows that every belief space $\Pi = (Y, \mathcal{Y}, \mathfrak{s}, (\pi_i)_{i \in N})$, where Y is a finite set, is equivalent to an Aumann model of incomplete information $(N, Y, (\mathcal{F}_i)_{i \in N}, \mathfrak{s}, (\mathbf{P}_i)_{i \in N})$ in which every player has a prior of his own.

Example 10.4   (*Continued*) Using Equation (10.10), we have

$$\mathbf{P}_{\text{I}} = \left[\tfrac{2}{3}(\omega_1), 0(\omega_2), \tfrac{1}{3}(\omega_3)\right], \quad \mathbf{P}_{\text{II}} = \left[\tfrac{1}{2}(\omega_1), \tfrac{1}{2}(\omega_2), 0(\omega_3)\right]. \tag{10.12}$$

In fact, the definition of $\mathbf{P}_i$ in Equation (10.10) can be replaced with any weighted average of the beliefs $(\pi_i(\cdot \mid \omega))_{\omega \in Y}$, where all the weights are positive. The probability distribution of Equation (10.7) corresponds to the weights $(y, x - y, 1 - x)$, where $y \in (0, x)$ (verify!). ◄

---

3 When the space of states of the world is infinite, additional technical assumptions are needed to ensure the existence of a prior distribution from which each player's beliefs can be derived.

Just as in an Aumann model of incomplete information, we can trace all levels of beliefs for each player at any state of the world in a belief space. For example, consider Example 10.4 and write out Player 1's beliefs at the state of the world ω_3. At that state, Player 1 ascribes probability 1 to the state of nature being s_2; this is his first-order belief. He ascribes probability 1 to the state of nature being s_2 and to Player 2 ascribing equal probability to the two possible states of nature; this is his second-order belief. Player 1's third-order belief at the state of the world ω_3 is as follows: Player 1 ascribes probability 1 to the state of nature being s_2, to Player 2 ascribing equal probability to the two states of nature, and to Player 2 believing that Player 1 ascribes probability 1 to the state of nature s_1. We can similarly describe the beliefs of every player, at any order, at every state of the world.

10.2 Belief and knowledge

One of the main elements of the Aumann model of incomplete information is the partitions $(\mathcal{F}_i)_{i \in N}$ defining the players' knowledge operators. In an Aumann model, the players' beliefs are derived from a common prior, given the information that the player has (i.e., the partition element $F_i(\omega)$). In contrast, in a belief space, a player's beliefs are given by the model itself. Since an Aumann model of incomplete information is a special case of a belief space, it is natural to ask whether a knowledge operator can be defined generally, in all belief spaces. As we saw in Equation (10.9), the beliefs $(\pi_i)_{i \in N}$ of the players define partitions $(\mathcal{F}_i)_{i \in N}$ of Y. A knowledge operator can then be defined using these partitions. When player i knows what the belief space Π is, he can indeed compute his partitions $(\mathcal{F}_i)_{i \in N}$ and the knowledge operators corresponding to these partitions. As the next example shows, knowledge based on these knowledge operators is not equivalent to belief with probability 1.

Example 10.5 Consider the belief space Π of a single player $N = \{I\}$ over a set of states of the world $S = \{s_1, s_2\}$, shown in Figure 10.1.

II	State of the world	$\mathfrak{s}(\cdot)$	$\pi_I(\cdot)$
	ω_1	s_1	$[1(\omega_1)]$
	ω_2	s_2	$[1(\omega_1)]$

Figure 10.1 The belief space Π in Example 10.5

In the belief space Π, the partition defined by Equation (10.9) contains a single element, and therefore the minimal knowledge element of Player I at every state of the world is $\{\omega_1, \omega_2\}$. In other words, at the state of the world ω_1 Player I does not know that the state of the world is ω_1. Thus, despite the fact that at the state of the world ω_1 Player I ascribes probability 1 to the state of the world ω_1, he does not know that this is the true state of the world. ◄

The assumption that a player knows the belief space Π is a strong assumption: at the state of the world ω_1 in Example 10.5 the player ascribes probability 1 to the state of the world ω_1. Perhaps he does not know that there is a state of the world ω_2? We will assume that the only information that a player has is his belief, and that he does not know what the belief space is. In particular, different players may have different realities. In such a case, when a player does not know Π, he cannot compute the partitions $(\mathcal{F}_i)_{i \in N}$ and the knowledge operators corresponding to these partitions, and therefore cannot compute the events that he knows.

Under these assumptions the natural operator to use in belief spaces is a belief operator and not a knowledge operator. Under a knowledge operator, if a player knows a certain fact it must be true. This requirement may not be satisfied by belief operators; a player may ascribe probability 1 to a "fact" that is actually false. After we define this operator and study its properties we will relate it to the knowledge operator in Aumann models of incomplete information.

Definition 10.6 *At the state of the world $\omega \in Y$, player $i \in N$ believes that an event A obtains if $\pi_i(A \mid \omega) = 1$. Denote*

$$B_i A := \{\omega \in Y : \pi_i(A \mid \omega) = 1\}. \tag{10.13}$$

At the state of the world ω player i believes that event A obtains if he ascribes probability 1 to A. The event $B_i A$ is the set of all states of the world at which player i believes event A obtains. The belief operator B_i satisfies four of the five properties of Kripke that a knowledge operator must satisfy (see page 337 and Exercise 10.8).

Theorem 10.7 *For each player $i \in N$, the belief operator B_i satisfies the following four properties:*

1. *$B_i Y = Y$: At each state of the world, player i believes that Y is the set of states of the world.*
2. *$B_i A \cap B_i C = B_i(A \cap C)$: If player i believes that event A obtains and he believes that event C obtains, then he believes that event $A \cap C$ obtains.*
3. *$B_i(B_i A) = B_i A$: If player i believes that event A obtains, then he believes that he believes that event A obtains.*
4. *$(B_i A)^c = B_i((B_i A)^c)$: If player i does not believe that event A obtains, then he believes that he does not believe that event A obtains.*

The knowledge operator K_i satisfies a fifth property: $K_i A \subseteq A$. This property is not necessarily satisfied by a belief operator: it is not always the case that $B_i A \subseteq A$. In other words, it is possible that $\omega \in B_i A$ but $\omega \notin A$. This means that a player may believe that the event A obtains despite the fact that the true state of the world is not in A; i.e., A does not obtain. This is the case in Example 10.4: for $A = \{\omega_1\}$, $B_1 A = \{\omega_1, \omega_2\}$: at the state of the world ω_2 the player believes that A obtains, despite the fact that $\omega_2 \notin A$.

The belief operator does satisfy the following additional property (Exercise 10.13). The analogous property for the knowledge operator is stated in Theorem 9.10 (page 337).

Theorem 10.8 *For each player $i \in N$, and any pair of events $A, C \subseteq Y$, if $A \subseteq C$, then $B_i A \subseteq B_i C$.*

In words, when a player believes that event A obtains, he also believes that every event containing A obtains.

Just as we defined the concept of common knowledge (Definition 9.2 on page 332), we can define the concept of common belief.

Definition 10.9 *Let $A \subseteq Y$ be an event and let $\omega \in Y$. The event A is* common belief *among the players at the state of the world ω if at that state of the world every player believes that A obtains, every player believes that every player believes that A obtains, and so on. In other words, for every finite sequence $i_1, i_2, \ldots, i_l$ of players in N,*

$$\omega \in B_{i_1} B_{i_2} \ldots B_{i_{l-1}} B_{i_l} A. \tag{10.14}$$

It follows from Definition 10.9 and Theorem 10.7(1) that, in particular, the event Y is common belief among the players at every state of the world $\omega \in Y$. The next theorem presents a sufficient condition for an event to be common belief among the players at a particular state of the world.

Theorem 10.10 *Let $\omega \in Y$ be a state of the world. Let $A \in \mathcal{Y}$ be an event satisfying the following two conditions:*

- *$\pi_i(A \mid \omega) = 1$ for every player $i \in N$.*
- *$\pi_i(A \mid \omega') = 1$ for every player $i \in N$ and every $\omega' \in A$.*

Then A is common belief among the players at ω.

Proof: The first condition implies that $\omega \in B_i A$, and the second condition implies that $A \subseteq B_i A$, for each player $i \in N$. From this, and from repeated application of Theorem 10.8, we get for every finite sequence $i_1, i_2, \ldots, i_l$ of players:

$$\omega \in B_{i_1} A \subseteq B_{i_1} B_{i_2} A \subseteq \cdots \subseteq B_{i_1} B_{i_2} \ldots B_{i_{l-1}} A \subseteq B_{i_1} B_{i_2} \ldots B_{i_{l-1}} B_{i_l} A.$$

It follows that at the state of the world ω event A is common belief among the players.   □

When a belief space is equivalent to an Aumann model of incomplete information, the concept of knowledge is a meaningful one, and the question naturally arises as to whether there is a relation between knowledge and belief in this case. As we now show, the answer to this question is positive. Let $\Pi = (Y, \mathcal{Y}, \mathfrak{s}, (\pi_i)_{i \in N})$ (where Y is a finite set of states of the world) be a belief space that is equivalent to an Aumann model of incomplete information. In particular, there exists a probability distribution $\mathbf{P}$ over Y satisfying $\mathbf{P}(\omega) > 0$ for all $\omega \in Y$, and there exist partitions $(\mathcal{F}_i)_{i \in N}$ of Y such that

$$\pi_i(\omega) = \mathbf{P}(\cdot \mid F_i(\omega)), \quad \forall i \in N, \forall \omega \in Y. \tag{10.15}$$

The partition $\mathcal{F}_i$ in the Aumann model coincides with the partition defined by Equation (10.9) for the belief space Π (Exercise 10.14); hence the knowledge operator in the Aumann model is the same operator as the belief operator in the belief space. We therefore have the following theorem:

Theorem 10.11 *Let Π be a belief space equivalent to an Aumann model of incomplete information. Then the belief operator in the belief space is the same operator as the knowledge operator in the Aumann model. For every $i \in N$, at the state of the world ω player i believes that event A obtains (in the belief space) if and only if he knows that event A obtains (in the Aumann model).*

Note that for this result to obtain, it must be the case that $P(\omega) > 0$ for every state of the world $\omega \in Y$ (Exercise 10.11).

If $\Pi = (Y, \mathcal{Y}, \mathfrak{s}, (\pi_i)_{i \in N})$ is a belief space satisfying the condition that for player $i \in N$, $B_i A \subseteq A$ for every event $A \subseteq Y$, then the operator B_i satisfies the five properties of Kripke, and is therefore a knowledge operator: there exists a partition $\mathcal{G}_i$ of Y such that B_i is the knowledge operator defined by $\mathcal{G}_i$ via Equation (9.2) on page 336 (Exercise 9.2, Chapter 9). Since this partition is simply the partition defined by Equation (10.9) (Exercise 10.9), the conclusion of Theorem 10.11 obtains in this case as well. We stress that this case is more general than the case in which a belief space is equivalent to an Aumann model of incomplete information, because this condition can be met in an Aumann model of incomplete information in which the players do not share a common prior (see Example 10.3). Nevertheless, in this case, the belief operator is also the same operator as the knowledge operator.

10.3 Examples of belief spaces

As stated above, the information that player i has at the state of the world ω is given by his belief $\pi_i(\omega)$. We shall refer to this belief as the player's *type*. A player's type is thus a probability distribution over Y.

Definition 10.12 *Let $\Pi = (Y, \mathcal{Y}, \mathfrak{s}, (\pi_i)_{i \in N})$ be a belief space. The* type *of player i at the state of the world ω is $\pi_i(\omega)$. The set of all types of player i in a belief space Π is denoted by T_i and called the* type set *of player i:*

$$T_i := \{\pi_i(\omega) : \omega \in Y\} \subseteq \Delta(Y). \tag{10.16}$$

The coherency requirement in Definition 10.1, and the definition of the belief operator B_i, together imply that at each state of the world ω, every player $i \in N$ believes that his type is $\pi_i(\omega)$:

$$\pi_i(\{\omega' \in Y : \pi_i(\omega') = \pi_i(\omega)\} \mid \omega) = 1. \tag{10.17}$$

We next present examples showing how situations of incomplete information can be modeled by belief spaces. We start with situations that can be modeled both by Aumann models of incomplete information, and by belief spaces.

Example 10.13 **Complete information** Suppose that a state of nature $s_0 \in S$ is common belief among the players in a finite set $N = \{1, 2, \ldots, n\}$. The following belief space corresponds to this situation, where the set of states of the world, $Y = \{\omega\}$, contains only one state, and all the players have the same beliefs:

State of the world	$\mathfrak{s}(\cdot)$	$\pi_1(\cdot), \ldots, \pi_n(\cdot)$
ω	s_0	$[1(\omega)]$

In this space, every player $i \in N$ has only one type, $T_i = \{[1(\omega)]\}$. The beliefs of the players can be calculated from the common prior $\mathbf{P}$ defined by $\mathbf{P}(\omega) = 1$, hence this belief space is also an Aumann model of incomplete information, with the trivial partition $\mathcal{F}_i = \{\{\omega\}\}$, for every player $i \in N$.

This situation can also be modeled by the following belief space, where $Y = \{\omega_1, \omega_2\}$:

State of the world	$\mathfrak{s}(\cdot)$	$\pi_1(\cdot), \ldots, \pi_n(\cdot)$
ω_1	s_0	$[1(\omega_1)]$
ω_2	s_0	$[1(\omega_2)]$

The two states of the world ω_1 and ω_2 are distinguished only by their names; they are identical from the perspective both of the state of nature associated with them and of the beliefs of the players about the state of nature: at both states of the world, the state of nature is s_0, and at both states that fact is common belief. This is an instance of *redundancy*: two states of the world describe the same situation. If we eliminate the redundancy, we recapitulate the former belief space.   ◀

Example 10.14 **Known lottery** The set of players is $N = \{1, \ldots, n\}$. The set of states of nature, $S = \{s_1, s_2\}$, contains two elements; a chance move chooses s_1 with probability $\frac{1}{3}$, and s_2 with probability $\frac{2}{3}$. This probability distribution is common belief among the players. The following belief space, where $Y = \{\omega_1, \omega_2\}$, corresponds to this situation:

State of the world	$\mathfrak{s}(\cdot)$	$\pi_1(\cdot), \ldots, \pi_n(\cdot)$
ω_1	s_1	$\left[\frac{1}{3}(\omega_1), \frac{2}{3}(\omega_2)\right]$
ω_2	s_2	$\left[\frac{1}{3}(\omega_1), \frac{2}{3}(\omega_2)\right]$

In this space, each player $i \in N$ has only one type, $T_i = \{[\frac{1}{3}(\omega_1), \frac{2}{3}(\omega_2)]\}$, and this fact is therefore common belief among the players. The beliefs of the players can be calculated from a common prior $\mathbf{P}$ defined by $\mathbf{P}(\omega_1) = \frac{1}{3}$ and $\mathbf{P}(\omega_2) = \frac{2}{3}$, and the partitions derived from the beliefs of the types, i.e., $\mathcal{F}_i = \{\{\omega_1, \omega_2\}\}$ for every player $i \in N$; hence this belief space is also an Aumann model of incomplete information.   ◀

Example 10.15 **Incomplete information on one side** There are two players, $N = \{I, II\}$, and two states of nature, $S = \{s_1, s_2\}$; a chance move chooses s_1 with probability p, and s_2 with probability $1 - p$. The state of the world that is chosen is known to Player I, but not to Player II. This description of the situation is common belief among the players. The following belief space, where $Y = \{\omega_1, \omega_2\}$, corresponds to this situation:

State of the world	$\mathfrak{s}(\cdot)$	$\pi_I(\cdot)$	$\pi_{II}(\cdot)$
ω_1	s_1	$[1(\omega_1)]$	$[p(\omega_1), (1-p)(\omega_2)]$
ω_2	s_2	$[1(\omega_2)]$	$[p(\omega_1), (1-p)(\omega_2)]$

In this belief space, Player II has only one type, $T_{II} = \{[p(\omega_1), (1-p)(\omega_2)]\}$, while Player I has two possible types, $T_I = \{[1(\omega_1)], [1(\omega_2)]\}$, because he knows the true state of nature. The beliefs of the players can be calculated from a common prior $\mathbf{P}$ given by $\mathbf{P}(\omega_1) = p$ and $\mathbf{P}(\omega_2) = 1 - p$, and the partition $\mathcal{F}_I = \{\{\omega_1\}, \{\omega_2\}\}$ (Player I knows which state of the world has been chosen) and $\mathcal{F}_{II} = \{Y\}$ (Player II does not know which state of the world has been chosen). Note that in this example, the belief operator is the same as the knowledge operator (in accordance with Theorem 10.11).   ◀

Example 10.16 **Incomplete information about the information of the other player**   This example, which is similar to Example 10.2 (on page 398), describes a situation in which one of the players knows the true state of nature, but is uncertain whether the other player knows the true state of nature. Consider a situation with two players, $N = \{I, II\}$. A state of nature s_1 or s_2 is chosen by tossing a fair coin. Player I is informed which state of nature has been chosen. If the chosen state of nature is s_2, only Player I is informed of that fact. If the chosen state of nature is s_1, the coin is tossed again, in order to determine whether or not Player II is to be informed that the chosen state of nature is s_1; Player I is not informed of the result of the second coin toss; hence in this situation, even though he knows the state of nature, he does not know whether or not Player II knows the state of nature. The belief space corresponding to this situation contains three states of the world $Y = \{\omega_1, \omega_2, \omega_3\}$ and is given by:

State of the world	$\mathfrak{s}(\cdot)$	$\pi_I(\cdot)$	$\pi_{II}(\cdot)$
ω_1	s_1	$\left[\frac{1}{2}(\omega_1), \frac{1}{2}(\omega_2)\right]$	$[1(\omega_1)]$
ω_2	s_1	$\left[\frac{1}{2}(\omega_1), \frac{1}{2}(\omega_2)\right]$	$\left[\frac{1}{3}(\omega_2), \frac{2}{3}(\omega_3)\right]$
ω_3	s_2	$[1(\omega_3)]$	$\left[\frac{1}{3}(\omega_2), \frac{2}{3}(\omega_3)\right]$

At the state of the world ω_1, the state of nature is s_1, and both Player I and Player II know this. At the state of the world ω_2, the state of nature is s_1, and Player I knows this, but Player II does not know this. The state of the world ω_3 corresponds to the situation in which the state of nature is s_2. Player I cannot distinguish between the states of the world ω_1 and ω_2. Player II cannot distinguish between the states of the world ω_2 and ω_3. The beliefs of the players can be derived from the probability distribution $\mathbf{P}$:

$$\mathbf{P}(\omega_1) = \tfrac{1}{4}, \quad \mathbf{P}(\omega_2) = \tfrac{1}{4}, \quad \mathbf{P}(\omega_3) = \tfrac{1}{2}, \tag{10.18}$$

given the partitions $\mathcal{F}_I = \{\{\omega_1, \omega_2\}, \{\omega_3\}\}$ and $\mathcal{F}_{II} = \{\{\omega_1\}, \{\omega_2, \omega_3\}\}$. Notice that, as required, at every state of the world ω, every player ascribes probability 1 to the states of the world at which his beliefs coincide with his beliefs at ω. In this belief space, each player has two possible types:

$$T_I = \left\{ \left[\tfrac{1}{2}(\omega_1), \tfrac{1}{2}(\omega_2)\right], [1(\omega_3)] \right\}, \tag{10.19}$$

$$T_{II} = \left\{ [1(\omega_1)], \left[\tfrac{1}{3}(\omega_2), \tfrac{2}{3}(\omega_3)\right] \right\}. \tag{10.20}$$

What information does Player I of type $[\tfrac{1}{2}(\omega_1), \tfrac{1}{2}(\omega_2)]$ lack (at the states of the world ω_1 and ω_2)? He knows that the state of nature is s_1, but he does not know whether Player II knows this: Player I ascribes probability $\tfrac{1}{2}$ to the state of the world being ω_1, at which Player II knows that the state of nature is s_1, and he ascribes probability $\tfrac{1}{2}$ to the state of the world being ω_2, at which Player II does not know what the true state of nature is. Player I's lack of information involves the information that Player II has. ◄

Example 10.17 **Incomplete information on two sides (the independent case)**   There are two players, $N = \{I, II\}$, and four states of nature, $S = \{s_{11}, s_{12}, s_{21}, s_{22}\}$. One of the states of nature is chosen, using the probability distribution p defined by $p(s_{11}) = p(s_{12}) = \tfrac{1}{6}, p(s_{21}) = p(s_{22}) = \tfrac{1}{3}$.

Each player has partial information about the chosen state of nature: Player I knows only the first coordinate of the chosen state, while Player II knows only the second coordinate. The belief space corresponding to this situation contains four states of the world, $Y = \{\omega_{11}, \omega_{12}, \omega_{21}, \omega_{22}\}$, and is given by:

State of the world	$\mathfrak{s}(\cdot)$	$\pi_{\mathrm{I}}(\cdot)$	$\pi_{\mathrm{II}}(\cdot)$
ω_{11}	s_{11}	$\left[\frac{1}{2}(\omega_{11}), \frac{1}{2}(\omega_{12})\right]$	$\left[\frac{1}{3}(\omega_{11}), \frac{2}{3}(\omega_{21})\right]$
ω_{12}	s_{12}	$\left[\frac{1}{2}(\omega_{11}), \frac{1}{2}(\omega_{12})\right]$	$\left[\frac{1}{3}(\omega_{12}), \frac{2}{3}(\omega_{22})\right]$
ω_{21}	s_{21}	$\left[\frac{1}{2}(\omega_{21}), \frac{1}{2}(\omega_{22})\right]$	$\left[\frac{1}{3}(\omega_{11}), \frac{2}{3}(\omega_{21})\right]$
ω_{22}	s_{22}	$\left[\frac{1}{2}(\omega_{21}), \frac{1}{2}(\omega_{22})\right]$	$\left[\frac{1}{3}(\omega_{12}), \frac{2}{3}(\omega_{22})\right]$

In this case, each player has two possible types:

$$T_{\mathrm{I}} = \{I_1, I_2\} = \left\{\left[\tfrac{1}{2}(\omega_{11}), \tfrac{1}{2}(\omega_{12})\right], \left[\tfrac{1}{2}(\omega_{21}), \tfrac{1}{2}(\omega_{22})\right]\right\}, \tag{10.21}$$

$$T_{\mathrm{II}} = \{II_1, II_2\} = \left\{\left[\tfrac{1}{3}(\omega_{11}), \tfrac{2}{3}(\omega_{21})\right], \left[\tfrac{1}{3}(\omega_{12}), \tfrac{2}{3}(\omega_{22})\right]\right\}. \tag{10.22}$$

Note that each player knows his own type: at each state of the world, each player ascribes positive probability only to those states of the world in which he has the same type. The beliefs of each player about the type of the other player are described in Figure 10.2.

	II_1	II_2
I_1	1/2	1/2
I_2	1/2	1/2

	II_1	II_2
I_1	1/3	1/3
I_2	2/3	2/3

The beliefs of Player I   The beliefs of Player II

Figure 10.2 The beliefs of each player about the type of the other player

The tables in Figure 10.2 state, for example, that Player I of type I_2 ascribes probability $\frac{1}{2}$ to Player II being of type II_1, and probability $\frac{1}{2}$ to his being of type II_2.

The beliefs of each player about the types of the other player do not depend on his own type, which is why this model is termed the "independent case." This is a Harsanyi model of incomplete information, in which the common prior p over the set of type vectors, $T = T_{\mathrm{I}} \times T_{\mathrm{II}}$, is the product distribution shown in Figure 10.3.

	II_1	II_2
I_1	1/6	1/6
I_2	1/3	1/3

Figure 10.3 The common prior in Example 10.17

The independence in this example is expressed in the fact that p is a product distribution over T_{I} and T_{II}. In summary, in this case the belief space Π is equivalent to a Harsanyi model of incomplete information. ◀

Example 10.18 Incomplete information on two sides (the dependent case) This example is similar to Example 10.17, but here the probability distribution p according to which the state of nature is chosen is given by $p(s_{11}) = 0.3, p(s_{12}) = 0.4, p(s_{21}) = 0.2, p(s_{22}) = 0.1$. As in Example 10.17, the corresponding belief space has four states of the world, $Y = \{\omega_{11}, \omega_{12}, \omega_{21}, \omega_{22}\}$, and is given by:

State of the world	$\mathfrak{s}(\cdot)$	$\pi_{\mathrm{I}}(\cdot)$	$\pi_{\mathrm{II}}(\cdot)$
ω_{11}	s_{11}	$\left[\frac{3}{7}(\omega_{11}), \frac{4}{7}(\omega_{12})\right]$	$\left[\frac{3}{5}(\omega_{11}), \frac{2}{5}(\omega_{21})\right]$
ω_{12}	s_{12}	$\left[\frac{3}{7}(\omega_{11}), \frac{4}{7}(\omega_{12})\right]$	$\left[\frac{4}{5}(\omega_{12}), \frac{1}{5}(\omega_{22})\right]$
ω_{21}	s_{21}	$\left[\frac{2}{3}(\omega_{21}), \frac{1}{3}(\omega_{22})\right]$	$\left[\frac{3}{5}(\omega_{11}), \frac{2}{5}(\omega_{21})\right]$
ω_{22}	s_{22}	$\left[\frac{2}{3}(\omega_{21}), \frac{1}{3}(\omega_{22})\right]$	$\left[\frac{4}{5}(\omega_{12}), \frac{1}{5}(\omega_{22})\right]$

The sets of type sets are

$$T_{\mathrm{I}} = \{I_1, I_2\} = \left\{\left[\tfrac{3}{7}(\omega_{11}), \tfrac{4}{7}(\omega_{12})\right], \left[\tfrac{2}{3}(\omega_{21}), \tfrac{1}{3}(\omega_{22})\right]\right\},$$

$$T_{\mathrm{II}} = \{II_1, II_2\} = \left\{\left[\tfrac{3}{5}(\omega_{11}), \tfrac{2}{5}(\omega_{21})\right], \left[\tfrac{4}{5}(\omega_{12})), \tfrac{1}{5}(\omega_{22})\right]\right\}.$$

The mutual beliefs of the players are described in Figure 10.4.

	II_1	II_2
I_1	3/7	4/7
I_2	2/3	1/3

	II_1	II_2
I_1	3/5	4/5
I_2	2/5	1/5

The beliefs of Player I   The beliefs of Player II

Figure 10.4 The beliefs of each player about the types of the other player

These beliefs correspond to a Harsanyi model with incomplete information, with the common prior p described in Figure 10.5.

	II_1	II_2
I_1	0.3	0.4
I_2	0.2	0.1

Figure 10.5 The common prior in Example 10.18

This prior distribution can be calculated from the mutual beliefs described in Figure 10.4 as follows. Denote $x = p(I_1, II_1)$. From the beliefs of type I_1, we get $p(I_1, II_2) = \frac{4}{3}x$; from the beliefs of type II_2, we get $p(I_2, II_2) = \frac{1}{3}x$; from the beliefs of type I_2, we get $p(I_2, II_1) = \frac{2}{3}x$. From the beliefs of type II_1, we get $p(I_1, II_1) = x$, which is what we started with. Since p is a probability distribution, $x + \frac{4}{3}x + \frac{1}{3}x + \frac{2}{3}x = 1$. Then $x = \frac{3}{10}$, and we have indeed shown that the common prior of the Harsanyi model is the probability distribution appearing in Figure 10.5.

The difference between this example and Example 10.17 is that in this case the common prior is not a product distribution over $T = T_{\mathrm{I}} \times T_{\mathrm{II}}$. Equivalently, the beliefs of one player about the types of the other player depend on his own type: Player I of type I_1 ascribes probability $\frac{3}{7}$ to Player II being of type II_1, while Player I of type I_2 ascribes probability $\frac{2}{3}$ to Player II being of type II_1.   ◀

Example 10.19 Inconsistent beliefs. This example studies a belief space in which the players hold inconsistent beliefs. This means that the beliefs cannot be derived from a common prior. Such a situation cannot be described by an Aumann model of incomplete information.

There are two players, $N = \{I, II\}$, and four states of nature, $S = \{s_{11}, s_{12}, s_{21}, s_{22}\}$. The corresponding belief space has four states of the world, $Y = \{\omega_{11}, \omega_{12}, \omega_{21}, \omega_{22}\}$:

State of the world	$\mathfrak{s}(\cdot)$	$\pi_{\mathrm{I}}(\cdot)$	$\pi_{\mathrm{II}}(\cdot)$
ω_{11}	s_{11}	$\left[\frac{3}{7}(\omega_{11}), \frac{4}{7}(\omega_{12})\right]$	$\left[\frac{1}{2}(\omega_{11}), \frac{1}{2}(\omega_{21})\right]$
ω_{12}	s_{12}	$\left[\frac{3}{7}(\omega_{11}), \frac{4}{7}(\omega_{12})\right]$	$\left[\frac{4}{5}(\omega_{12}), \frac{1}{5}(\omega_{22})\right]$
ω_{21}	s_{21}	$\left[\frac{2}{3}(\omega_{21}), \frac{1}{3}(\omega_{22})\right]$	$\left[\frac{1}{2}(\omega_{11}), \frac{1}{2}(\omega_{21})\right]$
ω_{22}	s_{22}	$\left[\frac{2}{3}(\omega_{21}), \frac{1}{3}(\omega_{22})\right]$	$\left[\frac{4}{5}(\omega_{12}), \frac{1}{5}(\omega_{22})\right]$

The type sets are

$$T_{\mathrm{I}} = \{I_1, I_2\} = \left\{\left[\frac{3}{7}(\omega_{11}), \frac{4}{7}(\omega_{12})\right], \left[\frac{2}{3}(\omega_{21}), \frac{1}{3}(\omega_{22})\right]\right\},$$

$$T_{\mathrm{II}} = \{II_1, II_2\} = \left\{\left[\frac{1}{2}(\omega_{11}), \frac{1}{2}(\omega_{21})\right], \left[\frac{4}{5}(\omega_{12}), \frac{1}{5}(\omega_{22})\right]\right\}.$$

The mutual beliefs of the players are described in Figure 10.6.

	II_1	II_2
I_1	3/7	4/7
I_2	2/3	1/3

	II_1	II_2
I_1	1/2	4/5
I_2	1/2	1/5

The beliefs of Player I   The beliefs of Player II

Figure 10.6 The beliefs of each player about the types of the other player

These mutual beliefs are the same beliefs as in Example 9.56 (page 376). As shown there, there does not exist a common prior in the Harsanyi model with these beliefs. Note that this example resembles Example 10.18, the only difference being the change of one of the types of Player II, namely, type II_1, from $[\frac{3}{5}(\omega_{11}), \frac{2}{5}(\omega_{21})]$ to $[\frac{1}{2}(\omega_{11}), \frac{1}{2}(\omega_{21})]$. These two situations, which are similar in their presentations as belief spaces, are in fact significantly different: one can be modeled by an Aumann or Harsanyi model of incomplete information, while the other cannot. ◀

In general, if there exists a probability distribution p such that at any state of the world ω in the support of p, the beliefs of the player are calculated as a conditional probability via

$$\pi_i(\omega) = p(\cdot \mid \{\omega' \in Y : \pi_i(\omega') = \pi_i(\omega)\}), \tag{10.23}$$

then p is called a *consistent distribution*, and every state of the world in the support of p is called a *consistent state of the world*. In that case, the collection of beliefs $(\pi_i)_{i \in N}$ is called a *consistent belief system* (see also Section 10.6 on page 424).

In the above example, all the states of the world in Y are inconsistent. Ensuring consistency requires the existence of certain relationships between the subjective probabilities of the players, and, therefore, the dimension of the set of consistent belief systems is lower than the dimension of the set of all mutual belief systems. For example, in the examples above containing two players and two types for each player, the mutual belief system of the types contains four probability distributions over $[0, 1]$; hence the set of mutual belief systems is isomorphic to $[0, 1]^4$. The consistency condition requires that any one of these four probability distributions be determined by the three others; hence the set of mutual belief systems is isomorphic to $[0, 1]^3$. In other words, within the set of all mutual belief systems, the relative dimension of the set of consistent belief systems is 0 (see Exercise 10.18).

Example 10.20 **Infinite type space** There are two players $N = \{I, II\}$ and the set of states of nature is $S = [0, 1]^2$. Player I is informed of the first coordinate of the chosen state of nature, while Player II is informed of the second coordinate. The beliefs of the players are as follows. If x is the value that Player I is informed of, he believes that the value Player II is informed of is taken from the uniform distribution over $[0.9x, 0.9x + 0.1]$. If y is the value that Player 2 is informed of, then if $y \leq \frac{1}{2}$, Player 2 believes that the value Player 1 is informed of is taken from the uniform distribution over $[0.7, 1]$, and if $y > \frac{1}{2}$, Player 2 believes that the value Player 1 is informed of is taken from the uniform distribution over $[0, 0.3]$.

A belief space that corresponds to this situation is:

- The set of states of the world is $Y = [0, 1]^2$. A state of the world is denoted by $\omega_{xy} = (x, y)$, where $0 \leq x, y \leq 1$. For every $(x, y) \in [0, 1]^2$, the equation $\mathfrak{s}(\omega_{xy}) = (x, y)$ holds.
- For every $x \in [0, 1]$, Player I's belief $\pi_I(\omega_{xy})$ is a uniform distribution over the set $\{(x, y) \in [0, 1]^2 : 0.9x \leq y \leq 0.9x + 0.1\}$, which is the interval $[(x, 0.9x), (x, 0.9x + 0.1)]$.
- If $y \leq \frac{1}{2}$ then Player II's belief $\pi_{II}(\omega_{xy})$ is the uniform distribution over the set $\{(x, y) \in [0, 1]^2 : 0.7 \leq x \leq 1\}$ (which is the interval $[(0.7, y), (1, y)]$), and if $y > \frac{1}{2}$ then the belief $\pi_{II}(\omega_{xy})$ is the uniform distribution over the set $\{(x, y) \in [0, 1]^2 : 0 \leq x \leq 0.3\}$ (which is the interval $[(0, y), (0.3, y)]$).

The type sets of the players are[4]

$$T_I = \{U[(x, 0.9x), (x, 0.9x + 0.1)] : 0 \leq x \leq 1\}, \tag{10.24}$$

$$T_{II} = \left\{U[(0.7, y), (1, y)] : 0 \leq y \leq \tfrac{1}{2}\right\} \bigcup \left\{U[(0, y), (0.3, y)] : \tfrac{1}{2} < y \leq 1\right\}. \tag{10.25}$$

The beliefs of the players in this example are inconsistent. At every state of the world, Player I believes that $|x - y| \leq 0.1$, while Player II believes that $|x - y| \geq 0.2$; there cannot be a common prior from which these two beliefs are both derived (Exercise 10.19). ◄

10.4 Belief subspaces

Definition 10.21 *Let* $\Pi = (Y, \mathcal{Y}, \mathfrak{s}, (\pi_i)_{i \in N})$ *be a belief space and let* $\tilde{Y} \in \mathcal{Y}$ *be a nonempty subset of the set of states of the world. The ordered vector* $\tilde{\Pi} = (\tilde{Y}, \mathcal{Y}_{|\tilde{Y}}, \mathfrak{s}, (\pi_i)_{i \in N})$ *is called*[5] *a belief subspace if*

$$\pi_i(\tilde{Y} \mid \omega) = 1, \quad \forall i \in N, \forall \omega \in \tilde{Y}. \tag{10.26}$$

In words, a belief subspace is a set of states of the world that is closed under the beliefs of the players. If the true state of the world ω is in the belief subspace $\tilde{Y}$, then the states of the world that are not in $\tilde{Y}$ are irrelevant to all the players, and this fact is common belief among them (Exercise 10.16). Later in this chapter, we will analyze games with incomplete information, where each player chooses his action as a function of his beliefs.

---

4 For $-\infty < a < b < \infty$, we denote the uniform distribution over $[a, b]$ by $U[a, b]$.
5 We denote the restriction of $\mathcal{Y}$ to $\tilde{Y}$ by $\mathcal{Y}_{|\tilde{Y}} = \{E \subseteq \tilde{Y} : E \in \mathcal{Y}\}$, and $\mathfrak{s}$ and $(\pi_i)_{i \in N}$ are the functions appearing in the definition of Π, restricted to $\tilde{Y}$.

In his strategic considerations, each player may ignore the states of the world that are not in the belief subspace that describes the situation he is in. For convenience, we will call both $\widetilde{Y}$ and $\widetilde{\Pi}$ belief subspaces of Π. If a belief space is derived from an Aumann model of incomplete information, then for every state of the world ω the common knowledge component $C(\omega)$ at the state of the world ω (see page 344) is a belief subspace (Exercise 10.17).

Example 10.22 Consider the following belief space, in which the set of players is $N = \{\mathrm{I}, \mathrm{II}\}$, the set of states of nature is $S = \{s_1, s_2, s_3\}$, and $Y = \{\omega_1, \omega_2, \omega_3\}$:

State of the world	$\mathfrak{s}(\cdot)$	$\pi_{\mathrm{I}}(\cdot)$	$\pi_{\mathrm{II}}(\cdot)$
ω_1	s_1	$\left[\frac{1}{2}(\omega_1), \frac{1}{2}(\omega_2)\right]$	$[1(\omega_1)]$
ω_2	s_2	$\left[\frac{1}{2}(\omega_1), \frac{1}{2}(\omega_2)\right]$	$[1(\omega_3)]$
ω_3	s_3	$[1(\omega_3)]$	$[1(\omega_3)]$

The subspace $\widetilde{Y} = \{\omega_3\}$ is a belief subspace, and it is the only strict subspace of Y that is a belief subspace (verify!). ◀

The next theorem states that the intersection of two belief subspaces of the same belief space is also a belief subspace. The proof of the theorem is left to the reader as an exercise (Exercise 10.29).

Theorem 10.23 *If* $\widetilde{\Pi}_1 = \left(\widetilde{Y}_1, \mathcal{Y}_{|\widetilde{Y}_1}, \mathfrak{s}, (\pi_i)_{i \in N}\right)$ *and* $\widetilde{\Pi}_2 = \left(\widetilde{Y}_2, \mathcal{Y}_{|\widetilde{Y}_2}, \mathfrak{s}, (\pi_i)_{i \in N}\right)$ *are two belief subspaces of the same belief space* $\Pi = (Y, \mathcal{Y}, \mathfrak{s}, (\pi_i)_{i \in N})$, *and if* $\widetilde{Y}_1 \cap \widetilde{Y}_2 \neq \emptyset$, *then* $\left(\widetilde{Y}_1 \cap \widetilde{Y}_2, \mathcal{Y}_{|\widetilde{Y}_1 \cap \widetilde{Y}_2}, \mathfrak{s}, (\pi_i)_{i \in N}\right)$ *is also a belief subspace.*

By definition, for every state of the world $\omega \in Y$, the space Y itself is a belief subspace containing ω; i.e., Y is a model of the situation: it can be used to describe the situation associated with ω. However, this may be a model that is "too large," in the sense that it contains states of the world that all the players deem to be irrelevant. The most "efficient" model is the smallest belief subspace (with respect to set inclusion) that contains ω.

Definition 10.24 *The minimal belief subspace* at a state of the world ω is the smallest belief subspace (with respect to set inclusion) that contains ω. We will denote the minimal subspace at ω (if such a space exists) by $\widetilde{\Pi}(\omega)$, and the set of states of the world of $\widetilde{\Pi}(\omega)$ we will denote by $\widetilde{Y}(\omega)$.

Theorem 10.23 implies that if there exists a minimal belief subspace, then it is unique (Exercise 10.30). Does every state of the world $\omega \in Y$ have a minimal belief subspace containing it? As the next theorem shows, the answer to this question is positive, when the set of states of the world is finite. The same holds true if the set of states of the world is countably infinite (Exercise 10.31).

Theorem 10.25 *Let* $\Pi = (Y, \mathcal{Y}, \mathfrak{s}, (\pi_i)_{i \in N})$ *be a belief space in which the set of states of the world* Y *is a finite set. For each state of the world* $\omega \in Y$, *there exists a unique minimal belief subspace containing* ω.

Proof: Π is a belief subspace; hence there exists at least one belief subspace containing ω. Since Y is a finite set, there is a finite number of belief subspaces containing ω. By repeated application of Theorem 10.23, the intersection of all the belief subspaces containing ω is a belief subspace containing ω, and it is the minimal belief subspace at ω.   □

As the next example shows, in more general spaces there may not exist a minimal belief space.

Example 10.26 Consider the one-player belief space in which $N = \{I\}$, the set of states of nature is $S = [0, 1]$, the set of states of the world is $Y = [0, 1]$, the σ-algebra $\mathcal{Y}$ is the σ-algebra of Borel sets, the function $\mathfrak{s}$ is given by $\mathfrak{s}(\omega) = \omega$ for each $\omega \in Y$, and the player's belief at each state of the world is the uniform distribution over $[0, 1]$. At each state of the world ω, every subset of states of the world $\tilde{Y} \subseteq Y$ whose Lebesgue measure is 1 is a belief subspace. Since there does not exist a minimal set containing ω whose Lebesgue measure is 1, it follows that there is no minimal belief subspace at any state of the world in this example.   ◄

Since player i does not know the true state of the world ω, and knows only his belief $\pi_i(\omega)$, he may not be able to calculate $\tilde{Y}(\omega)$. This point is elucidated in the next example.

Example 10.27 Figure 10.7 depicts a belief space with a set of players $N = \{I, II\}$, and a set of states of nature $S = \{s_1, s_2, s_3\}$. The set of states of the world is $Y = \{\omega_1, \omega_2, \omega_3\}$.

State of the world	$\mathfrak{s}(\cdot)$	$\pi_{\mathrm{I}}(\cdot)$	$\pi_{\mathrm{II}}(\cdot)$	$\tilde{Y}(\omega)$
ω_1	s_1	$[1(\omega_1)]$	$[1(\omega_1)]$	$\{\omega_1\}$
ω_2	s_2	$[1(\omega_1)]$	$[1(\omega_3)]$	Y
ω_3	s_3	$[1(\omega_3)]$	$[1(\omega_3)]$	$\{\omega_3\}$

Figure 10.7 The belief space in Example 10.27

At the state of the world ω_2, the players do not agree on the states of the world that are relevant to the situation: at this state of the world, Player I believes it is common belief that the state of nature is s_1, while Player II believes it is common belief that the state of nature is s_3. In fact, both of them are wrong, because the true state of nature is s_2.

The sets $\tilde{Y}_1 = \{\omega_1\}$ and $\tilde{Y}_3 = \{\omega_3\}$ are belief subspaces. At the state of the world ω_2, Player I believes that the state of the world is ω_1, and he therefore ascribes probability 1 to the minimal belief subspace being $\tilde{Y}_1$. Player II, in contrast, ascribes probability 1 at the state of the world ω_2 to the minimal belief subspace being $\tilde{Y}_3$. If the situation is a game situation, then at the state of the world ω_2 Player I will ignore in his strategic considerations the states of the world ω_2 and ω_3 and Player II will ignore the states of the world ω_1 and ω_2.   ◄

The last example leads to the following definition.

Definition 10.28 *Let* $\Pi = (Y, \mathcal{Y}, \mathfrak{s}, (\pi_i)_{i \in N})$ *be a belief space, and let* $\omega \in Y$ *be a state of the world. A belief subspace of player* i *at a state of the world* ω *is a belief subspace* $\tilde{\Pi} = (\tilde{Y}, \mathcal{Y}, \mathfrak{s}, (\pi_i)_{i \in N})$ *satisfying*

$$\pi_i(\tilde{Y} \mid \omega) = 1. \tag{10.27}$$

The condition in Equation (10.27) guarantees that at the state of the world ω, player i ascribes probability 1 to the true state of the world being in $\tilde{Y}$. Note that Y itself is a belief subspace for each player at each state of the world.

The next theorem states that the intersection of two belief subspaces of player i at the state of the world ω is a belief subspace of player i at ω.

Theorem 10.29 *If* $\tilde{\Pi}_1 = (\tilde{Y}_1, \mathcal{Y}_{|\tilde{Y}_1}, \mathfrak{s}, (\pi_i)_{i \in N})$ *and* $\tilde{\Pi}_2 = (\tilde{Y}_2, \mathcal{Y}_{|\tilde{Y}_2}, \mathfrak{s}, (\pi_i)_{i \in N})$ *are two belief subspaces of player i at a state of the world ω, then* $(\tilde{Y}_1 \cap \tilde{Y}_2, \mathcal{Y}_{|\tilde{Y}_1 \cap \tilde{Y}_2}, \mathfrak{s}, (\pi_i)_{i \in N})$ *is a belief subspace of player i at ω.*

Proof: We first establish that $\tilde{Y}_1 \cap \tilde{Y}_2 \neq \emptyset$. Since $\tilde{\Pi}_1$ is a belief subspace of player i at ω, it follows that $\pi_i(\tilde{Y}_1 \mid \omega) = 1$. We similarly deduce that $\pi_i(\tilde{Y}_2 \mid \omega) = 1$. Therefore,

$$\pi_i(\tilde{Y}_1 \cap \tilde{Y}_2 \mid \omega) = 1, \tag{10.28}$$

and, in particular, the set $\tilde{Y}_1 \cap \tilde{Y}_2$ is not empty. If follows from Theorem 10.23 that $(\tilde{Y}_1 \cap \tilde{Y}_2, \mathcal{Y}_{|\tilde{Y}_1 \cap \tilde{Y}_2}, \mathfrak{s}, (\pi_i)_{i \in N})$ is a belief subspace; hence this is a belief subspace of player i at the state of the world ω. $\square$

The smallest belief subspace of a player i (with respect to set inclusion) is called the *minimal belief subspace* of player i.

Definition 10.30 *Let* $\Pi = (Y, \mathcal{Y}, \mathfrak{s}, (\pi_i)_{i \in N})$ *be a belief space, and let* $\omega \in Y$ *be a state of the world. The* minimal belief subspace *of player i at ω is the smallest belief subspace of player i (with respect to set inclusion) at the state of the world ω.*

The minimal belief subspace of player i at a state of the world ω (if such a subspace exists) will be denoted by $\tilde{\Pi}_i(\omega)$, and the set of states of the world in $\tilde{\Pi}_i(\omega)$ will be denoted by $\tilde{Y}_i(\omega)$.

The next two examples show that the minimal belief subspaces of two players at a given state of the world may be different, and even disjoint.

Example 10.22 (*Continued*) The table in Figure 10.8 presents the belief space of Example 10.22, along with the minimal belief subspaces of the players. At the state of the world ω_2, the minimal belief subspace of Player I is $\tilde{Y}_I(\omega_2) = \{\omega_1, \omega_2, \omega_3\}$. It properly contains the minimal belief subspace of Player II, which is $\tilde{Y}_{II}(\omega_2) = \{\omega_3\}$.

State of the world	$\mathfrak{s}(\cdot)$	$\pi_I(\cdot)$	$\pi_{II}(\cdot)$	$\tilde{Y}_I(\omega)$	$\tilde{Y}_{II}(\omega)$
ω_1	s_1	$[\frac{1}{2}(\omega_1), \frac{1}{2}(\omega_2)]$	$[1(\omega_1)]$	Y	Y
ω_2	s_2	$[\frac{1}{2}(\omega_1), \frac{1}{2}(\omega_2)]$	$[1(\omega_3)]$	Y	$\{\omega_3\}$
ω_3	s_3	$[1(\omega_3)]$	$[1(\omega_3)]$	$\{\omega_3\}$	$\{\omega_3\}$

Figure 10.8 The belief space in Example 10.22, and the minimal belief subspaces of the players

◀

Example 10.27 (*Continued*) The table in Figure 10.9 presents the belief space of Example 10.27, along with the minimal belief subspaces of the players.

State of the world	$\mathfrak{s}(\cdot)$	$\pi_{\mathrm{I}}(\cdot)$	$\pi_{\mathrm{II}}(\cdot)$	$\tilde{Y}_{\mathrm{I}}(\omega)$	$\tilde{Y}_{\mathrm{II}}(\omega)$
ω_1	s_1	$[1(\omega_1)]$	$[1(\omega_1)]$	$\{\omega_1\}$	$\{\omega_1\}$
ω_2	s_2	$[1(\omega_1)]$	$[1(\omega_3)]$	$\{\omega_1\}$	$\{\omega_3\}$
ω_3	s_3	$[1(\omega_3)]$	$[1(\omega_3)]$	$\{\omega_3\}$	$\{\omega_3\}$

Figure 10.9 The belief space in Example 10.27, and the minimal belief subspaces of the players

As consideration of the table shows, the belief subspaces of the players at the state of the world ω_2 are disjoint. Note in addition that the state of the world ω_2 is not contained in the minimal belief subspaces of the two players at the state of the world ω_2, $\omega_2 \notin \tilde{Y}_{\mathrm{I}}(\omega_2)$ and $\omega_2 \notin \tilde{Y}_{\mathrm{II}}(\omega_2)$. ◄

The significance of $\tilde{Y}_i(\omega)$ is that, when player i is considering the situation that he faces at the state of the world ω, $\tilde{Y}_i(\omega)$ is the belief subspace that he deems relevant: player i believes that it is common belief among all the players that the state of the world is contained in $\tilde{Y}_i(\omega)$. Note the difference between the definitions of the minimal belief subspace $\tilde{Y}(\omega)$ and the minimal belief subspace of player i, $\tilde{Y}_i(\omega)$: while $\tilde{Y}_i(\omega)$ does not necessarily contain ω, as shown in Example 10.27, $\tilde{Y}(\omega)$ by definition must contain ω, because for an "objective" analysis of the game, the true state is of relevance for the situation; in particular, it affects the payoffs of the players.

The statement of the following theorem shows that there is a tight relationship between the minimal belief subspaces of different players.

Theorem 10.31 *Let $\Pi = (Y, \mathcal{Y}, \mathfrak{s}, (\pi_i)_{i \in N})$ be a belief space in which Y is a finite set. If $\omega' \in \tilde{Y}_i(\omega)$ then $\tilde{Y}_j(\omega') \subseteq \tilde{Y}_i(\omega)$ for every $j \in N$.*

In words, if at the state of the world ω, the belief subspace of player i contains another state of the world ω', then it also contains all the minimal belief subspaces of the other players at ω'.

Proof: We will show that for any player $j \in N$, every state of the world $\omega'' \in \tilde{Y}_j(\omega')$ is also contained in $\tilde{Y}_i(\omega)$. From the definition of the minimal belief subspace of player j, if $\omega'' \in \tilde{Y}_j(\omega')$, then every belief subspace $\tilde{Y}$ containing ω' and satisfying $\pi_j(\tilde{Y} \mid \omega') = 1$ contains ω''. Since $\tilde{Y}_i(\omega)$ is such a space, it too contains ω''. □

The next theorem states that if the set of states of the world is finite, and at the state of the world ω all the players ascribed positive probability to ω, then the minimal belief subspaces of all the players at ω are the same.

Theorem 10.32 *Let $\Pi = (Y, \mathcal{Y}, \mathfrak{s}, (\pi_i)_{i \in N})$ be a belief space in which Y is a finite set, and let $\omega \in Y$. If $\pi_i(\{\omega\} \mid \omega) > 0$ for each player $i \in N$, then $\tilde{Y}_i(\omega) = \tilde{Y}_j(\omega)$ for every pair of players i and j (hence $\tilde{Y}_i(\omega) = \tilde{Y}(\omega)$ for every $i \in N$).*

Proof: Let $i \in N$ be a player. Since $\pi_i(\{\omega\} \mid \omega) > 0$, it follows from Equation (10.27) in Definition 10.28 that $\omega \in \tilde{Y}_i(\omega)$. Then Theorem 10.31 implies that $\tilde{Y}_j(\omega) \subseteq \tilde{Y}_i(\omega)$ for every $j \in N$. Since this is true for any pair of players $i, j \in N$, the proof of the theorem is complete. ☐

The next theorem states that the minimal belief subspace at a state of the world ω is simply the union of the true state of the world ω and the minimal belief subspaces of the players at that state. The proof of the theorem is left to the reader (Exercise 10.32).

Theorem 10.33 *Let* $\Pi = (Y, \mathcal{Y}, \mathfrak{s}, (\pi_i)_{i \in N})$ *be a belief space in which Y is a finite set. Then for every state of the world $\omega \in Y$,*

$$\widetilde{Y}(\omega) = \{\omega\} \cup \left(\bigcup_{i \in N} \widetilde{Y}_i(\omega) \right). \tag{10.29}$$

Remark 10.34 *As shown in Example 10.26, when the set of states of the world has the cardinality of the continuum, the minimal belief subspace may not necessarily exist. If the set of states of the world is a topological space,[6] define the minimal belief subspace of a player as follows.*

A belief subspace is an ordered vector $\widetilde{\Pi} = (\widetilde{Y}, \mathcal{Y}_{|\widetilde{Y}}, \mathfrak{s}, (\pi_i)_{i \in N})$ *satisfying Equation (10.26), and also satisfying the property that $\widetilde{Y}$ is a closed set. Player i's minimal belief subspace at the state of the world ω is the belief subspace* $\widetilde{\Pi} = (\widetilde{Y}, \mathcal{Y}|\widetilde{Y}, \mathfrak{s}, (\pi_i)_{i \in N})$ *in which the set $\widetilde{Y}$ is the smallest closed subset (with respect to set inclusion) among all the belief subspaces satisfying Equation (10.27).* ◆

When the set of states of the world Y is finite, there exists a characterization of belief subspaces. Define a directed graph $G = (Y, E)$ in which the set of vertices is the set of states of the world Y, and there is a directed edge from ω_1 to ω_2 if and only if there exists a player $i \in N$ for whom $\pi_i(\{\omega_2\} \mid \omega_1) > 0$. A set of vertices C in a directed graph is called a *closed component* if for each vertex $\omega \in C$, every vertex connected to ω by a directed edge is also in C; i.e., if there exists an edge from ω to ω', then $\omega' \in C$.

The next theorem states that the set of belief subspaces is exactly the set of closed sets in the graph G. The proof of the theorem is left to the reader (Exercise 10.33).

Theorem 10.35 *Let* $\Pi = (Y, \mathcal{Y}, \mathfrak{s}, (\pi_i)_{i \in N})$ *be a belief space in which Y is a finite set of states of the world. A subset $\widetilde{Y}$ of Y is a belief subspace if and only if $\widetilde{Y}$ is a closed component in the graph G.*

Denote the minimal closed set containing ω by $C(\omega)$. This set contains the vertex ω, all the vertices that are connected to ω by way of directed edges emanating from ω, all vertices that are connected to those vertices by directed edges, and so on. Since the graph G is finite, this is a finite process, and therefore the set $C(\omega)$ is well defined. Together with the construction of the set $C(\omega)$, Theorem 10.35 provides a practical method for calculating belief subspaces and minimal belief subspaces of the players.

---

6 A space Y is called a *topological space* if there exists a family of subsets $\mathcal{T}$ that are called *open sets*: the empty set is contained in $\mathcal{T}$, the set Y is contained in $\mathcal{T}$, the union of any set of elements of $\mathcal{T}$ is in $\mathcal{T}$, and the intersection of a finite number of elements in $\mathcal{T}$ is also a set in $\mathcal{T}$. A set A in a topological space is called *closed* if it is the complement of an open set.

The next theorem provides a practical method of computing minimal belief subspaces at a particular state of the world. The proof of the theorem is left to the reader (Exercise 10.34).

Theorem 10.36 *Let* $\Pi = (Y, \mathcal{Y}, \mathfrak{s}, (\pi_i)_{i \in N})$ *be a belief space in which Y is a finite set, let* $\omega \in Y$, *and let* $i \in N$. *Then*

$$\widetilde{Y}_i(\omega) = \bigcup_{\{\omega' : \, \pi_i(\{\omega'\}|\omega) > 0\}} C(\omega'). \tag{10.30}$$

Recognizing his own beliefs, player i can compute his own minimal belief subspace. To see this, note that since he knows $\pi_i(\omega)$, he knows which states of the world are in the support of this probability distribution. Knowing the states of the world in the support, player i knows the beliefs of the other players at these states of the world; hence he knows which states of the world are in the supports of those beliefs. Player i can thus recursively construct the portion of the graph G relevant for computing $\widetilde{Y}_i(\omega)$. The construction is completed in a finite number of steps because Y is a finite set.

While player i can compute his minimal belief subspace $\widetilde{Y}_i(\omega)$ using his own beliefs, in order to compute the belief subspaces of the other players, $(\widetilde{Y}_j(\omega))_{j \neq i}$, he needs to know their beliefs. Since player i does not know the true state of the world ω, he does not know the beliefs of the other players at that state, which means that he cannot compute the minimal belief subspaces of the other players. In Example 10.22 (page 413), at the states of the world ω_2 and ω_3, the belief of Player II is $[1(\omega_3)]$; hence Player II cannot distinguish between the two states of the world based on his beliefs. The minimal belief subspaces of Player I at the two states of the world are different:

$$\widetilde{Y}_{\mathrm{I}}(\omega_2) = Y, \qquad \widetilde{Y}_{\mathrm{I}}(\omega_3) = \{\omega_3\}. \tag{10.31}$$

It follows that, based on his beliefs, Player II cannot know whether the minimal belief subspace of Player I is Y or $\{\omega_3\}$.

10.5 Games with incomplete information

So far, we have discussed the structure of the mutual beliefs of players, and largely ignored the other components of a game, namely, the actions and the payoffs. In this section, we will define games with incomplete information without a common prior, and the concept of Bayesian equilibrium in such games.

Definition 10.37 *A* game with incomplete information *is an ordered vector* $G = (N, S, (A_i)_{i \in N}, \Pi)$, *where:*

- *N is a finite set of players.*
- *S is a measurable space of states of nature. To avoid a surfeit of symbols, we will not mention the σ-algebra over S, or over other measurable sets that are defined below.*
- *A_i is a measurable set of possible actions of player i, for every $i \in N$.*
- *Each state of nature in S is a state game $s = (N, (A_i(s))_{i \in N}, (u_i(s))_{i \in N})$, where $A_i(s) \subseteq A_i$ is a nonempty measurable set of possible actions of player i, for each $i \in N$. We denote by $A(s) = \times_{i \in N} A_i(s)$ the set of vectors of possible actions in s. For each player*

$i \in N$ the function $u_i(s) : A(s) \to \mathbb{R}$ is a measurable function assigning a payoff to player i in the state game s for each vector of possible actions.

- $\Pi = (Y, \mathcal{Y}, \mathfrak{s}, (\pi_i)_{i \in N})$ is a belief space of the players N over the set of states of nature S, satisfying the following condition: for every pair of states of the world $\omega, \omega' \in Y$, if $\pi_i(\omega) = \pi_i(\omega')$, then $A_i(\mathfrak{s}(\omega)) = A_i(\mathfrak{s}(\omega'))$.

The last condition in Definition 10.37 implies that at each state of the world $\omega \in Y$, player i's set of possible actions $A_i(\mathfrak{s}(\omega))$ depends on ω, but only through his type $\pi_i(\omega)$. Since the player knows his own type, he knows the set of possible actions $A_i(\mathfrak{s}(\omega))$ available to him. Formally, consider the partition $\mathcal{F}_i$ of Y determined by player i's beliefs (see Equation (10.9) on page 400) given by the sets

$$F_i(\omega) = \{\omega' \in Y : \pi_i(\omega') = \pi_i(\omega)\}, \tag{10.32}$$

and the knowledge operator defined by this partition. Define the event $C_i(\omega) =$ "player i's set of actions is $A_i(\mathfrak{s}(\omega))$":

$$C_i(\omega) := \{\omega' \in Y : A_i(\mathfrak{s}(\omega')) = A_i(\mathfrak{s}(\omega))\}. \tag{10.33}$$

Then the last condition in Definition 10.37 guarantees that at each state of the world ω, player i knows $C_i(\omega)$, i.e., $F_i(\omega) \subseteq C_i(\omega)$ for each $\omega \in Y$. A game with incomplete information, therefore, is composed of a belief space Π, and a collection of state games, one for each state of nature in S. The information that each player i has at the state of the world ω is his type, $\pi_i(\omega)$. As required in the Harsanyi model of incomplete information, the set of actions available to a player must depend solely on his type. Every Harsanyi game with incomplete information (see Definition 9.39 on page 358) is a game with incomplete information according to Definition 10.37 (Exercise 10.48).

Player i's type set was denoted by

$$T_i := \{\pi_i(\omega) : \omega \in Y\}. \tag{10.34}$$

To define the expected payoff, we assume that the graph of the function $s \mapsto A(s)$, defined by $\mathrm{Graph}(A) := \{(s, a) : s \in S, a \in A(s)\} \subseteq S \times A$, is a measurable set. We similarly assume that for each player $i \in N$, the function $u_i : \mathrm{Graph}(A) \to \mathbb{R}$ is a measurable function.

Definition 10.38 *A behavior strategy of player i in a game with incomplete information $G = (N, S, (A_i)_{i \in N}, \Pi)$ is a measurable function $\sigma_i : Y \to \Delta(A_i)$, mapping every state of the world to a mixed action available at the stage game that corresponds to that state of the world,[7] and dependent solely on the type of the player. In other words, for each $\omega, \omega' \in Y$,*

---

7 Since a behavior strategy is a measurable function whose range is the space of mixed actions, we need to specify the σ-algebra over the space $\Delta(A_i)$ that we are using. The σ-algebra over this space is the σ-algebra induced by the weak topology (see Dunford and Schwartz [1999]). An alternative definition of a measurable function taking values in this space is: for each measurable set $C \subseteq A_i$, the function $\omega \mapsto \sigma_i(C \mid \omega)$ is a measurable function.

In an infinite space, the existence of a behavior strategy requires that the function $\omega \mapsto A_i(\mathfrak{s}(\omega))$ be measurable. Results appearing in Kuratowski and Ryll–Nardzewski [1965] imply that a sufficient condition for the existence of a behavior strategy is that (a) A_i is a complete metric space for every $i \in N$, (b) the function $\omega \mapsto A_i(\mathfrak{s}(\omega))$ is a measurable function, and (c) for each state of nature s, the set $A_i(s)$ is a closed set.

$$\sigma_i(\omega) \in \Delta(A_i(\mathfrak{s}(\omega))), \tag{10.35}$$

$$\pi_i(\omega) = \pi_i(\omega') \implies \sigma_i(\omega) = \sigma_i(\omega'). \tag{10.36}$$

Since the mixed action $\sigma_i(\omega)$ of player i depends solely on his type $t_i = \pi_i(\omega)$, it can also be denoted by $\sigma_i(t_i)$. Because the type sets of the players may be infinite, strategies must be measurable functions in order for us to calculate the expected payoff of a player given his type. Let $\sigma = (\sigma_i)_{i \in N}$ be a strategy vector. Denote by

$$\sigma(\omega) := (\sigma_i(\omega))_{i \in N} \in \underset{i \in N}{\times} \Delta(A_i(\mathfrak{s}(\omega))) \tag{10.37}$$

the vector of mixed actions of the players when the state of the world is ω. Player i's *payoff* under σ at the state of the world ω is[8]

$$\gamma_i(\sigma \mid \omega) = \int_Y U_i(\mathfrak{s}(\omega'); \sigma(\omega')) \mathrm{d}\pi_i(\omega' \mid \omega). \tag{10.38}$$

Since $\pi_i(\omega)$ is player i's belief at the state of the world ω about the states of the world $\omega' \in Y$, the integral of the payoff function with respect to this probability distribution describes the expected payoff of the player at the state of the world ω, based on his subjective beliefs, and given the other players' strategies.

To emphasize that the expected payoff of player i at the state of world ω depends on the mixed action implemented by player i at ω, and is independent of mixed actions that he implements at other states of the world, we sometimes write $\gamma_i(\sigma_i(\omega), \sigma_{-i} \mid \omega)$ instead of $\gamma_i(\sigma_i, \sigma_{-i} \mid \omega)$.

We will now define the concept of Bayesian equilibrium in games with incomplete information.

Definition 10.39 *A* Bayesian equilibrium *is a strategy vector* $\sigma^* = (\sigma_i^*)_{i \in N}$ *satisfying*

$$\gamma_i(\sigma^* \mid \omega) \geq \gamma_i(\sigma_i(\omega), \sigma_{-i}^* \mid \omega), \quad \forall i \in N, \forall \sigma_i(\omega) \in \Delta(A_i(\mathfrak{s}(\omega))), \forall \omega \in Y. \tag{10.39}$$

In other words, a Bayesian equilibrium is a strategy vector that satisfies the condition that based on his subjective beliefs, at no state of the world can a player profit by deviating from his strategy.

As the next theorem states, a strategy vector is a Bayesian equilibrium if no player of any type can profit by deviating to any other action. The theorem is a generalization of Corollary 5.8 (page 148). In our formulation of the theorem, we will use the following notation. Let $\sigma = (\sigma_j)_{j \in N}$ be a strategy vector. For each player $i \in N$, each state of the world $\omega \in Y$, and for each action $a_{i,\omega} \in A_i(\mathfrak{s}(\omega))$, denote by $(\sigma; a_{i,\omega})$ the strategy vector at which every player $j \neq i$ implements strategy σ_j, and player i plays action $a_{i,\omega}$ when his type is $\pi_i(\omega)$.

Theorem 10.40 *A strategy vector* $\sigma^* = (\sigma_i^*)_{i \in N}$ *is a Bayesian equilibrium if and only if for each player $i \in N$, for each state of the world $\omega \in Y$, and each action $a_{i,\omega} \in A_i(\mathfrak{s}(\omega))$,*

---

8 Recall that U_i is the multilinear extension of u_i; see Equation (5.9) on page 146.

$$\gamma_i(\sigma^* \mid \omega) \geq \gamma_i((\sigma^*; a_{i,\omega}) \mid \omega). \tag{10.40}$$

The proof of the theorem is left to the reader (Exercise 10.49).

Example 10.41 We consider a game that extends Example 10.19 (page 408), where beliefs are inconsistent. There are two players $N = \{I, II\}$, four states of nature $S = \{s_{11}, s_{12}, s_{21}, s_{22}\}$, and four states of the world $Y = \{\omega_{11}, \omega_{12}, \omega_{21}, \omega_{22}\}$. The beliefs of the players and the function s are given in Figure 10.10.

State of the world	$s(\cdot)$	$\pi_I(\cdot)$	$\pi_{II}(\cdot)$
ω_{11}	s_{11}	$[\frac{3}{7}(\omega_{11}), \frac{4}{7}(\omega_{12})]$	$[\frac{1}{2}(\omega_{11}), \frac{1}{2}(\omega_{21})]$
ω_{12}	s_{12}	$[\frac{3}{7}(\omega_{11}), \frac{4}{7}(\omega_{12})]$	$[\frac{4}{5}(\omega_{12}), \frac{1}{5}(\omega_{22})]$
ω_{21}	s_{21}	$[\frac{2}{3}(\omega_{21}), \frac{1}{3}(\omega_{22})]$	$[\frac{1}{2}(\omega_{11}), \frac{1}{2}(\omega_{21})]$
ω_{22}	s_{22}	$[\frac{2}{3}(\omega_{21}), \frac{1}{3}(\omega_{22})]$	$[\frac{4}{5}(\omega_{12}), \frac{1}{5}(\omega_{22})]$

Figure 10.10 The beliefs of the players and the function s in Example 10.41

The players' type sets are

$$T_I = \{I_1, I_2\} = \left\{ \left[\frac{3}{7}(\omega_{11}), \frac{4}{7}(\omega_{12}) \right], \left[\frac{2}{3}(\omega_{21}), \frac{1}{3}(\omega_{22}) \right] \right\}, \tag{10.41}$$

$$T_{II} = \{II_1, II_2\} = \left\{ \left[\frac{1}{2}(\omega_{11}), \frac{1}{2}(\omega_{21}) \right], \left[\frac{4}{5}(\omega_{12}), \frac{1}{5}(\omega_{22}) \right] \right\}. \tag{10.42}$$

The state games s_{11}, s_{12}, s_{21}, and s_{22} are given in Figure 10.11. A behavior strategy of Player I is a pair (x, y), defined as:

- Play the mixed action $[x(T), (1 - x)(B)]$ if your type is I_1.
- Play the mixed action $[y(T), (1 - y)(B)]$ if your type is I_2.

Similarly, a behavior strategy of Player II is a pair (z, t), defined as:

- Play the mixed action $[z(L), (1 - z)(R)]$ if your type is II_1.
- Play the mixed action $[t(L), (1 - t)(R)]$ if your type is II_2.

We will now find a Bayesian equilibrium satisfying $0 < x, y, z, t < 1$ (assuming one exists). In such an equilibrium, every player of each type must be indifferent between his two actions, given his beliefs about the type of the other player.

If the players are indifferent between their actions, then:

Player I of type I_1 is indifferent between B and T : $\frac{3}{7} \cdot 2z = \frac{3}{7}(1 - z) + \frac{4}{7}$;

Player I of type I_2 is indifferent between B and T : $\frac{1}{3} \cdot 2(1 - t) = \frac{2}{3}z$;

Player II of type II_1 is indifferent between R and L : $\frac{1}{2}(1 - y) = \frac{1}{2}x$;

Player II of type II_2 is indifferent between R and L : $\frac{4}{5}(1 - x) = \frac{1}{5}(y + 2(1 - y))$.

The solution to this system of equations is (verify!)

$$x = \tfrac{3}{5}, \quad y = \tfrac{2}{5}, \quad z = \tfrac{7}{9}, \quad t = \tfrac{2}{9}. \tag{10.43}$$

The mixed actions $[\frac{3}{5}(T), \frac{2}{5}(B)]$ for Player I of type I_1, and $[\frac{2}{5}(T), \frac{3}{5}(B)]$ for Player I of type I_2, and $[\frac{7}{9}(L), \frac{2}{9}(R)]$ for Player II of type II_1, and $[\frac{2}{9}(L), \frac{7}{9}(R)]$ for Player II of type II_2 therefore

	L	R
T	2, 0	0, 1
B	0, 0	1, 0

State game s_{11}

	L	R
T	0, 0	0, 0
B	1, 1	1, 0

State game s_{12}

	L	R
T	0, 0	0, 0
B	1, 1	0, 0

State game s_{21}

	L	R
T	0, 0	2, 1
B	0, 0	0, 2

State game s_{22}

Figure 10.11 The payoff functions in Example 10.41

form a Bayesian equilibrium of this game. This game has no "expected payoff," because there is no common prior distribution over Y. Nevertheless, one can speak about an "objective" expected payoff at each state of nature (calculated from the actions of the players at that state of nature). Denote by $\gamma_i(s)$ the payoff of player i at the state game s. Denote the payoff matrix of player i at the state game s_{kl} by $G_{i,kl}$. The payoff $\gamma_i(s_{kl})$, for example, can be represented in vector form:

$$\gamma_i(s_{11}) = (x, 1-x)G_{i,11} \begin{pmatrix} z \\ 1-z \end{pmatrix}. \tag{10.44}$$

A simple calculation gives the payoff of each player at each state of nature:

$$\gamma_I(\omega_{11}) = \left(\frac{3}{5}, \frac{2}{5}\right) G_{I,11} \begin{pmatrix} 7/9 \\ 2/9 \end{pmatrix} = \frac{46}{45}, \qquad \gamma_{II}(\omega_{11}) = \left(\frac{3}{5}, \frac{2}{5}\right) G_{I,11} \begin{pmatrix} 7/9 \\ 2/9 \end{pmatrix} = \frac{6}{45},$$

$$\gamma_I(\omega_{12}) = \left(\frac{3}{5}, \frac{2}{5}\right) G_{I,12} \begin{pmatrix} 2/9 \\ 7/9 \end{pmatrix} = \frac{18}{45}, \qquad \gamma_{II}(\omega_{12}) = \left(\frac{3}{5}, \frac{2}{5}\right) G_{I,12} \begin{pmatrix} 2/9 \\ 7/9 \end{pmatrix} = \frac{4}{45},$$

$$\gamma_I(\omega_{21}) = \left(\frac{2}{5}, \frac{3}{5}\right) G_{II,21} \begin{pmatrix} 7/9 \\ 2/9 \end{pmatrix} = \frac{21}{45}, \qquad \gamma_{II}(\omega_{21}) = \left(\frac{2}{5}, \frac{3}{5}\right) G_{II,21} \begin{pmatrix} 7/9 \\ 2/9 \end{pmatrix} = \frac{21}{45},$$

$$\gamma_I(\omega_{22}) = \left(\frac{2}{5}, \frac{3}{5}\right) G_{II,22} \begin{pmatrix} 2/9 \\ 7/9 \end{pmatrix} = \frac{28}{45}, \qquad \gamma_{II}(\omega_{22}) = \left(\frac{2}{5}, \frac{3}{5}\right) G_{II,22} \begin{pmatrix} 2/9 \\ 7/9 \end{pmatrix} = \frac{70}{45}.$$

Because the players do not know the true state game, the relevant expected payoff for a player is the subjective payoff he receives given his beliefs. For example, at the state of the world ω_{11} (or ω_{12}) Player I believes that the state of the world is ω_{11} with probability $\frac{3}{7}$, and ω_{12} with probability $\frac{4}{7}$. Player I therefore believes that the state game is G_{11} with probability $\frac{3}{7}$, and G_{12} with probability $\frac{4}{7}$. His subjective expected payoff is therefore $\frac{3}{7} \times \frac{46}{45} + \frac{4}{7} \times \frac{18}{45} = \frac{2}{3}$, and it is this payoff that he "expects" to receive at the state of the world ω_{11} (or ω_{12}). Similarly, at the state of the world ω_{21} (or ω_{22}), Player I "expects" to receive $\frac{2}{3} \times \frac{21}{45} + \frac{1}{3} \times \frac{28}{45} = \frac{14}{27}$. At ω_{11} (or ω_{21}) Player II "expects" to receive $\frac{1}{2} \times \frac{6}{45} + \frac{1}{2} \times \frac{21}{45} = \frac{3}{10}$. At ω_{12} (or ω_{22}) Player II "expects" to receive $\frac{4}{5} \times \frac{4}{45} + \frac{1}{5} \times \frac{70}{45} = \frac{86}{225}$.

◀

There are no general results concerning the existence of Bayesian equilibria in inconsistent models, but we do have the following result.

Theorem 10.42 *Let* $G = (N, S, (A_i)_{i \in N}, \Pi)$ *be a game with incomplete information, where Y is a finite set of states of the world, and each player i has a finite set of actions* A_i. *Then G has a Bayesian equilibrium in behavior strategies.*

Proof: To prove the theorem, we will define the agent-form game corresponding to G (see Definition 9.50, on page 364), and show that every Nash equilibrium of the agent-form game is a Bayesian equilibrium of G. Since Nash's Theorem (Theorem 5.10 on page 150) implies that there exists an equilibrium in the agent-form game, we will deduce that the given game G has a Bayesian equilibrium.

Recall that the type set of player i is denoted $T_i = \{\pi_i(\omega) : \omega \in Y\}$. The agent-form game corresponding to G is a strategic-form game $\Gamma = (\widehat{N}, (\widehat{S}_k)_{k \in \widehat{N}}, (\widehat{u}_k)_{k \in \widehat{N}})$, where:

- The set of players is $\widehat{N} = \{(i, t_i) : i \in N, t_i \in T_i\}$. In other words, each type of each player is a player in the agent-form game.
- The set of pure strategies of player $(i, t_i) \in \widehat{N}$ is $\widehat{S}_{(i,t_i)} := A_i(\mathfrak{s}(\omega))$, where ω is any state of the world satisfying $t_i = \pi_i(\omega)$.

A pure strategy $\sigma_{(i,t_i)}$ of player (i, t_i) in the agent-form game is a possible action of player i's type t_i in G. It follows that a pure strategy vector $\sigma = (\sigma_{(i,t_i)})_{(i,t_i) \in \widehat{N}}$ is a prescription for what each type of each player should play; hence it is, in fact, also a pure strategy vector in G, in which for each $i \in N$, the vector $(\sigma_{(i,t_i)})_{t_i \in T_i}$ is a pure strategy of player i. This means that the set of pure strategy vectors in G is equal to the set of strategy vectors in Γ, and the set of behavior strategy vectors in the game G equals the set of mixed strategy vectors in the game Γ.

- The payoff function of player (i, t_i) is

$$\widehat{u}_{(i,t_i)}(\widehat{\sigma}) = \gamma_i(\widehat{\sigma} \mid \omega), \tag{10.45}$$

where ω is any state of the world satisfying $t_i = \pi_i(\omega)$. Since $\gamma_i(\widehat{\sigma} \mid \omega)$ depends on ω only via $\pi_i(\omega)$, this expression depends only on t_i, and therefore $u_{(i,t_i)}(\widehat{\sigma})$ is well defined.

Because the set of states of the world Y is finite, we deduce that the set of players $\widehat{N}$ in Γ is also finite. Since every player i's set of actions A_i is finite, the agent-form game Γ satisfies the conditions of Nash's Theorem (see Theorem 5.10 on page 150); hence it has an equilibrium $\sigma^* = (\sigma^*_{(i,t_i)})_{(i,t_i) \in \widehat{N}}$ in mixed strategies. Since the set of behavior strategy vectors of G equals the set of mixed strategies of Γ, we can regard $\sigma^* = (\sigma^*_i(\cdot \mid t_i))_{i \in N, t_i \in T_i}$ as a vector of behavior strategies in G. The fact that σ^* is a Bayesian equilibrium then follows from the definition of the agent-form game, and because σ^* is a mixed strategy equilibrium of the agent-form game Γ. $\qquad \square$

The following examples look at games with incomplete information with infinite spaces of states of nature.

Example 10.43 **Sealed-bid first-price auction**[9]   An original van Gogh painting is being offered in a first-price sealed-bid auction, meaning that every buyer writes his bid on a slip of paper that is placed in a sealed envelope, which is then inserted into a box. After all buyers have submitted their bids, all of the envelopes in the box are opened and read. The buyer who has made the highest bid wins the painting, paying for it the amount that he offered. If more than one buyer bids the highest bid, a fair lottery is conducted among them to choose the winner. Every buyer has a private evaluation for the painting, which will be referred to as his private value for the object. This is the subjective value he ascribes to the painting; private values may differ from one buyer to the next.

Only two buyers take part in this auction, Elizabeth and Charles. Each of them knows his or her private value, but not the private value of the other buyer. Each buyer believes that the private value of the other buyer is uniformly distributed in the interval $[0, 1]$, and this fact is common belief among the buyers. This situation can be modeled as a game with incomplete information, in the following way:

- The set of players is $N = \{\text{Elizabeth}, \text{Charles}\}$.
- The set of states of nature is $S = \{s_{x,y} : 0 \leq x, y \leq 1\}$; The subscript x corresponds to Elizabeth's private value, and subscript y corresponds to Charles's private value.
- Player i's set of actions is $A_i(s) = [0, \infty)$; hence each player i can submit any nonnegative bid a_i. The pair of bids submitted in the envelopes is therefore (a_E, a_C).
- Elizabeth's payoff function is

$$u_E(s_{x,y}; a_E, a_C) = \begin{cases} x - a_E & \text{if } a_E > a_C, \\ \frac{1}{2}(x - a_E) & \text{if } a_E = a_C, \\ 0 & \text{if } a_E < a_C. \end{cases} \tag{10.46}$$

If Elizabeth wins the auction, her payoff is the difference between her private value and the amount of money she pays for the painting; if she does not win the auction, her payoff is 0. If both buyers submit the same bid, the winner of the auction is chosen at random between them, where each buyer has a probability of $\frac{1}{2}$ of being chosen (this can be accomplished, for example, by tossing a fair coin). It follows that in this case Elizabeth's payoff is half of the difference between her private value and the sum of money she pays for the painting. Charles's payoff function is defined similarly.

- The space of the states of the world is $Y = [0, 1]^2$ with the σ-algebra generated by the Borel sets.
- The function $\mathfrak{s} : Y \to S$ is defined by $\mathfrak{s}(x, y) = s_{x,y}$ for all $(x, y) \in Y$.
- For each state of the world $\omega = (x, y)$, Elizabeth's belief, $\pi_E(x, y)$, is the uniform distribution over the set $\{(x, \hat{y}) : \hat{y} \in [0, 1]\}$ and Charles's belief, $\pi_C(x, y)$, is the uniform distribution over the set $\{(\hat{x}, y) : \hat{x} \in [0, 1]\}$.

We will show that this game has a symmetric Bayesian equilibrium $\sigma^* = (\sigma_E^*, \sigma_C^*)$, in which both buyers make use of the same strategy: player i's bid is half of his private value. That is,

$$\sigma_E^*(x, y) = \frac{x}{2}, \quad \sigma_C^*(x, y) = \frac{y}{2}, \quad \forall (x, y) \in [0, 1]^2. \tag{10.47}$$

Suppose that Charles uses strategy σ_C^*. We will show that Elizabeth's best reply is to bid half of her private value. Elizabeth's expected payoff if her private value is x, and her bid is a_E, is

$$\gamma_E(a_E, \sigma_C^* \mid x) = \mathbf{P}\left(a_E > \frac{y}{2}\right) \times (x - a_E) \tag{10.48}$$

$$= \mathbf{P}(2a_E > y) \times (x - a_E) \tag{10.49}$$

$$= \min\{2a_E, 1\} \times (x - a_E). \tag{10.50}$$

---

9 Auction theory is studied in greater detail in Chapter 12.

As a function of a_E, this is a quadratic function over $a_E \in [0, \frac{1}{2}]$ (attaining a maximum at $a_E = \frac{x}{2}$), and a linear function with a negative slope for $a_E \geq \frac{1}{2}$. The graph of this function is shown in Figure 10.12.

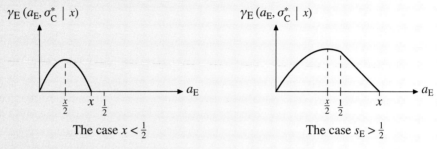

$$\gamma_E(a_E, \sigma_C^* \mid x) \qquad\qquad \gamma_E(a_E, \sigma_C^* \mid x)$$

The case $x < \frac{1}{2}$ The case $s_E > \frac{1}{2}$

Figure 10.12 Elizabeth's payoff function

In both cases, the function attains a maximum at the point $a_E = \frac{x}{2}$. It follows that $a_E^*(x) = \frac{x}{2}$ is the best reply to σ_C^*. Thus, $\sigma^* = (\sigma_E^*, \sigma_C^*)$ is a Bayesian equilibrium. ◀

Example 10.44 This is an example in which the beliefs of the players are inconsistent. There are two players $N = \{I, II\}$. The set of states of nature is $S = \{s_{x,y}: 0 < x, y < 1\}$; the state games in S are depicted in Figure 10.13.

	L	R
T	1, 0	0, 0
B	2, 1	1, −1

State game $s_{x,y}$ for $x > y$

	L	R
T	0, 0	0, 0
B	0, 0	0, 0

State game $s_{x,y}$ for $x = y$

	L	R
T	0, 1	1, 2
B	0, 0	−1, 1

State game $s_{x,y}$ for $x < y$

Figure 10.13 The state games in Example 10.44

The set of states of the world is $Y = (0, 1)^2$, and the function $\mathfrak{s}: Y \to S$ is defined by $\mathfrak{s}(x, y) = s_{x,y}$ for every $(x, y) \in Y$. Player I is told the first coordinate x of the state of the world, and Player II is told the second coordinate y of the state of the world. Given the value z that is told to a player, that player believes that the value told to the other player is uniformly distributed over the interval $(0, z)$. In other words, $\pi_I(x, y)$ is the uniform distribution over the line segment $((x, 0), (x, x))$ and $\pi_{II}(x, y)$ is the uniform distribution over the line segment $((0, y), (y, y))$.

At every state of the world, Player I believes that $x > y$; hence he believes that action B strictly dominates action T. In a similar way, at every state of the world Player II believes that $y > x$; hence he believes that action R strictly dominates action L. It follows that the only equilibrium is that where Player I, of any type, plays B, and Player II, of any type, plays R. The equilibrium payoff is then $(-1, 1)$ if $x < y$, $(1, -1)$ if $x > y$, and $(0, 0)$ if $x = y$. However, in every state of the world, each player believes that his payoff is 1. ◀

Example 10.45 We now consider a game similar to the game in Example 10.44, but with different state games, given in Figure 10.14; here, x represents the first coordinate of the state of nature, and y the second coordinate. Note that each player, after learning his type, knows his payoff function, but does not know the payoff function of the other player, even if he knows the strategy used by the other player, because he does not know the other player's type.

Player II

L   R

	L	R
T	$x, 0$	$0, y$
B	$0, 1$	$1, 0$

Player I

Figure 10.14 The state game $s_{(x,y)}$ in Example 10.45

We will seek a Bayesian equilibrium in which both players, of each type, use a completely mixed action. At such an equilibrium, every player of every type is indifferent between his two actions. Denote by $\sigma_I(x)$ the probability that Player I of type x, who has received the information x, will choose action T, and by $\sigma_{II}(y)$ the probability that Player II of type y, who has received the information y, will choose action L. Denote by U_x the uniform distribution over $[0, x]$. The payoff to Player I of type x if he plays the action T is then

$$\gamma_I(T, \sigma_{II} \mid x) = \int_{y=0}^{x} x\sigma_{II}(y)dU_x(y) = x\int_{y=0}^{x} \sigma_{II}(y)dU_x(y), \qquad (10.51)$$

and the payoff to Player I of type x if he plays the action B is then

$$\gamma_I(B, \sigma_{II} \mid x) = \int_{y=0}^{x} (1 - \sigma_{II}(y))dU_x(y) = 1 - \int_{y=0}^{x} \sigma_{II}(y)dU_x(y). \qquad (10.52)$$

Player I of type x is indifferent between T and B if these two quantities are equal to each other, i.e., if

$$(1 + x)\int_{y=0}^{x} \sigma_{II}(y)dU_x(y) = 1. \qquad (10.53)$$

The density function of the distribution U_x equals $\frac{1}{x}$ in the interval $[0, x]$, and it follows that in this interval $dU_x(y) = \frac{dy}{x}$. After inserting this equality in Equation (10.53) and moving terms from one side of the equal sign to the other, we get

$$\int_{y=0}^{x} \sigma_{II}(y)dy = \frac{x}{1+x}. \qquad (10.54)$$

Differentiating by x yields

$$\sigma_{II}(x) = \frac{1}{(1+x)^2}. \qquad (10.55)$$

By replacing the variable x by y, which is the information that Player II receives, we deduce that $\sigma_{II}(y) = \frac{1}{(1+y)^2}$ is a strategy of Player II that makes Player I of any type indifferent between his two actions. In Exercise 10.54, the reader is asked to conduct a similar calculation to find a strategy of Player I that makes Player II of any type indifferent between his two actions. When each player implements a strategy that makes the other player indifferent between his two actions, we obtain an equilibrium (why is this true?). ◄

10.6 The concept of consistency

The concept of consistency in belief spaces was defined on page 409. A consistent belief space is one in which the beliefs of the players are derived from a common prior p over the types. In this section, we will study this concept in greater detail. For simplicity, we will deal here only with finite belief spaces, but all the results of this section also hold in belief spaces with a countably infinite number of states of the world. The definitions and results can be generalized to infinite belief spaces, often requiring only adding appropriate technical conditions. Denote the support of $\pi_i(\omega)$ by $P_i(\omega)$:

$$P_i(\omega) := \mathrm{supp}(\pi_i(\omega)) \subseteq Y. \tag{10.56}$$

This is the set of states of the world that are possible, in player i's opinion, at the state of the world ω.

Definition 10.46 *Let* $\Pi = (Y, \mathcal{Y}, \mathfrak{s}, (\pi_i)_{i \in N})$ *be a belief space, where Y is a finite set. A belief subspace $\tilde{Y}$ is* consistent *if there exists a probability distribution p over $\tilde{Y}$ such that, for every event $A \subseteq \tilde{Y}$, for each player i, and for each $\omega \in \mathrm{supp}(p)$, $p(P_i(\omega))$ > 0 and*

$$\pi_i(A \mid \omega) = p(A \mid P_i(\omega)). \tag{10.57}$$

A probability distribution p satisfying Equation (10.57) for every event $A \subseteq \tilde{Y}$, for every player i and for every $\omega \in \mathrm{supp}(p)$, is called a consistent distribution *(over $\tilde{Y}$), or a* common prior.

   In words, the belief of player i at the state of the world ω is given by the conditional probability of p given the information $P_i(\omega)$ that the player has at ω. A consistent distribution, therefore, plays the same role as the common prior in the Aumann model of incomplete information.

   On page 409 we defined the concept of consistency by conditioning on the set $\{\omega' \in Y \colon \pi_i(\omega') = \pi_i(\omega)\}$ instead of the set $P_i(\omega)$ (see Equation (10.57)). The coherency requirement in the definition of a belief space guarantees that these two definitions are equivalent (Exercise 10.65).

   If p is a consistent distribution, then every state of the world $\omega \in \mathrm{supp}(p)$ is called a *consistent state of the world*. Every state of the world that is not consistent is called *inconsistent*.

Remark 10.47 *Let* $\Pi = (Y, \mathcal{Y}, \mathfrak{s}, (\pi_i)_{i \in N})$ *be a belief space, and let $\tilde{\Pi} = (\tilde{Y}, \mathcal{Y}, \mathfrak{s}, (\pi_i)_{i \in N})$ be a consistent belief subspace of Π. Then Π is also a consistent belief space. To see this, note that since $\tilde{\Pi}$ is a consistent belief subspace, there exists a consistent distribution $\tilde{p}$ over $\tilde{Y}$. In that case, define a probability distribution p over Y by*

$$p(\omega) = \begin{cases} \tilde{p}(\omega) & \text{if } \omega \in \tilde{Y}, \\ 0 & \text{if } \omega \notin \tilde{Y}. \end{cases} \tag{10.58}$$

This is a consistent distribution over Π (Exercise 10.64). ◆

   The next example elucidates the concepts of consistent distribution and consistent state of the world.

Example 10.48   Figure 10.15 depicts a belief space for the set of players $N = \{I, II\}$ over the set of states of nature $S = \{s_1, s_2\}$. In this belief space, the set of states of the world is $Y = \{\omega_1, \omega_2\}$.

State of the world	$s(\cdot)$	$\pi_I(\cdot)$	$\pi_{II}(\cdot)$
ω_1	s_1	$[1(\omega_1)]$	$[1(\omega_1)]$
ω_2	s_2	$[1(\omega_1)]$	$[1(\omega_2)]$

Figure 10.15 The belief space in Example 10.48

At the state of the world ω_1, the fact that the state of nature is s_1 is common belief among the players. At the state of the world ω_2, Player I believes that the fact that the state of nature is s_1 is common belief among the players, while Player II believes that the state of nature is s_2, and believes that Player I believes that the fact that the state of nature is s_1 is common belief among the players.

The belief subspace $\widetilde{Y} = \{\omega_1\}$ is a consistent belief subspace, with a consistent distribution $\widetilde{p} = [1(\omega_1)]$. Remark 10.47 shows that Π is also a consistent belief space, with consistent distribution $p = [1(\omega_1)]$. The state of the world ω_1 is contained in the support of p; therefore it is a consistent state of the world.

The state of the world ω_2, however, is inconsistent. Indeed, at that state of the world Player I ascribes probability 1 to the state of nature being s_1, while Player II ascribes probability 1 to the state of nature being s_2. There cannot, then, exist a probability distribution p from which these two beliefs can be derived (verify!).   ◄

Example 10.18   (*Continued*) Consider the event $A = \{\omega_{12}, \omega_{21}\}$ and the probability distribution p, as defined in Figure 10.5 on page 408. Then

$$\pi_I(A \mid \omega_{11}) = \tfrac{4}{7}, \tag{10.59}$$

$$p(A \mid P_I(\omega_{11})) = p(A \mid \{\omega_{11}, \omega_{12}\}) = \tfrac{4}{7}; \tag{10.60}$$

hence $\pi_I(A \mid \omega_{11}) = p(A \mid P_I(\omega))$. It can be shown that Equation (10.57) is satisfied for every event $A \subseteq Y$, for every player $i \in \{I, II\}$, and for every $\omega \in Y$ (Exercise 10.66); hence p is a consistent distribution.   ◄

Example 10.19   (*Continued*) The beliefs of the players are shown in Figure 10.6 on page 409. Consider the event $A = \{\omega_{12}, \omega_{21}\}$ and the probability distribution p defined in Figure 10.5 on page 408. Then

$$\pi_I(A \mid \omega_{11}) = \tfrac{4}{7}, \tag{10.61}$$

$$p(A \mid P_I(\omega_{11})) = p(A \mid \{\omega_{11}, \omega_{12}\}) = \tfrac{4}{7}. \tag{10.62}$$

On the other hand,

$$\pi_{II}(A \mid \omega_{11}) = \tfrac{1}{2}, \tag{10.63}$$

$$p(A \mid P_{II}(\omega_{11})) = p(A \mid \{\omega_{11}, \omega_{21}\}) = \tfrac{2}{5}; \tag{10.64}$$

hence $\pi_{II}(A \mid \omega_{11}) \neq p(A \mid P_{II}(\omega_{11}))$. It follows that p is not a consistent distribution. This is not surprising, since we proved that this belief space is not consistent.   ◄

It can be shown (Exercise 10.67) that the following definition is equivalent to the definition of a consistent distribution (see Definition 10.46).

Definition 10.49 *A probability distribution $p \in \Delta(Y)$ (over a finite set of states of the world Y) is called* consistent *if for each player $i \in N$,*

$$p = \sum_{\omega \in Y} \pi_i(\omega)p(\omega). \tag{10.65}$$

In other words,

$$p(\omega') = \sum_{\omega \in Y} \pi_i(\{\omega'\} \mid \omega)p(\omega), \quad \forall \omega' \in Y. \tag{10.66}$$

A probability distribution p is consistent if, for every player i, it is the average according to p of player i's types (recall that a type is a probability distribution over Y). This gives us a new angle from which to regard the consistency condition: in any consistent system of beliefs, we can find weights for the states of the world (a probability distribution p), such that the weighted average of the type of each player is the same for all the players, and this average is exactly the probability distribution p. (Equations (10.65) and (10.66) refer to sums, and not integrals, because of the assumption that the set of states of the world is finite.)

Example 10.18 (*Continued*) To ascertain that p is a consistent distribution according to Definition 10.49, we need to ascertain that Equation (10.65) is satisfied for each player $i \in N$. Each row in the table in Figure 10.16 describes a type of Player I at a state of the world. The right column shows the common prior, and the bottom row describes the weighted average of Player I's types.

	ω_{11}	ω_{12}	ω_{21}	ω_{22}	Probability
$\pi_1(\omega_{11})$	$\frac{3}{7}$	$\frac{4}{7}$	0	0	$\frac{3}{10}$
$\pi_1(\omega_{12})$	$\frac{3}{7}$	$\frac{4}{7}$	0	0	$\frac{4}{10}$
$\pi_1(\omega_{21})$	0	0	$\frac{2}{3}$	$\frac{1}{3}$	$\frac{2}{10}$
$\pi_1(\omega_{22})$	0	0	$\frac{2}{3}$	$\frac{1}{3}$	$\frac{1}{10}$
Average	$\frac{3}{10}$	$\frac{4}{10}$	$\frac{2}{10}$	$\frac{1}{10}$	

Figure 10.16 The probability that each type of Player I ascribes to each state of nature in Example 10.18

When we take the weighted average of each row of the table (i.e., compute the right-hand side of the equal sign in Equation (10.65)), we obtain the probability distribution p with which we started (listed in the left-most column). We obtain a similar result with respect to Player II (Exercise 10.68); hence p is a consistent distribution according to Definition 10.49. ◀

Definition 10.46 does not require the support of a consistent distribution p to be all of Y. The next theorem states, however, that the support of such a probability distribution is also a consistent belief subspace.

Theorem 10.50 *Let $\Pi = (Y, \mathcal{Y}, \mathfrak{s}, (\pi_i)_{i \in N})$ be a belief space in which Y is a finite set. If p is a consistent distribution over Y, then $\tilde{Y} = \operatorname{supp}(p)$ is a consistent belief subspace.*

The proof of Theorem 10.50 is left to the reader (Exercise 10.70). As the next example shows, it is possible for a consistent belief space to have several different consistent distributions.

Example 10.51 Consider the following belief space, with one player $N = \{I\}$, two states of nature $S = \{s_1, s_2\}$, and two states of the world $Y = \{\omega_1, \omega_2\}$, where:

State of the world	$\mathfrak{s}(\cdot)$	$\pi_I(\cdot)$
ω_1	s_1	$[1(\omega_1)]$
ω_2	s_2	$[1(\omega_2)]$

That is, at ω_1 the player believes that the state of nature is s_1, and at ω_2 he believes that the state of nature is s_2. For each $\lambda \in [0, 1]$, the probability distribution p^λ, defined as follows, is consistent (verify!):

$$p^\lambda(\omega_1) = \lambda, \quad p^\lambda(\omega_2) = 1 - \lambda. \tag{10.67}$$

◀

The belief space $Y = \{\omega_1, \omega_2\}$ in Example 10.51 properly contains two belief subspaces: $\{\omega_1\}$ and $\{\omega_2\}$. As the next theorem states, this is the only possible way in which multiple consistent distributions can arise.

Theorem 10.52 *Let* $\Pi = (Y, \mathcal{Y}, \mathfrak{s}, (\pi_i)_{i \in N})$ *be a consistent belief space in which Y is finite that does not properly contain a belief subspace. Then there exists a unique consistent probability distribution p whose support* $\mathrm{supp}(p)$ *is contained in Y.*

By definition, for each consistent belief subspace $\widetilde{Y}$ there exists a consistent distribution p satisfying $\mathrm{supp}(p) \subseteq \widetilde{Y}$. Theorem 10.52 states that if the belief subspace is minimal, then there exists a unique such probability distribution. It then follows from Theorem 10.50 that $\mathrm{supp}(p) = \widetilde{Y}$.

In order to prove Theorem 10.52, we will first prove the following auxiliary theorem. We adopt here the convention that $\frac{0}{0} = 1$.

Theorem 10.53 *Let* $(\alpha_k)_{k=1}^n$ *be nonnegative numbers, let* $(x_k, y_k)_{k=1}^n$ *be a sequence of pairs of positive numbers, and let* $C > 1$. *If* $\frac{x_k}{y_k} \leq C$ *for all* $i \in \{1, 2, \ldots, n\}$, *then* $\frac{\sum_{k=1}^n \alpha_k x_k}{\sum_{k=1}^n \alpha_k y_k} \leq C$. *If, in addition, there exists* $j \in \{1, 2, \ldots, n\}$ *such that* $\alpha_j > 0$, *and* $\frac{x_j}{y_j} < C$, *then* $\frac{\sum_{k=1}^n \alpha_k x_k}{\sum_{k=1}^n \alpha_k y_k} < C$.

Proof: If $\alpha_k = 0$ for each k, then both the numerator and the denominator in the expression $\frac{\sum_{k=1}^n \alpha_k x_k}{\sum_{k=1}^n \alpha_k y_k}$ are zero; hence their ratio equals 1, which is smaller than C. Suppose, therefore, that at least one of the numbers in $(\alpha_k)_{k=1}^n$ is positive. This implies that both the numerator and the denominator in the expression $\frac{\sum_{k=1}^n \alpha_k x_k}{\sum_{k=1}^n \alpha_k y_k}$ are positive.

Since $\frac{x_k}{y_k} \leq C$ for each $k \in \{1, 2, \ldots, n\}$, it follows that $x_k \leq Cy_k$. Because $(\alpha_k)_{k=1}^n$ are nonnegative numbers,

$$\sum_{k=1}^n \alpha_k x_k \leq C \sum_{k=1}^n \alpha_k y_k. \tag{10.68}$$

Since the sum on the right-hand side of the equation is positive, we can divide by that sum to get

$$\frac{\sum_{k=1}^n \alpha_k x_k}{\sum_{k=1}^n \alpha_k y_k} \leq C. \tag{10.69}$$

Next, suppose that there also exists $j \in \{1, 2, \ldots, n\}$ such that $\alpha_j > 0$ and $\frac{x_j}{y_j} < C$. In this case, we deduce that Equation (10.68) is satisfied as a strict inequality (verify!). It follows that Equation (10.69) is also satisfied as a strict inequality, which is what we sought to show. $\qquad\square$

Proof of Theorem 10.52: Let p and $\widehat{p}$ be two distinct consistent probability distributions, where the supports $\mathrm{supp}(p)$ and $\mathrm{supp}(\widehat{p})$ are contained in Y. Theorem 10.50 implies that $\mathrm{supp}(p)$ is a belief subspace. Since Y is a minimal belief subspace, it must be the case that $\mathrm{supp}(p) = Y$. We similarly deduce that $\mathrm{supp}(\widehat{p}) = Y$ and therefore in particular $\mathrm{supp}(\widehat{p}) = \mathrm{supp}(p)$. Denote $C := \max_{\omega \in \mathrm{supp}(p)} \frac{p(\omega)}{\widehat{p}(\omega)}$. Since $\mathrm{supp}(\widehat{p}) = Y$, the denominator $\widehat{p}(\omega)$ is positive for all $\omega \in Y$; therefore C is well defined.

Since p and $\widehat{p}$ are different probability distributions, it must be the case that $C > 1$. To see why, suppose that $C \leq 1$. Then $p(\omega) \leq \widehat{p}(\omega)$ for each $\omega \in Y$, and since $\sum_{\omega \in Y} p(\omega) = 1 = \sum_{\omega \in Y} \widehat{p}(\omega)$, we have $p(\omega) = \widehat{p}(\omega)$ for each $\omega \in \widehat{Y}$. Denote

$$A := \left\{ \omega \in Y : \frac{p(\omega)}{\widehat{p}(\omega)} = C \right\}. \tag{10.70}$$

We now show that Theorem 10.53 implies that $\mathrm{supp}(\pi_i(\omega')) \subseteq A$ for each $\omega' \in A$. Let $\omega' \in A$ be an element of A, and write out the expressions in Theorem 10.53 with $(\pi_i(\{\omega'\} \mid \omega))_{\omega \in Y}$ as the set of nonnegative numbers $(\alpha_k)_{k=1}^n$ and $(p(\omega))_{\omega \in Y}$ and $(\widehat{p}(\omega))_{\omega \in Y}$ as, respectively, the sets of positive numbers $(x_k)_{k=1}^n$ and $(y_k)_{k=1}^n$. Since p and $\widehat{p}$ are consistent distributions, with the aid of Definition 10.49, we get

$$\frac{\sum_k \alpha_k x_k}{\sum_k \alpha_k y_k} = \frac{\sum_\omega \pi_i(\{\omega'\} \mid \omega) p(\omega)}{\sum_\omega \pi_i(\{\omega'\} \mid \omega) \widehat{p}(\omega)} = \frac{p(\omega')}{\widehat{p}(\omega')}. \tag{10.71}$$

If $\mathrm{supp}(\pi_i(\omega'))$ were not contained in A, then there would be a state $\omega \in \mathrm{supp}(\pi_i(\omega'))$ satisfying $\frac{p(\omega)}{\widehat{p}(\omega)} < C$. Then Theorem 10.53 would in turn imply that $\frac{p(\omega')}{\widehat{p}(\omega')} < C$, i.e., $\omega' \notin A$, which would be a contradiction.

If follows that $\mathrm{supp}(\pi_i(\omega')) \subseteq A$ for each $\omega' \in A$; hence A is a belief subspace (see Definition 10.21 on page 410). Since Y is a minimal belief subspace, $A = Y$. We then deduce that $\frac{p(\omega)}{\widehat{p}(\omega)} = C > 1$ for each $\omega \in Y$, i.e., $p(\omega) > \widehat{p}(\omega)$. Summing over $\omega \in Y$, we get

$$1 = \sum_{\omega \in Y} p(\omega) > \sum_{\omega \in Y} \widehat{p}(\omega) = 1. \tag{10.72}$$

This contradiction establishes that $p = \widehat{p}$. $\qquad\square$

The consistency presented in this section is an "objective" concept, by which we mean objective from the perspective of an outside observer, who knows the belief space $\Pi = (Y, \mathcal{Y}, s, (\pi_i)_{i \in N})$ and can verify whether or not a given state of the world $\omega \in Y$

is consistent according to Definition 10.46. But what are the beliefs of the players about the consistency of a given state of the world? If a player believes that the state of the world is consistent, then he can describe the situation he is in as a Harsanyi game with incomplete information, and choose his actions by analyzing that game. The following theorem relates to this question.

Theorem 10.54 *Let* $\Pi = (Y, \mathcal{Y}, \mathfrak{s}, (\pi_i)_{i \in N})$ *be a belief space, where Y is a finite set, and let* $\omega \in Y$ *be a consistent state of the world. Then it is common belief among the players at* ω *that* ω *is consistent. In particular, every player at* ω *believes that* ω *is consistent.*

Proof: Since ω is a consistent state of the world, there exists a consistent distribution p over Y satisfying $p(\omega) > 0$. Since $p(\omega) > 0$, Equation (10.57) implies that for each player $i \in N$,

$$\pi_i(\{\omega\} \mid \omega) = p(\{\omega\} \mid P_i(\omega)) > 0. \tag{10.73}$$

It follows from Theorem 10.32 on page 414 that for each pair of players $i, j \in N$,

$$\widetilde{Y}_j(\omega) = \widetilde{Y}_i(\omega), \tag{10.74}$$

where $\widetilde{Y}_i(\omega)$ is the minimal belief space of player i at the state of the world ω (see Definition 10.30 on page 413). Note that $\omega \in \text{supp}(\pi_i(\omega))$ for each player $i \in N$; hence $\omega \in Y_i(\omega)$. Theorem 10.33 implies that $\widetilde{Y}_i(\omega) = \widetilde{Y}(\omega)$ for each $i \in N$, where $\widetilde{Y}(\omega)$ is the minimal belief space at the state of the world ω (see Definition 10.24 on page 411). Let $\widetilde{p}$ be the probability distribution p, conditioned on the set $\widetilde{Y}(\omega)$:

$$\widetilde{p}(\omega') = \frac{p(\omega')}{p(\widetilde{Y}(\omega))}, \quad \forall \omega' \in \widetilde{Y}(\omega). \tag{10.75}$$

Then $\widetilde{p}$ is a consistent distribution (Exercise 10.72). It follows that $\widetilde{Y}(\omega)$ is a consistent belief subspace. As stated after Definition 10.21 (page 410), every belief subspace is common belief at every state of the world contained in it; hence the event $\widetilde{Y}(\omega)$ is common belief among the players at the state of the world ω. In particular, it is common belief among the players at ω that ω is consistent. □

Every player i, based only on his own private information (i.e., his type), can construct the minimal belief subspace $\widetilde{Y}_i(\omega)$ that includes, according to his beliefs, all the states of the world that are relevant to the situation he is in. If the state of the world ω is consistent, then the belief subspace $\widetilde{Y}_i(\omega)$ is also consistent, and, since it is a minimal belief subspace, there is a unique consistent distribution p over it (Theorem 10.52), which the player can compute. In this case, the situation, according to player i's beliefs, is equivalent to a Harsanyi model of incomplete information. That model is constructed by first selecting a state of the world according to the consistent distribution p over $\widetilde{Y}_i(\omega)$; hence the situation, according to player i's beliefs, is equivalent to the interim stage, which is the point in time at which every player knows his partition element, which contains the true state of the world. Every Aumann model, or equivalently Harsanyi model, is but an auxiliary construction that can be made by each of the players. The entire model thus constructed, including the space of types (which is computed from the belief subspace $\widetilde{Y}_i(\omega)$), and the probability distribution used to choose the types (which is derived from the consistent distribution p), is based on the private information of the player. In addition, when ω is a consistent state of the world, Theorem 10.54 states that every player computes the same minimal belief space, and computes the same consistent distribution p, and it is common belief among the players that this is the case. In particular, all the players arrive at the same Aumann (or Harsanyi) model of incomplete information, and this model is common belief among them.

The next question that naturally arises is what are the beliefs of the players about the consistency of a given state of the world when that state of the world is inconsistent. As we will now show, in that case there are two possibilities: it is possible for a player to believe that the state of the world is inconsistent, and in some cases this may even be common belief among the players. However, it is also possible for a player (mistakenly) to believe that the state of the world is consistent, and it is even possible for all the players to believe that the state of the world is consistent, and for that fact to be common belief among the players.

Theorem 10.55 *Let* $\Pi = (Y, \mathcal{Y}, \mathfrak{s}, (\pi_i)_{i \in N})$ *be a belief space, where* Y *is a finite set, and let* $\omega \in Y$ *be an inconsistent state of the world. If* $\pi_i(\{\omega\} \mid \omega) > 0$, *then at the state of the world* ω *player* i *believes that the state of the world is inconsistent.*

Proof: The assumption that $\pi_i(\{\omega\} \mid \omega) > 0$ implies that $\omega \in \widetilde{Y}_i(\omega)$; hence $\widetilde{Y}_i(\omega)$ is a belief subspace containing ω. Since ω is an inconsistent state of the world, there does not exist a consistent distribution p over $\widetilde{Y}_i(\omega)$ satisfying $p(\omega) > 0$; hence player i, after calculating his minimal belief subspace $\widetilde{Y}_i(\omega)$, believes that the state of the world is inconsistent. $\square$

It follows from Theorem 10.55 that at an inconsistent state of the world ω, player i is liable (mistakenly) to believe that the state of the world is consistent only if he ascribes probability 0 to ω; that is, $\pi_i(\{\omega\} \mid \omega) = 0$. This happens in fact in Example 10.27 on page 412, in which the state of the world ω_2 is inconsistent, but at this state of the world, both players believe that the actual state of the world is consistent. In fact, in Example 10.27, at the state of the world ω_2 it is common belief among the players that the state of the world is consistent, even though it is inconsistent (Exercise 10.80).

In Example 10.19 on page 408, every state of the world is inconsistent; hence the fact that any given state of the world is inconsistent is common belief among the players at every state of the world. The next theorem generalizes this example, and presents a sufficient condition that guarantees that the fact that a given state of the world is inconsistent is common belief among the players.

Theorem 10.56 *Let* $\Pi = (Y, \mathcal{Y}, \mathfrak{s}, (\pi_i)_{i \in N})$ *be a belief space, where* Y *is a finite set, and let* $\omega \in Y$ *be an inconsistent state of the world. If* $\pi_i(\{\omega'\} \mid \omega') > 0$ *for every player* i *and every state of the world* ω' *in the minimal belief subspace* $\widetilde{Y}(\omega)$ *at* ω, *then the fact that the state of the world is inconsistent is common belief among the players at* ω, *and at every state of the world in* $\widetilde{Y}(\omega)$.

Proof: Because $\omega \in \widetilde{Y}(\omega)$, the assumption implies that $\pi_i(\{\omega\} \mid \omega) > 0$ for every player $i \in N$. By Theorem 10.32 (page 414), $\widetilde{Y}(\omega) = \widetilde{Y}_i(\omega)$ for each player $i \in N$. It then follows from Theorem 10.55 that at every state of the world $\omega' \in \widetilde{Y}(\omega)$, every player believes that the state of the world is inconsistent. In particular, it follows that at every state of the world $\omega' \in \tilde{Y}(\omega)$ it is common belief that the state of the world is inconsistent. $\square$

There are cases in which, at a given state of the world, every player believes that the state of the world is inconsistent, but this fact is not common belief among the players (Exercise 10.81). There are also cases in which some of the players believe that the state of the world is consistent while others believe that the state of the world is inconsistent (Exercise 10.82).

Most of the models of incomplete information used in the game theory literature are Harsanyi games. This means that nearly every model in published papers is described using a consistent belief system, despite the fact that, as we have seen, not only do inconsistent belief spaces exist, they comprise an "absolute majority" of situations of incomplete information – the set of consistent situations is a set of measure zero within the set of belief spaces. The reason that consistent models are ubiquitous in the literature is mainly because consistent models are presentable extensive-form games, while situations of inconsistent beliefs cannot be presented as either extensive-form or strategic-form games. This makes the mathematical study of such situations difficult. It should, however, be reiterated that the central solution concept – Bayesian equilibrium – is computable and applicable in both consistent and inconsistent situations.

10.7 Remarks

Example 10.16 (page 406) appears in Sorin and Zamir [1985], under the name "Lack of information on one-and-a-half sides." Results on Nash equilibria and Bayesian equilibria in games with incomplete information and general space of states of the world can be found in many papers. A partial list includes Milgrom and Weber [1985], Milgrom and Roberts [1990], van Zandt and Vives [2007], van Zandt [2007], and Vives [1990].

Exercises 10.37–10.40 are taken from Mertens and Zamir [1985]. The notion "belief with probability at least p" that appears in Exercise 10.15 was defined in Monderer and Samet [1989]. Discussion about the subject of probabilistic beliefs appeared in Gaifman [1986]. Exercise 10.62 is taken from van Zandt [2007].

The authors thank Yaron Azrieli, Aviad Heifetz, Dov Samet, and Eran Shmaya for their comments on this chapter.

10.8 Exercises

10.1 Let the set of players be $N = \{\mathrm{I}, \mathrm{II}\}$, the set of states of nature be $S = \{s_1, s_2\}$, and the set of states of the world be $Y = \{\omega_1, \omega_2, \omega_3\}$. The σ-algebra over Y is $\mathcal{Y} = \{\emptyset, \{1\}, \{2, 3\}, \{1, 2, 3\}\}$, and the function $\mathfrak{s}$ mapping the states of the world to the states of nature is given by

$$\mathfrak{s}(\omega_1) = s_1, \quad \mathfrak{s}(\omega_2) = \mathfrak{s}(\omega_3) = s_2. \tag{10.76}$$

For each of the following three belief functions, determine whether $(Y, \mathcal{Y}, \mathfrak{s}, (\pi_i)_{i \in N})$ is a belief space of N over S. Justify your answers.

(a) $\pi_I(\omega_1) = [1(\omega_1)]$, $\pi_I(\omega_2) = \pi_I(\omega_3) = [\frac{1}{3}(\omega_2), \frac{2}{3}(\omega_3)]$, $\pi_{II}(\omega_1) = \pi_{II}(\omega_2) = \pi_{II}(\omega_3) = [\frac{4}{7}(\omega_2), \frac{3}{7}(\omega_3)]$.

(b) $\pi_I(\omega_1) = \pi_I(\omega_2) = \pi_I(\omega_3) = [\frac{1}{4}(\omega_1), \frac{3}{4}(\omega_2)]$, $\pi_{II}(\omega_1) = [1(\omega_1)]$, $\pi_{II}(\omega_2) = \pi_{II}(\omega_3) = [\frac{1}{3}(\omega_2), \frac{2}{3}(\omega_3)]$.

(c) $\pi_I(\omega_1) = [\frac{1}{3}(\omega_1), \frac{1}{3}(\omega_2), \frac{1}{3}(\omega_3)]$, $\pi_I(\omega_2) = \pi_I(\omega_3) = [\frac{1}{6}(\omega_2), \frac{5}{6}(\omega_3)]$, $\pi_{II}(\omega_1) = [1(\omega_1)]$, $\pi_{II}(\omega_2) = \pi_{II}(\omega_3) = [1(\omega_3)]$.

10.2 Let $\Pi = (Y, \mathcal{Y}, \mathfrak{s}, (\pi_i)_{i \in N})$ and $\widehat{\Pi} = (\widehat{Y}, \widehat{\mathcal{Y}}, \widehat{\mathfrak{s}}, (\widehat{\pi}_i)_{i \in N})$ be two belief spaces satisfying $Y \cap \widehat{Y} = \emptyset$. Prove that $\widetilde{\Pi} = (\widetilde{Y}, \widetilde{\mathcal{Y}}, \widetilde{\mathfrak{s}}, (\widetilde{\pi}_i)_{i \in N})$, as defined below, is a belief space.[10]

- $\widetilde{Y} := Y \cup \widehat{Y}$.
- $\widetilde{\mathcal{Y}} := \{F \cup \widehat{F} : F \in \mathcal{Y}, \widehat{F} \in \widehat{\mathcal{Y}}\}$.
- $\widetilde{\mathfrak{s}}(\omega) = \mathfrak{s}(\omega)$ for every $\omega \in Y$ and $\widetilde{\mathfrak{s}}(\widehat{\omega}) = \widehat{\mathfrak{s}}(\widehat{\omega})$ for every $\widehat{\omega} \in \widehat{Y}$.
- $\widetilde{\pi}_i(\omega) = \pi_i(\omega)$ for every $\omega \in Y$ and $\widetilde{\pi}_i(\widehat{\omega}) = \widehat{\pi}_i(\widehat{\omega})$ for every $\widehat{\omega} \in \widehat{Y}$.

10.3 Prove Equation (10.11) on p. 400.

10.4 Minerva ascribes probability 0.7 to Hercules being able to lift a massive rock, and she believes that Hercules believes that he can lift the rock. Construct a belief space in which the described situation is represented by a state of the world and indicate that state (more than one answer is possible).

10.5 Minerva ascribes probability 0.7 to Hercules being able to lift a massive rock, and she believes that Hercules believes that he can lift the rock. Hercules, in contrast, believes that if he attempts to lift the rock he will fail to do so. Construct a belief space in which the described situation is represented by a state of the world and indicate that state (more than one answer is possible).

10.6 Eric believes that it is common belief among him and Jack that the New York Mets won the baseball World Series in 1969. Jack ascribes probability 0.5 to the New York Mets having won the World Series in 1969, and to Eric believing that it is common belief among the two of them that the New York Mets won the World Series in 1969. Jack also ascribes probability 0.5 to the New York Mets not having won the World Series in 1969, and to Eric believing that it is not common belief among the two of them that the New York Mets won the World Series in 1969. Construct a belief space in which the described situation is represented by a state of the world and indicate that state (more than one answer is possible).

10.7 (a) Using two states of the world describe the following situation, specifying how each state differs from the other: "Roger ascribes probability 0.4 to the Philadelphia Phillies winning the World Series."

----

[10] Every probability distribution π over the space Y can be regarded as a probability distribution over the space $Y \cup \widehat{Y}$ such that $\pi(\widehat{Y}) = 0$.

(b) Add to the two states of the world that you listed above two more states of the world, and use the four states to construct a belief space in which the following situation is represented as a state of the world: "Jimmy ascribes probability 0.3 to the Philadelphia Phillies winning the World Series and to Roger ascribing probability 0.4 to the Philadelphia Phillies winning the World Series, and Jimmy ascribes probability 0.7 to the Philadelphia Phillies not winning the World Series and to Jimmy ascribing 0.4 to the Philadelphia Phillies winning the World Series."

(c) Construct a belief space in which the following situation is represented by a state of the world and indicate that state.

Roger says:

- I ascribe probability 0.3 to "the Philadelphia Phillies will win the World Series, and Jimmy ascribes probability 0.3 to the Philadelphia Phillies winning the World Series and to my ascribing 0.4 to the Philadelphia Phillies winning the World Series, and Jimmy ascribes probability 0.7 to the Philadelphia Phillies not winning the World Series and to my ascribing 0.4 to the Philadelphia Phillies winning the World Series."

- I ascribe probability 0.2 to "the Philadelphia Phillies will win the World Series, and Jimmy ascribes probability 0.7 to the Philadelphia Phillies winning the World Series and to my ascribing 0.5 to the Philadelphia Phillies winning the World Series, and Jimmy ascribes probability 0.3 to the Philadelphia Phillies not winning the World Series and to my ascribing 0.5 to the Philadelphia Phillies winning the World Series."

- I ascribe probability 0.4 to "the Philadelphia Phillies will win the World Series, and Jimmy ascribes probability 0.2 to the Philadelphia Phillies winning the World Series and to my ascribing 0.1 to the Philadelphia Phillies winning the World Series, and Jimmy ascribes probability 0.8 to the Philadelphia Phillies not winning the World Series and to my ascribing 0.1 to the Philadelphia Phillies winning the World Series."

- I ascribe probability 0.1 to "the Philadelphia Phillies will win the World Series, and Jimmy ascribes probability 0.6 to the Philadelphia Phillies winning the World Series and to my ascribing 0.4 to the Philadelphia Phillies winning the World Series, and Jimmy ascribes probability 0.4 to the Philadelphia Phillies not winning the World Series and to my ascribing 0.3 to the Philadelphia Phillies winning the World Series."

10.8 Prove Theorem 10.7: player i's belief operator B_i (see Definition 10.6 on page 402) satisfies the following properties:

(a) $B_i Y = Y$: player i believes that Y is the set of all states of the world.
(b) $B_i A \cap B_i C = B_i (A \cap C)$: if player i believes that event A obtains, and that event C obtains, then he believes that event $A \cap C$ obtains.
(c) $B_i(B_i A) = B_i A$: if player i believes that event A obtains, then he believes that he believes that event A obtains.

(d) $(B_iA)^c = B_i((B_iA)^c)$: if player i does not believe that event A obtains, then he believes that he does not believe that event A obtains.

10.9 Let Π be a belief space equivalent to an Aumann model of incomplete information and let B_i be player i's belief operator in Π (see Definition 10.6 on page 402). Prove that the knowledge operator K_i that is defined by the partition via Equation (10.9) (page 400) is the same operator as the belief operator B_i.

10.10 In this exercise we show that the converse of the statement of Theorem 10.10 does not hold. Find an example of a belief space in which there exists a state of the world $\omega \in Y$, an event A that is common belief among the players at the state of the world ω, a player $i \in N$, and a state of the world $\omega' \in A$, such that $\pi_i(A \mid \omega') < 1$.

10.11 In this exercise we show that Theorem 10.11 on page 403 does not hold without the assumption that $\mathbf{P}(\omega) > 0$ for every state of the world $\omega \in Y$.

Prove that there exists an Aumann model of incomplete information in which the common prior $\mathbf{P}$ satisfies $\mathbf{P}(\omega) = 0$ in at least one state of the world $\omega \in Y$, such that the following claim holds: the knowledge operator in the Aumann model is not identical to the belief operator in the belief space Π equivalent to the Aumann model.

10.12 Describe in words the beliefs of the players about the state of nature and the beliefs of the other players about the state of nature in each of the states of the world in Example 10.4 (page 399).

10.13 Prove Theorem 10.8 (page 402): for each player $i \in N$ and every pair of events $A, C \subseteq Y$, if $A \subseteq C$, then $B_iA \subseteq B_iC$.

10.14 Let $\Pi = (Y, \mathcal{Y}, \mathfrak{s}, (\pi_i)_{i \in N})$ be a belief space equivalent to an Aumann model of incomplete information. Prove that the partition defined by Equation (10.9) (page 400) for the belief space Π is the same partition as the partition $\mathcal{F}_i$ in the equivalent Aumann model.

10.15 For every player $i \in N$ and every real number $p \in [0, 1]$, define B_i^p to be the operator mapping each set $E \in \mathcal{Y}$ to the set of states of the world at which player i ascribes to E probability equal to or greater than p:

$$B_i^p(E) := \{\omega \in Y : \pi_i(E \mid \omega) \geq p\}. \tag{10.77}$$

Which of the following properties are satisfied by B_i^p for $p \in [0, 1]$? For each property, either prove that it is satisfied, or present a counterexample. There may be different answers for different values of p.

(a) $B_i^p(Y) = Y$.
(b) $B_i^p(A) \subseteq A$.
(c) If $A \subseteq C$ then $B_i^p(A) \subseteq B_i^p(C)$.
(d) $B_i^p(B_i^p(A)) = B_i^p(A)$.
(e) $B_i^p((B_i^p(A))^c) = (B_i^p(A))^c$.

10.16 Prove that if $\widetilde{Y}$ is a belief subspace of a belief space $\Pi = (Y, \mathcal{Y}, \mathfrak{s}, (\pi_i)_{i \in N})$, then the event $\widetilde{Y}$ is common belief among the players at every state of the world $\omega \in \widetilde{Y}$.

10.17 Let $\Pi = (Y, \mathcal{Y}, \mathfrak{s}, (\pi_i)_{i \in N})$ be a belief space equivalent to an Aumann model of incomplete information. Prove that for each state of the world ω, the common knowledge component among the players at ω (see page 344) is a belief subspace.

10.18 Consider Example 10.19 (page 408), and suppose that the beliefs of the types in that example are as follows, where $x, y, z, w \in [0, 1]$. For which values of x, y, z, and w is the belief system of the players consistent?

	II_1	II_2
I_1	x	$1 - x$
I_2	y	$1 - y$

	II_1	II_2
I_1	z	w
I_2	$1 - z$	$1 - w$

The beliefs of Player I   The beliefs of Player II

10.19 Prove that the beliefs of the players in Example 10.20 (page 410) are inconsistent. Recall that when the set of states of the world is a topological space, we require that a belief subspace be a closed set (see Remark 10.34).

10.20 Consider the following belief space, where the set of players is $N = \{\text{I}, \text{II}\}$, and the set of states of nature is $S = \{s_1, s_2\}$.

State of the world	$\mathfrak{s}(\cdot)$	$\pi_{\text{I}}(\cdot)$	$\pi_{\text{II}}(\cdot)$
ω_1	s_1	$\left[\frac{2}{5}(\omega_1), \frac{3}{5}(\omega_2)\right]$	$[1(\omega_1)]$
ω_2	s_2	$\left[\frac{2}{5}(\omega_1), \frac{3}{5}(\omega_2)\right]$	$\left[\frac{3}{4}(\omega_2), \frac{1}{4}(\omega_3)\right]$
ω_3	s_2	$[1(\omega_1)]$	$\left[\frac{3}{4}(\omega_2), \frac{1}{4}(\omega_3)\right]$

(a) List the types of the two players at each state of the world in Y.
(b) Can the beliefs of the players be derived from a common prior? If so, what is that common prior? If not, justify your answer.

10.21 Boris believes that "it is common belief among me and Alex that Bruce Jenner won a gold medal at the Montreal Olympics," while Alex believes that "it is common belief among me and Boris that Bruce Jenner won a silver medal at the Montreal Olympics."

(a) Construct a belief space in which the described situation is represented by a state of the world and indicate that state.
(b) Prove that, in any belief space in which the set of states of the world is a finite set and contains a state ω describing the situation in this exercise, ω is not contained in the support of the beliefs of either Boris or Alex, at any state of the world. In other words, $\omega \notin \text{supp}(\pi_i(\omega'))$ for any state of the world ω', for $i \in \{\text{Boris}, \text{Alex}\}$.

10.22 Laocoön declares: "I ascribe probability 0.6 to the Greeks attacking us from within a wooden horse." Priam then declares: "I ascribe probability 0.7 to the Greeks attacking us from within a wooden horse." After Priam's declaration, is the fact that "Laocoön ascribes probability 0.6 to the Greeks attacking from within a wooden horse" common belief among the players? Justify your answer.

10.23 There are two players $N = \{I, II\}$, and two states of nature $S = \{s_1, s_2\}$. A chance move chooses the state of nature, where s_1 is chosen with probability 0.4, and s_2 is chosen with probability 0.6. Player I knows the true state of nature that has been chosen. A chance move selects a signal that is received by Player II. The signal depends on the state of nature, as follows: if the true state of nature is s_1, Player II receives signal R with probability 0.6, and signal L with probability 0.4; if the true state of nature is s_2, Player II receives signal M with probability 0.7, and signal L with probability 0.3. It follows that if Player II receives signal L, he does not know with certainty which state of nature has been chosen. If the state of nature that has been chosen is s_2, and Player II has received signal M, then Player I is informed of this with probability 0.2, and Player I is not informed of this with probability 0.8. This description is common belief among the players. Construct a belief space in which the described situation is represented by a state of the world and indicate that state.

10.24 Repeat Exercise 10.23, under the assumption that the players do not agree on the probability distribution according to which the state of nature is chosen; that is, there is no common prior over S: Player I believes that s_1 is chosen with probability 0.4, while Player II believes that s_1 is chosen with probability 0.5. The rest of the description of the situation is as in Exercise 10.23, and this description is common belief among the players.

10.25 John, Bob, and Ted meet at a party in which all the invitees are either novelists or poets (but no one is both a novelist and a poet). Every poet knows all the other poets, but no novelist knows any other attendee at the party, whether novelist or poet. Every novelist believes that one-quarter of the attendees are novelists. Construct a belief space describing the beliefs of John, Bob, and Ted about the others' profession.

10.26 Walter, Karl, and Ferdinand are on the road to Dallas. They arrive at a fork in the road; should they turn right or left? Type t_1 believes that "we should turn right, everyone here believes that we should turn right, everyone here believes that everyone here believes that we should turn right, etc.": in other words, that type believes that turning right is called for, and believes that this is common belief among the three. Type t_2 believes that "we should turn right, the two others believe that we should turn left, the two others believe that everyone here believes that we should turn left, the two others believe that everyone here believes that everyone here believes that we should turn left, etc.": in other words, that type believes that turning right is called for, but believes that the other two believe that they should turn left and that this fact is common belief among the three. Type t_3 does not know which way to turn, but believes that the two others know the right way to turn, and believes that the others believe that everyone knows the right way to turn: he believes "the probability that we should turn right is $\frac{1}{2}$, and the probability that we should turn left is $\frac{1}{2}$; if we should turn right, then the two others believe that we should turn right, and that this is common belief among everyone here, and if we should turn left, then the two others believe that we should turn left, and that this is common belief among everyone here." Walter's type is t_1, Karl's type is t_2, and Ferdinand's type is t_3.

(a) Construct a belief space in which the described situation is represented by a state of the world and indicate that state.

(b) What is the minimal belief subspace of each of the three players (at the state of the world in which Walter's type is t_1, Karl's type is t_2, and Ferdinand's type is t_3)?

10.27 Repeat Exercise 10.26, when all three players are of type t_3.

10.28 In this exercise we show that when there is no common prior, it is possible to find a lottery that satisfies the property that each player has a positive expectation of profiting from the lottery, using his subjective probability belief.

Let $\Pi = (Y, \mathcal{Y}, \mathsf{s}, (\pi_i)_{i \in N})$ be a belief space of the set of players $N = \{I, II\}$, where the set of states of the world Y is finite. For each $i \in N$, define a set P_i of probability distributions over Y as follows:

$$P_i := \left\{ \sum_{\omega \in Y} x_\omega \pi_i(\cdot \mid \omega) : \sum_{\omega \in Y} x_\omega = 1, x_\omega > 0 \;\; \forall \omega \in Y \right\} \subset \Delta(Y). \qquad (10.78)$$

This is the set of all convex combinations of the beliefs $(\pi_i(\cdot \mid \omega))_{\omega \in Y}$ of player i such that the weight given to every ω is positive.

(a) Prove that for every $p \in P_i$ and every $\omega \in Y$, the belief $\pi_i(\cdot \mid \omega)$ is the conditional probability distribution of p given $F_i(\omega)$ (for the definition of the set $F_i(\omega)$ see Equation (10.9) on page 400). In other words, if p were a common prior, the beliefs of player i would be given by π_i.

(b) Prove that the set P_i is a convex set in $\Delta(Y)$, for every $i \in N$.

(c) Prove that if there is no common prior, then P_I and P_{II} are disjoint sets.

(d) Using Exercise 24.45 (page 1002) prove that there exist $\alpha \in \mathbb{R}^{|Y|}$ and $\beta \in \mathbb{R}$ such that[11]

$$\langle \alpha, p_I \rangle > \beta > \langle \alpha, p_{II} \rangle, \quad \forall p_I \in P_I, \forall p_{II} \in P_{II}. \qquad (10.79)$$

(e) The beliefs of Players I and II about the state of the world are given by the probability distributions $(\pi_i)_{i \in N}$. The state of the world, while unknown to them today, will become known to them tomorrow. They decide that after the state of the world ω will be revealed to them, Player II will pay Player I the sum $\alpha(\omega) - \beta$. If this quantity is negative, the payment will be from Player I to Player II. Prove that, given his subjective beliefs, the expected payoff of each player under this procedure is positive.

---

11 The inner product is given by $\langle p, \alpha \rangle = \sum_{\omega \in Y} p(\omega) \alpha(\omega)$.

10.29 Prove Theorem 10.23 (page 411): given two belief subspaces $\tilde{\Pi}_1 = (\tilde{Y}_1, \mathcal{Y}_{|\tilde{Y}_1},$ $\mathfrak{s}, (\pi_i)_{i \in N})$ and $\tilde{\Pi}_2 = (\tilde{Y}_2, \mathcal{Y}_{|\tilde{Y}_2}, \mathfrak{s}, (\pi_i)_{i \in N})$ of a belief space $\Pi = (Y, \mathcal{Y}, \mathfrak{s}, (\pi_i)_{i \in N})$ satisfying $\tilde{Y}_1 \cap \tilde{Y}_2 \neq \emptyset$, prove that $(\tilde{Y}_1 \cap \tilde{Y}_2, \mathcal{Y}_{|\tilde{Y}_1 \cap \tilde{Y}_2}, \mathfrak{s}, (\pi_i)_{i \in N})$ is also a belief subspace of Π.

10.30 Prove that if there exists a minimal belief subspace, then it is unique.

10.31 Generalize Theorem 10.25 to the case in which the set of states of the world is countably infinite: let $\Pi = (Y, \mathcal{Y}, \mathfrak{s}, (\pi_i)_{i \in N})$ be a belief space in which the set of states of the world Y is countably infinite. Prove that there exists a minimal belief subspace at each state of the world $\omega \in Y$.

10.32 Prove Theorem 10.33 (page 415): let $\Pi = (Y, \mathcal{Y}, \mathfrak{s}, (\pi_i)_{i \in N})$ be a belief space, where Y is a finite set. Then for each state of the world $\omega \in Y$,

$$\tilde{Y}(\omega) = \{\omega\} \cup \left(\bigcup_{i \in N} \tilde{Y}_i(\omega) \right). \tag{10.80}$$

10.33 Prove Theorem 10.35 (page 415): let $\Pi = (Y, \mathcal{Y}, \mathfrak{s}, (\pi_i)_{i \in N})$ be a belief space, where Y is a finite set. Then the subset $\tilde{Y}$ of Y is a belief subspace if and only if $\tilde{Y}$ is a closed component in the graph G defined by Π.

10.34 Prove Theorem 10.36 (page 416): let $\Pi = (Y, \mathcal{Y}, \mathfrak{s}, (\pi_i)_{i \in N})$ be a belief space, where Y is a finite set, let $\omega \in Y$, and let $i \in N$. For each state of the world ω, let $C(\omega)$ be the minimal closed component containing ω in the graph corresponding to Π. Prove that

$$\tilde{Y}_i(\omega) = \bigcup_{\{\omega' : \pi_i(\{\omega'\}|\omega) > 0\}} C(\omega'). \tag{10.81}$$

10.35 Present an example of a belief space Π with three players, and a state of the world ω satisfying $\tilde{Y}_1(\omega) \supset \tilde{Y}_2(\omega) \supset \tilde{Y}_3(\omega)$ (where all the set inclusions are strict inclusions).

10.36 Prove or disprove the following. There exists a belief space $\Pi = (Y, \mathcal{Y}, \mathfrak{s}, (\pi_i)_{i \in N})$, where Y is a finite set, and there are two players, $i, j \in N$, such that there exists a state of the world $\omega \in Y$ satisfying the property that $\tilde{Y}_i(\omega) \cap \tilde{Y}_j(\omega)$ is nonempty and strictly included in both $\tilde{Y}_i(\omega)$ and $\tilde{Y}_j(\omega)$.

10.37 In this exercise, suppose there are four states of nature, $S = \{s_{11}, s_{12}, s_{21}, s_{22}\}$. The information that Player I receives is the first coordinate of the state of nature chosen, while the information that Player II receives is the second coordinate. The conditional probabilities of the players, given their respective informations, are given by the following table (the conditional probability of Player I appears in the left column, while the conditional probability of Player II appears in the top row of the table):

$$\begin{array}{c|cc}
 & \begin{pmatrix} \frac{3}{5} \\ \frac{2}{5} \end{pmatrix} & \begin{pmatrix} 0 \\ 1 \end{pmatrix} \\
\hline
(1,0) & s_{11} & s_{12} \\
\left(\frac{2}{3}, \frac{1}{3}\right) & s_{21} & s_{22}
\end{array}$$

The table is to be read as stating, e.g., that if Player I receives information indicating that the state of nature is contained in $\{s_{11}, s_{12}\}$, he believes with probability 1 that the state of nature is s_{11}.

(a) Construct a belief space in which the described situation is represented by a state of the world and indicate that state.

Suppose that the state of nature is s_{12}, and that ω is the corresponding state of the world. Answer the following questions:

(b) What are the minimal belief subspaces $\tilde{Y}_I(\omega)$ and $\tilde{Y}_{II}(\omega)$ of the players?
(c) Is $\tilde{Y}_I(\omega) = \tilde{Y}_{II}(\omega)$?
(d) Is there a common prior p over S such that the players agree that the state of the world has been chosen according to p?
(e) Is the state of the world ω ascribed positive probability by p?

10.38 Repeat Exercise 10.37, where this time there are nine states of nature $S = \{s_{11}, s_{12}, s_{13}, s_{21}, s_{22}, s_{23}, s_{31}, s_{32}, s_{33}\}$ and the beliefs of the players, given their information, are presented in the following table:

$$\begin{array}{c|ccc}
 & \begin{pmatrix} \frac{3}{5} \\ \frac{1}{5} \\ \frac{1}{5} \end{pmatrix} & \begin{pmatrix} 0 \\ 1 \\ 0 \end{pmatrix} & \begin{pmatrix} \frac{1}{3} \\ \frac{2}{3} \\ 0 \end{pmatrix} \\
\hline
(1,0,0) & s_{11} & s_{12} & s_{13} \\
\left(\frac{2}{3}, \frac{1}{3}, 0\right) & s_{21} & s_{22} & s_{23} \\
(0,0,1) & s_{31} & s_{32} & s_{33}
\end{array}$$

10.39 Repeat Exercise 10.37, but this time suppose that the beliefs of each player of each type are:

$$\begin{array}{c|cc}
 & \begin{pmatrix} 1 \\ 0 \end{pmatrix} & \begin{pmatrix} 0 \\ 1 \end{pmatrix} \\
\hline
(1,0) & s_{11} & s_{12} \\
(0,1) & s_{21} & s_{22}
\end{array}$$

Parts (b)–(e) of Exercise 10.37 relate to a situation in which the true state of nature is s_{12}. Can each player calculate the minimal belief subspace of the other player at each state of the world? Justify your answer.

10.40 Repeat Exercise 10.37, where S includes 20 states of nature, the true state of nature is s_{13}, and the beliefs of the players are given in the following table:

	$\begin{pmatrix}0\\1\\0\\0\end{pmatrix}$	$\begin{pmatrix}\frac{3}{5}\\\frac{2}{5}\\0\\0\end{pmatrix}$	$\begin{pmatrix}0\\0\\\frac{1}{2}\\\frac{1}{2}\end{pmatrix}$	$\begin{pmatrix}0\\0\\\frac{1}{2}\\\frac{1}{2}\end{pmatrix}$	$\begin{pmatrix}0\\0\\\frac{1}{3}\\\frac{2}{3}\end{pmatrix}$
$(1,0,0,0,0)$	s_{11}	s_{12}	s_{13}	s_{14}	s_{15}
$(\frac{1}{3},\frac{2}{3},0,0,0)$	s_{21}	s_{22}	s_{23}	s_{24}	s_{25}
$(0,0,0,\frac{1}{4},\frac{3}{4})$	s_{31}	s_{32}	s_{33}	s_{34}	s_{35}
$(0,0,0,\frac{1}{4},\frac{3}{4})$	s_{41}	s_{42}	s_{43}	s_{44}	s_{45}

10.41 Suppose there are two players $N = \{I, II\}$, and four states of nature $S = \{s_{11}, s_{12}, s_{21}, s_{22}\}$. Player I's information is the first coordinate of the state of nature, and Player II's information is the second coordinate. The beliefs of each player, given his information, about the other player's type are given by the following tables:

	II_1	II_2
I_1	$\frac{1}{4}$	$\frac{3}{4}$
I_2	$\frac{4}{9}$	$\frac{5}{9}$

The beliefs of Player I

	II_1	II_2
I_1	$\frac{1}{5}$	$\frac{3}{8}$
I_2	$\frac{4}{5}$	$\frac{5}{8}$

The beliefs of Player II

(a) Find a belief space describing this situation.

(b) Is this belief space consistent? If so, describe this situation as an Aumann model of incomplete information.

10.42 Repeat Exercise 10.41 for the following beliefs of the players:

	II_1	II_2
I_1	$\frac{1}{4}$	$\frac{3}{4}$
I_2	$\frac{1}{5}$	$\frac{4}{5}$

The beliefs of Player I

	II_1	II_2
I_1	$\frac{2}{3}$	$\frac{1}{2}$
I_2	$\frac{1}{3}$	$\frac{1}{2}$

The beliefs of Player II

10.43 Calculate the minimal belief subspaces of the two players at each state of the world in Example 10.20 (page 410). Recall that when the set of states of the world is a topological space, a belief subspace is required to be a closed set (Remark 10.34).

10.44 Prove or disprove: There exists a belief space in which the set of states of the world contains K states, and there are $2^K - 1$ different belief subspaces (in other words, every subset of states of the world, except for the empty set, constitutes a belief subspace).

10.45 Prove or disprove: There exists a belief space comprised of three states of the world and six different belief subspaces.

10.46 Prove or disprove: There exists a belief space with $N = \{\mathrm{I}, \mathrm{II}\}$ and a finite set of states of the world containing a state of the world ω such that $\tilde{Y}_{\mathrm{I}}(\omega) \not\supseteq \tilde{Y}_{\mathrm{II}}(\omega)$ and $\tilde{Y}_{\mathrm{II}}(\omega) \not\supseteq \tilde{Y}_{\mathrm{I}}(\omega)$.

10.47 Prove or disprove: For each $\omega \in Y$, and each player $i \in N$, the set $\tilde{Y}_i(\omega) \cup \{\omega\}$ is a belief subspace.

10.48 Prove that every Harsanyi game with incomplete information (see Definition 9.39 on page 358) is a game with incomplete information according to Definition 10.37 on page 416.

10.49 Prove Theorem 10.40 (page 418): the strategy vector $\sigma^* = (\sigma_i^*)_{i \in N}$ is a Bayesian equilibrium if and only if for each player $i \in N$, each state of the world $\omega \in Y$, and each action $a_{i,\omega} \in A_i(\omega)$,

$$\gamma_i(\sigma^* \mid \omega) \geq \gamma_i((\sigma^*; a_{i,\omega}) \mid \omega). \tag{10.82}$$

10.50 In this exercise we show that for studying the set of Bayesian equilibria, one may assume that the action sets of the players are independent of the state of nature.
Let $G = (N, S, (A_i)_{i \in N}, \Pi)$ be a game with incomplete information such that the payoff functions $(u_i)_{i \in N}$ are uniformly bounded from below:

$$M := \inf_{i \in N} \inf_{s \in S} \inf_{a \in A(s)} u_i(s; a) > -\infty. \tag{10.83}$$

Let $\hat{G} = (N, S, (A_i)_{i \in N}, \Pi)$ be the game with incomplete information defined as follows:

- The action sets of the players are independent of the state of nature: $A_i(s) = A_i$ for every player $i \in N$ and every state of nature $s \in S$.
- For each player $i \in N$, the payoff function $\hat{u}_i$ is a real-valued function defined over the set $A = \times_{i \in N} A_i$ and given by

$$\hat{u}_i(s; a) = \begin{cases} u_i(s; a) & a \in A(s), \\ M & a_i \in A_i(s), a \notin A(s), \\ M - 1 & a_i \notin A_i(s), \end{cases} \tag{10.84}$$

where $A(s) = \times_{i \in N} A_i(s)$. In other words, if at least one player $j \neq i$ chooses an action that is not in $A_j(s)$, while player i chooses an action in $A_i(s)$, player i receives payoff M, and if player i chooses an action that is not in $A_i(s)$, he receives a payoff that is less than M.

Prove that the set of Bayesian equilibria of the game G coincides with the set of Bayesian equilibria of the game $\hat{G}$.

10.51 Prove that there exists a Bayesian equilibrium (in behavior strategies) in every game with incomplete information in which the set of players is finite, the number of types of each player is countable, the number of actions of each type is finite, and the payoff functions are uniformly bounded.

10.52 In this exercise we generalize Corollary 4.27 (page 105) to Bayesian equilibria. Suppose that for every player i in a game with incomplete information there exists a strategy σ_i^* that weakly dominates all his other strategies. Prove that the strategy vector $\sigma^* = (\sigma_i^*)_{i \in N}$ is a Bayesian equilibrium.

10.53 This exercise presents an alternative proof of Theorem 10.42 (page 421), regarding the existence of Bayesian equilibria in finite games.

Let $G = (N, S, (A_i)_{i \in N}, \Pi)$ be a game with incomplete information where the set of actions $(A_i)_{i \in N}$ is a finite set, and $\Pi = (Y, \mathcal{Y}, \mathfrak{s}, (\pi_i)_{i \in N})$ is a belief space with a finite set of states of the world Y. Define a strategic-form game Γ, where the set of players is N, the set of player i's pure strategies is the set of functions σ_i that map each type of player i to an available action for that type, and player i's payoff function w_i is given by

$$w_i(\sigma) = \sum_{\omega \in Y} \gamma_i(\sigma \mid \omega). \tag{10.85}$$

(a) Prove that the game Γ has a Nash equilibrium in mixed strategies.
(b) Deduce that the game Γ has a Nash equilibrium in behavior strategies.
(c) Prove that the set of Nash equilibria in behavior strategies of the game Γ coincides with the set of Bayesian equilibria of the game G.

10.54 In Example 10.45 (page 423), find a strategy for Player I that guarantees that Player II, of any type, is indifferent between L and R.

10.55 Find a Bayesian equilibrium in pure strategies in the following two-player game. Are there any additional Bayesian equilibria?

The set of states of nature is $S = \{s_1, s_2\}$, the set of players is $N = \{I, II\}$, and the belief space is given by:

State of the world	$\mathfrak{s}(\cdot)$	$\pi_1(\cdot)$	$\pi_2(\cdot)$
ω_1	s_1	$[1(\omega_1)]$	$[1(\omega_1)]$
ω_2	s_1	$[1(\omega_1)]$	$[\frac{1}{2}(\omega_2), \frac{1}{2}(\omega_3)]$
ω_3	s_2	$[1(\omega_4)]$	$[\frac{1}{2}(\omega_2), \frac{1}{2}(\omega_3)]$
ω_4	s_2	$[1(\omega_4)]$	$[1(\omega_4)]$

The state games are as follows:

	L	R
T	0, 0	0, 1
B	$-10, 0$	1, 1

State game s_1

	L	R
T	1, 2	$-10, 0$
B	0, 2	0, 0

State game s_2

10.56 Find a Bayesian equilibrium in the game appearing in Exercise 9.39 (page 388), when each player has a different prior, as follows. The prior distribution of Player I is

$$p_I(I_1, II_1) = 0.4, \quad p_I(I_1, II_2) = 0.1, \quad p_I(I_2, II_1) = 0.2, \quad p_I(I_2, II_2) = 0.3.$$

The prior distribution of Player II is

$$p_{\mathrm{II}}(I_1, II_1) = 0.3, \quad p_{\mathrm{II}}(I_1, II_2) = 0.2,$$
$$p_{\mathrm{II}}(I_2, II_1) = 0.25, \quad p_{\mathrm{II}}(I_2, II_2) = 0.25.$$

Assume that these prior distributions are common knowledge among the players.

10.57 Ronald and Jimmy are betting on the result of a coin toss. Ronald ascribes probability $\frac{1}{3}$ to the event that the coin shows heads, while Jimmy ascribes probability $\frac{3}{4}$ to that event. The betting rules are as follows: Each of the two players writes on a slip of paper "heads" or "tails," with neither player knowing what the other player is writing. After they are done writing, they show each other what they have written. If both players wrote heads, or both players wrote tails, each of them receives a payoff of 0. If they have made mutually conflicting predictions, they toss the coin. The player who has made the correct prediction regarding the result of the coin toss receives $1 from the player who has made the incorrect prediction. This description is common knowledge among the two players.

(a) Depict this situation as a game with incomplete information.
(b) Are the beliefs of Ronald and Jimmy consistent? Justify your answer.
(c) If you answered the above question positively, find the common prior.
(d) Find a Bayesian equilibrium in this game (whether or not the beliefs of the players are consistent).

10.58 Find a Bayesian equilibrium in the game appearing in Exercise 9.50 (page 392).

10.59 In Exercise 9.42 (page 389), suppose that the players' beliefs are:

- Marc thinks that the probability of every possible value is $\frac{1}{3}$, and he believes that this is common belief among him and Nicolas.
- Nicolas knows that Marc's beliefs are as described above, but he also knows that the true value of the company is 11.

Answer the following questions:

(a) Can this situation be described as a Harsanyi game with incomplete information (with a common prior)? Justify your answer.
(b) Find a Bayesian equilibrium of the game.

10.60 Find all the Bayesian equilibria of the following two-player game with incomplete information. The set of states of nature is $S = \{s_1, s_2, s_3\}$, the set of players is $N = \{I, II\}$, the set of states of the world is $Y = \{\omega_1, \omega_2, \omega_3\}$, and the belief space is:

State of the world	$s(\cdot)$	$\pi_I(\cdot)$	$\pi_{II}(\cdot)$
ω_1	s_1	$\left[\frac{1}{2}(\omega_1), \frac{1}{2}(\omega_2)\right]$	$[1(\omega_1)]$
ω_2	s_2	$\left[\frac{1}{2}(\omega_1), \frac{1}{2}(\omega_2)\right]$	$[1(\omega_1)]$
ω_3	s_3	$[1(\omega_3)]$	$[1(\omega_3)]$

The state games are as follows:

	L	R
T	4, 0	1, 1
B	1, 2	3, 0

State game s_1

	L	R
T	0, 3	1, 5
B	1, 0	0, 2

State game s_2

	L	R
T	0, 0	6, 4
B	7, 5	2, 3

State game s_3

10.61 A Cournot game with inconsistent beliefs Each of two manufacturers $i \in \{I, II\}$ must determine the quantity of a product x_i to be manufactured (in thousands of units) for sale in the coming month. The unit price of the manufactured products depends on the total quantities both manufacturers produce, and is given by $p = 2 - x_I - x_{II}$. Each manufacturer knows his own unit production cost, but does not know the unit production cost of his rival. The unit production cost of manufacturer i may be high ($c_i = \frac{5}{4}$) or low ($c_i = \frac{3}{4}$). Manufacturer i's profit is $x_i(p - c_i)$.

The first manufacturer ascribes probability $\frac{2}{3}$ to the second manufacturer's costs being high (and probability $\frac{1}{3}$ to the second manufacturer's costs being low). The second manufacturer ascribes probability $\frac{3}{4}$ to the costs of both manufacturers being equal to each other (and probability $\frac{1}{4}$ to their costs being different).

Answer the following questions:

(a) Describe this situation as a game with incomplete information.
(b) Prove that the beliefs of the manufacturers are inconsistent.
(c) Find all Bayesian equilibria in pure strategies in this game.

10.62 This exercise shows that when the players agree that every state of the world may obtain, the game is equivalent to a game with a common prior.

Let $G = (N, S, (A_i)_{i \in N}, \Pi)$ be a game with incomplete information, where $s = (N, (A_i(s))_{i \in N}, (u_i(s))_{i \in N})$ for every $s \in S$, $\Pi = (Y, \mathcal{Y}, \mathfrak{s}, (\pi_i)_{i \in N})$, the set of states of the world Y is finite, the set of states of nature S equals the set of states of the world, $S = Y$ with $\mathfrak{s}(\omega) = \omega$, and each player i has a prior distribution $\mathbf{P}_i$ whose support is Y, and a partition $\mathcal{F}_i$ of Y such that $\pi_i(\omega) = \mathbf{P}_i(\omega \mid F_i(\omega))$, for every player i and every state of the world ω.

Let $\mathbf{P}$ be a probability distribution over Y whose support is Y. For each $s \in S$ define a state game $\hat{s} := (N, (A_i(s))_{i \in N}, (\hat{u}_i(s))_{i \in N})$, where $\hat{u}_i(a; \omega) := \frac{\mathbf{P}_i(\omega)}{\mathbf{P}(\omega)} u_i(a; \omega)$. Let $\hat{S}$ be the collection of all state games $\hat{s}$ defined in this way. Let $\hat{G} = (N, \hat{S}, (A_i)_{i \in N}, \hat{\Pi})$ be a game with incomplete information, where $\hat{\mathfrak{s}}(\omega) = \hat{\mathfrak{s}}(\omega)$, $\hat{\Pi} = (Y, \mathcal{Y}, \hat{\mathfrak{s}}, (\hat{\pi}_i)_{i \in N})$, and for every player $i \in N$ and every $\omega \in Y$, $\hat{\pi}_i(\omega) := \mathbf{P}(\omega \mid F_i(\omega))$. In words, the game $\hat{G}$ has a common prior equal to $\mathbf{P}$. Each player i's payoff function at the state of the world ω is his payoff function in the game G multiplied by the ratio $\frac{\mathbf{P}_i(\omega)}{\mathbf{P}(\omega)}$.

Prove that the set of Bayesian equilibria of the game G coincides with the set of Bayesian equilibria of the game $\hat{G}$.

10.63 In this exercise, we relate the set of Bayesian equilibria in a game G with incomplete information to the set of Bayesian equilibria when we restrict the game to a belief subspace of the belief space of G.

Let $G = (N, S, (A_i)_{i \in N}, \Pi)$ be a game with incomplete information, where $\Pi = (Y, \mathcal{Y}, \mathfrak{s}, (\pi_i)_{i \in N})$ is a belief space with a finite set of states of the world Y, and let $\widetilde{\Pi} = (\widetilde{Y}, \widetilde{\mathcal{Y}}_{|\widetilde{Y}}, \mathfrak{s}, (\pi_i)_{i \in N})$ be a belief subspace of Π.

(a) Prove that $\widetilde{G} = (N, S, (A_i)_{i \in N}, \widetilde{\Pi})$ is a game with incomplete information.
(b) Let σ^* be a Bayesian equilibrium of G. Prove that $\sigma^*_{|\widetilde{Y}}$, the strategy vector σ^* restricted to the states of the world in $\widetilde{Y}$, is a Bayesian equilibrium of the game $\widetilde{G}$.
(c) Let $\widetilde{\sigma}$ be a Bayesian equilibrium of $\widetilde{G}$. Prove that if the action sets $(A_i)_{i \in N}$ are finite, then there exists a Bayesian equilibrium σ^* of G satisfying $\widetilde{\sigma}_i(\omega) = \sigma_i^*(\omega)$ for each player $i \in N$ and each state of the world $\omega \in \widetilde{Y}$.

10.64 Prove that the probability distribution defined by Equation (10.58) on page 425 is consistent over the belief space described in Remark 10.47.

10.65 Prove that for probability distributions p over Y whose support is a finite set in Equation (10.57) one may condition on the set $\{\omega' \in Y : \pi_i(\omega') = \pi_i(\omega)\}$ instead of $P_i(\omega)$.

10.66 Prove that, in Example 10.18 (page 407), Equation (10.57) (page 425) is satisfied for each event $A \subseteq Y$, for each player i, and for each $\omega \in Y$.

10.67 Prove that the two definitions of a consistent distribution, Definition 10.46 (page 425) and Definition 10.49 (page 427), are equivalent.

10.68 Prove that Equation (10.65) on page 427 is satisfied for Player II in Example 10.18 (page 407).

10.69 Verify that Equation (10.65) on page 427 is satisfied in Example 10.17 (page 406).

10.70 Prove Theorem 10.50 (page 431): if the set of states of the world is finite, and if p is a consistent distribution, then $\widetilde{Y} = \text{supp}(p)$ is a consistent belief subspace.

10.71 Let $\widetilde{Y}_1$ and $\widetilde{Y}_2$ be two consistent belief subspaces of the same belief space Π, and let p_1 and p_2 be consistent distributions over these two subspaces, respectively. Assume that the set of states of the world Y is finite. Prove that the set $\widetilde{Y}_1 \cup \widetilde{Y}_2$ is also a consistent belief subspace, and that for each $\lambda \in [0, 1]$ the probability distribution $\lambda p_1 + (1 - \lambda)p_2$ is consistent. In addition, if for each $i \in \{1, 2\}$ we expand p_i to a probability distribution over Y by setting $p_i(\omega) = 0$ for every $\omega \notin \widetilde{Y}_i$, then for every $\lambda \in [0, 1]$ the probability distribution $\lambda p_1 + (1 - \lambda)p_2$ is consistent.

10.72 Let Π be a consistent belief space, and let p be a consistent distribution. Let $\omega \in Y$ be a state of the world satisfying $p(\widetilde{Y}(\omega)) > 0$. Prove that the probability distribution p conditioned on the set $\widetilde{Y}(\omega)$ is consistent. Deduce that $\widetilde{Y}(\omega)$ is a consistent belief subspace.

10.73 Prove or disprove: Every finite belief space has a consistent belief subspace.

10.74 Prove or disprove: If $\tilde{Y}_i(\omega)$ is inconsistent for some player $i \in N$, then $\tilde{Y}(\omega)$ is also inconsistent.

10.75 Prove or disprove: If $\tilde{Y}_i(\omega)$ is inconsistent for every player $i \in N$, then $\tilde{Y}(\omega)$ is also inconsistent.

10.76 Prove or disprove: If $\tilde{Y}(\omega)$ is inconsistent, then there exists a player $i \in N$ for whom $\tilde{Y}_i(\omega)$ is inconsistent.

10.77 Provide an example of a belief space Π with three players, which contains a state of the world ω, such that the minimal belief subspaces of the players at ω are inconsistent, and differ from each other.

10.78 Provide an example of a belief space Π with three players, which contains a state of the world ω, such that the minimal belief subspaces of two of the players at ω are consistent and differ from each other, but the minimal belief space of the third player is inconsistent.

10.79 Prove that if $\tilde{Y}$ is a minimal consistent belief subspace, and $\tilde{Y}'$ is an inconsistent belief subspace, then $\tilde{Y} \cap \tilde{Y}' = \emptyset$. Does the claim hold without the condition that $\tilde{Y}$ is minimal?

10.80 In Example 10.27 on page 412, show that at the state of the world ω_2, the fact that the state of the world is consistent is common belief among the players.

10.81 Consider the following belief space, where the set of players is $N = \{I, II\}$, the set of states of nature is $S = \{s_1, s_2\}$, the set of states of the world is $Y = \{\omega_1, \omega_2, \omega_3\}$, and the beliefs of the players are given by the following table:

State of the world	$s(\cdot)$	$\pi_I(\cdot)$	$\pi_{II}(\cdot)$
ω_1	s_1	$\left[\frac{1}{2}(\omega_1), \frac{1}{2}(\omega_2)\right]$	$[1(\omega_1)]$
ω_2	s_1	$\left[\frac{1}{2}(\omega_1), \frac{1}{2}(\omega_2)\right]$	$[1(\omega_3)]$
ω_3	s_2	$[1(\omega_3)]$	$[1(\omega_3)]$

(a) Prove that the state of the world ω_3 is the only consistent state of the world in Y.

(b) Prove that at the state of the world ω_2, Player II believes that the state of the world is consistent.

(c) Prove that at the state of the world ω_1, both players believe that the state of the world is inconsistent.

(d) Prove that at the state of the world ω_1, the fact that the state of the world is inconsistent is not common belief among the players.

10.82 Find an example of a belief space, where the set of players is $N = \{I, II\}$, and there is a state of the world at which Player I believes that the state of the world is consistent, while Player II believes the state of the world is inconsistent.

10.83 At the state of the world ω, Player I believes that the state of the world is consistent, while Player II believes the state of the world is inconsistent. Is it possible that ω is a consistent state of the world? Justify your answer.

10.84 Prove or disprove: If it is common belief among the players at the state of the world ω that the state of the world is consistent, then $\tilde{Y}_i(\omega) = \tilde{Y}_j(\omega)$ for every pair of players $i, j \in N$.

10.85 Find an example of a belief space where the set of players consists of two players, and there exists an inconsistent state of the world ω at which $\pi_i(\{\omega\} \mid \omega) = 0$, and each player i believes that the state of the world is inconsistent.

10.86 Prove that if player i believes at the state of the world ω that the state of the world is consistent, then he believes that every player believes that the state of the world is consistent. Deduce that in this case player i believes that it is common belief that the state of the world is consistent.

10.87 Two buyers are participating in a first-price auction. Each of them has a private value, located in $[0, 1]$. With regards to each of the following belief situations, in which the two buyers have symmetric beliefs, answer the following questions:

- Ascertain whether the beliefs of the buyers are consistent. Prove your reply.
- Find a Bayesian equilibrium.

(a) The buyer whose private value is x believes:

- If $x \in [0, \frac{1}{2}]$, the buyer believes that the private value of the other buyer is given by the uniform distribution over $[0, \frac{1}{2}]$.
- If $x \in (\frac{1}{2}, 1]$, the buyer believes that the private value of the other buyer is given by the uniform distribution over $[\frac{1}{2}, 1]$.

(b) A buyer whose private value is x believes:

- If $x \in [0, \frac{1}{2}]$, the buyer believes that the private value of the other buyer is given by the uniform distribution over $[\frac{1}{2}, 1]$.
- If $x \in (\frac{1}{2}, 1]$, the buyer believes that the private value of the other buyer is given by the uniform distribution over $[0, \frac{1}{2}]$.

11

The universal belief space

Chapter summary

In this chapter we construct the *universal belief space*, which is a belief space that contains all possible situations of incomplete information of a given set of players over a certain set of states of nature. The construction is carried out in a straightforward way. Starting from a given set of states of nature S and a set of players N we construct, step by step, the space of all possible hierarchies of beliefs of the players in N. The space of all possible hierarchies of beliefs of each player is proved to be a well-defined compact set T, called the *universal type space*. It is then proved that a type of a player is a joint probability distribution over the set S and the types of the other players. Finally, the universal belief space Ω is defined as the Cartesian product of S with n copies of T; that is, an element of Ω, called the *state of the world*, consists of a state of nature and a list of types, one for each player.

Chapters 9 and 10 focused on models of incomplete information and their properties. A belief space Π with a set of players N on a set of states of nature S is given by a set of states of the world Y and, for each state of the world $\omega \in Y$, a corresponding state of nature $\mathfrak{s}(\omega) \in S$ and a belief $\pi_i(\omega) \in \Delta(Y)$ for each player $i \in N$. As we saw, the players' beliefs determine hierarchies of beliefs over the states of nature, that is, beliefs about the state of nature, beliefs about beliefs about the state of nature, beliefs about beliefs about beliefs about the state of nature, and so on (see Example 9.28 on page 345 for an Aumann model of incomplete information, Example 9.43 on page 361 for a Harsanyi model of incomplete information, and page 401 for a hierarchy of beliefs in a more general belief space). The players' hierarchies of beliefs are thus derived from the model of incomplete information, and they are not an element of the model.

In reality, when individuals analyze a situation with incomplete information they do not write down a belief space. They do, however, have hierarchies of beliefs over the state of nature: an investor ascribes a certain probability to the event "the interest rate next year will be 3%," he ascribes a possibly different probability to the event "the interest rate next year will be 3% and the other investor ascribes probability at least 0.7 to the interest rate next year being 3%," and he similarly ascribes probabilities to events that involve higher levels of beliefs. It therefore seems more natural to have the belief hierarchies as part of the data of the situation. In other words, we wish to describe a situation of incomplete information by the set of states of nature S and the players' belief hierarchies on S. Does such a description correspond to a belief space as defined in Chapter 10? This chapter is devoted to the affirmative answer of this question: starting from belief hierarchies we will construct the belief space that yields these belief hierarchies.

We will first define the concept of a belief hierarchy of a player, and construct a space $\Omega = \Omega(N, S)$ containing all possible hierarchies of beliefs of the set of players N about the set of states of nature S. We will then prove that this space is a belief space. This will imply that every belief space of the set of players N on the set of states of nature S is a belief subspace of the space Ω. That is why the space Ω will be called the *universal belief space*.

In constructing the universal belief space Ω, we will assume that the space of states of nature S is a compact set in a metric space. This assumption is satisfied, in particular, when S is a finite set, or when it is a closed and bounded set in a finite-dimensional Euclidean space.

Remark 11.1 *As we will now show, the assumption that the space of states of nature is compact is not a strong assumption. Suppose that the players in N are facing a strategic-form game in which the set of actions of player i is A_i, which may be a finite or an infinite set. We argue that under mild assumptions, such a game can be presented as a point in a compact subset of a metric space. Denote by $A = \times_{i \in N} A_i$ the set of action vectors. Assume that the preference relation of each player satisfies the von Neumann–Morgenstern axioms, and that each player has a most-preferred and a least-preferred outcome (see Section 2.6 for a generalization of the von Neumann–Morgenstern axioms to infinite sets of outcomes). It follows that the preference relation of each player i can be presented by a bounded linear utility function u_i. Since the utility function of every player is determined up to a positive affine transformation, we may suppose that the utility function of each player takes values in the range $[0, 1]$.*

As we saw in Chapters 9 and 10, a state of nature is a state game in strategic form that the players face. Suppose for now that the set of actions A_i of player i is common knowledge among the players. Then a state of nature is described by a vector of utility functions $(u_i)_{i \in N}$, i.e., by an element in $S := [0, 1]^A$: a list of payoff vectors for each action vector.

When the sets of actions are finite, the set S is compact, i.e., the set of states of nature is a compact set. When the sets of actions are compact (not necessarily finite), the set of states of nature is a compact set if we consider only state games in which the utility functions of all players are Lipschitz functions with a given constant. ◆

Recall that for every set X in a topological space, $\Delta(X)$ is the space of all probability distributions over X. We endow $\Delta(X)$ with the weak-∗ topology. In the weak-∗ topology, a sequence of distributions $(\mu^j)_{j \in \mathbb{N}}$ converges to a probability distribution μ if and only if for every continuous function $f : X \to \mathbb{R}$,

$$\lim_{j \to \infty} \int_X f(x) \mathrm{d}\mu^j(x) = \int_X f(x) \mathrm{d}\mu(x). \tag{11.1}$$

This topology is a metric topology: there exists a metric over the set $\Delta(X)$ satisfying the property that the collection of open sets in the weak-∗ topology is identical with the collection of open sets generated by open balls in this metric.

A fundamental property of this topology, which we will often make use of, is the following theorem, which follows from Riestz's representation theorem.

Theorem 11.2 *If X is a compact set in a metric space, then $\Delta(X)$ is a compact metric space (in the weak-$*$ topology).*

For the proof of this theorem, see Conway [1990], Theorem V.3.1 and Claim III.5.4. Further properties of this topology will be presented, as needed, in the course of the chapter.

11.1 Belief hierarchies

We begin by constructing all the belief spaces in the most direct and general possible way. A player's belief is described by a distribution over the parameter about which he is uncertain, i.e., over the state of nature. Denote by X_k the space of all belief hierarchies of order k. In particular, X_1 includes all the possible beliefs of a player about the states of nature; X_2 includes all possible beliefs of a player about the state of nature, and on the beliefs of the other players about the state of nature; X_3 includes all the beliefs of order 1 and 2 and the beliefs about the second-order beliefs of all the other players, etc.

Definition 11.3 *The space of belief hierarchies of order k of a set of players N on the set of states of nature S is the space X_k defined inductively as follows:*

$$X_1 := \Delta(S), \tag{11.2}$$

and for every $k \geq 2$,

$$\begin{aligned} X_k : &= X_{k-1} \times \Delta\left(S \times (X_{k-1})^{n-1}\right) \\ &= X_{k-1} \times \Delta(S \times \underbrace{X_{k-1} \times X_{k-1} \times \cdots \times X_{k-1}}_{n-1 \text{ times}}). \end{aligned} \tag{11.3}$$

An element $\mu_k \in X_k$ is called a belief of order k, *or a* belief hierarchy of order k.

Every probability distribution over S can be a first-order belief of a player in a game. A second-order belief (or hierarchy) is a first-order belief and a joint distribution over the set of states of nature and the first-order beliefs of the other players. In general, a $(k+1)$-order belief includes a belief of order k and a joint distribution over the vectors of length n composed of a state of nature and the $n-1$ beliefs of order k of the other players. Note that the joint distribution over $S \times (X_k)^{n-1}$ is not necessarily a product distribution. This means that a player can believe that there is a correlation between the beliefs of order k of the other players, and between those beliefs and the state of nature. This can happen, for example, if the player believes that one or more of the other players knows the state of nature, or if some other players have common information on the state of nature.

Since the first component of a $(k+1)$-order belief is a k-order belief, and the first component of a k-order belief is a $(k-1)$-order belief, and so on, a $(k+1)$-order belief defines the player's beliefs of order $1, 2, \ldots, k$. This is the reason that a $(k+1)$-order belief is also called a "belief hierarchy of order $k+1$."

Example 11.4   Suppose that there are two players $N = \{\text{Benjamin, George}\}$, and two states of nature $S = \{s_1, s_2\}$. The space of belief hierarchies of order 1 of every player is $X_1 = \Delta(S)$, and a first-order belief is of the form $[p_1(s_1), (1 - p_1)(s_2)]$: "I ascribe probability p_1 to the state of nature being s_1, and probability $1 - p_1$ to the state of nature being s_2." A second-order belief is an element in $X_2 = X_1 \times \Delta(S \times X_1)$, for example, "I ascribe probability p_2 to the state of nature being s_1, probability $1 - p_2$ to the state of nature being s_2 (an element of X_1), probability α_1 to the state of nature being s_1 and the belief of the second player on the state of nature being $[q_1(s_1), (1 - q_1)(s_2)]$, probability α_2 to the state of nature being s_1 and the belief of the second player on the state of nature being $[q_2(s_1), (1 - q_2)(s_2)]$, and probability $1 - \alpha_1 - \alpha_2$ to the state of nature being s_2 and the belief of the second player on the state of nature being $[q_3(s_1), (1 - q_3)(s_2)]$ (this is an element in $\Delta(S \times X_1)$).

Note that each of these beliefs can be those of either Benjamin or George: the belief spaces, at any order, of the players are identical." ◀

While the concept of a belief hierarchy is an intuitive one, the detailed mathematical description of a belief hierarchy may be extremely cumbersome. Despite this, we can prove mathematical properties of belief hierarchies that will eventually enable us to construct the universal belief space, which is the space of all possible belief hierarchies.

Theorem 11.5   *For each $k \in \mathbb{N}$, the set X_k is a compact set in a metric space.*

Proof: The theorem is proved by induction on k. Because S is a compact set in a metric space, Theorem 11.2 implies that $X_1 = \Delta(S)$ is also a compact set in a metric space.

Let $k \geq 1$, and suppose by induction that X_k is a compact set. It follows that the set $S \times (X_k)^{n-1}$ is also compact, as the Cartesian product of compact sets in metric spaces. By Theorem 11.2 again, the set $\Delta(S \times (X_k)^{n-1})$ is a compact subset of a metric space in the weak-$*$ topology. We deduce that the set $X_{k+1} = X_k \times \Delta(S \times (X_k)^{n-1})$ as the Cartesian product of two compact sets in metric spaces is also a compact set in a metric space. □

A k-order belief of a player is an element of X_k. Can every element in X_k be an "acceptable" belief of a player? The answer to this question is negative.

Example 11.4   (*Continued*) In this example, where $N = \{\text{Benjamin, George}\}$ and $S = \{s_1, s_2\}$, an element in X_1 is of the form $[p_1(s_1), (1 - p_1)(s_2)]$, and every such element is an "acceptable" first-order belief of a player. We will show, however, that not every second-order belief is "acceptable."

A second-order belief of a player is a pair $\mu_2 = (\mu_1, \nu_1)$, where μ_1 is a first-order belief of the player, and ν_1 is a probability distribution over $S \times X_1$. In other words, ν_1 is a probability distribution over vectors of the form (s, ρ), where s is a state of nature, and ρ is a first-order belief of the other player.

Above, we gave an example of a second-order belief of a player where:

- The first-order belief is $\mu_1 = [p_2(s_1), (1 - p_2)(s_2)]$.
- The distribution ν_1 ascribes probability α_1 to the state of nature being s_1 and the first-order belief of the second player being $[q_1(s_1), (1 - q_1)(s_2)]$.
- The distribution ν_1 ascribes probability α_2 to the state of nature being s_1 and the first-order belief of the second player being $[q_2(s_1), (1 - q_2)(s_2)]$.
- The distribution ν_1 ascribes probability $1 - \alpha_1 - \alpha_2$ to the state of nature being s_2 and the first-order belief of the second player being $[q_3(s_1), (1 - q_3)(s_2)]$.

If a player's belief is "acceptable," we expect the player to be able to answer the question "what is the probability you ascribe to the state of nature being s_1?" When the second-order belief of the player is $\mu_2 = (\mu_1, v_1)$, he can answer this question in two different ways. On the one hand, μ_1 is a first-order belief; i.e., it is a probability distribution over S, so that the answer to our question is the probability that μ_1 ascribes to s_1. In the example above, that answer is p_2. On the other hand, v_1 is a probability distribution over $S \times X_1$, so that the answer to our question is the probability that the marginal distribution of v_1 over S ascribes to s_1. In the above example, that answer is $\alpha_1 + \alpha_2$. For the probability that the player ascribes to the state of nature s_1 to be well defined, we must require that $p_2 = \alpha_1 + \alpha_2$. In general, for a second-order belief of a player to be "acceptable," the marginal distribution of v_1 over S must coincide with μ_1, which is also a probability distribution over S.

Note that according to the player's second-order belief, the probability that the other player ascribes to the state of nature being s_1 is $\alpha_1 q_1 + \alpha_2 q_2 + (1 - \alpha_1 - \alpha_2)q_3$. It follows that even if the player's belief is "acceptable," i.e., if $p_2 = \alpha_1 + \alpha_2$, if $\alpha_1 q_1 + \alpha_2 q_2 + (1 - \alpha_1 - \alpha_2)q_3 \neq p_2$, then the player believes that the other player ascribes a probability to the state of nature being s_1 that is different from the probability that he himself ascribes to that event. Thus, the inequality $\alpha_1 q_1 + \alpha_2 q_2 + (1 - \alpha_1 - \alpha_2)q_3 \neq p_2$ does not mean that the player's belief is unacceptable, because the player may believe that the other player does not agree with him.   ◀

The condition $p_2 = \alpha_1 + \alpha_2$, which emerged in the above discussion, is a mathematical condition constraining the distributions that comprise a belief hierarchy. Its purpose is to ensure that the beliefs in a belief hierarchy do not contradict each other. This condition is called the *coherency condition*. To define the coherency condition precisely, denote by μ_{k+1} a belief hierarchy of order $k + 1$, i.e., an element in X_{k+1}, for every $k \geq 0$. We will present conditions that ensure that such a hierarchy is coherent.

Since by the inductive definition (Definition 11.3) an element of X_{k+1} is $\mu_{k+1} \in X_k \times \Delta(S \times (X_k)^{n-1})$, we write $\mu_{k+1} = (\mu_k, v_k)$, where $\mu_k \in X_k$ and $v_k \in \Delta(S \times X_k^{n-1})$. We similarly write $\mu_k = (\mu_{k-1}, v_{k-1})$, where $\mu_{k-1} \in X_{k-1}$ and $v_{k-1} \in \Delta(S \times (X_{k-1})^{n-1})$. Note that[1]

$$v_k \in \Delta\big(S \times (X_k)^{n-1}\big) = \Delta\big(S \times (X_{k-1} \times \Delta(S \times (X_{k-1})^{n-1}))^{n-1}\big)$$
$$= \Delta\big(S \times (X_{k-1})^{n-1} \times (\Delta(S \times (X_{k-1})^{n-1}))^{n-1}\big). \qquad (11.4)$$

The marginal distribution of v_k over $S \times (X_{k-1})^{n-1}$ is the player's belief about the $(k-1)$-order beliefs of the other players. For μ_{k+1} to be coherent, we require the marginal distribution of v_k over $S \times (X_{k-1})^{n-1}$ to be equal to the probability distribution v_{k-1} over $S \times (X_{k-1})^{n-1}$, which comprises part of μ_k. We also require that the players believe that the beliefs of the other players are coherent: v_k must ascribe probability 1 to the event that the lower-order beliefs of the other players are also coherent. These conditions together lead to the following inductive definition of Z_k, the set of all coherent belief hierarchies of order k (for each $k \in \mathbb{N}$).

---

1 The spaces $(S \times (X_{k-1})^{n-1})^{n-1}$ and $S \times (X_{k-1})^{n-1} \times \left(\Delta(S \times (X_{k-1})^{n-1})\right)^{n-1}$ in Equation (11.4) differ from each other in the order of the coordinates. Here and in the sequel we will relate to these spaces as if they were identical, identifying the corresponding coordinates in the two spaces.

Definition 11.6 *For each $k \in \mathbb{N}$, the space of coherent belief hierarchies of order k is the space Z_k defined inductively as follows:*

$$Z_1 := X_1 = \Delta(S), \tag{11.5}$$

$$Z_2 := \{\mu_2 = (\mu_1, \nu_1) \in Z_1 \times \Delta(S \times (Z_1)^{n-1}): \tag{11.6}$$

the marginal distribution of ν_1 over S equals μ_1}.

For each $k \geq 2$,

$$Z_{k+1} := \{\mu_{k+1} = (\mu_k, \nu_k) \in Z_k \times \Delta(S \times (Z_k)^{n-1}):$$

the marginal distribution of ν_k over $S \times (Z_{k-1})^{n-1}$ equals ν_{k-1} where $\mu_k = (\mu_{k-1}, \nu_{k-1})$}.

$$\tag{11.7}$$

An element in the set Z_k is called a coherent belief hierarchy of order k.

In words, every belief of order 1 of a player is coherent; a second-order belief hierarchy $\mu_2 = (\mu_1, \nu_1)$ is a coherent belief hierarchy if the marginal distribution of ν_1 over S equals μ_1; for $k \geq 2$, a $(k+1)$-order belief hierarchy $\mu_{k+1} = (\mu_k, \nu_k)$ is a coherent belief hierarchy of order $k + 1$ if:

- $\mu_k = (\mu_{k-1}, \nu_{k-1})$ is a coherent belief hierarchy of order k.
- ν_k is a probability distribution over $S \times (Z_k)^{n-1}$.
- The marginal distribution of ν_k over $S \times (X_{k-1})^{n-1}$ equals ν_{k-1}.

One can prove by induction that $Z_k \subseteq X_k$: every coherent belief hierarchy is a belief hierarchy (Exercise 11.3). As mentioned before, the coherency condition requires the beliefs of a player to be well defined. If the coherency condition is not met, then, for example, the probability that the player ascribes to event A may be $\frac{1}{3}$ according to his k-order belief, and $\frac{2}{5}$ according to his l-order belief. This is, of course, meaningless: the mathematical structure must reflect the intuition that the question "What is the probability that the player ascribes to an event A?" has an unequivocal answer. To understand the content of the coherency condition, note that a belief hierarchy of order k of any player defines a belief hierarchy for all orders l less than k for that player. Indeed, $\mu_k = (\mu_{k-1}, \nu_{k-1})$, where $\mu_{k-1} \in Z_{k-1}$ is the player's belief hierarchy of order $k - 1$ and $\nu_{k-1} \in \Delta(S \times (Z_{k-1})^{n-1})$ is that player's belief on the states of nature and on the belief hierarchies of order $k - 1$ of the other players. Similarly, $\mu_{k-1} = (\mu_{k-2}, \nu_{k-2})$, where $\mu_{k-2} \in Z_{k-2}$ is the players' belief hierarchy of order $k - 2$ and $\nu_{k-2} \in \Delta(S \times (Z_{k-2})^{n-1})$ is that player's belief about the states of nature and about the belief hierarchies of order $k - 2$ of the other players. Continuing in this way, we arrive at the conclusion that in effect a belief hierarchy of order k is equivalent to a vector

$$\mu_k = (\mu_1; \nu_1, \nu_2, \ldots, \nu_{k-1}), \quad k \geq 2, \tag{11.8}$$

where μ_1 is the player's belief about the state of nature, and $\nu_l \in \Delta(S \times (Z_l)^{n-1})$ is a probability distribution over the states of nature and the belief hierarchies of order l of the other players, for all $2 \leq l < k$. As the next theorem states, the coherency condition guarantees that all of these distributions "agree" with each other. The proof of the theorem is left to the reader (Exercise 11.6).

Theorem 11.7 *Let $\mu_k = (\mu_1; v_1, v_2, \ldots, v_{k-1}) \in Z_k$ be a coherent belief hierarchy of order k, and let l_1, l_2 be integers satisfying $1 \le l_1 \le l_2 \le k$. Then:*

1. *The marginal distribution of v_{l_1} over S equals μ_1.*
2. *The marginal distribution of v_{l_2} over $S \times (Z_{l_1})^{n-1}$ is v_{l_1}.*

The following theorem is a reformulation of Definition 11.6, and it details which pairs (μ_k, v_k) form coherent beliefs of order $k + 1$.

Theorem 11.8 *Let $\mu_k = (\mu_1; v_1, v_2, \ldots, v_{k-1}) \in Z_k$ be a coherent belief hierarchy of order k, and let $v_k \in \Delta(S \times (X_k)^{n-1})$. The pair (μ_k, v_k) is a coherent belief hierarchy of order $k + 1$ if and only if the following conditions are met:*

- v_k *ascribes probability 1 to $S \times (Z_k)^{n-1}$.*
- *For $k = 1$, the marginal distribution of v_1 over S is μ_1.*
- *For $k > 1$, the marginal distribution of v_k over $S \times (X_{k-1})^{n-1}$ equals v_{k-1}, where $\mu_k = (\mu_{k-1}, v_{k-1})$.*

From Theorem 11.8 it follows that if the belief of player i is coherent, then for every finite sequence of players $i_1, i_2, \ldots, i_l$, player i believes (ascribes probability 1) to i_1 believing that player i_2 believes ... that the belief hierarchy of order $k - l$ of player i_l is coherent.

Example 11.9 In this example we present a situation of incomplete information and write down the belief hierarchy of one of the players. Phil wonders what the color of the famous Shwezigon Pagoda in Burma is, and whether his brother Don knows what it is. The states of nature are the possible colors of the pagoda: s_b (blue), s_g (gold), s_p (purple), s_r (red), s_w (white), and so on. Phil does not know the color of the pagoda; he ascribes probability $\frac{1}{3}$ to the pagoda being red and probability $\frac{2}{3}$ to its being gold. Phil's first-order belief is therefore

$$\mu_1 = \left[\tfrac{1}{3}(s_r), \tfrac{2}{3}(s_g)\right] \in \Delta(S). \tag{11.9}$$

Phil also believes that if the pagoda is red, then Don ascribes probability $\frac{1}{2}$ to the pagoda being red and probability $\frac{1}{2}$ to its being blue. He also believes that if the pagoda is gold then Don ascribes probability 1 to its being gold. Phil's second-order belief is $\mu_2 = (\mu_1, v_1)$ where μ_1 is given by Equation (11.9) and

$$v_1 = \left[\tfrac{1}{3}\left(s_r, \left[\tfrac{1}{2}(s_r), \tfrac{1}{2}(s_b)\right]\right), \tfrac{2}{3}\left(s_g, 1[s_g]\right)\right] \in \Delta(S \times Z_1). \tag{11.10}$$

In addition, Phil believes that if the pagoda is red, then the following conditions are met:

- Don ascribes probability $\frac{1}{2}$ to "the pagoda is red, and Phil believes that the pagoda is purple."
- Don ascribes probability $\frac{1}{2}$ to "the pagoda is blue, and Phil believes that the pagoda is red."

Phil also believes that if the pagoda is gold, then Don ascribes probability 1 to "the pagoda is gold, and Phil ascribes probability 1 to the pagoda being white." Phil's third-order belief is $\mu_3 = (\mu_2, v_2)$ with μ_2 as defined above and

$$v_2 = \left[\tfrac{1}{3}\left(s_r, \left[\tfrac{1}{2}(s_r), \tfrac{1}{2}(s_b)\right], \left[\tfrac{1}{2}(s_r, [1(s_p)]), \tfrac{1}{2}(s_b, [1(s_r)])\right]\right), \tfrac{2}{3}(s_g, [1(s_g)], [1(s_g, [1(s_w)])])\right].$$

$$\tag{11.11}$$

v_2 is Phil's belief about Don's belief. In Equation (11.11), we see that Phil believes that if the state of nature is s_r, then Don's first-order belief is $[\frac{1}{2}(s_r), \frac{1}{2}(s_b)]$ and Don's second-order belief is $([\frac{1}{2}(s_r), \frac{1}{2}(s_b)], [\frac{1}{2}(s_r, [1(s_p)]), \frac{1}{2}(s_b, [1(s_r)])])$. Phil also believes that if the state of nature is s_g, then Don's first-order belief is $[1(s_g)]$ and Don's second-order belief is $([1(s_g)], [1(s_g, [1(s_w)])])$.

We can now check the meaning of the coherence condition in this example. First, Phil's belief is coherent:

- The marginal distribution of v_1 over S is μ_1.
- The projection of v_2 on $S \times Z_1$ is v_1.

Second, Phil believes that Don's belief is coherent. Indeed, the second-order belief that Phil ascribes to Don is coherent in both the states of nature s_r and s_g. Note that Phil indeed has beliefs about Don's beliefs, but Don's true beliefs are not expressed in Phil's belief about Don's beliefs; the latter may in fact differ from Phil's beliefs about Don's beliefs.   ◀

Does there exist a coherent belief hierarchy of order k for every k? Can every coherent belief hierarchy of order k be extended to a coherent belief hierarchy of order $k + 1$; in other words, given a coherent belief hierarchy μ_k of order k, can we find a coherent belief hierarchy μ_{k+1} of order $k + 1$ such that $\mu_{k+1} = (\mu_k, v_k)$? The answer to these questions is yes. With respect to the first question, if $s_0 \in S$ is a given state of nature, then the following sentence defines a coherent belief hierarchy order k (Exercise 11.7): "I ascribe probability 1 to the state of nature being s_0, I ascribe probability 1 to the other players ascribing probability 1 to the state of nature being s_0, I ascribe probability 1 to each of the other players ascribing probability 1 to each of the other players ascribing probability 1 to the state of nature being s_0, and so on, up to level k."

The proof that every coherent belief hierarchy of order k can be extended to a coherent belief hierarchy of order $k + 1$ is more complicated, and we will present it next. We start by showing that for every k, the set Z_k is compact.

Theorem 11.10 *For each $k \in \mathbb{N}$, the set Z_k is compact in X_k.*

Proof: The theorem is proved by induction on k. Start with $k = 1$. By definition, $Z_1 = \Delta(S)$, which is a compact set in a metric space (see the proof of Theorem 11.5).

Let $k \geq 1$, and suppose by induction that Z_k is a compact set in X_k. Since the set X_{k+1} is compact in a metric space (Theorem 11.5), to prove that Z_{k+1} is a compact set in X_{k+1} it suffices to prove that the set Z_{k+1} is a closed set. To this end we need to show that the limit of every convergent sequence of points in Z_{k+1} is also in Z_{k+1}. This follows from the following two well-known facts regarding the weak-* topology:

- Let $(\mu_n)_{n \in \mathbb{N}}$ be a sequence of probability distributions over a space X, which converges in the weak-* topology to a probability distribution μ, and satisfies, for a compact set $T \subseteq X$, the condition $\mu_n(T) = 1$ for all $n \in \mathbb{N}$. Then $\mu(T) = 1$ (this follows from Theorem 2.1 in Billingsley [1999]).
- Let $(\mu_n)_{n \in \mathbb{N}}$ be a sequence of probability distributions over a product space $X \times Y$ converging in the weak-* topology to a probability distribution μ. Denote by v^j the marginal distribution of μ^j over X, and by v the marginal distribution of μ over X. Then the sequence $(v_n)_{n \in \mathbb{N}}$ converges in the weak-* topology to v (see Theorem 2.8 in Billingsley [1999]).

Indeed, let $(\mu_{k+1}^j)_{j\in\mathbb{N}}$ be a sequence of points in Z_{k+1} converging to the limit μ_{k+1} in X_{k+1}. Denote $\mu_{k+1}^j = (\mu_k^j, \nu_k^j)$ and $\mu_{k+1} = (\mu_k, \nu_k)$. By Equation (11.8), μ_{k+1}^j ascribes probability 1 to $S \times (Z_k)^{n-1}$, and the marginal probability distribution of ν_k^j over $S \times (Z_k)^{n-1}$ is ν_{k-1}^j. By the two above-mentioned facts, these two properties also hold for the limits μ_k and ν_k. By Theorem 11.8, we deduce that $\mu_{k+1} \in Z_{k+1}$, which is what we needed to show. $\square$

We are now ready to prove that every coherent belief hierarchy $\mu_k \in Z_k$ of order k can be extended to a coherent belief hierarchy $\mu_{k+1} = (\mu_k, \nu_k) \in Z_{k+1}$. Since the set Z_1 is nonempty, it will follow from this in particular that for any $k \in \mathbb{N}$ the set Z_k is nonempty.

Theorem 11.11 *For any $k \in \mathbb{N}$ and every coherent belief hierarchy μ_k of order k there exists $\nu_k \in \Delta(S \times (Z_k)^{n-1})$ such that the pair (μ_k, ν_k) is a coherent belief hierarchy of order $k + 1$.*

We will in effect be proving that there exists a continuous function $h_k : Z_k \to \Delta(S \times (Z_k)^{n-1})$ such that $(\mu_k, h_k(\mu_k)) \in Z_{k+1}$ for every $\mu_k \in Z_k$. If we define a function $f_k : Z_k \to Z_{k+1}$ by

$$f_k(\mu_k) = (\mu_k, h_k(\mu_k)), \tag{11.12}$$

the function f_k will be a continuous function associating every coherent belief hierarchy of order k with a coherent belief hierarchy of order $k + 1$, such that the projection of f_k to the first coordinate is the identity function.

Proof: We prove the existence of the continuous function h_k by induction on k. We start with the case $k = 1$. Let $s_1 \in S$ be a state of nature. The distribution $[1(s_1)] \in \Delta(S)$ is a first-order belief hierarchy in which the player ascribes probability 1 to s_1. For each $\mu_1 \in Z_1 = \Delta(S)$, consider the product[2] distribution $\nu_1 := \mu_1 \otimes [1(s_1)]^{n-1}$ over $S \times (Z_1)^{n-1}$. The pair $\mu_2 := (\mu_1, \nu_1)$ is a second-order belief hierarchy: the player believes that the probability distribution of the state of nature is μ_1, and that each of the other players ascribes probability 1 to the state of nature being s_1.

Define a function $h_1 : Z_1 \to \Delta(S \times (Z_1)^{n-1})$ as follows:

$$h_1(\mu_1) := \mu_1 \otimes [1(s_1)]^{n-1}. \tag{11.13}$$

As we saw earlier, the pair $(\mu_1, h_1(\mu_1))$ is a coherent second-order belief hierarchy. Moreover, the function h_1 is continuous (why?). We have thus completed the proof for the case $k = 1$.

Suppose by induction that there exists a continuous function $h_k : Z_k \to \Delta(S \times (Z_k)^{n-1})$ satisfying $(\mu_k, h_k(\mu_k)) \in Z_{k+1}$ for all $\mu_k \in Z_k$. By Equation (11.12) this function defines a function $f_k : Z_k \to Z_{k+1}$. We now proceed to construct the function h_{k+1}.

---

2 When $\mu_1 \in \Delta(X_1)$ and $\mu_2 \in \Delta(X_2)$ are two probability distributions, the product distribution $\mu_1 \otimes \mu_2 \in \Delta(X_1 \times X_2)$ is the unique probability distribution over $X_1 \times X_2$ that satisfies $(\mu_1 \otimes \mu_2)(A_1 \times A_2) = \mu_1(A_1) \cdot \mu_2(A_2)$ for every pair of measurable sets A_1 in X_1 and A_2 in X_2.

For every $k \in \mathbb{N}$ set $Y_k := S \times (Z_k)^{n-1}$. For every coherent belief hierarchy of order $k+1$, $\mu_{k+1} = (\mu_k, \nu_k)$, the component ν_k is a probability distribution over $S \times (Z_k)^{n-1} = Y_k$. Note that

$$Y_{k+1} = S \times (Z_{k+1})^{n-1} \subseteq S \times (Z_k \times \Delta(S \times (Z_k)^{n-1}))^{n-1}$$

$$= S \times (Z_k)^{n-1} \times (\Delta(S \times (Z_k)^{n-1}))^{n-1} = Y_k \times (\Delta(Y_k))^{n-1}. \quad (11.14)$$

We will denote an element of Y_k by $(s, (\mu_{kj})_{j=1}^{n-1})$, where $\mu_{kj} \in Z_k$ for all $j = 1, 2, \ldots, n-1$. Using Equation (11.12), changing the order of the coordinates yields

$$\left(s, (f_k(\mu_{kj}))_{j=1}^{n-1}\right) = \left(s, (\mu_{kj}, h_k(\mu_{kj}))_{j=1}^{n-1}\right) = \left(s, (\mu_{kj})_{j=1}^{n-1}, (h_k(\mu_{kj}))_{j=1}^{n-1}\right); \quad (11.15)$$

i.e., the projection of $(s, (f_k(\mu_{kj}))_{j=1}^{n-1})$ on Y_k is $(s, (\mu_{kj})_{j=1}^{n-1})$.

For every measurable set $A \subseteq Y_k$, define a set $F_k(A) \subseteq Y_{k+1}$ as follows:

$$F_k(A) := \left\{\left(s, (f_k(\mu_{kj}))_{j=1}^{n-1}\right) : \left(s, (\mu_{kj})_{j=1}^{n-1}\right) \in A\right\} \subseteq Y_{k+1}. \quad (11.16)$$

This set includes all the coherent belief hierarchy vectors of order $k+1$ of the other players derived by expanding the coherent belief hierarchy vectors of order k contained in A by using f_k. By the induction assumption, $F_k(A)$ is not empty when $A \neq \emptyset$ (because $(s, (f_k(\mu_{kj})_{j=1}^{n-1})) \in F_k(A)$ for every $\mu_k \in A$) and is contained in $S \times (Z_{k+1})^{n-1}$.

Consider next the inverse function of F_k: for every measurable set $B \subseteq Y_{k+1}$ define

$$F_k^{-1}(B) := \left\{\left(s, (\mu_{kj})_{j=1}^{n-1}\right) : \left(s, (f_k(\mu_{kj})_{j=1}^{n-1})\right) \in B\right\} \subseteq Y_k. \quad (11.17)$$

This is the set of all elements of Y_k that are mapped by f_k to the elements of B. Since the function f_k is continuous, it is in particular a measurable function, and therefore the set $F_k^{-1}(B)$ is also measurable.[3] We next define an element $\nu_{k+1} \in \Delta(Y_{k+1})$ as follows: for every measurable set $B \subseteq Y_{k+1}$,

$$\nu_{k+1}(B) := \nu_k(F_k^{-1}(B)). \quad (11.18)$$

Define the function $h_{k+1} : Z_{k+1} \to \Delta(Y_{k+1})$ by

$$h_{k+1}(\mu_{k+1}) := \nu_{k+1}. \quad (11.19)$$

The probability distribution ν_{k+1} is a distribution over Y_{k+1}. By Equation (11.14), ν_{k+1} is also a probability distribution over the set $Y_k \times (\Delta(Y_k))^{n-1}$ whose support is Y_{k+1}. We need to check that the marginal distribution of ν_{k+1} over Y_k is ν_k. To do so, we consider a measurable set $A \subseteq Y_k$ and check that

$$\nu_{k+1}(A \times (\Delta(Y_k))^{n-1}) = \nu_k(A). \quad (11.20)$$

Now,

$$\nu_{k+1}(A \times (\Delta(Y_k))^{n-1}) = \nu_k(F_k^{-1}(A \times (\Delta(Y_k))^{n-1})) \quad (11.21)$$

$$= \nu_k\left(\left\{\left(s, (\mu_{kj})_{j=1}^{n-1}\right) : \left(s, f_k(\mu_{kj})_{j=1}^{n-1}\right) \in A \times (\Delta(Y_k))^{n-1}\right\}\right) \quad (11.22)$$

$$= \nu_k(A). \quad (11.23)$$

---

3 To show that the set $F_k^{-1}(B)$ is measurable, it suffices to show that the function f_k is a measurable function. We choose to show that this function is continuous because it is easier to do so than to show directly that it is measurable.

Finally, we show that h_{k+1} is a continuous function. Let $(\mu_{k+1}^l)_{l\in\mathbb{N}}$ be a sequence of probability distributions over Y_k converging to the limit μ_{k+1} in the weak-$*$ topology. Denote $v_{k+1}^l := h_{k+1}(\mu_{k+1}^l)$ and $v_{k+1} = h_{k+1}(\mu_{k+1})$. We need to show that for every continuous function $g: Y_{k+1} \to \mathbb{R}$,

$$\lim_{l\to\infty} \int_{S\times(Z_{k+1})^{n-1}} g\big(s, (\tilde{\mu}_{k+1,j})_{j=1}^{n-1}\big) \mathrm{d}v_{k+1}^l\big(s, (\tilde{\mu}_{k+1,j})_{j=1}^{n-1}\big)$$

$$= \int_{S\times(Z_{k+1})^{n-1}} g\big(s, (\tilde{\mu}_{k+1,j})_{j=1}^{n-1}\big) \mathrm{d}v_{k+1}\big(s, (\tilde{\mu}_{k+1,j})_{j=1}^{n-1}\big). \qquad (11.24)$$

This follows directly from $\mu_{k+1} = f_k(\mu_k)$, along with the fact that if g and f_k are continuous functions then the composition $g(s, (f(\mu_{k,j}))_{j=1}^{n-1})$ is a continuous function, where $\mu_{k+1,j} = (\mu_{k,j}, v_{k,j})$. $\square$

11.2 Types

The sequence $(Z_k)_{k=1}^{\infty}$ of the spaces of coherent belief hierarchies has a special structure. Define a projection $\rho: Z_{k+1} \to Z_k$ as follows: if $\mu_{k+1} = (\mu_k, v_k) \in Z_{k+1}$, then $\rho(\mu_{k+1}) := \mu_k$. Theorem 11.11 implies that $\rho(Z_{k+1}) = Z_k$. Such a structure is called a *projective structure*, and it enables us to define the projective limit as follows.

Definition 11.12 The projective limit[4] *of the sequence of the spaces $(Z_k)_{k=1}^{\infty}$ is the space T of all the sequences $(\mu_1, \mu_2, \ldots) \in \times_{k=1}^{\infty} Z_k$, where for every $k \in \mathbb{N}$ the belief hierarchy $\mu_k \in Z_k$ is the projection of the belief hierarchy $\mu_{k+1} \in Z_{k+1}$ on Z_k. In other words, there exists a distribution $v_k \in \Delta(S \times Z_k^{n-1})$ such that $\mu_{k+1} = (\mu_k, v_k)$. The projective limit T is called the* universal type space.

An element in the universal type space is a sequence of finite belief hierarchies, satisfying the condition that for each k, the belief hierarchy of order $k+1$ is an extension of the belief hierarchy of order k. Such an element is called a *type*, a term due to Harsanyi.

Definition 11.13 *An element $t = (\mu_1, \mu_2, \ldots) \in T$ is called a* type.

A player's type is sometimes called his "state of mind," since it contains answers to all questions regarding the player's beliefs (of any order) about the state of nature. A player's belief hierarchy defines his beliefs to all orders: his beliefs about the state of nature, his beliefs about the beliefs of the other players, his beliefs about their second-order beliefs, and so on. We assume that a player's type is all the relevant information that the player has about the situation, and in what follows we will relate to a type as all the information in a player's possession.

Let $t = (\mu_1, \mu_2, \ldots)$ be a player's type. Since the distribution μ_k is a coherent belief hierarchy of order k, as previously noted, it follows that for every list of players $i_1, i_2, \ldots, i_l$, the player believes that player i_1 believes that player i_2 believes that ... believes that player i_l's belief hierarchy of order $k - l$ is coherent. Since for every $k \in \mathbb{N}$,

---

4 The projective limit is also called the *inverse limit*. This definition is a special case of the more general definition of the projective limit of an infinite sequence of spaces on which a projective operator is defined, from which the name "projective limit" is derived.

the first component of μ_{k+1} is μ_k, a player of type t believes that the fact that "the players' beliefs are coherent" is common belief among the players (Definition 10.9 on page 403).

As the following example shows, when the set of players contains only one player, and there are two states of nature, the universal type space can be simply described. This observation is extended to any finite set of states of nature in Exercise 11.9.

Example 11.14 In this example, we will construct the universal type space when there is one player, $N = \{I\}$, and two states of nature, $S = \{s_1, s_2\}$. By definition,

$$X_1 = \Delta(S), \tag{11.25}$$

$$X_k = \Delta(S)^{k-1} \times \Delta(S) = (\Delta(S))^k, \quad \forall k \geq 2. \tag{11.26}$$

The coherency condition implies that the player's type (there is only one player here) is entirely determined by his first-order beliefs. The universal type space in this case is homeomorphic to the set $[0, 1]$: for every $p \in [0, 1]$, the element t_p corresponds to the type ascribing probability p to the state of nature s_1, and probability $1 - p$ to the state of nature s_2.   ◀

When the set of players contains two or more players, the mathematical structure of the universal type space is far more complicated, because in that case a second-order belief hierarchy is a distribution over distributions, a third-order belief hierarchy is a distribution over distributions over distributions, and so on. The only way to analyze universal type spaces tractably requires simplifying their mathematical description. We will therefore consider several mathematical properties of the universal type space T that will be useful towards that end. Since a type is an element of the product space $\times_{k=1}^{\infty} Z_k$, a natural topology over the universal type space, which we will use, is the topology induced by the product topology on this space.

Theorem 11.15 *The universal type space T is a compact space.*

Proof: As previously stated, every coherent belief hierarchy μ_k of order k uniquely defines an element

$$(\mu_1, \mu_2, \ldots, \mu_k) \in Z_1 \times Z_2 \times \cdots \times Z_k, \tag{11.27}$$

where μ_l is the projection of μ_k on Z_l for every l, $1 \leq l \leq k$. Denote by $T_k \subseteq Z_1 \times Z_2 \times \cdots \times Z_k$ the set containing all k-order coherent belief hierarchies and their projections. Z_k is a compact space for every $k \in \mathbb{N}$ (Theorem 11.10), and therefore the Cartesian product $Z_1 \times Z_2 \times \cdots \times Z_k$ is also compact. We will now show that $T_k \subseteq Z_1 \times Z_2 \times \cdots \times Z_k$ is a compact set. To see this, note that for every $l = 1, 2, \ldots, k$, the projection $\rho_{k,l} : Z_k \to Z_l$ is a continuous function; hence T_k, which is the image of the compact set Z_k under the continuous mapping $(\rho_{k,1}, \rho_{k,2}, \ldots, \rho_{k,k})$, is a compact set.

Tychonoff's Theorem (see, for example, Theorem I.8.5 in Dunford and Schwartz [1988]) states that the (finite or infinite) Cartesian product of compact spaces is a compact space in the product topology. It follows that

$$\widehat{T}_k := T_k \times Z_{k+1} \times Z_{k+2} \times \cdots \tag{11.28}$$

is also a compact set for every $k \in \mathbb{N}$. Since $T = \bigcap_{k \in \mathbb{N}} \widehat{T}_k$ we conclude that T, as the intersection of compact sets, is a compact set in $Z_1 \times Z_2 \times \cdots$.   □

The topology over T is the collection of open sets in T. In order to study the probability distributions over T, it is necessary first to define a σ-algebra over T. A natural σ-algebra is the σ-algebra of the Borel sets: this is the minimal σ-algebra over T that contains all the open sets in T. The next theorem provides us with another way of defining the type of a player. It says that the type of a player is a probability distribution over the states of nature and the types of the other players.

Theorem 11.16 *The universal type space T satisfies*[5]

$$T = \Delta(S \times T^{n-1}). \tag{11.29}$$

To be more precise, we will prove that there exists a natural homeomorphism[6] $\varphi : \Delta(S \times T^{n-1}) \to T$.

Proof: An element in T is a vector of the form $(\mu_1, \mu_2, \ldots)$, satisfying $\mu_k = \rho(\mu_{k+1})$ for all $k \in \mathbb{N}$.

In the proof we will use the following:

$$S \times T^{n-1} \subseteq S \times \underbrace{(Z_1 \times Z_2 \times \cdots) \times \cdots \times (Z_1 \times Z_2 \times \cdots)}_{n-1 \text{ times}}$$

$$= S \times (Z_1)^{n-1} \times (Z_2)^{n-1} \times \cdots . \tag{11.30}$$

Step 1: Definition of the function $\varphi : \Delta(S \times T^{n-1}) \to T$.
We will show that every distribution $\lambda \in \Delta(S \times T^{n-1})$ uniquely determines an element $(\mu_1, \mu_2, \ldots) \in T$. The belief hierarchies of all finite orders are defined as follows. Let μ_1 be the marginal distribution of λ over S. For each $k \geq 1$, let ν_k be the marginal distribution of λ over $S \times (Z_k)^{n-1}$ (see Equation (11.30)). Inductively define $\mu_{k+1} = (\mu_k, \nu_k)$ for each $k \geq 1$. To show that the resulting sequence $(\mu_1, \mu_2, \ldots)$ is a type in T, we need to show that for each $k \in \mathbb{N}$, the projection of μ_{k+1} on Z_k is μ_k, which follows from the definitions of ν_{k+1} and ν_k and from the fact that T contains only coherent types.

Step 2: The function φ is continuous.
The claim obtains because if $(\lambda^l)_{l\in\mathbb{N}}$ is a sequence of probability distributions defined over the probability space $X \times Y$ converging to λ in the weak-$*$ topology, and if μ^l is the marginal distribution of λ^l over X, then the sequence of distributions $(\mu^l)_{l\in\mathbb{N}}$ converges in the weak-$*$ topology to the marginal distribution μ of λ over X (see Theorem 2.8 in Billingsley [1999]).

Step 3: The function φ is injective.
We will show that λ can be reconstructed from $\varphi(\lambda)$, for each $\lambda \in \Delta(S \times T^{n-1})$. Denote $\varphi(\lambda) = (\mu_1, \mu_2, \ldots)$. Recall that $\mu_{k+1} = (\mu_k, \nu_k)$, where ν_k is a probability distribution over the space $S \times (Z_k)^{n-1}$. Because Z_k contains all the hierarchies of all orders $1, 2, \ldots, k$, it follows that ν_k is a probability distribution over the space $S \times (Z_1)^{n-1} \times (Z_2)^{n-1} \times \cdots \times (Z_{k-1})^{n-1}$. Since $\mu_k = (\mu_{k-1}, \nu_{k-1})$, the marginal distribution of ν_k over

---

[5] The σ-algebra over $S \times T^{n-1}$ is the product σ-algebra.
[6] A *homeomorphism* between two spaces X and Y is a continuous bijection $f : X \to Y$, whose inverse $f^{-1} : Y \to X$ is also continuous.

$S \times (Z_1)^{n-1} \times (Z_2)^{n-1} \times \cdots \times (Z_{k-2})^{n-1}$ is the probability distribution ν_{k-1}. From the Kolmogorov Extension Theorem (see, for example, Theorem II.3.4 in Shiryaev [1995]) it follows that there exists a unique distribution λ^* over the space $S \times (Z_1)^{n-1} \times (Z_2)^{n-1} \times \cdots$ satisfying the condition that for every $k \in \mathbb{N}$, the marginal distribution of λ^* over $S \times (Z_1)^{n-1} \times (Z_2)^{n-1} \times \cdots \times (Z_{k-1})^{n-1}$ is ν_k. Since the marginal distribution of λ^* over $S \times (Z_1)^{n-1} \times (Z_2)^{n-1} \times \cdots \times (Z_{k-1})^{n-1}$ equals the marginal distribution of λ over these spaces, the uniqueness of the extension implies that $\lambda = \lambda^*$.

Step 4: The function φ is surjective.
Let $(\mu_1, \mu_2, \ldots) \in T$ be a type. As we saw in Step 3, a type in T defines a unique distribution $\lambda \in \Delta(S \times T^{n-1})$. The reader is asked to ascertain that $\varphi(\lambda)$ equals $(\mu_1, \mu_2, \ldots)$.

Step 5: The function φ is a homeomorphism.
Every continuous, injective, and surjective function φ from a compact space to a Hausdorff space[7] is a homeomorphism (see Claim I.5.8 in Dunford and Schwartz [1988]). □

11.3 Definition of the universal belief space

Definition 11.17 *The* universal belief space *is*

$$\Omega = \Omega(N, S) = S \times T^n. \tag{11.31}$$

By definition, the universal belief space is determined by the set of states of nature and by the number of players. To understand the meaning of Definition 11.17, write Equation (11.31) in the following form:

$$\Omega = S \times \left(\underset{i \in N}{\times} T_i \right), \tag{11.32}$$

where $T_i = T$ for all $i \in N$. The space T_i is called *player i's type space*. It is the same space for all the players, and is the universal type space. An element of Ω is a *state of the world*, and denoted by ω to distinguish it from the states of nature, which are elements of S. A state of the world is therefore a vector

$$\omega = (\mathfrak{s}(\omega), t_1(\omega), t_2(\omega), \ldots, t_n(\omega)). \tag{11.33}$$

The first coordinate $\mathfrak{s}(\omega)$ is the state of nature at the state of the world ω, and $t_i(\omega)$ is player i's type at this state of the world. In other words, a state of the world is characterized by the state of nature $\mathfrak{s}(\omega)$, and the vector of types of the players, $(t_i(\omega))_{i \in N}$, at that state of the world. We will assume that all a player knows is his own type. While in the Aumann and Harsanyi models the belief hierarchies of the players can be computed at every state of the world, in the universal belief space these hierarchies are part of the data defining the state of the world: a state of the world consists of a state of nature and the players' belief hierarchies.

---

7 A topological space is a *Hausdorff* space if (a) every set containing a single point is closed, and (b) for every pair of distinct points there exist two disjoint and open sets, each of which contains one point but not the other. The space T is a Hausdorff space (Exercise 11.11).

Example 11.14   (*Continued*) We have seen that when $N = \{I\}$ and $S = \{s_1, s_2\}$, the universal type space T is homeomorphic to the interval $[0, 1]$. In this case, the universal belief space is $\Omega = \Omega(\{I\}, S) = S \times [0, 1]$. For every $p \in [0, 1]$, at the state of the world $\omega = (s_1, p)$, the state of nature is s_1, and the player ascribes probability p to the state of nature being s_1, and probability $1 - p$ to the state of nature being s_2. ◀

Remark 11.18 *As we saw in Theorem 11.16, a type $t_i(\omega) \in T = \Delta(S \times T^{n-1})$ is a probability distribution over the vectors of the state of nature and the list of the $n - 1$ types of the other players. Since $\Omega = (S \times (\times_{j \neq i} T_j)) \times T_i$, and because at every state of the world ω every player i knows his own type $t_i(\omega)$, we can regard $t_i(\omega)$ also as a probability distribution over Ω, where the marginal distribution over T_i is the degenerate distribution at the point $\{t_i(\omega)\}$. From here on, we will assume that $t_i(\omega)$ is indeed a probability distribution over Ω.* ◆

Recall that a belief space of the set of players N on the set of states of nature S is an ordered vector $\Pi = (Y, \mathcal{Y}, \mathfrak{s}, (\pi_i)_{i \in N})$, where $(Y, \mathcal{Y})$ is a measure space of states of the world, $\mathfrak{s} : Y \to S$ is a measurable function associating a state of nature with every state of the world, and $\pi_i : Y \to \Delta(Y)$ is a function associating a probability distribution over Y with every state of the world and every player $i \in N$, which satisfies the conditions of coherency and measurability. The next two theorems justify the name "universal belief space" that we gave to Ω: Theorem 11.19 states that Ω naturally defines a belief space, and Theorem 11.20 states that every belief space is a belief subspace of Ω. It follows that the space $\Omega(N, S)$ contains all the possible situations of incomplete information of a set of players N on a set of states of nature S.

Denote by $\mathcal{Y}^*$ the product σ-algebra over the set Ω defined by Equation (11.32).

Theorem 11.19 *The ordered vector $\Pi^* = (\Omega, \mathcal{Y}^*, \mathfrak{s}, (t_i)_{i \in N})$ is a belief space, where Ω is the universal belief space and $\mathfrak{s}$ and $(t_i)_{i \in N}$ are projections on the $n + 1$ coordinates of the state of the world (see Equation (11.33)).*

Proof: We will show that all the conditions defining a belief space are satisfied. The space $(\Omega, \mathcal{Y}^*)$ is a measurable space. Since $\mathcal{Y}^*$ is a σ-algebra, the functions $\mathfrak{s}$ and t_i are measurable functions.

We will next show that the functions $(t_i)_{i \in N}$ satisfy the coherency condition (see Definition 10.1 on page 397). As stated in Remark 11.18, for every player $i \in N$ and every $\omega \in \Omega$, the type $t_i(\omega)$ is a probability distribution over Ω. Since t_i is a measurable function, the set $\{\omega' \in \Omega : t_i(\omega') = t_i(\omega)\}$ is measurable, and by definition, the probability distribution $t_i(\omega)$ ascribes probability 1 to this set, showing that the coherency condition is satisfied.

Finally, we check that for every $i \in N$, the function t_i satisfies the measurability condition (see Definition 10.1 on page 397). To do so, we need to show that for every measurable set E in Ω, the function $t_i(E \mid \cdot) : \Omega \to [0, 1]$ is measurable. We prove this by showing that for every $x \in [0, 1]$, the set $G_x = \{\omega \in \Omega : t_i(E \mid \omega) > x\}$ is measurable. By the definition of the weak-$*$ topology, for every continuous function $f : \Omega \to \mathbb{R}$ and every $x \in [0, 1]$, the set

$$A_{f,x} := \left\{ \omega \in \Omega : \int_\Omega f(\omega') \mathrm{d}t_i(\omega' \mid \omega) > x \right\} \tag{11.34}$$

is measurable. Let $\mathcal{F}$ be the family of continuous functions $f : \Omega \to (0, \infty)$ satisfying the condition $f(\omega) > 1$ for all $\omega \in E$. Let $\mathcal{F}_0$ be a countable dense subset of $\mathcal{F}$ (why does such a set exist?). The intersection $\cap_{f \in \mathcal{F}_0} A_{f,x}$, as the intersection of a countable number of measurable sets, is measurable, and is equal to G_x (why?). $\qquad\square$

Theorem 11.20 *Every belief space Π of a set of players N on a set of states of nature S is a belief subspace (see Definition 10.21 on page 410) of the universal belief space $\Omega(N, S)$ defined in Theorem 11.19.*

To be precise, every belief space $\Pi = (Y, \mathcal{Y}, \mathfrak{s}, (\pi_i)_{i \in N})$ is homomorphic to a belief subspace of the belief space Π^*, in the following sense: the belief hierarchy of every player i at every state of the world $\omega \in Y$ equals his belief hierarchy at the state of the world in Π^* corresponding to ω, under the homomorphism.

Proof: Let $\Pi = (Y, \mathcal{Y}, \mathfrak{s}, (\pi_i)_{i \in N})$ be a belief space. As we stated on page 401, for every state of the world $\omega \in Y$ and every player $i \in N$, we can associate an infinite belief hierarchy that describes the beliefs of player i at the state of the world ω. Denote this belief hierarchy by $t_i(\omega)$. For each $\omega \in Y$, the vector $\varphi(\omega) := (\mathfrak{s}(\omega), t_1(\omega), t_2(\omega), \ldots, t_n(\omega))$ is a state of the world in the universal belief space. Note that if there are two states of the world $\omega, \omega' \in Y$ satisfying the conditions that the belief hierarchy of every player i in ω equals his belief hierarchy in ω', and if these two states of the world are associated with the same state of nature, then $\varphi(\omega) = \varphi(\omega')$ (this happens, for example, in the second belief space in Example 10.13 on page 404). The definition implies that the belief hierarchy of every player i at every state of the world $\omega \in Y$ equals his belief hierarchy in $\varphi(\omega)$. Consider the set

$$\widehat{Y} := \{\varphi(\omega) : \omega \in Y\} \subseteq \Omega. \tag{11.35}$$

It is left to the reader to check that the set $\widehat{Y}$ is a belief subspace of Π^* (Exercise 11.10). $\qquad\square$

Theorem 11.20 implies, for example, that in each of the examples in Section 10.3 (page 404), the belief space is a belief subspace of an appropriate universal belief space. For example, each of the belief spaces described in Examples 10.17 (page 406), 10.18 (page 407), and 10.19 (page 408) is a subspace of the universal belief space $\Omega(N, S)$, where $N = \{I, II\}$ and $S = \{s_{11}, s_{12}, s_{21}, s_{22}\}$.

11.4   Remarks

The universal belief space was first constructed and studied by Mertens and Zamir [1985]. Heifetz and Samet [1998] discuss a construction of the universal belief space using measure-theoretical tools, without any use of topological structures. Aumann [1999] constructs the universal belief space using a semantic approach. The reader interested in the weak-$*$ topology is directed to Dunford and Schwartz [1988] (Chapter V.12), Conway [1990], or Billingsley [1999].

The authors thank Yaron Azrieli, Aviad Heifetz, Dov Samet, Boaz Klartag, John Levy, and Eran Shmaya for their comments on this chapter.

11.5 Exercises

. . . .

11.1 Joshua and his army are planning to circle Jericho seven times. Will the wall come tumbling down? The king of Jericho reports that:

- I ascribe probability 0.8 to "the wall of the city will fall, and Joshua ascribes probability 0.6 to the wall falling."
- I ascribe probability 0.2 to "the wall of the city will not fall, and Joshua ascribes probability 0.5 to the wall falling."

Answer the following questions:

(a) What is the set of states of nature corresponding to the above description.

(b) What is the king's first-order belief? What is his second-order belief?

(c) Can Joshua's first-order belief be ascertained from the above description? Justify your answer.

11.2 Construct a belief space of the set of players $N = \{Don, Phil\}$ on the set of states of nature $S = \{s_b, s_g, s_p, s_r, s_w\}$ describing the situation in Example 11.9 (page 455), and indicate at which state of the world Phil's belief hierarchy of order 3 is the hierarchy described in the example. There may be more than one correct answer.

11.3 Prove that $Z_k \subseteq X_k$ for each $k \geq 1$: every coherent belief hierarchy of order k (Definition 11.6 on page 454) is a belief hierarchy of order k (Definition 11.3 on page 451).

11.4 Consider the following belief space, where the set of players is $N = \{I, II\}$, and the set of states of nature is $S = \{s_1, s_2\}$:

State of the world	$\mathfrak{s}(\cdot)$	$\pi_{\mathrm{I}}(\cdot)$	$\pi_{\mathrm{II}}(\cdot)$
ω_1	s_1	$[\frac{1}{2}(\omega_1), \frac{1}{2}(\omega_2)]$	$[1(\omega_1)]$
ω_2	s_2	$[\frac{1}{2}(\omega_1), \frac{1}{2}(\omega_2)]$	$[\frac{3}{4}(\omega_2), \frac{1}{4}(\omega_3)]$
ω_3	s_1	$[1(\omega_3)]$	$[\frac{3}{4}(\omega_2), \frac{1}{4}(\omega_3)]$

Write out the belief hierarchies of orders 1, 2, and 3 of Player I, at each state of the world.

11.5 Roger reports:

- I ascribe probability 0.3 to "the Philadelphia Phillies will win the World Series next year, Chris ascribes probability 0.4 to their winning the World Series and to me ascribing probability 0.4 that they will win the World Series, and Chris ascribes probability 0.6 to the Philadelphia Phillies not winning the World Series and to me ascribing probability 0.2 that they will win the World Series."
- I ascribe probability 0.2 to "the Philadelphia Phillies will win the World Series next year, Chris ascribes probability 0.4 to their winning the World Series and to me ascribing probability 0.5 that they will win the World Series, and Chris ascribes probability 0.6 to the Philadelphia Phillies not winning the World Series and to me ascribing probability 0.8 that they will win the World Series."

- I ascribe probability 0.4 to "the Philadelphia Phillies will win the World Series next year, Chris ascribes probability 0.2 to their winning the World Series and to me ascribing probability 0.1 that they will win the World Series, and Chris ascribes probability 0.8 to the Philadelphia Phillies not winning the World Series and to me ascribing probability 0.3 that they will win the World Series."
- I ascribe probability 0.1 to "the Philadelphia Phillies will win the World Series next year, Chris ascribes probability 0.6 to their winning the World Series and to me ascribing probability 0.4 that they will win the World Series, and Chris ascribes probability 0.4 to the Philadelphia Phillies not winning the World Series and to me ascribing probability 0.7 that they will win the World Series."

Answer the following questions:

(a) Construct a space of states of nature corresponding to the above description.
(b) What is Roger's first-order belief? What is his second-order belief? What is his third-order belief?

11.6 Prove Theorem 11.7: let $\mu_k = (\mu_1; v_1, v_2, \ldots, v_{k-1}) \in Z_k$ be a coherent belief hierarchy of order k and let l_1, l_2 be two integers such that $1 \le l_1 \le l_2 \le k$. Then:

(a) The marginal distribution of v_{l_1} over S equals μ_1.
(b) The marginal distribution of v_{l_2} over $S \times (Z_{l_1})^{n-1}$ is v_{l_1}.

11.7 Let $s_0 \in S$ be a state of nature. Prove that the following sentence defines a coherent belief hierarchy of order k: "I ascribe probability 1 to the state of nature being s_0, I ascribe probability 1 to all the other players ascribing probability 1 to the state of nature being s_0, I ascribe probability 1 to each of the other players ascribing probability 1 to every other player ascribing probability 1 to the state of nature being s_0, and so on, to level k."

11.8 There are two players, $N = \{I, II\}$, and the space of states of nature is $S = \{s_1, s_2\}$. Ascertain for each of the following belief hierarchies of Player I whether or not it is a coherent belief hierarchy (of some order). Justify your answer.

(a) I ascribe probability $\frac{1}{9}$ to the state of nature being s_1.
(b) • I ascribe probability $\frac{1}{2}$ to the state of nature being s_1.
   - I also ascribe probability $\frac{2}{3}$ to the state of nature being s_1 and to Player II ascribing probability $\frac{3}{4}$ to the state of nature being s_1.
   - I also ascribe probability $\frac{1}{3}$ to the state of nature being s_1 and to Player II ascribing probability 0 to the state of nature being s_1.
(c) • I ascribe probability $\frac{1}{2}$ to the state of nature being s_1.
   - I also ascribe probability $\frac{1}{3}$ to the state of nature being s_1 and to Player II ascribing probability $\frac{1}{4}$ to the state of nature being s_1.
   - I also ascribe probability $\frac{1}{6}$ to the state of nature being s_1 and to Player II ascribing probability $\frac{1}{2}$ to the state of nature being s_1.
   - I also ascribe probability $\frac{1}{2}$ to the state of nature being s_2 and to Player II ascribing probability $\frac{2}{3}$ to the state of nature being s_1.

(d) • I ascribe probability $\frac{1}{2}$ to the state of nature being s_1.

   • I also ascribe probability $\frac{1}{3}$ to the state of nature being s_1 and to Player II ascribing probability $\frac{1}{4}$ to the state of nature being s_1.

   • I also ascribe probability $\frac{1}{6}$ to the state of nature being s_1 and to Player II ascribing probability $\frac{1}{4}$ to the state of nature being s_1.

   • I also ascribe probability $\frac{1}{2}$ to the state of nature being s_2 and to Player II ascribing probability $\frac{2}{3}$ to the state of nature being s_1.

   • I also ascribe probability $\frac{1}{3}$ to the state of nature being s_2 and to Player II ascribing probability $\frac{1}{4}$ to the state of nature being s_1, and to me ascribing probability $\frac{2}{5}$ to the state of nature being s_1, and to Player II ascribing probability $\frac{3}{4}$ to the state of nature being s_2, and to me ascribing probability $\frac{4}{5}$ to the state of nature being s_1.

   • I also ascribe probability $\frac{1}{6}$ to the state of nature being s_1 and to Player II ascribing probability $\frac{1}{4}$ to the state of nature being s_1, and to me ascribing probability $\frac{3}{5}$ to the state of nature being s_1, and to Player II ascribing probability $\frac{3}{4}$ to the state of nature being s_2, and to me ascribing probability $\frac{3}{7}$ to the state of nature being s_1.

   • I also ascribe probability $\frac{1}{2}$ to the state of nature being s_2 and to Player II ascribing probability $\frac{1}{4}$ to the state of nature being s_1, and to me ascribing probability $\frac{4}{5}$ to the state of nature being s_1, and to Player II ascribing probability $\frac{3}{4}$ to the state of nature being s_2, and to me ascribing probability $\frac{2}{5}$ to the state of nature being s_1.

(e) • I ascribe probability $\frac{1}{2}$ to the state of nature being s_1.

   • I also ascribe probability $\frac{1}{3}$ to the state of nature being s_1 and to Player II ascribing probability $\frac{1}{4}$ to the state of nature being s_1.

   • I also ascribe probability $\frac{1}{6}$ to the state of nature being s_1 and to Player II ascribing probability $\frac{1}{2}$ to the state of nature being s_1.

   • I also ascribe probability $\frac{1}{2}$ to the state of nature being s_1 and to Player II ascribing probability $\frac{2}{3}$ to the state of nature being s_1.

   • I also ascribe probability $\frac{1}{2}$ to the state of nature being s_1 and to Player II ascribing probability $\frac{1}{3}$ to the state of nature being s_1, and to me ascribing probability $\frac{2}{5}$ to the state of nature being s_1, and to Player II ascribing probability $\frac{2}{3}$ to the state of nature being s_2, and to me ascribing probability $\frac{4}{5}$ to the state of nature being s_1.

   • I also ascribe probability $\frac{1}{2}$ to the state of nature being s_2 and to Player II ascribing probability $\frac{2}{3}$ to the state of nature being s_1, and to me ascribing probability $\frac{4}{5}$ to the state of nature being s_1, and to Player II ascribing probability $\frac{1}{3}$ to the state of nature being s_2, and to me ascribing probability $\frac{1}{5}$ to the state of nature being s_1.

(f) • I ascribe probability $\frac{1}{2}$ to the state of nature being s_1.

 • I also ascribe probability $\frac{1}{3}$ to the state of nature being s_1 and to Player II ascribing probability $\frac{1}{4}$ to the state of nature being s_1.

 • I also ascribe probability $\frac{1}{6}$ to the state of nature being s_1 and to Player II ascribing probability $\frac{1}{2}$ to the state of nature being s_1.

 • I also ascribe probability $\frac{1}{2}$ to the state of nature being s_2 and to Player II ascribing probability $\frac{2}{3}$ to the state of nature being s_1.

 • I also ascribe probability $\frac{1}{3}$ to the state of nature being s_1, and to Player II ascribing probability $\frac{1}{4}$ to the state of nature being s_1 and to me ascribing probability $\frac{2}{5}$ to the state of nature being s_1, and to Player II ascribing probability $\frac{3}{4}$ to the state of nature being s_2 and to me ascribing probability $\frac{4}{5}$ to the state of nature being s_1.

 • I also ascribe probability $\frac{1}{6}$ to the state of nature being s_1, and to Player II ascribing probability $\frac{1}{2}$ to the state of nature being s_1 and to me ascribing probability $\frac{4}{5}$ to the state of nature being s_1, and to Player II ascribing probability $\frac{1}{2}$ to the state of nature being s_2 and to me ascribing probability $\frac{3}{5}$ to the state of nature being s_1.

 • I also ascribe probability $\frac{1}{2}$ to the state of nature being s_2, and to Player II ascribing probability $\frac{2}{3}$ to the state of nature being s_1 and to me ascribing probability $\frac{2}{5}$ to the state of nature being s_1, and to Player II ascribing probability $\frac{1}{3}$ to the state of nature being s_2 and to me ascribing probability $\frac{1}{5}$ to the state of nature being s_1.

11.9 There is a single player $N = \{I\}$ and the set of states of nature is a finite set S. What is the universal type space in this case? What is the universal belief space $\Omega(N, S)$?

11.10 Complete the proof of Theorem 11.20 on page 464: prove that the set $\widehat{Y}$ that was defined in the proof of the theorem is a belief subspace of Π^*.

11.11 Prove that the universal type space T is a Hausdorff space.

12 Auctions

Chapter summary

In this chapter we present the theory of auctions, which is considered to be one of the most successful applications of game theory, and in particular of games with incomplete information. We mainly study symmetric auctions with independent private values and risk-neutral buyers. An auction is presented as a game with incomplete information and the main interest is in the (Bayesian) equilibrium of this game, that is, in the *bidding strategies* of the buyers and in the expected revenue of the seller. A hallmark of this theory is the *Revenue Equivalence Theorem*, which states that in any equilibrium of an auction method in which (a) the winner is the buyer with the highest valuation for the auctioned item, and (b) any buyer who assigns private value 0 to the auctioned item pays nothing, the expected revenue of the seller is independent of the auction method. This theorem implies that a wide range of auction methods yield the seller the same expected revenue. We also prove that the expected revenue to the seller increases if all buyers are risk averse, and it decreases if all buyers are risk seeking.

The theory is then extended to selling mechanisms. These are abstract mechanisms to sell items to buyers that include, e.g., post-auction bargaining between the seller and the buyers who placed the highest bids. We prove the *revelation principle* for selling mechanisms, which allows us to consider only a simple class of mechanisms, called *incentive-compatible direct selling mechanisms*. We then prove the Revenue Equivalence Theorem for selling mechanisms, and identify the selling mechanism that yields the seller the highest expected profit. This turns out to be a sealed-bid second-price auction with a reserve price.

Auctions and tenders are mechanisms for the buying and selling of objects by way of bids submitted by potential buyers, with the auctioned object sold to the highest bidder. Auctions have been known since antiquity. The earliest mention of auctions appears in the fifth century BCE, in the writings of Herodotus (Book One, Clio 194):

> When they arrive at Babylon in their voyage and have disposed of their cargo, they sell by auction the ribs of the boat and all the straw.

Herodotus also tells of a Babylonian custom of selling young women by public auction to men seeking wives (Book One, Clio 196). In 193 CE, the Roman emperor Pertinax was assassinated by his Praetorian Guard. In an attempt to win the support of the guard and be crowned the next emperor, Titus Flavius Sulpicianus offered to pay 20,000 sesterces to each member of the guard. Upon hearing of Sulpicianus's offer, Marcus Severus Didius Julianus countered with an offer of 25,000 sesterces to each member of the Praetorian guard, and ascended to the throne; in effect, the Roman Empire had been auctioned to the highest bidder. Julianus did not live long to enjoy the prize he had won; within three months, three other generals laid claim to the crown, and Julianus was beheaded.

Auctions and tenders are ubiquitous nowadays. A very partial list of examples of objects sold in this way includes Treasury bills, mining rights, objects of fine art, bottles of wine, and repossessed houses. A major milestone in the history of auctions was achieved in the 1995 auctioning of the rights to radio-spectrum frequencies in the United States, which resulted in the federal government pocketing an unprecedented profit of 8.7 billion dollars.

The main reasons for preferring auctions and tenders to other sales mechanisms are the speed with which deals are concluded, the revelation of information achieved by these mechanisms, and the prevention of improper conduct on the part of sales agents and purchasers (an especially important reason when the seller is a public body).

As we will show in this chapter, an auction is a special case of a game with incomplete information. Many of the games we encounter in daily life are highly complex. Even when the theory assures us that these games have equilibria, in most cases the equilibria are hard to compute, and it is therefore difficult to predict what buyers will do, or to advise them on the way to play. This is also true, in general, with respect to auctions. However, as we will show, under certain assumptions, it is possible to compute the equilibrium strategies in auctions, to describe how the equilibria will change if the parameters of the game are changed (e.g., the utility functions of the buyers), and to compare the expected outcomes (for both buyers and seller) when the rules of the game (or the auction method) are changed. The theory developed in this chapter provides insights useful for participating in auctions and designing auctions.

The theory of auctions is one of the most successful applications of game theory, and in particular of games with incomplete information. The theory is not simple, but it is very elegant. The combination of mathematical challenge with clear applicability makes the theory of auctions a central element of modern economic theory.

In the literature, auctions are classified in several ways:

- **Open-bid or sealed-bid auction.** In an open-bid auction, the buyers hear or see each other in real time, as bids are made, and are able immediately to offer counter bids. In a sealed-bid auction, all the buyers submit their bids simultaneously, and no buyer knows the offers made by the other buyers.

  Art objects are usually sold in open-bid auctions. Most public auctions conducted on the Web, and many large state-run auctions, such as the auctioning of radio-spectrum frequencies, are also open-bid auctions. In contrast, tenders for government contracts, and auctions for the sale of assets taken into receivership after a corporate bankruptcy, are usually conducted in sealed-bid auctions.

- **Private value or common value.** A buyer's assessment of the worth of an object offered for sale is called a *value*. The literature on auction theory distinguishes between *private values* and *common values*. When the value of an object for a buyer is a private value, it is independent of the value as assessed by the other buyers. A private value is always known ahead of time to the buyer, with no uncertainty.

When the value is a common value, it is identical for all the buyers, but is unknown. This occurs, for example, in tenders for oil-drilling rights, where there is uncertainty regarding the amount of oil that can be extracted from the oil field, and in tenders for real-estate development rights, where there is uncertainty regarding the potential demand for apartments, and the final price at which the apartments will be sold.

Most auctions share both characteristics to a certain extent: the value of any object, whether it is a valuable work of art or a drilling project, is never known with certainty. This unknown value is common among the buyers when measured in dollars and cents, but there is also a private component, determined by personal taste, financial resources, and the future plans of the buyer. When the object offered for sale is, for example, a real-estate development or oil-drilling rights, the expected financial revenue that the project will yield is the common value component. When the object is a Treasury bond or shares in a company, the difference between the sale price and the purchase price is the common value component. This component is common to all the buyers, but is unknown to them, and each buyer may have different information (or different assessments) regarding this value. The financial abilities of the buyer, his future plans, and other possibilities available to him, should he fail to win the auction, also affect the value of an object to the buyer. These factors differ from one buyer to another, and what influences one buyer usually has no effect on another. This is the private component of the value of an object for a buyer.

The literature includes general auction models that use general valuation functions, and take into account the possibility that the private information of the buyers regarding the common but unknown value of an object may be interdependent (see Milgrom and Weber [1982]).

- **Selling a single object or several objects.** Auctions differ with respect to the number of objects offered. Sometimes only one object is offered, such as a Chagall painting, a license to operate a television station for five years, or a letter from Marilyn Monroe to Elvis Presley. Sometimes, several copies of the same object are offered, such as batches of Treasury bonds, or shares in a company listed on the stock exchange. There are also cases in which several objects with different characteristics are offered at once. For example, in recent years some countries have conducted auctions of regional communication licenses (covering mobile telephone rights, broadcast radio rights, and so on), with licenses for different regions offered simultaneously.

In this chapter, we will focus on the case in which the buyers in an auction have independent private values, and only one object is offered for sale. This is the simplest case from the mathematical perspective. It is also historically the first case that was studied in the literature. Despite the simplicity of this model, the mathematical analysis is not trivial and the results are both elegant and applicable.

We close this introduction to the chapter with a remark on terminology. In previous chapters, the term "payoff" meant the expected payoff of a buyer. In this chapter, we will use the term "payment" to refer to the amount of money a buyer pays to the seller, and the term "profit" to denote the expected profit of the buyer, which is defined as the difference between the buyer's expected utility from receiving the object (the probability that he will win the auction times the utility he receives from winning the object) and the expected payment the buyer pays the seller.

12.1 Notation

The participants in the auctions will be called *buyers*. For every random variable X, denote its cumulative distribution function by F_X. That is,

$$F_X(c) = \mathbf{P}(X \le c), \quad \forall c \in \mathbb{R}. \tag{12.1}$$

If X is a continuous random variable, denote its density function by f_X. In this case,

$$F_X(c) = \int_{-\infty}^{c} f_X(x)\mathrm{d}x, \quad \forall c \in \mathbb{R}. \tag{12.2}$$

12.2 Common auction methods

The following list details the most common auction methods.

1. **Open-bid ascending auction (English auction).** This is the most common public auction. It is characterized by an auctioneer who publicly declares the price of the object offered for sale. The opening price is low, and as long as there are at least two buyers willing to pay the declared price, the auctioneer raises the price (either in discrete jumps, or in a continuous manner using a clock). Each buyer raises a hand as long as he is willing to pay the last price that the auctioneer has declared. The auction ends when all hands except one have been lowered, and the object is sold to the last buyer whose hand is still raised, at the last price declared by the auctioneer. If the auction ends in a draw (i.e., the last two or more buyers whose hands were raised drop out of the auction at the same time), a previously agreed rule (such as tossing a coin) is employed to determine who wins the object, which is then sold to the winner at the price that was current when they lowered their hands.

   Web-based auctions and auctions of works of art (such as those conducted at Sotheby's and Christie's) typically use this method.

2. **Open-bid descending auction (Dutch auction).** A Dutch auction operates in the reverse direction of the English auction. In this method, the auctioneer begins by declaring a very high price, higher than any buyer could be expected to pay. As long as no buyer is willing to pay the last declared price, the auctioneer lowers the declared price (either in discrete jumps or in a continuous manner using a clock), up to the point at which at least one buyer is willing to pay the declared price and indicates his readiness by raising his hand or pressing a button to stop the clock. If the price drops below a previously declared minimum, the auction is stopped, and the object on offer is not sold. Similarly to the English auction, a previously agreed rule is employed to determine who wins the auction if two or more buyers stop the clock at the same time.

   The flower auction at the Aalsmeer Flower Exchange, near Amsterdam, is conducted using this method.

3. **Sealed-bid first-price auction.** In this method, every buyer in the auction submits a sealed envelope containing the price he is willing to pay for the offered object. After all buyers have submitted their offers, the auctioneer opens the envelopes and reads

the offers they contain. The buyer who has submitted the highest bid wins the offered object, and pays the price that he has bid. A previously agreed rule determines how to resolve draws.

4. **Sealed-bid second-price auction (Vickery auction).** The sealed-bid second-price auction method is similar to the first-price sealed-bid auction method, except that the winner of the auction, i.e., the buyer who submitted the highest bid, pays the *second-highest* price among the bid prices for the offered object. A previously agreed-upon rule determines the winner in case of a draw, with the winner in this case paying what he bid (which is, in the case of a draw, also the second-highest bid).

We mention here in passing several sealed-bid auction methods that, despite being important, will not be studied in detail in this book. In each of these methods, the winner of the auction is the buyer who has submitted the highest bid (if several buyers have submitted the same highest bid, the winner is determined by a previously agreed-upon rule).

1. A **sealed-bid auction with a reserve price** is a sealed-bid auction in which every bid that is lower than a minimal price, as determined by the seller, is disqualified. In a sealed-bid first-price auction with a reserve price, the winner of the auction pays the highest bid for the object; in a sealed-bid second-price auction with a reserve price, the winner pays either the second-highest bid for the object or the reserve price, whichever is higher.

2. An **auction with an entry fee** is a sealed-bid auction in which every buyer must pay an entry fee for participating in the auction, whether or not he wins the auction. The winner of the auction also pays for the object he has won, in addition to the entry fee. In a sealed-bid first-price auction with an entry fee, the winner of the auction pays the highest bid for the object; in a sealed-bid second-price auction with an entry fee, the winner pays the second-highest bid for the object. In an auction with an entry fee, a buyer's strategy is composed of two components: whether or not to participate in the auction (and pay the entry fee), and if so, how high a bid to submit.

3. An **all-pay auction** is a sealed- or open-bid auction in which every buyer pays the amount of money he has bid, whether or not he has won the object for sale. All-pay auctions are appropriate models for competitions, such as arms races between countries, or research and development competitions between companies racing to be the first to market with a new innovation. In these cases, all the buyers in the race, or competition, end up paying the full amounts of their investments, whether or not they win.

12.3 Definition of a sealed-bid auction with private values

In a sealed-bid auction, every buyer submits a bid, and the rules of the auction determine who wins the object for sale, and the amounts of money that the buyers (the winner, and perhaps also the other buyers) must pay. The winner is usually the highest bidder, but it is possible to define auctions in which the winner is not necessarily the highest bidder.

Definition 12.1 *A* sealed-bid auction *(with independent private values) is a vector* $(N, (\mathbb{V}_i, F_i)_{i \in N}, p, C)$, *where:*

- $N = \{1, 2, \ldots, n\}$ *is the set of buyers.*
- $\mathbb{V}_i \subseteq \mathbb{R}$ *is the set of possible private values of buyer i, for each $i \in N$. Denote by $\mathbb{V}^N := \mathbb{V}_1 \times \mathbb{V}_2 \times \cdots \times \mathbb{V}_n$ the set of vectors of private value.*
- *For each buyer $i \in N$ there is a cumulative distribution function F_i over his set of private values $\mathbb{V}_i$.*
- $p : [0, \infty)^N \to \Delta(N)$ *is a function associating each vector of bids $b \in [0, \infty)^N$ with a distribution according to which the buyer who wins the auctioned object is identified.*[1]
- $C : N \times [0, \infty)^N \to \mathbb{R}^N$ *is a function determining the payment each buyer pays, for each vector of bids $b \in [0, \infty)^N$, depending on which buyer $i_* \in N$ is the winner.*

A sealed-bid auction is conducted as follows:

- The private value v_i of each buyer i is chosen randomly from the set $\mathbb{V}_i$, according to the cumulative distribution function F_i.
- Every buyer i learns his private value v_i, but not the private values of the other buyers.
- Every buyer i submits a bid $b_i \in [0, \infty)$ (depending on his private value v_i).
- The buyer who wins the auctioned object, i_*, is chosen according to the distribution $p(b_1, b_2, \ldots, b_n)$; the probability that buyer i wins the object is $p_i(b_1, b_2, \ldots, b_n)$.
- Every buyer i pays the sum $C_i(i_*; b_1, b_2, \ldots, b_n)$.

For simplicity we will sometimes denote an auction by (p, C) instead of $(N, (F_i)_{i \in N}, p, C)$. Note several points relating to this definition:

- The private values of the buyers are independent, and therefore the vector of private values $(v_1, v_2, \ldots, v_n)$ is drawn according to a product distribution, whose cumulative distribution function is $F^N := F_1 \times F_2 \times \cdots \times F_n$. A more general model would take into account the possibility of general joint distributions, thereby enabling the modeling of situations of interdependency between the private values of different buyers.
- In most of the auctions with which we are familiar, the winner of the auction is the highest bidder. In other words, if there is a buyer i such that $b_i > \max_{j \neq i} b_j$, then $p(b_1, b_2, \ldots, b_n)$ is a degenerate distribution ascribing probability 1 to buyer i. If two (or more) buyers submit the same highest bid, a previously agreed-upon rule is implemented to determine the winner. That rule may be deterministic (for example, among the buyers who have submitted the highest bid, the winner is the buyer who submitted his bid first), or probabilistic (for example, the winner may be determined by the toss of a fair coin).
- In the most familiar payment functions, the winner pays either the highest, or the second-highest bid for the auctioned object. The payment function in the definition of a sealed-bid auction is more general, and enables the modeling of entry-fee favoritism (e.g., incentives for certain sectors), and all-pay auctions. It also enables the modeling

---

1 Recall that $\Delta(N) := \{x \in [0, 1]^N : \sum_{i \in N} x_i = 1\}$ is the set of all probability distributions over the set of buyers $N = \{1, 2, \ldots, n\}$.

of auctions with less-familiar rules, such as third-price auctions, in which the winner pays the third-highest bid.

The private value of buyer i is a random variable whose cumulative distribution function is F_i. This random value is denoted by V_i. A sealed-bid auction can be presented as a Harsanyi game with incomplete information (see Section 9.4) in the following way:

- The set of players is the set of buyers $N = \{1, 2, \ldots, n\}$.
- Player i's set of types is $\mathbb{V}_i$.
- The distribution over the set of type vectors is a product distribution with cumulative distribution function $F^N = F_1 \times F_2 \times \cdots \times F_n$.
- For each type vector $v \in \mathbb{V}^N$, the state of the world is the state game s_v, where buyer i's set of actions is $[0, \infty)$ and for every action vector $x \in [0, \infty)^N$, buyer i's profit is

$$p_i(x)v_i - \sum_{i_* \in N} p_{i_*}(x)C_i(i_*; x). \tag{12.3}$$

In words, if buyer i is the winner, he receives v_i (his private value for the object), and he pays $C_i(i_*; x)$ in any event (whether or not he is the winner), where i_* is the winning buyer.

A formal definition of an open-bid auction depends on the specific method used in conducting the auction, and may be very complex. For example, in the most common open-bid auction method, the English auction, a buyer's decision on whether or not to stop bidding at a certain moment depends on the identities of the other buyers, both those who have already quit the auction, and those who are still bidding, and the prices at which those who have already quit chose to stop bidding. We will not present a formal definition of an open-bid auction in this book.

Example 12.1   **Sealed-bid second-price auction** In a sealed-bid second-price auction, the winner is the highest bidder. If several buyers have submitted the highest bid then each of them has the same probability of winning: denote by $N(x) = \{i \in N : x_i = \max_{j \in N} x_j\}$ the set of buyers who have submitted the highest bid, and by i_* the buyer who wins the auctioned object. Then:

$$p_i(x) = \begin{cases} 0 & i \notin N(x), \\ \frac{1}{|N(x)|} & i \in N(x), \end{cases} \tag{12.4}$$

$$C_i(i_*; x) = \begin{cases} 0 & i \neq i_*, \\ \max_{j \neq i} x_j & i = i_*. \end{cases} \tag{12.5}$$

Note that if at least two buyers have submitted the same highest bid, the auctioned object is sold at this highest bid; that is, if $|N(x)| \geq 2$, then $C_{i_*}(i_*; x) = \max_{j \in N} x_j$. ◀

A *pure strategy* of buyer i in a sealed-bid auction is a measurable function[2]

$$\beta_i : [0, \infty) \to [0, \infty). \tag{12.6}$$

....

2 Recall that for every subset $X \subseteq \mathbb{R}$, a real-valued function $f : X \to [0, \infty)$ is *measurable* if for each number $y \in [0, \infty)$, the set $f^{-1}([0, y]) = \{x \in X : f(x) \leq y\}$ is a measurable set.

If buyer i uses pure strategy β_i, then when his type is v_i he bids $\beta_i(v_i)$. If the buyers use the strategy vector $\beta = (\beta_i)_{i \in N}$, buyer i's expected profit is

$$u_i(\beta) = \int_{\mathbb{V}^N} \left(p_i(\beta_1(x_1), \ldots, \beta_n(x_n)) v_i - \sum_{i_* \in N} p_{i_*}(x) C_i(i_*; \beta_1(x_1), \ldots, \beta_n(x_n)) \right) dF^N(x).$$

(12.7)

The next theorem points out a connection between two of the auction methods described above.

Theorem 12.3 *The open-bid descending auction method is equivalent to the sealed-bid first-price auction method: both methods describe the same strategic-form game, with the same strategy sets and the same payoff functions.*

Proof: The set of (pure) strategies in a sealed-bid first-price auction, for each buyer i, is the set of all measurable functions $\beta_i : \mathbb{V}_i \to [0, \infty)$. This set is also the set of buyer i's strategies in an open descending auction. Indeed, a strategy of buyer i is a function detailing how he should play at each of his information sets. An open descending auction ends when the clock is stopped. Hence his only information consists of the current price. A strategy of buyer i then only needs to determine, for each of his possible private values, the announced price at which he will stop the clock (if no other buyer has stopped the clock before that price has been announced). In other words, every strategy of buyer i is a measurable function $\beta_i : [0, \infty) \to [0, \infty)$.

In both auctions, every strategy vector $\beta = (\beta_i)_{i \in N}$ leads to the same outcome in both auctions: in a sealed-bid first-price auction, the winning buyer is the one who submits the highest bid, $\max_{i \in N} \beta_i(v_i)$, and the price he pays for the auctioned object is his bid. In an open descending auction, the winning buyer is the one who stops the clock at the price $\max_{i \in N} \beta_i(v_i)$, and the price he pays for the auctioned object is that price. It follows that both types of auction correspond to the same strategic-form game. $\square$

Remark 12.4 *Note that this equivalence obtains without any assumption on the information that each buyer has regarding the other buyers, their preferences, and their identities, or even the number of other buyers. Similarly, it does not depend on the assumption that the private values of the buyers are independent.* ◆

We next present additional relations between auction methods based on the concept of equilibrium.

12.4 Equilibrium

Having defined games, buyers, strategies, and payoffs, we next introduce the concept of equilibrium. In actual fact, since an auction is a game with incomplete information (because the type of each buyer, which is his private value, is known to him but not to the other buyers), the concept of equilibrium introduced here is that of Bayesian equilibrium (see Definition 9.49 on page 364), corresponding to the interim stage, when each buyer knows his private value.

Let $\beta = (\beta_1, \beta_2, \ldots, \beta_n)$ be a strategy vector. Denote by

$$\beta_{-i}(x_{-i}) := (\beta_j(x_j))_{j \neq i} \tag{12.8}$$

the vector of bids of the buyers other than i, given their types and their strategies. Denote by $u_i(\beta; v_i)$ buyer i's expected profit under the strategy vector β, when his private value is v_i,

$$u_i(\beta; v_i) := \int_{\mathbb{V}_{-i}} (p_i(\beta_i(v_i), \beta_{-i}(x_{-i}))v_i$$
$$- \sum_{i_* \in N} p_{i_*}(\beta_i(v_i), \beta_{-i}(x_{-i})) C_i(i_*; \beta_i(v_i), \beta_{-i}(x_{-i}))) \, dF_{-i}(x_{-i}). \tag{12.9}$$

Here, $\mathbb{V}_{-i} := \times_{j \neq i} \mathbb{V}_j$ is the space of the vectors of the private values of all the buyers except for buyer i, and $F_{-i} := \times_{j \neq i} F_j$ is the cumulative distribution function of the multidimensional random variable $V_{-i} = (V_j)_{j \neq i}$.

Note that the expected profit $u_i(\beta; v_i)$ depends on β_i, buyer i's strategy, only via $\beta_i(v_i)$, the bid of buyer i with private value v_i. We denote by $u_i(b_i, \beta_{-i}; v_i)$ the expected profit of buyer i with private value v_i when he submits bid b_i and the other buyers use strategy vector β_{-i}.

Definition 12.5 *A strategy vector β^* is an* equilibrium *(or a* Bayesian equilibrium*) if for every buyer $i \in N$ and every private value $v_i \in \mathbb{V}_i$*

$$u_i(\beta^*; v_i) \geq u_i(b_i, \beta^*_{-i}; v_i), \quad \forall b_i \in [0, \infty). \tag{12.10}$$

In other words, β^* is an equilibrium if no buyer i with private value v_i can profit by deviating from his equilibrium bid $\beta_i^*(v_i)$ to another bid b_i.

Remark 12.6 *Analyzing auctions using mixed strategies is beyond the scope of this book. In the auctions covered in this chapter, the distribution of the private value of each buyer is continuous, and we will show that under appropriate assumptions, equilibria in pure strategies exist in these auctions. Note that if β^* is an equilibrium in pure strategies, then no buyer can increase his payoff by deviating to a mixed strategy. To see this, recall that a mixed strategy is a distribution over pure strategies. If the buyer could increase his payoff by deviating to a mixed strategy, then he could do the same by deviating to one of the pure strategies in the support of the mixed strategy. This shows that every equilibrium in pure strategies is also an equilibrium in mixed strategies. In general, however, it is possible for all the equilibria in an auction to be equilibria in completely mixed strategies (see for example Vickrey [1961]).* ♦

In Section 4.6 (page 91) we considered sealed-bid second-price auctions, and proved the following result (see Theorem 4.15 on page 92).

Theorem 12.7 *In a sealed-bid second-price auction, the strategy of buyer i in which he bids his private value weakly dominates all his other strategies.*

Remark 12.8 *As noted in Remark 12.4, Theorem 12.7 obtains under very few assumptions: we assume nothing regarding the behavior of the other buyers, the number of other buyers, or their identities. In other words, in a sealed-bid second-price auction, revealing* *your private value is a (weakly) dominant strategy. This is a great advantage that the sealed-bid second-price auction has over other auction methods: it incentivizes every buyer to reveal his true preferences, i.e., how much he truly is willing to pay for the object. From the seller's perspective, this is an advantage, because he need not be concerned that the buyers will conceal their preferences and act as if they value the object less than they really do. Another, secondary advantage for the seller is that if a buyer who submitted a high bid does not win the auction, the seller, knowing his true preferences, might be able to offer him a similar object.* ◆

An important consequence of Theorem 12.7 is:

Theorem 12.9 *In a sealed-bid second-price auction, the strategy vector in which every buyer's bid equals his private value is an equilibrium.*

Proof: As stated in Theorem 12.7, in a second-price auction, bidding the true value is a dominant strategy. Corollary 4.27 (page 105; see also Exercise 10.52 on page 442) states that a vector of dominant strategies is an equilibrium, and therefore this strategy vector is a Bayesian equilibrium. ☐

Although we have not defined a game corresponding to an open-bid ascending auction, and in particular not defined a strategy in such an auction, it is possible to regard a behavior under which the buyer lowers his hand and no longer participates in the auction when the declared price reaches his private value as a "strategy" in this type of auction. We will show that this is a dominant strategy for such a buyer. Since we have not presented the necessary definitions, the proof here is not a formal proof.

Theorem 12.10 *In an open ascending auction (English auction), the strategy of buyer i that calls on him to lower his hand when the declared price reaches his private value, weakly dominates all his other strategies.*

Proof: As long as the declared price is lower than buyer i's private value, he receives 0 with certainty if he quits the auction. On the other hand, if he continues to bid, he stands to receive a positive profit (and certainly cannot lose). When the declared price equals buyer i's private value, if he quits he receives 0 with certainty, but if he continues to bid he may win the auction and end up paying more for the object than he values it for. Here we are relying on the fact that buyer i knows his private value, and that this value is independent of the values of the other buyers, so that the information given by the timing that the other buyers choose for quitting the auction is irrelevant to his strategic considerations. ☐

Similarly to the proof of Theorem 12.9, and referring to Theorem 12.10, we can prove the following theorem.

Theorem 12.11 *In an open-bid ascending auction, the strategy vector in which every buyer lowers his hand when the declared price equals his private value is an equilibrium.*

Remark 12.12 *Note that in the dominant strategy equilibrium of the English auction established in Theorem 12.11, the winner of the object is the buyer with the highest private value and the selling price is the second highest private value. This is the same allocation* *and the same payment as in the dominant strategy equilibrium of the sealed-bid second-price auction established in Theorem 12.7.*   ♦

Remark 12.13 *There are other equilibria in sealed-bid second-price auctions, in addition to the equilibrium in which every buyer's bid equals his private value. For example, if the private values of two buyers are independent and uniformly distributed over the interval $[0, 1]$, the strategy vector in which buyer 1's bid is $b_1 = 1$ (for every private value v_1), and buyer 2's bid is $b_2 = 0$ (for every private value v_2), is an equilibrium (Exercise 12.4)*   ♦

12.5 The symmetric model with independent private values

In this section we will study models of sealed-bid auctions that satisfy the following assumptions:

(A1) Single object for sale: There is only one object offered for sale in the auction, and it is indivisible.

(A2) The seller is willing to sell the object at any nonnegative price.

(A3) There are n buyers, denoted by $1, 2, \ldots, n$.

(A4) Private values: All buyers have the same set of possible private values $\mathbb{V}$. This set can be a closed bounded interval $[0, \bar{v}]$ or the set of nonnegative numbers $[0, \infty)$. Every buyer knows his private value of the object. The random values $V_1, V_2, \ldots, V_n$ of the private values of the buyers are independent and identically distributed. Denote by F the common cumulative distribution function of the random variables V_i, $i = 1, 2, \ldots, n$. The support of this distribution is $\mathbb{V}$.

(A5) Continuity: For each i, the random variable V_i is continuous, and its density function, which we denote by f, is continuous and positive (this is the density function of the cumulative distribution function F of (A4)).

(A6) Risk neutrality: All the buyers are risk neutral, and therefore seek to maximize their expected profits.

We further assume that Assumptions (A1)–(A6) are common knowledge among the buyers (see Definition 9.17 on page 341). An auction model satisfying Assumptions (A1)–(A6) is called a *symmetric auction with independent private values*. This is the model studied in this section.

Since every buyer knows his own private value, any additional information, and in particular information regarding the private values of the other buyers, has no effect on his private value. That means that when buyer i's private value is v_i, then if he wins the auctioned object at price p, his profit is $v_i - p$, whether or not he knows the private values of the other buyers. In more general models in which buyers do not know with certainty the value of the auctioned object, the information a buyer has regarding the private values of the other buyers may be important to him, because it may be relevant to updating his own private value. Note that even if, after the auction is completed, the winner knows only that he has won, and not the details of the private values of the other buyers, he still obtains information about the other buyers' private values: he knows that the private values of the other buyers were sufficiently low for them not to submit bids higher than his bid.

The assumption that $V_1, V_2, \ldots, V_n$ are identically distributed is equivalent to the statement that prior to the random selection of the private values, the buyers are symmetric; each buyer, in his strategic considerations, assumes that all of the other buyers are similar to each other and to him.

12.5.1 Analyzing auctions: an example

Definition 12.14 *In a symmetric auction with independent private values, an equilibrium* $(\beta_1^*, \beta_2^*, \ldots, \beta_n^*)$ *is called a* symmetric equilibrium $\beta_i^* = \beta_j^*$ *for all* $1 \leq i, j \leq n$; *that is, all buyers implement the same strategy.*

When $\beta^* = (\beta_i^*)_{i \in N}$ is a symmetric equilibrium, we abuse notations and denote the common strategy also by β^*, that is, $\beta^* = \beta_i^*$ for every $i \in N$. Such a strategy is called a **symmetric equilibrium strategy**. We will denote by β_{-i}^* the vector of strategies in which all buyers except buyer i implement strategy β^*. We will sometimes denote the symmetric equilibrium strategy also by β_i^* when we want to focus on the strategy implemented by buyer i.

Example 12.15 **Two buyers with uniformly distributed private values**[3] Suppose that there are two buyers, and that V_i has uniform distribution over $[0, 1]$ for $i = 1, 2$ (and by Assumption (A4) V_1 and V_2 are independent). We will show that in a sealed-bid first-price auction the following strategy is a symmetric equilibrium:

$$\beta_i^*(v_i) = \frac{v_i}{2}, \quad i = 1, 2. \tag{12.11}$$

This equilibrium calls on each buyer to submit a bid that is half of his private value. Suppose that buyer 2 implements this strategy. Then if buyer 1's private value is v_1, and her submitted bid is b_1, her expected profit is

$$u_1(b_1, \beta_2^*; v_1) = u_1\left(b_1, \frac{V_2}{2}; v_1\right) \tag{12.12}$$

$$= \mathbf{P}\left(b_1 > \frac{V_2}{2}\right)(v_1 - b_1) \tag{12.13}$$

$$= \mathbf{P}(2b_1 > V_2)(v_1 - b_1) \tag{12.14}$$

$$= \min\{2b_1, 1\}(v_1 - b_1). \tag{12.15}$$

This function is quadratic over the interval $b_1 \in [0, \frac{1}{2}]$ (attaining its maximum at $b_1 = \frac{v_1}{2}$), and linear, with a negative slope, when $b_1 \geq \frac{1}{2}$. The graph of the function $b_1 \mapsto u_1(b_1, \beta_2^*; v_1)$ is shown in Figure 12.1 for the case $v_1 \leq \frac{1}{2}$ and the case $v_1 > \frac{1}{2}$.

In both cases, the function attains its maximum at the point $b_1 = \frac{v_1}{2}$. This implies that $b_1^*(v_1) = \frac{v_1}{2}$ is the best response to β_2^*, which in turn means that the strategy vector $\beta^* = (\beta_1^*, \beta_2^*)$ is a symmetric equilibrium.

We note that from our results so far we can observe that different auction methods have different equilibria:

- In the sealed-bid first-price auction in Example 12.15, a symmetric equilibrium is given by $\beta_i^*(v_i) = \frac{v_i}{2}$.

---

3 This example also appears on page 422 in Chapter 10.

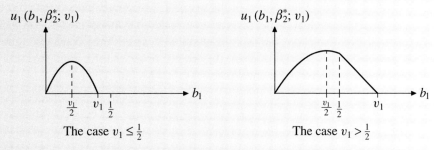

Figure 12.1 The payoff to buyer 1, as a function of b_1, when buyer 2 implements β_2^*

- In a sealed-bid second-price auction, a symmetric equilibrium is given by $\beta_i^*(v_i) = v_i$ (Theorem 12.9 and Exercise 12.3).

Which auction method is preferable from the perspective of the seller? To answer this question, we need to calculate the seller's expected revenue in each of the two auction methods. The seller's expected revenue equals the expected sale price. At the equilibrium that we have calculated, the expected sale price is

$$\mathbf{E}\left[\max\left\{\frac{V_1}{2}, \frac{V_2}{2}\right\}\right] = \frac{1}{2}\mathbf{E}[\max\{V_1, V_2\}]. \tag{12.16}$$

Denote $Z := \max\{V_1, V_2\}$. Since V_1 and V_2 are independent, and have uniform distribution over $[0, 1]$, the cumulative distribution function of Z is

$$F_Z(z) = \mathbf{P}(Z \le z) = \mathbf{P}(\max\{V_1, V_2\} \le z) = \mathbf{P}(V_1 \le z) \times \mathbf{P}(V_2 \le z) = z^2. \tag{12.17}$$

It follows that the density function of Z is

$$f_Z(z) = \begin{cases} 2z & \text{if } 0 \le z \le 1, \\ 0 & \text{otherwise.} \end{cases} \tag{12.18}$$

We deduce from this that the expected revenue is

$$\tfrac{1}{2}\mathbf{E}[Z] = \tfrac{1}{2}\int_0^1 z f_Z(z)\mathrm{d}z = \int_0^1 z^2\mathrm{d}z = \tfrac{1}{3}. \tag{12.19}$$

The seller's expected revenue in a sealed-bid second-price auction is given by $\mathbf{E}[\min\{V_1, V_2\}]$. Note that

$$\min\{V_1, V_2\} + \max\{V_1, V_2\} = V_1 + V_2, \tag{12.20}$$

and hence

$$\mathbf{E}[\min\{V_1, V_2\}] + \mathbf{E}[\max\{V_1, V_2\}] = \mathbf{E}[V_1] + \mathbf{E}[V_2] = \tfrac{1}{2} + \tfrac{1}{2} = 1. \tag{12.21}$$

We have already calculated that $\mathbf{E}[\max\{V_1, V_2\}] = \mathbf{E}[Z] = \tfrac{2}{3}$, so $\mathbf{E}[\min\{V_1, V_2\}] = \tfrac{1}{3}$. In other words, the seller's expected revenue in a sealed-bid second-price auction is $\tfrac{1}{3}$. ◀

Corollary 12.16 *In Example 12.15, in equilibrium, the expected revenue of the seller is the same, whether the auction method used is a sealed-bid first-price auction or second-price auction.*

This result is surprising at first sight, because one "would expect" that the seller would be better off selling the object at the price of the highest bid submitted, rather than the second-highest bid. However, buyers in a sealed-bid first-price auction will submit bids that are lower than those they would submit in a sealed-bid second-price auction, because in a sealed-bid first-price auction the winner pays what he bids, while in a sealed-bid second-price auction the winner pays less than his bid. The fact that these two opposing elements (on the one hand, the sale price in a sealed-bid first-price auction is the highest bid, while on the other hand, bids are lower in a sealed-bid first-price auction) cancel each other out and lead to the same expected revenue, is a mathematical result that is far from self-evident.

The equivalence between sealed-bid first-price auctions and open-bid descending auctions (Theorem 12.3), and the equivalence between the equilibrium payments in sealed-bid second-price auctions and open-bid ascending auctions (Remark 12.12), lead to the following corollary.

Corollary 12.17 *In Example 12.15, all four auction methods presented, the sealed-bid first price auction, sealed-bid second price auction, open-bid ascending auction and open-bid descending auction, yield the seller the same expected revenue in equilibrium.*

As we will see later, the equivalence of the expected profit in these four auction methods follows from a more general result (Theorem 12.23), called the Revenue Equivalence Theorem.

12.5.2 Equilibrium strategies

In this section, we will compute the equilibria of several auction methods.

Definition 12.18 *A symmetric equilibrium strategy β^* is* monotonically increasing *if the higher the private value, the higher the buyer's bid:*

$$v < v' \implies \beta^*(v) < \beta^*(v'), \quad \forall v, v' \in \mathbb{V}. \tag{12.22}$$

If β is a monotonically increasing symmetric equilibrium, the winner of the auction is the buyer with the highest private value. Since the distribution of V is continuous, the probability that two buyers have the same private value is 0. We proceed now to find monotonically increasing symmetric equilibria. Define

$$Y = \max\{V_2, V_3, \ldots, V_n\}. \tag{12.23}$$

This is a random variable, whose value equals the highest private value of buyers $2, \ldots, n$. From buyer 1's perspective, this is the highest private value of his competitors. In a monotonically increasing symmetric equilibrium, buyer 1 wins the auction if and only if $Y < V_1$. (As we previously stated, the event $Y = V_1$ has probability 0, so we ignore it, as it has no effect on the expected profit.)

The following theorem identifies a specific symmetric equilibrium, in symmetric auctions with independent private values.

Theorem 12.19 *In a symmetric auction with independent private values, the following strategy defines a symmetric equilibrium:*

$$\beta(v) := \mathbf{E}[Y \mid Y \leq v], \quad \forall v \in \mathbb{V}\setminus\{0\}, \tag{12.24}$$

and $\beta(0) := 0.$

Proof:
Step 1: β *is a monotonically increasing function.*
Recall that for every random variable X, and every pair of disjoint events A and B:

$$\mathbf{E}[X \mid A \cup B] = \mathbf{P}(A \mid A \cup B)\mathbf{E}[X \mid A] + \mathbf{P}(B \mid A \cup B)\mathbf{E}[X \mid B]. \tag{12.25}$$

Note that by the assumption that the density function f is positive (Assumption (A5)), it follows that Y is a continuous random variable with positive density function f_Y. Let v be an interior point of $\mathbb{V}_1$; that is, $v > 0$ and if $\mathbb{V} = [0, \bar{v}]$ is a bounded interval, then $v < \bar{v}$. For every $\delta > 0$ satisfying $v + \delta \in \mathbb{V}$,

$$\beta(v + \delta) = \mathbf{E}[Y \mid Y \leq v + \delta]$$
$$= \mathbf{P}(Y \leq v \mid Y \leq v + \delta) \times \mathbf{E}[Y \mid Y \leq v]$$
$$\quad + \mathbf{P}(v < Y \leq v + \delta \mid Y \leq v + \delta) \times \mathbf{E}[Y \mid v < Y \leq v + \delta]$$
$$= \frac{\mathbf{P}(Y \leq v)}{\mathbf{P}(Y \leq v + \delta)}\mathbf{E}[Y \mid Y \leq v]$$
$$\quad + \frac{\mathbf{P}(v < Y \leq v + \delta)}{\mathbf{P}(Y \leq v + \delta)}\mathbf{E}[Y \mid v < Y \leq v + \delta]. \tag{12.26}$$

Since the density function f_Y is positive, and since v is an interior point of $\mathbb{V}_1$,

$$\mathbf{E}[Y \mid Y \leq v] \leq v < \mathbf{E}[Y \mid v < Y \leq v + \delta]. \tag{12.27}$$

From Equation (12.26), we deduce that the $\beta(v + \delta)$ is the weighted average of two numbers, which, by Equation (12.27), satisfy the property that one is strictly greater than the other. Since the density function f_Y is positive, and since $v > 0$, the weights of both terms are positive. It follows that $\beta(v + \delta)$ is strictly greater than the minimal number among the two, which is, according to Equation (12.27), $\mathbf{E}[Y \mid Y \leq v]$, that is,

$$\beta(v + \delta) > \mathbf{E}[Y \mid Y \leq v] = \beta(v). \tag{12.28}$$

Therefore, β is an increasing function.

Step 2: β *is a continuous function.*
We will first show that β is continuous at $v = 0$. This obtains because for each $v \in \mathbb{V}$, $v > 0$,

$$0 \leq \beta(v) = \mathbf{E}[Y \mid Y \leq v] \leq v, \tag{12.29}$$

leading to $\lim_{v \to 0} \beta(v) = 0 = \beta(0)$. We now show that β is continuous at each point $v > 0$. By the definition of conditional expectation,

$$\beta(v) = \mathbf{E}[Y \mid Y \leq v] = \frac{\int_0^v yf_Y(y)dy}{\mathbf{P}(Y \leq v)} = \frac{1}{F_Y(v)}\int_0^v yf_Y(y)dy. \tag{12.30}$$

Since the random variable Y is continuous, the cumulative distribution function F_Y is a continuous function. Since the density function f_Y is positive for all $v > 0$, $F_Y(v) > 0$; the denominator is not zero. It follows that β is the quotient of two continuous functions of v in which the function in the denominator is non-zero for $v > 0$, and hence it is a continuous function.

Note that from Equation (12.30) we can deduce, by integrating by parts, that

$$F_Y(v)\mathbf{E}[Y \mid Y \le v] = \int_0^v y f_Y(y)\mathrm{d}y = v F_Y(v) - \int_0^v F_Y(y)\mathrm{d}y. \qquad (12.31)$$

This equation will be useful later in the proof.

Step 3: β is a symmetric equilibrium strategy.

Suppose that buyers $2, 3, \ldots, n$ all implement strategy β. We will show that in that case, buyer 1's best reply is the same strategy β. Let v_1 be buyer 1's private value. If $\mathbb{V} = [0, \bar{v}]$ is a bounded interval, suppose that $v < \bar{v}$, which occurs with probability 1 (why?). Since the function β is monotonically strictly increasing (Step 1) and continuous (Step 2), it has a continuous inverse β^{-1}.

Buyer 1's expected profit, when he bids b_1, is

$$u_1(b_1, \beta_{-1}; v_1) = \mathbf{P}(\beta(Y) < b_1)(v_1 - b_1). \qquad (12.32)$$

If buyer 1 bids $b_1 = 0$, with probability 1 he does not win the auction: since the density of Y is positive in the interval $\mathbb{V}$, the probability that $Y > 0$ is 1, and since β is monotonically increasing, with probability 1 another buyer bids more than 0. We deduce that $u_1(0, \beta_{-1}; v_1) = 0$.

If buyer 1 bids b_1 greater than or equal to his private value v_1, by Equation (12.32) his expected payoff is nonpositive:

$$u_1(b_1, \beta_{-1}; v_1) \le 0, \quad \forall b_1 \ge v_1. \qquad (12.33)$$

Since the density of V_i is positive in the set $\mathbb{V}$, the probability $\mathbf{P}(\beta(Y) < b_1)$ is positive for every $b_1 > 0$. It follows that in the domain $\mathbb{V} \setminus \{0\}$ the function $b_1 \mapsto u_1(b_1, \beta_{-1}; v_1)$ is the product of two positive functions and it is therefore a positive function. To summarize, we proved that $u_1(b_1, \beta_{-1}; v_1)$ is positive for $b_1 \in (0, v_1)$ and nonpositive for $b_1 \notin (0, v_1)$, and therefore the function $b_1 \mapsto u_1(b_1, \beta_{-1}; v_1)$, attains its maximum at an interior point of $[0, v_1]$. We next present the expected profit $u_1(b_1, \beta_{-1}; v_1)$ in a more useful form:

$$u_1(b_1, \beta_{-1}; v_1) = \mathbf{P}(\beta(Y) < b_1)(v_1 - b_1) \qquad (12.34)$$

$$= \mathbf{P}(Y < \beta^{-1}(b_1))(v_1 - b_1) \qquad (12.35)$$

$$= F_Y(\beta^{-1}(b_1)) \times (v_1 - \beta(\beta^{-1}(b_1))) \qquad (12.36)$$

$$= F_Y(\beta^{-1}(b_1)) \times (v_1 - \mathbf{E}[Y \mid Y \le \beta^{-1}(b_1)]). \qquad (12.37)$$

Let b_1 be an interior point of the interval $\beta(\mathbb{V})$, which is the image of β, and denote $z_1 := \beta^{-1}(b_1)$. Then $b_1 = \beta(z_1)$, and hence

$$u_1(\beta(z_1), \beta_{-1}; v_1) = F_Y(z_1) \times (v_1 - \mathbf{E}[Y \mid Y \le z_1]). \qquad (12.38)$$

Denote the right-hand side of Equation (12.38) by $h(z_1)$:

$$h(z_1) := F_Y(z_1) \times (v_1 - \mathbf{E}[Y \mid Y \leq z_1]) \qquad (12.39)$$

$$= F_Y(z_1)(v_1 - z_1) + F_Y(z_1)z_1 - F_Y(z_1)\mathbf{E}[Y \mid Y \leq z_1] \qquad (12.40)$$

$$= F_Y(z_1)(v_1 - z_1) + \int_0^{z_1} F_Y(y)dy, \qquad (12.41)$$

where Equation (12.41) follows from Equation (12.31).

To find the point $b_1 \in \mathbb{V}$ at which the maximum of $u_1(b_1, \beta_{-1}; v_1)$ is attained, it suffices to find the point $z_1 \in \mathbb{V}$ at which the maximum of $h(z_1)$ is attained. To do so, differentiate h; the function h is differentiable over the interval $(0, v_1)$, and its derivative is

$$h'(z_1) = f_Y(z_1)(v_1 - z_1) - F_Y(z_1) + F_Y(z_1) = f_Y(z_1)(v_1 - z_1). \qquad (12.42)$$

The derivative h' equals zero at a single point, $z_1 = v_1$, which is therefore the maximum of h. In other words, buyer 1's best reply, when his private value is v_1 and the other buyers implement strategy β, is $\beta^{-1}(b_1) = z_1 = v_1$, i.e., $b_1 = \beta(v_1)$. $\qquad \square$

In summary, our results on equilibrium strategies in sealed-bid first-price and second-price auctions are as follows:

Corollary 12.20 *In a symmetric sealed-bid auction with independent private values:*

- $\beta(v) = \mathbf{E}[Y \mid Y \leq v]$ *is a symmetric equilibrium strategy in the sealed-bid first-price auction.*
- $\beta(v) = v$ *is a symmetric equilibrium strategy in the sealed-bid second-price auction.*

Example 12.15 *(Continued)* When there are two buyers, with private values uniformly distributed over $[0, 1]$, $\beta(v) = \mathbf{E}[Y \mid Y \leq v] = \frac{v}{2}$. This is the symmetric equilibrium strategy we found on page 480. ◀

We next compute the expected profits of the buyers and the seller in these two auction methods.

Theorem 12.21 *In the symmetric equilibria given by Corollary 12.20, the expected payment that a buyer with private value v makes for the object is $F_Y(v) \times \mathbf{E}[Y \mid Y \leq v]$, in both sealed-bid first-price and second-price auctions.*

Proof: At equilibrium in a sealed-bid second-price auction, a buyer with private value v submits a bid of v. He wins the auction with probability $F_Y(v)$, and the expected amount he pays is $\mathbf{E}[Y \mid Y \leq v]$. His expected payment is therefore $F_Y(v) \times \mathbf{E}[Y \mid Y \leq v]$, as claimed above.

At equilibrium in a sealed-bid first-price auction, a buyer with private value v submits a bid of $\mathbf{E}[Y \mid Y \leq v]$. He wins the auction with probability $F_Y(v)$, and pays what he bid. His expected payment for the object is therefore also $F_Y(v) \times \mathbf{E}[Y \mid Y \leq v]$. $\qquad \square$

Corollary 12.22 *In a symmetric sealed-bid auction with independent private values, at the symmetric equilibrium, the expected revenue of a seller in both sealed-bid first-price and second-price auctions, is*

$$\pi = n \int_{\mathbb{V}} F_Y(v)\mathbf{E}[Y \mid Y \le v] f(v) dv. \tag{12.43}$$

Proof: The expected payment of a buyer with private value v is $F_Y(v)\mathbf{E}[Y \mid Y \le v]$. It follows that the expected payment made by each buyer is $\int_{\mathbb{V}} F_Y(v)\mathbf{E}[Y \mid Y \le v] f(v) dv$. Since the seller's expected revenue is the sum of the expected payments of the n buyers, the result follows. $\qquad\square$

12.5.3 The Revenue Equivalence Theorem

In the previous section, we saw that the symmetric and monotonically increasing equilibrium that we found in sealed-bid first-price and second-price auctions always yields the seller the same expected revenue. Is this coincidental, or is there a more general result implying this? As we shall see in the sequel, the Revenue Equivalence Theorem shows that there is indeed a more general result, ascertaining that the expected revenue of the seller is constant over a broad family of auction methods.

Recall that we denote by (p, C) a sealed-bid auction in which the winner is determined by the function p, and each buyer's payment is determined by the function C. Let $\beta : \mathbb{V} \to [0, \infty)$ be a monotonically increasing strategy. Denote by $e_i(v_i) = e(p, C, \beta; v_i)$ the expected payment that buyer i with private value v_i pays in auction method (p, C), when all the buyers implement strategy β:

$$e_i(v_i) := \int_{\mathbb{V}_{-i}} \sum_{i_* \in N} p_{i_*}(\beta(v_1), \beta(v_2), \dots, \beta(v_n)) C_i(i_*; \beta(v_1), \beta(v_2), \dots, \beta(v_n)) dF_{-i}(v_{-i}). \tag{12.44}$$

Theorem 12.23 *Let β be a symmetric and monotonically increasing equilibrium in a sealed-bid symmetric auction with independent private values satisfying the following properties: (a) the winner of the auction is the buyer with the highest private value, and (b) the expected payment made by a buyer with private value 0 is 0. Then*

$$e_i(v_i) = F_Y(v_i)\mathbf{E}[Y \mid Y \le v_i]. \tag{12.45}$$

Property (a) of the equilibrium is known as the "efficiency condition": an efficient auction is one in which, at equilibrium, the auctioned object is allocated to the buyer who most highly values it. Since the seller is willing to sell the auctioned object at any nonnegative price, and since the private values of the buyers are nonnegative, in an efficient auction the object is sold with probability 1. Under a symmetric and monotonically increasing equilibrium, the object is sold to the highest bidder.

The expression on the right-hand side of Equation (12.45) is independent of the auction methods, and depends solely on the distribution of Y, which is determined by the distribution of the private values of the buyers. Theorem 12.23 states therefore that the expected payment that a buyer with private value v makes is independent of the auction method, and depends only on the distribution of the private values of the buyers. It follows that if n risk-neutral buyers are asked whether they prefer to participate in a sealed-bid first-price auction, or a sealed-bid second-price auction, they have no reason to prefer one to the other.

By integrating Equation (12.45) over buyer types, we deduce that the seller's expected revenue is independent of the auction method:

Corollary 12.24 (The Revenue Equivalence Theorem) *In a symmetric sealed-bid auction with independent private values, let β be a symmetric and monotonically increasing equilibrium satisfying the following properties: (a) the winner is the buyer with the highest private value, and (b) the expected payment of each buyer with private value 0 is 0. Then the seller's expected revenue is*

$$\pi = n \int_{\mathbb{V}} e_i(v)f(v)dv, \tag{12.46}$$

where

$$e_i(v) = F_Y(v)\mathbf{E}[Y \mid Y \le v]. \tag{12.47}$$

Proof of Theorem 12.23: Since the private values are independent and identically distributed, the cumulative distribution function of Y is

$$F_Y = F^{n-1}. \tag{12.48}$$

Let β be a symmetric and monotonically increasing equilibrium strategy in a sealed-bid auction (p, C). Let $v_1 \in \mathbb{V}$ be a private value of buyer 1 (which is not 0 and is not $\bar{v}$ if $\mathbb{V} = [0, \bar{v}]$ is a bounded interval). If buyer 1 with private value v_1 deviates from the strategy and plays as if his private value is z_1, he wins only if z_1 is higher than the private values of the other buyers, and the probability of that occurring is $F_Y(z_1)$. His profit in this case is

$$u_1(\beta z_1, \beta_{-1}; v_1) = v_1 F_Y(z_1) - e_1(z_1). \tag{12.49}$$

Since β is an equilibrium, buyer 1's best reply is $z_1 = v_1$. In other words, the function $z_1 \mapsto u_1(\beta z_1, \beta_{-1}; v_1)$ attains its maximum at $z_1 = v_1$, which is an interior point of $\mathbb{V}$.

We next prove that the function e_1 is differentiable, and compute its derivative. Since the function $z_1 \mapsto u_1(\beta z_1, \beta_{-1}; v_1)$ attains its maximum at $z_1 = v_1$, for any pair of interior points v_1, z_1 in the interval $\mathbb{V}$ one has

$$v_1 F_Y(z_1) - e_1(z_1) = u_1(\beta z_1, \beta_{-1}; v_1) \le u_1(\beta v_1, \beta_{-1}; v_1) = v_1 F_Y(v_1) - e_1(v_1). \tag{12.50}$$

By exchanging the roles of z_1 and v_1, we deduce that for every pair of interior points v_1, z_1 in the interval $\mathbb{V}$ one has

$$z_1 F_Y(v_1) - e_1(v_1) = u_1(\beta v_1, \beta_{-1}; z_1) \le u_1(\beta z_1, \beta_{-1}; z_1) = z_1 F_Y(z_1) - e_1(z_1). \tag{12.51}$$

From Equations (12.50) and (12.51), by rearrangement, we have

$$e_1(v_1) - e_1(z_1) \le (F_Y(v_1) - F_Y(z_1))v_1, \tag{12.52}$$

$$e_1(v_1) - e_1(z_1) \ge (F_Y(v_1) - F_Y(z_1))z_1. \tag{12.53}$$

For $z_1 \neq v_1$, dividing Equations (12.52) and (12.53) by $v_1 - z_1$, and taking the limit as z_1 goes to v_1, we get

$$\lim_{z_1 \to v_1} \frac{e_1(v_1) - e_1(z_1)}{v_1 - z_1} = v_1 f_Y(v_1), \quad \forall v_1 \in V, v_1 \notin \{0, \bar{v}\}. \tag{12.54}$$

In particular, e_1 is a differentiable function and its derivative is $e_1'(v_1) = v_1 f_Y(v_1)$ for every $v_1 \in V_1$. Note that the derivative e_1' is independent of the auction method. Since $e_1(0) = 0$, by integration, for every $v_1 \in V$ (including the extreme points) we get

$$e_1(v_1) = e_1(0) + \int_0^{v_1} e_1'(y)\mathrm{d}y = \int_0^{v_1} y f_Y(y)\mathrm{d}y = F_Y(v_1)\mathbf{E}[Y \mid Y \leq v_1],$$

$$\tag{12.55}$$

which is what we wanted to prove. □

We now show how to use the Revenue Equivalence Theorem to find symmetric equilibrium strategies in various auctions.

Theorem 12.25 *Let β be a symmetric, monotonically increasing equilibrium strategy, satisfying $\beta(0) = 0$ in a symmetric sealed-bid first-price auction with independent private values. Then*

$$\beta(v) = \mathbf{E}[Y \mid Y \leq v]. \tag{12.56}$$

This theorem complements Theorem 12.19, where we proved that $\beta(v) = \mathbf{E}[Y \mid Y \leq v]$ is a symmetric equilibrium strategy that is monotonically increasing and satisfies $\beta(0) = 0$. Theorem 12.25 shows that this is the unique such symmetric equilibrium in sealed-bid first-price auctions.

Proof: Since the function β is monotonic, a buyer with private value v wins the auction if and only if his private value is higher than the private values of all the other buyers. It follows that the probability that a buyer with value v wins the auction is $F_Y(v)$. If he wins, he pays his bid, meaning that he pays $\beta(v)$. The expected payment that the buyer makes is therefore

$$e(v) = F_Y(v)\beta(v). \tag{12.57}$$

Since β satisfies the conditions of Theorem 12.23 (note that the condition that $\beta(0) = 0$ guarantees that at this equilibrium, $e(0) = 0$), Theorem 12.23 implies that

$$e(v) = F_Y(v)\mathbf{E}[Y \mid Y \leq v]. \tag{12.58}$$

Since $F_Y(v) > 0$ for every $v > 0$, from Equations (12.57) and (12.58) we get

$$\beta(v) = \mathbf{E}[Y \mid Y \leq v], \tag{12.59}$$

which is what we wanted to show. □

The following theorem exhibits the equilibrium of an all-pay auction in which every buyer pays the amount of his bid, whether or not he wins the auctioned object (see page 473).

Theorem 12.26 *Let β be a symmetric, monotonically increasing equilibrium strategy, satisfying $\beta(0) = 0$, in a symmetric sealed-bid all-pay auction with independent private values. Then*

$$\beta(v) = F_Y(v)\mathbf{E}[Y \mid Y \le v]. \tag{12.60}$$

Proof: In a sealed-bid all-pay auction, every buyer pays his bid, in any event, and it follows that the payment that a buyer with private value v makes is $e(v) = \beta(v)$. Since the conditions of Theorem 12.23 are guaranteed by the monotonicity of β and the condition $\beta(0) = 0$, we deduce that $e(v) = F_Y(v)\mathbf{E}[Y \mid Y \le v]$. It follows that $\beta(v) = F_Y(v)\mathbf{E}[Y \mid Y \le v]$, which is what we needed to prove. $\quad\square$

Example 12.15 *(Continued)* **A sealed-bid first-price auction with two buyers** Consider a sealed-bid first-price auction with two buyers, where the private values of the buyers are independent and uniformly distributed over $[0, 1]$. We will compute the following:

- $e(v)$, the expected payment of a buyer with a private value v.
- e, the buyer's expected payment, before he knows his private value.
- $E = ne$, the seller's expected revenue.

For each $v \in [0, 1]$, one has $F_Y(v) = v$ and $f_Y(v) = 1$, and we have seen that $\beta(v) = \mathbf{E}[Y \mid Y \le v] = \frac{v}{2}$. Therefore,

$$e(v) = F_Y(v)\mathbf{E}[Y \mid Y \le v] = \frac{v^2}{2}, \tag{12.61}$$

$$e = \int_0^1 \frac{v^2}{2}\,dv = \left.\frac{v^3}{6}\right]_0^1 = \tfrac{1}{6}, \tag{12.62}$$

$$\pi = 2\left(\tfrac{1}{6}\right) = \tfrac{1}{3}. \tag{12.63}$$

The seller's expected revenue π is $\tfrac{1}{3}$, as we computed directly on page 481. ◀

Example 12.27 **A sealed-bid first-price auction with an arbitrary number of buyers** Consider a symmetric sealed-bid first-price auction with $n \ge 2$ buyers. The private values of the buyers are independent and uniformly distributed over $[0, 1]$. Then $F_Y(v) = v^{n-1}$ and $f_Y(v) = (n-1)v^{n-2}$, for each $v \in [0, 1]$. By Theorem 12.26, the symmetric equilibrium strategy is

$$\beta(v) = \mathbf{E}[Y \mid Y \le v] = \frac{\int_0^v x f_Y(x)\,dx}{F_Y(v)} = \frac{\int_0^v (n-1)x^{n-1}\,dx}{v^{n-1}} = \frac{n-1}{n}v. \tag{12.64}$$

It follows that the expected payment of a buyer with private value v is

$$e(v) = F_Y(v)\mathbf{E}[Y \mid Y \le v] = \frac{n-1}{n}v^n. \tag{12.65}$$

The buyer's expected payment, before he knows his private value, is

$$e = \frac{n-1}{n}\int_0^1 v^n\,dv = \frac{n-1}{n}\frac{1}{n+1}, \tag{12.66}$$

and the seller's expected revenue is

$$\pi = ne = \frac{n-1}{n+1}. \tag{12.67}$$

This value converges to 1 as n increases to infinity. Since the seller's revenue equals the sale price, we deduce that the sale price converges to 1 as the number of buyers approaches infinity (explain intuitively why this should be expected). ◄

12.5.4 Entry fees

We have assumed, up to now, that participation in an auction is free, and that buyers therefore lose nothing in submitting bids. In this section, we explore, via examples, how adding entry fees for auctions may affect the strategies of buyers, and the seller's expected revenue.

Example 12.28   **Sealed-bid second-price auction with entry fee** Consider a sealed-bid second-price auction with entry fee $\lambda \in [0, 1]$. In such an auction, a buyer may decide not to participate; for example, he may decline to participate if his private value is lower than the entry free. If there is only one buyer submitting a bid, that buyer wins the auction and pays 0.

As in second-price auctions without entry fees, when a buyer decides to participate in a second-price auction with an entry fee, his bid will be his private value of the auctioned object. To formulate this claim precisely, denote the set of actions of each buyer by $A = \mathbb{R}_+ \cup \{\text{"no"}\}$, where "no" means "don't participate in the auction" and $x \in \mathbb{R}_+$ means "participate in the auction, pay the entry fee λ and bid the price x." A (pure) strategy of buyer i is a measurable function $\beta_i : V_i \to A$. That is, when buyer i's private value is v_i he implements action $\beta_i(v_i)$.

Theorem 12.29 *In a sealed-bid second-price auction with entry fee, for every strategy β_i of buyer i the following strategy $\widehat{\beta}_i$ weakly dominates β_i, if $\widehat{\beta}_i \neq \beta_i$,*

$$\widehat{\beta}_i(v) = \begin{cases} \text{"no"} & \beta_i(v) = \text{"no,"} \\ v & \beta_i(v) = x. \end{cases} \tag{12.68}$$

The proof of the theorem is similar to the proof of Theorem 4.15 (page 92); the proof is left to the reader (Exercise 12.22). Theorem 12.29 implies that to find an equilibrium in a sealed-bid second-price auction with entry fees, we have to find for each buyer the set of private values for which he will participate in the auction.

Suppose that there are two buyers, and that the private values V_1 and V_2 are independent and uniformly distributed over $[0, 1]$. Since the buyer knows his own private value before he submits his bid, if his private value is low, he will not participate in the auction. There must therefore exist a threshold value v_0 such that no buyer with a private value below v_0 will participate in the auction.

Suppose that buyer 1's private value equals the threshold $V_1 = v_0$. If the equilibrium is monotonic, this buyer will win the auction if and only if buyer 2 does not participate in the auction, since if buyer 2 participates, with probability 1 his private value V_2 is greater than v_0, and therefore buyer 2's bid is greater than buyer 1's private value v_0. It follows that $\mathbf{P}(\text{winning the auction} \mid v_0) = v_0$. On the other hand, when the private value of buyer 1 equals the threshold value v_0, he is indifferent between participating and not participating. The buyer's expected profit if he participates is

$$\mathbf{P}(\text{winning the auction} \mid v_0) \times v_0 - \lambda = (v_0)^2 - \lambda, \tag{12.69}$$

and his profit if he does not participate is 0; we deduce that $(v_0)^2 - \lambda = 0$, or $v_0 = \sqrt{\lambda}$. An equilibrium strategy in this game is therefore

$$\beta(v) = \begin{cases} \text{"Don't participate"} & \text{if } v < \sqrt{\lambda}, \\ v & \text{if } v \geq \sqrt{\lambda}. \end{cases} \tag{12.70}$$

The probability that each buyer will participate in the auction is $1 - \sqrt{\lambda}$.

To compute the seller's expected revenue, denote $V_{\max} = \max\{V_1, V_2\}$, and $V_{\min} = \min\{V_1, V_2\}$.

- If $V_{\min} \geq v_0$, both buyers participate in the auction, the seller receives 2λ as entry fee, and the sale price of the auctioned object is $V_{\min}$.
- If $V_{\max} < v_0$, no buyer will participate, and the seller's revenue is 0.
- If $V_{\min} < v_0 \leq V_{\max}$, only one buyer participates in the auction, the seller receives λ as entry fee, and the sale price of the auctioned object will be 0.

The seller's expected revenue, as a function of the entry fee λ, is therefore

$$\pi(\lambda) = \mathbf{P}(V_{\min} \geq v_0)(2\lambda + \mathbf{E}[V_{\min} \mid V_{\min} \geq v_0]) + \mathbf{P}(V_{\min} < v_0 \leq V_{\max}) \times \lambda. \tag{12.71}$$

Now,

$$F_{V_{\min}}(z) = \mathbf{P}(V_{\min} \leq z) = z + (1-z)z = z(2-z), \tag{12.72}$$

$$f_{V_{\min}}(z) = F'_{V_{\min}}(z) = 2(1-z), \tag{12.73}$$

$$\mathbf{P}(V_{\min} \geq v_0) = (1-v_0)^2, \tag{12.74}$$

$$\mathbf{P}(V_{\min} < v_0 \leq V_{\max}) = 2\mathbf{P}(V_1 < v_0 \leq V_2) = 2v_0(1-v_0), \tag{12.75}$$

$$\mathbf{E}[V_{\min} \mid V_{\min} \geq v_0] = \frac{1}{\mathbf{P}(V_{\min} \geq v_0)} \int_{v_0}^1 v f_{V_{\min}}(v) dv$$

$$= \frac{1}{(1-v_0)^2} \int_{v_0}^1 2v(1-v) dv = \frac{2v_0+1}{3}. \tag{12.76}$$

By inserting the values of Equations (12.74)–(12.76) in (12.71), and using the fact that $v_0 = \sqrt{\lambda}$, we get

$$\pi(\lambda) = (1-\sqrt{\lambda})^2 \left(2\lambda + \frac{2\sqrt{\lambda}+1}{3}\right) + 2\sqrt{\lambda}(1-\sqrt{\lambda}) \times \lambda \tag{12.77}$$

$$= \frac{(1-\sqrt{\lambda})}{3}((1-\sqrt{\lambda})(1+2\sqrt{\lambda}+6\lambda) + (6\lambda\sqrt{\lambda})) \tag{12.78}$$

$$= \frac{(1-\sqrt{\lambda})(4\lambda + \sqrt{\lambda} + 1)}{3}. \tag{12.79}$$

This is a concave function of λ, satisfying $\pi(0) = \frac{1}{3}$ and $\pi(1) = 0$. Differentiating the function π, we have:

$$\pi'(\lambda) = [(1-\sqrt{\lambda})(4\lambda + \sqrt{\lambda} + 1)]' = [1 + 3\lambda - 4\lambda^{\frac{3}{2}}]' = 3 - 6\sqrt{\lambda}. \tag{12.80}$$

The derivative π' vanishes at $\lambda^* = \frac{1}{4}$, where

$$\pi\left(\frac{1}{4}\right) = \frac{1}{3}\left(1 - \frac{1}{2}\right)\left(4 \cdot \frac{1}{4} + \frac{1}{2} + 1\right) = \frac{1}{3} \cdot \frac{1}{2} \cdot \frac{5}{2} = \frac{5}{12} > \frac{1}{3}. \tag{12.81}$$

Because $\pi(\frac{1}{4})$ is greater than $\pi(0)$ and greater than $\pi(1)$, the function π attains its maximum at the point $\lambda^* = \frac{1}{4}$, and hence the entry fee maximizing the seller's expected revenue is $\lambda^* = \frac{1}{4}$. We conclude that in this case, a sealed-bid second-price auction with entry fee $\frac{1}{4}$ yields the seller an expected revenue that is greater than what he can receive from a sealed-bid second-price auction without entry fees. ◄

Remark 12.30 *The fact that the seller's expected revenue from a sealed-bid second-price auction with entry fee is greater than his expected revenue from a sealed-bid second-price auction without entry fee does not contradict the Revenue Equivalence Theorem (Theorem 12.23), because the auction with entry fees does not satisfy the efficiency property: if both buyers have private values lower than the entry fee, the auctioned object is not sold, despite the fact that there is a buyer willing to pay for it.*　◆

12.6　The Envelope Theorem

Recall that, given the strategy of the other buyers β_{-i}, the profit of buyer i with private value v_i who submits a bid b_i, is $u_i(b_i, \beta_{-i}; v_i)$. The expected profit of the buyer is the difference between the product of the probability he will win the auction and his private value of the auctioned object, and his expected payment to the seller:

$$u_i(b_i, \beta_{-i}; v_i) = \mathbf{P}(\text{buyer } i \text{ wins the auction } \mid b_i, \beta_{-i}) \times v_i$$
$$- \mathbf{E}[\text{buyer } i\text{'s payment to the seller } \mid b_i, \beta_{-i}]. \tag{12.82}$$

Both the probability of winning the auction and buyer i's payment depend on the bid b_i that he submits (and the strategies of the other buyers), but not on his private value. The function $u_i(b_i, \beta_{-i}; v_i)$ is therefore linear in v_i. At equilibrium, the buyer's bid maximizes his expected profit. The buyer's profit at equilibrium is therefore

$$u_i^*(\beta_{-i}; v_i) := \max_{b_i \geq 0} u_i(b_i, \beta_{-i}; v_i). \tag{12.83}$$

This function is called the *upper envelope*, because if we draw the function $v_i \mapsto u_i(b_i, \beta_{-i}; v_i)$ for every b_i, then $u_i^*(\beta_{-i}; v_i)$ is the upper envelope of this family of linear functions. Figure 12.2 shows some of these linear functions $v_i \mapsto u_i(b_i, \beta_{-i}; v_i)$ for various values of b_i, along with the upper envelope. Denote by $b_i^*(v_i)$ a value of b_i at which the maximum of $u_i(b_i, \beta_{-i}; v_i)$ for a given v_i is obtained:

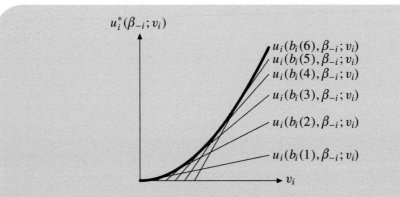

Figure 12.2 The function $u_i(b, \beta_{-i}; v_i)$, for different values of b_i and the upper envelope $u_i^*(\beta_{-i}; v_i)$ (the bold curve)

$$u_i^*(\beta_{-i}; v_i) = u_i(b_i^*(v_i), \beta_{-i}; v_i). \tag{12.84}$$

That is, b_i^* is a best reply of the buyer to the strategy vector β_{-i}. Assuming that the function u_i is differentiable[4] and the function $v_i \mapsto b_i^*(v_i)$ is also differentiable, the function $v_i \mapsto u_i^*(\beta_{-i}; v_i)$ is differentiable, and its derivative is

$$\frac{\partial u_i^*}{\partial v_i}(\beta_{-i}; v_i) = \frac{\partial u_i}{\partial v_i}(b_i, \beta_{-i}; v_i)_{|b_i=b_i^*(v_i)} + \frac{\partial u_i}{\partial b_i}(b_i, \beta_{-i}; v_i)_{|b_i=b_i^*(v_i)} \cdot \frac{db_i^*(v_i)}{dv_i}. \tag{12.85}$$

If for each private value v_i, $\frac{\partial u_i}{\partial b_i}(b_i, \beta_{-i}; v_i)_{|b_i=b_i^*(v_i)} = 0$ at the maximal point $b_i^*(v_i)$, then the second term is zero, leading to the following conclusion, called the Envelope Theorem, which has many applications in economics.

Theorem 12.31 (The Envelope Theorem) *Let b_i^* be a best response of buyer i to the strategy vector β_{-i} of the other buyers; i.e., b_i^* satisfies Equation (12.84). If the function $u_i(b_1, \beta_{-i}; v_i)$ is differentiable, and the function $v_i \mapsto b_i^*(v_i)$ is differentiable and satisfies $\frac{\partial u_i}{\partial b_i}(b_i, \beta_{-i}; v_i)_{|b_i=b_i^*(v_i)} = 0$ for every private value v_i, then*

$$\frac{\partial u_i^*}{\partial v_i}(\beta_{-i}; v_i) = \frac{\partial u_i}{\partial v_i}(b_i, \beta_{-i}; v_i)_{|b_i=b_i^*(v_i)}. \tag{12.86}$$

Remark 12.32 *The condition $\frac{\partial u_i}{\partial b_i}(b_i, \beta_{-i}; v_i)_{|b_i=b_i^*(v_i)} = 0$ holds if $0 < b_i^*(v_i) < \infty$ because this is the first-order condition for a local maximum. If follows that it is necessary to check that it holds only if the maximum is at an extreme point, i.e., only if $b_i^*(v_i) = 0$.* ◆

To apply the chain rule, the function $v_i \mapsto b_i^*(v_i)$ has to be differentiable. That means that the equilibrium strategy must be differentiable. A symmetric equilibrium β^* is called a *differentiable symmetric equilibrium* if the function β^* is differentiable.

Example 12.33 **Sealed-bid first-price auction** Consider a sealed-bid first-price auction with n buyers. Suppose that the private values of the buyers are independent of each other, that they are all in the unit interval $[0, 1]$, and that they share the same cumulative distribution function F. Assuming that there exists a monotonically increasing and differentiable symmetric equilibrium strategy β^*, we can compute it using the Envelope Theorem. Recall that β_{-i}^* is the strategy vector in which all the buyers, except for buyer i, use the strategy β^*. The expected profit of buyer i with private value v_i who submits a bid b_i is

$$u_i(b_i, \beta_{-i}^*; v_i) = \mathbf{P}(\text{the buyer wins the auction} \mid b_i, \beta_{-i}^*) \times (v_i - b_i) \tag{12.87}$$

$$= (F((\beta^*)^{-1}(b_i)))^{n-1} \times (v_i - b_i). \tag{12.88}$$

Since β^* is an equilibrium, $\beta_i^*(v_i)$ is the best response of buyer i with private value v_i to β_{-i}^*, and therefore $b_i^*(v_i) = \beta_i^*(v_i)$. If β is differentiable, then β^{-1} is also differentiable, and then $u_i(b_i, \beta_{-i}^*; v_i)$ is differentiable. Since the strategy β^* is monotonically increasing, and because $\beta^*(0) \geq 0$ and $\beta^*(1) \leq 1$, it follows that $0 \leq \beta^*(v_i) \leq 1$ for all $v_i \in (0, 1)$, and therefore $\frac{\partial u_i}{\partial b_i}(b_i, \beta_{-i}^*; v_i)_{|b_i=\beta_i^*(v_i)} = 0$. The Envelope Theorem implies that

---

4 A real-valued multi-variable function is *differentiable* if it is continuously differentiable (i.e., its derivative is continuous) with respect to each variable. This is equivalent to it being differentiable in every direction in the space of variables.

$$\frac{\partial u_i^*}{\partial v_i}(\beta_{-i}^*; v_i) = \frac{\partial u_i}{\partial v_i}(b_i, \beta_{-i}^*; v_i)_{|b_i = \beta_i^*(v_i)} = (F(v_i))^{n-1}. \tag{12.89}$$

Note that $u_i^*(\beta_{-i}^*; 0) = 0$, i.e., the profit of a buyer with private value 0 is 0. By integrating, we get

$$u_i^*(\beta_{-i}^*; v_i) = \int_0^{v_i} (F(x_i))^{n-1} \mathrm{d}x_i. \tag{12.90}$$

From this equation, along with Equation (12.88), for $b_i = b_i^*(v_i) = \beta^*(v_i)$, we get

$$(F(v_i))^{n-1}(v_i - \beta^*(v_i)) = \int_0^{v_i} (F(x_i))^{n-1} \mathrm{d}x_i. \tag{12.91}$$

After moving terms from one side of the equals sign to the other, we have

$$\beta^*(v_i) = v_i - \frac{\int_0^{v_i}(F(x_i))^{n-1}\mathrm{d}x_i}{(F(v_i))^{n-1}}. \tag{12.92}$$

In other words, if a monotonically increasing, differentiable, and symmetric equilibrium exists, it is necessarily given by Equation (12.92).

Recall that, according to Theorem 12.19, in a symmetric sealed-bid first-price auction with independent private values, the symmetric equilibrium is $\beta^*(v) = \mathbf{E}[Y \mid Y \leq v]$. It follows that in the case before us, in which the distribution of the private values of the buyers is the uniform distribution over $[0, 1]$, this expression must be equal to the expression given by Equation (12.92). The reader is asked to check directly that these two expressions indeed equal each other in Exercise 12.24. ◄

Example 12.34   **Sealed-bid first-price auction with a reserve price** An auction with a reserve price ρ is an auction in which every bid below ρ is invalid. Consider a sealed-bid first-price auction with a reserve price $\rho \in [0, 1]$ and two buyers whose private values are independent and uniformly distributed over $[0, 1]$. What is the symmetric equilibrium strategy β^*? A buyer with a private value lower than or equal to ρ cannot profit no matter what bid he makes. Using the Envelope Theorem we can find a symmetric, monotonically increasing and differentiable equilibrium strategy satisfying $\beta^*(v_1) = v_1$ for all $v_1 \in [0, \rho]$. This choice is arbitrary and it guarantees that a bid by a buyer whose private value is less than ρ is invalid.[5]

Step 1: $\rho \leq \beta^*(v_1) < v_1$ for all $v_1 \in (\rho, 1]$.
$u_1(b_1, \beta^*; v_1) = 0$ for all $b_1 < \rho$, and $u_1(b_1, \beta^*; v_1) \leq 0$ for all $b_1 \geq v_1$. For all $b_1 \in (\rho, v_1)$,

$$u_1(b_1, \beta^*; v_1) \geq \mathbf{P}(V_2 < \rho)(b_1 - \rho) > 0. \tag{12.93}$$

It follows that the maximum of the function $b_1 \mapsto u_1(b_1, \beta^*; v_1)$ is attained at a point in the interval $[\rho, v_1)$.

Step 2: $\rho < \beta^*(v_1) < v_1$ for all $v_1 \in (\rho, 1]$.
Suppose by contradiction that there exists $v_1 \in (\rho, 1]$ such that $\beta^*(v_1) = \rho$ and let $\widehat{v}_1 \in (\rho, v_1)$. Since β^* is a monotonic strategy,

$$\beta^*(\widehat{v}_1) < \beta^*(v_1) = \rho, \tag{12.94}$$

in contradiction to Step 1.

---

5 In this example we have two buyers, and therefore the vector β_{-1}^* of the strategies played in the symmetric equilibrium by all players except Player 1 is β^*. We therefore write β^* instead of β_{-1}^*.

Step 3: Computing β^*.
For $v_1 \in (\rho, 1]$ the maximum of the function $b_1 \mapsto u_1(b_1, \beta^*; v_1)$ is attained at a point in the interval (ρ, v_1), this is a local maximum, and since β^* is a differentiable function, $\frac{\partial u_1}{\partial b_1}(b_1, \beta^*; v_1)_{|b_1 = \beta^*(v_1)} = 0$.

By the Envelope Theorem:

$$\frac{\partial u_1^*}{\partial v_1}(\beta^*; v_1) = \frac{\partial u_1}{\partial v_1}(b_1, \beta^*; v_1)_{|b_1 = \beta^*(v_1)}. \tag{12.95}$$

Since the distribution of V_2 is the uniform distribution over $[0, 1]$, and since β^* is monotonically increasing,

$$u_1(b_1, \beta^*; v_1) = \mathbf{P}(\beta^*(V_2) < b_1) \times (v_1 - b_1) = (\beta^*)^{-1}(b_1) \times (v_1 - b_1). \tag{12.96}$$

Therefore,

$$\frac{\partial u_1}{\partial v_1}(b_1, \beta^*; v_1) = (\beta^*)^{-1}(b_1), \tag{12.97}$$

and Equations (12.82) and (12.95)–(12.97) imply that

$$\frac{\partial u_1^*}{\partial v_1}(\beta^*; v_1) = (\beta^*)^{-1}(\beta^*(v_1)) = v_1. \tag{12.98}$$

For $v_1 \le \rho$, the profit is zero: $u_1^*(\beta_{-1}^*; v_1) = 0$. By integration, we get

$$u_1^*(\beta^*; v_1) = \int_\rho^{v_1} \frac{\partial u_1^*}{\partial t_1}(\beta^*; t_1)\mathrm{d}t_1 = \int_\rho^{v_1} t_1 \mathrm{d}t_1 = \frac{(t_1)^2}{2}\Big|_\rho^{v_1} = \frac{(v_1)^2}{2} - \frac{\rho^2}{2}. \tag{12.99}$$

On the other hand, the buyer's profit $u_1^*(\beta^*; v_1)$ can be computed directly: in a symmetric, monotonically increasing equilibrium, buyer 1's profit is the probability that the private value of buyer 2 is lower than v_1 times the profit $(v_1 - \beta^*(v_1))$ if he wins:

$$u_1^*(\beta^*; v_1) = u_1(\beta^*(v_1), \beta^*; v_1) = v_1(v_1 - \beta^*(v_1)), \quad \forall v_1 \in (\rho, 1]. \tag{12.100}$$

From Equations (12.99) and (12.100) we conclude that

$$\beta^*(v_1) = \frac{v_1}{2} + \frac{\rho^2}{2v_1}, \quad \forall v_1 \in (\rho, 1]. \tag{12.101}$$

Step 4: Computing the seller's expected revenue.
We have shown that if there exists a monotonically increasing and differentiable symmetric equilibrium strategy in the interval $(\rho, 1]$, then that strategy is defined by Equation (12.101). The strategy that we found is indeed differentiable. To see that it is monotonically increasing, we look at its derivative:

$$(\beta^*)'(v_1) = \frac{1}{2} - \frac{\rho^2}{2(v_1)^2}, \quad \forall v_1 \in (\rho, 1]. \tag{12.102}$$

We see that for $v_1 \in (\rho, 1]$ it is indeed the case that $(\beta^*)'(v_1) > 0$.

Note that for $\rho = 0$ (an auction without a minimum price), by Equation (12.101), $\beta^*(v_1) = \frac{v_1}{2}$, which is the solution that we found for sealed-bid first-price auctions without a reserve price (Example 12.15 on page 480).

What is the seller's expected revenue? Computing this requires first computing each buyer's expected payment. Buyer 1's payment is 0 when $v_1 \le \rho$. If $v_1 > \rho$, he wins only if $v_1 > v_2$ (an event that occurs with probability v_1), and then he pays $\beta^*(v_1)$ (we are ignoring the possibility that $v_1 = v_2$, which occurs with probability 0). The expected payment of buyer 1 is, therefore,

$$e = \int_\rho^1 v_1 \beta^*(v_1) dv_1 = \int_\rho^1 v_1 \left(\frac{v_1}{2} + \frac{\rho^2}{2v_1} \right) dv_1 = \tfrac{1}{2} \left(\frac{(v_1)^3}{3} + \rho^2 v_1 \right) \Big|_\rho^1$$

$$= \tfrac{1}{6} + \tfrac{\rho^2}{2} - \tfrac{2}{3}\rho^3. \tag{12.103}$$

Since there are two buyers, the seller's expected revenue is

$$\pi(\rho) = 2e = \tfrac{1}{3} + \rho^2 - \tfrac{4}{3}\rho^3. \tag{12.104}$$

Note that $\pi(0) = \tfrac{1}{3}$: in a sealed-bid first-price auction without a reserve price, the seller's expected revenue is $\tfrac{1}{3}$. Similarly, $\pi(1) = 0$: when the reserve price is 1, with probability 1 no buyer wins the object and the seller's expected revenue is 0. What is the reserve price that maximizes the seller's expected payoff? To compute that, differentiate the function π, and set the derivative to 0:

$$0 = \pi'(\rho) = 2\rho - 4\rho^2. \tag{12.105}$$

It follows that the reserve price that maximizes the seller's expected revenue is $\rho = \tfrac{1}{2}$, at which the seller's expected revenue is $\pi(\tfrac{1}{2}) = \tfrac{5}{12}$. Since $\tfrac{5}{12} \geq \tfrac{1}{3}$, introducing a reserve price is beneficial for the seller. Note that $\tfrac{5}{12}$ is also the seller's expected revenue in a sealed-bid second-price auction with entry fee $\tfrac{1}{4}$ (see Example 12.28). ◀

12.7 Risk aversion

One of the underlying assumptions of our analysis so far has been that the buyers participating in auctions are risk neutral, and therefore their goal is to maximize their expected profits. What happens if we drop this assumption? In this section, we will see how risk-averse buyers behave in sealed-bid first-price and second-price auctions. We will consider auction models satisfying Assumptions (A1)–(A5), thus omitting the risk neutrality assumption (A6). For simplicity we maintain the term "symmetric auction with independent private values" for this model.

Suppose that the buyers satisfy the von Neumann–Morgenstern axioms with respect to their utility for money (for a review of utility theory, see Chapter 2). In addition, suppose that each buyer has the same monotonically increasing utility function for money, $U : \mathbb{R} \to \mathbb{R}$, satisfying $U(0) = 0$.

If buyer i's private value is v_i, and his bid is b_i, the buyer's profit is:

- 0, if he does not win the auction.
- $v_i - b_i$, if he wins.

If we denote by α_{b_i} the probability that the buyer wins the auction if he bids b_i, then when he bids b_i, he is effectively facing the lottery

$$[\alpha_{b_i}(v_i - b_i), (1 - \alpha_{b_i})(0)]. \tag{12.106}$$

Since the buyer's preference relation satisfies the von Neumann–Morgenstern axioms, and since $U(0) = 0$, his utility from this lottery is

$$U[\alpha_{b_i}(v_i - b_i), (1 - \alpha_{b_i})(0)] = \alpha_{b_i} U(v_i - b_i). \tag{12.107}$$

Recall (see Section 2.7 on page 23) that a buyer is *risk averse* if his utility function for money U is concave, is *risk neutral* if his utility function U is linear, and is *risk seeking* if his utility function U is convex.

In a sealed-bid second-price auction, the strategy

$$\beta(v) = v \tag{12.108}$$

still weakly dominates all other strategies, even if the buyers are risk averse (or risk seeking). The reasoning behind this is the same reasoning behind the similar conclusion we presented in the case of risk-neutral buyers, using the fact that U is monotonic (see Exercise 12.25). The situation is quite different in a sealed-bid first-price auction.

Theorem 12.35 *Consider a symmetric sealed-bid first-price auction with independent private values. Suppose that each buyer has the same utility function for money U that is monotonically increasing, differentiable, and strictly concave. Let γ be a monotonically increasing, differentiable, and symmetric equilibrium strategy satisfying $\gamma(0) = 0$. Then γ is the solution of the differential equation*

$$\gamma'(v) = (n-1) \times \frac{f(v)}{F(v)} \times \frac{U(v - \gamma(v))}{U'(v - \gamma(v))}, \quad \forall v > 0 \tag{12.109}$$

with initial condition $\gamma(0) = 0$.

Proof: Since γ is monotonically increasing, if buyer i bids b_i, and the other buyers implement strategy γ, the probability that buyer i wins the auction is $(F(\gamma^{-1}(b_i)))^{n-1}$. Since $U(0) = 0$, the buyer's utility is

$$u_i(b_i, \gamma_{-i}; v_i) = (F(\gamma^{-1}(b_i)))^{n-1} \times U(v_i - b_i). \tag{12.110}$$

We will first check that for $v_i > 0$, the maximum of this function is attained at a value b_i, which is in the interval $(0, v_i)$. This is accomplished by showing that $u_i(0, \gamma_{-i}; v_i) = u_i(v_i, \gamma_{-i}; v_i) = 0$ and $u_i(b_i, \gamma_{-i}; v_i) < 0$ for each $b_i > v_i$, while $u_i(b_i, \gamma_{-i}; v_i) > 0$ for each $b_i \in (0, v_i)$.

- If buyer i's bid is $b_i = v_i$, his utility from winning is 0, and therefore $u_i(v_i, \gamma_{-i}; v_i) = 0$.
- Since $\gamma(0) = 0$ it follows that $F(\gamma^{-1}(0)) = 0$, and therefore $u_i(0, \gamma_{-i}; v_i) = 0$.
- Since U is monotonically increasing and $U(0) = 0$, $v_i - b_i < 0$ for $b_i > v_i$, and therefore $U(v_i - b_i) < 0$. By Assumptions (A4) and (A5), $F(\gamma^{-1}(b_i)) > 0$ for every $b_i > v_i$, and therefore $u_i(b_i, \gamma_{-i}; v_i) < 0$ for every $b_i > v_i$.
- Finally, we show that $u_i(b_i, \gamma_{-i}; v_i) > 0$ for every $b_i \in (0, v_i)$. For every $b_i > 0$, since γ is monotonically increasing, $\gamma^{-1}(b_i) > 0$, and Assumptions (A4) and (A5) imply that $F(\gamma^{-1}(b_i)) > 0$. Since the utility function is monotonically increasing, $U(v_i - b_i) > 0$, and therefore $u_i(b_i, \gamma_{-i}; v_i) > 0$.

We deduce that the maximum of the function $b_i \mapsto u_i(b_i, \gamma_{-i}; v_i)$ is indeed attained at a point in the open interval $(0, v_i)$.

We next differentiate the function u_i in Equation (12.110) (which is differentiable because both U and γ are differentiable), yielding

$$\frac{\partial u_i}{\partial b_i}(b_i, \gamma_{-i}; v_i) = (n-1)\frac{f(\gamma^{-1}(b_i))}{\gamma'(\gamma^{-1}(b_i))}(F(\gamma^{-1}(b_i)))^{n-2}U(v_i - b_i)$$

$$- (F(\gamma^{-1}(b_i)))^{n-1}U'(v_i - b_i). \qquad (12.111)$$

Since the strategy γ is a symmetric equilibrium strategy, the maximum of this function is attained at $b_i = \gamma(v_i)$; and at that point, the derivative vanishes. Thus, by substituting $b_i = \gamma(v_i)$ in Equation (12.111) one has

$$0 = \frac{\partial u_i}{\partial b_i}(b_i, \gamma_{-i}; v_i)|_{b_i = \gamma(v_i)}$$

$$= (n-1)\frac{f(v_i)}{\gamma'(v_i)}(F(v_i))^{n-2}U(v_i - \gamma(v_i)) - (F(v_i))^{n-1}U'(v_i - \gamma(v_i)). \quad (12.112)$$

Because $v_i > 0$, and by Assumption (A5), $F(v_i) > 0$. Reducing the factor $(F(v_i))^{n-2}$ in Equation (12.112), and rearranging the remaining equation, yields Equation (12.109). □

We now prove that when all the buyers are risk averse and have the same utility function, the submitted bids in equilibrium are higher than the bids that would be submitted by risk-neutral buyers. The intuition behind this result is that risk-averse buyers are more concerned about not winning the auction, and therefore they submit higher bids than risk-neutral buyers.

Theorem 12.36 *Suppose that in a symmetric sealed-bid first-price auction with independent private values, each buyer's utility function U is monotonically increasing, differentiable, strictly concave, and satisfies $U(0) = 0$. Let γ be a monotonically increasing, differentiable, symmetric equilibrium strategy satisfying $\gamma(0) = 0$, and let β be monotonically increasing, differentiable, symmetric equilibrium strategy satisfying $\beta(0) = 0$ in the auction when the buyers are risk-neutral. Then $\gamma(v) > \beta(v)$ for each $v > 0$.*

Proof: Theorem 12.35 implies that

$$\gamma'(v) = (n-1)\frac{f(v)}{F(v)} \times \frac{U(v - \gamma(v))}{U'(v - \gamma(v))}, \quad \forall v > 0. \qquad (12.113)$$

Since the strategy β also satisfies the conditions of Theorem 12.35, this strategy, for risk-neutral buyers, satisfies Equation (12.113) with utility function $U(v) = v$:

$$\beta'(v) = (n-1)\frac{f(v)}{F(v)} \times (v - \beta(v)), \quad \forall v > 0. \qquad (12.114)$$

Since U is a strictly concave function, and $U(0) = 0$, it follows that $U'(v) < \frac{U(v)}{v}$ (see Figure 12.3), or equivalently, $\frac{U(v)}{U'(v)} > v$.

It follows that

$$\gamma'(v) = (n-1)\frac{f(v)}{F(v)} \times \frac{U(v - \gamma(v))}{U'(v - \gamma(v))} > (n-1)\frac{f(v)}{F(v)} \times (v - \gamma(v)). \qquad (12.115)$$

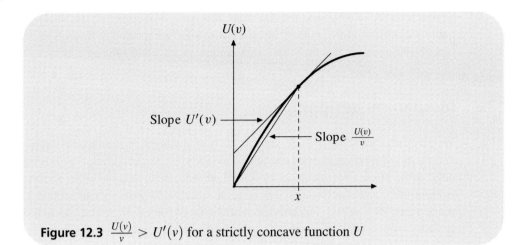

Figure 12.3 $\frac{U(v)}{v} > U'(v)$ for a strictly concave function U

To show that $\gamma(v) > \beta(v)$ for each $v > 0$, note that if $v_0 > 0$ satisfies $\gamma(v_0) \le \beta(v_0)$, then

$$\gamma'(v_0) > (n-1)\frac{f(v_0)}{F(v_0)} \times (v_0 - \gamma(v_0)) \tag{12.116}$$

$$\ge (n-1)\frac{f(v_0)}{F(v_0)} \times (v_0 - \beta(v_0)) = \beta'(v_0) > 0. \tag{12.117}$$

Define $\delta(v) := \gamma(v) - \beta(v)$ for all $v \in \mathbb{V}$. Equations (12.116) and (12.117) show that $\delta'(v) > 0$ for each $v > 0$ such that $\delta(v) \le 0$. It follows that if there exists $v_0 > 0$ such that $\delta(v_0) \le 0$, then $\delta(v) < 0$ for each $v \in [0, v_0)$. Since $\delta(0) = \gamma(0) - \beta(0) = 0$, there does not exist $v_0 > 0$ such that $\delta(v_0) \le 0$. In other words, $\gamma(v) > \beta(v)$ for each $v > 0$. □

In the model used in this section, in which all the buyers have the same utility function for money, the bids submitted by the buyers in the symmetric equilibrium of the sealed-bid first-price auctions are higher if all buyers are risk averse, which implies that the seller's expected revenue is higher. In contrast, in sealed-bid second-price auctions, the bids submitted by buyers in the symmetric equilibrium equal their private values, whether they are risk averse or risk neutral, and hence the seller's expected revenue is equal in either case. This leads to the following corollary.

Corollary 12.37 *In a symmetric sealed-bid auction with independent private values, when buyers are risk averse, and they all have the same monotonically increasing, differentiable, and strictly concave utility function, the seller's expected revenue in the symmetric equilibrium is higher in a sealed-bid first-price auction than in a sealed-bid second-price auction. In particular, this proves that the Revenue Equivalence Theorem does not apply when the buyers are risk averse.*

The converse corollary can similarly be proved for risk-seeking buyers (Exercise 12.26). In a symmetric sealed-bid auction with independent private values, when the buyers are risk seeking and they all have the same monotonically increasing, differentiable, and strictly convex utility functions, the seller's expected revenue in the symmetric equilibrium is lower in a first-price auction than in a second-price auction.

12.8 Mechanism design

We have presented up to now several auction methods, which we analyzed by computing an equilibrium in each auction, and studying its properties. The advantages and disadvantages of a particular auction method were then judged by the properties of its equilibrium. A natural question that arises is whether one can plan an auction method, or more generally a selling mechanism, that can be expected to yield a "desired outcome." In other words, what we seek is a selling mechanism whose equilibrium has "desired properties," such as efficiency and maximizing the revenue of the seller. In this section we will study mechanism design, a subject that focuses on these sorts of questions.

Definition 12.38 *A selling problem is a vector* $(N; (\mathbb{V}_i, f_i)_{i \in N})$ *such that:*

- $N = \{1, 2, \ldots, n\}$ *is a set of buyers.*
- $\mathbb{V}_i$ *is a bounded interval* $[0, \bar{v}]$ *or an infinite interval* $[0, \infty)$.
- $f_i : \mathbb{V}_i \to [0, \infty)$ *is a density function, i.e.,* $\int_{\mathbb{V}_i} f_i(v) dv = 1$.

A selling problem serves as a model for the following situation:

- A seller wishes to sell an indivisible object, whose value for the seller is normalized to be 0.
- The set of buyers is $N = \{1, 2, \ldots, n\}$. The buyers are all risk-neutral, and each seeks to maximize the expected value of his profit.
- The private value of buyer i is a random variable V_i with values in the interval $\mathbb{V}_i$. This is a continuous random variable whose density function is f_i. The random variables $(V_i)_{i \in N}$ are independent random variables that do not necessarily have the same distribution; we do not rule out the possibility that $f_i \neq f_j$ for different buyers i and j.
- Each buyer knows his private value and does not know the private values of the other buyers, but he knows the distributions of the random variables $(V_j)_{j \neq i}$.

Denote by $\mathbb{V}^N := \mathbb{V}_1 \times \mathbb{V}_2 \times \cdots \times \mathbb{V}_n$ the space of all possible vectors of private values. Since the private value of the buyers are independent, the joint density function of the vector $V = (V_1, V_2, \ldots, V_n)$ is

$$f_V(v) = \prod_{i \in N} f_i(v_i). \tag{12.118}$$

Denote:

$$f_{-i}(v_{-i}) := \prod_{j \neq i} f_j(v_j). \tag{12.119}$$

f_{-i} is the joint density function of $V_{-i} = (V_j)_{j\neq i}$. Since the private values are independent, this is also the marginal density of V over $\mathbb{V}_{-i}$, conditioned on V_i, where $\mathbb{V}_{-i} := \times_{j\neq i}\mathbb{V}_j$ is the set of all possible private value vectors of all the buyers except for buyer i.

Definition 12.39 *A selling mechanism for a selling problem* $(N, (\mathbb{V}_i, f_i)_{i\in N})$ *is a vector* $((\Theta_i, \widehat{q}_i, \widehat{\mu}_i)_{i\in N})$ *where, for each buyer* $i \in N$:

1. Θ_i *is a measurable space*[6] *of messages that buyer* i *can send to the seller. The space of the message vectors is* $\Theta = \Theta_1 \times \Theta_2 \times \cdots \times \Theta_n$.
2. $\widehat{q}_i : \Theta \to [0, 1]$ *is a function mapping each vector of messages to the probability that buyer* i *wins the object. (Necessarily,* $\sum_{i\in N} \widehat{q}_i(\theta) \leq 1$, *for every* $\theta \in \Theta$.*)*
3. $\widehat{\mu}_i : \Theta \to \mathbb{R}$ *is a function mapping every vector of messages to the payment that buyer* i *makes to the seller (whether or not he wins the object).*

If $\sum_{i\in N} \widehat{q}_i(\theta) < 1$ for a particular $\theta \in \Theta$, then when the message vector received by the seller is θ there is a positive probability that the object will not be sold (and will therefore remain in the possession of the seller).

Given a selling mechanism, we define the following game.

- The set of players (buyers) is N.
- Each buyer $i \in N$ chooses a message $\theta_i \in \Theta_i$. Denote $\theta = (\theta_1, \theta_2, \ldots, \theta_n)$.
- Buyer i wins the object with probability $\widehat{q}_i(\theta)$. The object remains in the possession of the seller with probability $1 - \sum_{i\in N} \widehat{q}_i(\theta)$.
- Every buyer i pays to the seller the amount $\widehat{\mu}_i(\theta)$.

The space of messages in a selling mechanism may be very complex: if the selling mechanism includes negotiations, the message space may include the buyer's first offer, his second offer to every counteroffer of the seller, and so on.

From now on we study selling mechanisms for a given selling problem.

Example 12.40 **Sealed-bid first-price auction** A sealed-bid first-price auction with risk-neutral buyers can be presented as a selling mechanism as follows:

- $\Theta_i = [0, \infty)$: Buyer i's message is a nonnegative number; this is buyer i's bid.
- Denote by

$$N(\theta) := |\{i \in N : \theta_i = \max_{j\in N} \theta_j\}| \qquad (12.120)$$

the number of buyers who submit the highest bid.[7]

$$\widehat{q}_i(\theta) = \begin{cases} \frac{1}{N(\theta)} & \text{if } \theta_i = \max_{j\in N} \theta_j, \\ 0 & \text{if } \theta_i < \max_{j\in N} \theta_j. \end{cases} \qquad (12.121)$$

- The payment that buyer i makes is

$$\widehat{\mu}_i(\theta) = \begin{cases} \frac{\theta_i}{N(\theta)} & \text{if } \theta_i = \max_{j\in N} \theta_j, \\ 0 & \text{if } \theta_i < \max_{j\in N} \theta_j. \end{cases} \qquad (12.122)$$

---

6 Recall that Θ_i is a *measurable space* if it has an associated σ-algebra, i.e., a collection of subsets of Θ_i containing the empty set that is closed under countable unions and set complementation.

7 Recall that for every finite set A, the number of elements in A is denoted by $|A|$.

This description differs from the auction descriptions we previously presented only in the payment that the buyer who submits the highest bid makes, and only in the case that several buyers submit the same bid. In the description of an auction as a selling mechanism, all the buyers who submitted the highest bid equally share the cost of that bid whether or not they finally get the object, while in the description on page 472, only the winner of the object pays its full price, which equals his bid. But this difference does not change the strategic considerations of the buyers: when there are several buyers submitting the same highest bid and the winner of the object is chosen from among them according to the uniform distribution, in both cases the expected payment that the buyer who wins the auction makes is the amount that he bid, divided by $N(\theta)$, and his probability of winning is $\frac{1}{N(\theta)}$. Since the buyers are risk-neutral and the goal of each buyer is to maximize his expected profit, the strategic considerations of the buyers, under both definitions, are unchanged. ◀

Example 12.41 **Sealed-bid second-price auction** Similar to a sealed-bid first-price auction, a sealed-bid second-price auction with risk-neutral buyers can also be presented as a selling mechanism. The only difference is in the payment function, $\widehat{\mu}$, which is given as follows:

$$\widehat{\mu}_i(\theta) = \begin{cases} \frac{\max_{j \neq i} \theta_j}{N(\theta)} & \text{if } \theta_i = \max_{j \in N} \theta_j, \\ 0 & \text{if } \theta_i < \max_{j \in N} \theta_j. \end{cases} \tag{12.123}$$

Again, $N(\theta)$ is the number of buyers who submitted the highest bid. ◀

As the following theorem states, every sealed-bid auction is an example of a selling mechanism. The proof of the theorem is left to the reader (Exercise 12.28).

Theorem 12.42 *Every sealed-bid auction with risk-neutral buyers can be presented as a selling mechanism.*

The game that corresponds to a selling mechanism is a Harsanyi game with incomplete information (see Definition 9.39 on page 358).

- The set of players is the set of buyers $N = \{1, 2, \ldots, n\}$.
- Player i's set of types is $\mathbb{V}_i$. Denote $\mathbb{V}^N := \times_{i \in N} \mathbb{V}_i$.
- The distribution of the set of type vectors is a product distribution, whose density is f_V.
- For each type vector $v \in \mathbb{V}^N$, the state of nature s_v is the state game defined by
  - player i's set of actions is Θ_i;
  - for each vector of actions $\theta \in \Theta$, buyer i's utility is

$$u_i(v; \theta) = \widehat{q}(\theta)v_i - \widehat{\mu}_i(\theta). \tag{12.124}$$

In other words, the buyer pays $\widehat{\mu}_i(\theta)$ in any event, and if he wins the auctioned object, he receives v_i, his value of the object.

A pure strategy for player i is a measurable function $\beta_i : \mathbb{V}_i \to \Theta_i$. For each strategy vector $\beta_{-i} = (\beta_j)_{j \neq i}$ of the other buyers, denote by $u_i(\theta_i, \beta_{-i}; v_i)$ buyer i's expected profit, when his private value is v_i, and he sends message θ_i:

$$u_i(\theta_i, \beta_{-i}; v_i)$$
$$= \int_{\mathbb{V}_{-i}} u_i(v_i; \beta_1(v_1), \ldots, \beta_{i-1}(v_{i-1}), \theta_i, \beta_{i+1}(v_{i+1}), \ldots, \beta_n(v_n)) f_{-i}(v) dv_{-i}.$$

$$\tag{12.125}$$

The definition of a Bayesian equilibrium of the game with incomplete information that corresponds to a selling mechanism is as follows (see Definition 9.49 on page 364).

Definition 12.43 *A vector $\beta = (\beta_1, \beta_2, \ldots, \beta_n)$ of strategies is a (Bayesian) equilibrium if for each buyer $i \in N$, and every private value $v_i \in \mathbb{V}_i$,*

$$u_i(\beta_i(v_i), \beta_{-i}; v_i) \geq u_i(\theta_i, \beta_{-i}; v_i), \quad \forall \theta_i \in \Theta_i. \tag{12.126}$$

A simple set of mechanisms is the set of direct selling mechanisms, in which the set of messages of each buyer is his set of private values.

Definition 12.44 *A selling mechanism $(\Theta_i, \widehat{q}_i, \widehat{\mu}_i)_{i \in N}$ is called direct if $\Theta_i = \mathbb{V}_i$ for each buyer $i \in N$.*

A direct selling mechanism is a mechanism in which every buyer is required to report a private value; he may report his true private value or make up any other value to report. We will denote a direct selling mechanism by $(\widehat{q}, \widehat{\mu})$ for short, where $\widehat{q} = (\widehat{q}_i)_{i \in N}$ and $\widehat{\mu} = (\widehat{\mu}_i)_{i \in N}$.

When a mechanism is direct, a possible strategy that a buyer may use is to report his true private value:

$$\beta_i^*(v_i) = v_i, \quad \forall v_i \in \mathbb{V}_i. \tag{12.127}$$

We refer to this as the "truth-telling" strategy.

Definition 12.45 *A direct selling mechanism $(\widehat{q}, \widehat{\mu})$ is* incentive compatible *if the vector $\beta^* = (\beta_i^*)_{i \in N}$ of truth-telling strategies $\beta_i^*(v_i) = v_i$ is an equilibrium.*

The reason we use the term "incentive compatible" is because if β^* is an equilibrium, then each buyer has an incentive to report his private value truthfully: he cannot profit by lying in reporting his private value. This property is analogous to the nonmanipulability property that we will discuss in Chapter 22, on social choice theory.

The direct selling mechanism depicted in Example 12.41 for a sealed-bid second-price auction is an incentive compatible mechanism, because in a sealed-bid second-price auction, the strategy vector β^* in which every buyer's bid equals his private value is an equilibrium. In contrast, the direct selling mechanism depicted in Example 12.40, corresponding to a sealed-bid first-price auction, is not incentive compatible, because in a sealed-bid first-price auction the strategy vector β^* is not an equilibrium. As the next example shows, when the buyers are symmetric, it is nevertheless possible to describe sealed-bid first-price auctions as incentive-compatible direct selling mechanisms.

Example 12.46 **Sealed-bid first-price auction: another representation as a selling mechanism** Consider a symmetric sealed-bid first-price auction that satisfies Assumptions (A4)–(A6). Let $\beta = (\beta_i)_{i \in N}$ be an equilibrium of the auction. Consider the following direct selling mechanism:

- $\Theta_i = [0, \infty)$: buyer i's message is a nonnegative number.
- The probability that buyer i wins the auctioned object is

$$\widehat{q}_i(\theta) = \begin{cases} \frac{1}{N(\theta)} & \text{if } \theta_i = \max_{j \in N} \theta_j, \\ 0 & \text{if } \theta_i < \max_{j \in N} \theta_j. \end{cases} \tag{12.128}$$

- The expected payment that buyer i makes is

$$\widehat{\mu}_i(\theta) = \begin{cases} \beta_i(\theta_i) & \text{if } \theta_i = \max_{j \in N} \theta_j, \\ 0 & \text{if } \theta_i < \max_{j \in N} \theta_j. \end{cases} \qquad (12.129)$$

In words, a buyer submitting the highest bid pays the expected sum that he would pay under equilibrium β when the private values are $(\theta_i)_{i \in N}$. Since β is an equilibrium, the strategy vector β^*, under which each buyer reports his private value, is an equilibrium in this selling mechanism, and therefore in particular this selling mechanism is incentive compatible. ◀

12.8.1 The revelation principle

The idea in Example 12.46 can be generalized to any selling mechanism: let $(\Theta_i, \widehat{q}_i, \widehat{\mu}_i)_{i \in N}$ be a selling mechanism, and let $\widehat{\beta}$ be an equilibrium of this mechanism. We can then define a direct selling mechanism (q, μ), as follows: if the buyers report the private values vector $v = (v_i)_{i \in N}$, the mechanism computes what message $\widehat{\beta}_i(v_i)$ the buyer would have sent in the original mechanism, and then proceeds exactly as that mechanism would have done under those messages: for each buyer $i \in N$,

$$q_i(v) := \widehat{q}_i(\widehat{\beta}_1(v_1), \dots, \widehat{\beta}_n(v_n)), \qquad (12.130)$$

$$\mu_i(v) := \widehat{\mu}_i(\widehat{\beta}_1(v_1), \dots, \widehat{\beta}_n(v_n)). \qquad (12.131)$$

The mechanism (q, μ) is schematically described in Figure 12.4. Since the strategy vector $\widehat{\beta}$ is an equilibrium of the mechanism $(\Theta_i, \widehat{q}_i, \widehat{\mu}_i)_{i \in N}$, the strategy vector β^* according to which every buyer reports his true private value is an equilibrium of the mechanism (q, μ). This leads to the following theorem, which is called the revelation principle.

Theorem 12.47 (Myerson [1979]) *Let $(\Theta_i, \widehat{q}_i, \widehat{\mu}_i)_{i \in N}$ be a selling mechanism, and let $\widehat{\beta}$ be an equilibrium of this mechanism. There exists an incentive-compatible direct selling mechanism (q, μ) satisfying that the outcome of the original mechanism under $\widehat{\beta}$ is identical to the outcome of (q, μ) under β^* (which is the truth-telling equilibrium):*

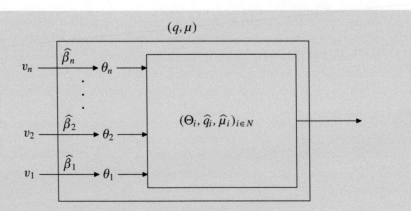

Figure 12.4 A selling mechanism, along with a θ incentive-compatible direct selling mechanism that is equivalent to it

$$\hat{q}\left(\hat{\beta}_1(v_1), \hat{\beta}_2(v_2), \ldots, \hat{\beta}_n(v_n)\right) = q(v_1, v_2, \ldots, v_n), \quad \forall(v_1, \ldots, v_n) \in \mathbb{V}, \quad (12.132)$$

$$\hat{\mu}\left(\hat{\beta}_1(v_1), \hat{\beta}_2(v_2), \ldots, \hat{\beta}_n(v_n)\right) = \mu(v_1, v_2, \ldots, v_n), \quad \forall(v_1, \ldots, v_n) \in \mathbb{V}. \quad (12.133)$$

The proof of the theorem is left to the reader as an exercise (Exercise 12.30). The theorem's importance stems from the fact that incentive-compatible direct selling mechanisms are simple and easy to work with, resulting in simpler mathematical analysis. The space of messages in a generic selling mechanism may be quite large, and the revelation principle simplifies the effort required to analyze selling mechanisms. It implies that it suffices to consider only incentive-compatible direct selling mechanisms, because every general selling mechanism has an incentive-compatible, direct mechanism that is equivalent to it in the sense of Theorem 12.47.

12.8.2 The Revenue Equivalence Theorem

In this section we prove a general Revenue Equivalence Theorem for selling mechanisms, which includes the Revenue Equivalence Theorem for auctions as a special case (Theorem 12.23 on page 486). To that end, we first introduce some new notation, and prove intermediate results.

Consider a direct selling mechanism (q, μ). When buyer i reports that his private value is x_i, and the other buyers report their true private values, the probability that buyer i wins the object is

$$Q_i(x_i) = \int_{\mathbb{V}_{-i}} q_i(x_i, v_{-i}) f_{-i}(v_{-i}) dv_{-i}, \quad (12.134)$$

and the expected payment he makes is

$$M_i(x_i) = \int_{\mathbb{V}_{-i}} \mu_i(x_i, v_{-i}) f_{-i}(v_{-i}) dv_{-i}. \quad (12.135)$$

Because the private value of the buyers are independent, these two quantities are independent of buyer i's true private value, and depend solely on the message x_i that he reports.

Buyer i's expected profit, when his true private value is v_i and he reports x_i, is

$$u_i(x_i, \beta^*_{-i}; v_i) = Q_i(x_i)v_i - M_i(x_i). \quad (12.136)$$

In other words, the buyer's expected profit is the probability that he wins the auction, times his private value, less the expected payment that he makes. Given this, the following equation is obtained:

$$u_i(x_i, \beta^*_{-i}; v_i) = Q_i(x_i)v_i - M_i(x_i) \quad (12.137)$$
$$= Q_i(x_i)x_i - M_i(x_i) + Q_i(x_i)(v_i - x_i) \quad (12.138)$$
$$= u_i(x_i, \beta^*_{-i}; x_i) + Q_i(x_i)(v_i - x_i). \quad (12.139)$$

Denote buyer i's expected profit when he reports his true private value by

$$W_i(v_i) = u_i(v_i, \beta^*_{-i}; v_i). \tag{12.140}$$

Inserting $x_i = v_i$ into Equation (12.136), one has

$$W_i(v_i) = Q_i(v_i)v_i - M_i(v_i). \tag{12.141}$$

Theorem 12.48 *A direct selling mechanism* (q, μ) *is incentive compatible if and only if*

$$W_i(v_i) \geq W_i(x_i) + Q_i(x_i)(v_i - x_i), \quad \forall i \in N, \forall v_i \in \mathbb{V}_i, \forall x_i \in \mathbb{V}_i. \tag{12.142}$$

Proof: A direct selling mechanism (q, μ) is incentive compatible if and only if equilibrium is attained when all buyers report their true private values. This means that for each buyer i, each private value $v_i \in \mathbb{V}_i$, and each possible report $x_i \in \mathbb{V}_i$,

$$u_i(v_i, \beta^*_{-i}; v_i) \geq u_i(x_i, \beta^*_{-i}; v_i). \tag{12.143}$$

Since $u_i(v_i, \beta^*_{-i}; v_i) = W_i(v_i)$ (Equation (12.140)), Equations (12.137)–(12.139) imply that Equation (12.143) is equivalent to

$$W_i(v_i) \geq u_i(x_i, \beta^*_{-i}; x_i) + Q_i(x_i)(v_i - x_i) = W_i(x_i) + Q_i(x_i)(v_i - x_i). \tag{12.144}$$

In other words, (q, μ) is incentive compatible if and only if Equation (12.144) obtains, which is what we needed to prove. $\square$

The following theorem yields an explicit formula for computing a buyer's expected profit in an incentive-compatible direct selling mechanism.

Theorem 12.49 *Let* (q, μ) *be an incentive-compatible direct selling mechanism. Then for each* $v_i \in \mathbb{V}_i$,

$$W_i(v_i) = W_i(0) + \int_0^{v_i} Q_i(t_i)dt_i \tag{12.145}$$

$$= -M_i(0) + \int_0^{v_i} Q_i(t_i)dt_i. \tag{12.146}$$

We see from Equation (12.146) that buyer i's expected profit depends on the payment he makes for the object, M_i, only through $M_i(0)$ – the sum that he pays when the private value that he reports is 0. Inserting Equation (12.141) into Equation (12.146), one gets

$$M_i(v_i) = M_i(0) + Q_i(v_i)v_i - \int_0^{v_i} Q_i(t_i)dt_i. \tag{12.147}$$

This equation is an explicit formula for a buyer's expected payment under the truth-telling equilibrium β^* as a function of $M_i(0)$, and of his probability of winning.

Proof of Theorem 12.49: Note that if Equation (12.145) is satisfied, then Equation (12.146) also holds, since

$$W_i(0) = u_i(0, \beta^*_{-i}; 0) = Q_i(0) \times 0 - M_i(0) = -M_i(0). \tag{12.148}$$

To prove Equation (12.145), we first prove that the function Q_i is monotonically nondecreasing. Since (q, μ) is an incentive-compatible mechanism, Theorem 12.48 implies that

$$W_i(v_i) - W_i(x_i) \geq Q_i(x_i)(v_i - x_i), \quad \forall i \in N, \forall v_i \in \mathbb{V}_i, \forall x_i \in \mathbb{V}_i. \tag{12.149}$$

In particular:

$$W_i(v_i) - W_i(x_i) \geq Q_i(x_i)(v_i - x_i), \quad \forall v_i \geq x_i. \tag{12.150}$$

Reversing the roles of x_i and v_i in Equation (12.149), and reinserting $v_i \geq x_i$, one gets

$$W_i(x_i) - W_i(v_i) \geq Q_i(v_i)(x_i - v_i), \quad \forall v_i \geq x_i. \tag{12.151}$$

Multiplying both sides of the inequality sign in this equation by -1 yields:

$$W_i(v_i) - W_i(x_i) \leq Q_i(v_i)(v_i - x_i), \quad \forall v_i \geq x_i. \tag{12.152}$$

Note the resemblance between the inequalities in Equations (12.150) and (12.152): the only difference is the argument of Q_i, and the direction of the inequality sign. Equations (12.150) and (12.152) imply that for each x_i and v_i,

$$Q_i(x_i)(v_i - x_i) \leq W_i(v_i) - W_i(x_i) \leq Q_i(v_i)(v_i - x_i), \quad \forall v_i \geq x_i. \tag{12.153}$$

For $v_i > x_i$, we can divide Equation (12.153) by $v_i - x_i$, which yields

$$\text{If } v_i > x_i \text{ then } Q_i(v_i) \geq Q_i(x_i). \tag{12.154}$$

That is, the function Q_i is a monotonically nondecreasing function, and is therefore in particular integrable.

We next turn to the proof that Equation (12.145) is satisfied. Let $v_i \in \mathbb{V}_i$, $v_i > 0$, and consider the integral $\int_0^{v_i} Q_i(t_i)dt_i$ as the limit of Riemann sums of the function Q_i. Divide the interval $[0, v_i]$ into L intervals of length $\delta = \frac{v_i}{L}$; denote by $z^k = (k+1)\delta$ the rightmost (upper) end of the k-th interval, and by $x^k = k\delta$ its leftmost (lower) end. Inserting $v_i = z^k$ and $x_i = x^k$ in Equation (12.153) and summing over $k = 0, 1, \ldots, L - 1$ yields

$$\sum_{k=0}^{L-1} Q_i(x^k)(z^k - x^k) \leq \sum_{k=0}^{L-1}(W_i(z^k) - W_i(x^k)) \leq \sum_{k=0}^{L-1} Q_i(z^k)(z^k - x^k). \tag{12.155}$$

The middle series is a telescopic series that sums to $W_i(v_i) - W_i(0)$. The left series is a Riemann sum, where the value of the function is taken to be its value at the leftmost end of each interval, and the right series is a Riemann sum, where the value of the function is taken to be its value at the rightmost end of the interval. By increasing L (letting δ approach 0), both the right series and the left series converge to $\int_0^{v_i} Q_i(t_i)dt_i$, which yields

$$\int_0^{v_i} Q_i(t_i)dt_i = W_i(v_i) - W_i(0), \tag{12.156}$$

and hence Equation (12.145) is satisfied. $\square$

Corollary 12.50 *Let (q, μ) and $(\tilde{q}, \tilde{\mu})$ be two incentive-compatible direct selling mechanisms defined over the same selling problem $(N, (\mathbb{V}_i, f_i)_{i \in N})$ and satisfying:*

- $q = \tilde{q}$: the rule determining the winner is identical in both mechanisms.
- $\mu_i(0, v_{-i}) = \tilde{\mu}_i(0, v_{-i})$: a buyer who reports that his private value is 0 pays the same sum in both mechanisms.

Then at the truth-telling equilibrium β^* the expected profit of each buyer is the same in both mechanisms:

$$u_i(v_i, \beta^*_{-i}; v_i) = \tilde{u}_i(v_i, \beta^*_{-i}; v_i), \tag{12.157}$$

where $\tilde{u}_i(v_i, \beta^*_{-i}; v_i)$ is seller i's expected revenue under equilibrium β^* using the selling mechanism $(\tilde{q}, \tilde{\mu})$.

Proof: Since both mechanisms apply identical rules for determining the winner, the probability that a buyer with private value v_i wins is equal in both mechanisms: the second term in Equation (12.146) is therefore the same in both mechanisms. Since in both cases a buyer who reports 0 pays the same amount, the first term in Equation (12.146) is also the same in both mechanisms. Equation (12.146) therefore implies that the expected profit of each buyer is equal in both mechanisms. □

Since every auction is, in particular, a selling mechanism, Corollary 12.50 implies the Revenue Equivalence Theorem (Corollary 12.24, page 487) as the reader is asked to prove in Exercise 12.31.

12.9) Individually rational mechanisms

A direct selling mechanism is called individually rational if at the truth-telling equilibrium β^*, the expected profit of each buyer is nonnegative.

Definition 12.51 *A direct selling mechanism is called* individually rational *if $W_i(v_i) \geq 0$ for each buyer i and for every $v_i \in \mathbb{V}_i$.*

If $W_i(v_i) < 0$, buyer i with private value v_i will not want to participate, because by doing so he is liable to lose. Therefore, assuming that the equilibrium β^* is attained, a buyer cannot lose by participating in a sale by way of a direct and individually rational selling mechanism.

Theorem 12.52 *An incentive-compatible direct selling mechanism is individually rational if and only if $M_i(0) \leq 0$, for each buyer $i \in N$.*

Proof: From Equations (12.145) and (12.146):

$$W_i(v_i) = -M_i(0) + \int_0^{v_i} Q_i(t_i)\mathrm{d}t. \tag{12.158}$$

Since the function Q_i is nonnegative, the right-hand side of the equation is minimal when $v_i = 0$. That is, $W_i(v_i)$ is minimal at $v_i = 0$. Therefore, the mechanism is individually rational if and only if $0 \leq W_i(0) = -M_i(0)$, that is, if and only if $M_i(0) \leq 0$, for each buyer $i \in N$, which is what we needed to prove. □

12.10 Finding the optimal mechanism

In this section, we will find the incentive-compatible and individually rational mechanism that maximizes the seller's expected revenue. We will assume the following condition, which is similar to Assumption (A5):

(B) For every buyer i, the density function f_i of buyer i's private values is positive over the interval $\mathbb{V}_i$.

Remark 12.53 *Changing a density function at a finite (or countable) number of points does not affect the distribution. Therefore, if a density function is zero at a finite number of points, it can be changed to satisfy Assumption (B).* ◆

Define, for each buyer i, a function $c_i : \mathbb{V}_i \to \mathbb{R}$ as follows:

$$c_i(v_i) = v_i - \frac{1 - F_i(v_i)}{f_i(v_i)}. \tag{12.159}$$

This function depends only on the distribution of the buyer's private values. From Assumption (B), the function c_i is well defined over the interval $\mathbb{V}_i$.

Example 12.54 **The private value is uniformly distributed over** $[0, 1]$ Since $f_i(v_i) = 1$ and $F_i(v_i) = v_i$, for each $v_i \in [0, 1]$:

$$c_i(v_i) = v_i - \frac{1 - v_i}{1} = 2v_i - 1. \tag{12.160}$$

◀

Example 12.55 **The distribution of the private values over** $[0, 1]$ **is given by the cumulative distribution function** $F_i(v_i) = v_i(2 - v_i)$ In this case, $f_i(v_i) = 2(1 - v_i)$, and therefore

$$c_i(v_i) = v_i - \frac{1 - v_i(2 - v_i)}{2(1 - v_i)} = \frac{3v_i - 1}{2}. \tag{12.161}$$

◀

We will first prove the following claim:

Theorem 12.56 $\mathbf{E}[c_i(V_i)] = 0$ *for each buyer $i \in N$.*

Proof:

$$\mathbf{E}[c_i(V_i)] = \int_{\mathbb{V}_i} \left(v_i - \frac{1 - F_i(v_i)}{f_i(v_i)} \right) f_i(v_i) \mathrm{d}v_i$$

$$= \mathbf{E}[V_i] - \int_{\mathbb{V}_i} (1 - F_i(v_i)) \mathrm{d}v_i = 0, \tag{12.162}$$

where the last equality obtains because for every nonnegative random variable,

$$\mathbf{E}[X] = \int_0^\infty (1 - F_X(x)) \mathrm{d}x. \tag{12.163}$$

□

Using the functions $(c_i)_{i \in N}$, we define a direct selling mechanism (q^*, μ^*).

Definition 12.57 *Define the direct mechanism (q^*, μ^*) as follows:*

$$q_i^*(v) = \begin{cases} 0 & c_i(v_i) \leq 0, \\ 0 & c_i(v_i) < \max_{j \in N} c_j(v_j), \\ \frac{1}{|\{l: c_l(v_l) = \max_{j \in N} c_j(v_j)\}|} & c_i(v_i) = \max_{j \in N} c_j(v_j) > 0. \end{cases} \quad (12.164)$$

$$\mu_i^*(v) = v_i q_i^*(v) - \int_0^{v_i} q_i^*(t_i, v_{-i}) dt_i. \quad (12.165)$$

In other words, buyer i wins the object (with positive probability) only if $c_i(v_i)$ is positive and maximal.

First, we will show that if the function c_i is monotonically nondecreasing, then the mechanism (q^*, μ^*) is incentive compatible and individually rational. Then we will show that, if c_i is monotonically nondecreasing, (q^*, μ^*) maximize the seller's expected revenue among the incentive-compatible and individually rational direct selling mechanisms.

Theorem 12.58 *If for each buyer $i \in N$ the function c_i is monotonically nondecreasing, then the direct mechanism (q^*, μ^*) is incentive compatible and individually rational.*

Proof: In the direct mechanism (q^*, μ^*), when each buyer reports his true private value, for each buyer i with private value v_i denote by $Q_i^*(v_i)$ buyer i's probability of winning the object, by $M_i^*(v_i)$ the expected payment that buyer i makes, and by $U_i^*(v_i)$ his expected profit in this case. Also denote by $u_i^*(x_i, \beta_{-i}^*; v_i)$ the expected profit of buyer i with private value v_i if he reports x_i while all other buyers truthfully report their private value.

Step 1: The function Q_i^* is nondecreasing: $Q_i^*(t_i) \geq Q_i^*(x_i)$ for all $t_i \geq x_i$.
Since the function c_i is nondecreasing, the definition of q^* (Equation (12.164)) implies that the greater the buyer's private value, the greater his probability of winning, i.e., for each buyer i, for any $t_i \geq x_i$ and for any $v_{-i} \in V_{-i}$,

$$q_i^*(t_i, v_{-i}) \geq q_i^*(x_i, v_{-i}). \quad (12.166)$$

Integrating over V_{-i} yields

$$\int_{V_{-i}} q_i^*(t_i, v_{-i}) f_{-i}(v_{-i}) dv_{-i} \geq \int_{V_{-i}} q_i^*(x_i, v_{-i}) f_{-i}(v_{-i}) dv_{-i}. \quad (12.167)$$

By the definition of Q_i^* (see Equation (12.134)),

$$Q_i^*(t_i) \geq Q_i^*(x_i), \quad \forall i \in N, \forall t_i \geq x_i. \quad (12.168)$$

Step 2: $u_i^*(x_i, \beta_{-i}^*; v_i) = Q_i^*(x_i)(v_i - x_i) + \int_0^{x_i} Q_i^*(t_i) dt_i$ for each $i \in N$ and every $x_i \in V_i$.
By definition (see Equation (12.136)),

$$u_i^*(x_i, \beta_{-i}^*; v_i) = Q_i^*(x_i) v_i - M_i^*(x_i), \quad (12.169)$$

and

$$M_i^*(x_i) = \int_{\mathbb{V}_{-i}} \mu_i^*(x_i, v_{-i}) f_{-i}(v_{-i}) dv_{-i} \tag{12.170}$$

$$= \int_{\mathbb{V}_{-i}} \left(x_i q_i^*(x_i, v_{-i}) - \int_0^{x_i} q_i^*(t_i, v_{-i}) dt_i \right) f_{-i}(v_{-i}) dv_{-i}$$

$$= x_i Q_i^*(x_i) - \int_0^{x_i} Q_i^*(t_i) dt_i,$$

where the first equality follows from Equation (12.135), the second equality follows from the definition of μ^* (Equation (12.165)), and the third equality follows from the definition of Q_i^*, and changing the order of integration. Inserting this equation into Equation (12.169), one has

$$u_i^*(x_i, \beta_{-i}^*; v_i) = Q_i^*(x_i)(v_i - x_i) + \int_0^{x_i} Q_i^*(t_i) dt_i, \tag{12.171}$$

as claimed. This equation obtains for every $x_i \in \mathbb{V}_i$, and in particular, for $x_i = v_i$, it becomes $u_i^*(v_i, \beta_{-i}^*; v_i) = \int_0^{v_i} Q_i^*(t_i) dt_i$.

Step 3: The mechanism (q^*, μ^*) is an incentive-compatible direct selling mechanism. The mechanism is incentive compatible if and only if reporting the truth is an equilibrium:

$$u_i^*(v_i, \beta_{-i}^*; v_i) \geq u_i^*(x_i, \beta_{-i}^*; v_i), \quad \forall v_i, x_i \in \mathbb{V}_i. \tag{12.172}$$

By substituting the expression for $u_i^*(x_i, \beta_{-i}^*; v_i)$ obtained in Equation (12.171) into both the left-hand side and the right-hand side of (12.172), we deduce that the mechanism is incentive compatible if and only if

$$Q_i^*(x_i)(v_i - x_i) + \int_0^{x_i} Q_i^*(t_i) dt_i \leq \int_0^{v_i} Q_i^*(t_i) dt_i, \quad \forall v_i, x_i \in \mathbb{V}_i. \tag{12.173}$$

The last equation holds if and only if

$$Q_i^*(x_i)(v_i - x_i) \leq \int_{x_i}^{v_i} Q_i^*(t_i) dt_i, \quad \forall v_i, x_i \in \mathbb{V}_i. \tag{12.174}$$

By Step 1 the function Q_i^* is nondecreasing. Thus, if $x_i \leq v_i$ then $Q_i^*(x_i) \leq Q_i^*(t)$ for all $t \in [x_i, v_i]$, and therefore

$$Q_i^*(x_i)(v_i - x_i) = \int_{x_i}^{v_i} Q_i^*(x_i) dt_i \leq \int_{x_i}^{v_i} Q_i^*(t_i) dt_i \tag{12.175}$$

and Equation (12.174) holds. If $x_i > v_i$,

$$Q_i^*(x_i)(x_i - v_i) = \int_{v_i}^{x_i} Q_i^*(x_i) dt_i \geq \int_{v_i}^{x_i} Q_i^*(t_i) dt_i, \tag{12.176}$$

and therefore

$$Q_i^*(x_i)(v_i - x_i) = -Q_i^*(x_i)(x_i - v_i) \leq -\int_{v_i}^{x_i} Q_i^*(t_i) dt_i = \int_{x_i}^{v_i} Q_i^*(t_i) dt_i,$$

and Equation (12.174) also holds.

Step 4: The mechanism (q^*, μ^*) is individually rational.

Since the mechanism is direct and incentive compatible, by Theorem 12.52 it suffices to show that $M_i^*(0) \leq 0$ for every buyer $i \in N$. By Equation (12.165), for every $v_{-i} \in \mathbb{V}_{-i}$,

$$\mu_i^*(0, v_{-i}) = 0 \cdot q_i^*(0, v_{-i}) + \int_0^0 q_i^*(t_i, v_{-i})dt_i = 0. \tag{12.177}$$

It follows that

$$M_i^*(0) = \int_{\mathbb{V}_{-i}} \mu_i^*(0, v_{-i})f_{-i}(v_{-i})dv_{-i} = 0, \tag{12.178}$$

and therefore in particular $M_i^*(0) \leq 0$.   □

The next theorem shows that if the functions $(c_i)_{i \in N}$ are monotonically nondecreasing, then the mechanism (q^*, μ^*) is optimal from the seller's perspective.

Theorem 12.59 *Consider the selling problem* $(N, (\mathbb{V}_i, f_i)_{i \in N})$ *and suppose that the functions* $(c_i)_{i \in N}$ *defined by Equation (12.159) are monotonically nondecreasing. Then the mechanism* (q^*, μ^*) *defined by Equations (12.164) and (12.165) maximizes the seller's expected revenue within all incentive-compatible, individually rational direct selling mechanisms.*

Proof: The seller's revenue is the sum of the payments made by the buyers. His expected revenue, which we will denote by π, is therefore

$$\pi = \sum_{i \in N} \mathbf{E}[M_i(V_i)]. \tag{12.179}$$

From[8] Equation (12.147),

$$\mathbf{E}[M_i(V_i)] = \int_0^{\bar{v}_i} M_i(v_i)f_i(v_i)dv_i$$

$$= M_i(0) + \int_0^{\bar{v}_i} Q_i(v_i)v_i f_i(v_i)dv_i$$

$$- \int_0^{\bar{v}_i} \left(\int_0^{v_i} Q_i(t_i)dt_i \right) f_i(v_i)dv_i. \tag{12.180}$$

Changing the order of integration in the last term, and using the fact that $F_i(\bar{v}_i) = 1$, yields:

$$\int_0^{\bar{v}_i} \left(\int_0^{v_i} Q_i(t_i)dt_i \right) f_i(v_i)dv_i = \int_0^{\bar{v}_i} \left(\int_{t_i}^{\bar{v}_i} Q_i(t_i)f_i(v_i)dv_i \right) dt_i$$

$$= \int_0^{\bar{v}_i} Q_i(t_i)(1 - F_i(t_i))dt_i. \tag{12.181}$$

---

8 When $\mathbb{V}_i$ is not bounded we denote $\bar{v}_i = \infty$ and $F_i(\bar{v}_i) := \lim_{v_i \to \infty} F_i(v_i)$.

It follows that

$$E[M_i(V_i)] = M_i(0) + \int_0^{\bar{v}_i} Q_i(v_i)v_if_i(v_i)dv_i - \int_0^{\bar{v}_i} Q_i(t_i)(1 - F_i(t_i))dt_i \qquad (12.182)$$

$$= M_i(0) + \int_0^{\bar{v}_i} Q_i(v_i)f_i(v_i)\left(v_i - \frac{1 - F_i(v_i)}{f_i(v_i)}\right)dv_i \qquad (12.183)$$

$$= M_i(0) + \int_0^{\bar{v}_i} Q_i(v_i)c_i(v_i)f_i(v_i)dv_i \qquad (12.184)$$

$$= M_i(0) + \int_{\mathbb{V}^N} q_i(v)c_i(v_i)f_V(v)dv. \qquad (12.185)$$

Equation (12.184) follows from the definition of c_i, and Equation (12.185) holds by Equation (12.134) (page 505) together with the fact that the private values are independent. By summing over $i \in N$, we deduce that the seller should maximize the quantity

$$\pi = \sum_{i \in N} M_i(0) + \int_{\mathbb{V}^N}\left(\sum_{i \in N} q_i(v)c_i(v_i)\right)f_V(v)dv. \qquad (12.186)$$

The first term depends only on $(M_i(0))_{i \in N}$, i.e., only on $(\mu_i)_{i \in N}$, and the second term depends only on $(q_i)_{i \in N}$. To maximize π it therefore suffices to maximize each term separately.

Start with the second term. For each $v \in \mathbb{V}$, consider $\sum_{i \in N} q_i(v)c_i(v_i)$. What are the coefficients $(q_i(v))_{i \in N}$ that maximize this sum?

- If $c_i(v_i) < 0$ for every $i \in N$, the sum is maximized when $q_i(v) = 0$ for each $i \in N$.
- If $\max_{i \in N} c_i(v_i) \geq 0$, the maximum of the sum (under the constraint $\sum_{i \in N} q_i(v) \leq 1$) is $\max_{i \in N} c_i(v_i)$: give positive weights (summing to 1) only to those buyers for whom $c_i(v_i)$ is maximal.

Since $(q_i^*)_{i \in N}$ have been defined to satisfy these conditions (see Equation (12.164)), it follows that the second term in Equation (12.186) is maximal for $q = q^*$. We next turn to the first term in Equation (12.186). By Theorem 12.52, $M_i(0) \leq 0$ for every individually rational direct selling mechanism. Therefore, the first term is not greater than 0. As we proved in Step 4 above (Equation (12.178)), $M_i^*(0) = 0$ for all $i \in N$, and therefore μ^* maximizes the first term in Equation (12.186). The definition of $(\mu_i^*)_{i \in N}$ implies that $M_i^*(0) = 0$. It follows that there is no incentive-compatible direct selling mechanism that yields the seller an expected revenue greater than his expected revenue yielded by (q^*, μ^*). □

Example 12.60 **Private values distributed over different intervals** Suppose that there are two buyers, where buyer 1's private value is uniformly distributed over $[0, 1]$, and buyer 2's private value is uniformly distributed over $[0, 2]$. As we saw in Example 12.54, $c_1(v_1) = 2v_1 - 1$, and therefore $c_1(v_1) < 0$ if and only if $v_1 < \frac{1}{2}$. For buyer 2, $f_2(v_2) = \frac{1}{2}$ and $F_2(v_2) = \frac{v_2}{2}$, and therefore $c_2(v_2) = v_2 - \frac{1 - v_2/2}{1/2} = 2v_2 - 2$. It follows that $c_2(v_2) < 0$ if and only if $v_2 < 1$. Since

$$c_1(v_1) > c_2(v_2) \iff 2v_1 - 1 > 2v_2 - 2 \iff v_1 > v_2 - \frac{1}{2}, \qquad (12.187)$$

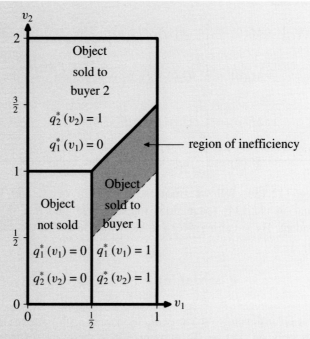

Figure 12.5 The function q^* in Example 12.60

the optimal allocation rule q^* is defined as follows:

- If $v_1 < \frac{1}{2}$ and $v_2 < 1$, the object is not sold ($q_i^*(v_i) = 0$ for $i = 1, 2$).
- If $v_1 \geq \frac{1}{2}$ and $v_1 > v_2 - \frac{1}{2}$, buyer 1 wins the object, ($q_1^*(v_1) = 1$ and $q_2^*(v_2) = 0$).
- If $v_2 > 1$ and $v_2 > v_1 + \frac{1}{2}$, buyer 2 wins the object, ($q_2^*(v_2) = 1$ and $q_1^*(v_1) = 0$).
- If $v_1 \geq \frac{1}{2}$, $v_2 \geq 1$ and $v_1 = v_2 - \frac{1}{2}$, each buyer wins the object with probability $\frac{1}{2}$, ($q_1^*(v_1) = q_2^*(v_2) = \frac{1}{2}$).

To compute the payment function we first compute

$$
\int_0^{v_1} q_1^*(t_1, v_2)\,dt_1 = \begin{cases} 0 & v_1 < \frac{1}{2}, \\ 0 & v_1 < v_2 - \frac{1}{2}, \\ v_1 - \max\left\{\frac{1}{2}, v_2 - \frac{1}{2}\right\} & v_1 \geq \frac{1}{2} \text{ and } v_1 \geq v_2 - \frac{1}{2}. \end{cases} \tag{12.188}
$$

$$
\int_0^{v_2} q_2^*(v_1, t_2)\,dt_2 = \begin{cases} 0 & v_2 < 1, \\ 0 & v_2 < v_1 + \frac{1}{2}, \\ v_2 - \max\left\{1, v_1 + \frac{1}{2}\right\} & v_1 \geq 1 \text{ and } v_2 \geq v_1 + \frac{1}{2}. \end{cases} \tag{12.189}
$$

Equation (12.165) yields

$$
\mu_1^*(v_1, v_2) = \begin{cases} 0 & \text{Buyer 1 does not win,} \\ \max\left\{\frac{1}{2}, v_2 - \frac{1}{2}\right\} & \text{Buyer 1 wins.} \end{cases} \tag{12.190}
$$

$$
\mu_2^*(v_1, v_2) = \begin{cases} 0 & \text{Buyer 2 does not win,} \\ \max\left\{1, v_1 + \frac{1}{2}\right\} & \text{Buyer 2 wins.} \end{cases} \tag{12.191}
$$

Note that in this case, each buyer has a different minimum price: $\frac{1}{2}$ for buyer 1 and 1 for buyer 2. Note also that when $\frac{1}{2} < v_1 < v_2 < v_1 + \frac{1}{2}$ (the shaded area in Figure 12.5), buyer 1 wins the object, despite the fact that his private value is less than buyer 2's private value. In other words, the selling mechanism that maximizes the seller's expected revenue is not efficient: the winner is not necessarily the buyer with the highest private value.   ◄

When private values are independent and identically distributed, Theorem 12.59 leads to the following corollary.

Corollary 12.61 *If the private values of the buyers are independent and identically distributed, and if the functions $(c_i)_{i \in N}$ are monotonically nondecreasing, the incentive-compatible direct selling mechanism that maximizes the seller's expected revenue is a sealed-bid second-price auction with a reserve price.*

Proof: Since the private values of the buyers are identically distributed, $c_i = c_j =: c$ for every pair of buyers i, j. The function c is monotonically nondecreasing, and therefore a buyer for whom $c(v_i)$ is maximal is one whose private value v_i is maximal. Denote

$$\rho^* = \inf\{t_i \in \mathbb{V}_i : c_i(t_i) > 0\}, \tag{12.192}$$

which is independent of i, since $\mathbb{V}_i = \mathbb{V}_j$ for all $i, j \in N$.

To simplify the analysis, suppose that c_i is a continuous function, and therefore $c_i(\rho^*) = 0$. By the definition of q^* (Equation (12.164)), the buyer who wins the object is the one who submits the highest bid, as long as that bid is greater than ρ^*:

$$q_i^*(v_i) = \begin{cases} 0 & \text{if } v_i \leq \rho^* \text{ or } v_i < \max_{j \neq i} v_j, \\ \frac{1}{|\{l: \, v_l = \max_{j \in N} v_j\}|} & \text{if } v_i > \rho^* \text{ and } v_i = \max_{j \in N} v_j. \end{cases} \tag{12.193}$$

We next calculate $\mu^*(v_i) = v_i q_i^*(v_i) - \int_0^{v_i} q_i^*(t_i, v_{-i}) \mathrm{d}t_i$ (see Equation (12.165) on page 510):

- If $v_i \leq \rho^*$ or $v_i < \max_{j \neq i} v_j$, then $q_i^*(v_i) = 0$, and $q_i^*(t_i) = 0$ for each $t_i \in [0, v_i)$, and hence in this case

$$\mu_i^*(v_i) = v_i q_i^*(v_i) - \int_0^{v_i} q_i^*(t_i, v_{-i}) \mathrm{d}t_i = 0. \tag{12.194}$$

In other words, a buyer whose bid is lower than the highest bid or less than or equal to ρ^* pays nothing.
- If $v_i > \rho^*$ and $v_i \geq \max_{j \neq i} v_j$, then $q_i^*(v_i) = \frac{1}{|\{i: \, v_i = \max_{j \in N} v_j\}|}$, and $q_i^*(t_i) = 0$ for all $t_i \in [0, v_i)$. Hence, in this case,

$$\mu_i^*(v_i) = v_i q_i^*(v_i) - \int_0^{v_i} q_i^*(t_i, v_{-i}) \mathrm{d}t_i = \frac{v_i}{|\{l: \, v_l = \max_{j \in N} v_j\}|}. \tag{12.195}$$

In words, all the buyers who bid the maximum bid, provided it is at least ρ^*, equally share the payment to the seller.

In summary,

$$\mu^*(v_i) = v_i q_i^*(v_i) - \int_0^{v_i} q_i^*(t_i, v_{-i}) dt_i$$

$$= \begin{cases} 0 & v_i < \rho^* \text{ or } v_i < \max_{j \in N} v_j, \\ \dfrac{\max_{j \neq i} v_j}{|\{i : c_i(v_i) = \max_{j \in N} c_j(v_j)\}|} & v_i \geq \rho^* \text{ and } v_i = \max_{j \in N} v_j. \end{cases} \qquad (12.196)$$

In other words, (q^*, μ^*) is a sealed-bid second-price auction with a reserve price ρ^*. □

12.11 Remarks

The first use of game theory to study auctions was accomplished by economist William Vickrey [1961, 1962]. Vickrey, 1914–96, was awarded the Nobel Memorial Prize in Economics in 1996 for his contributions to the study of incentives when buyers have different information, and the implications incentives have on auction theory. The results in Section 12.7 are based on Holt [1980].

In this chapter we studied symmetric sealed-bid auctions with independent private values. The theory of asymmetric sealed-bid auctions and sealed-bid auctions in which the private values of the buyers are not independent is mathematically complex. The interested reader is directed to Milgrom and Weber [1982], Lebrun [1999], Maskin and Riley [2000], Fibich, Gavious, and Sela [2004], Reny and Zamir [2004], and Kaplan and Zamir [2011, 2012].

The significance of mechanism design in economic theory was recognized by the Nobel Prize Committee in 2007, when it awarded the prize to three researchers who were instrumental in developing mechanism design, Leonid Hurwicz, Eric Maskin, and Roger Myerson. The revelation principle was proved by Myerson [1979], and the structure of the optimal mechanism was proved by Myerson [1981]. The reader interested in further deepening his understanding of auction theory and mechanism design is directed to Krishna [2002], Milgrom [2004], or Klemperer [2004].

Exercise 12.1 is based on Wolfstetter [1996]. Exercise 12.7 is based on Engelbrecht-Wiggans, Milgrom, and Weber [1983]. Exercise 12.10 is based on Blume and Heidhues [2004]. Exercises 12.19 and 12.42 are based on examples that appear in Krishna [2002]. Exercises 12.20 and 12.21 are based on Kaplan and Zamir [2012].

The authors wish to thank Vijay Krishna for answering questions during the composition of this chapter. Many thanks are due to the students in the Topics in Game Theory course that was conducted at Tel Aviv University in 2005, for their many comments on this chapter, with special thanks going to Ronen Eldan and Ayala Mashiah-Yaakovi.

12.12 Exercises

In each of the exercises in this chapter, assume that buyers are risk neutral, unless it is explicitly noted otherwise.

12.1 Selling an object at the monopoly price Andrew is interested in selling a rare car (whose value in his eyes we will normalize to 0). Assume there are n buyers and that buyer i's private value of the car, V_i, is uniformly distributed over $[0, 1]$. The private values of the buyers are independent.

Instead of conducting an auction, Andrew intends on setting a price for the car, publicizing this price, and selling the car only to buyers who are willing to pay this price; if no buyer is willing to pay the price, the car will not be sold, and if more than one buyer is willing to pay the price, the car will be sold to one of them based on a fair lottery that gives each of them equal probability of winning.

Answer the following questions:

(a) Find Andrew's expected revenue as a function of the price x that he sets.
(b) Find the price x^* that maximizes Andrew's expected revenue.
(c) What is the maximal expected revenue that Andrew can obtain, as a function of n?
(d) Compare Andrew's maximal revenue to his revenue in the symmetric equilibrium if he sells the car by way of a sealed-bid first-price auction. For which values of n does a sealed-bid first-price auction yield a higher revenue?

12.2 (a) Explain what a buyer in an open-bid decreasing auction knows when the current announced price is x that he did not know prior to the auction.
(b) Explain what a buyer in an open-bid increasing auction knows when the current announced price is x that he did not know prior to the auction.

12.3 Prove that in a symmetric sealed-bid second-price auction with independent private values the only monotonically increasing, symmetric equilibrium is the equilibrium in which every buyer submits a bid equal to his private value.

12.4 Suppose that $\mathbb{V} = [0, \bar{v}]$ is a bounded interval. Show that in a symmetric sealed-bid second-price auction with independent private values the strategy vector under which buyer 1 bids $\bar{v}$ and all the other buyers bid 0 is an (asymmetric) equilibrium. Is it also an equilibrium in a sealed-bid first-price auction? Justify your answer. Is there an equilibrium in an open-bid ascending auction that is analogous to this equilibrium?

12.5 Consider a sealed-bid second-price auction where the private values of the buyers are independent and identically distributed with the uniform distribution over $[0, 1]$. Show that the strategy under which a buyer bids his private value does not strictly dominate all his other strategies.

12.6 Brent and Stuart are the only buyers in a sealed-bid first-price auction of medical devices. Brent knows that Stuart's private value is uniformly distributed over $[0, 2]$, and that Stuart's strategy is $\beta(v) = \frac{v^2}{3} + \frac{v}{3}$.

(a) What is Brent's optimal strategy?
(b) What is Brent's expected payment if he implements this optimal strategy (as a function of his own private value)?

12.7 A single indivisible object is sold in a first-price auction between two buyers, 1 and 2. The value of the object v is common (the same) to both buyers but it is uncertain; it has a uniform distribution in $[0, 1]$. Buyer 1 knows the (realized) value

v while buyer 2 only knows that it is uniformly distributed in $[0, 1]$ (and that buyer 1 knows the realized value).

(a) Prove that the following pair of strategies is a Nash equilibrium: buyer 1 bids $v/2$ and buyer 2 plays a mixed strategy, choosing the bid by the uniform distribution on $[0, 1/2]$.

(b) Calculate the expected profit to each buyer.

12.8 (a) Suppose that the private values of two buyers in a sealed-bid first-price auction are independent and uniformly distributed over the set $\{0, 1, 2\}$. In other words, each buyer has three possible private values. The bids in the auction must be nonnegative integers. Find all the equilibria.

(b) Find all the equilibria, under the same assumptions, when the auction is a sealed-bid second-price auction.

(c) Compare the seller's expected revenue under both auction methods. What have you discovered?

12.9 Denote by E^I the seller's revenue in a sealed-bid first-price auction, and by E^{II} the seller's revenue in a sealed-bid second-price auction. Find the variance of E^I and of E^{II} when there are n buyers, whose private values are independent and uniformly distributed over $[0, 1]$. Which of the two is the lesser?

12.10 Consider a sealed-bid second-price auction with n buyers whose private values are independent and uniformly distributed over $[0, 1]$. Prove that the following pair of strategies is an asymmetric equilibrium:

$$\beta_1^*(v) = \begin{cases} v & v \geq \frac{1}{2}, \\ \frac{1}{2} & v < \frac{1}{2}, \end{cases} \qquad \beta_2^*(v) = \begin{cases} v & v \geq \frac{1}{2}, \\ 0 & v < \frac{1}{2}. \end{cases}$$

12.11 Consider a sealed-bid first-price auction with three buyers, where the private values of the buyers are independent and uniformly distributed over $[0, 2]$.

(a) Find a symmetric equilibrium of the game.

(b) What is the seller's expected revenue?

12.12 Prove that in a symmetric sealed-bid auction with independent private values the random variable $Y = \max\{V_2, V_3, \ldots, V_n\}$ is a continuous random variable and its density function f_Y is a positive function.

12.13 Which of the following auction methods satisfy the conditions of the Revenue Equivalence Theorem (Corollary 12.24 on page 487): sealed-bid first-price auctions (see Example 12.15 on page 480), sealed-bid second-price auctions, sealed-bid first-price auctions with a reserve price (see Example 12.34 on page 494), sealed-bid second-price auctions with a reserve price, sealed-bid second-price auctions with entry fees (see Example 12.28 on page 490)? When only some of the conditions are satisfied, specify which conditions are not satisfied, and justify your answer.

12.14 Compute the seller's expected revenue in a sealed-bid second-price auction with a reserve price ρ, in which there are two buyers whose private values are independent and uniformly distributed over $[0, 1]$. Compare the results here with the results we computed for sealed-bid first-price auctions with a reserve price ρ (Equation (12.104) on page 496).

12.15 (a) Compute the seller's expected revenue in a sealed-bid first-price auction with a reserve price ρ, with n buyers whose private values are independent and uniformly distributed over $[0, 1]$.

(b) What is the reserve price ρ^* that maximizes the seller's expected revenue?

(c) Repeat items (a) and (b) for a sealed-bid second-price auction with a reserve price ρ.

(d) Did you obtain the same results in both cases? Explain why.

(e) Compare the expected revenue computed here with the expected revenue of a seller who is selling the object by setting the monopoly price (see Exercise 12.1). Which expected revenue is higher?

(f) What does the optimal reserve price in items (b) and (c) above converge to when the number of buyers increases to infinity?

12.16 Consider a symmetric sealed-bid first-price auction with independent private values that are distributed uniformly in $[0, 1]$ and n buyers whose cumulative distribution function F is given by $F(v) = v^2$. Find the symmetric equilibrium, compute $e_i(v_i)$ (the expected payment of buyer i if his private value is v_i), compute e_i (the payment that buyer i makes), and compute π (the seller's expected revenue).

12.17 Repeat Exercise 12.16 when the cumulative distribution function of each buyer i's private value is $F_i(v) = v^3$.

12.18 Repeat Exercise 12.17 when the auction method conducted is a sealed-bid first-price auction with entry fee λ.

12.19 In this exercise, using Theorem 12.23 (page 486), compute a symmetric equilibrium β in a sealed-bid third-price auction, with n buyers whose private values are independent; each V_i has uniform distribution over $[0, 1]$. The winner of this auction is the buyer submitting the highest bid, and he pays the third-highest bid.[9] If several buyers have submitted the highest bid, the winner is chosen from among them by a fair lottery granting each equal probability of winning.

---

9 If only two buyers have submitted the highest bid, the next-highest bid is the sum of money that the winner pays for the auctioned object. If three buyers have submitted the highest bid, that bid is the amount of money the winner pays for the auctioned object.

Denote the highest bid from among $V_2, V_3, \ldots, V_n$ by Y, and the second-highest bid from among $V_2, V_3, \ldots, V_n$ by W. Denote by F the cumulative distribution function of V_i, and by f its density function.

(a) Prove that for every $v_1 \in (0, 1]$, the conditional cumulative distribution function of W, given $Y \leq v_1$, is

$$F_{(W|Y \leq v_1)}(w)$$

$$= (F(w))^{n-2} \times \frac{(n-1)F(v_1) - (n-2)F(w)}{(F(v_1))^{n-1}}, \quad \forall w \in [0, v_1]. \tag{12.197}$$

(b) Compute the conditional density function $f_{(W|Y \leq v_1)}$.
(c) Denote

$$h(y) = (n-2)(F(y))^{n-3}f(y), \quad \forall y \in [0, 1]. \tag{12.198}$$

The expected payment of buyer 1 with private value $v_1 \in (0, 1]$ is given by $F_Y(v_1)\mathbf{E}[\beta(W) \mid Y \leq v_1]$. Using the Revenue Equivalence Theorem conclude from this that

$$\int_0^{v_1} \beta(y)(n-1)h(y)(F(v_1) - F(y))dy = \int_0^{v_1} yf_Y(y)dy, \quad \forall v_1 \in (0, 1]. \tag{12.199}$$

(d) Differentiate Equation (12.199) by v_1, and show that

$$\int_0^{v_1} \beta(y)h(y)dy = v_1(F(v_1))^{n-2}, \quad \forall v_1 \in (0, 1). \tag{12.200}$$

(e) Differentiate Equation (12.200) by v_1, and show that the solution to this equation is

$$\beta(v_1) = v_1 + \frac{F(v_1)}{(n-2)f(v_1)}, \quad \forall v_1 \in (0, 1). \tag{12.201}$$

(f) What are the conditions that the density function f should satisfy to ensure that the strategy β satisfies the conditions of Theorem 12.23 on page 486?
(g) Do the computations done so far show that the strategy β is a symmetric equilibrium, or should this issue be checked directly?

12.20 Consider a sealed-bid first-price auction with two buyers whose private values are independent; the private value of buyer 1 has uniform distribution over the interval $[0, 3]$, and the private value of buyer 2 has uniform distribution over the interval $[3, 4]$. Answer the following questions:

(a) Prove that the following pair of strategies form an equilibrium

$$\beta_1(v_1) = 1 + \frac{v_1}{2}, \tag{12.202}$$

$$\beta_2(v_2) = \frac{1}{2} + \frac{v_2}{2}. \tag{12.203}$$

(b) Is the probability that buyer 2 wins the auction equal to 1?

(c) Compute the seller's expected revenue if the buyers implement the strategies (β_1, β_2).

(d) Compute the seller's expected revenue if the object is sold by a sealed-bid second-price auction (instead of a sealed-bid first price auction) and every bidder bids his private value.

12.21 Consider a sealed-bid first-price auction with two buyers whose private values are independent; the private value of buyer 1 has uniform distribution over the interval $[0, m+z]$, and the private value of buyer 2 has uniform distribution over the interval $[\frac{3m}{2}, \frac{3m}{2} + z]$, where $m, z > 0$. Show that the following pair of strategies form an equilibrium:

$$\beta_1(v_1) = \frac{v_1}{2} + \frac{m}{2}, \tag{12.204}$$

$$\beta_2(v_2) = \frac{v_2}{2} + \frac{m}{4}. \tag{12.205}$$

Note that these equilibrium strategies are independent of z. This is a generalization of Exercise 12.20 (which is the special case in which $m = 2, z = 1$).

12.22 Prove Theorem 12.29 (page 490): in a sealed-bid second-price auction with a reserve price, for each buyer strategy β the following strategy $\widehat{\beta}$ weakly dominates β, if $\widehat{\beta} \neq \beta$:

$$\widehat{\beta}(v) = \begin{cases} \text{"no"} & \beta(v) = \text{"no,"} \\ v & \beta(v) = x. \end{cases} \tag{12.206}$$

12.23 Consider a sealed-bid second-price auction with two buyers, whose private values are independent; buyer 1's private value is uniformly distributed over $[0, 1]$, and buyer 2's private value is uniformly distributed over $[0, 2]$.

(a) For each buyer, find all weakly dominant strategies.

(b) Consider the equilibrium in which every buyer bids his private value. What is the probability that buyer 1 wins the auction, under this equilibrium? What is the seller's expected revenue in this case?

(c) Prove that at any equilibrium $\beta = (\beta_1, \beta_2)$ satisfying $\beta_1(v) = \beta_2(v)$ for all $v \in [0, 1]$, one has $\beta_1(v) = \beta_2(v) = v$ for all $v \in [0, 1]$.

(d) Are there equilibria at which a buyer, whose private value v_i is less than 1, does not submit the bid $\beta_i(v_i) = v_i$?

12.24 (a) Prove that if F is a cumulative distribution function over $[0, 1]$, and if Y is the maximum of $n - 1$ independent random variables with cumulative distribution function F, then

$$\mathbf{E}[Y \mid Y \leq v] = v - \frac{\int_0^v (F(x))^{n-1} dx}{(F(v))^{n-1}}. \tag{12.207}$$

Hint: Differentiate the function $x(F(x))^{n-1}$.

(b) Use Equation (12.207) to write explicitly the symmetric equilibrium β^* in a symmetric sealed-bid first-price auction with independent private values with n buyers when $\mathbb{V} = [0, 1]$ and (a) $F(x) = x$ and (b) $F(x) = x^2$.

12.25 Prove that in a sealed-bid second-price auction, the strategy under which a buyer submits a bid equal to his private value weakly dominates all his other strategies, also when the buyer is risk averse or risk seeking.

12.26 Prove that in a symmetric sealed-bid auction with independent private values in which all the buyers are risk seeking, and have the same strictly convex, differentiable, and monotonically increasing utility function, the seller's expected revenue is lower in a sealed-bid first-price auction than in a sealed-bid second-price auction.

12.27 Suppose that in a symmetric sealed-bid first-price auction there are n buyers whose private values are independent. Suppose further that the utility function of all buyers is $U(x) = x^c$.

(a) Find the values c for which the buyers are risk averse, risk neutral, and risk seeking.

(b) Prove that a symmetric equilibrium γ must satisfy the following differential equation:

$$\gamma'(x) = \frac{n-1}{c} \frac{f(x)}{F(x)} (x - \gamma(x)). \tag{12.208}$$

(c) Show that the following strategy is a symmetric equilibrium:

$$\gamma(v) = v - \frac{\int_0^v F^{\frac{n-1}{c}}(x)dx}{F^{\frac{n-1}{c}}(v)}. \tag{12.209}$$

(d) Compute the symmetric equilibrium γ for the case that F is the uniform distribution over $[0, 1]$.

(e) Compare the strategy that you found for arbitrary c with the symmetric equilibrium in the case in which the buyers are risk neutral (see Exercise 12.24). Ascertain that risk-averse buyers submit higher bids than risk-neutral buyers, and that risk-seeking buyers submit lower bids than risk-neutral buyers.

(f) What is the seller's expected revenue as a function of c? Is this an increasing function?

This exercise shows that a symmetric equilibrium in a sealed-bid first-price auction with n buyers, where the utility function of each buyer is $U(x) = x^c$, is also a symmetric equilibrium in the same auction with $\frac{n-1}{c} + 1$ risk-neutral buyers.[10] In other words, a risk-averse buyer behaves like a risk-neutral buyer in an auction with more buyers, and therefore increases his bid.

---

10 Under the assumption that $\frac{n-1}{c}$ is an integer.

12.28 Prove Theorem 12.42 on page 502: every sealed-bid auction with risk-neutral buyers can be presented as a selling mechanism.

12.29 Can there be more than one equilibrium for an incentive-compatible direct selling mechanism? If your answer is yes, present an example. If not, justify your answer. If your answer is yes, do all these equilibria yield the same expected revenue for the seller? Justify your answer.

12.30 Prove the revelation principle (Theorem 12.47 on page 504): let $(\Theta_i, \hat{q}_i, \hat{\mu}_i)_{i \in N}$ be a selling mechanism, and $\hat{\beta}$ be an equilibrium of this mechanism. Then the outcome of this mechanism under $\hat{\beta}$ is identical to the outcome under β^* (the equilibrium when all buyers reveal their true values) in mechanism (q, μ), defined by Equations (12.132) and (12.133).

12.31 Let (p, C) and $(\tilde{p}, \tilde{C})$ be two symmetric sealed-bid auctions with independent private values defined over the same set N of risk-neutral buyers. Suppose that in both auctions the winner of the auction is the buyer who submits the highest bid. and a buyer who submits a bid of 0 pays nothing. Let β and $\tilde{\beta}$ be symmetric and monotonically increasing equilibrium strategies in (p, C) and in $(\tilde{p}, \tilde{C})$, respectively (for the same distributions of private values). Using Corollary 12.50 (page 507), prove that the seller's expected revenue is the same under both equilibria, and the buyer's expected profit given his private value is also identical in both auctions.

12.32 Consider the following cumulative distribution function, where $k \in \mathbb{N}$:

$$F_i(v_i) = (v_i)^k, \quad 0 \le v \le 1. \tag{12.210}$$

Compute the function c_i (see Equation (12.159) on page 509). For which values k is the function c_i monotonically increasing?

12.33 Suppose that V_i is distributed according to the exponential distribution with parameter λ (i.e., $V_i = [0, \infty)$ and $f_i(v_i) = \lambda e^{-\lambda v_i}$ for each $v_i \ge 0$). Compute the function c_i. Is c_i monotonically increasing?

12.34 For each of the following auctions and their respective equilibria β, construct an incentive-compatible direct selling mechanism whose truth-telling equilibrium β^* is equivalent to the equilibrium β.

(a) Auction method: sealed-bid second-price auction; equilibrium $\beta = (\beta_i)_{i \in N}$, where $\beta_i(v_i) = v_i$ for each buyer i and each $v_i \in V_i$.
(b) Auction method: a sealed-bid second-price auction in which $V_i = [0, 1]$ for every buyer i, equilibrium $\beta = (\beta_i)_{i \in N}$ where $\beta_1(v_1) = 1$ for all $v_1 \in [0, 1]$ and $\beta_i(v_i) = 0$ for each buyer $i \ne 1$ and all $v_1 \in [0, 1]$.
(c) Auction method: sealed-bid first-price auction with $n = 2$, and the private values of the buyers are independent and uniformly distributed over $[0, 1]$; equilibrium $\beta = (\beta_i)_{i=1,2}$, given by $\beta_i(v_i) = \frac{v_i}{2}$.

(d) Auction method: sealed-bid first-price auction with a reserve price ρ and two buyers whose private values are independent and uniformly distributed over the interval $[0, 1]$; equilibrium given in Example 12.34 (page 494).

12.35 Suppose that there are n buyers whose private values are independent and uniformly distributed over $[0, 1]$. Answer the following questions:

(a) What is the individually rational, incentive-compatible direct selling mechanism that maximizes the seller's expected revenue?

(b) In this mechanism, what is each buyer's probability of winning the object, assuming that each buyer reports his true private value?

(c) What is the seller's expected revenue in this case?

12.36 Repeat Exercise 12.35 for the case in which there are two buyers, and their private values V_1 and V_2 are independent; V_1 is uniformly distributed over $[0, 2]$ and V_2 is uniformly distributed over $[0, 3]$.

12.37 Partition the following list of auction methods into groups, each of which contains methods whose symmetric equilibrium yields the same expected revenue for the seller. In all these methods consider the symmetric case with independent private values and a symmetric and monotonic increasing equilibrium.

(a) Sealed-bid first-price auction.

(b) Sealed-bid first-price auction with a reserve price ρ.

(c) Sealed-bid first-price auction with an entry fee λ.

(d) Sealed-bid second-price auction.

(e) Sealed-bid second-price auction with a reserve price ρ.

(f) Sealed-bid second-price auction with an entry fee λ.

(g) Sealed-bid third-price auction (in which the winning buyer is the one who submits the highest bid, and the price he pays for the object is the third-highest price bid. See Exercise 12.19).

(h) Sealed-bid all-pay auction.

(i) Sealed-bid all-pay auction with a reserve price ρ.

12.38 Among the auction methods listed in Exercise 12.37, do there exist methods in which a buyer's submitted bid in an equilibrium may be greater than his private value? Justify your answer.

12.39 Suppose that there are n buyers participating in an auction, where the private values $V_1, V_2, \ldots, V_n$ are independent and identically distributed, with the cumulative distribution function $F_i(v_i) = (v_i)^2$ for $v \in [0, 1]$. Which auction maximizes the seller's expected revenue? What is the seller's expected revenue in that auction?

12.40 Suppose there are n buyers participating in an auction, where the private values $V_1, V_2, \ldots, V_n$ are independent and identically distributed, with the cumulative distribution function

$$F_i(v_i) = \tfrac{1}{2}v_i + \tfrac{1}{2}(v_i)^2, \quad v_i \in [0, 1]. \tag{12.211}$$

Answer the following questions:

(a) Which auction maximizes the seller's expected revenue?
(b) What is the seller's expected revenue in this auction? (To answer this, it suffices to write the formula for the seller's expected revenue, and specify the values of the variables. There is no need to compute the formula explicitly.)
(c) Is the seller's expected revenue monotonically increasing as the number of buyers in the auction increases? Justify your answer.

12.41 Suppose there are n buyers participating in an auction, where the private values $V_1, V_2, \ldots, V_n$ are independent and for each $i \in \{1, 2, \ldots, n\}$, v_i is uniformly distributed over $[0, \bar{v}_i]$. Suppose further that $\bar{v}_1 < \bar{v}_2 < \cdots < \bar{v}_n$. Answer the following questions:

(a) Which selling mechanism maximizes the seller's expected revenue?
(b) What is the seller's expected revenue under this mechanism?
(c) What is the probability that buyer n wins the object under this mechanism?

In the last two items, it suffices to write down the appropriate formula, with no need to solve it explicitly.

12.42 This exercise explores the case in which the number of buyers in an auction is unknown.

Suppose that there are N potential buyers whose private values $V_1, V_2, \ldots, V_N$ are independent and have identical continuous distribution over $[0, 1]$. Denote by F the common cumulative distribution function.

The number of buyers participating in this auction is unknown to any of the participating buyers. Each buyer ascribes probability p_n to the event that there are n participating buyers, in addition to himself, where $\sum_{n=0}^{N-1} p_n = 1$. Note that each buyer has the same belief about the distribution of the number of buyers in the auction.

(a) Find a symmetric equilibrium of this situation when the selling takes place by way of a sealed-bid second-price auction. Explain why this is an equilibrium.
(b) Denote $G^{(n)}(z) = (F(z))^n$. Prove that the expected payment to the seller of a participating buyer with a private value v is,

$$\sum_{n=0}^{N-1} p_n G^{(n)}(v) \mathbf{E}\big[Y_1^{(n)} \mid Y_1^{(n)} < v\big], \tag{12.212}$$

where $Y_1^{(n)}$ is the maximum of n independent random variables sharing the same cumulative distribution function F.

(c) Prove the Revenue Equivalence Theorem in this case: consider a symmetric sealed-bid auction with independent private values, and let β be a monotonically increasing symmetric equilibrium satisfying the assumptions that (a) the winner is the buyer submitting the highest bid, and (b) the expected payment of a buyer whose private value is 0, is 0. Then the expected payment of a buyer whose private value is v is given by Equation (12.212).

(d) Compute a symmetric equilibrium strategy when the selling takes place by way of a sealed-bid first-price auction.

(e) Explain how Theorem 12.59 (page 512) can be used to show that the optimal selling mechanism in this case is a sealed-bid second-price auction with a reserve price.

13 Repeated games

Chapter summary

In this chapter we present the model of repeated games. A repeated game consists of a base game, which is a game in strategic form, that is repeated either finitely or infinitely many times. We present three variants of this model:

- The finitely repeated game, in which each player attempts to maximize his average payoff.
- The infinitely repeated game, in which each player attempts to maximize his long-run average payoff.
- The infinitely repeated game, in which each player attempts to maximize his discounted payoff.

For each of these models we prove a *Folk Theorem*, which states that under some technical conditions the set of equilibrium payoffs is (or approximates) the set of feasible and individually rational payoffs of the base game.

We then extend the Folk Theorems to uniform equilibria for discounted infinitely repeated games and to uniform ε-equilibria for finitely repeated games. The former is a strategy vector that is an equilibrium in the discounted game, for every discount factor sufficiently close to 1, and the latter is a strategy vector that is an ε-equilibrium in all sufficiently long finite games.

In the previous chapters, we dealt with one-stage games, which model situations where the interaction between the players takes place only once, and once completed, it has no effect on future interactions between the players. In many cases, interaction between players does not end after only one encounter; players often meet each other many times, either playing the same game over and over again, or playing different games. There are many examples of situations that can be modeled as multistage interactions: a printing office buys paper from a paper manufacturer every quarter; a tennis player buys a pair of tennis shoes from a shop in his town every time his old ones wear out; baseball teams play each other several times every season. When players repeatedly encounter each other in strategic situations, behavioral phenomena emerge that are not present in one-stage games.

- The very fact that the players encounter each other repeatedly gives them an opportunity to cooperate, by conditioning their actions in every stage on what happened in previous stages. A player can threaten his opponent with the threat "if you do not cooperate now, in the future I will take actions that harm you," and he can carry out this threat, thus "punishing" his opponent. For example, the manager of a printing office can inform a paper manufacturer that if the price of the paper he purchases is not reduced by 10% in the future, he will no longer buy paper from that manufacturer.

- Repeated games enable players to develop reputations. A sporting goods shop can develop a reputation as a quality shop, or a discount store.

In this chapter, we present the model of repeated games. This is a simple model of games in which players play the same base game time and again. In particular, the set of players, the actions available to the players, and their payoff functions do not change over time, and are independent of past actions. This assumption is, of course, highly restrictive, and it is often unrealistic: in the example above, new paper manufacturers enter the market, existing manufacturers leave the market, there are periodic changes in the price of paper, and the quantity of paper that printers need changes over time. This simple model, however, enables us to understand some of the phenomena observed in multistage interactions. The more general model, where the actions of the players and their payoff functions may change from one stage to another, is called the model of "stochastic games." The reader interested in learning more about stochastic games is directed to Filar and Vrieze [1997] and Neyman and Sorin [2003].

13.1　The model

A repeated game is constructed out of the base game Γ that defines it, i.e., the game that the players play at each stage. We will assume that the base game is given in strategic form $\Gamma = (N, (S_i)_{i \in N}, (u_i)_{i \in N})$, where $N = \{1, 2, \ldots, n\}$ is the set of players, S_i is the set of actions[1] available to player i, and $u_i : S \to \mathbb{R}$ is the payoff function of player i in the base game, where $S = S_1 \times S_2 \times \cdots \times S_n$ is the set of action vectors.

In repeated games, the players encounter each other again and again, playing the same strategic-form game Γ each time. The complete description of a repeated game needs to include the number of stages that the game is played. In addition, since the players receive a payoff at each stage, we need to specify how the players value the sequence of payoffs that they receive, i.e., how each player compares each payoff sequence to another payoff sequence. We will consider three cases:

- The game lasts a finite number of stages T, and every player wants to maximize his average payoff.
- The game lasts an infinite number of stages, and every player wants to maximize the upper limit of his average payoffs.
- The game lasts an infinite number of stages, and each player wants to maximize the time-discounted sum of his payoffs.

Denote by

$$M := \max_{i \in N} \max_{s \in S} |u_i(s)| \tag{13.1}$$

---

1 In this chapter we will call the elements of S_i "actions," and reserve the term "strategy" for strategies in the repeated game.

the maximal absolute value of the payoffs received by the players in one stage. Recall that the set of distributions over a set S_i is $\Sigma_i = \Delta(S_i)$, the product set of these sets is $\Sigma = \Sigma_1 \times \Sigma_2 \times \cdots \times \Sigma_n$, and $U_i : \Sigma \to \mathbb{R}$ is the mixed extension of the payoff functions u_i (defined over S; see page 146).

By definition, a strategy instructs a player how to play throughout the game. The definition of a strategy in finite repeated games, and infinitely repeated games, will be presented when these games are defined.

13.2 Examples

The following example will be referenced often, for illustrating definitions, and explaining claims in this chapter.

Example 13.1 **Repeated Prisoner's Dilemma** Recall that the Prisoner's Dilemma is a one-stage two-player game, depicted in Figure 13.1.

Player II

		D	C
Player I	D	1, 1	4, 0
	C	0, 4	3, 3

Figure 13.1 The one-stage Prisoner's Dilemma

For both players, action D strictly dominates action C, so the only equilibrium of the base game is (D, D).

Consider the case in which the players play the Prisoner's Dilemma twice, and the second time the game is played, they both know which actions were chosen the previous time they played the game. When this situation is depicted as an extensive-form game (see Figure 13.2), the game tree has information sets representing the fact that at each stage the players choose their actions simultaneously. In Figure 13.2, the total payoff of each player in the two stages is indicated by the leaves of the game tree, where the upper number is the total payoff of Player I, and the lower number is the total payoff of Player II. In this figure, and several other figures in this chapter, the depicted tree "grows" from top to bottom, rather than left to right, for the sake of saving space on the page.

What are the equilibria of this game? A direct inspection reveals that the strategy vector in which the players repeat the one-stage equilibrium (D, D) at both stages is an equilibrium of the two-stage game. This is a special case of a general claim that states that every strategy vector where in every stage the players play an equilibrium of the base game is an equilibrium of the T-stage game (Theorem 13.6).

We argue now that at every equilibrium of the two-stage repeated game, the players play (D, D) in both stages. To see this, suppose instead that there exists an equilibrium at which, with positive probability, the players do not play (D, D) at some stage. Let $t \in \{1, 2\}$ be the last stage in which there is positive probability that the players will not play (D, D), and suppose that in this event, Player I does not play D in stage t. This means that if the game continues after stage t, the players will play (D, D). We will show that this strategy cannot be an equilibrium strategy.

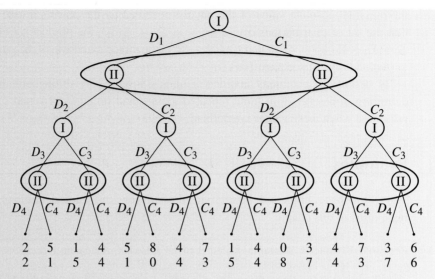

Figure 13.2 The two-stage Prisoner's Dilemma, represented as an extensive-form game

Case 1: t = 1. Consider the strategy of Player I at which he plays D in both stages. We will show that this strategy grants him a higher payoff. Since D strictly dominates C, Player I's payoff rises if he switches from C to D in the first stage. And since, by assumption, after stage t the players play (D, D) (since stage t is the last stage in which they may not play (D, D)), Player I's payoff in the second stage was supposed to be 1. By playing D in the second stage, Player I's payoff is either 1 or 4 (depending on whether Player II plays D or C);[2] in either case, Player I cannot lose in the second stage. The sum total of Player I's payoffs therefore rises.

Case 2: t = 2. Consider the strategy of Player I at which he plays in the first stage what the original strategy tells him to play, and in the second stage he plays D. Player I's payoff in the first stage does not change, but because D strictly dominates C, his payoff in the second stage does increase. The sum total of Player I's payoffs therefore increases.

Note that despite the fact that at every equilibrium of the two-stage repeated game the players play (D, D) in every stage, it is possible that at equilibrium, the strategy C is used off the equilibrium path; that is, if a player does deviate from the equilibrium strategy, the other player may play C with positive probability. For example, consider the following strategy σ_1:

- Play D in the first stage.
- In the second stage, play as follows: if in the first stage the other player played D, play D in the second stage; otherwise play $[\frac{1}{8}(C), \frac{7}{8}(D)]$ in the second stage.

Direct inspection shows that the strategy vector (σ_1, σ_1), in which both players play strategy σ_1, is an equilibrium of the two-stage repeated game.

By the same rationale used here to show that in the two-stage repeated Prisoner's Dilemma at equilibrium the players play (D, D) in both stages, it can be shown that in the T-stage repeated Prisoner's Dilemma, at equilibrium, the players play (D, D) in every stage (Exercise 13.6). ◄

---

2 Even if $t = 1$ is the last stage in which one of the players plays C with positive probability, it is still possible that if both players play D in the first stage, then Player II will play C in the second stage with positive probability. To see this, consider the following strategy vector. In the first stage, both players play C. In the second stage, Player I plays D, and Player II plays D if Player I played C in the first stage, and he plays C if Player I played D in the first stage. In this case, if neither player deviates, the players play (C, C) in the first stage, and (D, D) in the second stage; but if Player I plays D in the first stage, then Player II plays C in the second stage.

As we saw, in the finitely repeated Prisoner's Dilemma, at every equilibrium the players play (D, D) in every stage. Does this extend to every repeated game? That is, does every equilibrium strategy of a repeated game call on the players to play a one-stage equilibrium in every stage? The following example shows that the answer is negative: in general, the set of equilibria of repeated games is a much richer set.

Example 13.2 **Repeated Prisoner's Dilemma, with the possibility of punishment** Consider the two-player game given in Figure 13.3, where each player has three possible actions.

	D	C	P
D	1, 1	4, 0	−1, 0
C	0, 4	3, 3	−1, 0
P	0, −1	0, −1	−2, −2

Figure 13.3 The repeated Prisoner's Dilemma, with the possibility of punishment

This game is similar to the Prisoner's Dilemma in Example 13.1, with the addition of a third action P to each player, yielding low payoffs for both players. Note that action P (which stands for Punishment) is strictly dominated by action D, and therefore by Theorem 4.35 (page 108) we can eliminate it without changing the set of equilibria of the base game. After eliminating P for both players, we are left with the one-stage Prisoner's Dilemma, whose only equilibrium is (D, D). It follows that the only equilibrium of the base game in Figure 13.3 is (D, D).

As previously stated, when the players play an equilibrium of the base game in every stage, the resulting strategy vector is an equilibrium of the repeated game. It follows that in the two-stage repeated game in this example, playing (D, D) in both stages is an equilibrium. In contrast with the standard repeated Prisoner's Dilemma, there are additional equilibria in this repeated game. The strategy vector at which both players play the following strategy is an equilibrium:

- Play C in the first stage.
- If your opponent played C in the first stage, play D in the second stage. Otherwise, play P in the second stage.

If both players play this strategy, they will both play C in the first stage, and D in the second stage, and each player's total payoff will be 4 (in contrast to the total payoff 2 that they receive under the equilibrium of playing (D, D) in both stages). Since action D weakly dominates both of the other actions, no player can gain by deviating from D in the second stage alone. A player who deviates in the first stage from C to D gets a payoff of 4 in the first stage, but he will then get at most -1 in the second stage (because his opponent will play P in the second stage), and so in sum total he loses: his total payoff when he deviates is 3, which is less than his total payoff of 4 at the equilibrium. By deviating to P in the first stage, the deviator also loses.

This example illustrates that in a repeated game, the players can threaten each other, by adopting strategies that call on them to punish a player in later stages, if at some stage that player deviates from a particular action. The greater the number of stages in the repeated game, the greater opportunity players have to punish each other. In general, this increases the number of equilibria.

The last equilibrium in this example is not a subgame perfect equilibrium (see Section 7.1 on page 263), since the use of the action P is not part of an equilibrium in the subgame starting in the second stage. We will see later in this chapter that repeated games may have additional equilibria that are subgame perfect.

Note that there is a proliferation of pure strategies in repeated games, compared to one-stage games. For example, in the one-stage game in Figure 13.3, every player has three pure strategies, D, C, and P. In the two-stage game, every player has $3 \times 3^9 = 3^{10} = 59{,}049$ pure strategies: there are three actions available to the player in the first stage, and in the second stage his strategy is given by a function from the pair of actions played in the first stage, i.e., from $\{D, C, P\}^2$ to $\{D, C, P\}$. In the three-stage repeated game, every player has $3 \times 3^9 \times (3^{3^4}) = 3^{91}$ pure strategies: the number of possible strategies in the first two stages is as calculated above, and in the third stage the player's strategy is given by a function from $\{D, C, P\}^4$ to $\{D, C, P\}$: for every pair of actions that were played in the first two stages, the player needs to decide what to play in the third stage. ◀

In general, the size of each player's space of strategies grows super-exponentially with the number of stages in the repeated game (Exercise 13.1). This growth has two consequences. A positive consequence is that it leads to complex and interesting equilibria. In Example 13.2, we found an equilibrium that grants a higher average payoff to the two players than their payoff when they repeat the only equilibrium of the one-stage game. A negative consequence is that, due to the complications inherent in the proliferation of strategies, it becomes practically impossible to find all the equilibria of repeated games with many stages. For this reason, we will not attempt to compute all equilibria of repeated games. We will instead look for asymptotic results, as the number of repetitions grows; we will seek approximations to the set of equilibrium payoffs, without trying to find all possible equilibrium payoffs; and we will be interested in special equilibria that can easily be described.

13.3 The T-stage repeated game

In this section we will study the equilibria of a T-stage repeated game Γ_T that is based on a strategic-form game Γ. Our goal is to characterize the limit set of equilibrium payoffs as T goes to infinity. We will also construct, for each vector x in the limit set of equilibrium payoffs, and for each sufficiently large natural number T, an equilibrium in the T-stage repeated game that yields a payoff close to x.

13.3.1 Histories and strategies

Since players encounter each other repeatedly in repeated games, they gather information as the game progresses. The information available to every player at stage $t + 1$ is the actions played by all the players in the first t stages of the game. We will therefore define, for every $t \geq 0$, the *set of t-stage histories* as

$$H(t) := S^t = \underbrace{S \times S \times \cdots \times S}_{t \text{ times}}. \tag{13.2}$$

For $t = 0$, we identify $H(0) := \{\emptyset\}$, where $\emptyset$ is the history at the start of the game, which contains no actions. A history in $H(t)$ will sometimes be denoted by h^t, and sometimes by $(s^1, s^2, \ldots, s^t)$, where $s^j = (s_i^j)_{i \in N}$ is the vector of actions played in stage j.

A behavior strategy for player i is an action plan that instructs the player which mixed action to play after every possible history.

Definition 13.3 *A* behavior strategy *for player i in a T-stage game is a function associating a mixed action with each history of length less than T*

$$\tau_i : \bigcup_{t=0}^{T-1} H(t) \to \Sigma_i. \tag{13.3}$$

The set of behavior strategies of player i in a T-stage game is denoted by $\mathcal{B}_i^T$.

Equivalently, we can define a behavior strategy of player i as a sequence $\tau_i = (\tau_i^t)_{t=0}^{T-1}$ of functions, where $\tau_i^{t+1} : H(t) \to \Sigma_i$ instructs the player what to play in stage t, for each $t \in \{0, 1, \ldots, T-1\}$.

Remark 13.4 *When a T-stage repeated game is depicted as an extensive-form game, a pure strategy is a function $\tau_i : \bigcup_{t=0}^{T-1} H(t) \to S_i$. A mixed strategy is a distribution over pure strategies (Definition 5.3 on page 146). We have assumed that every player knows which actions were played at all previous stages; i.e., every player has perfect recall (see Definition 6.13 on page 242). By Kuhn's Theorem (Theorem 6.16 on page 246) it follows that every mixed strategy is equivalent to a behavior strategy, and we can therefore consider only behavior strategies, which are more convenient to use in this chapter.* ♦

Example 13.1 (*Continued*) Consider the two-stage Prisoner's Dilemma. Two (behavior) strategies are written in Figure 13.4, one for each player. The notation $\tau_\mathrm{I}(DC) = \left[\frac{2}{3}(D), \frac{1}{3}(C)\right]$ means that after history DC (which occurs if in the first stage Player I plays D, and Player II plays C), Player I plays the mixed action $\left[\frac{2}{3}(D), \frac{1}{3}(C)\right]$ in the second stage.

$$\begin{aligned}
\tau_\mathrm{I}(\phi) &= \left[\tfrac{1}{2}(D), \tfrac{1}{2}(C)\right], & \tau_\mathrm{II}(\phi) &= C, \\
\tau_\mathrm{I}(DD) &= D, & \tau_\mathrm{II}(DD) &= \left[\tfrac{3}{4}(D), \tfrac{1}{4}(C)\right], \\
\tau_\mathrm{I}(DC) &= \left[\tfrac{2}{3}(D), \tfrac{1}{3}(C)\right], & \tau_\mathrm{II}(DC) &= \left[\tfrac{1}{2}(D), \tfrac{1}{2}(C)\right], \\
\tau_\mathrm{I}(CD) &= \left[\tfrac{1}{4}(D), \tfrac{3}{4}(C)\right], & \tau_\mathrm{II}(CD) &= C, \\
\tau_\mathrm{I}(CC) &= C. & \tau_\mathrm{II}(CC) &= D.
\end{aligned}$$

Figure 13.4 Strategies for both players in the two-stage Prisoner's Dilemma

◄

Given the strategies $(\tau_i)_{i \in N}$ of the players, denote by $\tau = (\tau_1, \tau_2, \ldots, \tau_n)$ the vector of the players' strategies. Denote by $\tau_i(s_i)$ the probability that player i plays action s_i in the first stage, and by $\tau_i(s_i \mid s^1, \ldots, s^{t-1})$ the conditional probability that player i plays action s_i in stage t, given that the players have played $(s^1, \ldots, s^{t-1})$ in the first $t-1$ stages.

Example 13.1 (*Continued*) If the players play according to the strategies τ_I and τ_II that we defined in Figure 13.4 in the two-stage Prisoner's Dilemma, we can associate with every branch in the game tree the probability that it will be chosen in a play of the game. These probabilities are shown in Figure 13.5.

The figure also shows, by each leaf of the game tree, the probability that the leaf will be arrived at if the players play strategies τ_{I} and τ_{II}.

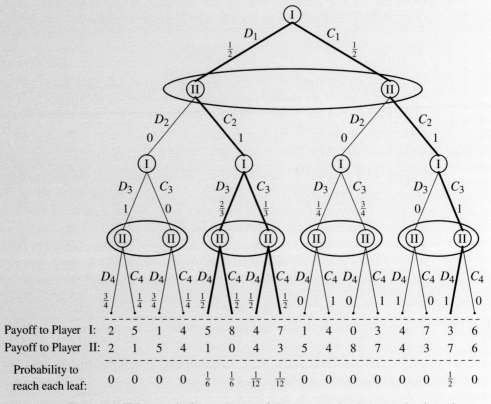

Payoff to Player I:	2	5	1	4	5	8	4	7	1	4	0	3	4	7	3	6
Payoff to Player II:	2	1	5	4	1	0	4	3	5	4	8	7	4	3	7	6

Probability to reach each leaf:	0	0	0	0	$\frac{1}{6}$	$\frac{1}{6}$	$\frac{1}{12}$	$\frac{1}{12}$	0	0	0	0	0	0	$\frac{1}{2}$	0

Figure 13.5 The probabilities attached to each play of the game, under the strategies $(\tau_{\mathrm{I}}, \tau_{\mathrm{II}})$

◀

The collection of all the possible plays of the T-stage game is $S^T = H(T)$. As can be seen in Figure 13.5, every strategy vector τ naturally induces a probability measure $\mathbf{P}_\tau$ over $H(T)$. The probability of every play of the game $(s^1, s^2, \ldots, s^T)$ is the probability that if the players play according to strategy τ, the resulting play of the game will be this history. Formally, for every action vector $s^1 = (s_1^1, \ldots, s_n^1) \in S$, define

$$\mathbf{P}_\tau(s^1) = \tau_1(s_1^1) \times \tau_2(s_2^1) \times \cdots \times \tau_n(s_n^1). \tag{13.4}$$

This is the probability that the action vector played in the first stage is s^1, and it equals the product of the probability that every player i plays action s_i^1. More generally, for every t, $2 \le t \le T$, and every finite history $(s^1, s^2, \ldots, s^t) \in S^t$, define by induction

$$\mathbf{P}_\tau(s^1, s^2, \ldots, s^t) = \mathbf{P}_\tau(s^1, s^2, \ldots, s^{t-1}) \times \tau_1(s_1^t \mid s^1, s^2, \ldots, s^{t-1})$$
$$\times \tau_2(s_2^t \mid s^1, s^2, \ldots, s^{t-1}) \times \cdots \times \tau_n(s_n^t \mid s^1, s^2, \ldots, s^{t-1}).$$

This means that the probability that under τ the players play the action vector $s^1, s^2, \ldots, s^t$ in the first t stages is the probability that the players play $s^1, s^2, \ldots, s^{t-1}$ in the first $t - 1$ stages, times the conditional probability that they play the action vector s^t in stage t, given that they played $s^1, s^2, \ldots, s^{t-1}$ in the first $t - 1$ stages. This formula for $\mathbf{P}_\tau$ expresses the fact that the mixed action that a player implements in any given stage can depend on the actions that he or other players played in previous stages, but the random choices of the players made simultaneously in each stage are independent of each other. The case in which there may be correlation between the actions chosen by the players was addressed in Chapter 8, where we studied the concept of correlated equilibrium.

13.3.2 Payoffs and equilibria

In repeated games, the players receive a payoff in every stage of the game. Denote the payoff received by player i in stage t by u_i^t, and denote the vector of payoffs to the players in stage t by $u^t = (u_1^t, \ldots, u_n^t)$. Then, during the course of a play of the game, player i receives the sequence of payoffs $(u_i^1, u_i^2, \ldots, u_i^T)$. We assume that every player seeks to maximize the sum total of these payoffs or, equivalently, seeks to maximize the average of these payoffs.

As previously noted, every strategy vector τ induces a probability measure $\mathbf{P}_\tau$ over $H(T)$. Denote the corresponding expectation operator by $\mathbf{E}_\tau$; i.e., for every function $f : H(T) \to \mathbb{R}$, the expectation of f under $\mathbf{P}_\tau$ is denoted by $\mathbf{E}_\tau[f]$:

$$\mathbf{E}_\tau[f] = \sum_{(s^1, \ldots, s^T) \in H(T)} \mathbf{P}_\tau(s^1, \ldots, s^T) f(s^1, \ldots, s^T). \tag{13.5}$$

Player i's expected payoff in stage t, under the strategy vector τ, is $\mathbf{E}_\tau[u_i^t]$. Denote player i's average expected payoff in the first T stages under strategy vector τ by

$$\gamma_i^T(\tau) := \mathbf{E}_\tau\left[\frac{1}{T} \sum_{t=1}^T u_i^t\right] = \frac{1}{T} \sum_{t=1}^T \mathbf{E}_\tau(u_i^t). \tag{13.6}$$

Example 13.1 (*Continued*) Figure 13.5 provides the probability to every play of the game under the strategy pair (τ_I, τ_{II}). The table in Figure 13.6 presents the plays of the game that are obtained with positive probability in the left column, the probability that each play is obtained in the middle column, and the payoff to the players, under that play of the game, in the right column. Each play of the game is written from left to right, with the actions implemented by the players in the first stage appearing first, followed by the actions implemented by the players in the second stage. Player I's action appears to the left of Player II's action.

Play of the Game	Probability	Payoff
$(D, C), (D, D)$	$\frac{1}{6}$	$(5, 1)$
$(D, C), (D, C)$	$\frac{1}{6}$	$(8, 0)$
$(D, C), (C, D)$	$\frac{1}{12}$	$(4, 4)$
$(D, C), (C, C)$	$\frac{1}{12}$	$(7, 3)$
$(C, C), (C, D)$	$\frac{1}{2}$	$(3, 7)$

Figure 13.6 The probability of every play of the game, and the corresponding payoff, under the strategy pair (τ_I, τ_{II})

It follows that the expected payoff of the two players is

$$\tfrac{1}{6} \times (5,1) + \tfrac{1}{6} \times (8,0) + \tfrac{1}{12} \times (4,4) + \tfrac{1}{12} \times (7,3) + \tfrac{1}{2} \times (3,7) = \left(4\tfrac{7}{12}, 4\tfrac{1}{4}\right). \qquad (13.7)$$

◀

Definition 13.5 *Let* $\Gamma = (N, (S_i)_{i\in N}, (u_i)_{i\in N})$ *be a base game. The T-stage game* Γ_T *corresponding to* Γ *is the game* $\Gamma_T = (N, (\mathcal{B}_i^T)_{i\in N}, (\gamma_i^T)_{i\in N})$.

The strategy vector $\tau^* = (\tau_1^*, \ldots, \tau_n^*)$ is a (Nash) equilibrium of Γ_T if for each player $i \in N$, and each strategy $\tau_i \in \mathcal{B}_i^T$,

$$\gamma_i^T(\tau^*) \geq \gamma_i^T(\tau_i, \tau_{-i}^*). \qquad (13.8)$$

The vector $\gamma^T(\tau^*)$ is called an *equilibrium payoff* of the repeated game Γ_T.

The following theorem states that a strategy vector at which in each stage the players play a one-stage equilibrium is an equilibrium of the *T*-stage game.

Theorem 13.6 *Let* $\Gamma = (N, (S_i)_{i\in N}, (u_i)_{i\in N})$ *be a base game, and let* Γ_T *be its corresponding repeated T-stage game. Let* $\sigma^1, \sigma^2, \ldots, \sigma^T$ *be equilibria of* Γ *(not necessarily different equilibria). Then the strategy vector* τ^* *in* Γ_T, *at which in each stage* t, $1 \leq t \leq T$, *every player* $i \in N$ *plays the mixed action* σ_i^t, *is an equilibrium.*

Proof: The strategy vector τ^* is an equilibrium, because neither player can profit by deviating. No player can profit in a stage in which he deviates from equilibrium, because by definition in such a stage the players implement an equilibrium of the base game. In addition, his deviation in any stage cannot influence the future actions of the other players, because they are playing according to a strategy that depends only on the stage t, not on the history h^t.

Formally, let $i \in N$ be a player, and let τ_i be any strategy of player i in Γ_T. We will show that $\gamma_i^T(\tau_i, \tau_{-i}^*) \leq \gamma_i^T(\tau^*)$; i.e., player i does not profit by deviating from τ_i^* to τ_i.

For each t, $1 \leq t \leq T$, the mixed action vector σ^t is an equilibrium of Γ. Therefore, for each history $h^{t-1} \in H(t-1)$,

$$U_i(\sigma^t) \geq U_i\big(\tau_i(h^{t-1}), \sigma_{-i}^t\big). \qquad (13.9)$$

This implies that

$$\mathbf{E}_{\tau_i, \tau_{-i}^*}\left[u_i^t\right] = \sum_{h^{t-1} \in H(t-1)} \mathbf{P}_{\tau_i, \tau_{-i}^*}(h^{t-1}) U_i(\tau_i(h^{t-1}), \tau_{-i}^*(h^{t-1})) \qquad (13.10)$$

$$= \sum_{h^{t-1} \in H(t-1)} \mathbf{P}_{\tau_i, \tau_{-i}^*}(h^{t-1}) U_i\big(\tau_i(h^{t-1}), \sigma_{-i}^t\big) \qquad (13.11)$$

$$\leq \sum_{h^{t-1} \in H(t-1)} \mathbf{P}_{\tau_i, \tau_{-i}^*}(h^{t-1}) U_i(\sigma^t) \qquad (13.12)$$

$$= U_i(\sigma^t) \sum_{h^{t-1} \in H(t-1)} \mathbf{P}_{\tau_i, \tau_{-i}^*}(h^{t-1}) = U_i(\sigma^t). \qquad (13.13)$$

The last equality follows from the fact that the sum total of the probabilities of all $(t-1)$-stage histories is 1, and therefore $\mathbf{E}_{\tau_i, \tau^*_{-i}}[u^t_i] \leq u_i(\sigma^t)$. Averaging over the T stages of the game shows that $\gamma^T_i(\tau_i, \tau^*_{-i}) \leq \gamma^T_i(\tau^*)$, which is what we wanted to show. Since $\gamma^T_i(\tau_i, \tau^*_{-i}) \leq \gamma^T_i(\tau^*)$ for every strategy τ_i of player i, and for every player i, we deduce that τ^* is an equilibrium. □

By repeating the same equilibrium in every stage, we get the following corollary:

Corollary 13.7 *Let Γ be a base game, and let Γ_T be the corresponding repeated T-stage game. Every equilibrium payoff of Γ is also an equilibrium payoff of Γ_T.*

13.3.3 The minmax value

Recall that U_i is the multilinear extension of u_i (Equation (5.9), page 146). The minmax value of player i in the base game Γ is (Equation (4.50), page 112):

$$\bar{v}_i = \min_{\sigma_{-i} \in \times_{j \neq i} \Sigma_j} \max_{\sigma_i \in \Sigma_i} U_i(\sigma_i, \sigma_{-i}). \qquad (13.14)$$

This is the value that the players $N \setminus \{i\}$ cannot prevent player i from attaining: for any vector of mixed actions σ_{-i} they implement, player i can receive at least $\max_{\sigma_i \in \Sigma_i} U_i(\sigma_i, \sigma_{-i})$, which is at least $\bar{v}_i$. Every mixed strategy vector σ_{-i} satisfying

$$\bar{v}_i = \max_{\sigma_i \in \Sigma_i} U_i(\sigma_i, \sigma_{-i}) \qquad (13.15)$$

is called a *punishment strategy vector* against player i, because if the players $N \setminus \{i\}$ play σ_{-i}, they guarantee that player i's average payoff will not exceed $\bar{v}_i$. Similarly to what we saw in Equation (5.25) (page 150), for every mixed action vector $\sigma_{-i} \in \Sigma_{-i}$ there exists a pure action $s'_i \in S_i$ of player i satisfying $U_i(s'_i, \sigma_{-i}) \geq \bar{v}_i$ (why?).

The next theorem states that at every equilibrium of the repeated game, the payoff to each player i is at least $\bar{v}_i$. The discussion above and the proof of the theorem imply that the minmax value of each player i in the T-stage game is $\bar{v}_i$ (Exercise 13.8).

Theorem 13.8 *Let τ^* be an equilibrium of Γ_T. Then $\gamma^T_i(\tau^*) \geq \bar{v}_i$ for each player $i \in N$.*

Proof: We will show that for every strategy vector τ (not necessarily an equilibrium vector) there exists a strategy τ^*_i of player i (which depends on τ_{-i}) satisfying $\gamma^T_i(\tau^*_i, \tau_{-i}) \geq \bar{v}_i$. It follows, in particular, that if τ is an equilibrium, then

$$\gamma^T_i(\tau) \geq \gamma^T_i(\tau^*_i, \tau_{-i}) \geq \bar{v}_i, \qquad (13.16)$$

which is what the theorem claims. We now construct such a strategy τ^*_i explicitly, for any given τ_{-i}. Recall that when τ is a strategy vector, $\tau_j(h)$ is the mixed action that player j plays after history h, and $\tau_{-i}(h) = (\tau_j(h))_{j \neq i}$ is the mixed action vector that the players $N \setminus \{i\}$ play after history h. As previously noted, for every history $h \in \bigcup^{T-1}_{t=0} H(t)$ there is an action $s'_i(h) \in S_i$ such that $U_i(s'_i(h), \tau_{-i}(h)) \geq \bar{v}_i$. Let τ^*_i be a strategy of player i under which, after every history h, he plays the action $s'_i(h)$. Then for every $t \in \{1, 2, \ldots, T\}$,

$$\mathbf{E}_{\tau^*_i, \tau_{-i}}[u^t_i] = \sum_{h^{t-1} \in H(t-1)} \mathbf{P}_{\tau^*_i, \tau_{-i}}(h^{t-1}) U_i(\tau^*_i(h^{t-1}), \tau_{-i}(h^{t-1})) \qquad (13.17)$$

$$= \sum_{h^{t-1} \in H(t-1)} \mathbf{P}_{\tau_i^*, \tau_{-i}}(h^{t-1}) U_i(s_i'(h^{t-1}), \tau_{-i}(h^{t-1})) \tag{13.18}$$

$$\geq \sum_{h^{t-1} \in H(t-1)} \mathbf{P}_{\tau_i^*, \tau_{-i}}(h^{t-1}) \bar{v}_i = \bar{v}_i. \tag{13.19}$$

The last equality follows from the fact that the sum total of the probabilities of all the possible histories at time period t is 1. In words, the expected payoff in stage t is at least $\bar{v}_i$. By averaging over the T stages of the game, we conclude that the expected average of the payoffs is at least $\bar{v}_i$:

$$\gamma_i^T(\tau_i^*, \tau_{-i}) = \frac{1}{T} \sum_{t=1}^{T} \mathbf{E}_{\tau_i^*, \tau_{-i}}[u_i^t] \geq \frac{1}{T} \sum_{t=1}^{T} \bar{v}_i = \bar{v}_i, \tag{13.20}$$

which is what we wanted to show.   □

Define a set of payoff vectors V by

$$V := \left\{ x \in \mathbb{R}^N : x_i \geq \bar{v}_i \text{ for each player } i \in N \right\}. \tag{13.21}$$

This is the set of payoff vectors at which every player receives at least his minmax value. The set is called the set of *individually rational payoffs*. Theorem 13.8 implies that the set of equilibrium payoffs is contained in V.

13.4   Characterization of the set of equilibrium payoffs of the *T*-stage repeated game

For every set of vectors $\{x_1, \ldots, x_K\}$ in $\mathbb{R}^N$, denote by $\text{conv}\{x_1, \ldots, x_K\}$ the smallest convex set that contains $\{x_1, \ldots, x_K\}$.

The players play some action vector s in S in each stage; hence the payoff vector in each stage is one of the vectors $\{u(s), s \in S\}$. In particular, the average payoff of the players, which is equal to $\frac{1}{T} \sum_{t=1}^{T} u(s^t)$, is necessarily located in the convex hull of these vectors (because it is a weighted average of the vectors in this set), which we denote by F:

$$F := \text{conv}\{u(s), s \in S\}. \tag{13.22}$$

This set is called the *set of feasible payoffs*. We thus have $\gamma^T(\tau) \in F$ for every strategy vector τ.

Using the last remark, and Theorem 13.8, we deduce that the set of equilibrium payoffs is contained in the set $F \cap V$ of feasible and individually rational payoff vectors. As we now show, if the base game satisfies a certain technical condition, then for every feasible and individually rational payoff vector x there exists an equilibrium payoff vector of the T-stage game that is close to it, for sufficiently large T. The technical condition that is needed here is that, for every player i, it is possible to find an equilibrium of the base game at which the payoff to player i is strictly greater than his minmax value.

Theorem 13.9 (The Folk Theorem[3]) *Suppose that for every player $i \in N$ there exists an equilibrium $\beta(i)$ in the base game $\Gamma = (N, (S_i)_{i \in N}, (u_i)_{i \in N})$ satisfying $u_i(\beta(i)) > \bar{v}_i$. Then for every $\varepsilon > 0$ there exists $T_0 \in \mathbb{N}$ such that for every $T \geq T_0$, and every feasible and individually rational payoff vector $x \in F \cap V$, there exists an equilibrium τ^* of the T-stage game Γ_T whose corresponding payoff is ε-close to x (in the maximum norm[4]):*

$$||\gamma^T(\tau^*) - x||_\infty < \varepsilon. \tag{13.23}$$

Under every equilibrium β of the base game, $u_i(\beta) \geq \bar{v}_i$ for every player i (as implied by Theorem 13.8 for $T = 1$). The condition of the theorem requires furthermore that, for every player i, there exists an equilibrium at which that inequality is a strict inequality.

Remark 13.10 *One can choose the minimal length T_0 in Theorem 13.9 to be independent of x. To see this, note that since $F \cap V$ is a compact set, given ε there exists a finite set $x^1, x^2, \ldots, x^J$ of vectors in $F \cap V$ such that the distance between each vector $x \in F$ and at least one of the vectors $x^1, x^2, \ldots, x^J$ is below $\frac{\varepsilon}{2}$:*

$$\max_{x \in F \cap V} \min_{1 \leq j \leq J} ||x - x^j||_\infty \leq \frac{\varepsilon}{2}. \tag{13.24}$$

Denote by $T_0(x^j, \frac{\varepsilon}{2})$ the size of T_0 in Theorem 13.9 corresponding to x^j and $\frac{\varepsilon}{2}$. Let $x \in F \cap V$, and let $j_0 \in \{1, 2, \ldots, J\}$ be an index satisfying $||x - x^{j_0}||_\infty \leq \frac{\varepsilon}{2}$. By the triangle inequality, every equilibrium τ of the T-stage repeated game satisfying $||\gamma^T(\tau) - x^{j_0}||_\infty \leq \frac{\varepsilon}{2}$ also satisfies $||\gamma^T(\tau) - x||_\infty \leq \varepsilon$. It follows that the statement of Theorem 13.9 holds for x and ε with $T_0 := \max_{1 \leq j \leq J} T_0(x^j, \frac{\varepsilon}{2})$, and this T_0 is independent of x. ◆

13.4.1   Proof of the Folk Theorem: example

Before we prove the theorem, we present an example that illustrates the proof. Consider the two-player game in Figure 13.7 (this is the game of Chicken; see Example 8.3 on page 314).

The minmax value of both players is 2. The punishment strategy against Player I is R, and the punishment strategy against Player II is B. The game has two equilibria in pure strategies, (T, R) and (B, L), with payoffs $(2, 7)$ and $(7, 2)$ respectively (we will not use the equilibrium in mixed strategies). If we denote

$$\beta(I) = (B, L), \quad \beta(II) = (T, R), \tag{13.25}$$

we deduce that the condition of Theorem 13.9 holds (because $u_i(\beta(i)) = 7 > 2 = \bar{v}_i$ for $i \in \{I, II\}$).

The payoff vector $(3, 3)$ is in F, since $(3, 3) = \frac{1}{2}(0, 0) + \frac{1}{2}(6, 6)$. It is also in V, because both of its coordinates are greater than or equal to 2, which is the minmax value of both

3 The name of the Folk Theorem is borrowed from the analogous theorem (see Theorem 13.17) for infinitely repeated games, which was well known in the scientific community for many years, despite the fact that it was not formally published in any journal article, and hence it was called a "folk theorem." The theorem is now usually ascribed to Aumann and Shapley [1994]. The Folk Theorem for finite games, Theorem 13.9, was proved by Benoit and Krishna [1985].

4 The maximum norm over $\mathbb{R}^n$ is defined as follows: $||x||_\infty = \max_{i=1,2,\ldots,n} |x_i|$ for each vector $x \in \mathbb{R}^n$.

Figure 13.7 The payoff matrix of the game of Chicken

Player I's actions	T	B	T	B	•	•	•	T	B	B	T
Player II's actions	L	R	L	R	•	•	•	L	R	L	R
Stage	1	2	3	4	•	•	•	97	98	99	100
Player I's payoff	6	0	6	0	•	•	•	6	0	7	2
Player II's payoff	6	0	6	0	•	•	•	6	0	2	7

Figure 13.8 An equilibrium in the 100-stage game of Chicken

players. It is therefore in $F \cap V$. We will now construct an equilibrium of the 100-stage game, whose average payoff is close to $(3, 3)$.

If the players play (T, L) in odd-numbered stages (yielding the payoff $(6, 6)$ in every odd-numbered stage) and play (B, R) in even-numbered stages (yielding the payoff $(0, 0)$ in every even-numbered stage), the average payoff is $(3, 3)$. This does not yet constitute an equilibrium, because every player can profit by deviating at every stage. Because this sequence of actions is deterministic, any deviation from it is immediately detected, and the other player can then implement the punishment strategy. The punishment strategy guarantees that the deviating player receives at most 2 in every stage after the deviation, which is less than the average of 3 that he can receive if he avoids deviating.

Because the repeated game in this case is finite, a threat to implement a punishment strategy is effective only if there are sufficiently many stages left to guarantee that the loss imposed on a deviating player is greater than the reward he stands to gain by deviating. If, for example, a player deviates in the last stage, he cannot be punished because there are no more stages, and he therefore stands to gain by such a deviation. This detail has to be taken into consideration in constructing an equilibrium.

We now describe a strategy vector defined by a basic plan of action and a punishment strategy. The basic plan of action is depicted in Figure 13.8, and consists of 49 cycles, each comprised of two stages, along with a tail-end that is also comprised of two stages.

In the first 98 stages, the players alternately play the action vectors (T, L) and (B, R), thereby guaranteeing that the average payoffs in these stages is $(3, 3)$, with the average payoff in all 100 stages close to $(3, 3)$. In these stages, they play according to a deterministic plan of action; hence if one of them deviates from this plan, the other immediately takes note of this deviation. Once one player deviates at a certain stage, the other player implements the punishment strategy against the deviator, from the next stage on: if Player II deviates, Player I plays B from the next stage to the end of the play of the game.

If Player I deviates, Player II plays R from the next stage to the end of the play of the game. In the last two stages of the basic plan of action, the players play the pure strategy equilibria $\beta(\mathrm{I})$ and $\beta(\mathrm{II})$ (in that order).

We now show that this strategy vector is an equilibrium yielding an average payoff that is close to $(3,3)$. Indeed, if the players follow this strategy vector, the average payoff is

$$\tfrac{49}{100}(6,6) + \tfrac{49}{100}(0,0) + \tfrac{1}{100}(7,2) + \tfrac{1}{100}(2,7) = (3.03, 3.03), \tag{13.26}$$

which is close to $(3,3)$.

We next turn to ascertaining that Player I cannot gain by deviating (ascertaining that Player II cannot gain by deviating is conducted in a similar way). In each of the last two stages (the tail-end of the action plan), the two players play an equilibrium of the base game, and therefore Player I cannot gain by deviating in those stages. Suppose, therefore, that Player I deviated during one of the first 98 stages. In the cycle at which he deviates for the first time, he can gain at most 3, relative to the payoff he would receive at that cycle by following the basic action plan. To see this, note that if he deviates in the second stage of the cycle (playing T instead of B), he gains 2 at that stage. If he deviates in the first stage of the cycle (playing B instead of T), he gains 1 at that stage, and if he then plays T instead of B in the second stage of the cycle he gains 2 at that stage, and in total he gains 3 at that cycle ($7 + 2$ instead of $6 + 0$ according to the basic plan). In each of the following cycles he loses (because he receives at most 2 in every stage of the cycle, instead of receiving 6 in the first stage and 0 in the second stage of the cycle, as he would receive under the basic plan of action). Finally, at stage 100 he loses 5: he will receive at most 2 rather than the 7 that he receives in the basic plan of action. In sum total, the deviation leads to a loss of at least $5 - 3 = 2$, relative to the payoff he would receive by following the basic action plan, and therefore Player I cannot gain by deviating.

In the construction depicted here, we have split the stages into cycles of length 2, because the payoff $(3,3)$ is the average of two payoff vectors of the matrix. If we had wanted to construct an equilibrium with a payoff that is, say, close to $(3\tfrac{1}{2}, 4\tfrac{3}{4})$ (which is also in $F \cap V$), then, since $(3\tfrac{1}{2}, 4\tfrac{3}{4}) = \tfrac{1}{4}(0,0) + \tfrac{1}{2}(6,6) + \tfrac{1}{4}(2,7)$, we would have constructed an equilibrium using cycles of length 4: except for the last stages, the players would repeatedly play the action vectors

$$(B,R), (T,L), (T,L), (T,R). \tag{13.27}$$

We can mimic the construction above whenever the target payoff can be obtained as the weighted average of the payoff vectors in the matrix, with rational weights. Since the target payoff is in F, it can always be obtained as a weighted average of payoffs. If the weights are irrational, we need to approximate them using rational weights.

The role of the tail-end (the last two stages in the above example) is to guarantee that a deviating player loses. During the course of the tail-end, the players cyclically play the equilibria $\beta(1), \dots, \beta(n)$. The expected payoff of each player i under each of these equilibria is greater than or equal to $\overline{v}_i$ (because they are equilibria) and under $\beta(i)$ it is strictly greater than $\overline{v}_i$. That is why, if the other players punish player i by reducing his payoff to $\overline{v}_i$, he loses in the tail-end. The tail-end needs to be sufficiently long for the total loss to be greater than the maximal gain that a player can obtain by deviating. On the other hand, the tail-end needs to be sufficiently short, relative to the length of the game, for the overall payoff to be close to the target payoff (which is the average payoff in a single cycle).

In the formulation of the Folk Theorem, the equilibrium payoff does not equal the target payoff x; the best we can do is obtain a payoff that is close to it. This stems from two reasons:

1. The existence of the tail-end, in which the payoff is not the target payoff.
2. It may be the case that x cannot be expressed as the weighted average of payoff vectors of the matrix using rational weights, which then requires approximating these weights using rational weights.

13.4.2 Detailed proof of the Folk Theorem

We will now generalize the construction in the example of the previous section to all repeated games. For every real number c, denote by $\lceil c \rceil$ the least integer that is greater than or equal to c, and by $\lfloor c \rfloor$ the greatest integer that is less than or equal to c. Recall that $M = \max_{i \in N} \max_{s \in S} |u_i(s)|$ is the maximal payoff of the game (in absolute value).

Denote $\delta_i = u_i(\beta(i)) - \bar{v}_i > 0$ and

$$\delta = \min \left\{ \min_{i \in N} \delta_i, \tfrac{1}{2} \right\} > 0. \tag{13.28}$$

Step 1: We assume w.l.o.g. that $x_i \geq \bar{v}_i + \frac{\varepsilon \delta}{4M}$ for every $i \in N$.

Define a vector $y \in \mathbb{R}^N$ by

$$y := \left(1 - \tfrac{\varepsilon}{4nM}\right) x + \tfrac{\varepsilon}{4M} \sum_{i=1}^{n} u(\beta(i)). \tag{13.29}$$

Since y is a convex combination of vectors in F, we have $y \in F$. For every player $i \in N$ we have (a) $x_i \geq \bar{v}_i$, (b) $u_i(\beta(j)) \geq \bar{v}_i$ for every $j \in N$, and (c) $u_i(\beta(i)) \geq \bar{v}_i + \delta$, and therefore $y_i \geq \bar{v}_i + \frac{\varepsilon \delta}{4M}$. In addition, for every player $i \in N$ we have

$$|y_i - x_i| \leq 2nM \tfrac{\varepsilon}{4nM} = \tfrac{\varepsilon}{2}. \tag{13.30}$$

Fix now $\varepsilon > 0$ and suppose that we proved that there is $T_0 \in \mathbb{N}$ such that for every $T \geq T_0$ and every payoff vector $y \in F$ that satisfies $y_i \geq \bar{v}_i + \frac{\varepsilon}{2}$ there is an equilibrium τ^* in the T-stage game that satisfies $\|\gamma^T(\tau^*) - y\|_\infty < \frac{\varepsilon}{2}$. By the triangle inequality and Equation (13.30) we have $\|\gamma^T(\tau^*) - x\|_\infty < \varepsilon$ and therefore Theorem 13.9 will be proven.

Step 2: Determining the cycle length.

We first show that every vector in F can be approximated by a weighted average of the vectors $(u(s))_{s \in S}$, with rational weights sharing the same denominator. The proof of the following theorem is left to the reader (Exercise 13.14).

Theorem 13.11 *For every $K \in \mathbb{N}$ and every vector $x \in F$ there are nonnegative integers $(k_s)_{s \in S}$ summing to K satisfying*

$$\left\| \sum_{s \in S} \frac{k_s}{K} u(s) - x \right\|_\infty \leq \frac{M \times |S|}{K}. \tag{13.31}$$

For $\varepsilon > 0$ and $x \in F \cap V$, let K be a natural number satisfying $K \geq \frac{4M^2 \times |S|}{\varepsilon \delta}$ and let $(k_s)_{s \in S}$ be nonnegative integers summing to K satisfying Equation (13.31). If the players implement cycles of length K, and in each cycle they play each action vector $s \in S$ exactly k_s times, then the average payoff over the course of the cycle is $\sum_{s \in S} \frac{k_s}{K} u(s)$, and the distance between this average payoff and x is at most $\frac{M \times |S|}{K}$. Because $x_i \geq \bar{v}_i + \frac{\varepsilon \delta}{4M}$ it follows that the average payoff of player i along one cycle is at least $\bar{v}_i$.

Step 3: Defining the strategy vector τ^*.
We next define a strategy vector τ^* of the T-stage game, which depends on two variables, R and L, to be defined later. The T stages of the game are divided into R cycles of length K and a tail of length L:

$$T = RK + L. \tag{13.32}$$

These variables will be set in such a way that the following two properties are satisfied: R will be sufficiently large for the average payoff according to τ^* to be close to x, and L will be sufficiently large for τ^* to be an equilibrium. In each cycle, the players play every action vector $s \in S$ exactly k_s times. In the tail-end, the players cycle through the equilibria $\beta(1), \ldots, \beta(n)$. In other words, each player j plays the mixed action $\beta_j(1)$ in the first stage, and in stages $n + 1$, $2n + 1$, etc., of the tail-end; he plays the mixed action $\beta_j(2)$ in the second stage, and in stages $n + 2$, $2n + 2$, etc., of the tail-end, and so on.

The basic plan that we have defined for the first RK stages is deterministic: the players do not choose their actions randomly in these stages. It follows that if a player deviates from the basic plan in one of the first RK stages, this deviation is detected by the other players. In this case, from the next stage on, the other players punish the deviator: at every subsequent stage they implement a punishment strategy vector against the deviator. If a player deviates for the first time in one of the L final stages, the other players do not punish him, and instead continue cycling through the equilibria $\{\beta(i)\}_{i \in N}$.

Step 4: The constraints on R and L needed to ensure that the distance between the average payoff under τ^* and x is at most ε.
Suppose that the players implement the strategy vector τ^*. Given the choice of $(k_s)_{s \in S}$, the distance between the average payoff in every cycle of length K and x is at most $\frac{M \times |S|}{K}$. This also holds true for any integer number of repetitions of the cycle. By the choice of K and since $\delta \leq \frac{1}{2}$, one has $\frac{M \times |S|}{K} \leq \frac{\varepsilon}{2}$, and hence the distance between the average payoff in the first RK stages and x is at most $\frac{\varepsilon}{2}$. If the length of the tail-end L is small relative to RK, the average payoff in the entire game will be close to x. We will ascertain that if

$$L \leq \frac{KR\varepsilon}{4M}, \tag{13.33}$$

then the distance between the average payoff in the entire game and x is at most ε. Indeed, the distance between the average payoff in the first RK stages and x is at most $\frac{\varepsilon}{2}$, and the distance between the average payoff in the last L stages and x is at most $2M$. Therefore the average payoff in the entire game is within ε of x, as long as

$$\frac{RK\frac{\varepsilon}{2} + 2ML}{T} \leq \varepsilon. \tag{13.34}$$

Since $T = RK + L > RK$, it suffices to require that

$$\frac{RK\frac{\varepsilon}{2} + 2ML}{RK} \leq \varepsilon, \tag{13.35}$$

and this inequality is equivalent to Equation (13.33).

Step 5: τ^* is an equilibrium.
Suppose that player i first deviates from the basic plan at stage t_0. We will ascertain here that his average payoff cannot increase by such a deviation.

Suppose first that t_0 is in the tail-end: $t_0 > RK$. Since throughout the tail the players play an equilibrium of the base game at every stage, player i cannot increase his average payoff by such a deviation.

Suppose next that $t_0 \leq RK$. Then player i's deviation triggers a punishment strategy against him from stage $t_0 + 1$. It follows that from stage $t_0 + 1$ player i's payoff at each stage is at most his minmax value $\bar{v}_i$. If $L \geq n$, by the condition that $u_i(\beta(i)) > \bar{v}_i$ we deduce that at each n consecutive stages in the tail-end, player i loses by the deviation at least $u_i(\beta(i)) - \bar{v}_i$, relative to his payoff at the equilibrium strategy. Denote $\delta_i = u_i(\beta(i)) - \bar{v}_i > 0$, and $\delta = \min_{i \in N} \delta_i > 0$.

The maximal profit that player i can gain by deviating up to stage RK is $2KM$: because the payoffs are between $-M$ and M, player i can gain at most $2M$ by deviating in any single stage; hence in a cycle in which he deviates, a player can gain[5] at most $2KM$. The player cannot gain in any of the subsequent cycles, because the average payoff in a cycle under the equilibrium strategy is at least $\bar{v}_i$, while if a player deviates, he receives at most $\bar{v}_i$.

For a punishment to be effective, we need to require that the tail-end be sufficiently long to ensure that the losses at the tail-end exceed the possible gains in the cycle in which the deviation occurred:

$$\delta \left\lfloor \frac{L}{n} \right\rfloor > 2KM. \tag{13.36}$$

In this calculation, we have rounded down L/n. In every n stages of the tail-end, every player is punished only once. If L is not divisible by n, some of the players are punished $\lfloor \frac{L}{n} \rfloor$ times, and some are punished $\lceil \frac{L}{n} \rceil$ times.

---

[5] If a player deviates at any stage, from the next stage on his one-stage expected payoff is at most his minmax value, but it is possible that in the basic plan during the cycle there may be stages in which his payoff is less than his minmax value. For example, in the equilibrium constructed in the example in Section 13.4.1 (page 539), in the even stages the payoff to each player is 0, while the minmax value of each player is 2. It is therefore possible for a player to gain at more than one stage by deviating.

Equation (13.36) gives us the required minimal length of the tail-end

$$L > n\left(1 + \frac{2KM}{\delta}\right).\tag{13.37}$$

The length of the tail-end, L, cannot be constant for all T, because $T - L$ needs to be divisible by K. It suffices to use tail-ends whose length is at least $n\left(1 + \frac{2KM}{\delta}\right)$, and at most $n\left(1 + \frac{2KM}{\delta}\right) + K$.

Step 6: Establishing T_0.

The length of the game, T, satisfies $T = RK + L$. From Equation (13.33), we need to require that $R \geq \frac{4ML}{K\varepsilon}$, i.e., $T = RK + L \geq L\left(1 + \frac{4M}{\varepsilon}\right)$. This, along with Equation (13.37), implies that the length of the game must satisfy

$$T > n\left(1 + \frac{2KM}{\delta}\right)\left(1 + \frac{4M}{\varepsilon}\right).\tag{13.38}$$

We can therefore set T_0 to be the value of the right-hand side of Equation (13.38). This concludes the proof of Theorem 13.9.

Remark 13.12 *As mentioned above, the only equilibrium payoff in the finitely repeated Prisoner's Dilemma is* $(1,1)$. *This does not contradict Theorem 13.9, because the conditions of the theorem do not hold in this case: the only equilibrium of the one-stage Prisoner's Dilemma is* (D,D), *and the payoff to both players at this equilibrium is* 1, *which is the minmax value of both players. The proof of the uniqueness of the equilibrium payoff in the T-stage Prisoner's Dilemma is based on the existence of a last stage in the game. In the next section we will study repeated games of infinite length, and show that in that case, the repeated Prisoner's Dilemma has more than one equilibrium payoff.* ◆

13.5   Infinitely repeated games

As noted above, the strategy vector constructed in the previous section is highly dependent on the length of the game: it cannot be implemented unless the players know the length of the game. However, it is often the case that the length of a repeated game is not known ahead of time. For example, the owner of a tennis-goods shop does not know if or when he will sell his shop, tennis players do not know when they will stop playing tennis, nor if or when they will move to another town. Infinitely repeated games can serve to model finite but extremely long repeated games, in which (a) the number of stages is unknown, (b) the players ascribe no importance to the last stage of the game, or (c) at every stage the players believe that the game will continue for several more stages.

In this section, we will present a model of infinitely repeated games, and characterize the set of equilibria of such games. The definitions in this section are analogous to the definitions in the section on T-stage games. As the next example shows, extending games to an infinite number of repetitions leads to new equilibrium payoffs: payoff vectors that cannot be obtained as limits of sequences of equilibrium payoffs in finite games whose lengths increase to infinity.

Example 13.1 (*Continued*) Recall the repeated Prisoner's Dilemma, given by the payoff matrix in Figure 13.9.

Player II

		D	C
	D	1, 1	4, 0
Player I	C	0, 4	3, 3

Figure 13.9 The Prisoner's Dilemma

Consider the repeated Prisoner's Dilemma in the case where the players repeat playing the basic game ad infinitum. In this case, every player receives an infinite sequence of payoffs: one payoff per stage of the game. We will assume that every player strives to maximize the limit of the average payoff he receives. Certain technical issues, such as what happens when the limit of the average payoffs does not exist, will be temporarily ignored (we will consider this issue later in this chapter). Whereas the only equilibrium payoff of the T-stage repeated game is $(1, 1)$, in the infinitely repeated game there are additional equilibrium payoffs.

Let us look, for example, at the following strategy: in the first stage play C. In every subsequent stage, if the other player chose C in every stage since the game started, choose C in the current stage; otherwise choose D. This is an unforgiving strategy that is called the grim-trigger strategy: as long as the opponent cooperates, you also cooperate, but if he fails to cooperate once, defect forever from that point on in the game. When both players implement this strategy, no player has an incentive to deviate. To see why, note that at this strategy vector, every player receives 3 in each stage; hence every player's average payoff is 3. If a player deviates at some stage and plays D, he receives 4 in that stage, instead of 3, but from that stage on, the other player plays D, and then the most that the deviating player receives in every stage is 1. In particular, the limit of the average payoff of the deviating player is at most 1. Thus, the payoff vector $(3, 3)$ is an equilibrium payoff of the infinitely repeated game, despite not being an equilibrium payoff of the T-stage game. ◄

Definition 13.13 *A behavior strategy for player i (in the infinitely repeated game) is a function mapping every finite history to a mixed action:*

$$\tau_i : \bigcup_{t=0}^{\infty} H(t) \rightarrow \Sigma_i. \tag{13.39}$$

The collection of all of player i's strategies in the infinitely repeated game is denoted by $\mathcal{B}_i^{\infty}$.

Remark 13.14 *If $\tau_i(h) \in S_i$ for every finite history $h \in \bigcup_{t=1}^{\infty} H(t)$, then the strategy τ_i is a pure strategy. Note that even when the sets of actions of the players are finite, the set of pure strategies available to them has the cardinality of the continuum.* ◆

Denote by $H(\infty)$ the collection of all possible plays of the infinitely repeated game:

$$H(\infty) = S^{\mathbb{N}}. \tag{13.40}$$

An element of this set is an infinite sequence $(s^1, s^2, \ldots)$ of action vectors, where $s^t = (s_i^t)_{i \in N}$ is the action vector of the players in stage t. The results in Section 6.4 (page 249) show that every vector of behavior strategies $\tau = (\tau_i)_{i \in N}$ induces a probability distribution $\mathbf{P}_\tau$ over the set $H(\infty)$ (which, together with the σ-algebra of cylinder sets forms a measurable space; see Section 6.4 for the definitions of these notions). We denote by $\mathbf{E}_\tau$ the expectation operator that corresponds to the probability distribution $\mathbf{P}_\tau$.

To define an infinitely repeated game, we need to define, in addition to the sets of strategies of the players, their payoff functions. One way to try doing this is by taking the limit of Equation (13.6) as T goes to infinity, but this limit may not necessarily exist. In this section, we will define infinitely repeated games, and equilibria in infinitely repeated games, without explicitly defining payoff functions in such games. In the next section we will define discounted payoff functions for infinitely repeated games, and study the corresponding equilibrium notion, which turns out to be different from the equilibrium concept presented in this section.

Definition 13.15 *Let $\Gamma = (N, (S_i)_{i \in N}, (u_i)_{i \in N})$ be a game in strategic form. The infinitely repeated game Γ_∞ corresponding to Γ is the game whose set of players is N, and each player i's set of strategies is $\mathcal{B}_i^\infty$.*

For every stage $t \in \mathbb{N}$, and every player $i \in N$, denote by u_i^t player i's payoff in stage t. We next define the concept of the equilibrium of Γ_∞.

Definition 13.16 *A strategy vector τ^* is an equilibrium (of the infinitely repeated game Γ_∞), with a corresponding equilibrium payoff $x \in \mathbb{R}^N$, if with probability 1 according to $\mathbf{P}_{\tau^*}$, for each player $i \in N$, the limit*

$$\lim_{T \to \infty} \frac{1}{T} \sum_{t=1}^{T} u_i^t \tag{13.41}$$

exists, and for each strategy τ_i of player i,

$$\mathbf{E}_{\tau^*} \left(\lim_{T \to \infty} \frac{1}{T} \sum_{t=1}^{T} u_i^t \right) = x_i \geq \mathbf{E}_{\tau_i, \tau_{-i}^*} \left(\limsup_{T \to \infty} \frac{1}{T} \sum_{t=1}^{T} u_i^t \right). \tag{13.42}$$

In words, a strategy vector τ^* is an equilibrium, with payoff x if (a) the average payoff under τ^* converges, (b) the expectation of its limit is x, and (c) no player can profit by deviating. Since there is no guarantee that every deviation leads to a well-defined limit of the average payoffs, we require that the expectation of the limit superior of the average payoffs after a deviation be not greater than the equilibrium payoff.

The following theorem characterizes the set of equilibrium payoffs of the infinitely repeated game.

Theorem 13.17 (The Folk Theorem for the infinitely repeated game Γ_∞) *The set of equilibrium payoffs of Γ_∞ is the set $F \cap V$.*

That is, every payoff vector that is in the convex hull of the payoffs $\{u(s), s \in S\}$ and is individually rational (i.e., that is not less than the minmax value $\bar{v}_i$ for each player i, which a player cannot be prevented from attaining) is an equilibrium payoff.

Note that the Folk Theorem for Γ_∞ and the Folk Theorem for Γ_T differ in two respects. First, in Γ_∞ we need not approximate a payoff to within ε; exact payoffs can be obtained. Second, in the finite repeated game, we required that for every player i there

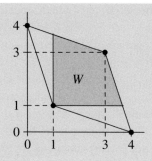

Figure 13.10 The set of equilibrium payoffs of the infinitely repeated Prisoner's Dilemma

exists an equilibrium of the base game that gives player i a payoff that is strictly greater than his minmax value; this requirement is not needed for the Folk Theorem for Γ_∞. The differences between these two theorems are illustrated in the repeated Prisoner's Dilemma. In that example, for every $T \in \mathbb{N}$ the only equilibrium payoff of Γ_T is $(1, 1)$ (see Example 13.1 on page 529), while according to Theorem 13.17, the set of equilibrium payoffs of Γ_∞ is the set W, shown in Figure 13.10.

Example 13.1 (*Continued*) Consider again the repeated Prisoner's Dilemma of Figure 13.9. We will show that $(1, 2)$, for example, is an equilibrium payoff of the infinitely repeated game. We do so by constructing an equilibrium leading to this payoff. Note first that

$$(1, 2) = \tfrac{5}{8}(1, 1) + \tfrac{1}{8}(3, 3) + \tfrac{2}{8}(0, 4). \tag{13.43}$$

Define the pair of strategies $\tau^* = (\tau_\mathrm{I}^*, \tau_\mathrm{II}^*)$ that repeatedly cycle through the action vectors

$$(D, D), (D, D), (D, D), (D, D), (D, D), (C, C), (C, C), (C, D), \tag{13.44}$$

unless a player deviates, in which case the other player switches to the punishment action D. Formally:

- Player I repeatedly cycles through the actions D, D, D, D, D, C, C, C.
- Player II repeatedly cycles through the actions D, D, D, D, D, C, C, D.
- If one of the players deviates, and fails to play the action he is supposed to play under this plan, the other player chooses D in every subsequent stage of the game, forever.

Direct inspection shows that τ^* is an equilibrium of the infinitely repeated game. By Equation (13.43) the average payoff at this equilibrium converges to $(1, 2)$.

We can similarly obtain every payoff vector in $F \cap V$ that is representable as a weighted average of the vectors $(u(s))_{s\in S}$, with rational weights, as an equilibrium payoff of the infinitely repeated game.

When a payoff vector $x \in F \cap V$ cannot be represented as a weighted average with rational weights, we can use Theorem 13.11 to approximate x by way of a weighted average with rational weights. In other words, for every $k \in \mathbb{N}$ we can find rational coefficients $(\lambda_s(k))_{s\in S}$ with denominator k such that

$$\left| x - \sum_{s\in S} \lambda_s(k)u(s) \right| < \frac{1}{k}. \tag{13.45}$$

In this case, in the basic action plan, the players play in blocks, where the k-th block has k stages: in the first block the players play to obtain the average $\sum_{s\in S} \lambda_s(1)u(s)$, in the second block they play to obtain the average $\sum_{s\in S} \lambda_s(2)u(s)$, and so on. Recall that for every sequence $(z^k)_{k\in\mathbb{N}}$ of real numbers converging in the limit to z, the sequence of averages $(\frac{1}{n}\sum_{k=1}^{n} z^k)_{n\in\mathbb{N}}$ also converges to z. Since the average payoff of the k-th block approaches x as k increases, the average payoff of the infinitely repeated game approaches x.

If one of the players deviates, the other player plays D in every stage from that stage on, forever, and hence no player can profit by deviating.   ◄

The construction of the equilibrium strategy in the above example can be generalized to any repeated game, thus proving Theorem 13.17. The proof is left to the reader (Exercise 13.24).

As stated at the beginning of this section, one reason to study infinitely repeated games is to obtain insights into very long finitely repeated games. To present the connection between infinitely repeated games and finite games, we define the concept of ε-equilibrium of finite games.

Definition 13.18 *Let $\varepsilon > 0$, and let $T \in \mathbb{N}$. A strategy vector τ^* is an ε-equilibrium of Γ_T if for each player $i \in N$ and any strategy $\tau_i \in \mathcal{B}_i^T$,*

$$\gamma_i^T(\tau^*) \geq \gamma_i^T(\tau_i, \tau_{-i}^*) - \varepsilon. \tag{13.46}$$

If τ^* is an ε-equilibrium of Γ_T, it is perhaps possible for a player to profit by deviating, but his profit will be no greater than ε. The smaller ε is, the less motivation a player has to deviate. When $\varepsilon = 0$, we recapitulate the definition of equilibrium, in which case no player has any motivation to deviate. If there is a cost for deviating, and the cost exceeds ε, then even at an ε-equilibrium, deviating is unprofitable. In this sense, ε-equilibria satisfy the property of being "almost stable," where "almost" is measured by ε.

For every strategy vector τ in Γ_∞, and every $T \in \mathbb{N}$, we can define the restriction of τ to the first T stages of the game. To avoid a plethora of symbols, we will denote such a restricted strategy vector by the same symbol, τ.

A stronger formulation of the Folk Theorem for Γ_∞ relates the equilibria of the infinitely repeated game to ε-equilibria in long finitely repeated games. The proof of the theorem is left to the reader (Exercise 13.26).

Theorem 13.19 *For every $\varepsilon > 0$ and every vector $x \in F \cap V$ there exist a strategy vector τ in Γ_∞ and $T_0 \in \mathbb{N}$ that satisfy the following:*

1. τ is an equilibrium of Γ_∞ with corresponding equilibrium payoff x.
2. τ is an ε-equilibrium of Γ_T, for all $T \geq T_0$.

Example 13.1 (*Continued*) On page 529, we saw that the only equilibrium payoff of the T-stage repeated Prisoner's Dilemma is $(1, 1)$. It follows that for every payoff vector $x \in F \cap V$ that is not $(1, 1)$, the corresponding strategy vector τ constructed on page 548, which is an equilibrium of the infinitely repeated game, is not an equilibrium of the T-stage repeated game, for any $T \in \mathbb{N}$. However, for every $\varepsilon > 0$, for T sufficiently large, the strategy vector τ is an ε-equilibrium of the T-stage repeated game with an average payoff close to x. In other words, every payoff vector $x \in F \cap V$ can be supported by an ε-equilibrium in the T-stage repeated game, provided T is large enough (Exercise 13.25).   ◄

As the following example shows, it is not the case that every equilibrium of Γ_∞ is an ε-equilibrium of every sufficiently long finitely repeated game.

Example 13.20　Consider the two-player zero-sum game in Figure 13.11.

Player II

		L	R
	T	0	-1
Player I	B	1	0

Figure 13.11　The base game in Example 13.20

The pure action B strictly dominates T, and R strictly dominates L. Elimination of strictly dominated actions reveals that the value of the (finitely or infinitely) repeated game is 0.

Consider the following pair of strategies $\tau^* = (\tau_{\mathrm{I}}^*, \tau_{\mathrm{II}}^*)$ in the infinitely repeated game:

- τ_{I}^* instructs Player I to play T up to stage $(t_{\mathrm{II}})^2$ and to play B thereafter, where t_{II} is the first stage in which Player II plays R ($t_{\mathrm{II}} = \infty$ if Player II plays L in every stage).
- τ_{II}^* instructs Player II to play L up to stage $(t_{\mathrm{I}})^2$ and to play R thereafter, where t_{I} is the first stage in which Player I plays B ($t_{\mathrm{I}} = \infty$ if Player II plays T at every stage).

Thus, Player I plays T and checks whether Player II plays L (in which case the payoff is 0). As long as Player II plays L, Player I plays T. If at a certain stage (which we denote by t_{II}) Player II first plays R, Player I continues to play T for several stages (up to stage $(t_{\mathrm{II}})^2$) and from that stage on he punishes Player II by playing B in every subsequent stage. Player II's strategy is defined similarly, all things being equal.

At strategy vector τ^*, the players play (T, L) in every stage, and the payoff, in the infinitely repeated game, is 0. If one of the players (say Player I) deviates he may receive the higher payoff of 1 for several stages (the stages between t_{I} and $(t_{\mathrm{I}})^2$), but afterwards he can receive at most 0 in every stage. The upper limit of the average payoff of Player I in Γ_∞ is therefore less than or equal to 0 even when he deviates: he cannot profit by deviating. In particular, $(\tau_{\mathrm{I}}^*, \tau_{\mathrm{II}}^*)$ is an equilibrium of the infinitely repeated game.

However, in finite games, $(\tau_{\mathrm{I}}^*, \tau_{\mathrm{II}}^*)$ is not an ε-equilibrium for ε close to 0: for example, in the 99-stage repeated game, if Player I deviates from τ_{I}^*, and plays B from stage 10 onwards, his average payoff is $\frac{90}{99}$. It follows that a deviation yields Player I a profit of $\frac{90}{99}$. In general, in the T-stage game, playing against strategy τ_{II}^*, Player I has a deviation yielding him a payoff of $\frac{T - \lceil \sqrt{T} \rceil}{T}$ (Exercise 13.27). Similarly, playing against strategy τ_{I}^*, Player II has a deviation yielding him a payoff of $-\frac{T - \lceil \sqrt{T} \rceil}{T}$. It follows that when ε is sufficiently small, $(\tau_{\mathrm{I}}^*, \tau_{\mathrm{II}}^*)$ is not an ε-equilibrium in any finite repeated game Γ_T, for large T. ◄

13.6　The discounted game

In the definition of the T-stage game, we assumed that every player seeks to maximize his average expected payoff at every stage of the game, or, equivalently, that every player seeks to maximize the expected sum of his payoffs. This means that if, say, John receives $10,000 today, and Paul receives $10,000 in a year from now, their situations are considered identical. Such an assumption is not appealing: in reality, if John invests his $10,000 in a bank account yielding, say, 5% annual interest, he will have $10,500 in one year, and thus will be better off than Paul. This is the reason that economic models usually assume that players maximize not the sum of their payoffs over time, but the discounted sum of their payoffs, where the discount rate takes into account the interest that players can receive over time for their money.

Discounted repeated games are presented in this section. For mathematical convenience, we will consider only infinitely repeated games. The assumption that all games are infinite is applicable in realistic models, because when payoffs are time-discounted, payoffs in far-off stages have a negligible effect on the discounted sum of the payoffs. We will study the equilibria of such games, and compare them to the equilibria of the finitely and infinitely repeated games presented in the previous sections.

Definition 13.21 *Let $\lambda \in [0, 1)$ be a real number, and let $\tau = (\tau_i)_{i \in N}$ be a strategy vector in an infinitely repeated game. The λ-discounted payoff to player i under strategy vector τ is*

$$\gamma_i^\lambda(\tau) := \mathbf{E}_\tau \left[(1 - \lambda) \sum_{t=1}^{\infty} \lambda^{t-1} u_i^t \right]. \tag{13.47}$$

The constant λ is called the discount factor.

The coefficient λ^{t-1} that multiplies the stage payoff u_i^t in Equation (15.17) expresses the fact that a payoff of $1 tomorrow is equivalent to a payoff of $\lambda today, a payoff of $1 in two days is equivalent to a payoff of $\lambda^2 today, and so on. Since $(1 - \lambda) \sum_{t=1}^{\infty} \lambda^{t-1} = 1$, the discounted payoff is the weighted average of the daily payoffs, where the weights decrease exponentially. When $\lambda = 0$, players' payoffs in Γ_λ equal their payoffs in the first stage of the game, and the discounted repeated game is essentially equivalent to the (one-stage) base game. When λ is close to zero, $1 - \lambda$ (the weight associated with the first stage) is large relative to λ (the total weight associated with the payoffs in the subsequent stages), and the first-stage payoff is the most important one: players attach more importance to today's payoff, and are willing to forgo high payoffs in the future. When λ is close to 1, the weight associated with stage t is very close to that of stage $t + 1$, and hence the players exhibit "patience": each player evaluates tomorrow's payoff almost as much as he evaluates today's payoff.

Since the sum total of the weights is 1, the λ-discounted payoff γ_i^λ may be viewed as an "expected payoff per stage." This can be seen in two different ways:

1. If the payoffs are 1 in each stage, we want the "average payoff" per stage to be 1, and indeed the discounted sum in this case is $(1 - \lambda) \sum_{t=1}^{\infty} \lambda^{t-1} = 1$.
2. We can also interpret the discount factor λ as the probability that the game will continue to the next stage. In other words, at every stage there is probability $1 - \lambda$ that the game will end, and probability λ that the game will continue. It follows that $\frac{1}{1-\lambda}$ is the expected number of stages to the end of the game, and the probability that the

game will get to stage t is λ^{t-1}. With this interpretation, the sum on the right-hand side of Equation (15.17) is the total expected payoff in the game divided by the expected number of stages.

Finally, since the definition in Equation (15.17) captures the per-stage payoff to player i, it allows us to compare equilibrium payoffs in discounted games, for different discount factors, and to compare these payoffs with equilibrium payoffs in finitely and infinitely repeated games.

Example 13.1 (*Continued*) Consider the strategy pair τ^* defined on Page 540, in which the players repeat the 8 action pairs

$$(D,D),(D,D),(D,D),(D,D),(D,D),(C,C),(C,D),(C,D).$$

The discounted payoff under the strategy pair τ^* is

$$\gamma^\lambda(\tau^*) = (1-\lambda)((1,1)(1+\lambda+\lambda^2+\lambda^3+\lambda^4)+(3,3)\lambda^5 \qquad (13.48)$$

$$+ (0,4)(\lambda^6+\lambda^7))(1+\lambda^8+\lambda^{16}+\cdots) \qquad (13.49)$$

$$= \tfrac{1-\lambda}{1-\lambda^8}\left((1,1)\tfrac{1-\lambda^5}{1-\lambda}+(3,3)\lambda^5+(0,4)\tfrac{\lambda^6(1-\lambda^2)}{1-\lambda}\right) \qquad (13.50)$$

$$= \left(\tfrac{1-2\lambda^5-3\lambda^6}{1-\lambda^8}, \tfrac{1+2\lambda^5+\lambda^6-4\lambda^8}{1-\lambda^8}\right). \qquad (13.51)$$

The reader can verify that by L'hôpital's rule $\lim_{\lambda\to 1}\gamma^\lambda(\tau^*) = (1,2)$, which is the average payoff on one cycle.   ◀

Definition 13.22 *Let* $\Gamma = (N,(S_i)_{i\in N},(u_i)_{i\in N})$ *be a base game, and let* $\lambda \in [0,1)$. *The* discounted game Γ_λ *(with discount factor* λ*) corresponding to* Γ *is the game* $\Gamma_\lambda = (N,(\mathcal{B}_i^\infty)_{i\in N},(\gamma_i^\lambda)_{i\in N})$.

It follows that a strategy vector τ^* is an equilibrium of Γ_λ if for each player $i \in N$ and each strategy τ_i,

$$\gamma_i^\lambda(\tau^*) \geq \gamma_i^\lambda(\tau_i,\tau^*_{-i}). \qquad (13.52)$$

In this case, the vector $\gamma_i^\lambda(\tau^*)$ is an *equilibrium payoff* of Γ_λ. The minmax value of each player i in Γ_λ is his minmax value in the base game Γ (Exercise 13.32), and an equilibrium payoff of a player is at least his minmax value (Theorem 5.42 on page 179). Therefore, $\gamma_i^\lambda(\tau^*) \geq \bar{v}_i$ for each player $i \in N$.

So far we have seen two ways to model long repeated games, using the infinitely repeated game Γ_∞ and using finite repeated games with duration T that increases to infinity. As we have seen in point 2 above, in a λ-discounted model we can interpret the quantity $\frac{1}{1-\lambda}$ as the expected duration of the game. Since this quantity goes to infinity as λ goes to 1, a third way to model a long repeated game is by λ-discounted games with a discount factor λ that goes to 1. A natural question that arises concerns the limit set of the set of λ-discounted equilibrium payoffs as λ goes to 1. In view of the Folk Theorem for infinitely repeated games, can we prove an analogue result for discounted games, that is, is it true that every vector $x \in F \cap V$ is the limit of λ-discounted equilibrium payoffs, as the discount factor goes to 1? The following example shows that this is not the case.

Example 13.23   Consider the three-player base game given in Figure 13.12, in which Player I has three actions $\{T, M, B\}$, Player II has two actions $\{L, R\}$, and Player III is a dummy player who has only one action, which has no effect on the payoffs (and is not mentioned throughout the example).

Player II

		L	R
	T	0, 2, 5	0, 0, 0
Player I	M	0, 1, 0	2, 0, 5
	B	1, 1, 0	1, 1, 0

Figure 13.12 The base game in Example 13.23

The minmax values of the players are 1, 1, and 0 respectively, and the set $F \cap V$ of the feasible and individually rational payoffs is the line segment $[(1, 1, 0) - (1, 1, 5)]$ (verify!). We will now show that $(1, 1, 0)$ is the only equilibrium payoff in the discounted game Γ_λ, for any discount factor $\lambda \in [0, 1)$.

Let τ^* be an equilibrium of the discounted game Γ_λ. The vector $\gamma^\lambda(\tau^*)$ is feasible and individually rational (why?) and therefore $\gamma_I^\lambda(\tau^*) = \gamma_{II}^\lambda(\tau^*) = 1$. It is left to show that $\gamma_{III}^\lambda(\tau^*) = 0$. Since the entries in the payoff matrix in which Player III's payoff is nonzero are (T, L) and (M, R), it is enough to show that under τ^* these entries are played at every stage with probability 0. To do that we will show that under τ^* at every stage Player I plays B with probability 1.

The sum of payoffs of Players I and II in all entries of the payoff matrix is at most 2. Since the discounted payoff is a weighted average of the stage payoffs with positive weights for every stage, and since $\gamma_I^\lambda(\tau^*) + \gamma_{II}^\lambda(\tau^*) = 2$, under τ^* the sum of payoffs of Players I and II in all stages is 2:

$$\mathbf{E}_{\tau^*}[u_I^t + u_{II}^t] = 2, \quad \forall t \in \mathbb{N}.$$

Since the sum of payoffs for Players I and II at (M, L) and (T, R) is strictly less than 2, it follows that these two entries are not chosen under τ^*: if one of these entries would be chosen at some stage with positive probability, it would imply that $\gamma_I^\lambda(\tau^*) + \gamma_{II}^\lambda(\tau^*) < 2$, a contradiction.

For any $t \geq 0$ and any history $h^t \in H(t)$, denote by $\gamma_i^\lambda(\tau^* \mid h^t)$ the conditional discounted future payoff of player i (from stage $t + 1$ on) given the history h^t, under the equilibrium τ^*:

$$\gamma_i^\lambda(\tau^* \mid h^t) := \mathbf{E}_{\tau^*}\left[(1 - \lambda) \sum_{j=1}^\infty \lambda^{j-1} u_i^{t+j} \mid h^t\right]. \tag{13.53}$$

The arguments provided above show that $\gamma_i^\lambda(\tau^* \mid h^t) = 1$ for $i \in \{I, II\}$ and every history h^t that has positive probability under τ^*. To prove that $\gamma_{III}^\lambda(\tau^*) = 0$ we will show that the pairs of actions (T, L) and (M, R) are chosen under τ^* with probability 0. We prove this claim only for the pair of actions (T, L).

Let $t \geq 0$ and $h^t \in H(t)$ a history that occurs under τ^* with positive probability, and assume to the contrary that $\tau_I^*(T \mid h^t) > 0$ and $\tau_{II}^*(L \mid h^t) > 0$. Since the action pairs (M, L) and (T, R) are chosen under τ^* with probability 0, we necessarily have $\tau_I^*(M \mid h^t) = 0$ and $\tau_{II}^*(R \mid h^t) = 0$. It follows that $\tau_{II}^*(L \mid h^t) = 1$ and $\tau_I^*(B \mid h^t) = 1 - \tau_I^*(T \mid h^t)$. Set $\alpha := \tau_I^*(B \mid h^t)$. Then

$$1 = \gamma_{\text{II}}^\lambda(\tau^* \mid h^t) \tag{13.54}$$

$$= \alpha \left((1 - \lambda) \times 2 + \lambda \times \gamma_{\text{II}}^\lambda(\tau^* \mid (h^t, (T, L))) \right)$$
$$+ (1 - \alpha) \left((1 - \lambda) \times 1 + \lambda \times \gamma_{\text{II}}^\lambda(\tau^* \mid (h^t, (B, L))) \right) \tag{13.55}$$

$$= \alpha \left((1 - \lambda) \times 2 + \lambda \times 1 \right) + (1 - \alpha) \left((1 - \lambda) \times 1 + \lambda \times 1 \right), \tag{13.56}$$

which implies that $\alpha = 0$, in contradiction to our assumption that $\alpha > 0$. This proves that the action pair (T, L) is played with probability 0 under τ^*, and similarly the action pair (M, L) is played with probability 0 under τ^*. This concludes the proof that $\gamma^\lambda(\tau^*) = (1, 1, 0)$.

The fact that at the only equilibrium payoff every player's payoff is his minmax value is a coincidence. Indeed, replacing the payoffs 5 in Figure 13.12 by (-5) does not affect our proof that $(1, 1, 0)$ is the only equilibrium payoff, while the minmax value of Player III changes to (-5). ◀

The Folk Theorem for finitely repeated games required a technical condition on the base game: for every player i there exists an equilibrium $\beta(i)$ of the base game that yields player i a payoff higher than his minmax value. In our construction of equilibria in the repeated game, the mixed actions $(\beta(i))_{i=1}^n$ were played in the last stages of the game, to ensure that a player who deviates along the play will lose when punished. To obtain a Folk Theorem for discounted games one also needs a technical condition on the base game for the same purpose. The condition that we will require is weaker than the one that appears in the Folk Theorem for finite games (Exercise 13.42).

Theorem 13.24 (The Folk Theorem for discounted games) *Let Γ be a base game in which there exists a vector $\widehat{x} \in F \cap V$ that satisfies $\widehat{x}_i > \overline{v}_i$ for every player $i \in N$. For every $\varepsilon > 0$ there exists $\lambda_0 \in [0, 1)$ such that for every $\lambda \in [\lambda_0, 1)$ and every vector $x \in F \cap V$, there exists an equilibrium τ^* of Γ_λ satisfying[6]*

$$\|\gamma^\lambda(\tau^*) - x\|_\infty < \varepsilon. \tag{13.57}$$

The condition that appears in the statement of the theorem ensures that there is a convex combination of the entries of the payoff matrix, using rational weights, that is close to x, and yields each player a payoff that is strictly higher than his minmax value. If, as we did in the proof of Theorem 13.17, we construct a strategy vector with a basic plan in which the players play according to this convex combination, then, for λ sufficiently close to 1, for every t, the λ-discounted payoff of every player, from stage t on, is strictly higher than his minmax value, allowing the players to punish a deviator. The reader is asked to complete the details of the proof (Exercise 13.43).

13.7 Subgame perfectness

We have proved the Folk Theorems (Theorems 13.9, 13.17, 13.19, and 13.24) for the concept of Nash equilibrium. The constructions used to prove these theorems consist of a basic plan of action supplemented with a punishment phase that is triggered as soon as

---

6 Recall that the maximum norm over $\mathbb{R}^n$ is defined as $\|x\|_\infty = \max_{i=1,2,\dots,n} |x_i|$ for every vector $x \in \mathbb{R}^n$.

some player deviates from the the basic plan. If player i is the first player to deviate from the basic plan and he does so at stage t, then from stage $t+1$ on all other players play a minmax mixed action vector σ_{-i} that keeps player i's stage payoff to at most his minmax value $\bar{v}_i$. These are called *grim-trigger* strategies, reflecting the fact that the punishment continues forever as soon as it is triggered.

A punishment may be costly for some punishers; that is, some players in $N\setminus\{i\}$ may suffer low payoffs while using the minmax mixed action vector σ_{-i}. For example, in Game D of Exercise 13.12 (page 567), the players may construct an equilibrium in the game Γ_∞ that yields a payoff of $(2, 3)$, yet when Player I punishes Player II, Player I's payoff goes down to 1 (or 0), lower than his minmax value, which is 2. This observation means that an equilibrium that uses grim-trigger strategies is not necessarily subgame perfect: the punishment play that starts at stage $t+1$ may not be an equilibrium of the subgame that starts at stage $t+1$. Since in practice a player may be reluctant to follow a strategy that yields him a low payoff, players may refuse to implement such an equilibrium. This leads to the question of whether the Folk Theorems can be sustained by subgame perfect equilibria rather than by Nash equilibria.

The answer to this question is essentially affirmative. Several authors have proved variants of the Folk Theorems for subgame perfect equilibria. We bring here, without proofs, two such important results. The first is the (slightly weaker) analogue of Theorem 13.17 (page 547) for the infinitely repeated game Γ_∞.

Theorem 13.25 (Aumann and Shapley [1994]) *The set of subgame perfect equilibrium payoffs of Γ_∞ is the set $F \cap V$.*

The idea of the proof is to modify the punishment phase. Instead of having the punishment last forever, the punishment that follows a deviation is of finite length, and, once the punishment phase ends, the players resume the equilibrium play as if no deviation had occurred. If the payoff $x \in F \cap V$ that is implemented satisfies $x_i > \bar{v}_i$ for every player $i \in I$, then by setting the punishment phase to be sufficiently long, the construction ensures that a deviation is not profitable. If $x_i = \bar{v}_i$ for some player i, then to ensure that a deviation is not profitable the length of the punishment phase increases when a player deviates more than once; that is, the length $l_{k,i}$ of the punishment phase against the k-th deviation of player i satisfies $l_{k,i} < l_{k+1,i}$ for every $k \in \mathbb{N}$. The proof of the theorem is left for the reader in Exercise 13.44.

The following is the analogue of the Folk Theorem for discounted games (Theorem 13.24 on page 554). The proof of the result is left for the reader (Exercise 13.45).

Theorem 13.26 (Fudenberg and Maskin [1986]) *Let Γ be a base game in which there exists a vector $\widehat{x} \in F \cap V$ that satisfies $\widehat{x}_i > \bar{v}_i$ for every player $i \in N$. For every $\varepsilon > 0$ there exists $\lambda_0 \in [0, 1)$ such that for every $\lambda \in [\lambda_0, 1)$ and every vector $x \in F \cap V$, there exists a subgame perfect equilibrium τ^* of Γ_λ satisfying*

$$\|\gamma^\lambda(\tau^*) - x\|_\infty < \varepsilon. \tag{13.58}$$

Unlike in the proof of Theorem 13.25, to prove Theorem 13.26 we can construct a cyclic base play that yields a discounted payoff close to x. The punishment following a deviation will then also be of finite length, as in the proofs of Theorem 13.24.

13.8 Uniform equilibrium

As we said before, players may not always know the number of stages a repeated game will have:

- A young professional baseball player knows that at a certain age he will retire from the sport, but does not know exactly when that day will come.
- We are all players in "the game of life," whose length is unknown and differs among the players.

Similarly, players do not always know the discount factor of the game:

- Although the prime interest rate is common knowledge, we do not know what the interest rate will be next year, in two years, or a decade from today.
- Suppose the government is interested in selling a state-owned company. What discount rate should be used? Computing a reasonable discount rate in such cases can be very complicated.

In the examples above, the discount rate and the exact length of the game are unknown. How should a player play in this case? In this section we will present concepts enabling us to study this question, and to arrive at results that are independent of the exact value of the discount factor, or the exact length of the game. To do so, we introduce the concept of *uniform equilibrium*, first for discounted games, then for finite games, and later we will see the relation between the two.

Definition 13.27 *A strategy vector τ^* is called a* uniform equilibrium for discounted games *if $\lim_{\lambda \to 1} \gamma^{\lambda}(\tau^*)$ exists, and there exists $\lambda_0 \in [0, 1)$ such that τ^* is an equilibrium of Γ_{λ} for every discount factor $\lambda \in [\lambda_0, 1)$. The limit $\lim_{\lambda \to 1} \gamma^{\lambda}(\tau^*)$ is called a* uniform equilibrium payoff for discounted games.

τ^* is therefore a uniform equilibrium for discounted games if it is an equilibrium of every game in which the discount factor is sufficiently close to 1; that is, the players are sufficiently patient.

Do uniform equilibria for discounted games exist? As we will see (Theorem 13.29), there are many uniform equilibria for discounted games.

Example 13.28   Consider the two-player game in Figure 13.13.

Player II

		L	R
Player I	T	3, 1	0, 0
	B	1, 2	4, 3

Figure 13.13 The payoff matrix of the game in Example 13.28

The minmax value of Player I is $\overline{v}_I = 2$, and the punishment strategy against him is $[\frac{2}{3}(L), \frac{1}{3}(R)]$. Player II's minmax value is $\overline{v}_{II} = 1$, and the punishment strategy against him is T. We will show that in the example above,

$$\left(3\tfrac{1}{2}, 2\tfrac{5}{8}\right) = \tfrac{7}{8} \times (4,3) + \tfrac{1}{8} \times (0,0) \tag{13.59}$$

is a uniform equilibrium payoff for discounted games. To do so, we will show that the following pair of strategies is a discounted equilibrium for every discount factor sufficiently close to 1:

- Player I plays B at the first stage, and as long as Player II plays R, Player I repeatedly cycles through the following sequence of actions: B, B, B, B, B, B, B, T (the action B played at the first stage is the beginning of the first cycle).
- Player II plays R at the first stage, and as long as Player I cycles through the sequence of actions B, B, B, B, B, B, B, T, Player II plays R.

If neither player deviates from this strategy, the discounted sum of the payoffs of the first eight stages of the game is

$$(1 + \lambda + \lambda^2 + \cdots + \lambda^6)(4,3) + \lambda^7(0,0) = \frac{1 - \lambda^7}{1 - \lambda} \cdot (4,3). \tag{13.60}$$

Therefore, the discounted payoff is

$$(1 - \lambda)((4,3) + \lambda(4,3) + \lambda^2(4,3) + \cdots + \lambda^6(4,3) + \lambda^7(0,0) + \lambda^8(4,3)$$
$$+ \lambda^9(4,3) + \cdots + \lambda^{14}(4,3) + \lambda^{15}(0,0) + \cdots)$$

$$= (1 - \lambda) \times \frac{1 - \lambda^7}{1 - \lambda}(1 + \lambda^8 + \lambda^{16} + \cdots) \cdot (4,3) \tag{13.61}$$

$$= \frac{1 - \lambda^7}{1 - \lambda^8} \cdot (4,3). \tag{13.62}$$

Applying L'Hôpital's Rule, the limit of this value, as λ approaches 1, is

$$\lim_{\lambda \to 1}\left(\frac{1 - \lambda^7}{1 - \lambda^8} \cdot (4,3)\right) = \left(\lim_{\lambda \to 1}\frac{-7\lambda^6}{-8\lambda^7}\right) \times (4,3) = \tfrac{7}{8} \times (4,3) = \left(3\tfrac{1}{2}, 2\tfrac{5}{8}\right). \tag{13.63}$$

Neither player can profit by deviating in the stages in which the players play (B, R), because in these stages each receives his maximal possible payoffs. To guarantee that neither player can profit by deviating in the stages in which the players play (T, R), we add the following punishments:

- If Player II deviates for the first time in stage t, from stage $t + 1$ onwards Player I always plays T (which is Player I's punishment strategy against Player II).
- If Player I deviates for the first time in stage t, from stage $t + 1$ onwards Player II always plays the mixed action $[\tfrac{2}{3}(L), \tfrac{1}{2}(R)]$ (which is Player II's punishment strategy against Player I).

We next seek discount factors λ for which this strategy vector is a λ-discounted equilibrium. If Player I deviates in stage t, where the players are supposed to play (T, R), he receives in that stage a payoff of 4 instead of 0, for a net profit of 4. In contrast, from the next stage onwards, his expected payoff is 2. Player I's λ-discounted payoff from stage t onwards is therefore[7]

$$(1 - \lambda)(4 + \lambda \times 2 + \lambda^2 \times 2 + \lambda^3 \times 2 + \cdots) = 4(1 - \lambda) + 2\lambda = 4 - 2\lambda. \tag{13.64}$$

....

7 For all $a, b \in \mathbb{R}$, $(1 - \lambda)\left(\lambda^{t-1}a + \lambda^{tb} + \lambda^{t+1}b + \cdots\right) = \lambda^{t-1}((1 - \lambda)a + \lambda b)$.

If Player I had not deviated in stage t, his discounted payoff from stage t onwards would be

$$(1 - \lambda) \times 0 + \lambda \times \frac{1 - \lambda^7}{1 - \lambda^8} \times 4, \tag{13.65}$$

because if in stage t the players are supposed to play (T, R), then a new cycle of length 8 begins in stage $t + 1$, and therefore the λ-discounted payoff from stage $t + 1$ onwards equals (up to multiplication by λ^t) the λ-discounted payoff from the first stage. The deviation is unprofitable only if the payoff, when no deviation occurs, is greater than or equal to the payoff when a deviation occurs:

$$\lambda \times \frac{1 - \lambda^7}{1 - \lambda^8} \times 4 \geq 4 - 2\lambda. \tag{13.66}$$

Multiplying both sides of the expression by $1 - \lambda^8$, we deduce that the following must hold:

$$4\lambda - 4\lambda^8 \geq 4 - 4\lambda^8 - 2\lambda + 2\lambda^9. \tag{13.67}$$

For $\lambda = 1$, both sides of the expression equal zero. Differentiating the left-hand side and setting $\lambda = 1$ yields $4 - 32 = -28$, while differentiating the right-hand side and setting $\lambda = 1$ yields $-32 - 2 + 18 = -16$. Therefore, an interval $(\lambda_0, 1)$ exists such that for every discount factor λ in the interval, the left-hand side of Equation (13.67) is greater than the right-hand side of Equation (13.67). One can check that the inequality in Equation (13.67) holds as a strict inequality for every $\lambda \in (0.615, 1)$.

If Player II deviates in stage t, where the players are supposed to play (T, R), he receives a payoff of 1 instead of 0 in that stage, for a net profit of 1. In contrast, from that stage onwards his payoff is bounded by 1. It follows that the λ-discounted payoff of Player II from stage t onwards is at most 1. In contrast, if Player II does not deviate, his payoff from stage t onwards is $(1 - \lambda) \times 0 + \lambda \times \frac{1-\lambda^7}{1-\lambda^8} \times 3$. Deviating is not profitable if

$$(1 - \lambda) \times 0 + \lambda \times \frac{1 - \lambda^7}{1 - \lambda^8} \times 3 \geq 1. \tag{13.68}$$

It can be shown that this holds for all $\lambda \geq 0.334$. We deduce from this that the pair of strategies defined above form a λ-discounted equilibrium for all $\lambda > \max\{0.334, 0.615\} = 0.615$; hence it is a uniform equilibrium for discounted games. ◀

Theorem 13.29 (The Folk Theorem for uniform equilibrium in discounted games)
Let Γ be a base game in which there exists a vector $\widehat{x} \in F \cap V$ that satisfies $\widehat{x}_i > \overline{v}_i$ for every player $i \in N$. For every $\varepsilon > 0$, and every $x \in F \cap V$, there exists a strategy vector τ^* in the discounted repeated game such that:

1. τ^* is a uniform equilibrium for discounted games.
2. $\|\lim_{\lambda \to 1} \gamma^\lambda(\tau^*) - x\|_\infty < \varepsilon$.

In words, for each $x \in F \cap V$ there exists a uniform equilibrium for discounted games τ^* satisfying the property that the limit of discounted payoffs $\lim_{\lambda \to 1} \gamma^\lambda(\tau^*)$ is approximately x. The strategy vector τ^* satisfying the conditions of the theorem, similarly to the case in the proof of Theorem 13.17 (page 547), is of the grim-trigger type, with a basic plan that ensures that the payoff vector is close to x. The complete proof of this theorem is left to the reader (Exercise 13.47).

The concept of uniform equilibrium can also be defined for long finite games. We will see in Theorem 13.34 that the two concepts of uniform equilibrium are related.

Definition 13.30 *Let* $\varepsilon \geq 0$. *A strategy vector* τ^* *in an infinitely repeated game is a uniform* ε-*equilibrium for finite games if the limit* $\lim_{T\to\infty} \gamma^T(\tau^*)$ *exists, and there exists* $T_0 \in \mathbb{N}$ *such that* τ^* *is an* ε-*equilibrium of* Γ_T, *for every* $T \geq T_0$. *The limit* $\lim_{T\to\infty} \gamma^T(\tau^*)$ *is called a uniform* ε-*equilibrium payoff.*

At every uniform 0-equilibrium for finite games (i.e., the case in which $\varepsilon = 0$), from some stage onwards, in every stage, the players play an equilibrium of the base game (Exercise 13.51). Consequently, the set of uniform 0-equilibrium payoffs is the convex hull of the set of Nash equilibrium payoffs of the base game. For $\varepsilon > 0$, however, the set of uniform ε-equilibrium payoffs is much larger; that is, the Folk Theorem holds.

Theorem 13.31 (The Folk Theorem for uniform equilibrium in finite games) *For every* $\varepsilon > 0$, *and every* $x \in F \cap V$, *there exists a strategy vector* τ^* *such that:*

1. τ^* *is a uniform* ε-*equilibrium for finite games:*
2. $\| \lim_{T\to\infty} \gamma^T(\tau^*) - x \|_\infty < \varepsilon$.

The proof of the theorem, which is similar to the proof of Theorem 13.17 (page 547), is left to the reader (Exercise 13.52).

We now turn our attention to comparing the concepts of uniform equilibrium for discounted games and uniform ε-equilibrium for finite games. For this purpose, we will first find a connection between finite averages and discounted sums.

Theorem 13.32 *Let* $(x_t)_{t=1}^\infty$ *be a bounded sequence of numbers. Denote the average of the first* T *elements of this sequence by*

$$S_T = \frac{1}{T} \sum_{t=1}^T x_t, \qquad \forall T \in \mathbb{N}, \tag{13.69}$$

and the discounted sum by

$$A(\lambda) = (1-\lambda) \sum_{t=1}^\infty \lambda^{t-1} x_t, \qquad \forall \lambda \in [0,1). \tag{13.70}$$

Also denote

$$\alpha_T(\lambda) = (1-\lambda)^2 \lambda^{T-1} T, \qquad \forall T \in \mathbb{N}, \forall \lambda \in [0,1). \tag{13.71}$$

Then, for all $\lambda \in [0,1)$,

$$A(\lambda) = \sum_{T=1}^\infty \alpha_T(\lambda) S_T. \tag{13.72}$$

Note that $\sum_{T=1}^\infty \alpha_T(\lambda) = 1$:

$$\sum_{T=1}^\infty \alpha_T(\lambda) = (1-\lambda)^2 \sum_{T=1}^\infty T\lambda^{T-1} \tag{13.73}$$

$$= (1 - \lambda)^2 \frac{\mathrm{d}}{\mathrm{d}\lambda} \left(\sum_{T=1}^{\infty} \lambda^T \right) \tag{13.74}$$

$$= (1 - \lambda)^2 \frac{\mathrm{d}}{\mathrm{d}\lambda} \left(\frac{1}{1 - \lambda} \right) = 1, \tag{13.75}$$

where Equation (13.74) follows from the Bounded Convergence Theorem (see Theorem 16.4 in Billingsley [1999]). Thus, Equation (13.72) states that $A(\lambda)$ is a weighted average of $(S_T)_{T \in \mathbb{N}}$.

Proof: The proof of the theorem is accomplished by the following sequence of equalities:

$$A(\lambda) = (1 - \lambda) \sum_{t=1}^{\infty} \lambda^{t-1} x_t \tag{13.76}$$

$$= (1 - \lambda) \sum_{t=1}^{\infty} \left(\sum_{k=t}^{\infty} (\lambda^{k-1} - \lambda^k) \right) x_t \tag{13.77}$$

$$= (1 - \lambda) \sum_{k=1}^{\infty} \left((\lambda^{k-1} - \lambda^k) \sum_{t=1}^{k} x_t \right) \tag{13.78}$$

$$= \sum_{k=1}^{\infty} \left((1 - \lambda)(\lambda^{k-1} - \lambda^k) k S_k \right) \tag{13.79}$$

$$= \sum_{k=1}^{\infty} (1 - \lambda)^2 \lambda^{k-1} k S_k \tag{13.80}$$

$$= \sum_{k=1}^{\infty} \alpha_k(\lambda) S_k. \tag{13.81}$$

Equation (13.78) follows by changing the order of summation (why can the order of summation be changed in this case?), and Equation (13.78) follows from Equation (13.69). □

The next theorem is a consequence of Theorem 13.32.

Theorem 13.33 (Hardy and Littlewood) *Every bounded sequence of real numbers* $(x_t)_{t=1}^{\infty}$ *satisfies*

$$\liminf_{T \to \infty} \frac{1}{T} \sum_{t=1}^{T} x_t \leq \liminf_{\lambda \to 1} \sum_{t=1}^{\infty} (1 - \lambda) \lambda^{t-1} x_t \tag{13.82}$$

$$\leq \limsup_{\lambda \to 1} \sum_{t=1}^{\infty} (1 - \lambda) \lambda^{t-1} x_t \tag{13.83}$$

$$\leq \limsup_{T \to \infty} \frac{1}{T} \sum_{t=1}^{T} x_t. \tag{13.84}$$

In particular, if the limit $\lim_{T\to\infty} \frac{1}{T}\sum_{t=1}^{T} x_t$ *exists, then the limit* $\lim_{\lambda\to 1}\sum_{t=1}^{\infty}(1 - \lambda)\lambda^{t-1}x_t$ *also exists, and both limits are equal.*

Using the notation of Theorem 13.32, Theorem 13.33 states that

$$\liminf_{T\to\infty} S_T \leq \liminf_{\lambda\to 1} A(\lambda) \leq \limsup_{\lambda\to 1} A(\lambda) \leq \limsup_{T\to\infty} S_T. \tag{13.85}$$

Proof: We will prove Equation (13.84):

$$\limsup_{\lambda\to 1} \sum_{t=1}^{\infty}(1-\lambda)\lambda^{t-1}x_t \leq \limsup_{T\to\infty} \frac{1}{T}\sum_{t=1}^{T} x_t. \tag{13.86}$$

The proof of Equation (13.82) can be accomplished in a similar manner, or by considering the sequence $(y_t)_{t\in\mathbb{N}}$ defined by $y_t := -x_t$ for every $t \in \mathbb{N}$. Equation (13.83) requires no proof. Theorem 13.32 implies that for all $T_0 \in \mathbb{N}$,

$$A(\lambda) = \sum_{T=1}^{\infty} \alpha_T(\lambda)S_T = \sum_{T=1}^{T_0-1} \alpha_T(\lambda)S_T + \sum_{T=T_0}^{\infty} \alpha_T(\lambda)S_T. \tag{13.87}$$

Denote $C := \limsup_{T\to\infty} S_T$, and let $\varepsilon > 0$ be any positive real number. Let T_0 be sufficiently large such that $S_T \leq C + \varepsilon$ for all $T \geq T_0$. Note that

$$\sum_{T=1}^{T_0} \alpha_T(\lambda) = (1-\lambda)^2 \sum_{T=1}^{T_0} \lambda^{T-1}T < (1-\lambda)^2(T_0)^2, \tag{13.88}$$

where the last inequality follows from the fact that $\lambda \in [0, 1)$. In particular, when λ approaches 1 the sum $\sum_{T=1}^{T_0-1} \alpha_T(\lambda)$ approaches 0, and therefore the first sum in Equation (13.87) also converges to 0. The second sum is bounded by $C + \varepsilon$. We therefore have

$$\limsup_{\lambda\to 1} A(\lambda) \leq C + \varepsilon = \limsup_{T\to\infty} S_T + \varepsilon. \tag{13.89}$$

Since this inequality holds for all $\varepsilon > 0$, we deduce that $\limsup_{\lambda\to 1} A(\lambda) \leq \limsup_{T\to\infty} S_T$, which is what we wanted to prove. □

Analogously to the definition for finite games (Definition 13.18), a strategy vector τ^* is an ε-equilibrium in the discounted game Γ_λ if no player can profit more than ε by deviating:

$$\gamma_i^\lambda(\tau^*) \geq \gamma_i^\lambda(\tau_i, \tau_{-i}^*) - \varepsilon, \quad \forall i \in N, \forall \tau_i \in \mathcal{B}_i^\infty. \tag{13.90}$$

A strategy vector τ^* is a *uniform ε-equilibrium for discounted games* if there is $\lambda_0 \in [0, 1)$ such that for every $\lambda \in [\lambda_0, 1)$, the strategy vector τ^* is an ε-equilibrium of the λ-discounted game.

Theorem 13.33 enables us to establish the following connection between uniform ε-equilibria for finite games and uniform ε-equilibria for discounted games.

Theorem 13.34 *If τ^* is a uniform ε-equilibrium for finite games, then for every $\delta > 0$ it is a uniform $(\varepsilon + \delta)$-equilibrium for discounted games.*

$$\gamma_i^\lambda(\tau^*) \geq \gamma_i^\lambda(\tau_i, \tau_{-i}^*) - \varepsilon - 2\delta. \tag{13.91}$$

Proof: Let τ^* be a uniform ε-equilibrium for finite games, and let $\delta > 0$. Recall that M is a bound on the payoffs of the base game, and denote by $C := \lim_{T \to \infty} \gamma_i^T(\tau^*)$ the limit of the payoffs in the finite games. By Theorem 13.33,

$$C = \lim_{\lambda \to 1} \gamma_i^\lambda(\tau^*). \tag{13.92}$$

Let T_0 be sufficiently large such that for each $T \geq T_0$, one has (a) the strategy vector τ^* is an ε-equilibrium of the T-stage game, and (b) $|C_i - \gamma_i^T(\tau^*)| < \delta$.

Let λ_0 be sufficiently close to 1 such that $\sum_{T=1}^{T_0} \alpha_T(\lambda_0) \leq \frac{\delta}{M}$ (see Equation (13.88)). Let i be a player, and let τ_i be a strategy of player i. We will show that for λ sufficiently close to 1, player i cannot profit more than $\varepsilon + \delta$ by deviating to any strategy τ_i. Denote the expected payoff in stage t, when player i deviates to τ_i, by

$$x_t = \mathbf{E}_{\tau_i, \tau_{-i}^*}[u_i(a_t)]. \tag{13.93}$$

The average of $x_1, x_2, \ldots, x_T$ equals the payoff under (τ_i, τ_{-i}^*) in the T-stage game:

$$\gamma_i^T(\tau_i, \tau_{-i}^*) = \frac{\sum_{t=1}^{T} x_t}{T}. \tag{13.94}$$

For each $\lambda \in [\lambda_0, 1)$,

$$\gamma_i^\lambda(\tau_i, \tau_{-i}^*) = \sum_{T=1}^{\infty} \alpha_T(\lambda) \gamma_i^T(\tau_i, \tau_{-i}^*) \tag{13.95}$$

$$= \sum_{T=1}^{T_0-1} \alpha_T(\lambda) \gamma_i^T(\tau_i, \tau_{-i}^*) + \sum_{T=T_0}^{\infty} \alpha_T(\lambda) \gamma_i^T(\tau_i, \tau_{-i}^*) \tag{13.96}$$

$$\leq \delta + \sum_{T=T_0}^{\infty} \alpha_T(\lambda) \gamma_i^T(\tau_i, \tau_{-i}^*) \tag{13.97}$$

$$\leq \delta + \sum_{T=T_0}^{\infty} \alpha_T(\lambda) \gamma_i^T(\tau^*) + \varepsilon \tag{13.98}$$

$$\leq \delta + C + \delta + \varepsilon \tag{13.99}$$

$$= \lim_{\lambda \to 1} \gamma_i^\lambda(\tau^*) + \varepsilon + 2\delta. \tag{13.100}$$

Equation (13.95) holds by Theorem 13.32, Equation (13.97) holds because $\lambda \in [\lambda_0, 1)$ and by the choice of λ_0, and Equation (13.98) holds because τ^* is an ε-equilibrium for every $T \geq T_0$. Equation (13.99) holds because $|C_i - \gamma_i^T(\tau^*)| < \delta$ for every $T \geq T_0$, and Equation (13.100) follows from Equation (13.92). It follows that τ^* is an $(\varepsilon + 2\delta)$-equilibrium of the λ-discounted game, and this holds for all $\lambda \in [\lambda_0, 1)$. $\qquad \square$

We have already seen in Example 13.20 that an equilibrium of Γ_∞ is not necessarily an ε-equilibrium of long finite games, and therefore not necessarily a uniform ε-equilibrium for finite games. The following example shows that a uniform equilibrium for discounted games is not necessarily a uniform ε-equilibrium for finite games, or an equilibrium of Γ_∞.

Example 13.35   Let $(x_t)_{t=1}^\infty$ be a sequence of zeros and ones satisfying

$$\limsup_{T\to\infty} \frac{\sum_{t=1}^T x_t}{T} > \limsup_{\lambda\to 1}(1-\lambda)\sum_{t=1}^\infty \lambda^{t-1}x_t. \tag{13.101}$$

For details on how to construct such a sequence, see Exercise 13.53. Let c be a real number satisfying

$$\limsup_{T\to\infty} \frac{\sum_{t=1}^T x_t}{T} > c > \limsup_{\lambda\to 1}(1-\lambda)\sum_{t=1}^\infty \lambda^{t-1}x_t. \tag{13.102}$$

Consider the two-player game in Figure 13.14. In this game, the payoff to Player II is 2, under every action vector. As we will now show, $(c, 2)$ is a uniform equilibrium payoff of discounted repeated games, but is not a uniform ε-equilibrium payoff of finite games, for $\varepsilon > 0$ sufficiently small. Since under every circumstance Player II receives 2 in every stage of the repeated game, to prove that a pair of strategies is an equilibrium it is sufficient to show that Player I cannot profit by deviating.

		Player II		
		D	E	F
Player I	A	0, 2	0, 2	c, 2
	B	0, 2	1, 2	c, 2

Figure 13.14 The payoff matrix of the game in Example 13.35

Define the following strategy σ_{II} of Player II:

- In the first stage, play F.
- If in the first stage Player I played A, play F in all of the remaining stages of the game.
- If in the first stage Player I played B, play D or E in all of the remaining stages of the game, according to the above-mentioned sequence $(x_t)_{t=1}^\infty$: if $x_t = 0$, play D in stage t, and if $x_t = 1$, play E in stage t.

The strategy σ_{II} does not depend on Player I's actions after the first stage. For Player I, therefore, every strategy σ_{I} is weakly dominated by the strategy in which Player I's action in the first stage is the same as that of σ_{I}, and from the second stage onwards his action is always B. It follows that Player I's best reply to σ_{II} is either σ_{I}^A, where Player I plays A in the first stage, and B in every other stage, or σ_{I}^B, where he plays B in every stage, including the first stage.

The strategy vector $(\sigma_{\mathrm{I}}^A, \sigma_{\mathrm{II}})$ is a uniform equilibrium for discounted games with payoff $(c, 2)$. To see this, note that since $\gamma_{\mathrm{I}}^\lambda(\sigma_{\mathrm{I}}^A, \sigma_{\mathrm{II}}) = c$, while $\gamma_{\mathrm{I}}^\lambda(\sigma_{\mathrm{I}}^B, \sigma_{\mathrm{II}}) = (1-\lambda)\sum_{t=1}^\infty \lambda^{t-1}x_t$, Equation (13.102) implies that for a discount factor sufficiently close to 1, one has $\gamma_{\mathrm{I}}^\lambda(\sigma_{\mathrm{I}}^A, \sigma_{\mathrm{II}}) > \gamma_{\mathrm{I}}^\lambda(\sigma_{\mathrm{I}}^B, \sigma_{\mathrm{II}})$, and therefore Player I has no profitable deviation.

We next show that $(\sigma_I^A, \sigma_{II})$ is not a uniform ε-equilibrium for finite games, for $\varepsilon > 0$ sufficiently small. Set $\varepsilon_0 := \frac{1}{2}\left(\limsup_{T \to \infty} \frac{\sum_{t=1}^{T} x_t}{T} - c\right)$. We will show that there exists an increasing sequence $(T_k)_{k \in \mathbb{N}}$ such that $(\sigma_I^A, \sigma_{II})$ is not an ε-equilibrium of the T_k-stage game, for every $k \in \mathbb{N}$ and every $\varepsilon \in (0, \varepsilon_0)$. By Equation (13.102), there exists an increasing sequence $(T_k)_{k \in \mathbb{N}}$ such that for every $k \in \mathbb{N}$,

$$\gamma_I^{T_k}(\sigma_I^B, \sigma_{II}) = \frac{\sum_{t=1}^{T_k} x_t}{T_k} > c + \varepsilon_0 > c = \gamma_I^{T_k}(\sigma_I^A, \sigma_{II}). \tag{13.103}$$

Therefore, for every $k \in \mathbb{N}$, by deviating in the T_k-stage game to σ_I^B, Player I's profit is more than ε_0. It follows that $(\sigma_I^A, \sigma_{II})$ is not an ε-equilibrium in Γ_{T_k} for every $k \in \mathbb{N}$ and every $\varepsilon \in (0, \varepsilon_0]$. We further note that it follows from this discussion that $(\sigma_I^A, \sigma_{II})$ is also not an equilibrium in the infinitely repeated game (Exercise 13.55). ◄

13.9　Discussion

There is a wealth of literature on repeated games, and many variations of this model have been studied. One line of inquiry has focused on the subject of punishment. The equilibrium strategies we have defined in this section are unforgiving: once a player deviates, he is punished by the other player for the rest of the game. Because a punishment strategy is liable to lower the payoff of not only the player who is being punished but also other players in the game, it is reasonable to ask whether players whose interests are harmed by a punishment strategy will join in implementing it. Considerations such as these have led to the study of subgame perfect equilibria in repeated games (for a discussion on the notion of subgame perfect equilibrium in an extensive-form game, see Section 7.1 on page 263). In repeated games, a strategy vector τ^* is a subgame perfect equilibrium if after every finite history (whether or not the players arrive at that history if they implement τ^*), the play of the game that ensues from that stage onwards is an equilibrium of the subgame starting at that point. A proof of the Folk Theorem under this definition of equilibrium appears in Aumann and Shapley [1994], Rubinstein [1979], Fudenberg and Maskin [1986], and Gossner [1995]. Rubinstein [1979] proved the Folk Theorem with subgame perfect equilibria for the infinitely repeated game with a different valuation criterion, known as the *overtaking criterion*.

There are several other variations on the theme of repeated games that have been studied in the literature. These include what happens when: (1) players do not observe the actions implemented by other players, and instead receive only a signal that depends on the actions of all the players (see, e.g., Lehrer [1989], [1990], and [1992], and Gossner and Tomala [2007]); (2) players do not know their payoff functions (see, e.g., Megiddo [1980]); and (3) at the start of the game, a payoff function is chosen from a set of possible payoff functions, and the players receive partial information regarding which payoff function is chosen (see Aumann and Maschler [1995] and Section 14.7 on page 598).

13.10 Remarks

Exercise 13.7 is based on a result appearing in Benoit and Krishna [1985]. Exercise 13.35 is based on Rubinstein [1982]. Exercise 13.39 is based on Neyman [1985]. Exercise 13.53 is based on Liggett and Lippman [1969]. Exercise 13.54 is based on Example H.1 in Filar and Vrieze [1997]. The game appearing in Exercise 15.2 is known as the Big Match. It was first described in Gillette [1957], and was extensively studied in Blackwell and Ferguson [1968].

A review on repeated games with complete information can be found in Sorin 1992]. For a presentation of repeated games with incomplete information see Aumann and Maschler [1995] and Sorin [2002]. For a presentation of repeated games with private monitoring see Mailath and Samuelson [2006]. More information on Tauberian Theorems, of which Theorem 13.33 (page 560) is an example, can be found in Korevaar [2004].

The authors thank Abraham Neyman for clarifications provided during the composition of this chapter.

13.11 Exercises

13.1 Compute the number of pure strategies a player has in a T-stage game with n players, where the number of actions of each player i in the base game is $|S_i| = k_i$.

13.2 Artemis and Diana are avid hunters. They devote Tuesdays to their shared hobby. On Monday evening, each of them separately writes, on a slip of paper, whether or not he or she will go hunting, and whether he or she wants to be the lead hunter, or the second hunter. They then meet and each reads what the other wrote. If at least one of the two is not interested in going hunting, or both of them want the same role (lead hunter or second hunter), they do not go hunting on Tuesday. If they are both interested in a hunt, one of them wants to be the lead hunter, and the other wants to be second hunter, they do go hunting on Tuesday.

The utility of being lead hunter is 2. The utility of being second hunter is 1, and the utility of not going hunting is 0. Answer the following questions for this situation of repeated interaction:

(a) Write down the base game for this situation.
(b) Find all the equilibria of the one-stage game (the base game).
(c) Find all the equilibria of the two-stage game.

13.3 Repeat Exercise 13.2 for the following situation. Mark and Jim are neighbors, and are employed in the same place of work. They start work at the same hour every day, but their working day ends at different hours. Each has the option of going to work by train, or by bus. Every morning, each of them decides the mode of transportion by which he will get to work that day. Each of them "gains" 5 when they travel to work together, and each "gains" 0 if they travel by different modes of transportation. Taking the bus costs 1, and taking the train costs 2. Mark enjoys a 50% reduction on train tickets. The utility each of them receives is the difference between what he gains during the ride to work, and the cost of the ticket. For example, Jim's utility from taking the bus with Mark is 4.

13.4 Repeat Exercise 13.2 for the following situation. There are two pubs in a neighborhood. Three friends, Andrew, Mike, and Ron, like to cap off their working days with a beer at the pub. Each of them gains a utility of 2 when drinking with only one other friend, a utility of 1 when the three drink together, and a utility of 0 when drinking alone. Every day each of them independently decides which of the two pubs in the neighborhood he will go to, for a drink.

13.5 Prove or disprove the following claim: let τ be a strategy vector in Γ_T where, for each history h, the mixed action vector $\tau(h)$ is an equilibrium of the base game Γ. Then τ is an equilibrium of the game Γ_T. Compare this result with Theorem 13.6 (page 536), where the equilibrium of the base game that is played at any stage is independent of the history.

13.6 Prove that at every equilibrium of the T-stage Prisoner's Dilemma, both players play D in every stage.

13.7 Let $\Gamma = (N, (S_i)_{i \in N}, (u_i)_{i \in N})$ be a game in strategic form that has a unique equilibrium, and let Γ_T be the T-stage repeated game corresponding to Γ. Prove that Γ_T has a unique subgame perfect equilibrium. Is it possible for Γ_T to have an additional Nash equilibrium? Justify your answer.

13.8 Prove that the minmax value of each player i in the T-stage repeated game is equal to his minmax value $\overline{v}_i$ in the base game.

13.9 In the following two-player zero-sum game (see Figure 13.15), find the value of the T-stage repeated game, and the optimal strategies of the two players for every $T \in \mathbb{N}$. What is the limit of the values of the T-stage games, as T goes to infinity? Player I's set of actions is $A_I = \{T, B\}$, and Player II's set of actions is $A_{II} = \{L, R\}$.

- If the players choose the pair of actions (T, L), Player II pays Player I the sum of $1, and the players play the repeated game in Figure 13.15(A).

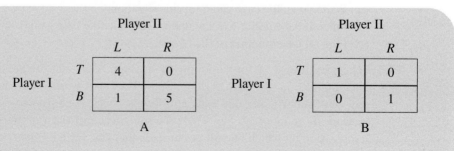

Figure 13.15 The payoff matrix of the game in Exercise 13.9

- If the players choose the pair of actions (T, R), Player II pays Player I the sum of $4, and the players play the repeated game in Figure 13.15(B).
- If the players choose the pair of actions (B, L), Player II pays Player I the sum of $2, and the players play the repeated game in Figure 13.15(B).
- If the players choose the pair of actions (B, R), Player II pays Player I the sum of $0, and the players play the repeated game in Figure 13.15(A).

13.10 In this exercise, we will prove that the payoff received by a player in a T-stage repeated game is a linear function of the probabilities under which he chooses his pure strategies.

(a) Let $\tau_i^1, \ldots, \tau_i^L$ be all the pure strategies of player i in the T-stage repeated game. Prove that for every behavior strategy τ_i of player i (see Definition 13.3 on page 533) in the repeated game, there exist nonnegative numbers $\alpha_1, \ldots, \alpha_L$, whose sum is 1, such that for each strategy vector τ_{-i} of the other players,

$$\gamma_i^T(\tau_i, \tau_{-i}) = \sum_{l=1}^{L} \alpha_l \gamma_i^T(\iota_i^l, \tau_{-i}). \tag{13.104}$$

(b) What are the coefficients $(\alpha_l)_{l=1}^L$?

13.11 Consider the following base game.

Player II

		L	R
	T	$-1, 3$	$4, 0$
Player I	B	$1, -1$	$0, 2$

What is the limit of the average payoffs in the infinitely repeated game corresponding to this game, when the players implement the following strategies?

(a) In even stages, Player I plays T, and in odd stages he plays B. In stages divisible by 3 Player II plays L, and in all other stages he plays R.

(b) In even stages, Player I plays T, and in odd stages he plays B. Player II plays as follows. In the first stage he plays L. At any other stage he plays R if Player I played T in the previous stage; otherwise he plays the mixed action $[\frac{1}{4}(L), \frac{3}{4}(R)]$ in the current stage.

(c) Player I plays $[\frac{2}{3}(T), \frac{1}{3}(B)]$ in every stage. Player II plays as follows. In the first stage he plays L. At any other stage he plays R if Player I played T in the previous stage; otherwise he plays the mixed action $[\frac{1}{4}(L), \frac{3}{4}(R)]$ in the current stage.

13.12 For each of the infinitely repeated games corresponding to the following base games, plot on the same graph in $\mathbb{R}^2$ the sets F and $F \cap V$, where the x-axis represents Player I's payoff, and the y-axis represents Player II's payoff.

Player II

	L	R
T	−1, 1	1, −1
B	1, −1	−1, 1

Player I

Game A

Player II

	L	R
T	6, 6	2, 7
B	7, 2	0, 0

Player I

Game B

Player II

	L	C	R
T	0, 0	2, 4	4, 2
M	4, 2	0, 0	2, 4
B	2, 4	4, 2	0, 0

Player I

Game C

Player II

	L	R
T	4, 2	2, 3
B	1, 0	0, 1

Player I

Game D

13.13 The following base game is a three-player game in which Player I chooses a row (*T* or *B*), Player II chooses a column (*L* or *R*), and Player III chooses a matrix (*W* or *E*). Is $(3, 3, \frac{1}{2})$ an equilibrium payoff in the infinitely repeated game? If the answer is yes, describe an equilibrium that corresponds to this payoff vector. If not, justify your answer.

	L	R
T	6, 6, 1	2, 7, 0
B	7, 2, 0	0, 0, 1

W

	L	R
T	0, 5, 0	5, 0, 1
B	5, 0, 1	0, 5, 0

E

Hint: Find an upper bound to the minmax value of each player and use the Folk Theorem.

13.14 Prove Theorem 13.11 on page 542: for every $K \in \mathbb{N}$ and every vector $x \in F$ there are nonnegative integers $(k_s)_{s \in S}$ summing to K satisfying

$$\left\| \sum_{s \in S} \frac{k_s}{K} u(s) - x \right\|_{\infty} \leq \frac{M \times |S|}{K}. \tag{13.105}$$

13.15 Suppose that each player i in a two-player zero-sum base game Γ has a unique optimal mixed strategy x_i. Prove that in the T-stage repeated game Γ_T, at each equilibrium in behavior strategies, at each stage each player implements the mixed strategy x_i.

13.16 In the 1,000,000-stage repeated game of the following base game, describe an equilibrium whose payoff is within 0.01 of $(5, 6)$, and an equilibrium whose payoff is within 0.01 of $(4, 3)$.

Player II

	L	R
T	6, 6	2, 7
B	7, 2	0, 0

Player I (rows), Player II (columns)

13.17 Consider the infinitely repeated game of the following base game:

Player II

	L	R
T	4, 6	2, 8
B	7, 3	1, 0

Player I (rows), Player II (columns)

Suppose that, in this game, Player I implements the following strategy σ_1. In the first stage, he plays the mixed action $\left[\frac{2}{3}(T), \frac{1}{3}(B)\right]$. In every stage $t > 1$, he plays a mixed action that is determined by the action that Player II played in the previous stage: if in stage t Player II played L, then in stage $t+1$ Player I plays the mixed action $\left[\frac{1}{2}(T), \frac{1}{2}(B)\right]$, while if in stage t Player II played R, then in stage $t+1$ Player I plays the mixed action $\left[\frac{3}{4}(T), \frac{1}{4}(B)\right]$.

Player II is considering which of the following four strategies to implement: (a) play L in every stage, (b) play R in every stage, (c) play L in odd stages, and R in even stages, (d) play R in odd stages, and L in even stages.

What is the limit of the average payoffs of each of the players when Player I implements strategy σ_1 and Player II implements each of the above four strategies?

13.18 For the base game in Exercise 13.16 describe an equilibrium of the infinitely repeated game that yields a payoff of $\left(4\frac{1}{3}, 2\frac{1}{3}\right)$.

13.19 For each of the following base games determine whether or not $(2, 1)$ is an equilibrium payoff of the corresponding infinitely repeated game. If it is an equilibrium payoff, describe an equilibrium leading to that payoff. If not, justify your answer. In these games, Player I is the row player and Player II is the column player.

	L	R
T	0, 0	2, 2
B	1, 1	0, 0

Game A

	L	R
T	1, 3	4, 0
B	2, 0	0, 1

Game B

	L	R
T	1, 3	4, 0
B	3, 0	1, 1

Game C

	L	M	R
T	0, 1	1, 0	3, 1
B	3, 1	0, 2	0, 3

Game D

13.20 In the infinitely repeated game of the following base game, describe an equilibrium leading to the payoff $\left(2, 3\frac{2}{3}\right)$.

Player II

	L	R
T	1, 4	2, 5
B	0, 1	3, 2

Player I — T/B rows

13.21 In the following three-player base game Γ Player I chooses the row (T or B), Player II chooses the column (L or R), and Player III chooses the matrix (W or E).

	L	R
T	1, 0, 2	1, 1, 0
B	3, 0, 3	3, 2, 1

W

	L	R
T	2, 0, 0	2, 1, 2
B	1, 2, 1	1, 2, 3

E

(a) Compute the minmax values of the three players.

(b) Does the game satisfy the conditions of Theorem 13.9 on page 531?

(c) Describe an equilibrium in the 1000-stage repeated game whose payoff is within 0.1 of $(2, 1, 2\frac{1}{2})$.

(d) Describe an equilibrium in the infinitely repeated game whose payoff is $(2, 1, 2\frac{1}{2})$.

13.22 One of the payoffs in the following base game is a parameter labeled x. For every $x \in [0, 1]$ find the set of equilibrium payoffs in the infinitely repeated game based on this game.

	L	R
T	1, 1	0, 2
B	0, 1	$x, \frac{3}{2}$

13.23 Find an example of an infinitely repeated game, and a strategy vector τ in this game satisfying (a) τ is an equilibrium for every finite game Γ_T with a corresponding payoff of $\gamma^T(\tau)$ and (b) the limit $\lim_{T \to \infty} \gamma^T(\tau)$ does not exist.

13.24 Prove the Folk Theorem for infinitely repeated games (Theorem 13.17 on page 547).

Guidance: For each $K \in \mathbb{N}$, approximate x by a weighted average of vectors in the payoff matrix, with weights that are nonnegative and rational, with denominator K. Construct a strategy vector in which the players play in blocks, such that the length of the K-th block is K stages, and in the K-th block the players play in such a way that the average of the payoffs is approximately x. If, at a certain stage, a player deviates from the action he is supposed to play at that stage, he is punished from the next stage onwards by a punishment strategy.

13.25 Prove directly that the statement of Theorem 13.19 (page 549) holds with respect to the strategy vector τ^* defined in Example 13.1 (page 548): τ^* is an ε-equilibrium of the T-stage game, for every T sufficiently large.

13.26 Prove the strong formulation of the Folk Theorem for infinitely repeated games (Theorem 13.19 on page 549).

13.27 In the game in Example 13.20, prove that for every $T \in \mathbb{N}$, Player I has a strategy in Γ_T yielding the payoff $\frac{T-\lceil \sqrt{T} \rceil}{T}$ when Player II uses the strategy τ_{II}^* defined in the example.

13.28 Let N be a set of players, and let $(S_i)_{i \in N}$ be finite sets of actions of the players. Let $u : S \to \mathbb{R}^N$ and $u' : S \to \mathbb{R}^N$ be two payoff functions. Consider a variation of the repeated game, in which in odd stages the payoff function is u, and in even stages the payoff function is u'.

    (a) Write the analogous theorem to Theorem 13.9 in this model.
    (b) Write the analogous theorem to Theorem 13.17 in this model.

13.29 Repeat Exercise 13.28, under the following variation of the game: in each stage, one of the payoff functions is chosen randomly (each payoff function is chosen with probability $\frac{1}{2}$, independently of the payoff functions and the actions of the players in previous stages), and the players are informed of the chosen payoff functions before they choose their actions in each stage.

13.30 Repeat Exercise 13.29 for the case where the players are not informed of the payoff function chosen in each stage.

13.31 Repeat Exercise 13.29 for the case where only Player 1 is informed of the payoff function chosen in each stage (with the other players not informed of the chosen payoff function).

13.32 Prove that for every discount factor $\lambda \in [0, 1)$, the minmax value of each player i in the λ-discounted game Γ_λ is equal to his minmax value in the base game Γ.

13.33 Compute the λ-discounted payoff in each of the three cases (a), (b), (c) of Exercise 13.11.

13.34 **Cartel game** A cartel is an association of players who coordinate their actions in order to attain better results than the players could attain if they acted individually. In this exercise we will show that players can indeed profit by forming a cartel, and check whether a cartel can be stable.

    Consider the following Cournot competition (see Example 4.23 on page 99): there are n luxury car manufacturers. The manufacturing cost of each car is \$100,000 (for each manufacturer) and the consumer price of each such car is \$200,000 $- \sum_{i=1}^{n} x_i$, where x_i is the number of cars manufactured annually by manufacturer i. For computational ease, we assume below that x_i can be any nonnegative real number (not necessarily an integer). Answer the following questions:

(a) Describe the situation as a strategic-form game, where a pure strategy of each manufacturer is the number of cars he manufactures annually.

(b) Prove that this game has a unique symmetric equilibrium (that is, an equilibrium x in which $x_i = x_j$ for all i and j), at which $x_i = \frac{100,000}{n+1}$.

(c) Suppose that the manufacturers decide to form a cartel, and to determine jointly the number of cars that each of them will manufacture, in order to maximize the profit of each of them. Prove that to maximize this profit, the manufacturers need to manufacture collectively 50,000 cars; hence if they divide this number equally between them they will each manufacture $\frac{50,000}{n}$ cars. In other words, the cartel limits the number of cars manufactured by each member to a number that is lower than the number of cars manufactured at equilibrium (assuming that $n > 1$). Show that despite the lower manufacturing numbers, the profit of each manufacturer under the cartel's quotas is higher than his profit at the equilibrium strategy.

(d) Consider next the discounted repeated game of the above-described base game. Is the strategy vector at which each manufacturer manufactures $\frac{50,000}{n}$ cars in each stage an equilibrium of Γ_λ, for every $\lambda \in [0, 1)$? Justify your answer.

(e) For each manufacturer i define a strategy τ_i as follows:

- In the first stage, manufacture $\frac{50,000}{n}$ cars.
- For each $t > 1$, the number of cars to manufacture in stage t is determined as follows:
    - if in each of the previous stages every manufacturer manufactured $\frac{50,000}{n}$ cars, manufacture $\frac{50,000}{n}$ cars in stage t;
    - otherwise, manufacture $\frac{100,000}{n+1}$ cars in stage t.

For which value of n, and which discount factor λ, is the strategy vector $\tau = (\tau_i)_{i=1}^{n}$ an equilibrium of the game Γ_λ? What can we conclude regarding the stability of cartels, given these results?

(f) Are there similarities between the repeated Prisoner's Dilemma (see Example 13.1 on page 529) and the cartel game of this exercise? If so, what are they? Which equilibria of the repeated Prisoner's Dilemma correspond to the equilibria described in items (b) and (e) of this exercise?

13.35 Alternating offers game Barack and Joe can together implement a project that will jointly yield them a profit of $100. How should they divide this sum of money between them? They decide to implement the following mechanism: Barack will offer Joe a split of $(x, 100 - x)$, where x is a number in the interval $[0, 100]$, signifying the amount of money that Barack will receive under this offer. Joe may accept or reject this offer. If he accepts, this will be the final split. If he rejects the offer, the next day he proposes a counteroffer $(y, 100 - y)$, where y is a number in the interval $[0, 100]$, signifying the amount of money that Barack will receive, under this offer. Barack may accept or reject this offer. If he accepts, this will be the final split. If he rejects the offer, the next day he proposes a counteroffer, and so on. Every delay in implementing the project reduces the profit they will receive: if the two of them agree on a division of the money $(x, 100 - x)$ on day n, Barack's payoff is $\beta^{n-1} \times x$, and Joe's payoff is $\beta^{n-1} \times (100 - x)$, where $\beta \in (0, 1)$ is the discount factor in the game (in other words, $100(\frac{1}{\beta} - 1)$ is the daily interest rate in the game).

Depict this situation as an extensive-form game, and find all the subgame perfect equilibria of the game.

13.36 In the two-player zero-sum game in Exercise 13.9, find the value of the discounted game, and the optimal strategy of both players for any discount factor $\lambda \in [0, 1)$. What is the limit of the discounted values, as the discount factor converges to 1? Is the limit equal to the limit you computed in Exercise 13.9 for the values of the T-stage game?

13.37 Find an example of a repeated game, and a strategy vector τ, such that (a) τ is an equilibrium of the discounted game for every $\lambda \in [0, 1)$, and (b) the limit $\lim_{\lambda \to 1} \gamma^\lambda(\tau)$ does not exist.

13.38 Suppose two players are playing the repeated Prisoner's Dilemma. Prove that if the discount factor λ is sufficiently close to 1, the strategy vector at which the players implement the grim-trigger strategy, i.e., every player plays C as long as the other player plays C, and otherwise plays D, is a λ-discounted equilibrium.

13.39 A strategy in an infinitely repeated game has *recall k* if the action a player chooses in stage t depends only on the actions that were played in stages $t - 1, t - 2, \ldots$, $t - k$ (and is independent of the actions played in earlier stages, and of the number of the stages t). Formally, a strategy τ_i has recall k if for every $t, \hat{t} \geq k$ we have $\tau_i(a^1, a^2, \ldots, a^{t-1}) = \tau_i(\hat{a}^1, \hat{a}^2, \ldots, \hat{a}^{\hat{t}-1})$ whenever $(a^{t-k}, a^{t-k+1}, \cdots, a^{t-1}) = (\hat{a}^{\hat{t}-k}, \hat{a}^{\hat{t}-k+1}, \cdots, \hat{a}^{\hat{t}-1})$.

(a) How many pure strategies of recall k has each player got?

(b) Can the grim-trigger strategy be implemented by a pure strategy with recall k? Justify your answer.

(c) Prove that in the T-stage repeated Prisoner's Dilemma, when the players are limited to playing only strategies with recall k (where $k + 1 < T$), $(3, 3)$ is an equilibrium payoff.

(d) For which triples k, l, and T is $(3, 3)$ an equilibrium payoff in the T-stage repeated Prisoner's Dilemma, where Player I is limited to strategies with recall k, and Player II is limited to strategies with recall l?

13.40 Suppose two players are playing the repeated Prisoner's Dilemma with an unknown number of stages; after each stage, a lottery is conducted, such that with probability $1 - \beta$ the game ends with no further stages conducted, and with probability β the game continues to another stage, where $\beta \in [0, 1)$ is a given real number. Each player's goal is to maximize the sum total of payoffs received over all the stages of the game.

Prove that if β is sufficiently close to 1, the strategy vector in which at the first stage every player plays C, and in each subsequent stage each player plays C if the other player played C in the previous stage, and he plays D otherwise, is an equilibrium. This strategy is called the Tit-for-Tat strategy.

13.41 In this exercise, we will show that in a discounted two-player zero-sum game in which the discount factors of the two players are different from each other, the payoff to each player at every equilibrium is the value of the base game. Consider the two-player zero-sum repeated game based on the following base game:

	L	R
T	$-1, 1$	$1, -1$
B	$1, -1$	$-1, 1$

Assume that the discount factor of Player I is λ throughout this exercise (except in section (j)), and that the discount factor of Player II is λ^2, where $\lambda \in [0, 1)$. Answer the following questions:

(a) What is the value in mixed strategies v of the base game?

(b) What is the discounted payoff to each player under the following pair of strategies, as a function of the parameter $t_0 \in \mathbb{N}$:

- Player I plays T in each stage of the game.
- Player II plays L in the first t_0 stages, and always R afterwards.

(c) Find t_0 such that the sum of the payoffs of the two players is maximized. What is the sum of the payoffs for this t_0? In the solution here, assume that t_0 may be any nonnegative real number.

(d) Prove that the pair of strategies in which Player I plays the mixed action $[\frac{1}{2}(T), \frac{1}{2}(B)]$ at each stage, and Player II plays the mixed action $[\frac{1}{2}(L), \frac{1}{2}(R)]$ at each stage, is an equilibrium in this discounted game.

Let $\tau^* = (\tau_{\mathrm{I}}^*, \tau_{\mathrm{II}}^*)$ be any equilibrium of this discounted game. For $t_0 \in \mathbb{N}$, denote by $A(\lambda, t_0)$ the λ-discounted payoff under strategy vector τ^* starting from stage t_0:

$$A(\lambda, t_0) = (1 - \lambda) \sum_{t=t_0}^{\infty} \mathbf{E}_{\tau^*}[u^t]\lambda^{t-t_0}. \qquad (13.106)$$

(e) Prove that for every $t_0 \in \mathbb{N}$, the following holds: $A(\lambda, t_0) \geq v$ and $A(\lambda^2, t_0) \leq v$.

(f) Prove that for every $t_0 \in \mathbb{N}$ and every $\lambda \in [0, 1)$, the following holds:

$$A(\lambda, t_0) = \frac{\lambda}{1 + \lambda} A(\lambda^2, t_0) + \frac{1 - \lambda}{1 + \lambda} \sum_{k=0}^{\infty} \lambda^k A(\lambda^2, t_0 + k). \qquad (13.107)$$

(g) Deduce from the last two items that $A(\lambda, t_0) = v$ for every $t_0 \in \mathbb{N}$, and from this further deduce that $\mathbf{E}_{\tau^*}[u^t] = 0$ for every $t \in \mathbb{N}$.

(h) Prove that at each equilibrium of this discounted game, the discounted payoff of each player is v.

(i) Does the result of item (c) contradict the result of item (h)? Explain.

(j) Generalize the result of item (h) to any discounted game and any pair of discount factors: if $\tau^* = (\tau_I^*, \tau_{II}^*)$ is an equilibrium of a two-player zero-sum game in which the discount factor of Player I is λ_I and the discount factor of Player II is λ_{II}, then $A(\lambda_i, t_0) = v$ for $i \in \{I, II\}$, for every $t_0 \in \mathbb{N}$, where v is the value in mixed strategies of the base game. In particular, at any equilibrium, the discounted payoff of each player (at his discount factor) is the value of the base game.

13.42 Prove that the condition in Theorem 13.9 (page 539) implies the condition in Theorem 13.24 (page 554): if for every player i there exists an equilibrium $\beta(i)$ in the base game for which $U_i(\beta(i)) > \overline{v}_i$, then there exists a vector $\widehat{x} \in F \cap V$ satisfying $x_i > \overline{v}_i$ for every $i \in N$.

13.43 Prove the Folk Theorem for discounted games (Theorem 13.24 on page 554).

13.44 Prove Theorem 13.25: the set of subgame perfect equilibrium payoffs of Γ_∞ is the set $F \cap V$.

13.45 Prove the Folk Theorem 13.26 regarding the characterization of the set of subgame perfect discounted equilibrium payoffs in an infinitely repeated game.

13.46 Show (by finding appropriate strategy vectors) that the payoff vectors mentioned in Exercises 13.20 and 13.21 are payoffs of uniform equilibria for discounted games.

13.47 Prove the Folk Theorem for uniform equilibrium in discounted games (Theorem 13.29 on page 558).

13.48 In this exercise, we define the uniform value of two-player zero-sum games. Let Γ be a two-player zero-sum base game. The real number v is called the *uniform value* (for the finite games $(\Gamma_T)_{T \in \mathbb{N}}$) if for each $\varepsilon > 0$ there exist strategies τ_I^* of Player I and τ_{II}^* of Player II in Γ_∞, and an integer T_0, such that the following condition is satisfied: for each $T \geq T_0$, and each pair of strategies (τ_I, τ_{II}) in Γ_T,

$$\gamma^T(\tau_I, \tau_{II}^*) \leq v + \varepsilon, \text{ and } \gamma^T(\tau_I^*, \tau_{II}) \geq v - \varepsilon. \tag{13.108}$$

Prove that the uniform value for finite games equals the value of the base game.

13.49 Repeat Exercise 13.46 for uniform ε-equilibria for finite games, for every $\varepsilon > 0$.

13.50 Let E_T be the set of equilibrium payoffs of a T-stage repeated game Γ_T.

(a) Prove that $E_T \subseteq E_{kT}$ for every $T \in \mathbb{N}$ and for every $k \in \mathbb{N}$.
(b) Prove[8] that $\frac{T}{T+1} E_T + \frac{1}{T+1} E_1 \subseteq E_{T+1}$ for every $T \in \mathbb{N}$.
(c) For every set $S \subseteq \mathbb{R}^k$, the set $\overline{S}$ denotes the closure of S: the smallest closed set containing S. Let

$$E_\infty := \limsup_{T \to \infty} E_T = \bigcap_{T \in \mathbb{N}} \bigcup_{k \geq t} \overline{E_k} \tag{13.109}$$

---

8 For every pair of sets S_1 and S_2 in $\mathbb{R}^k$, and every real number α, the sets αS_1 and $S_1 + S_2$ are defined by $\alpha S_1 := \{\alpha x : x \in S_1\}$ and $S_1 + S_2 := \{x + y : x \in S_1, \ y \in S_2\}$.

The set E_∞ is the upper limit of the sets $(E_T)_{T\in\mathbb{N}}$, and it includes all the partial limits of the sequences $(x_t)_{t\in\mathbb{N}}$, where $x_t \in E_t$ for each $t \in \mathbb{N}$.

Prove, using items (a) and (b), that $E_T \subseteq E_\infty$ for every $T \in \mathbb{N}$, and in particular that E_∞ is not empty. Furthermore, prove that for every $x \in E_\infty$ and every $\varepsilon > 0$, there exists $T_0 \in \mathbb{N}$ such that for every $T \geq T_0$ there exists $y \in E_T$ satisfying $\|x - y\|_\infty \leq \varepsilon$. In other words, the sets $(E_T)_{T\in\mathbb{N}}$ "approach" E_∞ as T goes to infinity.

13.51 Prove that in every uniform 0-equilibrium for finite games, from some stage onwards the players play an equilibrium of the base game at each stage.

13.52 Prove the Folk Theorem for uniform equilibrium in finite games (Theorem 13.31 on page 559).

13.53 In this exercise we prove the existence of a sequence $(x_t)_{t=1}^\infty$ of zeros and ones satisfying

$$\liminf_{T\to\infty} \frac{\sum_{k=1}^T x_k}{T} < \liminf_{\lambda\to 1}(1 - \lambda) \sum_{t=1}^\infty \lambda^{t-1} x_t. \tag{13.110}$$

Let $(q_t)_{t\in\mathbb{N}}$ be a sequence of natural numbers. Define a sequence $(p_t)_{t\in\mathbb{N}}$ as follows:

$$p_1 := 0, \tag{13.111}$$

$$p_t := q_1 + q_2 + \cdots + q_{t-1}. \tag{13.112}$$

Define a sequence $(x_t)_{t\in\mathbb{N}}$ as follows:

$$x_t = \begin{cases} 1 & \text{when there exists } k \text{ such that } 2p_k < t \leq 2p_k + q_k, \\ 0 & \text{otherwise.} \end{cases} \tag{13.113}$$

In words, the first q_1 elements of the sequence $(x_t)_{t\in\mathbb{N}}$ equal 1, the next q_1 elements of the sequence equal 0, the next q_2 elements of the sequence equal 1, the next q_2 elements of the sequence equal 0, and so on.

(a) Prove that $\liminf_{T\to\infty} \frac{\sum_{k=1}^T x_k}{T} = \frac{1}{2}$.

(b) Denote $A(\lambda) = (1 - \lambda) \sum_{t=1}^\infty \lambda^{t-1} x_t$. Prove that $A(\lambda) = \sum_{k=1}^\infty \lambda^{2p_k}(1 - \lambda^{q_k})$.

(c) Denote $\alpha_k = \lambda^{p_k} - \lambda^{p_{k+1}}$ for every $k \in \mathbb{N}$. Using item (b) above, prove that

$$A(\lambda) = \frac{1}{2}\left(\sum_{k=1}^\infty (\alpha_k)^2 + 1\right). \tag{13.114}$$

(d) Let $\varepsilon \in (0, \frac{1}{4})$, and define $c := \frac{\ln(\varepsilon)}{\ln(1-\sqrt{\varepsilon})}$. Prove that $c > 2$.

(e) Suppose that the sequence $(q_t)_{t\in\mathbb{N}}$ satisfies $q_k > \frac{2p_k}{c-2}$ for every $k \in \mathbb{N}$. Define

$$a_k := \frac{|\ln(1 - \sqrt{\varepsilon})|}{q_k}, \quad b_k := \frac{|\ln(\varepsilon)|}{2p_k}. \tag{13.115}$$

Prove that $\lim_{k\to\infty} b_k = 0$, and that for every $k \in \mathbb{N}$, (a) $b_{k+1} < b_k$ for every $k \in \mathbb{N}$, (b) $cq_k > 2p_k + 2q_k$, and (c) $a_k < b_{k+1}$.

(f) Prove, with the aid of item (e) above, that $\bigcup_{k\in\mathbb{N}}(a_k, b_k) = (0, \infty)$. Deduce that for every $\lambda \in [0, 1)$ there exists $k(\lambda) \in \mathbb{N}$ satisfying $a_{k(\lambda)} \le |\ln(\lambda)| < b_{k(\lambda)}$.

(g) Using Equation (13.115), prove that $\varepsilon < \lambda^{2p_k(\lambda)}$, and $1 - \sqrt{\varepsilon} \ge \lambda^{q_k(\lambda)}$. Deduce that

$$(\alpha_k)^2 = \lambda^{2p_k(\lambda)}\left(1 - \lambda^{q_k(\lambda)}\right)^2 > \varepsilon^2. \tag{13.116}$$

(h) Deduce, with the aid of item (c) above, that $\liminf_{\lambda\to 1} A(\lambda) \ge \frac{\varepsilon^2+1}{2}$.

(i) Deduce that Equation (13.110) holds for the sequence $(x_t)_{t\in\mathbb{N}}$ defined in item (d) above.

(j) Construct a sequence $(y_t)_{t=1}^{\infty}$ of zeros and ones satisfying

$$\limsup_{T\to\infty} \frac{\sum_{t=1}^{T} y_t}{T} > \limsup_{\lambda\to 1}(1-\lambda)\sum_{t=1}^{\infty}\lambda^{t-1}y_t. \tag{13.117}$$

Such a sequence was used in Example 13.35.

13.54 Consider the following sequence $(x_t)_{t\in\mathbb{N}}$: $1, -1, 2, -2, 3, -3, \ldots$, i.e., $x_{2t} = -t$, and $x_{2t-1} = t$ for every $t \in \mathbb{N}$. Compute $\limsup_{T\to\infty}\frac{\sum_{k=1}^{T}x_k}{T}$, $\liminf_{T\to\infty}\frac{\sum_{k=1}^{T}x_k}{T}$ and $\lim_{\lambda\to 1}(1-\lambda)\sum_{t=1}^{\infty}\lambda^{t-1}x_t$.

13.55 Prove that the strategy vector $(\sigma_{\mathrm{I}}^A, \sigma_{\mathrm{II}})$ defined in Example 13.35 (page 563) is not an equilibrium of the infinitely repeated game.

13.56 David and Tom play the following game, over T stages. In each stage David chooses a color, either red or yellow, and Tom guesses which color David chose. If Tom guesses "red," he pays David one dollar if he guessed incorrectly, and receives one dollar from David if he guessed correctly. If, however, Tom guesses "yellow," he pays David a dollar in that stage and in every subsequent stage of the game if he guessed incorrectly, and he receives a dollar from David in that stage and in every subsequent stage of the game if he guessed correctly.

Note that this is not a repeated game, because if the first time that Tom guesses "yellow" is in stage t, the payoffs in all the stages after t depend on Tom's choice in stage t.

(a) Prove that the only equilibrium payoff when $T = 1$ is $(0, 0)$.
(b) Prove that the only equilibrium payoff when $T = 2$ is $(0, 0)$.
(c) Prove that the only equilibrium payoff for every T is $(0, 0)$.

13.57 Consider the game in Exercise 15.2 with $T = \infty$. Let x and y be two numbers in the interval $[0, 1]$. Suppose that in each stage David chooses "red" with probability x and "yellow" with probability $1 - x$, and in each stage Tom guesses "red" with probability y and "yellow" with probability $1 - y$.

(a) Compute the expected λ-discounted payoff in this infinite game as a function of x and y, for each $\lambda \in [0, 1)$.
(b) Conclude that, if the players are restricted to these i.i.d. strategies, $(0, 0)$ is a λ-discounted equilibrium payoff, for each $\lambda \in [0, 1)$. What are the corresponding equilibrium strategies?

14 Repeated games with vector payoffs

Chapter summary

This chapter is devoted to a theory of repeated games with vector payoffs, known as the theory of *approachability*, developed by Blackwell in 1956. Blackwell considered two-player repeated games in which the outcome is an *m*-dimensional vector of attributes, and the goal of each player is to control the average vector of attributes. The goal can be either to *approach* a given target set $S \subseteq \mathbb{R}^m$, that is, to ensure that the distance between the vector of average attributes and the target set S converges to 0, or to *exclude* the target set S, that is, to ensure that the distance between the vector of average attributes and S remains bounded away from 0. If a player can approach the target set we say that the set is *approachable* by the player, whereas if the player can exclude the target set we say that it is *excludable* by that player. Clearly, a set cannot be both approachable by one player and excludable by the other player.

We provide a geometric condition that ensures that a set is approachable by a player, and show that any convex set is either approachable by one player or excludable by the other player.

Two applications of the theory of approachability are provided: it is used, respectively, to construct an optimal strategy for the uninformed player in two-player zero-sum repeated games with incomplete information on one side, and to construct a no-regret strategy in sequential decision problems with experts.

In Chapter 13 we studied repeated games in which the payoff to each player in every stage was a real number representing the player's utility. In this chapter we will look at two-player repeated games in which the outcome in every stage is not a pair of payoffs, but a vector in the *m*-dimensional Euclidean space $\mathbb{R}^m$. These games correspond to situations in which the outcome of an interaction between the players is comprised of several incommensurable factors. For example, an employment contract between an employee and an employer may specify the number of hours the employee is to commit to the job; the salary the employee will receive; and the number of days of annual leave granted to the employee. As we saw in Chapter 2 on utility theory, under certain assumptions it is possible to associate each outcome with a real number representing the utility of the outcome, thereby translating the situation into a game with payoffs in real numbers. But we may not know the players' utility functions. In addition, we may at times be interested in controlling each variable separately, as is done for example in physics problems, where pressure and temperature may be controlled separately. The model of repeated games with vector payoffs was first presented by Blackwell [1956]. The first part of this chapter is based on that paper.

When the outcome of an interaction to each player is a payoff, each player tries to maximize the average of the payoffs he receives. When the outcome is a vector in $\mathbb{R}^m$, maximizing one coordinate may come at the expense of another coordinate. We therefore speak of target sets in the space of vector payoffs: each player tries either to cause the average of his payoffs to approach a target set (i.e., a certain subset of $\mathbb{R}^m$) or to exclude a target set.

In Chapters 9 and 10 we studied Bayesian games; these are games with incomplete information whose payoffs depend on the state of nature, which can have a finite number of values. In Section 14.7 (page 598) we will study two-player zero-sum repeated games with incomplete information regarding the state of nature using the model of repeated games with vector payoffs: every pair of actions in such a game is associated with a vector of payoffs composed of the payoff for each possible state of nature. In this way, we can monitor the average payoff for every possible state of nature, even if the state of nature is not known by all the players. An example of such an application appears in Section 14.7 (page 598). In Section 14.8 (page 608), we will present an additional application of the model of repeated games with vector payoffs to the study of dynamic decision problems with experts.

14.1 Notation

In this chapter we will work in $\mathbb{R}^m$, the m-dimensional Euclidean space. We will sometimes term $x \in \mathbb{R}^m$ a "vector," and sometimes a "point." The zero vector in $\mathbb{R}^m$ is denoted by $\vec{0}$.

Recall that for a finite set A, we denote by $\Delta(A)$ the set of probability distributions over A. The inner product in $\mathbb{R}^m$ is denoted as follows. For every pair of vectors $x, y \in \mathbb{R}^m$,

$$\langle x, y \rangle := \sum_{l=1}^{m} x_l y_l. \tag{14.1}$$

The inner product is symmetric, $\langle x, y \rangle = \langle y, x \rangle$, and *bilinear*; i.e., it is a linear function in each of its variables. That is, for every $\alpha, \beta \in \mathbb{R}$ and every $x, x_1, x_2, y, y_1, y_2 \in \mathbb{R}^m$,

$$\langle \alpha x_1 + \beta x_2, y \rangle = \alpha \langle x_1, y \rangle + \beta \langle x_2, y \rangle, \tag{14.2}$$

and

$$\langle x, \alpha y_1 + \beta y_2 \rangle = \alpha \langle x, y_1 \rangle + \beta \langle x, y_2 \rangle. \tag{14.3}$$

The norm of a vector $x \in \mathbb{R}^m$, denoted by $||x||$, is the Euclidean norm, given by

$$||x|| := \langle x, x \rangle^{1/2} = \sqrt{\sum_{l=1}^{m} (x_l)^2}, \tag{14.4}$$

and the distance function between vectors is

$$d(x, y) := ||x - y|| = \langle x - y, x - y \rangle^{1/2} = \sqrt{\sum_{l=1}^{m} (x_l - y_l)^2}. \tag{14.5}$$

If $C \subseteq \mathbb{R}^m$ is a set, and $x \in \mathbb{R}^m$ is a vector, the distance between x and C is given by

$$d(x, C) := \inf_{y \in C} d(x, y). \tag{14.6}$$

It follows that the distance between a point x and a set C equals the distance between x and the closure of C, and $d(x, C) = 0$ for every x in the closure of C. The triangle inequality states that

$$d(x, y) + d(y, z) \geq d(x, z), \quad \forall x, y, z \in \mathbb{R}^m. \tag{14.7}$$

Equivalently,

$$||x|| + ||y|| \geq ||x + y||. \tag{14.8}$$

The Cauchy–Schwarz inequality states that

$$||x||^2 ||y||^2 \geq \langle x, y \rangle^2. \tag{14.9}$$

The following inequalities also hold (Equation (14.11) follows from the Cauchy–Schwarz inequality):[1]

$$d(x + y, x + z) = d(y, z), \quad \forall x, y, z \in \mathbb{R}^m, \tag{14.10}$$

$$d(x + y, z + w) \leq d(x, z) + d(y, w), \quad \forall x, y, z, w \in \mathbb{R}^m, \tag{14.11}$$

$$d(\alpha x, \alpha y) = \alpha d(x, y), \quad \forall x, y \in \mathbb{R}^m, \forall \alpha > 0, \tag{14.12}$$

$$d(x, y) \leq 2M\sqrt{m}, \quad \forall M > 0, \forall x, y \in [-M, M]^m. \tag{14.13}$$

If $C \subseteq \mathbb{R}^m$ is a set, and $x, y \in \mathbb{R}^m$ are vectors, then (Exercise 14.1)

$$d(x, C) \leq d(x, y) + d(y, C). \tag{14.14}$$

All the vectors are considered to be row vectors. If x is a row vector, then $x^\top$ is the corresponding column vector.

Since we are studying two-player games, for every player $k \in \{1, 2\}$, we will denote by $-k$ the player who is not player k. In particular, the notation σ_{-k} denotes a strategy of the player who is not k.

---

1 For every set $A \subseteq \mathbb{R}$, and natural number m, the set $A^m \subseteq \mathbb{R}^m$ is defined as follows:

$$A^m = \underbrace{A \times A \times \cdots \times A}_{m \text{ times}} = \{(x_1, x_2, \ldots, x_m) \in \mathbb{R}^m : x_i \in A, \quad i = 1, 2, \ldots, m\}.$$

14.2 The model

Definition 14.1 *A repeated (two-player) game with (m-dimensional) vector payoffs is given by two action sets* $\mathcal{I} = \{1, 2, \ldots, I\}$ *and* $\mathcal{J} = \{1, 2, \ldots, J\}$ *of Players 1 and 2, respectively,*[2] *and a payoff function* $u : \mathcal{I} \times \mathcal{J} \to \mathbb{R}^m$.

As previously stated, the vectors in $\mathbb{R}^m$ are not necessarily payoffs; they are various attributes of the outcome of the game. Despite this, we use the term "payoff function" for u, both for convenience and because of the analogy to games with scalar payoffs (the case $m = 1$). It will sometimes be convenient to present the payoff function u as a matrix of order $I \times J$, whose elements are vectors in $\mathbb{R}^m$.

The game proceeds in stages as follows. In stage t $(t = 1, 2, \ldots)$, each one of the players chooses an action: Player 1 chooses action $i^t \in \mathcal{I}$, and Player 2 chooses action $j^t \in \mathcal{J}$. As in the model of repeated games, we will assume that every player knows what the other player chose in previous stages. A behavior strategy of Player 1 is a function associating a mixed action with each history of actions

$$\sigma_1 : \bigcup_{t=1}^{\infty} (\mathcal{I} \times \mathcal{J})^{t-1} \to \Delta(\mathcal{I}). \tag{14.15}$$

Similarly, a behavior strategy of Player 2 is a function

$$\sigma_2 : \bigcup_{t=1}^{\infty} (\mathcal{I} \times \mathcal{J})^{t-1} \to \Delta(\mathcal{J}). \tag{14.16}$$

Kuhn's Theorem for infinite games (Theorem 6.26 on page 253) states that every mixed strategy has an equivalent behavior strategy and vice versa. It therefore suffices to consider only behavior strategies here, because they are more natural than mixed strategies. The word *strategy* in this chapter will be short-hand for "behavior strategy."

By Theorem 6.23 (page 253), every pair of strategies (σ_1, σ_2) induces a probability measure $\mathbf{P}_{\sigma_1, \sigma_2}$ over the set of infinite plays, i.e., over $(\mathcal{I} \times \mathcal{J})^{\mathbb{N}}$. The expectation operator corresponding to this probability distribution is denoted by $\mathbf{E}_{\sigma_1, \sigma_2}$.

Denote the payoff in stage t by $g^t = u(i^t, j^t) \in \mathbb{R}^m$, and the average payoff up to stage T by[3]

$$\overline{g}^T = \frac{1}{T} \sum_{t=1}^{T} g^t = \frac{1}{T} \sum_{t=1}^{T} u(i^t, j^t) \in \mathbb{R}^m. \tag{14.17}$$

We next define the concept of an approachable set, the central concept of this chapter.

---

2 For convenience, we use in this chapter the notation $\mathcal{I}$ and $\mathcal{J}$ for the action sets of the players, instead of A_1 and A_2.

3 While in one-stage games the payoff is defined to be the expected payoff according to the mixed actions of the players, in repeated games the payoff in each stage t is the actual payoff $u(i^t, j^t)$ of that stage (and not the expected payoff according to the mixed actions at that stage). In this chapter we will be interested in the average payoff $\overline{g}^T$, as opposed to its expectation.

Definition 14.2 *A nonempty set $C \subseteq \mathbb{R}^m$ is called* approachable *by player k if there exists a strategy σ_k of player k such that for every $\varepsilon > 0$ there exists $T \in \mathbb{N}$ such that for every strategy σ_{-k} of the other player*

$$\mathbf{P}_{\sigma_k,\sigma_{-k}}(d(\overline{g}^t, C) < \varepsilon, \quad \forall t \geq T) > 1 - \varepsilon. \tag{14.18}$$

In this case we say that σ_k approaches C *for player k.*

A set is approachable by a player if that player can guarantee that for any strategy used by the other player, the average payoff approaches the set with probability 1 uniformly. In particular, this implies that

$$\mathbf{P}_{\sigma_k,\sigma_{-k}}\left(\lim_{t \to \infty} d(\overline{g}^t, C) = 0 \right) = 1. \tag{14.19}$$

The convergence of the average payoff to C is uniform; i.e., the rate at which the average payoff approaches this set (meaning the ratio between ε and t in Equation (14.18)) is independent of the strategy used by the rival player.

The dual to Definition 14.2 relates to the situation in which player k can guarantee that the distance between the average payoff and the target set is positive and bounded away from 0.

Definition 14.3 *A nonempty set $C \subseteq \mathbb{R}^m$ is called* excludable *by player k if there exists $\delta > 0$ such that the set $\{x \in \mathbb{R}^m : d(x, C) \geq \delta\}$ is approachable by player k. If the strategy σ_k of player k approaches the set $\{x \in \mathbb{R}^m : d(x, C) \geq \delta\}$ for some $\delta > 0$, we say that σ_k* excludes *the set C for player k.*

14.3   Examples

When $m = 1$, the outcome at each stage is a real number. If we interpret this number as the payoff to Player 1, and the negative of this number as the payoff to Player 2, then this model is equivalent to the model of repeated two-player zero-sum games. If v is the value of the one-stage game, then $[v, \infty)$ is an approachable set for Player 1, and $(-\infty, v]$ is an approachable set for Player 2. The players' approaching strategies are stationary strategies, in which each player plays an optimal strategy of the one-stage game at each stage (independently of the history of play). It follows that for every $\delta > 0$, the set $(-\infty, v - \delta]$ is an excludable set for Player 1, and the set $[v + \delta, \infty)$ is an excludable set for Player 2. This example shows that one may regard the model of repeated games with vector payoffs as a generalization of the model of two-player zero-sum games. Blackwell [1956], in fact, presented his model in such a way.

Example 14.4   Consider a game where $m = 2$, each player has two possible actions, and the payoff function u is given by the matrix in Figure 14.1.

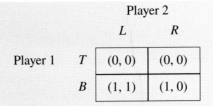

Figure 14.1 The game in Example 14.4

The set $C_1 = \{(0,0)\}$, containing only the vector $(0,0)$ (see Figure 14.2), is approachable by Player 1: if Player 1 plays T in every stage, he guarantees that the average payoff is $(0,0)$.

The set $C_2 = \{(1,x): 0 \leq x \leq 1\}$ (see Figure 14.2) is also approachable by Player 1: if Player 1 plays B in every stage, he guarantees that the average payoff is in C_2.

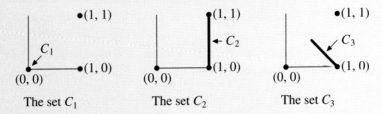

Figure 14.2 Three sets approachable by Player 1 in Example 14.4

It is also interesting to note that the set $C_3 = \left\{(x, 1-x): \frac{1}{2} \leq x \leq 1\right\}$ (see Figure 14.2) is also approachable by Player 1. The following strategy of Player 1 guarantees that the average payoff approaches this set:

- If $\overline{g}^{t-1}$, the average payoff up to stage $t-1$, is located above the diagonal $x_1 + x_2 = 1$, i.e., if $\overline{g}_1^{t-1} + \overline{g}_2^{t-1} \geq 1$, then play T in stage t.
- If $\overline{g}^{t-1}$, the average payoff up to stage $t-1$, is located below the diagonal $x_1 + x_2 = 1$, i.e., if $\overline{g}_1^{t-1} + \overline{g}_2^{t-1} < 1$, then play B in stage t.

In Exercise 14.8 we present a guided proof of the fact that the set C_3 is indeed approachable by Player 1. ◄

14.4 Connections between approachable and excludable sets

The following claims, whose proofs are left to the reader, state several simple properties that follow from the definitions (Exercise 14.4).

Theorem 14.5 *The following two claims hold:*

1. *If strategy σ_k approaches a set C for player k, then it approaches the closure of C for that player.*
2. *If strategy σ_k excludes a set C for player k, then it excludes the closure of C for that player.*

Let $M \geq 1$ be a bound on the norm of the payoffs in the game

$$\|u(i,j)\| \leq M, \quad \forall i \in \mathcal{I}, \forall j \in \mathcal{J}. \tag{14.20}$$

In particular, $||u(i^t, j^t)|| \leq M$, in every stage t. The triangle inequality implies that

$$||\bar{g}^T|| \leq M, \quad \forall T \in \mathbb{N}. \tag{14.21}$$

In words, the average payoff is located in the ball with radius M around the origin. Therefore, if the average payoff approaches a particular set, it must approach the intersection of that set and the ball of radius M around the origin. Similarly, if a player can guarantee that the distance between the average payoff and a particular set is positive and bounded away from 0, then he can guarantee that the distance between the average payoff and the intersection of that set and the ball of radius M around the origin is positive and bounded away from 0. This insight is expressed in the next theorem, whose proof is left to the reader (Exercise 14.5).

Theorem 14.6 *The following two claims hold:*

1. *A closed set C is approachable by a player if and only if the set $\{x \in C : ||x|| \leq M\}$ is approachable by the player.*
2. *A closed set C is excludable by a player if and only if the set $\{x \in C : ||x|| \leq M\}$ is excludable by the player.*

The following theorem relates to sets containing approachable sets, and to subsets of excludable sets (Exercise 14.6).

Theorem 14.7 *The following two claims hold:*

1. *If strategy σ_k approaches a set C for player k, then it approaches every superset of C for that player.*
2. *If strategy σ_k excludes a set C for player k, then it excludes every subset of C for that player.*

We close this section with the following theorem (Exercise 14.7).

Theorem 14.8 *A set C cannot be both approachable by one player and excludable by the other player.*

Theorem 14.8 expresses the opposing interests of the players in this model, as in the model of two-player zero-sum games. In the next section we will present a geometric condition for the approachability of a set, which we then use to prove that every closed and convex set is either approachable by one player, or excludable by the other player.

14.5) A geometric condition for the approachability of a set

If in stage t Player 1 plays the mixed action p and Player 2 plays the mixed action q, then the expected payoff in that stage is[4]

$$U(p, q) := \sum_{i,j} p_i u(i, j) q_j, \tag{14.22}$$

---

[4] Here, and in the rest of this chapter, a sum $\sum_{i,j}$ will be understood to mean the double sum $\sum_{i \in \mathcal{I}} \sum_{j \in \mathcal{J}}$.

which is a vector in $\mathbb{R}^m$. For every mixed action $p \in \Delta(\mathcal{I})$ of Player 1, define the set

$$R_1(p) := \{U(p,q) : q \in \Delta(\mathcal{J})\} = \left\{ \sum_{i,j} p_i u(i,j) q_j : q \in \Delta(\mathcal{J}) \right\} \subseteq \mathbb{R}^m. \qquad (14.23)$$

Thus, if Player 1 plays the mixed action p, the expected payoff in the current stage is in the set $R_1(p)$. As we will show (Theorem 14.19, page 594), for every $p \in \Delta(\mathcal{I})$, the strategy of Player 1 in which he plays the mixed action p in every stage approaches the set $R_1(p)$. The reason for this is that when Player 1 implements the mixed action p in every stage, the expected payoff in each stage is located in $R_1(p)$, independently of the action implemented by Player 2. Since the set $R_1(p)$ is convex, it follows that for every $T \in \mathbb{N}$ the expectation of the average payoff up to stage T is also in $R_1(p)$. As we will later show this further implies, by way of a variation of the strong law of large numbers, that the average payoff $\bar{g}^T$ approaches $R_1(p)$ as T increases to infinity.

Similarly, for every mixed action $q \in \Delta(\mathcal{J})$ of Player 2, defines

$$R_2(q) := \{U(p,q) : p \in \Delta(\mathcal{I})\} = \left\{ \sum_{i,j} p_i u(i,j) q_j : p \in \Delta(\mathcal{I}) \right\} \subseteq \mathbb{R}^m. \qquad (14.24)$$

Just as for $R_1(p)$, for every $q \in \Delta(\mathcal{J})$, the strategy of Player 2 in which he plays the mixed action q in every stage approaches the set $R_2(q)$ (Theorem 14.19, page 594).

Example 14.9 Consider the game with two-dimensional payoffs in Figure 14.3.

Player 2

		L	R
Player 1	T	(3, 0)	(5, 2)
	B	(0, 1)	(4, 4)

Figure 14.3 The game in Example 14.9

Figure 14.4 depicts the sets $R_1(p)$ and $R_2(q)$ for several values of p and q. For simplicity, when Player 1 has two actions, T and B, we will identify every number p in the interval $[0, 1]$ with the mixed action $[p(T), (1 - p)(B)]$. When Player 2 has two actions, L and R, we will identify every number q in the interval $[0, 1]$ with the mixed action $[q(L), (1 - q)(R)]$.

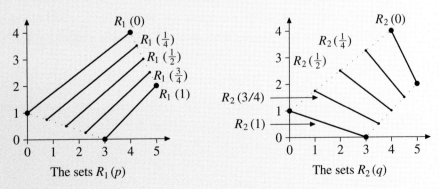

Figure 14.4 The sets $R_1(p)$ and $R_2(q)$ in Example 14.9

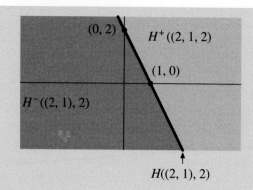

Figure 14.5 The hyperplane $H((2,1),2)$ in $\mathbb{R}^2$, which is the line $2x_1 + x_2 = 2$

Definition 14.10 *A hyperplane $H(\alpha,\beta)$ in $\mathbb{R}^m$ is defined by*

$$H(\alpha,\beta) := \{x \in \mathbb{R}^m : \langle \alpha, x \rangle = \beta\}, \tag{14.25}$$

where $\alpha \in \mathbb{R}^m \setminus \{\vec{0}\}$ and $\beta \in \mathbb{R}$.

Denote

$$H^+(\alpha,\beta) = \{x \in \mathbb{R}^m : \langle x, \alpha \rangle \geq \beta\} \tag{14.26}$$

and

$$H^-(\alpha,\beta) = \{x \in \mathbb{R}^m : \langle x, \alpha \rangle \leq \beta\}. \tag{14.27}$$

$H^+(\alpha,\beta)$ and $H^-(\alpha,\beta)$ are the *half-spaces* defined by the hyperplane $H(\alpha,\beta)$. Note that $H^+(\alpha,\beta) \cap H^-(\alpha,\beta) = H(\alpha,\beta)$. Figure 14.5 depicts the hyperplane $H((2,1),2)$ in $\mathbb{R}^2$, and the two corresponding half-spaces.

By definition (see Corollary 14.25),

$$H^+(\alpha,\beta) = H^-(-\alpha,-\beta). \tag{14.28}$$

For every $x, y \in \mathbb{R}^m$, the hyperplane $H(x - y, \langle x - y, y \rangle)$ is the hyperplane passing through the point y, and perpendicular to the line passing through x and y (Exercise 24.35 on page 1000). For example, in the case $m = 2$ described in Figure 14.6, the slope of the line passing through x and y is $\frac{y_2 - x_2}{y_1 - x_1}$. We now show that the slope of the hyperplane $H(x - y, \langle x - y, y \rangle)$, which in this case is a line, is $-\frac{y_1 - x_1}{y_2 - x_2}$, and therefore this line is perpendicular to the line passing through x and y. Choose a point $z = (z_1, z_2) \neq y$ on the hyperplane $H(x - y, \langle x - y, y \rangle)$. Then z satisfies

$$z_1(x_1 - y_1) + z_2(x_2 - y_2) = \langle x - y, y \rangle = (x_1 - y_1)y_1 + (x_2 - y_2)y_2. \tag{14.29}$$

This further implies that the slope of the line connecting z and y, which is the hyperplane H, is

$$\frac{z_2 - y_2}{z_1 - y_1} = -\frac{x_1 - y_1}{x_2 - y_2}, \tag{14.30}$$

which is what we needed to show.

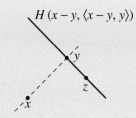

Figure 14.6 The hyperplane $H(y - x, \langle y - x, y \rangle)$

Definition 14.11 *Let $C \subseteq \mathbb{R}^m$ be a set, and let $x \notin C$ be a point in $\mathbb{R}^m$. A hyperplane $H(\alpha, \beta)$ is said to* separate *x from C if:*

1. $x \in H^+(\alpha, \beta) \setminus H(\alpha, \beta)$ *and* $C \subseteq H^-(\alpha, \beta)$, *or*
2. $x \in H^-(\alpha, \beta) \setminus H(\alpha, \beta)$ *and* $C \subseteq H^+(\alpha, \beta)$.

In words, a hyperplane $H(\alpha, \beta)$ separates x from C if (i) $\langle x, \alpha \rangle > \beta$ and $\langle y, \alpha \rangle \leq \beta$ for all $y \in C$, or (ii) $\langle x, \alpha \rangle < \beta$ and $\langle y, \alpha \rangle \geq \beta$ for all $y \in C$.

As in Chapter 13, denote by F the convex hull of all possible one-stage payoffs:

$$F = \operatorname{conv}\{u(i,j), (i,j) \in \mathcal{I} \times \mathcal{J}\}. \tag{14.31}$$

Note that the average payoff $\overline{g}^t$, as a weighted average of vectors in the convex set $\{u(i,j), (i,j) \in \mathcal{I} \times \mathcal{J}\}$, is necessarily in the set F.

As previously noted, it will follow that the set $R_1(p)$ will be proved to be approachable by Player 1, for every $p \in \Delta(\mathcal{I})$. By Theorem 14.7, any half-space containing at least one of the sets $(R_1(p))_{p \in \Delta(\mathcal{I})}$ is also approachable by Player 1. This observation leads to the concept of a "B-set." A set C is a B-set for Player 1 if each half-space in a certain collection of half-spaces contains a set $R_1(p)$ for some $p \in \Delta(\mathcal{I})$.

Definition 14.12 *A closed set $C \subseteq \mathbb{R}^m$ is a B-set for Player 1 if for every point $x \in F \setminus C$ there exist a point $y = y(x, C) \in C$ and a mixed action $p = p(x, C) \in \Delta(\mathcal{I})$ of Player 1 satisfying:*

1. *y is a point in C that is closest to x:*

$$d(x, y) = d(x, C). \tag{14.32}$$

2. *The hyperplane $H(y - x, \langle y - x, y \rangle)$ separates x from $R_1(p)$:*

$$R_1(p) \subseteq H^+(y - x, \langle y - x, y \rangle), \tag{14.33}$$

$$x \in H^-(y - x, \langle y - x, y \rangle) \setminus H(y - x, \langle y - x, y \rangle). \tag{14.34}$$

Remark 14.13 *The hyperplane $H(y-x, \langle y-x, y \rangle)$ satisfies the following three properties (Exercise 24.35 on page 1000):*

1. *$y \in H(y - x, \langle y - x, y \rangle)$.*
2. *This hyperplane is perpendicular to $y - x$, that is, $\langle y - x, z - y \rangle = 0$ for all $z \in H(y - x, \langle y - x, y \rangle)$.*

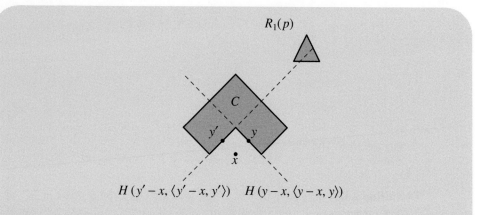

Figure 14.7 The hyperplane $H(y - x, \langle y - x, y \rangle)$ separates x from $R_1(p)$

3. y *is the point in* $H(y - x, \langle y - x, y \rangle)$ *that is closest to* x, *that is*, $\langle z - x, z - x \rangle > \langle y - x, y - x \rangle$ *for all* $z \in H(y - x, \langle y - x, y \rangle)$, $z \neq y$.

Similarly, for a given hyperplane H *and a point* $x \notin H$, *if* $y \in H$ *is the point in* H *that is closest to* x, *then* $H = H(y - x, \langle y - x, y \rangle)$ *(Exercise 24.36 on page 1000).*   ◆

Note that the condition in Definition 14.12 requires that for every x there exist a point y and a mixed action p of Player 1 satisfying (a) and (b); for a given mixed action p, it is not the case that every point y satisfying (a) also satisfies (b). In Figure 4.7, there are two points y, y' in C that are the closest points to x. The hyperplane $H(y - x, \langle y - x, y \rangle)$, containing y, separates x from $R_1(p)$. In contrast, the hyperplane $H(y' - x, \langle y' - x, y' \rangle)$ does not separate x from $R_1(p)$.

The definition of a B-set for Player 2 is analogous to Definition 14.12: a set C is a B-set for Player 2 if for each point $x \in F \backslash C$ there exists a mixed action $q \in \Delta(\mathcal{J})$ of Player 2 such that the hyperplane $H(y - x, \langle y - x, y \rangle)$ separates x from $R_2(q)$, where $y \in C$ is a point in C that is closest to x. The following theorem presents a geometric condition that guarantees the approachability of a set by a particular player.

Theorem 14.14 (Blackwell [1956]) *If a set* C *is a B-set for player* k, *then it is approachable by player* k.

The converse may not hold: there are sets approachable by a player k that are not B-sets for player k (Exercise 14.15).

The intuition behind the proof (for Player 1) is depicted in Figure 14.8. Consider the strategy of Player 1 under which he plays the mixed action $p(\overline{g}^t, C)$ in every stage t. The hyperplane identified by the definition of a B-set is the hyperplane tangent to C at the point $y = y(\overline{g}^t, C)$ in C that is closest to x. Suppose that $\overline{g}^t$, the average payoff up to stage t is outside C, and let $p = p(\overline{g}^t, C)$ be the mixed action of Player 1, respectively, satisfying conditions (1) and (2) in Definition 14.12, for $x = \overline{g}^t$. If Player 1 plays the mixed action p, the expected payoff in stage $t + 1$, denoted in the figure by f^{t+1}, is in $R_1(p)$, and therefore the expected value of $\overline{g}^{t+1}$ is located on the line connecting $\overline{g}^t$ with f^{t+1}. We will show that the expected distance $d(\overline{g}^{t+1}, C)$ is smaller than $d(\overline{g}^t, C)$; i.e.,

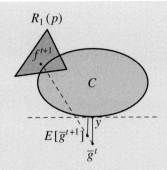

Figure 14.8 The idea behind the proof of Theorem 14.14

the expected distance between $\bar{g}^{t+1}$ and C is smaller than the distance between $\bar{g}^t$ and C. Finally, we will show that if the expected distance to C goes to 0, the distance itself also goes to 0, with probability 1.

We now turn to the formal proof of the theorem.

Proof: We will prove the theorem for Player 1. The proof for Player 2 is similar. From Theorem 14.6 (page 584) we may assume without loss of generality that for every $y \in C$,

$$||y|| \leq M, \tag{14.35}$$

and, in particular, the absolute value of every coordinate of y is less than or equal to M. We will first define a strategy σ_1^* for Player 1, and then prove that it guarantees that the average payoff approaches the set C. In the first stage, the strategy σ_1^* chooses any action. For each $t \geq 1$ the strategy σ_1^* instructs Player 1 to play as follows in stage $t + 1$:

- If $\bar{g}^t \in C$, the definition of σ_1^* is immaterial (play any action).
- If $\bar{g}^t \notin C$, the strategy σ_1^* instructs the player to choose the mixed action $p(\bar{g}^t, C)$ (as defined in Definition 14.12).

Denote by $d^t = d(\bar{g}^t, C)$ the distance between the average payoff up to stage t and the set C. We wish to show that for every strategy σ_2 of Player 2, the distance d^t converges to zero, with probability 1, and that the rate of convergence can be bounded, independently of the strategy of Player 2.

Lemma 14.15 *For every strategy σ_2 of Player 2, and for every $t \in \mathbb{N}$,*

$$\mathbf{E}_{\sigma_1^*,\sigma_2}\left[(d^t)^2\right] \leq \frac{4M^2}{t}. \tag{14.36}$$

Proof: We will prove the claim by induction on t. Since the payoffs are bounded by M, one has $d^t = d(\bar{g}^t, C) \leq 2M$ for all $t \in \mathbb{N}$: the distance between the average payoff and the set C is not greater than twice the maximal payoff. Since $M \geq 1$, Equation (14.36) holds, for $t = 1$.

Assume by induction that Equation (14.36) holds for t; we will prove that it holds for $t + 1$. The average payoff up to stage $t + 1$ is a weighted average (i) of the average payoff up to stage t, and (ii) of the payoff in stage $t + 1$:

$$\bar{g}^{t+1} = \frac{1}{t+1} \sum_{l=1}^{t+1} g^l = \frac{t}{t+1} \times \frac{1}{t} \sum_{l=1}^{t} g^l + \frac{1}{t+1} g^{t+1} = \frac{t}{t+1} \bar{g}^t + \frac{1}{t+1} g^{t+1}. \quad (14.37)$$

We wish to show that the expected value of d^{t+1}, the distance between $\bar{g}^{t+1}$ and C, shrinks. If $\bar{g}^t \in C$, then $y^t = \bar{g}^t$. If $\bar{g}^t \notin C$, denote by p^t the mixed action that Player 1 plays in stage $t+1$. Since $y^t \in C$, one has $d(\bar{g}^{t+1}, C) \leq d(\bar{g}^{t+1}, y^t)$, leading to

$$(d^{t+1})^2 = (d(\bar{g}^{t+1}, C))^2 \leq (d(\bar{g}^{t+1}, y^t))^2 = ||y^t - \bar{g}^{t+1}||^2. \quad (14.38)$$

By Equation (14.37), the right-hand side of Equation (14.38) is

$$\left|\left| \frac{t}{t+1}(y^t - \bar{g}^t) + \frac{1}{t+1}(y^t - g^{t+1}) \right|\right|^2. \quad (14.39)$$

Since $d^t = ||y^t - \bar{g}^t||$ and $||y^t - g^{t+1}|| \leq 2M$, using Equations (14.38) and (14.39), this implies that

$$(d^{t+1})^2 \leq \left(\frac{t}{t+1} \right)^2 (d^t)^2 + \frac{4M^2}{(t+1)^2} + \frac{2t}{(t+1)^2} \langle y^t - g^{t+1}, y^t - \bar{g}^t \rangle. \quad (14.40)$$

Taking conditional expectation in both sides of Equation (14.40), conditioned on the history h^t up to stage t yields

$$\mathbf{E}_{\sigma_1^*, \sigma_2}[(d^{t+1})^2 \mid h^t]$$

$$\leq \left(\frac{t}{t+1} \right)^2 \mathbf{E}_{\sigma_1^*, \sigma_2}[(d^t)^2 \mid h^t] + \frac{4M^2}{(t+1)^2} + \frac{2t}{(t+1)^2} \mathbf{E}_{\sigma_1^*, \sigma_2}[\langle y^t - g^{t+1}, y^t - \bar{g}^t \rangle \mid h^t].$$
$$(14.41)$$

We now show that the third element on the right-hand side of Equation (14.41) is nonpositive. If $\bar{g}^t \in C$, then $y^t = \bar{g}^t$, in which case the third element equals 0. If $\bar{g}^t \notin C$, then, because C is a B-set for Player 1, it follows from the definition of p^t that $R_1(p^t) \subset H^+(y^t - \bar{g}^t, \langle y^t - \bar{g}^t, y^t \rangle)$. Since in stage $t+1$, Player 1 plays mixed action p^t, the expected payoff in stage $t+1$, which is $\mathbf{E}_{\sigma_1^*, \sigma_2}[g^{t+1} \mid h^t]$, is located in $R_1(p^t)$, and therefore in $H^+(y^t - \bar{g}^t, \langle y^t - \bar{g}^t, y^t \rangle)$. It follows that

$$\langle y^t - \bar{g}^t, \mathbf{E}_{\sigma_1^*, \sigma_2}[g^{t+1} \mid h^t] \rangle \geq \langle y^t - \bar{g}^t, y^t \rangle. \quad (14.42)$$

Since the inner product is symmetric and bilinear, and since the average payoff $\bar{g}^t$ and the point y^t are determined given the history h^t, we get

$$\mathbf{E}_{\sigma_1^*, \sigma_2}[\langle y^t - g^{t+1}, y^t - \bar{g}^t \rangle \mid h^t]$$

$$= \langle y^t - \mathbf{E}_{\sigma_1^*, \sigma_2}[g^{t+1} \mid h^t], y^t - \bar{g}^t \rangle$$

$$= \langle y^t - \mathbf{E}_{\sigma_1^*, \sigma_2}[g^{t+1} \mid h^t], y^t \rangle - \langle y^t - \mathbf{E}_{\sigma_1^*, \sigma_2}[g^{t+1} \mid h^t], \bar{g}^t \rangle \leq 0. \quad (14.43)$$

Since the third element on the right-hand side of Equation (14.41) is nonpositive, we get

$$\mathbf{E}_{\sigma_1^*,\sigma_2}[(d^{t+1})^2 \mid h^t] \le \left(\frac{t}{t+1}\right)^2 \mathbf{E}_{\sigma_1^*,\sigma_2}[(d^t)^2] + \frac{4M^2}{(t+1)^2}. \tag{14.44}$$

Taking the expectation over h^t of the conditional expectation on the left-hand side yields

$$\mathbf{E}_{\sigma_1^*,\sigma_2}[(d^{t+1})^2] = \mathbf{E}_{\sigma_1^*,\sigma_2}\left[\mathbf{E}_{\sigma_1^*,\sigma_2}[(d^{t+1})^2 \mid h^t]\right] \le \left(\frac{t}{t+1}\right)^2 \mathbf{E}_{\sigma_1^*,\sigma_2}[(d^t)^2] + \frac{4M^2}{(t+1)^2}. \tag{14.45}$$

By the inductive hypothesis, $\mathbf{E}_{\sigma_1^*,\sigma_2}[(d^t)^2] \le \frac{4M^2}{t}$, and therefore

$$\mathbf{E}_{\sigma_1^*,\sigma_2}[(d^{t+1})^2] \le \left(\frac{t}{t+1}\right)^2 \frac{4M^2}{t} + \frac{4M^2}{(t+1)^2} = \frac{4M^2}{t+1}, \tag{14.46}$$

which is what we wanted to show. $\square$

Recall that Markov's inequality states that for every nonnegative random variable X, and for every $c > 0$,

$$\mathbf{P}(X \ge c) \le \frac{\mathbf{E}(X)}{c}. \tag{14.47}$$

By Lemma 14.15, and the Markov inequality (with $c = \frac{2M}{\sqrt{t}}$), we deduce that the probability that d^t is large is small (for large t):

Corollary 14.16 *For every strategy σ_2 of Player 2,*

$$\mathbf{P}_{\sigma_1^*,\sigma_2}\left((d^t)^2 \ge \frac{2M}{\sqrt{t}}\right) \le \frac{2M}{\sqrt{t}}, \tag{14.48}$$

and therefore

$$\mathbf{P}_{\sigma_1^*,\sigma_2}\left(d^t \ge \frac{\sqrt{2M}}{t^{1/4}}\right) \le \frac{2M}{\sqrt{t}}. \tag{14.49}$$

This corollary relates to the distance between $\bar{g}^t$ and the set C in stage t. We are interested in showing that this distance is small for large t, i.e., that there exists T sufficiently large such that from stage T onwards, the distance d^t remains small. In other words, while in Lemma 14.15 we show that the expected value of the random variables $(d^t)_{t \in \mathbb{N}}$ converges to 0, and therefore the sequence $(d^t)_{t \in \mathbb{N}}$ converges in probability to 0, we now wish to show that convergence occurs almost surely. Although this can be proved using the strong law of large numbers for uncorrelated random variables, we will present a direct proof of convergence, without appealing to the law of large numbers.

Lemma 14.17 *For every $\varepsilon > 0$, there exists a number T sufficiently large such that for every strategy σ_2 of Player 2,*

$$\mathbf{P}_{\sigma_1^*,\sigma_2}(d^t < \varepsilon, \ \forall t \ge T) > 1 - \varepsilon. \tag{14.50}$$

In particular, this implies that the set C is approachable by Player 1. Therefore, proving Lemma 14.17 will complete the proof of Theorem 14.14.

Proof: Let $\varepsilon > 0$. By[5] Equation (14.49), for $t = l^3$,

$$\mathbf{P}_{\sigma_1^*,\sigma_2}\left(d^{l^3} \geq \frac{\sqrt{2M}}{l^{3/4}}\right) \leq \frac{2M}{l^{3/2}}. \tag{14.51}$$

Let $L \in \mathbb{N}$. Summing Equation (14.51) over $l \geq L$ yields

$$\mathbf{P}_{\sigma_1^*,\sigma_2}\left(d^{l^3} \geq \frac{\sqrt{2M}}{l^{3/4}} \text{ for some } l \geq L\right) \leq 2M \sum_{l=L}^{\infty} \frac{1}{l^{3/2}}. \tag{14.52}$$

Consider the complement of the event on the left-hand side in Equation (14.52):

$$\mathbf{P}_{\sigma_1^*,\sigma_2}\left(d^{l^3} < \frac{\sqrt{2M}}{l^{3/4}}, \quad \forall l \geq L\right) \geq 1 - 2M \sum_{l=L}^{\infty} \frac{1}{l^{3/2}}. \tag{14.53}$$

Since the series $\sum_{l=1}^{\infty} \frac{1}{l^{3/2}}$ converges, there exists L_0 sufficiently large for $1 - 2M \sum_{l=L_0}^{\infty} \frac{1}{l^{3/2}} \geq 1 - \varepsilon$. For the remainder of the proof, we will also require that $L_0 \geq 7$.

We next prove the following lemma.

Lemma 14.18 *If* $d^{l^3} < \frac{\sqrt{2M}}{l^{3/4}}$ *for every* $l \geq L_0$, *then* $d^t < \frac{19M\sqrt{m}}{t^{1/4}}$ *for every* $t \geq (L_0)^3$.

We will first show that Lemma 14.17 follows from Lemma 14.18. From Lemma 14.18, and Equation (14.53), one has

$$\mathbf{P}_{\sigma_1^*,\sigma_2}\left(d^t < \frac{19M\sqrt{m}}{t^{1/4}}, \quad \forall t \geq (L_0)^3\right) \geq 1 - \varepsilon, \tag{14.54}$$

from which Lemma 14.17 follows (what is the T that should be used in Lemma 14.17?).

We next turn to the proof of Lemma 14.18. Let $t \geq (L_0)^3$, and let $l \geq L_0$ be the only integer satisfying

$$l^3 \leq t < (l+1)^3. \tag{14.55}$$

We start by proving two inequalities that will be needed later.

Fact 1: $\frac{1}{l^{3/4}} \leq \frac{2}{t^{1/4}}$ for all $l \geq L_0$.

Since $l \geq 7$, one has $\left(\frac{l+1}{l}\right)^3 \leq \left(\frac{8}{7}\right)^3 < 2$, so it follows from Equation (14.55) that $\frac{t}{2} < \frac{(l+1)^3}{2} < l^3$. Therefore,

$$\frac{1}{l^{3/4}} = \frac{1}{(l^3)^{1/4}} < \frac{1}{\left(\frac{t}{2}\right)^{1/4}} < \frac{2}{t^{1/4}}. \tag{14.56}$$

---

5 As will shortly be clear, the reason for setting $t = l^3$ is to ensure that the bound on the right-hand side of Equation (14.51) is a convergent series.

Fact 2: $\frac{t-l^3}{t} \leq \frac{8}{t^{1/3}}$.

Based on the definition of l (Equation (14.55)),

$$\frac{t-l^3}{t} \leq \frac{(l+1)^3 - l^3}{l^3} = \frac{3l^2 + 3l + 1}{l^3} \leq \frac{7l^2}{l^3} = \frac{7}{l} \leq \frac{8}{l+1} < \frac{8}{t^{1/3}}, \tag{14.57}$$

where the inequality $\frac{7}{l} \leq \frac{8}{l+1}$ holds because $l \geq 7$.

Finally, the average payoff up to stage t satisfies

$$\bar{g}^t = \frac{1}{t}\sum_{n=1}^{t} g^n = \frac{1}{t}\sum_{n=1}^{l^3} g^n + \frac{1}{t}\sum_{n=l^3+1}^{t} g^n = \frac{l^3}{t}\bar{g}^{l^3} + \frac{1}{t}\sum_{n=l^3+1}^{t} g^n. \tag{14.58}$$

Since $d(x+y, x+z) = d(y,z)$ (Equation (14.10) on page 580), one has

$$d(\bar{g}^t, \bar{g}^{l^3}) = d\left(\frac{l^3}{t}\bar{g}^{l^3} + \frac{1}{t}\sum_{n=l^3+1}^{t} g^n, \bar{g}^{l^3}\right) = d\left(\frac{1}{t}\sum_{n=l^3+1}^{t} g^n, \frac{t-l^3}{t}\bar{g}^{l^3}\right)$$

$$= d\left(\frac{1}{t}\sum_{n=l^3+1}^{t} g^n, \frac{1}{t}\sum_{n=l^3+1}^{t} \bar{g}^{l^3}\right). \tag{14.59}$$

Using properties of the distance relation (Equations (14.11)–(14.13) on page 580) one has

$$d(\bar{g}^t, \bar{g}^{l^3}) \leq \frac{1}{t}\sum_{n=l^3+1}^{t} d(g^n, \bar{g}^{l^3}) \leq 2M\sqrt{m}\,\frac{t-l^3}{t}. \tag{14.60}$$

Therefore,

$$d^t = d(\bar{g}^t, C) \tag{14.61}$$

$$\leq d(\bar{g}^t, \bar{g}^{l^3}) + d(\bar{g}^{l^3}, C) \tag{14.62}$$

$$\leq 2M\sqrt{m}\,\frac{t-l^3}{t} + d^{l^3} \tag{14.63}$$

$$\leq 2M\sqrt{m}\,\frac{t-l^3}{t} + \frac{\sqrt{2M}}{l^{3/4}} \tag{14.64}$$

$$\leq \frac{16M\sqrt{m}}{t^{1/3}} + \frac{2\sqrt{2M}}{t^{1/4}} \leq \frac{19M\sqrt{m}}{t^{1/4}}. \tag{14.65}$$

Equation (14.62) follows from the triangle inequality (Equation (14.7)), Equation (14.63) follows from (14.60), Equation (14.64) follows from the assumption that $d^{l^3} \leq \frac{\sqrt{2M}}{l^{3/4}}$, and Equation (14.65) follows from Facts 1 and 2. This completes the proof of Lemma 14.18, and with it the proof of Lemma 14.17. □

Conclusion of the proof of Blackwell's Theorem (Theorem 14.14): Lemma 14.17 implies that the strategy σ_1^* guarantees with probability 1 that the distance between the average payoff $\bar{g}^t$ and the set C converges to 0 with probability 1, and therefore C is an approachable set by Player 1, which is what we wanted to prove. □

14.6 Characterizations of convex approachable sets

In the various applications making use of approachable sets, the target set is convex (we will consider two such applications later in this chapter). In this section, we will show that convex approachable sets have several simple characterizations.

Since for every mixed action p of Player 1, the set $R_1(p)$ is convex, there is a unique point $y \in R_1(p)$ that is closest to x. By the Separating Hyperplane Theorem (Theorem 24.39 on page 990), for every $x \in F \backslash R_1(p)$, the hyperplane $H(x - y, \langle x - y, y \rangle)$ separates x from $R_1(p)$, where y is the point in $R_1(p)$ closest to x. It follows that $R_1(p)$ is a B-set for Player 1, and Blackwell's Theorem (Theorem 14.14 on page 588) implies that it is an approachable set by Player 1. Moreover, the strategy under which Player 1 plays the mixed action p in every stage approaches $R_1(p)$. A similar result holds for sets $R_2(q)$ and Player 2. This leads to the following theorem:

Theorem 14.19 *For every $p \in \Delta(\mathcal{I})$, the strategy of Player 1 in which he plays the mixed action p in every stage approaches the set $R_1(p)$. For every $q \in \Delta(\mathcal{J})$, the strategy of Player 2 in which he plays the mixed action q in every stage approaches the set $R_2(q)$.*

Theorem 14.19 has the following corollary.

Corollary 14.20 *Let C be a closed set. If there exists $p \in \Delta(\mathcal{I})$ such that $C \cap R_1(p) = \emptyset$, then the set C is excludable by Player 1. If there exists $q \in \Delta(\mathcal{J})$ such that $C \cap R_2(q) = \emptyset$, then the set C is excludable by Player 2.*

The following theorem is a result in the theory of convex sets.

Theorem 14.21 *Let H^+ be a half-space. If for every $p \in \Delta(\mathcal{I})$ the set $R_1(p)$ is not contained in H^+, then there exists $q \in \Delta(\mathcal{J})$ such that $R_2(q) \cap H^+ = \emptyset$.*

The proof we present here applies von Neumann's Minmax Theorem (Theorem 5.11 on page 150).

Proof: Let $H^+ = H^+(\alpha, \beta) = \{x \in \mathbb{R}^m : \langle \alpha, x \rangle \geq \beta\}$. Define a two-player zero-sum game in strategic form G with the set of players $\{1, 2\}$, such that the set of pure strategies of Player 1 is $\mathcal{I}$, the set of pure strategies of Player 2 is $\mathcal{J}$, and the payoff function (for Player 1) is given by $w(i, j) = \langle \alpha, u(i, j) \rangle$. Denote by $W(p, q)$ the multilinear extension of w:

$$W(p, q) = \sum_{i=1}^{I} \sum_{j=1}^{J} p_i q_j w(i, j) = \langle \alpha, U(p, q) \rangle, \qquad (14.66)$$

where U is the bilinear extension of u. By von Neumann's Theorem (Theorem 5.11 on page 150) this game has a value v. By assumption, for every mixed strategy $p \in \Delta(\mathcal{I})$ of Player 1 in the game G, there exists a mixed strategy $q \in \Delta(\mathcal{J})$ of Player 2 in G such that $U(p, q) \notin H^+$, and therefore $W(p, q)$, the payoff in G, satisfies

$$W(p, q) = \langle \alpha, U(p, q) \rangle < \beta. \qquad (14.67)$$

It follows that the value v of G is less than β. Let q^* be an optimal strategy of Player 2 in G. Then $W(p, q^*) \leq v < \beta$ for every $p \in \Delta(\mathcal{I})$. It follows that $R_2(q^*) \cap H^+ = \emptyset$, as required. $\qquad \square$

The next theorem presents conditions guaranteeing the approachability of a half-space.

Theorem 14.22 *Let H^+ be a half-space, and let $p^* \in \Delta(\mathcal{I})$ be a mixed action of Player 1. The following conditions are equivalent:*

(a) $R_1(p^*) \subseteq H^+$.

(b) H^+ *is a B-set for Player 1, and for every* $x \in F\backslash H^+$, *the mixed action* $p(x, H) = p^*$ *satisfies condition (2) of Definition 14.12 (page 587).*

(c) *The strategy of Player 1 that plays the mixed action* p^* *in every stage approaches* H^+ *for Player 1.*

Proof: Let $H^+ = H^+(\alpha, \beta) = \{x \in \mathbb{R}^m : \langle \alpha, x \rangle \geq \beta\}$. We start by proving that (a) implies (b).[6] Let $x \in F\backslash H^+$, and let $y \in H^+$ be the point in H^+ closest to x. We will show that conditions (1) and (2) in Definition 14.12 (page 587) hold with $p(x, H^+) = p^*$. Since x is a point in $F\backslash H^+$, it will follow that H^+ is a B-set for Player 1. Since $x \notin H^+(\alpha, \beta)$, the hyperplane $H(\alpha, \beta)$ separates x and $H^+(\alpha, \beta)$, and it contains the point y. It follows (see Remark 14.13) that $H(\alpha, \beta) = H(y - x, \langle y - x, y \rangle)$. Since condition (a) holds, $R_1(p^*) \subseteq H^+(\alpha, \beta) = H^+(y - x, \langle y - x, y \rangle)$. Because this is true for all $x \in F\backslash H^+$, we deduce that H^+ is a B-set for Player 1.

We next prove that (b) implies (c). Suppose, then, that condition (b) holds. By Blackwell's Theorem (Theorem 14.14 on page 588), H^+ is an approachable set. The strategy that we constructed in the proof of Blackwell's Theorem, under which Player 1 guarantees that the average payoff approaches H^+, is the strategy in which in every stage t he plays the mixed action $p(\overline{g}_{t-1}, H^+)$, where $\overline{g}_{t-1}$ is the average payoff up to stage t. Since $p(x, H) = p^*$ for every $x \in F\backslash H^+$, the strategy σ^* approaches H^+, and therefore condition (c) holds.

Finally, we prove that (c) implies (a). Let $q \in \Delta(\mathcal{J})$ be a mixed action of Player 2, and let τ be the strategy that plays the mixed action q in every stage. By the strong law of large numbers, the average payoffs under (σ^*, τ) converge to $U(p^*, q)$ with probability 1. Since σ^* approaches H^+, it follows that $U(p^*, q) \in H^+$. Since $R_1(p^*) = \{U(p^*, q) : q \in \Delta(\mathcal{J})\}$, and since $U(p^*, q) \in H^+$ for every $q \in \Delta(J)$, we deduce that $R_1(p^*) \subseteq H^+$, i.e., condition (a) holds. □

A *stationary strategy* of player k is a strategy that plays the same mixed action in every stage, regardless of past choices of the two players.

Corollary 14.23 *A half-space H^+ is approachable by a player if and only if the player has a stationary strategy that approaches the set.*

Proof: We prove the result for Player 1. Clearly, if Player 1 has a stationary strategy that approaches H^+, then H^+ is approachable by him. We need to prove, therefore, that if H^+ is approachable by Player 1, then Player 1 has a stationary strategy that approaches H^+. Suppose, by contradiction, that Player 1 has no stationary strategy approaching H^+. By Theorem 14.22, $R_1(p) \nsubseteq H^+$ for every $p \in \Delta(\mathcal{I})$. By Theorem 14.21, there exists a $q \in \Delta(\mathcal{J})$ such that $R_2(q) \cap H = \emptyset$. By Corollary 14.20, H is excludable by

---

6 Another way to prove this is as follows: as previously stated, the set $R_1(p^*)$ is convex, and a B-set for Player 1. The half-space H^+ is a convex set containing $R_1(p^*)$, and therefore it is also a B-set (Exercise 14.11). Note that by Theorem 14.19, (a) implies (c).

Player 2. Since a set cannot be both approachable by Player 1 and excludable by Player 2 (Theorem 14.8 on page 584), we deduce that H^+ is not approachable by Player 1, contradicting the assumption. This contradiction implies that Player 1 has a stationary strategy guaranteeing that the average payoff approaches H^+, which is what we wanted to show. $\qquad\square$

The next theorem is, in a sense, a generalization of Theorem 14.22 to convex sets.

Theorem 14.24 *For every closed and convex set $C \subseteq \mathbb{R}^m$, the following conditions are equivalent:*

(a) For every half-space H^+ containing C, there exists $p \in \Delta(\mathcal{I})$ satisfying $R_1(p) \subseteq H^+$.
(b) The set C is a B-set for Player 1.
(c) The set C is approachable by Player 1.

Proof: We start by proving that (a) implies (b). Let $x \in F \backslash C$. Since C is closed and convex, there exists a unique point y in C closest to x. The Separating Hyperplane Theorem (Theorem 24.39 on page 990), implies that the hyperplane $H^+ := H^+(y - x, \langle y - x, y \rangle)$ separates x from C. In particular, the half-space H^+ contains C, and by (a), there exists $p \in \Delta(\mathcal{I})$ such that $R_1(p) \subseteq H^+$. We deduce from this that for every $x \in F \backslash C$ there exists $p \in \Delta(\mathcal{I})$ such that the hyperplane $H(y-x, \langle y-x, y \rangle)$ separates x from $R_1(p)$, and therefore C is a B-set for Player 1.

By Blackwell's Theorem (Theorem 14.14 on page 588), (b) implies (c).

Finally, we prove that (c) implies (a). Since C is approachable by Player 1, and since every set containing an approachable set is also approachable (Theorem 14.7 on page 584), it follows that every half-space H^+ containing C is approachable by Player 1. Corollary 14.23, and Theorem 14.22, imply that for every half-space H^+ containing C there exists $p \in \Delta(\mathcal{I})$ satisfying $R_1(p) \subseteq H^+$, and therefore condition (a) holds. $\qquad\square$

By Theorem 14.8 (page 584), a set approachable by one player is not excludable by the other player. For convex sets, the converse statement also obtains.

Theorem 14.25 *A closed and convex set that is not approachable by one player is excludable by the other player.*

Proof: Let C be a convex and closed set that is not approachable by one of the players, say Player 1. By Theorem 14.24 (the negation of condition (a)), there exists a half-space H^+ containing C, such that for every $p \in \Delta(\mathcal{I})$, one has $R_1(p) \nsubseteq H^+$. By Theorem 14.21, there exists $q \in \Delta(\mathcal{J})$ such that $R_2(q) \cap H^+ = \emptyset$. Since H^+ contains C, it follows in particular that $R_2(q) \cap C = \emptyset$. By Corollary 14.20, it follows that C is excludable by Player 2. $\qquad\square$

Theorem 14.25 holds only for convex sets. Example 14.4 below presents a set that is not convex, and is neither approachable by Player 1, nor excludable by Player 2.

For every vector $\alpha \in \mathbb{R}^m$, let G_α be the two-player zero-sum game (with real-valued payoffs) in which Player 1's set of pure strategies is $\mathcal{I}$, Player 2's set of pure strategies is $\mathcal{J}$, and the payoff function is

$$U[\alpha]_{i,j} = \langle \alpha, u(i,j) \rangle. \tag{14.68}$$

In words, using the linear transformation given by the vector α, we convert the vector payoff into a real-valued payoff. Denote the value of the game G_α by $\text{val}(G_\alpha)$.

The following corollary presents a relatively simple criterion for checking whether a convex and compact set is approachable by Player 1.

Corollary 14.26 *A compact and convex set C is approachable by Player 1 if and only if*

$$\text{val}(G_\alpha) \geq \min_{x \in C}\langle \alpha, x \rangle, \quad \forall \alpha \in \mathbb{R}^m. \tag{14.69}$$

Proof: We first prove that there exists a mixed action $p \in \Delta(\mathcal{I})$ such that $R_1(p) \subseteq H^+(\alpha, \beta)$ if and only if $\text{val}(G_\alpha) \geq \beta$. The property $R_1(p) \subseteq H^+(\alpha, \beta)$ holds if and only if $U(p, q) \in H^+(\alpha, \beta)$ for all $q \in \Delta(\mathcal{J})$, that is, if and only if $U_\alpha(p, q) = \langle \alpha, U(p, q) \rangle \geq \beta$. In other words, the mixed action p guarantees that the payoff of the game G_α is at least β. The existence of such a mixed action p is therefore equivalent to $\text{val}(G_\alpha) \geq \beta$.

For each $\alpha \in \mathbb{R}^m$ define

$$\beta_\alpha := \min_{x \in C}\langle \alpha, x \rangle. \tag{14.70}$$

The minimum is attained because C is a compact set. It follows by definition that $C \subseteq H^+(\alpha, \beta_\alpha)$ for all $\alpha \in \mathbb{R}^m$. In addition, $C \subseteq H^+(\alpha, \beta)$ if and only if $\beta \leq \beta_\alpha$.

In conclusion, C is an approachable set for Player 1 if and only if for every half-space $H^+(\alpha, \beta)$ containing it there exists $p \in \Delta(\mathcal{I})$ satisfying $R_1(p) \subseteq H^+(\alpha, \beta)$ (Theorem 14.24). Since $C \subseteq H^+(\alpha, \beta)$ if and only if $\beta \leq \beta_\alpha$, this holds if and only if for all $\alpha \in \mathbb{R}^m$ there exists $p \in \Delta(\mathcal{I})$ satisfying $R_1(p) \subseteq H^+(\alpha, \beta)$ for all $\beta \leq \beta_\alpha$. Since $H^+(\alpha, \beta) \supseteq H^+(\alpha, \beta_\alpha)$ when $\beta \leq \beta_\alpha$, this holds if and only if for all $\alpha \in \mathbb{R}^m$ there exists $p \in \Delta(\mathcal{I})$ satisfying $R_1(p) \subseteq H^+(\alpha, \beta_\alpha)$, and this, as we have shown, is equivalent to $\text{val}(G_\alpha) \geq \beta_\alpha = \min_{x \in C}\langle \alpha, x \rangle$. □

Remark 14.27 *The proof of Corollary 14.26 relies on the compactness of the set C to ensure that the minimum on the right-hand side of Equation (14.69) is attained. If the set C is not compact, yet the minimum on the right-hand side of Equation (14.69) is attained for every $\alpha \in \mathbb{R}^m$, Corollary 14.26 holds for the set C. If there exists $\alpha \in \mathbb{R}^m$ for which the minimum on the right-hand side of Equation (14.69) is not attained, Corollary 14.26 holds if we replace the minimum by an infimum (Exercise 14.23).* ◆

As we previously mentioned, Theorem 14.25, which states that every compact and convex set is either approachable by Player 1 or excludable by Player 2, does not hold for a set that is not convex. Indeed, we will now present an example of a nonconvex set C that is neither approachable by Player 1, nor excludable by Player 2.

Example 14.14 (*Continued*) The vector payoffs in this example are given by the matrix in Figure 14.9.

Player 2

		L	R
Player 1	T	(0, 0)	(0, 0)
	B	(1, 1)	(1, 0)

Figure 14.9 The game in Example 14.4

Define sets C_a, C_b, and C as follows (see Figure 14.10):

$$C_a := \left\{ \left(\tfrac{1}{2}, y \right) : 0 \le y \le \tfrac{1}{4} \right\}, C_b := \left\{ (1, y) : \tfrac{1}{4} \le y \le 1 \right\}, \tag{14.71}$$

and

$$C := C_a \cup C_b. \tag{14.72}$$

Figure 14.10 The sets C_a and C_b

We first show that Player 2 can prevent the average payoff from remaining near C, implying that C is not approachable by Player 1. Indeed, Player 2 can achieve this using the following strategy:

- If the average payoff is close to C_b, and in particular $\overline{g}_1^t$ is close to 1 (for example $\overline{g}_1^t \ge 0.9$), Player 2 plays the action R a sufficiently large number of times to make the value of the second coordinate fall (approaching 0 as t increases), and therefore the average payoff moves away from C_b.
- If the average payoff is close to C_a, and in particular $\overline{g}_1^t$ is close to $\tfrac{1}{2}$ (for example $0.4 \le \overline{g}_1^t \le 0.6$), Player 2 plays L a sufficiently large number of times to make the average payoff move towards the diagonal $x_1 = x_2$, and thus move away from C_a.
- If the average payoff is far from C (for example $0.6 < \overline{g}_1^t < 0.9$, or $\overline{g}_1^t < 0.4$), Player 2 can play any action.

We will now show that for every t, Player 1 can guarantee that in stage $2t$ the average payoff will be in C, leading to the conclusion that the set C is not excludable by Player 2.

- In the first t stages, Player 1 plays B. In particular,

$$\overline{g}^t \in \{(1, x) : 0 \le x \le 1\}. \tag{14.73}$$

- If $\overline{g}_2^t \ge \tfrac{1}{2}$, Player 1 plays B in the next t stages. In particular, $\overline{g}_1^{2t} = 1$, and $\overline{g}_2^{2t} \ge \tfrac{1}{2}\overline{g}_2^t \ge \tfrac{1}{4}$, and therefore $\overline{g}^{2t} \in C_b \subset C$.
- If $\overline{g}_2^t < \tfrac{1}{2}$, Player 1 plays T in the next t stages. In particular, $\overline{g}^{2t} = \tfrac{1}{2}\overline{g}^t$, i.e., $\overline{g}_1^{2t} = \tfrac{1}{2}$ and $\overline{g}_2^{2t} = \tfrac{1}{2}\overline{g}_2^t < \tfrac{1}{4}$. It follows that $\overline{g}^{2t} \in C_a \subset C$.

In conclusion, we have proved that C is not approachable by Player 1, and not excludable by Player 2. ◀

14.7 Application 1: Repeated games with incomplete information

Repeated games with incomplete information were first investigated by Aumann and Maschler in 1967. As the name implies, these games combine the model of repeated games (Chapter 13) with the model of games with incomplete information (Chapter 9). In such games, the payoff matrix is chosen randomly at the start of the game, and the players have different information regarding which matrix was chosen. As in all games with incomplete information, in choosing his action a player needs to take into account the state of knowledge of the other players, because a player's actions may reveal to the others some of the information he has. Because the game is repeated, the process of information revelation and information gathering becomes part of the strategic considerations of the players. In such games, the use of information means choosing an action based on the information that a player has regarding the payoff matrix. If the players know the actions taken by other players in earlier stages, the use of information may reveal information to the other players. A natural question that arises here is whether a player should use the information he has (and thus reveal it to the others), not use it, or make only partial use of it. All three cases are possible: in this section we will see an example in which it is not to a player's advantage to reveal the information he has. Exercise 14.30 presents an example in which it is to a player's advantage to reveal all of the information he has, and Exercise 14.32 presents an example in which it is to a player's advantage to reveal only part of the information he has.

In this section we will not present a full methodological development of the subject. We will content ourselves instead with one example that exemplifies the use of repeated games with vector payoffs in the analysis of repeated games with incomplete information. The example is from Aumann and Maschler [1995]; the interested reader is encouraged to read this book for an introduction to the subject. A guided proof of the characterization of the value of two-player zero-sum repeated games with incomplete information for one player appears in Exercise 14.33.

Two players 1 and 2 play a zero-sum repeated game G, where each player has two actions: Player 1's set of actions is $\mathcal{I} = \{T, B\}$, and Player 2's set of actions is $\mathcal{J} = \{L, R\}$. As in the model of games with incomplete information, the payoff here depends on the state of nature s, which can take one of two values, $s = 1$ or $s = 2$. Each state of nature is a state game. The two state games appear in Figure 14.11. The state of nature is chosen by a fair coin toss at the beginning of the game: the probability that the chosen state is $s = 1$ is $\frac{1}{2}$. Player 1 (the row player) is informed which state of nature is chosen, but Player 2 (the column player) does not have this information. After the state of nature is chosen, and Player 1 is informed of the chosen state of nature, the two players play the infinitely repeated game whose payoff function corresponds to the chosen state of nature. At each stage t, the players know the actions chosen in all previous stages, but do not know what payoffs they have received. Player 1, however, can determine what the payoffs have been, because he knows both the actions chosen and the payoff matrix. This description of the situation is common knowledge among the players. Since Player 1 knows the true state of nature, but Player 2 does not, this game is called a repeated game with incomplete information for Player 2.

Denote the payoff matrices in Figure 14.11 by A^s, $s = 1, 2$, and denote their elements by $(a_{i,j}^s)_{i \in \mathcal{I}, j \in \mathcal{J}}$.

The game presented here is a game with perfect recall (Definition 6.13 on page 242) and therefore by Theorem 6.26 (page 253) it follows that every mixed strategy has an equivalent behavior strategy and vice versa. In this section we will assume that the set of strategies of every player is his set of behavior strategies. For convenience we will denote a behavior strategy of player i by σ_i instead of b_i, and the set of behavior strategies of player i will be denoted by $\mathcal{B}_i$. The information available to Player 1 in stage t is the state

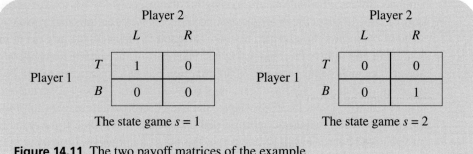

Figure 14.11 The two payoff matrices of the example

of nature and the sequence of actions of the players up to stage t. It follows that Player 1's behavior strategy is the function

$$\sigma_1 : \bigcup_{t \in \mathbb{N}} (\{1, 2\} \times \mathcal{I}^{t-1} \times \mathcal{J}^{t-1}) \to \Delta(\mathcal{I}). \tag{14.74}$$

In stage t, Player 2 does not know the state of nature and therefore the information available to him in stage t is the sequence of actions up to that stage. It follows that a behavior strategy of Player 2 is the function

$$\sigma_2 : \bigcup_{t \in \mathbb{N}} (\mathcal{I}^{t-1} \times \mathcal{J}^{t-1}) \to \Delta(\mathcal{J}). \tag{14.75}$$

We next define the uniform value of the game. In Chapter 13 we saw that in infinite games payoff functions are not always defined for every pair of strategies (σ_1, σ_2). As done there, we define the concept of uniform value without defining the payoff function. The definition is analogous to the definition of the uniform equilibrium we gave in Chapter 13 (Definition 13.30 on page 559), and it holds for every repeated game with incomplete information. Denote by i^t and j^t the actions chosen by the players in stage t.

Definition 14.28 *A strategy σ_1^* of Player 1 guarantees the real number v_1 if there exists an integer T_0 such that for every $T \geq T_0$ and every strategy $\sigma_2 \in \mathcal{B}_2$,*

$$\mathbf{E}_{\sigma_1^*, \sigma_2} \left[\frac{1}{T} \sum_{t=1}^{T} a_{i^t, j^t}^s \right] \geq v_1. \tag{14.76}$$

A strategy σ_2^* of Player 2 guarantees the real number v_2 if there exists an integer T_0 such that for every $T \geq T_0$ and every strategy $\sigma_1 \in \mathcal{B}_1$,

$$\mathbf{E}_{\sigma_1, \sigma_2^*} \left[\frac{1}{T} \sum_{t=1}^{T} a_{i^t, j^t}^s \right] \leq v_2. \tag{14.77}$$

A real number v is called the uniform value *of the game G if for every $\varepsilon > 0$ Player 1 has a strategy guaranteeing him $v - \varepsilon$ and Player 2 has a strategy guaranteeing him $v + \varepsilon$. A strategy σ_1^* of Player 1 guaranteeing $v - \varepsilon$ for all $\varepsilon > 0$ is called an* optimal strategy *of Player 1. An optimal strategy of Player 2 is defined similarly.*

Remark 14.29 *In Definition 14.28 we defined the uniform value when the sets of strategies of the two players are $\mathcal{B}_1$ and $\mathcal{B}_2$. This concept can be defined when the sets of strategies of the players are not necessarily $\mathcal{B}_1$ and $\mathcal{B}_2$ but subsets of them.* ◆

As we will later show, the proof that Player 2 can guarantee $v + \varepsilon$ is closely related to the fact that a particular set in a repeated game with vector payoffs corresponding to G is approachable by Player 2.

Remark 14.30 *We emphasize that the state of nature is chosen only once, at the start of the game, and does not change during the course of the play of the game.* ◆

Remark 14.31 *The assumption that the players cannot see the payoffs they receive in every stage is intended to enable us to concentrate on the information directly revealed by the actions chosen by the players, and to neutralize information about the state of nature obtained indirectly by way of the payoffs. In a more general model, the information given to each player after each stage may be any item of information, and may include the payoff given to the players in each stage. The formal definition of a more general model of repeated games with incomplete information, and results pertaining to such a model, can be found in Zamir [1992].* ◆

Remark 14.32 *The definition of a repeated game with incomplete information for Player 2 can be generalized to any number of states of nature, as follows. A (two-player zero-sum) repeated game with incomplete information on one side is given by a finite set S of states of nature, where each state of nature is associated with a (two-player zero-sum) state game in strategic form G_s, in each of which Player 1's action set is $\mathcal{I}$, and Player 2's action set is $\mathcal{J}$. A state of nature is chosen according to a distribution $p \in \Delta(S)$, which is common knowledge among the players. The chosen state of nature is made known to Player 1, but not to Player 2. After the state of nature has been chosen and told to Player 1, the players play the (finite or infinite) repeated game whose payoff function corresponds to the chosen state of nature. At every stage t, the players know the actions that have been chosen in the previous stages, but they do not know what payoffs they have received in those stages.* ◆

As the following theorem states, if the uniform value exists, then it equals the limit of the values of the finitely repeated games, as the repetition length grows to infinity.

Theorem 14.33 *Denote by v^T the value in behavior strategies of the T-stage game Γ_T, i.e., the two-player zero-sum game whose payoff function is*

$$\gamma^T(\sigma_1, \sigma_2) = \mathbf{E}_{\sigma_1, \sigma_2} \left[\frac{1}{T} \sum_{t=1}^{T} a_{i^t j^t}^s \right]. \tag{14.78}$$

If the uniform value v exists, then $v = \lim_{T \to \infty} v^T$.

Note that v^T, the value of the game Γ_T, exists for every T. Indeed, since the number of pure strategies of every player in this game is finite, by the Minmax Theorem (Theorem 5.11 on page 150) this game has a value in mixed strategies.

Proof: Let v be the uniform value of the game, and let $\varepsilon > 0$. Let σ_1^* and σ_2^* be strategies for each player, respectively, and let T_0 be a natural number such that for every $T \geq T_0$, and for every pair of strategies (σ_1, σ_2), Equations (14.76) and (14.77) hold. By Equation (14.77), for[7] every $T \geq T_0$,

$$v^T = \max_{\sigma_1 \in \mathcal{B}_1^T} \min_{\sigma_2 \in \mathcal{B}_2^T} \gamma^T(\sigma_1, \sigma_2) \tag{14.79}$$

$$\geq \min_{\sigma_2 \in \mathcal{B}_2^T} \gamma^T(\sigma_1^*, \sigma_2) \geq v - \varepsilon. \tag{14.80}$$

We similarly deduce from Equation (14.76) that $v^T \leq v + \varepsilon$ for every $T \geq T_0$. Since these inequalities hold for every $\varepsilon > 0$, one has $\lim_{T \to \infty} v^T = v$, as claimed. $\square$

Remark 14.34 *In Chapter 13 on repeated games, we defined the concept of uniform ε-equilibrium for finite games. By restricting this concept to two-player zero-sum games, we defined the concept of uniform value defined in this section (see Exercise 13.48 on page 575). Recall that the value of the T-stage repeated game Γ_T equals the value of the one-stage (base) game for every $T \in \mathbb{N}$ (Exercise 13.8 on page 566), and that the uniform value equals the value of the one-stage (base) game (Exercise 13.48 on page 575). In particular, Theorem 14.33 holds for repeated games with complete information. Furthermore, in repeated games with complete information the uniform value coincides with the value of the one-stage (base) game. As we will see shortly this does not necessarily hold in repeated games with incomplete information.* ◆

In the game described above, Player 1 has information that Player 2 lacks – knowledge of the chosen state of nature. What is the "best" way for him to use this information? We will first show that if Player 1 ignores the information he has regarding the chosen state of nature, he cannot guarantee more than $\frac{1}{4}$, while if Player 2 ignores the information revealed by the actions of Player 1, he cannot guarantee less than $\frac{1}{2}$.

Denote by $\mathcal{B}_1^*$ the set of behavior strategies of Player 1 in the repeated game that do not use the information he has regarding the state of nature, i.e., the mixed actions played in each stage that are independent of s (and depend only on the actions of the players in previous stages).

Proposition 14.35 *The uniform value of the game with the sets of strategies $\mathcal{B}_1^*$ and $\mathcal{B}_2$ is $\frac{1}{4}$.*

Proof: If Player 1 ignores his information on the state of nature, the players actually play the repeated game with the average payoff matrices appearing in Figure 14.12.

Indeed, if Player 1 does not use the information in his possession on the state of nature, the game is equivalent to the game in which the player does not know the state of nature. In that game, the expected payoff in each stage is given by the matrix appearing in Figure 14.12. The value in mixed strategies of the one-stage game, as well as the uniform value of the repeated game, is $\frac{1}{4}$ (verify!). $\square$

---

7 The set of behavior strategies of player i in the game Γ_T is denoted by $\mathcal{B}_i^T$.

Figure 14.12 The matrix of average payoffs

As the following claim shows, if Player 2 does not use the information revealed by the actions of Player 1, he cannot guarantee less than $\frac{1}{2}$. Denote by $\mathcal{B}_2^*$ the set of strategies of Player 2 in the repeated game that are independent of the history of the actions of Player 1.

Proposition 14.36 *The uniform value of the game with sets of strategies $\mathcal{B}_1^*$ and $\mathcal{B}_2$ is $\frac{1}{2}$.*

Proof: To show that the uniform value of the game is $\frac{1}{2}$, we will construct strategies for the two players that guarantee this value. Consider first the following strategy σ_2^* of Player 2: in each stage, play the mixed action $[\frac{1}{2}(L), \frac{1}{2}(R)]$. For every strategy σ_1 of Player 1, the expected payoff in each stage is at most $\frac{1}{2}$, and therefore the strategy σ_2^* guarantees $\frac{1}{2}$ for Player 2.

Consider next the following strategy σ_1^* of Player 1: if $s = 1$, play T in every stage; if $s = 2$, play B in every stage. The mixed action that Player 2 plays in stage t is independent of the action played by Player 1 in the previous stages. Denote this mixed action by y^t (which may depend on the actions played by Player 2 in previous stages); this is the probability of playing L in stage t. For every strategy σ_2 of Player 2,

$$\mathbf{E}_{\sigma_1^*,\sigma_2}\left[\frac{1}{T}\sum_{t=1}^{T} a_{i^t,j^t}^s\right] = \mathbf{E}_{\sigma_1^*,\sigma_2}\left[\frac{1}{T}\sum_{t=1}^{T}\left(\mathbf{1}_{\{s=1\}}y^t + \mathbf{1}_{\{s=2\}}(1-y^t)\right)\right] \tag{14.81}$$

$$= \mathbf{P}(s=1)\mathbf{E}_{\sigma_1^*,\sigma_2}\left[\frac{1}{T}\sum_{t=1}^{T} y^t\right] + \mathbf{P}(s=2)\mathbf{E}_{\sigma_1^*,\sigma_2}\left[\frac{1}{T}(1-y^t)\right] \tag{14.82}$$

$$= \tfrac{1}{2}\mathbf{E}_{\sigma_1^*,\sigma_2}\left[\tfrac{1}{T}\sum_{t=1}^{T} y^t\right] + \tfrac{1}{2}\mathbf{E}_{\sigma_1^*,\sigma_2}\left[\tfrac{1}{T}(1-y^t)\right] \tag{14.83}$$

$$= \mathbf{E}_{\sigma_1^*,\sigma_2}\left[\frac{1}{T}\sum_{t=1}^{T}\frac{1}{2}\right] = \frac{1}{2}. \tag{14.84}$$

Since the strategy σ_1^* of Player 1 guarantees $\frac{1}{2}$, it guarantees $\frac{1}{2} - \varepsilon$ for all $\varepsilon > 0$. Since the strategy σ_2^* of Player 2 guarantees $\frac{1}{2}$, it guarantees $\frac{1}{2} + \varepsilon$ for all $\varepsilon > 0$. It follows that the uniform value of the game is indeed $\frac{1}{2}$. $\qquad\square$

Can Player 1 guarantee more than $\frac{1}{4}$ by using the information he has? If the game is a one-stage game, the answer is affirmative: the strategy under which Player 1 plays T

if $s = 1$ and B if $s = 2$ guarantees him $\frac{1}{2}$ (Exercise 14.28). Intuitively, it might seem that in the repeated game, if the state of nature is $s = 1$, Player 1 would want to play T more often, while if the state of nature is $s = 2$, he would want to play B more often. But in the repeated game, this strategy is not necessarily a good one, because it reveals the state of nature to Player 2: if Player 2 notices that Player 1 plays T more often, he will ascribe greater probability to the event that the payoff matrix corresponds to $s = 1$ and therefore he will increase the probability that he will play R, while if he notices that Player 1 plays B more often, he will increase the probability that he will play L. As the following proposition shows, in the long run, even when he uses the information he has, Player 1 cannot guarantee that the average payoff will be significantly higher than $\frac{1}{4}$. To prove this proposition, we use tools we developed for approachable sets.

Proposition 14.37 *The uniform value of the game G (with sets of strategies $\mathcal{B}_1$ and $\mathcal{B}_2$) is $\frac{1}{4}$.*

Proof: In Proposition 14.35, we saw that Player 1 can guarantee $\frac{1}{4}$. It remains to show that Player 2 can guarantee $\frac{1}{4} + \varepsilon$ for every $\varepsilon > 0$. To do so, consider the repeated game with two-dimensional vector payoffs G_V, where the sets of actions are $\mathcal{I} = \{T, B\}$ and $\mathcal{J} = \{L, R\}$, and the two coordinates of the payoff represent the payoff in each of the two states of nature (see Figure 14.13).

In this game, the set of possible payoffs is $F = \text{conv}\{(0, 0), (0, 1), (1, 0)\}$ (see Figure 14.14). Define a set C as follows:

$$C = \left[0, \tfrac{1}{4}\right]^2 = \left[0, \tfrac{1}{4}\right] \times \left[0, \tfrac{1}{4}\right] = \left\{(x, y): 0 \leq x \leq \tfrac{1}{4}, 0 \leq y \leq \tfrac{1}{4}\right\}. \qquad (14.85)$$

The proposition will be proved by proving the following two claims:

Claim 14.38 *The set C is approachable by Player 2 in the repeated game G_V.*

Claim 14.39 *If the set C is approachable by Player 2 in the repeated game G_V, then the uniform value of the game G is $\frac{1}{4}$.*

We begin by proving the second claim.

Proof of Claim 14.39: Suppose that the set C is approachable by Player 2 in the game G_V, and denote by σ_2^* his strategy that approaches this set. Then for every $\varepsilon > 0$ there exists $T \in \mathbb{N}$ such that for every strategy σ_1 of Player 1 in the game G_V:

$$\mathbf{P}_{\sigma_1, \sigma_2^*}\left(d(\overline{g}^t, C) < \varepsilon, \quad \forall t \geq T\right) > 1 - \varepsilon. \qquad (14.86)$$

	L	R
T	$(1, 0)$	$(0, 0)$
B	$(0, 0)$	$(0, 1)$

Figure 14.13 The matrix of vector payoffs in the game G_V

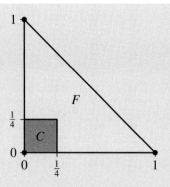

Figure 14.14 The sets F and C of the example

Since C is the square $[0, \frac{1}{4}]^2$, if x is close to C, the coordinates x_1 and x_2 cannot be much greater than $\frac{1}{4}$:

$$\mathbf{P}_{\sigma_1, \sigma_2^*} \left(\bar{g}_1^t < \tfrac{1}{4} + \varepsilon, \quad \forall t \geq T \right) > 1 - \varepsilon, \tag{14.87}$$

$$\mathbf{P}_{\sigma_1, \sigma_2^*} \left(\bar{g}_2^t < \tfrac{1}{4} + \varepsilon, \quad \forall t \geq T \right) > 1 - \varepsilon. \tag{14.88}$$

Since Player 2 does not know the state of nature, the strategy σ_2^* in G_V is also a strategy in the game G. Player 1, in contrast, knows the state of nature, and so his strategy σ_1 in G is essentially composed of two "sub-strategies," each of which is a strategy in G_V: the strategy σ_1^1 that he plays if the state of nature is $s = 1$, and the strategy σ_1^2 that he plays if the state of nature is $s = 2$.

Equations (14.87) and (14.88) hold for every strategy σ_1 of Player 1, and in particular for the strategies σ_1^1 and σ_1^2. Inserting the strategy σ_1^1 in Equation (14.87) and the strategy σ_1^2 in Equation (14.88) yields

$$\mathbf{P}_{\sigma_1^1, \sigma_2^*} \left(\bar{g}_1^t < \tfrac{1}{4} + \varepsilon, \quad \forall t \geq T \right) > 1 - \varepsilon, \tag{14.89}$$

$$\mathbf{P}_{\sigma_1^2, \sigma_2^*} \left(\bar{g}_2^t < \tfrac{1}{4} + \varepsilon, \quad \forall t \geq T \right) > 1 - \varepsilon. \tag{14.90}$$

Equation (14.89) states that when $s = 1$, with probability close to 1, the average payoff when Player 1 plays according to strategy σ_1^1 cannot be much more than $\frac{1}{4}$. Equation (14.90) says the same is true when $s = 2$ for the strategy σ_1^2. Equations (14.89) and (14.90) imply that for every $t \geq T$

$$\mathbf{E}_{\sigma_1, \sigma_2^*} [\bar{g}^t] \leq (1 - \varepsilon) \left(\tfrac{1}{4} + \varepsilon \right) + \varepsilon \leq \tfrac{1}{4} + 2\varepsilon. \tag{14.91}$$

It follows that the strategy σ_2 of Player 2 guarantees $\frac{1}{4} + \varepsilon$ for all $\varepsilon > 0$, and therefore the uniform value of the game is $\frac{1}{4}$. $\qquad \square$

Proof of Claim 14.38: Recall that $R_2(q)$ is the set in which the expected payoffs are located when Player 2 plays the mixed action $[q(L), (1 - q)(R)]$ in each stage (see Equation (14.24)). In the game G_V,

$$R_2(q) = \text{conv}\{(q, 0), (0, 1 - q)\}. \tag{14.92}$$

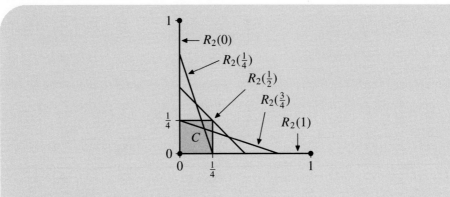

Figure 14.15 The set C and five of the sets $R_2(q)$

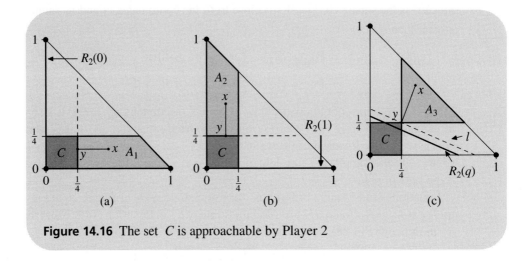

Figure 14.16 The set C is approachable by Player 2

Figure 14.15 shows the set C and the sets $R_2(q)$ for five values of q.

We now check that C is a B-set for Player 2 in the game G_V. Let x be a vector payoff in $F\backslash C$. If $\frac{1}{4} \leq x_1 \leq 1 - x_2$, and $0 \leq x_2 \leq \frac{1}{4}$ (the area labeled A_1 in Figure 14.16(a)), the point in C closest to x is $y = (\frac{1}{4}, x_2)$, the hyperplane separating x from C passes through this point, and perpendicular to the line interval xy is the line $x_1 = \frac{1}{4}$, which separates x from $R_2(0)$. If $0 \leq x_1 \leq \frac{1}{4}$ and $\frac{1}{4} \leq x_2 \leq 1 - x_1$ (the area labeled A_2 in Figure 14.16(b)), the point in C closest to x is $y = (x_1, \frac{1}{4})$, the hyperplane separating x from C passes through this point, and perpendicular to the line interval xy is the line $x_2 = \frac{1}{4}$, which separates x from $R_2(1)$.

If $x_1 \geq \frac{1}{4}$, $x_2 \geq \frac{1}{4}$, and $x_1 + x_2 \leq 1$ (the area labeled A_3 in Figure 14.16(c)), the point C closest to x is $y = (\frac{1}{4}, \frac{1}{4})$. The hyperplane l separating x from C passing through this point and perpendicular to the line interval xy can be calculated using similar triangles. In Figure 14.17, which is a more detailed view of Figure 14.16(c), we see that the triangles xyz, yab, and dyc are similar triangles. Since the lengths of the sides xz and yz are known (these lengths are $x_2 - \frac{1}{4}$ and $x_1 - \frac{1}{4}$ respectively), and since

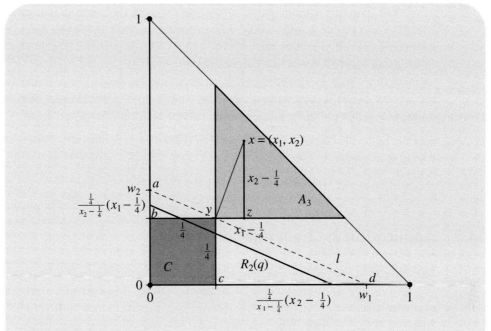

Figure 14.17 The hyperplane l separating x and $R_2(q)$

the lengths of the sides by and cy are also known (they are both $\frac{1}{4}$), one can calculate the lengths of the sides ab and cd, deducing that the hyperplane l is the line passing through the points $(0, w_2)$ and $(w_1, 0)$, where $w_2 = \frac{1}{4} + \frac{\frac{1}{4}}{x_2 - \frac{1}{4}}\left(x_1 - \frac{1}{4}\right)$ and $w_1 = \frac{1}{4} + \frac{\frac{1}{4}}{x_1 - \frac{1}{4}}\left(x_2 - \frac{1}{4}\right)$. Since $a^2 + b^2 \geq 2ab$ for every $a, b \in \mathbb{R}$,

$$w_1 + w_2 = \frac{1}{2} + \frac{1}{4}\frac{\left(x_1 - \frac{1}{4}\right)^2 + \left(x_2 - \frac{1}{4}\right)^2}{\left(x_1 - \frac{1}{4}\right)^2\left(x_2 - \frac{1}{4}\right)^2} \geq \frac{1}{2} + \frac{1}{2} = 1. \tag{14.93}$$

Defining

$$q = \frac{w_1}{w_1 + w_2} = \frac{x_2 - \frac{1}{4}}{x_1 + x_2 - \frac{1}{2}}, \tag{14.94}$$

we get that $R_2(q)$ is parallel to the line l (see Figure 14.16(c)); therefore the line l separates $R_2(q)$ from x. In summary, we showed that C is indeed a B-set for Player 2. □

The proof of Proposition 14.37 is complete. □

Using the proof of the last claim, we can now describe an optimal strategy for Player 2:

- If $\bar{g}^t \in C$, play any action.
- If $\bar{g}^t \in A_1$ play R.
- If $\bar{g}^t \in A_2$ play L.
- If $\bar{g}^t \in A_3$ play the mixed action $[q(L), (1 - q)(R)]$, where q is defined in Equation (14.94).

In the first case, the average payoff up to that stage of the game is not greater than $\frac{1}{4}$, whether $s = 1$ or $s = 2$, and so Player 2 can play any action. In the second case, if $s = 1$, the average payoff is greater than $\frac{1}{4}$, while if $s = 2$, the payoff is not greater than $\frac{1}{4}$. It follows that Player 2 needs to guarantee that the average payoff is reduced if $s = 1$, and therefore must play R. The third case is analogous to the second case. In the fourth case, the average payoff is greater than $\frac{1}{4}$, whether $s = 1$ or $s = 2$. In this case, Player 2 plays a mixed action that guarantees that (in expectation) both coordinates go down. The greater the ratio $\frac{\overline{g}_1^t}{\overline{g}_2^t}$ is, the more the average payoff when $s = 1$ is greater than the average payoff when $s = 2$; therefore the probability that Player 2 plays R grows. Note that this strategy depends on the history only by way of the average payoff over the course of the game up to that stage.

14.8 Application 2: Challenge the expert

In this section, we present a second application of the theory developed in this chapter, this time to the dynamic process of decision making. Most of us seek the advice of experts: statesmen and government leaders employ experts in many different fields: media advisers, policy advisers, and legal advisers; investors listen to the advice of financial advisers; the person-in-the-street listens to the weather forecast to decide what to wear tomorrow, and where to go on a trip. It is sometimes the case that a decision maker has several different advisers, and needs to decide whose advice to take: government leaders often have multiple staffs working for them; banks employ many financial advisers, and on different television channels one may see weather forecasters using different models for weather prediction. A decision maker's problems are not resolved if he has many experts at his disposal – the problem has just been transformed: the problem now is not which decision to take, but which expert to heed.

In this section we will consider the problem of dynamic decision making. By this, we mean that in each stage, the decision maker needs to adopt the advice of one expert, out of a group of experts, and then choose the action recommended by that expert. In each stage the decision maker receives a payoff ($=$ utility) that is determined by the action chosen, and the "state of nature," i.e., the environment in which the action is taken. The payoff to an investor depends both on the specific investment chosen, and on the behavior of the market; the payoff to a head of state depends on his or her actions, and on the actions of other heads of state.

We further assume that it is unknown how the state of nature changes, or, alternatively, that the way the state of nature changes is so complex that the cost or the time investment required for computing it is vast. In addition, we suppose that the actions chosen by the decision maker do not change the way the state of nature changes. This is a reasonable assumption to make with respect to a person deciding what he or she will wear based on the weather forecast, or a person deciding where to invest $10,000, in accordance with advice received from a financial expert, but is not reasonable for a head of state, whose decision may influence the decisions of other heads of state.

Suppose that the goal of a decision maker is to be at least as good as each one of the advisers. In other words, the decision maker is interested in ensuring that his average payoff is no less than the average payoff of a person who from the start picks one of the advisers, and always listens to his or her advice. If this is possible, it means that the decision maker's performance is at least as good as that of the best expert.

14.8.1 The model

With the general presentation of the problem behind us, we turn our attention to the formal definitions.

Definition 14.40 *A decision problem with experts is given by:*

- *A finite set S of states of nature.*
- *A finite set A of actions.*
- *A payoff function $u : A \times S \to \mathbb{R}$.*
- *A finite set E of experts.*

The interpretation we give to this model is as follows. In every stage $t \in \mathbb{N}$, the state of nature s^t is one of the states in S, and each expert $e \in E$ recommends[8] an action $a_e^t \in A$. The decision maker, who does not know what is the true state of nature, must choose one expert from E. If the decision maker chooses expert e, and the state of nature is $s \in S$, the decision maker receives the payoff $u(a_e^t, s^t)$. We assume that the decision maker learns what the state of nature is after choosing the expert whose recommendation he followed.[9] We do not assume anything regarding the information that the experts have: it is possible that they have full or partial information about the states of nature $(s^t)_{t \in \mathbb{N}}$, they may receive information from time to time about future states of nature, and some may have full or partial information about the advice given by the other experts.

For every distribution $\alpha \in \Delta(A)$ over the set of actions, define

$$U(\alpha, s) := \sum_{a \in A} \alpha(a) u(a, s). \tag{14.95}$$

This is the expected payoff if the state of nature is s and the action that is chosen by the probability distribution is α.

The information that the decision maker has in stage t includes the states of nature in the past (in stages $1, 2, \ldots, t-1$), the expert chosen in each past stage, and the recommendations of the experts in each past stage. The set of all possible histories in stage t is

$$H(t) := (S \times E \times A^{|E|})^{t-1}. \tag{14.96}$$

Denote a history in $H(t)$ by $h^t = (s^1, e^1, a^1, \ldots, s^{t-1}, e^{t-1}, a^{t-1})$, where $a^j = (a_e^j)_{e \in E}$ is the vector composed of the recommendations of the experts in stage j.

---

8 For simplicity, we assume that each expert recommends an action, rather than a lottery over the actions. The results presented in this section hold if we assume that each expert recommends a mixed action in each stage; the only difference is that the proofs become more complex.

9 For the analysis we present here, all we need to assume is that the decision maker knows the payoff received in each stage, and what payoff he would have received if he had followed the recommendation of each other expert.

Definition 14.41 *A decision maker's (behavior)* strategy *in a decision problem with experts is a function*

$$\sigma : \bigcup_{t=1}^{\infty} H(t) \to \Delta(E). \tag{14.97}$$

In other words, in every stage, the decision maker needs to choose, based on his past choices and the performances of the experts in the past, one expert, and to implement the action recommended by that expert. The decision maker may choose an expert in each stage by lottery. If the decision maker adopts strategy σ, after history $h^t = (s^1, e^1, a^1, \ldots, s^{t-1}, e^{t-1}, a^{t-1})$ he chooses one of the experts in E using the probability distribution $\sigma(h^t)$: $\sigma(e; h^t)$ is the probability that expert e is chosen. Since in stage t expert e recommends the action a_e^t, the average payoff that the decision maker receives up to stage T is

$$\frac{1}{T} \sum_{t=1}^{T} \sum_{e \in E} \sigma(e; h^t) u(a_e^t, s^t) = \sum_{e \in E} \left(\frac{1}{T} \sum_{t=1}^{T} \sigma(e; h^t) u(a_e^t, s^t) \right), \tag{14.98}$$

where s^t is the state of nature in stage t, and h^t is the history up to stage t. If the decision maker would follow the recommendation of a particular expert e, his average payoff up to stage T would be

$$\frac{1}{T} \sum_{t=1}^{T} u(a_e^t, s^t). \tag{14.99}$$

We are using here the assumption that the action implemented by the decision maker does not affect the way that the state of nature changes, and therefore if $(s^t)_{t \in \mathbb{N}}$ is the sequence of states of nature that obtain when the decision maker implements strategy σ, that same sequence would obtain if he were always to choose expert e. The decision maker's goal is to attain a performance at least as good as the performance of any one of the experts.

Definition 14.42 *A decision maker's strategy σ is a* no-regret strategy *if for each expert $e \in E$, and each sequence $(s^1, s^2, \ldots)$ of states of nature,*

$$\mathbf{P}_\sigma \left(\liminf_{T \to \infty} \left(\frac{1}{T} \sum_{t=1}^{T} u(a_{e^t}^t, s^t) - \frac{1}{T} \sum_{t=1}^{T} u(a_e^t, s^t) \right) \geq 0 \right) = 1. \tag{14.100}$$

In words, a strategy is a no-regret strategy if, with probability 1, the decision maker does not regret the way he played: his performance is at least as good as the hypothetical performance of any expert, independently of the way the state of nature changes. If a decision maker has a no-regret strategy, he can pride himself on making decisions at least as good as each expert.

Remark 14.43 *Although the model we have presented here is a single-player model, where the single player is the decision maker, it is convenient to think of this situation as including an additional player, Nature, who chooses the state of nature, and we imagine that Nature seeks to reduce the decision maker's payoff as much as possible. By doing so, we have defined a two-player zero-sum repeated game.* ◆

Does a no-regret strategy exist? If so, can we construct it, or must we content ourselves with proving its theoretical existence, without finding a no-regret strategy in a practical way? Using the theory of approachability developed in this chapter, we will prove the following theorem.

Theorem 14.44 *The decision maker has a no-regret strategy.*

In addition, we will construct this strategy in a way that can easily be programmed into a computer.

14.8.2 Existence of a no-regret strategy: a special case

Recall that for every finite set X the number of elements in X is denoted by $|X|$. We first present a proof in the simple case where there are exactly $|A|$ experts. Each expert is identified with the action that he recommends in each stage. In other words, for every action $a \in A$ there is an expert e such that $a_e^t = a$ in every stage t. We will later show how the proof needs to be changed for the general case. Since the recommendations of the experts are fixed, we can define a strategy to be a function associating for each $t \in \mathbb{N}$, each sequence of length $t - 1$ of actions chosen by the decision maker in the past, and each sequence of length $t - 1$ of states of nature, with a probability distribution over the set of actions.

Define an auxiliary game with vector payoffs G_V as follows. In the auxiliary game, Player 1 represents the decision maker whose set of actions is A, and Player 2 represents Nature, whose set of actions is S. The payoffs are $|A|$-dimensional and the payoff function w is defined as follows: the vector payoff $w(a, s) = (w_b(a, s))_{b \in A}$ that obtains when Player 1 implements action a and Player 2 implements s is given by

$$w_b(a, s) := u(a, s) - u(b, s). \tag{14.101}$$

This is the difference between the payoff received by the decision maker if he chooses action a (based on the recommendation of expert a, who always recommends action a) and the payoff received by the decision maker if he chooses action b (based on the recommendation of expert b, who always recommends action b).

A strategy for Player 1 in this auxiliary game with vector payoffs is a function

$$\hat{\sigma} : \bigcup_{t=1}^{\infty} (A \times S)^{t-1} \to \Delta(A). \tag{14.102}$$

In words, a strategy associates every finite sequence of actions chosen by Player 1 and states of nature chosen by Player 2 with a mixed action. As previously noted, $\hat{\sigma}$ is a strategy in the decision problem with experts, in the special case.

Denote by

$$C = \{x \in \mathbb{R}^A : x_i \geq 0 \quad \forall i \in A\} \tag{14.103}$$

the nonnegative orthant in $\mathbb{R}^A$. To prove that there exists a no-regret strategy, and to describe such a strategy in detail, we will prove the following theorems.

Theorem 14.45 *The set C is approachable by Player 1 in the auxiliary game with vector payoffs G_V.*

Theorem 14.46 *Every strategy σ of Player 1 that approaches the set C in G_V is a no-regret strategy for the decision maker in the decision problem with experts.*

We will first show that these two theorems prove Theorem 14.44. We will then proceed to prove them.

By Theorem 14.45, the set C is approachable by Player 1 in the game G_V by a strategy in the auxiliary game that approaches C. By Theorem 14.46, the strategy σ is a no-regret strategy for the decision maker in the decision problem with experts, and Theorem 14.44 is proved.

Proof of Theorem 14.45: For every $\pi \in \mathbb{R}^A$ define a two-player zero-sum one-stage game $\widehat{G}_\pi$ in which the set of pure strategies of Player 1 is A, the set of pure strategies of Player 2 is S, and the payoff function $\widehat{W}_\pi$ is defined by

$$\widehat{W}_\pi = \langle \pi, w(a, s) \rangle. \tag{14.104}$$

We will show that for every $\pi \in \mathbb{R}^A$,

$$\mathrm{val}(\widehat{G}_\pi) \geq \inf_{x \in C} \langle \pi, x \rangle, \tag{14.105}$$

and Theorem 14.45 then follows from this equation and Corollary 14.26 on page 597, because the set C is convex.

If $\pi = \vec{0}$, both sides of Equation (14.105) are zero, and the inequality holds. If there exists an index a such that $\pi_a < 0$, then the right-hand side of Equation (14.105) is $-\infty$. To see this, for each $k \in \mathbb{N}$ denote by x^k the vector $(0, \ldots, 0, k, 0, \ldots, 0)$, all of whose coordinates are 0, except for coordinate a, which equals k. Since $x^k \in C$,

$$\inf_{x \in C} \langle \pi, x \rangle \leq \inf_{k \in \mathbb{N}} \langle \pi, x^k \rangle = -\infty. \tag{14.106}$$

In contrast, the left-hand side of Equation (14.105) is finite, being the value of a two-player zero-sum game. The inequality in Equation (14.105) therefore holds in this case.

It remains to check the case where all the coordinates of π are nonnegative, and at least one of them is strictly positive. Since both sides of Equation (14.105) are linear in π (i.e., $\mathrm{val}(\widehat{G}_{\lambda\pi}) = \lambda\,\mathrm{val}(\widehat{G}_\pi)$ and $\langle \lambda\pi, x \rangle = \lambda\langle \pi, x \rangle$ for every $\lambda > 0$), by multiplying both sides of Equation (14.105) by $\lambda = \frac{1}{\sum_{a \in A} \pi_a}$, which is a positive value, we may assume without loss of generality that $\sum_{a \in A} \pi_a = 1$, and then we may interpret π as a mixed strategy of Player 1. We will show that in this case

$$\mathrm{val}(\widehat{G}_\pi) \geq 0 \geq \inf_{x \in R} \langle \pi, x \rangle. \tag{14.107}$$

The right-hand inequality in Equation (14.107) holds, because $\vec{0} \in C$, and therefore

$$\inf_{x \in C} \langle \pi, x \rangle \leq \langle \pi, \vec{0} \rangle = 0. \tag{14.108}$$

We next turn our attention to the proof of the left-hand inequality of Equation (14.107). Denote by $\mathbf{1}_s \in \mathbb{R}^S$ the column vector in which the coordinate s equals 1, and all the other coordinates equal 0. For each $s \in S$ the vector $\mathbf{1}_s$ corresponds to the pure strategy s of Player 2. We now show that $\widehat{W}_\pi(\pi, \mathbf{1}_s) \geq 0$ for each $s \in S$.

$$\widehat{W}_\pi(\pi, \mathbf{1}_s) = \sum_{e \in E} \pi(e) \sum_{e' \in E} \pi(e')(u(e, s) - u(e', s)) \tag{14.109}$$

$$= \sum_{e \in E} \pi(e) \left(u(e, s) - \sum_{e' \in E} \pi(e')u(e', s) \right) \tag{14.110}$$

$$= \sum_{e \in E} \pi(e)u(e, s) - \sum_{e' \in E} \pi(e')u(e', s) = 0. \tag{14.111}$$

It follows that $\widehat{W}_\pi(\pi, y) = 0$ for every mixed action $y \in \Delta(S)$. In other words, the mixed strategy π guarantees Player 1 the payoff 0; therefore $\mathrm{val}(\widehat{G}_\pi) \geq 0$, which is the left-hand inequality in Equation (14.105). $\square$

Proof of Theorem 14.46: Let σ be a strategy of Player 1 in the auxiliary game G_V that approaches C. Then for every $\varepsilon > 0$, there exists $T_0 \in \mathbb{N}$ such that for every strategy τ of Player 2 in G_V,

$$\mathbf{P}_{\sigma,\tau}\left(d\left(\frac{1}{T} \sum_{t=1}^{T} w(a^t, s^t), C \right) \leq \varepsilon \quad \forall T \geq T_0 \right) > 1 - c. \tag{14.112}$$

This equation implies that

$$\mathbf{P}_{\sigma,\tau}\left(\lim_{T \to \infty} d\left(\frac{1}{T} \sum_{t=1}^{T} w(a^t, s^t), C \right) = 0 \right) = 1. \tag{14.113}$$

Since $w_b(a, s) = u(a, s) - u(b, s)$, and since C is the nonnegative orthant, we deduce that for every $b \in A$,

$$\mathbf{P}_{\sigma,\tau}\left(\liminf_{T \to \infty} \left(\frac{1}{T} \sum_{t=1}^{T} u(a^t, s^t) - \frac{1}{T} \sum_{t=1}^{T} u(b, s^t) \right) \geq 0 \right) = 1. \tag{14.114}$$

This equation holds for every strategy τ of Player 2, and in particular for every sequence of states $(s^1, s^2, \ldots)$ (constituting a pure strategy) in which Player 2 plays the action s^t in stage t. This states precisely that σ is a no-regret strategy. $\square$

14.8.3 Existence of a no-regret strategy: the general case

We now show how the proof of Theorem 14.44 needs to be changed when we do not assume that $E = A$ and that for every action $a \in A$ there exists an expert recommending that action.

Two changes are implemented in the definition of the game G_V. First of all, since the set of experts is E, the set of actions of Player 1 is E (and not A). Secondly, since the recommendations of the experts change from stage to stage, the payoff function W is also dependent on the stage t. For every $e \in E$ and $s \in S$, and every stage t, the vector $w^t(e, s)$ is in $\mathbb{R}^E$, and is defined by

$$W_{e'}^t(e, s) = u\left(a_e^t, s\right) - u\left(a_{e'}^t, s\right). \tag{14.115}$$

The rest of the proof of Theorem 14.45 is similar to the proof above, with the only difference being that now π is a vector in $\mathbb{R}^E$, and when $\pi_e \geq 0$ for all $e \in E$ and

$\sum_{e \in E} \pi_e = 1$, we interpret the vector π as a mixed action of Player 1 (Exercise 14.34). The proof of Theorem 14.46 needs to be adapted to the case in which the payoffs change during the game (Exercise 14.27).

14.9 Discussion

In this chapter, we described a model of two-player repeated games with vector payoffs. The central concept of the model is that of a set approachable by a player. We gave a geometric sufficient condition for a closed set to be approachable: every closed set containing a B-set for a player is approachable by him. Lehrer [2003] generalizes Blackwell's Theorem (Theorem 14.14 on page 588) to the case in which the payoffs are in an infinite-dimensional space rather than an m-dimensional space.

Hou [1971] proves the following theorem:

Theorem 14.47 *A closed set C is approachable by player k if and only if it contains a B-set for player k.*

Another proof of the same theorem, arrived at independently, appears in Spinat [2002]. Since the set C is excludable by a player if and only if there exists $\delta > 0$ such that the set $\{x \in \mathbb{R}: d(x, C) \geq \delta\}$ is approachable by him, Theorems 14.14 and 14.47 provide a geometric characterization of excludable sets.

Every closed and convex set is either approachable by one of the players, or excludable by the other player (Theorem 14.25, page 596). We saw an example of a set C that is neither approachable by Player 1 nor excludable by Player 2 (this set is necessarily not convex). In that example, although the set C is not approachable by Player 1, for every t sufficiently large, Player 2 has a strategy guaranteeing that the average payoff in stage t is close to C. A set satisfying this property is called "weakly approachable" by Player 1.

Definition 14.48 *A set S is* weakly approachable *by player k if for every $\varepsilon > 0$ there exists $T \in \mathbb{N}$ such that for every $t \geq T$ there exists a strategy σ_k of player k (that depends on t) satisfying the property that for every strategy σ_{-k} of the other player*

$$\mathbf{E}_{\sigma_k, \sigma_{-k}}(d(\overline{g}^t, C)) \leq \varepsilon. \tag{14.116}$$

A set S is weakly excludable *by player k if there exists $\delta > 0$ such that the set $\{x \in \mathbb{R}^m: d(x, S) \geq \delta\}$ is weakly approachable by player k.*

The difference between the concept of "approachability" and the concept of "weak approachability" is subtle: the concept of "approachability" requires the existence of a strategy guaranteeing that the average payoff up to stage t is close to C for all $t \geq T$ (i.e., the same strategy is good for all stages $t \geq T$), while in the concept of "weak approachability" the strategy can depend on t (and it may be the case that there is no strategy that is good for all $t \geq T$, if the set is not approachable).

The definitions imply that every set approachable by one of the players is weakly approachable by that player, and every set excludable by one of the players is weakly excludable by that player. Vieille [1992] shows that every set is either weakly approachable by Player 1 or weakly excludable by Player 2. Compare this to Theorem

14.25 (page 596), with respect to the concepts of approachable and excludable sets, where a similar statement holds only for closed and convex sets.

In Section 14.7 (page 598), we used repeated games with vector payoffs to analyze a repeated game with incomplete information on one side. A similar analysis for general two-player zero-sum games with incomplete information for Player 2 and a finite set of states of nature is conducted by Aumann and Maschler [1995], who use repeated games with vector payoffs to show that the uniform value $v(p)$ of a repeated game with incomplete information for Player 2 is the smallest concave function that is greater than or equal to $u(p)$, where $u(p)$ is the value of the one-stage game in which the state of nature is chosen by the distribution p, and Player 1 does not make use of the information he has regarding the state of nature (equivalently, this is the game in which neither player knows the true state of nature). They also show that a strategy guaranteeing Player 2 the payoff $v(p) + \varepsilon$ is the strategy that approaches a proper set in an auxiliary repeated game with vector payoffs. They also construct a simple strategy for Player 1, guaranteeing him $v(p)$ (Exercise 14.31).

A geometric characterization of equilibria in two-player repeated games with incomplete information on one side that are not zero-sum appears in Hart [1986] (see also Aumann and Hart [1986]), and the existence of equilibria in these games is proved by Sorin [1983] for games with two states of nature, and by Simon, Spież, and Toruńczyk [1995] for games with an arbitrary number of states of nature. The existence of the value and equilibria in games with different information structures is studied in Kohlberg and Zamir [1974], Forges [1982], and Neyman and Sorin [1997, 1998], among others.

The first study of no-regret strategies was conducted by Hannan [1957]. The connection between no-regret strategies and the concept of approachable sets was first made by Hart and Mas-Colell [2000]. Several studies, including Foster and Vohra [1997] and Fudenberg and Levine [1999], define no-regret in a stronger form than the one presented here. Rustichini [1999], Lugosi, Mannor, and Stoltz [2007], and Lehrer and Solan [2007] studied no-regret strategies under which the decision maker does not know the true state of nature, but receives information that depends on the state of nature and the chosen action. No-regret strategies and their applications are covered in detail in Cesa-Bianchi and Lugosi [2006].

A characterization of approachable sets and excludable sets, where one of the players is restricted to strategies with finite memories, is given by Lehrer and Solan [2006, 2008] (such strategies are mentioned in Exercise 13.39, on page 573).

14.10   Remarks

A definition equivalent to that of a B-set, for convex sets, is given in Hart and Mas-Colell [2000]. Exercise 14.17 is adapted from Bernstein, Mannor, and Shimkin [2014]. Exercise 14.25 is based on Lehrer [2002], who calls the condition appearing there "the principle of approachability." Exercise 14.30 is based on an example in Chapter I.3 in Aumann and Maschler [1995], and Exercise 14.31 is based on Example IV.4.1 in that book. Exercise 14.32 is based on Zamir [1992]. Exercise 14.38 is based on Lehrer and Solan [2007].

14.11 Exercises

14.1 Let (X, d) be a metric space and let C be a subset of X. Prove that for each $x, y \in X$,

$$d(x, C) \leq d(x, y) + d(y, C). \tag{14.117}$$

14.2 Prove Markov's inequality: for every nonnegative random variable X, and every $c > 0$,

$$\mathbf{P}(X \geq c) \leq \frac{\mathbf{E}(X)}{c}. \tag{14.118}$$

14.3 Describe the following situation as a repeated game with vector payoffs, where Player 1 is M. Goriot, and Player 2 represents his daughters. At the start of every month, Anastasia and Delphine decide how to relate to their father, M. Goriot, that month: will they ignore his existence or pay him a visit now and again? M. Goriot, for his part, decides whether to give his daughters a generous, or a stingy, monthly allowance. If M. Goriot decides to be generous, he gives Anastasia 10 francs at the end of the month, and Delphine 12 francs, if his daughters have not visited him that month; and he gives Anastasia 18 francs at the end of the month, and Delphine 16 francs, if they have visited him. If M. Goriot decides to be stingy, he gives Anastasia 3 francs at the end of the month, and Delphine 2 francs, if his daughters have not visited him that month; and he gives Anastasia 5 francs at the end of the month, and Delphine 8 francs, if they have visited him.

14.4 Prove the following two claims:

(a) If strategy σ_k approaches a set C for player k, then it approaches the closure of C for that player.

(b) If strategy σ_k excludes a set C for player k, then it excludes the closure of C for that player.

14.5 Prove that the following two claims hold for any closed set $C \subseteq \mathbb{R}^m$ (recall that M is the maximal payoff of the game, in absolute value):

(a) C is approachable by a player if and only if the set $\{x \in C : \|x\| \leq M\}$ is approachable by the other player.

(b) C is excludable by a player if and only if the set $\{x \in C : \|x\| \leq M\}$ is excludable by the player.

(c) Show that if C is not closed, item (a) above does not necessarily hold.

14.6 Prove the following claims:

(a) If strategy σ_k approaches a set C for player k, then it approaches every superset of C for that player.

(b) If strategy σ_k excludes a set C for player k, then it excludes every subset of C for that player.

14.7 Prove Theorem 14.8 on page 584: a set cannot be both approachable by one player and excludable by the other player.

14.8 In this exercise we will prove that the set C_3 defined in Example 14.4, page 582 (see Figure 14.4) is approachable by Player 1, using the strategy described there.

(a) Prove that if $\bar{g}^{t-1}$ is above the diagonal $x_1 + x_2 = 1$, then $d(\bar{g}^t, \vec{0}) \le d(\bar{g}^{t-1}, \vec{0}) - \frac{1}{2t}$.

(b) Prove that if $\bar{g}^{t-1}$ is under the diagonal $x_1 + x_2 = 1$, then $d(\bar{g}^t, C_2) \le (1 - \frac{1}{2t}) d(\bar{g}^{t-1}, C_2)$.

(c) Using the fact that the series $\sum_{t=1}^{\infty} \frac{1}{t}$ diverges, and that the sequence $\{\frac{1}{t}\}$ converges to 0, deduce that $\lim_{t \to \infty} d(\bar{g}^t, C_3) = 0$.

14.9 For each of the following sentences, find an example in which the claim of the sentence obtains:

(a) The sets C_1 and C_2 are approachable by Player 1, but the set $C_1 \cap C_2$ is excludable by Player 2.

(b) The set C_1 is approachable by Player 1, the set C_2 is excludable by Player 2, and the set $C_1 \setminus C_2 := C_1 \cap (C_2)^c$ is excludable by Player 2.

(c) The sets C_1 and C_2 are excludable by Player 2, but the set $C_1 \cup C_2$ is approachable by Player 1.

14.10 Consider the following two-player game, with payoffs in $\mathbb{R}^2$:

Player 2

		L	R
	T	$(-1, 1)$	$(1, -1)$
Player 1			
	B	$(2, 2)$	$(-1, -1)$

(a) Draw the sets $R_1(p)$ and $R_2(q)$, for each p and q.

(b) Prove that the following two sets are approachable by Player 1:

$$C_1 = [(1, -1), (-1, 1)], \tag{14.119}$$

$$C_2 = [(0, 0), (2, 2)] \cup [(0, 0), (1, -1)]. \tag{14.120}$$

(c) Prove that the following three sets are not approachable by Player 1:

$$C_3 = [(-1, 1), (2, 2)], \tag{14.121}$$

$$C_4 = [(0, 0), (-1, 1)] \cup [(0, 0), (-1, -1)], \tag{14.122}$$

$$C_5 = \left\{ (x, \tfrac{1}{2}) : -\infty < x < \infty \right\}. \tag{14.123}$$

14.11 Let C_1 be a closed and convex set in $\mathbb{R}^m$ and let C_2 be a closed and convex set containing C_1. Prove that if C_1 is a B-set for a certain player, then C_2 is also a B-set for that player.

14.12 In this exercise, we will show that Exercise 14.11 does not hold without the condition that C_2 and C_2 are convex sets. Consider the game presented in Exercise 14.10.

(a) Prove that the set $C_1 = [(0,0), (2,2)] \cup [(0,0), (1,-1)]$ is a B-set for Player 1.
(b) Prove that for $\varepsilon > 0$ sufficiently small, the set C_ε, which is the union of C_1 with the triangle whose vertices are $(0,0)$, $(\varepsilon, \varepsilon)$, and $(\varepsilon, -\varepsilon)$, is not a B-set for Player 1.

14.13 Answer the following questions for each one of the games below, whose payoffs are in $\mathbb{R}^2$.

(a) Draw the sets $R_1(p)$ and $R_2(q)$, for every p and q.
(b) Find four B-sets for Player 1.
(c) Find four B-sets for Player 2.

Player 2

		L	R
	T	(0, 1)	(0, 4)
Player 1	B	(2, −1)	(1, 1)

Game A

Player 2

		L	R
	T	(0, 0)	(2, 2)
Player 1	B	(3, 1)	(1, 1)

Game B

14.14 Answer the following questions for the game below, whose payoffs are in $\mathbb{R}^2$.

Player 2

		L	R
	T	(1, 0)	(0, 4)
Player 1	B	(0, 2)	(3, 1)

(a) Draw the sets $R_1(p)$ and $R_2(q)$, for every p and q.
(b) Which of the following sets is a B-set for Player 1, which one is a B-set for Player 2, and which one is neither? Justify your answers.

- $C_1 = [(1,0), (0,4)]$.
- $C_2 = [(0,4), (\frac{6}{11}, \frac{20}{11})] \cup [(0,2), (\frac{6}{11}, \frac{20}{11})]$.
- $C_3 = [(3,1), (\frac{6}{11}, \frac{20}{11})] \cup [(1,1), (\frac{6}{11}, \frac{20}{11})]$.
- $C_4 = \{(\frac{6}{11}, \frac{20}{11})\}$.

14.15 Theorem 14.14 (on page 588) states that every B-set for a player is also an approachable set for that player, and Theorem 14.47 (page 614) states that every approachable set for a player contains a B-set for that player. In this exercise, we show that an approachable set for a player may not be a B-set for that player.
Consider the game appearing in Example 14.4 (page 582).

(a) Prove that the set C, which is the union of two intervals, $[(0,0), (\frac{1}{2},0)]$ and $[(\frac{1}{2},0), (1, \frac{1}{2})]$ (see the accompanying figure), is not a B-set for Player 1.
(b) Find a B-set for Player 1 contained in C, and deduce that C is indeed an approachable set for Player 1. Prove that the set that you have found is a B-set for Player 1.

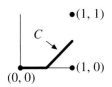

14.16 Prove that a closed and convex set C is approachable by Player 1 if and only if $C \cap R_2(q) \neq \emptyset$ for every $q \in \Delta(\mathcal{J})$.

14.17 Consider the following game where the payoffs are scalars:

Player 2

		L	R
	T	2	0
Player 1	B	0	-2

Let $C := [1, 2] \cup [-1, -2]$.

(a) Prove that $C \cap R_2(q) \neq \emptyset$ for every $q \in \Delta(\mathcal{J})$.

(b) Prove that C is not approachable by Player 1. Explain why this result does not contradict Exercise 14.16.

(c) Prove that C is excludable by Player 2.

14.18 In this exercise we will prove von Neumann's Theorem (Theorem 5.11 on page 150) using results proved in this chapter. Let $\Gamma = (N, S_1, S_2, u)$ be a two-player zero-sum game. Denote by $\underline{v}_1 = \max_{\sigma_1 \in \Delta(S_1)} \min_{\sigma_2 \in \Delta(S_2)} U_1(\sigma_1, \sigma_2)$ (respectively $\overline{v}_1 = \min_{\sigma_2 \in \Delta(S_2)} \max_{\sigma_1 \in \Delta(S_1)} U_1(\sigma_1, \sigma_2)$) the maxmin (respectively minmax) value in mixed strategies. Consider the game to be a game with one-dimensional vector payoffs, and define the sets $C = [\overline{v}_1, \infty)$ and $D = (-\infty, \underline{v}_1]$.

(a) Prove (without using von Neumann's Theorem) that C is approachable by Player 1.

(b) Prove (without using von Neumann's Theorem) that D is approachable by Player 2.

(c) Using the fact that $\overline{v}_1 \geq \underline{v}_1$ (Exercise 4.34 on page 136), deduce that $\overline{v}_1 = \underline{v}_1$.

14.19 Let $(Y_i)_{i=1}^{\infty}$ be a sequence of random variables, $Y_i \in [0, 1]$ for every $i \in N$. Let $(X_i)_{i=1}^{\infty}$ be a sequence of independent random variables, with Bernoulli distribution with parameter p, where $p \in (0, 1)$. In other words, $\mathbf{P}(X_i = 1) = p$, and $\mathbf{P}(X_i = 0) = 1 - p$.

(a) Prove that[10]

$$\mathbf{P}\left(\lim_{n \to \infty} \left(\frac{1}{n} \sum_{i=1}^{n} Y_i - \frac{\sum_{\{i: X_i = 1\}} Y_i}{|\{i: X_i = 1\}|} \right) = 0 \right) = 1. \qquad (14.124)$$

---

10 Recall that for every finite set X we denote by $|X|$ the number of elements it contains.

In words, for n sufficiently large, the average of the first n elements in the sequence $(Y_i)_{i=1}^{\infty}$ is close to the average of independently chosen elements: every element is chosen with probability p.

(b) Prove that Equation (14.124) holds, even when Y_i depends on $X_1, X_2, \ldots, X_{i-1}$ (but is independent of $(X_j)_{j \geq i}$) for each $i \in \{1, 2, \ldots, n\}$.

Guidance: Consider the following game with vector payoffs in $\mathbb{R}^4$:

Player 2

		1	0
Player 1	1	$(1, 0, 0, 0)$	$(0, 1, 0, 0)$
	0	$(0, 0, 1, 0)$	$(0, 0, 0, 1)$

Interpret Y_n as the mixed action of Player 2 in stage n, and X_n as the pure action of Player 1 in stage n. Prove that the strategy of Player 1, under which he plays action 1 with probability p, and action 0 with probability $1 - p$ (independently of previous choices) in each stage, approaches the set

$$C := \{(yp, (1 - y)p, y(1 - p), (1 - y)(1 - p)): 0 \leq y \leq 1\} \tag{14.125}$$

$$= \{y(p, 0, 1 - p, 0) + (1 - y)(0, p, 0, 1 - p): 0 \leq y \leq 1\}. \tag{14.126}$$

Prove that the fact that C is approachable by Player 1 using the above-described strategy implies Equation (14.124) (in item (a)). Deduce the claim in item (b) from this.

14.20 Prove that Blackwell's Theorem (Theorem 14.14 on page 588) obtains even when for every $i \in \mathcal{I}$ and $j \in \mathcal{J}$, the payoff is a random variable $X(i, j)$ taking values in $\mathbb{R}^m$ with expectation $u(i, j)$, and Player 1 observes, after every stage t, the value of $X(i^t, j^t)$ and the action j^t of Player 2.

14.21 State the analogous corollary to Corollary 14.26 on page 597 for Player 2. Justify your answer.

14.22 Prove that a compact and convex set $C \subseteq \mathbb{R}^m$ is approachable by Player 1 if and only if $C \cap H_2(q) \neq \emptyset$ for every $q \in \Delta(\mathcal{J})$.

14.23 Prove Corollary 14.26 for closed and convex sets that are not compact: a closed and convex set C is approachable by Player 1 if and only if

$$\mathrm{val}(G_\alpha) \geq \inf_{x \in C} \langle \alpha, x \rangle, \quad \forall \alpha \in \mathbb{R}^m. \tag{14.127}$$

14.24 Consider the following two-player game with payoffs in $\mathbb{R}^2$:

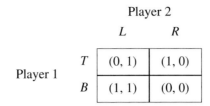

Player 2

		L	R
Player 1	T	(0, 1)	(1, 0)
	B	(1, 1)	(0, 0)

(a) Write down the payoff function U_π in the game G_π for every $\pi = (\pi_1, \pi_2) \in \mathbb{R}^2$ (for the definition of U_π see Equation (14.68) on page 596).
(b) Draw the graph of the function $\mathrm{val}(G_\pi)$. That is, on the two-dimensional plane, where the x axis is identified with π_1, and the y axis is identified with π_2, draw $\mathrm{val}(G_{\pi_1, \pi_2})$ at each point.
(c) For the following sets C, compute the value of $\min_{x \in C} \langle \pi, x \rangle$ as a function of π, and determine which of them are approachable by Player 1.

  (i) $C_1 = \{(\frac{1}{2}, \frac{1}{2})\}$.
  (ii) $C_2 = [(0, 1), (1, 0)]$.
  (iii) $C_3 = [(0, 1), (0, 0)]$.
  (iv) C_4 is the triangle whose vertices are $(1, 1)$, $(1, 0)$, and $(\frac{1}{2}, \frac{1}{2})$.
  (v) C_5 is the parallelogram whose vertices are $(\frac{1}{2}, 1)$, $(\frac{1}{4}, 1)$, $(\frac{1}{2}, 0)$, and $(\frac{3}{4}, 0)$.

14.25 The principle of approachability In this exercise, we will present the geometric principle behind Blackwell's Theorem. Let $C \subset \mathbb{R}^m$ be a compact and convex set, and let $(x^t)_{t \in \mathbb{N}}$ be a bounded sequence of vectors in $\mathbb{R}^m$. Denote by $\overline{x}^t = \frac{1}{t} \sum_{j=1}^t x^j$ the average of the first t elements in the sequence $(x^t)_{t \in \mathbb{N}}$ and denote by $y(\overline{x}^t, C)$ the point in C that is closest to $\overline{x}^t$. Assume that for each t, the following inequality holds:

$$\langle \overline{x}^t - y(\overline{x}^t, C), x^{t+1} - y(\overline{x}^t, C) \rangle \leq 0, \quad \forall t \in \mathbb{N}. \tag{14.128}$$

(a) Prove that if $\overline{x}^t \notin C$, then Equation (14.128) holds if and only if the hyperplane tangent to C at $y(\overline{x}^t, C)$ separates x^{t+1} from $\overline{x}^t$.
(b) Prove that $\lim_{t \to \infty} d(\overline{x}^t, y(\overline{x}^t, C)) = 0$: the distance of the average $\overline{x}^t$ from C converges to 0.
(c) Explain why this exercise generalizes Blackwell's Theorem for compact and convex sets.

Guidance: See the last part of the proof of Lemma 14.15. For item (c) substitute $x^t = u(i^t, j^t)$.

14.26 Let C be a compact and convex set in $\mathbb{R}^m$. Let $(x^t)_{t=1}^\infty$ be a sequence of points in C satisfying

$$\langle \overline{x}^t, x^{t+1} \rangle \leq \langle \overline{x}^t, z \rangle, \quad \forall z \in C. \tag{14.129}$$

Prove that $\lim_{t\to\infty} d(\overline{x}^t, \text{argmin}_{z\in C}\langle z, z\rangle) = 0$: the sequence of averages $(\overline{x}^t)_{t=1}^{\infty}$ converges to the point minimizing $\langle z, z\rangle$ in C.

Guidance: Show, using the convexity of C, that the set $\text{argmin}_{z\in C}\langle z, z\rangle$ contains a single point y. This is the point in C closest to the origin. Apply the principle of approachability (Exercise 14.25) to the set $\text{argmin}_{z\in C}\langle z, z\rangle$.

14.27 Let $M > 0$. For every $k \in \mathbb{N}$, let $u(k) : \mathcal{I} \times \mathcal{J} \to [-M, M]^m$ be a vector payoff function, and let $G(k)$ be the repeated game whose payoff function is $u(k)$. Let $\widehat{G}$ be the game in which the payoffs change from one stage to another: the payoffs in stage k are given by the function $u(k)$. Answer the following questions:

(a) Let $C \subseteq \mathbb{R}^m$ be a convex and closed set. Prove that if for every $k \in \mathbb{N}$ the set C is a B-set for Player 1 in $G(k)$, then C is approachable by Player 1 in the game $\widehat{G}$.

(b) Show by example that the result in the previous item does not necessarily hold if C is not convex.

14.28 Consider the game described in Section 14.7 (page 598).

(a) Prove that the value of the one-stage game is $\frac{1}{2}$.

(b) Prove the value of the two-stage game is $\frac{3}{8}$.

(c) Denote by v^T the value of the T-stage repeated game. Prove that $\lim_{T\to\infty} v^T = \frac{1}{4}$.

Guidance: For item (c), use the fact that the uniform value of the game (Definition 14.28 on page 600) is $\frac{1}{4}$.

14.29 This exercise presents a generalization of the repeated game with incomplete information for Player 2 in Section 14.7 (page 598) to the case where the state of nature s is chosen by a probability distribution: $\mathbf{P}(s = 1) = p$ and $\mathbf{P}(s = 2) = 1 - p$, where $p \in [0, 1]$. Denote by $v(p)$ the uniform value of the game. We will prove that $v(p) = p(1 - p)$ for every $p \in [0, 1]$.

(a) Prove that $v(0) = v(1) = 0$.

(b) Prove that Player 1, knowing s, can guarantee $p(1 - p)$ by not using his information, and playing the same mixed action in every stage. What mixed action will he choose?

(c) Define $C := \text{conv}\{(0, 0), (\frac{1-p}{2}, 0), (0, \frac{p}{2}), (\frac{1-p}{2}, \frac{p}{2})\}$. Prove that if C is approachable by Player 2, then $v(p) \leq p(1 - p)$.

(d) Prove that C is approachable by Player 2.

(e) Deduce that $v(p) = p(1 - p)$ for every $p \in [0, 1]$.

(f) For every $\varepsilon > 0$, find a strategy for Player 2 that guarantees $p(1 - p) + \varepsilon$.

14.30 In this exercise, we present an example of a repeated game with incomplete information for Player 2, in which, under the optimal strategy, Player 1 reveals all the information in his possession. Consider the repeated game with incomplete information, as defined in Section 14.7 (page 598), with the following state games:

Player 2

	L	R
T	−1	0
B	0	0

Player 1

The state game $s = 1$

Player 2

	L	R
T	0	0
B	0	−1

Player 1

The state game $s = 2$

The state of nature is chosen using the distribution: $\mathbf{P}(s = 1) = p$ and $\mathbf{P}(s = 2) = 1 - p$, where $0 \leq p \leq 1$.

(a) Denote by $w(p)$ the value of the game in which Player 1 is restricted to playing the strategies in $\mathcal{B}_1^*$; in other words, he does not make use of his information regarding the state of nature. Prove that $w(p) = -p(1 - p)$.

(b) For each player, find a strategy guaranteeing him 0 in the repeated game. Deduce that the uniform value of the game is $v(p) = 0$, for every $p \in [0, 1]$, and explain how Player 1 uses the information in his possession.

14.31 Repeat Exercise 14.30, using the following payoff functions:

Player 2

	L	R
T	2	0
B	0	1

Player 1

The state game $s = 1$

Player 2

	L	R
T	1	0
B	0	2

Player 1

The state game $s = 2$

(a) Prove that $w(p) = \frac{(2-p)(1+p)}{3}$.

(b) Write out the corresponding repeated game with vector payoffs G_V.

(c) Sketch, in the plane, the sets F and $R_2(q)$ for $q \in [0, 1]$.

(d) Prove that for all $p \in [0, 1]$, the set

$$C := \text{conv} \left\{ (0, 0), \left(0, \frac{p^2 + 2}{3} \right), \right.$$

$$\left. \left(\frac{p^2 - 2p + 3}{3}, 0 \right), \left(\frac{p^2 - 2p + 3}{3}, \frac{p^2 + 2}{3} \right) \right\} \tag{14.130}$$

is a B-set for Player 2 in the game G_V.

(e) What is $v(p)$, the uniform value of the repeated game, for every $p \in [0, 1]$? Justify your answer.

Guidance: To prove that C is a B-set for Player 2 in the game G_V, divide the points in F into three sets: $A_1 := \{x \in F : x_1 \leq \frac{p^2 - 2p + 3}{3}\}$, $A_2 := \{x \in F : x_2 \leq \frac{p^2 + 2}{3}\}$, and $A_3 := F\backslash(A_1 \cup A_2)$. The q corresponding to $x \in A_1$ in the definition of the B-set (of Player 2) is $q = \frac{p^2+2}{3}$; the q corresponding to $x \in A_2$ in the definition of the B-set (of Player 2) is $q = \frac{p^2-2p+3}{3}$. For $x \in A_3$, compute the supporting line of C at the point $(\frac{p^2-2p+3}{3}, \frac{p^2+2}{3})$ that is the perpendicular to the line connecting x to that point, and show that there is a q such that this supporting line separates x from $R_2(q)$.

14.32 In this exercise, we present an example of a repeated game with incomplete information for Player 2 in which, under the optimal strategy, Player 1 reveals only some of the information in his possession. Consider the repeated game with incomplete information for Player 2, where Player 1 has two actions $\mathcal{I} = \{T, B\}$, Player 2 has three actions $\mathcal{J} = \{L, M, R\}$, and there are two states of nature $S = \{1, 2\}$. The state of nature is chosen by the toss of a fair coin: $\mathbf{P}(s = 1) = \mathbf{P}(s = 2) = \frac{1}{2}$, and the state games are given by the following tables:

Player 2

	L	M	R
T	4	0	2
B	4	0	-2

Player 1 (left table)

The state game $s = 1$

Player 2

	L	M	R
T	0	4	-2
B	0	4	2

Player 1 (right table)

The state game $s = 2$

(a) Prove that when Player 1 does not use the information in his possession, he can guarantee at most 0; that is, the value of the game in which Player 1's set of strategies is $\mathcal{B}_1^*$, and Player 2's set of strategies is $\mathcal{B}_2$, is 0.

(b) Prove that when Player 2 also knows the state of nature, the value of the game is 0.

(c) Returning to the game in which only Player 1 knows the state of nature, define the strategy $\hat{\sigma}_1$ of Player 1 as follows:

- In the first stage, if $s = 1$, play the mixed action $[\frac{3}{4}(T), \frac{1}{4}(B)]$. If $s = 2$, play the mixed action $[\frac{1}{4}(T), \frac{3}{4}(B)]$.
- In each stage $t > 1$, repeat the action that was played in the first stage; i.e., play either T in every stage, or B in every stage, according to the result of the lottery in the first stage.

Compute the conditional probability $\mathbf{P}(s = 1 \mid i^1 = T)$ that the state of the world is $s = 1$, given that Player 1 played T in the first stage. Compute also $\mathbf{P}(s = 1 \mid i^1 = B)$.

(d) Show that for every strategy of Player 2, the conditional expectation of the average payoff $\overline{g}^t$, given the action of Player 1 in the first stage, is at least 1. Deduce that Player 1 can guarantee at least 1 in the infinitely repeated game.

(e) Prove that if the set $C = [0, 1]^2$ is approachable by Player 2, then the uniform value of the game is at most 1.

(f) Draw, in the plane, the set of possible payoffs F and the sets $R_2(0, 0, 1)$, $R_2(0, 1, 0)$, $R_2(1, 0, 0)$, $R_2(\frac{1}{2}, \frac{1}{2}, 0)$, and $R_2(\frac{1}{2}, 0, \frac{1}{2})$.

(g) Prove that C is approachable by Player 2. Note that when checking the condition in the definition of a B-set, one needs to distinguish between points on the diagonal $x_1 = x_2$ and points below the diagonal.

(h) In which stages of the game does Player 1 reveal information on the state of nature? Does he ever entirely reveal the state of nature?

14.33 In this exercise, we generalize the results presented in Section 14.7 (page 598), and Exercises 14.30, 14.31, and 14.32, to two-player zero-sum infinitely repeated games with incomplete information on one side. Consider the following game:

- There are K state games (states of nature). In all state games, the set of actions of Player 1 is $\mathcal{I} = \{1, 2, \ldots, I\}$, and the set of actions of Player 2 is $\mathcal{J} = \{1, 2, \ldots, J\}$. The payoff function in state game k is u_k; $u_k(i, j)$ is the payoff that Player 2 pays Player 1 when the state of nature is the matrix u_k, and the pair of actions chosen is (i, j). Denote $S = \{1, 2, \ldots, K\}$.
- The game begins with a move of chance that selects one of the payoff matrices according to the probability distribution $p = (p_k)_{k=1}^K$, which is common knowledge among the players.
- Player 1 knows which state game has been chosen, but Player 2 does not have this information.
- In each stage, the two players choose their actions simultaneously: Player 1 chooses an action in $\mathcal{I}$, and Player 2 chooses an action in $\mathcal{J}$.
- In each stage t, when coming to choose an action, each player knows the actions chosen by both players in the previous stages. The players are not informed of their payoffs after each stage (although Player 1, knowing the state game and the actions chosen, can calculate the payoffs, while Player 2 cannot do so).
- This description of the game is common knowledge among the players.

For every distribution $p \in \Delta(S)$, denote the game described above by $G(p)$, denote by $v(p)$ the value of $G(p)$, if the game has a value, and denote by $D(p)$ the one-stage game in which the payoff matrix is chosen according to the distribution p, and neither Player 1 nor Player 2 knows which matrix has been chosen. The game $D(p)$ is a one-stage game, and therefore its value exists. Denote this value by $w(p)$.

Let cavw be the smallest concave function that is pointwise greater than or equal to w. In other words:

$$(\text{cav}w)(q) \geq w(q), \quad \forall q \in \Delta(S). \tag{14.131}$$

In this exercise, we will prove that the value $v(p)$ exists, and equals $(\text{cav}w)(p)$, and we will construct the players' optimal strategies.

We first prove that Player 1 can guarantee this value.

(a) Show that for every $p \in \Delta(S)$, Player 1 can guarantee $w(p)$ in $G(p)$ (find a strategy of Player 1 that guarantees this value).

(b) Let $p^1, p^2, \ldots, p^L \in \Delta(S)$, and let $\alpha = (\alpha_l)_{l=1}^L$ be a distribution over $\{1, 2, \ldots, L\}$ satisfying $p = \sum_{l=1}^L \alpha_l p^l$. Consider the following strategy σ_1^* of

Player 1: if u_{k_0} is the payoff function that has been selected in the chance move at the beginning of the game, randomly choose $l_0 \in \{1, 2, \ldots, L\}$ according to the following distribution $\lambda^{k_0} = (\lambda_1^{k_0}, \lambda_2^{k_0}, \ldots, \lambda_L^{k_0})$:

$$\lambda_l^{k_0} = \frac{\alpha_l p_{k_0}^l}{\sum_{l'=1}^{L} \alpha_{l'} p_{k_0}^{l'}} = \frac{\alpha_l p_{k_0}^l}{p_{k_0}}. \tag{14.132}$$

In each stage of the game, play the optimal strategy in the game $D(p^{l_0})$.

We will prove that this strategy guarantees Player 1 the payoff $\sum_{l=1}^{L} \alpha_l w(p^l)$ in $G(p)$.

To accomplish this, consider the game $G'(p)$, a variation of $G(p)$, where Player 2 is informed of the index l_0 that Player 1 chose. Show that after Player 2 knows l_0, the conditional probability that the chosen payoff matrix is u_k, given l_0, equals $p_k^{l_0}$. Deduce from this that in $G'(p)$, the strategy σ_1^* guarantees Player 1 the[11] payoff $\sum_{l=1}^{L} \alpha_l w(p^l)$.

(c) Using the fact that in the game $G(p)$, Player 2 has fewer strategies than he has in $G'(p)$ (because he has more information in $G'(p)$), deduce, with the help of Exercise 4.27 (page 134), that in $G(p)$, the strategy σ_1^* guarantees Player 1 the payoff $\sum_{l=1}^{L} \alpha_l w(p^l)$.

(d) Deduce that Player 1 can guarantee $(\text{cav} w)(p)$ in $G(p)$.

We now prove that Player 2 can also guarantee $(\text{cav} w)(p)$ in $G(p)$. Define an auxiliary game with vector payoffs G_V, where the sets of actions of the players are $\mathcal{I}$ and $\mathcal{J}$ respectively, and the matrix of vector payoffs is

$$u(i, j) = (u_1(i, j), u_2(i, j), \ldots, u_K(i, j)) \in \mathbb{R}^K. \tag{14.133}$$

Define

$$Z := \{z \in \mathbb{R}^K : \langle q, z \rangle \geq w(q), \quad \forall q \in \Delta(S)\}. \tag{14.134}$$

The significance of Z stems from the following claim:

(e) Prove that $(\text{cav} w)(p) = \min_{z \in Z} \langle p, z \rangle$.

For every $z \in Z$, define

$$M_z := z - \mathbb{R}_+^K = \{x \in \mathbb{R}^K : x_k \leq z_k \ \forall k \in S\}. \tag{14.135}$$

As we will see, the set M_z is approachable by Player 2 in G_V, and this is the set corresponding to the rectangles C defined in Equation (14.85) (page 604), and in Exercises 14.31 and 14.32.

---

[11] The lottery that chooses l_0 has the property that the conditional distribution over S, after the lottery, will be one of the probability distributions $p^1, p^2, \ldots, p^L$ with probabilities $\alpha_1, \alpha_2, \ldots, \alpha_L$, respectively. It follows that if for any l_0 chosen, Player 1 can guarantee $w(p^{l_0})$, then he can guarantee $\sum_{l=1}^{L} \alpha_l w(p^l)$ in $G(p)$. This random choice is the only stage in which Player 1 uses the knowledge he has regarding the payoff matrix that has been chosen. After l_0 has been chosen, Player 1 plays, in every stage, an optimal strategy in $G(p^{l_0})$, independently of the true payoff matrix u_{k_0}, and thus he does not reveal any additional information about the chosen payoff matrix in those stages.

(f) Prove that the set M_z is approachable by Player 2 in G_V if and only if for every $\pi \in \mathbb{R}^K$,

$$\max_{y \in \Delta(\mathcal{J})} \min_{x \in \Delta(I)} U_\pi(x, y) \geq \min_{z' \in M_z} \langle \pi, z' \rangle. \tag{14.136}$$

Guidance: Use Corollary 14.26 (page 597), reversing the roles of the players.

(g) Prove that Equation (14.136) obtains for $\pi = \vec{0}$.

(h) Let $\pi \neq \vec{0}$ satisfy the property that there exists $k \in S$ such that $\pi_k > 0$. Prove that the right-hand side of Equation (14.136) equals $-\infty$, while the left-hand side is finite, and therefore Equation (14.136) obtains.

(i) We now show that $z \in Z$ if and only if Equation (14.136) holds for every $\pi \neq \vec{0}$ satisfying $\pi_k \leq 0$ for all $k \in S$. Let $\pi \neq \vec{0}$ satisfy $\pi_k \leq 0$ for all $k \in S$. Define $\hat{q}_k = \frac{\pi_k}{\sum_{k'=1}^K \pi_{k'}}$. Show that $\hat{q} = (\hat{q}_k)_{k=1}^K \in \Delta(S)$.

(j) Prove that Equation (14.136) obtains for π if and only if the following equation obtains:

$$\min_{y \in \Delta(\mathcal{J})} \max_{x \in \Delta(I)} U_{\hat{q}}(x, y) \leq \max_{z' \in M_z} \langle \hat{q}, z' \rangle. \tag{14.137}$$

(k) Prove that the right-hand side of Equation (14.137) equals $\langle q, z \rangle$.

(l) Prove that the left-hand side of Equation (14.137) equals $w(\hat{q})$.

(m) Deduce that $z \in Z$ if and only if M_z is approachable by Player 2 in G_V.

(n) Let $z_0 \in Z$ satisfy $\langle p, z_0 \rangle = \min_{z \in Z} \langle p, z \rangle$. Deduce that M_{z_0} is approachable by Player 2 in G_V.

(o) Prove that the strategy of Player 2 that approaches M_{z_0} in G_V guarantees him $(\text{cavw})(p)$ in $G(p)$.

14.34 We proved Theorem 14.44 (page 611) for the case in which $|E| = |A|$, and every expert recommends one action in every stage. Prove the theorem for any set E of experts.

Guidance: Use Exercise 14.27.

14.35 In this exercise we consider a decision problem *without* experts. A strategy σ of a decision maker in a decision problem is a *no-regret strategy* if for every action $\hat{a} \in A$, and every sequence $(s^1, s^2, \ldots)$ of states of nature,

$$\mathbf{P}_\sigma \left(\liminf_{T \to \infty} \left(\frac{1}{T} \sum_{t=1}^T u(a^t, s^t) - \frac{1}{T} \sum_{t=1}^T u(\hat{a}, s^t) \right) \geq 0 \right) = 1. \tag{14.138}$$

Prove that there exists a no-regret strategy in every decision problem.

Guidance: Show that this problem may be described as a decision problem with experts, and use Theorem 14.44 (page 611) to prove the claim.

14.36 In this exercise, we present Blackwell's proof of Theorem 14.44 (page 611), which states that there exists a no-regret strategy when there are $|A|$ experts, and each of them is identified with one action (as was assumed in Section 14.8.2, on page 611).

Consider a decision problem with experts, where $E = A$, and for every action $a \in A$ there exists an expert $e \in E$ such that $a_e^t = a$ for every $t \in \mathbb{N}$. Define a game with vector payoffs, where the set of actions of Player 1 is A, the set of actions of Player 2 is S, and the payoffs are $(|S| + 1)$-dimensional vectors $(w(s, a))_{a \in A}^{s \in S}$, where $w(s, a) = ((w_{s'}(s, a))_{s' \in S}, U(s, a))$, defined as follows:

$$
\begin{aligned}
w_{s'}(s, a) &= 1 & s' &= s, \\
w_{s'}(s, a) &= 0 & s' &\neq s.
\end{aligned}
\tag{14.139}
$$

Define a set $C \subseteq \mathbb{R}^{|S|+1}$ as follows:

$$
C := \{(q, x) \in \Delta(S) \times \mathbb{R} : x \geq \max_{p \in \Delta(A)} U(p, q)\}.
\tag{14.140}
$$

(a) Prove that C is a convex set.
(b) Prove that C is not excludable by Player 2.
(c) Deduce that C is approachable by Player 1, and prove that every strategy of Player 1 that approaches C is a no-regret strategy: if Player 1 plays this strategy, then with probability 1

$$
\liminf_{t \to \infty} u(\overline{x}^t, \overline{y}^t) - \max_{a \in A} U(a, \overline{y}^t) \geq 0.
\tag{14.141}
$$

14.37 In this exercise, we present an alternative proof to the proof given in Exercise 14.36. Repeat Exercise 14.36 for the game where the set of actions of Player 1 is A, the set of actions of Player 2 is S, and the payoffs are $(|S| \times |A|)$-dimensional vectors $(w(s, a))_{a \in A}^{s \in S}$, with $w(s, a) = (w_{s',a'}(s, a))_{a' \in A}^{s' \in S}$ defined as follows:

$$
\begin{aligned}
w_{s',a'}(s, a) &= 1 & (s', a') &= (s, a), \\
w_{s',a'}(s, a) &= 0 & (s', a') &\neq (s, a),
\end{aligned}
\tag{14.142}
$$

and for the following set C:

$$
C := \{q \in \Delta(S \times A) : U(\mathbf{1}_a, q_{|a}) \geq \max_{p \in \Delta(A)} U(p, q_{|a}), \quad \forall a \in A\},
\tag{14.143}
$$

where U is the multilinear extension of u, and for every action $a \in A$, $q_{|a}$ is the conditional distribution over S given a, with this conditional distribution defined by

$$
q_{|a}(s) := \begin{cases} \frac{q(s,a)}{\sum_{s' \in S} q(s',a)} & \text{if } \sum_{s' \in S} q(s', a) > 0, \\ 0 & \text{if } \sum_{s' \in S} q(s', a) = 0. \end{cases}
\tag{14.144}
$$

14.38 Let S be a finite set of states of nature, and let A be a finite set of actions available to a decision maker. Let $F : \Delta(S) \to 2^A$ be a set-valued function with nonempty values associating each $y \in \Delta(S)$ with a set $F(y) \subseteq A$ and satisfying the property that for every $a \in A$, the set $F^{-1}(a) := \{y \in \Delta(S) : a \in F(y)\}$ is closed and convex. When the state of nature is chosen according to y, the best actions, from the perspective of the decision maker, are those in $F(y)$. Define a game with $(|A| \times |S|)$-dimensional vector payoffs as follows: the payoff $u(a, s)$ that is attained when the state of nature is s, and the action chosen is a, is the unit vector whose value is 0 at every coordinate except the coordinate (a, s), where its value is 1. Denote this vector by $\mathbf{1}_{as} \in \mathbb{R}^{|A| \times |S|}$. Define a set $C \subset \mathbb{R}^{|S| \times |A|}$ as follows:

$$C := \operatorname{conv}\left\{\sum_{s \in S} y_s \mathbf{1}_{as}, a \in A, y \in F^{-1}(a)\right\}. \tag{14.145}$$

(a) Prove that the set C is a convex set.
(b) Prove that C is approachable by Player 1.
(c) Let n_a^t be the number of stages, up to t, in which the action a is chosen, and let y_a^t be the empirical distribution of the states of nature in all stages up to stage t in which the action a is chosen:

$$n_a^t := |\{j \le t: a^j = a\}|, \quad y_a^t(s) := \frac{1}{n_a^t}|\{j \le t: s^j = s, a^j = a\}|.$$

Prove that if the decision maker plays a strategy that approaches C, and if $\liminf_{t \to \infty} \frac{n_a^t}{t} > 0$, then $\lim_{t \to \infty} d(y_a^t, F^{-1}(a)) = 0$. In other words, if the density of the stages where the action a is chosen is positive, then the empirical distribution of the states of nature in the stages in which the action a is chosen approaches $F^{-1}(a)$, which is the set of distributions for which a is the best response in the decision maker's opinion.

14.39 Morris notices that in the proof of Theorem 14.45 (page 611), in order to prove that $\operatorname{val}(\widehat{G}_\pi) \ge \inf_{x \in C}\langle \pi, x\rangle$ for every $\pi \in \mathbb{R}^A$, the only fact that is used is that the vectors $\vec{0}$ and $(x^k)_{k \in \mathbb{N}}$ are in the nonnegative quadrant of $\mathbb{R}$. Morris therefore claims that every set containing these vectors is approachable in the auxiliary game. Is Morris correct? If not, what is his error?

14.40 In this exercise we show that the theory of approachability developed in this chapter is related to the concept of correlated equilibrium (Chapter 8): if each player in a strategic-form game G follows a strategy that approaches a certain target set in a proper auxiliary game, then the empirical play converges to the set of correlated equilibria of the game G.

Let $G = (N, (S_i)_{i \in N}, (u_i)_{i \in N})$ be a two-player game in strategic form, and denote by $E_c \subseteq \Delta(S_1 \times S_2)$ the set of correlated equilibria of this game. Recall that every pair of mixed actions $(\sigma_1, \sigma_2) \in \Sigma_1 \times \Sigma_2$ induces a probability distribution p_{σ_1, σ_2} in $\Delta(S_1 \times S_2)$ by (see Equation (8.10) on page 319)

$$p_{\sigma_1, \sigma_2}(s_1, s_2) := \sigma_1(s_1) \cdot \sigma_2(s_2), \quad \forall s_1 \in S_1, \forall s_2 \in S_2. \tag{14.146}$$

When $\sigma_1 = [1(s_1)]$ is a pure strategy, we denote p_{σ_1, σ_2} by p_{s_1, σ_2}. Similarly, when $\sigma_2 = [1(s_2)]$ is a pure strategy, we denote p_{σ_1, σ_2} by p_{σ_1, s_2}.

(a) For every $s_1 \in S_1$ define

$$\Sigma_2(s_1) := \{\sigma_2 \in \Sigma_2: u_1(s_1, \sigma_2) = \max_{t_1 \in S_1} u_1(t_1, \sigma_2)\}. \tag{14.147}$$

That is, $\Sigma_2(s_1)$ is the set of all mixed actions of Player 2 for which s_1 is a best response. Prove that the set $\Sigma_2(s_1)$ is a closed and convex subset of Σ_2.

(b) Consider the following repeated game with vector payoffs Γ:

- The set of players is $N = \{1, 2\}$.
- The sets of actions are $\mathcal{I} = S_1$ and $\mathcal{J} = S_2$.
- The payoffs are $|S_1| \cdot |S_2|$-dimensional. The payoff vector at the entry (s_1, s_2) is a unit vector whose coordinate (s_1, s_2) is equal to 1, and all other coordinates are 0.

Note that the strategy sets of the players are the same in G and in Γ. Define

$$C_1(s_1) := \{p_{s_1, \sigma_2} : \sigma_2 \in \Sigma_2(s_1)\} \subseteq \Delta(S_1 \times S_2), \tag{14.148}$$

and let $C_1 := \text{conv}(\cup_{s_1 \in S_1} C_1(s_1))$. Prove that the set C_1 is approachable by Player 1.

(c) Prove that for every $p \in C_1$, every $s_1 \in S_1$, and every $s_1' \in S_1$,

$$\sum_{s_2 \in S_2} p(s_1, s_2) u_1(s_1, s_2) \geq \sum_{s_2 \in S_2} p(s_1, s_2) u_1(s_1', s_2) \tag{14.149}$$

(compare this equation with Equation (8.9) on page 318).

(d) Define the analogue sets for Player 2: for every $s_2 \in S_2$ let

$$\Sigma_1(s_2) := \{\sigma_1 \in \Sigma_1 : u_2(\sigma_1, s_2) = \max_{t_2 \in S_2} u_2(\sigma_1, t_2)\}, \tag{14.150}$$

$$C_2(s_2) := \{p_{\sigma_1, s_2} : \sigma_1 \in \Sigma_1(s_2)\} \subseteq \Delta(S_1 \times S_2), \tag{14.151}$$

$$C_2 := \text{conv}(\cup_{s_2 \in S_2} C_2(s_2)). \tag{14.152}$$

Prove that the set C_2 is approachable by Player 2.

(e) Let σ_1^* be a strategy of Player 1 that approaches C_1 in Γ and let σ_2^* be a strategy of Player 2 that approaches C_2 in Γ. Prove that under (σ_1^*, σ_2^*) the average play converges to the set of correlated equilibria of the original game in strategic form. That is,

$$P_{\sigma_1^*, \sigma_2^*}\left(\lim_{N \to \infty} d(p_N, E_c) = 0\right) = 1, \tag{14.153}$$

where $p_N \in \Delta(S_1 \times S_2)$ is the empirical play up to stage N:

$$p_N(s_1, s_2) := \frac{1}{N} \#\{n \leq N : (a_1^n, a_2^n) = (s_1, s_2)\}. \tag{14.154}$$

(f) Can you generalize the result to n-player games in strategic form?

14.41 Prove that a set cannot be weakly approachable by Player 1 and also weakly excludable by Player 2.

15 Stochastic games

Chapter summary

In this chapter we present the model of *stochastic games*, which is a generalization of the model of repeated games for the case where the available sets of actions and the payoff functions may change over time by a random process determined by the players' actions. We study the concept of Nash equilibrium both for the finite-stage game and for the discounted infinite-stage game. For the finite-stage game we construct a *subgame perfect* Nash equilibrium using *backward induction*. For the discounted infinite-stage game we apply *fixed-point theorems* to prove the existence of both the value and optimal *stationary* strategies in two-player zero-sum games. We similarly prove the existence of a Nash equilibrium in *stationary* strategies in general non-zero-sum games.

In Chapter 13 we studied repeated games in which the same players repeatedly play the same stage game. Players often interact again and again in a changing environment. Football teams may play against each other several times in a season in different competitions with different positions in the league. A salesperson may represent different companies and consequently provide different goods or services and negotiate with different purchasers as time goes by. The life of a couple changes over the years from courtship to marriage to raising kids to sending the kids to college; throughout life their commitments change as well.

To capture such situations of repeated interactions, we consider in this chapter repeated games in which the base game changes from stage to stage according to both the players' actions and some "exogenous" random factors. This model, called a *stochastic game*, was first presented by Lloyd Shapley in 1953. Similarly to what we did in Chapter 13, we will study in this chapter both the finite T-stage game and the discounted infinite-stage game. We will construct Nash equilibria for the T-stage game using *backward induction* and prove the existence of Nash equilibrium for the discounted infinite-stage game. We will see that in the discounted infinite-stage stochastic game players have *stationary* equilibrium strategies, which are strategies in which the action of a player, at every given stage in the game, depends only on the current base game and not on the whole history of the play.

15.1   The model

. . . .

A stochastic game is a repeated game in which the base game changes from stage to stage. The strategic game in a certain stage, which defines the sets of actions and the payoff functions of the players are called the *state of the game* (or *state* for short).

Definition 15.1 *A* stochastic game *is an ordered quintuple* $\Gamma = (N, Z, (A_i(z))_{i \in N, z \in Z}, (u_i)_{i \in N}, q)$ *in which*

- *N is a finite set of players.*
- *Z is a finite set of states.*
- *For each player $i \in N$ and every state $z \in Z$, the finite set $A_i(z)$ is the set of actions available to player i in state z. For each state z denote by $A(z)$ the set of vectors of actions available for the players in state z:*

$$A(z) := \underset{i \in N}{\times} A_i(z). \tag{15.1}$$

Define

$$\Lambda := \{(z, a): z \in Z, a \in A(z)\}. \tag{15.2}$$

This is the set of all pairs (state, action vector) possible in the game.
- *For each player $i \in N$, the function $u_i : \Lambda \to \mathbb{R}$ is the payoff function of player i. Denote by $u_i(z, a)$ the payoff to player i in state z when the players are taking actions $a \in A(z)$.*
- *$q : \Lambda \to \Delta(Z)$ is the* transition function, *that is, a function assigning to every state $z \in Z$ and to every action vector $a \in A(z)$ a probability distribution $q(z, a) \in \Delta(Z)$ on the set of states Z.*

The stochastic game is played as follows: the game starts at an initial state $z^1 \in Z$. Each player $i \in N$ chooses an action $a_i^1 \in A_i(z^1)$. This choice is made by all players simultaneously. Each player i receives a payoff $u_i(z^1, a^1)$, where $a^1 = (a_i^1)_{i \in N}$, and a new state z^2 is chosen according to the probability distribution $q(\cdot \mid z^1, a^1)$. At each stage $t > 1$ the current state z^t is told to the players. The players simultaneously choose actions; each player $i \in N$ chooses an action $a_i^t \in A_i(z^t)$, receives a payoff $u_i(z^t, a^t)$, where $a^t = (a_i^t)_{i \in N}$, and a new state z^{t+1} is chosen according to the probability distribution $q(z^t, a^t)$. In other words, if the state at stage t is z and the players play the action vector a, then the probability that the new state z^{t+1} at stage $t + 1$ is z' is given by

$$\mathbf{P}(z^{t+1} = z' \mid z^t = z, a^t = a) = q(z' \mid z, a). \tag{15.3}$$

For a given initial state z^1, a stochastic game is a game in extensive form with an infinite game tree (see Section 6.4). Therefore, a stochastic game as given by Definition 15.1 is a collection of $|Z|$ extensive-form games with infinite game trees.

Example 15.2 **Repeated games** Every repeated game is a stochastic game in which the set of states Z consists of a single state. ◀

Example 15.3 **Finite games in strategic form** Every finite game in strategic form is a stochastic game. To see this, consider the game given in Figure 15.1.

Player II

		L	R
	T	6, 6	2, 7
Player I	B	7, 2	0, 0

Figure 15.1 The game in strategic form in Example 15.3.

In Figure 15.2 we describe this game as a stochastic game with two states.

	L	R
T	6, 6 z_1	2, 7 z_1
B	7, 2 z_1	0, 0 z_1

state z_0

0, 0 z_1

state z_1

Figure 15.2 The stochastic game corresponding to the game in Figure 15.1

In Figure 15.3 each state is described by a payoff matrix: the rows are the actions of Player I and the columns are the actions of Player II. The transition function is given at the top-right corner of each cell. In this game, all transitions are deterministic and the indication at the top-right corner of a cell is the next state reached when that pair of actions is played. For example, if in state z_0 Player I plays T and Player II plays R, then the payoff to Player I is 2, the payoff to Player II is 7, and the next state is z_1.

In the stochastic game in Figure 15.2, when the initial state is $z^1 = z_0$, at the first stage the players play the strategic-form game that appears in Figure 15.1, and from the second stage on the payoff to each player is 0. ◀

Example 15.4 In this example we present a simplified situation of fishing. Two fishermen fish at a lake where the quantity of fish can be "high" or "low." Every day, each fisherman decides whether to fish on a large scale, using many nets, or fish on a small scale, using a few nets. On each day, before choosing an action, each fisherman knows whether the quantity of fish in the lake is high or low. The amount of fish collected by each fisherman, which depends on his action, on the other fisherman's action, and on the quantity of fish in the lake on that day, is given in Figure 15.3.

Quantity of fish in the lake	How many nets you use	How many nets the other uses	Weight of fish you collect (tons)
High	Many	Many	7
High	Many	Few	8
High	Few	Many	4
High	Few	Few	5
Low	Many	Many	5
Low	Many	Few	6
Low	Few	Many	2
Low	Few	Few	3

Figure 15.3 The payoffs in Example 15.4

The quantity of fish in the lake changes from day to day according to the intensity of the fishing of the two fishermen, as given in Figure 15.4.

Quantity of fish in the lake	Total intensity of fishing (total number of nets)	Quantity of fish the following day
High	Both use many nets	Low
High	One uses many nets and one uses few nets	High with probability $\frac{2}{3}$, Low with probability $\frac{1}{3}$
High	Both use few nets	High
Low	Both use many nets	Low
Low	One uses many nets and one uses few nets	High with probability $\frac{1}{2}$, Low with probability $\frac{1}{2}$
Low	Both use few nets	High

Figure 15.4 The change in the quantity of fish following the fishermen's actions

This situation can be described as a stochastic game in the following way:

- The players are the two fishermen, $N = \{1, 2\}$.
- The set of states is $Z = \{z_h, z_\ell\}$, where z_h corresponds to a *high* quantity of fish in the lake and z_ℓ corresponds to a *low* quantity of fish in the lake.
- At each state z, each player i has two actions $A_i(z) = \{a_m, a_f\}$, where a_m corresponds to using *many* nets and a_f corresponds to using *few* nets.
- The transition probabilities and the payoff functions are given in Figure 15.5.

Clearly this is a very simplified description and in a real situation of this kind the number of states and actions will typically be much larger. For example, the quantity of fish in the lake is not just "high" or "low"; in general, the quantity is unknown to the fishermen, and the set of actions available to the fishermen is also richer.

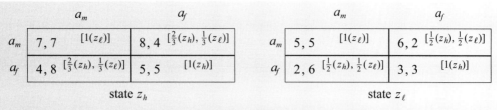

Figure 15.5 The stochastic game corresponding to the game in Example 15.4

◀

In the stochastic game presented in Figure 15.2, the state z_1 has the property that once it is reached, the play remains in that state in all future stages. Such a state is called an *absorbing state*.

Definition 15.5 *A state* $z \in Z$ *in a stochastic game is called an* absorbing state *if* $q(z \mid z, a) = 1$ *for every* $a \in A(z)$.

Example 15.6 Consider the situation in which at the first stage ($t = 1$) two players are playing the two-player strategic-form game in Example 15.3, and from the second stage on ($t \geq 2$), the payoffs to the players at each stage are the same as their payoff at stage $t = 1$. This game can be presented as the stochastic game with five states in Figure 15.6.

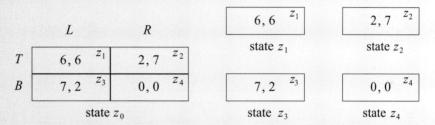

Figure 15.6 The stochastic game in Example 15.6

In this game, all states except one (state z_0) are absorbing. A game in which all states but one are absorbing is called an *absorbing game*. In this example, in each absorbing state every player has only one action and the constant payoff is equal to the payoff in the cell in state z_0 that leads to it. Therefore, rather than the detailed description used in Figure 15.6, we use the shorter description that appears in Figure 15.7.

Player II

		L	R
Player I	T	6, 6*	2, 7*
	B	7, 2*	0, 0*

state z_0

Figure 15.7 Short description of the stochastic game in Figure 15.6

The asterisks indicate two things: (a) a transition to absorbing states, and (b) the payoff written in an asterisked entry is both the stage payoff and the payoff in the absorbing state that this entry leads to. For example, the asterisk in the cell (T, L) indicates that if the actions T and L are played in state z_0, then the payoff at the current stage, as well as in all future stages, is $(6, 6)$.   ◄

15.2 The *T*-stage stochastic game

In this section we study the T-stage stochastic game. Just like the T-stage repeated game, the T-stage stochastic game is played for T stages, the utility of a player is his average payoff over the T stages, and each player tries to maximize his expected utility.

Given the initial state z^1, the T-stage stochastic game is a finite extensive-form game in which the probabilities of the chance moves are derived from the transition function q, and the information sets capture the fact that players choose their actions simultaneously: when choosing an action at stage t, a player does not know the choices of the other players. Thus, to every stochastic game correspond $|Z|$ finite extensive-form games, one for each initial state.

15.2.1 Histories and strategies

We assume that at each stage t, in addition to the current state, a player knows the sequence of states that were visited in all previous stages of the play, as well as the actions taken by all players at those stages. We refer to this whole package of information as the *history* of the play at stage t. The set of all *t-stage histories* is therefore

$$H(t) := \Lambda^{t-1} \times Z, \tag{15.4}$$

where Λ is defined in Equation (15.2) and Λ^0 is the set that contains only the empty history. A t-stage history is thus a sequence $h = (z^1, a^1, z^2, a^2, \dots, z^{t-1}, a^{t-1}, z^t)$. The set of all possible *finite histories* in the T-stage stochastic game is the set

$$H^T := \cup_{t=1}^T H(t). \tag{15.5}$$

As in repeated games, a probability distribution over the set of actions $A_i(z)$ is called a *mixed action*, and to emphasize the distinction between actions and mixed actions we call the former *pure actions*. For each player $i \in N$, a history in H^T corresponds to an information set of that player in the extensive-form representation of the stochastic T-stage game. Therefore a behavior strategy of a player is a function assigning to each finite history in H^T a mixed action available to the player at the last state of that history.

Definition 15.7 A behavior strategy *of player i is a function* τ_i *assigning to each history* $h = (z^1, a^1, z^2, a^2, \dots, z^{t-1}, a^{t-1}, z^t) \in H^T$ *a mixed action* $\tau_i(h) \in \Delta(A_i(z^t))$ *available to player i in state* z^t.

We note that a strategy prescribes the actions of a player for *every* initial state z^1, and not just for a specific initial state.

We denote by $\mathcal{B}_i^T$ the set of all behavior strategies of player i in the T-stage stochastic game. Since every initial state $z \in Z$ determines a finite extensive-form game, a behavior strategy in the stochastic game consists of $|Z|$ behavior strategies, one for each of the extensive-form games corresponding to the $|Z|$ possible initial states.

Remark 15.8 *A pure strategy of player i is a function τ_i that assigns an action $\tau_i(h) \in A_i(z^t)$ to each history $h = (z^1, a^1, z^2, a^2, \ldots, z^{t-1}, a^{t-1}, z^t) \in H^T$. In particular, a pure strategy is a behavior strategy. Since a mixed strategy is a probability distribution over the set of pure strategies (see Definition 5.2 on page 145), and since a stochastic game is a game with perfect recall (explain why), it follows from Kuhn's Theorem (see Theorem 4.49 on page 118) that every mixed strategy has a strategically equivalent behavior strategy (and vice versa). Therefore we shall confine our study to behavior strategies, which are more natural and more convenient to work with in the model of stochastic games.* ◆

A play in the T-stage stochastic game is a sequence of T pairs (state, action vector), namely, an element of Λ^T. Since the set of states Z and the sets of actions $(A_i(z))_{i\in N, z\in Z}$ are finite sets, the set of plays is also a finite set. As we saw in Chapter 13, each vector of behavior strategies $\tau = (\tau_i)_{i\in N}$, together with the initial state z^1, induces a probability distribution $P_{z^1,\tau}$ on the set of plays Λ^T. This probability is given by the following expression: for every play $(z^1, a^1, z^2, a^2, \ldots, z^T, a^T) \in \Lambda^T$,

$$\mathbf{P}_{z^1,\tau}(z^1, a^1, z^2, a^2, \ldots, z^T, a^T) \tag{15.6}$$

$$= \left(\prod_{t=1}^{T} \prod_{i\in N} \tau_i(z^1, a^1, \ldots, z^{t-1}, a^{t-1}, z^t)(a_i^t) \right) \cdot \left(\prod_{t=1}^{T-1} q(z^{t+1} \mid z^t, a^t) \right).$$

The expectation with respect to the probability distribution $P_{z^1,\tau}$ is denoted by $\mathbf{E}_{z^1,\tau}$.

Example 15.4 **The fishermen game** (*Continued*) The set of one-stage histories is the set of initial states $\{z_h, z_\ell\}$. A two-stage history is a quadruple (z^1, a_1^1, a_2^1, z^2), where each of the variables can have two values. Therefore there are 16 two-stage histories. Notice that in our example four of these histories have probability 0, namely, the histories $(z_\ell, a_f, a_f, z_\ell)$, (z_h, a_f, a_f, z_ℓ), (z_ℓ, a_m, a_m, z_h), and (z_h, a_m, a_m, z_h).

An example of behavior strategies of the players in the two-stage stochastic game appears in Figure 15.8.

$$\tau_1(z_\ell) = [1(a_m)], \qquad \tau_2(z_\ell) = [1(a_m)],$$
$$\tau_1(z_h) = [\tfrac{1}{4}(a_f), \tfrac{3}{4}(a_m)], \qquad \tau_2(z_h) = [1(a_m)],$$
$$\tau_1(z_\ell, a_m, a_m, z_\ell) = [\tfrac{1}{4}(a_f), \tfrac{3}{4}(a_m)], \qquad \tau_2(z_\ell, a_m, a_m, z_\ell) = [\tfrac{2}{5}(a_f), \tfrac{3}{5}(a_m)],$$
$$\tau_1(z_\ell, a_m, a_m, z_h) = [\tfrac{1}{2}(a_f), \tfrac{1}{2}(a_m)], \qquad \tau_2(z_\ell, a_m, a_m, z_h) = [\tfrac{1}{5}(a_f), \tfrac{4}{5}(a_m)],$$
$$\tau_1(z_\ell, a_m, a_f, z_\ell) = [\tfrac{1}{2}(a_f), \tfrac{1}{2}(a_m)], \qquad \tau_2(z_\ell, a_m, a_f, z_\ell) = [\tfrac{1}{3}(a_f), \tfrac{1}{2}(a_m)],$$
$$\tau_1(z_\ell, a_m, a_f, z_h) = [1(a_f)], \qquad \tau_2(z_\ell, a_m, a_f, z_h) = [\tfrac{2}{3}(a_f), \tfrac{1}{3}(a_m)],$$
$$\tau_1(z_\ell, a_f, a_m, z_\ell) = [\tfrac{1}{3}(a_f), \tfrac{2}{3}(a_m)], \qquad \tau_2(z_\ell, a_f, a_m, z_\ell) = [\tfrac{1}{2}(a_f), \tfrac{1}{2}(a_m)],$$
$$\tau_1(z_\ell, a_f, a_m, z_h) = [\tfrac{1}{8}(a_f), \tfrac{7}{8}(a_m)], \qquad \tau_2(z_\ell, a_f, a_m, z_h) = [\tfrac{4}{9}(a_f), \tfrac{5}{9}(a_m)],$$
$$\tau_1(z_\ell, a_f, a_f, z_\ell) = [1(a_3)], \qquad \tau_2(z_\ell, a_f, a_f, z_\ell) = [\tfrac{2}{3}(a_f), \tfrac{1}{3}(a_m)],$$
$$\tau_1(z_\ell, a_f, a_f, z_h) = [\tfrac{3}{4}(a_f), \tfrac{1}{4}(a_m)], \qquad \tau_2(z_\ell, a_f, a_f, z_h) = [1(a_m)],$$
$$\tau_1(z_h, a_m, a_m, z_\ell) = [1(a_f)], \qquad \tau_2(z_h, a_m, a_m, z_\ell) = [1(a_m)],$$
$$\tau_1(z_h, a_m, a_m, z_h) = [1(a_m)], \qquad \tau_2(z_h, a_m, a_m, z_h) = [1(a_f)],$$
$$\tau_1(z_h, a_m, a_f, z_\ell) = [\tfrac{4}{7}(a_f), \tfrac{3}{7}(a_m)], \qquad \tau_2(z_h, a_m, a_f, z_\ell) = [1(a_m)],$$
$$\tau_1(z_h, a_m, a_f, z_h) = [\tfrac{8}{9}(a_f), \tfrac{1}{9}(a_m)], \qquad \tau_2(z_h, a_m, a_f, z_h) = [\tfrac{2}{7}(a_f), \tfrac{5}{7}(a_m)],$$
$$\tau_1(z_h, a_f, a_m, z_\ell) = [\tfrac{1}{7}(a_f), \tfrac{6}{7}(a_m)], \qquad \tau_2(z_h, a_f, a_m, z_\ell) = [\tfrac{4}{5}(a_f), \tfrac{1}{5}(a_m)],$$
$$\tau_1(z_h, a_f, a_m, z_h) = [1(a_m)], \qquad \tau_2(z_h, a_f, a_m, z_h) = [\tfrac{2}{3}(a_f), \tfrac{1}{3}(a_m)],$$
$$\tau_1(z_h, a_f, a_f, z_\ell) = [1(a_f)], \qquad \tau_2(z_h, a_f, a_f, z_\ell) = [1(a_m)],$$
$$\tau_1(z_h, a_f, a_f, z_h) = [1(a_f)], \qquad \tau_2(z_h, a_f, a_f, z_h) = [1(a_m)].$$

Figure 15.8 Possible behavior strategies in the two-stage game in Example 15.4

For every initial state, this vector of strategies induces a probability distribution on the set of three-stage histories. In Figure 15.9 we present the probabilities corresponding to a few such histories (verify!).

Initial state	History	Probability
z_h	$(z_h, a_f, a_m, z_h, a_f, a_m)$	0
z_h	$(z_h, a_f, a_m, z_\ell, a_f, a_m)$	$\frac{1}{420}$
z_h	$(z_h, a_f, a_m, z_h, a_m, a_f)$	$\frac{1}{9}$
z_ℓ	$(z_\ell, a_m, a_m, z_\ell, a_f, a_f)$	$\frac{1}{10}$

Figure 15.9 Probabilities of some histories induced by the strategies (τ_1, τ_2) defined in Figure 15.8

◄

15.2.2 Payoffs and equilibrium

The payoff u_i^t to player i at stage t depends (only) on the state z^t and the actions a^t of all the players at that stage: $u_i^t := u_i(z^t, a^t)$. The vector of all the players' payoffs at stage t is $u^t = (u_i^t)_{i \in N}$. We denote by $\gamma_i^T(z^1, \tau)$ the expected average payoff to player i in the T stages of the game, when the initial state is z^1 and the vector of strategies chosen by the players is τ:

$$\gamma_i^T(z^1, \tau) := \mathbf{E}_{z^1, \tau} \left[\frac{1}{T} \sum_{t=1}^{T} u_i^t \right] = \frac{1}{T} \sum_{t=1}^{T} \mathbf{E}_{z^1, \tau}[u_i^t]. \tag{15.7}$$

Definition 15.9 *The T-stage stochastic game with initial state z^1 is the strategic-form game* $\Gamma^T(z^1) := (N, (\mathcal{B}_i^T)_{i \in N}, (\gamma_i^T(z^1, \cdot))_{i \in N})$.

The solution concept that we will apply to the T-stage stochastic game is a Nash equilibrium (Definition 4.17 on page 96).

Definition 15.10 *Let $z^1 \in Z$ be the initial state; the vector of strategies $\tau^* = (\tau_i^*)_{i \in N}$ is an equilibrium of the T-stage stochastic game with initial state z^1 if it is an equilibrium of the game $\Gamma^T(z^1)$. That is,*

$$\gamma_i^T(z^1, \tau^*) \geq \gamma_i^T(z^1, \tau_i, \tau_{-i}^*) \tag{15.8}$$

for every player $i \in N$ and every behavior strategy $\tau_i \in \mathcal{B}_i^T$.

Definition 15.11 *A strategy vector $\tau^* = (\tau_i^*)_{i \in N}$ is an equilibrium of the T-stage game if it is an equilibrium for every initial state $z^1 \in Z$.*

It follows from these definitions that if the T-stage game has an equilibrium τ^*, then for every $z^1 \in Z$ the T-stage stochastic game with initial state z^1 has an equilibrium (namely, the strategy vector τ^*). The converse is also true: if for every initial state z^1 there is an equilibrium τ^{z^1} of the game $\Gamma^T(z^1)$, then we can define an equilibrium τ^* for the T-stage game as follows (Exercise 15.4): for every player $i \in N$ and every history $h = (z^1, a^1, z^2, a^2, \ldots, z^t) \in H^T$,

$$\tau_i^*(h) := \tau_i^{z^1}(h). \tag{15.9}$$

Because the set of states, the set of players, and the set of actions are all finite sets, the set H^T of finite histories in the T-stage stochastic game is a finite set. Thus, the set of pure strategies of each player in the T-stage stochastic game is also finite. Therefore, given an initial state z^1, the stochastic game with initial state z^1 can be presented as a strategic-form game with a finite number of players and a finite number of pure strategies. It follows from Nash's Theorem (Theorem 5.10 on page 150) that every T-stage stochastic game with initial state $z^1 \in Z$ has an equilibrium in mixed strategies. Since the stochastic game is a game with perfect recall, it follows from Kuhn's Theorem that it also has a Nash equilibrium in behavior strategies. We conclude that for every $z^1 \in Z$, the T-stage stochastic game with initial state z^1 has a Nash equilibrium in behavior strategies, and from the above discussion we deduce the following result:

Theorem 15.12 *Every T-stage stochastic game has a Nash equilibrium in behavior strategies.*

15.2.3   Construction of an equilibrium of the *T*-stage stochastic game

The T-stage stochastic game with initial state z^1 is a finite extensive-form game in which a node corresponding to a t-stage history $h = (z^1, a^1, z^2, a^2, \ldots, z^{t-1}, a^{t-1}, z^t) \in H^T$ is the initial node of a subgame, which is the $(T - t + 1)$-stage stochastic game $\Gamma^{T-t+1}(z^t)$. This subgame describes the continuation of the game after the history h. This observation reflects the "memory-free" nature of stochastic games: the current state and the number of remaining stages are sufficient to describe the strategic situation of the players, and the preceding history does not affect the remaining game, although it is known to the players and can affect the way they choose their actions.

In Section 7.1 we saw a way to construct recursively an equilibrium for finite extensive-form games: find an equilibrium of the smallest subgames, replace each such subgame by its equilibrium outcome, and proceed recursively to find an equilibrium of the resulting new game. This procedure can be applied to the T-stage stochastic game, as illustrated by the following example.

Example 15.13   Consider the stochastic game in Figure 15.10. This game has only one state, z_0, and therefore it is a repeated game.

Player II

	L	R
T	$(2,2)$ ^{z_0}	$(0,0)$ ^{z_0}
B	$(0,0)$ ^{z_0}	$(1,1)$ ^{z_0}

Player I, with rows T and B; z_0 below.

Figure 15.10 The game in Example 15.13

Let us find an equilibrium of the two-stage game. According to the backward induction procedure, we should first find all equilibria of the one-stage game, then assign to each two-stage history one of the equilibria of the one-stage game, and finally find an equilibrium in the one-stage game obtained when fixing the second-stage actions (to be the history-dependent one-stage equilibrium we assigned).

There are three equilibria of the one-stage game:

- (T, L) with payoff $(2, 2)$.
- (B, R) with payoff $(1, 1)$.
- $([\frac{1}{3}(T), \frac{2}{3}(B)], [\frac{1}{3}(L), \frac{2}{3}(R)])$ with payoff $(\frac{2}{3}, \frac{2}{3})$.

We can now assign an equilibrium $\tau^* = (\tau_1^*, \tau_2^*)$ to each of the four possible two-stage histories. For example:

$$\tau_1^*(z_0, T, L, z_0) = [\frac{1}{3}(T), \frac{2}{3}(B)], \qquad \tau_2^*(z_0, T, L, z_0) = [\frac{1}{3}(L), \frac{2}{3}(R)],$$
$$\tau_1^*(z_0, T, R, z_0) = T, \qquad \tau_2^*(z_0, T, R, z_0) = L,$$
$$\tau_1^*(z_0, B, L, z_0) = B, \qquad \tau_2^*(z_0, B, L, z_0) = R,$$
$$\tau_1^*(z_0, B, R, z_0) = T, \qquad \tau_2^*(z_0, B, R, z_0) = L.$$

Once the second-stage actions of the players are fixed according to τ^*, the situation at the beginning of the two-stage game is equivalent to that of the one-stage game described in Figure 15.11. Here the payoff is the average of the payoffs in the two stages.

	L	R
T	$(\frac{4}{3}, \frac{4}{3})$	$(1, 1)$
B	$(\frac{1}{2}, \frac{1}{2})$	$(\frac{3}{2}, \frac{3}{2})$

z_0

Figure 15.11 The game the players face in the first stage when τ^* is played at the second stage

This game has three equilibria:

- (T, L) with payoff $(\frac{4}{3}, \frac{4}{3})$.
- (B, R) with payoff $(\frac{3}{2}, \frac{3}{2})$.
- $([\frac{3}{4}(T), \frac{1}{4}(B)], [\frac{3}{8}(R), \frac{5}{8}(R)])$ with payoff $(\frac{9}{8}, \frac{9}{8})$.

In the two-stage equilibrium each of these mixed-action vectors can be played in the first stage. For example, one way to define τ^* in the first stage so that it constitutes an equilibrium of the two-stage game is

$$\tau_1^*(z_0) = [\frac{3}{4}(T), \frac{1}{4}(B)], \qquad \tau_2^*(z_0) = [\frac{3}{8}(R), \frac{5}{8}(R)].$$

◀

We now provide an example of the construction of an equilibrium in two-player zero-sum T-stage stochastic games. As we saw in Section 4.12, in two-player zero-sum games all equilibria are composed of optimal strategies, and the unique equilibrium payoff to Player I is the value of the game. The value of a two-player zero-sum T-stage stochastic game with initial state z is denoted by $v^T(z)$.

Example 15.14   The game given in Figure 15.12 is a two-player zero-sum absorbing game with three states.

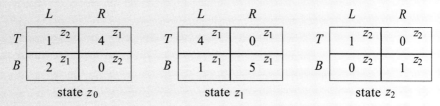

Figure 15.12 The stochastic game in Example 15.14

As in Example 15.3, the transition function in this game is deterministic. States z_1 and z_2 are absorbing and the only equilibrium payoff in each of them is the value of the game in that state (why?). Therefore, for every $T \in \mathbb{N}$, the value of the T-stage stochastic game with initial state z_1 or z_2 is

$$v^T(z_1) = 2.5 \quad \text{and} \quad v^T(z_2) = 0.5. \tag{15.10}$$

In computing the value of the T-stage stochastic game with initial state z_0, we note that at stage 2 the play will be in state z_1 or z_2 and will remain at that state until stage T, as both states z_1 and z_2 are absorbing. Therefore, by Equation (15.10), the total payoff in equilibrium in the last $(T-1)$ stages is either $2.5(T-1)$, if the transition at the first stage is to state z_1, or $0.5(T-1)$, if the transition at the first stage is to state z_2. Since the payoff in the T-stage stochastic game is the average payoff in all T stages, it follows that to find the value of the T-stage stochastic game with initial state z_0 we need to consider the one-stage two-player zero-sum game given in Figure 15.14.

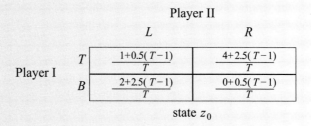

Figure 15.13 The one-stage game played in state z_0 after folding the last $(T-1)$ stages[1]

The value of this game, which can be calculated using the indifference principle (Theorem 5.18 on page 158), is $\frac{8+14.5(T-1)+6(T-1)^2}{T(5+4(T-1))}$, and the (only) optimal strategies of Players I and II are $[x(T), (1-x)(B)]$ and $[y(L), (1-y)(R)]$, respectively, with

$$x = \frac{2+2(T-1)}{5+4(T-1)} \quad \text{and} \quad y = \frac{4+2(T-1)}{5+4(T-1)}.$$

◀

---

1 For a description of the process of folding a game tree, see page 255.

15.2.4 Markovian equilibrium

Recall that when a stochastic game is presented as an extensive-form game, the continuation game following a history $h = (z^1, a^1, z^2, a^2, \ldots, z^{t-1}, a^{t-1}, z^t)$ is $\Gamma^{T-t+1}(z^t)$. It follows that two histories $h = (z^1, a^1, z^2, a^2, \ldots, z^{t-1}, a^{t-1}, z^t)$ and $\widehat{h} = (\widehat{z}^1, \widehat{a}^1, \widehat{z}^2, \widehat{a}^2, \ldots, \widehat{z}^{t-1}, \widehat{a}^{t-1}, \widehat{z}^t)$ of the same length t and with the same last state, that is, $z^t = \widehat{z}^t$, define equivalent subgames. A strategy that chooses the same action in every two nodes that define equivalent subgames is called *Markovian*.

Definition 15.15 *A Markovian strategy of player i is a behavior strategy $\tau_i \in \mathcal{B}_i^T$ satisfying $\tau_i(h) = \tau_i(\widehat{h})$ for every $t \in \{1, 2, \ldots, T\}$ and for every two histories $h = (z^1, a^1, z^2, a^2, \ldots, z^{t-1}, a^{t-1}, z^t)$ and $\widehat{h} = (\widehat{z}^1, \widehat{a}^1, \widehat{z}^2, \widehat{a}^2, \ldots, \widehat{z}^{t-1}, \widehat{a}^{t-1}, \widehat{z}^t)$ with $z^t = \widehat{z}^t$.*

Thus, a Markovian strategy is a behavior strategy in which the mixed action at stage t depends only on the value of t and the current state, z^t, but not on the history that led to that state. By Theorem 5.18 on page 158, every finite extensive-form game with perfect recall has a subgame perfect equilibrium that can be constructed using backward induction. Such an equilibrium can be constructed so that players use the same mixed action in every two nodes that correspond to equivalent subgames, thereby producing a subgame perfect equilibrium in Markovian strategies. We thus conclude the following result, whose proof is left to the reader (Exercise 15.5):

Theorem 15.16 *Every T-stage stochastic game has an equilibrium in Markovian strategies.*

The equilibrium we constructed in Example 15.13 for the two-stage game is not Markovian (explain why). By Theorem 15.16 there exists a Markovian equilibrium in this example. To construct such an equilibrium all we have to do is choose for every two-stage history the same equilibrium in the corresponding one-stage game. For example, with regard to Example 15.13, the strategy vector that appears in Figure 15.14 is a Markovian equilibrium of the two-stage stochastic game (verify).

The construction of the Markovian equilibrium by backward induction is based on the following auxiliary game.

Definition 15.17 *Given a vector $w = (w_i(z))_{i \in N, z \in Z} \in \mathbb{R}^{N \times Z}$ and a state $z \in Z$, define a strategic-form game $G(z; w)$ as follows: the set of players is N, for each player $i \in N$ the set of pure strategies is $A_i(z)$, and his payoff function is given by*

$$\tau_1^*(z_0) = T, \qquad\qquad \tau_2^*(z_0) = L,$$
$$\tau_1^*(z_0, T, L, z_0) = B, \qquad \tau_2^*(z_0, T, L, z_0) = R,$$
$$\tau_1^*(z_0, T, R, z_0) = B, \qquad \tau_2^*(z_0, T, R, z_0) = R,$$
$$\tau_1^*(z_0, B, L, z_0) = B, \qquad \tau_2^*(z_0, B, L, z_0) = R,$$
$$\tau_1^*(z_0, B, R, z_0) = B, \qquad \tau_2^*(z_0, B, R, z_0) = R.$$

Figure 15.14 A Markovian equilibrium in the two-stage game in Example 15.14

$$\varphi_i(a) := u_i(a) + \sum_{z' \in Z} q(z' \mid z, a) w_i(z'), \quad \forall a \in A(z). \tag{15.11}$$

The game $G(z; w) = (N, (A_i(z))_{i \in N}, (\varphi_i)_{i \in N})$ captures the situation in state z in the stochastic game, where w stands for the total payoff from the next stage on: if the state at the next stage is z', then the sum of payoffs (rather than the average payoff) to player i from that stage until the end of the game will be $w_i(z')$.

In the construction of an equilibrium in the T-stage stochastic game by backward induction, we needed to find the equilibrium actions in stage t, for every $t = 1, 2, \ldots, T$. To that end we considered the strategic-form game played in state z^t, where the payoff was the weighted average of the current stage payoff (with weight $\frac{1}{T-t+1}$) and the equilibrium payoff in the last $(T - t)$ stages (with weight $\frac{T-t}{T-t+1}$). Since the set of equilibria does not change when multiplying all payoffs in the game by a constant, this is equivalent to considering the strategic-form game played in state z^t, where the payoff is the sum of the current stage payoff and the total equilibrium payoff in the last $(T - t)$ stages. This game is the game $G(z^t, w)$, where $w(z)$ is the total (and not the average) equilibrium payoff vector of the subgame $\Gamma^{T-t}(z)$, for every $z \subset Z$. This leads us to the following result, whose proof is left for the reader as an exercise (Exercise 15.8).

Theorem 15.18 *Let τ^* be a vector of Markovian strategies in the T-stage stochastic game satisfying the following properties: for every history $h = (z^1, a^1, \ldots, z^t) \in H^T$, the vector of mixed actions $(\tau_i^*(h))_{i \in N}$ is an equilibrium in the game $G(z^t; w)$, where $w(z) := (T - t)\gamma^{T-t}(z; \tau')$ for every $z \in Z$ and τ' is the vector of strategies induced by τ^* from stage $(t + 1)$ on; that is, $w(z)$ is $(T - t)$ times the payoff vector induced by τ^* in the subgame starting at stage $(t + 1)$ in state z. Then τ^* is a subgame perfect Markovian equilibrium for every initial state.*

15.3 The infinite discounted game

In Section 13.6 we discussed discounted infinitely repeated games and established results about the equilibria of these games. In this section we study the discounted infinite stochastic game and prove two main results.

(i) For every discount factor $0 < \lambda \leq 1$, every two-player zero-sum discounted infinite stochastic game has a value and each player has a "simple" optimal strategy, called a *stationary strategy*. This is a Markovian strategy in which the mixed action at stage t depends only on the state z^t and not on the stage of the game t.

(ii) Every discounted infinite stochastic game has an equilibrium in stationary strategies.

Although (i) follows from (ii), we will prove both results for two reasons.

- Historically, (i) was proved before (ii) and was the trigger that opened the field of stochastic games.
- The mathematical tools needed to prove (i) are much simpler than those needed to prove (ii) and can therefore be studied independently, without relying on (ii).

15.3.1 Histories, strategies, equilibrium payoffs

The set of *finite histories* in the infinite game is the set of all t-stage histories, for all $t \in \mathbb{N}$:

$$H^\infty := \cup_{t \in \mathbb{N}} H(t). \tag{15.12}$$

The set of *plays* is denoted by $H(\infty)$:

$$H(\infty) := \Lambda^\infty. \tag{15.13}$$

We encountered infinite plays in Sections 6.4 and 13.6. As we did there, we define the *σ-algebra of the cylinder sets* over the set of plays: every finite history $h = (z^1, a^1, z^2, a^2, \ldots, z^{t-1}, a^{t-1}, z^t) \in H^\infty$ defines a cylinder set $C(h)$, which is the set of all plays in $H(\infty)$ that start with h:

$$C(h) = \{\widehat{h}^\infty = (\widehat{z}^1, \widehat{a}^1, \widehat{z}^2, \widehat{a}^2, \ldots) : \widehat{z}^1 = z^1, \widehat{a}^1 = a^1, \ldots, \widehat{z}^t = z^t\}. \tag{15.14}$$

Denote by $\mathcal{H}$ the σ-algebra on $H(\infty)$ generated by the cylinder sets. The pair $(H(\infty), \mathcal{H})$ is a *measurable space*.[2]

We now turn to the definition of strategies in the infinite game. The definition is analogous to Definition 15.15 for the T-stage game and to Definition 13.13 for infinitely repeated games.

Definition 15.19 A behavior strategy *of player i in the infinite stochastic game is a function τ_i assigning to each finite history $h = (z^1, a^1, z^2, a^2, \ldots, z^{t-1}, a^{t-1}, z^t) \in H^\infty$ a probability distribution, $\tau_i(h) \in \Delta(A_i(z^t))$, over the set of actions of player i in state z^t. Denote by $\mathcal{B}_i^\infty$ the set of behavior strategies of player i in the infinite stochastic game.*

Similar to the discussion in Chapter 13, every vector of behavior strategies $\tau = (\tau_i)_{i \in N}$ and every initial state z^1 induce a probability distribution $\mathbf{P}_{z^1, \tau}$ over the measurable space $(H(\infty), \mathcal{H})$ given by

$$\mathbf{P}_{z^1, \tau}(C(z^1)) = 1, \tag{15.15}$$

$$\mathbf{P}_{z^1, \tau}(C(h, a^{t+1}, z^{t+1})) =$$

$$\mathbf{P}_{z^1, \tau}(C(h)) \cdot \left(\prod_{i \in N} \tau_i(a_i^{t+1} \mid h) \right) \cdot q(z^{t+1} \mid z^t, a^{t+1}). \tag{15.16}$$

The expectation operator with respect to $\mathbf{P}_{z^1, \tau}$ is denoted by $\mathbf{E}_{z^1, \tau}$. The discounted payoff in the infinite stochastic game is now defined analogously to the discounted payoff in repeated games (Definition 13.21 on page 551).

Definition 15.20 *Let $\lambda \in [0, 1)$ be a real number and let $\tau = (\tau_i)_{i \in N}$ be a vector of behavior strategies in the infinite stochastic game. The λ-discounted payoff to player i in the infinite stochastic game with initial state z^1 under the strategy vector τ is*

$$\gamma_i^\lambda(z^1, \tau) := \mathbf{E}_{z^1, \tau} \left[(1 - \lambda) \sum_{t=1}^\infty \lambda^{t-1} u_i^t \right] = (1 - \lambda) \sum_{t=1}^\infty \lambda^{t-1} \mathbf{E}_{z^1, \tau} \left[u_i^t \right]. \tag{15.17}$$

The real number λ is called a discount factor.

---

2 For the definition of a measurable space, see page 237.

Definition 15.21 *The λ-discounted infinite stochastic game* with initial state z^1 is the *strategic-form game* $\Gamma^\lambda(z^1) := (N, (\mathcal{B}_i^\infty)_{i \in N}, (\gamma_i^\lambda)_{i \in N})$.

We now extend the concept of Nash equilibrium to discounted infinite stochastic games.

Definition 15.22 *A strategy vector τ^* is a λ-discounted equilibrium for the initial state z^1 if it is a Nash equilibrium of the strategic-form game $\Gamma^\lambda(z^1)$. In that case, the vector $\gamma^\lambda(z^1, \tau^*)$ is a λ-discounted equilibrium payoff for the initial state z^1. The strategy vector τ^* is a λ-discounted equilibrium if it is a λ-discounted equilibrium for every initial state $z^1 \in Z$. In that case, the vector $(\gamma^\lambda(z^1, \tau^*))_{z^1 \in Z}$ is a λ-discounted equilibrium payoff.*

Thus, a strategy vector τ^* is a λ-discounted equilibrium if for every player $i \in N$, every strategy τ_i of that player, and every initial state $z^1 \in Z$, we have

$$\gamma_i^\lambda(z^1, \tau^*) \geq \gamma_i^\lambda(z^1, \tau_i, \tau_{-i}^*). \tag{15.18}$$

If for every state $z \in Z$ there is a Nash equilibrium τ^z of $\Gamma^\lambda(z)$, which is the discounted stochastic game with discount factor λ and initial state z, then we can construct a Nash equilibrium for the λ-discounted stochastic game, just like we did for the T-stage stochastic game.

Remark 15.23 *In the following sections we will prove the existence of a λ-discounted equilibrium of the infinite stochastic game in stationary strategies. The existence of λ-discounted equilibria (not necessarily in stationary strategies) follows from the existence of Nash equilibria in finite strategic-form games. Indeed, define the following metric on the set $\mathcal{B}_i^\infty$ of behavior strategies of player i:*

$$d_i(\tau_i, \widehat{\tau}_i) := \sum_{t=1}^\infty \frac{1}{2^t |H(t)|} \sum_{h \in H(t)} ||\tau_i(h) - \widehat{\tau}_i(h)||_1, \tag{15.19}$$

where for each $x \in \mathbb{R}^m$ we denote by $||x||_1 := \sum_{j=1}^m |x_j|$ the l_1-norm of x. The set $\mathcal{B}_i^\infty$ is a compact set in this metric (why?). Define now the following metric on $\mathcal{B}^\infty := \times_{i \in N} \mathcal{B}_i^\infty$: for every two strategy vectors $\tau = (\tau_i)_{i \in N}$ and $\widehat{\tau} = (\widehat{\tau}_i)_{i \in N}$,

$$d(\tau, \widehat{\tau}) := \sum_{i \in N} d_i(\tau_i, \widehat{\tau}_i). \tag{15.20}$$

For every initial state z^1, every discount factor $\lambda \in [0, 1)$, and every player i, the payoff function $\gamma_i^\lambda(z^1, \cdot)$ is continuous in the metric $d(\cdot, \cdot)$. For $k \in \mathbb{N}$, consider the k-stage λ-discounted stochastic game. This is the game that terminates at stage k with the payoff function

$$\gamma_i^{\lambda,k}(z^1, \tau) := \mathbf{E}_{z^1, \tau}\left[(1 - \lambda) \sum_{t=1}^k \lambda^{t-1} u_i^t\right]. \tag{15.21}$$

This is a finite game and therefore, by Theorem 5.10 on page 150, it has a Nash equilibrium in behavior strategies $\tau^*(k)$. Since $\mathcal{B}^\infty$ is a compact set, the sequence $(\tau^*(k))_{k \in \mathbb{N}}$ has a converging subsequence with limit $\tau^*(\infty)$. Since the payoff functions are continuous in the metric $d(\cdot, \cdot)$, this limit is a λ-discounted equilibrium of the infinite game. The reader is requested to fill in the details of the proof in Exercise 15.25. ◆

15.3.2 Stationary strategies

In the T-stage stochastic game, the subgame following the history $h = (z^1, a^1, \ldots, z^{t-1}, a^{t-1}, z^t)$ is a $(T - t + 1)$-stage stochastic game with initial state z^t. This subgame is determined by its initial state, z^t, and the number of remaining stages until the end of the game, $(T - t + 1)$. We defined a Markovian strategy as a strategy in which the player uses the same mixed action in every two equivalent subgames. Therefore, a Markovian strategy of a player assigns a mixed action to every state $z \in Z$ and every number $(T - t + 1)$ of the remaining stages. In the infinite game, all subgames have infinite length and therefore two histories ending with the same state define equivalent subgames even when the histories have different lengths. It follows that the analogue of a Markovian strategy in the infinite game is a strategy that assigns a mixed action to each state $z \in Z$. This observation leads to the following definition.

Definition 15.24 *A behavior strategy τ_i of player i in an infinite stochastic game is a stationary strategy if for every finite history $h = (z^1, a^1, z^2, a^2, \ldots, z^{t-1}, a^{t-1}, z^t) \in H^\infty$, the mixed action $\tau_i(h)$ depends only on the state z^t.*

In other words, the strategy τ_i is stationary if for every two histories $h = (z^1, a^1, z^2, a^2, \ldots, z^{t-1}, a^{t-1}, z^t) \in H^\infty$ and $\widehat{h^t} = (\widehat{z}^1, \widehat{a}^1, \widehat{z}^2, \widehat{a}^2, \ldots, \widehat{z}^{t-1}, \widehat{a}^{t-1}, \widehat{z}^t) \in H^\infty$, if $z^t = \widehat{z}^t$ then $\tau_i(h) = \tau_i(\widehat{h^t})$. In particular, every Markovian strategy is a stationary strategy.

A stationary strategy of a player is given by $|Z|$ probability distributions: for every state $z \in Z$, the strategy specifies the probability distribution according to which the player chooses his (pure) action whenever the play visits state z. We therefore denote a stationary strategy of player i by a vector $\sigma_i = (\sigma_i(z))_{z \in Z}$, where $\sigma_i(z) \in \Delta(A_i(z))$, and we denote a vector of stationary strategies of all players by $\sigma = (\sigma_i)_{i \in N} \in \bigtimes_{i \in N} \bigtimes_{z \in Z} \Delta(A_i(z))$. The probability that under the stationary strategy σ_i player i plays the action a_i in state z is denoted by $\sigma_i(z; a_i)$. The mixed extension of the stage payoff function is given by

$$U_i(z, \sigma(z)) := \sum_{a \in A(z)} \left(u_i(a) \prod_{i \in N} \sigma_i(z; a_i) \right), \quad \forall z \in Z, \forall \sigma(z) \in \bigtimes_{i \in N} \Delta(A_i(z)). \quad (15.22)$$

Similarly, the mixed extension of the transition function q, still denoted by q, is

$$q(z' \mid z, \sigma(z)) := \sum_{a \in A(z)} \left(q(z' \mid z, a) \prod_{i \in N} \sigma_i(z; a_i) \right), \quad \forall z, z' \in Z, \forall \sigma(z) \in \bigtimes_{i \in N} \Delta(A_i(z)).$$

$$(15.23)$$

The following theorem asserts that when the vector $\sigma = (\sigma_i)_{i \in N}$ of stationary strategies is played, the (expected) payoffs to the players can be computed by solving a system of linear equations.

Theorem 15.25 *Let $\sigma = (\sigma_i)_{i \in N}$ be a vector of stationary strategies, and let $\lambda \in [0, 1)$ be a discount factor. The vector of λ-discounted payoffs $(\gamma_i^\lambda(z, \sigma))_{z \in Z}$ to player i is the unique solution of the following system of $|Z|$ linear equations in the variables $(y_z)_{z \in Z}$:*

$$y_z = (1 - \lambda)U_i(z, \sigma(z)) + \lambda \sum_{z' \in Z} q(z' \mid z, \sigma(z))y_{z'}, \quad \forall z \in Z. \tag{15.24}$$

Proof: We first prove that $(\gamma_i^\lambda(z, x))_{z \in Z}$ is a solution of Equation (15.24). Indeed, recall that u_i^t is the payoff to player i at stage t. The expected λ-discounted payoff to player i at the initial state z is

$$\gamma_i^\lambda(z, \sigma) = \mathbf{E}_{z,\sigma}\left[(1 - \lambda)\sum_{t=1}^\infty \lambda^{t-1}u_i^t\right] \tag{15.25}$$

$$= (1 - \lambda)\mathbf{E}_{z,\sigma}\left[u_i^1\right] + \mathbf{E}_{z,\tau}\left[(1 - \lambda)\sum_{t=2}^\infty \lambda^{t-1}u_i^t\right]. \tag{15.26}$$

The term $\mathbf{E}_{z,\sigma}\left[u_i^1\right]$ is the expected payoff in the first stage, which is equal to $U_i(z, \sigma(z))$. The second term, $\mathbf{E}_{z,\sigma}\left[(1 - \lambda)\sum_{t=2}^\infty \lambda^{t-1}u_i^t\right]$, is the expected payoff from the second stage on, given that the initial state is z and the players play the vector of stationary strategies σ. By the law of total expectation, this quantity is equal to the expectation with respect to z^2, the state at stage 2, of the conditional expected payoff given z^2:

$$\mathbf{E}_{z,\sigma}\left[(1 - \lambda)\sum_{t=2}^\infty \lambda^{t-1}u_i^t\right] = \mathbf{E}_{z,\sigma}\left[\mathbf{E}_{z^2,\sigma}\left[(1 - \lambda)\sum_{t=2}^\infty \lambda^{t-1}u_i^t \mid z^2\right]\right]. \tag{15.27}$$

We note that

$$\mathbf{E}_{z^2,\sigma}\left[(1 - \lambda)\sum_{t=2}^\infty \lambda^{t-1}u_i^t \mid z^2\right] = \lambda\mathbf{E}_{z^2,\sigma}\left[(1 - \lambda)\sum_{t=1}^\infty \lambda^{t-1}u_i^{t+1} \mid z^2\right] \tag{15.28}$$

$$= \lambda\gamma_i^\lambda(z^2, \sigma), \tag{15.29}$$

where Equation (15.29) follows from the fact that σ is a vector of stationary strategies. Taking expectation with respect to z^2 yields

$$\mathbf{E}_{z,\sigma}\left[(1 - \lambda)\sum_{t=2}^\infty \lambda^{t-1}u_i^t\right] = \lambda\mathbf{E}_{z,\sigma}\left[\gamma_i^\lambda(z^2, \sigma)\right]. \tag{15.30}$$

To compute the expectation with respect to z^2 in Equation (15.30) we recall that the probability that $z^2 = z'$, given that the initial state is z, is $q(z' \mid z, \sigma(z))$. Therefore,

$$\gamma_i^\lambda(z, \sigma) = (1 - \lambda)U_i(z, \sigma(z)) + \lambda \sum_{z' \in Z} q(z' \mid z, \sigma(z))\gamma_i^\lambda(z', \sigma), \tag{15.31}$$

which proves that the vector $(\gamma_i^\lambda(z, x))_{z \in Z}$ is a solution of Equation (15.24).

We now prove that Equation (15.24) has a unique solution. Assume by contradiction that there are two distinct solutions: $y = (y_z)_{z \in Z}$ and $\widehat{y} = (\widehat{y}_z)_{z \in Z}$. Let $z_0 \in Z$ be the state for which the difference $|y_z - \widehat{y}_z|$ is maximal:

$$|y_{z_0} - \widehat{y}_{z_0}| = \max_{z \in Z} |y_z - \widehat{y}_z|. \tag{15.32}$$

Denote this difference by $c := |y_{z_0} - \widehat{y}_{z_0}|$ and without loss of generality assume that $y_{z_0} \geq \widehat{y}_{z_0}$. Since the solutions y and $\widehat{y}$ are different, we have $c > 0$. Now,

$$c = y_{z_0} - \widehat{y}_{z_0} \tag{15.33}$$

$$= \left((1 - \lambda)U_i(z_0, \sigma(z_0)) + \lambda \sum_{z' \in Z} q(z' \mid z_0, \sigma(z_0))y_{z'} \right) \tag{15.34}$$

$$- \left((1 - \lambda)U_i(z_0, \sigma(z_0)) + \lambda \sum_{z' \in Z} q(z' \mid z_0, \sigma(z_0))\widehat{y}_{z'} \right)$$

$$= \lambda \sum_{z' \in Z} q(z' \mid z_0, \sigma(z_0)) \, (y_{z'} - \widehat{y}_{z'}) \tag{15.35}$$

$$\leq \lambda \sum_{z' \in Z} q(z' \mid z_0, \sigma(z_0))c \tag{15.36}$$

$$= \lambda c \sum_{z' \in Z} q(z' \mid z_0, \sigma(z_0)) = \lambda c < c, \tag{15.37}$$

since $\lambda < 1$. This contradiction proves the uniqueness of the solution of Equation (15.24), completing the proof of the theorem. $\qquad\qquad\square$

The following is an equivalent representation of Equation (15.24) that is useful in applications:

$$y_z = \sum_{a \in A(z)} \left(\prod_{i \in N} \sigma_i(z; a) \cdot \left((1 - \lambda)U_i(z, a) + \lambda \sum_{z' \in Z} q(z' \mid z, a)y_{z'} \right) \right), \quad \forall z \in Z. \tag{15.38}$$

When the cell that corresponds to action vector a in state z leads to an absorbing state z' where each player has a single action, the solution y of Equation (15.24) satisfies that $y_{z'}$ is the payoff in the unique cell in state z'. If in some state z there is an action a that leads to state z' with probability 1, and if the stage payoff $u(z, a)$ is equal to $y_{z'}$, then the term $(1 - \lambda)U_i(z, a) + \lambda \sum_{z' \in Z} q(z' \mid z, a)y_{z'}$ is equal to $y_{z'}$. This observation will be useful in the computation performed in the next example.

Example 15.26   Consider the absorbing game given in Figure 15.15.

Player II

	L	R	
T	$0, 0^{z_0}$	$7, 2\ ^*$	α
B	$2, 7\ ^*$	$6, 6\ ^*$	$1 - \alpha$
	β	$1 - \beta$	

Player I is at left; state z_0.

Figure 15.15 The game in Example 15.26 together with the stationary strategies of the players

Since in every absorbing state each player has one action, a stationary strategy of a player is given by the mixed action the player uses in state z_0. Consider the stationary strategies $\sigma_I = [\alpha(T), (1-\alpha)(B)]$ for Player I and $\sigma_{II} = [\beta(L), (1-\beta)(R)]$ for Player II. By Theorem 15.25, for $i = I, II$, the λ-discounted payoff $\gamma_i(z_0; \sigma_I, \sigma_{II})$ satisfies the following equations:

$$\gamma_I(z_0; \sigma_I, \sigma_{II}) = \lambda\alpha\beta\gamma_1(z_0; \sigma_I, \sigma_{II}) \tag{15.39}$$
$$+ 7\alpha(1-\beta) + 2(1-\alpha)\beta + 6(1-\alpha)(1-\beta),$$

$$\gamma_{II}(z_0; \sigma_I, \sigma_{II}) = \lambda\alpha\beta\gamma_2(z_0; \sigma_I, \sigma_{II}) \tag{15.40}$$
$$+ 2\alpha(1-\beta) + 7(1-\alpha)\beta + 6(1-\alpha)(1-\beta),$$

from which we obtain

$$\gamma_I(z_0; \sigma_I, \sigma_{II}) = \frac{7\alpha(1-\beta) + 2(1-\alpha)\beta + 6(1-\alpha)(1-\beta)}{1 - \lambda\alpha\beta}, \tag{15.41}$$

$$\gamma_{II}(z_0; \sigma_I, \sigma_{II}) = \frac{2\alpha(1-\beta) + 7(1-\alpha)\beta + 6(1-\alpha)(1-\beta)}{1 - \lambda\alpha\beta}. \tag{15.42}$$

◀

Remark 15.27 *Theorem 15.25 shows that the quantities $(\gamma_i(z; \sigma_I, \sigma_{II}))_{z\in Z}$ are a solution of a system of linear equations with coefficients that are multilinear in λ, $(\sigma_I(z; a_I))_{z\in Z, a_I\in A_I(z)}$, and $(\sigma_{II}(z; a_{II}))_{z\in Z, a_{II}\in A_{II}(z)}$. By Cramer's rule this implies that the payoff function $(\lambda, \sigma_I, \sigma_{II}) \mapsto \gamma_i(z_0; \sigma_I, \sigma_{II})$ is a rational function in its parameters, as can be seen in Equations (15.41) and (15.42).* ◆

15.3.3 The game $G^\lambda(z; w)$

In Definition 15.17 (page 642) we defined the game $G(z; w)$ for every state $z \in Z$ and every vector $w \in \mathbb{R}^Z$. We now provide a variant of this definition that is more convenient for the discounted game.

Definition 15.28 *Let $\lambda \in [0, 1)$ be a discount factor, let $z \in Z$ be a state, and let $w = (w_i(z))_{i\in N, z\in Z} \in \mathbb{R}^{N\times Z}$ be a vector of $|N| \cdot |Z|$ real numbers. The game $G^\lambda(z; w)$ is the game in strategic form in which the set of players is N, the set of pure strategies of every player $i \in N$ is $A_i(z)$, and the payoff function of every player i is*

$$u_i^\lambda(a) := (1 - \lambda)u_i(z, a) + \lambda \sum_{z'\in Z} q(z' \mid z, a)w_i(z'), \quad \forall a \in A(z). \tag{15.43}$$

The payoff function reflects the discounted nature of the stochastic game: it is the sum of two components that have different weights: the stage payoff has a weight $(1 - \lambda)$, and the future payoff, represented by the vector w, has a weight λ.

Denote by $U_i^\lambda(z; w; \cdot)$ the mixed extension of u_i^λ, namely

$$U_i^\lambda(z; w; \sigma(z)) = (1 - \lambda)U_i(z, \sigma(z)) + \lambda \sum_{z'\in Z} q(z'|z, \sigma(z))w_i(z'), \quad \forall \sigma(z) \in \underset{i\in N}{\times} \Delta(A_i(z)).$$

$$\tag{15.44}$$

The following lemma relates the games $G^\lambda(z; w)$ to the payoff under a strategy vector in the λ-discounted stochastic game.

Lemma 15.29 *Let $\lambda \in [0, 1)$ be a discount factor, let $z \in Z$ be a state, let $w = (w_i(z))_{i \in N, z \in Z} \in \mathbb{R}^{N \times Z}$ be a vector of real numbers, and let $i \in N$ be a player. Let τ be a vector of strategies in the stochastic game (not necessarily stationary) satisfying the following inequality for every finite history $h = (z^1, a^1, z^2, a^2, \ldots, z^{t-1}, a^{t-1}, z^t) \in H^\infty$:*

$$w_i(z^t) \leq U_i^\lambda(z^t; w; \tau(h)). \tag{15.45}$$

Then

$$w_i(z^1) \leq \gamma_i^\lambda(z^1, \tau). \tag{15.46}$$

The right-hand side of Equation (15.45) is the payoff to player i in the auxiliary game $G^\lambda(z^t; w)$ under the vector of mixed actions $\tau(h)$. This is equal to the payoff to the player after the finite history h if, from the next stage on, his payoff is $w_i(z^{t+1})$. Thus, the above lemma asserts that if after each finite history h the vector of strategies τ guarantees player i a payoff of at least $w_i(z^t)$, provided that from the next stage on his payoff is $w_i(z^{t+1})$, then the strategy vector τ guarantees that the payoff to player i in the λ-discounted stochastic game is at least $w_i(z^1)$.

Proof: By Equation (15.45), for every history $h = (z^1, a^1, z^2, a^2, \ldots, z^{t-1}, a^{t-1}, z^t) \in H^\infty$ we have

$$w_i(z^t) \leq U_i^\lambda(z^t; w; \tau(h)) = \mathbf{E}_{z^1, \tau}[(1 - \lambda)u_i(z^t, a^t) + \lambda w_i(z^{t+1}) \mid h]. \tag{15.47}$$

Since Equation (15.47) holds for every finite history h of length t, and every initial state $z^1 \in Z$, we can take expectation of both sides with respect to the probability distribution $P_{z^1, \tau}$ over the histories of length t and obtain

$$\mathbf{E}_{z^1, \tau}[w_i(z^t)] \leq \mathbf{E}_{z^1, \tau}[\mathbf{E}_{z^1, \tau}[(1 - \lambda)u_i(z^t, a^t) + \lambda w_i(z^{t+1}) \mid h]]. \tag{15.48}$$

By the law of total expectation, the right-hand side of Equation (15.48) is equal to $\mathbf{E}_{z^1, \tau}[(1 - \lambda)u_i(z^t, a^t) + \lambda w_i(z^{t+1})]$. Therefore,

$$\mathbf{E}_{z^1, \tau}[w_i(z^t)] \leq \mathbf{E}_{z^1, \tau}[(1 - \lambda)u_i(z^t, a^t) + \lambda w_i(z^{t+1})] \tag{15.49}$$

$$= \mathbf{E}_{z^1, \tau}[(1 - \lambda)u_i(z^t, a^t)] + \lambda \mathbf{E}_{z^1, \tau}[w_i(z^{t+1})]. \tag{15.50}$$

Moving the second term on the right-hand side in Equation (15.50) to the left-hand side of the inequality and multiplying both sides by λ^{t-1}, we obtain

$$\lambda^{t-1}\mathbf{E}_{z^1, \tau}[w_i(z^t)] - \lambda^t \mathbf{E}_{z^1, \tau}[w_i(z^{t+1})] \leq \lambda^{t-1}\mathbf{E}_{z^1, \tau}[(1 - \lambda)u_i(z^t, a^t)]. \tag{15.51}$$

Summing up the telescopic sequence on the left-hand side of Equation (15.51) over $t \in \mathbb{N}$ we obtain

$$\sum_{t=1}^{\infty} \left(\lambda^{t-1}\mathbf{E}_{z^1, \tau}[w_i(z^t)] - \lambda^t \mathbf{E}_{z^1, \tau}[w_i(z^{t+1})] \right) = \mathbf{E}_{z^1, \tau}[w_i(z^1)] = w_i(z^1). \tag{15.52}$$

Summing up the right-hand side of Equation (15.51) over $t \in \mathbb{N}$ we obtain

$$\sum_{t=1}^{\infty} \lambda^{t-1} \mathbf{E}_{z^1, \tau} [(1-\lambda) u_i(z^t, a^t)] = \mathbf{E}_{z^1, \tau} \left[(1-\lambda) \sum_{t \in \mathbb{N}} \lambda^{t-1} u_i(z^t, a^t) \right] \quad (15.53)$$

$$= \gamma_i^{\lambda}(z^1, \tau). \quad (15.54)$$

Equation (15.46) follows from Equations (15.51)–(15.54), concluding the proof of the lemma.   □

If, in the condition of Theorem 15.29, which is in Equation (15.45), we reverse the direction of the inequality, then in the conclusion of the theorem, i.e., in Equation (15.46), the direction of the inequality will be reversed as well, yielding an upper bound for the payoffs to player i. We thus conclude with the following lemma.

Lemma 15.30 *Let $\lambda \in [0, 1)$ be a discount factor, let $z \in Z$ be a state, and let $w = (w_i(z))_{i \in N, z \in Z} \in \mathbb{R}^{N \times Z}$ be a vector of real numbers. If the vector of strategies τ (not necessarily stationary) satisfies*

$$w_i(z^t) \geq U_i^{\lambda}(z^t; w; \tau(h)), \quad \forall h = (z^1, a^1, z^2, a^2, \dots, z^{t-1}, a^{t-1}, z^t) \in H^{\infty}, \quad (15.55)$$

then

$$w_i(z^1) \geq \gamma_i^{\lambda}(z^1, \tau). \quad (15.56)$$

If the vector of strategies satisfies

$$w_i(z^t) = U_i^{\lambda}(z^t; w; \tau(h)), \quad \forall h = (z^1, a^1, z^2, a^2, \dots, z^{t-1}, a^{t-1}, z^t) \in H^{\infty}, \quad (15.57)$$

then

$$w_i(z^1) = \gamma_i^{\lambda}(z^1, \tau). \quad (15.58)$$

15.3.4   Two-player zero-sum games

In Section 4.11 we defined the *minmax* and *maxmin* values of two-player zero-sum games in strategic form. If these two quantities coincide, the common value is called the value of the game. A strategy that guarantees to a player the value of the game is called an optimal strategy.

In a λ-discounted infinite stochastic game each player has an infinite number of pure strategies and therefore we cannot deduce from the results in Chapter 4 the existence of the value for two-player zero-sum λ-discounted infinite stochastic games. In this section we generalize the definitions of the value and optimal strategies as well as the results for these concepts to two-player zero-sum discounted stochastic games. Since the payoffs in a stochastic game depend on the initial state, the definitions have to be adjusted accordingly. We will prove that every two-player zero-sum λ-discounted stochastic game has a value for each initial state. Furthermore, we will present a functional equation that has to be satisfied by these values. This equation is often useful for computing the values for the various initial states.

Recall that in a two-player zero-sum game we omit the index of the player from the payoff, and therefore the stage payoff is denoted by $u(z, a)$, the mixed extension is denoted by $U(z, \sigma(z))$, and the payoff that Player I maximizes and Player II minimizes is denoted by $\gamma^\lambda(z^1, \tau_I, \tau_{II})$.

Definition 15.31 *Let $\lambda \in [0, 1)$. The λ-discounted minmax value for the initial state z^1, denoted by $\bar{v}^\lambda(z^1)$, is given by*

$$\bar{v}^\lambda(z^1) := \min_{\tau_{II} \in \mathcal{B}_{II}^\infty} \max_{\tau_I \in \mathcal{B}_I^\infty} \gamma^\lambda(z^1, \tau_I, \tau_{II}). \tag{15.59}$$

A strategy τ_{II} of Player II that attains the minimum in Equation (15.59) is called a minmax strategy of Player II for the initial state z^1. The λ-discounted maxmin value for the initial state z^1, denoted by $\underline{v}^\lambda(z^1)$, is given by

$$\underline{v}^\lambda(z^1) := \max_{\tau_I \in \mathcal{B}_I^\infty} \min_{\tau_{II} \in \mathcal{B}_{II}^\infty} \gamma^\lambda(z^1, \tau_I, \tau_{II}). \tag{15.60}$$

A strategy τ_I of Player I that attains the maximum in Equation (15.60) is called a minmax strategy of Player I for the initial state z^1. When $\bar{v}^\lambda(z^1) = \underline{v}^\lambda(z^1)$ we denote the common quantity by $v^\lambda(z^1)$ and call it the value of the discounted stochastic game with initial state z^1. In this case the minmax strategy of Player II for the initial state z^1 and the maxmin strategy of Player I for the initial state z^1 are called optimal strategies for this state.

When the value exists for every initial state, we denote the vector of values by $v^\lambda := (v^\lambda(z))_{z \in Z}$ and call it the *value* of the stochastic game. In that case, a strategy of a player that is optimal for all initial states is called an *optimal strategy*.

The main result in this section is the following.

Theorem 15.32 (Shapley [1953b]) *For every $\lambda \in [0, 1)$ the value of the two-player zero-sum λ-discounted infinite stochastic game exists. Furthermore, each player has a stationary optimal strategy, and the value $v^\lambda = (v^\lambda(z))_{z \in Z}$ is the unique solution of the following system of equations:*

$$v^\lambda(z) = \text{val}(G^\lambda(z; v^\lambda)), \quad z \in Z. \tag{15.61}$$

The following example uses Theorem 15.32 to compute the value of a two-player zero-sum λ-discounted infinite stochastic game.

Example 15.33 Consider the two-player zero-sum discounted infinite absorbing game that appears in Figure 15.16.

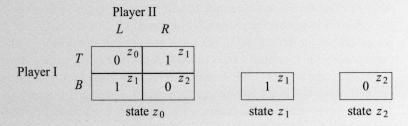

Figure 15.16 The game in Example 15.33

Although states z_1 and z_2 are absorbing states, for ease of computation we will not use the concise notation (with asterisked cells). The games $G^\lambda(z; v^\lambda)$ for the three states are given in Figure 15.17 (see Equation (15.43)).

	L	R
T	$\lambda v^\lambda(z_0)$	$(1-\lambda)+\lambda v^\lambda(z^1)$
B	$(1-\lambda)+\lambda v^\lambda(z^1)$	$\lambda v^\lambda(z_2)$

Game $G^\lambda(z_0; v^\lambda)$

$$\boxed{(1-\lambda)+\lambda v^\lambda(z^1)}$$

Game $G^\lambda(z_1; v^\lambda)$

$$\boxed{\lambda v^\lambda(z_2)}$$

Game $G^\lambda(z_2; v^\lambda)$

Figure 15.17 The games $(G^\lambda(z; v^\lambda))_{z\in Z}$ in Example 15.33

Let us now solve Equation (15.61) for this game. We start with the two absorbing states. The value of the game $G^\lambda(z_2; v^\lambda)$ is $\lambda v^\lambda(z_2)$ (why?). Therefore, Equation (15.61) for state z_2 is

$$v^\lambda(z_2) = \text{val}(G^\lambda(z_2; v^\lambda)) = \lambda v^\lambda(z_2). \tag{15.62}$$

Since $\lambda > 0$, this implies that $v^\lambda(z_2) = 0$, which is the expected result: if the initial state is absorbing with payoff 0, then the payoff will be 0 in all stages, and therefore the discounted value is 0. Similarly, for the initial state z_1 we get

$$v^\lambda(z_1) = \text{val}(G^\lambda(z_1; v^\lambda)) = 1 - \lambda + \lambda v^\lambda(z_1). \tag{15.63}$$

Since $\lambda < 1$, the only solution for this equation is $v^\lambda(z_1) = 1$, which is, once again, the expected result.

The computation of the value for the initial states z_1 and z_2 leads to the following more general observation (Exercise 15.12):

Theorem 15.34 *Let z be an absorbing state in a two-player zero-sum stochastic game. Then for every discount factor $\lambda \in [0, 1)$, the quantity $v^\lambda(z)$ is equal to $\text{val}(\Gamma^1(z))$, the value of the one-stage game with initial state z.*

We now turn to compute $v^\lambda(z_0)$, the discounted value when the initial state is z_0. Substituting $v^\lambda(z_1) = 1$ and $v^\lambda(z_2) = 0$ in the game $G^\lambda(z_0; v^\lambda)$, we obtain the game described in Figure 15.18.

Player II

		L	R
Player I	T	$\lambda v^\lambda(z_0)$	1
	B	1	0

Figure 15.18 The auxiliary game $G^\lambda(z_0; v^\lambda)$ in Example 15.33

In this game each player has a unique optimal strategy, which is completely mixed (why?). The pair of optimal strategies forms an equilibrium (Theorem 4.44 on page 115), and can therefore be identified by the indifference principle (Theorem 5.18 on page 158). Let $[y(L), (1-y)(R)]$ be the optimal strategy of Player II (the column player). Then the payoff to Player I is $y\lambda v^\lambda(z_0) + (1-y)$

if he plays T and y if he plays B. These payoffs are equal to his equilibrium payoff, which is the value of the game $v^\lambda(z_0)$. Therefore,

$$y\lambda v^\lambda(z_0) + (1-y) = y = v^\lambda(z_0). \tag{15.64}$$

We obtained two equations in the two variables y and $v^\lambda(z_0)$. Substituting the second equation $y = v^\lambda(z_0)$ into the first yields the following quadratic equation for $v^\lambda(z_0)$ (verify!):

$$\lambda(v^\lambda(z_0))^2 - 2v^\lambda(z_0) + 1 = 0, \tag{15.65}$$

which has two solutions:

$$v^\lambda(z_0) = \frac{2\pm\sqrt{4-4\lambda}}{2\lambda} = \frac{1\pm\sqrt{1-\lambda}}{\lambda}. \tag{15.66}$$

Since all payoffs in the game are 0 or 1, the value of the game is between 0 and 1 (Exercise 15.13). We conclude that the value of the λ-discounted stochastic game with initial state z_0 is $v^\lambda(z_0) = \frac{1-\sqrt{1-\lambda}}{\lambda}$. In Exercise 15.14 the reader is asked to compute the stationary optimal strategies for the two players.   ◀

Remark 15.35 *Example 15.33 shows that the value of the λ-discounted stochastic game may depend on the discount factor λ. This example also shows that the value may not be in the field of the data of the game (payoffs, discount factor, and transition probabilities). Indeed, the payoffs and probabilities in Example 15.33 are integers, and in particular they are in the field of rational numbers. If, for example, the discount factor is the rational number $\lambda = \frac{1}{2}$, then the value of the game with initial state z_0 is $v^\lambda(z_0) = 2 - \sqrt{2}$, which is an irrational number. This stands in sharp contrast to the situation in finite games in strategic form, where the value of the game is in the same field of the data of the game. This is so because in finite strategic-form games the value is a solution of a linear programming problem (see Section 5.2.5 on page 162), which always lies in the same field as the coefficients of the problem.*   ◆

15.3.5 Contraction mapping

For the proof of Theorem 15.32 we will need the concept of *contraction mapping*.

Definition 15.36 *A function $f : \mathbb{R}^m \to \mathbb{R}^m$ is called a* contraction mapping *if there is a real number $\rho \in [0, 1)$ satisfying*[3]

$$\|f(x) - f(y)\|_\infty \le \rho\|x - y\|_\infty, \quad \forall x, y \in \mathbb{R}^m. \tag{15.67}$$

The number ρ is called the contraction constant *of f.*

Remark 15.37 *The concept of contraction mapping is defined for every metric space (X, d): a function $f : X \to X$ is a* contraction mapping *if there is $\rho \in [0, 1)$ satisfying $d(f(x), f(y)) \le \rho d(x, y)$ for every $x, y \in X$. The results proven in this section hold for every metric space.*   ◆

---

[3] Recall that the maximum norm in $\mathbb{R}^m$ is defined as follows:

$$\|x\|_\infty := \max_{i\in\{1,2,\ldots,m\}} |x_i|, \quad \forall x = (x_1, x_2, \ldots, x_m) \in \mathbb{R}^m. \tag{15.68}$$

It follows from the definition that a contraction mapping is a Lipschitz function, and in particular it is a continuous function. For the sake of completeness we prove this result.

Lemma 15.38 *Every contraction mapping is a continuous function.*

Proof: Let $f : \mathbb{R}^m \to \mathbb{R}^m$ be a contraction mapping with a contraction constant $\rho \in [0, 1)$. Let $(x_k)_{k \in \mathbb{N}}$ be a sequence converging to a limit x^*. Since f is a contraction mapping,

$$||f(x_k) - f(x^*)||_\infty \leq \rho ||x_k - x^*||, \quad \forall k \in \mathbb{N}. \tag{15.69}$$

Since the sequence $(x_k)_{k \in \mathbb{N}}$ converges to x^*,

$$\lim_{k \to \infty} ||f(x_k) - f(x^*)||_\infty \leq \rho \lim_{k \to \infty} ||x_k - x^*|| = 0. \tag{15.70}$$

Since this holds for every converging sequence $(x_k)_{k \in \mathbb{N}}$, it follows that f is continuous. $\square$

Brouwer's Fixed Point Theorem (Theorem 5.23 on page 164) asserts that every continuous function from a compact set in a Euclidian space to itself has a fixed point. Since $\mathbb{R}^m$ is not compact, Brouwer's Fixed Point Theorem cannot be applied to show that a contraction mapping $f : \mathbb{R}^m \to \mathbb{R}^m$ has a fixed point. The following fixed point theorem asserts that every contraction mapping has a unique fixed point.

Theorem 15.39 (Banach [1922]) *Every contraction mapping $f : \mathbb{R}^m \to \mathbb{R}^m$ has a unique fixed point; that is, there is a unique point $x^* \in \mathbb{R}^m$ satisfying $f(x^*) = x^*$.*

Proof: Step 1: The function f has at most one fixed point.
Let $x \in \mathbb{R}^m$ and $y \in \mathbb{R}^m$ be two fixed points of f, that is, $f(x) = x$ and $f(y) = y$. Since f is a contraction mapping, we have

$$||x - y||_\infty = ||f(x) - f(y)||_\infty \leq \rho ||x - y||_\infty. \tag{15.71}$$

Since $\rho < 1$, it follows that $||x - y||_\infty = 0$, implying $x = y$. We conclude that every contraction mapping f has at most one fixed point, as claimed.

Step 2: The function f has at least one fixed point.
Let x_0 be a point in $\mathbb{R}^m$ and define the sequence $(x_k)_{k \in \mathbb{N}}$ of points in $\mathbb{R}^m$ in the following way:

$$x_{k+1} := f(x_k). \tag{15.72}$$

We claim that for every $k \geq 0$, we have

$$||x_{k+1} - x_k||_\infty \leq \rho^k ||x_1 - x_0||_\infty. \tag{15.73}$$

We prove this by induction on k. For $k = 0$, both sides are equal. For $k > 0$,

$$||x_{k+1} - x_k||_\infty = ||f(x_k) - f(x_{k-1})||_\infty \tag{15.74}$$

$$\leq \rho ||x_k - x_{k-1}||_\infty \tag{15.75}$$

$$\leq \rho \cdot \rho^{k-1} ||x_1 - x_0||_\infty = \rho^k ||x_1 - x_0||_\infty, \tag{15.76}$$

where Equation (15.76) follows from the induction hypothesis. A consequence of Equation (15.73) is that the sequence $(x_k)_{k \in \mathbb{N}}$ is a Cauchy sequence; that is, for every $\varepsilon > 0$ there is $K \in \mathbb{N}$ such that for every $k \geq K$ and for every $r \in \mathbb{N}$, we have $\|x_k - x_{k+r}\|_\infty \leq \varepsilon$. Indeed, by Equation (15.73) and the triangle inequality, we get

$$\|x_k - x_{k+r}\|_\infty \leq \sum_{l=0}^{r-1} \|x_{k+l} - x_{k+l+1}\|_\infty \tag{15.77}$$

$$\leq \sum_{l=0}^{r-1} \rho^{k+l} \|x_1 - x_0\|_\infty \tag{15.78}$$

$$= \|x_1 - x_0\|_\infty \sum_{l=0}^{r-1} \rho^{k+l} \tag{15.79}$$

$$= \frac{\rho^k}{1-\rho} \|x_1 - x_0\|_\infty. \tag{15.80}$$

Therefore, for every $\varepsilon > 0$, let $K \in \mathbb{N}$ be such that $\frac{\rho^K}{1-\rho} \|x_1 - x_0\|_\infty \leq \varepsilon$; then for every $k \geq K$ and every $r \in \mathbb{N}$, we have $\|x_k - x_{k+r}\|_\infty \leq \varepsilon$, proving that $(x_k)_{k \in \mathbb{N}}$ is a Cauchy sequence. Consequently, this sequence has a limit x^*. We finally prove that the limit x^* is a fixed point of f. Indeed, this follows from the definition of the sequence and the continuity of f:

$$f(x^*) = f\left(\lim_{k \to \infty} x_k\right) = \lim_{k \to \infty} f(x_k) = \lim_{k \to \infty} x_{k+1} = x^*. \tag{15.81}$$

$\square$

Proof of Theorem 15.32: *Step 1:* Definition of a contraction mapping $T : \mathbb{R}^{|Z|} \to \mathbb{R}^{|Z|}$.
Define the function $T : \mathbb{R}^{|Z|} \to \mathbb{R}^{|Z|}$ as follows:

$$T_z(w) := \mathrm{val}(G^\lambda(z; w)), \quad \forall w \in \mathbb{R}^{|Z|}. \tag{15.82}$$

That is, for every vector $w \in \mathbb{R}^{|Z|}$, the z coordinate of $T(w)$ is the value of the auxiliary game $G^\lambda(z; w)$. The function T is called the *Shapley operator*. We now prove that it is a contraction mapping. Let w and $\widehat{w}$ be two vectors in $\mathbb{R}^{|Z|}$. From the definition of T and Exercise 5.41 in Chapter 5 (page 214), it follows that

$$|T_z(w) - T_z(\widehat{w})| = \left|\mathrm{val}(G^\lambda(z; w)) - \mathrm{val}(G^\lambda(z; \widehat{w}))\right| \tag{15.83}$$

$$\leq \|U^\lambda(z; w; \cdot) - U^\lambda(z; \widehat{w}; \cdot)\|_\infty. \tag{15.84}$$

Recall that for every vector of actions $a \in A(z)$,

$$U^\lambda(z; w; a) = (1 - \lambda)u(z, a) + \lambda \sum_{z' \in Z} q(z' \mid z, a)w(z'), \quad \forall z \in A(z), \tag{15.85}$$

$$U^\lambda(z; \widehat{w}; a) = (1 - \lambda)u(z, a) + \lambda \sum_{z' \in Z} q(z' \mid z, a)\widehat{w}(z'), \quad \forall z \in A(z). \tag{15.86}$$

By the triangle inequality we therefore obtain

$$|T_z(w) - T_z(\widehat{w})| \leq ||U^\lambda(z; w; \cdot) - U^\lambda(z; \widehat{w}; \cdot)||_\infty \tag{15.87}$$

$$= \max_{a \in A(z)} \left| \left((1 - \lambda)u(z, a) + \lambda \sum_{z' \in Z} q(z' \mid z, a)w(z')\right) \right. \tag{15.88}$$

$$\left. - \left((1 - \lambda)u(z, a) + \lambda \sum_{z' \in Z} q(z' \mid z, a)\widehat{w}(z')\right) \right| \tag{15.89}$$

$$= \lambda \max_{a \in A(z)} \left| \sum_{z' \in Z} q(z' \mid z, a)w(z') - \sum_{z' \in Z} q(z' \mid z, a)\widehat{w}(z') \right| \tag{15.90}$$

$$\leq \lambda \max_{a \in A(z)} \sum_{z' \in Z} q(z' \mid z, a)|w(z') - \widehat{w}(z')| \tag{15.91}$$

$$\leq \lambda \max_{a \in A(z)} \sum_{z' \in Z} q(z' \mid z, a)||w - \widehat{w}||_\infty \tag{15.92}$$

$$= \lambda||w - \widehat{w}||_\infty \max_{a \in A(z)} \sum_{z' \in Z} q(z' \mid z, a) \tag{15.93}$$

$$= \lambda||w - \widehat{w}||_\infty \max_{a \in A(z)} 1 \tag{15.94}$$

$$= \lambda||w - \widehat{w}||_\infty, \tag{15.95}$$

proving that T is indeed a contraction mapping with contraction constant λ. By Theorem 15.39 the function T has a unique fixed point w^*. We shall prove that $w^*(z)$ is the value of the λ-discounted stochastic game with initial state z.

Step 2: $\underline{v}^\lambda(z) \geq w^*(z)$ for every state $z \in Z$.
We shall prove that Player I has a stationary strategy τ_I^* satisfying

$$\gamma^\lambda(z; \tau_I^*, \tau_{II}) \geq w^*(z), \quad \forall \tau_{II} \in \mathcal{B}_{II}, \forall z \in Z, \tag{15.96}$$

which implies the claimed inequality, since

$$\underline{v}^\lambda(z) = \max_{\tau_I \in \mathcal{B}_I} \min_{\tau_{II} \in \mathcal{B}_{II}} \gamma^\lambda(z; \tau_I, \tau_{II}) \geq \min_{\tau_{II} \in \mathcal{B}_{II}} \gamma^\lambda(z; \tau_I^*, \tau_{II}) \geq w^*(z), \quad \forall z \in Z. \tag{15.97}$$

By the definition of T and since w^* is a fixed point of T,

$$w^*(z) = T_z(w^*) = \mathrm{val}(G^\lambda(z; w^*)). \tag{15.98}$$

Let $\sigma_{I,z} \in \Delta(A_I(z))$ be an optimal mixed strategy[4] of Player I in the strategic-form game $G^\lambda(z; w^*)$. That is, for every mixed action $\sigma_{II,z} \in \Delta(A_{II}(z))$ of Player II in the game $G^\lambda(z; w^*)$, the payoff in that game under the pair of actions $(\sigma_{I,z}, \sigma_{II,z})$ is at least $w^*(z)$:

$$U^\lambda(z; w^*; \sigma_{I,z}, \sigma_{II,z}) \geq w^*(z). \tag{15.99}$$

. . . .

4 A mixed strategy in the game $G^\lambda(z; w^*)$ is a mixed action in the stochastic game.

Let τ_{I}^* be the stationary strategy of Player I that at every stage t chooses the mixed action σ_{I,z^t}, that is,

$$\tau_{\mathrm{I}}^*(h) := \sigma_{\mathrm{I},z}, \quad \forall h = (z^1, a^1, z^2, \ldots, z^{t-1}, z^{t-1}, z^t) \in H^\infty. \tag{15.100}$$

The conditions of Lemma 15.30 are satisfied (why?) and therefore $\gamma^\lambda(z, \tau_{\mathrm{I}}^*, \tau_{\mathrm{II}}) \geq w^*(z)$ for every strategy τ_{II} of Player II, as desired.

Step 3: $\bar{v}^\lambda(z) \leq w^*(z)$ for every state $z \in Z$.
The proof of this step is analogous to that of Step 2. For every state $z \in Z$, let $\sigma_{\mathrm{II},z} \in \Delta(A_{\mathrm{II}}(z))$ be a mixed optimal strategy of Player II in the game $G^\lambda(z; w^*)$. This means that for every mixed action $\sigma_{\mathrm{I},z} \in \Delta(A_{\mathrm{I}}(z))$ of Player I, the payoff in the game $G^\lambda(z; w^*)$ under the pair of mixed actions $(\sigma_{\mathrm{I},z}, \sigma_{\mathrm{II},z})$ is at most $w^*(z)$:

$$U^\lambda(z; w^*; \sigma_{\mathrm{I},z}, \sigma_{\mathrm{II},z}) \leq w^*(z). \tag{15.101}$$

Let τ_{II}^* be the stationary strategy of Player II that at stage t chooses the mixed action σ_{II,z^t}:

$$\tau_{\mathrm{II}}^*(h) := \sigma_{\mathrm{II},z^t}, \quad \forall h = (z^1, a^1, z^2, \cdots, z^{t-1}, z^{t-1}, z^t) \in H^\infty. \tag{15.102}$$

The conditions of Lemma 15.30 on page 651 are satisfied, and hence we get $\gamma^\lambda(z, \tau_{\mathrm{I}}, \tau_{\mathrm{II}}^*) \leq w^*(z)$ for every strategy τ_{I} of Player I. It follows that

$$\bar{v}^\lambda(z) = \min_{\tau_{\mathrm{II}} \in \mathcal{B}_{\mathrm{II}}} \max_{\tau_{\mathrm{I}} \in \mathcal{B}_{\mathrm{I}}} \gamma^\lambda(z; \tau_{\mathrm{I}}, \tau_{\mathrm{II}}) \leq \max_{\tau_{\mathrm{I}} \in \mathcal{B}_{\mathrm{I}}} \gamma^\lambda(z; \tau_{\mathrm{I}}, \tau_{\mathrm{II}}^*) \leq w^*(z), \tag{15.103}$$

as claimed.

Step 4: $w^*(z) = \underline{v}^\lambda(z) = \bar{v}^\lambda(z)$.
Let $z \in Z$ be a state. Since $\underline{v}^\lambda(z) \leq \bar{v}^\lambda(z)$, it follows from Steps 2 and 3 that

$$w^*(z) \leq \underline{v}^\lambda(z) \leq \bar{v}^\lambda(z) \leq w^*(z), \tag{15.104}$$

from which follows the claimed equality.

Thus we have proved that for every initial state z, the value $v^\lambda(z)$ of the discounted stochastic game with initial state z exists and is equal to $w^*(z)$. The strategy τ_{I}^* defined in Step 2 guarantees that when the initial state is z the payoff is at least $w^*(z)$, and therefore this is a stationary optimal strategy of Player I. Similarly, the strategy τ_{II}^* defined in Step 3 guarantees that when the initial state is z the payoff is at most $w^*(z)$, and therefore this is a stationary optimal strategy of Player II. Finally, since w^* is a fixed point of T, we have

$$v^\lambda(z) = w^*(z) = T_z(w^*) = \mathrm{val}(G^\lambda(z; w^*)) = \mathrm{val}(G^\lambda(z; v^\lambda)), \quad \forall z \in Z, \tag{15.105}$$

and since w^* is the unique fixed point of T, the value $v^\lambda(z)$ is the unique solution of this system of equations, as claimed by the last part of the theorem. $\qquad\square$

As a consequence of Shapley's Theorem (Theorem 15.32 on page 652) and Lemma 15.29 we have the following characterization of stationary optimal strategies in two-player zero-sum discounted stochastic games. The proof is left as an exercise for the reader (Exercise 15.32).

Theorem 15.40 *Let τ_i be a strategy of Player i, $i \in \{I, II\}$, that has the following property: for every finite history $h = (z^1, a^1, z^2, a^2, \ldots, z^{t-1}, a^{t-1}, z^t) \in H^\infty$, the mixed action $\tau_i(h)$ is an optimal strategy in the strategic-form game $G^\lambda(z^t; v^\lambda)$. Then, τ_i is an optimal strategy of Player i in the discounted stochastic game.*

15.3.6 Generalization to any number of players

In this section we generalize Shapley's Theorem to games with any number of players: every λ-discounted stochastic game has an equilibrium in stationary strategies. Furthermore, we show that the payoff vector corresponding to such an equilibrium satisfies a certain set of equations.

Theorem 15.41 (Fink [1964]) *For every discount factor $\lambda \in [0, 1)$, every λ-discounted stochastic game has an equilibrium in stationary strategies.*

The proof of this theorem is analogous to the proof of Nash's Theorem (Theorem 5.10 on page 150), except that instead of applying Brouwer's Fixed Point Theorem we apply Kakutani's Fixed Point Theorem (Theorem 24.32 on page 985). To prove Theorem 15.41, we first define a certain mapping and prove that it satisfies the conditions of Kakutani's Fixed Point Theorem, and therefore has a fixed point. We then prove that every fixed point of this mapping is an equilibrium of the discounted stochastic game.

Proof: Step 1: Defining a set Q in a Euclidian space.

Let $M := \max_{(z,a) \in \Lambda, i \in N} |u_i(z, a)|$. This is the maximum absolute value of payoffs in the game. Let $m := \sum_{i \in N, z \in Z} |A_i(z)| + n|Z|$, and define a set $Q \subseteq \mathbb{R}^m$ by

$$Q := \left(\underset{i \in N, z \in Z}{\times} \Delta(A_i(z)) \right) \times [-M, M]^{n|Z|}. \tag{15.106}$$

The set Q is a Cartesian product of two sets, $\times_{i \in N, z \in Z} \Delta(A_i(z))$ and $[-M, M]^{n|Z|}$. The set of all stationary strategies of player i is $\times_{z \in Z} \Delta(A_i(z))$, and therefore the first set in the product is the set of all vectors of stationary strategies. The set $[-M, M]^{n|Z|}$ is the set of all functions $w : Z \to [-M, M]^N$, that is, all functions that assign a real number between $-M$ and M to each state $z \in Z$ and every player i. Points in Q are written as pairs (σ, w), where $\sigma \in \times_{i \in N, z \in Z} \Delta(A_i(z))$ is a vector of stationary strategies and $w : Z \to [-M, M]^N$ can be interpreted as $|Z|$ payoff vectors in $[-M, M]^N$ (a payoff to each one of the n players), one for each state $z \in Z$.

The set Q is a nonempty, convex, and compact set (see Exercises 5.1, 5.2, and 5.3 in Chapter 5).

Step 2: Defining a correspondence F from Q to Q.

Recall that a correspondence is a multivalued function; that is, a correspondence F from Q to Q is a function $F : Q \to 2^Q$ assigning a subset of Q to every point $(\sigma, w) \in Q$.

Let (σ, w) be a point in Q. This means that σ is a stationary strategy profile. For every $i \in N$ and every $z \in Z$, denote by $\sigma_i(z)$ the mixed action for player i in state z under σ, and by $\sigma(z) = (\sigma_i(z))_{i \in N}$ the mixed action vector played under σ in state z. For every state

$z \in Z$, consider the strategic-form game $G^\lambda(z; w)$ and denote by $J_{i,z}(\sigma, w)$ the set of best replies of player i to the vector of mixed actions $\sigma_{-i}(z) = (\sigma_j(z))_{j \neq i}$ in this game:

$$J_{i,z}(\sigma, w) := \left\{ \tilde{\sigma}_i(z) \in \Delta(A_i(z)) : U_i^\lambda(z; w; \tilde{\sigma}_i(z), \sigma_{-i}(z)) \right. \tag{15.107}$$

$$= \max_{\sigma_i'(z) \in \Delta(A_i(z))} \left. U_i^\lambda(z; w; \sigma_i'(z), \sigma_{-i}(z)) \right\}.$$

The set $J_{i,z}(\sigma, w)$ is nonempty, convex, and compact (why?). Denote by $L_{i,z}(\sigma, w)$ the set containing a single real number: the payoff to player i in the game $G^\lambda(z; w)$ under the vector of strategies $\sigma(z)$:

$$L_{i,z}(\sigma, w) := \left\{ U_i^\lambda(z; w; \sigma(z)) \right\}. \tag{15.108}$$

Since the set $L_{i,z}(\sigma, w)$ consists of a single element, it is also nonempty, convex, and compact. Finally, define

$$F(\sigma, w) := \left(\underset{i \in N, z \in Z}{\times} J_{i,z}(\sigma, w) \right) \times \left(\underset{i \in N, z \in Z}{\times} L_{i,z}(\sigma, w) \right) \subseteq Q. \tag{15.109}$$

As a Cartesian product of convex, compact, and nonempty sets, the set $F(\sigma, w)$ is also convex, compact, and nonempty (see Exercises 5.1, 5.2, and 5.3 in Chapter 5).

Step 3: The correspondence F is upper semi-continuous.
To prove that the correspondence F is upper semi-continuous we show that the limit of a converging sequence of points in the graph of F is also a point in the graph of F.
  A point in the graph of F is denoted by $(\sigma, w, \tilde{\sigma}, c)$, where:

- The pair (σ, w) is in Q, i.e., $\sigma \in \times_{i \in N, z \in Z} \Delta(A_i(z))$ and $w : Z \to \mathbb{R}^N$.
- $\tilde{\sigma} = (\tilde{\sigma}_i(z))_{i \in N, z \in Z} \in \times_{i,z} \Delta(A_i(z))$ and $\tilde{\sigma}_i(z)$ is a best reply of player i to the vector of mixed actions $\sigma_{-i}(z)$ in the game $G^\lambda(z; w)$.
- $c = (c_{i,z})_{i \in N, z \in Z} \in [-M, M]^{n|Z|}$ and $c_{i,z} = U_i^\lambda(z; w; \sigma(z))$.

Let $(\sigma^k, w^k, \tilde{\sigma}^k, c^k)_{k \in \mathbb{N}}$ be a sequence of points in the graph of F converging to $(\sigma^*, w^*, y^*, c^*)$, i.e., for every $k \in \mathbb{N}$:

- The pair (σ^k, w^k) is in Q, i.e., $\sigma^k \in \times_{i \in N, z \in Z} \Delta(A_i(z))$ and $w^k : Z \to \mathbb{R}^N$.
- $\tilde{\sigma}_{i,z}^k$ is a best reply of player i to the vector of mixed actions $\sigma_{-i}^k(z)$ in the game $G^\lambda(z; w^k)$.
- $c_{i,z}^k = U_i^\lambda(z; w^k; \sigma^k(z))$.

Since $\sigma_{-i}^*(z) = \lim_{k \to \infty} \sigma_{-i}^k(z)$ and $\tilde{\sigma}_{i,z}^* = \lim_{k \to \infty} y_{i,z}^k$, it follows from the continuity of the payoff function that $\tilde{\sigma}_{i,z}^*$ is a best reply of player i to the vector of mixed actions $\sigma_{-i}^*(z)$ in the game $G^\lambda(z; w^*)$. For the same reason, $\lim_{k \to \infty} U_i^\lambda(z; w^k; \sigma^k(z)) = U_i^\lambda(z; w^*; \sigma^*(z))$, and therefore $\lim_{k \to \infty} L_{i,z}(\sigma^k, w^k) = L_{i,z}(\sigma^*, w^*)$ for every player $i \in N$ and every state $z \in Z$, implying that $(\sigma^*, w^*, \tilde{\sigma}^*, c^*)$ is in the graph of F, as claimed.

Step 4: Applying Kakutani's Fixed Point Theorem.

The correspondence F satisfies the conditions of Kakutani's Fixed Point Theorem (Theorem 24.32 on page 985), and therefore has a fixed point (σ^*, w^*). To complete the proof we show now that if (σ^*, w^*) is a fixed point of F then the strategy vector σ^* is a stationary equilibrium in the λ-discounted stochastic game and w^* is the corresponding equilibrium payoff.

Denote $w^* = (w^*_{i,z})_{i \in N, z \in Z}$. Since $w^*_{i,z} = U^\lambda_i(z; w^*; \sigma^*(z))$ for every player $i \in N$ and every state $z \in Z$, it follows from Lemma 15.30 on page 651 that

$$\gamma^\lambda_i(z, \sigma^*) = w^*_{i,z}, \quad \forall i \in N, \forall z \in Z. \tag{15.110}$$

That is, w^* is the payoff vector corresponding to the vector of stationary strategies σ^*. Let τ_i be any strategy (not necessarily stationary) of player i. Since $\sigma^*_i(z)$ is a best reply of player i to $\sigma^*_{-i}(z)$ in the game $G^\lambda(z; w^*)$, for every history $h = (z^1, a^1, z^2, a^2, \ldots, z^t) \in H^\infty$ we have

$$U^\lambda_i(z^t; w^*_{z^t}; \tau_i(h), \sigma^*_{-i}(z)) \le U^\lambda_i(z^t; w^*_{z^t}; \sigma^*_i(z^t), \sigma^*_{-i}(z^t)) = w^*_{i,z^t}, \quad \forall i \in N. \tag{15.111}$$

From Lemma 15.29 on page 650 it follows that for every player $i \in N$ and every strategy τ_i of that player,

$$\gamma^\lambda_i(z; \tau_i, \sigma^*_{-i}) \le w^*_{i,z} = \gamma^\lambda_i(z; \sigma^*), \tag{15.112}$$

i.e., no player i has a profitable deviation from σ^*_i. Therefore, the vector of stationary strategies σ^* is indeed an equilibrium of the λ-discounted stochastic game. $\square$

15.4 Remarks

In Example 15.33 we computed the function $\lambda \mapsto v^\lambda(z)$ for every state z and found that this function is the ratio of two polynomials in $\sqrt{1 - \lambda}$. This result is not accidental: for every stochastic game and every initial state z, the interval $[0, 1)$ is divided into a finite number of subintervals such that on each subinterval, the function $\lambda \mapsto v^\lambda(z)$ is the ratio of two polynomials in fractional powers of $(1 - \lambda)$. This general result was proved by Bewley and Kohlberg [1976]. In particular, it implies that $\lim_{\lambda \to 1} v^\lambda(z)$ exists for every initial state $z \in Z$.

For repeated games we defined the concept of uniform ε-equilibrium (see Section 13.8 on page 537). A strategy vector τ^* in a repeated game is a *uniform ε-equilibrium for discounted games* if it is an ε-equilibrium in the λ-discounted repeated game for every discount factor λ close enough to 1. The analogous concept for two-player zero-sum stochastic games was defined by Mertens and Neyman [1981], who also proved its existence. The analogous concept for multiplayer stochastic games is called *uniform ε-equilibrium for discounted games*. Vieille [2000a, b] proved that every two-player non-zero-sum stochastic game has a uniform equilibrium, and Solan [1999] proved a similar result for three-player absorbing games. The existence of a uniform equilibrium for general stochastic games with three or more players is an open question. The existence of a *uniform correlated ε-equilibrium for discounted games*, which is an analogous concept based on the concept of correlated equilibrium (see Chapter 8), was proved by Solan and Vieille [2002] for all stochastic games.

The "Big Match" game that appears in Exercise 15.2 was first presented by Gillette [1957], and is the first nontrivial two-player zero-sum stochastic game for which the uniform value has been calculated. A deep and detailed discussion of the game in Exercise 15.24 can be found in Flesch, Thuijsman and Vrieze [1997]. We are grateful to Tristan Tomala for contributing Exercise 15.36.

15.5) Exercises

15.1 Present the following situation as a stochastic game. The United States and Russia are competing for military superiority. Each of the two countries can lead in military power, but they can also be equal in military power. The "utility" of leading in military power is 10, while the "utility" of being inferior is -10. The "utility" of equal power is 0 for both countries. Every year both countries decide their military budget independently and simultaneously: a high budget of 10 or a low budget of 4. The total utility of a country in a given year is its utility from the mutual position minus the military budget of that year. In a year during which both countries make equal investments in armaments, the relative position of strength is maintained till the following year. In a year during which one country invests more than its rival, that country improves its position the following year with probability 0.6 and remains in the same position with probability 0.4 (that is, if it was inferior that year, with probability 0.6 it will tie the following year and with probability 0.4 it will remain inferior; if it was a tie that year, with probability 0.6 it will lead the following year and with probability 0.4 it will remain a tie; if it was leading that year, with probability 1 it will lead also the following year).

15.2 (The Big Match game) David and Tom play the following game over T stages. In each stage David chooses a color, either red or yellow, and Tom guesses which color David chose. If Tom guesses "red," he pays David one dollar if he guessed incorrectly, and receives one dollar from David if he guessed correctly. If, however, Tom guesses "yellow," he pays David a dollar in that stage and in every subsequent stage of the game if he guessed incorrectly, and he receives a dollar from David in that stage and in every subsequent stage of the game if he guessed correctly.

Note that this is not a repeated game, because if the first time that Tom guesses "yellow" is in stage t, the payoffs in all the stages after t depend on Tom's choice in stage t.

(a) Present the game as a stochastic game and specify its initial state.
(b) Present the game in the shortened description where absorbing states are indicated by asterisks.
(c) Prove that the only equilibrium payoff at the initial state when $T = 1$ is 0.
(d) Prove that the only equilibrium payoff at the initial state when $T = 2$ is 0.
(e) Prove that for every $T \in \mathbb{N}$, the only equilibrium payoff at the initial state is 0.

15.3 Present the two-stage stochastic game in Example 15.14 (on page 641) with the initial state z_0 as an extensive-form game.

15.4 Given a stochastic game, for every initial state $z^1 \in Z$ let τ^{z^1} be an equilibrium of the T-stage game with this initial state. Define the vector of strategies $\tau^* = (\tau_i^*)_{i \in N}$ by

$$\tau_i^*(h) := \tau_i^{z^1}(h), \quad \forall h = (z^1, a^1, \dots, z^t) \in H^T. \tag{15.113}$$

Prove that the strategy vector τ^* is an equilibrium of the T-stage game.

15.5 Prove Theorem 15.16: every T-stage stochastic game has an equilibrium in Markovian strategies.

15.6 Find all Markovian equilibria in the following two-stage two-player stochastic game when the initial state is z_0.

	L	R
T	$0, 0^{z_0}$	$3, 2^{z_1}$
B	$2, 1^{z_1}$	$0, 0^{z_0}$

state z_0

	L	R
T	$0, 0^{z_0}$	$1, 2^{z_0}$
B	$3, 1^{z_1}$	$0, 0^{z_1}$

state z_1

15.7 Prove that the set of equilibria of a T-stage stochastic game is a closed set.

15.8 Prove Theorem 15.18.

15.9 In the stochastic game described in the figure below there are three states denoted by z_0, z_1, and z_2. The states z_1 and z_2 are absorbing states. The transition probabilities are deterministic; that is, the probability distribution $q(z, a)$ assigns probability 1 to the state written in the upper-right corner of the corresponding cell. For the initial state z_0, find all equilibria of the T-stage game for $T = 1, 2$, and find all equilibrium payoffs in the T-stage game for $T = 3$.

	L	R
T	$0, 0^{z_0}$	$-1, -1^{z_1}$
B	$-1, -1^{z_1}$	$0, 0^{z_2}$

state z_0

| $-1, -1^{z_1}$ |

state z_1

| $0, 0^{z_2}$ |

state z_2

15.10 In the stochastic game described in the figure below there are three states denoted by z_0, z_1, and z_2. The states z_1 and z_2 are absorbing states. The transition probabilities are deterministic; that is, the probability distribution $q(z, a)$ assigns probability 1 to the state written in the upper-right corner of the corresponding cell. For the initial state z_0 find all equilibrium payoffs in the one-stage and two-stage games. Note that there are infinitely many equilibria.

	L	R
T	2, 4 $\quad^{z_0}$	5, 1 $\quad^{z_2}$
B	8, 0 $\quad^{z_1}$	2, 3 $\quad^{z_0}$

state z_0

| 0, 8 $\quad^{z_1}$ |

state z_1

| 3, 8 $\quad^{z_2}$ |

state z_2

15.11 A two-player zero-sum stochastic game is *symmetric* if the following conditions are satisfied for every state $z \in Z$:

(a) The two players have the same set of actions in state z, which we denote by $A(z)$, that is, $A_{\mathrm{I}}(z) = A_{\mathrm{II}}(z) = A(z)$.

(b) The payoff matrix in state z is anti-symmetric:

$$u(z, a_{\mathrm{I}}, a_{\mathrm{II}}) = -u(z, a_{\mathrm{II}}, a_{\mathrm{I}}), \quad \forall a_{\mathrm{I}}, a_{\mathrm{II}} \in A(z). \tag{15.114}$$

(c) The transition probabilities are symmetric:

$$q(z, a_{\mathrm{I}}, a_{\mathrm{II}}) = q(z, a_{\mathrm{II}}, a_{\mathrm{I}}), \quad \forall a_{\mathrm{I}}, a_{\mathrm{II}} \in A(z). \tag{15.115}$$

Prove by induction on T that the value of a two-player zero-sum symmetric stochastic T-stage game is 0 for every initial state.

15.12 Prove Theorem 15.34 on page 653: let z be an absorbing state in a two-player zero-sum stochastic game. Then, for every discount factor $\lambda \in [0, 1)$, the quantity $v^\lambda(z)$ is equal to $\mathrm{val}(\Gamma^1(z))$, the value of the one-stage game in state z.

15.13 Given a two-player zero-sum stochastic game, denote the minimal payoff in the game by $m := \min_{(z,a) \in \Lambda} u(z, a)$ and the maximal payoff in the game by $M := \max_{(z,a) \in \Lambda} u(z, a)$. Prove that for every state $z \in Z$ and for every discount factor $\lambda \in [0, 1)$, the value $v^\lambda(z)$ of the discounted stochastic game with initial state z satisfies $m \le v^\lambda(z) \le M$.

15.14 Find λ-discounted optimal strategies for the two players in Example 15.34.

15.15 In the stochastic game described in the figure below there are four states denoted by z_0, z_1, z_2, and z_3. The states z_1, z_2, and z_3 are absorbing states. The transition probabilities are deterministic; that is, the probability distribution $q(z, a)$ assigns probability 1 to the state written in the upper-right corner of the corresponding cell.

	L	R
T	0 $\quad^{z_0}$	1 $\quad^{z_3}$
B	2 $\quad^{z_1}$	0 $\quad^{z_2}$

state z_0

| 1 $\quad^{z_1}$ |

state z_1

| 0 $\quad^{z_2}$ |

state z_2

| 3 $\quad^{z_3}$ |

state z_3

(a) Prove that for every discount factor λ, the *maxmin* value of the λ-discounted game with initial state z_0 is positive.

(b) Prove that Player I has no stationary optimal strategy that chooses a pure action in state z_0.

(c) For every discount factor $\lambda \in [0, 1)$, compute the λ-discounted value and stationary optimal strategies for the two players.

15.16 In the stochastic game presented below, there are two non-absorbing states. The transition probabilities are deterministic; that is, the probability distribution $q(z, a)$ assigns probability 1 to the state written in the upper-right corner of the corresponding cell.

	L	R
T	0 z_1	0 z_2
B	0 z_2	1 z_3

state z_0

	L	R
T	0 z_0	1 z_3
B	1 z_3	0 z_2

state z_1

0 z_2

state z_2

1 z_3

state z_3

(a) Prove that for every discount factor λ, the λ-discounted value of the stochastic game with initial state z_0 or z_1 is a positive number less than 1.

(b) Prove that Player I does not have a stationary optimal strategy that chooses a pure action in state z_0 or in state z_1.

(c) For every discount factor $\lambda \in [0, 1)$, compute the λ-discounted value of the game and stationary optimal strategies for the players.

15.17 In the stochastic game described in the figure below there are four states denoted by z_0, z_1, z_2, and z_3. The states z_2 and z_3 are absorbing states. The transition probabilities are deterministic; that is, the probability distribution $q(z, a)$ assigns probability 1 to the state written in the upper-right corner of the corresponding cell.

	L	R
T	1 z_0	1 z_1
B	1 z_1	1 z_2

state z_0

	L	R
T	-1 z_1	-1 z_0
B	-1 z_0	-1 z_3

state z_1

1 z_2

state z_2

-1 z_3

state z_3

(a) Prove that $v^\lambda(z_0) = -v^\lambda(z_1)$.

(b) Prove that $v^\lambda(z_0) > 0$.

(c) Conclude that the stationary optimal strategies of both players involve completely mixed actions in both states z_0 and z_1, and compute the λ-discounted value for every discount factor $\lambda \in [0, 1)$.

15.18 Let τ_I be an optimal strategy of Player I in a T-stage two-player zero-sum stochastic game. Is it necessarily true that for every history $h \in H^T$ the mixed action $\tau_I(h)$ is an optimal strategy in the one-stage game in the current state? Explain your answer.

15.19 Let τ_I be a stationary strategy of Player I in a two-player zero-sum stochastic game satisfying the following condition: for every state $z \in Z$ the mixed action $\tau_I(z)$ is not optimal in the game $G^\lambda(z; v^\lambda)$. Prove that for every initial state, the strategy τ_I is not an optimal strategy in the stochastic game.

15.20 Using Shapley's Theorem (Theorem 15.32 on page 652), prove that in a repeated two-player zero-sum game, for every discount factor the value of the discounted game is equal to the value of the one-stage game.

15.21 A (finite) *directed graph* is a pair (V, E), where V is a finite set of *vertices* (or *nodes*) and E is a finite set of *directed edges*. In other words, $E \subseteq V \times V$ and an element $e = (v_1, v_2) \in E$ is a directed edge from vertex v_1 to vertex v_2. A *game on a graph* is a two-player zero-sum game given by

- A directed graph (V, E) with the property that $(v, v) \in E$ for each vertex $v \in V$. In other words, from every vertex v there is a directed edge to v itself.
- A function $i : V \to \{I, II\}$ assigning each vertex to one of the players.
- A function $u : V \to \mathbb{R}$ assigning a payoff to each vertex.
- An initial vertex $v^1 \in V$.

The game is played in stages as follows:

- At every stage the play is at one of the vertices, with v^1 being the initial vertex.
- At stage $t \in \mathbb{N}$ the following takes place:
  – Player II pays Player I the amount of $u(v^t)$, where v^t is the vertex at stage t.
  – Player $i(v^t)$ chooses an edge starting at v^t, say the edge $(v^t, \hat{v})$.
  – Stage t is terminated, and the state for the next stage, stage $(t+1)$, is $v^{t+1} := \hat{v}$.

Answer the following questions:

(a) Describe the game on a graph as a stochastic game.
(b) Prove that for every $\lambda \in [0, 1)$, each player has a λ-discounted optimal strategy that is pure and stationary.
(c) Assume that the two players follow optimal pure stationary strategies. Is it necessarily true that there exist a vertex v^* and a stage $t_0 \in \mathbb{N}$ such that $v^t = v^*$ for all $t \geq t_0$? Provide a counterexample showing that this is not necessarily true.

15.22 In this exercise we generalize one part of Shapley's Theorem (Theorem 15.32 on page 652) to games with any number of players. Let $(N, Z, (A_i)_{i \in N}, (u_i)_{i \in N}, q)$ be a stochastic game. The λ-*discounted maxmin value* of player i in state z is

$$\underline{v}_i^\lambda(z) = \sup_{\tau_i \in \mathcal{B}_i^\infty} \inf_{\tau_{-i} \in \mathcal{B}_{-i}^\infty} \gamma_i^\lambda(z, \tau_i, \tau_{-i}). \tag{15.116}$$

Prove that every player i has a stationary strategy τ_i^* satisfying

$$\gamma_i^\lambda(z, \tau_i^*, \tau_{-i}) \geq \underline{v}_i^\lambda(z), \quad \forall z \in Z, \forall \tau_{-i} \in \mathcal{B}_i^\infty. \tag{15.117}$$

15.23 In this exercise we generalize another part of Shapley's Theorem (Theorem 15.32 on page 652) to games with any number of players. Let $(N, Z, (A_i)_{i \in N}, (u_i)_{i \in N}, q)$ be a stochastic game. The λ-*discounted minmax value* of player i in state z is

$$\bar{v}_i^\lambda(z) = \inf_{\tau_{-i} \in \mathcal{B}_{-i}^\infty} \sup_{\tau_i \in \mathcal{B}_i^\infty} \gamma_i^\lambda(z, \tau_i, \tau_{-i}). \tag{15.118}$$

Prove that there exists a stationary strategy vector τ_{-i}^* satisfying

$$\gamma_i^\lambda(z, \tau_i, \tau_{-i}^*) \leq \bar{v}_i^\lambda, \quad \forall z \in Z, \forall \tau_i \in \mathcal{B}_i^\infty. \tag{15.119}$$

15.24 The stochastic game described in the figure below is a three-player game in which Player I chooses a row (T or B), Player II chooses a column (L or R), and Player III chooses a matrix (W or E). Recall that $*$ in the upper-right corner of a cell indicates a transition to an absorbing state with payoffs equal to the payoffs in that cell.

	W			E	
	L	R		L	R
T	$0,0,0$ ^{z0}	$0,1,3$ *	T	$3,0,1$ *	$1,1,0$ *
B	$1,3,0$ *	$1,0,1$ *	B	$0,1,1$ *	$0,0,0$ *

state z_0

For every discount factor $\lambda \in [0,1)$, find a symmetric λ-discounted equilibrium; that is, find a number $p_\lambda \in [0,1]$ such that the vector of stationary strategies $([p_\lambda(T),(1-p_\lambda)(B)],[p_\lambda(L),(1-p_\lambda)(R)],[p_\lambda(W),(1-p_\lambda)(E)])$ is a λ-discounted equilibrium.

15.25 Theorem 15.41 on page 659 states that every discounted stochastic game has an equilibrium in stationary strategies. The proof of this result uses a fixed point theorem on the product space $\left(\times_{i\in N} \times_{z\in Z} \Delta(A_i(z))\right) \times \mathbb{R}^{|I|\times|Z|}$. In this exercise we prove a weaker result using Nash's Theorem for finite games, which was discussed in Remark 15.23 on page 645: we prove that every stochastic game has a λ-discounted equilibrium, not necessarily in stationary strategies, for every discount factor $\lambda \in [0,1)$. The proof is based on the finiteness of the game: the set of states, the set of players, and the sets of actions are all finite sets. Yet the most crucial property that is used is the finiteness of the discounted payoff: since $\lambda < 1$, the contribution of the payoffs in the distant future to the discounted payoff is negligible; the contribution of the payoffs after stage t is bounded by $M(1-\lambda)(\lambda^t + \lambda^{t+1} + \cdots) = M\lambda^t$, where M is the maximal payoff in absolute values, and this bound is small when t is large.

Fix a discount factor $\lambda \in [0,1)$.

(a) Prove that the set $\mathcal{B}_i^\infty$ is a compact set in the metric d_i defined in Equation (15.19).

(b) Prove that for every state $z^1 \in Z$, the function $\tau \mapsto \gamma_i^\lambda(z^1, \tau)$ is a continuous function in the metric d defined in Equation (15.20).

(c) For every initial state $z^1 \in Z$ and every $k \in \mathbb{N}$, let $\widehat{\Gamma}^{k,\lambda}(z^1)$ be the game in which the player set is N, the strategy set of each player i is $\mathcal{B}_i^\infty$, and the payoff function is the k-th-stage payoff defined in Equation (15.21). Prove that the game $\widehat{\Gamma}^{k,\lambda}(z^1)$ has an equilibrium $\tau^k(z^1)$.

(d) Prove that the sequence $(\tau^k(z^1))_{k \in \mathbb{N}}$ has a converging subsequence, and denote by $\tau^*(z^1)$ the limit point of such a subsequence.

(e) Prove that the vector of strategies $\tau^*(z^1)$ is a λ-discounted equilibrium of the stochastic game with initial state z^1.

15.26 The following game is a two-player zero-sum absorbing game in which, in the non-absorbing state z_0, each player has three pure actions.

Player II

		L	I	R
	T	$0 \quad {}^{z_0}$	$0 \quad {}^{z_0}$	$1 \quad {}^*$
Player I	M	$0 \quad {}^{z_0}$	$1 \quad {}^*$	$0 \quad {}^*$
	B	$1 \quad {}^*$	$0 \quad {}^*$	$0 \quad {}^*$

state z_0

(a) Prove that the λ-discounted maxmin value is positive.

(b) Prove that the optimal stationary strategy of Player I (in the non-absorbing state z_0) is completely mixed; that is, each of the three pure actions T, M, and B is played with positive probability.

(c) Compute the λ-discounted value of the game, as well as optimal strategies for the two players.

15.27 The following game is a two-player zero-sum stochastic game with non-deterministic transitions and one absorbing state.

	L		R	
T	1	$[0.6(z_0), 0.4(z_1)]$	1	$[0.3(z_0), 0.7(z_1)]$
B	0	$[0.4(z_0), 0.6(z_1)]$	2	$[0.5(z_0), 0.5(z_1)]$

state z_0

	L
T	$0 \quad {}^{z_1}$

state z_1

For every discount factor $\lambda \in [0, 1)$, compute the λ-discounted value of the game and stationary optimal strategies for the players.

15.28 Repeat Exercise 15.27 for the following game:

	L		R	
T	3	$[0.6(z_0), 0.4(z_1)]$	1	$[0.3(z_0), 0.7(z_1)]$
B	0	$[0.4(z_0), 0.6(z_1)]$	2	$[0.5(z_0), 0.5(z_1)]$

state z_0

	L
T	$0 \quad {}^{z_1}$

state z_1

15.29 In Exercise 15.11 we proved that the value of a two-player zero-sum symmetric T-stage stochastic game is 0, for every initial state. Prove that, in such games, for every discount factor and every initial state, the discounted value is 0 as well.

15.30 A stochastic game with a single player is called a *Markov decision process*. In such games, every equilibrium strategy is called an *optimal strategy*. Answer the following questions about a Markovian decision process.

(a) Prove that for every discount factor $\lambda \in [0, 1)$, the player has an optimal strategy that is stationary and pure.

(b) Prove that for every stationary strategy σ and every initial state z^1, the payoff function $\lambda \mapsto \gamma^\lambda(z^1, \sigma)$ is a rational function in λ; that is, it is the ratio of two polynomials in λ.

(c) Prove that there is a pure stationary strategy σ that is λ-discounted optimal for every discount factor λ close enough to 1. Such a strategy is called a *Blackwell optimal strategy*.

15.31 Generalize Shapley's Theorem (Theorem 15.32 on page 652) to the case where the state space is a countable set, each player has a finite number of actions in each state, and the payoff functions of all players are bounded.

15.32 Prove Theorem 15.40 on page 659: in a two-player zero-sum stochastic game, if a strategy τ_I of Player I is such that for every finite history $h = (z^1, a^1, z^2, a^2, \ldots, z^{t-1}, a^{t-1}, z^t) \in H^\infty$, the mixed action $\tau_I(h)$ is an optimal strategy in the game $G^\lambda(z^t; v^\lambda)$, then τ_I is an optimal strategy of Player I in the stochastic game. Is the converse of this result also true? Prove or provide a counterexample.

15.33 Prove that in a two-player zero-sum stochastic game, a pair of strategies (τ_I, τ_{II}) is a subgame perfect equilibrium[5] if and only if for every finite history $h = (z^1, a^1, z^2, a^2, \ldots, z^{t-1}, a^{t-1}, z^t) \in H^\infty$, the mixed action $\tau_I(h)$ is an optimal strategy of Player I in the game $G_\lambda(z^t; v^\lambda)$ and the mixed action $\tau_{II}(h)$ is an optimal strategy of Player II in this game.

15.34 Exercises 15.34–15.38 are dedicated to stochastic games with perfect information. An infinite stochastic game has *perfect information* if each one of the $|Z|$ extensive-form games assigned to it, one for every initial state, has perfect information. Answer the following questions:

(a) Prove that the λ-discounted infinite stochastic game has perfect information if and only if in every state $z \in Z$, the action set of all players but one is a singleton; that is, for every $z \in Z$ there is $i_z \in I$ such that $|A_i(z)| = 1$ for every player $i \neq i_z$.

(b) Prove that in every two-player zero-sum λ-discounted stochastic game with perfect information, each player has a pure optimal strategy.

---

5 For the definition of a subgame perfect equilibrium, see Chapter 7.

15.35 Consider a two-player zero-sum stochastic game with perfect information.

(a) Prove that for every pair of strategies (τ_I, τ_{II}) and for every initial state $z \in Z$, the function $\lambda \mapsto \gamma^\lambda(z, \tau_I, \tau_{II})$ is a *rational function*; that is, it is the ratio of two polynomials in λ.

(b) Prove that for every stationary strategy τ_{II} of Player II and for every discount factor λ, Player I has a best reply that is a stationary pure strategy.

(c) Use the fact that Player II has a finite number of pure stationary strategies to conclude that there is a pure stationary strategy τ_I of Player I and a discount factor $\lambda_0 \in [0, 1)$ such that τ_I is a λ-discounted optimal strategy for every $\lambda \in (\lambda_0, 1)$.

15.36 In this exercise we show that the result in Exercise 15.35 does not hold for non-zero-sum games; that is, a two-player non-zero-sum stochastic game with perfect information may not have a stationary equilibrium in pure strategies.

Consider the following two-player stochastic game with perfect information where $|A_2(z_1)| = |A_1(z_2)| = 1$. Show that for every discount factor $\lambda \in [0, 1)$ there is a unique λ-discounted equilibrium in stationary strategies, and this equilibrium is not pure.

Player II

			L	R
Player I	T	2,1 $\quad z_2$	3,2 $\quad z_1$	1,2 $\quad z_2$
	B	2,3 $\quad z_1$		

state z_1 ··· state z_2

15.37 Prove that in a stochastic game with any number of players and with perfect information, the λ-discounted maxmin value of player i in state z is equal to player i's λ-discounted minmax value in that state. For the definitions of the maxmin value and the minmax value, see Equations (15.116) and (15.118), respectively.

15.38 Consider a stochastic game with perfect information and fix a discount factor $\lambda \in [0, 1)$.

(a) Prove that each player i has a pure stationary strategy τ_i^* that guarantees him the maxmin value in any state, that is,

$$\gamma_i^\lambda(z, \tau_i^*, \tau_{-i}) \geq \underline{v}_i^\lambda, \quad \forall z \in Z, \forall \tau_{-i} \in \mathcal{B}_{-i}^\infty. \tag{15.120}$$

(b) Prove that for every player i there is a vector of pure stationary strategies of the other players $\tilde{\tau}_{-i}^i = (\tilde{\tau}_j^i)_{j \neq i}$ that guarantees that player i's payoff will be no more than his minmax value:

$$\gamma_i^\lambda(z, \tau_i, \tilde{\tau}_{-i}^i) \leq \bar{v}_i^\lambda, \quad \forall z \in Z, \forall \tau_i \in \mathcal{B}_i^\infty. \tag{15.121}$$

(c) Prove that the following vector of strategies is a λ-discounted equilibrium:

- Each player i plays the strategy τ_i^*, as long as no other player $j \in N$ has deviated from his strategy τ_j^*.
- As soon as some player deviates from this plan, say at stage t player i_0 deviates from the strategy $\tau_{i_0}^*$, all the other players play $\tilde{\tau}_j^{i_0}$ from stage $(t+1)$ on.

Hint: Use Exercises 15.22, 15.23, and 15.37.

15.39 A state $\hat{z}$ is *recurrent* if for every strategy vector τ and every state $z \in Z$, the probability of eventually reaching $\hat{z}$ under τ when the initial state is z is 1:

$$\mathbf{P}_{z,\tau}\left(\bigcup_{t=1}^{\infty}\{z^t = \hat{z}\}\right) = 1, \quad \forall z \in Z, \forall \tau \in \mathcal{B}^{\infty}. \tag{15.122}$$

A stochastic game is called a *recurrent game* if it has a recurrent state.

(a) Is it true that in a recurrent game every state is recurrent? Prove or provide a counterexample.
(b) Prove that if $\hat{z}$ is a recurrent state in a stochastic game, then for every $\varepsilon > 0$ there exists $T_0 \in \mathbb{N}$ that satisfies

$$\mathbf{P}_{z,\tau}(z^t = \hat{z} \text{ for some } t \in \{1, 2, \ldots, T_0\}) \geq 1 - \varepsilon, \quad \forall z \in Z, \forall \tau \in \mathcal{B}^{\infty}. \tag{15.123}$$

(c) Prove that in a recurrent two-player zero-sum stochastic game, the limit $\lim_{\lambda \to 1} v^\lambda(z)$ is independent of the initial state z.

15.40 For every discount factor $\lambda \in [0, 1)$, find a λ-discounted equilibrium of the following two-player absorbing game:

Player II

		L		R	
		L		R	
Player I	T	1, 0	z_0	0, 1	z_0
	B	0, 2	*	1, 0	*

state z_0

15.41 In the following two-player stochastic game there are two non-absorbing states, z_1 and z_2.

	L		R			L		R	
T	0, 0	z_2	1, 3	*	T	0, 0	z_1	0, 0	*
B	1, 3	*	3, 1	*	B	0, 0	*	3, 1	*

state z_1　　　　　　　　　　　　state z_2

(a) For every discount factor $\lambda \in [0, 1)$, find a λ-discounted equilibrium in which in state z_2 the players play (T, L).

(b) For every discount factor $\lambda \in [0, 1)$, find a λ-discounted equilibrium in which in state z_2 the players play (B, R).

15.42 Let us generalize the model of stochastic games by allowing different discount factors for different players. That is, for every player $i \in N$ there is a discount factor $\lambda_i \in [0, 1)$ and the payoff to player i given the strategy vector τ and the initial state z^1 is $\gamma_i^{\lambda_i}(z^1, \tau)$. Prove that in this generalized model there exists a discounted equilibrium in stationary strategies for every vector of discount factors $(\lambda_i)_{i \in N}$.

16 Bargaining games

Chapter summary

In this chapter we present bargaining games, which model situations in which two or more players bargain toward an agreed-upon outcome. The set of all possible outcomes is called the *feasible set* and each outcome can be attained only by the unanimous agreement of all players. Different players typically prefer different outcomes, which explains the bargaining aspect of the model. A default outcome, called the *disagreement point*, is realized if the players fail to reach an agreement.

A solution concept for bargaining games is a function that assigns to every bargaining game an outcome that can be looked at as the outcome that would be recommended to the players by an arbitrator or a judge. We list several desirable properties that a solution concept for two-player bargaining games could satisfy and provide the unique solution concept that satisfies all these properties, namely, the *Nash solution* for bargaining games. Variants of the Nash solution, like the Kalai–Smorodinsky solution, are obtained by imposing a different set of properties that a solution concept should satisfy. Finally, the model and some of the results are extended to bargaining games with more than two players.

It is frequently the case that two (or more) parties conduct negotiations over an issue, with the payoff to each party dependent on the outcome of the negotiation process. Examples include negotiations between employers and employees on working conditions, nations negotiating trade treaties, and company executives negotiating corporate mergers and acquisitions. In each of these cases, there is a range of outcomes available, if only the parties can come to an agreement and cooperate. Sometimes negotiations do not lead to an agreement. Employees can leave their place of work, countries can impose high tariffs, hurting mutual trade, and negotiations on mergers and acquisitions can fail, with no acquisition taking place. Such bargaining situations are typically not zero-sum: if two countries fail to agree on a trade treaty, for example, they may both suffer from decreased trade.

We will model bargaining games between two parties using a set $S \subseteq \mathbb{R}^2$, and a vector $d \in \mathbb{R}^2$. A point $x = (x_1, x_2) \in S$ represents a potential bargaining outcome expressed in units of utility, where x_i is player i's utility from the bargaining outcome, or in units of money. (Utility theory was presented in Chapter 2.) The set S thus represents the collection of possible bargaining outcomes, and the vector d represents the outcomes in the case where no agreement emerges from the bargaining process. The model presented in this chapter was introduced and first studied by Nash [1950a].

Before we continue, let us consider two simple examples of bargaining games.

Example 16.1 Suppose two players are to divide between them a potential profit of $100. If the players come to an agreement, they divide the money based on their agreement; if they fail to agree, neither of them receives anything. This is a simple model for a situation in which the abilities of the players are complementary and both players are needed to produced a profit; examples of such situations include an investor and the holder of a patent, and an investor and a landowner.

Figure 16.1(a) depicts this game graphically. The set of possible agreements is the interval

$$S = \{(x, 100 - x): 0 \le x \le 100\}, \tag{16.1}$$

and the vector of disagreement $d = (0, 0)$. The first coordinate represents the outcome for Player 1, and the second coordinate represents the outcome for Player 2. If the outcomes are interpreted in dollars, and if the two players are of similar economic status, it is reasonable for them to divide the $100 equally.

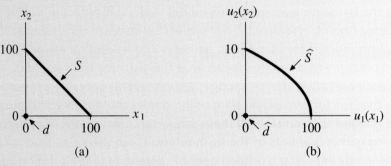

Figure 16.1 Graphic presentation of the bargaining game in Example 16.1, in dollars (a) and in utility units (b)

Suppose now that Player 1's utility from money is $u_1(x) = x$, and Player 2's utility from money is $u_2(x) = \sqrt{x}$. In utility units, the set of possible outcomes is

$$\widehat{S} = \{(x, \sqrt{100 - x}): 0 \le x \le 100\}, \tag{16.2}$$

and the disagreement point is $\widehat{d} = (0, 0)$ (see Figure 16.1(b)). How will they now divide the $100? ◀

As we can see, the set of possible agreements can be described in various ways, depending on the units in which results are measured. Which of the two depictions is preferable? We will not answer this question in this chapter, but instead only check which agreements can reasonably be expected, once the units in which outcomes are measured have been set.

Example 16.2 Larry and Sergey can, by cooperating, attain a potential profit of $100. They need to agree on dividing this sum between them. If they cannot come to an agreement, they will not cooperate, there will be no profit, and neither will receive any payoff. If they come to an agreement, they will cooperate, and divide the money according to the agreement. However, Larry will be required to pay tax at a rate of 50% of his share of the profit, whereas Sergey will be taxed at a rate of only 30% of his share. In this case, the disagreement point is $d = (0, 0)$, and the set of possible agreements is the interval S between $(50, 0)$ and $(0, 70)$ (see Figure 16.2).

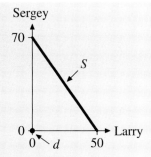

Figure 16.2 Graphic presentation of the bargaining game in Example 16.2

◀

Even rational players may sometimes fail to reach a compromise. This is why players on occasion turn to an arbitrator, to determine a fair agreement. How should an arbitrator decide which is the fairest agreement among all the possible agreements? Under any proposed agreement, a party to the agreement who receives less than he would receive under his optimal agreement can claim that the arbitrator is unfair! For the arbitrator to be able to explain how he arrived at the proposed agreement and defend his proposal, he needs to base his method of choosing the agreement on principles agreeable to both players, and show how his proposed agreement follows from those principles. It is also desirable for the principles to determine an agreement in such a way that any other suggested agreement would fail to satisfy one or more of the principles.

The following principles, which we present in an intuitive manner, are examples of principles that can be used to guide arbitrators:

- Symmetry: If the two players are equal both in their abilities and in how disagreement will affect them (a formal definition of this concept appears later in this chapter; see Definition 16.5), then under the arbitrator's proposed agreement, both players receive the same payoff.
- Efficiency: There does not exist a possible agreement that is better for both players than the proposed agreement.

Suppose that the arbitrator lists principles according to which he plans to choose a proposed agreement. He then needs to find a function that associates every bargaining game with a proposed agreement. Such a function will be called a "solution concept." The list of principles will be expressed as a list of mathematical properties to be satisfied by this function.

If the arbitrator chooses a list of desired principles that is too long, he may discover that there is no solution concept that satisfies every principle. If the list is too short, there may be many solution concepts that satisfy all the principles. In such a case, the arbitrator needs to find a way to choose one solution concept out of the many possible solution concepts, which is tantamount to adding another principle to the list. When there is exactly one solution concept that satisfies all the principles, the arbitrator can propose one agreement for every bargaining game, and defend his choice.

In his mathematical model, Nash presented several desired properties, and pointed to a unique solution concept that satisfies all those properties. We will present Nash's properties, and then introduce two more properties and the solution concepts that follow from them. This approach to finding a solution concept based on a list of properties is called the *axiomatic approach*, and the properties underlying the associated solution concept are often called *axioms*.

16.1 Notation

Let $x, y \in \mathbb{R}^m$ be two vectors. Denote $x \geq y$ if $x_i \geq y_i$ for all $i \in \{1, 2, \ldots, m\}$. Denote $x > y$ if $x \geq y$ and $x \neq y$. Denote $x \gg y$ if $x_i > y_i$ for all $i \in \{1, 2, \ldots, m\}$.

Given vectors $x, y \in \mathbb{R}^m$, $c \in \mathbb{R}$ and sets $S, T \subseteq \mathbb{R}^m$ define

$$x + y := (x_1 + y_1, x_2 + y_2, \ldots, x_m + y_m), \tag{16.3}$$

$$xy := (x_1 y_1, x_2 y_2, \ldots, x_m y_m), \tag{16.4}$$

$$cx := (cx_1, cx_2, \ldots, cx_m), \tag{16.5}$$

$$cS := \{cx \colon x \in S\}, \tag{16.6}$$

$$x + S := \{x + s \colon s \in S\}, \tag{16.7}$$

$$xS := \{xs \colon s \in S\}, \tag{16.8}$$

$$S + T := \{x + y \colon x \in S, y \in T\}. \tag{16.9}$$

If $x^1, x^2, \ldots, x^n$ are vectors in $\mathbb{R}^m$, denote by $\text{conv}\{x^1, x^2, \ldots, x^n\}$ the smallest convex set in $\mathbb{R}^m$ (using the set inclusion relation) containing the points $x^1, x^2, \ldots, x^n$. For example, if x, y, and z are three points in the plane and are not colinear, then $\text{conv}\{x, y, z\}$ is the triangle whose vertices are x, y, and z.

Given a compact set $S \subset \mathbb{R}^2$, and a continuous function $f : S \to \mathbb{R}$, denote by

$$\text{argmax}_{\{x \in S\}} f(x) := \{x \in S \colon f(x) \geq f(y) \quad \forall y \in S\} \tag{16.10}$$

the set of points in S at which the maximum of f is attained.

16.2 The model

Definition 16.3 *A bargaining game is an ordered pair* (S, d) *in which:*

- $S \subseteq \mathbb{R}^2$ *is a nonempty, compact, and convex set, called the* set of alternatives.
- $d = (d_1, d_2) \in S$ *is called the* disagreement point *(or conflict point).*
- *There exists an alternative* $x = (x_1, x_2) \in S$ *satisfying* $x \gg d$.

Denote the collection of all bargaining games by $\mathcal{F}$.

We interpret a bargaining game as a situation in which two players need to agree on an alternative $x = (x_1, x_2) \in S$. If they come to such an agreement, Player 1's payoff is x_1, and Player 2's payoff is x_2. If the players cannot come to an agreement, the outcome of

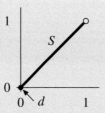

Figure 16.3 A bargaining game in which S is not closed

the game is d; i.e., Player 1's payoff is d_1, and Player 2's payoff is d_2. The assumptions appearing in the definition of a bargaining game are justified as follows:

- The set of alternatives S is bounded; i.e., the maximal and minimal outcomes of each player are bounded.
- The set of alternatives S is closed, and therefore, the boundary of every sequence of possible outcomes in S is also in S. Without this assumption, it may be the case that there is no optimal solution. For example, if the set of alternatives is $S = \{(x_1, x_1) : 0 \leq x_1 < 1\}$, a half-closed and half-open interval, the players do not have a most-preferred alternative: for every proposed solution, there is a solution that is closer than it to $(1, 1)$, and is therefore more preferred by both (see Figure 16.3).
- The set of alternatives S is convex; i.e., a weighted average of possible alternatives is also an alternative. This is a reasonable assumption when we relate to outcomes as linear von Neumann–Morgenstern utilities (see Chapter 2), and the players can conduct lotteries over two (or more) alternatives. For example, a lottery that chooses one possible outcome with probability $\frac{1}{3}$, and another outcome with probability $\frac{2}{3}$, is also a possible outcome of a bargaining process.
- We assume that there exists an alternative $x \in S$ such that $x \gg d$, to avoid dealing with degenerate cases in which there is no possibility that both players can profit from an agreement. Such cases require separate proofs (Exercise 16.12).

Definition 16.4 *A solution concept is a function φ associating every bargaining game $(S, d) \in \mathcal{F}$ with an alternative $\varphi(S, d) \in S$.*

The interpretation we give to a solution concept φ is that if two players are playing a bargaining game (S, d), the point $\varphi(S, d)$ is the alternative that an arbitrator will propose that the players accept as an agreement.

16.3   Properties of the Nash solution

In this section, we present several properties that one can require from solution concepts of bargaining games. These properties were first proposed by John Nash in 1953, and they are the mathematical expression of principles that could guide an arbitrator who is called upon to propose a bargaining agreement.[1] In the next section, we will show that there exists a unique solution concept satisfying these properties. We will then critique some of these properties, and present alternative properties (which are also open to critique), leading to other solution concepts to the bargaining game.

16.3.1 Symmetry

Definition 16.5 *A bargaining game* $(S, d) \in \mathcal{F}$ *is* symmetric *if the following two properties are satisfied:*

- $d_1 = d_2$ *(the disagreement point is symmetric).*
- *If* $x = (x_1, x_2) \in S$, *then* $(x_2, x_1) \in S$.

Geometrically, symmetry implies that S is symmetric with respect to the main diagonal in $\mathbb{R}^2$, where the disagreement point is located. The symmetry property forbids the arbitrator from giving preference to one party over the other when the game is symmetric.

Definition 16.6 *A solution concept* φ *is* symmetric *(or satisfies the symmetry property) if for every symmetric bargaining game* $(S, d) \in \mathcal{F}$ *the vector* $\varphi(S, d) = (\varphi_1(S, d), \varphi_2(S, d))$ *satisfies* $\varphi_1(S, d) = \varphi_2(S, d)$.

16.3.2 Efficiency

The goal of bargaining is to improve the situations of the players. We therefore do not want to propose an alternative that can be improved upon, that is, that is strictly preferred by one player and does not harm the interests of the other player. If such an alternative exists, the arbitrator will prefer it to the proposed alternative.

Definition 16.7 *An alternative* $x \in S$ *is called an* efficient point *of S if there does not exist an alternative* $y \in S$, $y \neq x$, *such that* $y \geq x$.

Denote by $PO(S)$ the set of efficient points[2] of S.

Definition 16.8 *A solution concept* φ *is* efficient *(or satisfies the* efficiency *property) if* $\varphi(S, d) \in PO(S)$ *for each bargaining game* $(S, d) \in \mathcal{F}$.

Definition 16.9 *An alternative* $x \in S$ *is called* weakly efficient *in S if there is no alternative in S that is strictly preferred to x by both players; in other words, there is no alternative* $y \in S$ *satisfying* $y \gg x$.

Denote the set of weakly efficient points in S by $PO^W(S)$. It follows by definition that $PO(S) \subseteq PO^W(S)$ for each set $S \subseteq \mathbb{R}^2$; as the following example shows, this set inclusion can be a proper inclusion.

---

1 These properties are also called the Nash axioms in the literature.

2 *PO* stands for Pareto optimum, named after the Italian economist Vilfredo Pareto (1848–1923). In his 1906 book, *Manuale di Economia Politica*, Pareto developed the idea that a distribution of resources in a society is nonoptimal if it is possible to increase at least one person's welfare without decreasing the welfare of any other individual.

Example 16.10   Consider the bargaining game in Figure 16.4. The set of possible outcomes that cannot be improved from the perspective of at least one player, i.e., $PO(S)$, appears in bold in part A. The set of possible outcomes that cannot be improved from the perspective of both players, i.e., $PO^W(S)$, appears in bold in part B. For example, the outcome $(30, 100)$ is inefficient, since the outcome $(40, 100)$ is better from the perspective of Player 1. On the other hand, there is no outcome that is strictly better for both players than $(30, 100)$. In other words, $(30, 100) \in PO^W(S)$, but $(30, 100) \notin PO(S)$.

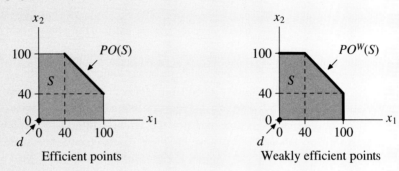

Figure 16.4   The efficient points of S in Example 16.10

Definition 16.11   *A solution concept φ is* weakly efficient *if $\varphi(S, d) \in PO^W(S)$ for each bargaining game $(S, d) \in \mathcal{F}$.*

The sets $PO(S)$ and $PO^W(S)$ are on the boundary of S, and therefore $\varphi(S, d)$ is on the boundary of S whenever φ is an efficient or a weakly efficient solution concept.

16.3.3   Covariance under positive affine transformations

When the axes of a bargaining game represent monetary payoffs, it is reasonable to require that the solution concept be *independent of the units of measurement*. In other words, if we measure the payoff to one player in cents instead of dollars, we get a different bargaining game (in which the coordinate corresponding to each point is larger by a factor of 100). In this case, we want the coordinate corresponding to the solution to change by the same ratio.

Another possible property to adopt is *covariance under translations*. This property implies that if we add a constant to each one of a certain player's payoffs, the solution will change by the same constant: the amount of money that each player has at the start of the bargaining process should not change the profit that each player gets by bargaining.

Definition 16.12   *A solution concept φ is* covariant under changes in the units of measurement *if for each bargaining game $(S, d) \in \mathcal{F}$, and every vector $a \in \mathbb{R}^2$ such that $a \gg 0$,*

$$\varphi(aS, ad) = a\varphi(S, d) = (a_1\varphi_1(S, d), a_2\varphi_2(S, d)). \tag{16.11}$$

A solution concept φ is covariant under translations *if for each bargaining game $(S, d) \in \mathcal{F}$, and every vector $b = (b_1, b_2) \in \mathbb{R}^2$,*

$$\varphi(S + b, d + b) = \varphi(S, d) + b = (\varphi_1(S, d) + b_1, \varphi_2(S, d) + b_2). \tag{16.12}$$

We combine these two properties into one, the property of covariance under positive affine transformations. Recall that a positive affine transformation in the plane is a function $x \mapsto ax + b$, where $a, b \in \mathbb{R}^2$, and $a \gg 0$.

Definition 16.13 *A solution concept φ is covariant under positive affine transformations if for every bargaining game $(S, d) \in \mathcal{F}$, for every vector $a \in \mathbb{R}^2$ such that $a \gg 0$, and for every vector $b \in \mathbb{R}^2$,*

$$\varphi(aS + b, ad + b) = a\varphi(S, d) + b. \tag{16.13}$$

While covariance under multiplication by $a \gg 0$ (change of units) is reasonable when considering bargaining over money, covariance under translations is open to critique because the amount of money a player has does, in general, affect his attitude towards any extra money over which the players are bargaining. If we wish to take this into consideration, we need to consider not the amount of money a player gets, but his utility from this amount of money. In other words, covariance under positive affine transformations is a natural assumption when the alternatives are expressed as pairs of utilities: the utility of each player from the alternative. As we saw in the chapter on the theory of utility (Chapter 2), von Neumann–Morgenstern utility functions are determined only up to positive affine transformations, so that we need to impose the condition that solution concepts to bargaining games be independent of the particular representation chosen for the players' utility functions.

16.3.4 Independence of irrelevant alternatives (IIA)

Suppose that $S \subseteq T$ and $\varphi(T, d) \in S$ (see Figure 16.5); i.e., in the bargaining process of the game (T, d), the players have checked all the alternatives in T and decided that the best alternative is $\varphi(T, d)$, which happens to be located in S. What happens if the set of possible alternatives is now restricted to S? One could make the case that the players will still choose $\varphi(T, d)$, because if there were a better alternative in S, that alternative would also be available in the game (T, d), and that alternative should then have been chosen, rather than $\varphi(T, d)$.

Definition 16.14 *A solution concept φ satisfies the property of* independence of irrelevant alternatives *(IIA) if for every bargaining game $(T, d) \in \mathcal{F}$, and every subset $S \subseteq T$,*

$$\varphi(T, d) \in S \implies \varphi(S, d) = \varphi(T, d). \tag{16.14}$$

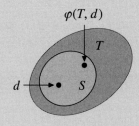

Figure 16.5 Independence of irrelevant alternatives

As we see in the intuitive "justification" presented above, this property is reasonable when a solution concept is supposed to reflect the "best" outcome: if the alternative $\varphi(T, d)$ that is the best alternative out of all the alternatives in T is in S, then if we delete the alternatives in $T\backslash S$, it will still be the best alternative. If, however, a solution concept is supposed to reflect the outcome of a compromise between the players, then it is possible to claim that even an alternative that is not chosen may influence the solution concept. In such cases, the independence of irrelevant alternatives is open to critique.

16.4 Existence and uniqueness of the Nash solution

In this section, we prove the existence of a unique solution concept that satisfies the properties of symmetry, efficiency, covariance under positive affine transformations, and independence of irrelevant alternatives. We will also present a formula for computing this solution for every bargaining game in $\mathcal{F}$.

An alternative $x \in S$ is *individually rational* in S if $x \geq d$. Since $d \in S$, the set of individually rational alternatives is not empty. If x is not individually rational in S, then at least one player strictly prefers d to x, and since each player can enforce the condition that the bargaining outcome is d, it is reasonable to suppose that such an alternative x will not be the end result of the bargaining process.

Theorem 16.15 *There exists a unique solution concept $\mathcal{N}$ for the family $\mathcal{F}$ satisfying symmetry, efficiency, covariance under positive affine transformations, and independence of irrelevant alternatives. The solution $\mathcal{N}(S, d)$ of the bargaining game (S, d) is the individually rational alternative x in S that maximizes the area of the rectangle whose bottom left vertex is d, and whose top right vertex is x (see Figure 16.6).*

The point $\mathcal{N}(S, d)$ is called the *Nash agreement point* (or the *Nash solution*) of the bargaining game (S, d). Note that for every $x \in S$ satisfying $x \geq d$, the area of the rectangle whose bottom left vertex is d, and whose top right vertex is x, is given by the product $(x_1 - d_1)(x_2 - d_2)$. The product $(x_1 - d_1)(x_2 - d_2)$ is called the *Nash product*. We will denote it here by $f(x)$.

We will prove the theorem in three steps. We first show that for every bargaining game in the family $\mathcal{F}$, there exists a unique alternative maximizing the area of this rectangle.

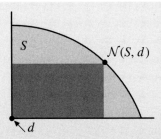

Figure 16.6 The Nash solution (the darkened rectangle is the rectangle of maximal area)

Lemma 16.16 *For every bargaining game* $(S, d) \in \mathcal{F}$ *there exists a unique point in the set*

$$\mathrm{argmax}_{\{x \in S, x \geq d\}} (x_1 - d_1)(x_2 - d_2). \tag{16.15}$$

Proof of Lemma 16.16: If we translate all the points in the plane by adding $-d$ to each point, we get the bargaining game $(S - d, (0, 0))$. Since the area of a rectangle is unchanged by translation, the points at which the Nash product is maximized for the bargaining game (S, d) are translated to the points at which the Nash product is maximized in the bargaining game $(S - d, (0, 0))$. We can therefore assume that, without loss of generality, $d = (0, 0)$, and then

$$f(x) = x_1 x_2. \tag{16.16}$$

The set of individually rational points in S, which we denote by $D := \{x \in S, x \geq d\}$, is the intersection of the compact and convex set S with the closed and convex set $\{x \in \mathbb{R}^2 : x \geq d\}$, so that it, too, is compact and convex. As we already noted, the set D is nonempty because it contains the disagreement point d.

Since the function f is continuous, and the set D is compact, there exists at least one point y in D at which the maximum is attained. Suppose by contradiction that there exist two distinct points y and z in D at which the maximum of f is attained. In particular,

$$y_1 y_2 = z_1 z_2. \tag{16.17}$$

Define

$$w := \tfrac{1}{2} y + \tfrac{1}{2} z. \tag{16.18}$$

Since D is convex, and $y, z \in D$, it follows that $w \in D$. We will show that

$$f(w) > f(y), \tag{16.19}$$

contradicting the fact that the Nash product is maximized at y (and at z). The assumption that $y \neq z$ therefore leads to a contradiction, hence $y = z$, and we will be able to conclude that the Nash product is maximized at a unique point.

One way to prove Equation (16.19) is to note that for every $c > 0$ the function $x_2 = \frac{c}{x_1}$ is strictly convex. For $c = y_1 y_2$, both $(y, f(y))$ and $(z, f(z))$ are on the graph of the function, and therefore $(w, f(w))$ is above the graph. In particular, $w_1 w_2 > c = y_1 y_2$.

A direct proof of the claim is as follows. In Figure 16.7, the points y and z are noted, with A, B, C, and D denoting four rectangular areas. From the figure we see that

$$y_1 z_2 + z_1 y_2 = A + 2B + C + D > A + 2B + C = y_1 y_2 + z_1 z_2. \tag{16.20}$$

Thus we have

$$f(w) = w_1 w_2 = \left(\tfrac{1}{2} y_1 + \tfrac{1}{2} z_1\right)\left(\tfrac{1}{2} y_2 + \tfrac{1}{2} z_2\right) \tag{16.21}$$

$$= \tfrac{1}{4} y_1 y_2 + \tfrac{1}{4} y_1 z_2 + \tfrac{1}{4} z_1 y_2 + \tfrac{1}{4} z_1 z_2 \tag{16.22}$$

$$> \tfrac{1}{4} y_1 y_2 + \tfrac{1}{4} y_1 y_2 + \tfrac{1}{4} z_1 z_2 + \tfrac{1}{4} z_1 z_2 \tag{16.23}$$

$$= \tfrac{1}{2} y_1 y_2 + \tfrac{1}{2} z_1 z_2 = f(y), \tag{16.24}$$

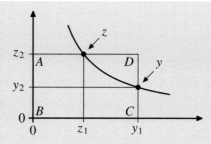

Figure 16.7 The areas of the rectangles defined by y and z are equal

where Equation (16.23) follows from Equation (16.20) and Equation (16.24) follows from Equation (16.17). In summary, $f(w) > f(y)$, which is the desired contradiction. ☐

From Lemma 16.16, the function $\mathcal{N}$ defined by

$$\mathcal{N}(S, d) := \text{argmax}_{\{x \in S, x \geq d\}} (x_1 - d_1)(x_2 - d_2) \tag{16.25}$$

is well defined and single-valued and is therefore a solution concept. Since there exists $x \in S$ satisfying $x \gg d$, one has $\max_{\{x \in S, x \geq d\}} f(x) > 0$, and therefore $\mathcal{N}(S, d) \gg d$.

We next show that this solution concept satisfies the four properties of Theorem 16.15.

Lemma 16.17 *The solution concept $\mathcal{N}$ satisfies the properties of symmetry, efficiency, covariance under positive affine transformations, and independence of irrelevant alternatives.*

Proof: $\mathcal{N}$ satisfies symmetry: Let (S, d) be a symmetric bargaining game, and let

$$y^* := \mathcal{N}(S, d) = \text{argmax}_{\{x \in S, x \geq d\}} (x_1 - d_1)(x_2 - d_2). \tag{16.26}$$

Denote by z the point $z = (y_2^*, y_1^*)$. Since S is symmetric, and $y^* \in S$, we deduce that $z \in S$. Since $d_1 = d_2$, the area of the rectangle defined by y^* and d equals the area of the rectangle defined by z and d (see Figure 16.8):

$$f(y^*) = (y_1^* - d_1)(y_2^* - d_2) = (z_2 - d_1)(z_1 - d_2) = (z_1 - d_1)(z_2 - d_2) = f(z). \tag{16.27}$$

By Lemma 16.16, the maximum of f over S is attained at a unique point. Therefore $y^* = z$, leading to $y_1^* = y_2^*$, as required.

$\mathcal{N}$ satisfies efficiency: If y is not efficient in S then there exists $z \in S$ satisfying (a) $z \geq y$ and (b) $z \neq y$. Then the area of the rectangle defined by z and d is strictly greater than the area of the rectangle defined by y and d, and therefore $\mathcal{N}(S, d) \neq y$ (see Figure 16.8).

$\mathcal{N}$ satisfies covariance under positive affine transformations: The maximum of the function f over $\{x \in S, x \geq d\}$ is attained at the point $\mathcal{N}(S, d)$. Applying the positive affine transformation $x \mapsto ax + b$ to the plane combines a translation with multiplication by a positive constant at every coordinate. A translation does not change the area of a rectangle, and multiplication by $a = (a_1, a_2)$ multiplies the area of the rectangle by

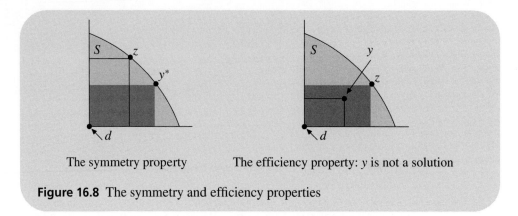

The symmetry property   The efficiency property: y is not a solution

Figure 16.8 The symmetry and efficiency properties

$a_1 a_2$. It follows that if prior to the application of the transformation the Nash product maximizes at y, then after the application of the transformation $x \mapsto ax + b$ the Nash product maximizes at $ay + b$.

$\mathcal{N}$ *satisfies independence of irrelevant alternatives:* This follows from a general fact: let $S \subseteq T$, let $g : T \to \mathbb{R}$ be a function, and let $w \in \operatorname{argmax}_{\{x \in T, x \geq d\}} g(x)$. If $w \in S$, then $w \in \operatorname{argmax}_{\{x \in S, x \geq d\}} g(x)$ (explain why the claim that $\mathcal{N}$ satisfies independence of irrelevant alternatives follows from this general fact). To see why this claim holds, note that since $w \in S$ and $S \subseteq T$,

$$\max_{\{x \in S, x \geq d\}} g(x) \geq g(w) = \max_{\{x \in T, x \geq d\}} g(x) \geq \max_{\{x \in S, x \geq d\}} g(x). \tag{16.28}$$

It follows that

$$\max_{\{x \in T, x \geq d\}} g(x) = \max_{\{x \in S, x \geq d\}} g(x), \tag{16.29}$$

and therefore $w \in \operatorname{argmax}_{\{x \in S, x \geq d\}} g(x)$. □

To complete the proof of Theorem 16.15, we need to prove the uniqueness of the solution concept.

Lemma 16.18 *Every solution concept φ satisfying symmetry, efficiency, covariance under positive affine transformations, and independence of irrelevant alternatives is identical to the solution concept $\mathcal{N}$ defined by Equation (16.25).*

Proof: Let φ be a solution concept satisfying the four properties of the statement of the theorem. Let (S, d) be a bargaining game in $\mathcal{F}$, and denote $y^* := \mathcal{N}(S, d)$. We will show that $\varphi(S, d) = y^*$.

Step 1: Applying a positive affine transformation L.
Since there is an alternative x in S such that $x \gg d$, the point $\mathcal{N}(S, d) = y^* \in \{z \in S : z \geq d\}$ at which the Nash product is maximized satisfies $y^* \gg d$. We can therefore define a positive affine transformation L over the plane shifting d to the origin, and y^* to $(1, 1)$ (see Figure 16.9). This function is given by

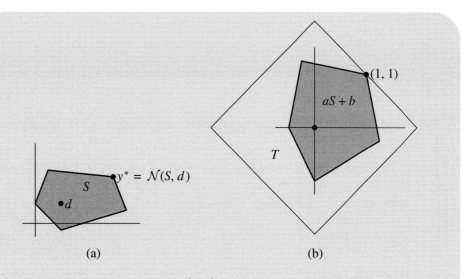

Figure 16.9 The bargaining game (S, d) (a) and the game obtained by implementation of the positive affine transformation L, along with the symmetric square T (b)

$$L(x_1, x_2) = \left(\frac{x_1 - d_1}{y_1^* - d_1}, \frac{x_2 - d_2}{y_2^* - d_2} \right).$$ (16.30)

Since $y_1^* > d_1$ and $y_2^* > d_2$, the denominators in the definition of L are positive. The function L is of the form $L = ax + b$, where $a_1 = \frac{1}{y_1^* - d_1} > 0$, $a_2 = \frac{1}{y_2^* - d_2} > 0$, $b_1 = -\frac{d_1}{y_1^* - d_1}$, and $b_2 = -\frac{d_2}{y_2^* - d_2}$. Since the solution concept $\mathcal{N}$ satisfies covariance under positive affine transformations,

$$\mathcal{N}(aS + b, (0,0)) = \mathcal{N}(aS + b, ad + b) = ay^* + b = (1,1).$$ (16.31)

Step 2: $x_1 + x_2 \leq 2$ for every $x \in aS + b$.
Let $x \in aS + b$. Since S is convex, the set $aS + b$ is also convex (Exercise 16.7). Therefore, since both x and $(1, 1)$ are in $aS + b$, the interval connecting x and $(1, 1)$ is also in $aS + b$. In other words, for every $\varepsilon \in [0, 1]$, the point z^ε defined by

$$z^\varepsilon := (1 - \varepsilon)(1, 1) + \varepsilon x = (1 + \varepsilon(x_1 - 1), 1 + \varepsilon(x_2 - 1))$$ (16.32)

is in $aS + b$. If ε is sufficiently close to 0 then $z^\varepsilon \geq (0,0)$, and therefore z^ε is one of the points in the set $\{w \in aS + b, w \geq (0,0)\}$. It follows that for each such ε,

$$f(z^\varepsilon) \leq \max_{\{w \in aS + b, w \geq (0,0)\}} f(w) = f(\mathcal{N}(aS + b, (0,0))) = f((1,1)) = 1.$$ (16.33)

Hence

$$1 \geq f(z^\varepsilon) = z_1^\varepsilon z_2^\varepsilon = 1 + \varepsilon(x_1 + x_2 - 2) + \varepsilon^2(x_1 - 1)(x_2 - 1)$$ (16.34)

$$= 1 + \varepsilon(x_1 + x_2 - 2 + \varepsilon(x_1 - 1)(x_2 - 1)).$$ (16.35)

Therefore, for every $\varepsilon > 0$ sufficiently small,

$$0 \geq \varepsilon(x_1 + x_2 - 2 + \varepsilon(x_1 - 1)(x_2 - 1)), \tag{16.36}$$

leading to the conclusion that

$$2 + \varepsilon(x_1 - 1)(x_2 - 1) \geq x_1 + x_2. \tag{16.37}$$

Taking the limit as ε approaches 0 yields $2 \geq x_1 + x_2$, which is what we wanted to show.

Step 3: $\varphi(S, d) = \mathcal{N}(S, d)$.
Let T be a symmetric square relative to the diagonal $x_1 = x_2$ that contains $aS + b$, with one side along the line $x_1 + x_2 = 2$ (see Figure 16.9(b)). Since $aS + b$ is compact (and thus bounded), such a square exists. By the symmetry and efficiency of φ, one has $\varphi(T, (0,0)) = (1, 1)$. Since the solution concept φ satisfies independence of irrelevant alternatives, and since $aS + b$ is a subset of T containing $(1, 1)$, it follows that $\varphi(aS + b, (0,0)) = (1, 1)$. Since the solution concept φ satisfies covariance under positive affine transformations, one can implement the inverse transformation L^{-1} to deduce that $\varphi(S, d) = y^*$. Since $y^* = \mathcal{N}(S, d)$, we conclude that $\varphi(S, d) = \mathcal{N}(S, d)$, as required. □

16.5 Another characterization of the Nash solution

In this section, we present another geometric characterization of the solution concept $\mathcal{N}$ defined in Equation (16.25).

Definition 16.19 *Let S be a closed and convex set in $\mathbb{R}^2$, and let x be an alternative on the boundary of S. A supporting line of S at x is any line through x such that the set S lies in one of the closed half-planes defined by it.*

By a general theorem from the theory of convex sets (the Separating Hyperplane Theorem; see Section 24.2, page 989), for every convex set $S \subseteq \mathbb{R}^2$ and every point x on the boundary S there exists a supporting line of S at x.

If the boundary of S is smooth at a point x, there exists a unique supporting line of S at x, which is the tangent line to S at x. If, in contrast, x is a "corner" of S, there are several supporting lines at x (see Figure 16.10).

Recall that since the Nash solution is an efficient solution concept, $\mathcal{N}(S, d) \in PO(S)$: the Nash solution is in the boundary of S.

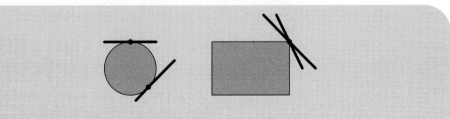

Figure 16.10 Examples of supporting lines of closed and convex sets

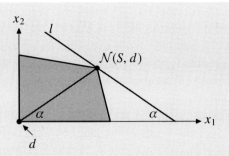

Figure 16.11 The second characterization of the Nash solution

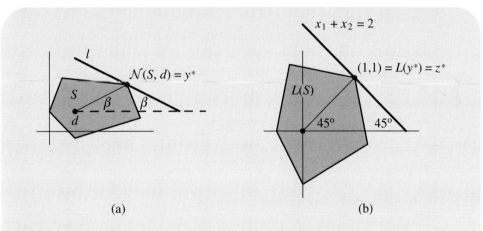

(a)   (b)

Figure 16.12 Proof of Theorem 16.20. The bargaining game prior to the implementation of L (a), and after the implementation of L (b)

Theorem 16.20 *For every bargaining game $(S, d) \in \mathcal{F}$, one has $\mathcal{N}(S, d) = y$ if and only if (a) $y \in PO(S)$, (b) $y \gg d$, and (c) there exists a supporting line l of S at y, such that the triangle whose vertices are d, y, and the intersection point of l with the line $x_2 = d_2$ is an equilateral triangle, whose base is the line $x_2 = d_2$ (see Figure 16.11).*

In other words, the angle between the line connecting d with $\mathcal{N}(S, d)$ and the x_1-axis equals the angle between the supporting line l and the x_1-axis.

Proof: Given a bargaining game $(S, d) \in \mathcal{F}$, denote $y^* := \mathcal{N}(S, d)$. In the proof of Lemma 16.18, we saw that there exists a positive affine transformation L such that $L(d) = (0, 0)$ and $z^* := L(y^*) = (1, 1)$. We also proved there that the set $L(S)$, the image of S under the transformation L, is a subset of the half-plane $x_1 + x_2 \leq 2$, and therefore the line $x_1 + x_2 = 2$ is a supporting line of $L(S)$ at z^* (see Figure 16.12(b)). In addition, the angle between the line connecting z^* and d, and the x_1-axis, is $45°$, and this is also the angle between the line $x_1 + x_2 = 2$ and the x_1-axis. It follows that the triangle whose vertices are $L(d)$, z^*, and the intersection of the line $x_1 + x_2 = 2$ with the x_1-axis is an equilateral triangle.

The inverse transformation L^{-1} maps the supporting line $x_1 + x_2 = 2$ of $L(S)$ at $z^* = L(y^*)$ to the supporting line l of S at y^* (see Exercise 16.6), and $(1,1)$ to $\mathcal{N}(S, d)$ (see Figure 16.12). Similarly, a positive affine transformation maps an equilateral triangle whose base is the line $x_2 = d_2$ to an equilateral triangle (whose base is parallel to the x_1-axis; Exercise 16.11). It follows that S has a supporting line at y^* defining an equilateral triangle, as required.

We now prove the opposite direction; i.e., we will show that if there is an efficient point $y \in S$, $y \gg d$, and a supporting line l of S at y defining an equilateral triangle, then necessarily $y = \mathcal{N}(S, d)$. Since $y \gg d$, there is an affine transformation L, $L(x) = ax + b$ where $a \gg 0$, mapping d to $(0, 0)$, y to $(1, 1)$, and l to the supporting line of $aS + b$ at $ay + b$. In addition, the triangle formed by the line connecting $ad + b = (0, 0)$ with $ay + b = (1, 1)$, the image of the supporting line $al + b$, and the axis $x_1 = 0$, is an equilateral triangle.

The angle between the line connecting $(0, 0)$ to $(1, 1)$ and the x_1-axis is $45°$. Since the triangle we described is an equilateral triangle, the line $al + b$ also intersects the x_1-axis at a $45°$ angle, and it is therefore the line $x_1 + x_2 = 2$. The point that maximizes the Nash product in the triangle whose vertices are $(0, 0)$, $(2, 0)$, and $(0, 2)$ is $(1, 1)$, and since this point is in the set $aS + b$, it follows that $\mathcal{N}(aS + b, (0, 0)) = (1, 1)$. Therefore, $y = \mathcal{N}(S, d)$, which is what we wanted to show. $\square$

In the next two subsections we present applications of this characterization of the Nash solution.

16.5.1 Interpersonal comparison of utilities

In the previous sections, we described the Nash point as a solution concept based on several properties. This solution concept, similar to every solution concept in game theory, is convincing only insofar as the properties characterizing it are convincing. In the case of the Nash solution, the property of independence of irrelevant alternatives is open to critique (see Sections 16.3.4 (page 680) and 16.7 (page 691)). This motivates interest in the question of whether the solution concept can be characterized in a different manner. Shapley [1969] proposed such a characterization, based on the following two properties:

- **Egalitarianism:**[3] At the solution point, the profit in utility units, relative to the disagreement point, is the same for both players.
- **Utilitarianism:**[4] The players will choose an alternative that maximizes the sum of their profits (in utility units), relative to the disagreement point.

The main difficulty in applying these properties is that within the framework of the von Neumann–Morgenstern utility theory (Chapter 2), a player's utility function is determined only up to a positive affine transformation, so there is no way to compare or add together

---

3 Shapley used the term "equitability" for this concept.
4 Shapley used the term "efficiency" for this concept.

the utilities of different players. This is called the "interpersonal comparison of utilities" problem in the literature.

Shapley's approach to this problem is that although it is impossible to compare utilities between the players over all games, in every particular game we can regard the alternative which the players finally agree upon as a reflection of the exchange rate between their utilities that emerged in the bargaining process. In particular, Shapley's suggestion is that the minus of the slope c of the supporting line[5] at the agreement point should be considered the exchange rate between the utility of the second player and the utility of the first player. The reasoning behind this suggestion is that at this point, slightly moving the agreement point within the set of efficient points $PO(S)$ yields approximately c units of profit/loss to the second player, with a unit of loss/profit to the first player (prove that this is true).

We next present Shapley's characterization of the Nash solution.

Definition 16.21 *An alternative* $x = (x_1, x_2) \in S$ *is a* solution *of a bargaining game* (S, d) *if there exists a positive number* c *satisfying:*

- *Egalitarianism:* $x_2 - d_2 = c(x_1 - d_1)$.
- *Utilitarianism:* $x \in \operatorname{argmax}_{y \in S}\{(y_2 - d_2) + c(y_1 - d_1)\}$.

Shapley's characterization states that the only possible candidate for a solution concept of the bargaining game, according to this definition, is the Nash solution. In that case, the constant c is minus the slope of a supporting line to S at the Nash point.

Theorem 16.22 *Let* $(S, d) \in \mathcal{F}$ *be a bargaining game such that for each efficient point satisfying* $y \gg d$ *there exists a unique tangent to* S *at* y. *Then there exists a unique alternative* $x \in S$ *that is a solution of the game according to Definition 16.21. Furthermore, this alternative is* $x = \mathcal{N}(S, d)$.

The proof of this theorem is accomplished using Theorem 16.20, and is left to the reader (Exercise 16.17).

16.5.2 The status quo region

Given a bargaining game (S, d), we ask what are the disagreement points that, with the same feasible set S, yield the same solution. That is, what is the collection of all the points $\widehat{d}$ such that $\mathcal{N}(S, \widehat{d}) = \mathcal{N}(S, d)$? By Theorem 16.20, if S has a unique supporting line at the point $\mathcal{N}(S, d)$, then the point $\widehat{d}$ satisfies this condition if and only if it is located on the ray emanating from $\mathcal{N}(S, d)$ and passing through d (see Figure 16.13(a)).

If there are several supporting lines for S at the point $\mathcal{N}(S, d)$, then $\widehat{d}$ may be located on any ray emanating from $\mathcal{N}(S, d)$, forming, along with one of the supporting lines, an equilateral triangle whose base is on the axis $x_2 = d_2$ (the darkened area in Figure 16.14(b)). This line (or region) is called the *status quo line* (or *status quo region*).

Suppose that in the current situation, the players are at point d. Both players are interested in signing an agreement that will improve this situation. The set of alternatives

---

5 For simplicity, we assume here that S has a unique supporting line at the agreement point.

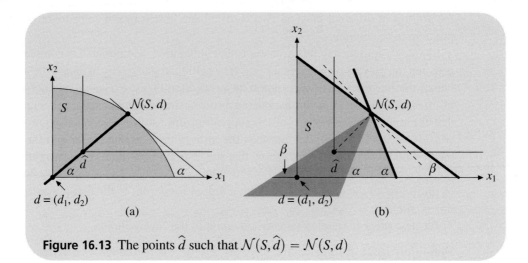

Figure 16.13 The points $\widehat{d}$ such that $\mathcal{N}(S,\widehat{d}) = \mathcal{N}(S,d)$

S represents the possible situations to which the players can move. Since the players believe in the Nash solution, they have an interest in following a process that will move them to $y^* = \mathcal{N}(S,d)$. For various reasons (for example, the players may not trust each other) they want to arrive at the Nash point by way of a series of interim agreements that will not change the balance of power; none of the players will have a reason to object to the common goal of reaching y^* throughout the process. Since the two parties believe in the Nash solution, we require that y^* continue to be the Nash solution in all the interim stages, where the disagreement point is the situation in the interim stage. This property is satisfied when the interim states are on the status quo line (or in the status quo region). As long as the interim state is on this line (or in this region) y^* is the Nash solution of the changing bargaining problem throughout the process.

16.6 The minimality of the properties of the Nash solution

In the previous section, we showed that there exists a unique solution concept satisfying the four properties of the Nash solution. We will show here that if one of these properties is left out, uniqueness is lost. In the following examples, for each property in turn, we will exhibit a solution concept for the family $\mathcal{F}$ with respect to which that property fails to hold, but the other three properties do hold. Since the Nash solution satisfies all four properties, it will follow that for every set of three of the four properties there exist at least two solution concepts satisfying these three properties.

Example 16.23 Leaving out efficiency Let φ be the solution concept that coincides with the disagreement point:

$$\varphi(S,d) := d.$$

Out of the four Nash properties, the only property that this solution concept does not satisfy is efficiency (Exercise 16.1). ◀

Example 16.24 **Leaving out symmetry: preferring one player to another** Define a solution concept φ as follows:

$$\varphi(S,d) := \mathrm{argmax}_{\{x \in PO(S):\, x \geq d\}} x_1. \tag{16.38}$$

This solution is Player 1's most-preferred alternative among the efficient and individually rational alternatives. Out of the four Nash properties, the only property that this solution concept does not satisfy is symmetry (Exercise 16.2).   ◀

Example 16.25 **Leaving out covariance under positive affine transformations** For every angle $0° < \alpha < 90°$ let $\lambda_\alpha(S,d)$ be the highest point in S on the line emanating from the disagreement point d at angle α relative to the line $x_2 = d_2$ (see Figure 16.14).

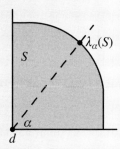

Figure 16.14 The solution concept λ_α

The solution concept $\lambda_{45°}(S,d)$ satisfies all the Nash properties except for covariance under positive affine transformations (Exercise 16.3).   ◀

Example 16.26 **Leaving out independence of irrelevant alternatives** Define a solution concept φ as follows. If there exists a positive affine transformation L satisfying the property that $(L(S), L(d))$ is a symmetric bargaining game, then $\varphi(S,d) := \mathcal{N}(S,d)$. Otherwise, $\varphi(S,d) := \mathrm{argmax}_{\{x \in PO(S):\, x \geq d\}} x_1$ is the best efficient and individually rational alternative for Player 1. Out of the four Nash properties, the only one that this solution concept fails to satisfy is independence of irrelevant alternatives (Exercise 16.4).   ◀

16.7 Critiques of the properties of the Nash solution

We have seen that if one seeks a solution concept satisfying symmetry, efficiency, covariance under positive affine transformations, and independence of irrelevant alternatives, the only solution concept one obtains is the Nash solution. But are these properties reasonable? Can an arbitrator who believes in these properties persuade the contending players that these are reasonable properties upon which to base his decisions? It is easy to make a case for efficiency, because it is reasonable for the players to agree to improve one player's situation if doing so does not come at the expense of the other player.

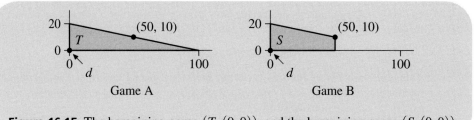

Figure 16.15 The bargaining game $(T, (0,0))$, and the bargaining game $(S, (0,0))$

Covariance under affine transformations, in contrast, is open to criticism, because changing the location of the disagreement point d and the set of alternatives S may give rise to new claims on the part of the players. For example, when two players of approximately equal abilities are negotiating the division of $1,000, the symmetric solution ($500, $500) seems reasonable. If, in contrast, one of the players is very wealthy, there may be two opposite influences on the outcome of the bargaining process: on one hand, it may appear more just for the person who is more in need of the money to receive a greater share, with his justification being that an additional $500 will have little effect on the wealthy player's condition, but is significant for a poor player. On the other hand, a wealthy player can exploit this fact to his advantage: he can hold out for a greater share of the money, knowing that if negotiations fail and the players walk away with nothing, this state of affairs will be harder on the poor player, who therefore has greater incentive to yield to the wealthy player's demands out of fear of being left with nothing. As we stated above, covariance under affine transformations is necessary when outcomes are stated in units of utility.

The property that has drawn the greatest share of attention is the property of independence of irrelevant alternatives. The next example is taken from Luce and Raiffa [1957]. Consider the two bargaining games in Figure 16.15.

Nash's solution for both bargaining games is $(50, 10)$. We do not dispute that this solution appears reasonable for the game $(T, (0,0))$ (Game A), but we will present a case here that the solution appears unreasonable for the game $(S, (0,0))$ (Game B). Suppose that both players accept $(50, 10)$ as a fair solution for the game $(T, (0,0))$, and then turn to playing $(S, (0,0))$. Player 2 can now claim that alternative $(50, 10)$ is unreasonable: in the bargaining game $(T, (0,0))$ both players compromise to some extent to arrive at the outcome $(50, 10)$, but in contrast, in the bargaining game $(S, (0,0))$, the outcome $(50, 10)$ gives Player 1 his highest possible payoff, while Player 2 does not receive his highest possible payoff. It is therefore reasonable for Player 2 to demand more than 10, by claiming that Player 1 should also compromise and receive less than he would from his best alternative.

Another critique of the Nash solution arises from the following example, given by Kalai and Smorodinsky [1975]. Let S_1 and S_2 be the two compact and convex sets in the plane defined by:

- S_1 is the convex hull of the points $(0,0), (0,1), (1,0), (0.75, 0.75)$ (the darkly shaded area in Figure 16.16).

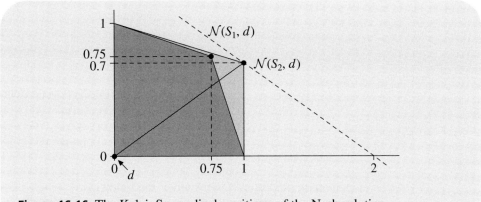

Figure 16.16 The Kalai–Smorodinsky critique of the Nash solution

- S_2 is the convex hull of the points $(0,0), (0,1), (1,0), (1,0.7)$ (the lightly shaded area in Figure 16.16).

The set S_2 contains the set S_1. In addition, both players are better off in the bargaining game $(S_2, (0,0))$ than in the bargaining game $(S_1, (0,0))$: for every point $x \in S_1$ (except for the points $(1,0)$ and $(0,1)$), there is a point $y \in S_2$ satisfying $y \gg x$. In this sense, by playing $(S_2, (0,0))$, the players are both in an improved situation, and Kalai and Smorodinsky therefore claim that one should expect the solution of $(S_2, (0,0))$ to be better for both players than the solution of $(S_1, (0,0))$.

Since the bargaining game $(S_1, (0,0))$ is symmetric, $\mathcal{N}(S_1, (0,0)) = (0.75, 0.75)$. By drawing an equilateral triangle whose vertices are $(0,0), (1,0.7), (2,0)$ (see Figure 16.16) and using Theorem 16.20, we deduce that $\mathcal{N}(S_2, (0,0)) = (1, 0.7)$. Notice that under $\mathcal{N}$, Player 2's situation is worsened in going from $(S_1, (0,0))$ to $(S_2, (0,0))$ (in S_1 he receives 0.75, as opposed to 0.7 in S_2). At the same time, this critique is not unequivocal, because although both players are better off, one may argue that in a certain sense Player 1's situation is "more improved" than Player 2's, because the set of efficient points has "moved more to the right than upwards."

Additional critiques that have been applied to the Nash solution are presented in Exercises 16.21 and 16.22. Despite these critiques, the Nash solution is still regarded as the most important solution concept for bargaining games. It is more frequently applied than other proposed solution concepts, which are also open to critique.

16.8 Monotonicity properties

Up to now, we have dealt with solution concepts defined over the family $\mathcal{F}$ of bargaining games. In this section, we will consider solution concepts defined over other families of bargaining games. Our goal will be to replace the property of independence of irrelevant alternatives with a different property, a monotonicity property. We will present two different monotonicity properties, and study the solution concepts implied by each of them.

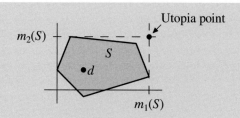

Figure 16.17 The definition of $m_1(S)$ and $m_2(S)$

The first monotonicity property we will study is the following.

Definition 16.27 *A solution concept φ satisfies* full monotonicity *over a family $\mathcal{F}_0$ of bargaining games if for every pair of bargaining games (S,d) and (T,d) in $\mathcal{F}_0$ such that $S \subseteq T$,*

$$\varphi(S,d) \leq \varphi(T,d). \tag{16.39}$$

The full monotonicity property is satisfied if adding more possible outcomes does not make a player's situation worse. The second monotonicity property is more complex. For every compact set $S \subset \mathbb{R}^2$, define

$$m_1(S) := \max\{x_1 \in \mathbb{R} : \text{ there exists } x_2 \in \mathbb{R} \text{ such that } (x_1, x_2) \in S\}, \tag{16.40}$$

and

$$m_2(S) := \max\{x_2 \in \mathbb{R} : \text{ there exists } x_1 \in \mathbb{R} \text{ such that } (x_1, x_2) \in S\}. \tag{16.41}$$

The maximal payoff that Player 1 can possibly get is $m_1(S)$, and $m_2(S)$ is the maximal payoff that Player 2 can get (see Figure 16.17). The point $(m_1(S), m_2(S))$ is called the *utopia point* of the game. This point is typically not in S, as in Figure 16.17.

The second monotonicity property is, in a sense, a weaker version of full monotonicity.

Definition 16.28 *A solution concept φ satisfies* limited monotonicity *over a family $\mathcal{F}_0$ of bargaining games if for every pair of bargaining games (S,d) and (T,d) in $\mathcal{F}_0$ satisfying (a) $S \subseteq T$, (b) $m_1(S) = m_1(T)$, and (c) $m_2(S) = m_2(T)$, it is the case that*

$$\varphi(S,d) \leq \varphi(T,d). \tag{16.42}$$

A solution concept φ which satisfies full monotonicity also satisfies limited monotonicity. As the example in Figure 16.16 shows, the Nash solution does not satisfy limited monotonicity over the family of games $\mathcal{F}$, since in that example $S_1 \subset S_2$, $m_1(S_1) = m_1(S_2) = 1$, $m_2(S_1) = m_2(S_2) = 1$, and $\mathcal{N}(S_2, d) \not\geq \mathcal{N}(S_1, d)$.

Denote by $\mathcal{F}_0$ the family of bargaining games (S,d) satisfying:

1. The set S is compact and convex.
2. The disagreement point is $d = (0,0)$.
3. $x \geq (0,0)$ for every $x \in S$, and there exists $x \in S$ such that $x \gg (0,0)$.

4. **Comprehensiveness:** If $x \in S$, then the rectangle defined by $(0,0)$ and x is also contained in S:

$$[0, x_1] \times [0, x_2] \subseteq S, \quad \forall x \in S. \tag{16.43}$$

We already encountered the first condition in the definition of the family of bargaining games $\mathcal{F}$. The second condition states that if the players cannot arrive at a compromise, neither of them gets anything. This assumption imposes no loss of generality if we add the property of covariance under translations. The third condition states that every alternative in S is weakly preferred to the disagreement point; any other alternative would be rejected by one of the players, and therefore we can omit it from S. The fourth condition is equivalent to enabling the players to throw away (or donate to charity) some of their profits from the bargaining process.

Since the disagreement point is $(0,0)$, it suffices to denote the bargaining games in $\mathcal{F}_0$ by S, instead of (S, d). By the definition of a bargaining game, there exists $x \in S$ satisfying $x \gg d = (0,0)$. It follows that $m_1(S) > 0$, $m_2(S) > 0$, and $S \subseteq [0, m_1(S)] \times [0, m_2(S)]$.

In this section we will focus on bargaining games in $\mathcal{F}_0$. A solution concept over $\mathcal{F}_0$ is a function associating every bargaining game S in this family with an alternative in S.

Definition 16.29 *A solution concept φ satisfies (first-order) homogeneity if for every bargaining game S and every real number $c > 0$,*

$$\varphi(cS) = c\varphi(S). \tag{16.44}$$

This property is a weakening of the property of independence of units of measurement, because it requires covariance only for every linear transformation that multiplies both coordinates by the same constant.

Definition 16.30 *A solution concept φ satisfies strict individual rationality if for every bargaining game S,*

$$\varphi(S) \gg (0,0). \tag{16.45}$$

This property requires that each player obtain a strictly positive profit relative to the disagreement point. Because there exists $x \in S$ satisfying $x \gg (0,0)$, it is reasonable to require that both players profit from cooperation.

For every angle $0° < \alpha < 90°$, define a solution λ_α over the family $\mathcal{F}_0$ as follows: $\lambda_\alpha(S)$ is the highest point in S on the ray emanating from the disagreement point $(0,0)$ at angle α, relative to the axis $x_2 = 0$ (see Figure 16.18).

For every $0° < \alpha < 90°$, the solution λ_α satisfies weak efficiency, homogeneity, strict individual rationality, and full monotonicity. In addition, if $\alpha = 45°$, the solution λ_α also satisfies symmetry (Exercise 16.23). The next theorem, due to Kalai [1977], shows that these are all the solution concepts satisfying these properties.

Theorem 16.31 *Let φ be a solution concept over $\mathcal{F}_0$ satisfying weak efficiency, homogeneity, strict individual rationality, and full monotonicity. Then there exists an angle $0° < \alpha < 90°$ such that $\varphi = \lambda_\alpha$.*

Proof: Let φ be a solution concept satisfying the four properties of the statement of the theorem.

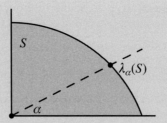

Figure 16.18 The solution λ_α

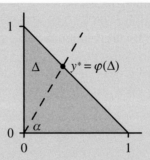

Figure 16.19 The definitions of $y^* = \varphi(\Delta)$ and the angle α

Step 1: Defining α.

Define the set $\Delta \subset \mathbb{R}^2$ as follows:

$$\Delta = \{x \in [0,1]^2 : x_1 + x_2 \le 1\}. \tag{16.46}$$

Denote $y^* := \varphi(\Delta)$ (see Figure 16.19). Since φ satisfies weak efficiency and strict individual rationality, the solution $y^* = \varphi(\Delta)$ is in the interior of the interval connecting $(0,1)$ with $(1,0)$.

Let $\alpha = \arctan(\frac{y_2^*}{y_1^*})$ be the angle of the line connecting $(0,0)$ with y^* (see Figure 16.19). Then $\varphi(\Delta) = y^* = \lambda_\alpha(\Delta)$. We will prove that $\varphi(S) = \lambda_\alpha(S)$ for every $S \in \mathcal{F}_0$. For the rest of the proof, we fix $S \in \mathcal{F}_0$.

Step 2: $\varphi(S) \ge \lambda_\alpha(S)$.

Recall that $\varphi(\Delta) = y^* = (y_1^*, y_2^*) \gg (0,0)$. For every $\varepsilon \in (0, \min\{\frac{1}{y_1^*} - 1, \frac{1}{y_2^*} - 1\})$, consider the convex set V_ε whose extreme points are $(0,0), (0, y_2^*(1 + \varepsilon)), y^*, (y_1^*(1 + \varepsilon), 0)$ (see Figure 16.20). Since $\varepsilon < \frac{1}{y_1^*} - 1$ and $\varepsilon < \frac{1}{y_2^*} - 1$, we deduce that $V_\varepsilon \subseteq \Delta$.

We now show that $\varphi(V_\varepsilon) = y^*$. Since φ satisfies full monotonicity, $\varphi(V_\varepsilon) \le \varphi(\Delta) = y^*$. Since φ satisfies weak efficiency, $\varphi(V_\varepsilon)$ is an efficient point of V_ε. But the only weakly efficient point x in V_ε satisfying $x \le y^*$ is y^*, and therefore $\varphi(V_\varepsilon) = y^*$.

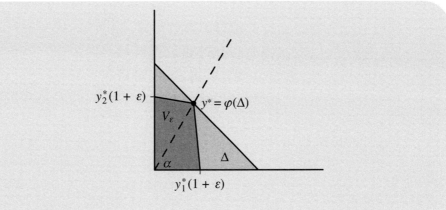

Figure 16.20 The set V_ε

Denote $z^* := \lambda_\alpha(S)$. Since y^* and z^* are both points on the line emanating from $(0,0)$ and forming an angle α with the axis $x_2 = 0$,

$$\frac{y_1^*(1+\varepsilon)}{y_2^*(1+\varepsilon)} = \frac{y_1^*}{y_2^*} = \frac{z_1^*}{z_2^*}. \tag{16.47}$$

Denote $c_\varepsilon := \dfrac{z_1^*}{y_1^*(1+\varepsilon)} = \dfrac{z_2^*}{y_2^*(1+\varepsilon)}$. We deduce

$$c_\varepsilon y_1^*(1+\varepsilon) = z_1^*, \qquad c_\varepsilon y_2^*(1+\varepsilon) = z_2^*. \tag{16.48}$$

Denote

$$z_\varepsilon = c_\varepsilon y^* = \frac{z^*}{1+\varepsilon}. \tag{16.49}$$

The set $c_\varepsilon V_\varepsilon$ and the point z_ε are depicted in Figure 16.21. Note that since S is a comprehensive set, it follows that $c_\varepsilon V_\varepsilon \subseteq S$.

Since the solution concept φ satisfies homogeneity,

$$\varphi(c_\varepsilon V_\varepsilon) = c_\varepsilon \varphi(V_\varepsilon) = c_\varepsilon y^* = z_\varepsilon = \frac{z^*}{1+\varepsilon}. \tag{16.50}$$

Since the solution concept φ satisfies full monotonicity, and $c_\varepsilon V_\varepsilon \subseteq S$, we deduce that $\varphi(S) \geq \frac{z^*}{1+\varepsilon}$. This inequality holds for every $\varepsilon > 0$ that is sufficiently small. Letting ε converge to 0 yields $\varphi(S) \geq z^* = \lambda_\alpha(S)$, which is what we wanted to show.

In the example in Figure 16.21 there exists only one weakly efficient point in S that is greater than or equal to $\lambda_\alpha(S)$, and therefore in this case $\varphi(S) = \lambda_\alpha(S)$. As can be seen in Figure 16.22, when the boundary of S is parallel to one of the axes, there may be several weakly efficient points in S that are greater than or equal to $\lambda_\alpha(S)$. We will now deal with this case.

Step 3: $\varphi(S) = \lambda_\alpha(S)$.
Let $\varepsilon > 0$, and define $z_\varepsilon^* = (1+\varepsilon)z^*$. Let S^* be the smallest convex and comprehensive set containing S and z_ε^* (see Figure 16.22).

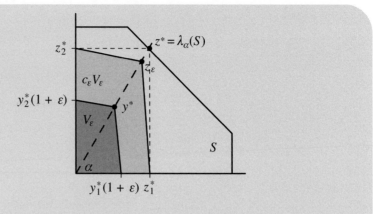

Figure 16.21 The set $c_\varepsilon V_\varepsilon$ and the point z_ε

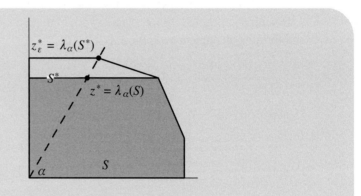

Figure 16.22 The set S (in gray) and the set S^*

From what we showed in Step 2, $\varphi(S^*) \geq \lambda_\alpha(S^*)$. As the only weakly efficient point in S^* that is greater than or equal to $\lambda_\alpha(S^*)$ is $\lambda_\alpha(S^*)$ itself, we deduce that

$$\varphi(S^*) = \lambda_\alpha(S^*) = z_\varepsilon^* = z^*(1 + \varepsilon). \tag{16.51}$$

Since $S \subset S^*$, and since φ satisfies full monotonicity,

$$\varphi(S) \leq \varphi(S^*) = z^*(1 + \varepsilon), \tag{16.52}$$

and this inequality holds for all $\varepsilon > 0$. Letting ε converge to 0 yields

$$\varphi(S) \leq z^* = \lambda_\alpha(S). \tag{16.53}$$

Together with the result of Step 2, we conclude that $\varphi(S) = \lambda_\alpha(S)$, which is what we wanted to show. $\qquad\Box$

The next theorem, which is proved in Kalai and Smorodinsky [1974], characterizes the solution concept obtained from the limited monotonicity property.

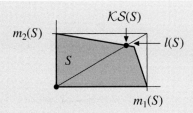

Figure 16.23 The Kalai–Smorodinsky solution

Theorem 16.32 *There exists a unique solution concept $\mathcal{KS}$ over the family $\mathcal{F}_0$ satisfying symmetry, efficiency, independence of the units of measurement, and limited monotonicity. That solution is the highest point located in S and on the line $l(S)$ connecting the disagreement point $(0,0)$ with the utopia point $(m_1(S), m_2(S))$ (see Figure 16.23).*

The alternative $\mathcal{KS}(S)$ is called the *Kalai–Smorodinsky solution* or the *Kalai–Smorodinsky agreement point.*

Proof: The $\mathcal{KS}$ solution is well defined: Denote by $l(S)$ the line that passes through the disagreement point $(0,0)$ and the utopia point $(m_1(S), m_2(S))$. Since there exists $x \in S$ satisfying $x \gg (0,0)$, necessarily $m_1(S) > 0$ and $m_2(S) > 0$. It follows that $l(S)$ is a strictly increasing line. Since $(0,0)$ is on the line $l(S)$, there exists at least one point in S on this line. Since S is compact, the highest point in S that is on $l(S)$ is well defined, and located in S. Denote this point by $\mathcal{KS}(S)$. In particular, $\mathcal{KS}$ is a solution concept over the family $\mathcal{F}_0$.

$\mathcal{KS}$ satisfies symmetry: If S is a symmetric bargaining game, then $m_1(S) = m_2(S)$. In particular, the line $l(S)$ is the diagonal $x_1 = x_2$, and therefore the point $\mathcal{KS}(S)$, located on this line, satisfies $\mathcal{KS}_1(S) = \mathcal{KS}_2(S)$. We deduce from this that the solution $\mathcal{KS}$ satisfies symmetry.

$\mathcal{KS}$ satisfies efficiency: Let $S \in \mathcal{F}_0$. Denoting $x^* = \mathcal{KS}(S)$, we will show that x^* is an efficient point; i.e., there does not exist y in S satisfying $y \geq x^*$ and $y \neq x^*$.

If x^* is inefficient, there is $y \in S$ satisfying one of the following three properties:

1. $y \gg x^*$,
2. $y_1 > x_1^*$ and $y_2 = x_2^*$, or
3. $y_1 = x_1^*$ and $y_2 > x_2^*$.

Case 1: There exists $y \in S$ satisfying $y \gg x^*$ (see Figure 16.24(a)).

Since S is comprehensive, the rectangle defined by $(0,0)$ and y is contained in S, and therefore x^* is in the interior of S. In particular, x^* is not the highest point in S on the line $l(S)$, contradicting its definition. It follows that this case is impossible.

Case 2: $y_1 > x_1^*$ and $y_2 = x_2^*$.
Since $m_i(S) \geq x_i^*$ for $i = 1, 2$, we can distinguish between two alternatives: $m_2(S) > x_2^*$ (see Figure 16.24(b)) and $m_2(S) = x_2^*$ (see Figure 16.24(c)).

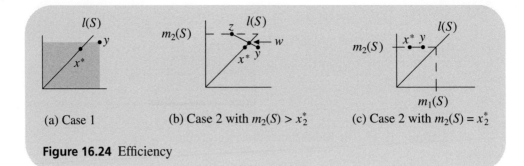

Figure 16.24 Efficiency

If $m_2(S) > x_2^*$, then there exists $z \in S$ satisfying $z_2 = m_2(S) > x_2^*$. Since S is convex, the interval connecting y with z is contained in S. But this interval contains a point w satisfying $w \gg x^*$, which is impossible, as shown in Case 1.

As we saw in Case 1, if $m_2(S) = x_2^*$, then since $y_1 > x_1^*$, necessarily $m_1(S) > x_1^*$. It follows that the line $l(S)$ is located under x^*, and does not pass through it, contradicting the definition of $\mathcal{KS}(S)$, so that this case, too, is impossible.

Case 3: $y_1 = x_1^*$ and $y_2 > x_2^*$.
This case is similar to Case 2, switching the roles of the players, and is therefore impossible.

$\mathcal{KS}$ satisfies independence of units of measurement: Let S be a bargaining game in $\mathcal{F}_0$. Denote $x^* := \mathcal{KS}(S)$. Let $a \in \mathbb{R}^2$ such that $a \gg (0,0)$. We will show that $\mathcal{KS}(aS) = ax^*$. Since $a_1 > 0$ and $a_2 > 0$, it follows by definition that $m_i(aS) = a_i m_i(S)$ for $i = 1, 2$. Therefore, under the positive affine transformation $x \mapsto ax$ the line $l(S)$ is mapped to the line $l(aS)$. In particular, ax^* is located on the line $l(aS)$. Since $a \gg (0,0)$, we deduce that $az \gg ax^*$ for every $z \in S$ if and only if $z \gg x^*$. Since x^* is the highest point in S on the line $l(S)$, we obtain that ax^* is the highest point in aS on the line $l(aS)$, which is what we wanted to show.

$\mathcal{KS}$ satisfies limited monotonicity: Let S and T be two bargaining games in $\mathcal{F}_0$ satisfying $m_1(S) = m_1(T)$, $m_2(S) = m_2(T)$, and $S \subseteq T$.
Since $m_1(S) = m_1(T)$ and $m_2(S) = m_2(T)$, one has $l(S) = l(T)$, and since $S \subseteq T$, the highest point in T on this line is not below the highest point in S on the line.

$\mathcal{KS}$ is the only solution satisfying these properties: Let φ be a solution concept satisfying symmetry, efficiency, independence of units of measurement, and limited monotonicity. We will prove that $\varphi = \mathcal{KS}$.
Let S be a bargaining game in $\mathcal{F}_0$, and denote $x^* := \mathcal{KS}(S)$. Let T be the following set (see Figure 16.25):

$$T := \text{conv}\{(0,0), (0, m_2(S)), x^*, (m_1(S), 0)\}. \tag{16.54}$$

The set T is contained in S. To see this, note that the point $(0,0)$ is a disagreement point and is therefore in S. Since S is comprehensive, the points $(0, m_2(S))$ and $(m_1(S), 0)$ are also in S, and by the definition of the Kalai–Smorodinsky solution the point x^* is in S. Finally, the set S is convex and therefore T is contained in S. Furthermore, $\mathcal{KS}(T) = \mathcal{KS}(S) = x^*$ (why?).

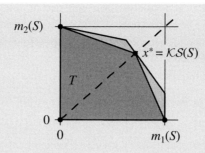

Figure 16.25 The sets T (in dark gray) and S (in light and dark gray)

Since φ and $\mathcal{KS}$ satisfy independence of units of measurement, symmetry, and efficiency, $\varphi(T) = \mathcal{KS}(T)$ (Exercise 16.10). Since φ and $\mathcal{KS}$ satisfy limited monotonicity,

$$\varphi(S) \geq \varphi(T) = \mathcal{KS}(T) = \mathcal{KS}(S) = x^*. \tag{16.55}$$

Since $\mathcal{KS}$ is efficient, the only alternative in S that is greater than or equal to x^* is x^* itself. Therefore, $\varphi(S) = x^* = \mathcal{KS}(S)$, which is what we wanted to show.   □

16.9 Bargaining games with more than two players

In the previous sections we concentrated on bargaining games with two players. But there are cases in which more than two players conduct negotiations. Examples include the distribution of government ministries among governing coalitions in parliamentary democracies, and the financing of joint projects.

Definition 16.33 *A bargaining game is a triple (N, S, d), where:*

- *N is a finite set of players.*
- *$S \subseteq \mathbb{R}^N$ is a nonempty, compact, and convex set of alternatives.*
- *$d \in \mathbb{R}^N$ is a disagreement point.*
- *There exists $x \in S$ satisfying $x \gg d$.*

Denote by $\mathcal{F}^N$ the family of bargaining games (N, S, d) with the set of players N, and by $\mathcal{F}^* = \cup_{\{N \subset \mathbb{N}\}} \mathcal{F}^N$ the family of all bargaining games with a finite number of players. As in the case of two players, a *solution concept for bargaining games over the set of players N* is a function associating each bargaining game $(N, S, d) \in \mathcal{F}^N$ with an alternative $\varphi(N, S, d) \in S$, and a *solution concept* (for the collection of all bargaining games with an arbitrary number of players) is a function associating every bargaining game $(N, S, d) \in \mathcal{F}^*$ with an alternative $\varphi(N, S, d) \in S$.

This model has the following interpretation: an alternative in S is the outcome of a bargaining process if and only if all the players agree to cooperate. In other words, in this model no proper subset of N can obtain an outcome in S except for d. A model that takes into account the possibility that various proper subcoalitions of N can on their own obtain an outcome that is preferred by their members will be presented in Chapter 17.

We now specify the properties we will use in studying bargaining games with more than two players. The definitions of efficiency, covariance under positive affine transformations, and independence of irrelevant alternatives are analogous to the definitions in Section 16.3 (page 677).

We next define the concept of symmetry for this case.

Definition 16.34 *A bargaining game* $(N, S, d) \in \mathcal{F}^*$ *is called a* symmetric game *if:*

- $d_i = d_j$ *for every pair of players* $i, j \in N$: *the disagreement point is symmetric.*
- $(x_{\pi(i)})_{i \in N} \in S$ *for every alternative* $x \in S$ *and every permutation* π *of* N.

A solution concept φ satisfies symmetry if $\varphi_i(N, S, d) = \varphi_j(N, S, d)$ for every symmetric bargaining game $(N, S, d) \in \mathcal{F}^*$, and every pair of players $i, j \in N$.

Theorem 16.15 (page 681) can be generalized to the case in which there are more than two players:

Theorem 16.35 *There exists a unique solution concept* $\mathcal{N}^*$ *for the family of bargaining games* $\mathcal{F}^*$ *satisfying the properties of symmetry, efficiency, covariance under positive affine transformations, and independence of irrelevant alternatives. For every bargaining game* $(N, S, d) \in \mathcal{F}^*$, *the point* $\mathcal{N}^*(N, S, d)$ *is the vector* x *in* S *satisfying* $x \gg d$ *that maximizes the product* $\prod_{i \in N}(x_i - d_i)$.

The proof is analogous to the proof in the case $|N| = 2$ (Exercise 16.28).

Another property of a solution concept, which appears in various contexts, is the property of consistency.

Definition 16.36 *A solution concept* φ *satisfies* consistency *if for every bargaining game* $(N, S, d) \in \mathcal{F}^*$, *and every nonempty set of players* $I \subset N$, $(\varphi_i(I, S, d))_{i \in I}$ *is the solution of the bargaining game* $(I, \widehat{S}, \widehat{d})$ *in which:*

- $\widehat{d}_i = d_i$ *for every* $i \in I$: *The disagreement point is derived from the disagreement point of the original game.*
- $\widehat{S} = \{(x_i)_{i \in I} \in \mathbb{R}^I : ((x_i)_{i \in I}, (\varphi_j(N, S, d))_{j \notin I}) \in S\}$. *The set of alternatives is the set of all alternatives in* S *at which all the players who are not in* I *get the outcome offered to them under the solution concept* φ.

A solution concept satisfies consistency if after the bargaining game has ended, every set of players who decide to go to arbitration and renegotiate only the shares of the members of that set discover that the arbitrator (who acts according to the solution concept φ) will not change the outcome they previously attained. The consistency property is the only property we have presented that involves games with different numbers of players.

A permutation π of the set of players N defines a mapping $\pi : \mathbb{R}^N \to \mathbb{R}^N$ by

$$\pi(x) := (x_{\pi(i)})_{i \in N}. \tag{16.56}$$

For a set $S \subseteq \mathbb{R}^N$ define

$$\pi(S) := \{\pi(x) : x \in S\}. \tag{16.57}$$

The bargaining game $(N, \pi(S), \pi(d))$ is the game (N, S, d), in which the names of the players have been changed according to the permutation π.

A solution concept satisfies anonymity if when the names of the players are changed, the proposed solution concept changes accordingly. Such a solution concept cannot discriminate between the players solely because of their names.

Definition 16.37 *A solution concept φ satisfies* anonymity *if for every bargaining game $(N, S, d) \in \mathcal{F}^*$, and every permutation π of the set of players N,*

$$\varphi_{\pi(i)}(\pi(S), \pi(d)) = \varphi_i(S, d), \quad \forall i \in N.$$

This property is also called independence of the names of the players *in the literature.*

Denote by $\mathcal{F}_0^*$ the family of bargaining games (N, S, d) satisfying:

1. The set of players N is a finite set.
2. The disagreement point is $d = \vec{0} := (0, 0, \ldots, 0)$.
3. The set S is a nonempty, compact, and convex set in $\mathbb{R}^N$.
4. $x \geq \vec{0}$ for every $x \in S$, and there exists $x \in S$ such that $x \gg \vec{0}$.
5. *Comprehensiveness:* If $x \in S$, then the n-dimensional rectangle defined by d and x is also contained in S:

$$\underset{i \in N}{\times} [d_i, x_i] \subseteq S, \quad \forall x \in S. \tag{16.58}$$

Note that every solution concept that satisfies anonymity also satisfies symmetry. The following theorem is proved in Lensberg [1988].

Theorem 16.38 *The only solution concept for the family of bargaining games $\mathcal{F}_0^*$ that satisfies efficiency, anonymity, covariance under positive affine transformations, and consistency is the Nash solution $\mathcal{N}^*$.*

This characterization does not use the independence of irrelevant alternatives property. Thus, when restricted to the family of bargaining games $\mathcal{F}_0^*$, adding the consistency property, which is meaningless when $|N| = 2$, makes independence of irrelevant alternatives superfluous. Since the Nash solution $\mathcal{N}^*$ satisfies the independence of irrelevant alternatives property, one deduces that this property follows from the other properties characterizing the Nash solution $\mathcal{N}^*$.

16.10 Remarks

A discussion of the influence risk aversion has on the outcomes of bargaining games (see Exercise 16.20) can be found in Kihlstrom et al. [1981]. The difficulty pointed out in Exercise 16.21 was first noted in Perles and Maschler [1981], which suggests an alternative solution concept that overcomes this difficulty.

16.11) Exercises

16.1 Prove that the solution concept defined in Example 16.23 (page 690) satisfies the properties of symmetry, covariance under positive affine transformations, and independence of irrelevant alternatives, but does not satisfy efficiency.

16.2 Prove that the solution concept defined in Example 16.24 (page 691) satisfies the properties of efficiency, covariance under positive affine transformations, and independence of irrelevant alternatives, but does not satisfy symmetry.

16.3 Prove that the following solution concept φ satisfies the properties of efficiency, symmetry, and independence of irrelevant alternatives, but does not satisfy the property of covariance under affine transformations: $\varphi(S, d)$ is the efficient point in S that is closest to $\lambda_{45^\circ}(S, d)$ (see Example 16.25 on page 691).

16.4 Prove that the solution concept defined in Example 16.26 (page 691) satisfies the properties of efficiency, symmetry, and covariance under positive affine transformations, but does not satisfy the property of independence of irrelevant alternatives.

16.5 Let (S, c) be a bargaining game, and let (T, d) be the image of (S, c) under the positive affine transformation $x \mapsto ax + b$ on $\mathbb{R}^2$; that is, $T = aS + b$ and $d = ac + b$. Prove that the set $\mathrm{argmax}_{y \in T}(y_1 - d_1)(y_2 - d_2)$ is the image of the set $\mathrm{argmax}_{x \in S}(x_1 - c_1)(x_2 - c_2)$ under this transformation.

16.6 Let $S \subset \mathbb{R}^2$, let $x \in S$ be an alternative on the boundary of S, and let l be a supporting line[6] of S at x. Let $x \mapsto ax + b$ be a positive affine transformation on $\mathbb{R}^2$. Prove that the line $al + b$ is a supporting line of the set $aS + b$ at the point $ax + b$.

16.7 Let $S \subset \mathbb{R}^2$ be a convex set, and let $a, b \in \mathbb{R}^2$. Prove that the set $aS + b$ is convex.

16.8 Let φ be a solution concept (for $\mathcal{F}$) satisfying symmetry and efficiency. Prove that for every symmetric bargaining game (S, d), the outcome $\varphi(S, d)$ is the highest point on the line $x_1 = x_2$ that is also in S (in other words, the point in S and on the line $x_1 = x_2$ for which x_1 is maximal).

16.9 Let φ be a solution concept (for $\mathcal{F}$) satisfying symmetry, efficiency, and independence of the units of measurement. Let $a, b > 0$ be positive numbers, and let S be the triangle whose vertices are $(0, 0)$, $(a, 0)$, and $(0, b)$. Prove that $\varphi(S, (0, 0)) = \left(\frac{a}{2}, \frac{b}{2}\right)$.

16.10 Let φ be a solution concept (for $\mathcal{F}$) satisfying symmetry, efficiency, and independence of the units of measurement. Let $a, b > 0$ be positive numbers, and let $x = (x_1, x_2)$ be a point on the ray emanating from $(0, 0)$ and passing through (a, b), satisfying $x_1 > \frac{a}{2}$. Let S be the quadrangle whose vertices are $(0, 0)$, $(a, 0)$, $(0, b)$, and x. Prove that $\varphi(S, (0, 0)) = x$.

---

6 Here we are identifying the line l with the set of points contained in it: the line l defined by the equation $\alpha x_1 + \beta x_2 = \gamma$ is identified with the collection of points $\{x \in \mathbb{R}^2 : \alpha x_1 + \beta x_2 = \gamma\}$.

16.11 Prove that under a positive affine transformation of the plane, an equilateral triangle whose base is the x_1-axis is transformed into an equilateral triangle whose base is parallel to the x_1-axis.

16.12 A *set solution concept* for a family of bargaining games $\widetilde{\mathcal{F}}$ is a function φ associating every bargaining game (S,d) in $\widetilde{\mathcal{F}}$ with a subset of S (which may contain more than a single point). Let $f : \mathbb{R}^4 \to \mathbb{R}$ be a function. Define a set solution concept φ as follows:

$$\varphi(S,d) = \mathrm{argmax}_{x \in S} f(d,x). \tag{16.59}$$

(a) Give an example of a function f for which $\varphi(S,d)$ is not always a single point.
(b) Prove that φ satisfies independence of irrelevant alternatives. In other words, if $T \supseteq S$ and $x \in \varphi(T,d) \cap S$, then $x \in \varphi(S,d)$.

16.13 Let φ_1 and φ_2 be two solution concepts for the family of bargaining games $\mathcal{F}$. Define another solution concept φ for the family of bargaining games $\mathcal{F}$ as follows:

$$\varphi(S,d) = \tfrac{1}{2}\varphi_1(S,d) + \tfrac{1}{2}\varphi_2(S,d). \tag{16.60}$$

For each of the following properties, prove or disprove the following claim: if φ_1 and φ_2 satisfy the property, then the solution concept φ also satisfies the same property.

(a) Symmetry.
(b) Efficiency.
(c) Independence of irrelevant alternatives.
(d) Covariance under positive affine transformations.

16.14 Two players are to divide $2,000 between them. The utility functions of the players are the amounts of money they receive: $u_1(x) = u_2(x) = x$. If they cannot come to agreement, neither of them receives anything. For the following cases, describe the bargaining game derived from the given situation, in utility units, and find its Nash solution of the game.

(a) Given any division which the players agree upon, the first player receives his full share under the agreed division, and the second player pays a tax of 40%.
(b) Repeat the situation in the previous item, but assume that the second player pays a tax of 60%.
(c) The first player pays a tax of 20%, and the second pays a tax of 30%.

16.15 Two players are to divide $2,000 between them. The utility function of the first player is $u_1(x) = x$. The utility function of the second player is $u_2(x) = \sqrt{x}$. For each of the following two situations, describe the bargaining game derived from the situation, in utility units, and find its Nash solution.

(a) If the two players cannot come to an agreement, neither of them receives any payoff.

(b) If the two players cannot come to an agreement, the first one receives $16, and the second receives $49 (note that in this case the disagreement point in the utility space is $(16, 7)$).

16.16 Find the Nash solution for the bargaining game in which

$$S = \left\{ x \in \mathbb{R}^2 : \frac{x_1^2}{16^2} + \frac{x_2^2}{20^2} \leq 1 \right\}, \tag{16.61}$$

and

(a) The disagreement point is $(0, 0)$.
(b) The disagreement point is $(10, 0)$.

16.17 Prove Theorem 16.22 on page 689: for every bargaining game (S, d), the only alternative that constitutes a solution concept according to Definition 16.21 (page 689) is the Nash solution $\mathcal{N}(S, d)$. Moreover, the constant c equals minus the slope of the supporting line of S at the point $\mathcal{N}(S, d)$.

16.18 Let $(S, d) \in \mathcal{F}$ be a bargaining game.

(a) Prove that there exists a unique efficient alternative in S minimizing the absolute value $|(x_1 - d_1) - (x_2 - d_2)|$. Denote this alternative by x^*.

Let Y be the collection of efficient alternatives y in S satisfying the property that the sum of their coordinates $y_1 + y_2$ is maximal.

(b) Show that the Nash solution $\mathcal{N}(S, d)$ is on the efficient boundary between x^* and the point in Y that is closest to x. In particular, if $x^* \in Y$ then $x^* = \mathcal{N}(S, d)$.

16.19 Let $(S, d) \in \mathcal{F}$ be a bargaining game. Denote by $x_2 = g(x_1)$ the equation defining the north-east boundary of S. Prove that if g is strictly concave and twice differentiable, then the point $x^* = \mathcal{N}(S, d)$ is the only efficient point x in S satisfying $-g'(x_1)(x_1 - d_1) = (x_2 - d_2)$.

16.20 Suppose two players have utility functions for money given by

$$u_1(x) = x^{\alpha_1}, \quad u_2(x) = x^{\alpha_2}, \tag{16.62}$$

where $0 < \alpha_1 < \alpha_2 < 1$. The Arrow–Pratt risk aversion index of player i is $r_{u_i}(x) := -\frac{u_i''(x)}{u_i'(x)}$ (see Exercise 2.28 on page 37 for an explanation of this index).

(a) Are the players risk seeking or risk averse? In other words, are their utility functions convex or concave?
(b) Player i is more risk averse than player j if $r_{u_i}(x) \geq r_{u_j}(x)$ for every x. Which of the two players is more risk averse?
(c) The players are to divide between them a potential profit of A dollars, but this profit can only be realized if the players can come to agreement on how to divide it. What is the Nash solution of this bargaining game, when the outcomes are in units of utility? Which of the players receives the greater payoff?

(d) What is the effect of risk aversion on the Nash outcome of a bargaining game in this example?

16.21 Two bargaining games, $(S, (0,0))$ and $(T, (0,0))$, are given by

$$S = \{x \in \mathbb{R}_+^2 : 2x_1 + x_2 \le 100\}, \qquad (16.63)$$

$$T = \{x \in \mathbb{R}_+^2 : x_1 + 2x_2 \le 100\}. \qquad (16.64)$$

David and Jonathan face the following situation. With probability $\frac{1}{2}$, they will negotiate tomorrow over the bargaining game $(S, (0,0))$, and with probability $\frac{1}{2}$, they will negotiate over the bargaining game $(T, (0,0))$.

David and Jonathan believe in the Nash solution, but they do not know which bargaining game they will play. Jonathan proposes that they apply the Nash solution in each of the two bargaining games (when it is reached), and therefore their expected utility is

$$\tfrac{1}{2}\mathcal{N}(S, (0,0)) + \tfrac{1}{2}\mathcal{N}(T, (0,0)). \qquad (16.65)$$

David counterproposes as follows: since the probability that they will negotiate over each of the bargaining games is $\frac{1}{2}$, the players are actually facing the bargaining game $(\frac{1}{2}S + \frac{1}{2}T, (0,0))$, where the set $\frac{1}{2}S + \frac{1}{2}T$ is defined by

$$\tfrac{1}{2}S + \tfrac{1}{2}T = \left\{ \tfrac{1}{2}x + \tfrac{1}{2}y : x \in S, y \in T \right\}. \qquad (16.66)$$

They should therefore implement the Nash solution over the game $(\frac{1}{2}S + \frac{1}{2}T, (0,0))$, which then should be

$$N\left(\tfrac{1}{2}S + \tfrac{1}{2}T, (0,0)\right). \qquad (16.67)$$

To compute the set $\frac{1}{2}S + \frac{1}{2}T$, draw the set $\frac{1}{2}S$, and "slide" the set $\frac{1}{2}T$ along its efficient points (see Figure 16.26(c)).

Compute $\frac{1}{2}\mathcal{N}(S, (0,0)) + \frac{1}{2}\mathcal{N}(T, (0,0))$, and $\mathcal{N}\left(\frac{1}{2}S + \frac{1}{2}T, (0,0)\right)$. Did you get the same result in both cases?

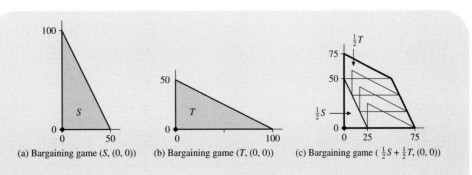

(a) Bargaining game $(S, (0, 0))$ (b) Bargaining game $(T, (0, 0))$ (c) Bargaining game $(\frac{1}{2}S + \frac{1}{2}T, (0, 0))$

Figure 16.26 The bargaining games $(S, (0,0))$, $(T, (0,0))$, and $(\frac{1}{2}S + \frac{1}{2}T, (0,0))$

16.22 Repeat Exercise 16.21 for the following bargaining games $(S, (0,0))$ and $(T, (0,0))$:

$$S = \{x \in \mathbb{R}^2_+ : x_1 + x_2 \leq 4\}, \tag{16.68}$$

$$T = \{x \in \mathbb{R}^2_+ : x_1 + x_2 \leq 5, \tfrac{3}{4}x_1 + x_2 \leq 4\}. \tag{16.69}$$

16.23 Prove that for every $0° < \alpha < 90°$, the solution λ_α defined on page 691 satisfies weak efficiency, homogeneity, strict individual rationality, and full monotonicity. In addition, if $\alpha = 45°$, the solution λ_α satisfies symmetry.

16.24 Prove the minimality of the set of properties characterizing the solution concept λ_α, as listed in Theorem 16.31 (page 695). In other words, prove (by examples) that for every three properties out of the four properties mentioned in the statement of Theorem 16.31 there exists a solution concept satisfying all three properties, but not the fourth.

16.25 Solve Exercises 16.14 and 16.15, assuming the players accept the Kalai–Smorodinsky solution, not the Nash solution. To convert the bargaining game (S, d) in $\mathcal{F}$ to a bargaining game in $\mathcal{F}_0$ (over which the Kalai–Smorodinsky solution is defined), apply the positive affine transformation $x \mapsto x - d$ and remove all the points y that do not satisfy $y \geq (0,0)$.

16.26 Solve Exercises 16.21 and 16.22, assuming the players accept the Kalai–Smorodinsky solution, rather than the Nash solution. To convert the bargaining game (S, d) in $\mathcal{F}$ to a bargaining game in $\mathcal{F}_0$ (over which the Kalai–Smorodinsky solution is defined), apply the positive affine transformation $x \mapsto x - d$ and remove all the points y that do not satisfy $y \geq (0,0)$.

16.27 Prove the minimality of the set of properties defining the Kalai–Smorodinsky solution. In other words, prove (by examples) that for any set of three of the four properties characterizing the solution concept, there exists a solution concept over $\mathcal{F}_0$ that satisfies those three properties, but not the fourth property.

16.28 Prove Theorem 16.35 (page 702), which characterizes the Nash solution for bargaining games with any number of players.
Hint: Look at the function $\ln(\prod_{i=1}^n (x_i - d_i))$.

17 Coalitional games with transferable utility

Chapter summary

Coalitional games model situations in which players may cooperate to achieve their goals. It is assumed that every set of players can form a coalition and engage in a binding agreement that yields them a certain amount of profit. The maximal amount that a coalition can generate through cooperation is called the *worth* of the coalition.

In this and subsequent chapters we ask which coalitions of players will form, and, if the players are partitioned into a certain collection of coalitions, how each coalition will divide its worth. Specifically, in this chapter we present the model of coalitional games, and introduce various classes of coalitional games: revenue games, cost games, simple games, weighted majority games, market games, sequencing games, spanning tree games, and cost-sharing games. We define the notion of strategic equivalence between games.

We then turn to define the notion of a solution concept. A *single-valued solution concept* is a function that assigns to each coalitional game a vector in $\mathbb{R}^N$ indicating the amount each player receives. A *set solution concept* is a function that assigns to each coalitional game a set of vectors in $\mathbb{R}^N$. Single-valued solution concepts model a judge or an arbitrator who has to recommend to the players how to divide the worth of the coalition among its members. A set solution concept may indicate which divisions are more likely than others.

Finally, using barycentric coordinates, we introduce a graphic representation of three-player coalitional games.

The games we studied in the previous chapters, with the exception of Chapter 16, were characterized by the assumption that each player acted independently of the actions of the other players. Even if there is nothing preventing correlation of actions between the players and no limit on the information being exchanged among them, and even when there is an observer who can give the players recommendations on which actions to choose (as in the chapter on correlated equilibria, Chapter 8), correlations and recommendations are not binding on the players: a player always has the option of choosing any action from the set of actions available to him. For that reason, such games are called *noncooperative games*. In this chapter and the following chapters we will study *cooperative games*. Cooperative games model situations in which the players may conclude binding agreements that impose a particular action or series of actions on each player. The bargaining games that we studied in Chapter 16 are examples of cooperative games, since the players can agree and commit themselves to choosing a particular outcome from the set of possible alternatives S: they can sign an agreement binding them to implement the actions required to obtain this outcome. The subject of this chapter and the next four chapters is cooperative games with a finite number of players. The concept of Nash equilibrium as it is applied to strategic-form and extensive-form games is insufficient for analyzing such games because every agreement, being a binding agreement, constitutes an equilibrium

Cooperative game theory therefore concentrates on questions such as which sets of players (coalitions) will agree to conclude binding agreements? Which agreements can reasonably be expected to be arrived at by players (and which are not reasonable)? Which agreements can reasonably be proposed to the players by an arbitrator or a judge? For this reason, cooperative games are also called *coalitional games*, to underscore the fact that the situations modeled by cooperative games involve issues related to the formation of coalitions by the players.

As in noncooperative game theory, in cooperative game theory a player may be a person, corporation, nation, and so on. The only requirement is that players be capable of arriving at decisions, and committing to those decisions. In addition, when a coalition is formed, the coalition must be able to undertake commitments binding on all its members. We will see that cooperative games can be used to study situations in which the "players" are more abstract objects, such as roads, flights, political parties, and so on.

In this chapter, and Chapters 18, 19, 20, and 21, we will concentrate on *finite games with transferable utilities*. Such games involve a finite number of players, and every coalition is associated with a sum that it can guarantee for itself.

Definition 17.1 *A coalitional game with transferable utility (TU game) is a pair* $(N; v)$ *such that:*[1]

- $N = \{1, 2, \ldots, n\}$ *is a finite set of players. A subset of N is called a* coalition. *The collection of all the coalitions is denoted by* 2^N.
- $v : 2^N \to \mathbb{R}$ *is a function associating every coalition S with a real number $v(S)$, satisfying $v(\emptyset) = 0$. This function is called the* coalitional function *of the game.*[2]

The real number $v(S)$ is called the *worth of the coalition S*. The significance of this is that if the members of S agree to form the coalition S, then as a result they can produce (or expect to receive) the sum of $v(S)$ units of money, independently of the actions of the players who are not members of S.

The fact that $v(S)$ is a real number is an expression of two assumptions of the model:

- The utilities of all the players can be measured in a common unit, such as monetary units.
- Utility (money) can be tranferred between the players.

Under these assumptions, we can summarize the worth of each coalition using a single number $v(S)$, which is the amount of utility (= money) that a coalition S can produce

---

1 Such games are also called *coalitional games with side payments* in the literature.
2 The function v is also called the *characteristic function* of the game.

by cooperation among its members. Situations in which a coalition creates utilities that cannot be transferred between the members of the coalition, such as reputation, prestige, political influence, and so on, are not dealt with by this model, and are instead described by coalitional functions without transferable utility. An example of such a model is the bargaining game discussed in Chapter 16.

In contrast to the commonplace meaning of the term "coalition," for mathematical convenience a set containing only one player, and similarly the empty set $\emptyset$, will each be called a coalition. As we saw in the definition of coalitional games, it is standard to set the worth of the empty coalition at 0.

Under the interpretation used here, a coalitional game is sometimes called a *profit game*. We may also be interested in what is termed a *cost game*, in which the worth of a coalition S is the sum that the members of the coalition must pay. An example of a cost game is given by a set of townships that wish to pave a network of roads, where the worth of a coalition is the cost of paving a network of roads connecting only the townships in that coalition. The coalitional function in a cost game is denoted by c: it is the function associating each coalition S with the costs $c(S)$ that the members of S will bear if they agree to form a coalition. It is again mathematically convenient to define $c(\emptyset) = 0$.

The term "forming a coalition" is given to varying interpretations, depending on the situation one wishes to model. The property common to all coalition formations is the fact that the members of a coalition agree to join the coalition, and commit to their roles within it. A coalition cannot form without the agreement of all its members.

We remark that when we say that coalitions S and T are formed, we mean that they are disjoint: $S \cap T = \emptyset$. If one or more players participate in two coalitions S and T, it is meaningless to say that S and T are formed.

A coalitional game model $(N; v)$ (or $(N; c)$) always includes a basic assumption: the money gained (or paid) by a coalition S, if it is formed, does not depend on the behavior of players who are not in S, nor on other coalitions that may form. This assumption greatly restricts the applicability of the model. For example, in an economic analysis of oligopoly, in which a set of manufacturers forms a coalition, the coalitional game model cannot take into account the effects of coalitions of players formed outside of the oligopoly on the oligopoly's profits. There exists a more general model called a *game in partition function form*, which is not considered in this book, that takes into account the possibility that the profit of every coalition S may depend on the partition into coalitions of the players who are not members of S.

17.1　Examples

In this section, we present several situations that can be analyzed as coalitional games.

17.1.1　Profit games

Profit games are games in which players profit according to the coalitions they form. For example, imagine a situation with three entrepreneurs: Orville, Ron, and Wilbur. Orville has ideas for various new inventions and patents, and he estimates his profits from these inventions to be $170,000 per year. Ron has a sharp business sense, and is interested in forming a business consultancy, which he estimates can yield profits of $150,000 per year. Wilbur, an excellent salesman, is interested in forming a sales company, which he estimates can yield profits of $180,000 per year. The three entrepreneurs recognize that their talents are complementary, and that if they work together, they can profit more than if they each work separately. Ron can advise Orville regarding which patents command the greatest market demand, so they estimate that together they can gain profits of $350,000 per year. Wilbur can sell Orville's inventions, so they estimate that together they can gain profits of $380,000 per year. Ron and Wilbur together can form a business consulting and sales corporation, which they estimate can gain profits of $360,000 per year. If all three of them work together, Ron can tell Orville which inventions will enjoy the greatest market demand, and then Wilbur can sell those inventions; the estimated profits of all three working together is $560,000 per year.

The entrepreneurs understand that it is to their advantage to work together, but it is not so immediately clear how they ought to divide among them the profits of a joint company, should they form one, because the contribution of each entrepreneur is different from that of the others, and the profit each one can earn working alone also differs from one entrepreneur to the next.

The coalitional game that corresponds to this situation (with payoffs in dollars) is as follows:[3]

$$v(\emptyset) = 0,$$
$$v(\text{Wilbur}) = 180,000,$$
$$v(\text{Orville}) = 170,000,$$
$$v(\text{Ron}) = 150,000,$$
$$v(\text{Orville, Wilbur}) = 380,000,$$
$$v(\text{Ron, Wilbur}) = 360,000,$$
$$v(\text{Orville, Ron}) = 350,000,$$
$$v(\text{Orville, Wilbur, Ron}) = 560,000.$$

17.1.2 Cost games

Cost games are similar to profit games, but the worth of a coalition in a cost game represents the price the coalition members must pay if the coalition were to form. We present an example of a cost game.

Sweden, Norway, and Finland are interested in constructing a dam for generating 3 gigawatts of electricity; each country will receive one-third of the electricity generated by the dam. The cost of constructing the dam is $180 million. The question the leaders of the three nations need to decide is how to divide that cost between them. Since each country will receive one-third of the generated electricity, it is reasonable to require that each one also contribute one-third of the construction costs. But suppose that it is discovered that there is a river inside Sweden appropriate for a smaller dam, that can generate 2 gigwatts

---

[3] For simplicity, we will write $v(\text{Orville, Wilbur})$ instead of $v(\{\text{Orville, Wilbur}\})$.

of electricity, at a construction cost of $100 million. Sweden then claims that if the three countries agree to share the cost of the larger dam equally, with each paying $60 million, then Sweden would be better off building a smaller dam with either Norway or Finland, with each paying $50 million. But Finland and Norway can also build a smaller dam generating 2 gigawatts together, at a cost of $130 million. Any country that fails to join the two other countries in a joint dam-constructing project will have no choice but to build a 1 gigawatt electricity-generating plant alone. The cost of constructing such a plant is $80 million for Sweden, $90 million for Norway, and $70 million for Finland.

Given this, how should the three countries divide the cost of constructing a large dam between them?

The coalitional game corresponding to this situation is the following. Let $c(S)$ represent the cost in millions of dollars for coalition S to provide a gigawatt of electricity to each member country (costs are listed in millions of dollars).

$$c(\emptyset) = 0,$$
$$c(\text{Finland}) = 70,$$
$$c(\text{Sweden}) = 80,$$
$$c(\text{Norway}) = 90,$$
$$c(\text{Sweden, Finland}) = 100,$$
$$c(\text{Sweden, Norway}) = 100,$$
$$c(\text{Norway, Finland}) = 130,$$
$$c(\text{Sweden, Norway, Finland}) = 180.$$

17.1.3 Simple games

A coalitional game is simple if the worth of any coalition is either 0 or 1.

Definition 17.2 *A coalitional game* $(N; v)$ *is called* simple *if for each coalition S, either* $v(S) = 0$, *or* $v(S) = 1$.

In a simple game, a coalition S is called *winning* if $v(S) = 1$, and is called *losing* if $v(S) = 0$. It is sometimes convenient to represent simple games by indicating the family of winning coalitions $\mathcal{W} = \{S \subseteq N : v(S) = 1\}$.

Simple games can model committee votes, including cases in which the voting rule is not necessarily majority rule. We interpret $v(S) = 1$ as meaning that the coalition S can pass a motion, and $v(S) = 0$ as meaning that the coalition S cannot pass a motion on its own. For example, the United Nations Security Council has 5 permanent members, and 10 nonpermanent members. Every permanent member can cast a veto on any Security Council resolution, and adopting a resolution requires the support of a majority of 9 council members. Ignoring the possibility of abstention in votes, this means that for a resolution to be adopted by the council it needs the support of all 5 permanent members, and at least 4 nonpermanent members. The coalitional function v corresponding to this game is

$$v(S) = \begin{cases} 1 & \text{if } |S| \geq 9 \text{ and } S \text{ contains all the permanent members,} \\ 0 & \text{for any other coalition } S. \end{cases} \quad (17.1)$$

Another example is the legislative process in the United States. Passing a bill into law in the United States requires the signature of the President of the United States, and a simple majority in both the Senate (composed of 100 Senators) and the House of Representatives (composed of 435 members), or alternatively the two-thirds majority in both the Senate and the House of Representatives required to override a presidential veto. In Exercise 17.2, the reader is asked to write down the coalitional game corresponding to this situation. In this example, $v(S)$ is not measured in units of money, but rather in terms of "governance," or "victory," or "the power to make decisions," and $v(S)$ takes the values of either 0 or 1.

17.1.4 Weighted majority games

Weighted majority games are a special case of simple games. In the British Parliament's House of Commons, for example, which is comprised of 650 members, a coalition requires a majority of 326 members to form a government. Suppose there are three parties represented, the first with 282 seats, the second with 260 seats, and the third with 108 seats.

Denote by 1 the "worth" of being the governing coalition and by 0 the "worth" of being in the opposition. The coalitional game corresponding to this situation is a three-player game. Since no single party has 326 seats or more, no party alone can form a governing coalition. Therefore,

$$v(1) = v(2) = v(3) = 0.$$

Since every pair of parties together has more than 326 seats, each pair of parties may form a governing coalition, and all three parties together may form a governing coalition. Therefore,

$$v(1,2) = v(1,3) = v(2,3) = v(1,2,3) = 1.$$

Note that although each party has a different number of parliament members, when this situation is presented as a coalitional game, the parties have entirely symmetric roles. We now define the family of weighted majority games.

Definition 17.3 *A coalitional game* $(N; v)$ *is a* weighted majority game *if there exists a quota* $q \geq 0$ *and nonnegative real weights* $(w_i)_{i \in N}$, *one for each player, such that the worth of each nonempty coalition S is*

$$v(S) = \begin{cases} 1 & \text{if } \sum_{i \in S} w_i \geq q, \\ 0 & \text{if } \sum_{i \in S} w_i < q. \end{cases} \quad (17.2)$$

A weighted majority game is denoted by $[q; w_1, w_2, \ldots, w_n]$. The example above with the three parties in the British House of Commons is the weighted majority game $[326; 282, 260, 108]$. Every weighted majority game is a simple game, but not every simple game can be represented as a weighted majority game (Exercise 17.10).

17.1.5 Market games

Market games are games arising from economic situations. Consider five traders, three of whom arrive to market with 100 liters of gin apiece, and two others with 100 liters of tonic apiece. Assuming that customers are interested solely in cocktails of equal parts gin and tonic, the traders recognize that they must cooperate with each other. The price for a cocktail composed of equal parts gin and tonic is $100 per liter.

Denoting the set of traders with gin by G, and the set of traders with tonic by T, the coalitional game corresponding to this situation is given by the following coalitional function:[4,5]

$$v(S) = 20,000 \times \min\{|S \cap G|, |S \cap T|\}. \tag{17.3}$$

The formal definition and analysis of market games appear in Section 18.4 (page 750).

17.1.6 Sequencing games

Sequencing games are games in which players are to be ordered in a particular sequence; every player prefers being placed earlier in the queue to being placed later in it.

Consider three customers, Eileen, Barbara, and Gail, who seek to hire an architect. The following table presents the placements in the queue of each customer in the architect's schedule book, the amount of time the architect needs to devote to each customer, and the financial loss of each customer from every day lost until the completion of the architectural job she wishes to accomplish.

Number in the queue	Name	Time to completion of job	Loss per day (in dollars)
1	Eileen	3	2,000
2	Barbara	4	1,500
3	Gail	2	3,000

The current sequencing of the architect's work leads to a loss of $3 \times \$2,000 = \$6,000$ for Eileen, a loss of $7 \times \$1,500 = \$10,500$ for Barbara, and a loss of $9 \times \$3,000 = \$27,000$ for Gail. But if Barbara and Gail were to exchange places in the queue, Gail's loss would fall to $5 \times \$3,000 = \$15,000$, while Barbara's loss would rise to $9 \times \$1,500 = \$13,500$. The sum of their losses together, however, falls by $9,000 (from $37,500 to $28,500); hence if Gail were to compensate Barbara for this by paying her, say, $5,000, both of them would profit from the new scheduling. Eileen and Gail cannot switch places unilaterally: such a switch would affect Barbara, and could not be accomplished without her consent.

We can similarly compute the optimal scheduling of jobs that can be arrived at by changing the ordering of Eileen, Barbara, and Gail's jobs, as well as the gain achievable by each coalition of two or three players. The coalitional function corresponding to the sequencing game is:

---

4 For every coalition S, $|S|$ denotes the number of members of coalition S.
5 The constant 20,000 is the worth of a cocktail composed of 100 liters of gin and 100 liters of tonic.

$$v(\text{Eileen}) = 0,$$
$$v(\text{Barbara}) = 0,$$
$$v(\text{Gail}) = 0,$$
$$v(\text{Eileen, Barbara}) = 0,$$
$$v(\text{Eileen, Gail}) = 0,$$
$$v(\text{Barbara, Gail}) = 9{,}000,$$
$$v(\text{Eileen, Gail, Barbara}) = 14{,}000.$$

In general, a sequencing game is given by an ordering of the sets of players, the amount of time that needs to be devoted to each player, and the cost per day borne by each player until the completion of the job he needs accomplished. We call a reordering of the players *feasible* for coalition S if under both orderings (the new ordering and the original ordering) the amount of time needed for completing the job of every player who is not a member of S is unchanged. For example, the ordering [1: Gail, 2: Barbara, 3: Eileen] is feasible for the coalition {Eileen, Barbara, Gail}, but is not feasible for the coalition {Eileen, Gail}. Every sequencing game corresponds to a coalitional game in which the worth of coalition S is the amount of money that the members of the coalition can save by forming the optimal feasible ordering (for S).

17.1.7 Spanning tree games

We will give a formal presentation of spanning tree games in Section 18.8. In this section, we present one example of such games.

Suppose that local authorities have decided to connect three villages, Amherst, Belchertown, and Conway, to a single sewage system. The chief engineer of the project knows that directly connecting each village to the central drainage point into the sewage line is not necessarily the most cost-effective method: for example, it may be more cost-effective to connect only Conway to the central drainage point, and connect the other two villages to Conway. The table in Figure 17.1 depicts the cost of laying a sewage pipe between every pair of villages, and the cost in millions of dollars of connecting each village to the drainage point.

These costs are graphically depicted in Figure 17.2.

After crunching the numbers, the chief engineer concludes that the most cost-effective solution is to connect Amherst and Belchertown directly to the main sewage line,

	Amherst	Belchertown	Conway
Central drainage point	2	1	4
Amherst	0	4	3
Belchertown	4	0	2
Conway	3	2	0

Figure 17.1 Costs of laying sewage pipes

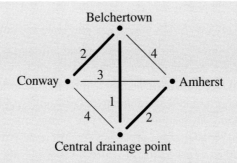

Figure 17.2 A graphical presentation of the costs of laying sewage pipes

and to connect Conway to Belchertown (see Figure 17.2, and check that this is the least expensive connection option). The total cost of this project is $5,000,000. The next question is how to divide this cost between the three villages. If the residents of Belchertown are asked to bear a third of the cost, $1,666,666, they may well claim that the cost of connecting them directly to the central drainage point is only $1,000,000. Why should they then subsidize the other villages?

The coalitional game corresponding to this situation, in which the worth of each coalition is the minimal cost of connecting the members of that coalition, directly or indirectly via other villages, to the central drainage point, is:

$$c(\text{Amherst}) = 2,$$
$$c(\text{Belchertown}) = 1,$$
$$c(\text{Conway}) = 4,$$
$$c(\text{Amherst, Belchertown}) = 3,$$
$$c(\text{Amherst, Conway}) = 5,$$
$$c(\text{Belchertown, Conway}) = 3,$$
$$c(\text{Amherst, Belchertown, Conway}) = 5.$$

In general, spanning tree games are games based on a connected graph, one of whose vertices is called the *source*, each player is associated with a node, and every edge of the graph is associated with a nonnegative cost. The cost $c(S)$ of a coalition S is the minimal cost of a collection of edges connecting all the members of S to the source. Since the collection of edges that attains the minimal cost is a tree (containing no circular paths), these games are called *spanning tree games*.

17.1.8 Cost-sharing games

Cost-sharing games model situations in which the cost of a service is to be divided among different users, where different users need different amounts of that service.

An example of such a situation, as presented in Littlechild [1974], is the construction of landing and takeoff runways in airports. Suppose an airport authority intends to construct a new landing runway in an international airport, and needs to decide:

1. The length of a new runway.
2. The price to charge every airplane using the new runway.

The longer the runway, the greater the construction cost, the more land that needs to be appropriated, and the greater the maintenance costs. On the other hand, if the runway is insufficiently long, large airplanes will be unable to land or take off. Charging every airplane an equal amount per landing and takeoff seems unfair: why should airplanes capable of landing on a shorter runway pay as much as airplanes needing a long runway? Why should the smaller airplanes subsidize the needs of the large airplanes? This situation can be depicted as a cost game, in which a set of players is a set of flights, and the worth of a coalition is the cost of a landing and takeoff runway that is sufficiently long to satisfy the needs of all the flights in the coalition.

This is an example in which the "players" are not decision makers in the usual sense, but rather takeoffs and landings. The real decision makers, of course, are airline executives, but it is more convenient to model takeoffs and landings as players in the game, because the relevant information for the problem we are solving is related to the price of takeoffs and landings. This game is discussed in greater detail in Exercise 19.18 (page 825).

17.2 Strategic equivalence

The descriptions presented in the examples above do not uniquely define the coalitional functions of their corresponding games. For example, the worth of a coalition in the cost game presented in Section 17.1.1 can be calculated in British pounds instead of American dollars, using an exchange rate. A different perspective on the situation takes into account all the incomes of all the entrepreneurs. For example, if Wilbur has an income of $10,000 from renting a house he owns, while Orville and Ron have incomes of $5,000 and $4,000 from other endeavors, the coalitional function can be rewritten to take into account the total income of each member of every coalition. The different games obtained this way can all be considered to be equivalent from the perspectives of the players, because the income every entrepreneur draws from his other endeavors should not affect his income from joining a coalition with other players. We now present a formal definition of this sort of equivalence.

Let $(N; v)$ be a coalitional game, and let $a > 0$. The game $(N; w)$ defined by

$$w(S) = av(S), \quad \forall S \subseteq N \tag{17.4}$$

is the game derived from $(N; v)$ by changing the units of measurement of the worth of each coalition, by the exchange rate a. Suppose that in addition to changing the units of measurement, we give the sum b_i to every player i, independently of the coalition he joins (b_i can also be a negative value). If every coalition takes into account the extra sums thus received by every one of its members, we get the game $(N; u)$, whose coalitional function is given by

$$u(S) = av(S) + \sum_{i \in S} b_i, \quad \forall S \subseteq N. \tag{17.5}$$

We next introduce some convenient notation. For every coalition S, let $\mathbb{R}^S$ be an $|S|$-dimensional Euclidean space, where every axis is associated with one of the players in coalition S. In other words, if $x \in \mathbb{R}^S$ we denote the coordinates of x by $(x_i)_{i \in S}$.

For every vector $x \in \mathbb{R}^N$, define

$$x(S) := \sum_{i \in S} x_i, \quad \emptyset \neq S \subseteq N, \tag{17.6}$$

$$x(\emptyset) := 0. \tag{17.7}$$

In general, x_i denotes the amount of money that player i receives (or pays in a cost game). It follows that the quantity $x(S)$ is the sum of the payments received by members of coalition S.

Definition 17.4 *A coalitional game* $(N; w)$ *is strategically equivalent to the game* $(N; v)$ *if there exists a positive number* a, *and a vector* $b \in \mathbb{R}^N$, *such that for every coalition* $S \subseteq N$:

$$w(S) = av(S) + \sum_{i \in S} b_i = av(S) + b(S). \tag{17.8}$$

In other words, $(N; w)$ is derived from $(N; v)$ by changing the units of measurement, and adding a constant sum that every player receives or pays at the start of the game.

Theorem 17.5 *The strategic equivalence relation is an equivalence relation; i.e., it is reflexive, symmetric, and transitive.*[6]

Proof: To show that $(N; v)$ is equivalent to itself, in order to prove reflexivity, set $a = 1$ and $b = (0, 0, \ldots, 0)$.

We next show that the strategic equivalence relation is symmetric; i.e., if $(N; w)$ is strategically equivalent to $(N; v)$, then $(N; v)$ is strategically equivalent to $(N; w)$. To see this, if $w(S) = av(S) + b(S)$ for every $S \subseteq N$, where $a > 0$, then

$$v(S) = \frac{1}{a} w(S) + \sum_{i \in S} \frac{-b_i}{a}. \tag{17.9}$$

In other words, $v(S) = \tilde{a}w(S) + \tilde{b}(S)$, where $\tilde{a} = \frac{1}{a} > 0$ and $\tilde{b}_i = -\frac{b_i}{a}$ for every $i \in N$.

We complete the proof by showing that the strategic equivalence relation is transitive. Suppose that $(N; v)$ is strategically equivalent to $(N; w)$, and $(N; w)$ is strategically equivalent to $(N; u)$, i.e., there exist $a, a' > 0$ and $b, b' \in \mathbb{R}^N$ such that

$$v(S) = aw(S) + b(S), \quad w(S) = a'u(S) + b'(S), \quad \forall S \subseteq N. \tag{17.10}$$

Then

$$v(S) = aw(S) + b(S), \quad w(S) = a'u(S) + b'(S), \tag{17.11}$$

....

6 A binary relation P over a set X is *reflexive* if aPa for all $a \in X$. It is *symmetric* if aPb implies bPa. It is *transitive* if aPb and bPc imply aPc.

where $a, a' > 0$. Then

$$v(S) = aw(S) + b(S) = aa'u(S) + (ab' + b)(S). \tag{17.12}$$

In other words, $v(S) = \tilde{a}u(S) + \tilde{b}(S)$, where $\tilde{a} = aa' > 0$ and $\tilde{b}_i = ab'_i + b_i$ for every $i \in N$. This means that $(N; v)$ is strategically equivalent to $(N; u)$.   □

Definition 17.6 *The game* $(N; v)$ *is* 0−1 *normalized if* $v(i) = 0$ *for every player* $i \in N$ *and* $v(N) = 1$. *The game is* 0−0 *normalized if* $v(i) = 0$ *for every player* $i \in N$ *and* $v(N) = 0$. *The game is* 0−(−1) *normalized if* $v(i) = 0$ *for every player* $i \in N$ *and* $v(N) = -1$.

The next theorem states that every coalitional game is strategically equivalent to a 0−1, or 0−0, or 0−(−1) normalized game. The proof of the theorem is left to the reader (Exercise 17.18).

Theorem 17.7 *Let* $(N; v)$ *be a coalitional game.*

1. $(N; v)$ *is strategically equivalent to a* 0−1 *normalized game if and only if* $v(N) > \sum_{i \in N} v(i)$.
2. $(N; v)$ *is strategically equivalent to a* 0−0 *normalized game if and only if* $v(N) = \sum_{i \in N} v(i)$.
3. $(N; v)$ *is strategically equivalent to a* 0−(−1) *normalized game if and only if* $v(N) < \sum_{i \in N} v(i)$.

A coalitional game $(N; v)$ is called 0-*normalized* if $v(i) = 0$ for every $i \in N$. By Theorem 17.7, every game is strategically equivalent to a 0-normalized game.

17.3 A game as a vector in a Euclidean space

Denote the set of nonempty coalitions by $\mathcal{P}(N) := \{S \subseteq N, S \neq \emptyset\}$. The space of coalitional games with the set of players N, G_N, is equivalent[7] to the $(2^n - 1)$-dimensional Euclidean space $\mathbb{R}^{\mathcal{P}(N)}$: a coalitional game $(N; v)$ is associated with a point $z = (z_S)_{S \in \mathcal{P}(N)} \in \mathbb{R}^{\mathcal{P}(N)}$ if and only if $v(S) = z_S$ for each coalition $S \in \mathcal{P}(N)$. The space $\mathbb{R}^{\mathcal{P}(N)}$ is a vector space: a game can be multiplied by a constant, and two games can be added together. The equivalence between $\mathbb{R}^{\mathcal{P}(N)}$ and G_N induces a vector space structure on G_N. For every coalitional function v and every real number α, define the coalitional function αv as follows:

$$(\alpha v)(S) := \alpha v(S), \quad \forall S \subseteq N. \tag{17.13}$$

For every pair of coalitional functions v and w, define the coalitional function $v + w$ as follows:

$$(v + w)(S) := v(S) + w(S), \quad \forall S \subseteq N. \tag{17.14}$$

---

7 Note that when a point in $\mathbb{R}^{\mathcal{P}(N)}$ is written as a vector with $2^n - 1$ elements, it is necessary to state which coalition is associated with each coordinate.

When α is positive, multiplying by α can be interpreted as changing the units of measurement by α. The game $(N; v + w)$ can be interpreted as a situation in which the players are playing two games $(N; v)$ and $(N; w)$, and the worth of each coalition is the sum of the worth of the coalition in both games. This definition applies to situations in which (a) both the games $(N; v)$ and $(N; w)$ are related to each other, in the sense that every coalition formed in one is also formed in the other, and (b) the worth of a coalition formed in one game does not affect its worth in the other game, and therefore $(v + w)(S) := v(S) + w(S)$ for every coalition S.

17.4 Special families of games

Up until now we have not imposed any conditions on the coalitional function v. But these functions sometimes satisfy properties that have implications for the solutions of the game. We now present several such properties.

Definition 17.8 *A coalitional game $(N; v)$ is* superadditive *if for any pair of disjoint coalitions S and T,*

$$v(S) + v(T) \leq v(S \cup T). \tag{17.15}$$

A superadditive game is one in which two disjoint coalitions that choose to merge can obtain at least what they could obtain if they instead were to work separately. This property makes the formation of large coalitions an advantage in superadditive games; there is "positive pressure" to form the grand coalition N. Although this is not an unequivocal determination, as we will see in Example 17.12, superadditivity serves as a justification for the assumption that the grand coalition N will be formed, and many solution concepts therefore focus mainly on this case.

The corresponding definition for cost games is as follows.

Definition 17.9 *A cost game $(N; c)$ is* superadditive *if for every pair of disjoint coalitions S and T,*

$$c(S \cup T) \leq c(S) + c(T). \tag{17.16}$$

The assumption of superadditivity appears natural at first, but there are examples in which it does not obtain: in some cases, merging coalitions can be detrimental to the aims they seek to achieve, for political, legal, personal, or other reasons. For example, the merger of several large companies is liable to lead to a cartel, which is illegal, or to bureaucratic bloating that can reduce efficiency.

Definition 17.10 *A coalitional game $(N; v)$ is* monotonic *if for any pair of coalitions S and T, such that $S \subseteq T$,*

$$v(S) \leq v(T). \tag{17.17}$$

In monotonic games, as a coalition grows larger its worth is not reduced. Although there may superficially appear to be a resemblance between the definitions of superadditive games and monotonic games, the two concepts are significantly different.

A monotonic game is not necessarily superadditive, and a superadditive game is not necessarily monotonic (Exercise 17.22). In addition, while superadditivity is invariant under strategic equivalence (Exercise 17.23), monotonicity is not invariant under strategic invariance, since every game is strategically equivalent to a monotonic game (Exercise 17.25). The following example depicts two games that are strategically equivalent; one is monotonic, and the other is not monotonic.

Example 17.11 Consider two three-player games $(N; v)$ and $(N; w)$ with the following coalitional functions:

$$v(S) = |S|, \forall S \subseteq N, \tag{17.18}$$

$$w(S) = -|S|, \forall S \subseteq N. \tag{17.19}$$

The coalitional game $(N; v)$ is monotonic, and the coalitional game $(N; w)$ is not monotonic. Yet the two games are strategically equivalent. To see this, let $a = 1$ and let $b \in \mathbb{R}^3$ be defined by $b = (-2, -2, -2)$. Then

$$w(S) = -|S| = |S| - 2|S| = av(S) + b(S). \tag{17.20}$$

◄

17.5 Solution concepts

. . . .

The main questions that are the focus of coalitional game theory include:

1. What happens when the players play the game? What coalitions will form, and if a coalition S is formed, how does it divide the worth $v(S)$ among its members?
2. What would a judge or an arbitrator recommend that the players do?

The answers to these two questions are quite different. The question regarding the coalitional structure that the players can be expected to form is a difficult one, and will not be addressed in this book. We will often assume that the grand coalition N is formed and ask how the players will divide among them the worth $v(N)$. The answer to this question is generally a set solution, i.e., a solution that contains several possible payoff vectors, according to which the players may choose to divide $v(N)$ among them. On the other hand, a recommendation of a judge or an arbitrator is usually a point solution, i.e., a single payoff vector.

Example 17.12 **Majority game** Let $(N; v)$ be the three-player coalitional game in which $N = \{1, 2, 3\}$, and the coalitional function v is given by

$$v(1) = v(2) = v(3) = 0, \qquad v(1, 2) = v(1, 3) = v(2, 3) = v(1, 2, 3) = 1.$$

What can we expect to happen in this game? It is reasonable to suppose that a coalition of two players will form and that, given the symmetry between the players, the members of the coalition will divide the worth equally among themselves. This leads to one of the following payoff vectors in the set

$$\left\{ \left(\tfrac{1}{2}, \tfrac{1}{2}, 0 \right), \left(\tfrac{1}{2}, 0, \tfrac{1}{2} \right), \left(0, \tfrac{1}{2}, \tfrac{1}{2} \right) \right\}. \tag{17.21}$$

Without more information about the players, it is not possible to know which payoff vector will finally be chosen.

In contrast, if the players were to approach an arbitrator and ask him to determine how to divide the sum 1 that they can achieve, given the symmetry between the players it is reasonable to expect that the arbitrator will recommend a split of $(\frac{1}{3}, \frac{1}{3}, \frac{1}{3})$. We can therefore regard the three outcomes $\left\{(\frac{1}{2}, \frac{1}{2}, 0), (\frac{1}{2}, 0, \frac{1}{2}), (0, \frac{1}{2}, \frac{1}{2})\right\}$ as a set solution to the game, while $(\frac{1}{3}, \frac{1}{3}, \frac{1}{3})$ is a point solution. ◄

The simple majority game in Example 17.12 is superadditive (verify!), but there is a high likelihood in this game that the grand coalition N will not form.

Definition 17.13 *Let $\mathcal{U}$ be a family of coalitional games (over any set of players). A solution concept (over $\mathcal{U}$) is a function φ associating every game $(N; v) \in \mathcal{U}$ with a subset $\varphi(N; v)$ of $\mathbb{R}^N$. A solution concept is called a* point solution *if for every coalitional game $(N; v) \in \mathcal{U}$, the set $\varphi(N; v)$ contains only one element.*

Note that in Definition 17.13, it is possible for a particular game $(N; v)$ to satisfy $\varphi(N; v) = \emptyset$.

Sometimes the players form the grand coalition N, and sometimes several coalitions are formed instead. Both the set solutions and the point solutions that we will see in the examples below depend on the coalitional structures that are formed.

Definition 17.14 *A* coalitional structure *is a partition $\mathcal{B}$ of the set of players N.*

In other words, a coalitional structure is a collection of disjoint and nonempty sets whose union is N. Examples of coalitional structures for a set of players $N = \{1, 2, 3, 4\}$ include:

All the players play as isolated individuals: $\mathcal{B} = \{\{1\}, \{2\}, \{3\}, \{4\}\}$.
Two two-player coalitions form: $\mathcal{B} = \{\{1, 2\}, \{3, 4\}\}$.
Players 2 and 3 form a coalition: $\mathcal{B} = \{\{1\}, \{2, 3\}, \{4\}\}$.
All the players form the grand coalition: $\mathcal{B} = \{\{1, 2, 3, 4\}\}$.

A point solution offers a single solution to every game, given the coalitional structure: for every coalition S in a coalitional structure, it offers one and only one way to divide the worth $v(S)$ among the members of the coalition. A set solution offers a set of vector payoffs for every game and every coalitional structure. We use the notation $\varphi(N; v; \mathcal{B})$ to denote a (set or point) solution, when $\mathcal{B}$ is the coalitional structure that is formed. When the coalitional structure that is formed contains only the coalition N, i.e., $\mathcal{B} = \{N\}$, we will omit the explicit denotation of the coalitional structure and instead write $\varphi(N; v)$.

Definition 17.15 *Let $(N; v)$ be a game, and let $\mathcal{B}$ be a coalitional structure. A vector $x \in \mathbb{R}^N$ is called* efficient[8] *for the coalitional structure $\mathcal{B}$ if for every coalition $S \in \mathcal{B}$,*

$$x(S) = v(S). \tag{17.22}$$

---

8 The efficiency property is sometimes also called *social rationality*.

A vector x is called individually rational *if for every player i ∈ N,*

$$x_i \geq v(i). \tag{17.23}$$

When the players divide into coalitions, forming a coalitional structure $\mathcal{B}$, it is reasonable to suppose that each coalition $S \in \mathcal{B}$ will divide its worth $v(S)$ among its members: the members of the coalition cannot divide among themselves more than the sum $v(S)$ available to the coalition, and there is no point in dividing less than $v(S)$, because then part of the worth $v(S)$ available to the coalition is wasted. Therefore, if x_i is the sum that player i receives (or pays), it is reasonable that $\sum_{i \in S} x_i = v(S)$ holds for every coalition $S \in \mathcal{B}$. In that case, the vector $x = (x_i)_{i \in N}$ is efficient for a coalitional structure $\mathcal{B}$. Since every player can guarantee for himself $v(i)$ if he does not join any coalition, it is reasonable to suppose that every player will demand at least that sum. In other words, $x_i \geq v(i)$: this is the *individual rationality* property of the vector x.

This leads to the definition of the set of imputations as the set of all efficient and individually rational payoffs.

Definition 17.16 *Let $(N; v)$ be a coalitional game, and let $\mathcal{B}$ be a coalitional structure. An* imputation *for the coalitional structure $\mathcal{B}$ is a vector $x \in \mathbb{R}^N$ that is efficient for the coalitional structure $\mathcal{B}$, and individually rational. The set of all imputations for the coalitional structure $\mathcal{B}$ is denoted by $X(\mathcal{B}; v)$.*

When the coalitional structure is $\mathcal{B} = \{N\}$ we will say for short "imputation" instead of "imputation for the coalitional structure $\{N\}$," and write $X(N; v)$ instead of $X(\{N\}; v)$. Note that the set $X(\mathcal{B}; v)$ is compact in $\mathbb{R}^N$ (see Exercise 17.32).

When there are two players $N = \{1, 2\}$, the set of imputations is

$$X(N; v) = \{x \in \mathbb{R}^N : x_1 \geq v(1), x_2 \geq v(2), x_1 + x_2 = v(1,2)\}. \tag{17.24}$$

This set can be empty (if $v(1) + v(2) > v(1,2)$), an isolated point (if $v(1) + v(2) = v(1,2)$), or an interval (if $v(1) + v(2) < v(1,2)$). In the last case, the extreme points of the interval are $(v(1), v(1,2) - v(1))$ and $(v(1,2) - v(2), v(2))$.

Example 17.17 Let $N = \{1, 2, 3\}$, and let the coalitional function be

$$v(1) = v(2) = v(3) = 0, \quad v(1,2) = 2, \quad v(1,3) = 3, \quad v(2,3) = 4, \quad v(1,2,3) = 7.$$

The set of imputations is given by the triangle whose vertices are $(7, 0, 0)$, $(0, 7, 0)$, and $(0, 0, 7)$ (see Figure 17.3(a)). The sets of imputations for the coalitional structures containing two sets are intervals (see Figure 17.3(b)).

For the coalitional structure $\{\{1\}, \{2\}, \{3\}\}$, the only imputation is $(0, 0, 0)$. The collections of imputations for coalitional structures containing two sets are the interval (see Figure 17.3(b)):

$$X(\{\{1,2\}, \{3\}\}; v) = [(0,2,0), (2,0,0)], \tag{17.25}$$

$$X(\{\{1,3\}, \{2\}\}; v) = [(0,0,3), (3,0,0)], \tag{17.26}$$

$$X(\{\{2,3\}, \{1\}\}; v) = [(0,4,0), (0,0,4)]. \tag{17.27}$$

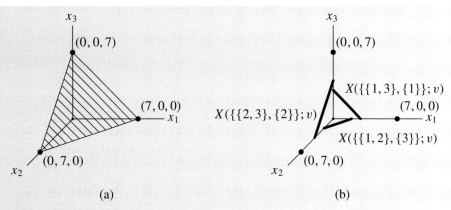

Figure 17.3 The set of imputations of all the coalitional structures in Example 17.17

The set of imputations may be empty: this happens if there is a coalition $S \in \mathcal{B}$ such that $\sum_{i \in S} v(i) > v(S)$.

Let N be a set of players, and $\mathcal{B}$ be a coalitional structure. One possible solution concept is

$$\varphi(N; v; \mathcal{B}) := X(\mathcal{B}; v). \tag{17.28}$$

This is the set of all possible individually rational and efficient outcomes. In other words, if $x \notin X(\mathcal{B}; v)$, it is not reasonable for the players to divide among themselves the sum they receive according to x. This is a weak solution: in many games the set $X(\mathcal{B}; v)$ is very large (as in Example 17.17). When the set $X(\mathcal{B}; v)$ is empty, it is unclear whether or not the coalitional structure $\mathcal{B}$ will be formed, and if it is formed, this solution concept provides no prediction regarding the outcome of the game.

17.6 Geometric representation of the set of imputations

As we saw in Example 17.17, although the set of imputations is a subset of $\mathbb{R}^N$, the efficiency constraint $(\sum_{i=1}^n x_i = x(N) = v(N))$ implies that this set is located in an $(n-1)$-dimensional subspace. Since a large part of our intuition comes from graphical representations of figures, and the smaller the dimension of the space in which they are displayed, the easier it is to present them, it is more convenient to present the set of imputations in $\mathbb{R}^{n-1}$. This advantage is especially pronounced in three-player games, because in that case the set of imputations is a triangle in $\mathbb{R}^3$, which can be more conveniently presented in $\mathbb{R}^2$ (see Figure 17.4).

The set of all imputations in which one coordinate is fixed is a straight line parallel to the corresponding side of the triangle. Figure 17.5 depicts (in both $\mathbb{R}^3$ and $\mathbb{R}^2$) the set of imputations x in Example 17.17 satisfying $x_2 \geq 3$. This is also the set of imputations x in Example 17.17 satisfying $x_1 + x_3 \leq 4$.

In a 0-normalized three-player game it is convenient to present the set of imputations as an equilateral triangle in $\mathbb{R}^2$ whose height is $v(N)$ (as opposed to its height in $\mathbb{R}^3$, which

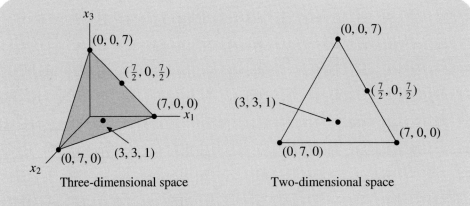

Three-dimensional space   Two-dimensional space

Figure 17.4 The set of imputations in Example 17.18

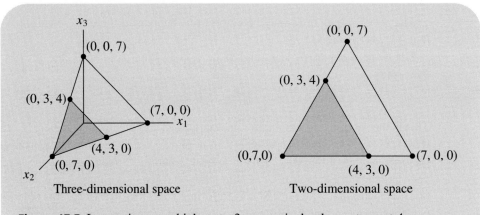

Three-dimensional space   Two-dimensional space

Figure 17.5 Imputations at which $x_2 \geq 3$, or, equivalently, $x_1 + x_3 \leq 4$

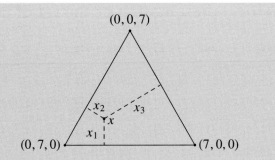

Figure 17.6 The barycentric coordinates of x: the distances of the point x from the three sides of the triangle

is $\frac{\sqrt{3}}{2} v(N)$; check that this is true). The sides of the triangle will be labeled by the names of the three players, 1, 2, and 3. A point in the triangle will be denoted by $x = (x_1, x_2, x_3)$, where x_i is the distance of the point from the side labeled i, for $i \in \{1, 2, 3\}$. Recall that in

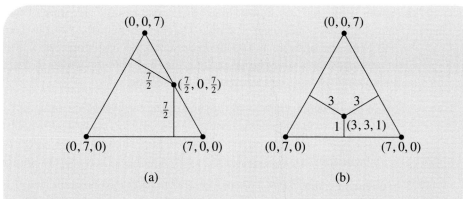

Figure 17.7 The sum of the distances of every point from the sides of a triangle equals the height of the triangle

an equilateral triangle, the sum of the distances of each point from the three sides of the triangle equals the height of the triangle (see Exercise 17.36). It follows that the vertices of the triangle are $(v(N), 0, 0)$, $(0, v(N), 0)$, and $(0, 0, v(N))$, and every point in the triangle satisfies $x_1 + x_2 + x_3 = v(N)$ (see Figures 17.6 and 17.7). Similarly, every point in the triangle corresponds to an efficient imputation because the game is 0-normalized and the distance of the point from each one of the sides of the triangle is nonnegative, hence $x_i \geq 0 = v(i)$. This coordinate system is called the *barycentric coordinate* system, and it can be generalized to any number of players. For further discussion of this topic, see Section 24.1 (page 962). Barycentric coordinates have the following physical interpretation. If we place weights x_1, x_2, and x_3 respectively at the three vertices $(v(N), 0, 0)$, $(0, v(N), 0)$, and $(0, 0, v(N))$ of the triangle, the center of mass of the system will be the point $x = (x_1, x_2, x_3)$. The word barycenter means "center of mass," which is where the term barycentric coordinates comes from.

17.7 Remarks

Simple games and weighted majority games were first introduced in von Neumann and Morgenstern [1944]. Market games were first introduced in Shapley and Shubik [1963]. Sequencing games were first introduced in Curiel et al. [1989]. Spanning tree games were first introduced in Claus and Kleitman [1973] and in Bird [1976]. Exercise 17.6 is taken from Tamir [1991]. We thank Yonatan Elhanani and Yotam Gafni for bringing the game in Exercise 17.11 to our attention.

17.8 Exercises

17.1 By finding the appropriate weights, show that the United Nations Security Council game described by Equation (17.1) (page 714) is a weighted majority game.

17.2 Passing a bill into law in the United States requires the signature of the President of the United States, and a simple majority in both the Senate (composed of 100 Senators) and the House of Representatives (composed of 435 members), or alternatively a two-thirds majority in both the Senate and the House of Representatives required to override a presidential veto.

(a) Write down the coalitional function of the corresponding game.

(b) Is this a weighted majority game? If you answer yes, write down the quota and weights of the game. If you answer no, prove that it is not a weighted majority game.

17.3 Sequencing game Don, a painter, is hired to paint the houses of Henry, Ethan, and Tom. The following table depicts the sequential ordering of each client in Don's schedule book, the amount of time required to paint his house, and the loss he suffers from every day that passes until work is completed.

Sequential ordering	Name	Time required	Daily loss in dollars
1	Henry	5	200
2	Ethan	3	550
3	Tom	4	400

Write down the coalitional function of the corresponding sequencing game in which the worth of a coalition is the sum of money that the members of the coalition can save by changing their ordering in a feasible way in Don's schedule book.

17.4 Write down the coalitional functions in each of the following weighted majority games:

(a) $[4; 3, 2, 1, 1]$.

(b) $[5; 3, 2, 1, 1]$.

(c) $[4; 3, 1, 1, 1]$.

(d) $[39; 7, 7, 7, 7, 7, 1, 1, 1, 1, 1, 1, 1, 1, 1, 1]$.

17.5 The board of directors of a certain company contains four members (including the chairman of the board). A motion is passed by the board only if the chairman approves it, and it is supported by a majority of the board (i.e., gets at least three votes). Write down the coalitional function of the corresponding game.

17.6 Spanning tree games The following figure depicts a network of roads connecting the capital city, Washington, with three nearby towns, Bethesda, Silver Spring, and McLean. The towns are responsible for maintaining the roads between themselves and the capital. The maintenance cost of every segment of road is listed as a unit.

In the figure, a large dot indicates a vertex at which a town is located, and a small dot indicates a vertex at which no town is located.

Define $c(S)$ as the minimal cost required for all the towns in coalition S to be connected with the capital. Write down the coalitional function.

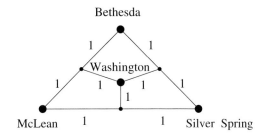

17.7 Repeat Exercise 17.6 for each of the following networks. The maintenance cost of each road segment is indicated next to it.

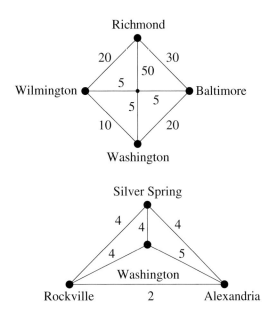

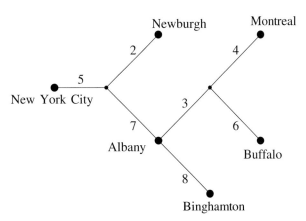

17.8 Prove that the following weighted majority games share the same coalitional function, and therefore they are different representations of the same game.

$$[2; 1, 1, 1], \quad [9; 8, 2, 7], \quad [9; 8, 1, 8].$$

17.9 The representation $[2; 1, 1, 1]$ of the game in Exercise 17.8 has the property that the sum of the weights equals the quota 2 in every *minimal winning* coalition, that is, a winning coalition such that every one of its proper subsets is not winning. These weights are called *homogeneous weights*, and the representation is called a *homogeneous representation*.

In general, weights $w_1, w_2, \ldots, w_n$ are called *homogeneous weights* if there exists a real number q such that in the weighted majority game $[q; w_1, w_2, \ldots, w_n]$ the equality $\sum_{i \in S} w_i = q$ holds for every minimal winning coalition S. This representation is called a *homogeneous representation*.

For each of the following weighted majority games determine whether it has a homogeneous representation. If yes, write it down. If no, explain why.

(a) $[10; 9, 1, 2, 3, 4]$.
(b) $[8; 5, 4, 2]$.
(c) $[9; 7, 5, 3, 1]$.
(d) $[10; 7, 5, 3, 1]$.

17.10 A projective game with seven players Consider a simple game with seven players, with winning coalitions:

$$\{1, 2, 4\}, \{2, 3, 5\}, \{1, 3, 6\}, \{3, 4, 7\}, \{1, 5, 7\}, \{2, 6, 7\}, \{4, 5, 6\},$$

and every coalition containing at least one of these winning coalitions. The game is presented graphically in the following figure. Each winning coalition must contain three players who are either all along one of the straight lines, or all on the circle.

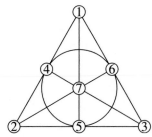

Prove that this game cannot be represented as a weighted majority game.

17.11 Let $(N; v)$ be the simple game where $N = \{1, 2, 3, 4\}$ and the winning coalitions are $\{1, 2\}, \{3, 4\}$, and every coalition that contains one of these two coalitions. Prove that $(N; v)$ is not a weighted majority game.

17.12 A player i in a simple game $(N; v)$ is called a *veto player* if $v(S) = 0$ for every coalition S that does not contain i. The player is called a *dictator* if $v(S) = 1$ if and only if $i \in S$.

(a) Prove that in a simple game satisfying the property that $v(S) + v(N \backslash S) = 1$ for every coalition $S \subseteq N$, there exists at most one veto player, and that player is a dictator.

(b) Find a simple three-player game satisfying $v(S) + v(N \backslash S) = 1$ for every coalition $S \subseteq N$ that has no veto player.

17.13 Market game A set of merchants $N_1 = \{1, 2\}$ sell their wares in the market. Each merchant has an "initial endowment" $(0, \frac{1}{2})$: the first number represents the amount of gin the merchant has and the second number the amount of tonic the merchant has. A second set of merchants $N_2 = \{3, 4, 5\}$ also sells in the same market, and each member of this set has an initial endowment of $(1, 0)$. The total bundle available to a coalition $S \subseteq N_1 \cup N_2$ is

$$\left(|S \cap N_2|, \tfrac{1}{2} |S \cap N_1| \right),$$

where $|R|$ denotes the number of members of coalition R.

Consumers will only buy cocktails containing equal parts gin and tonic. The net profit from selling α units of cocktail is α dollars. Describe this situation as a coalitional game, and write down in detail the coalitional function.

17.14 Repeat Exercise 17.13, but assume that the initial endowment of the merchants in N_1 is $(0, \frac{2}{3})$.

17.15 Are the following three-player games strategically equivalent? Justify your answer.

$$v(1) = 6, \quad v(2) = 5, \quad v(3) = 8, \quad v(1, 2) = 10, \quad v(1, 3) = 20,$$
$$v(2, 3) = 50, \quad v(1, 2, 3) = 80,$$
$$w(1) = 13, \quad w(2) = 10, \quad w(3) = 19, \quad w(1, 2) = 25, \quad w(1, 3) = 55,$$
$$w(2, 3) = 140, \quad w(1, 2, 3) = 235.$$

17.16 Let $(N; v)$ be the coalitional game with $N = \{1, 2, 3\}$ and the following coalitional function:

$$v(1) = 3, \quad v(2) = 6, \quad v(3) = 8, \quad v(1, 2) = 12, \quad v(1, 3) = 15,$$
$$v(2, 3) = 18, \quad v(1, 2, 3) = 80.$$

Write down a $0-1$ normalized coalitional game $(N; w)$ that is strategically equivalent to $(N; v)$.

17.17 What is the coalitional function of the game derived from

$$v(1) = 20, \quad v(2) = 30, \quad v(3) = 50, \quad v(1, 2) = 10, \quad v(1, 3) = 15,$$
$$v(2, 3) = 40, \quad v(1, 2, 3) = 5$$

if each player is given an initial sum of \$1,000?

17.18 Prove Theorem 17.7 (page 720): let $(N; v)$ be a coalitional game. Then

(a) $(N; v)$ is strategically equivalent to a $0-1$ normalized game if and only if $v(N) > \sum_{i \in N} v(i)$.

(b) $(N; v)$ is strategically equivalent to a $0-0$ normalized game if and only if $v(N) = \sum_{i \in N} v(i)$.

(c) $(N; v)$ is strategically equivalent to a $0-(-1)$ normalized game if and only if $v(N) < \sum_{i \in N} v(i)$.

17.19 Describe the family of all superadditive games in which the set of players is $N = \{1, 2\}$.

17.20 Let $(N; v)$ be a coalitional game with a set of players $N = \{1, 2, 3\}$ and coalitional function

$$v(S) = \begin{cases} 0 & \text{if } S = \emptyset, \\ 1 & \text{if } S = \{1\}, \{2\}, \\ 2 & \text{if } S = \{3\}, \\ 4 & \text{if } |S| = 2, \\ 5 & \text{if } |S| = 3. \end{cases}$$

(a) Is $(N; v)$ a superadditive game?

(b) What is the set of imputations of this game?

17.21 Prove that the convex combination of superadditive games is also superadditive. In other words, if $(N; v)$ and $(N; w)$ are superadditive games, and if $0 \leq \lambda \leq 1$, then the game $(N, \lambda v + (1 - \lambda)w)$ defined by

$$(\lambda v + (1 - \lambda)w)(S) := \lambda v(S) + (1 - \lambda)w(S) \qquad (17.29)$$

is also superadditive.

17.22 Give an example of a monotonic game that is not superadditive, and an example of a superadditive game that is not monotonic.

17.23 Prove that every game that is strategically equivalent to a superadditive game is itself superadditive.

17.24 Prove that a convex combination of monotonic games is also monotonic. In other words, if $(N; v)$ and $(N; w)$ are monotonic games, and if $0 \leq \lambda \leq 1$, then the game $(N, \lambda v + (1 - \lambda)w)$ defined by

$$(\lambda v + (1 - \lambda)w)(S) := \lambda v(S) + (1 - \lambda)w(S) \qquad (17.30)$$

is also monotonic.

17.25 (a) Is the three-player game $(N; v)$ in which v is given by

$$v(1) = 3, \quad v(2) = 13, \quad v(3) = 4, \quad v(1, 2) = 12, \quad v(1, 3) = 15,$$
$$v(2, 3) = 1, \quad v(1, 2, 3) = 10$$

monotonic? Justify your answer.

(b) Find a monotonic game that is strategically equivalent to $(N; v)$.

(c) Prove that every game is strategically equivalent to a monotonic game. It follows that the property of monotonicity is not invariant under strategic equivalence.

17.26 Let $(N; v)$ be a nonnegative coalitional game, i.e., $v(S) \geq 0$ for every coalition $S \subseteq N$.

(a) Prove that if $(N; v)$ is superadditive then $(N; v)$ is monotonic.
(b) Show by example that the converse does not hold: it is possible for $(N; v)$ to be monotonic but not superadditive.

17.27 The 0-*normalization* of a coalitional game $(N; v)$ is a coalitional game $(N; w)$ that is strategically equivalent to $(N; v)$ and satisfies $w(i) = 0$ for every player $i \in N$. A coalitional game is called 0-*monotonic* if its 0-normalization is a monotonic game.

(a) Which of the following monotonic games with set of players $N = \{1, 2, 3\}$ is 0-monotonic?

(i) $v(1) = 5$, $v(2) = 8$, $v(3) = 15$, $v(1, 2) = 10$, $v(1, 3) = 30$, $v(2, 3) = 50$, $v(1, 2, 3) = 80$.
(ii) $v(1) = 5$, $v(2) = -2$, $v(3) = 7$, $v(1, 2) = 9$, $v(1, 3) = 30$, $v(2, 3) = 17$, $v(1, 2, 3) = 30$.

(b) Give an example of a coalitional game that is not monotonic, but is 0-monotonic.

17.28 Prove that a coalitional game $(N; v)$ is 0-monotonic if and only if $v(S \cup \{i\}) \geq v(S) + v(i)$ for every coalition S and every player $i \notin S$.

17.29 Let $(N; v)$ be a coalitional game. The *superadditive cover* of $(N; v)$ is the coalitional game $(N; w)$ satisfying the properties:

- $(N; w)$ is a superadditive game.
- $w(S) \geq v(S)$ for every coalition S.
- Every game $(N; u)$ satisfying the previous two properties also satisfies $u(S) \geq w(S)$ for every coalition S.

Find the superadditive cover of the following game, whose set of players is $N = \{1, 2, 3\}$:

$$v(1) = 3, \quad v(2) = 5, \quad v(3) = 7, \quad v(1, 2) = 6, \quad v(1, 3) = 8,$$
$$v(2, 3) = 10, \quad v(1, 2, 3) = 13.$$

17.30 Let $(N; v)$ be a coalitional game. The *monotonic cover* of $(N; v)$ is the coalitional game $(N; w)$ satisfying the properties:

- $(N; w)$ is a monotonic game.
- $w(S) \geq v(S)$ for every coalition S.
- Every game $(N; u)$ satisfying the above two properties also satisfies $u(S) \geq w(S)$ for every coalition S.

Prove that the monotonic cover $(N; w)$ of the game $(N; v)$ satisfies

$$w(S) = \max_{T \subseteq S} v(T). \tag{17.31}$$

17.31 (a) How many different coalitional structures can there be in a three-player game? Write down all of them.

   (b) How many different coalitional structures can there be in a four-player game? Write down all of them.

17.32 Prove that for every coalitional game $(N; v)$ and every coalitional structure $\mathcal{B}$, the set of imputations $X(\mathcal{B}; v)$ is convex and compact.

17.33 Prove that for every coalitional game $(N; v)$ there exists a coalitional structure $\mathcal{B}$ for which the set of imputations $X(\mathcal{B}; v)$ is nonempty.

17.34 (a) Write down the set of imputations of the three-player game in which

$$v(1) = 3, \quad v(2) = 5, \quad v(3) = 7, \quad v(1,2) = 6, \quad v(1,3) = 12,$$
$$v(2,3) = 15, \quad v(1,2,3) = 10$$

for all coalitional structures.

   (b) Repeat part (a) when $v(1,2,3) = 13$.

   (c) Repeat part (a) when $v(1,2,3) = 34$.

17.35 Let $(N; v)$ and $(N; w)$ be two coalitional games with the same set of players. Let $x \in X(\mathcal{B}; v)$ and $y \in X(\mathcal{B}; w)$. Does $x + y \in X(\mathcal{B}; v + w)$ necessarily hold? Does $x - y \in X(\mathcal{B}; v - w)$ necessarily hold? If you answer yes to either question, provide a proof. If you answer no, present a counterexample.

17.36 Suppose that you are given an equilateral triangle, with x being a point in the triangle. Denote by x_1, x_2, x_3 the distance of the point x from each side of the triangle, respectively (see accompanying figure).

   (a) Prove that $x_1 + x_2 + x_3 = k$, where k is the height of the triangle.

   (b) Prove that this is true even if the point is located in the plane of the triangle, but not necessarily in the triangle, where the distance from the point to the side of the triangle is negative if the line on which the side lies separates the triangle from the point (in the accompanying diagram, y_1 and y_2 are positive and y_3 is negative).

   (c) Describe a similar property in one-dimensional line segments.

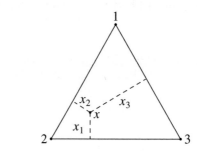

18 The core

Chapter summary

This chapter presents the *core*, which is the most important set solution concept for coalitional games. The core consists of all coalitionally rational imputations: for every imputation in the core and every coalition, the total amount that the members of the coalition receive according to that imputation is at least the worth of the coalition.

The core of a coalitional game may be empty. A condition that characterizes coalitional games with a nonempty core is provided in Section 18.3. A game satisfying this condition is called a *balanced* game and the Bondareva–Shapley Theorem states that the core of a coalitional game is nonempty if and only if the game is balanced. This characterization is used in Section 18.4 to prove that every market game has a nonempty core. A game is called *totally balanced* if the cores of all its subgames are nonempty. It is proved that a game is totally balanced if and only if it is a market game. Similarly, a game is totally balanced if and only if it is the minimum of finitely many additive games.

In Section 18.6 it is proved that the core is a consistent solution concept with respect to the Davis–Maschler definition of a reduced game; that is, for every imputation in the core and every coalition, the restriction of the imputation to that coalition is in the core of the Davis–Maschler reduced game to that coalition.

We introduce two families of coalitional games, *spanning tree games* and *flow games*, and by identifying imputations in the core we prove that games in both families possess a nonempty core.

Finally, in Section 18.10 the notion of the core is extended to any coalitional structure, and we establish a relation between the core of the coalitional game for a coalition structure and the core of the superadditive cover of the game.

Having previously defined what a solution concept in the context of coalitional games means, we proceed by introducing the core, which is a central solution concept for this class of games.

Suppose that the coalition formed by the players is the grand coalition N, and that the players now need to decide how to divide among themselves the worth of the coalition, $v(N)$. As explained on page 724, it is reasonable to assume that this will lead to an imputation in $X(N; v) = \{x \in \mathbb{R}^N : x(N) = v(N), x_i \geq v(i) \ \forall i \in N\}$. In most cases, there will be a continuum of alternative imputations, and it is natural to ask which imputations are more likely to be implemented. If x is an imputation according to which the players divide up $v(N)$, one reasonable assumption is that $x(S) \geq v(S)$ for every[1] coalition S; in words, the total sum received by the players in S should be at least $v(S)$. If this inequality does not hold, the members of S have an incentive to form their own separate coalition and attain $v(S)$, which they can then divide among themselves in such a way that every member i of S receives more than x_i, for example, by dividing the excess $v(S) - x(S)$ equally among the members of the coalition. The concept of the core is based on this idea: the core contains all the imputations x satisfying the property that for every coalition S, the members of S collectively receive at least $v(S)$.

18.1 Definition of the core

Definition 18.1 *Let* $(N; v)$ *be a coalitional game. An imputation* $x \in X(N; v)$ *is coalitionally rational if for every coalition* $S \subseteq N$

$$x(S) \geq v(S). \tag{18.1}$$

Definition 18.2 *The* core *of a coalitional game* $(N; v)$, *denoted by* $C(N; v)$, *is the collection of all coalitionally rational imputations,*

$$C(N; v) := \{x \in X(N; v): x(S) \geq v(S), \quad \forall S \subseteq N\}. \tag{18.2}$$

The case where the players do not form the grand coalition N but instead divide up into several coalitions is dealt with in Section 18.10 (page 780).

When working with cost games, we reverse the inequalities in the definition of the core:

$$C(N; c) := \{x \in X(N; c): x(S) \leq c(S), \quad \forall S \subseteq N\}, \tag{18.3}$$

where $X(N; c)$ is the set of imputations in the game $(N; c)$,

$$X(N; c) := \{x \in \mathbb{R}^N : x(N) = c(N), x_i \leq c(i), \quad \forall i \in N\}. \tag{18.4}$$

Some simple properties of the core are detailed in the next theorem.

Theorem 18.3 *The core of a coalitional game is the intersection of a finite number of half-spaces, and is therefore a convex set. In addition, the core is a compact set.*

A compact set that is the intersection of a finite number of half-spaces is called a *polytope*. It follows from Theorem 18.3 that the core of a coalitional game is a polytope.

Proof: For each coalition S the set $\{x \in \mathbb{R}^N : x(S) \geq v(S)\}$ is a closed half-space. The core is the intersection of $2^n - 1$ half-spaces $\{x \in \mathbb{R}^N : x(S) \geq v(S)\}$, for all $\emptyset \neq S \subseteq N$, and the half-spaces $\{x \in \mathbb{R}^N : x(N) \leq v(N)\}$.

Every half-space is convex, and the intersection of convex sets is convex. The core is therefore a convex set. Every half-space is closed, and the intersection of closed sets is closed. The core is therefore a closed set. Finally, since the core is a subset of $X(N; v)$, it is bounded. A closed and bounded set is compact. $\qquad\square$

---

1 Recall that for $x \in \mathbb{R}^N$ we defined $x(S) := \sum_{i \in S} x_i$ for every nonempty coalition S, and $x(\emptyset) := 0$.

Example 18.4 In this example we consider four coalitional games, each with the set of players $N = \{1, 2, 3\}$, that are distinguished from each other solely by the worth of coalition $\{1, 3\}$.

First game

$$v(1) = v(2) = v(3) = 0, \quad v(1, 2) = v(2, 3) = 1, \quad v(1, 3) = 2, \quad v(1, 2, 3) = 3.$$

The set of imputations is the triangle whose vertices are $(3, 0, 0)$, $(0, 3, 0)$, and $(0, 0, 3)$. An imputation $x = (x_1, x_2, x_3)$ is in the core of this game if and only if

$$x_1 + x_2 + x_3 = 3, \tag{18.5}$$
$$x_1 + x_2 \geq 1, \tag{18.6}$$
$$x_1 + x_3 \geq 2, \tag{18.7}$$
$$x_2 + x_3 \geq 1, \tag{18.8}$$
$$x_1, x_2, x_3 \geq 0. \tag{18.9}$$

The set of solutions to this system of equations, which forms a trapezoid, is depicted in Figure 18.1. The plane in which the figure lies is given by $x_1 + x_2 + x_3 = 3$ in $\mathbb{R}^3$, and the labels in the figure refer to coordinates in $\mathbb{R}^3$.

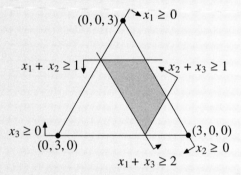

Figure 18.1 First game: the core of the game, and the inequalities defining it

The condition $x_1 + x_2 \geq 1$ is equivalent to the condition $x_3 \leq 2$, because $x_1 + x_2 + x_3 = 3$ and this corresponds to a line parallel to the side $(3, 0, 0)$–$(0, 3, 0)$ of the triangle in Figure 18.1. The rest of the inequalities can be treated similarly.

Second game

If the worth of the coalition $\{1, 3\}$ is changed to $v(1, 3) = 1$, the core becomes the hexagon appearing in Figure 18.2.

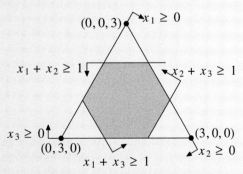

Figure 18.2 Second game: the core of the game, and the inequalities defining it

Third game

If the worth of the coalition $\{1,3\}$ is changed to $v(1,3) = 3$, the core becomes the one-dimensional line segment appearing in Figure 18.3.

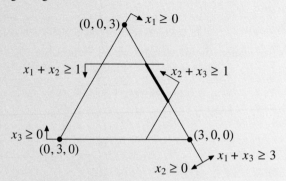

Figure 18.3 Third game: the core of the game, and the inequalities defining it

Fourth game

If the worth of the coalition $\{1,3\}$ is changed to $v(1,3) = 4$, the core is the empty set.

The above examples do not exhaust all the geometric possibilities of the core. In the following example we exhibit a coalitional game whose core includes a single point. The core of a three-player game may also be a triangle, a parallelogram, or a pentagon (Exercise 18.2).   ◀

Example 18.5 The gloves game Consider a three-player game in which the coalitional function is defined as follows:

$$v(1) = v(2) = v(3) = v(1,2) = 0, \quad v(1,3) = v(2,3) = v(1,2,3) = 1.$$

This game is called the "gloves game" because it corresponds to a situation in which Players 1 and 2 each have only a right-handed glove, Player 3 has only a left-handed glove, and the worth of a coalition equals the number of complementary pairs of gloves that it can form.

In this game, the set of imputations is given by the triangle whose vertices are $(1,0,0)$, $(0,1,0)$, and $(0,0,1)$, and the core contains a single imputation, $(0,0,1)$. To see this, if $x = (x_1, x_2, x_3)$ is in the core, then in particular $x_1 + x_2 + x_3 = 1$, $x_1 \geq 0$, $x_2 \geq 0$, and $x_3 \geq 0$. In addition, $x_2 + x_3 \geq v(2,3) = 1$, and using the efficiency condition $x_1 + x_2 + x_3 = 1$, one deduces that $x_1 \leq 0$. This implies that $x_1 = 0$. Similarly, $x_2 = 0$.

For an intuitive explanation of why the core contains only the imputation $(0,0,1)$, note that there is a surplus of right-handed gloves. This leads to a competition that greatly reduces their value: if, for example, Player 3 and Player 1 form a coalition in which Player 1 receives $\alpha > 0$ out of the quantity of 1 that the coalition can attain, Player 2 receives nothing. Player 2 will therefore be willing to form a coalition with Player 3 in return for a payoff that is less than α, say, $\frac{\alpha}{2}$. Knowing this, Player 1 will express readiness to form a coalition with Player 3 for an even smaller payoff, such as $\frac{\alpha}{4}$, and so on.   ◀

Example 18.6 The simple majority game Consider a simple majority game with three players, where the coalitional function is defined as follows (see Example 17.12 on page 722):

$$v(1) = v(2) = v(3) = 0, \quad v(1,2) = v(1,3) = v(2,3) = v(1,2,3) = 1.$$

In this game, again, the set of imputations is given by the triangle whose vertices are $(1,0,0)$, $(0,1,0)$, and $(0,0,1)$. In this case, the core is empty. To see this, for x to be in the core, it must be the case that $x_1 + x_2 \geq 1$, $x_1 + x_3 \geq 1$, and $x_2 + x_3 \geq 1$. Summing these three inequalities we deduce that $x_1 + x_2 + x_3 \geq \frac{3}{2}$, which contradicts the efficiency requirement $x_1 + x_2 + x_3 = 1$. ◄

Theorem 18.7 *The core of a coalitional game is covariant under strategic equivalence,*[2] *i.e., for every $a > 0$, and every $b \in \mathbb{R}^N$,*

$$\mathcal{C}(N; av + b) = a\mathcal{C}(N; v) + b. \tag{18.10}$$

As a corollary of Theorem 18.7, we deduce the following corollary.

Corollary 18.8 *The existence of a nonempty core is invariant under strategic equivalence.*

Proof of Theorem 18.7: Let $(N; u)$ be a coalitional game that is strategically equivalent to $(N; v)$: there exist $a > 0$ and $b \in \mathbb{R}^N$ such that

$$u(S) = av(S) + b(S), \quad \forall S \subseteq N. \tag{18.11}$$

Let $x \in \mathcal{C}(N; v)$. We will show that $ax + b \in \mathcal{C}(N; u)$. Since $x \in \mathcal{C}(N; v)$,

$$x(S) \geq v(S), \quad \forall S \subseteq N, \tag{18.12}$$

$$x(N) = v(N). \tag{18.13}$$

Since $a > 0$,

$$ax(S) + b(S) \geq av(S) + b(S) = u(S), \quad \forall S \subseteq N, \tag{18.14}$$

$$ax(N) + b(N) = av(N) + b(N) = u(N). \tag{18.15}$$

In other words, $ax + b \in \mathcal{C}(N; u)$, and we have therefore shown that $a\mathcal{C}(N; v) + b \subseteq \mathcal{C}(N; u)$.

To show the opposite inclusion, note that since the strategic equivalence relation is symmetric, $(N; v)$ is strategically equivalent to $(N; u)$: indeed, $v = \frac{1}{a}u - \frac{b}{a}$. From the first part, $\frac{1}{a}\mathcal{C}(N; u) - \frac{b}{a} \subseteq \mathcal{C}(N; v)$. By multiplying both sides of the equal sign by a and adding b to both sides, we get $\mathcal{C}(N; v) \subseteq a\mathcal{C}(N; v) + b$. □

Since the core may in some cases be empty, it is natural to ask whether it is possible to characterize the games that have nonempty cores, or at least identify interesting families of games whose core is nonempty. This question is answered in the following sections.

18.2 Balanced collections of coalitions

We begin by seeking a necessary condition for the existence of a nonempty core in three-player games. Suppose $(N; v)$ is a coalitional game with three players, $N = \{1, 2, 3\}$. An imputation x is in the core if and only if the following inequalities hold:

---

2 Recall that for every set $C \subseteq \mathbb{R}^N$, every $a > 0$, and every $b \in \mathbb{R}^N$, the sets aC and $C + b$ are defined by $aC := \{ax : x \in C\}$ and $C + b := \{x + b : x \in C\}$.

$$x_1 + x_2 + x_3 = v(1, 2, 3), \tag{18.16}$$

$$x_1 + x_2 \quad\;\; \geq v(1, 2), \tag{18.17}$$

$$x_1 \qquad + x_3 \geq v(1, 3), \tag{18.18}$$

$$x_2 + x_3 \geq v(2, 3), \tag{18.19}$$

$$x_1 \qquad\qquad \geq v(1), \tag{18.20}$$

$$x_2 \qquad\; \geq v(2), \tag{18.21}$$

$$x_3 \geq v(3). \tag{18.22}$$

We look for necessary conditions that the function v must meet for this system to have a solution. Suppose, therefore, that the core is not empty; i.e., Equations (18.16)–(18.22) have a solution. Combining the inequalities in Equations (18.20), (18.21), and (18.22) and using Equation (18.16) yields the following necessary condition:

$$v(1, 2, 3) \geq v(1) + v(2) + v(3). \tag{18.23}$$

Combining the inequalities in Equations (18.17) and (18.22), and using Equation (18.16), yields the following necessary condition:

$$v(1, 2, 3) \geq v(1, 2) + v(3). \tag{18.24}$$

We similarly derive the following two inequalities:

$$v(1, 2, 3) \geq v(1, 3) + v(2), \tag{18.25}$$

$$v(1, 2, 3) \geq v(2, 3) + v(1). \tag{18.26}$$

Combining the inequalities in Equations (18.17), (18.18), and (18.19), and using Equation (18.16), yields the following necessary condition:

$$v(1, 2, 3) \geq \tfrac{1}{2}v(1, 2) + \tfrac{1}{2}v(1, 3) + \tfrac{1}{2}v(2, 3). \tag{18.27}$$

With a little effort (Exercise 18.19) we can prove that if Equations (18.23)–(18.27) hold then there is a solution to the system of Equations (18.16)–(18.22), and therefore the core is nonempty. In other words, these equations constitute necessary and sufficient conditions for the core of a three-player game to be nonempty. Our goal now is to generalize this result to any number of players. To this end, let us look closely at these inequalities.

The inequalities in Equations (18.23)–(18.27) impose the requirement that $v(N)$ be "sufficiently large." The right-hand sides of these equations all contain collections of coalitions multiplied by various coefficients. This is summarized in the following table:

	Collection of coalitions	Coefficients
Equation (18.23)	$\{\{1\}, \{2\}, \{3\}\}$	$1, 1, 1$
Equation (18.24)	$\{\{1, 2\}, \{3\}\}$	$1, 1$
Equation (18.25)	$\{\{1, 3\}, \{2\}\}$	$1, 1$
Equation (18.26)	$\{\{2, 3\}, \{1\}\}$	$1, 1$
Equation (18.27)	$\{\{1, 2\}, \{1, 3\}, \{2, 3\}\}$	$\tfrac{1}{2}, \tfrac{1}{2}, \tfrac{1}{2}$

The first four collections are partitions of the set of players $\{1, 2, 3\}$, that is, a collection of disjoint coalitions whose union is $\{1, 2, 3\}$. The fifth collection, in contrast, does not satisfy this condition; it corresponds to the inequality (18.27), which at this stage in our exposition does not yet have a clear interpretation. From the way that the first four inequalities in Equations (18.23), (18.24), (18.25), and (18.26) are obtained here, we can perceive a necessary condition for the nonemptiness of the core: for every partition $\{S_1, S_2, \ldots, S_k\}$ of N, it must be the case that

$$v(N) \geq v(S_1) + v(S_2) + \cdots + v(S_k). \tag{18.28}$$

Indeed, this inequality holds from the combination of the inequalities $x(S_i) \geq v(S_i)$ for $i = 1, \ldots, k$, and the use of the efficiency requirement $x(N) = v(N)$. This is a form of superadditivity, but it does not imply that $(N; v)$ is necessarily superadditive, because the condition applies only to partitions of N. Focusing again on the five collections in the above table, we will try to find a property common to all of them. To this end, we define the following two concepts that will be used in the sequel.

Definition 18.9 *For every coalition S, the* incidence vector *of the coalition is the vector* $\chi^S \in \mathbb{R}^N$ *defined as follows:*

$$\chi_i^S = \begin{cases} 1 & \text{if } i \in S, \\ 0 & \text{if } i \notin S. \end{cases} \tag{18.29}$$

Definition 18.10 *Let $\mathcal{D} = \{S_1, S_2, \ldots, S_k\}$ be a collection of nonempty coalitions. The* incidence matrix *of $\mathcal{D}$ is the matrix with k rows (one for each coalition in the collection) and n columns (one per player), such that the i-th row is the incidence vector of coalition S_i.*

In words, the (i, j)-th entry of the incidence matrix contains 1 if player j is a member of coalition S_i, and 0 if he is not a member of the coalition.

The incidence matrices of the five collections of coalitions mentioned earlier appear in Figure 18.4, with the corresponding coefficients appearing alongside each matrix. For example, the second matrix, corresponding to Equation (18.24) and the collection of coalitions $\{\{1, 2\}, \{3\}\}$, has two rows: the first is the vector $(1, 1, 0)$, which is the incidence vector of the coalition $\{1, 2\}$, and the second is the vector $(0, 0, 1)$, which is the incidence vector of the coalition $\{3\}$.

One can see that in each collection of coalitions, the inner product of each column of the incidence matrix with the column of coefficients is 1. A collection of coalitions that has a vector of positive coefficients satisfying this property is called a *balanced collection*. The coefficients are then called *balancing coefficients*.

Definition 18.11 *A collection of coalitions $\mathcal{D}$ is a* balanced collection *if there exists a vector of positive numbers $(\delta_S)_{S \in \mathcal{D}}$ such that*

$$\sum_{\{S \in \mathcal{D} : i \in S\}} \delta_S = 1, \quad \forall i \in N. \tag{18.30}$$

The vector $(\delta_S)_{S \in \mathcal{D}}$ is a vector of balancing weights *of the collection. If all we require is for the coefficients $(\delta_S)_{S \in \mathcal{D}}$ to be nonnegative, then the corresponding collection of*

Equation	Coalition	Incidence matrix	Coefficients
Equation (18.23)	{1} {2} {3}	$\begin{pmatrix} 1 & 0 & 0 \\ 0 & 1 & 0 \\ 0 & 0 & 1 \end{pmatrix}$	1 1 1
Equation (18.24)	{1, 2} {3}	$\begin{pmatrix} 1 & 1 & 0 \\ 0 & 0 & 1 \end{pmatrix}$	1 1
Equation (18.25)	{1, 3} {2}	$\begin{pmatrix} 1 & 0 & 1 \\ 0 & 1 & 0 \end{pmatrix}$	1 1
Equation (18.26)	{2, 3} {1}	$\begin{pmatrix} 0 & 1 & 1 \\ 1 & 0 & 0 \end{pmatrix}$	1 1
Equation (18.27)	{1, 2} {1, 3} {2, 3}	$\begin{pmatrix} 1 & 1 & 0 \\ 1 & 0 & 1 \\ 0 & 1 & 1 \end{pmatrix}$	$\frac{1}{2}$ $\frac{1}{2}$ $\frac{1}{2}$

Figure 18.4 The incidence matrices for balanced collections of coalitions in three-player games

coalitions is called weakly balanced, and the coefficients $(\delta_S)_{S \in \mathcal{D}}$ are called weakly balancing weights.

In vector notation, we can define a balanced collection of coalitions using the incidence vectors, as follows: a collection $\mathcal{D}$ of coalitions is balanced with balancing weights $(\delta_S)_{S \in \mathcal{D}}$ if

$$\sum_{S \in \mathcal{D}} \delta_S \chi^S = \chi^N, \quad \text{and} \quad \delta_S > 0 \quad \forall S \in \mathcal{D}. \tag{18.31}$$

The collection is weakly balanced if $\delta_S > 0$ is replaced by $\delta_S \geq 0$ in Equation (18.31). By definition it follows that every balanced collection is weakly balanced, and therefore a collection that is not weakly balanced is not balanced. Note that every partition of N constitutes a balanced collection with weight 1 for every coalition in the partition. This is because Equation (18.30) holds in this case, since every player $i \in N$ appears in one and only one coalition in the partition, and therefore the sum on the left-hand side of the equation is 1 for every player $i \in N$. The other direction does not obtain: it is not true that every balanced collection is a partition. For example, the fifth collection in Figure 18.4, corresponding to Equation (18.27), is a balanced collection that is not a partition.

The concept of a balanced collection, in fact, may be regarded as a generalization of the concept of a partition: suppose that the players could divide their time among the various coalitions; each player i can determine what part of his time he will devote to each coalition to which he belongs. For example, a partition $\mathcal{B}$ corresponds to the situation in which every player i belonging to a coalition S in $\mathcal{B}$ devotes all his time to this coalition. The balanced collection $\mathcal{D}$, with balancing coefficients $(\delta_S)_{S \in \mathcal{D}}$, corresponds to a situation in which every player i devotes δ_S of his time to the coalition S, for every coalition S in $\mathcal{D}$ to which he belongs. The condition $\sum_{\{S \in \mathcal{D}: i \in S\}} \delta_S = 1$ guarantees that no player will be idle (it will not be the case that $\sum_{\{S \in \mathcal{D}:\ i \in S\}} \delta_S < 1$), and that no player "puts in overtime hours" (it will not be the case that $\sum_{\{S \in \mathcal{D}:\ i \in S\}} \delta_S > 1$). Every coalition S in the collection will form for a time period δ_S (out of 1), which is the amount of time that each member of the coalition devotes to the coalition.

Example 18.12 **Balanced collections in three-player games** Suppose that $N = \{1, 2, 3\}$. As we saw above, the following collections are balanced collections: $\mathcal{D}_1 = \{\{1\}, \{2\}, \{3\}\}$ with the balancing weights $\delta_{\{1\}} = \delta_{\{2\}} = \delta_{\{3\}} = 1$; $\mathcal{D}_2 = \{\{1, 2\}, \{1, 3\}, \{2, 3\}\}$ with the balancing weights $\delta_{\{1,2\}} = \delta_{\{1,3\}} = \delta_{\{2,3\}} = \frac{1}{2}$. We will show that the collection $\mathcal{D} = \{\{1\}, \{2\}, \{3\}, \{1, 2\}, \{1, 3\}, \{2, 3\}\}$, which is the union of the collections $\mathcal{D}_1$ and $\mathcal{D}_2$, is also a balanced collection. In fact, this collection has an infinite number of vectors of balancing weights:

$$\delta_{\{1\}} = \delta_{\{2\}} = \delta_{\{3\}} = \lambda, \quad \delta_{\{1,2\}} = \delta_{\{1,3\}} = \delta_{\{2,3\}} = \tfrac{1}{2}(1 - \lambda), \tag{18.32}$$

where $0 < \lambda < 1$.

This indicates a general way to construct a balanced collection out of two other balanced collections: if $\mathcal{D}_1$ and $\mathcal{D}_2$ are two balanced collections, then their union $\mathcal{D}_1 \cup \mathcal{D}_2$ is also a balanced collection. This follows because if $(\delta_S^1)_{S \in \mathcal{D}_1}$ and $(\delta_S^2)_{S \in \mathcal{D}_2}$ are vectors of balancing weights of the two collections, then for every $0 < \lambda < 1$, the vector of weights $(\delta_S^*)_{S \in \mathcal{D}_1 \cup \mathcal{D}_2}$ defined by

$$\delta_S^* = \begin{cases} \lambda \delta_S^1 & \text{if } S \in \mathcal{D}_1 \setminus \mathcal{D}_2, \\ (1 - \lambda) \delta_S^2 & \text{if } S \in \mathcal{D}_2 \setminus \mathcal{D}_1, \\ \lambda \delta_S^1 + (1 - \lambda) \delta_S^2 & \text{if } S \in \mathcal{D}_1 \cap \mathcal{D}_2, \end{cases} \tag{18.33}$$

is a vector of balancing weights for $\mathcal{D}_1 \cup \mathcal{D}_2$ (Exercise 18.20).

The collection $\mathcal{D} = \{\{1, 2\}, \{1, 3\}\}$ is neither balanced, nor weakly balanced. To see this, note that if $(\delta_S)_{S \in \mathcal{D}}$ were a vector of weakly balancing weights for $\mathcal{D}$, then by Equation (18.30), for $i = 1$ one has $\delta_{\{1,2\}} + \delta_{\{1,3\}} = 1$ while for $i = 2$ one has $\delta_{\{1,2\}} = 1$, and for $i = 3$ one has $\delta_{\{1,3\}} = 1$. There is no nonnegative solution for these three equations.

The collection $\mathcal{D} = \{\{1, 3\}, \{2, 3\}, \{1\}\}$ is not balanced, but it is weakly balanced. To see this, note that if $(\delta_S)_{S \in \mathcal{D}}$ were a vector of balancing weights for $\mathcal{D}$, then by Equation (18.30) applied to $i = 2$ one has $\delta_{\{2,3\}} = 1$. From Equation (18.30) applied to $i = 3$ it then follows that one has $\delta_{\{1,3\}} = 0$, but for a balanced collection, all the coefficients must be positive numbers. This collection is, however, weakly balanced, with balancing weights $\delta_{\{2,3\}} = \delta_{\{1\}} = 1$, $\delta_{\{1,3\}} = 0$. ◄

Example 18.13 When $N = \{1, 2, 3, 4\}$, the collection $\{\{1, 2\}, \{2, 3\}, \{1, 3, 4\}, \{4\}\}$ is a balanced collection, with balancing weights

$$\delta_{\{1,2\}} = \delta_{\{1,3\}} = \delta_{\{1,3,4\}} = \delta_{\{4\}} = \tfrac{1}{2}. \tag{18.34}$$

In contrast, the collection $\{\{1, 2\}, \{1, 3\}, \{1, 3, 4\}, \{4\}\}$ is not weakly balanced (why?). ◄

As previously noted, every balanced collection is in particular weakly balanced. Given a weakly balanced collection, one can obtain a balanced collection by removing every coalition whose weight is 0. If $(\delta_S)_{S \in \mathcal{D}}$ is a vector of weakly balancing weights for the collection $\mathcal{D}$, then the collection $\mathcal{T}$ defined as follows is a balanced collection, with balancing weights $(\delta_S)_{S \in \mathcal{T}}$:

$$\mathcal{T} = \{S \in \mathcal{D}:\ \delta_S > 0\}. \tag{18.35}$$

18.3 The Bondareva–Shapley Theorem

Bondareva [1963] and Shapley [1967] independently proved the following theorem, which provides a necessary and sufficient condition for the existence of a nonempty core.

Theorem 18.14 (Bondareva, Shapley) *A necessary and sufficient condition for the core of a coalitional game* $(N; v)$ *to be nonempty is for every balanced collection* $\mathcal{D}$ *of coalitions, and every vector of balancing weights* $(\delta_S)_{S \in \mathcal{D}}$ *for* $\mathcal{D}$, *to satisfy*

$$v(N) \geq \sum_{S \in \mathcal{D}} \delta_S v(S). \tag{18.36}$$

This condition is called the *Bondareva–Shapley condition*, or the *balancing condition*. A coalitional game satisfying the Bondareva–Shapley condition is called a *balanced game*, and the Bondareva–Shapley Theorem can therefore be reformulated as stating that the core of a coalitional game is nonempty if and only if the game is balanced.

Remark 18.15 *The Bondareva–Shapley Theorem holds when the words "balanced collection" are replaced by "weakly balanced collection" in its statement, because the inequality* (18.36) *holds for every balanced collection if and only if it holds for every weakly balanced collection (explain why).* ◆

The Bondareva–Shapley Theorem is not very useful for checking whether the core of a particular game is empty; it is usually more convenient to solve directly the inequalities defining the core. The theorem is useful when one wishes to prove that all the games in a particular class of games have nonempty cores. An example of such a class of games is that of market games, which we will see in Section 18.4 (page 750).

The following claim will be useful for the proof.

Lemma 18.16 *A collection of coalitions* $\mathcal{D}$ *is balanced with balancing weights* $(\delta_S)_{S \in \mathcal{D}}$ *if and only if for every vector* $x \in \mathbb{R}^N$

$$\sum_{S \in \mathcal{D}} \delta_S x(S) = x(N). \tag{18.37}$$

Proof: Assume first that $\mathcal{D}$ is a balanced collection of coalitions with balanced weights $(\delta_S)_{S \in \mathcal{D}}$, and let $x \in \mathbb{R}^N$. Then

$$\sum_{S \in \mathcal{D}} \delta_S x(S) = \sum_{S \in \mathcal{D}} \left(\delta_S \sum_{i \in S} x_i \right) \tag{18.38}$$

$$= \sum_{i \in N} \left(x_i \sum_{\{S \in \mathcal{D} : i \in S\}} \delta_S \right) \tag{18.39}$$

$$= \sum_{i \in N} x_i = x(N), \tag{18.40}$$

where Equation (18.38) follows from the definition of $x(S)$, Equation (18.39) follows from changing the order of summation, and Equation (18.40) holds because $(\delta_S)_{S \in \mathcal{D}}$ is a vector of balanced weights of $\mathcal{D}$ (Equation (18.30)).

Suppose now that there exists a vector of positive numbers $(\delta_S)_{S \in \mathcal{D}}$ such that Equation (18.37) holds for every $x \in \mathbb{R}^N$. We will show that $\mathcal{D}$ is a balanced collection of coalitions with balancing weights $(\delta_S)_{S \in \mathcal{D}}$. To do so, we need to show that $\sum_{\{S \in \mathcal{D}:\ i \in S\}} \delta_S = 1$ for every player $i \in N$. This equality holds by setting $x = \chi^{\{i\}}$ in Equation (18.37). $\qquad\square$

As we showed above, the property of having a nonempty core is invariant under strategic equivalence (Corollary 18.8). The following theorem states that the balancing property is also invariant under strategic equivalence.

Theorem 18.17 *Let $(N; v)$ and $(N; u)$ be two coalitional games with the same set of players satisfying the condition that $u = av + b$, where $a > 0$ and $b \in \mathbb{R}^N$. The game $(N; v)$ is balanced if and only if the game $(N; u)$ is balanced.*

Proof: It suffices to prove that if the game $(N; v)$ is balanced then the game $(N; u)$ is also balanced (why?). Suppose that $(N; v)$ is balanced, and let $\mathcal{D}$ be a balanced collection with balancing weights $(\delta_S)_{S \in \mathcal{D}}$. Then

$$v(N) \geq \sum_{S \in \mathcal{D}} \delta_S v(S). \tag{18.41}$$

Lemma 18.16 implies that $\sum_{S \in \mathcal{D}} \delta_S b(S) = b(N)$. Since $a > 0$, for every balanced collection $\mathcal{D}$ with balancing weights $(\delta_S)_{S \in \mathcal{D}}$ one has

$$\sum_{S \in \mathcal{D}} \delta_S u(S) = \sum_{S \in \mathcal{D}} \delta_S(av(S) + b(S)) \tag{18.42}$$

$$= a \sum_{S \in \mathcal{D}} \delta_S v(S) + \sum_{S \in \mathcal{D}} \delta_S b(S) \tag{18.43}$$

$$\leq av(N) + b(N) = u(N). \tag{18.44}$$

Since this inequality holds for every balanced collection of coalitions $\mathcal{D}$ with balancing weights $(\delta_S)_{S \in \mathcal{D}}$, it follows that the game $(N; u)$ is balanced. $\qquad\square$

We will present two different proofs of the Bondareva–Shapley Theorem: one proof is based on the Minmax Theorem, and the other proof is based on the Duality Theorem from linear programming. Sections 18.3.1 and 18.3.2 are devoted to proving Theorem 18.14 using the Minmax Theorem. The other proof will be presented in Section 18.3.3.

18.3.1 The Bondareva–Shapley condition is a necessary condition for the nonemptiness of the core

Let $x \in \mathcal{C}(N; v)$ be an imputation in the core of the coalitional game $(N; v)$. In particular, $x(N) = v(N)$ and $x(S) \geq v(S)$ for every coalition $S \subseteq N$.

Let $\mathcal{D}$ be a balanced collection of coalitions with balancing weights $(\delta_S)_{S \in \mathcal{D}}$. We will show that Equation (18.36) holds.

The balancing weights are nonnegative (they are, in fact, positive), and therefore one has

$$\delta_S v(S) \leq \delta_S x(S), \quad \forall S \in \mathcal{D}. \tag{18.45}$$

Summing this equation over all $S \in \mathcal{D}$ and making use of Lemma 18.16 and the fact that $x(N) = v(N)$ yields

$$\sum_{S \in \mathcal{D}} \delta_S v(S) \le \sum_{S \in \mathcal{D}} \delta_S x(S) = x(N) = v(N). \tag{18.46}$$

This means that Equation (18.36) holds.

18.3.2 The Bondareva–Shapley condition is a sufficient condition for the nonemptiness of the core

The proof of the other direction of the Bondareva–Shapley Theorem is more complicated, and relies on the Minmax Theorem. By Theorem 18.17, the balancing condition is invariant under strategic equivalence, and by Theorem 18.7, the property of having a nonempty core is also invariant under strategic equivalence. Since every game is strategically equivalent to either a $0-1$, $0-0$, or $0-(-1)$ normalized game (Theorem 17.7 on page 720), it suffices to prove this direction of the theorem for each of these three cases. In each case, the proof is by contradiction; we will assume that the game has an empty core, and prove that it is not balanced.

The proof for 0–1 normalized games:

Step 1: Defining the auxiliary game.
We will define an auxiliary two-player zero-sum strategic-form game that will be used throughout the proof of this case. The players in this game are denoted Player I and Player II. The set of (pure) strategies of Player I is $\{1, 2, \ldots, n\}$. We interpret this as Player I choosing a player in the coalitional game $(N; v)$. The set of (pure) strategies of Player II is $\{S \subseteq N : v(S) > 0\}$, the collection of coalitions of positive worth in the coalitional game $(N; v)$. Since the game is $0-1$ normalized, $v(N) = 1$, and therefore there is at least one such coalition. The payoffs in the auxiliary game are

$$u(i, S) = \begin{cases} \frac{1}{v(S)} & \text{if } i \in S, \\ 0 & \text{if } i \notin S. \end{cases} \tag{18.47}$$

In words, Player II pays Player I the sum $\frac{1}{v(S)}$ if the player i chosen by Player I is in the coalition S chosen by Player II; otherwise he pays him 0.   ☐

Example 18.18   Suppose that $N = \{1, 2, 3\}$, and that the coalitional function is

$$v(1) = v(2) = v(3) = 0, \quad v(1, 2) = \tfrac{1}{3}, \quad v(1, 3) = v(2, 3) = \tfrac{1}{2}, \quad v(1, 2, 3) = 1.$$

Then the payoff matrix in the auxiliary game is shown in Figure 18.5.

Player II

		$\{1, 2\}$	$\{1, 3\}$	$\{2, 3\}$	$\{1, 2, 3\}$
	1	3	2	0	1
Player I	2	3	0	2	1
	3	0	2	2	1

Figure 18.5 The payoff matrix for Example 18.18

The game defined above is a zero-sum game, in which each player has a finite number of pure strategies. It therefore follows from the Minmax Theorem (see Theorem 5.11 on page 150) that the game has a value in mixed strategies. Denote this value by λ.

Step 2: Proving that the value λ of the auxiliary game is positive.

Since every column contains at least one positive entry, Player I's mixed strategy $(\frac{1}{n}, \frac{1}{n}, \ldots, \frac{1}{n})$, in which he chooses every pure strategy with equal probability, guarantees him a positive payoff that is at least $\frac{1}{n} \min \left\{ \frac{1}{v(S)} : v(S) > 0 \right\}$. It follows that the value of the game in mixed strategies is positive.

Step 3: Proving that the value λ of the auxiliary game is less than 1.

We will prove this by showing that Player I cannot guarantee himself an expected payoff of 1. Let $x = (x_1, x_2, \ldots, x_n)$ be a mixed strategy of Player I. Since the game $(N; v)$ is 0–1 normalized, the strategy x is also an imputation in this game. Because the core is empty, x cannot be contained in the core, and therefore there exists a coalition S such that $v(S) > x(S) \geq 0$ (the inequality $x(S) \geq 0$ holds because x is a probability distribution, and therefore every coordinate of x is nonnegative).

Since $v(S) > 0$, it follows that S is a pure strategy for Player II in the auxiliary game that we have constructed. The expected payoff, when Player I plays the mixed strategy x and Player II plays the pure strategy S, is

$$u(x, S) = \sum_{i \in S} x_i u(i, S) = \sum_{i \in S} \frac{x_i}{v(S)} = \frac{x(S)}{v(S)} < 1. \tag{18.48}$$

We deduce from this that for every mixed strategy of Player I, there is a pure strategy of Player II guaranteeing that the payoff will be less than 1. By Equation (5.25) (page 150) it then follows that $\lambda < 1$, as claimed.

Step 4: The coalitional game $(N; v)$ is not balanced. That is, there exists a balanced collection $\mathcal{D}$, with balancing weights $(\delta_S)_{S \in \mathcal{D}}$, satisfying

$$v(N) < \sum_{S \in \mathcal{D}} \delta_S v(S). \tag{18.49}$$

A mixed strategy of Player II in the auxiliary game is a probability distribution over coalitions with positive worth. Let $y = (y_S)_{\{S: v(S) > 0\}}$ be an optimal strategy of Player II in the auxiliary game. Such a strategy guarantees that the expected payoff will be at most λ, for every mixed strategy of Player I.

Consider the following collection of coalitions:

$$\mathcal{D} = \{S \subseteq N : v(S) > 0\} \cup \{\{1\}, \{2\}, \ldots, \{n\}\}, \tag{18.50}$$

with weights

$$\delta_S = \frac{y_S}{\lambda v(S)}, \quad v(S) > 0, \tag{18.51}$$

$$\delta_{\{i\}} = 1 - \sum_{\{S \subseteq N : i \in S, v(S) > 0\}} \delta_S, \quad \forall i \in N. \tag{18.52}$$

Since the game is 0–1 normalized, $v(i) = 0$, and therefore no coalition appears more than once in $\mathcal{D}$.

We next show that $\mathcal{D}$ is a weakly balanced collection with balancing weights $(\delta_S)_{S \in \mathcal{D}}$ defined by Equations (18.51) and (18.52). To do so, we need to show that the sum of the weights of the coalitions containing each player i equals 1, and that the weights are nonnegative.

The definition of δ_S implies that for every player $i \in N$,

$$\sum_{\{S \subseteq N : i \in S, v(S) > 0\}} \delta_S + \delta_{\{i\}} = 1, \tag{18.53}$$

and the first property therefore obtains. We next show that the weights are nonnegative. By Equation (18.51), for every coalition S such that $v(S) > 0$, the weight δ_S is the quotient of the nonnegative number y_S and the positive number $\lambda v(S)$, and is therefore nonnegative. As for the weights $(\delta_{\{i\}})_{i \in N}$,

$$\sum_{\{S \subseteq N : i \in S, v(S) > 0\}} \delta_S = \frac{1}{\lambda} \sum_{\{S \subseteq N : i \in S, v(S) > 0\}} \frac{y_S}{v(S)} = \frac{1}{\lambda} u(i, y) \leq \frac{1}{\lambda} = 1, \tag{18.54}$$

where the inequality follows from the fact that y is an optimal strategy for Player II in the auxiliary game whose value is λ. By definition of $\delta_{\{i\}}$ (see Equation (18.52)), we deduce that $\delta_{\{i\}} \geq 0$, which is what we wanted to show.

We next show that the Bondareva–Shapley condition is not satisfied by the weakly balanced collection $\mathcal{D}$ and by the weights $(\delta_S)_{S \in \mathcal{D}}$. Indeed,

$$\sum_{S \in \mathcal{D}} \delta_S v(S) = \sum_{j \in N} \delta_{\{j\}} v(j) + \sum_{\{S \subseteq N : v(S) > 0\}} \delta_S v(S) \tag{18.55}$$

$$= 0 + \sum_{\{S \subseteq N : v(S) > 0\}} \frac{y_S}{\lambda v(S)} v(S) \tag{18.56}$$

$$= \frac{1}{\lambda} \sum_{\{S \subseteq N : v(S) > 0\}} y_S = \frac{1}{\lambda} \cdot 1 > 1 = v(N). \tag{18.57}$$

In other words, $v(N) < \sum_{S \in \mathcal{D}} \delta_S v(S)$. Removing from $\mathcal{D}$ all the coalitions whose weight is 0, we are left with a balanced collection that does not satisfy the Bondareva–Shapley condition. We have shown that if the core is empty, the game is not balanced, and this completes the proof that the Bondareva–Shapley condition is a necessary condition for the nonemptiness of the core, in the case of 0–1 normalized games.

The proof for 0–0 normalized games: We will now show that if a coalitional game $(N; v)$ is 0–0 normalized and has an empty core, then it is not balanced. When a coalitional game is 0–0 normalized, the only imputation is $x = (0, 0, \ldots, 0)$. It therefore follows that if the core is empty, there exists a coalition S satisfying $v(S) > 0$. Denote by $\{i_1, i_2, \ldots, i_{n-|S|}\}$ the set of players who are not in S, i.e., $N = S \cup \{i_1, i_2, \ldots, i_{n-|S|}\}$. Define the collection of coalitions

$$\mathcal{D} = \{S, \{i_1\}, \{i_2\}, \ldots, \{i_{n-|S|}\}\}. \tag{18.58}$$

This is a partition of N, and the collection is therefore balanced with balancing weights

$$\delta_R = 1, \quad \forall R \in \mathcal{D}. \tag{18.59}$$

But

$$\sum_{R \in \mathcal{D}} \delta_R v(R) = v(S) + \sum_{i \notin S} v(i) = v(S) > 0 = v(N), \tag{18.60}$$

and the game is therefore not balanced.

The proof for 0–(−1) normalized games

The core of a 0–(−1) normalized game is empty, because there is no vector $x \in \mathbb{R}^N$ satisfying $x_i \geq v(i) = 0$ and $\sum_{i \in N} x_i = v(N) = -1$. It follows that to prove the sufficiency of the Bondareva–Shapley condition in this case, we need to show that every 0–(−1) normalized game is not balanced. Indeed, consider the balanced collection $\{\{1\}, \{2\}, \ldots, \{n\}\}$, with balancing weights $\delta_{\{i\}} = 1$ for every $i \in N$. Since $\sum_{i \in N} \delta_{\{i\}} v(i) = 0 > -1 = v(N)$, the game is not balanced. We have shown that the Bondareva–Shapley Theorem holds for 0–0 normalized games, 0–1 normalized games, and 0–(−1) normalized games, thus concluding the proof of the theorem. $\square$

18.3.3 A proof of the Bondareva–Shapley Theorem using linear programming

The Bondareva–Shapley Theorem (Theorem 18.14) can be proved using the Duality Theorem of linear programming. A brief review of linear programming appears in Section 24.3 (page 991).

Denote by $\mathcal{P}(N) := \{S \subseteq N, S \neq \emptyset\}$ the collection of nonempty coalitions. Denote by P the collection of all weights weakly balancing $\mathcal{P}(N)$,

$$P := \left\{ \delta = (\delta_S)_{S \in \mathcal{P}(N)} : \delta_S \geq 0 \ \ \forall S \in \mathcal{P}(N), \ \sum_{S \in \mathcal{P}(N)} \delta_S \chi^S = \chi^N \right\}. \tag{18.61}$$

This set is a polytope in the space $\mathbb{R}^{2^n - 1}$, and is nonempty: it contains, for example, the vector δ in which $\delta_{\{i\}} = 1$ for every $i \in N$, and $\delta_S = 0$ for every S containing at least two players.

The following theorem is equivalent to Theorem 18.14 (Exercise 18.28).

Theorem 18.19 (Bondareva, Shapley, second formulation) *A necessary and sufficient condition for the nonemptiness of the core of a coalitional game $(N; v)$ is that*

$$v(N) \geq \sum_{S \in \mathcal{P}(N)} \delta_S v(S), \quad \forall \delta = (\delta_S)_{S \in \mathcal{P}(N)} \in P. \tag{18.62}$$

Proof of Theorem 18.19 using linear programming: The proof is conducted in steps. We will define a linear program and show that its set of feasible solutions is bounded and nonempty. By the Duality Theorem of linear programming we will deduce that the value of the linear program, Z_P, is equal to the value of its dual program, Z_D. We will prove that the core is nonempty if and only if $Z_D \leq v(N)$, and conclude by proving that $Z_P \leq v(N)$ if and only if Equation (18.62) holds.

Step 1: Defining a linear program.

Consider the following linear program with the variables $(\delta_S)_{S\in\mathcal{P}(N)}$:

$$\text{Compute:} \quad Z_P := \max \sum_{S\in\mathcal{P}(N)} \delta_S v(S),$$
$$\text{subject to:} \quad \sum_{\{S:\, i\in S\}} \delta_S = 1, \quad \forall i \in N,$$
$$\delta_S \geq 0, \quad \forall S \in \mathcal{P}(N).$$

The set of feasible solutions of this linear program is the set P defined in Equation (18.61). As previously noted, this set is compact and nonempty; hence Z_P is finite.

Step 2: The dual problem.

The dual problem is the following problem with the variables $(x_i)_{i\in N}$ (verify!):

$$\text{Compute:} \quad Z_D := \min x(N),$$
$$\text{subject to:} \quad x(S) \geq v(S), \quad \forall S \in \mathcal{P}(N).$$

As already shown, Z_P is finite, and therefore the Duality Theorem of linear programming (Theorem 24.46 on page 995) implies that Z_D is also finite, and equals Z_P.

Step 3: If the core is not empty, then $Z_D \leq v(N)$.

Let x be a vector in the core. Then $x(S) \geq v(S)$ for every coalition S, and therefore x satisfies all the constraints of the dual problem. The value of the objective function at x is $x(N) = v(N)$; hence $Z_D \leq v(N)$.

Step 4: If $Z_D \leq v(N)$, then the core is not empty.

Let x be a feasible solution of the dual problem at which the minimum is attained, i.e., $x(N) = Z_D$. Since x satisfies the constraints of the dual problem, it is coalitionally rational. We show that $x(N) = v(N)$. Since $Z_D \leq v(N)$, it follows that $x(N) = \sum_{i\in N} x_i = Z_D \leq v(N)$. For $S = N$, the constraint $x(S) \geq v(S)$ is $x(N) \geq v(N)$, so that we deduce that $x(N) = v(N)$. It follows that x is in the core, and therefore the core is not empty.

Step 5: $Z_P \leq v(N)$ if and only if Equation (18.62) holds.

$Z_P \leq v(N)$ if and only if $\sum_{\{S\in\mathcal{P}(N):\, i\in S\}} \delta_S v(S) \leq v(N)$ for every feasible solution $\delta = (\delta_S)_{S\in\mathcal{P}(N)}$, i.e., if and only if Equation (18.62) holds. □

18.4 Market games

In this section, we will concentrate on coalitional games that naturally arise in the study of economics and apply the Bondareva–Shapley Theorem to prove the nonemptiness of the core of these games. The economic model we will study is the model of a market with a set of producers $N = \{1, 2, \ldots, n\}$ who trade l commodities. The set of commodities is denoted by $L = \{1, 2, \ldots, l\}$. The goods produced can be of different types: metals, water, human resources, consultation hours, etc. We will assume that the final goods that the producers offer have fixed prices in the market, and it is therefore convenient to analyze production as if it involves the production of money.

Denote the nonnegative real numbers by $\mathbb{R}_+ := [0, \infty)$. A vector of commodities is denoted by $x = (x_j)_{j=1}^{L} \in \mathbb{R}_+^L$; i.e., we assume that the quantity of each commodity is nonnegative. Such a vector x is called a *bundle*. The bundle of producer i will be denoted by x_i, and the quantity of commodity j in this bundle will be denoted by $x_{i,j}$.

Each producer has at his disposal a "production technology" represented by a production function $u_i : \mathbb{R}_+^L \to \mathbb{R}$: if $x_i \in \mathbb{R}_+^L$ is the bundle of commodities owned by producer i, then that producer can produce the sum of money $u_i(x_i)$. Since the production technologies may differ from one producer to another, their production functions may also differ. We also assume that every producer i has an initial endowment that is a bundle $a_i \in \mathbb{R}_+^L$ of goods, and the producers can trade goods between each other.

If coalition S is formed, the members of S trade commodities among themselves, with the goal of maximizing the money that they can produce. In other words, if the coalition S is formed, the total bundle of goods available to the coalition is $a(S) := \sum_{i \in S} a_i \in \mathbb{R}_+^L$. The coalition can allocate to each of its members a bundle $x_i \in \mathbb{R}_+^L$, subject to the constraint

$$x(S) = \sum_{i \in S} x_i = \sum_{i \in S} a_i = a(S). \tag{18.63}$$

Hence, by this reallocation of commodities, the members of the coalition can together produce an amount of money equal to $\sum_{i \in S} u_i(x_i)$.

Formally, a market is defined as follows:

Definition 18.20 *A* market *is given by a vector* $(N, L, (a_i, u_i)_{i \in N})$, *where:*

- $N = \{1, 2, \ldots, n\}$ *is the set of producers.*
- $L = \{1, 2, \ldots, l\}$ *is the set of commodities.*
- *For every* $i \in N$, $a_i \in \mathbb{R}_+^L$ *is the initial endowment of producer* i.
- *For every* $i \in N$, $u_i : \mathbb{R}_+^L \to \mathbb{R}$ *is the production function of producer* i.

The assumption that $a_i \in \mathbb{R}_+^L$ for every $i \in N$ implies that there is a finite amount of each commodity in the market.

Definition 18.21 *An* allocation *for a coalition* S *is a collection of bundles of commodities* $(x_i)_{i \in S}$, *where* $x_i \in \mathbb{R}_+^L$ *for every producer* $i \in N$, *satisfying* $x(S) = a(S)$.

In words, an allocation is a redistribution of the commodities available to the members of S in their initial endowments. Denote by X^S the set of allocations for coalition S:

$$X^S := \{(x_i)_{i \in S} : x_i \in \mathbb{R}_+^L \ \forall i \in S, \ x(S) = a(S)\} \subseteq \mathbb{R}_+^{S \times L}. \tag{18.64}$$

Theorem 18.22 *For every coalition* S, *the set* X^S *is compact.*

Proof: We need to show that X^S is a closed and bounded set. The set X^S is bounded because the total quantity of commodities in the market is bounded: if $x \in X^S$, then

$$0 \le x_{i,j} \le \sum_{i \in N} a_{i,j}, \quad \forall i \in N, \forall j \in L. \tag{18.65}$$

To show that X^S is a closed set, note that every half-space is closed. The set X^S defined by Equation (18.64) is the intersection of half-spaces and therefore closed. $\square$

Every market can be associated with a coalitional game, in which the set of players is the set of producers $N = \{1, 2, \ldots, n\}$, and the worth of each nonempty coalition $S \subseteq N$ is

$$v(S) = \max\left\{\sum_{i\in S} u_i(x_i) : x = (x_i)_{i\in S} \in X^S\right\}. \tag{18.66}$$

In words, the worth of coalition S is the maximal sum of money that its members can produce if they trade commodities among themselves (without involving the players who are not in S). The coalitional game $(N; v)$ so defined is *the market game derived from the market* $(N, L, (a_i, u_i)_{i\in N})$.

The first question to answer is whether $v(S)$ is well defined, i.e., whether the maximum in Equation (18.66) is attained.

Theorem 18.23 *If for every $i \in N$ the production function u_i is continuous, then the maximum at Equation (18.66) is attained for every coalition S.*

Proof: Since all production functions $(u_i)_{i\in N}$ are continuous, the function $\sum_{i\in S} u_i$, as the sum of a finite number of continuous functions, is also a continuous function. Since the maximum of a continuous function over a compact set is always attained, and since the set X^S is compact (Theorem 18.22), we deduce that the maximum at Equation (18.66) is attained. $\square$

Example 18.24 Consider the following market:
- $N = \{1, 2, 3\}$; the market contains three producers.
- $L = \{1, 2\}$; there are two commodities.
- The initial endowments of the producers are

$$a_1 = (1, 0), \quad a_2 = (0, 1), \quad a_3 = (2, 2).$$

- The production functions of the producers are

$$u_1(x_1) = x_{1,1} + x_{1,2}, \quad u_2(x_2) = x_{2,1} + 2x_{2,2}, \quad u_3(x_3) = \sqrt{x_{3,1}} + \sqrt{x_{3,2}}.$$

The game derived from this market is given as follows. If a coalition contains only one producer, $S = \{i\}$, then the only bundle in X^S is a_i, the initial endowment of producer i. Therefore,

$$v(1) = 1, \quad v(2) = 2, \quad v(3) = 2\sqrt{2}.$$

We will compute $v(1, 2, 3)$, and leave the computations of $v(1, 2)$, $v(1, 3)$, and $v(2, 3)$ to the reader (Exercise 18.36). Note that $a_1 + a_2 + a_3 = (3, 3)$. Every unit of commodity 1 contributes equally to the production functions of producers 1 and 2, and every unit of commodity 2 contributes to the production function of producer 2 twice as much as it contributes to producer 1. No production loss therefore occurs if nothing is given to producer 1; every quantity of commodities we give him can be given instead to producer 2 without lessening total production at all. If we therefore set the bundle of producer 1 as $x_1 = (0, 0)$, and denote by $x_2 = (x_{2,1}, x_{2,2})$ the bundle to producer 2, and by $x_3 = (3 - x_{2,1}, 3 - x_{2,2})$ the bundle to producer 3, then

$$v(1, 2, 3) = \max\left\{x_{2,1} + 2x_{2,2} + \sqrt{3 - x_{2,1}} + \sqrt{3 - x_{2,2}} : 0 \le x_{2,1} \le 3, 0 \le x_{2,2} \le 3\right\}.$$

By differentiating the function $x_{2,1} + 2x_{2,2} + \sqrt{3 - x_{2,1}} + \sqrt{3 - x_{2,2}}$ and equating its directional derivatives to 0, we deduce that the optimal allocation is

$$x_1 = (0, 0), \quad x_2 = \left(2\tfrac{3}{4}, 2\tfrac{15}{16}\right), \quad x_3 = \left(\tfrac{1}{4}, \tfrac{1}{4}\right),$$

and that the worth of the grand coalition $\{1, 2, 3\}$ is the value of the maximum, which is $v(1, 2, 3) = 9\tfrac{5}{8}$. It can be shown (Exercise 18.36) that the coalitional function of the market game derived from the market in this example is

$$v(1) = 1, \quad v(2) = 2, \quad v(3) = 2\sqrt{2}, \quad v(1,2) = 3, \quad v(1,3) = 5\tfrac{1}{2},$$
$$v(2,3) = 8\tfrac{3}{8}, \quad v(1,2,3) = 9\tfrac{5}{8}.$$

◄

Definition 18.25 *A coalitional game* $(N; v)$ *is a* market game *if there exist a positive number l, and for every player* $i \in N$ *an initial endowment* $a_i \in \mathbb{R}_+^L$, *and a continuous and concave production function* $u_i : \mathbb{R}_+^L \to \mathbb{R}$, *where* $L = \{1, 2, \ldots, l\}$, *such that Equation (18.66) is satisfied*[3] *for every coalition* $S \in \mathcal{P}(N)$.

In other words, a market game is a coalitional game derived from a market in which the production functions are continuous and concave. The assumption that the production functions are continuous and concave is part of the definition of a market game. The proof of the following theorem is left to the reader (Exercise 18.38).

Theorem 18.26 *If* $(N; v)$ *is a market game, then every coalitional game that is strategically equivalent to* $(N; v)$ *is also a market game.*

Theorem 18.27 (Shapley and Shubik [1969]) *The core of a market game is nonempty.*

Proof: The proof of this theorem relies on the Bondareva–Shapley Theorem; we will prove that every market game is a balanced game. For every coalition S, choose an imputation $x^S = (x_i^S)_{i \in S} \in \mathbb{R}_+^{S \times L}$ at which the maximum in Equation (18.66) is attained. This is possible due to Theorem 18.23. Then:

- $x_i^S \in \mathbb{R}_+^L$ for every player i,
- $x^S(S) = \sum_{i \in S} x_i^S = a(S)$,
- and $\sum_{i \in S} u_i(x_i^S) = v(S)$.

Let $\delta = (\delta_S)_{S \in \mathcal{P}(N)} \in P$ be a vector[4] that weakly balances $\mathcal{P}(N)$. We need to show that

$$v(N) \geq \sum_{S \in \mathcal{P}(N)} \delta_S v(S). \tag{18.67}$$

For every $i \in N$ denote

$$z_i := \sum_{\{S \in \mathcal{P}(N) : \, i \in S\}} \delta_S x_i^S \in \mathbb{R}_+^L. \tag{18.68}$$

Equation (18.68) is a weighted average with weights $(\delta_S)_{\{S \in \mathcal{P}(N) : \, i \in S\}}$ of the bundles $(x_i^S)_{\{S \in \mathcal{P}(N) : \, i \in S\}}$ allocated to producer i in each coalition S in which he participates. We first show that $z = (z_i)_{i \in N}$ is a feasible bundle, i.e., that $z(N) = a(N)$. Note that by the definition of z_i,

---

3 Recall that $\mathcal{P}(N) = \{S \subseteq N : S \neq \emptyset\}$ is the collection of all the nonempty coalitions in N.
4 Recall that P is the set of all vectors that weakly balance $\mathcal{P}(N)$ (see Equation (18.61) on page 749).

$$z(N) = \sum_{i \in N} z_i = \sum_{i \in N} \sum_{\{S \in \mathcal{P}(N): i \in S\}} \delta_S x_i^S. \tag{18.69}$$

By changing the order of summation,

$$z(N) = \sum_{S \in \mathcal{P}(N)} \sum_{i \in S} \delta_S x_i^S = \sum_{S \in \mathcal{P}(N)} \left(\delta_S \sum_{i \in S} x_i^S \right) = \sum_{S \in \mathcal{P}(N)} \delta_S x^S(S). \tag{18.70}$$

Since $x^S(S) = a(S)$, by changing the order of summation, one has

$$z(N) = \sum_{S \in \mathcal{P}(N)} \delta_S a(S) = \sum_{S \in \mathcal{P}(N)} \left(\delta_S \sum_{i \in S} a_i \right) = \sum_{i \in N} \left(a_i \sum_{\{S \in \mathcal{P}(N): i \in S\}} \delta_S \right). \tag{18.71}$$

Since δ is a vector of balancing weights, $\sum_{\{S \in \mathcal{P}(N): i \in S\}} \delta_S = 1$ for every player $i \in N$, and therefore

$$z(N) = \sum_{i \in N} a_i = a(N); \tag{18.72}$$

that is, z is indeed a feasible bundle. By this, and from the definition of the function v (Equation (18.66)), we deduce that

$$v(N) \geq \sum_{i \in N} u_i(z_i). \tag{18.73}$$

Next, based on Equation (18.68),

$$v(N) \geq \sum_{i \in N} u_i(z_i) \tag{18.74}$$

$$= \sum_{i \in N} u_i \left(\sum_{\{S \in \mathcal{P}(N): i \in S\}} \delta_S x_i^S \right) \tag{18.75}$$

$$\geq \sum_{i \in N} \sum_{\{S \in \mathcal{P}(N): i \in S\}} \delta_S u_i \left(x_i^S \right) \tag{18.76}$$

$$= \sum_{S \in \mathcal{P}(N)} \sum_{i \in S} \delta_S u_i \left(x_i^S \right) \tag{18.77}$$

$$= \sum_{S \in \mathcal{P}(N)} \left(\delta_S \sum_{i \in S} u_i \left(x_i^S \right) \right) \tag{18.78}$$

$$= \sum_{S \in \mathcal{P}(N)} \delta_S v(S), \tag{18.79}$$

where Equation (18.76) follows from the concavity of the functions $(u_i)_{i \in N}$, Equation (18.78) follows from changing the order of summation, and Equation (18.79) holds because $v(S) = \sum_{i \in N} u_i(x_i^S)$. It follows that the game is balanced, and therefore the core is nonempty, which is what we wanted to show. $\square$

Let $(N, L, (a_i, u_i)_{i \in N})$ be a market, and let $(N; v)$ be the market game derived from it. Suppose that some of the producers leave the market, and that the only producers left are the members of the coalition S. This yields a new market, $(S, L, (a_i, u_i)_{i \in S})$. What is the market game derived from this market? If we denote this game by $(S; \tilde{v})$, then for every coalition $T \subseteq S$ one has

$$\tilde{v}(T) = \max \left\{ \sum_{i \in T} u_i(x_i) : x_i \in \mathbb{R}_+^L \ \forall i \in T, x(T) = a(T) \right\} = v(T). \qquad (18.80)$$

In other words, $\tilde{v}$ is the function v restricted to the members of S. This distinction motivates the following definition.

Definition 18.28 *Let $(N; v)$ be a coalitional game, and let $S \subseteq N$ be a nonempty set of players. The* subgame *$(S; v)$ is the coalitional game where:*

- *The set of players is S.*
- *The coalitional function is the function v restricted to the coalitions contained in S.*

The game $(S; v)$ is also called the game *$(N; v)$ restricted to S.*

An immediate corollary of the above discussion and Theorem 18.27 is:

Corollary 18.29 *If $(N; v)$ is a market game, then every subgame $(S; v)$ of $(N; v)$ is a market game, and in particular its core is nonempty.*

Indeed, if $(N, L, (a_i, u_i)_{i \in N})$ is a market from which the coalitional game $(N; v)$ is derived, then the same market restricted to the members of S, that is, the market $(S, L, (a_i, u_i)_{i \in S})$, is a market from which the game $(S; v)$ is derived.

Definition 18.30 *A coalitional game $(N; v)$ is* totally balanced *if the core of every subgame of $(N; v)$ is nonempty.*

We can reformulate Corollary 18.29 as follows:

Theorem 18.31 (Shapley and Shubik [1969]) *Every market game is totally balanced.*

Example 18.32 Let $(N; v)$ be a coalitional game, where $N = \{1, 2, 3\}$ and the coalitional function v is given by

$$v(1) = v(2) = v(3) = 10, \quad v(1,2) = v(1,3) = v(2,3) = 15, \quad v(1,2,3) = 90.$$

This game has a nonempty core. To see this, note, for example, that the vector $x = (30, 30, 30)$ is in the core of the game. On the other hand, the game restricted to the coalition $\{1, 2\}$ is the game $(\{1, 2\}, \tilde{v})$ where

$$\tilde{v}(1) = \tilde{v}(2) = 10, \quad \tilde{v}(1,2) = 15,$$

and the core of this game is empty. If follows therefore that the game $(N; v)$ is balanced, but not totally balanced. By Corollary 18.29, we deduce that $(N; v)$ is not a market game: there is no market from which this game can be derived.   ◀

18.4.1 The balanced cover of a coalitional game

Let $(N; v)$ be a coalitional game. The inequalities in the Bondareva–Shapley condition indicate that if $v(N)$ is sufficiently large, then the core of the game is not empty. It follows that when the core is empty, by enlarging $v(N)$ we may obtain a new game whose core is not empty, and differs from $(N; v)$ only in the worth of the grand coalition N. How large must the worth of the grand coalition N be for the core of the new game to be nonempty?

By the Bondareva–Shapley Theorem (Theorem 18.19 on page 749), it suffices to increase to be at least $\max\{\sum_{S\in\mathcal{P}(N)} \delta_S v(S): \delta \in P\}$.

Definition 18.33 *The* balanced cover *of a coalitional game* $(N; v)$ *is the coalitional game* $(N; \tilde{v})$ *defined by*

$$\tilde{v}(S) := \begin{cases} v(S) & \text{if } S \neq N, \\ \max\left\{\sum_{S\in\mathcal{P}(N)} \delta_S v(S): \delta \in P\right\} & \text{if } S = N. \end{cases} \tag{18.81}$$

Theorem 18.34 *The coalitional game* $(N; v)$ *has a nonempty core if and only if* $\tilde{v}(N) = v(N)$, *where* $(N; \tilde{v})$ *is the balanced cover of* $(N; v)$.

Proof: We first show that $\tilde{v}(N) \geq v(N)$, whether or not the core is empty: $\{N\}$ is a balanced collection with the balancing weight $\delta_N = 1$; hence $\tilde{v}(N) \geq 1 \cdot v(N) = v(N)$.

To complete the proof, we will show that $v(N) \geq \tilde{v}(N)$ if and only if the core is not empty. By the Bondareva–Shapley Theorem (see Theorem 18.14) the core of a coalitional game is nonempty if and only if $v(N) \geq \sum_{S\in\mathcal{P}(N)} \delta_S v(S)$ for every $\delta \in P$, i.e., if and only if

$$v(N) \geq \max\left\{ \sum_{S\in\mathcal{P}(N)} \delta_S v(S): \delta \in P \right\} = \tilde{v}(N), \tag{18.82}$$

which is what we wanted to show. □

Example 18.32 shows that a balanced game need not be totally balanced. To obtain a totally balanced game, one needs to guarantee that for every coalition S the worth $v(S)$ is sufficiently large so that the game restricted to S is balanced. How much must the worth of each coalition be increased for the resulting game to be totally balanced, or equivalently for the core of every subgame to be nonempty? Applying the same reasoning we applied to the coalition N to every nonempty coalition S, we deduce that the worth of every coalition S must be at least

$$\max\left\{ \sum_{\{R\subseteq S, R\neq\emptyset\}} \delta_R v(R): \sum_{\{R\subseteq S, R\neq\emptyset\}} \delta_R \chi^R = \chi^S, \delta_R \geq 0 \ \ \forall R \subseteq S \right\}. \tag{18.83}$$

Definition 18.35 *The* totally balanced cover *of a coalitional game* $(N; v)$ *is the coalitional game* $(N; \hat{v})$ *defined as follows. For every nonempty coalition* $S \subseteq N$,

$$\hat{v}(S) := \max\left\{ \sum_{\{R\subseteq S, R\neq\emptyset\}} \delta_R v(R): \sum_{\{R\subseteq S, R\neq\emptyset\}} \delta_R \chi^R = \chi^S, \delta_R \geq 0 \ \ \forall R \subseteq S \right\} \tag{18.84}$$

and $\hat{v}(\emptyset) := 0$.

We can now characterize when a coalitional game is totally balanced.

Theorem 18.36 *A coalitional game* $(N; v)$ *is totally balanced if and only if* $\hat{v}(S) = v(S)$ *for every coalition* $S \subseteq N$, *where the function* $\hat{v}$ *is defined by Equation (18.84).*

Proof: The game $(N; v)$ is totally balanced if and only if for every nonempty coalition $S \subseteq N$ the coalitional game $(S; v)$ is balanced. Suppose that $S \subseteq N$ is a nonempty coalition. Theorem 18.34 implies that the game $(S; v)$ is balanced if and only if

$$v(S) = \max \left\{ \sum_{R \in \mathcal{P}(N)} \delta_R v(R) : \delta \in P \right\} = \widehat{v}(S). \tag{18.85}$$

Since $v(\emptyset) = 0 = \widehat{v}(\emptyset)$, it follows that the game $(N; v)$ is totally balanced if and only if $v(S) = \widehat{v}(S)$ for every coalition $S \subseteq N$, as claimed. $\qquad\square$

18.4.2 Every totally balanced game is a market game

Corollary 18.29 states that the core of every subgame of a market game is nonempty. As Example 18.32 shows, there are games with nonempty cores that are not market games. We can now prove the following theorem, which is the converse to Corollary 18.29.

Theorem 18.37 *Every totally balanced game is a market game.*

Proof: Let $(N; v)$ be a totally balanced game. We need to show that $(N; v)$ is a market game. To do so, we will define a market and show that $(N; v)$ is the market game derived from this market.

If $(N; v)$ is a totally balanced game, then every coalitional game strategically equivalent to $(N; v)$ is also totally balanced. It therefore suffices to prove the theorem for 0-normalized games. Recall that a coalitional game $(N; v)$ is 0-normalized if $v(i) = 0$ for every player $i \in N$.

Step 1: Defining the market.
Let $(N; v)$ be a totally balanced and 0-normalized game. We will construct a market in which both the set of producers and the set of commodities are the set of players N; i.e., $N = L = \{1, 2, \ldots, n\}$. The space of bundles is therefore $\mathbb{R}^N_+$, with every coordinate associated with the name of a player. The initial endowment of player i is one unit of the commodity "associated with him," that is,

$$a_i := \chi^{\{i\}}, \quad \forall i \in N. \tag{18.86}$$

If we interpret the commodities as the labor time of the various players (over a certain time period), then the initial endowment of player i is the amount of labor time that he can give, namely one unit. In particular, we deduce that the sum total of commodities that the members of each coalition S have is

$$a(S) = \chi^S, \quad \forall S \subseteq N. \tag{18.87}$$

Define a production function $u \colon \mathbb{R}^N_+ \to \mathbb{R}$, as follows:

$$u(x) := \max \left\{ \sum_{S \in \mathcal{P}(N)} \delta_S v(S) : \sum_{S \in \mathcal{P}(N)} \delta_S \chi^S = x, \delta_S \geq 0 \ \forall S \subseteq N \right\}. \tag{18.88}$$

We can interpret this production function as follows. For every coalition S, there exists an economic activity yielding the income $v(S)$ for every unit of time that the members of S

(all together) give to that activity. If every player $i \in S$ gives δ_S of his time to the economic activity of coalition S, then the coalition S is active δ_S of the time, and produces $\delta_S v(S)$. In this case, all the coalitions together can produce the total profit of $\sum_{S \in \mathcal{P}(N)} \delta_S v(S)$. If the vector $x = (x_i)_{i \in N}$ represents the amount of time that each player has, then the constraint on the amount of time that the players of the different coalitions have is $\sum_{S \in \mathcal{P}(N)} \delta_S \chi^S = x$. Under this interpretation, $u(x)$ is the maximum that the players can produce together when the amount of time available to each player i is x_i.

Note that the function u is well defined: the set

$$\left\{ \sum_{S \in \mathcal{P}(N)} \delta_S \chi^S = x, \delta_S \geq 0 \quad \forall S \subseteq N \right\}$$

is not empty since it contains the vector $(\delta_S)_{S \in \mathcal{P}(N)}$ that is defined by

$$\delta_S := \begin{cases} x_i & S = \{i\}, \\ 0 & |S| \geq 2. \end{cases} \tag{18.89}$$

The function u is defined to be the production function of every player:

$$u_i(x) := u(x), \quad \forall i \in N. \tag{18.90}$$

A useful property of the function u is:

Lemma 18.38 $u(x + y) \geq u(x) + u(y)$ *for every* $x, y \in \mathbb{R}^N_+$.

Proof: Denote by $\alpha = (\alpha_T)_{T \in \mathcal{P}(N)}$ the weight vector at which the maximum is attained in the definition of $u(x)$,

$$u(x) = \sum_{T \subseteq N} \alpha_T v(T), \quad \alpha_T \geq 0 \ \forall T \subseteq N, \quad \sum_{T \subseteq N} \alpha_T \chi^T = x,$$

and by $\beta = (\beta_T)_{T \in \mathcal{P}(N)}$ the weight vector at which the maximum is attained in the definition of $u(y)$,

$$u(y) = \sum_{T \subseteq N} \beta_T v(T), \quad \beta_T \geq 0 \ \forall T \subseteq N, \quad \sum_{T \subseteq N} \beta_T \chi^T = y.$$

Denote

$$\gamma_T := \alpha_T + \beta_T.$$

Since for every coalition T, $\alpha_T, \beta_T \geq 0$, it follows that $\gamma_T \geq 0$. Moreover,

$$\sum_{T \subseteq N} \gamma_T \chi^T = \sum_{T \subseteq N} \alpha_T \chi^T + \sum_{T \subseteq N} \beta_T \chi^T = x + y.$$

We therefore have that $\gamma = (\gamma_T)_{T \subseteq N}$ is one of the elements in the maximization in the definition of $u(x + y)$, and therefore

$$u(x + y) \geq \sum_{T \subseteq N} \gamma_T v(T) = \sum_{T \subseteq N} \alpha_T v(T) + \sum_{T \subseteq N} \beta_T v(T)$$

$$= u(x) + u(y), \tag{18.91}$$

which is what we wanted to show. □

The production function u is a homogeneous function: for all $\alpha > 0$ and all $x \in \mathbb{R}^N_+$,

$$u(\alpha x) = \alpha u(x) \tag{18.92}$$

(check that this is true). Using this fact and Lemma 18.38 we deduce the following corollary.

Corollary 18.39 *The production function u defined in Equation (18.88) is a concave function.*

The market we have constructed is therefore the market in which:

- The set of players is N.
- The set of commodities is N.
- The initial endowment of player i is $a_i = \chi^{\{i\}}$.
- The production function $u_i(x)$ is the same for all players $i \in N$, and is given by Equation (18.88).

This market is called the *direct market* corresponding to the coalitional game $(N; v)$. The definition of a market game requires the production function to be continuous and concave. The concavity of the function u follows from Corollary 18.39 while the proof of its continuity is left to the reader (Exercise 18.40).

Step 2: $u(\chi^S) = v(S)$ for every coalition S.
For $x = \chi^S$, Equation (18.88) is equivalent to the definition of $\widehat{v}(S)$ (see Equation (18.84)), i.e., $u(\chi^S) = \widehat{v}(S)$. We have assumed that $(N; v)$ is a totally balanced game, and therefore by Theorem 18.36, $\widehat{v} = v$. It follows that $u(\chi^S) = v(S)$ for every coalition S.

Step 3: Deriving the market game corresponding to the market we have defined.
Having defined the market, we need to prove that the market game derived from it, denoted by $(N; w)$, is the coalitional game $(N; v)$ we started with. In other words, we need to prove that $w(S) = v(S)$ for every $S \subseteq N$, where $w(S)$ is given by

$$w(S) := \max \left\{ \sum_{i \in S} u(x_i) : x(S) = a(S) = \chi^S, x_i \in \mathbb{R}^N_+ \right\}. \tag{18.93}$$

We will show that $w(S) \geq v(S)$ and $w(S) \leq v(S)$ for every coalition S.
One possible allocation of $a(S)$ among the members of S is to give the entire set of commodities to one of the players, i.e., $\widehat{x} = (\widehat{x}_i)_{i \in S}$, where $\widehat{x}_{i_0} = \chi^S$ for some player $i_0 \in S$ and $\widehat{x}_i = \vec{0}$ for every $i \in S \setminus \{i_0\}$, where $\vec{0}$ is the vector in $\mathbb{R}^L_+$ all of whose coordinates are 0. By Step 2 this leads to

$$w(S) \geq \sum_{i \in S} u(\widehat{x}_i) = u(\chi^S) = v(S). \tag{18.94}$$

To prove that $w(S) \leq v(S)$, let $x^* = (x_i^*)_{i \in S}$ be an allocation under which the maximum in the definition of $w(S)$ is attained. By Lemma 18.38 (generalized to any finite number of sums), and by Step 2,

$$w(S) = \sum_{i \in S} u(x_i^*) \leq u\left(\sum_{i \in S} x_i^*\right) = u(\chi^S) = v(S). \tag{18.95}$$

This completes the proof of Theorem 18.37. □

Theorems 18.31 and 18.37 imply the following theorem.

Theorem 18.40 *A coalitional game $(N; v)$ is a market game if and only if it is totally balanced.*

18.5) Additive games

In this section we study a family of coalitional games called *additive games* (also called *inessential games*), and show how they are related to totally balanced games.

Definition 18.41 *A coalitional game $(N; v)$ is additive if*

$$v(S) = \sum_{i \in S} v(i) \tag{18.96}$$

for every nonempty coalition S.

Theorem 18.42 *Every additive game is totally balanced.*

Proof: We will show that for every coalition S, the vector $x = (x_i)_{i \in S}$ defined by $x_i = v(i)$ is in the core of the subgame $(S; v)$, and therefore the core of every subgame is nonempty; hence the game is totally balanced.

For every coalition $R \subseteq S$,

$$x(R) = \sum_{i \in R} x_i = v(R), \tag{18.97}$$

and therefore the vector x is coalitionally rational. By plugging $R = S$ into Equation (18.97), we deduce that it is also an efficient vector in the game $(S; v)$. This implies that x is indeed in the core of the game $(S; v)$. □

Theorem 18.43 *Let $(N; v)$ and $(N; u)$ be totally balanced games over the same set of players. Define a coalitional game $(N; w)$ by*

$$w(S) = \min\{v(S), u(S)\}, \quad \forall S \subseteq N. \tag{18.98}$$

Then $(N; w)$ is also a totally balanced game.

Proof: Let $S \subseteq N$ be a nonempty coalition. We will prove that the core of the game $(S; w)$ is nonempty. Suppose without loss of generality that $u(S) \leq v(S)$, and therefore $w(S) = u(S)$. Since the game $(N; u)$ is totally balanced, the core of the subgame $(S; u)$ is nonempty. Let $x \in C(S; u)$ be an imputation in the core of this game. We will show that $x \in C(S; w)$. Since x is an imputation in $(S; u)$,

$$x(S) = u(S) = w(S). \tag{18.99}$$

Since x is a coalitionally rational imputation in the game $(S; u)$, for every $R \subseteq S$,

$$x(R) \geq u(R) \geq w(R). \tag{18.100}$$

Hence x is coalitionally rational in $(S; w)$, and therefore $x \in C(S; w)$; the core of the game $(S; w)$ is nonempty, which is what we wanted to show.   □

Theorem 18.44 *A coalitional game* $(N; v)$ *is totally balanced if and only if it is the minimum of a finite number of additive games.*

Proof: Step 1: The minimum of a finite number of additive games is a totally balanced game.
By Theorem 18.42 every additive game is totally balanced, and using Theorem 18.43, one obtains by induction over k that the minimum of k totally balanced games is totally balanced.

We now show that every totally balanced game is the minimum of a finite number of additive games. Let $(N; v)$ be a totally balanced game. We will define, for every coalition $S \subseteq N$, a corresponding additive game $(N; v^S)$, and we will show that $v = \min_{S \subseteq N} v^S$.

Step 2: The definition of the games $(N; v^S)$ for $S \subseteq N$.
Since $(N; v)$ is a totally balanced game, for every coalition S, the core of $(S; v)$ is nonempty. Choose an imputation $x^S = (x_i^S)_{i \in S} \in C(S; v)$. In particular,

$$x_i^S \geq v(i), \quad \forall i \in S, \tag{18.101}$$

and

$$\sum_{i \in S} x_i^S = v(S). \tag{18.102}$$

Denote $M = 2 \max\{|v(S)|, S \subseteq N\}$. For every coalition $S \subseteq N$, expand the vector x^S to a vector in $\mathbb{R}^N$ by defining

$$x_i^S = M, \quad \forall i \notin S. \tag{18.103}$$

Note that for $S = \emptyset$, one has $x_i^\emptyset = M$, for every player $i \in N$.
For every coalition $S \subseteq N$, construct an additive game $(N; v^S)$ using the vector x^S, as follows:

$$v^S(R) := \sum_{i \in R} x_i^S, \quad R \subseteq N, R \neq \emptyset, \tag{18.104}$$

$$v^S(\emptyset) := 0. \tag{18.105}$$

By its definition, the game $(N; v^S)$ is additive.

Step 3: $v^S(R) \geq v(R)$ for every pair of coalitions S and R in N.
Consider the following chain of equalities and inequalities:

$$v^S(R) = \sum_{i \in R} x_i^S \tag{18.106}$$

$$= \sum_{i \in R \cap S} x_i^S + \sum_{i \in R \setminus S} x_i^S \tag{18.107}$$

$$\geq v(R \cap S) + \sum_{i \in R \setminus S} x_i^S \tag{18.108}$$

$$= v(R \cap S) + |R \setminus S| M. \tag{18.109}$$

Inequality (18.108) follows from the fact that x^S is in the core of the subgame $(S; v)$, and Equation (18.109) follows from the fact that $x_i^S = M$ for every $i \notin S$.

If $R \subseteq S$, then $R \cap S = R$ and $|R \setminus S| = 0$, and it follows from Equations (18.106)–(18.109) that $v^S(R) \geq v(R)$. If $R \nsubseteq S$ then $|R \setminus S| \geq 1$. By the choice of M, one has $M \geq v(R) - v(R \cap S)$, and, therefore,

$$v^S(R) \geq v(R \cap S) + |R \setminus S| M \geq v(R \cap S) + M \geq v(R). \tag{18.110}$$

Step 4: $\min_{S \subseteq N} v^S(R) = v(R)$ for every coalition $R \subseteq N$.
From Step 3 we know that $\min_{S \subseteq N} v^S(R) \geq v(R)$, and by Equations (18.102) and (18.104),

$$v^R(R) = \sum_{i \in R} x_i^R = v(R). \tag{18.111}$$

Therefore, we also have that $\min_{S \subseteq N} v^S(R) \leq v^R(R) = v(R)$. We deduce that $\min_{S \subseteq N} v^S(R) = v(R)$, which completes the proof. $\square$

By Theorems 18.40 and 18.44, we deduce the following corollary.

Corollary 18.45 *A coalitional game $(N; v)$ is a market game if and only if it is the minimum of a finite number of additive games.*

18.6 The consistency property of the core

Consider the three-player coalitional game appearing in Example 18.4:

$$v(1) = v(2) = v(3) = 0, \quad v(1,2) = v(2,3) = 1, \quad v(1,3) = 2, \quad v(1,2,3) = 3.$$

As we saw in Figure 18.1, the imputation $(2, \frac{1}{2}, \frac{1}{2})$ is in the core of this game. Suppose that the players decide to divide the worth of the grand coalition, 3, on the basis of this vector. Suppose now that Player 3 leaves with his share, $\frac{1}{2}$. Can the issue of dividing the total share of $2\frac{1}{2}$ by Players 1 and 2 be open to rediscussion? To answer this question, we will attempt to describe the new situation between players $\{1, 2\}$ as a new game. What is this new game? What is its core? Is $(2, \frac{1}{2})$ in it?

One way to define the new game is as follows.

Definition 18.46 *Let* $(N; v)$ *be a coalitional game, let S be a nonempty coalition, and let x be an efficient vector in* $\mathbb{R}^N$ *(so that* $x(N) = v(N)$*). The Davis–Maschler reduced game to S relative to x, denoted by* $(S; w_S^x)$*, is the coalitional game with the set of players S and a coalitional function*

$$
w_S^x(R) = \begin{cases} \max_{Q \subseteq N \setminus S}(v(R \cup Q) - x(Q)) & \emptyset \neq R \subset S, \\ x(S) & R = S, \\ 0 & R = \emptyset. \end{cases} \tag{18.112}
$$

The idea behind this definition is the following. $w_S^x(S)$, the sum that the players in S divide among themselves, should equal $x(S)$, which is the total sum that they receive according to x. Since we are defining a coalitional game, we must require that $w_S^x(\emptyset) = 0$. For each coalition R, $\emptyset \neq R \subset S$, when the members of R come to assess what their coalition is worth, they may add partners outside S, as long as they give these partners what they are allocated according to the original vector x. If they choose the set of partners Q, they will generate a worth $v(R \cup Q)$, will pay the members of Q the amount $x(Q)$, and hence be left with $v(R \cup Q) - x(Q)$. The definition assumes that the members of R will choose those partners so as to maximize this amount.

The amount $w_S^x(R)$ is a virtual worth associated with each coalition separately: if two coalitions R_1 and R_2 try to realize their worths under w_S^x and choose as partners Q_1 and Q_2, they may discover that Q_1 and Q_2 are not disjoint sets, which would mean that at least one of the coalitions will be unable to realize its worth. For this reason, it is important in every application to consider carefully the details of the reduced game, and check whether it fits the intended application.

Definition 18.47 *A set solution concept* φ *satisfies the* Davis–Maschler reduced game property *if for every coalitional game* $(N; v)$*, for every nonempty coalition* $S \subseteq N$*, and for every vector* $x \in \varphi(N; v)$*,*

$$
(x_i)_{i \in S} \in \varphi(S; w_S^x). \tag{18.113}
$$

The reduced game property is a consistency property: if the players believe in the solution concept φ, then every set of players S considering redistributing $\sum_{i \in S} x_i$ among its members will refrain from doing so, because the vector $(x_i)_{i \in S}$ is in the solution φ of the game reduced to S.

Theorem 18.48 *The core satisfies the Davis–Maschler reduced game property.*

Proof: Let x be a point in the core of the coalitional game $(N; v)$, and let S be a nonempty coalition. We will show that $(x_i)_{i \in S}$ is in the core of $(S; w_S^x)$. To do so, we need to show that $x(R) \geq w_S^x(R)$ for every $\emptyset \neq R \subset S$, and that $w_S^x(S) = x(S)$.

The second requirement is satisfied by the definition of the Davis–Maschler reduced game. To prove the first requirement, let $R \subset S$ be a nonempty coalition. We want to show that $x(R) \geq w_S^x(R)$. By the definition of $w_S^x(R)$, there exists a coalition $Q \subseteq N \setminus S$ such that $w_S^x(R) = v(R \cup Q) - x(Q)$. Then we have

$$
w_S^x(R) = v(R \cup Q) - x(Q) = v(R \cup Q) - x(R \cup Q) + x(R). \tag{18.114}
$$

The vector x is in the core of $(N; v)$, hence $x(R \cup Q) \geq v(R \cup Q)$, and therefore

$$x(R) \geq w_S^x(R), \tag{18.115}$$

which is what we wanted to prove. □

Given a solution concept φ, we can ask the converse question: let $x \in \mathbb{R}^N$ be an efficient vector in the game $(N; v)$. If it is known that $(x_i, x_j) \in \varphi(\{i,j\}; w_{\{i,j\}}^x)$ for every pair of players $i \neq j$, does it follow that $x \in \varphi(N; v)$. If the answer to this question is always affirmative, the solution concept φ is said to satisfy the converse reduced game property.

Definition 18.49 *A set-valued solution concept φ satisfies the Davis–Maschler converse reduced game property if for every coalitional game $(N; v)$, every preimputation $x \in X^0(N; v)$ that satisfies*

$$(x_i, x_j) \in \varphi\left(\{i,j\}; w_{\{i,j\}}^x\right), \quad \forall i, j \in N, i \neq j \tag{18.116}$$

also satisfies $x \in \varphi(N; v)$.

Having this property satisfied is useful in many cases, when one is seeking to calculate the solution φ to some game by considering two-player games (which are simpler than games involving more than two players).

Theorem 18.50 *The core satisfies the Davis–Maschler converse reduced game property.*

Proof: Let $(N; v)$ be a coalitional game, and let $x \in X^0(N; v)$ be a preimputation satisfying, for every pair of players $i \neq j$,

$$(x_i, x_j) \in \mathcal{C}\left(\{i,j\}; w_{\{i,j\}}^x\right). \tag{18.117}$$

To show that x is in the core of the game $(N; v)$ we need to prove that $x(S) \geq v(S)$ for every coalition $S \subseteq N$. Note that $x(\emptyset) = 0 = v(\emptyset)$. Since x is a preimputation, $x(N) = v(N)$. Let $S \subset N$ be a nonempty coalition. Let $i \in S$ and $j \notin S$. Since (x_i, x_j) is in the core of $(\{i,j\}; w_{\{i,j\}}^x)$,

$$x_i \geq w_{\{i,j\}}^x(i). \tag{18.118}$$

By the definition of $w_{\{i,j\}}^x$,

$$x_i \geq w_{\{i,j\}}^x(i) = \max_{Q \subseteq N \setminus \{i,j\}} (v(\{i\} \cup Q) - x(Q)). \tag{18.119}$$

Set $Q = S \setminus \{i\}$. Then Q contains neither i nor j, and it is therefore one of the elements of the maximization in Equation (18.119). This further yields

$$x_i \geq v(\{i\} \cup Q) - x(Q) = v(S) - x(S \setminus \{i\}). \tag{18.120}$$

We deduce from this that

$$x(S) = x_i + x(S \setminus \{i\}) \geq v(S), \tag{18.121}$$

which is what we needed to show. □

18.7 Convex games

The class of convex games was first defined in Shapley [1971].

Definition 18.51 *A coalitional game $(N; v)$ is* convex *if for every pair of coalitions S and T the following holds:*

$$v(S) + v(T) \leq v(S \cup T) + v(S \cap T). \qquad (18.122)$$

Recall that a superadditive game (Definition 17.8 on page 721) is a coalitional game in which Equation (18.122) holds for every pair of disjoint coalitions S and T, while in a convex game this equation holds for every pair of coalitions S and T. It follows that every convex game is superadditive. This means that the set of convex games is a subset of the set of superadditive games. In fact, it is a proper subset of the set of superadditive games (Exercise 18.45).

The corresponding definition for cost games is the following.

Definition 18.52 *A cost game $(N; c)$ is* convex *if for every pair of coalitions S and T the following holds:*

$$c(S) + c(T) \geq c(S \cup T) + c(S \cap T). \qquad (18.123)$$

Remark 18.53 *If $(N; v)$ is a convex game then for every coalition $S \subseteq N$, the subgame $(S; v)$ restricted to the players in S is also a convex game (Exercise 18.46).*   ◆

Convex games are characterized by the property that players have an incentive to join large coalitions. The mathematical formulation of this idea is expressed in the following theorem.

Theorem 18.54 *For any coalitional game $(N; v)$, the following conditions are equivalent:*

1. *$(N; v)$ is a convex game.*
2. *For every $S \subseteq T \subseteq N$ and every $R \subseteq N \backslash T$,*

$$v(S \cup R) - v(S) \leq v(T \cup R) - v(T). \qquad (18.124)$$

3. *For every $S \subseteq T \subseteq N$ and every $i \in N \backslash T$,*

$$v(S \cup \{i\}) - v(S) \leq v(T \cup \{i\}) - v(T). \qquad (18.125)$$

In words, the theorem states that a coalitional game is convex if and only if the marginal contribution of any fixed player i, or of any fixed set of players R, to coalition S rises as more players join S.

Proof: We first prove that Condition 1 implies Condition 2. Suppose that $(N; v)$ is a convex game, that S and T are two coalitions satisfying $S \subseteq T \subseteq N$, and that $R \subseteq N \backslash T$. By Condition 1 the game is convex, and therefore

$$v(S \cup R) + v(T) \leq v(S \cup T \cup R) + v((S \cup R) \cap T). \qquad (18.126)$$

Since $S \cup R \cup T = T \cup R$ and $(S \cup R) \cap T = S$ we have

$$v(S \cup R) + v(T) \leq v(T \cup R) + v(S), \qquad (18.127)$$

Figure 18.6 The sets S and T in the proof of Theorem 18.54

and hence

$$v(S \cup R) - v(S) \leq v(T \cup R) - v(T), \tag{18.128}$$

which is what we needed to show.

That Condition 2 implies Condition 3 is clear: set $R = \{i\}$.

Finally, we show that Condition 3 implies Condition 1. Let S and T be two coalitions. If $S \subseteq T$, then Equation (18.122) holds with equality (explain why). Suppose now that S is not contained in T. Define $A := S \cap T$ and $C := S \setminus T$ (see Figure 18.6). Since S is not contained in T, the set C is nonempty. Let $C = \{i_1, i_2, \ldots, i_k\}$.

Since $T \supseteq A$, $T \cup \{i_1, \ldots, i_l\} \supseteq A \cup \{i_1, \ldots, i_l\}$ for every $l = 0, 1, \ldots, k-1$. Moreover, $i_{l+1} \notin T \cup \{i_1, \ldots, i_l\}$. By Condition 3, for every $l = 0, 1, \ldots, k-1$,

$$v(T \cup \{i_1, \ldots, i_l, i_{l+1}\}) - v(T \cup \{i_1, \ldots, i_l\})$$
$$\geq v(A \cup \{i_1, \ldots, i_l, i_{l+1}\}) - v(A \cup \{i_1, \ldots, i_l\}).$$

Summing this equation for $l = 0, 1, \ldots, k-1$ yields

$$v(T \cup C) - v(T) \geq v(A \cup C) - v(A). \tag{18.129}$$

Since $T \cup C = T \cup S$, $A \cup C = S$, and $A = S \cap T$, we obtain

$$v(S \cup T) + v(S \cap T) \geq v(S) + v(T). \tag{18.130}$$

Since this inequality holds for every two coalitions S and T, the game is convex. This concludes the proof of Theorem 18.54. $\qquad\square$

We next show that the core of a convex game is nonempty. We will show this by identifying a particular imputation that is in the core (actually, we will identify several imputations in the core).

Theorem 18.55 *Let $(N; v)$ be a convex game, and let x be the imputation*

$$x_1 = v(1), \tag{18.131}$$

$$x_2 = v(1, 2) - v(1), \tag{18.132}$$

$$\ldots$$

$$x_n = v(1, 2, \ldots, n) - v(1, 2, \ldots, n-1). \tag{18.133}$$

Then the vector x is in the core of $(N; v)$.

Proof: First, note that x is an efficient vector:

$$\sum_{i \in N} x_i = v(1) + (v(1,2) - v(1)) + (v(1,2,3) - v(1,2)) + \cdots + (v(1,2,\ldots,n)$$

$$- v(1,2,\ldots,n-1))$$
$$= v(1,2,\ldots,n) = v(N).$$

We next show that $x(S) \geq v(S)$ for every coalition $S \subseteq N$. Let $S = \{i_1, i_2, \ldots, i_k\}$ be a coalition and suppose that $i_1 < i_2 < \cdots < i_k$. Then $\{i_1, i_2, \ldots, i_{j-1}\} \subseteq \{1, 2, \ldots, i_j - 1\}$ for every $j \in \{1, 2, \ldots, k\}$. Theorem 18.54 implies that

$$v(1,2,\ldots,i_j) - v(1,2,\ldots,i_j - 1) \geq v(i_1,i_2,\ldots,i_j) - v(i_1,i_2,\ldots,i_{j-1}).$$

Hence

$$x(S) = \sum_{j=1}^{k} x_{i_j} \tag{18.134}$$

$$= (v(1,2,\ldots,i_1) - v(1,2,\ldots,i_1 - 1)) + (v(1,2,\ldots,i_2)$$
$$- v(1,2,\ldots,i_2 - 1)) + \cdots + (v(1,2,\ldots,i_k) - v(1,2,\ldots,i_k - 1)) \tag{18.135}$$

$$\geq (v(i_1) - v(\emptyset)) + (v(i_1,i_2) - v(i_1)) + \cdots + (v(i_1,i_2,\ldots,i_k) - v(i_1,i_2,\ldots,i_{k-1})) \tag{18.136}$$

$$= v(i_1,i_2,\ldots,i_k) = v(S), \tag{18.137}$$

as claimed. $\square$

Remark 18.56 *In the proof of Theorem 18.55, we proved that*

$$(v(1), v(1,2) - v(1), \ldots, v(1,2,\ldots,n) - v(1,2,\ldots,n-1))$$

is an imputation in the core of the coalitional game $(N;v)$. In that case, we considered the players according to the ordering $1, 2, \ldots, n$. But the same result obtains under any ordering of the players. In other words, given any ordering $\pi = (i_1, i_2, \ldots, i_n)$ of the players, the following is an imputation in the core of the game $(N;v)$:

$$w^{\pi} := (v(i_1), v(i_1, i_2) - v(i_1), v(i_1, i_2, i_3) - v(i_1, i_2), \ldots, v(N) - v(N \setminus \{i_n\})).$$

$$\tag{18.138}$$

This imputation corresponds to the following description: the players enter a room one after the other, according to the ordering π. Each player receives the marginal contribution that he provides to the coalition of players who have entered the room before him. The imputation that is arrived at through this process is w^{π}, and it is in the core of the game.   ♦

Definition 18.57 *The convex hull of the imputations $\{w^{\pi} : \pi$ is a permutation of $N\}$ is called the* Weber set *of the coalitional game $(N;v)$.*

Since the core is a convex set, Theorem 18.55 and Remark 18.56 imply the following theorem.

Theorem 18.58 *In a convex game, the core contains the Weber set.*

Remark 18.59 *Using the Separating Hyperplane Theorem (Theorem 24.39 on page 990), one can prove that the Weber set always contains the core (see Weber [1988] and Derks [1992]). It therefore follows that in a convex game the core coincides with the Weber set.* ◆

The Weber set is a polytope in which there are at most $n!$ vertices, equal to the number of permutations of n players. When $w^{\pi_1} = w^{\pi_2}$ for two different permutations, the number of vertices in this polytope is less than $n!$.

Theorem 18.55 has implications for the geometry of the core in convex games. The core is defined as the intersection of the half-spaces $\{x \in \mathbb{R}^N : x(S) \geq v(S)\}$ for each coalition S, and the hyperplane $\{x \in \mathbb{R}^N : x(N) = v(N)\}$. There are games in which the core does not touch some of the hyperplanes $\{x \in \mathbb{R}^N : x(S) = v(S)\}$ defining the half-spaces (see, for example, Figure 18.3, in which the core does not touch the hyperplane $x_1 = 0$). As the next theorem shows, this cannot happen in convex games.

Theorem 18.60 *Let $(N; v)$ be a convex game. Then for every coalition S there exists an imputation $x \in \mathcal{C}(N; v)$ satisfying $x(S) = v(S)$.*

Proof: Order the players such that the elements of S appear first. In other words, denote $S = \{i_1, i_2, \ldots, i_k\}$ and consider the following ordering, in which the players in S appear before the players not in S:

$$\pi = (i_1, i_2, \ldots, i_s, i_{s+1}, \ldots, i_n). \tag{18.139}$$

The imputation w^π is given by

$$w^\pi = (v(i_1), v(i_1, i_2) - v(i_1), \cdots, v(N) - v(N \setminus \{i_n\}))$$

and it satisfies

$$w^\pi(S) = v(S). \tag{18.140}$$

As argued in Remark 18.56, w^π is in the core, thus completing the proof. □

We have so far presented two families of games in which the core is nonempty. Using the Bondareva–Shapley Theorem we proved that the core of a market game is never empty. In convex games we explicitly find points that are in the core. The next section deals with another family of games with a nonempty core, and we will again explicitly find points in the core.

18.8 Spanning tree games

Spanning tree games were introduced in Section 17.1.7 (page 716). Denote by $\mathbb{R}_{++} := (0, \infty)$ the set of positive real numbers.

Definition 18.61 *A spanning tree system is a vector (N, V, E, v^0, a), where:*

- $N = \{1, 2, \ldots, n\}$ *is the set of players.*

- (V, E) *is a finite connected (undirected) graph*[5] *where the set of vertices is* $V = N \cup \{v^0\}$ *and the set of edges is* E. *The vertex* v^0 *is called the* initial vertex *or the* source.
- $a : E \to \mathbb{R}_{++}$ *is a function associating each edge* $e \in E$ *with a cost* $a(e)$ *that is greater than* 0.

Example 18.62 Figure 18.7 depicts a spanning tree system with four players, Detroit, Lansing, Grand Rapids, and Ann Arbor. The graph has five vertices and five edges. The cost associated with each edge is indicated near that edge, and the player associated with each vertex is similarly indicated near the vertex.

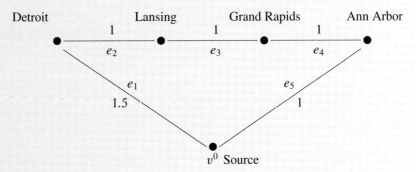

Figure 18.7 The spanning tree system in Example 18.62

A spanning tree system can describe various networks, such as a road network system connecting towns, or a computer network system. Under this interpretation, every player is either a town or a computer that needs to be connected to a source, which is a central city or a central computer connected to the Internet. The cost associated with each edge is the cost of constructing or maintaining the corresponding connection in the network.

Every spanning tree system can be associated with a *spanning tree game* $(N; c)$, in which the set of players is N and $c(S)$ is the minimal cost of connecting all the members of S to the source v^0, defined as follows. For each coalition S, a spanning graph for S is a collection of edges that contains, for each i in S, a path leading from vertex i to the source v^0. The total cost of this collection is the sum of costs of the edges in the collection. From among all the spanning graphs for S we choose a spanning graph whose cost is minimal (there may be several such collections). This graph must be a tree, i.e., an acyclic graph (why?). We will denote this spanning tree by (V^S, E^S) and call it the *minimal-cost spanning tree of coalition* S. The total cost of this collection is the cost $c(S)$ of coalition S in the game $(N; c)$.

---

5 Directed graphs were defined in Definition 3.2 (page 41). An *undirected* graph is a pair (V, E) where V is a finite set of vertices and E is a set of undirected edges; each edge is a subset of V of size 2.

Example 18.62 (*Continued*) The following table (Figure 18.8) depicts several coalitions, the minimal-cost spanning tree corresponding to each coalition, and the cost of constructing the tree.

Coalition	Minimal-cost tree	Total cost
{Detroit}	e_1	1.5
{Grand Rapids}	e_4, e_5	2
{Detroit, Lansing}	e_1, e_2	2.5
{Detroit, Ann Arbor}	e_1, e_5	2.5
{Detroit, Grand Rapids}	e_1, e_2, e_3	3.5
{Detroit, Grand Rapids}	e_1, e_4, e_5	3.5
{Detroit, Grand Rapids, Lansing, Ann Arbor}	e_2, e_3, e_4, e_5	4

Figure 18.8 The minimal-cost tree and its total cost for several coalitions in Example 18.62

The minimal-cost spanning tree for the coalition {Grand Rapids} contains Ann Arbor; Ann Arbor is therefore a "free rider," i.e., it gains connection to the source despite not being a member of the coalition. As the case of the coalition {Detroit} shows, the set of edges in the graph (V^S, E^S) may be disjoint from the set of edges in the graph (V^N, E^N). ◄

A connected graph over a set V of $n + 1$ vertices is a tree (i.e., an acyclic graph) if and only if it contains n edges (Exercise 18.55). The minimal-cost tree (V^N, E^N) therefore contains n edges. Such a tree contains a path from each vertex i to the source. Denote by $e(i)$ the first edge in the path from vertex i to the source. Then $e(i) \neq e(j)$ for every pair of distinct vertices i and j, and hence $E^N = \{e(i), i \in N\}$ and $V^N = N \cup \{v^0\}$. In Example 18.62, $e(\text{Detroit}) = e_2$, $e(\text{Lansing}) = e_3$, $e(\text{Grand Rapids}) = e_4$, and $e(\text{Ann Arbor}) = e_5$.

Theorem 18.63 *Let (N, V, E, v^0, a) be a spanning tree system. Then the core of the corresponding spanning tree game is nonempty. Moreover, the imputation x defined by*

$$x_i := a(e(i)), \quad \forall i \in N \tag{18.141}$$

is in the core of the game, where for each player $i \in N$, $e(i)$ is the first edge on the path from vertex i to the source in the minimal[6] cost spanning tree-for the coalition N.

Proof: We will show that x is efficient and coalitionally rational. Since $E^N = \{e(i)\}_{i \in N}$, one has $c(N) = \sum_{i \in N} a(e(i)) = x(N)$, and therefore x is an efficient imputation. We next show that $x(S) \leq c(S)$ for every coalition S. Let S be a coalition. Consider the set of edges

$$E^* = E^S \cup \{e(i): i \in N \backslash S\}. \tag{18.142}$$

---

6 Since the definition of $\{e(i)\}_{i \in N}$ depends on the minimal-cost spanning tree, when there are several minimal-cost spanning trees, one particular minimal-cost spanning tree needs to be chosen, and with respect to that tree one defines $\{e(i)\}_{i \in N}$. The theorem holds true for any choice of a minimal-cost spanning tree.

Coalition S	E^S	$\{e(i): i \notin S\}$	E^*
{Detroit}	e_1	e_3, e_4, e_5	$\{e_1, e_3, e_4, e_5\}$
{Grand Rapids}	e_4, e_5	e_2, e_3, e_5	$\{e_2, e_3, e_4, e_5\}$
{Detroit, Lansing}	e_1, e_2	e_4, e_5	$\{e_1, e_2, e_4, e_5\}$
{Detroit, Ann Arbor}	e_1, e_5	e_3, e_4	$\{e_1, e_3, e_4, e_5\}$
{Detroit, Grand Rapids}	e_1, e_2, e_3	e_3, e_5	$\{e_1, e_2, e_3, e_5\}$
{Detroit, Grand Rapids, Lansing, Ann Arbor}	e_2, e_3, e_4, e_5	$\emptyset$	$\{e_2, e_3, e_4, e_5\}$

Figure 18.9 The set of edges E^* for several coalitions in Example 18.62

This set contains all the edges of the minimal-cost spanning tree of coalition S, and for every player who is not in S, it contains the edge emanating from him in the direction of the source in the minimal-cost spanning tree of the coalition N.

The table in Figure 18.8 illustrates the set E^* in the spanning tree system depicted in Figure 18.9 for various coalitions.

The coalition {Detroit, Grand Rapids} has two minimal-cost spanning trees. We have chosen one of them arbitrarily.

We will show that (V, E^*) is a spanning graph; in such a graph, every vertex is connected to the source.[7] Indeed, since the collection of edges E^* contains all the edges of E^S, and since (V^S, E^S) is the minimal-cost spanning tree for S, every vertex in S is connected to the source by a path in E^S (and therefore by a path in E^*). Let v_1 be a player in $N \setminus S$. The edge $e(v_1)$ is in E^*, and connects v_1 to another vertex in the graph, v_2. If $v_2 = v^0$ is the source, v_1 is connected to the source by an edge in E^*. If v_2 is a player in S, then since every vertex in S is connected to the source by a path in E^*, v_1 is also connected to the source by a path in E^*. If not, then neither of these possibilities holds, the edge $e(v_2)$ is in E^*, and it connects v_2 to vertex v_3. Continue the process with v_3. In the k-th stage of the process, a sequence of vertices $v_1, v_2, v_3, \ldots, v_k$, which are players in $N \setminus S$, is obtained such that the edge $e(v_l)$ is in E^* and connects v_l with v_{l+1} for every $l = 1, 2, \ldots, k - 1$. If v_k is the source, or is contained in S, then v_1 is connected to the source via edges in E^*. Otherwise, the sequence can be extended by adding the vertex v_{k+1} that $e(v_k)$ leads to from v_k.

Since the graph has a finite number of vertices, either this process has an end, or is cyclical. If the process is cyclical, there exist positive integers l and k, $l < k$, such that $v_k = v_l$. Then the set of edges $\{e(v_l), e(v_{l+1}), \ldots, e(v_{k-1})\}$ contained in E^N is a cycle, in contradiction to E^N being a tree. The process must therefore end, meaning that for some k the vertex v_k is either the source or is in S. Since every vertex in S is connected to the source by edges in E^*, it follows that the vertex v_1 is connected to the source by edges in E^*.

---

7 In fact, $(V; E^*)$ is a spanning tree, because it is a connected graph containing n edges and $n + 1$ vertices, and hence a tree (Exercise 18.55).

Since the graph (V, E^*) is a spanning tree for the coalition N, its cost is greater than or equal to $c(N)$. The cost of the edges of this graph equal $c(S) + \sum_{i \notin S} a(e(i))$, and, therefore,

$$x(N) = c(N) \leq c(S) + \sum_{i \notin S} a(e(i)) = c(S) + \sum_{i \notin S} x_i. \tag{18.143}$$

This implies,

$$x(S) = \sum_{i \in S} x_i \leq c(S), \tag{18.144}$$

which is what we needed to show. $\qquad \square$

18.9 Flow games

In the previous section we studied spanning tree games in which the worth of each coalition is given by the cost of the minimal-cost spanning tree connecting all the members of the coalition to the source. Another class of games derived from graphs is the class of flow games. A flow game is given by a directed graph in which every edge has a maximal capacity and is controlled by one of the players. The graph contains two distinguished vertices, a source and a sink, and the goal of the players is to direct as great a flow as possible from the source to the sink.

Definition 18.64 *A* flow problem *is described by a vector* $F = (V, E, v^0, v^1, c, N, I)$ *where:*

- *(V, E) is a directed graph: V is a set of vertices, and E is a set of directed edges, i.e., a set of pairs of vertices $(v, v') \in V \times V$.*
- *$v^0, v^1 \in V$ are two distinguished vertices. v^0 is called the* source *and v^1 is called the* sink.
- *$c : E \to \mathbb{R}_{++}$ is a function associating each edge with a positive number, which represents the maximal* capacity *of the edge.*
- *N is the set of players.*
- *$I : E \to N$ is a function associating each edge with a player who controls it.*

A flow problem can be thought of as follows. The directed graph describes a toll road system (consisting of one-way roads) leading from one point (a residential area) to another point (a commercial district). Each road has a maximal capacity, and different roads are controlled by different operators.

Example 18.65 Figure 18.10 depicts a flow problem. In this problem, the set of players is $N = \{1, 2, 3\}$, and each edge is labeled (in an adjacent circle) with the player who controls that edge, along with its maximal capacity.

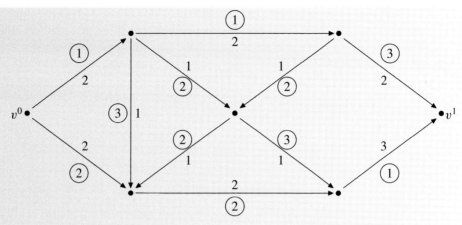

Figure 18.10 The flow problem in Example 18.65

◀

Definition 18.66 *Let $F = (V, E, v^0, v^1, c, N, I)$ be a flow problem. A* flow *is a function $f : E \to \mathbb{R}_+$ associating each edge in the graph with a positive nonnegative real number and satisfying the following conditions:*

1. *$f(e) \leq c(e)$ for every edge $f \in E$: the flow in each edge is not greater than the maximal capacity of the edge.*

2. *$\sum_{\{u \in V \setminus \{v\} : (u,v) \in E\}} f(u, v) = \sum_{\{u \in V \setminus \{v\} : (v,u) \in E\}} f(v, u)$ for every vertex $v \in V \setminus \{v^0, v^1\}$.*

The magnitude[8] *of a flow f, denoted by $M(f)$, is the total flow arriving at the sink:*

$$M(f) := \sum_{\{u \in V \setminus \{v^1\} : (u,v^1) \in E\}} f(u, v^1). \tag{18.145}$$

Since the capacity of each edge is finite, and because one cannot push more flow through an edge than its maximal capacity, the magnitude of the flow is bounded by $\sum_{(u,v^1) \in E} c(u, v^1)$. The flow whose magnitude is maximal (among all possible flows) is called the *maximal flow*.

Every flow problem may be described as a coalitional game in which the worth of a coalition S is the maximal amount of flow that the members of S can carry from source to sink without the assistance of players who are not members of S, i.e., the maximal magnitude in the flow problem $F_{|S} = (V, E_{|S}, v^0, v^1, c, S, I)$, where the set of players is S and the set of edges $E_{|S}$ consists of the edges in E controlled by the members of S, that is, $E_{|S} = I^{-1}(S)$.

Definition 18.67 *The coalitional game $(N; v)$ corresponding to the flow problem $F = (V, E, v^0, v^1, c, N, I)$ is the game in which the worth $v(S)$ of a coalition S is the magnitude of the maximal flow of the flow problem $F_{|S}$. A coalitional game $(N; v)$ corresponding to some flow problem is called a* flow game.

....

8 We use the term "magnitude of a flow" instead of the term "value of a flow" because the term "value" has several other meanings in the game theory literature.

Returning to our interpretation of a flow problem as a system of toll roads, and of the capacity as the maximal number of cars that can pass through a road per hour, the flow that the members of S can carry is equal to the maximal number of cars that can pass from v^0 to v^1 per hour by using only roads controlled by the members of S.

Example 18.65 (*Continued*) The flow game corresponding to the flow problem is the following game $(N; u)$ (verify!):

$$u(1) = 0, \qquad u(2) = 0, \qquad u(3) = 0,$$
$$u(1,2) = 2, \qquad u(1,3) = 2, \qquad u(2,3) = 0, \qquad u(1,2,3) = 4.$$

◀

The next theorem states that if $(N; v)$ is a flow game corresponding to a flow problem F, then $(S; v)$, the game restricted to coalition S, is the flow game corresponding to the flow problem $F_{|S}$. The proof of the theorem is left to the reader (Exercise 18.62).

Theorem 18.68 *Let* $F = (V, E, v^0, v^1, c, N, I)$ *be a flow problem, let* $(N; v)$ *be the corresponding flow game, and let* S *be a coalition. Then the flow game corresponding to* $F_{|S}$ *is* $(S; v)$.

In particular, it follows from this theorem that the subgame of a flow game is a flow game. The next theorem is the main result of this section.

Theorem 18.69 *A coalitional game is totally balanced if and only if it is a flow game.*

The theorem is proved in several steps. To prove that every totally balanced game is a flow game, we will prove that every additive game is a flow game (Theorem 18.70), and that the minimum of every two flow games is a flow game (Theorem 18.71). Since every totally balanced game is the minimum of additive games (Theorem 18.44), it follows that every totally balanced game is a flow game (Corollary 18.72). To prove the converse direction, which states that every flow game is a totally balanced game, we will make use of the Ford–Fulkerson Theorem from graph theory (Theorem 18.74).

Theorem 18.70 *Every additive game is a flow game.*

Proof: Let $a = (a_i)_{i \in N} \in \mathbb{R}^N$, and let $(N; v)$ be the additive game corresponding to a, i.e., $v(S) = \sum_{i \in S} a_i$ for every nonempty coalition S. Then $(N; v)$ is the flow game corresponding to the flow problem depicted in Figure 18.11.

This flow problem has two nodes, the source v^0 and the sink v^1, and n edges, with each edge corresponding to one player, and the capacity of the edge corresponding to player i is equal to a_i. The magnitude of the maximal flow from v^0 to v^1 that use only edges controlled by coalition S is

$$\sum_{i \in S} a_i = v(S), \tag{18.146}$$

and therefore $(N; v)$ is indeed the game corresponding to this flow problem.   □

Theorem 18.71 *The minimum of two flow games over the same set of players is a flow game.*

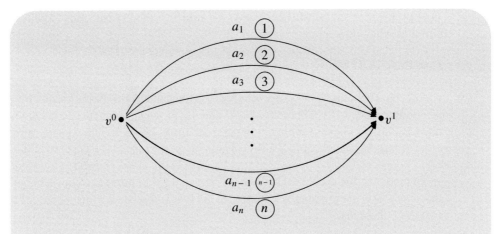

Figure 18.11 The flow problem corresponding to an additive game

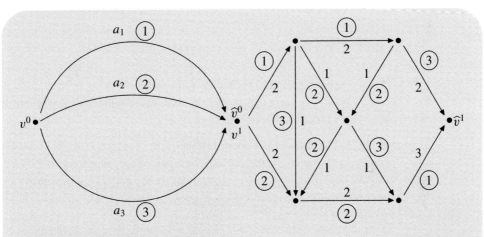

Figure 18.12 The flow problem in Figures 18.11 (with $n = 3$) and 18.10 connected in series

Proof: Let $(N; v)$ and $(N; \hat{v})$ be two flow games, and consider two flow problems corresponding to these flow games: $F = (V, E, v^0, v^1, c, N, I)$ and $\hat{F} = (\hat{V}, \hat{E}, \hat{v}^0, \hat{v}^1, \hat{c}, N, \hat{I})$. Construct a new flow problem by connecting in series these two flow problems (and identifying v^1 with $\hat{v}^0$).

If, e.g., F is the flow problem depicted in Figure 18.11 (for $n = 3$) and $\hat{F}$ is the flow problem depicted in Figure 18.10, the resulting new flow problem is depicted in Figure 18.12.

Since $v(S)$ is the magnitude of the maximal flow from v^0 to v^1 that uses only the edges controlled by members of coalition S, and $\hat{v}(S)$ is the magnitude of the maximal flow from $\hat{v}^0$ to $\hat{v}^1$ that uses only the edges controlled by members of this coalition, it follows that the magnitude of the maximal flow from v^0 to $\hat{v}^1$ that uses only the edges controlled by members of S is $\min\{v(S), \hat{v}(S)\}$. We deduce that the flow game corresponding to this flow problem is $(N; u)$, in which $u(S) = \min\{v(S), \hat{v}(S)\}$ for every coalition $S \subseteq N$, which is what we wanted to show. $\qquad\square$

Corollary 18.72 *Every totally balanced game is a flow game.*

Proof: By Theorem 18.44, every totally balanced game is the minimum of a finite number of additive games. By Theorems 18.70 and 18.71 (using induction over the number of players) the minimum of a finite number of additive games is a flow game. It follows that every totally balanced game is a flow game. $\qquad\square$

To complete the proof of Theorem 18.69, we need to prove the converse, i.e., to show that every flow game is totally balanced. This is accomplished using a new definition, and two more theorems.

Definition 18.73 *Let $F = (V, E, v^0, v^1, c, N, I)$ be a flow problem. A cut is a set of edges whose removal from the graph will prevent a flow with positive magnitude between v^0 and v^1. The capacity of a cut is the sum of the capacities of the edges in the cut.*

In other words, a subset A of E is a cut if the maximal magnitude in the flow problem $F = (V, E \setminus A, v^0, v^1, c, N, I)$ is 0. The capacity of a cut A will be denoted by $C(A) := \sum_{(u,v) \in A} c(u, v)$.

If $A \subseteq E$ is a set of edges, and if there exists a path from v^0 to v^1 that does not contain any edge in A, then A is not a cut. It follows that if a set of edges A is a cut, then every path from v^0 to v^1 contains at least one edge of A.

Theorem 18.74 (Ford and Fulkerson [1956]) *Let $(V, E, v^0, v^1, c, N, I)$ be a flow problem. The capacity of any cut is greater than or equal to the magnitude of the maximal flow of the flow problem. Moreover, there exists a cut whose capacity equals the magnitude of the maximal flow of the flow problem.*

Proof: For every flow f and every two sets of vertices $X, Y \subseteq V$, define

$$f(X, Y) = \sum \{f(u, v) : (u, v) \in E, u \in X, v \in Y\}$$
$$- \sum \{f(u, v) : (u, v) \in E, u \in Y, v \in X\}. \qquad (18.147)$$

This is the difference between the total flow in the edges connecting the vertices in X to the vertices Y to the total flow in the edges connecting the vertices in Y to the vertices in X. This function has several useful properties:

1. $f(X, X) = 0$ for every set of vertices $X \subseteq V$.
2. $f(X_1 \cup X_2, Y) = f(X_1, Y) + f(X_2, Y)$ for all $Y \subseteq V$ and every pair of disjoint sets $X_1, X_2 \subseteq V$.
3. $f(V, \{v^1\}) = M(f)$.
4. $f(V, \{v\}) = 0$ for every vertex $v \in V \setminus \{v^0, v^1\}$.

The first two properties follow from the definition of $f(\cdot, \cdot)$ and the last two properties follow from the definition of a flow. Recall that for every set $X \subseteq V$, the complement of X is $X^c := V \setminus X$.

We next prove that for every flow f and every set X satisfying $v^0 \in X$ and $v^1 \notin X$,

$$M(f) = f(X, X^c). \tag{18.148}$$

Indeed, from Property (2) of $f(\cdot, \cdot)$,

$$f(X, X^c) = f(V, X^c) - f(X^c, X^c) \tag{18.149}$$

$$= \sum_{v \in X^c \setminus \{v^1\}} f(V, \{v\}) + f(V, \{v^1\}) - f(X^c, X^c) \tag{18.150}$$

$$= M(f). \tag{18.151}$$

To obtain Equation (18.151) note that $f(X^c, X^c)$ equals 0 by Property (1) of $f(\cdot, \cdot)$, and $\sum_{v \in X^c \setminus \{v^1\}} f(V, \{v\})$ equals 0 by Properties (4) and (2) of $f(\cdot, \cdot)$, since $X^c \setminus \{v^1\} \subseteq V \setminus \{v^0, v^1\}$.

For any cut A let $X(A)$ be the set of vertices containing the source v^0 and every vertex $v \in V$ such that there exists a path from v^0 to v that does not contain any edge in A. By the definition of a cut, we deduce that $v^1 \notin X(A)$.

Note that if $u \in X(A)$, $v \notin X(A)$, and $(u, v) \in E$, then $(u, v) \in A$. Indeed, since $u \in X(A)$ there exists a path from the source v^0 to u that does not contain any edge in A. If the edge (u, v) were not in A, there would be a path from v^0 to v that does not contain any edge in A, but this contradicts the fact that $v \notin X(A)$. In particular,

$$\{(u, v) \in E : u \in X(A), v \notin X(A)\} \subseteq A. \tag{18.152}$$

Therefore,

$$f(X(A), (X(A))^c) = \sum \{f(u, v) : (u, v) \in E, u \in X(A), v \notin X(A)\}$$

$$- \sum \{f(u, v) : (u, v) \in E, u \notin X(A), v \in X(A)\} \tag{18.153}$$

$$\leq \sum \{f(u, v) : (u, v) \in E, u \in X(A), v \notin X(A)\} \tag{18.154}$$

$$\leq \sum_{(u,v) \in A} f(u, v) \tag{18.155}$$

$$\leq \sum_{(u,v) \in A} c(u, v) = C(A), \tag{18.156}$$

where the inequality (18.155) follows from Equation (18.152). Using Equations (18.149)–(18.151) and (18.153)–(18.156), we deduce that for every flow f and every cut A,

$$M(f) \leq C(A). \tag{18.157}$$

This leads to

$$\max_f M(f) \leq \min_A C(A), \tag{18.158}$$

where the maximum is taken over all flows and the minimum is over all cuts. The minimum is attained because the number of cuts in the graph is finite, and the maximum is attained because the set of flows is compact and the function $f \mapsto M(f)$ is continuous. That completes the proof of the first part of Theorem 18.74.

To prove the second part of the theorem, let f^* be a maximal flow. We will show that there exists a cut A such that $M(f^*) = C(A)$. Such a cut A is in particular a cut with minimal capacity.

Define a graph $\widehat{G} = (V, \widehat{E})$ as follows. The edge (u, v) is in $\widehat{E}$ if and only if at least one of the following two conditions holds:

- The edge (u, v) is in E, and $f^*(u, v) < c(u, v)$.
- The edge (v, u) is in E, and $f^*(v, u) > 0$.

In words, if the flow in edge (u, v) is less than its maximal capacity (and therefore more flow can be added to that edge), then we add the edge (u, v) to $\widehat{E}$. If the flow in edges (u, v) is positive (and therefore flow can be removed from that edge), we add the edge in the opposite direction, (v, u), to $\widehat{E}$. In particular, it follows that the set of edges $\widehat{E}$ is nonempty.

We first claim that the graph $\widehat{G}$ contains no path from v^0 to v^1. Suppose by contradiction that there exists such a path σ. Denote

$$\varepsilon := \min \Big\{ \min\{ c(u, v) - f(u, v) \colon (u, v) \in E, (u, v) \in \widehat{E}, f^*(u, v) < c(u, v) \},$$

$$\min\{ f^*(v, u) \colon (v, u) \in E, (u, v) \in \widehat{E}, f^*(v, u) > 0 \} \Big\} > 0. \qquad (18.159)$$

If the set $\{(u, v) \in E, (u, v) \in \widehat{E}, f^*(u, v) < c(u, v)\}$ is empty, then the first internal minimum on the right-hand side of Equation (18.159) is ∞, and if the set $\{(v, u) \in E, (u, v) \in \widehat{E}, f^*(v, u) > 0\}$ is empty, then the second internal minimum is ∞. Since at least one of these two sets is nonempty, ε is a positive number.

Define a function $\widehat{f} \colon E \to \mathbb{R}_+$ as follows:

$$\widehat{f}(u, v) = \begin{cases} f^*(u, v) & (u, v) \text{ is not in the path } \sigma, \\ f^*(u, v) + \varepsilon & f^*(u, v) < c(u, v) \text{ and } (u, v) \text{ in the path } \sigma, \\ f^*(u, v) - \varepsilon & f^*(u, v) > 0 \text{ and } (v, u) \text{ in the path } \sigma. \end{cases} \qquad (18.160)$$

Since σ is a path from v^0 to v^1 in $\widehat{G}$, the function $\widehat{f}$ is a flow in G, and its magnitude is $M(f^*) + \varepsilon$ (Exercise 18.63). This contradicts the fact that f^* is a maximal flow.

Let X be a set containing v^0 and every vertex v such that there is a path from v^0 to v in the graph $\widehat{G}$. Since there is no path from v^0 to v^1 we deduce that $v^1 \notin X$. Let A be the following cut (why is this a cut?):

$$A := \{(u, v) \in E \colon u \in X, v \notin X\}. \qquad (18.161)$$

Let $u \in X$ and $v \notin X$. Note that $(u, v) \notin \widehat{E}$ by the definition of X. Therefore, if $(u, v) \in E$, then necessarily $f^*(u, v) = c(u, v)$, and if $(v, u) \in E$, then necessarily $f^*(v, u) = 0$. Therefore,

$$M(f^*) = f^*(X, X^c) \tag{18.162}$$

$$= \sum \{f^*(u, v) : (u, v) \in E, u \in X, v \in X^c\}$$

$$- \sum \{f^*(u, v) : (u, v) \in E, u \in X^c, v \in X\} \tag{18.163}$$

$$= \sum \{c(u, v) : (u, v) \in E, u \in X, v \in X^c\} = C(A). \tag{18.164}$$

This completes the proof of Theorem 18.74. □

If $(N; v)$ is a flow game corresponding to the flow problem $(V, E, v^0, v^1, c, N, I)$, then the magnitude of the maximal flow in the graph is $v(N)$. The Ford–Fulkerson Theorem implies that the minimal capacity of a cut in the problem equals $v(N)$.

We now complete the proof of Theorem 18.69 by proving the following theorem.

Theorem 18.75 *Every flow game is a totally balanced game.*

Proof: Let $(N; v)$ be a flow game. We first show that the core of the game $(N; v)$ is nonempty. Let $F = (V, E, v^0, v^1, c, N, I)$ be a flow problem corresponding to $(N; v)$. Let A be a cut of minimal capacity in the flow problem F. For each player $i \in N$, denote by c_i the sum of the capacities of all the edges in A controlled by player i,

$$c_i = \sum_{\{e \in A : I(e) = i\}} c(e). \tag{18.165}$$

We will show that the imputation $c = (c_i)_{i \in N}$ is in the core of $(N; v)$. The worth $v(N)$ of coalition N is the magnitude of the maximal flow, which equals the capacity of the minimal cut A by the Ford–Fulkerson Theorem (Theorem 18.74):

$$v(N) = \sum_{i \in N} c_i. \tag{18.166}$$

Thus, c is an efficient vector. We next show that $v(S) \geq \sum_{i \in S} c_i$ for every nonempty coalition $S \subseteq N$. Fix then a nonempty coalition S, and define $A_{|S} = \{e \in A : I(e) \in S\}$. These are all the edges in the cut that are controlled by the players in S. The collection $A_{|S}$ is a cut of $F_{|S}$, because every path from v^0 to v^1 using only edges controlled by the members of S must use an edge in $A_{|S}$. By definition, $v(S)$ is the magnitude of the maximal flow in $F_{|S}$, and by the first part of the Ford–Fulkerson Theorem, this quantity is at most the capacity of any cut. It follows that

$$v(S) \leq \sum_{e \in A_{|S}} c(e) = \sum_{i \in S} c_i. \tag{18.167}$$

Since this inequality holds for every nonempty coalition $S \subseteq N$, the vector c is coalitionally rational, and since it is efficient, it is in the core of the game $(N; v)$.

We have therefore proved that the core of every flow game is nonempty. Since every subgame of a flow game is a flow game (Theorem 18.68), it follows that the core of every subgame of a flow game is nonempty, and therefore the game $(N; v)$ is totally balanced. □

Using Theorem 18.40 (page 760), Theorem 18.44 (page 761), and Theorem 18.69 (page 774), we deduce the following corollary.

Corollary 18.76 *The following statements are equivalent for a coalitional game* $(N; v)$:

- $(N; v)$ *is totally balanced.*
- $(N; v)$ *is a market game.*
- $(N; v)$ *is the minimum of a finite number of additive games.*
- $(N; v)$ *is a flow game.*

18.10 The core for general coalitional structures

In this section, we extend the solution concept of the core to cover cases in which the grand coalition N is not formed, and instead players are partitioned into several disjoint coalitions. When several disjoint coalitions are formed, the members of each coalition divide the worth of that coalition among themselves.

Recall that a coalitional structure is a partition $\mathcal{B}$ of the set of players N. In other words, $\mathcal{B}$ is a set of disjoint sets whose union is N. The set of imputations for a coalitional structure $\mathcal{B}$ is the set

$$X(\mathcal{B}; v) := \{x \in \mathbb{R}^N : x(B) = v(B) \quad \forall B \in \mathcal{B}, \quad x_i \geq v(i) \quad \forall i \in N\}. \tag{18.168}$$

In words, an imputation for the coalitional structure $\mathcal{B}$ is an individually rational vector at which the total payoff to the members of each coalition B in the coalitional structure is equal to $v(B)$, the amount that the members of B can obtain on their own.

Definition 18.77 *The* core *of a coalitional game* $(N; v)$ *for a coalitional structure* $\mathcal{B}$ *is the set*

$$C(N; v; \mathcal{B}) := \{x \in X(\mathcal{B}; v) : x(S) \geq v(S) \quad \forall S \subseteq N\}. \tag{18.169}$$

This is the set of imputations for $\mathcal{B}$, such that no coalition of players can profit by forming and producing its worth. The coalitional rationality condition applies to all coalitions, not only to the subcoalitions of the coalitions in $\mathcal{B}$. For $\mathcal{B} = \{N\}$, the set $C(N; v; \mathcal{B})$ is the core of the game $(N; v)$ defined in Equation (18.2) on page 736.

A useful concept for the characterization of the core for coalitional structures is the superadditive cover of a coalitional game.

Definition 18.78 *Let* $(N; v)$ *be a coalitional game. The* superadditive cover *of* $(N; v)$ *is the game* $(N; v^*)$ *defined by*

$$v^*(S) := \max_{\mathcal{T}} \sum_{T \in \mathcal{T}} v(T), \tag{18.170}$$

where the maximization is taken over all the partitions $\mathcal{T}$ *of* S.

The idea behind this definition is as follows. Suppose that the members of S are interested in maximizing the total amount they generate, without taking into account the players who are not in S. In that case they will separate into several subcoalitions in a way that maximizes the sum total of the worth of these subcoalitions. The quantity $v^*(S)$ is precisely this maximal sum.

Note that $v(S) \leq v^*(S)$ for every coalition S, with equality between these two worths for every $S \subseteq N$, if the game is superadditive. Also, $v^*(i) = v(i)$ for every player $i \in N$.

Theorem 18.79 *Let $(N; v)$ be a coalitional game.*

1. *The game $(N; v^*)$ is superadditive.*
2. *The game $(N; v^*)$ is the smallest superadditive game that is larger than $(N; v)$: for every superadditive game $(N; w)$ satisfying $w(S) \geq v(S)$ for every coalition S, $w(S) \geq v^*(S)$ for every coalition S.*
3. *The game $(N; v)$ is superadditive if and only if $v^* = v$.*

The proof of the theorem is left to the reader (Exercise 18.67). The next theorem characterizes the core for a general coalitional structure $\mathcal{B}$.

Theorem 18.80 *Let $(N; v)$ be a coalitional game with a coalitional structure $\mathcal{B}$. Then,*

$$C(N; v; \mathcal{B}) = C(N; v^*) \cap X(\mathcal{B}; v). \tag{18.171}$$

The theorem states that to compute the core for a given coalitional structure, and in particular for the coalitional structure $\mathcal{B} = \{N\}$, it suffices to compute the core of the superadditive cover of $(N; v)$, and the set of imputations for $\mathcal{B}$, and to take the intersection of these two sets. We deduce from this that it suffices to compute the core only for superadditive games.

Proof: We first prove that $C(N; v; \mathcal{B}) \supseteq C(N; v^*) \cap X(\mathcal{B}; v)$. Let $x \in C(N; v^*) \cap X(\mathcal{B}; v)$. In particular, $x \in X(\mathcal{B}; v)$, and therefore to prove that $x \in C(N; v; \mathcal{B})$, we need to prove that for every coalition S,

$$x(S) \geq v(S). \tag{18.172}$$

Since $x \in C(N; v^*)$,

$$x(S) \geq v^*(S) \geq v(S), \tag{18.173}$$

which is what we needed to show.

We next prove that $C(N; v; \mathcal{B}) \subseteq C(N; v^*) \cap X(\mathcal{B}; v)$. Let $x \in C(N; v; \mathcal{B})$. In particular, $x \in X(\mathcal{B}; v)$. To show that $x \in C(N; v^*)$, we need to show that (a) $x(N) = v^*(N)$, and (b) $x(S) \geq v^*(S)$ for every coalition S.

Let $S \subseteq N$ be a coalition. Then there is a partition $\mathcal{T} = \{T_1, \ldots, T_K\}$ of S such that

$$v^*(S) = \sum_{k=1}^{K} v(T_K). \tag{18.174}$$

Since $x \in C(N; v; \mathcal{B})$,

$$x(T_K) \geq v(T_K), \quad \forall k \in \{1, 2, \ldots, K\}, \tag{18.175}$$

and, therefore,

$$x(S) = \sum_{k=1}^{K} x(T_K) \geq \sum_{k=1}^{K} v(T_K) = v^*(S). \tag{18.176}$$

It follows that $x(S) \geq v^*(S)$ for every coalition $S \subseteq N$. We set $S = N$, to deduce

$$x(N) \geq v^*(N). \tag{18.177}$$

Since $x \in X(\mathcal{B}; v)$, and since v^* is the superadditive cover of $(N; v)$,

$$x(N) = \sum_{B \in \mathcal{B}} x(B) = \sum_{B \in \mathcal{B}} v(B) \leq v^*(N). \tag{18.178}$$

Equations (18.177) and (18.178) imply that $x(N) = v^*(N)$. This completes the proof. $\square$

The last theorems lead to the following corollary.

Corollary 18.81 *Let $(N; v)$ be a coalitional game with a coalitional structure $\mathcal{B}$. If $v^*(N) = \sum_{B \in \mathcal{B}} v(B)$, then $\mathcal{C}(N; v; \mathcal{B}) = \mathcal{C}(N; v^*)$. If $v^*(N) > \sum_{B \in \mathcal{B}} v(B)$, then $\mathcal{C}(N; v; \mathcal{B})$ is empty.*

This corollary further leads to the conclusion that if the core of the superadditive cover $(N; v^*)$ is empty, then the core relative to any coalitional structure is also empty. This fact can also be deduced from Theorem 18.80. Similarly, if the core of $(N; v^*)$ is nonempty, then the core is nonempty only for coalitional structures $\mathcal{B}$ satisfying $v^*(N) = \sum_{B \in \mathcal{B}} v(B)$. The coalitional structures in which the core is nonempty are precisely those structures in which the sum $\sum_{B \in \mathcal{B}} v(B)$ attains its maximum, i.e., the "optimal" partition of the set of all players.

Proof of Corollary 18.81: If $v^*(N) > \sum_{B \in \mathcal{B}} v(B)$, then $\mathcal{C}(N; v^*)$ and $X(\mathcal{B}; v)$ are disjoint, since every imputation $x \in \mathcal{C}(N; v^*)$ satisfies $\sum_{i \in N} x_i = v^*(N)$, while every imputation $x \in X(\mathcal{B}; v)$ satisfies $\sum_{i \in N} x_i = \sum_{B \in \mathcal{B}} x(B) = \sum_{B \in \mathcal{B}} v(B)$. By Theorem 18.80, $\mathcal{C}(N; v; \mathcal{B})$ is empty.

If $v^*(N) = \sum_{B \in \mathcal{B}} v(B)$, then $\mathcal{C}(N; v^*) \subseteq X(\mathcal{B}; v)$, because every imputation $x \in \mathcal{C}(N; v^*)$ satisfies

$$\sum_{B \in \mathcal{B}} x(B) = \sum_{i \in N} x_i = v^*(N) = \sum_{B \in \mathcal{B}} v(B), \tag{18.179}$$

and

$$x_i \geq v^*(i) = v(i), \quad \forall i \in N. \tag{18.180}$$

Since $x \in \mathcal{C}(N; v^*)$,

$$x(B) \geq v^*(B) \geq v(B). \tag{18.181}$$

Equations (18.179) and (18.181) imply that $x(B) = v(B)$ for every $B \in \mathcal{B}$, and therefore $x \in X(\mathcal{B}; v)$. Since $\mathcal{C}(N; v^*) \subseteq X(\mathcal{B}; v)$, Theorem 18.80 then implies that $\mathcal{C}(N; v; \mathcal{B}) = \mathcal{C}(N; v^*)$. $\square$

18.11 Remarks

The concept of a balanced collection was introduced in Shapley [1967]. The proof appearing in Section 18.3.2 showing that the Bondareva–Shapley condition implies that the core is nonempty is due to Robert J. Aumann. Other proofs of this result appear in Bondareva [1963] and Shapley [1967]. The Weber set was introduced in Weber [1988].

Theorem 18.63 was first proved in Bird [1976]. The proof presented in this chapter is from Granot and Huberman [1981]. The results in Section 18.9 (page 772) and Exercise 18.64 are from Kalai and Zemel [1982b].

The definition of the reduced game to coalition S relative to preimputation x was introduced in Davis and Maschler [1965]. A different definition of the concept of a reduced game was introduced by Hart and Mas-Colell; we study the Hart–Mas-Colell reduced game in Chapter 19. The concept of a reasonable solution (Exercise 18.16) was introduced in Milnor [1952]. Exercise 18.17 is based on Huberman [1980]. The result in the exercise first appeared in Gillies [1953, 1959]. Exercise 18.18 is based on Schmeidler [1972]. The ε-core appearing in Exercise 18.33 was introduced in Shapley and Shubik [1966]. The intuitive meaning of this concept is that a deviation by members of a coalition S that leads to its formation requires information and imposes a cost, and the players will therefore not deviate to form a coalition S unless the profit from deviating is greater than this cost. The least core, and its geometric analysis, were introduced in Maschler et al. [1979]. Exercise 18.41 is from Kalai and Zemel [1982a]. Exercise 18.43 is from Aumann and Dréze [1975]. Exercise 18.57 is from Tamir [1991].

18.12 Exercises

18.1 Prove that the core is a convex set. That is, show that for any two imputations x, y in the core of a coalitional game $(N; v)$, and for all $\alpha \in [0, 1]$, the imputation $\alpha x + (1 - \alpha)y$ is also in the core of the game $(N; v)$.

18.2 (a) Give an example of a three-player coalitional game whose core is a triangle.
   (b) Give an example of a three-player coalitional game whose core is a parallelogram.
   (c) Give an example of a three-player coalitional game whose core is a pentagon.

18.3 Give an example of a monotonic game with an empty core.

18.4 Give an example of a superadditive game with an empty core.

18.5 Draw the cores of the following coalitional games. These games are 0-normalized, and in all of them $N = \{1, 2, 3\}$ and $v(N) = 90$.

   (a) $v(1, 2) = 20, v(1, 3) = 30, v(2, 3) = 10$.
   (b) $v(1, 2) = 30, v(1, 3) = 10, v(2, 3) = 80$.
   (c) $v(1, 2) = 10, v(1, 3) = 20, v(2, 3) = 70$.
   (d) $v(1, 2) = 50, v(1, 3) = 50, v(2, 3) = 50$.
   (e) $v(1, 2) = 70, v(1, 3) = 80, v(2, 3) = 60$.

18.6 Draw the core of the following three-player coalitional game:

$$v(1) = 5, \quad v(2) = 10, \quad v(3) = 20, \quad v(1, 2) = 50, \quad v(1, 3) = 70,$$
$$v(2, 3) = 50, \quad v(1, 2, 3) = 90.$$

18.7 Players i, j are *symmetric players* if for every coalition S that does not include any one of them,

$$v(S \cup \{i\}) = v(S \cup \{j\}).$$ (18.182)

(a) Prove that the symmetry relation between two players is transitive: if i and j are symmetric players, and j and k are symmetric players, then i and k are symmetric players.

(b) Show that if the core is nonempty, then there exists an imputation x in the core that grants every pair of symmetric players the same payoff, i.e., $x_i = x_j$ for every pair of symmetric players i, j.

18.8 Let $(a_i)_{i \in N}$ be nonnegative real numbers. Let v be the coalitional function

$$v(S) = \begin{cases} 0 & \text{if } |S| \le k, \\ \sum_{i \in S} a_i & \text{if } |S| > k. \end{cases}$$ (18.183)

Compute the core of the game $(N; v)$ for every $k = 0, 1, \ldots, n$.

18.9 Prove that a three-player 0-normalized game whose core is nonempty, and satisfying $v(S) \ge 0$ for every coalition S, is monotonic. Is this true also for games with more than three players? Justify your answer. Does it hold true without the condition that $v(S) \ge 0$ for every coalition? Justify your answer.

18.10 A player i in a coalitional game $(N; v)$ is a *null player* if for every coalition S,

$$v(S \cup \{i\}) = v(S).$$ (18.184)

In particular, by setting $S = \emptyset$, this implies that if player i is a null player then $v(i) = 0$. Show that if the core is nonempty, then $x_i = 0$ for every imputation x in the core, and every null player i.

18.11 Let $(N; v)$ be a coalitional game satisfying the strong symmetry property: for every permutation π over the set of players, and every coalition $S \subseteq N$,

$$v(S) = v(\pi(S)),$$ (18.185)

where

$$\pi(S) = \{\pi(i) : i \in S\}.$$ (18.186)

Prove the following claims:

(a) The core of the game is nonempty if and only if for every coalition $S \subseteq N$,

$$v(S) \le \frac{|S|}{n} v(N).$$ (18.187)

(b) If the core of the game is nonempty, and there exists a coalition $\emptyset \ne S \subset N$ satisfying $v(S) = \frac{|S|}{n} v(N)$, then the core contains only the imputation

$$\left(\frac{v(N)}{n}, \ldots, \frac{v(N)}{n} \right).$$ (18.188)

18.12 A player i in a simple game is a *veto player* if $v(S) = 0$ for every coalition S that does not contain i.

(a) Show that the core of a simple game satisfying $v(N) = 1$ contains every imputation x satisfying $x_i = 0$ for every player i who is not a veto player, and does not contain any other imputation. In other words, the only imputations in the core are those in which the set of veto players divide the worth of the grand coalition, $v(N)$, between them.

(b) Using part (a), find the core of the gloves game (Example 18.5 on page 738).

(c) Consider a simple majority game in which a coalition wins if and only if it has at least $\frac{n+1}{2}$ votes; that is, for every coalition $S \subseteq N$,

$$
v(S) = \begin{cases} 1 & \text{if } |S| \geq \frac{n+1}{2}, \\ 0 & \text{if } |S| < \frac{n+1}{2}. \end{cases}
\tag{18.189}
$$

What is the core of this game?

(d) What is the core of a simple coalitional game without veto players?

18.13 A *buyer–seller game* is a coalitional game in which the set of players N is the union of a set of buyers B and a set of sellers S (with these two sets disjoint from each other). The payoff function is defined by

$$
v(T) := \min\{|T \cap B|, |T \cap S|\}, \quad \forall T \subseteq N.
\tag{18.190}
$$

Compute the core of this game. Check your answer against the gloves game (Example 18.5 on page 738).

18.14 Compute the core of the cost game $(N; c)$ in which $N = \{1, 2, 3, 4\}$ and the coalitional function c is

$$
c(S) = \begin{cases} 0 & S = \emptyset, \\ 2 & \text{if } |S| = 2 \text{ or } |S| = 1, \\ 4 & \text{if } |S| = 3 \text{ or } |S| = 4. \end{cases}
\tag{18.191}
$$

18.15 Define the *dual game* of a coalitional game $(N; v)$ to be the coalitional game $(N; v^*)$ where

$$
v^*(S) = v(N) - v(N \setminus S), \quad \forall S \subseteq N.
\tag{18.192}
$$

Is the core of a coalitional game $(N; v)$ nonempty if and only if the core of its dual $(N; v^*)$ is nonempty? Either prove this claim, or provide a counterexample.

18.16 Prove that every imputation x in the core of a coalitional game $(N; v)$ satisfies

$$
x_i \leq \max_{S \subseteq N \setminus \{i\}} \{v(S \cup \{i\}) - v(S)\}, \quad \forall i \in N.
\tag{18.193}
$$

A solution satisfying this property is called a *reasonable solution*.

18.17 In this exercise, we will show that to compute the core of a coalitional game it suffices to know the worth of only some of the coalitions.

A coalition S is *inessential* in a coalitional game $(N; v)$ if there exists a partition $S_1, S_2, \ldots, S_r$ of S into nonempty coalitions such that $r \geq 2$ and $v(S) \leq \sum_{j=1}^{r} v(S_j)$. A coalition S that is not inessential is an *essential* coalition.

(a) Prove that if S is an inessential coalition, then there exists a partition $(S_j)_{j=1}^{r}$ of S into essential coalitions such that $v(S) \leq \sum_{j=1}^{r} v(S_j)$.

(b) Prove that an imputation x is in the core of the game $(N; v)$ if and only if (a) $x(N) = v(N)$, and (b) $x(S) \geq v(S)$ for every essential coalition S.

Let $(N; v)$ and $(N; u)$ be two coalitional games satisfying $v(S) = u(S)$ for every essential coalition S in $(N; v)$ or in $(N; u)$. Prove the following claims:

(c) A coalition S is essential in the game $(N; v)$ if and only if it is essential in the game $(N; u)$.

(d) Deduce that if $v(N) = u(N)$, then $\mathcal{C}(N; v) = \mathcal{C}(N; u)$.

(e) Prove that if the cores of the games $(N; v)$ and $(N; u)$ are nonempty, then $v(N) = u(N)$, and therefore by part (d), $\mathcal{C}(N; v) = \mathcal{C}(N; u)$.

(f) Show by example that it is possible for the core of the game $(N; v)$ to be nonempty while the core of the game $(N; u)$ is empty. In this case show, using part (d) above, that $v(N) \neq u(N)$.

18.18 A coalitional game $(N; v)$ with a nonempty core $\mathcal{C}(N; v)$ is an *exact game* if every coalition S satisfies $v(S) = \min_{x \in \mathcal{C}(N;v)} x(S)$. In other words, the worth of every coalition S equals the minimal total payoff, among the imputations in the core, that the members of S can get working together. In this exercise, we will show that for every game $(N; v)$ with a nonempty core there exists an exact game whose core equals the core of the original game $(N; v)$. In other words, the core of a coalitional game is also the core of an exact game. Moreover, we will show that every convex game is an exact game.

Let $(N; v)$ be a coalitional game with a nonempty core $\mathcal{C}(N; v)$. For every coalition $S \subseteq N$, define

$$v^E(S) := \min_{x \in \mathcal{C}(N;v)} x(S). \tag{18.194}$$

Answer the following questions:

(a) Prove that $v^E(S) \geq v(S)$ for every coalition $S \subseteq N$.

(b) Prove that $v^E(N) = v(N)$.

(c) Prove that $\mathcal{C}(N; v) = \mathcal{C}(N; v^E)$. Deduce that the coalitional game $(N; v^E)$ is exact.

18.19 Prove that if Equations (18.23)–(18.27) hold for a coalitional game $(N; v)$, where $N = \{1, 2, 3\}$, then the game has a nonempty core.

Guidance: Show that if $v(1, 2) + v(1, 3) \geq v(N) + v(1)$, then the imputation

$$(v(1, 2) + v(1, 3) - v(N), v(N) - v(1, 3), v(N) - v(1, 2)) \tag{18.195}$$

is in the core. If $v(1, 2) + v(1, 3) < v(N) + v(1)$ and $v(1, 3) \geq v(1) + v(3)$, then the imputation

$$(v(1), v(N) - v(1,3), v(1,3) - v(1)) \tag{18.196}$$

is in the core. If $v(1,2) + v(1,3) < v(N) + v(1)$ and $v(1,3) < v(1) + v(3)$, then the imputation

$$(v(1), v(N) - v(1) - v(3), v(3)) \tag{18.197}$$

is in the core.

18.20 Prove that if $\mathcal{D}_1$ and $\mathcal{D}_2$ are two balanced collections, then their union $\mathcal{D}_1 \cup \mathcal{D}_2$ is also a balanced collection.

18.21 Let $\mathcal{D}$ be a balanced collection of coalitions. Suppose that there is a player i contained in every coalition in $\mathcal{D}$. Prove that $\mathcal{D}$ contains a single coalition, $\mathcal{D} = \{N\}$.

18.22 Let $\mathcal{D}$ be a balanced collection of coalitions, and let $S \in \mathcal{D}$. Prove that there is a minimal balanced collection $\mathcal{T} \subseteq \mathcal{D}$ containing S. Deduce that $\mathcal{D}$ is the union of all the minimal balanced collections contained in $\mathcal{D}$.

18.23 Given a balanced collection $\mathcal{D}$ that is not minimal, and any coalition $S \in \mathcal{D}$, does there exist a minimal balanced collection $\mathcal{T} \subseteq \mathcal{D}$ that does not contain S? If so, prove it. If not, provide a counterexample.

18.24 Show that if $\mathcal{D}$ is a minimal balanced collection of coalitions, then the vectors $\{\chi^S, S \in \mathcal{D}\}$ (which are vectors in $\mathbb{R}^N$) are linearly independent.

18.25 Suppose that $|N| = 4$.

(a) Prove that $\{\{1\}, \{2\}, \{3\}, \{3,4\}, \{1,3,4\}\}$ is not a balanced collection.
(b) Prove that $\{\{1,2\}, \{1,3\}, \{1,4\}, \{3\}, \{4\}, \{2,3,4\}\}$ is a balanced collection, but is not a minimal balanced collection.

18.26 Prove or disprove the following:

(a) If $\mathcal{D}$ is a balanced collection of coalitions that is not minimal, then it has an infinite set of balancing weights.
(b) If $\mathcal{D}$ is a weakly balanced collection of coalitions that is not minimal, then it has an infinite set of balancing weights.

18.27 Show that if $N = \{1, 2, 3\}$, then the only minimal balanced collections of coalitions are: (a) $\{\{1,2,3\}\}$, (b) $\{\{1\}, \{2\}, \{3\}\}$, (c) $\{\{1,2\}, \{3\}\}$, (d) $\{\{1,3\}, \{2\}\}$, (e) $\{\{2,3\}, \{1\}\}$, (f) $\{\{1,2\}, \{1,3\}, \{2,3\}\}$.

18.28 Prove that the two formulations of the Bondareva–Shapley Theorem, Theorem 18.14 (page 744) and Theorem 18.19 (page 749), are equivalent. To do so, show that the following two conditions are equivalent:

- Equation (18.36) holds for every balanced collection of coalitions $\mathcal{D}$ with balancing weights $(\delta_S)_{S \in \mathcal{D}}$.
- Equation (18.62) holds for every $\delta \in P$.

18.29 Prove that the coalitional game $(\{1,2,3,4\}; v)$, in which v is defined by

$$v(S) = \begin{cases} 0 & \text{if } |S| = 1, \\ 30 & \text{if } |S| = 2, \\ 0 & \text{if } |S| = 3, \\ 50 & \text{if } |S| = 4, \end{cases} \qquad (18.198)$$

has an empty core.

Guidance: Find a balanced collection of coalitions that does not satisfy the Bondareva–Shapley condition.

18.30 In the following games, how large must $v(1,2,3)$ be for the game $(\{1,2,3\}, v)$ to have a nonempty core?

(a) $v(1) = 12, v(2) = 10, v(3) = 20, v(1,2) = 20, v(1,3) = 50, v(2,3) = 70$.
(b) $v(1) = 30, v(2) = 40, v(3) = 70, v(1,2) = 10, v(1,3) = 20, v(2,3) = 5$.

18.31 The totally balanced cover of a coalitional game $(N; v)$ is the minimal totally balanced coalitional game $(N; w)$ greater than or equal to $(N; v)$. In other words:

(a) $(N; w)$ is a totally balanced game.
(b) $w(S) \geq v(S)$ for every coalition $S \subseteq N$.
(c) Every totally balanced coalition $(N; u)$ satisfying $u(S) \geq v(S)$ for every coalition $S \subseteq N$ also satisfies $u(S) \geq w(S)$ for every coalition $S \subseteq N$.

What is the totally balanced cover of the two games in Exercise 18.30? (For $v(1,2,3)$ insert the worths you found in Exercise 18.30.)

18.32 Prove that a minimally balanced collection of coalitions contains at most n coalitions.

18.33 Let $(N; v)$ be a coalitional game. For any real number ε, define the ε-*core* of the game as follows:

$$\mathcal{C}_\varepsilon(N; v) = \{x \in \mathbb{R}^N : x(N) = v(N), x(S) \geq v(S) - \varepsilon \quad \forall S \subset N; S \neq \emptyset\}.$$

Note that for $\varepsilon = 0$, the ε-core $\mathcal{C}_0(N; v)$ is the core of the game. Denote $\varepsilon_0 = \inf\{\varepsilon \in \mathbb{R} : \mathcal{C}_\varepsilon(N; v) \neq \emptyset\}$. The set $\mathcal{C}_{\varepsilon_0}(N; v)$ is the *least core* of the game $(N; v)$.

(a) Prove that for every $\varepsilon \in \mathbb{R}$, the set $\mathcal{C}_\varepsilon(N; v)$ is a polytope; i.e., it is a compact set defined by the intersection of a finite number of half-spaces.
(b) Prove that the least core $\mathcal{C}_{\varepsilon_0}(N; v)$ is nonempty.

Finding the least core of a three-player coalitional game can be accomplished graphically as follows. Draw the space of payoffs, and the half-spaces $\{x \in \mathbb{R}^N : x(S) \geq v(S)\}$ defining the core. For example, the game

$$v(1) = v(2) = v(3) = 0, \quad v(1,2) = 2, \quad v(1,3) = 3, \quad v(2,3) = 7, \quad v(1,2,3) = 9$$

yields the following picture:

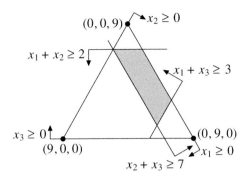

The core (which is the ε-core for $\varepsilon = 0$) is nonempty, and therefore to obtain the least core, we need to decrease ε. All the half-spaces appearing in the figure will then be moved in parallel in the direction of the arrow at a constant rate (with all the half-spaces moving at the same rate). As can be seen in the following figure, the least core is obtained at $\varepsilon_* = -1$, and is the interval whose ends are $(1, 5, 3)$ and $(1, 2, 6)$.

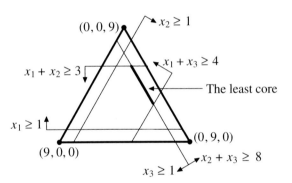

3. Find the least core of each of the following games. Note that if the core is empty, then the least core is obtained at a positive ε.

(i) $v(1) = v(2) = v(3) = 0$, $v(1,2) = 2$, $v(1,3) = 8$, $v(2,3) = 3$, $v(1,2,3) = 12$.

(ii) $v(1) = 6$, $v(2) = 5$, $v(3) = 4$, $v(1,2) = 2$, $v(1,3) = 4$, $v(2,3) = 3$, $v(1,2,3) = 12$.

(iii) $v(1) = v(2) = v(3) = 0$, $v(1,2) = 8$, $v(1,3) = 8$, $v(2,3) = 8$, $v(1,2,3) = 12$.

(iv) $v(1) = v(2) = v(3) = 0$, $v(1,2) = 3$, $v(1,3) = 6$, $v(2,3) = 2$, $v(1,2,3) = 12$.

(v) $v(1) = v(2) = v(3) = 0$, $v(1,2) = 12$, $v(1,3) = 15$, $v(2,3) = 12$, $v(1,2,3) = 12$.

18.34 Let $(N; v)$ and $(N; w)$ be two coalitional games satisfying $v(N) = w(N)$ and $v(S) \geq w(S)$ for every coalition $S \subseteq N$. Prove or disprove each of the following two claims:

(a) If $C(N; v) \neq \emptyset$ then $C(N; w) \neq \emptyset$.
(b) If $C(N; w) \neq \emptyset$ then $C(N; v) \neq \emptyset$.

18.35 Prove that if $(N; v)$ is a market game, then every game that is strategically equivalent to $(N; v)$ is also a market game.

18.36 Complete the computation of the market game derived from the market in Example 18.24 (page 752).

18.37 (a) Prove that a coalitional game $(N; v)$, where $N = \{1, 2\}$ and the coalitional function v is defined by

$$v(1) = v(2) = 1, v(1, 2) = 3, \tag{18.199}$$

is a market game.
(b) Find a market such that $(N; v)$ is the market game derived from it.

18.38 Let $(N; v)$ be a coalitional game, and let $(N; w)$ be a coalitional game strategically equivalent to it. Give direct proofs of the following claims:

(a) The game $(N; v)$ is a market game if and only if the game $(N; w)$ is a market game.
(b) The game $(N; v)$ is totally balanced if and only if the game $(N; w)$ is totally balanced.

18.39 Consider the following coalitional game $(N; v)$ where the set of players is $N = \{1, 2, 3\}$, and the coalitional function is

$$v(S) = \begin{cases} 0 & \text{if } |S| = 1, \\ 1 & \text{if } |S| = 2, \\ 2 & \text{if } |S| = 3. \end{cases} \tag{18.200}$$

Show in a direct way that this game is totally balanced, and find a market from which this game can be derived.

18.40 Let $\varepsilon > 0$, let $x \in \mathbb{R}^N$, and let $(\delta_S)_{\{S \subseteq N, S \neq \emptyset\}}$ be nonnegative weights satisfying $\sum_{\{S \subseteq N, S \neq \emptyset\}} \delta_S \chi^S = x$. Let $y \in \mathbb{R}^N$ be a vector satisfying $|x_i - y_i| < \varepsilon$ for all $i \in N$. Prove that there exists a collection of nonnegative weights $(\mu_S)_{\{S \subseteq N, S \neq \emptyset\}}$ satisfying (a) $\sum_{\{S \subseteq N, S \neq \emptyset\}} \mu_S \chi^S = y$ and (b) $|\delta_S - \mu_S| < 2^{|N|}\varepsilon$.

Deduce that the function u defined in Equation (18.88) (page 757) is a continuous function.

Guidance: First, define $\widehat{\mu}_S := \max\{\delta_S - \varepsilon, 0\}$ for every nonempty coalition S, and show that $\sum_{\{S \subseteq N, S \neq \emptyset\}} \widehat{\mu}_S \chi^S$ is approximately x. The vector $(\mu_S)_{\{S \subseteq N, S \neq \emptyset\}}$ equals the vector $(\widehat{\mu}_S)_{\{S \subseteq N, S \neq \emptyset\}}$, except for coalitions containing only one player.

18.41 Let $N = \{1, 2, \ldots, n\}$ be a set of players. A collection $(Y_S)_{\{S \subseteq N, S \neq \emptyset\}}$ of subsets of $\mathbb{R}^d$ is *balanced* relative to N if for every balanced collection of coalitions $\mathcal{D}$ with balancing weights $(\delta_S)_{S \in \mathcal{D}}$, and every list of points $(y_S)_{\{S \subseteq N, S \neq \emptyset\}}$ such that $y_S \in Y_S$ for every $S \in \mathcal{D}$, one has $\sum_{S \in \mathcal{D}} \delta_S y_S \in Y_N$. The collection $(Y_S)_{\{S \subseteq N, S \neq \emptyset\}}$ is *totally balanced* if for every nonempty coalition T, the collection $(Y_S)_{S \subseteq T, S \neq \emptyset}$ is balanced relative to T.

Let $\{B_1, B_2, \ldots, B_n\}$ be a partition of the set $\{1, 2, \ldots, d\}$. For each coalition S define

$$R_S := \{y \in \mathbb{R}^d : y_j = 0 \quad \forall j \notin \cup_{i \in S} B_i\}. \tag{18.201}$$

Regard the variables $(y_j)_{j \in B_i}$ as variables under the control of player i. The set R_S denotes the possible values of the variables $(y_j)_{j=1}^d$, when the players who are not in S set all the variables under their control to 0.

Let $f : \mathbb{R}^d \to \mathbb{R}$ be a concave function, and let $(Y_S)_{\{S \subseteq N, S \neq \emptyset\}}$ be a collection of compact, nonempty subsets of $\mathbb{R}^d$ satisfying $R_S \subseteq Y_S$ for every nonempty coalition S. Define a coalitional game $(N; v)$ by

$$v(S) := \max_{y \in Y_S} f(y). \tag{18.202}$$

(a) Prove that if the collection $(Y_S)_{\{S \subseteq N, S \neq \emptyset\}}$ is totally balanced, then $(N; v)$ is a totally balanced game.

(b) Show that for every market game $(N; v)$ there exist a natural number $d \in \mathbb{N}$, a partition $\{B_1, B_2, \ldots, B_n\}$ of $\{1, 2, \ldots, d\}$, a concave function $f : \mathbb{R}^d \to \mathbb{R}$, and a totally balanced collection $(Y_S)_{\{S \subseteq N, S \neq \emptyset\}}$ of compact, nonempty subsets of $\mathbb{R}^d$ satisfying $R_S \subseteq Y_S$ for every nonempty coalition S, such that $v(S) = \max_{y \in Y_S} f(y)$.

18.42 Find the cores for all the coalitional structures of all the games in Exercise 18.5, under the assumption that $v(N) = 60$ (and not $v(N) = 90$, as stated in the exercise).

18.43 Let $(N; v)$ be a coalitional game with a coalitional structure $\mathcal{B}$. Let k and l be two players who are members of different coalitions in $\mathcal{B}$. Prove that if k and l are symmetric players, i.e., $v(S \cup \{k\}) = v(S \cup \{l\})$ for every coalition S that does not contain either of them, then for every imputation x in the core of the game with coalitional structure $\mathcal{B}$, one has $x_k = x_l$.

18.44 Prove that every additive game is convex.

18.45 Find a superadditive game that is not convex.

18.46 Prove that a subgame of a convex game is a convex game. Deduce that every subgame of a convex game has a nonempty core, and that every convex game is totally balanced.

18.47 Let $(N; v)$ be a convex game whose core contains exactly one imputation. Prove that $(N; v)$ is an additive game; i.e., $v(S) = \sum_{i \in S} v(i)$ for every coalition S.
Hint: Make use of Remark 18.56 on page 767.

18.48 Let N be a set of players, let p_0 be a probability distribution over N, and let $\mathcal{B}$ be a partition of N into disjoint sets. Define a coalitional game $(N; v)$ by

$$v(S) := \sum_{\{B \in \mathcal{B}, B \subseteq S\}} \sum_{i \in B} p_0(i). \tag{18.203}$$

In words, $v(S)$ is the sum of the probabilities associated with the atoms of $\mathcal{B}$ that are contained in S. Let $C(p_0)$ be a set of probability distributions over N that are identical with p_0 over the elements of $\mathcal{B}$,

$$C(p_0) := \left\{ p \in \Delta(N) \colon \sum_{i \in B} p_i = \sum_{i \in B} p_0(i) \quad \forall B \in \mathcal{B} \right\}. \tag{18.204}$$

Prove the following claims:

(a) $v(N) = 1$ and $v(i) \geq 0$ for all $i \in N$. Deduce that the set of imputations $X(\mathcal{B}; v)$ is a subset of $\Delta(N)$. When does this inclusion hold as an equality?
(b) $(N; v)$ is a convex game.
(c) The core of $(N; v)$ equals $C(p_0)$.

18.49 Prove that if the coalitional game $(N; v)$ is strategically equivalent to the coalitional game $(N; w)$, and if $(N; v)$ is a convex game, then $(N; w)$ is also a convex game.

18.50 Let N be a set of players, and let $f : N \to \mathbb{R}$ be a function. The function f is a *convex* function[9] if for every three natural numbers k, m, l satisfying $k \leq m \leq l$ and $k < l$,

$$f(m) \leq \frac{l - m}{l - k} f(k) + \frac{m - k}{l - k} f(l). \tag{18.205}$$

Let N be a set of players, and let $f : N \to \mathbb{R}$ be a function. Define a coalitional game $(N; v)$ by

$$v(S) := f(|S|). \tag{18.206}$$

Prove that $(N; v)$ is a convex game if and only if f is a convex function.

18.51 The *monotonic cover* of a coalitional game $(N; v)$ is the coalitional game $(N; \tilde{v})$ defined by

$$\tilde{v}(S) := \max_{R \subseteq S} v(R). \tag{18.207}$$

Prove that the monotonic cover of a convex game is a convex game.

18.52 Find a coalitional game that is not convex, and has a nonempty core that does not contain the Weber set.

18.53 Find a coalitional game in which all the vectors w^π defined in Equation (18.138) (page 767) are identical: $w^{\pi_1} = w^{\pi_2}$ for every pair of permuations π_1 and π_2 of the set of players N.

---

9 This is the discrete analogue to the definition of a convex function over $\mathbb{R}$, since $\frac{l-m}{l-k}k + \frac{m-k}{l-k}l = m$. Recall that a real-valued function g is convex if $g(\alpha x + (1 - \alpha)y) \leq \alpha g(x) + (1 - \alpha)g(y)$ for all x, y and for all $\alpha \in [0, 1]$.

18.54 Write out the coalitional function of the spanning tree game corresponding to Example 18.62 (page 769). Is this a convex game?

18.55 Prove that a connected graph over a set V with $n + 1$ vertices is a tree (that is, it is acyclic) if and only if it contains n edges.

18.56 A spanning tree system (N, V, E, v^0, a), where (V, E) is a tree (i.e., a connected acyclic graph), is called a *tree system*. Prove that the spanning tree game corresponding to such a system is a convex game.

18.57 In Section 18.8 we defined a spanning tree system (N, V, E, v^0, a) in which every vertex that is not the source is associated with a player in N. In this exercise we will assume that some of the vertices are unmanned, i.e., $V \supseteq N \cup \{v^0\}$. In this case, as in the standard case, the spanning tree game $(N; c)$ corresponding to the spanning tree system is a cost game in which the worth $c(S)$ of each coalition S is the cost of the minimal-cost spanning tree of the coalition.

(a) Write out the spanning tree game corresponding to the following spanning tree system:

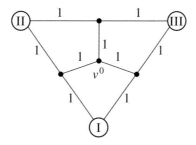

(b) Prove that the core of this game is empty.

18.58 A *bankruptcy problem* is given by $n + 1$ nonnegative numbers $[E; d_1, d_2, \ldots, d_n]$. Here E represents the assets of a bankrupt individual or corporation, and $N = \{1, 2, \ldots, n\}$ is the set of creditors, with each creditor i owed a debt of d_i. It is assumed that $E < \sum_{i=1}^n d_i$ (otherwise every creditor can be paid off in full, and there is no bankruptcy problem to be considered).

This problem can be analyzed using a mathematical model in several different ways. One way, as presented in O'Neill [1982], depicts the problem as a coalitional game $(N; v)$, where the set of players is the set of creditors, and the coalitional function is

$$v(S) := \max \left\{ E - \sum_{i \notin S} d_i, 0 \right\}. \qquad (18.208)$$

Prove that this game is convex, and deduce that it has a nonempty core.
Explanation: The intuition behind this definition is as follows. When a coalition S intends on forming, it computes what it can gain for its members. The coalition

takes into account the worst-case scenario, in which all the creditors who are not members of S get paid all the debt they are owed in full, if the worth of E enables this.

18.59 Let $[E; d_1, d_2, \ldots, d_n]$ be a bankruptcy problem, and let x be an imputation that divides the assets of the bankrupt estate among the creditors proportionally to the debt that is owed to each of them:

$$x_i = \frac{d_i}{\sum_{j=1}^{n} d_j} \cdot E. \tag{18.209}$$

Is x in the core of the game defined in Exercise 18.58?

18.60 Let $[E; d_1, d_2, \ldots, d_n]$ be a bankruptcy problem, and let $(N; v)$ be the coalitional game corresponding to this problem, as defined in Exercise 18.58. Let $x = (x_1, x_2, \ldots, x_n)$ be an imputation in the core of $(N; v)$, and let S be a nonempty coalition. Let $\Gamma = [x(S); (d_i)_{i \in S}]$ be the bankruptcy problem restricted to the creditors in S, given the imputation x. Denote by $(S; x_S^w)$ the reduced game of $(N; v)$ to coalition S relative to x. Prove that $(S; w_S^x)$ is the game corresponding to the bankruptcy problem Γ.

In other words, this exercise states that for every imputation x in the core, the game corresponding to the bankruptcy problem for coalition S at the point x is the reduced game to S relative to x.

18.61 Let φ be the solution concept to the collection of bankruptcy problems that divides the asset E among the creditors proportionally to the debt owed to them:

$$\varphi_i(E; d_1, d_2, \ldots, d_n) := \frac{d_i}{\sum_{j=1}^{n} d_j} \cdot E. \tag{18.210}$$

Does this solution concept satisfy the Davis–Maschler reduced game property (see page 763)?

18.62 Prove Theorem 18.68 on page 774.

18.63 Prove that the function $\widehat{f}$ that is defined in Equation (18.160) (page 778) is a flow in the graph G, and its magnitude is $M(f^*) + \varepsilon$.

18.64 In Section 18.9 we defined a flow problem in which each edge is controlled by one of the players. In this exercise we consider a flow problem $(V, E, v^0, v^1, c, N, I)$ in which some of the edges are "public edges"; that is, the function I is a function from E to $N \cup \{*\}$. If $I(e) = *$ we say that e is a *public edge*.

The worth of a coalition S is the maximal magnitude of the flow that can pass from v^0 to v^1 using the edges controlled by the members of S and the public edges. Answer the following questions.

(a) Construct a flow problem with public edges such that the core of the corresponding flow game is empty.

(b) Prove that every flow game corresponding to a flow problem with public edges is a monotonic game. In addition, show that for every monotonic game $(N; v)$

there is a flow problem in which there may be public edges such that $(N; v)$ is the flow game corresponding to this flow problem.

18.65 Write out the superadditive cover of the games in Exercise 18.5.

18.66 Draw the core of the game in Exercise 18.6, with respect to each possible coalitional structure.

18.67 Prove Theorem 18.79 on page 781.

18.68 Let $x \in C(N; v; \mathcal{B})$ and $y \in C(N; w; \mathcal{B})$. Is $x + y \in C(N; v + w; \mathcal{B})$? Is $x - y \in C(N; v - w; \mathcal{B})$? For each claim, either prove it, or provide a counterexample.

18.69 Prove or disprove: for every coalitional game $(N; v)$ there exists a coalitional structure $\mathcal{B}$ such that $C(N; v; \mathcal{B}) \neq \emptyset$.

18.70 Let $(N; v)$ be a coalitional game, let (N, v^*) be its superadditive cover, and let $(N; \tilde{v})$ be its monotonic cover (see Definition 18.78 for the definition of the superadditive cover, and Exercise 18.51 for the definition of the monotonic cover). Is one of the quantities $v(N)$, $v^*(N)$, and $\tilde{v}(N)$ always greater than or equal to one of the other quantities? Justify your answer.

The Shapley value

Chapter summary

This chapter presents the Shapley value, which is one of the two most important single-valued solution concepts for coalitional games. It assigns to every coalitional game an imputation, which represents the payoff that each player can expect to obtain from participating in the game. The Shapley value is defined by an axiomatic approach: it is the unique solution concept that satisfies the efficiency, symmetry, null player, and additivity properties. An explicit formula is provided for the Shapley value of a coalitional game, as a linear function of the worths of the various coalitions. A second characterization, due to Peyton Young, involves a marginality property that replaces the additivity and null player properties.

The Shapley value of a convex game turns out to be an element of the core of the game, which implies in particular that the core of a convex game is nonempty. Similar to the core, the Shapley value is consistent: it satisfies a reduced game property, with respect to the Hart–Mas-Colell definition of the reduced game.

When applied to simple games, the Shapley value is known as the Shapley–Shubik power index and it is widely used in political science as a measure of the power distribution in committees.

This chapter studies the *Shapley value*, a single-valued solution concept for coalitional games first introduced in Shapley [1953a]. Shapley's original goal was to answer the question "How much would a player be willing to pay for participating in a game?" Plainly, the answer to that question depends on how much a player expects to receive when he comes to play the game.

Assuming that the grand coalition N will be formed, how will the worth $v(N)$ be divided among the members of the coalition? If one may "expect" that player i will receive the sum φ_i, that sum will be called "player i's value in the game." We will also interpret φ_i as the sum that it is "reasonable" for player i to receive if the grand coalition N is formed.

Shapley proposed a solution concept that satisfies several properties, which have come to be known as the Shapley properties (or axioms). We leave it to the reader to judge to what extent the properties put forward by Shapley reflect his original goal. The properties may also be applicable to a fair judge who is hired to advise the players on how to divide their profit among themselves after forming the grand coalition.

19.1 The Shapley properties

We start by presenting Shapley's properties, also sometimes called "axioms," as they form the basis of a theory developed from them.

Recall that a single-valued solution concept φ is a function associating every coalitional game $(N; v)$ and every coalitional structure $\mathcal{B}$ with an imputation $\varphi(N; v; \mathcal{B}) \in \mathbb{R}^N$. In this chapter, we will restrict our attention to a coalitional structure containing only one coalition, the grand coalition $\mathcal{B} = \{N\}$, and therefore omit mentioning the coalitional structure in the notation for solution concepts. As we have seen, every game with a set of players N is a vector[1] $z = (z_S)_{S \subseteq N} \in \mathbb{R}^{\mathcal{P}(N)}$ satisfying $z_\emptyset = 0$. It follows that for a fixed set of players, a single-valued solution concept is a function φ defined over the set $\{z \in \mathbb{R}^{\mathcal{P}(N)} : z_\emptyset = 0\}$, which is a $(2^n - 1)$-dimensional subspace of $\mathbb{R}^{\mathcal{P}(N)}$. The function φ associates every game in this subspace with an n-dimensional vector in $\mathbb{R}^N$. In other words, a single-valued solution concept is an infinite sequence of functions, one for each set of players N.

Definition 19.1 *Let φ be a single-valued solution concept, let $(N; v)$ be a coalitional game, and let $i \in N$ be a player. Then $\varphi_i(N; v)$ is called the* value *of player i in $(N; v)$ according to φ.*

19.1.1 Efficiency

The first property we present here is the efficiency property, which requires that the sum total that all the players expect to get equals $v(N)$, the worth of the grand coalition N.

Definition 19.2 *A solution concept φ satisfies* efficiency *if for every coalitional game $(N; v)$,*

$$\sum_{i \in N} \varphi_i(N; v) = v(N). \tag{19.1}$$

If we assume that the coalition that will form is the grand coalition N, then the sum total that the players expect to receive is $v(N)$, the total amount available to them, and it is reasonable to assume that rational players will divide the entire sum total, without "wasting" any part of it.

19.1.2 Symmetry

The next property is the symmetry property, which is essentially a "non-discrimination" property, because it states that two players with the same standing in the game (who differ only in their names) should expect the same amount.

Definition 19.3 *Let $(N; v)$ be a coalitional game, and let $i, j \in N$. Players i and j are* symmetric players *if for every coalition $S \subseteq N \setminus \{i, j\}$ (which contains neither i nor j as members),*

---

1 $\mathcal{P}(N)$ is the collection of all subsets of the set of players N.

$$v(S \cup \{i\}) = v(S \cup \{j\}). \tag{19.2}$$

Symmetric players give the same marginal contribution to every coalition that does not contain them, and they are therefore identical from a strategic perspective. Adding player i to a coalition is equivalent to adding player j to that coalition.

Definition 19.4 *A solution concept φ satisfies* symmetry[2] *if for every coalitional game $(N; v)$ and every pair of symmetric players i and j in the game:*

$$\varphi_i(N; v) = \varphi_j(N; v). \tag{19.3}$$

The symmetry property requires that the solution concept be independent of the names of the players if their contributions to every coalition are equal. Two such players ought to get the same share of $v(N)$, and therefore ought to be willing to pay the same sum for participating in the game. This property is a reasonable one to adopt when there are no other differences between the players, stemming from social standing, age, personality, and so on.

19.1.3 Covariance under strategic equivalence

Another reasonable property to apply is covariance under strategic equivalence (see Section 17.2 on page 718).

Definition 19.5 *A solution concept φ satisfies* covariance under strategic equivalence *if for every coalitional game $(N; v)$, every positive real number a, every vector $b \in \mathbb{R}^N$, and every player $i \in N$,*[3]

$$\varphi_i(N, av + b) = a\varphi_i(N; v) + b_i. \tag{19.4}$$

19.1.4 The null player property

The next property is the null player property, which states that if a player contributes nothing to any coalition he joins, then he should not expect to receive a positive amount for participating in the game.

Definition 19.6 *A player i is called a* null *player in a game $(N; v)$ if for every coalition $S \subseteq N$, including the empty coalition, one has*[4]

$$v(S) = v(S \cup \{i\}). \tag{19.5}$$

A null player contributes nothing to any coalition he chooses to join. In particular, if i is a null player, then $v(i) = 0$.

----

2 This property is sometimes called the *equal treatment property*.

3 Recall that for every coalitional game $(N; v)$, for every $a > 0$, and for every $b \in \mathbb{R}^N$, the coalitional function $av + b$ is defined by

$$(av + b)(S) := av(S) + b(S).$$

4 If a coalition S contains player i then this equality holds trivially, because then $S \cup \{i\} = S$.

Definition 19.7 *A solution concept φ satisfies the* null player property *if for every coalitional game $(N; v)$ and every null player i in the game,*

$$\varphi_i(N; v) = 0. \tag{19.6}$$

19.1.5 Additivity property

The next property looks at a pair of coalitional games with the same set of players, and connects the solution of those two games to the solution of their sum.[5]

Definition 19.8 *A solution concept φ satisfies* additivity *if for every pair of coalitional games $(N; v)$ and $(N; w)$,*

$$\varphi(N; v + w) = \varphi(N; v) + \varphi(N; w). \tag{19.7}$$

The additivity property is justified as follows: suppose that the same set of players participate in the two coalitional games $(N; v)$ and $(N; w)$. The amount that player i expects to receive in $(N; v)$ is $\varphi_i(N; v)$, and the amount that he expects to receive in $(N; w)$ is $\varphi_i(N; w)$. If the two games are independent, we may regard this situation as a single game in which each coalition S, if it forms, receives $v(S) + w(S)$. Additivity states that player i should expect to receive $\varphi_i(N; v) + \varphi_i(N; w)$ in the game $(N; v + w)$.

This justification depends on the answer to the question: "To what extent is the single game $(N; v + w)$ equivalent to playing both $(N; v)$ and $(N; w)$?" In other words, to what extent are the two games indeed independent of each other? If we accept the additivity property, then the sum of the expectations of the players in the game $(N; v + w)$ is the sum of their expectations in the games $(N; v)$ and $(N; w)$. But is the "strength" of a player in the game $(N; v + w)$ equal to the sum of his "strengths" in each of the games $(N; v)$ and $(N; w)$? It is possible, for example, that one player may be willing to give up a bit in the game $(N; v)$ in exchange for receiving much more in the game $(N; w)$.

Another interpretation that can be adduced in justification of the additivity property is that the players play only one of the games, $(N; v)$ or $(N; w)$, each with probability $\frac{1}{2}$. In this case, they will expect to receive in the combined game $\frac{1}{2}\varphi(N; v) + \frac{1}{2}\varphi(N; w)$. The worth of a coalition in the combined game is then $\frac{1}{2}v(S) + \frac{1}{2}w(S)$, yielding the requirement that $\varphi(N; \frac{1}{2}v + \frac{1}{2}w) = \frac{1}{2}\varphi(N; v) + \frac{1}{2}\varphi(N; w)$, which, together with the covariance under strategic equivalence, is equivalent to the definition of the additivity property. This justification assumes that the utility that the players receive from the lottery conducted to choose the game equals the expected utility under the lottery, but in practice this does not always hold. Since the additivity property reflects assumptions that do not hold in all situations, it has been criticized. There is therefore some interest in characterizing the Shapley value using a system of properties that does not include the additivity property. We will present such a characterization in Section 19.5.

---

[5] If $(N; v)$ and $(N; w)$ are two games, their sum is $(N; v + w)$, defined by $(v + w)(S) := v(S) + w(S)$ for every coalition $S \subseteq N$.

19.2 Solutions satisfying some of the Shapley properties

In this section, we present several solutions, and check which of the Shapley properties they satisfy.

Example 19.9 Consider the solution concept ψ defined by

$$\psi_i(N; v) := v(i). \tag{19.8}$$

This solution concept satisfies additivity, symmetry, the null player property, and covariance under strategic equivalence. It does not, however, satisfy efficiency (Exercise 19.1). ◄

Example 19.10 A player i is called a *dummy player* if $v(S \cup \{i\}) = v(S) + v(i)$ for every coalition $S \subseteq N \setminus \{i\}$. Every null player is a dummy player. Denote by $d(v)$ the number of dummy players. Consider the solution concept ψ defined by

$$\psi_i(N; v) := \begin{cases} v(i) + \dfrac{v(N) - \sum_{j \in N} v(j)}{n - d(v)} & \text{if } i \text{ is not a dummy player,} \\ v(i) & \text{if } i \text{ is a dummy player.} \end{cases} \tag{19.9}$$

This solution concept satisfies efficiency, symmetry, covariance under strategic equivalence, and the null player property. It does not, however, satisfy additivity (Exercise 19.2).

Here is an example that shows that this solution concept does not satisfy additivity. Consider the following two three-player games:

$$v(1) = v(2) = v(3) = v(1, 2) = v(1, 3) = 0, \quad v(2, 3) = v(1, 2, 3) = 1, \tag{19.10}$$

and

$$u(1) = u(2) = u(3) = u(1, 3) = 0, \quad u(1, 2) = u(2, 3) = u(1, 2, 3) = 1. \tag{19.11}$$

In the game $(N; v)$, only Player 1 is a dummy player, and in the game $(N; u)$ there is no dummy player. Therefore,

$$\psi(N; v) = \left(0, \tfrac{1}{2}, \tfrac{1}{2}\right), \qquad \psi(N; u) = \left(\tfrac{1}{3}, \tfrac{1}{3}, \tfrac{1}{3}\right). \tag{19.12}$$

The game $(N; v + u)$ is the game

$$(v + u)(1) = (v + u)(2) = (v + u)(3) = u(1, 3) = 0, \quad (v + u)(1, 2) = 1,$$
$$(v + u)(2, 3) = (v + u)(1, 2, 3) = 2.$$

There is no dummy player in this game, and therefore

$$\psi(N; v + u) = \left(\tfrac{2}{3}, \tfrac{2}{3}, \tfrac{2}{3}\right) \neq \left(\tfrac{1}{3}, \tfrac{5}{6}, \tfrac{5}{6}\right) = \psi(N; v) + \psi(N; u). \tag{19.13}$$

In other words, φ does not satisfy additivity. ◄

Example 19.11 Consider the solution concept ψ defined by

$$\psi_i(N; v) := \max_{\{S: \, i \notin S\}} (v(S \cup \{i\}) - v(S)). \tag{19.14}$$

This is the maximal marginal contribution that player i can give to any coalition. This solution concept satisfies symmetry, the null player property, and covariance under strategic equivalence. It does not, however, satisfy efficiency and additivity (Exercise 19.3).

We first show that ψ does not satisfy efficiency. To this end, define the following three-player game $(N; w)$:

$$w(1) = 0, \quad w(2) = w(3) = w(1,2) = w(1,3) = w(2,3) = w(1,2,3) = 1. \tag{19.15}$$

Applying Equation (19.14) yields

$$\psi(N; w) = (0, 1, 1). \tag{19.16}$$

Since $\sum_{i=1}^{3} \psi_i(N; w) = 2 \neq 1 = w(N)$, the solution concept ψ does not satisfy efficiency.

We next show that ψ does not satisfy additivity. Let $(N; v)$ be the game defined in Equation (19.10). Then

$$\psi(N; v) = (0, 1, 1). \tag{19.17}$$

The sum $v + w$ is the coalitional function given by

$$(v + w)(1) = 0, \tag{19.18}$$

$$(v + w)(2) = (v + w)(3) = (v + w)(1,2) = (v + w)(1,3) = 1, \tag{19.19}$$

$$(v + w)(2, 3) = (v + w)(1, 2, 3) = 2, \tag{19.20}$$

and therefore

$$\psi(N; v + w) = (0, 1, 1) \neq (0, 1, 1) + (0, 1, 1) = \psi(N; v) + \psi(N; w), \tag{19.21}$$

from which we deduce that ψ does not satisfy additivity. ◀

Example 19.12 Consider the solution concept ψ defined by

$$\psi_i(N; v) := v(\{1, 2, \ldots, i\}) - v(\{1, 2, \ldots, i - 1\}). \tag{19.22}$$

This solution concept satisfies efficiency, additivity, the null player property, and covariance under strategic equivalence. It does not satisfy symmetry (Exercise 19.4). To show that this solution concept does not satisfy symmetry, note that for the game $(N; v)$ defined in Equation (19.10)

$$\psi(N; v) = (0, 0, 1), \tag{19.23}$$

even though Players 2 and 3 are symmetric players in this game. ◀

In the last example, we assumed the existence of a particular ordering of the players, namely, $1, 2, \ldots, n$. Clearly, this solution concept can be defined using any arbitrary ordering of the players. Denote by $\Pi(N)$ the set of all permutations of the set of players N (recall that the number of players is $n = |N|$). The set $\Pi(N)$ then contains $n!$ permutations. For every permutation $\pi \in \Pi(N)$, define

$$P_i(\pi) := \{j \in N : \pi(j) < \pi(i)\}. \tag{19.24}$$

This is the set of players ahead of player i when the players are ordered according to permutation π. Note that $P_i(\pi) = \emptyset$ if and only if $\pi(i) = 1$. Similarly, $P_i(\pi)$ contains only one element (which is $\pi^{-1}(1)$) if and only if $\pi(i) = 2$. Generally,

$$P_i(\pi) \cup \{i\} = P_k(\pi) \text{ if and only if } \pi(k) = \pi(i) + 1. \tag{19.25}$$

For every permutation $\pi \in \Pi(N)$, define a solution concept ψ^π as follows:

$$\psi_i^\pi(N; v) := v(P_i(\pi) \cup \{i\}) - v(P_i(\pi)). \tag{19.26}$$

As in Example 19.12, this solution concept satisfies efficiency, additivity, the null player property, and covariance under strategic equivalence. It does not satisfy symmetry.

19.3 The definition and characterization of the Shapley value

Are there solution concepts that satisfy efficiency, additivity, the null player property, and symmetry? Shapley [1953a] proved that this is indeed the case, and furthermore that there is a unique such solution concept.

Theorem 19.13 (Shapley [1953a]) *There is a unique solution concept satisfying efficiency, additivity, the null player property, and symmetry.*

Shapley provided an explicit formula for computing this solution concept. In Example 19.12, we saw that for every permutation $\pi \in \Pi(N)$, the solution concept ψ^π satisfies all the Shapley properties except symmetry. To define a solution concept that in addition satisfies symmetry, we average the solution concepts ψ^π over all permutations of the set of players N.

Definition 19.14 *The* Shapley value *is the solution concept* Sh *defined as follows:*

$$\text{Sh}_i(N; v) := \frac{1}{n!} \sum_{\pi \in \Pi(N)} (v(P_i(\pi) \cup \{i\}) - v(P_i(\pi))), \quad \forall i \in N. \tag{19.27}$$

Using the solution concept ψ^π defined in Equation (19.26), one may write Equation (19.27) as follows:

$$\text{Sh}(N; v) := \frac{1}{n!} \sum_{\pi \in \Pi(N)} \psi^\pi(N; v). \tag{19.28}$$

Before proceeding to the proof that the Shapley value Sh satisfies the above-listed properties, we present a probabilistic interpretation of Equation (19.27). Suppose that the players enter a room one at a time. Each player, upon entry, receives his marginal contribution to the set composed of the players who entered the room before him; i.e., if S is the set of players already in the room as player i enters, player i receives $v(S \cup \{i\}) - v(S)$. If the ordering under which the players enter the room is chosen randomly, with every ordering given equal probability of being chosen, then the expected payoff of player i is given by Equation (19.27).

Theorem 19.15 *The Shapley value is the only single-valued solution concept satisfying efficiency, additivity, the null player property, and symmetry.*

Remark 19.16 *In Exercise 19.12, we show that there exist subfamilies of the class of coalitional games over which one may define a solution concept different from the Shapley value and that satisfies efficiency, additivity, the null player property, and symmetry. Theorem 19.15, however, shows that the Shapley value is the only solution concept defined over all coalitional games that satisfies these four properties.* ◆

We now present a formulation equivalent to Equation (19.27). Let i be a player, and S be an arbitrary coalition that does not include player i. What is the number of permutations π for which $P_i(\pi) = S$? For $P_i(\pi)$ to equal S, we must require that the players in S enter the room before player i under the permutation π, then player i, and after him the players in $N\backslash(S \cup \{i\})$. The number of different ways that the players in S can be ordered is $S!$, and the number of different ways that the players in $N\backslash(S \cup \{i\})$ can be ordered is $(n - |S| - 1)!$. It follows that the number of permutations π under which $P_i(\pi) = S$ is $|S|! \times (n - |S| - 1)!$. This shows that the Shapley value of player i can be computed as follows.

Theorem 19.17 *The Shapley value is given by the following equation:*

$$\mathrm{Sh}_i(N; v) = \sum_{S \subseteq N\backslash\{i\}} \frac{|S|! \times (n - |S| - 1)!}{n!} (v(S \cup \{i\}) - v(S)). \tag{19.29}$$

We begin the proof of Theorem 19.15 by ascertaining that the Shapley value satisfies the four properties listed in the statement of the theorem.

Claim 19.18 *The Shapley value satisfies efficiency, additivity, the null player property, and symmetry. Furthermore, it satisfies covariance under strategic equivalence.*

Proof: Since

$$\mathrm{Sh}(N; v) = \frac{1}{n!} \sum_{\pi \in \Pi(N)} \psi^\pi(N; v), \tag{19.30}$$

and since for each permutation π, the solution concept ψ^π satisfies additivity, the null player property, and covariance under strategic equivalence, the Shapley value, as the average of these solution concepts, also satisfies the same list of properties (Exercise 19.6).

We now show that the Shapley value satisfies symmetry. Let i and j be two symmetric players. Define a function $f : \Pi(N) \to \Pi(N)$ that maps each permutation over the set of players to another permutation as follows. For every permutation π, the permutation $f(\pi)$ is identical to π except that it swaps player i with player j:

$$(f(\pi))(k) = \begin{cases} \pi(j) & \text{if } k = i, \\ \pi(i) & \text{if } k = j, \\ \pi(k) & \text{if } k \notin \{i, j\}. \end{cases} \tag{19.31}$$

Another way of saying this is that $f(\pi)$ is the composition of π with the permutation that swaps i with j and leaves all the other players in their place. The function f is bijective[6] (explain why).

We next show that if i and j are symmetric players, then the permutation π satisfies

$$v(P_i(\pi) \cup \{i\}) - v(P_i(\pi)) = v(P_j(f(\pi)) \cup \{j\}) - v(P_j(f(\pi))). \tag{19.32}$$

----

6 A function $f : A \to B$ is *bijective* if it is one-to-one and onto.

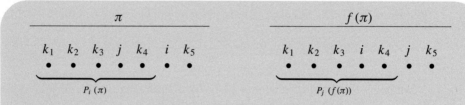

Figure 19.1 The case in which player i appears before player j under permutation π

$$
\begin{array}{l}
\overline{}\;\pi\;\overline{} \\
k_1 \quad k_2 \quad k_3 \quad j \quad k_4 \quad i \quad k_5 \\
\underbrace{\bullet \quad \bullet \quad \bullet \quad \bullet \quad \bullet}_{P_i(\pi)} \quad \bullet \quad \bullet
\end{array}
\qquad
\begin{array}{l}
\overline{}\;f(\pi)\;\overline{} \\
k_1 \quad k_2 \quad k_3 \quad i \quad k_4 \quad j \quad k_5 \\
\underbrace{\bullet \quad \bullet \quad \bullet \quad \bullet \quad \bullet}_{P_j(f(\pi))} \quad \bullet \quad \bullet
\end{array}
$$

Figure 19.2 The case in which player i appears after player j under permutation π

Case 1: Player i appears before player j under permutation π, i.e., $j \notin P_i(\pi)$.
In this case, $P_i(\pi) = P_j(f(\pi))$ (see Figure 19.1), and in particular $v(P_i(\pi)) = v(P_j(f(\pi)))$. Since i and j are symmetric players, and since $P_i(\pi)$ contains neither i nor j, $v(P_i(\pi) \cup \{i\}) = v(P_j(f(\pi)) \cup \{j\})$. These two equalities together imply Equation (19.32).

Case 2: Player i appears after player j under permutation π, i.e., $j \in P_i(\pi)$.
In this case, $P_i(\pi) \cup \{i\} = P_j(f(\pi)) \cup \{j\}$ (see Figure 19.2), and in particular $v(P_i(\pi) \cup \{i\}) = v(P_j(f(\pi)) \cup \{j\})$. Similarly, $P_i(\pi)\backslash\{j\} = P_j(f(\pi))\backslash\{i\}$. Since i and j are symmetric players, $v((P_i(\pi)\backslash\{j\}) \cup \{j\}) = v((P_j(f(\pi))\backslash\{i\}) \cup \{i\})$, i.e., $v(P_i(\pi)) = v(P_j(f(\pi)))$. These two equalities together imply that Equation (19.32) holds in this case as well.

Since f is bijective,

$$\{f(\pi)\colon \pi \in \Pi(N)\} = \Pi(N). \tag{19.33}$$

Therefore,

$$\mathrm{Sh}_i(N; v) = \frac{1}{n!} \sum_{\pi \in \Pi(N)} \left(v(P_i(\pi) \cup \{i\}) - v(P_i(\pi)) \right) \tag{19.34}$$

$$= \frac{1}{n!} \sum_{\pi \in \Pi(N)} \left(v(P_j(f(\pi)) \cup \{j\}) - v(P_j(f(\pi))) \right) \tag{19.35}$$

$$= \frac{1}{n!} \sum_{\mu \in \Pi(N)} \left(v(P_j(\mu) \cup \{j\}) - v(P_j(\mu)) \right) \tag{19.36}$$

$$= \mathrm{Sh}_j(N; v), \tag{19.37}$$

where Equation (19.35) follows from Equation (19.32) and Equation (19.36) follows from setting $\mu = f(\pi)$ and from using Equation (19.33). This shows that the Shapley value Sh satisfies symmetry, which is what we wanted to prove, completing the proof of Claim 19.18. $\square$

We next prove the uniqueness claim in Theorem 19.15. Define, for every nonempty coalition T, a simple game called the *carrier game over* T. In the carrier game over T, a coalition is a winning coalition (with worth 1) if and only if it contains T.

Definition 19.19 *Let* $T \subseteq N$ *be a nonempty coalition. The* carrier game *over* T *is the simple game* $(N; u_T)$ *defined as follows. For each coalition* $S \subseteq N$,

$$u_T(S) := \begin{cases} 1 & \text{if } T \subseteq S, \\ 0 & \text{otherwise.} \end{cases} \tag{19.38}$$

Theorem 19.20 *Every game* $(N; v)$ *is a linear combination of carrier games.*

Proof: Recall that the space of the coalitional games over the set of players N is a vector space of dimension $2^n - 1$. The number of carrier games equals the number of nonempty coalitions in N, namely, $2^n - 1$. To prove the theorem, it suffices to show that the carrier games are linearly independent over $\mathbb{R}^{2^n-1}$; this will imply that they form a linear basis of the space of games. Indeed, every set of $2^n - 1$ independent vectors in a vector space of dimension $2^n - 1$ is a basis for that space, and therefore every element of the vector space can be written as a linear combination of the basis elements.

Suppose, by contradiction, that the carrier games are linearly dependent. Then there exists a linear combination of carrier games with non-zero coefficients that sums to the zero vector. In other words, there exist real numbers $(\alpha_T)_{\{T \subseteq N, T \neq \emptyset\}}$, not all zero, such that

$$\sum_{\{T \subseteq N, T \neq \emptyset\}} \alpha_T u_T(S) = 0, \quad \forall S \subseteq N. \tag{19.39}$$

Let $\mathcal{T} = \{T \subseteq N : T \neq \emptyset, \alpha_T \neq 0\}$ be the set of all coalitions with non-zero coefficients in the linear combination in Equation (19.39). Since we assumed that not all coefficients are zero, the set $\mathcal{T}$ is nonempty. Let $S_0 \in \mathcal{T}$ be a minimal coalition in $\mathcal{T}$; i.e., there is no coalition in $\mathcal{T}$ strictly contained in S_0. We will show that $\sum_{\{T \subseteq N, T \neq \emptyset\}} \alpha_T u_T(S_0) \neq 0$, in contradiction to Equation (19.39). Note that

$$\sum_{\{T \subseteq N, T \neq \emptyset\}} \alpha_T u_T(S_0) = \sum_{\{T \subset S_0, T \neq \emptyset\}} \alpha_T u_T(S_0) + \alpha_{S_0} u_{S_0}(S_0) + \sum_{T \nsubseteq S_0} \alpha_T u_T(S_0). \tag{19.40}$$

$\alpha_T = 0$ for every T satisfying $T \subset S_0$, since S_0 is a minimal coalition in $\mathcal{T}$. For every T satisfying $T \nsubseteq S_0$, the definition of a carrier game implies that $u_T(S_0) = 0$. Therefore,

$$\sum_{\{T \subseteq N, T \neq \emptyset\}} \alpha_T u_T(S_0) = \alpha_{S_0} u_{S_0}(S_0) = \alpha_{S_0} \neq 0, \tag{19.41}$$

which is what we wanted to show. The contradiction implies that the assumption that the carrier games are linearly dependent is false; i.e., they are linearly independent. $\square$

The next theorem states that every solution concept satisfying efficiency, symmetry, and the null player property is uniquely determined for every game that is the product of a carrier game by a scalar.

Theorem 19.21 *Let T be a nonempty coalition, and let α be a real number. Define a game $(N; u_{T,\alpha})$ as follows:*

$$u_{T,\alpha}(S) = \begin{cases} \alpha & \text{if } T \subseteq S, \\ 0 & \text{otherwise.} \end{cases} \tag{19.42}$$

If φ is a solution concept satisfying efficiency, symmetry, and the null player property, then

$$\varphi_i(N; u_{T,\alpha}) = \begin{cases} \frac{\alpha}{|T|} & \text{if } i \in T, \\ 0 & \text{if } i \notin T. \end{cases} \tag{19.43}$$

Proof: In the game $(N; u_{T,\alpha})$, every player $i \notin T$ is a null player, and every pair of players in T are symmetric. The claim of the theorem then follows from the assumption that φ satisfies efficiency, symmetry, and the null player property. □

Proof of Theorem 19.15: By Claim 19.18, the Shapley value Sh satisfies additivity, efficiency, symmetry, and the null player property. All that remains is to show that the Shapley value is the unique solution concept satisfying these properties. Let φ therefore be a solution concept satisfying these properties; we will show that $\varphi = $ Sh. Let $(N; v)$ be a coalitional game. Theorem 19.20 implies that v is a sum of games of the form u_{T,α_T} for coalitions T in the collection $\{T \subseteq N, T \neq \emptyset\}$. In other words, there exist real numbers $(\alpha_T)_{\{T \subseteq N, T \neq \emptyset\}}$ such that

$$v(S) = \sum_{\{T \subseteq N, T \neq \emptyset\}} u_{T,\alpha_T}(S). \tag{19.44}$$

By Theorem 19.21, since both φ and Sh satisfy symmetry, efficiency, and the null player property,

$$\varphi(N; u_{T,\alpha_T}) = \text{Sh}(N; u_{T,\alpha_T}), \quad \forall T \subseteq N, T \neq \emptyset. \tag{19.45}$$

Since both φ and Sh satisfy additivity,

$$\varphi(N; v) = \sum_{\{T \subseteq N, T \neq \emptyset\}} \varphi(N; u_{T,\alpha_T}) = \sum_{\{T \subseteq N, T \neq \emptyset\}} \text{Sh}(N; u_{T,\alpha_T}) = \text{Sh}(N; v). \tag{19.46}$$

Because this is true for every game $(N; v)$, we conclude that $\varphi = $ Sh. In other words, every solution satisfying additivity, efficiency, symmetry, and the null player property is identical to the Shapley value. This concludes the proof of Theorem 19.15. □

19.4 Examples

In this section we compute the Shapley value in several examples.

Example 19.22 A two-player bargaining game Let $(N; v)$ be a two-player game with the following coalitional function:

$$v(1) = v(2) = 0, \quad v(1,2) = 1. \tag{19.47}$$

Since the two players are symmetric, $\text{Sh}_1(N; v) = \text{Sh}_2(N; v)$, the efficiency property implies that the Shapley value is

$$\text{Sh}(N; v) = \left(\tfrac{1}{2}, \tfrac{1}{2} \right). \tag{19.48}$$

◀

Example 19.23 A simple majority game with n players Let $(N; v)$ be an n-player game with the following coalitional function:

$$v(S) = \begin{cases} 0 & \text{if } |S| \le \tfrac{n}{2}, \\ 1 & \text{if } |S| > \tfrac{n}{2}. \end{cases} \tag{19.49}$$

Since all the players are symmetric, $\text{Sh}_i(N; v) = \text{Sh}_j(N; v)$ for every pair of players $i, j \in N$, and applying the efficiency property yields

$$\text{Sh}(N; v) = \left(\tfrac{1}{n}, \tfrac{1}{n}, \ldots, \tfrac{1}{n} \right). \tag{19.50}$$

◀

Example 19.24 The gloves game Let $(N; v)$ be a three-player game with the following coalitional function:

$$v(1) = v(2) = v(3) = v(1,2) = 0, \quad v(1,3) = v(2,3) = v(1,2,3) = 1. \tag{19.51}$$

We previously saw this game in Example 18.5 on page 738, where we found that its core solely contains the imputation $(0, 0, 1)$. We next compute the Shapley value of the game. To this end, we use Equation (19.27). For every permutation of N (there are six such permutations) we list the marginal contribution of each player:

Permutation	Contribution of Player 1	Contribution of Player 2	Contribution of Player 3
$(1,2,3)$	$v(1) - v(\emptyset) = 0$	$v(1,2) - v(1) = 0$	$v(1,2,3) - v(1,2) = 1$
$(1,3,2)$	$v(1) - v(\emptyset) = 0$	$v(1,2,3) - v(1,3) = 0$	$v(1,3) - v(1) = 1$
$(2,1,3)$	$v(1,2) - v(2) = 0$	$v(2) - v(\emptyset) = 0$	$v(1,2,3) - v(1,2) = 1$
$(2,3,1)$	$v(1,2,3) - v(2,3) = 0$	$v(2) - v(\emptyset) = 0$	$v(2,3) - v(2) = 1$
$(3,1,2)$	$v(1,3) - v(3) = 1$	$v(1,2,3) - v(1,3) = 0$	$v(3) - v(\emptyset) = 0$
$(3,2,1)$	$v(1,2,3) - v(2,3) = 0$	$v(2,3) - v(3) = 1$	$v(3) - v(\emptyset) = 0$

Summing the contribution of each player, and dividing by the number of permutations, 6, yields the Shapley value:

$$\text{Sh}(N; v) = \left(\tfrac{1}{6}, \tfrac{1}{6}, \tfrac{2}{3} \right). \tag{19.52}$$

This imputation emphasizes the fact that although Player 3 is the strongest player here, holding the left glove, the Shapley value of the other players is not zero, in contrast to the core of the gloves game.

Note that in this computation, it sufficed to compute only one of the three columns, say the Shapley value of Player 1, and to use that to deduce the Shapley values of Players 2 and 3. (Explain why this is true. Which properties did you use in your explanation?)

The core of this game contains only one imputation, $(0, 0, 1)$ (see Example 18.5 on page 738), and therefore even when the core is nonempty, the Shapley value may be outside the core. ◄

19.5 An alternative characterization of the Shapley value

The characterization of the Shapley value presented in the previous section relies on the additivity property. The motivation behind this property may be unpersuasive, and there are many cases in which it is unclear why additivity is a reasonable assumption. In this section we present a characterization of the Shapley value that does not use the additivity property. We first present several new properties, and then show that they can be used to characterize the Shapley value.

19.5.1 The marginality property

The property of monotonicity of marginal contributions requires that if a player contributes to each coalition in a game $(N; v)$ no less than he contributes to the same coalition in another game $(N; w)$ with the same set of players, then his value in $(N; v)$ is at least as great as his value in $(N; w)$.

Definition 19.25 *A solution concept φ satisfies* monotonicity of marginal contributions *if for every pair of games $(N; v)$ and $(N; w)$ with the same set of players, and for each player $i \in N$, if*

$$v(S \cup \{i\}) - v(S) \geq w(S \cup \{i\}) - w(S), \quad \forall S \subseteq N \setminus \{i\}, \tag{19.53}$$

then

$$\varphi_i(N; v) \geq \varphi_i(N; w). \tag{19.54}$$

The property of monotonicity of marginal contributions implies the property of marginality, defined as follows.

Definition 19.26 *A solution concept φ satisfies* marginality *if for every pair of games $(N; v)$ and $(N; w)$ with the same set of players, and for every player i, if*

$$v(S \cup \{i\}) - v(S) = w(S \cup \{i\}) - w(S), \quad \forall S \subseteq N \setminus \{i\}, \tag{19.55}$$

then

$$\varphi_i(N; v) = \varphi_i(N; w). \tag{19.56}$$

This property imposes the property that the value of a player depends only on his marginal contribution to each coalition, and is independent of the marginal contributions of the other players to all possible coalitions.

Theorem 19.27 *The Shapley value satisfies monotonicity of marginal contributions, and it therefore also satisfies marginality.*

The proof of Theorem 19.27 follows from the fact that by definition (see Definition 19.14) the Shapley value of player i is the weighted average of his marginal contributions to all possible coalitions. The next theorem connects several properties.

Theorem 19.28 *Every solution concept φ satisfying efficiency, symmetry, and marginality also satisfies the null player property.*

Proof: Let φ be a solution concept satisfying efficiency, symmetry, and marginality. We will show that φ also satisfies the null player property.

Let $(N; v)$ be a coalitional game, and let i be a null player in this game. Denote by z the zero game that is defined by $z(S) = 0$ for every coalition S. In $(N; z)$, all the players are symmetric, and the properties of efficiency and symmetry then imply that

$$\varphi_j(N; z) = 0 \quad \forall j \in N. \tag{19.57}$$

Since player i is a null player, one has

$$v(S \cup \{i\}) - v(S) = 0 = z(S \cup \{i\}) - z(S) \quad \forall S \subseteq N. \tag{19.58}$$

We deduce from this that the vector of marginal contributions of player i in $(N; v)$ equals his vector of marginal contributions in $(N; z)$. Marginality then implies that $\varphi_i(N; v) = \varphi_i(N; z) = 0$. $\qquad\square$

19.5.2 The second characterization of the Shapley value

The next theorem, which was proved in Young [1985], provides a second characterization of the Shapley value, replacing the properties of additivity and null player in the previous characterization with marginality.

Theorem 19.29 (Young [1985]) *The Shapley value is the unique single-valued solution concept satisfying efficiency, symmetry, and marginality.*

Proof: We have already seen (Claim 19.18 on page 803, and Theorem 19.27) that the Shapley value satisfies the three properties in the statement of the theorem. To prove the other direction of the claim of the theorem, we need to show that every solution concept φ satisfying efficiency, symmetry, and marginality is the Shapley value. The proof relies on the following definitions.

For every coalitional game $(N; v)$, denote

$$I(N; v) = \{S \subseteq N : \exists T \subseteq S, v(T) \neq 0\}. \tag{19.59}$$

A coalition S is not in $I(N; v)$ if and only if its worth, and the worth of all its subcoalitions, is 0. It follows that if S is a minimal coalition in $I(N; v)$ (i.e., none of its subcoalitions are in $I(N; v)$), then $v(S) \neq 0$, and the worth of all the subcoalitions of S is 0.

Given a game $(N; v)$, define for each coalition S a game $(N; v^S)$ as follows:

$$v^S(T) = v(S \cap T), \quad \forall T \subseteq N. \tag{19.60}$$

Every player $i \notin S$ is a null player in $(N; v^S)$. To see this, note that $S \cap (T \cup \{i\}) = S \cap T$, because $i \notin S$, and therefore

$$v^S(T \cup \{i\}) = v(S \cap (T \cup \{i\})) = v(S \cap T) = v^S(T). \tag{19.61}$$

Claim 19.30 *Let S be a coalition in $I(N; v)$. Then $I(N; v - v^S) \subset I(N; v)$.*

Proof of Claim 19.30: We first show that $I(N; v - v^S) \subseteq I(N; v)$. If $T \in I(N; v - v^S)$, then there exists a subcoalition $R \subseteq T$ satisfying

$$0 \neq (v - v^S)(R) = v(R) - v^S(R) = v(R) - v(R \cap S). \tag{19.62}$$

Therefore, either $v(R) \neq 0$, or $v(R \cap S) \neq 0$ (or both inequalities hold). Since $R \subseteq T$, both R and $R \cap S$ are subsets of T. It follows that T has at least one subset whose worth is not 0, and therefore $T \in I(N; v)$, which is what we wanted to show.

To show that $I(N; v - v^S) \neq I(N; v)$, we will show that $S \notin I(N; v - v^S)$. Indeed, for every coalition $T \subseteq S$,

$$(v - v^S)(S) = v(S) - v(S \cap S) = v(S) - v(S) = 0. \tag{19.63}$$

From this we deduce that S is not in $I(N; v - v^S)$, which is what we wanted to show. $\square$

To prove uniqueness in Theorem 19.29, let φ be a solution concept satisfying efficiency, symmetry, and marginality. We will show that $\varphi = $ Sh. By Theorem 19.28, the solution concept φ also satisfies the null player property.

The proof of uniqueness will be an inductive proof over $|I(N; v)|$, the number of elements in $I(N; v)$. If $|I(N; v)| = 0$, then $v(S) = 0$ for every coalition S, and then all the players are null players. Since both φ and Sh satisfy the null player property, $\varphi_i(N; v) = 0 = \text{Sh}_i(N; v)$ for every player $i \in N$.

Assume by induction that $\varphi(N; v) = \text{Sh}(N; v)$ for every game $(N; v)$ satisfying $|I(N; v)| < k$, and let $(N; v)$ be a game satisfying $|I(N; v)| = k$. Denote by $\hat{S}$ the set formed by the intersection of all the coalitions in $I(N; v)$, i.e.,

$$\hat{S} = \cap_{S \in I(N; v)} S. \tag{19.64}$$

Step 1: $\text{Sh}_i(N; v) = \varphi_i(N; v)$ for each $i \notin \hat{S}$.
Let $i \notin \hat{S}$. Then there exists a coalition $S \in I(N; v)$ that does not contain i. By Claim 19.30,

$$|I(N; v - v^S)| < |I(N; v)| = k, \tag{19.65}$$

and the inductive hypothesis then implies that

$$\varphi_j(N; v - v^S) = \text{Sh}_j(N; v - v^S) \quad \forall j \in N. \tag{19.66}$$

We next compute the marginal contribution of player i in $(N; v - v^S)$, and show that it equals the marginal contribution of that player in $(N; v)$. For every coalition $T \subseteq N \setminus \{i\}$,

$$(v - v^S)(T \cup \{i\}) = v(T \cup \{i\}) - v^S(T \cup \{i\}) \tag{19.67}$$

$$= v(T \cup \{i\}) - v(S \cap (T \cup \{i\})) \tag{19.68}$$

$$= v(T \cup \{i\}) - v(S \cap T) \tag{19.69}$$

$$= v(T \cup \{i\}) - v^S(T), \tag{19.70}$$

and, therefore,

$$(v - v^S)(T \cup \{i\}) - (v - v^S)(T) = v(T \cup \{i\}) - v^S(T) - v(T) + v^S(T)$$

$$= v(T \cup \{i\}) - v(T). \tag{19.71}$$

By assumption, φ satisfies marginality. By Theorem 19.27, the Shapley value Sh also satisfies marginality. It follows that $\varphi_i(N; v) = \varphi_i(N; v - v^S)$ and $\text{Sh}_i(N; v) = \text{Sh}_i(N; v - v^S)$. Using Equation (19.66), we get

$$\varphi_i(N; v) = \text{Sh}_i(N; v), \quad \forall i \notin \widehat{S}. \tag{19.72}$$

Step 2: $\text{Sh}_i(N; v) = \varphi_i(N; v)$ for each $i \in \widehat{S}$.

If $\widehat{S} = \emptyset$, the conclusion follows vacuously.

If $|\widehat{S}| = 1$, the conclusion follows from Step 1 and the fact that both the Shapley value Sh and the solution concept φ are efficient. Suppose, therefore, that $\widehat{S}$ contains at least two players.

We first show that every coalition T that does not contain $\widehat{S}$ satisfies $v(T) = 0$. Indeed, by the definition of $I(N; v)$, if $v(T) \neq 0$ then $T \in I(N; v)$. In particular, T must then contain $\widehat{S}$, which is the intersection of all the coalitions in $I(N; v)$, contradicting the fact that T does not contain $\widehat{S}$.

We now show that any pair of players in $\widehat{S}$ are symmetric players. Let $i, j \in \widehat{S}$ be two different players. For every coalition T that contains neither player i nor player j, both the coalitions $T \cup \{i\}$ and $T \cup \{j\}$ do not contain $\widehat{S}$, and therefore $v(T \cup \{i\}) = 0 = v(T \cup \{j\})$. Since this equality holds for every coalition T that contains neither i nor j, these players are symmetric, which is what we wanted to show.

Since both φ and Sh satisfy symmetry,

$$\varphi_i(N; v) = \varphi_j(N; v), \quad \text{Sh}_i(N; v) = \text{Sh}_j(N; v), \quad \forall i, j \in \widehat{S}. \tag{19.73}$$

Because we know from the previous step that $\varphi_k(N; v) = \text{Sh}_k(N; v)$ for every player $k \notin \widehat{S}$, and since both φ and Sh satisfy efficiency,

$$\sum_{k \in \widehat{S}} \varphi_k(N; v) = v(N) - \sum_{k \notin \widehat{S}} \varphi_k(N; v) = v(N) - \sum_{k \notin \widehat{S}} \text{Sh}_k(N; v) = \sum_{k \in \widehat{S}} \text{Sh}_k(N; v). \tag{19.74}$$

Equations (19.73) and (19.74) imply that for every player $j \in \widehat{S}$,

$$\varphi_j(N; v) = \frac{1}{|\widehat{S}|} \sum_{k \in \widehat{S}} \varphi_k(N; v) = \frac{1}{|\widehat{S}|} \sum_{k \in \widehat{S}} \text{Sh}_k(N; v) = \text{Sh}_j(N; v). \tag{19.75}$$

This completes the proof of the theorem. $\qquad\square$

19.6 Application: the Shapley–Shubik power index

The Shapley value can be used to measure the power of each member in a decision-making process. This application of the Shapley value was developed by Shapley and Shubik in 1954, and is called the Shapley–Shubik power index.

In this section, we will concentrate on simple monotonic games. Recall that simple games are coalitional games in which the worth of each coalition is 0 or 1. A simple game is monotonic if when the worth of a coalition is 1, the worth of every coalition containing it is also 1. These games can model decision-making in collectives containing several decision makers. $v(S) = 1$ if the members of the coalition S can impose a decision even when the other players are opposed to their decision. In this case, we say that the coalition S is a *winning* coalition. In contrast, $v(S) = 0$ if the members of S cannot impose their decisions on the other decision makers. In this case, we say that the coalition S is a *losing* coalition. In particular, in a simple monotonic game, a subcoalition of a losing coalition is also a losing coalition, and a coalition containing a winning coalition is also a winning coalition.

Here are three examples of simple monotonic games:

1. Simple majority games (see Example 19.23).
2. Unanimity games, in which a decision is accepted only if all the players agree to accept it:

$$v(S) = \begin{cases} 1 & \text{if } S = N, \\ 0 & \text{otherwise.} \end{cases} \tag{19.76}$$

3. Dictatorship games, in which a single player decides whether or not to accept or reject a decision; i.e., there exists a player i_0 such that

$$v(S) = \begin{cases} 1 & \text{if } i_0 \in S, \\ 0 & \text{if } i_0 \notin S. \end{cases} \tag{19.77}$$

Definition 19.31 *The* Shapley–Shubik power index *is the function associating each simple monotonic game with its Shapley value. The i-th coordinate of this vector is called the* power index *of player i.*

In a simple monotonic game, the Shapley value has a particularly simple form. In this case, $v(S \cup \{i\}) - v(S)$ either has the value 0 (if S and $S \cup \{i\}$ are both winning coalitions or both losing coalitions) or 1 (if S is a losing coalition, and $S \cup \{i\}$ is a winning coalition). By Theorem 19.17 on page 803, the Shapley value can therefore be written as follows:

$$\text{Sh}_i(N; v) = \sum_{\{S \subseteq N \,:\, S \cup \{i\} \text{winning}, S \text{ losing}\}} \frac{|S|! \times (n - |S| - 1)!}{n!}. \tag{19.78}$$

In what sense can one say that the Shapley–Shubik power index measures the power of a player in a game? Suppose that a set of individuals N make decisions by voting on them, and the outcome of a vote is determined by a simple monotonic game. Then, for every ordering $(i_1, i_2, \ldots, i_n)$ of the players, there is precisely one player such that the set of all the players before him in the sequence are a losing coalition, and his joining the coalition changes it into a winning coalition. Such a player is called a *pivot player*.

Suppose that a proposed decision is being voted on. The proposal induces an ordering of the players, according to their opinions regarding the proposal; the first player in this ordering is the most enthusiastic supporter of the proposal, the last player in this ordering is the most vociferous opponent of the proposal, and the players in between these two are ordered by decreasing support. The most enthusiastic supporter and the most vociferous opponent vie for the support of the other players for their positions.

Assume that all the players are exposed to the same arguments for and against the proposed decision. If the pivot player supports and votes in favor of the proposal, since all the players before him in the ordering support it to an equal or greater extent than he, they too will vote for it, and the proposal will be accepted. If, in contrast, the pivot player votes against the proposal, since all the players after him in the ordering are less enthusiastic about it than he, they too will vote against it, and the proposal will be rejected. It follows that the arguments for and against the proposed decision will be directed at the pivot player, whose vote will be the deciding vote, and his power flows from this.

When the number of proposals to be decided upon is large, and they induce all possible orderings of the players with equal probabilities, the Shapley–Shubik power index of player i is the probability that player i will be a pivot player. In this sense, the index does measure the power of each player. If the proposals to be decided upon do not induce all possible orderings of the players with equal probabilities, the Shapley–Shubik power index lacks a clear justification, and variations of this index need to be defined.

19.6.1 The power index of the United Nations Security Council

The United Nations Security Council, the most important body in the international political system, was formed in the aftermath of the Second World War. At the time, it was composed of five permanent members[7] and six nonpermanent members. The council's original charter established that a resolution could be adopted only if it received supporting votes from at least seven members. In addition, every permanent member was granted veto power over any resolution. Ignoring the possibility of a council member abstaining from a vote, it followed that for a resolution to be passed by the Security Council, it had to be supported by all five permanent members and at least two nonpermanent members.

The veto power in the hands of the permanent members of the council was the target of criticism over the years by observers who objected to the "unbalanced power" it gives the permanent members relative to the nonpermanent members. The chorus of criticism led to a restructuring of the Security Council in 1965, giving the council the structure it maintains to this day. Under the new council structure, four nonpermanent members were added to the body, and the number of supporting members required for the adoption of a resolution was raised to nine, including, as before, all five permanent members. It was claimed that both the increase in the number of nonpermanent members, from six to ten, and the fact that adoption of a resolution now required at least four nonpermanent members in addition to the five permanent members, as opposed to a minimum of two nonpermanent members in the previous structure, significantly changed the balance of power in the council. Can this claim be sustained?

The Shapley–Shubik power index enables us to explore this question in a quantified manner. To do so, we compute the Shapley value of the members of the Security Council under both structures, prior to 1965 and after 1965, and then check what change, if any, occurred in the Shapley value as a result of the 1965 restructuring. The pre-1965 structure of the Security Council can be described by a coalitional game. If we denote by P the set of permanent members of the council, and by NP the set of nonpermanent members, the resulting game is a simple game in which the set of players is given by $N := P \cup NP$, and the coalitional function (ignoring the possibility of abstentions) is given by

$$v(S) = \begin{cases} 1 & \text{if } S \supset P \text{ and } |S| \geq 7, \\ 0 & \text{otherwise.} \end{cases} \qquad (19.79)$$

---

7 The United States, the United Kingdom, the Union of the Soviet Socialist Republics, China, and France.

In this coalitional function all the members of P are symmetric and all the members of NP are symmetric, and hence only two Shapley values need to be computed: the Shapley value of a member of P and the Shapley value of a member of NP. Let us first compute the Shapley value of a nonpermanent member $i \in NP$ using Equation (19.78). For every $i \in NP$ there are five coalitions S that are not winning coalitions but satisfy the property that $S \cup \{i\}$ is a winning coalition, namely, the coalitions containing the five permanent members along with one nonpermanent member other than i. The size of each such coalition is $|S| = 6$, and therefore Equation (19.78) enables us to compute the Shapley value of each nonpermanent member, which is

$$5 \times \frac{6! \times 4!}{11!} = \frac{1}{462} = 0.0021645. \tag{19.80}$$

Since every pair of nonpermanent members is symmetric, each nonpermanent member has the same Shapley value. It follows that the sum of the Shapley values of the six nonpermanent members is

$$6 \times \frac{1}{462} = \frac{6}{462} \approx 0.013. \tag{19.81}$$

Since the Shapley value satisfies efficiency, the sum of the Shapley values of the five permanent members is $1 - \frac{6}{462} = \frac{456}{462} \approx 0.987$. Furthermore, since every pair of permanent members is symmetric, the Shapley value of each permanent member is $\frac{1}{5} \cdot \frac{456}{462} = \frac{91.2}{462} = 0.1974$. Note the immense ratio $1 : \frac{456}{5} = 1 : 91.2$ between the power of a permanent member and the power of a nonpermanent member.

The simple game corresponding to the structure of the post-1965 Security Council is given by the following coalitional game, where the set R now contains ten players:

$$v(S) = \begin{cases} 1 & \text{if } S \supset P \text{ and } |S| \geq 9, \\ 0 & \text{otherwise.} \end{cases} \tag{19.82}$$

We now compute the Shapley value of a nonpermanent member i in this game. The number of coalitions S that are not winning coalitions but satisfy the property that $S \cup \{i\}$ is a winning coalition is $\binom{9}{3}$, because, in addition to the five permanent members, such a coalition must contain three out of the nine nonpermanent members different from i. Since such a coalition contains eight players, applying Equation (19.78) gives us the Shapley value of a nonpermanent member, which is

$$\binom{9}{3} \times \frac{8! \times 6!}{15!} = \frac{4}{2145} = 0.001865. \tag{19.83}$$

The power of all the nonpermanent members together is $\frac{40}{2145} \approx 0.0186$. This enables us to deduce that the Shapley value of each permanent member is

$$\frac{1}{5} \left(1 - 10 \times \frac{4}{2145} \right) = \frac{421}{2145} = 0.1963. \tag{19.84}$$

The change in the total power of the permanent members dropped from 0.987 to $\frac{2105}{2145} \approx 0.9814$ as a result of the restructuring of the Security Council, but the relative power ratio between pairs of members moved in a negative direction for the nonpermanent members: while the power of every permanent member fell relatively marginally (by about half a percent), the power of each nonpermanent member fell by 14%. The ratio between the power of a permanent member to a nonpermanent member rose to $1 : 105\frac{1}{4}$.

If one accepts the Shapley value as a reasonable index of power, the conclusion of this computation is that the restructuring of the Security Council in 1965 did not significantly change the basic balance of power on the council: almost all the power in the Council was and remained in the hands of the veto-wielding permanent members. Measuring power under a different index, the Banzhaf power index (see Exercise 19.29) results in the conclusion that the power of the permanent members fell to a greater extent after the restructuring, but even under the Banzhaf power index the power of the permanent members was still much higher than the power of the nonpermanent members. It is therefore not surprising that complaints about the imbalance of power on the Security Council continue to be heard, with suggested changes in the composition of the council and its voting rules regularly raised by members of the United Nations.

19.7 Convex games

Recall that a game $(N; v)$ is convex if for every pair of coalitions $S, T \subseteq N$,

$$v(S) + v(T) \leq v(S \cup T) + v(S \cap T). \tag{19.85}$$

In Theorem 18.55 (page 766) we proved that the core of such a game is never empty. In this section we will show that the Shapley value of a convex game is in the core of the game.

Theorem 19.32 *If $(N; v)$ is a convex game, then the Shapley value is in the core of the game.*

Proof: For every permutation $\pi \in \Pi(N)$, denote by w^π the vector in $\mathbb{R}^N$ such that for every $i \in \{1, 2, \ldots, n\}$, its i-th coordinate is[8]

$$w_i^\pi = v(P_i(\pi) \cap \{i\}) - v(P_i(\pi)). \tag{19.86}$$

By Theorem 18.55 (page 766), for every $\pi \in \Pi(N)$, the imputation w^π is in the core of $(N; v)$. By Equation (19.27), the Shapley value is the average of the vectors $(w^\pi)_{\pi \in \Pi(N)}$:

$$\text{Sh}(N; v) = \sum_{\pi \in \Pi(N)} \frac{1}{n!} w^\pi. \tag{19.87}$$

Since the core is a convex set (Theorem 18.3 on page 736), we conclude that the Shapley value is in the core. $\square$

In Remark 18.59 (page 768) we noted that in a convex game the core equals the convex hull of the imputations defined by Equation (19.86). Since some of these vectors may be equal to each other, the Shapley value is not necessarily the core's center of mass.

---

[8] Recall that $P_i(\pi)$ denotes the set of players preceding player i according to the permutation π.

19.8) The consistency of the Shapley value

In the previous chapter on the core (see page 762), we defined the Davis–Maschler reduced game, and showed that the core satisfies the consistency property: if x is a point in the core of a game $(N; v)$, then for every nonempty coalition $S \subseteq N$, the vector $(x_i)_{i \in S}$ is a point in the core of the Davis–Maschler reduced game $(S; v_S)$. In this section, we prove that a similar property also holds for the Shapley value, but the definition of the reduced game is different in this case; it is the one introduced in Hart and Mas-Colell [1989]. Furthermore, we will prove that the reduced game property can be used to characterize the Shapley value axiomatically, similarly to the way that it can be used to characterize the nucleolus axiomatically (see Section 21.5 on page 863). Both of these single-valued solution concepts have the same system of characterizing axioms, but the definition of the reduced game differs between the two of them. It follows that if we have to choose between these two solution concepts, we can check which definition of a reduced game is more appropriate to the situation at hand.

Definition 19.33 *Let φ be a single-valued solution concept, let $(N; v)$ be a coalitional game, and let S be a nonempty coalition. The* Hart–Mas-Colell reduced game *over S relative to φ is the game $(S; \tilde{v}_{S,\varphi})$, with the following coalitional function:*[9]

$$\tilde{v}_{S,\varphi}(R) = v(R \cup S^c) - \sum_{i \in S^c} \varphi_i(R \cup S^c; v), \quad \forall R \subseteq S, R \neq \emptyset, \tag{19.88}$$

$$\tilde{v}_{S,\varphi}(\emptyset) = 0. \tag{19.89}$$

The idea behind the definition is that when a coalition R is formed in the reduced game over S, it adds as partners in the coalition all the players in S^c, computes how much each player should receive according to the solution concept φ in the reduced game, over the set of players $R \cup S^c$, and gives the players in S^c their shares in the solution. What remains after the members of S^c receive their share is the worth of the coalition R in the reduced game $\tilde{v}_{S,\varphi}$.

Remark 19.34 *Recall that when S is a nonempty coalition and x is an individually rational vector in $\mathbb{R}^N$ the Davis–Maschler reduced game over S relative to x, denoted by $(S; w_S^x)$, is the game with the set of players S in which the coalitional function is*

$$w_S^x(R) = \begin{cases} \max_{Q \subseteq N \setminus S}(v(R \cup Q) - x(Q)) & \emptyset \neq R \subset S, \\ x(S) & R = S, \\ 0 & R = \emptyset. \end{cases} \tag{19.90}$$

There are two differences between the Davis–Maschler reduced game and the Hart–Mas-Colell reduced game:

1. *The Hart–Mas-Colell reduced game is appropriate only for single-valued solution concepts, while the Davis–Maschler reduced game is appropriate for single-valued and set-valued solution concepts because it is defined in relation to each imputation in the solution.*

---

9 We alternatively use the notation S^c and $N \setminus S$ to denote the complement coalition of S.

2. *In the definition of the Hart–Mas-Colell reduced game, the members of R must add all the players who are not members of S as partners, while in the Davis–Maschler reduced game they may choose as partners the most beneficial subset, from their perspective, of the players in S^c.* ♦

Example 19.35 **The reduced game of the carrier game** Recall that for every nonempty coalition T the carrier game over T is the game $(N; u_T)$ (see Definition 19.19) in which

$$u_T(R) = \begin{cases} 1 & \text{if } R \supseteq T, \\ 0 & \text{if } R \not\supseteq T. \end{cases} \tag{19.91}$$

By Theorem 19.21 (page 806) the Shapley value of the carrier game u_T is

$$\text{Sh}_i(N; u_T) = \begin{cases} \frac{1}{|T|} & \text{if } i \in T, \\ 0 & \text{if } i \notin T. \end{cases} \tag{19.92}$$

Let $S \subseteq N$ be a nonempty coalition. We will compute the Hart–Mas-Colell reduced game over S relative to the Shapley value Sh.

Case 1: $S \cap T = \emptyset$.
Let $R \subseteq S$. Then $R \subseteq N \backslash T$, and therefore every player in R is a null player. Since $R \cup S^c \supseteq S^c \supseteq T$,

$$u_T(R \cup S^c) = 1 = \sum_{i \in T} \text{Sh}_i(R \cup S^c; u_T) = \sum_{i \in S^c} \text{Sh}_i(R \cup S^c; u_T). \tag{19.93}$$

Therefore

$$\tilde{u}_{S,\text{Sh}}(R) = v(R \cup S^c) - \sum_{i \in S^c} \text{Sh}_i(R \cup S^c; u_T) = 0, \tag{19.94}$$

which implies that the reduced game over S of the carrier game T is the zero game.

Case 2: $S \cap T \neq \emptyset$.
Let $R \subseteq S$ be a nonempty coalition. If $R \supseteq S \cap T$ then $R \cup S^c \supseteq T$ (see Figure 19.3), and therefore $u_T(R \cup S^c) = 1$. The calculation of the Shapley value of the carrier game of T yields that $\sum_{i \notin S} \text{Sh}_i(R \cup S^c; u_T) = \frac{|T \backslash S|}{|T|}$.

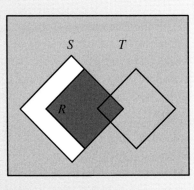

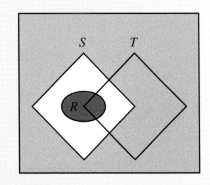

$$R \cup S^c \supseteq T \qquad\qquad R \cup S^c \not\supseteq T$$

Figure 19.3 The case $S \cap T \neq \emptyset$

If $R \not\supseteq S \cap T$, then $R \cup S^c \not\supseteq T$ (see Figure 19.3), and therefore the game $(R \cup S^c; u_T)$ is the zero game.

We deduce from this that $\tilde{u}_{T,S,\mathrm{Sh}}$, the Hart–Mas-Colell reduced game of u_T, is given by

$$\tilde{u}_{T,S,\mathrm{Sh}}(R) = \begin{cases} 1 - \frac{|T \setminus S|}{|T|} & R \supseteq S \cap T, \\ 0 & R \not\supseteq S \cap T. \end{cases} \tag{19.95}$$

Note that in this case, all the players in $S \cap T$ are symmetric, and all the players not in $S \cap T$ are null players. ◄

A solution concept φ is called *linear* if for every pair of coalitional games $(N; v)$ and $(N; u)$ with the same set of players and every pair of real numbers α and β,

$$\varphi_i(N; \alpha u + \beta v) = \alpha \varphi_i(N; u) + \beta \varphi_i(N; v), \quad \forall i \in N. \tag{19.96}$$

The Shapley value is a linear solution concept (Exercise 19.8).

The following result follows from the definitions and is left to the reader as an exercise (Exercise 19.35). It states that the correspondence between a coalitional game and its reduced game relative to a linear solution concept φ is a linear function.

Theorem 19.36 *Let φ be a linear solution concept. Then for every pair of coalitional games $(N; v)$ and $(N; u)$ and for every pair of real numbers α and β,*

$$\tilde{w}_{S,\varphi} = \alpha \tilde{u}_{S,\varphi} + \beta \tilde{v}_{S,\varphi}, \tag{19.97}$$

for every nonempty coalition $S \subseteq N$, where $w = \alpha u + \beta v$.

Definition 19.37 *A single-valued solution concept φ is said to be* consistent relative to the Hart–Mas-Colell reduced game *if for every game $(N; v)$, every nonempty coalition S, and every player $i \in S$,*

$$\varphi_i(N; v) = \varphi_i(S; \tilde{v}_{S,\varphi}). \tag{19.98}$$

Theorem 19.38 *The Shapley value is consistent relative to the Hart–Mas-Colell reduced game: for every game $(N; v)$, and every nonempty coalition S,*

$$\mathrm{Sh}_i(N; v) = \mathrm{Sh}_i(S; \tilde{v}_{S,\mathrm{Sh}}), \quad \forall i \in S. \tag{19.99}$$

Proof: Denote by $\tilde{G}$ the set of games satisfying Equation (19.99). We need to show that $\tilde{G}$ contains the set of all games. This is accomplished in two steps. In the first step, we prove that Equation (19.99) holds for the set of carrier games, which forms a basis for the vector space of all games. In the second step we show, using Theorem 19.36, that a linear combination of games satisfying Equation (19.99) also satisfies that equation.

Step 1: $\tilde{G}$ contains the set of all carrier games.
Let T be a nonempty coalition. We will show that $(N; u_T)$ is in $\tilde{G}$. Let $S \subseteq N$ be a nonempty coalition. If $S \cap T = \emptyset$, the left-hand side of Equation (19.99) equals 0 because the players in S are null players in the game $(N; u_T)$. We showed in Example 19.35 that the reduced game $\tilde{u}_{T,S,\mathrm{Sh}}$ is the zero game, and therefore the Shapley value of all the players in S is 0. Thus, Equation (19.99) holds, with both sides being 0.

Suppose now that $S \cap T \neq \emptyset$. As we showed in Example 19.35, in the reduced game $\tilde{u}_{T,S,\mathrm{Sh}}$, players who are not in $S \cap T$ are null players and all the players in $S \cap T$ are symmetric. Therefore, the Shapley value of the reduced game $\tilde{u}_{T,S,\mathrm{Sh}}$ is

$$\mathrm{Sh}_i(S; \tilde{u}_{T,S,\mathrm{Sh}}) = \begin{cases} \frac{1}{|T|} & \text{if } i \in S \cap T, \\ 0 & \text{if } i \in S \setminus T. \end{cases} \tag{19.100}$$

By Theorem 19.21 we deduce that in this case Equation (19.99) also holds.

Step 2: $\tilde{G}$ contains the space of all games.
Let $(N; v)$ be a coalitional game, and let $S \subseteq N$ be a nonempty coalition. We will show that Equation (19.99) is satisfied for $(N; v)$ and $S \subseteq N$. By Theorem 19.20 (page 805) every game is equal to a linear combination of carrier games. There therefore exist real numbers $(\alpha_T)_{\{T \subseteq N, T \neq \emptyset\}}$ such that

$$v = \sum_{\{T \subseteq N, T \neq \emptyset\}} \alpha_T u_T. \tag{19.101}$$

Since the Shapley value is a linear solution concept, it follows in particular that

$$\mathrm{Sh}_i(N; v) = \sum_{\{T \subseteq N, T \neq \emptyset\}} \alpha_T \mathrm{Sh}_i(N; u_T), \quad \forall i \in S. \tag{19.102}$$

Since Equation (19.99) holds for all carrier games, we deduce that

$$\mathrm{Sh}_i(N; v) = \sum_{\{T \subseteq N, T \neq \emptyset\}} \alpha_T \mathrm{Sh}_i(S; \tilde{u}_{T,S,\mathrm{Sh}}), \quad \forall i \in S. \tag{19.103}$$

Using once again the fact that the Shapley value is a linear solution concept yields

$$\mathrm{Sh}_i(N; v) = \mathrm{Sh}_i \left(S; \sum_{\{T \subseteq N, T \neq \emptyset\}} \alpha_T \tilde{u}_{T,S,\mathrm{Sh}} \right), \quad \forall i \in S. \tag{19.104}$$

To complete this proof we need to show that

$$\mathrm{Sh}_i \left(S; \sum_{\{T \subseteq N, T \neq \emptyset\}} \alpha_T \tilde{u}_{T,S,\mathrm{Sh}} \right) = \mathrm{Sh}_i(S; \tilde{v}_{S,\mathrm{Sh}}), \quad \forall i \in S, \tag{19.105}$$

and for this purpose, it suffices to show (again using the linearity of Sh) that

$$\sum_{\{T \subseteq N, T \neq \emptyset\}} \alpha_T \tilde{u}_{T,S,\mathrm{Sh}} = \tilde{v}_{S,\mathrm{Sh}}. \tag{19.106}$$

From Theorem 19.36, the function associating each game with its reduced game is linear, and this equality therefore holds. □

Theorem 19.39 *The Shapley value is the unique single-valued solution concept satisfying efficiency, symmetry, and covariance under strategic equivalence, and is also consistent relative to the Hart–Mas-Colell reduced game.*

In comparison with Theorem 19.15 (page 802), the properties of additivity and the null player are replaced in Theorem 19.39 by the properties of covariance under strategic equivalence and consistent relative to the Hart–Mas-Colell reduced game.

Proof: Let φ be a single-valued solution concept satisfying efficiency, symmetry, and covariance under strategic equivalence, which is also consistent relative to the Hart–Mas-Colell reduced game. We will show that φ coincides with the Shapley value Sh. The proof is accomplished by induction over the number of players n.

Step 1: $n = 1$.
When $N = \{1\}$, since both the Shapley value and φ satisfy efficiency,

$$\varphi_1(N;v) = v(1) = \text{Sh}_1(N;v). \tag{19.107}$$

Step 2: $n = 2$.
For two-player games, every single-valued solution concept φ satisfying efficiency, covariance under strategic equivalence, and symmetry is given by (see Exercise 19.5)

$$\varphi_1(N;v) = v(1) + \frac{v(1,2) - v(1) - v(2)}{2}, \tag{19.108}$$

$$\varphi_2(N;v) = v(2) + \frac{v(1,2) - v(1) - v(2)}{2}. \tag{19.109}$$

Since both the Shapley value and φ satisfy these properties, we deduce that

$$\varphi_i(N;v) = \text{Sh}_i(N;v), \quad i = 1, 2. \tag{19.110}$$

Note that by Equations (19.108) and (19.109)

$$\varphi_1(N;v) - \varphi_2(N;v) = v(1) - v(2) = \text{Sh}_1(N;v) - \text{Sh}_2(N;v). \tag{19.111}$$

Step 3: $n > 2$.
Assume by induction that for every k-player game $(K;u)$, such that $2 \leqslant k < n$, $\varphi(K;u) = \text{Sh}(K;u)$. Let $(N;v)$ be an n-player game. We will prove that $\varphi(N;v) = \text{Sh}(N;v)$. Let i and j be two players, and let $S := \{i,j\}$. Since $\{i\} \cup S^c = N\backslash\{j\}$ and $\{j\} \cup S^c = N\backslash\{i\}$, the Hart–Mas-Colell reduced game over S relative to φ is the game $(\{i,j\}; \tilde{v}_{S,\varphi})$ given by the following coalitional function:

$$\tilde{v}_{S,\varphi}(i) = v(N\backslash\{j\}) - \sum_{k \neq i,j} \varphi_k(N\backslash\{j\}; v), \tag{19.112}$$

$$\tilde{v}_{S,\varphi}(j) = v(N\backslash\{i\}) - \sum_{k \neq i,j} \varphi_k(N\backslash\{i\}; v). \tag{19.113}$$

Similarly, the Hart–Mas-Colell reduced game over S relative to Sh is the game $(\{i,j\}; \tilde{v}_{S,\text{Sh}})$ with the following coalitional function:

$$\tilde{v}_{S,\text{Sh}}(i) = v(N\backslash\{j\}) - \sum_{k \neq i,j} \text{Sh}_k(N\backslash\{j\}; v), \tag{19.114}$$

$$\tilde{v}_{S,\text{Sh}}(j) = v(N\backslash\{i\}) - \sum_{k \neq i,j} \text{Sh}_k(N\backslash\{i\}; v). \tag{19.115}$$

The inductive hypothesis, applied to the $(n-1)$-player games $(N\setminus\{i\}; v)$ and $(N\setminus\{j\}; v)$, and Equations (19.112)–(19.115), together yield

$$\varphi_k(N\setminus\{i\}; v) = \operatorname{Sh}_k(N\setminus\{i\}; v), \quad \forall k \neq i, \tag{19.116}$$

$$\varphi_k(N\setminus\{j\}; v) = \operatorname{Sh}_k(N\setminus\{j\}; v), \quad \forall k \neq j. \tag{19.117}$$

By Equations (19.112) and (19.113):

$$\tilde{v}_{S,\varphi}(i) = \tilde{v}_{S,\operatorname{Sh}}(i), \tag{19.118}$$

$$\tilde{v}_{S,\varphi}(j) = \tilde{v}_{S,\operatorname{Sh}}(j). \tag{19.119}$$

Applying Equation (19.111) to the reduced game over S, one has

$$\varphi_i(S, \tilde{v}_{S,\varphi}) - \varphi_j(S, \tilde{v}_{S,\varphi}) = \tilde{v}_{S,\varphi}(i) - \tilde{v}_{S,\varphi}(j), \tag{19.120}$$

$$\operatorname{Sh}_i(S, \tilde{v}_{S,\operatorname{Sh}}) - \operatorname{Sh}_j(S, \tilde{v}_{S,\operatorname{Sh}}) = \tilde{v}_{S,\operatorname{Sh}}(i) - \tilde{v}_{S,\operatorname{Sh}}(j). \tag{19.121}$$

By Equations (19.118) and (19.119), the right-hand side of Equation (19.120) equals the right-hand side of Equation (19.121), and therefore

$$\varphi_i(S, \tilde{v}_{S,\varphi}) - \varphi_j(S, \tilde{v}_{S,\varphi}) = \operatorname{Sh}_i(S, \tilde{v}_{S,\operatorname{Sh}}) - \operatorname{Sh}_j(S, \tilde{v}_{S,\operatorname{Sh}}). \tag{19.122}$$

By Theorem 19.38, the Shapley value is consistent relative to the Hart–Mas-Colell reduced game, and therefore

$$\operatorname{Sh}_k(S, \tilde{v}_{S,\operatorname{Sh}}) = \operatorname{Sh}_k(N; v), \quad \forall k \in \{i, j\}. \tag{19.123}$$

Since φ is consistent relative to the Hart–Mas-Colell reduced game, one has

$$\varphi_k(S, \tilde{v}_{S,\varphi}) = \varphi_k(N; v), \quad \forall k \in \{i, j\}. \tag{19.124}$$

Inserting this into Equation (19.122) yields

$$\varphi_i(N; v) - \varphi_j(N; v) = \operatorname{Sh}_i(N; v) - \operatorname{Sh}_j(N; v). \tag{19.125}$$

Since i and j are arbitrary players, Equation (19.125) holds for any pair of players $i, j \in N$. Since both the Shapley value and φ satisfy efficiency,

$$\sum_{k \in N} \varphi_k(N; v) = v(N) = \sum_{k \in N} \operatorname{Sh}_k(N; v). \tag{19.126}$$

Summing Equation (19.125) over $j \in N$, and using Equation (19.126), yields

$$n\varphi_i(N; v) - v(N) = n\operatorname{Sh}_i(N; v) - v(N). \tag{19.127}$$

This further implies that for every player $i \in N$,

$$\varphi_i(N; v) = \operatorname{Sh}_i(N; v). \tag{19.128}$$

This completes the inductive step, and the proof that $\varphi = \operatorname{Sh}$. $\square$

19.9　Remarks

The proof of Theorem 19.29 (page 809) presented in this section is from Neyman [1989]. The concept of consistency presented in this chapter first appeared in Hart and Mas-Colell [1989], who proved that the Shapley value is consistent.

　The potential function in Exercise 19.28 was introduced in Hart and Mas-Colell [1989]. The interested reader is directed to Felsenthal and Machover [1998] for an insightful discussion of the Shapley–Shubik power index and the Banzhaf power index (see Exercise 19.29). The interested reader is similarly directed to Aumann and Shapley [1974] for a thorough exposition of the Shapley value in games with a continuum of players.

19.10　Exercises

19.1 Prove that the solution concept defined in Example 19.9 (page 800) satisfies additivity, symmetry, the null player property, and covariance under strategic equivalence, but does not satisfy efficiency.

19.2 Prove that the solution concept defined in Example 19.10 (page 800) satisfies efficiency, symmetry, the null player property, and covariance under strategic equivalence.

19.3 Prove that the solution concept defined in Example 19.11 (page 800) satisfies the null player property, symmetry, and covariance under strategic equivalence.

19.4 Prove that the solution concept defined in Example 19.12 (page 801) satisfies efficiency, additivity, the null player property, and covariance under strategic equivalence.

19.5 Prove that when restricted to two-player games, every single-valued solution concept φ satisfying efficiency, covariance under strategic equivalence, and symmetry is given by the following equations:

$$\varphi_1(N;v) = v(1) + \frac{v(1,2) - v(1) - v(2)}{2} = \frac{v(1,2) + v(1) - v(2)}{2}, \quad (19.129)$$

$$\varphi_2(N;v) = v(2) + \frac{v(1,2) - v(1) - v(2)}{2} = \frac{v(1,2) - v(1) + v(2)}{2}. \quad (19.130)$$

19.6 Let ψ^1 and ψ^2 be two solution concepts both satisfying symmetry, efficiency, the null player property, and covariance under strategic equivalence, and let $\lambda \in [0,1]$. Define a solution concept ψ by $\psi := \lambda\psi^1 + (1-\lambda)\psi^2$. Prove that ψ also satisfies symmetry, efficiency, the null player property, and covariance under strategic equivalence.

19.7 Decompose the following game $(N; v)$ as a linear combination of carrier games. The set of players is $N = \{1, 2, 3, 4\}$, and the coalitional function is

$$v(1) = 6, \quad v(2) = 12, \quad v(3) = 0, \quad v(4) = 18,$$

$$v(1, 2) = 24, \quad v(1, 3) = 48, \quad v(1, 4) = 60, \quad v(2, 3) = 12,$$

$$v(2, 4) = 32, \quad v(3, 4) = 38,$$

$$v(1, 2, 3) = 120, \quad v(1, 2, 4) = 89, \quad v(1, 3, 4) = 150,$$

$$v(2, 3, 4) = 179, \quad v(1, 2, 3, 4) = 240.$$

19.8 Prove that the Shapley value is a linear solution concept: for every list of K games $((N; v_k))_{k=1}^{K}$, and every list of K real numbers $(\alpha_k)_{k=1}^{K}$:

$$\mathrm{Sh}\left(N; \sum_{k=1}^{K} \alpha_k v_k\right) = \sum_{k=1}^{K} \alpha_k \mathrm{Sh}(N; v_k). \tag{19.131}$$

19.9 In Theorem 19.15 (page 802), can any one of the properties (efficiency, symmetry, null player, or additivity) be replaced by covariance under strategic equivalence, while maintaining the conclusion of the theorem? Prove your answer.

19.10 In the proof of Theorem 19.15 we used the fact that the $2^n - 1$ carrier games form a basis to the space of games. Another set of coalitional functions over the set of players N that form a basis for the space of games is the set $\{w_T, \emptyset \subset T \subseteq N\}$, where $w_T(S) = 1$ if and only if $T = S$. Explain why this basis was not used in the proof of Theorem 19.15.

19.11 A solution concept φ satisfies *anonymity* if for every coalitional game $(N; v)$, every permutation π of the set N, and every player $i \in N$,

$$\varphi_{\pi(i)}(N; \pi(v)) = \varphi_i(N; v), \tag{19.132}$$

where $\pi(v)$ is the coalitional function that is defined by

$$\pi(v)(S) := v(\pi^{-1}(S)) \tag{19.133}$$

and $\pi(S) = \{\pi(i) : i \in S\}$ (see Definition 16.37 on page 652).
Prove that the Shapley value satisfies anonymity.

19.12 A single-valued solution concept is a function associating an imputation with every coalitional game. One may also define solution concepts that are only defined for a subset of the class of coalitional games. Let $\mathcal{F}$ be a subset of the class of coalitional games. A *single-valued solution concept for $\mathcal{F}$* is a function associating an imputation with each coalitional game in $\mathcal{F}$. The Shapley value is the only solution concept satisfying the four properties proposed by Shapley for the class of all coalitional games. In this exercise, we show that there exist families of coalitional games over which solution concepts different from the Shapley value that nevertheless satisfy Shapley's four properties can be defined.

A family $\mathcal{F}$ of coalitional games is called *additively closed* if for every pair of coalitional games $(N; v)$ and $(N; u)$ in $\mathcal{F}$, the game $(N; v + u)$ is also in $\mathcal{F}$.

Find a family of coalitional games that is additively closed and a single-valued solution concept defined over that family that satisfies the four Shapley properties but is not the Shapley value.

Explain why this exercise does not contradict Theorem 19.15 on page 802.

19.13 A coalitional game $(N; v)$ is called *additive* if every coalition S satisfies $v(S) = \sum_{i \in S} v(i)$. What is the Shapley value of each player i in an additive game?

19.14 Let $a \in \mathbb{R}^N$ be a vector. Compute the Shapley value of the coalitional game $(N; v)$ defined as follows:

$$v(S) := \left(\sum_{i \in S} a_i \right)^2, \quad \emptyset \neq S \subseteq N. \tag{19.134}$$

19.15 In this exercise, we present an algorithm for computing a solution concept. Given a coalitional game $(N; v)$:

(a) Choose a coalition whose worth is not 0, and divide this worth equally among the members of the coalition (this is called the *dividend* given to the members of the coalition).

(b) Subtract the worth of this coalition from the worth of every coalition containing it, or equal to it. This defines a new coalitional function (where subtracting a negative number is understood to be equivalent to adding the absolute value of that number).

(c) Repeat this process until there are no more coalitions whose worth is not 0.

For example, consider the game $(N; v)$ defined by the set of players $N = \{1, 2, 3\}$, and the coalitional function

$$v(1) = 6, \quad v(2) = 12, \quad v(3) = 18, \quad v(1, 2) = 30, \quad v(1, 3) = 60,$$
$$v(2, 3) = 90, \quad v(1, 2, 3) = 120.$$

The following table summarizes a stage of the algorithm in each row, and includes the coalitional function at the beginning of that stage, the chosen coalition (whose worth is not 0), and the payoff given to each player at that stage. The last line presents the sum total of all payoffs received by each player.

Stage	1	2	3	1,2	1,3	2,3	1,2,3	Coalition	1	2	3
1	6	12	18	30	60	90	120	1,2	15	15	0
2	6	12	18	0	60	90	90	2	0	12	0
3	6	0	18	−12	60	78	78	1,3	30	0	30
4	6	0	18	−12	0	78	18	1	6	0	0
5	0	0	18	−18	−6	78	12	3	0	0	18
6	0	0	0	−18	−24	60	−6	1,2,3	−2	−2	−2
7	0	0	0	−18	−24	60	0	1,2	−9	−9	0
8	0	0	0	0	−24	60	18	1,3	−12	0	−12
9	0	0	0	0	0	60	42	2,3	0	30	30
10	0	0	0	0	0	0	−18	1,2,3	−6	−6	−6
11	0	0	0	0	0	0	0				
									22	40	58

Prove the following claims:

(a) This process always terminates.
(b) The total payoffs received by the players are the Shapley value of the game (and are therefore independent of the order in which the coalitions are chosen).

Remark 19.40 *The algorithm terminates in the least number of steps if we first choose the coalitions containing only one player, then the coalitions containing two players each, and so on. This process was first presented by John Harsanyi.* ◆

19.16 Compute the Shapley value of the game in Exercise 19.7, using the algorithm described in Exercise 19.15.

19.17 For every game $(N; v)$, define the *dual game* $(N; v^*)$ as follows:

$$v^*(S) = v(N) - v(N \backslash S). \tag{19.135}$$

Prove the following claims:

(a) If $(N; v^*)$ is the dual game to $(N; v)$, then $(N; v)$ is the dual game to $(N; v^*)$.
(b) $\mathrm{Sh}(N; v) = \mathrm{Sh}(N; v^*)$.

19.18 The maintenance costs of airport runways are usually charged to the airlines landing planes at that airport. But light planes require shorter runways than heavy planes, and this raises the question of how to determine a fair allocation of maintenance costs among airlines with different types of planes.

Define a cost game $(N; c)$, where N is the set of all planes landing at an airport, and $c(S)$, for each coalition S, is the maintenance cost of the shortest runway that can accommodate all the planes in the coalition.

The following figure depicts an example in which eight planes, labeled A, B, C, D, E, F, G, and H land at an airport on a daily basis. Each plane requires the entire length of the runway up to (and including) the interval on which it is located in the figure. For example, plane F needs the first three segments of the runway. The weekly maintenance costs of each runway segment appear at the bottom of the figure. For example, $c(A, D, E) = 3{,}200$, $c(A) = 2{,}000$, and $c(C, F, G) = 5{,}100$.

Start of runway	A, B	C, D, E	F	G, H	End of runway
	2,000	1,200	900	1,000	

Prove that if the Shapley value of this game is used to determine the allocation of costs, then the maintenance cost of each runway segment is borne equally by the planes using that segment.

For example, in the above figure,

$$\mathrm{Sh}_A(N; c) = \frac{2{,}000}{8} = 250, \tag{19.136}$$

$$\mathrm{Sh}_F(N; c) = \frac{2{,}000}{8} + \frac{1{,}200}{6} + \frac{900}{3} = 750. \tag{19.137}$$

19.19 This exercise considers maintenance costs associated with a road network connecting villages to a central township. The network is depicted as a tree, with the central township at the root of the tree. Each village is associated with a node of the tree, and there are additional nodes of the tree that represent road intersections. The villages vary in their numbers of inhabitants. An example appears in the following figure, which depicts six villages and two intersections; the number of inhabitants in each village appears in the figure, near that village's name, and each segment of road connecting two intersections, or connecting the township to an intersection, is labeled with that segment's maintenance cost.

A cost game $(N; c)$ is derived from the network, where N is the set of residents in all the villages (in this example $|N| = 200$), and for each coalition $S \subseteq N$, $c(S)$ is the maintenance cost of the minimal subtree required to maintain the network of roads connecting all the members in S to the central township.

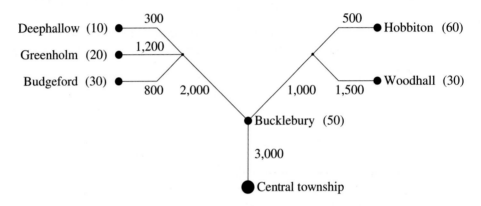

Prove that if the Shapley value of such a game is used to determine the allocation of costs, then the maintenance cost of each road segment is borne equally by all the people using that segment. For example, in the figure above, the Shapley value of every resident of Hobbiton is

$$\frac{500}{60} + \frac{1,000}{90} + \frac{3,000}{200} = 34\tfrac{4}{9}. \qquad (19.138)$$

19.20 For every pair of games over the same set of players $(N; v)$ and $(N; w)$, define the maximum game $(N; v \vee w)$ as follows:

$$(v \vee w)(S) = \max\{v(S), w(S)\}, \quad \forall S \subseteq N, \qquad (19.139)$$

and the minimum game $(N; v \wedge w)$ by

$$(v \wedge w)(S) = \min\{v(S), w(S)\}, \quad \forall S \subseteq N. \qquad (19.140)$$

Suppose that $(N; v)$ and $(N; w)$ are two weighted majority games (see Section 17.1.4). Are the games $(N; v \vee w)$ and $(N; v \wedge w)$ also weighted majority games?

19.21 Let $(N; v)$ and $(N; w)$ be two coalitional games over the same set of players. Does $\mathrm{Sh}_i(N; v \vee w) \geq \mathrm{Sh}_i(N; v)$ hold for every player $i \in N$? Either prove this statement or provide a counterexample. For the definition of the game $(N; v \vee w)$, see Exercise 19.20.

19.22 Let Σ_N be the set of simple monotonic games over a set of players N.

(a) Prove that if $(N; v), (N; w) \in \Sigma_N$ then $(N; v \vee w)$ and $(N; v \wedge w)$ are also games in Σ_N.

Since a sum of games in Σ_N is not necessarily in Σ_N, the additivity property is not applicable to this family of games. This motivated Dubey [1975] to define the following *valuation property*. A solution concept φ over Σ_N satisfies the *valuation property* if for every pair[10] of games $(N; v)$ and $(N; w)$ in Σ_N,

$$\varphi(N; v) + \varphi(N; w) = \varphi(N; v \wedge w) + \varphi(N; v \vee w). \tag{19.141}$$

(b) Prove that the Shapley value is the unique solution concept over Σ_N satisfying efficiency, symmetry, the null player property, and the valuation property.

19.23 Let $(a_i)_{i \in N}$ be real numbers. Let v be the following coalitional function:

$$v(S) = \begin{cases} 0 & \text{if } |S| \leq k, \\ \sum_{i \in S} a_i & \text{if } |S| > k. \end{cases} \tag{19.142}$$

Compute the Shapley value of the game $(N; v)$ for every $k = 0, 1, \ldots, n$.

19.24 Consider a weighted majority game with four players, with quota $q = \frac{1}{2}$, and weights $(0.1, 0.2, 0.3, 0.4)$ (see Section 17.4, page 721, for a discussion on weighted majority games).

(a) Write down the coalitional game corresponding to this weighted majority game.
(b) Compute the Shapley value of the game.
(c) Compute the core of the game.

19.25 Compute the Shapley value of the weighted majority game with $N + 1$ players, weights $(\frac{N}{3}, 1, 1, 1, \ldots, 1)$, and quota $q = \frac{N}{2}$. Suppose that N is divisible by 6. What is the limit of the Shapley value of the player with weight $\frac{N}{3}$ as N goes to infinity?

19.26 Compute the Shapley value of the weighted majority game with $N + 2$ players, weights $(\frac{N}{3}, \frac{N}{3}, 1, 1, 1, \ldots, 1)$, and quota $q = \frac{5N}{6}$. Suppose that N is divisible by 6. What is the limit of the Shapley value of each player with weight $\frac{N}{3}$ as N goes to infinity?

19.27 Compute the Shapley value of the weighted majority game with $N + 2$ players, weights $(\frac{N}{3}, \frac{N}{3}, 1, 1, 1, \ldots, 1)$, and quota $q = N$. Suppose that N is divisible by 6. What is the limit of the Shapley value of each player with weight $\frac{N}{3}$ as N goes to infinity?

10 For the definition of the games $v \wedge w$ and $v \vee w$, see Exercise 19.20.

19.28 Let U be a nonempty set of players. Denote by Γ_U^* the family of coalitional games $(N; v)$ such that $N \subseteq U$, i.e., those games in which the set of players is taken from U.

Let $P : \Gamma_U^* \to \mathbb{R}$ be a function associating each game in Γ_U^* with a real number.

Definition 19.41 *For every game $(N; v) \in \Gamma_U^*$, the marginal contribution of player i in N to the game $(N; v)$ relative to P is*

$$D_i P(N; v) := \begin{cases} P(N; v) & \text{if } |N| = 1, \\ P(N; v) - P(N\setminus\{i\}; v) & \text{if } |N| \geq 2. \end{cases} \tag{19.143}$$

In Equation (19.143), $(N\setminus\{i\}; v)$ is the game in which the set of players is $N\setminus\{i\}$, and the coalitional function is the function v restricted to this set of players.

Definition 19.42 *A function $P : \Gamma_U^* \to \mathbb{R}$ is called a* potential function *over Γ_U^* if for every $(N; v) \in \Gamma_U^*$ the sum of the marginal contributions equals $v(N)$:*

$$\sum_{i \in N} D_i P(N; v) = v(N). \tag{19.144}$$

Prove the following claims:

(a) For every nonempty set of players U, there is a unique potential function $P : \Gamma_U^* \to \mathbb{R}$.
(b) If P is a potential function, then for every game $(N; v) \in \Gamma_U^*$, and every $i \in N$,

$$D_i P(N; v) = \text{Sh}_i(N; v). \tag{19.145}$$

19.29 Let $(N; v)$ be a simple monotonic game satisfying $v(N) = 1$. For each player i, define $B_i(N; v)$ to be the number[11] of coalitions S satisfying $v(S) = 0$ and $v(S \cup \{i\}) = 1$. The *Banzhaf value* of player i is defined to be

$$\text{BZ}_i(N; v) := \frac{B_i(N; v)}{\sum_{j \in N} B_j(N; v)}. \tag{19.146}$$

Similarly to the Shapley–Shubik power index, the Banzhaf value also constitutes a power index, measuring the relative power of each player.

(a) Which of the following properties are satisfied by the Banzhaf value: efficiency, the null player property, additivity, marginality, symmetry?
(b) Compute the Banzhaf value of the game in Exercise 19.24.
(c) Find a formula for the Banzhaf value of the games in Exercises 19.25 and 19.26.
(d) Compute the Banzhaf value of the members of the United Nations Security Council, both in its pre-1965 structure and in its post-1965 structure (see Section 19.6.1 on page 813).

19.30 A cost game $(N; c)$ is called *convex* if

$$c(S) + c(T) \geq c(S \cup T) + c(S \cap T), \quad \forall S, T \subseteq N. \tag{19.147}$$

---

11 Such a coalition S is called a *swing* for player i.

Prove that this property is equivalent to the following property:

$$c(S \cup \{i\}) - c(S) \geq c(T \cup \{i\}) - c(T), \quad \forall i \in N, \forall S \subseteq T \subseteq N \setminus \{i\}. \quad (19.148)$$

Prove that the airport game in Exercise 19.18 is a convex cost game.

19.31 Construct a road network game, as in Exercise 19.19, for which the corresponding cost game is not convex.

Hint: Construct a road network in which the villages and the central township are geographically situated on a circle.

19.32 Let i be a null player in a coalitional game $(N; v)$. Compute the Hart–Mas-Colell reduced game over $N \setminus \{i\}$ relative to the Shapley value Sh.

19.33 Let $(N; v)$ be an additive game (for the definition of an additive game, see Exercise 19.13) and let S be a nonempty coalition. Compute the Hart–Mas-Colell reduced game over S relative to the Shapley value Sh.

19.34 Let $(N; v)$ be a coalitional game, and let $(N; v^*)$ be its dual game (for the definition of a dual game, see Exercise 19.17). For a nonempty coalition S, write down the coalition function of the Hart–Mas-Colell reduced game of $(N; v^*)$ over S relative to the Shapley value Sh, in terms of v and $\tilde{v}_{S,\mathrm{Sh}}$.

19.35 Prove that for every linear solution concept φ and for every nonempty coalition $S \subseteq N$, the function that assigns to each coalition game its Hart–Mas-Colell reduced game over S relative to φ is a linear function. That is, for every pair of coalitional games $(N; v)$ and $(N; u)$ and for every pair of real numbers α and β,

$$\tilde{w}_{S,\varphi} = \alpha \tilde{u}_{S,\varphi} + \beta \tilde{v}_{S,\varphi}. \quad (19.149)$$

The bargaining set

Chapter summary

In this chapter we present the bargaining set, which is a set solution concept for coalitional games. The idea behind the bargaining set is that when the players consider how to divide the worth of a coalition among themselves, a player who is unsatisfied with the suggested imputation can object to it. An *objection*, which is directed against another player, roughly claims: "I deserve more than my suggested share and you should transfer part of your suggested share to me because ..." The player against whom the objection is made may or may not have a *counterobjection*. An objection that meets with no counterobjection is a *justified objection*. The bargaining set consists of all imputations in which no player has a justified objection against any other player.

It follows from the definition of an objection that in any imputation in the core no player has an objection, and therefore the core is always a subset of the bargaining set. It is proved that contrary to the core, the bargaining set is never empty. In convex games the bargaining set coincides with the core.

In Chapter 18 we noted that the core, as a solution concept for coalitional games, suffers from a significant drawback: in many cases, the conditions that the core must satisfy are too strong, and as a result, there is no imputation that satisfies all of them. Consequently, in many games the core is the empty set. In this chapter, we present another solution concept, termed "the bargaining set," which imposes weaker conditions, and yields a recommended solution for every coalitional structure, provided that there exists at least one feasible imputation for that structure.

Example 20.1 An advertising agency seeks two celebrities to star in an advertising campaign. Three celebrities, Anna, Ben, and Carl, are approached, with the intention that two of them will be chosen for the advertising campaign. The advertising agency is persuaded that an advertisement depicting a man and a woman is generally more effective than one depicting two men, and it therefore offers a pair of celebrities comprised of a man and a woman $1,000,000, and offers a pair comprised of two men only $500,000. This situation may be depicted as a game in coalitional form (all payoffs are in thousands of dollars).

$$v(\emptyset) = 0,$$
$$v(\text{Anna}) = v(\text{Ben}) = v(\text{Carl}) = 0,$$
$$v(\text{Ben}, \text{Carl}) = 500,$$
$$v(\text{Anna}, \text{Ben}) = v(\text{Anna}, \text{Carl}) = 1,000,$$
$$v(\text{Anna}, \text{Ben}, \text{Carl}) = 0.$$

Remark 20.2 *We define* $v(\text{Anna, Ben, Carl}) = 0$ *because the advertising campaign cannot include three celebrities. We could alternatively define* $v(\text{Anna, Ben, Carl}) = 1,000$*, with all three celebrities forming a coalition that sends only two of them to be photographed for the advertisements.* ♦

Which coalition will be formed? Suppose that Anna and Ben form a coalition, without Carl's participation. How will they divide the $1,000,000 they are paid?

It is readily verified that this game has an empty core for any coalitional structure (the core is empty also if we set $v(\text{Anna, Ben, Carl}) = 1,000$). Experiments conducted using games similar to this game indicate that the players usually raise offers and counteroffers, in the hope of being included in the coalition that eventually forms. A typical bargaining process looks something like this (see Maschler [1978] and Kahan and Rapoport [1984]):

			Imputation		
Stage	Offer	Coalitional Structure	Anna	Ben	Carl
1	Ben	{Carl}, {Anna, Ben}	500	500	0
2	Carl	{Ben}, {Anna, Carl}	600	0	400
3	Ben	{Carl}, {Anna, Ben}	700	300	0
4	Carl	{Ben}, {Anna, Carl}	800	0	200
5	Ben	{Anna}, {Carl, Ben}	0	250	250
6	Anna	{Carl}, {Anna, Ben}	740	260	0
7	Carl	{Ben}, {Anna, Carl}	750	0	250

After this bargaining process is completed, Anna and Carl form a coalition, dividing the $1,000,000 they are paid among them as ($750,000, $250,000).

Experimental evidence indicates that the results of bargaining processes in this game are usually very close to one of the following imputations (again, in thousands of dollars in the order (Anna, Ben, Carl)):[1]

$$(750, 250, 0), \quad (750, 0, 250), \quad (0, 250, 250),$$

with slight variations in various directions, since a person who sees he is about to be left out is usually willing to yield a bit in the bargaining process to increase his chance of being included in a two-player coalition. Some experimental evidence indicates that each one of the above imputations is the average of payoffs obtained when the appropriate coalitional structure is formed. There are other empirical results pointing to more equitable outcomes, perhaps because Anna stands to lose more than the other players if she is not included in a two-player coalition, resulting in greater willingness on her part to yield in the bargaining process.

What characterizes these outcomes, and how can they be generalized to a solution concept? To answer this question, we first look at an imputation that is not included in the above set. For example, suppose that Anna proposes that she and Ben form a coalition, and offers to divide the money according to the imputation

$$x = (800, 200, 0).$$

Ben can be expected to be dissatisfied with this offer. He tells Anna that she should give him some of the 800 that she suggests for herself, because otherwise he will approach Carl with an offer to form a coalition {Ben, Carl}, with the imputation:

$$y = (0, 250, 250).$$

---

1 Other possible foreseeable outcomes are presented later in this chapter.

Carl will certainly agree to such an offer, and both Ben and Carl profit more from y than from x. We term the pair $(\{Ben, Carl\}, y)$ an *objection of Ben against Anna at x*.

Anna may respond by saying that she also has an objection to x: Ben needs to give her an even share greater than 800 since she can approach Carl and offer to form the coalition $\{Anna, Carl\}$, with the imputation:

$$z = (810, 0, 190).$$

The pair $(\{Anna, Carl\}, z)$ is an objection of Anna against Ben at x. But there is a difference between these objections: Ben's objection is *justified*, while Anna's objection is unjustified.

Why is Anna's objection unjustified? Suppose that Anna approaches Carl with the suggestion that they form a coalition and divide the money according to imputation z. Ben can prevent this from happening by offering to form a coalition with Carl and dividing the money according to y. Both Ben and Carl stand to gain from this: Ben receives 250 (instead of the 200 he receives according to x), and Carl receives 250 (instead of the 190 Anna promises him under z). Anna has no chance of realizing her objection $(\{Anna, Carl\}, z)$, and we therefore regard it as unrealistic. In this case, we say that $(\{Ben, Carl\}, y)$ is a *counterobjection of Ben to Anna's objection z*.

Why is Ben's objection justified? Because Anna has no counterobjection to it. Suppose that Ben indeed offers to form a coalition with Carl and divide the money according to y. To prevent this from happening, Anna must suggest forming a coalition with Carl, with an imputation giving Carl at least 250. But then all she will have left for herself is at most 750 – less than the 800 she received under x. In other words, Anna cannot defend the 800 she receives under x, and therefore Ben's objection against Anna is justified.

If the coalition $\{Anna, Ben\}$ is formed, we claim that neither Anna nor Ben has a justified objection to the imputation $\hat{x} = (750, 250, 0)$. For example, if Anna objects to $\hat{x}$ by proposing to form the coalition $\{Anna, Carl\}$ with an imputation $(750 + \varepsilon, 0, 250 - \varepsilon)$, where $\varepsilon > 0$, then as a counterobjection Ben can suggest the coalition $\{Ben, Carl\}$ with the imputation $(0, 250, 250)$. If Ben objects to $\hat{x}$ by proposing the coalition $\{Ben, Carl\}$ with an imputation $(0, 250 + \varepsilon, 250 - \varepsilon)$, Anna can counterobject by proposing to form the coalition $\{Anna, Carl\}$ with the imputation $(750, 0, 250)$.

For the coalitional structure $\{\{Anna, Ben\}, \{Carl\}\}$, the imputation $\hat{x} = (750, 250, 0)$ is the only imputation at which every objection of one player against another player in the same coalition can be met with a counterobjection (Exercise 20.7).   ◄

20.1   Definition of the bargaining set

We are now ready for the formal presentation of the bargaining set. Let $(N; v)$ be a coalitional game. Recall that for every vector $x \in \mathbb{R}^N$ we set $x(\emptyset) = 0$, and for every nonempty coalition $S \subseteq N$ we have denoted $x(S) = \sum_{i \in S} x_i$. Recall also that a coalitional structure $\mathcal{B}$ is a partition of the set of players into disjoint, nonempty coalitions whose union is N, and $X(\mathcal{B}; v)$ is the set of imputations relative to $\mathcal{B}$:

$$X(\mathcal{B}; v) := \{x \in \mathbb{R}^N : x(B) = v(B) \ \forall B \in \mathcal{B}, \quad x_i \geq v(i) \ \forall i \in N\}. \tag{20.1}$$

An imputation in $X(\mathcal{B}; v)$ is therefore a way to divide the worth of each coalition in $\mathcal{B}$ among its members, where each player receives at least what he can get by himself.

Definition 20.3 *Let $x \in X(\mathcal{B}; v)$ be an imputation, and let $k \neq l$ be two players belonging to the same coalition in $\mathcal{B}$. An objection of player k against player l at x is a pair (C, y) such that:*

form $k \to l$ on the left-hand side, which express that that line contains the conditions that must be met for player k to fail to have a justified objection against player l).

$1 \to 2$	$x_1 + x_3 \geq v(\{1,3\})$	$x_2 = v(2)$	$v(\{1,3\}) - x_1 \leq v(\{2,3\}) - x_2$
$2 \to 1$	$x_2 + x_3 \geq v(\{2,3\})$	$x_1 = v(1)$	$v(\{2,3\}) - x_2 \leq v(\{1,3\}) - x_1$

$$(20.17)$$

A larger system is needed for the coalitional structure $\{N\}$. A payoff vector $x \in X(\{N\}; v)$ is in the bargaining set relative to the coalitional structure $\{N\}$ if and only if it satisfies at least one expression in each line in the following system (as before, each line is specified by $l \leftarrow k$ and contains the conditions necessary for player k to fail to have a justified objection against player l):

$1 \to 2$	$x_1 + x_3 \geq v(1,3)$	$x_2 = v(2)$	$v(1,3) - x_1 \leq v(2,3) - x_2$
$2 \to 1$	$x_2 + x_3 \geq v(2,3)$	$x_1 = v(1)$	$v(2,3) - x_2 \leq v(1,3) - x_1$
$1 \to 3$	$x_1 + x_2 \geq v(1,2)$	$x_3 = v(3)$	$v(1,2) - x_1 \leq v(2,3) - x_3$
$3 \to 1$	$x_2 + x_3 \geq v(2,3)$	$x_1 = v(1)$	$v(2,3) - x_3 \leq v(1,2) - x_1$
$2 \to 3$	$x_1 + x_2 \geq v(1,2)$	$x_3 = v(3)$	$v(1,2) - x_2 \leq v(1,3) - x_3$
$3 \to 2$	$x_1 + x_3 \geq v(1,3)$	$x_2 = v(2)$	$v(1,3) - x_3 \leq v(1,2) - x_2$

$$(20.18)$$

Checking whether a particular vector x is in the bargaining set is relatively easy to do; it involves checking that at most 22 conditions are met (explain why). Computing the entire bargaining set requires solving 3^6 systems each with 10 linear equations (equalities and inequalities; explain why). The following theorem, whose proof is left to the reader (Exercise 20.11), shows that when a three-player game is 0-monotonic,[2] computing the bargaining set is simplified.

Theorem 20.16 *In a 0-monotonic, three-player game, the bargaining set for the coalitional structure $\{N\}$ coincides with the core, if the core is nonempty, and it contains only one imputation, if the core is empty.*

Computing the bargaining set for a three-player game that is not 0-monotonic is a problem with high computational complexity. This complexity is vastly increased when there are four or more players, because then for every objection of player k against player l we need to list the conditions negating the possibility of the formation of a counterobjection for each subset $N\setminus\{k,l\}$. For example, to determine if a particular point x is in the bargaining set for the coalitional structure $\{N\}$ in a four-player game, it suffices to check 197 simple inequalities. But computing all the points in the bargaining set directly requires solving 150^{12} systems, each one containing 41 inequalities. To date there is no known practical method for computing the bargaining set in games with a large number of players, which is why indirect methods are often used to compute the bargaining set for specific families of games.

---

2 A coalitional game is 0-*monotonic* if its 0-normalization is monotonic, or, equivalently, if $v(S \cup \{i\}) \geq v(S) + v(i)$ for every coalition S and every player $i \notin S$ (Exercise 17.28 on page 733).

The set of solutions for a system of weak linear inequalities is an intersection of a finite number of half-spaces and is therefore a closed and convex set. The bargaining set is contained in the set of vector payoffs, which is a compact set. This leads to the following theorem, whose proof is left to the reader (Exercise 20.21).

Theorem 20.17 *For every coalitional game* $(N; v)$ *and every coalitional structure* $\mathcal{B}$, *the bargaining set* $\mathcal{M}(N; v; \mathcal{B})$ *is a finite union of polytopes.*[3]

Another property of the bargaining set that is a corollary of our discussion so far is:

Theorem 20.18 *When the values of the coalitional functions are all in a subfield of the real numbers (such as the field of the rational numbers), then all the vertices of the polytopes determining the bargaining set have coordinates in that subfield.*

The reason this theorem holds is that the operations required to solve a finite system of linear equations are multiplying and dividing the coefficients in the equations, and application of those operators always yields results in the same field in which the coefficients are located.

The main significance of the bargaining set is that it may be regarded as a set of suggested ways of dividing the worth of the coalition among its members, which is applicable also in cases in which the core is empty, because, as the next theorem states, the bargaining set is not empty provided that the set of imputation is not empty.

Theorem 20.19 *For every game in coalitional form* $(N; v)$ *and every coalitional*[4] *structure* $\mathcal{B}$, *if* $X(\mathcal{B}; v) \neq \emptyset$, *then* $\mathcal{M}(N; v; \mathcal{B}) \neq \emptyset$.

We will prove this theorem for the coalitional structure $\{N\}$. The proof of the general case appears in the chapter on the nucleolus (Theorem 21.21 on page 861), where we show that the nucleolus is always contained in the bargaining set, and the nonemptiness of the nucleolus follows from simple considerations involving continuous functions defined on compact sets.

The proof presented here is important both because of its contribution to the understanding of the structure of the bargaining set, and because it can be extended to a proof of the nonemptiness of the bargaining set in games without transferable utility, where the proof using the nucleolus is not applicable. The proof makes use of the following definition and two theorems.

Definition 20.20 *Let* $(N; v)$ *be a coalitional game, let* k *and* l *be two players, and let* $x \in X(N; v)$. *We say that player* k *is* stronger *than player* l *at* x, *denoted by* $k >_x l$, *if player* k *has a justified objection against player* l *at* x *(relative to the coalitional structure* $\{N\}$).

The following example shows that the "stronger than" relation is not necessarily transitive.

---

3 Recall that a polytope is a compact set that is the intersection of a finite number of half-spaces.
4 Since by definition $\mathcal{M}(N; v; \mathcal{B})$ is contained in $X(\mathcal{B}; v)$, if $X(\mathcal{B}; v) = \emptyset$, then $\mathcal{M}(N; v; \mathcal{B}) = \emptyset$.

Example 20.21 Let $(N; v)$ be a coalitional game where $N = \{1, 2, 3, 4, 5\}$, and the coalitional function is

$$v(1, 2, 3, 4, 5) = v(1, 2, 3) = v(2, 4, 5) = 30, \tag{20.19}$$

$$v(1, 4) = 40, \tag{20.20}$$

$$v(3, 5) = 20, \tag{20.21}$$

$$v(S) = 0, \quad \text{for every other coalition } S. \tag{20.22}$$

Consider the imputation $x = (10, 10, 10, 0, 0) \in X(N; v)$. At x:

- $(\{1, 4\}, (11, 0, 0, 29, 0))$ is a justified objection of Player 1 against Player 2 (check!). It follows that $1 >_x 2$.
- $(\{2, 4, 5\}, (0, 11, 0, 1, 18))$ is a justified objection of Player 2 against Player 3 (check!). It follows that $2 >_x 3$.
- We now show that $1 \not>_x 3$, leading to the conclusion that the "stronger than" relation is not transitive. The only way that Player 1 can raise an objection against Player 3 involves the coalition $\{1, 4\}$. But for every such objection, Player 3 can respond with a counterobjection $(0, 0, 10, 0, 10)$, with coalition $\{3, 5\}$.

The last item also shows that $3 \not>_x 1$. This indicates that although the "stronger than" relation is not transitive, it is likely to be acyclic, and in fact this is true, as stated in the next theorem. ◀

Theorem 20.22 *The relation $>_x$ is acyclic, i.e., if $1 >_x 2 >_x 3 >_x \cdots >_x t - 1 >_x t$, then it $t >_x 1$ does not hold.*

Proof: Suppose by contradiction that $1 >_x 2 >_x 3 >_x \cdots >_x t - 1 >_x t$ and $t >_x 1$. Suppose that the justified objections used in the above sequence involve coalitions $S_1, S_2, \ldots, S_t$, respectively; i.e., S_i is the coalition that player i uses for his justified objection against player $i + 1$, for $i = 1, 2, \ldots, t - 1$, and S_t is the coalition that player t uses for his objection against Player 1.

Consider the excesses $e(S_1, x), e(S_2, x), \ldots, e(S_t, x)$. Since the coalitions $S_1, S_2, \ldots, S_t$ are used in justified objections, these excesses must be positive. Relabel the names of the players in such a way that $e(S_t, x)$ is the maximal excess among these excesses (there may be several indices i at which this maximum is attained). Then coalition S_t cannot include Player 1 as a member, since it is used in an objection against him.

We show by induction that the coalition S_t includes players $\{1, 2, \ldots, t\}$. This contradicts the fact, just mentioned, that it cannot include Player 1. The contradiction establishes what we wanted to show, namely, that $>_x$ is an acyclic relation.

Since S_t is used in an objection of player t, it must include that player as a member. Suppose by induction that S_t contains players $\{i + 1, i + 2, \ldots, t\}$. We show that it must include player i as well. To do so, we make use of Theorem 20.14 on page 835: the coalition S_i is used in a justified objection of player i against player $i + 1$ and by the inductive hypothesis the coalition S_t contains player $i + 1$. If $i \notin S_t$ were to hold, it would follow from Theorem 20.14 that $e(S_t, x) < e(S_i, x)$ in contradiction to the assumption that $e(S_t, x)$ is the maximal excess among the excesses $(e(S_j, x))_{j=1}^t$. Hence $i \in S_t$, completing the inductive step of the proof and the proof of the theorem. □

The next theorem is a corollary of an important theorem in topology known as the KKM Theorem (after Knaster–Kuratowski–Mazurkiewicz). A proof of this theorem appears in Section 24.1.4 (page 987). A different proof, using Brouwer's Fixed Point Theorem, is given as a guided exercise (Exercise 24.31 page 999).

Theorem 20.23 (KKM) *Consider the* $(n-1)$*-dimensional simplex*

$$X(n) = \left\{ x \in \mathbb{R}^n \colon \sum_{i=1}^{n} x_i = 1, x_i \geq 0 \quad i = 1, \ldots, n \right\}. \tag{20.23}$$

Let $X_1, X_2, \ldots, X_n$ *be compact subsets of* $X(n)$ *satisfying*

$$\{x \in X(n) \colon x_i = 0\} \subseteq X_i, \quad i = 1, \ldots, n, \tag{20.24}$$

and whose union is $X(n)$:

$$\bigcup_{i=1}^{n} X_i = X(n). \tag{20.25}$$

Then their intersection is nonempty:

$$\bigcap_{i=1}^{n} X_i \neq \emptyset. \tag{20.26}$$

Recall that we are assuming in this section that the coalitional structure is $\{N\}$. For every pair of players k and l, denote by Y_{kl} the set of vector payoffs at which player k has a justified objection against player l:

$$Y_{kl} := \{x \in X(N; v) \colon k >_x l\}. \tag{20.27}$$

Theorem 20.24 *The set* Y_{kl} *is relatively open*[5] *in* $X(N; v)$.

Proof: Let $x \in Y_{kl}$. We will show that every imputation located in a small neighborhood of x is also in Y_{kl}. Towards that goal we will prove that if (C, y) is a justified objection of player k against player l at x then (C, y) is also a justified objection of player k against player l at every payoff vector in a sufficiently small neighborhood of x.

We will first prove that (C, y) is an objection of player k against player l at each payoff vector in a sufficiently small neighborhood of x. Denote $\delta := \min_{i \in C}(y_i - x_i)$. Since (C, y) is a justified objection of player k against player l at x, it is an objection and therefore $\delta > 0$. By Definition 20.3, (C, y) is an objection of player k against player l at every payoff vector $\hat{x}$ satisfying $|\hat{x}_i - x_i| < \delta$ for all $i \in C$.

We now prove that there exists a sufficiently small neighborhood of x satisfying the property that at every vector in that neighborhood (C, y) is a justified objection of player k against player l. Suppose by contradiction that this is not true. Then there exists a sequence $(x^m)_{m \in \mathbb{N}}$ of payoff vectors converging to x such that (C, y) is not a justified objection of player k against player l at x^m, for all $m \in \mathbb{N}$. In other words, for every $m \in \mathbb{N}$ there exists a counterobjection (D^m, z^m) of player l against player k at x^m to the objection (C, y):

- $l \in D^m$, $k \notin D^m$ and $z^m(D^m) = v(D^m)$.

---

[5] That is, Y_{kl} is the intersection of an open set in $\mathbb{R}^N$ with $X(N; v)$.

- $z_i^m \geq x_i^m$ for all $i \in D^m \backslash C$.
- $z_i^m \geq y_i$ for all $i \in D^m \cap C$.

Since the number of coalitions is finite, there is a coalition D^* appearing an infinite number of times in the sequence $(D^m)_{m \in \mathbb{N}}$. The set of payoff vectors is compact and therefore every subsequence of the sequence (z^m) has a subsequence converging to the limit z^*. By taking the limit in the subsequence we deduce that:

- $l \in D^*$, $k \notin D^*$ and $z^*(D^*) = v(D^*)$.
- $z_i^* \geq x_i^*$ for all $i \in D^* \backslash C$.
- $z_i^* \geq y_i$ for all $i \in D^* \cap C$.

It follows that (D^*, z^*) is a counterobjection of player l against player k at x to the objection (C, y), and therefore (C, y) is not a justified objection, contradicting our assumption. This contradiction proves that the set Y_{kl} is a relatively open set in $X(N; v)$. □

We turn now to the proof of Theorem 20.19, which states that for the coalitional structure $\{N\}$ the bargaining set is not empty provided that the set of imputations is not empty.

Proof of Theorem 20.19 in the case that $\mathcal{B} = \{N\}$: The bargaining set is covariant under strategic equivalence (Exercise 20.6). By Theorem 17.7 (page 720) we may assume without loss of generality that the game is 0–0, 0–1, or 0–(-1) normalized.

We will first deal with the interesting case in which the game is 0–1 normalized, and then treat the other two cases, where the proof is rather simple.

When the game is 0–1 normalized, the set of imputations for the coalitional structure $\{N\}$ is

$$X(N; v) = \left\{ x \in \mathbb{R}^N : \sum_{i=1}^n x_i = 1, x_i \geq 0 \quad i = 1, \ldots, n \right\}. \tag{20.28}$$

This is an $(n - 1)$-dimensional simplex. Define n subsets of the simplex by:

$$X_i := \{ x \in X(N; v) : \text{there is no justified objection against player } i \text{ at } x \}. \tag{20.29}$$

Claim 20.25 X_i *contains the set* $\{ x \in X(N; v) : x_i = 0 \}$, *for all* $i = 1, 2, \ldots, n$.

Proof: If $x_i = 0$, the pair $(\{i\}, 0)$ constitutes a counterobjection of player i to any objection raised against him. □

Claim 20.26 $\cup_{i=1}^n X_i = X(N; v)$.

Proof: Suppose by contradiction that there exists a point x in $X(N; v)$ that is not in $\cup_{i=1}^n X_i$. Let j be any player. Since $x \notin X_j$, at x there is a player k_j who has a justified objection against j, that is, $k_j >_x j$. This holds for every player j, and in particular, there is a player j_1 such that $j_1 >_x 1$, there is a player j_2 such that $j_2 >_x j_1$, there is a player j_3 such that $j_3 >_x j_2$, and so on. Since the number of players is finite, the sequence $(j_m)_{m=1}^\infty$ must contain a player who appears at least twice; i.e., there exist m and l satisfying $j_m = j_{m+l}$. In particular,

$$j_m >_x j_{m+1} >_x j_{m+2} >_x \cdots >_x j_{m+l-1} >_x j_{m+l} = j_m.$$

The existence of such a sequence contradicts the fact that the relation $>_x$ is acyclic (Theorem 20.22). The contradiction proves that our starting assumption was false, and hence $\cup_{i=1}^n X_i = X(N; v)$. $\qquad\square$

Claim 20.27 *For every i, the set X_i is closed.*

Proof: X_i is a set of imputations at which there are no justified objections against player i. The complement $X(N; v) \setminus X_i$ is therefore the set of imputations at which at least one player has a justified objection against player i; i.e.,

$$X(N; v) \setminus X_i = \bigcup_{\{k:\, k \neq i\}} Y_{ki}. \qquad (20.30)$$

By Theorem 20.24, the sets $(X_{ki})_{i \in N}$ are all relatively open in $X(N; v)$. Therefore $X(N; v) \setminus X_i$, as the union of relatively open sets, is itself relatively open in $X(N; v)$, and thus its complement X_i is relatively closed in $X(N; v)$. Since the set $X(N; v)$ is closed in $\mathbb{R}^N$ it follows that X_i is also a closed set in $\mathbb{R}^N$, as claimed. $\qquad\square$

These three claims show that the sets $\{X_1, X_2, \ldots, X_n\}$ satisfy the conditions of the KKM Theorem (Theorem 20.23), and their intersection is therefore nonempty. This intersection is the bargaining set,

$$\bigcap_{i=1}^n X_i = \mathcal{M}(N; v; \{N\}), \qquad (20.31)$$

since $x \in \bigcap_{i=1}^n X_i$ if and only if no player has a justified objection at x against any other player. This completes the proof in the case that the game is 0–1 normalized.

If the game is 0–0 normalized, the only imputation in $X(\{N\}; v)$ is $(0, 0, \ldots, 0)$. This imputation is in the bargaining set, because there are no objections that can be raised by any player against any other player (explain why).

If the game is 0–(-1) normalized, the set $X(\{N\}; v)$ is empty, and the statement of the theorem holds vacuously. This completes the proof of Theorem 20.19 for the coalitional structure $\mathcal{B} = \{N\}$. $\qquad\square$

20.4 The bargaining set in convex games

There are several classes of games in which it is known that the bargaining set for the coalitional structure $\{N\}$ coincides with the core. This property, when it holds, constitutes a strong recommendation for choosing a point in the core as the solution to such a game, because at every imputation that is not in the core, there is a player who has a justified objection against another player. We prove in this section that in convex games the core and the bargaining set coincide for the coalitional structure $\mathcal{B} = \{N\}$. Recall that for this coalition structure we use the short notation $C(N; v)$ for $C(N; v; \{N\})$. For the definition of a convex game see Definition 18.51 (page 765).

Theorem 20.28 *For every convex game* $(N; v)$

$$C(N; v) = \mathcal{M}(N; v; \{N\}). \tag{20.32}$$

Proof: By Theorem 20.12 on page 834, we know that $C(N; v) \subseteq \mathcal{M}(N; v; \{N\})$, and we therefore need to show that $C(N; v) \supseteq \mathcal{M}(N; v; \{N\})$. Let $x \notin C(N; v)$ be an imputation that is not in the core. We need to show that it is not in the bargaining set, i.e., there is a justified objection at x.

Since the vector x is fixed throughout the proof, we denote by $e(S) = e(S, x) = v(S) - x(S)$ the excess of the coalition S at x. The function e associates each coalition with a real number, the excess, and we can therefore view $(N; e)$ as a coalitional game, namely, the game in which the worth of each coalition is its excess at x. We first show that $(N; e)$ is a convex game. To see this, note that

$$e(A) + e(B) = v(A) + v(B) - x(A) - x(B) \tag{20.33}$$

$$\leqslant v(A \cup B) + v(A \cap B) - x(A \cup B) - x(A \cap B) \tag{20.34}$$

$$= e(A \cup B) + e(A \cap B). \tag{20.35}$$

The inequality in Equation (20.34) holds because $(N; v)$ is a convex game, and $x(A) + x(B) = x(A \cup B) + x(A \cap B)$. Next, define the game $(N; \hat{e})$ to be the monotonic cover of the game $(N; e)$, that is,

$$\hat{e}(S) = \max_{R \subseteq S} e(R). \tag{20.36}$$

We will show that $(N; \hat{e})$ is also a convex game. In fact, the proof we provide is valid for any convex game and thus proves that the monotonic cover of any convex game is a convex game. Let S and T be two coalitions. Denote by R and R' the coalitions at which the maximum is attained in the definition of $\hat{e}(S)$ and $\hat{e}(T)$ respectively:

$$\hat{e}(S) = \max_{P \subseteq S} e(P): = e(R), \tag{20.37}$$

$$\hat{e}(T) = \max_{P' \subseteq T} e(P'): = e(R'). \tag{20.38}$$

Then

$$\hat{e}(S) + \hat{e}(T) = e(R) + e(R'). \tag{20.39}$$

Since $(N; e)$ is a convex game,

$$e(R) + e(R') \leqslant e(R \cup R') + e(R \cap R'). \tag{20.40}$$

Since $R \cup R' \subseteq S \cup T$ and $R \cap R' \subseteq S \cap T$,

$$e(R \cup R') + e(R \cap R') \leqslant \max_{P \subseteq S \cup T} e(P) + \max_{P \subseteq S \cap T} e(P) = \hat{e}(S \cup T) + \hat{e}(S \cap T).$$

$$\tag{20.41}$$

Using Equations (20.39)–(20.41) we deduce that

$$\hat{e}(S) + \hat{e}(T) \leqslant \hat{e}(S \cup T) + \hat{e}(S \cap T). \tag{20.42}$$

Since this inequality holds for every S and T, the game $(N; \hat{e})$ is indeed convex.

From among all the coalitions C that have maximal excess at x choose one, C^*, that is maximal with respect to set inclusion:

$$e(S) \leqslant e(C^*), \quad \forall S \subseteq N, \tag{20.43}$$

$$e(S) < e(C^*), \quad \forall S \text{ such that } C^* \subset S \subseteq N. \tag{20.44}$$

Since the imputation x is not in the core, there exists a coalition S such that $v(S) > x(S)$, i.e., $e(S) > 0$. Since $e(C^*)$ is maximal,

$$\hat{e}(C^*) = \max_{P \subseteq C^*} e(P) = e(C^*) > 0. \tag{20.45}$$

Consider the game $(C^*; \hat{e})$, which is the restriction of the game $(N; \hat{e})$ to the players in C^*. This is a convex game, because it is a subgame of a convex game (Exercise 18.46 on page 791). In particular, its core is not empty (Theorem 18.55 on page 766). Let $y \in \mathcal{C}(C^*; \hat{e})$ be an imputation in the core of this game. This imputation satisfies

$$y(C^*) = \hat{e}(C^*) = e(C^*), \tag{20.46}$$

$$y(R) \geqslant \hat{e}(R) \geqslant e(R), \quad \forall R \subset C^*. \tag{20.47}$$

In particular, for $R = \{i\}$,

$$y_i \geqslant \hat{e}(i) = \max\{e(i), e(\emptyset)\} \geq e(\emptyset) = 0. \tag{20.48}$$

In words, every imputation in the core of $(C^*; \hat{e})$ is nonnegative (in all its coordinates).

We will now show that there is a player $k \in C^*$ for whom (C^*, y) is a justified objection against every player $l \notin C^*$. Since $y(C^*) = \hat{e}(C^*) > 0$, there is a player $k \in C^*$ such that $y_k > 0$. By Equation (20.45) one has $e(C^*) > 0 = e(N)$, and therefore $C^* \neq N$. In particular, there exists a player $l \notin C^*$. We will show that player k has a justified objection against player l at x.

Let $\varepsilon > 0$ be sufficiently small such that

$$y_k > (|C^*| - 1)\varepsilon. \tag{20.49}$$

Define:

$$z_i = x_i + y_i + \varepsilon, \quad \forall i \in C^* \backslash \{k\}, \tag{20.50}$$

$$z_k = x_k + y_k - (|C^*| - 1)\varepsilon. \tag{20.51}$$

Then $z_i > x_i$ for every $i \in C^*$, and by Equation (20.46)

$$z(C^*) = x(C^*) + y(C^*) = x(C^*) + e(C^*) = v(C^*). \tag{20.52}$$

It follows that $(C^*; z)$ is an objection of player k against player l. We will show that this objection is justified. To do so, choose an arbitrary coalition D containing player l but not player k. For a counterobjection, player l must give each player i in $D \cap C^*$ at least z_i, and every player i in $D \backslash C^*$ at least x_i. But this is impossible, since

$$z(D \cap C^*) + x(D \backslash C^*) = z(D \cap C^*) + x(D) - x(D \cap C^*) \qquad (20.53)$$
$$\geqslant y(D \cap C^*) + x(D) \qquad (20.54)$$
$$\geqslant \widehat{e}(D \cap C) + x(D) \qquad (20.55)$$
$$\geq e(D \cap C^*) + x(D) \qquad (20.56)$$
$$\geqslant e(D) + e(C^*) - e(D \cup C^*) + x(D) \qquad (20.57)$$
$$> e(D) + x(D) \qquad (20.58)$$
$$= v(D). \qquad (20.59)$$

Equation (20.54) holds by Equation (20.50) and since $k \notin D \cap C^*$, Equation (20.55) holds because $y \in \mathcal{C}(C^*; \widehat{e})$ and $\widehat{e}(S) \geq e(S)$ for every $S \subseteq C^*$, Equation (20.57) holds because $(C^*; e)$ is a convex game, and the inequality in Equation (20.58) holds because the choice of C^* necessarily implies that $e(C^*) > e(D \cup C^*)$ (since $D \cup C^* \supset C^*$, which follows from player l being contained in $D \cup C^*$ but not in C^*).

It follows that D cannot be used for a counterobjection. Since this is true for any coalition D containing player l but not player k, the objection (C^*, y) is justified. We have shown that the imputation x, which is not in the core, is also not in the bargaining set, and therefore $\mathcal{C}(N; v) \supseteq \mathcal{M}(N; v; \{N\})$, which is what we wanted to show. $\qquad \square$

20.5 Discussion

The following iterative procedure, which identifies an imputation in the bargaining set, is due to Stearns [1968]. Let $(N; v)$ be a coalitional game such that $X(N; v) \neq \emptyset$. Start at an arbitrary imputation $x^0 \in X(N; v)$. If it is in the bargaining set, the procedure terminates successfully. Otherwise, at x^0 there exists a player who has a justified objection against another player. It can readily be checked that if player k_0 has a justified objection against player l_0, then there exists a minimal positive number $\delta_{k_0, l_0}(x^0)$ such that the transfer of $\delta_{k_0, l_0}(x^0)$ from the payoff of player l_0 to that of player k_0 yields an imputation in which player k_0 no longer has a justified objection against player l_0. Choose one of the justified objections at x^0, and implement such a transfer of payoffs. This leads to a new imputation x^1. Repeat the process on x^1: if there are justified objections at this imputation, choose one of them, say a justified objection of player k_1 against player l_1, and create a new imputation x^2 by transferring the sum $\delta_{k_1, l_1}(x^1)$ from the payoff of player l_1 to that of player k_1, and so on.

If the process terminates successfully after a finite number of steps, we have found an imputation in the bargaining set. It is possible, however, that the resulting sequence is infinite. In such a case it can be shown that the sequence converges, but not necessarily to an imputation in the bargaining set: for example, there may be Players 1, 2, and 3 who, throughout the iterative procedure, transfer smaller and smaller amounts of payoff between each other, but Player 4 has a justified objection against Player 5 at every step of the procedure that is never canceled by a transfer between them. If, however, we ensure that in the above-described procedure there are an infinite number of times at which the transfers that are implemented are those where $\delta_{k_m, l_m}(x^m)$ is maximal, then the sequence $(x^m)_{m=1}^\infty$ converges to an imputation in the bargaining set.

This can be viewed as a dynamic justification for our interpretation of a justified objection as a demand by one player to receive a "transfer payment" from another player.

20.6) Remarks

The first variant of the bargaining set was presented in Aumann and Maschler [1964]. The variant of the bargaining set presented in this chapter first appeared in Davis and Maschler [1967], who also proved that the bargaining set is nonempty relative to the coalitional structure $\{N\}$. Peleg [1967] generalized this result to any coalitional structure.

Exercise 20.19 is from Peleg and Sudhölter [2003], page 74, Example 4.1.19. Exercise 20.20 is a special case of a more general theorem proved in Solymosi [1999].

20.7) Exercises

20.1 Prove Theorem 20.5 on page 833: for the coalitional structure $\{N\}$ the core is the set of all imputations in $X(N; v)$ at which no player has an objection against any other player.

20.2 Prove Theorem 20.6 on page 833: for every coalitional structure $\mathcal{B}$, when the core relative to this coalitional structure is not empty, the core is the set of all imputations in $X(\mathcal{B}; v)$ at which no player has an objection against any other player.

20.3 In this exercise, we show that Theorem 20.6 does not hold without the condition that the core is nonempty. Let $(N; v)$ be a two-player coalitional game with payoff function

$$v(1) = v(2) = 0, \quad v(1, 2) = 1, \tag{20.60}$$

and let $\mathcal{B} = \{\{1\}, \{2\}\}$.

(a) Show that the core relative to the coalitional structure $\mathcal{B}$ is empty.
(b) Find an imputation in $X(\mathcal{B}; v)$ that is in the bargaining set $\mathcal{M}(N; v; \mathcal{B})$.

20.4 Prove that if player k has a justified objection against player l at x, then player l does not have a justified objection against player k at x.

20.5 Prove that in a three-player coalitional game $(N; v)$, if for an imputation x none of the three equations in (20.16) holds, then Player 1 has a justified objection against Player 2.

20.6 Prove that the bargaining set is covariant under strategic equivalence. In other words, if $(N; v)$ and $(N; w)$ are two coalitional games with the same set of players, and if there exist $a > 0$ and $b \in \mathbb{R}^N$ such that

$$w(S) = av(S) + b(S), \quad \forall S \subseteq N, \tag{20.61}$$

then for every coalitional structure $\mathcal{B}$,

$$x \in \mathcal{M}(N; v; \mathcal{B}) \iff ax + b \in \mathcal{M}(N; w; \mathcal{B}). \tag{20.62}$$

20.7 Show that in Example 20.1 (page 830) for every coalitional structure the bargaining set contains a single payoff vector, which is the corresponding payoff vector in the table on page 834.

20.8 For $N = \{1, 2, 3\}$, compute the bargaining set of the coalitional game $(N; v)$ relative to the coalitional structure $\{\{1, 2\}, \{3\}\}$, for each of the following coalitional functions:

(a) $v(1) = v(2) = v(3) = 0$, $\quad v(1, 2) = 40$, $\quad v(1, 3) = 50$, $\quad v(2, 3) = 60$, $v(1, 2, 3) = 100$.

(b) $v(1) = v(2) = v(3) = 0$, $\quad v(1, 2) = 80$, $\quad v(1, 3) = 20$, $\quad v(2, 3) = 30$, $v(1, 2, 3) = 100$.

20.9 Repeat Exercise 20.8 for the coalitional structure $\{N\}$.

20.10 Compute the bargaining set of the game "My Aunt and I" presented in Exercise 21.21 on page 894 for the coalitional structure $\{\{1, 2\}, \{3\}, \{4\}, \{5\}\}$, where the Players 1 and 2 are my aunt and I, respectively.

20.11 Prove Theorem 20.16 on page 837: in a 0-monotonic three-player game, for the coalitional structure $\{N\}$, the bargaining set coincides with the core if the core is nonempty, and is a single point if the core is empty.

20.12 Prove that in Definition 20.7 (page 833), the inequality in Condition 4 can be replaced by a strict inequality. In other words, if at x player k has a justified objection against player l, then he has a justified objection against player l also if in the definition of a justified objection the inequalities in Condition 4 are replaced by strict inequalities. Note that the justified objection may be different, under the different definitions.

20.13 Give an example in which the bargaining set is empty if strict inequalities are required in Condition 3 of Definition 20.7 (page 833).

20.14 Let $N = \{1, 2, 3, 4\}$. Write down a list of conditions guaranteeing that in the coalitional structure $\{N\}$ Player 1 has no justified objection against Player 2.
Comment: The 12 permutations of this list of conditions, along with the requirement that the imputation be in $X(\{N\}; v)$, determine the bargaining set relative to this coalitional structure.

20.15 **The gloves game** Two sellers go to the market. Each has a left-hand glove. At the same time, three other sellers come to the market, each of whom has a right-hand glove. Only pairs of gloves, each pair containing a right-hand glove and a left-hand glove, can be sold to customers. The net profit from selling one pair of gloves is $10.

(a) Write down this game's coalitional function.

(b) Compute the bargaining set of this game relative to the coalitional structure $\{N\}$.

20.16 Consider the market game (as described in Exercise 17.13 on page 731) in which the initial endowment of each member of $N_1 = \{1,2\}$ is $(1,0)$, the initial endowment of each member of $N_2 = \{3,4,5\}$ is $(0,\frac{1}{2})$ and for each coalition S,

$$v(S) = \min \left\{ |S \cap N_1|, \tfrac{1}{2}|S \cap N_2| \right\}. \tag{20.63}$$

(a) Prove that $(0,0,\frac{1}{2},\frac{1}{2},\frac{1}{2})$ is the only vector in the core of this game relative to the coalitional structure $\mathcal{B} = \{N\}$.

(b) Prove that the bargaining set relative to the coalitional structure $\{N\}$ is

$$\left\{ (\alpha,\alpha,\beta,\beta,\beta) : 0 \le \alpha \le \tfrac{3}{4}, \beta = \tfrac{1}{2} - \tfrac{2}{3}\alpha \right\}. \tag{20.64}$$

(c) Explain why points in the bargaining set that are not in the core may be more reasonable than points in the core, in this example.

20.17 Compute the core and the bargaining set relative to the coalitional structure $\{N\}$ in a game similar to the market game of Exercise 20.16, but where the initial endowment of the members of N_2 is $(0,1)$. What is the relationship between the results obtained for market games in this exercise and Exercise 20.16, and the results obtained for the gloves game in Exercise 20.15.

20.18 Find a game $(N;v)$, a coalitional structure, and an imputation x such that: (a) $1 >_x 3$, (b) $1 \sim_x 2$, and (c) $2 \sim_x 3$, where the notation $k \sim_x l$ means that the players k and l are members of the same coalition in the coalitional structure, and neither of them has a justified objection against the other.

20.19 In the weighted majority game $[3; 1,1,1,1,1,0]$ with six players, Player 6 is a null player. Prove that despite this, the vector $(\frac{1}{7},\frac{1}{7},\frac{1}{7},\frac{1}{7},\frac{1}{7},\frac{2}{7})$ is in the bargaining set relative to the coalitional structure $\{N\}$. What is the intuitive explanation for the fact that a null player can obtain a positive payoff in the bargaining set?

20.20 A simple coalitional game $(N;v)$ is called a *veto control game* if there is a player i such that $v(S) = 0$ for every coalition that does not contain i. Prove that given a monotonic, veto control game, the core relative to the coalitional structure $\{N\}$ coincides with the bargaining set relative to the same coalitional structure (see also Exercise 18.12 on page 785).

20.21 Prove Theorem 20.17 (page 838): in a coalitional game, for every coalitional structure, the bargaining set is a finite union of polytopes.

20.22 The statement of Theorem 20.28 is formulated for the coalitional structure $\mathcal{B} = \{N\}$. Where was this used in the proof of the theorem?

Chapter summary

This chapter is devoted to the study of the *nucleolus*, which is, like the Shapley value, a single-point solution concept for coalitional games. The notion that underlies the nucleolus is that of *excess*: the excess of a coalition at a vector x in $\mathbb{R}^N$ is the difference between the worth of the coalition and the total amount that the members of the coalition receive according to x. When the excess is positive, the members of the coalition are not content with the total amount that they together receive at x, which is less than the worth of the coalition. Each vector x in $\mathbb{R}^N$ corresponds to a vector of 2^N excesses of all coalitions. The nucleolus of a coalitional game relative to a set of vectors in $\mathbb{R}^N$ consists of the vectors in that set whose vector of excesses are minimal in the *lexicographic order*. It is proved that the nucleolus relative to any compact set is nonempty and if the set is also convex, then the nucleolus relative to that set consists of a single vector.

The nucleolus of the game is the nucleolus relative to the set of imputations, that is, the set of efficient and individually rational vectors. The *prenucleolus* of a coalitional game is its nucleolus relative to the set of preimputations, that is, the set of all efficient vectors. Both the nucleolus and the prenucleolus are defined for any coalition structure.

The prenucleolus of a coalitional game is characterized in Section 21.5 in terms of balanced collections of coalitions. This characterization is used to prove that the prenucleolus is a consistent solution concept; that is, it satisfies the Davis–Maschler reduced game property. In Section 21.7 we show that for a weighted majority game, the nucleolus is the unique representation of the game that satisfies some desirable properties.

In Section 21.8 the nucleolus is applied to bankruptcy problems. The Babylonian Talmud (a Jewish text that records rabbinic discussions held between the second and fifth centuries AD) presents a solution concept for bankruptcy problems suggested by Rabbi Nathan. We prove that for each bankruptcy problem one can define a coalitional game whose nucleolus coincides with the Rabbi Nathan solution of the bankruptcy problem.

> In this chapter we present the nucleolus, a solution concept for coalitional games that, like the Shapley value, is a single-valued solution that exists for every coalitional game. The nucleolus was first defined in Schmeidler [1969]. We consider coalitional games $(N; v)$ with a set of players $N = \{1, 2, \ldots, n\}$. As before, for every vector $x \in \mathbb{R}^N$ we denote

$$\begin{cases} x(S) := \sum_{i \in S} x_i, & \emptyset \subset S \subseteq N, \\ x(\emptyset) := 0. \end{cases} \tag{21.1}$$

21.1 Definition of the nucleolus

Definition 21.1 *For every vector $x \in \mathbb{R}^N$, and every coalition $S \subseteq N$,*

$$e(S, x) := v(S) - x(S) \tag{21.2}$$

is called the excess *of coalition S at x.*

When x_i is a payoff to player i, the excess $e(S, x)$ measures how dissatisfied the members of S are with the vector x. If the excess is positive, the members of S are not satisfied with x, because they could band together to form S, obtain $v(S)$, and then divide that sum in such a way that each member of S receives more than he receives under x. The smaller the excess, the less the members of S are dissatisfied. When the excess is negative, the members of S, as a coalition, are satisfied with x, and the more negative the excess is, the more satisfied they are, because collectively they are receiving at x more than they could receive working together as a coalition.

Recall that the set of imputations of the coalitional game $(N; v)$ is the set $X(N; v)$ defined by

$$X(N; v) := \{ x \in \mathbb{R}^N : x(N) = v(N), \quad x_i \geq v(i) \quad \forall i \in N \}. \tag{21.3}$$

This is the set of vectors that are *efficient*, that is, satisfy $x(N) = v(N)$, and *individually rational*, that is, satisfy $x_i \geq v(i)$ for every player $i \in N$. The core is the set of imputations satisfying in addition *coalitional rationality*, that is, $x(S) \geq v(S)$ for every coalition $S \subseteq N$. This can be expressed using the notion of excess, as follows:

$$C(N; v) = \{ x \in \mathbb{R}^N : x(N) = v(N), \quad e(S, x) \leq 0 \quad \forall S \subseteq N \}. \tag{21.4}$$

When the core is empty, then given any imputation, there will be at least one coalition with positive excess. In that case, we may wish to minimize the excesses as much as possible. The nucleolus proposes a way of achieving this end. We proceed to define it.

Given a vector $x \in \mathbb{R}^N$, we compute the excess of all the coalitions at x, and we write them in decreasing order from left to right,

$$\theta(x) = (e(S_1, x), e(S_2, x), \ldots, e(S_{2^n}, x)), \tag{21.5}$$

where $\{ S_1, S_2, \ldots, S_{2^n} \}$ are all the coalitions, indexed such that

$$e(S_1, x) \geq e(S_2, x) \geq \ldots \geq e(S_{2^n}, x). \tag{21.6}$$

Two elements in this sequence are $e(\emptyset, x)$ and $e(N, x)$. By definition $v(\emptyset) = 0$ for every coalitional game $(N; v)$, and $x(\emptyset) = 0$ for every $x \in \mathbb{R}^N$. It follows that $e(\emptyset, x) = 0$ for every coalitional game $(N; v)$ and every vector $x \in \mathbb{R}^N$. Also, $e(N, x) = 0$ for every efficient vector $x \in \mathbb{R}^N$.

Note that this indexing of the coalitions is determined only up to equality of excesses. If for example $e(S_k, x) = e(S_l, x)$, then swapping S_k and S_l will not change the vector $\theta(x)$. When passing to another vector $\theta(y)$, a different letter must be used to denote the coalitions,

$$\theta(y) = (e(R_1, y), e(R_2, y), \ldots, e(R_{2^n}, y)), \tag{21.7}$$

where the coalitions $(R_k)_{k=1}^{2^n}$ are ordered in decreasing excess order, and the ordering is a permutation of the previous ordering. To avoid relabeling the coalitions every time we consider a different imputation, denote the k-th coordinate of $\theta(x)$ by $\theta_k(x)$, without writing explicitly the corresponding coalition at the k-th coordinate, and write the vector $\theta(x)$ as

$$\theta(x) = (\theta_1(x), \theta_2(x), \ldots, \theta_{2^n}(x)), \tag{21.8}$$

where

$$\theta_1(x) \geq \theta_2(x) \geq \ldots \geq \theta_{2^n}(x). \tag{21.9}$$

We have thus defined 2^n functions $\theta_k : \mathbb{R}^N \to \mathbb{R}$ for $k \in \{1, 2, \ldots, 2^n\}$, where $\theta_k(x)$ is the k-th coordinate of $\theta(x)$. Note that there may be cases in which $\theta(x) = \theta(y)$, even though $x \neq y$ (explain why).

To minimize the excesses we compare any two vectors $\theta(x)$ and $\theta(y)$ lexicographically.

Definition 21.2 *Let* $a = (a_1, a_2, \ldots, a_d)$ *and* $b = (b_1, b_2, \ldots, b_d)$ *be two vectors in* $\mathbb{R}^d$. *Then* $a \succsim_L b$ *if either* $a = b$, *or there exists an integer* k, $1 \leq k \leq d$, *such that* $a_k > b_k$, *and* $a_i = b_i$ *for every* $1 \leq i < k$. *This order relation is termed the* lexicographic order.

As usual, the strong order $\succ_L$ derived from $\succsim_L$ is $a \succ_L b$ if $a \succsim_L b$ and $b \not\succsim_L a$. It follows that $a \succ_L b$ if $a \neq b$ and the first coordinate at which a differs from b is greater in a than in b. Moreover, $a \approx_L b$ if and only if $a = b$.

The lexicographic relation is reflexive, transitive, and complete, but not continuous (Exercise 21.4): there exists a sequence $(a^n)_{n\in\mathbb{N}}$ of vectors in $\mathbb{R}^d$ converging to a (in the Euclidean metric) and a vector b such that $a^n <_L b$ for all $n \in \mathbb{N}$, but $a \succ_L b$.

Example 21.3 The gloves game (see Example 18.5, page 738) Consider the following three-player coalitional game, with the coalitional function given by

$$v(1) = v(2) = v(3) = v(1,2) = 0, \quad v(1,3) = v(2,3) = v(1,2,3) = 1. \tag{21.10}$$

Computing the excesses with respect to the vectors $x = (\frac{1}{3}, \frac{1}{3}, \frac{1}{3})$, $y = (0, 0, 1)$, $z = (\frac{1}{6}, \frac{1}{3}, \frac{1}{2})$, and $w = (-\frac{1}{3}, \frac{1}{3}, 1)$ yields the table shown in Figure 21.1

S	$e(S, x)$	$e(S, y)$	$e(S, z)$	$e(S, w)$
$\emptyset$	0	0	0	0
$\{1\}$	$-\frac{1}{3}$	0	$-\frac{1}{6}$	$\frac{1}{3}$
$\{2\}$	$-\frac{1}{3}$	0	$-\frac{1}{3}$	$-\frac{1}{3}$
$\{3\}$	$-\frac{1}{3}$	-1	$-\frac{1}{2}$	-1
$\{1, 2\}$	$-\frac{2}{3}$	0	$-\frac{1}{2}$	0
$\{1, 3\}$	$\frac{1}{3}$	0	$\frac{1}{3}$	$\frac{1}{3}$
$\{2, 3\}$	$\frac{1}{3}$	0	$\frac{1}{6}$	$-\frac{1}{3}$
$\{1, 2, 3\}$	0	0	0	0

Figure 21.1 The excesses of all coalitions at x, y, z, and w

Writing the excesses in decreasing order gives

$$\theta(x) = \left(\tfrac{1}{3}, \tfrac{1}{3}, 0, 0, -\tfrac{1}{3}, -\tfrac{1}{3}, -\tfrac{1}{3}, -\tfrac{2}{3} \right), \tag{21.11}$$

$$\theta(y) = (0, 0, 0, 0, 0, 0, 0, -1), \tag{21.12}$$

$$\theta(z) = \left(\tfrac{1}{3}, \tfrac{1}{6}, 0, 0, -\tfrac{1}{6}, -\tfrac{1}{3}, -\tfrac{1}{2}, -\tfrac{1}{2} \right), \tag{21.13}$$

$$\theta(w) = \left(\tfrac{1}{3}, \tfrac{1}{3}, 0, 0, 0, -\tfrac{1}{3}, -\tfrac{1}{3}, -1 \right). \tag{21.14}$$

Therefore,

$$\theta(y) <_L \theta(z) <_L \theta(x) <_L \theta(w). \tag{21.15}$$

It can be proved that the vector y satisfies $\theta(y) <_L \theta(u)$ for every imputation $u \in X(N; v)$ (Exercise 21.7). ◄

Definition 21.4 *Let $(N; v)$ be a coalitional game and let $K \subseteq \mathbb{R}^N$. The* nucleolus *of the game $(N; v)$ relative to K is the set*

$$\mathcal{N}(N; v; K) := \{x \in K : \theta(x) \precsim_L \theta(y), \quad \forall y \in K\}. \tag{21.16}$$

The nucleolus emerges as the solution that an arbitrator would recommend for dividing the quantity $v(N)$ among the players if he uses the following procedure: he first seeks the imputations x such that $\theta_1(x)$ is minimal; since $\theta_1(x)$ measures the magnitude of the maximal complaint against x, the arbitrator wishes to minimize it. After accomplishing this, from among the vectors minimizing the maximal complaint, the arbitrator turns to seeking those vectors that minimize the second-highest complaint, $\theta_2(x)$, and so on.

If the set K is not compact, there may not be a vector x in K that is minimal in the lexicographic order, and therefore the nucleolus may be empty (Exercise 21.8). We will later prove the converse direction; if K is compact, the nucleolus relative to K is not empty (Corollary 21.10). In this section we study the nucleolus relative to some sets K that are not necessarily compact, such as closed sets that may not be bounded. The first set we will consider is the set of imputations $X(N; v)$, defined in Equation (21.3). If we drop the requirement of individual rationality in Equation (21.3), we get the set $X^0(N; v)$ of *preimputations*:

$$X^0(N; v) := \{x \in \mathbb{R}^N : x(N) = v(N)\}. \tag{21.17}$$

This is an unbounded set that contains the set of imputations: $X(N; v) \subset X^0(N; v)$. We can similarly define the sets of imputations and preimputations for any coalitional structure $\mathcal{B}$:

$$X(\mathcal{B}; v) := \{x \in \mathbb{R}^N : x(B) = v(B) \quad \forall B \in \mathcal{B}, \quad x_i \geq v(i) \quad \forall i \in N\}, \tag{21.18}$$

$$X^0(\mathcal{B}; v) := \{x \in \mathbb{R}^N : x(B) = v(B) \quad \forall B \in \mathcal{B}\}. \tag{21.19}$$

Remark 21.5 *Note that every vector x in either $X(\mathcal{B}; v)$ or $X^0(\mathcal{B}; v)$ satisfies $x(N) = \sum_{B \in \mathcal{B}} v(B)$: the sum of the coordinates is the same for all vectors in both sets.* ♦

Definition 21.6 *The* **nucleolus** *of a coalitional game* $(N; v)$ *is the nucleolus relative to the set of imputations* $X(N; v)$, *that is,* $\mathcal{N}(N; v; X(N; v))$. *The* **prenucleolus** *of a game is the nucleolus relative to the set of preimputations* $X^0(N; v)$; *i.e., it is the set* $\mathcal{N}(N; v; X^0(N; v))$. *For every coalitional structure* $\mathcal{B}$, *the* **nucleolus** *for* $\mathcal{B}$ *is the nucleolus relative to the set of imputations* $X(\mathcal{B}; v)$, *i.e.,* $\mathcal{N}(N; v; X(\mathcal{B}; v))$, *and the* **prenucleolus** *for* $\mathcal{B}$ *is the nucleolus relative to the set of preimputations* $X^0(\mathcal{B}; v)$, *i.e.,* $\mathcal{N}(N; v; X^0(\mathcal{B}; v))$.

For the sake of simplifying the notation, we will henceforth write $\mathcal{N}(N; v)$ in place of $\mathcal{N}(N; v; X(N; v))$, and call that the nucleolus of the game $(N; v)$. Similarly, we will write $\mathcal{PN}(N; v)$ in place of $\mathcal{N}(N; v; X^0(N; v))$ and call that the prenucleolus of the game $(N; v)$. For every coalitional structure $\mathcal{B}$, we will write $\mathcal{N}(N; v; \mathcal{B})$ and $\mathcal{PN}(N; v; \mathcal{B})$ in place of $\mathcal{N}(N; v; X(\mathcal{B}; v))$ and $\mathcal{N}(N; v; X^0(\mathcal{B}; v))$, and call them the nucleolus and the prenucleolus, respectively, of the game $(N; v)$ for the coalitional structure $\mathcal{B}$.

21.2 Nonemptiness and uniqueness of the nucleolus

We start by showing that if the set K is compact, then the nucleolus is nonempty. To this end we express $\theta_k(x)$ as the maximum of the minimum of the excesses.

Theorem 21.7 *For every k, $1 \le k \le 2^n$,*

$$\theta_k(x) = \max_{\text{different } S_1,\dots,S_k} \min\{e(S_1, x), \dots, e(S_k, x)\}. \tag{21.20}$$

For $k = 1$, Equation (21.20) takes the following form:

$$\theta_1(x) = \max_{S \subseteq N} e(S, x), \tag{21.21}$$

which is an expression of the fact that $\theta_1(x)$ is the maximal excess at x. The interpretation of the right-hand side of Equation (21.20) is that for every k different coalitions $S_1, S_2, \dots, S_k$, we compute the minimum among all their excesses at x. This yields a list of $\binom{2^n}{k}$ numbers. The maximum among these numbers is $\theta_k(x)$ (the k-th element of $\theta(x)$).

We will prove the theorem for the special case of $k = 2$. For $k > 2$ the proof is left to the reader (Exercise 21.11).

Proof: For $k = 2$, the statement of the theorem can be formulated more generally. Let A be a finite set of real numbers. Then the second greatest element[1] in A is $\max_{\{x,y\in A,x\neq y\}} \min\{x, y\}$.

To see this, denote the elements of A as $a_1, a_2, \dots, a_K$, and assume without loss of generality that

$$a_1 \ge a_2 \ge a_3 \ge \cdots \ge a_K. \tag{21.22}$$

The second greatest element in A is a_2. We will show that $\max_{\{x,y\in A,x\neq y\}} \min\{x, y\} = a_2$. Note that $\min\{a_i, a_j\} \le a_2$ for every pair of distinct elements $a_i, a_j \in A$, with equality if and only if $\{a_i, a_j\} = \{a_1, a_2\}$. Thus, $\max_{\{x,y\in A,x\neq y\}} \min\{x, y\} = a_2$, as claimed. $\square$

---

1 Here we mean the weakly second-greatest element, i.e., when arranging the elements in decreasing order. It may happen that the greatest element is equal to the second-greatest element.

Corollary 21.8 *For every* $k = 1, 2, \ldots, 2^n$, *the function* θ_k *is continuous.*

Proof: For every coalition $S \subseteq N$ the function $e(S, x) = v(S) - x(S)$ is linear in x, and therefore in particular it is a continuous function. Since the minimum of a finite number of continuous functions is a continuous function, we deduce that the function $x \mapsto \min\{e(S_1, x), \ldots, e(S_k, x)\}$ is continuous for every set of k coalitions $\{S_1, \ldots, S_k\}$. Since the maximum of a finite number of continuous functions is also a continuous function, by Equation (21.20) θ_k is a continuous function. □

Theorem 21.9 *For every coalitional game* $(N; v)$ *and any nonempty and compact set* $K \subseteq \mathbb{R}^N$, *the nucleolus of the game* $(N; v)$ *relative to* K *is a nonempty compact set.*

Proof: Since θ_1 is a continuous function, the set

$$X_1 := \left\{ x \in K : \theta_1(x) = \min_{y \in K} \theta_1(y) \right\} \tag{21.23}$$

is compact and nonempty (Exercise 21.3). Define X_k for $2 \le k \le 2^n$ inductively by

$$X_k := \left\{ x \in X_{k-1} : \theta_k(x) = \min_{y \in X_{k-1}} \theta_k(y) \right\}. \tag{21.24}$$

We prove by induction over k that the sets $(X_k)_{k=2}^{2^n}$ are compact and nonempty. Suppose that the set X_{k-1} is compact and nonempty. Since θ_k is a continuous function, by applying the inductive hypothesis, we deduce that the set X_k is also compact and nonempty. To conclude the proof, note that X_{2^n} is the nucleolus of the game. □

The set $X(\mathcal{B}; v)$ of imputations for the coalitional structure $\mathcal{B}$ is compact. It is nonempty if $v(B) \ge \sum_{i \in B} v(i)$ for every coalition $B \in \mathcal{B}$. We therefore have the following corollary.

Corollary 21.10 *The nucleolus* $\mathcal{N}(N; v; \mathcal{B})$ *of a coalitional game* $(N; v)$ *for any coalitional structure* $\mathcal{B}$ *is a compact set. If* $v(B) \ge \sum_{i \in B} v(i)$ *for every coalition* $B \in \mathcal{B}$, *then* $\mathcal{N}(N; v; \mathcal{B})$ *is also nonempty.*

Theorem 21.11 *Let* $(N; v)$ *be a coalitional game, and let* $K \subseteq \mathbb{R}^N$ *be a nonempty closed set satisfying the following property: there exists a real number* c *such that*

$$\sum_{i \in N} x_i = c, \quad \forall x \in K. \tag{21.25}$$

Then $\mathcal{N}(N; v; K)$ *is a nonempty compact set.*

A set K satisfying the property described by Equation (21.25) may not be bounded, and therefore may not be compact. In particular, Equation (21.25) holds for the closed set $X^0(\mathcal{B}; v)$ of preimputations for any coalitional structure $\mathcal{B}$ (Remark 21.5), and we deduce the following corollary.

Corollary 21.12 *The prenucleolus of a coalitional game, for any coalitional structure, is a nonempty compact set.*

Proof of Theorem 21.11: The outline of the proof proceeds as follows. We will choose a point $y \in K$, and use it to define a compact set $\widetilde{K}$ that is contained in K, contains y, and satisfies $\theta(y) <_L \theta(z)$ for every $z \in K \backslash \tilde{K}$. Since $\tilde{K}$ is nonempty and compact, the nucleolus relative to $\tilde{K}$ is a nonempty and compact set (Theorem 21.9). Since for every x in the nucleolus relative to $\tilde{K}$, the vector $\theta(x)$ is less than or equal to $\theta(y)$ in the lexicographic order, which is less than $\theta(z)$, for all $z \in K \backslash \tilde{K}$, it follows that the nucleolus relative to $\tilde{K}$ equals the nucleolus relative to K, and therefore the latter is also nonempty and compact.

We now turn to the construction of the set $\tilde{K}$. Let $y \in K$, and denote

$$\mu = \theta_1(y) = \max_{S \subseteq N} e(S, y). \tag{21.26}$$

Define

$$\tilde{K} = \left\{ x \in K : \max_{S \subseteq N} e(S, x) \le \mu \right\}. \tag{21.27}$$

By definition, $\tilde{K} \subseteq K$, and $y \in \tilde{K}$, and hence the set $\tilde{K}$ is nonempty. If $z \in K \backslash \tilde{K}$ then $\theta_1(z) = \max_{T \subseteq N} e(T, z) > \mu = \theta_1(y)$, and hence $\theta(y) <_L \theta(z)$.

Finally, we show that the set $\tilde{K}$ is compact. Since $\tilde{K}$ is defined by weak linear inequalities, it is a closed set. We will show that $\tilde{K}$ is also bounded. Let $x \in \tilde{K}$. By the definition of μ, one has $e(S, x) \le \mu$ for every coalition $S \subseteq N$. Setting $S = \{i\}$ yields

$$\mu \ge e(\{i\}, x) = v(i) - x_i, \tag{21.28}$$

and therefore $x_i \ge v(i) - \mu$ for every $i \in N$. On the other hand, since $\sum_{i \in N} x_i = c$,

$$x_i = c - \sum_{\{j : j \ne i\}} x_j \le c - \sum_{\{j : j \ne i\}} (v(j) - \mu) = c + |N - 1|\mu - \sum_{\{j : j \ne i\}} v(j). \tag{21.29}$$

To summarize, the set $\tilde{K}$ is contained in the following product of intervals:

$$\tilde{K} \subseteq \underset{i \in N}{\times} \left[v(i) - \mu, c + |N - 1|\mu - \sum_{\{j : j \ne i\}} v(j) \right]; \tag{21.30}$$

hence $\tilde{K}$ is a bounded set. □

Theorem 21.13 *Let $(N; v)$ be a coalitional game and let $K \subseteq \mathbb{R}^N$ be a convex set. Then $\mathcal{N}(N; v; K)$ contains at most one point.*

Proof: Let x and y be two points in the nucleolus. We will prove that $x = y$. Denote

$$\theta(x) = (e(S_1, x), e(S_2, x), \ldots, e(S_{2^n}, x)), \tag{21.31}$$

$$\theta(y) = (e(R_1, y), e(R_2, y), \ldots, e(R_{2^n}, y)), \tag{21.32}$$

and

$$\theta\left(\frac{x + y}{2}\right) = \left(e\left(T_1, \frac{x + y}{2}\right), e\left(T_2, \frac{x + y}{2}\right), \ldots, e\left(T_{2^n}, \frac{x + y}{2}\right) \right). \tag{21.33}$$

Since x and y are in the nucleolus, by definition $\theta(x) \approx_L \theta(y)$, and therefore $\theta(x) = \theta(y)$, i.e.,

$$\theta_k(x) = \theta_k(y), \quad 1 \le k \le 2^n. \tag{21.34}$$

Since K is a convex set, $\frac{x+y}{2}$ is also in K. For every coalition $T \subseteq N$,

$$2e\left(T, \frac{x+y}{2}\right) = 2v(T) - (x+y)(T) = e(T, x) + e(T, y), \tag{21.35}$$

and therefore

$$2\theta\left(\frac{x+y}{2}\right) = (e(T_1, x) + e(T_1, y), e(T_2, x) + e(T_2, y), \ldots, e(T_{2^n}, x) + e(T_{2^n}, y)). \tag{21.36}$$

Since S_1 maximizes the excess at x we deduce that

$$e(T_1, x) \le e(S_1, x), \tag{21.37}$$

and since R_1 maximizes the excess at y,

$$e(T_1, y) \le e(R_1, y). \tag{21.38}$$

Since $e(S_1, x) = e(R_1, y)$ (Equation (21.34)), Equations (21.36), (21.37), and (21.38) imply that

$$e\left(T_1, \frac{x+y}{2}\right) = \frac{e(T_1, x) + e(T_1, y)}{2} \le e(S_1, x). \tag{21.39}$$

If $e(T_1, \frac{x+y}{2}) < e(S_1, x)$, then $\theta(\frac{x+y}{2}) <_L \theta(x)$, contradicting the assumption that x is in the nucleolus. It follows that $e(T_1, \frac{x+y}{2}) = e(S_1, x)$, and therefore

$$e(T_1, x) + e(T_1, y) = e(S_1, x) + e(R_1, y). \tag{21.40}$$

Using Equations (21.37) and (21.38) we deduce that $e(T_1, x) = e(S_1, x)$ and $e(T_1, y) = e(R_1, y)$, and therefore T_1 maximizes the excess at x and at y; i.e., by changing the order of the coalitions, one can write

$$\theta(x) = (e(T_1, x), e(S'_2, x), \ldots, e(S'_{2^n}, x)), \tag{21.41}$$

and

$$\theta(y) = (e(T_1, y), e(R'_2, y), \ldots, e(R'_{2^n}, y)), \tag{21.42}$$

where $T_1, S'_2, \ldots, S'_{2^n}$ are obtained from $S_1, S_2, \ldots, S_{2^n}$, by swapping S_1 with T_1. A similar statement holds for $T_1, R'_2, \ldots, R'_{2^n}$. Continuing by induction, for every k such that $1 \le k \le 2^n$, we show that $e(T_k, x) = e(S_k, x)$ and $e(T_k, y) = e(R_k, y)$. In other words,

$$e(T, x) = e(T, y), \quad \forall T \subseteq N. \tag{21.43}$$

In particular setting $T = \{i\}$, we deduce that for every player $i \in N$,

$$v(i) - x_i = e(\{i\}, x) = e(\{i\}, y) = v(i) - y_i, \tag{21.44}$$

and therefore $x_i = y_i$. This means that $x = y$, which is what we needed to show. $\square$

When K is not a convex set, the nucleolus may contain more than one point (Exercise 21.14).

Corollary 21.14 *For every coalitional structure, the prenucleolus of a coalitional game $(N; v)$ for that coalitional structure consists of a single preimputation. If the set of imputations for the coalitional structure is nonempty, then the nucleolus for this coalitional structure consists of a single imputation as well.*

Proof: Since the set $X^0(\mathcal{B}; v)$ is convex for every coalitional structure $\mathcal{B}$, the claim for the prenucleolus follows from Corollary 21.12 and Theorem 21.13. Since the set $X(\mathcal{B}; v)$ is convex for every coalitional structure $\mathcal{B}$, the claim for the nucleolus follows from Corollary 21.10 and Theorem 21.13. □

As the nucleolus contains a single vector if it is not empty, and the prenucleolus always contains a single vector, we call these two vectors respectively "the nucleolus" and "the prenucleolus" of the game, and view them as vectors in $\mathbb{R}^N$. The i-th coordinates of these vectors are denoted by $\mathcal{N}_i(N; v)$ and $\mathcal{PN}_i(N; v)$ respectively. Similarly, for every coalitional structure $\mathcal{B}$ we call the single vector contained in the nucleolus (if it is nonempty) and in the prenucleolus for $\mathcal{B}$ "the nucleolus for $\mathcal{B}$" and "the prenucleolus for $\mathcal{B}$," and we view them as vectors in $\mathbb{R}^N$.

The nucleolus and the prenucleolus may not coincide (Exercise 21.15). As the next theorem states, when the prenucleolus of a game is an imputation, then the nucleolus and the prenucleolus coincide.

Theorem 21.15 *For every coalitional structure $\mathcal{B}$, if the prenucleolus x^* of a coalitional game $(N; v)$ for $\mathcal{B}$ is individually rational, i.e., $x_i^* \geq v(i)$ for all $i \in N$, then x^* is also the nucleolus of $(N; v)$ for $\mathcal{B}$.*

Proof: Let x^* be the prenucleolus of the game $(N; v)$ for $\mathcal{B}$. Since by assumption this vector is individually rational, it is in $X(\mathcal{B}; v)$. Because every imputation is also in particular a preimputation, $\theta(x^*) \precsim_L \theta(x)$ for every $x \in X(N; v)$. It follows that the vector x^* is also the nucleolus of the game $(N; v)$ for $\mathcal{B}$. □

21.3 Properties of the nucleolus

We have seen two single-valued solution concepts for coalitional games, the Shapley value and the nucleolus (or prenucleolus). We will now study what these two solution concepts have in common, and what properties distinguish them. This analysis may prove useful in determining which solution concept is more appropriate for each specific application.

Theorem 21.16 *The nucleolus is covariant under strategic equivalence. That is, for every coalitional game $(N; v)$, every set $K \subseteq \mathbb{R}^N$, every $a > 0$, and every $b \in \mathbb{R}^N$,*

$$\mathcal{N}(N; v; aK + b) = a\mathcal{N}(N; v; K) + b. \tag{21.45}$$

This theorem, whose proof is left to the reader as an exercise (Exercise 21.17), parallels the covariance under strategic equivalence of the Shapley value (Claim 19.18, page 803).

The next theorem states that for every coalitional structure $\mathcal{B}$, symmetric players who are members of the same coalition in $\mathcal{B}$ receive equal payoffs in the nucleolus and in the prenucleolus for $\mathcal{B}$. Recall that players i and j are symmetric players if $v(S \cup \{i\}) = v(S \cup \{j\})$ for every coalition S that contains neither player i nor player j. This theorem parallels the symmetry property of the Shapley value (Claim 19.18, page 803).

Theorem 21.17 *Let $(N; v)$ be a coalitional game and let $\mathcal{B}$ be a coalitional structure, and let i and j be symmetric players who are members of the same coalition in $\mathcal{B}$. Then $\mathcal{N}_i(N; v; \mathcal{B}) = \mathcal{N}_j(N; v; \mathcal{B})$ and $\mathcal{PN}_i(N; v; \mathcal{B}) = \mathcal{PN}_j(N; v; \mathcal{B})$.*

Proof: Let i and j be symmetric players in the same coalition in $\mathcal{B}$; i.e., there exists a coalition $B \in \mathcal{B}$ such that $i, j \in B$. Denote $x^* = \mathcal{N}(N; v; \mathcal{B})$, and let y be the vector obtained from x^* by swapping the payoffs of players i by j:

$$y_k = \begin{cases} x_i^* & \text{if } k = j, \\ x_j^* & \text{if } k = i, \\ x_k^* & \text{if } k \notin \{i, j\}. \end{cases} \tag{21.46}$$

Since players i and j are in the same coalition in $\mathcal{B}$, and since $x^* \in X(\mathcal{B}; v)$, it follows that $y \in X(\mathcal{B}; v)$. We will show that $\theta(x^*) \approx_L \theta(y)$, and therefore y is also minimal in the lexicographic order. In particular, y is also in the nucleolus. Since the nucleolus (or the prenucleolus) contains a single vector, it must be that $x^* = y$, and in particular $x_i^* = x_j^*$.

To show that $\theta(x^*) \approx_L \theta(y)$, define a bijection φ from the set of coalitions to itself:

$$\varphi(S) = \begin{cases} S, & \text{if } i \in S, \quad j \in S, \\ S, & \text{if } i \notin S, \quad j \notin S, \\ (S \setminus \{i\}) \cup \{j\}, & \text{if } i \in S, \quad j \notin S, \\ (S \setminus \{j\}) \cup \{i\}, & \text{if } i \notin S, \quad j \in S. \end{cases} \tag{21.47}$$

Since players i and j are symmetric, $v(\varphi(S)) = v(S)$ for every coalition $S \subseteq N$. The definitions of φ and y imply that $e(S, x^*) = e(\varphi(S), y)$ for every coalition $S \subseteq N$. Therefore the sets of excesses with respect to x^* and y are equal:

$$\{e(S, x^*) : S \subseteq N\} = \{e(S, y) : S \subseteq N\}. \tag{21.48}$$

Thus, arranging the collections of excesses at x^* and at y in decreasing order yields the same vector, and hence $\theta(x^*) \approx_L \theta(y)$. $\qquad\square$

Theorems 21.16 and 21.17 enable one to write explicitly a formula for the nucleolus of two-player games.

Theorem 21.18 *Let $(N; v)$ be a two-player coalitional game. If $v(1, 2) \geq v(1) + v(2)$, then the nucleolus is*

$$\left(\frac{v(1, 2) + v(1) - v(2)}{2}, \frac{v(1, 2) - v(1) + v(2)}{2} \right). \tag{21.49}$$

This imputation is called the *standard solution* of the game. To prove Theorem 21.18 one uses the fact that the nucleolus is symmetric and covariant under strategic equivalence. The condition $v(1, 2) \geq v(1) + v(2)$ guarantees that the set of imputations $X(N; v)$ is nonempty, thereby ensuring that the nucleolus is nonempty. Since the prenucleolus and the Shapley value are also symmetric solution concepts that are covariant under strategic equivalence, Equation (21.49) characterizes these two solution concepts in two-player coalitional games. The condition $v(1, 2) \geq v(1) + v(2)$ is, however, not needed for their characterizations, since they are defined for all coalitional games.

Theorem 21.19 *Let $i \in N$ be a null player in a coalitional game $(N; v)$. Then under both the nucleolus and the prenucleolus, player i's payoff is 0; i.e., $\mathcal{N}_i(N; v) = \mathcal{PN}_i(N; v) = 0$.*

This theorem does not hold for general coalitional structures (Exercise 21.16).

Proof: Let i be a null player in the coalitional game $(N; v)$. We will first prove the claim for the nucleolus x^*. Suppose by contradiction that $x_i^* \neq 0$. Since $x^* \in X(N; v)$, one has $x_i^* \geq v(i) = 0$, and since $x_i^* \neq 0$, it follows that $x_i^* > 0$. We will show that by transferring a small amount from player i to all the other players, it is possible to create an imputation y satisfying $\theta(y) <_L \theta(x^*)$, thereby contradicting the assumption that x^* is the nucleolus. Since i is a null player, it follows that for every coalition T that does not contain i,

$$e(T \cup \{i\}, x^*) = v(T \cup \{i\}) - x^*(T \cup \{i\}) \tag{21.50}$$

$$= v(T) - x^*(T) - x_i^* \tag{21.51}$$

$$= e(T, x^*) - x_i^*. \tag{21.52}$$

Since $e(N; x^*) = 0$, Equations (21.50)–(21.52) for $T = N \setminus \{i\}$ imply that

$$\theta_1(x^*) \geq e(N \setminus \{i\}, x^*) = e(N, x^*) + x_i^* = x_i^* > 0. \tag{21.53}$$

Let y be the vector derived from x^* by having player i transfer an amount $\frac{x_i^*}{n}$ to every other player:

$$y_j = \begin{cases} \frac{x_i^*}{n} & \text{if } j = i, \\ x_j^* + \frac{x_i^*}{n} & \text{if } j \neq i. \end{cases} \tag{21.54}$$

Since x^* is an imputation, it follows that y is also an imputation (why?). To prove that $\theta(y) <_L \theta(x^*)$ we will show that $\theta_1(y) < \theta_1(x^*)$. To this end we will prove that $e(T, y) < \theta_1(x^*)$ for every coalition $T \subseteq N$.

For the coalition $T = \emptyset$ we have

$$e(\emptyset, y) = 0 < \theta_1(x^*). \tag{21.55}$$

For every nonempty coalition T that does not contain player i we have

$$e(T, y) = e(T, x^*) - \frac{|T|}{n} x_i^* < e(T, x^*) \leq \theta_1(x^*). \tag{21.56}$$

From Equations (21.50)–(21.52) we deduce that $e(T, y) = e(T \setminus \{i\}) - x_i^*$ for every coalition T that contains player i, and, therefore,

$$e(T, y) = e(T, x^*) + \frac{n - |T|}{n} x_i^* = e(T \setminus \{i\}, x^*) - \frac{|T|}{n} x_i^* \tag{21.57}$$

$$\leq \theta_1(x^*) - \frac{|T|}{n} x_i^* < \theta_1(x^*). \tag{21.58}$$

We thus proved that $\theta_1(y) = \max_{T \subseteq N} e(T, y) < \theta_1(x^*)$, thereby contradicting the fact that x^* is the nucleolus.

Suppose now that x^* is the prenucleolus, and assume by way of contradiction that $x_i^* \neq 0$. If $x_i^* > 0$ we obtain a contradiction as in the case of the nucleolus. Suppose then that $x_i^* < 0$. We will prove that in this case as well the vector y defined in Equation (21.54) satisfies $\theta(y) <_L \theta(x^*)$. Since $x_i^* < 0$, the vector y is derived from x^* by having every other player transfer to player i the amount $\frac{|x_i^*|}{n}$. Since x^* is a preimputation, y is a preimputation as well. Since player i is a null player,

$$\theta_1(x^*) \geq e(\{i\}, x_i^*) = -x_i^* > 0. \tag{21.59}$$

For the coalition $T = N$ we have $e(N, y) = 0 < \theta_1(x^*)$. For every coalition T that does not contain player i we have $|T| < n$, and by Equations (21.50)–(21.52), we also have $e(T, x^*) = e(T \cup \{i\}, x^*) + x_i^*$. Therefore,

$$e(T, y) = e(T, x^*) - \frac{|T|}{n} x_i^* = e(T \cup \{i\}, x^*) + \frac{n - |T|}{n} x_i^* < e(T \cup \{i\}, x^*) \leq \theta_1(x^*). \tag{21.60}$$

For every coalition T that contains player i and is not N we have

$$e(T, y) = e(T, x^*) + \frac{n - |T|}{n} x_i^* < e(T, x^*) \leq \theta_1(x^*). \tag{21.61}$$

Therefore also in this case $\theta_1(y) = \max_{T \subseteq N} e(T, y) < \theta_1(x^*)$, contradicting the fact that x^* is the prenucleolus. $\qquad\square$

The Shapley value is the only single-valued solution concept satisfying the properties of efficiency, symmetry, null player, and additivity. Both the nucleolus and the prenucleolus satisfy the properties of efficiency, symmetry, and null player. If we show that the Shapley value differs from the nucleolus and the prenucleolus, then it will follow that the nucleolus and prenucleolus do not satisfy additivity. Indeed, there are examples of coalitional games in which the nucleolus and the prenucleolus differ from the Shapley value, such as the gloves game (Examples 18.5 and 19.24), where the nucleolus and the prenucleolus are $(0, 0, 1)$, while the Shapley value is $(\frac{1}{6}, \frac{1}{6}, \frac{2}{3})$.

An important property shared by the nucleolus and the prenucleolus is that both of them are in the core, if the core is nonempty. This property does not hold for the Shapley value (Example 19.24, page 807), another proof that the Shapley value does not coincide with the nucleolus and the prenucleolus.

Theorem 21.20 *If the core of a coalitional game $(N; v)$ for the coalitional structure $\mathcal{B}$ is nonempty, then the nucleolus for $\mathcal{B}$ is in the core, and it coincides with the prenucleolus for $\mathcal{B}$.*

Proof: Let x be an imputation in the core of a coalitional game $(N; v)$ for the coalitional structure $\mathcal{B}$, and let x^* be the prenucleolus for $\mathcal{B}$. Since x is in the core, $x(S) \geq v(S)$ for every coalition S, and therefore

$$e(S, x) = v(S) - x(S) \leq 0, \quad \forall S \subseteq N. \tag{21.62}$$

This implies that $\theta_1(x) \leq 0$. Since x^* is the prenucleolus, $\theta(x^*) \precsim_L \theta(x)$. Hence $\theta_1(x^*) \leq \theta_1(x) \leq 0$. By definition, $\theta_1(x^*) = \max_{S \subseteq N} e(S, x^*)$, and therefore for every coalition $S \subseteq N$ we have $e(S, x^*) \leq 0$; i.e., $x^*(S) \geq v(S)$, and therefore x^* is in the core.

Since x^* is in the core, $x_i^* \geq v(i)$, and therefore $x^* \in X(N; v)$. By Theorem 21.15, x^* is also the nucleolus. □

As the next theorem shows, the nucleolus is also in the bargaining set (the bargaining set is studied in Chapter 20).

Theorem 21.21 *The nucleolus of a coalitional game $(N; v)$ for any coalitional structure $\mathcal{B}$ is in the bargaining set for $\mathcal{B}$:*

$$\mathcal{N}(N; v; \mathcal{B}) \in \mathcal{M}(N; v; \mathcal{B}). \tag{21.63}$$

Proof: If the core is nonempty, then Theorems 21.20 and 20.12 (page 834) imply that

$$\mathcal{N}(N; v; \mathcal{B}) \in \mathcal{C}(N; v; \mathcal{B}) \subseteq \mathcal{M}(N; v; \mathcal{B}). \tag{21.64}$$

Suppose that the core $\mathcal{C}(N; v; \mathcal{B})$ is empty. Let $x^* = \mathcal{N}(N; v; \mathcal{B})$ be the nucleolus for the coalitional structure $\mathcal{B}$. In particular $x^* \notin \mathcal{C}(N; v; \mathcal{B})$, and therefore $\theta_1(x^*) > 0$ (Exercise 21.26). If $x^* \notin \mathcal{M}(N; v; \mathcal{B})$, then there is a player k who has a justified objection at x^* against player l, where players k and l are in the same coalition of $\mathcal{B}$.

Since player k has an objection at x^* against player l, there is a coalition S containing player k and not player l with positive excess. Since S is a justified objection against player l, all the coalitions containing player l but not player k have less excess (Theorem 20.14, page 835).

Order the coalitions by decreasing excess at x^*. Denote by a the maximal excess of the coalitions containing player k and not player l. Denote by b the maximal excess of the coalitions containing player l and not player k. All the coalitions whose excesses are greater than a either contain both player k and player l, or contain neither k nor l (Figure 21.2). Denote $\delta := \min\{a - b, x_l^* - v(l)\}$. As we showed previously, $a > b$.

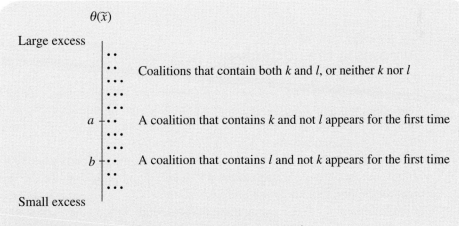

Figure 21.2 The coalitions and ordered excesses at x^*

Since player k has a justified objection against player l, it must be the case that $x_l^* > v(l)$; otherwise player l would have a counterobjection using the coalition $\{l\}$. We deduce that $\delta > 0$.

Define a vector y derived from x^* by transferring from player l to player k the amount of $\frac{\delta}{2}$:

$$
y_i = \begin{cases}
x_i^* & \text{if } i \notin \{l, k\}, \\
x_i^* - \frac{\delta}{2} & \text{if } i = l, \\
x_i^* + \frac{\delta}{2} & \text{if } i = k.
\end{cases} \tag{21.65}
$$

We first prove that y is an imputation. Since $y(N) = x^*(N) = v(N)$ it follows that y is an efficient vector. Since the imputation x^* is individually rational, $y_i \geq x_i^* \geq v(i)$ for every player $i \neq l$. As for player $i = l$, since by the definition of δ we have $x_l^* \geq v(l) + \delta$,

$$
y_l = x_l^* - \frac{\delta}{2} \geq v(l) + \frac{\delta}{2} > v(l). \tag{21.66}
$$

Hence y is also an individually rational vector, and therefore an imputation.

What is the relationship between $\theta(x^*)$ and $\theta(y)$?

- The excess of the coalitions containing both k and l, and of the coalitions that contain neither player k nor player l, do not change in passing from x^* to y.
- The excesses of coalitions containing player k but not player l are reduced by $\frac{\delta}{2}$.
- The excesses of coalitions containing player l but not player k are increased by $\frac{\delta}{2}$.

The excesses of coalitions whose excess is above a in Figure 21.2 do not change. The excess of at least one coalition at height a is reduced by a positive amount. The only coalitions whose excesses can increase are those with excesses b or less. By the definition of δ, these excesses do not exceed a. We conclude that this transfer has decreased the vector of the excesses in lexicographic order: $\theta(y) <_L \theta(x^*)$. This contradicts the fact that x^* is the nucleolus. The contradiction follows from the assumption that $x^* \notin \mathcal{M}(N; v; \mathcal{B})$, and hence the claim that $x^* \in \mathcal{M}(N; v; \mathcal{B})$ is proved. □

21.4 Computing the nucleolus

In this section, we present a procedure for computing the nucleolus $\mathcal{N}(N; v)$ by solving a sequence of linear programs. The complexity of the algorithm is exponential in the number n of players, and therefore it is useful only for small games. A brief review of linear programming appears in Section 24.3 (page 991).

The procedure is based on the conditions an imputation must satisfy to be the nucleolus; it finds an imputation x whose vector of excesses $\theta(x)$ is minimal in the lexicographic order. In the first step, the procedure finds all the vectors whose maximal excess $\theta_1(x)$ is as small as possible. From among these the procedure finds all the vectors whose second-largest excess is as small as possible, and so on. As the length of the vector of excesses is finite, the procedure eventually halts and yields an imputation, which is the nucleolus.

Step 1: Minimizing the maximal excess

Solve the following linear program with unknowns $x_1, x_2, \ldots, x_n, t$:

$$
\begin{array}{ll}
\text{Compute:} & \min t, \\
\text{subject to:} & e(S, x) \leq t, \quad \forall S \subseteq N, \\
& x(N) = v(N), \\
& x_i \geq v(i), \quad \forall i \in N.
\end{array}
\qquad (21.67)
$$

Denote by θ_1 the value of this program, and by X_1 the set of vectors at which the minimum of the excesses is attained:

$$
X_1 := \{ x \in X(N; v) \colon e(S, x) \leq \theta_1, \quad \forall S \subseteq N \}. \qquad (21.68)
$$

Denote by Σ_1 the set of all coalitions at which the maximal excess θ_1 is attained at all $x \in X_1$:

$$
\Sigma_1 := \{ S \subseteq N \colon e(S, x) = \theta_1, \quad \forall x \in X_1 \}. \qquad (21.69)
$$

The set Σ_1 is nonempty. To see this, note that by the definition of θ_1, we have $e(S, x) \leq \theta_1$ for every $x \in X_1$, and for every coalition S. If Σ_1 were empty, then for every coalition $S \subseteq N$ there would exist a vector $x^S \in X_1$ satisfying $e(S, x^S) < \theta_1$. But then the average $y := \frac{1}{2^n} \sum_{S \subseteq N} x^S$ would satisfy $e(S, y) < \theta_1$ for every coalition S (Exercise 21.32), contradicting the definition of θ_1.

Step 2: Minimizing the second-largest excess

Solve the following linear program with unknowns $x_1, x_2, \ldots, x_n, t$:

$$
\begin{array}{ll}
\text{Compute:} & \min t, \\
\text{subject to:} & e(S, x) = \theta_1, \quad \forall S \in \Sigma_1, \\
& e(S, x) \leq t, \quad \forall S \notin \Sigma_1, \\
& x(N) = v(N), \\
& x_i \geq v(i), \quad \forall i \in N.
\end{array}
\qquad (21.70)
$$

Denote the value of this program by θ_2, by X_2 the set of all vectors at which the minimum is attained, and by Σ_2 the set of all coalitions (a) that are not in Σ_1, and (b) at which the value θ_2 is attained for all $x \in X_2$. As before, Σ_2 is not empty.

Continue implementing this procedure iteratively in a similar manner to define disjoint collections of coalitions $\Sigma_3, \Sigma_4, \ldots$. Since these collections are disjoint, there exists $L > 0$ such that Σ_L is nonempty, and the union $\cup_{l=1}^{L} \Sigma_l$ contains all the coalitions. The set of imputations X_L contains a single vector, the nucleolus of the game. The reader is asked to prove that the algorithm indeed calculates the nucleolus in Exercise 21.31.

21.5 Characterizing the prenucleolus

· ·

In this section, we prove a theorem that can be used to check whether a preimputation x is the prenucleolus of a coalitional game $(N; v)$ by considering only the vector of excesses $\theta(x)$, without comparing it to $\theta(y)$ for $y \neq x$.

Definition 21.22 *A system of equalities and inequalities is* tight *if it has at least one solution, and at every solution of the system every inequality obtains as an equality.*

Example 21.23 The following system of inequalities is tight:

$$x + y \leq 7, \tag{21.71}$$
$$x + 2y \geq 7, \tag{21.72}$$
$$x \geq 7, \tag{21.73}$$

because the only solution of this system is $x = 7, y = 0$, and in this solution all inequalities hold as equalities. In contrast, the following system is not tight:

$$x + y \leq 7, \tag{21.74}$$
$$x + 2y \geq 7, \tag{21.75}$$
$$x \geq 6, \tag{21.76}$$

because $x = 7, y = 0$ is a solution of the system at which the third inequality does not obtain as an equality. ◄

The next theorem characterizes balanced collections of coalitions using tight systems of equations. We first recall the definition of a balanced collection of coalitions (Definition 18.11, page 741).

Definition 21.24 *A collection $\mathcal{D}$ of coalitions is* balanced *if there exist positive numbers $(\delta_S)_{S \in \mathcal{D}}$ satisfying*

$$\sum_{\{S \in \mathcal{D}: \, i \in S\}} \delta_S = 1, \quad \forall i \in N. \tag{21.77}$$

The vector $(\delta_S)_{S \in \mathcal{D}}$ is called a vector of balancing weights *of $\mathcal{D}$.*

Theorem 21.25 *A collection $\mathcal{D}$ of subsets of N is a balanced collection if and only if the following system of equations, with $|N|$ unknowns $(y_i)_{i \in N}$, is tight:*

$$\begin{cases} y(N) = 0, \\ y(S) \geqslant 0, & \forall S \in \mathcal{D}. \end{cases} \tag{21.78}$$

Example 21.26 Suppose that $N = \{1, 2, 3\}$. The system of equations (21.78) corresponding to the balanced collection $\mathcal{D} = \{\{1, 2\}, \{1, 3\}, \{2, 3\}\}$ is

$$y_1 + y_2 + y_3 = 0, \tag{21.79}$$
$$y_1 + y_2 \geq 0, \tag{21.80}$$
$$y_1 + y_3 \geq 0, \tag{21.81}$$
$$y_2 + y_3 \geq 0. \tag{21.82}$$

The only solution of this system is $y_1 = y_2 = y_3 = 0$ (verify!), in which the inequalities obtain as equalities, and hence this system is tight.

The system of equations corresponding to the balanced collection $\mathcal{D} = \{\{1\}, \{2, 3\}\}$ is

$$y_1 + y_2 + y_3 = 0, \tag{21.83}$$

$$y_1 \geq 0, \tag{21.84}$$

$$y_2 + y_3 \geq 0. \tag{21.85}$$

All the solutions of this system are of the form $y_1 = 0, y_3 = -y_2$ (verify!), in which the inequalities obtain as equalities, and hence this system is tight as well.

The system of equations corresponding to the collection $\mathcal{D} = \{\{1, 2\}, \{1, 2, 3\}\}$ is

$$y_1 + y_2 + y_3 = 0, \tag{21.86}$$

$$y_1 + y_2 \geq 0, \tag{21.87}$$

$$y_1 + y_2 + y_3 \geq 0. \tag{21.88}$$

One solution to this system is $y_1 = y_2 = 1, y_3 = -2$ (verify!). In this solution not all the inequalities hold as equalities (since $y_1 + y_2 > 0$), and hence the system is not tight. Indeed, the collection $\mathcal{D}$ is not balanced (verify), in accordance with Theorem 21.25. ◄

We now present the proof of Theorem 21.25, which uses the Duality Theorem from the theory of linear programming (Theorem 24.46, page 995).

Proof of Theorem 21.25: Suppose first that $\mathcal{D}$ is a balanced collection, and that $(\delta_S)_{S \in \mathcal{D}}$ is a vector of balancing weights of $\mathcal{D}$. We will show that the system of equations (21.78) is tight.

The zero vector ($y_i = 0$ for all i) is a solution of the system of equations (21.78), and the system therefore has at least one solution. We will show that at every solution y of this system, all inequalities obtain as equalities. Let y be a vector in $\mathbb{R}^N$ satisfying the system of equations (21.78). By Lemma 18.16 (page 744),

$$\sum_{S \in \mathcal{D}} \delta_S y(S) = y(N) = 0. \tag{21.89}$$

Since $\delta_S > 0$ and $y(S) \geq 0$ for every coalition $S \in \mathcal{D}$, it follows that $y(S) = 0$ for every $S \in \mathcal{D}$. Thus, the system of equations is tight.

Next, suppose that the system of equations (21.78) is tight. We will show that the collection $\mathcal{D}$ is a balanced collection of coalitions. Consider the following linear program with unknowns $(\beta_S)_{S \in \mathcal{D}}, \gamma, \delta$:

Compute: $Z_P := \max 0,$

subject to: $\sum_{\{S \in \mathcal{D} : i \in S\}} \beta_S + \gamma - \delta = \sum_{\{S \in \mathcal{D} : i \in S\}} (-1), \forall i \in N,$
    $\beta_S \geq 0, \quad \forall S \in \mathcal{D}, \tag{21.90}$
    $\gamma \geq 0,$
    $\delta \geq 0.$

To construct a vector of balancing weights for $\mathcal{D}$ we will use the optimal solution to program (21.90). Since the objective function is the zero function, showing the existence of an optimal solution only requires showing that there exists a solution to this linear program. This is achieved by checking the dual linear program. The dual linear program is the following program with unknowns $(y_i)_{i \in N}$ (verify!):

Compute: $Z_D := \min \sum_{S \in \mathcal{D}} (-y(S))$,

subject to: $y(S) \geq 0$, $\forall S \in \mathcal{D}$,

$\qquad\qquad y(N) \geq 0$,

$\qquad\qquad -y(N) \geq 0$. $\qquad\qquad\qquad\qquad$ (21.91)

Since $y = \vec{0}$ is a solution of the dual linear program (21.91), the set of possible solutions of that linear program is nonempty. The system of constraints of program (21.91) is system (21.78). Since system (21.78) is tight, at every solution of the dual linear program the constraints obtain with equality, and therefore $Z_D = 0$. By the Duality Theorem (Theorem 24.46, page 995) the set of possible solutions of program (21.90) is nonempty (and $Z_P = Z_D = 0$). Let $((\beta_S)_{S \in \mathcal{D}}, \gamma, \delta)$ be a solution of the primal linear program (21.90). Write the first constraint in this program as

$$\sum_{\{S \in \mathcal{D}: \, i \in S\}} (1 + \beta_S) = \delta - \gamma, \quad \forall i \in N. \qquad (21.92)$$

Since $\beta_S \geq 0$ for every $S \in \mathcal{D}$, the left-hand side of this equation is positive (for all $i \in N$), and therefore the right-hand side is also positive, that is, $\delta - \gamma > 0$. Define

$$\lambda_S := \frac{1 + \beta_S}{\delta - \gamma}, \quad \forall S \in \mathcal{D}. \qquad (21.93)$$

Then $(\lambda_S)_{S \in \mathcal{D}}$ is a vector of positive numbers satisfying

$$\sum_{\{S \in \mathcal{D}: \, i \in S\}} \lambda_S = 1, \quad \forall i \in N, \qquad (21.94)$$

which implies that the collection $\mathcal{D}$ is balanced with the vector of balancing weights $(\lambda_S)_{S \in \mathcal{D}}$. $\qquad\qquad\qquad\qquad\qquad\qquad\qquad\qquad\qquad\qquad\qquad$ □

Definition 21.27 *Let $(N; v)$ be a coalitional game, and let $x \in X^0(N; v)$ be a preimputation. For every $\alpha \in \mathbb{R}$, denote by $\mathcal{D}(\alpha, x)$ the collection of nonempty coalitions S satisfying $e(S, x) \geq \alpha$:*

$$\mathcal{D}(\alpha, x) := \{ S \subset N : S \neq \emptyset, e(S, x) \geq \alpha \}. \qquad (21.95)$$

The collection of coalition $\mathcal{D}(\alpha, x)$ is related to the vector $\theta(x)$ in the following way. Denote the different values of the excesses at x by $a_1, a_2, \ldots, a_p$, where $a_1 > a_2 > \cdots > a_p$. Then,

$$\theta(x) = (a_1, a_1, \ldots, a_1, a_2, \ldots, a_2, \ldots, a_p, \ldots, a_p). \qquad (21.96)$$

Note that since $e(N, x) = e(\emptyset, x) = 0$ we necessarily have $a_p \leq 0$. In this notation,

$$\mathcal{D}(a_1, x) \subset \mathcal{D}(a_2, x) \subset \cdots \subset \mathcal{D}(a_p, x) = \{ S : S \subset N, S \neq \emptyset \}, \qquad (21.97)$$

the collection $\mathcal{D}(a_1, x)$ contains all coalitions with maximal excess at x (that is, with excess a_1), the collection $\mathcal{D}(a_2, x)$ contains all coalitions whose excess at x is either a_1 or

a_2, etc. For every α for which this collection is nonempty, this collection is one of the p collections $(\mathcal{D}(a_k, x))_{k=1}^p$, since

$$\mathcal{D}(\alpha, x) = \begin{cases} \emptyset & \alpha > a_1, \\ \mathcal{D}(a_k, x) & a_{k+1} < \alpha \le a_k, \\ \{S : S \subset N, S \ne \emptyset\} & \alpha \le a_p. \end{cases} \qquad (21.98)$$

Theorem 21.28 *If x^* is the prenucleolus of a coalitional game $(N; v)$, then for every $\alpha \in \mathbb{R}$ such that the collection $\mathcal{D}(\alpha, x^*)$ is nonempty, the following system of equations is tight:*

$$y(N) = 0, \qquad (21.99)$$

$$y(S) \ge 0, \quad \forall S \in \mathcal{D}(\alpha, x^*). \qquad (21.100)$$

Conversely, if for the vector $x \in X^0(N; v)$, and for every $\alpha \in \mathbb{R}$ for which the collection $\mathcal{D}(\alpha, x)$ is nonempty, the following system of equations is tight:

$$y(N) = 0, \qquad (21.101)$$

$$y(S) \ge 0, \quad \forall S \in \mathcal{D}(\alpha, x), \qquad (21.102)$$

then x is the prenucleolus of the game.

Proof:
Step 1: If x^* is the prenucleolus, then the system (21.99)–(21.100) is tight, for every α such that $\mathcal{D}(\alpha, x^*) \ne \emptyset$.

Suppose that x^* is the prenucleolus, and let $\alpha \in \mathbb{R}$ satisfy $\mathcal{D}(\alpha, x^*) \ne \emptyset$. To show that the system (21.99)–(21.100) is tight, define for every $\varepsilon > 0$ and every solution y of the system (21.99)–(21.100) a vector $z_\varepsilon \in \mathbb{R}^N$ by

$$z_\varepsilon := x^* + \varepsilon y. \qquad (21.103)$$

Since $y(N) = 0$,

$$z_\varepsilon(N) = x^*(N) + \varepsilon y(N) = x^*(N) = v(N), \qquad (21.104)$$

and therefore $z_\varepsilon \in X^0(N; v)$. Since $\lim_{\varepsilon \to 0} z_\varepsilon = x^*$ it follows that for every coalition $S \subseteq N$ we have $\lim_{\varepsilon \to 0} e(S, z_\varepsilon) = e(S, x^*)$. If $S \in \mathcal{D}(\alpha, x^*)$ and $T \notin \mathcal{D}(\alpha, x^*)$, then $e(S, x^*) \ge \alpha > e(T, x^*)$. It follows that for $\varepsilon > 0$ sufficiently small, $e(S, z_\varepsilon) > e(T, z_\varepsilon)$. Choose ε to be small enough for the inequality $e(S, z_\varepsilon) > e(T, z_\varepsilon)$ to hold for all $S \in \mathcal{D}(\alpha, x^*)$ and all $T \notin \mathcal{D}(\alpha, x^*)$. Since $y(S) \ge 0$ for every coalition $S \in \mathcal{D}(\alpha, x^*)$, the excess of every such coalition S satisfies

$$e(S, z_\varepsilon) = v(S) - (x^*(S) + \varepsilon y(S)) = e(S, x^*) - \varepsilon y(S) \le e(S, x^*). \qquad (21.105)$$

We have therefore shown that for $\varepsilon > 0$ sufficiently small,

$$e(S, z_\varepsilon) \le e(S, x^*), \forall S \in \mathcal{D}(\alpha, x^*), \qquad (21.106)$$

$$e(T, z_\varepsilon) < e(S, z_\varepsilon), \forall S \in \mathcal{D}(\alpha, x^*), T \notin \mathcal{D}(\alpha, x^*). \qquad (21.107)$$

If one of the inequalities in Equation (21.106) were a strict inequality, then $\theta(z_\varepsilon) \prec_L \theta(x^*)$ would hold, which is impossible since x^* is the prenucleolus. This leads to the conclusion that every inequality in (21.106) holds as an equality, and this and Equation (21.105) imply that $y(S) = 0$ for every coalition $S \in \mathcal{D}(\alpha, x^*)$. In particular, the system of equations (21.99)–(21.100) is tight.

Step 2: If the system of equations (21.101)–(21.102) is tight for every α such that $\mathcal{D}(\alpha, x) \neq \emptyset$, then x is the prenucleolus.

Let $x \in X^0(N; v)$ satisfy the property that the system of equations (21.101)–(21.102) is tight for every α such that $\mathcal{D}(\alpha, x) \neq \emptyset$. Let x^* be the prenucleolus. We need to prove that $x = x^*$. We will show that $\theta(x^*) = \theta(x)$, which, by the uniqueness of the prenucleolus, implies that $x = x^*$.

Denote the excesses of the coalitions at the preimputation x by $a_1, a_2, \ldots, a_p$, where $a_1 > a_2 > \cdots > a_p$. In other words,

$$\theta(x) = (a_1, a_1, \ldots, a_1, a_2, \ldots, a_2, \ldots, a_p, \ldots, a_p). \tag{21.108}$$

In this notation, $\mathcal{D}(a_1, x) \subset \mathcal{D}(a_2, x) \subset \cdots \subset \mathcal{D}(a_p, x) = \{S \subset N, S \neq \emptyset\}$. Let $a_0 > a_1$. Then $\mathcal{D}(a_0, x) = \emptyset$. We will prove by induction over t that $\mathcal{D}(a_t, x) = \mathcal{D}(a_t, x^*)$ for every $t = 0, 1, \ldots, p$, and $e(S, x) = e(S, x^*)$ for every $S \in \mathcal{D}(a_t, x)$. Since $\mathcal{D}(a_p, x) = \{S \subset N, S \neq \emptyset\}$, $e(\emptyset, x) = 0 = e(\emptyset, x^*)$, and $e(N, x) = 0 = e(N, x^*)$, this implies that $\theta(x) = \theta(x^*)$.

The case $t = 0$

$\mathcal{D}(a_0, x) = \emptyset$, because $a_0 > a_1$. Since x^* is the prenucleolus, it follows that for every coalition S,

$$e(S, x^*) \leq \theta_1(x^*) \leq \theta_1(x) = a_1 < a_0, \tag{21.109}$$

and therefore $\mathcal{D}(a_0, x^*) = \emptyset = \mathcal{D}(a_0, x)$.

The case $t \geq 1$

Assume as the induction hypothesis that $\mathcal{D}(a_{t-1}, x) = \mathcal{D}(a_{t-1}, x^*)$, and that $e(S, x) = e(S, x^*)$ for every coalition $S \in \mathcal{D}(a_{t-1}, x)$.

Denote by l_{t-1} the number of coalitions in $\mathcal{D}(a_{t-1}, x)$, and by $\hat{l}_t$ the number of coalitions S satisfying $e(S, x) = a_t$. By the induction hypothesis, the first l_{t-1} coordinates of $\theta(x)$ equal the first l_{t-1} coordinates of $\theta(x^*)$, and the next $\hat{l}_t$ coordinates in the vector $\theta(x)$ equal a_t. Since $\theta(x^*) \preceq_L \theta(x)$, it follows that $e(S, x^*) \leq a_t$ for every coalition S that is not in $\mathcal{D}(a_{t-1}, x^*)$.

Define $y := x^* - x \in \mathbb{R}^N$. Then for every coalition $S \subseteq N$,

$$e(S, x) - e(S, x^*) = (v(S) - x(S)) - (v(S) - x^*(S)) = x^*(S) - x(S) = y(S). \tag{21.110}$$

Moreover, since both x^* and x are preimputations,

$$y(N) = x^*(N) - x(N) = v(N) - v(N) = 0. \tag{21.111}$$

Consider the following system of equations:

$$y(N) = 0, \tag{21.112}$$

$$y(S) \geq 0, \quad \forall S \in \mathcal{D}(a_t, x). \tag{21.113}$$

This system of equations is the system (21.101)–(21.102) for $\alpha = a_t$, and therefore it is tight. The vector $y = x^* - x$ is a solution of this system of equations. To see this, note that by the induction hypothesis, $e(S, x) = e(S, x^*)$ for every coalition $S \in \mathcal{D}(a_{t-1}, x)$, and by Equation (21.110), $y(S) = 0$ for every such coalition. As we saw earlier, $e(S, x) = a_t \geq e(S, x^*)$ for every $S \in \mathcal{D}(a_t, x) \backslash \mathcal{D}(a_{t-1}, x)$. Finally, $y(N) = 0$ by Equation (21.111). Because system (21.112)–(21.113) is tight, $y(S) = 0$ for every coalition $S \in \mathcal{D}(a_t, x)$, and therefore using Equation (21.110) one has

$$0 = y(S) = e(S, x) - e(S, x^*), \quad \forall S \in \mathcal{D}(a_t, x). \tag{21.114}$$

This implies that $\mathcal{D}(a_t, x) \subseteq \mathcal{D}(a_t, x^*)$, and that

$$\theta_{l_{t-1}+1}(x^*) = \theta_{l_{t-1}+2}(x^*) = \cdots = \theta_{l_{t-1}+\hat{l}_t}(x^*) = a_t. \tag{21.115}$$

It remains to prove that $\mathcal{D}(a_t, x) = \mathcal{D}(a_t, x^*)$. Since $\theta_{l_{t-1}+\hat{l}_t+1}(x) = a_{t+1}$, and since $\theta(x^*) \precsim_L \theta(x)$, we deduce that

$$\theta_{l_{t-1}+\hat{l}_t+1}(x^*) \leq \theta_{l_{t-1}+\hat{l}_t+1}(x) = a_{t+1} < a_t, \tag{21.116}$$

which implies that the set of coalitions whose excesses at x equal a_t equals the set of coalitions whose excesses at x^* equal a_t. We conclude that $\mathcal{D}(a_t, x) = \mathcal{D}(a_t, x^*)$, completing the proof of the inductive step, and the proof of Theorem 21.28.   □

The next theorem is an immediate corollary of Theorems 21.25 and 21.28.

Theorem 21.29 (Kohlberg) *A necessary and sufficient condition for x^* to be the prenucleolus of a coalitional game $(N; v)$ is for $\mathcal{D}(\alpha, x)$ to be a balanced collection for every $\alpha \in \mathbb{R}$ for which this collection is nonempty.*

With regard to the nucleolus, Kohlberg's Theorem is more complicated. We present the theorem here without proof.

Theorem 21.30 *Denote by $\mathcal{D}_0 = \{\{i\} : i \in N\}$ the collection of all coalitions containing only one player. A necessary and sufficient condition for x^* to be the nucleolus of a coalitional game $(N; v)$ is that, for every α such that $\mathcal{D}(\alpha, x^*)$ is nonempty, the collection $\mathcal{D}(\alpha, x^*) \cup \mathcal{D}_0$ is a weakly balanced collection of coalitions[2] with positive coefficients for the coalitions in $\mathcal{D}(\alpha, x^*)$.*

The nucleolus and the prenucleolus coincide in a large class of games that includes most games studied in applications.

Definition 21.31 *A coalitional game $(N; v)$ is 0-monotonic if its 0-normalization is a monotonic game, or equivalently (Exercise 17.28, page 733), if*

$$v(S \cup \{i\}) \geq v(S) + v(i), \quad \forall S \subset N, \forall i \notin S. \tag{21.117}$$

Every superadditive game (Definition 17.8, page 721), as well as every convex game (Definition 18.51, page 765), is a 0-monotonic game.

Theorem 21.32 *In 0-monotonic games, the nucleolus and the prenucleolus coincide.*

To prove this last theorem, we need the following theorem.

---

2 Recall that a collection $\mathcal{D}$ of coalitions is weakly balanced if there are nonnegative numbers $(\alpha_S)_{S \in \mathcal{D}}$ such that $\sum_{S \in \mathcal{D}} \alpha_S \chi^S = \chi^N$.

Theorem 21.33 *Let $i \in N$ be a player, and let $\mathcal{D}$ be a balanced collection of coalitions such that player i is a member of every coalition in $\mathcal{D}$. Then $\mathcal{D}$ contains only one coalition, namely, $\mathcal{D} = \{N\}$.*

Proof: Let $(\delta_D)_{D \in \mathcal{D}}$ be a vector of balancing weights of $\mathcal{D}$. Then $\sum_{\{S \in \mathcal{D}:\, j \in S\}} \delta_D = 1$ for each player $j \in N$. Since player i is a member of every coalition in $\mathcal{D}$, by setting $j = i$ we deduce that $\sum_{S \in \mathcal{D}} \delta_D = 1$. Let j be any player in N. Since all the weights $(\delta_D)_{D \in \mathcal{D}}$ are positive,

$$1 = \sum_{\{S \in \mathcal{D}:\, j \in D\}} \delta_D \leq \sum_{S \in \mathcal{D}} \delta_D = 1. \tag{21.118}$$

It follows that $\sum_{\{S \in \mathcal{D}:\, j \in D\}} \delta_D = \sum_{S \in \mathcal{D}} \delta_D$, and since all the weights are positive, $\{S \in \mathcal{D}: j \in D\} = \mathcal{D}$; that is, every player j is a member of every coalition in $\mathcal{D}$. Since every coalition in the collection may appear only once, $\mathcal{D} = \{N\}$, as claimed. $\qquad\square$

Proof of Theorem 21.32: Let $(N; v)$ be a 0-monotonic game, and let x^* be its prenucleolus. We will show that the prenucleolus is individually rational: $x_i^* \geq v(i)$ for every $i \in N$, and it therefore coincides with the nucleolus (Theorem 21.15, page 857).

Suppose by contradiction that there exists a player i for whom $x_i^* < v(i)$. Then for every $S \subseteq N \setminus \{i\}$,

$$e\left(S \cup \{i\}, x^*\right) = v\left(S \cup \{i\}\right) - x^*\left(S \cup \{i\}\right) \tag{21.119}$$

$$= v\left(S \cup \{i\}\right) - x^*(S) - x_i^* \tag{21.120}$$

$$\geq v(S) + v(i) - x^*(S) - x_i^* \tag{21.121}$$

$$= e(S, x^*) + \left(v(i) - x_i^*\right) \tag{21.122}$$

$$> e(S, x^*). \tag{21.123}$$

Equation (21.121) holds because the game is 0-monotonic, and Equation (21.123) holds because by assumption $x_i^* < v(i)$. Thus, player i is a member of every coalition with maximal excess. Let $\mathcal{D}$ be the set of all such coalitions. By Kohlberg's Theorem (Theorem 21.29), this is a balanced collection, and player i is a member of every coalition in it. By Theorem 21.33, $\mathcal{D} = \{N\}$. However, since x^* is the prenucleolus, it satisfies $v(N) = x^*(N)$, and therefore $e(N, x^*) = 0$. Since $\mathcal{D}$ contains the coalitions with maximal excess, the excesses of all the other coalitions must be strictly less than 0. In particular,

$$0 > e(\{i\}, x^*) = v(i) - x_i^*, \tag{21.124}$$

which contradicts the assumption that $x_i^* < v(i)$. This contradiction proves that $x_i^* \geq v(i)$ for every player i, which is what we wanted to show. $\qquad\square$

21.6 The consistency of the nucleolus

In Chapter 19, we showed that the Shapley value satisfies the property of consistency with respect to the Hart–Mas-Colell reduced game. In this section, we prove that the prenucleolus satisfies the property of consistency, with respect to the other notion of reduced game, the Davis–Maschler reduced game, which we discussed in Chapter 18. We begin by recalling the definition of a Davis–Maschler reduced game, and the definition of consistency.

Definition 21.34 *Let $(N; v)$ be a coalitional game, let S be a nonempty coalition, and let $x \in \mathbb{R}^N$ be a preimputation. The* Davis–Maschler reduced game *to coalition S at x, denoted by $(S; w_S^x)$, is the coalitional game with the set of players S, and a coalitional function w_S^x defined by*

$$
w_S^x(R) = \begin{cases} \max_{Q \subseteq S^c} (v(R \cup Q) - x(Q)) & \emptyset \neq R \subset S, \\ x(S) & R = S, \\ 0 & R = \emptyset. \end{cases} \tag{21.125}
$$

Definition 21.35 *A solution concept φ satisfies the* Davis–Maschler reduced game property *if for every game coalitional $(N; v)$, for every nonempty coalition $S \subseteq N$, and for every vector $x \in \varphi(N; v)$,*

$$
(x_i)_{i \in S} \in \varphi\left(S; w_S^x\right). \tag{21.126}
$$

Theorem 21.36 *The prenucleolus satisfies the Davis–Maschler reduced game property.*

Proof: Let $(N; v)$ be a coalitional game, let x^* be the prenucleolus of the game $(N; v)$, and let S be a nonempty coalition. Denote the restriction of x^* to the coalition S by

$$
x_S^* := (x_i^*)_{i \in S}. \tag{21.127}
$$

These are the coordinates of the members of S in the prenucleolus. For each coalition $R \subseteq S$, denote by $e(R, x^*; v)$ the excess of coalition R at x^* in the game $(N; v)$, and by $e(R, x_S^*; w_S^{x^*})$ the excess of this coalition at x_S^* in the reduced game $(S; w_S^{x^*})$.

To check that x_S^* is the prenucleolus of the reduced game $(S; w_S^{x^*})$, we must first ascertain that x_S^* is a preimputation of this game. By the definition of the reduced game $w_S^{x^*}(S) = x^*(S)$, and therefore $x_S^* \in X^0(S; w_S^{x^*})$.

For every $\alpha \in \mathbb{R}$, define

$$
\mathcal{D}_w^S(\alpha, x_S^*) := \left\{ R \subset S \colon R \neq \emptyset, \ e\left(R, x_S^*; w_S^{x^*}\right) \geq \alpha \right\}. \tag{21.128}
$$

The collection of coalitions $\mathcal{D}_w^S$ is the analogue, in the reduced game, to the collection of coalitions whose excess at x^* in the original game is greater than or equal to α, which is

$$
\mathcal{D}_v(\alpha, x^*) = \{ R \subset N \colon R \neq \emptyset, \ e(R, x^*; v) \geq \alpha \}. \tag{21.129}
$$

We now compare $\mathcal{D}_w^S(\alpha, x_S^*)$ and $\mathcal{D}_v(\alpha, x_S^*)$. For every coalition R in $\mathcal{D}_w^S(\alpha, x_S^*)$, $R \notin \{\emptyset, S\}$,

$$
e\left(R, x_S^*; w_S^{x^*}\right) = w_S^{x^*}(R) - x^*(R) \tag{21.130}
$$

$$
= \max_{Q \subseteq S^c} (v(R \cup Q) - x^*(Q)) - x^*(R) \tag{21.131}
$$

$$
= e(R \cup Q_R, x^*; v). \tag{21.132}
$$

Here, $Q_R \subseteq S^c$ is the coalition at which the maximum of Equation (21.131) is attained. Therefore, if $\mathcal{D}_w^S(\alpha, x_S^*)$ is nonempty, then $\mathcal{D}_v(\alpha, x^*)$ is also nonempty, because if $R \in \mathcal{D}_w^S(\alpha, x_S^*)$, then $R \cup Q_R \in \mathcal{D}_v(\alpha, x^*)$.

In the other direction, suppose that $T \in \mathcal{D}_v(\alpha, x^*)$. Denote $R = T \cap S$. Then $T = R \cup (T \setminus S)$. If R is neither the empty set nor the set S, then

$$e\left(R, x_S^*; w_S^{x^*}\right) = w_S^{x^*}(R) - x^*(R) \tag{21.133}$$

$$= \max_{Q \subseteq S^c} \left(v(R \cup Q) - x^*(Q)\right) - x^*(R) \tag{21.134}$$

$$\geq v(R \cup (T \setminus S)) - x^*(T \setminus S) - x^*(R) \tag{21.135}$$

$$= e(R \cup (T \setminus S), x^*; v) \tag{21.136}$$

$$= e(T, x^*; v) \geq \alpha, \tag{21.137}$$

where Equation (21.135) holds because $Q = T \setminus S$ is one of the coalitions in the maximization in Equation (21.134). In particular, $R \in \mathcal{D}_w^S(\alpha, x_S^*)$. Summarizing what we have proved so far: for every $\alpha \in \mathbb{R}$,

- if $R \in \mathcal{D}_w^S(\alpha, x_S^*)$, there exists a coalition T containing R satisfying $T \in \mathcal{D}_v(\alpha, x^*)$ and $T \cap S = R$;
- if $T \in \mathcal{D}_v(\alpha, x^*)$, and if $\emptyset \neq T \cap S \subset S$, then $T \cap S \in \mathcal{D}_w^S(\alpha, x_S^*)$ (and if $T \cap S$ is empty or equal to S, then $e(T \cap S, x_S^*; w_S^{x^*}) = 0$).

By the above, the collection $\mathcal{D}_w^S(\alpha, x_S^*)$ is derivable from the collection $\mathcal{D}_v(\alpha, x^*)$ by removing players who are not members of S from every coalition. This act of removing players may leave only the coalition S, or the empty coalition, and in those cases these coalitions must be removed, because by definition $\mathcal{D}_w^S(\alpha, x_S^*)$ does not contain these coalitions. It may happen, of course, that a coalition R emerges several times during this process. In that case, only one copy of that coalition is included in $\mathcal{D}_w^S(\alpha, x_S^*)$.

By Kohlberg's Theorem (Theorem 21.29), since x^* is the prenucleolus, $\mathcal{D}_v(\alpha, x^*)$ is a balanced collection for every $\alpha \in \mathbb{R}$ for which the collection $\mathcal{D}_v(\alpha, x^*)$ is not empty. Removing players who are not in S from the balanced collection $\mathcal{D}_v(\alpha, x^*)$ leaves either an empty collection or a nonempty collection that is also balanced (as follows from Definition 21.24). It follows that $\mathcal{D}_w^S(\alpha, x_S^*)$ is a balanced collection, for every $\alpha \in \mathbb{R}$, if it is not empty, and then Kohlberg's Theorem implies that x_S^* is the prenucleolus of the reduced game. $\qquad\square$

The consistency of the nucleolus is a more complex issue than the consistency of the prenucleolus. First of all, in a game reduced to a coalition S with respect to the nucleolus, the set of imputations may be empty, in which case the nucleolus is also empty.

Example 21.37 Consider the three-player simple majority game $(N; v)$; i.e., $N = \{1, 2, 3\}$ and the coalitional function is

$$v(S) = \begin{cases} 1 & |S| \geq 2, \\ 0 & |S| \leq 1. \end{cases} \tag{21.138}$$

Since every pair of players is symmetric, the nucleolus is $x^* = (\frac{1}{3}, \frac{1}{3}, \frac{1}{3})$. The Davis–Maschler reduced game to the coalition $S = \{1, 2\}$ at the nucleolus x^* is the game $(S; w_S^{x^*})$ where

$$w_S^{x^*}(1) = w_S^{x^*}(2) = w_S^{x^*}(1, 2) = \tfrac{2}{3} \qquad (21.139)$$

(check that this is true). Since $w_S^{x^*}(1) + w_S^{x^*}(2) > w_S^{x^*}(1, 2)$, the set of imputations $X(S; w_S^{x^*})$ is empty, and the nucleolus of the game $(S; w_S^{x^*})$ is therefore empty.   ◀

Example 21.27 shows that the nucleolus does not satisfy the Davis–Maschler reduced game property over the family of all games. For the reduced game property to be meaningful in this context, we need to restrict our attention to coalitional games $(N; v)$ that satisfy $X(S; w_S^{x^*}) \neq \emptyset$ for every nonempty coalition S, where x^* is the nucleolus of the game.

By Theorem 21.32, in 0-monotonic games the prenucleolus and the nucleolus coincide. The following theorem states that the nucleolus satisfies the Davis–Maschler reduced game property over the family of 0-monotonic games that satisfy the condition that for every nonempty coalition S, the game $(S; w_S^{x^*})$ is also 0-monotonic.

Theorem 21.38 *Let $(N; v)$ be a 0-monotonic game, with nucleolus x^*. If for each coalition $S \subseteq N$ the Davis–Maschler reduced game $(S; w_S^{x^*})$ is 0-monotonic, then x_S^* is the nucleolus of the game $(S; w_S^{x^*})$.*

Proof: By Theorem 21.32, x^* is the prenucleolus of the game $(N; v)$. By Theorem 21.36, x_S^* is the prenucleolus of the reduced game $(S; w_S^{x^*})$. Since this game is 0-monotonic, by Theorem 21.32 x_S^* is also the nucleolus of the reduced game.   □

21.7 Weighted majority games

In this section we study the nucleolus in a large class of simple games, the class of weighted majority games, which are pervasive in the study of elections and committee decision-making. We start by recalling the definition of a simple game.

Definition 21.39 *A coalitional game $(N; v)$ is a* simple game *if the worth of every coalition is 0 or 1; i.e., $v(S) \in \{0, 1\}$ for every coalition $S \subseteq N$.*

Definition 21.40 *In a simple game $(N; v)$:*

- *A coalition S is a* winning *coalition if $v(S) = 1$.*
- *A coalition S is a* losing *coalition if $v(S) = 0$.*
- *A coalition S is a* minimal winning *coalition if it is a winning coalition, and every one of its proper subcoalitions is a losing coalition.*

A simple game is *monotonic* if $v(S) = 1$ and $T \supseteq S$ implies that $v(T) = 1$. When a game is simple and monotonic, it is determined by the set of its minimal winning coalitions, which we denote by $\mathcal{W}^m$.

Definition 21.41 *A coalitional game $(N; v)$ is a* constant-sum game *if it satisfies*

$$v(S) + v(S^c) = v(N), \quad \forall S \subseteq N. \qquad (21.140)$$

In this section, we concentrate on a subclass of the class of simple games: the class of simple strong games.

Definition 21.42 *A simple game* $(N; v)$ *is* strong *if it is monotonic, constant sum, and satisfies* $v(N) = 1$.

By Equation (21.140), in a simple strong game the complement of a winning coalition is a losing coalition, and vice versa.

The class of weighted majority games is a proper subclass of the class of simple games.

Definition 21.43 *A simple game* $(N; v)$ *is a* weighted majority game *if there exist nonnegative numbers* $q, w_1, w_2, \ldots, w_n$ *such that*

$$v(S) = 1 \quad \Longleftrightarrow \quad w(S) \geq q, \tag{21.141}$$

$$v(S) = 0 \quad \Longleftrightarrow \quad w(S) < q, \tag{21.142}$$

where $w(S) = \sum_{i \in S} w_i$. *The quantity* q *is the* quota, *and* w_i *is the* weight *of player* i, *for every* $i \in N$. *We denote the weighted majority game by* $[q; w]$, *where* $w = (w_1, w_2, \ldots, w_n)$, *and call* $[q; w]$ *a* representation *of the game* $(N; v)$.

By definition, a weighted majority game is simple and monotonic, but not every simple and monotonic game is a weighted majority game, even if it is constant sum (see the example of a projective game, Exercise 17.10 on page 730). As mentioned in Chapter 17, weighted majority games are generally the appropriate type of games to use for modeling elections or majority decision-making. The players in these models may be political parties, where the weight of each player is the fraction of the seats in the parliament occupied by that party. The quota is determined by the specific rules used for adopting a decision. For example, if a majority of $\frac{2}{3}$ is required to pass a decision, then q is $\frac{2}{3}$ of the members of parliament. If only a simple majority is required, then q is the smallest integer that is greater than half the number of members of parliament.

By multiplying the quota and all the weights by the same positive constant, we obtain another representation of the same game; such a multiplication does not affect the coalitional function v of the game. A weighted majority game therefore has many possible representations. The next example shows that a game may also have different representations that cannot be derived from each other by multiplication by a positive constant.

Example 21.44 Consider the following simple majority game $(N; v)$ in which $N = \{1, 2, 3\}$ and the coalitional function is given by

$$v(1) = v(2) = v(3) = 0, \quad v(1, 2) = v(1, 3) = v(2, 3) = v(1, 2, 3) = 1. \tag{21.143}$$

This game has many possible representations, such as, for example, $[3; 2, 2, 2]$, $[5; 4, 4, 1]$, and $[6; 3, 4, 5]$ (check that each of these is indeed a representation of the game). Which of these representations seems the most "natural"? Since the game is symmetric, one may regard the representation $[3; 2, 2, 2]$ as the most natural. This representation has the property that the total weight of the members of every minimal winning coalition is the same (in this case, this total weight is 4). ◀

This property of a natural representation can be generalized as follows.

Definition 21.45 *A representation* $[q; w_1, w_2, \ldots, w_n]$ *of a weighted majority game* $(N; v)$ *is a* homogeneous representation *if the sum* $\sum_{i \in S} w_i$ *is the same for every minimal winning coalition* $S \in \mathcal{W}^m$.

In Example 21.44, the representation $[3; 2, 2, 2]$ is homogeneous, while the representations $[5; 4, 4, 1]$ and $[6; 3, 4, 5]$ are not homogeneous. The representation $[4; 2, 2, 2]$ is yet another homogeneous representation of the same game.

Not every weighted majority game has a homogeneous representation. For example, the game $[5; 2, 2, 2, 1, 1, 1]$ is a game without a homogeneous representation (Exercise 21.41).

Definition 21.46 *A weighted majority game* $(N; v)$ *is* homogeneous *if it has a homogeneous representation.*

The goal of this section is to prove that in every constant-sum weighted majority game, the nucleolus is a set of weights for a representation of the game, and in fact that representation is homogeneous if the game is homogeneous.

Definition 21.47 *A representation* $[q; w]$ *of a weighted majority game* $(N; v)$ *is* normalized *if* $\sum_{i=1}^{n} w_i = 1$.

If a game has a representation, it has a normalized representation. Normalizing the three representations of the game in Example 21.44 shows that a game may have several normalized representations. Note that if $[q; w]$ is a homogeneous representation of a game, then its normalization is also a homogeneous representation of the same game. It follows, in particular, that every homogeneous game has a normalized homogeneous representation. A homogeneous game can have several normalized representations. For example, for every $q \in (\frac{1}{3}, \frac{2}{3}]$, $[q; \frac{1}{3}, \frac{1}{3}, \frac{1}{3}]$ is a normalized representation of the coalitional game in Example 21.44. As the following example shows, a game may have different normalized homogeneous representations that differ from each other by their weights.

Example 21.48 **Dictator game** Let $(N; v)$ be a simple strong game, and suppose that there is a player i such that $v(i) = 1$. Since the game is both monotonic and constant sum,

$$v(S) = 1 \quad \Longleftrightarrow \quad i \in S. \tag{21.144}$$

The only minimal winning coalition of the game is $\{i\}$: $\mathcal{W}^m = \{\{i\}\}$.

The game has several normalized homogeneous representations: for every $q \in (\frac{1}{2}, 1]$, every representation $[q; w]$ satisfying (a) $w_i = q$ and (b) $\sum_{j \in N} w_j = 1$ is a normalized homogeneous representation of the game. In such a game, all the players in the set $N \setminus \{i\}$ are null players. The only normalized vector of weights in which the weight of each null player is zero is

$$w_j = \begin{cases} 1 & \text{if } j = i, \\ 0 & \text{if } j \neq i. \end{cases} \tag{21.145}$$

Therefore, all the normalized homogeneous representations of the game have the form $[q; w]$, where $q \in (0, 1]$. The vector of weights w is both the Shapley value and the nucleolus of the game, since under both solution concepts null players receive 0. This is also the only vector in the core. ◄

Let $[q; w_1, w_2, \ldots, w_n]$ be a constant-sum weighted majority game. If we increase the quota to $\min_{S \in \mathcal{W}^m} w(S)$, we get another representation of the same game, different from the original one when $q \neq \min_{S \in \mathcal{W}^m} w(S)$ (Exercise 21.43). This is the maximal quota that does not change the set of winning coalitions. This motivates the following definition:

Definition 21.49 *Let $(N; v)$ be a simple game, and let $w \in \mathbb{R}^N$ be a vector. Define*

$$q(w) := \min_{S \in \mathcal{W}^m} w(S). \tag{21.146}$$

Note that $q(w)$ depends on the coalitional function v, since v determines the set of minimal winning coalitions. Since the quota $q(w)$ is determined by the weights, when we say that w is a representation of the game, we will mean that $[q(w); w]$ is a representation. When $[q(w); w]$ is a homogeneous representation, then $w(S) = q(w)$ for every minimal winning coalition S.

Given a simple strong game $(N; v)$, every imputation $x \in X(N; v)$ defines a weighted majority game $[q(x); x]$. As a weighted majority game, this game is simple and monotonic but not necessarily a constant-sum game (Exercises 21.44 and 21.45). In particular, the weighted majority game $[q(x); x]$ is not necessarily a representation of the game $(N; v)$ with which we started. We would like to know for which imputations the weighted majority game $[q(x); x]$ is a representation of the original game $(N; v)$.

Theorem 21.50 *Let $(N; v)$ be a simple strong game, and let $x \in X(N; v)$. Then $[q(x); x]$ is a representation of $(N; v)$ if and only if $q(x) > \frac{1}{2}$.*

Proof: Since $x \in X(N; v)$, it follows in particular that $x(N) = \sum_{i \in N} x_i = v(N) = 1$. Suppose first that $[q(x); x]$ is a representation of $(N; v)$. In other words, a coalition is a winning coalition if and only if the total weight of its members is greater than or equal to $q(x)$. We will show that $q(x) > \frac{1}{2}$. Let S_* be a minimal winning coalition in which $q(x)$ is attained, i.e., $x(S_*) = q(x)$. Since S_* is a winning coalition, and since a simple strong game is a constant-sum game, the complementary coalition S_*^c is a losing coalition and hence $x(S_*^c) < q(x)$. One deduces from this that

$$q(x) > x(S_*^c) = 1 - x(S_*) = 1 - q(x), \tag{21.147}$$

and therefore $q(x) > \frac{1}{2}$, as we wanted to show.

Suppose next that $q(x) > \frac{1}{2}$. We will show that $[q(x); x]$ is a representation of $(N; v)$. For this, we need to show that $v(S) = 1$ if and only if $x(S) \geq q(x)$. If S is a winning coalition, then it must contain a minimal winning coalition, and hence $x(S) \geq q(x)$. On the other hand, if S is a losing coalition, since the game is constant sum, S^c is a winning coalition, hence $x(S^c) \geq q(x)$, and then

$$x(S) = x(N) - x(S^c) = 1 - x(S^c) \leq 1 - q(x) < \frac{1}{2} < q(x). \tag{21.148}$$

We proved that if S is a losing coalition, then $x(S) < q(x)$, and therefore if $x(S) \geq q(x)$ then $v(S) = 1$, as required. $\qquad \square$

Theorem 21.51 *Let $(N; v)$ be a simple strong game and let $x^* = \mathcal{N}(N; v)$ be the nucleolus of the game. Then $q(x^*) \geq q(x)$ for all $x \in X(N; v)$.*

Proof: Let $x \in X(N; v)$. Since x^* is the nucleolus, $\theta_1(x^*) \leq \theta_1(x)$, i.e.,

$$\max_{S \subseteq N} e(S, x^*) \leq \max_{S \subseteq N} e(S, x). \tag{21.149}$$

Now,

$$\max_{S \subseteq N} e(S, x) = \max \left\{ \max_{\{S: \, v(S)=1\}} e(S, x), \, \max_{\{S: \, v(S)=0\}} e(S, x) \right\} \tag{21.150}$$

$$= \max_{\{S: \, v(S)=1\}} e(S, x) \tag{21.151}$$

$$= \max_{\{S: \, v(S)=1\}} (1 - x(S)) \tag{21.152}$$

$$= \max_{S \in \mathcal{W}^m} (1 - x(S)) \tag{21.153}$$

$$= 1 - \min_{S \in \mathcal{W}^m} x(S) \tag{21.154}$$

$$= 1 - q(x). \tag{21.155}$$

Equation 21.151 holds because $\max_{\{S: \, v(S)=1\}} (v(S) - x(S)) \geq 0$ (since N is a winning coalition with excess 0), and on the other hand $\max_{\{S: \, v(S)=0\}} e(S, x) \leq 0$ (since for a losing coalition $v(S) = 0$ and $x(S) \geq 0$, because $x \in X(N; v)$). Equation (21.153) holds because $x_i \geq 0$ for all players (since $x \in X(N; v)$), and therefore maximizing $1 - x(S)$ over all winning coalitions is equivalent to maximizing this quantity over all minimal winning coalitions. By setting $x = x^*$ in Equations (21.150)–(21.155) we get $\max_{S \subseteq N} e(S, x^*) = 1 - q(x^*)$. By Equation (21.149) we obtain

$$q(x^*) = 1 - \max_{S \subseteq N} e(S, x^*) \geq 1 - \max_{S \subseteq N} e(S, x) = q(x), \tag{21.156}$$

as claimed. □

The next theorem states that the nucleolus is a normalized representation of strong weighted majority games.

Theorem 21.52 *Let $(N; v)$ be a strong weighted majority game, and let x^* be its nucleolus. Then $[q(x^*); x^*]$ is a normalized representation of the game $(N; v)$.*

Proof: Let $[q; w]$ be a normalized representation of $(N; v)$. Then $q(w) > \frac{1}{2}$ by Theorem 21.50, and $q(x^*) \geq q(w)$ by Theorem 21.51; hence $q(x^*) > \frac{1}{2}$. Since $x^*(N) = v(N) = 1$, we may again use Theorem 21.50, to conclude that $[q(x^*); x^*]$ is a normalized representation of the game. □

Theorem 21.53 *Let $(N; v)$ be a homogeneous weighted majority game satisfying $v(N) = 1$. Then it has a homogeneous representation in which the weight of each null player is 0.*

Proof: Let $[q; w]$ be a homogeneous representation of the game. Then $q(w) = w(S)$ for every minimal winning coalition S. Let D be the set of null players. Define a quota $\hat{q}$ and a vector of weights $\hat{w}$ in which the weight of null players is 0 as follows:

$$\widehat{q} := q(w), \tag{21.157}$$

$$\widehat{w}_i := \begin{cases} w_i & i \notin D, \\ 0 & i \in D. \end{cases} \tag{21.158}$$

We will ascertain that $[\widehat{q}; \widehat{w}]$ is a homogeneous representation of the game. To this end, we will check that $\widehat{w}(S) = \widehat{q}$ for every minimal winning coalition S. Indeed, since a minimal winning coalition cannot contain a null player, it follows that for every minimal winning coalition S:

$$\widehat{w}(S) = \sum_{i \in S} w_i = q(w) = \widehat{q}. \tag{21.159}$$

□

Theorem 21.54 *Let $(N; v)$ be a homogeneous and constant-sum weighted majority game satisfying $v(N) = 1$. Then the nucleolus is the only homogeneous normalized representation in which the weight of every null player is 0.*

Proof: If there is a player i such that $v(i) = 1$, then i is a dictator (explain why). As we saw in Example 21.48, the nucleolus in that case is the only normalized representation in which the weight of every null player is 0. We will therefore consider the case in which $v(i) = 0$ for every player i.

Since $v(i) = 0$ for each player i, and since $v(N) = 1$, the set of imputations $X(N; v)$ is nonempty, and hence, by Corollary 21.14, the nucleolus is a nonempty set that contains a single vector x^*.

Denote by D the set of all the null players in the game. Since the game is homogeneous, it has a homogeneous representation. By Theorem 21.53, the game has a homogeneous representation in which the weight of every null player is 0. Denote that representation by $[q(y); y]$. Then $y(S) = q(y)$ for every minimal winning coalition $S \in \mathcal{W}^m$. Define a polytope P as follows:[3]

$$P := \{x \in \mathbb{R}^n : x_i \geq v(i), \ \forall i \in N, x(N) = v(N),$$
$$x(S) \geq q(y) \ \forall S \in \mathcal{W}^m, \ x_i = 0 \ \forall i \in D\}. \tag{21.160}$$

The first two conditions in the definition of P guarantee that P is contained in $X(N; v)$. Since the game is a weighted majority game, if $x \in P$ then $x(S) \geq q(y)$ for every winning coalition $S \subseteq N$. Since y is a homogeneous representation in which the weight of every null player is 0, $y \in P$, and in particular $y \in X(N; v)$.

We next show that the nucleolus, x^*, is also in P. Since $x^* \in X(N; v)$, the vector x^* satisfies the first two conditions in the definition of P. By Theorem 21.52, the nucleolus is a representation of the game. By Theorem 21.51 one has $x^*(S) \geq q(x^*) \geq q(y)$ for every $S \in \mathcal{W}^m$. Finally, since the nucleolus satisfies the null player property (Theorem 21.19, page 859), $x_i^* = 0$ for every player $i \in D$, thus proving that indeed $x^* \in P$.

---

3 Recall that a *polytope* in $\mathbb{R}^n$ is the convex hull of a finite number of points in $\mathbb{R}^n$.

We will now show that the set P contains only one vector, and that in particular $y = x^*$. This will imply that the nucleolus is the unique homogeneous representation in which the weight of every null player is 0. If the set P contains at least two imputations, then in particular it has at least two extreme points, and one of them, z, must be distinct from y. This then implies that some of the inequalities defining P that did not obtain as equalities for y obtain as equalities for z. Since for y, all inequalities of the form $x^*(S) \geq q(y)$ obtain as equalities, at least one of the inequalities $x_i \geq v(i)$ obtains as an equality for z and as a strict inequality for y. This necessarily occurs for $i \notin D$, since $y_i = 0 = v(i)$ for every $i \in D$.

Let j be a player who is not in D, and for whom $z_j = 0$. Since j is not a null player, there is a coalition S such that $v(S) = 0$ and $v(S \cup \{j\}) = 1$. Let S_0 be a minimal coalition (with respect to set inclusion) such that this property holds. Then $S_0 \cup \{j\} \in \mathcal{W}^m$ (verify this). Since the coalition S_0 is a losing coalition, and since the game is constant sum, the complementary coalition S_0^c, containing j, is a winning coalition. Hence

$$q(y) \leq z(S_0^c) = 1 - z(S_0) = 1 - z(S_0 \cup \{j\}) \leq 1 - q(y). \tag{21.161}$$

The first inequality holds because $z(T) \geq q(y)$ for every winning coalition T, and S_0^c is a winning coalition. The last inequality holds for the same reason, and because $S_0 \cup \{j\}$ is a winning coalition. The second equality holds because $z_j = 0$. Equation (21.161) implies that $q(y) \leq \frac{1}{2}$, contradicting Theorem 21.50. The contradiction proves that P contains a single imputation, as we wanted to show.   □

21.8 The bankruptcy problem

Many legislators have contended with the issue of the best way to divide the assets of a bankrupt entity among the creditors, given that the total sum of the debts owed by the bankrupt entity is greater than the available assets. To date, various bankruptcy rules apply in different societies. In the Babylonian Talmud,[4] in Chapter Ten of Tractate Kethubot, the following item appears, attributed to Rabbi Nathan:

If a man who was married to three wives died, and the *kethubah*[5] of one was a *maneh*,[6] of the other two hundred *zuz*, and of the third three hundred *zuz*, and the estate [was worth] only one *maneh*, [the sum] is divided equally. If the estate [was worth] two hundred *zuz* [the claimant] of the *maneh* receives fifty *zuz* [and the claimants respectively] of the two hundred and three hundred *zuz* [receive each] three gold *denarii*.[7] If the estate [was worth] three hundred *zuz*, [the claimant]

4 The Babylonian Talmud is a Jewish text that records rabbinic discussions on Jewish law, ethics, customs, and philosophy held between the second and fifth centuries AD. The quotations below are taken from The Babylonian Talmud, translated and edited by Rabbi Dr. Isidore Epstein, Soncino Press, London. Available at: http://www.halakhah.com.

5 The *kethubah* is the traditional Jewish wedding document, and it specifies promises the groom makes to the bride, including the amount of money to be given to her in the event of the annulment of the marriage, either by the death of the husband or divorce.

6 The basic monetary unit in this passage is *zuz*, which was an ancient Near Eastern silver coin. One *maneh* is equivalent to 100 *zuz*.

7 The *denarium* (plural *denarii*) was an ancient Roman coin. One gold *denarium* was equivalent to 25 *zuz*. Therefore, 3 gold *denarii* were equivalent to 75 *zuz*, and 6 gold *denarii* were equivalent to 150 *zuz*.

of the *maneh* receives fifty *zuz* and [the claimant] of the two hundred *zuz* [receives] a *maneh*, while [the claimant] of the three hundred *zuz* [receives] six gold *denarii*.

The Talmud's prescription of division of the estate (in units of *zuz*) is summarized in the following table. To simplify the analysis, we will call the first wife Anne, the second wife Betty, and the third wife Carol.

		Anne	Betty	Carol
	Debt:	100	200	300
The Estate	100	$33\frac{1}{3}$	$33\frac{1}{3}$	$33\frac{1}{3}$
	200	50	75	75
	300	50	100	150

The idea behind this seemingly strange division of the estate appears to be unclear. When the size of the estate is small, the creditors divide the assets equally among them; when the size of the estate is large, the creditors divide the assets proportionally to their claims; and when the size of the estate is intermediate, the division seems inexplicable.

In this section, we relate the above Talmudic bankruptcy division recommendation to the nucleolus of an appropriate game in coalitional form. We begin by considering yet another passage from the Babylonian Talmud, appearing in Tractate Baba Metzia, Chapter 1, Mishnah 1:

Two [persons appearing before a court] hold a garment. One of them says, "I found it," and the other says "I found it"; one of them says "it is all mine" and the other says, "it is all mine." Then the one shall swear that his share in it is not less than half, and the other shall swear that his share in it is not less than half, and [the value of the garment] shall then be divided between them. If one says "it is all mine" and the other says "half of it is mine," he who says "it is all mine" shall swear that his share in it is not less than three quarters, and he who says "half of it is mine" shall swear that his share in it is not less than a quarter. The former then receives three quarters.

In other words, the Talmud here is recommending that if two parties each claim one hundred percent ownership of an asset, the asset should be divided among them equally. If one party claims one hundred percent ownership of an asset, and the other party claims only fifty percent ownership, then the division should be $\frac{3}{4} : \frac{1}{4}$.

The logic behind this Talmudic passage is clear. If both parties have an equal claim to the asset, by symmetry they should divide it equally. If, in contrast, one party claims all the asset, and the second party claims only half of the asset, then in effect both parties agree that at least one half of the asset belongs to the first party, and therefore there can be no dispute that the first party should get at least half of the asset. With respect to the second half of the asset, the claimants are symmetric, and therefore that half should be divided equally.

In the general case, if a person claims that his share in an asset is p, while another person claims that his share of the same asset is q (where $0 \leq p \leq 1$, $0 \leq q \leq 1$, and $p + q > 1$), the first person receives, by this reasoning, $(1 - q) + \frac{p+q-1}{2}$ of the asset, and the second person[8] receives $(1 - p) + \frac{p+q-1}{2}$. This solution for two-creditor bankruptcy problems is called the "contested garment" solution.

21.8.1 The model

Definition 21.55 *A bankruptcy problem is given by:*

1. *a set of players $N = \{1, 2, \ldots, n\}$,*
2. *for each player $i \in N$, a nonnegative real number $d_i \in \mathbb{R}_+$,*
3. *and a nonnegative real number $E \in \mathbb{R}_+$ such that $E < \sum_{i \in N} d_i$.*

We interpret N to be a set of creditors, E to be the total worth of the assets of a bankrupt entity, and d_i to be the amount of money that the bankrupt entity owes creditor i. Under this interpretation, the condition $E < \sum_{i \in N} d_i$ states that the debtor lacks sufficient capital to repay his debts. If this inequality does not hold, then the debtor can pay all that he owes, and he cannot justifiably be declared bankrupt. A bankruptcy problem will be denoted by $[E; d_1, \ldots, d_n]$, or by $[E; d]$ for short, where $d = (d_1, d_2, \ldots, d_n)$.

Definition 21.56 *An allocation for a bankruptcy problem $[E; d_1, \ldots, d_n]$ is a vector $x \in \mathbb{R}_+^N$ satisfying $x(N) = E$.*

An allocation is thus a suggested way of dividing the assets of the bankrupt entity among the creditors.

Definition 21.57 *A solution concept for bankruptcy problems is a function φ associating every bankruptcy problem $[E; d_1, \ldots, d_n]$ with an allocation.*

21.8.2 The case $n = 2$

The Babylonian Talmud, in its passage on the "contested garment," suggests a solution for every two-creditor bankruptcy problem $[E; d_1, d_2]$. Suppose, without loss of generality, that $d_2 \geq d_1$.

If $d_1 \geq E$, then each creditor is in effect claiming that the entire asset belongs to him, and the asset should therefore be divided equally between them. This yields the allocation

$$\left(\frac{E}{2}, \frac{E}{2} \right).$$
(21.162)

If $d_1 \leq E \leq d_2$, then the first creditor agrees that $E - d_1$ of the estate belongs to the second creditor, with both creditors claiming ownership over the remainder. This yields the allocation

$$\left(\frac{d_1}{2}, E - \frac{d_1}{2} \right).$$
(21.163)

---

8 There is another passage in the Babylonian Talmud (Tractate Yevamoth, page 38) in which this reasoning is applied. There, one party claims 50% of an asset, and a second party claims $66\frac{2}{3}\%$ of the same asset. The Talmud then instructs the first party to yield 50% of the asset to the second party, and instructs the second party to yield $33\frac{1}{3}\%$ of the asset to the first party, with the two parties then dividing the remainder equally between them.

Finally, we analyze the case where $d_1 \leq d_2 \leq E$ (and $d_1 + d_2 > E$). In this case, the first creditor agrees that $E - d_1$ belongs to the second creditor, and the second creditor agrees that $E - d_2$ belongs to the first creditor. That leaves the remainder under dispute, i.e.,

$$E - (E - d_1) - (E - d_2) = d_1 + d_2 - E, \tag{21.164}$$

which is then divided equally between the creditors. The resulting allocation is thus

$$\left(\frac{E + d_1 - d_2}{2}, \frac{E + d_2 - d_1}{2} \right). \tag{21.165}$$

This discussion can be summarized as follows. Define a function f associating a vector in $\mathbb{R}^2$ to every two-creditor bankruptcy problem $[E; d_1, d_2]$ as follows:

$$f(E; d_1, d_2) = \begin{cases} \left(\frac{E}{2}, \frac{E}{2} \right) & \text{if } E \leq d_2, d_1, \\ \left(\frac{d_1}{2}, E - \frac{d_1}{2} \right) & \text{if } d_1 \leq E \leq d_2, \\ \left(E - \frac{d_2}{2}, \frac{d_2}{2} \right) & \text{if } d_2 \leq E \leq d_1, \\ \left(\frac{E + d_1 - d_2}{2}, \frac{E + d_2 - d_1}{2} \right) & \text{if } d_2, d_1 \leq E. \end{cases} \tag{21.166}$$

The Babylonian Talmud, in Tractate Baba Metzia, states that if the debt owed to the two creditors is d_1 and d_2 respectively, and the assets of the bankrupt entity sum to E, then the first creditor receives $f_1(E; d_1, d_2)$, and the second creditor receives $f_2(E; d_1, d_2)$. Note that $f_1(E; d_1, d_2) + f_2(E; d_1, d_2) = E$ for every d_1 and d_2. The function f is continuous in E, d_1, d_2. Moreover, for fixed d_1 and d_2 the functions $E \mapsto f_1(E; d_1, d_2)$ and $E \mapsto f_2(E; d_1, d_2)$ are monotonic and nondecreasing (see the example in Figure 21.3).

Figure 21.4 depicts an implementation of the function f using "communicating vessels" composed of containers and pipes. The claims of the creditors (i.e., the debts owned by the bankrupt entity) are depicted by containers of unit base area, where the claim of d_i is represented by two containers of height $\frac{d_i}{2}$, one "on the ground," and the other "hanging from the ceiling"; the two containers are connected by a dimensionless pipe, with the two containers touching the ground also connected by a dimensionless pipe.

To compute $f_1(E; d_1, d_2)$ and $f_2(E; d_1, d_2)$, we let a volume of liquid equal to E flow into the system. By the communicating vessels law, the height of the liquid on both sides of the system must be equal. The volume of liquid on the left side represents the payment

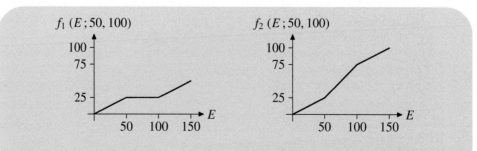

Figure 21.3 The functions $E \mapsto f_1(E; 50, 100)$ and $E \mapsto f_2(E; 50, 100)$

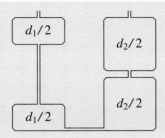

Figure 21.4 A physical manifestation of the "contested garment" solution

given to the first creditor, and the volume of liquid on the right side represents the payment given to the second creditor. When the volume of liquid flowing is at most d_1, the amount of liquid is divided equally between the two sides. After a volume of d_1 has entered the system, every additional volume of liquid flowing in, up to the amount $d_2 - d_1$, will be added only to the right side. After a volume of d_2 has entered the system, every additional volume of liquid flowing in will be divided equally between the two sides of the system.

21.8.3 The case $n > 2$

When there are more than two creditors, we will find a solution concept based on the "contested garment" solution, using the *principle of consistency*. This principle relates to the following situation. Suppose that n creditors, faced with a bankruptcy problem $[E; d_1, \ldots, d_n]$, divide the estate between them using the solution concept φ. Creditor i and creditor j can now unite their shares $\varphi_i(E; d_1, \ldots, d_n) + \varphi_j(E; d_1, \ldots, d_n)$, and divide this sum between them using the "contested garment" solution. A solution concept φ is consistent with the "contested garment" solution if for every two creditors i and j, after uniting their shares and applying the "contested garment" solution to the two-creditor problem that involves the two of them, they end up with the same shares allocated to them originally, namely, $\varphi_i(E; d_1, \ldots, d_n)$ and $\varphi_j(E; d_1, \ldots, d_n)$.

Consider the example of the three widows mentioned in the Babylonian Talmud's Tractate Kethubot. When the estate is 200, Anne, Betty, and Carol receive 50, 75, and 75 respectively. Together, Anne and Betty receive 125. If they divide this sum between them according to the "contested garment" solution (Equation (21.166)), then Anne gets

$$f_1(125; 100, 200) = 50, \qquad (21.167)$$

and Betty gets

$$f_2(125; 100, 200) = 75. \qquad (21.168)$$

These sums are identical to the sums that the women receive according to the Talmud. If Betty and Carol were to divide the 150 that they have together received according to the "contested garment" solution, Betty gets

$$f_1(150; 200, 300) = 75, \qquad (21.169)$$

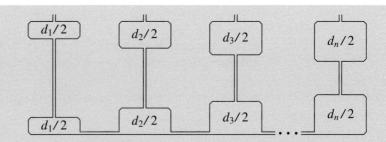

Figure 21.5 A physical implementation of the consistent solution

and Carol gets

$$f_2(150; 200, 300) = 75. \qquad (21.170)$$

A similar result is obtained if we change the value of the estate to 300 or decrease it to 100. We therefore see that the Talmud's recommended division of the estate of the man with three wives is consistent with the "contested garment" solution.

We are now ready to give a formal definition of the principle of consistency with the "contested garment" solution.

Definition 21.58 *A solution concept* φ *is consistent with the "contested garment" solution if for every bankruptcy problem* $[E; d_1, \ldots, d_n]$ *and every two creditors i and* $j, i \neq j$,

$$f_1(x; d_i, d_j) = \varphi_i(E; d_1, \ldots, d_n), \qquad (21.171)$$

where $x = \varphi_i(E; d_1, \ldots, d_n) + \varphi_j(E; d_1, \ldots, d_n)$.

Theorem 21.59 *There exists a unique solution concept that is consistent with the "contested garment" solution.*

The unique solution concept satisfying Theorem 21.59 is called the *Rabbi Nathan solution*.

Proof: Step 1: There exists at least one solution concept consistent with the "contested garment" solution.

Suppose, without loss of generality, that $d_1 \leq d_2 \leq \cdots \leq d_n$. We will construct a system of containers similar to the one constructed in Figure 21.4, with the containers ordered by increasing size from left to right (see Figure 21.5).

Pour liquid of volume E into this system of containers. Denote by x_i the amount of liquid in container i (in both its parts), $i \in \{1, 2, \ldots, n\}$. Then $x_1 + x_2 + \cdots + x_n = E$, and this system therefore defines a solution $(x_1, x_2, \ldots, x_n)$ to the bankruptcy problem, which we will call the "containers solution." If we restrict ourselves to two of the containers, i and j, the amount $x_i + x_j$ is divided between the two containers in accordance with the case $n = 2$, which is the physical implementation of the "contested garment" solution. The containers solution therefore defines a solution concept consistent with the "contested garment" solution, which is what we needed to show.

Step 2: There is at most one solution concept consistent with the "contested garment" solution.

Let φ be a solution concept to the bankruptcy problem consistent with the "contested garment" solution. We will show that φ coincides with the above-described containers solution. Let $[E; d_1, \ldots, d_n]$ be a bankruptcy problem, and consider the corresponding system of containers (see Figure 21.5). Disconnect all horizontal pipes between the containers and pour into container i a volume of liquid equal to $\varphi_i(E; d_1, \ldots, d_n)$. Since the solution concept φ is consistent with the "contested garment" solution, it follows that for every pair of containers, the liquid attains the same height. To see this, note that consistency with the "contested garment" solution implies that for every pair of containers i and j, if we construct a system containing only the containers i and j connected by a horizontal pipe (as in Figure 21.4), into which we pour liquid of volume $\varphi_i(E; d_1, \ldots, d_n) + \varphi_j(E; d_1, \ldots, d_n)$, the height of the liquid in both containers will be identical, the amount of liquid in container i being $\varphi_i(E; d_1, \ldots, d_n)$, and the amount of liquid in container j being $\varphi_j(E; d_1, \ldots, d_n)$.

It follows that the height of the liquid is the same in all n containers; hence if we open the horizontal pipes the height of the liquid in the containers will remain the same. After doing so, we arrive at the system depicted in Figure 21.5. In other words, $\varphi_i(E; d_1, \ldots, d_n)$ equals the amount creditor i receives in the containers solution, and therefore φ coincides with the containers solution. In particular, the containers solution is the unique solution concept that is consistent with the "contested garment" solution. $\square$

Using the physical system described above in the proof of the theorem, and considering money to be a continuous variable, we can describe the Rabbi Nathan solution to a bankruptcy problem $[E; d]$ as follows:

- Divide (in a continuous manner) the money equally only among the creditors who have not yet received half of their claims; a creditor who has already received half of his claim stops receiving any more money until all creditors receive half of their claims.
- Once each creditor has received half of his claim, we continue to give money (in a continuous manner) to the creditor with the maximal remaining claim, until there are two creditors left with maximal remaining claims.
- We continue to give money (in a continuous manner) to the two creditors with the maximal remaining claims, until there are three creditors left with maximal remaining claims, and so on.

Exercise 21.53 provides an explicit formula for the Rabbi Nathan solution.

21.8.4 The nucleolus of a bankruptcy problem

For every nonempty set of creditors S, denote by $d(S) := \sum_{i \in S} d_i$ the sum of their claims according to d, and set $d(\emptyset) := 0$. For every bankruptcy problem $[E; d_1, d_2, \ldots, d_n]$ define a game $(N; v)$ where the set of players is the set of creditors, and the coalitional function is defined as follows:

$$v(S) := \max \{E - d(S^c), 0\}, \quad \forall S \subseteq N. \tag{21.172}$$

The quantity $v(S)$ is the part of E that is not in dispute, i.e., the part of E that remains to the members of S if every member of $S^c = N \setminus S$ gets his whole claim. If $d(S^c) \geq E$, then nothing remains for the members of S that is under dispute, and then $v(S) = 0$. Note that $v(N) = E$ and $v(\emptyset) = 0$.

Example 21.60   **The case of two creditors**   Let $[E; d_1, d_2]$ be a bankruptcy problem with two creditors. The game corresponding to this problem is

$$
\begin{array}{llll}
v(1) = 0, & v(2) = 0, & v(1,2) = E & \text{if } E \leq d_1, d_2, \\
v(1) = E - d_2, & v(2) = 0, & v(1,2) = E & \text{if } d_2 < E \leq d_1, \\
v(1) = 0, & v(2) = E - d_1, & v(1,2) = E & \text{if } d_1 < E \leq d_2, \\
v(1) = E - d_2, & v(2) = E - d_1, & v(1,2) = E & \text{if } d_1, d_2 < E.
\end{array}
\tag{21.173}
$$

The nucleolus of this game (as given in Theorem 21.18, page 858) coincides with the "contested garment" solution, which we computed in Section 21.8.2 on page 881 (verify!).   ◀

The conclusion of Example 21.60 is summarized in the following theorem.

Theorem 21.61 *When* $n = 2$, *the "contested garment" solution coincides with the nucleolus of the coalitional game* $(N; v)$ *defined in Equation (21.172).*

The rest of this section is devoted to proving that when the number of creditors is greater than two, the nucleolus coincides with the Rabbi Nathan solution. The proof is conducted in several steps. We first prove that the game defined in Equation (21.172) is 0-monotonic (Theorem 21.62). Then we prove that for every imputation x in the game $(N; v)$, and for every nonempty coalition T, the game corresponding to the bankruptcy problem $[x(T); (d_i)_{i \in T}]$ in which the set of creditors is T and the estate is $x(T)$ is the Davis–Maschler reduced game of the game $(N; v)$ (Theorem 21.63). By Theorem 21.38 (page 873), it follows that the nucleolus is a consistent solution concept in the set of coalitional games corresponding to a bankruptcy problem. Since in two-player games the nucleolus and the Rabbi Nathan solution coincide, it follows that these two solution concepts coincide in every coalitional game corresponding to a bankruptcy problem.

Theorem 21.62 *For every bankruptcy game* $[E; d]$, *the coalitional game* $(N; v)$ *defined by Equation (21.172) is 0-monotonic.*

Proof: To prove that the game $(N; v)$ is 0-monotonic, we need to prove that for every coalition $S \subset N$ and every player $i \notin S$,

$$
v(S \cup \{i\}) \geq v(S) + v(i).
\tag{21.174}
$$

By the definition of the coalitional function v, the game $(N; v)$ is monotonic (verify!). If $v(i) = 0$ or $v(S) = 0$, then by the monotonicity of the game $(N; v)$ it follows that Equation (21.174) holds. Suppose therefore that $v(i) > 0$ and $v(S) > 0$. In particular,

$$
0 < v(i) = E - d(N \setminus \{i\}) < d_i,
\tag{21.175}
$$

where the right-hand side inequality follows from the assumption that $d(N) > E$, and

$$
0 < v(S) = E - d(N \setminus \{S\}).
\tag{21.176}
$$

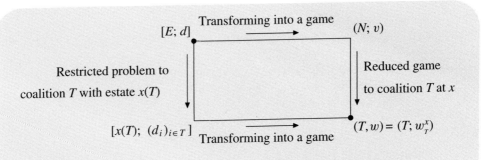

Figure 21.6 The commutative diagram according to Theorem 21.63

Therefore

$$v(S \cup \{i\}) \geq E - d((S \cup \{i\})^c) \tag{21.177}$$

$$= E - d(S^c) + d_i \tag{21.178}$$

$$> v(S) + v(i), \tag{21.179}$$

where Equation (21.177) holds[9] by the definition of v, and Equation (21.179) holds by Equations (21.175) and (21.176). □

Theorem 21.63 *Let* $(N;v)$ *be the coalitional game corresponding to a bankruptcy problem* $[E; (d_i)_{i \in N}]$. *Let* x *be a vector satisfying* $x(N) = E$ *and* $0 \leq x_i \leq d_i$ *for every* $i \in N$, *and let* $T \subseteq N$ *be a nonempty coalition. Let* $[x(T), (d_i)_{i \in T}]$ *be the bankruptcy problem restricted to* T *with estate* $x(T)$, *and let* $(T;w)$ *be the corresponding coalitional game. Then* $(T;w) = (T;w_T^x)$, *where* $(T;w_T^x)$ *is the Davis–Maschler reduced game of* $(N;v)$ *to coalition* T *at* x.

The theorem implies that the diagram in Figure 21.6 is commutative.

In words, the same game $(T;w)$ is derived under both of the following procedures: (a) converting the bankruptcy problem $[E; d]$ to a game, and then reducing it to the coalition T at x; (b) restricting the bankruptcy problem to the coalition T, with estate $\hat{E} = x(T)$, and then converting that bankruptcy problem to a game.

Proof of Theorem 21.63: We want to prove that $w_T^x = w$ holds for the coalition T, i.e., $w_T^x(R) = w(R)$ for every coalition $R \subseteq T$.

Step 1: $w_T^x(T) = w(T)$ *and* $w_T^x(\emptyset) = w(\emptyset)$.
For every $c \in \mathbb{R}$, denote $c_+ = \max\{c, 0\}$, and note that

$$a_+ - b_+ \leq (a - b)_+. \tag{21.180}$$

In this notation, $v(S) = \max\{E - d(S^c), 0\} = (E - d(S^c))_+$ for every coalition $S \subseteq N$, and $w(R) = (x(T) - d(T \setminus R))_+$, for every coalition $R \subseteq T$.

---

9 Actually, since $0 < v(S) \leq v(S \cup \{i\})$, Equation (21.177) holds with equality.

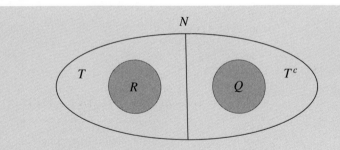

Figure 21.7 A depiction of the equality $N \setminus Q = R \cup (N \setminus (R \cup Q))$

Since $(T; w)$ is the game corresponding to a reduced bankruptcy problem,

$$w(T) = x(T), \quad w(\emptyset) = 0. \tag{21.181}$$

The equality $w(\emptyset) = 0$ holds because $x_i \leq d_i$ for every i, and therefore $w(\emptyset) = (x(T) - d(T))_+ = 0$. Since $(T; w_T^x)$ is a Davis–Maschler reduced game to T at x,

$$w_T^x(T) = x(T), \quad w_T^x(\emptyset) = 0. \tag{21.182}$$

From Equations (21.181) and (21.182) one obtains

$$w(T) = w_T^x(T), \quad w(\emptyset) = w_T^x(\emptyset), \tag{21.183}$$

which is what we wanted to show.

Step 2: $w_T^x(R) \leq w(R)$ for every coalition $R \subset T$.
Let Q be a coalition contained in T^c at which the maximum in the definition of $w_T^x(R)$ is attained,

$$w_T^x(R) = v(R \cup Q) - x(Q) = (E - d(N \setminus (R \cup Q)))_+ - x(Q). \tag{21.184}$$

Since $R \subset T$ and $Q \subseteq T^c$ one has that $N \setminus Q = R \cup (N \setminus (R \cup Q))$ (see Figure 21.7).
  $x(Q) \geq 0$ implies that $x(Q) = (x(Q))_+$, and therefore by Equations (21.184) and (21.180),

$$w_T^x(R) = (E - d(N \setminus (R \cup Q)))_+ - x(Q)_+ \tag{21.185}$$

$$\leq (E - d(N \setminus (R \cup Q)) - x(Q))_+ \tag{21.186}$$

$$= (x(N) - d(N \setminus (R \cup Q)) - x(Q))_+. \tag{21.187}$$

Because $x(N) - x(Q) = x(N \setminus Q) = x(T) + x(T^c \setminus Q)$, along with $d(N \setminus (R \cup Q)) = d(T \setminus R) + d(T^c \setminus Q)$, one has

$$w_T^x(R) \leq (x(T) + x(T^c \setminus Q) - d(T \setminus R) - d(T^c \setminus Q))_+. \tag{21.188}$$

Since $x_i \leq d_i$ for every player i, the difference $x(T^c \setminus Q) - d(T^c \setminus Q)$ is nonpositive; therefore,

$$w_T^x(R) \leq (x(T) - d(T \setminus R))_+ = w(R). \tag{21.189}$$

Step 3: $w_T^x(R) \geq w(R)$ for every coalition $R \subset T$.

Let $R \subset T$ be a coalition. By the definition of the reduced game, for $Q = N \backslash T$,

$$w_T^x(R) \geq v(R \cup (N \backslash T)) - x(N \backslash T) \tag{21.190}$$

$$= (E - d(T \backslash R))_+ - x(N \backslash T) \tag{21.191}$$

$$= (E - d(T \backslash R))_+ - x(N) + x(T) \tag{21.192}$$

$$= (E - d(T \backslash R))_+ - E + x(T) \tag{21.193}$$

$$\geq E - d(T \backslash R) - E + x(T) \tag{21.194}$$

$$= x(T) - d(T \backslash R). \tag{21.195}$$

By the definition of the reduced game, for $Q = \emptyset$,

$$w_T^x(R) \geq v(R) = (E - d(N \backslash R))_+ \geq 0. \tag{21.196}$$

By Equations (21.195) and (21.196),

$$w_T^x(R) \geq (x(T) - d(T \backslash R))_+ = w(R). \tag{21.197}$$

We deduce that $w_T^x(R) = w(R)$ for every coalition $R \subseteq T$, thus concluding the proof. $\square$

Theorem 21.64 *Let $(N; v)$ be the coalitional game corresponding to a bankruptcy problem $[E; d]$, and let x^* be its nucleolus. Then for every coalition $T \subseteq N$ the Davis–Maschler reduced game to the coalition T relative to x^*, i.e., the game $(T; w_T^{x^*})$, is 0-monotonic.*

Proof: We first show that $0 \leq x_i^* \leq d_i$ for all $i \in N$. The game $(N; v)$ is a convex game (Exercise 21.55), and in particular its core is nonempty (Theorem 18.55, page 766). It follows that the nucleolus x^* lies in the core of the game (Theorem 21.20, page 860). Therefore,

$$x_i^* \geq v(i) = (E - d(N \backslash \{i\}))_+ \geq 0. \tag{21.198}$$

Since $x^*(N) = E$, and since x^* is in the core, it follows that for every player i,

$$E - x_i^* = x^*(N \backslash \{i\}) \geq v(N \backslash \{i\}) = (E - d_i)_+ \geq E - d_i, \tag{21.199}$$

yielding the conclusion $x_i^* \leq d_i$, as claimed.

By Theorem 21.63 it follows that $(T; w_T^{x^*})$ is the game corresponding to the bankruptcy problem $[x^*(T); (d_i)_{i \in T}]$ and therefore by Theorem 21.62 this is a 0-monotonic game. $\square$

By Theorem 21.38 (page 873), the previous results deliver the following corollary, which states that the nucleolus satisfies the reduced game property over the family of games corresponding to the bankruptcy problem.

Corollary 21.65 *Let $(N; v)$ be the coalitional game corresponding to the bankruptcy problem $[E; d]$, let x^* be its nucleolus, and let $T \subseteq N$ be a nonempty coalition. Then $(x^*)_{i \in T}$ is the nucleolus of the game $(T; w_T^{x^*})$.*

We are ready to formulate and prove the central theorem of this section:

Theorem 21.66 *Let* $[E; d_1, d_2, \ldots, d_n]$ *be a bankruptcy problem, and let* $(N; v)$ *be the coalitional game defined by Equation (21.172). Then the Rabbi Nathan solution to the bankruptcy problem coincides with the nucleolus of the game* $(N; v)$.

Proof: Define a solution concept φ to the bankruptcy problem as follows. For every bankruptcy problem $[E; d]$, $\varphi(E; d)$ is the nucleolus of the game $(N; v)$ corresponding to $[E; d]$. We have to prove that φ coincides with the Rabbi Nathan solution.

By Corollary 21.65, for every coalition $T = \{i, j\}$ where i and j are distinct players, the nucleolus of the game $(T; w_T^{x^*})$ is (x_i^*, x_j^*). By Theorem 21.61, (x_i^*, x_j^*) is the "contested garment" solution of the problem $[x(T); d_i, d_j]$. It follows that the solution concept φ is consistent with the "contested garment" solution. Since the Rabbi Nathan solution is the only solution concept for the family of bankruptcy problems consistent with the "contested garment" solution, the nucleolus of the game $(N; v)$ coincides with the Rabbi Nathan solution. This concludes the proof of the theorem. $\square$

21.9 Discussion

In the chapter on the Shapley value, we proved that the Shapley value is the only single-valued solution concept satisfying the properties of efficiency, symmetry, covariance under strategic equivalence, and consistency relative to the Hart–Mas-Colell reduced game (Theorem 19.39, page 819). Sobolev [1975] shows that the same principles characterize the prenucleolus, if we replace Hart and Mas-Colell's notion of the reduced game by that of Davis and Maschler.[10] This shows that an arbitrator who is thinking of recommending the Shapley value or the prenucleolus as a solution concept should first consider both the Davis–Maschler reduced game and the Hart–Mas-Colell reduced game, and see which one is more appropriate for the given situation.

For defining the coalitional game corresponding to a bankruptcy problem, it is possible to consider other coalitional functions than that given in Equation (21.172), as for example

$$w(S) := E - \sum_{i \in S^c} d_i, \quad \forall S \subseteq N. \tag{21.200}$$

This coalitional function is appropriate for situations in which the debt must be paid, and creditors might pay out of their own pocket other creditors who have higher claims. It can be shown (Exercise 21.56) that in this case, if x is the Shapley value of the game, then the Hart–Mas-Colell reduced game $(S; w_S^x)$ coincides with the game corresponding to the restricted bankruptcy problem $[x(S); (d_i)_{i \in S}]$. Therefore, in such situations, it may be more appropriate to use the Shapley value. In summary, the system of properties characterizing single-valued solution concepts can be of use in deciding which solution is appropriate in a given situation.

A solution for the bankruptcy problem is *consistent* if, after some of the creditors leave the game, taking with them the amounts allocated to them under the solution, and the rest

---

10 Sobolev used the property of anonymity (independence from changing the names of the players), which is a stronger assumption than symmetry. Orshan [1993] showed that assuming symmetry is sufficient for the result.

of the creditors then contend with the resulting restricted bankruptcy problem where the amount to be divided is what remains after the other creditors have left, they discover that the solution to the restricted problem gives each of them exactly what he received under the original problem.

Definition 21.67 *A solution concept for a bankruptcy problem φ is consistent if for every bankruptcy problem $[E; d]$, and every set of creditors $T \subseteq N$,*

$$\varphi_i(E; d) = \varphi_i(x; (d_j)_{j \in T}), \quad \forall i \in T, \tag{21.201}$$

where $x = \sum_{j \in T} \varphi_j(E; d)$.

The Rabbi Nathan solution is consistent (Exercise 21.57), and several other consistent solutions exist (such as the proportional division solution). Kaminski [2000] proves that every consistent solution for bankruptcy problems can be described by a system of containers of various sizes, and that the converse also holds; i.e., every system of containers defines a consistent solution.

21.10 Remarks

The procedure presented in this chapter for computing the nucleolus was suggested by Bezalel Peleg, and first appeared in Kopelowitz [1967]. The results in Section 21.5 (page 863) are from Kohlberg [1971]. The proof of Theorem 21.25 (page 864) presented here is from Peleg and Sudhölter [2003].

Weighted majority games were first defined in von Neumann and Morgenstern [1944]. That book also presents an example of a game without a homogeneous representation. Isbell [1959] posed the question of whether it is possible to choose, among all the representations of a weighted majority game, one normalized representation that is, in a certain sense, the most "natural" representation. Isbell did not formally define the term "natural representation," but required the following property that such a representation should satisfy: if a game is homogeneous, then the "natural" representation thus chosen must be homogeneous. The answer to this question, appearing in Theorem 21.54 (page 878), was given by Peleg [1968], and extended to a larger class of games by Sudhölter [1996].

The explanation of the Talmudic passages presented in this chapter is based on Aumann and Maschler [1985]. The implementation of the solution using a system of containers was first suggested by Kaminski [2000], although the use of systems of containers for finding equilibria goes back as far as Fisher [1891].

Exercise 21.16 is Example 5.6.3 in Peleg and Sudhölter [2003]. The game "My Aunt and I," as presented in Exercise 21.21, first appeared in Davis [1965]. That article includes a report on correspondence that Davis and Maschler conducted with several researchers on the question "how will my aunt and one of my brothers divide the profit that will accrue to them if they form the coalition {aunt, brother}?" Various answers were given to this question. The game was included in an empirical study of twelve games, with the results of that study appearing in Selten and Schuster [1968]. Exercise 21.28 is based on Maschler et al. [1979].

21.11 Exercises

21.1 Is the function $x \mapsto \sum_{S \subseteq N} e(S, x)$ constant on the set of preimputations $X^0(N; v)$? Prove this claim, or show that it is incorrect.

21.2 Prove that the lexicographic relation is transitive.

21.3 Let $K \subseteq \mathbb{R}^n$, and let $f : \mathbb{R}^n \to \mathbb{R}$ be a function. Denote the set of points in K at which the minimum of f is attained by

$$\operatorname{argmin}_{x \in K} f(x) = \left\{ y \in K : f(y) = \min_{z \in K} f(z) \right\}. \qquad (21.202)$$

Prove that if K is a compact set and f is a continuous function, then the set $\operatorname{argmin}_{x \in K} f(x)$ is compact and nonempty.

21.4 Find a sequence of vectors $(x^n)_{n=1}^{\infty}$ in $\mathbb{R}^2$ converging to x, and a vector $y \in \mathbb{R}^2$ such that (a) $x^n >_L y$ for all $n \in \mathbb{N}$, but (b) $x <_L y$.

21.5 Consider the three-player coalitional game with the following coalitional function:

$$v(1) = 0, \quad v(2) = 1, \quad v(3) = 4, \quad v(1,2) = 2, \quad v(1,3) = 6,$$
$$v(2,3) = -1, \quad v(1,2,3) = 5. \qquad (21.203)$$

(a) Compute $\theta((1, 1, 3))$, $\theta((1, 3, 1))$, and $\theta((3, 1, 1))$.
(b) Arrange the three vectors in decreasing lexicographic order.

21.6 Let $x, y \in X(N; v)$ be imputations, and suppose that $\theta(x) \succsim_L \theta(y)$. Denote $z = \frac{1}{2}x + \frac{1}{2}y$. Is it necessarily true that $\theta(x) \succsim_L \theta(z) \succsim_L \theta(y)$? Either prove this statement, or provide a counterexample.

21.7 (a) Prove that in the gloves game (Example 21.3) the imputation $y = (0, 0, 1)$ satisfies $\theta(y) <_L \theta(u)$ for every $u \in X(N; v)$, $u \neq y$.
(b) Prove that this imputation also satisfies $\theta(y) <_L \theta(u)$ for every $u \in X^0(N; v)$, $u \neq y$.

21.8 (a) Find a two-player coalitional game $(N; v)$, and a bounded set K that is not closed, such that the nucleolus $\mathcal{N}(N; v; K)$ is the empty set.
(b) Find a two-player coalitional game $(N; v)$, and a closed and unbounded set K, such that the nucleolus $\mathcal{N}(N; v; K)$ is the empty set.

21.9 Let $(N; v)$ be a coalitional game satisfying the following property: there is an imputation $x \in X(N; v)$ such that all the excesses at x are nonnegative.

(a) Prove that x is the only imputation in the game, and in particular it is the nucleolus.
(b) Is x necessarily also the prenucleolus? Either prove this statement, or provide a counterexample.

21.10 Player i in a coalitional game $(N; v)$ is a *dummy player* if

$$v(S \cup \{i\}) = v(S) + v(i), \quad \forall S \subseteq N \setminus \{i\}. \tag{21.204}$$

Prove that if player i is a dummy player in a game $(N; v)$ then under both the nucleolus and the prenucleolus, player i's payoff is $v(i)$, that is, $\mathcal{N}_i(N; v) = v(i)$ and $\mathcal{PN}_i(N; v) = v(i)$.

21.11 Complete the proof of Theorem 21.7 (page 853): prove that for every k, $2 \le k \le 2^n$,

$$\theta_k(x) = \max_{\substack{\text{different } S_1, \dots, S_k}} \min\{e(S_1, x), \dots, e(S_k, x)\}. \tag{21.205}$$

21.12 Compute the nucleolus of the three-player coalitional game with the following coalitional function:

$$v(1) = v(2) = v(3) = v(2,3) = 0, \quad v(1,2) = v(1,3) = v(1,2,3) = 1. \tag{21.206}$$

21.13 Compute the prenucleolus of the three-player coalitional game with the following coalitional function:

$$v(1) = v(2) = v(3) = v(2,3) = 0, \quad v(1,2) = v(1,3) = v(1,2,3) = -1. \tag{21.207}$$

21.14 Let $(N; v)$ be the three-player coalitional game with the following coalitional function:

$$v(S) = 0 \iff |S| \le 1, \tag{21.208}$$
$$v(S) = 1 \iff |S| \ge 2. \tag{21.209}$$

Let K be the triangle in $\mathbb{R}^3$ whose vertices are $(1,0,0)$, $(0,1,0)$, and $(0,0,1)$, and let K_0 be its boundary. Compute the nucleolus of the game $(N; v)$ relative to K and relative to K_0.

21.15 Compute the nucleolus and the prenucleolus of the three-player coalitional game $(N; v)$ in which $v(1,2) = 1$ and $v(S) = 0$ for every other coalition S. Does the nucleolus coincide with the prenucleolus?

21.16 Let $(N; v)$ be a five-player coalitional game with the following coalitional function:

$$v(S) = \begin{cases} 1 & \text{if } S = \{1,2\} \text{ or } S = \{1,2,5\}, \\ 2 & \text{if } S = \{3,4\} \text{ or } S = \{3,4,5\}, \\ 0 & \text{for any other coalition } S. \end{cases} \tag{21.210}$$

Answer the following questions:

(a) Are there null players in this game? If so, which players are null players?
(b) Prove that the nucleolus and the prenucleolus for the coalitional structure $\mathcal{B} = \{\{1,2,5\}, \{3\}, \{4\}\}$ are

$$\mathcal{N}(N; v) = \mathcal{PN}(N; v) = (0,0,0,0,1). \tag{21.211}$$

21.17 Prove that the nucleolus is covariant under strategic equivalence: for every coalitional game $(N; v)$, for every set $K \subseteq \mathbb{R}^N$, for every $a > 0$, and every set $b \in \mathbb{R}^N$,

$$\mathcal{N}(N; av + b; aK + b) = a\mathcal{N}(N; v; K) + b. \tag{21.212}$$

21.18 Find a two-player coalitional game $(N; v)$, and a V-shaped set K, i.e., a set that is the union of two line segments sharing an edge point, such that the nucleolus of $(N; v)$ relative to K is the two edge points of K.

21.19 Compute the nucleolus of the weighted majority game $[q; 2, 2, 3, 3]$ for every quota $q > 0$.

21.20 Compute the nucleolus of the coalitional game $(N; v)$ where $N = \{1, 2, 3, 4\}$ and the coalitional function v is given by

$$v(S) = \begin{cases} i & \text{if } S = \{i\}, \\ 0 & \text{otherwise.} \end{cases} \tag{21.213}$$

21.21 My Aunt and I Auntie Betty can complete a certain job together with me or with any of my three brothers, with the payment for the work being \$1,000, but she must choose one of the four of us. All four of us brothers together (without Auntie Betty) can also complete the same job.

(a) Describe this situation as a coalitional game.
(b) Compute the nucleolus of the game for the coalitional structure $\mathcal{B} = \{N\}$.
(c) Compute the nucleolus of the game for the coalitional structure

$$\mathcal{B} = \{\{\text{Auntie Betty, Me}\}, \{\text{Brother } A\}, \{\text{Brother } B\}, \{\text{Brother } C\}\}. \tag{21.214}$$

21.22 Define the nucleolus of a cost game $(N; c)$.

21.23 Compute the core and the nucleolus of the following spanning tree game (see Section 17.1.7, page 716). v^0 is the central point to which Players I, II, and III, who are physically located at the vertices of a triangle (as depicted in the next figure), wish to connect. The cost associated with every edge in the figure is one unit.

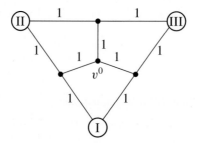

21.24 Let $K \subseteq \mathbb{R}^N$ be a closed set satisfying the following property: there exists a real number c such that $\sum_{i \in N} x_i \leq c$ for all $x \in K$. Prove that the nucleolus relative to K is nonempty.

21.25 Let $(N; v)$ be a coalitional game, let $(c_i)_{i \in N}$ be a collection of positive real numbers, let $c \in \mathbb{R}$, and let $K := \{x \in \mathbb{R}^N : \sum_{i \in N} c_i x_i \leq c\} \subseteq \mathbb{R}^N$. Prove that the set $\mathcal{N}(N; v; K)$ contains exactly one point.

21.26 Prove that the vector $x \in X(\mathcal{B}; v)$ is in the core $\mathcal{C}(N; v; \mathcal{B})$ if and only if $\theta_1(x) \leq 0$.

21.27 Prove that if the ε-core $\mathcal{C}_\varepsilon(N; v)$ is nonempty, then $\mathcal{N}(N; v) \subseteq \mathcal{C}_\varepsilon(N; v)$. Deduce that the nucleolus is contained in the minimal core, and that if the core is nonempty, then the nucleolus is contained in the core. For the definition of $\mathcal{C}_\varepsilon(N; v)$ and the minimal core, see Exercise 18.33 on page 788.

21.28 The nucleolus of a three-player coalitional game can be computed as follows.[11] First, find the minimal core of the game (see Exercise 18.33 on page 788). The minimal core is defined by linear inequalities corresponding to the various coalitions. The inequality corresponding to the coalition S corresponds to the line H_S. Changing the value of ε then corresponds to parallel displacement of these lines. In the process of reducing the value of ε, some of the lines H_S cannot be displaced without causing the ε-core to become empty. These lines are then left unmoved in the process, while other lines are moved as the value of ε is reduced. Every time a line is encountered such that continuing to move it will cause the ε-core to be empty, that line is no longer moved. This process is continued until only one point remains, which is the nucleolus.

For example, in the game in Exercise 18.33 (page 788) the minimal core is on the line defined by $x_1 = 1$, and the boundary points of the minimal core are located at $(1, 5, 3)$ and $(1, 2, 6)$. Move the constraints $x_1 + x_3$ and $x_1 + x_2$ (and x_1 and x_2) another unit and a half, until they meet, yielding the nucleolus $(1, 3\frac{1}{2}, 4\frac{1}{2})$.

(a) Prove that this process indeed finds the nucleolus.
(b) Compute, using this process, the nucleolus in the games in Exercise 18.33 (page 788).

21.29 Suppose that $(N; v)$ is a coalitional game such that the set of imputations $X(N; v)$ is nonempty, and such that the nucleolus x^* differs from the prenucleolus $\widehat{x}$. Prove that the nucleolus is located on the boundary of the set $X(N; v)$.
Hint: Show that if the nucleolus is not on the boundary of $X(N; v)$, then there is a point $z = \alpha x^* + (1 - \alpha)\widehat{x} \in X(N; v)$, where $\alpha \in (0, 1)$, and use the ideas presented in the proof of Theorem 21.13 (page 855).

21.30 Prove that the nucleolus is independent of the names given to the players; i.e., if $\pi : N \to N$ is a permutation of N, and the coalitional games $(N; v)$ and $(N; w)$ satisfy $w(S) = v(\pi(S))$ for every $S \subseteq N$, and if x^{*v} and x^{*w} are the nucleoli of these games, then $x_i^w = x_{\pi(i)}^v$ for every player $i \in N$.

21.31 Prove that the algorithm described in Section 21.4 (page 862) is well defined (i.e., show that there exists L for which the sets $\Sigma_1, \Sigma_2, \ldots, \Sigma_L$ are nonempty and the union $\cup_{l=1}^{L} \Sigma_l$ contains all the coalitions), and show that X_L contains only one point, which is the nucleolus.

Guidance: show that the nucleolus is contained in each of the sets $X_1, X_2, \ldots, X_L$.

21.32 Let $x_1, x_2, \ldots, x_L$ be imputations in the game $(N; v)$ that include the nucleolus. Suppose that $\theta_1(x_l) = \theta_1(x_{l'})$ for every l, l' satisfying $1 \le l, l' \le L$, and denote $\Sigma_1 := \{S \subseteq N : e(S, x_l) = \theta_1(x_l) \ \forall l \in \{1, 2, \ldots, L\}\}$. Prove that the collection of coalitions Σ_1 is nonempty.

21.33 Give an example of a monotonic game that is not 0-monotonic.

21.34 Show that a simple, constant-sum game need not be 0-monotonic.

21.35 Prove that every convex game is 0-monotonic.

21.36 Show that every null player is a dummy player, but there are dummy players that are not null players.

21.37 Using Theorem 21.29 (page 869), prove that the imputation $x = \left(\frac{1}{3}, \frac{1}{3}, \frac{1}{3}\right)$ is not the prenucleolus of the gloves game that appears in Example 21.3 and that the prenucleolus of this game is $y = (0, 0, 1)$.

21.38 Eilon contacts Michael, claiming that the second direction in the proof of Theorem 21.28 on page 867 (if the system of equations given by Equations (21.99) and (21.100) is tight for x, then x is the nucleolus) does not hold: "Denote the nucleolus by x^*, and let x be an imputation," explains Eilon. "Denote $y = x^* - x$. Then $y(N) = 0$. Let α_1 be the greatest value of the excesses at $\theta(x^*)$. Then for every coalition S,

$$y(S) = (x^* - x)(S) = e(S, x) - e(S, x^*). \tag{21.215}$$

Since x^* is the nucleolus, and since α_1 is the greatest value of the excesses, it must be the case that $e(S, x) \ge 0$ for every coalition $S \in \mathcal{D}(\alpha_1, x^*)$. In other words, $y(S) \ge 0$ for every such coalition. Since in the first part of the theorem, it is proved that relative to the nucleolus, the system of equations is tight, one deduces that $y(S) = 0$ for every $S \in \mathcal{D}(\alpha_1, x^*)$. Continuing by induction to the next level, one concludes that $y(S) = 0$ for every coalition S, which implies that $x = x^*$. But this cannot hold since x was chosen arbitrarily."

Is Eilon correct? If not, where is the flaw in his argument?

21.39 Find a weighted majority game that is not constant sum, and satisfies the property that if S is a winning coalition, then S^c is a losing coalition.

21.40 Find a weighted majority game that is not constant sum, satisfying the property that if S is a losing coalition, then S^c is a winning coalition.

21.41 Prove that the game $[5; 2, 2, 2, 1, 1, 1]$ does not have a homogeneous representation.

21.42 Prove that if $[q; w_1, w_2, \ldots, w_n]$ and $[\widehat{q}; \widehat{w}_1, \widehat{w}_2, \ldots, \widehat{w}_n]$ are two representations of the same simple game, then $[q + \widehat{q}; w_1 + \widehat{w}_1, w_2 + \widehat{w}_2, \ldots, w_n + \widehat{w}_n]$ is also a representation of that game.

21.43 Prove that if $[q; w]$ is a representation of a weighted majority game $(N; v)$, then $[q(w); w]$ is also a representation of that game.

21.44 Let $(N; v)$ be a simple strong game, and let $x \in X(N; v)$ be an imputation. Recall that $q(x) := \min_{S \in \mathcal{W}^m} x(S)$. Show by example that the game $[q(x); x]$ is not necessarily a simple strong game. Which property in the definition of a simple strong game may not hold?

21.45 Let $(N; v)$ be a coalitional game with $N = \{1, 2, 3\}$ and a coalitional function given by

$$v(S) = \begin{cases} 1 & |S| \geq 2, \\ 0 & |S| \leq 1. \end{cases} \qquad (21.216)$$

Answer the following questions:

(a) Is the game $(N; v)$ a simple strong game?
(b) For which imputations $x \in X(N; v)$ is $[q(x); x]$ a simple strong game?
(c) For which imputations $x \in X(N; v)$ does the game $[q(x); x]$ represent the game $(N; v)$?

21.46 Find the Rabbi Nathan solution of the following bankruptcy problems:

(a) There are four wives, who are owed 100, 200, 300, and 400, respectively, out of an estate of 350.
(b) There are four wives, who are owed 100, 200, 300, and 400, respectively, out of an estate of 720.
(c) There are five wives, who are owed 60, 120, 180, 240, and 300, respectively, out of an estate of 600.

21.47 Prove directly that the function f defined in Equation (21.166) is continuous, its first coordinate is monotonically nondecreasing in d_1 for every fixed d_2, and its second coordinate is monotonically nondecreasing in d_2 for every fixed d_1.

21.48 Which of the following properties are satisfied by the Rabbi Nathan solution to bankruptcy problems? (For each property, provide either a proof or a counter-example.)

(a) Symmetry (creditors with identical claims receive identical payments).
(a) Null player (a creditor with a claim of 0 receives nothing).
(c) Covariance under strategic equivalence: for every $a > 0$ and every $b \in \mathbb{R}^N$ that satisfy $ad_i + b_i > 0$ for every $i \in N$ we have

$$\varphi \left(aE + \sum_{i \in N} b_i; ad_1 + b_1, \ldots, ad_n + b_n \right) = a\varphi(E; d_1, \ldots, d_n) + b.$$

$$(21.217)$$

(d) Additivity:

$$\varphi(E; d_1, \ldots, d_n) + \varphi(\tilde{E}; \tilde{d}_1, \ldots, \tilde{d}_n) = \varphi(E + \tilde{E}; d_1 + \tilde{d}_1, \ldots, d_n + \tilde{d}_n).$$

$$(21.218)$$

21.49 Jeff owes Sam $140, and owes Harry $80. Jeff declares bankruptcy, because he has only $100, and the decision of how to divide his $100 between Harry and Sam comes before a court.

The court is composed of a three-judge panel, John, Clarence, and Ruth. John is convinced that the most proper division is $[40 : 60]$, using the following reasoning. "There is no dispute over the first $20," he claims, "because both agree that they go to Sam. Regarding the remaining 80, both parties have legitimate claims, and they must therefore divide that sum equally between them."

Clarence, in contrast, claims that the most proper division is $[20 : 80]$, explaining: "Suppose each of them could take the amount owed to him, $80 to Harry and $140 to Sam. That would lead to a deficit of $120. This deficit should be divided equally between the creditors; i.e., each of them should yield $60 of what he claims."[12]

Ruth claims that the most proper division is $[44.44 : 55.55]$, since "The total sum should be divided proportionally to the debts owed: Harry should get $\frac{80}{80+140} \times 100$, not a penny more or less."

For each judge, describe a solution concept to bankruptcy problems with n creditors that is consistent with his or her solution for the bankruptcy problem with two creditors.

21.50 Define the following solution concept φ to bankruptcy problems by

$$\varphi_i(E; d_1, d_2, \ldots, d_n) := \frac{d_1}{d_1 + d_2 + \cdots + d_n} \times E.$$

$$(21.219)$$

This is the proportional division between the creditors.

(a) Construct a system of containers that implements this solution.
(b) Prove that this is a consistent solution concept.
(c) Which of the properties listed in Exercise 21.48 are satisfied by this solution?

21.51 Repeat Exercise 21.50, using the following solution concept: divide the estate in a continuous manner equally between the creditors, until one (or more) of the creditors has received his or her entire claim. Continue to divide the remaining amount of money between the remaining creditors, until one (or more) of the creditors has received his or her entire claim, and so on, until all the money in the estate runs out.

---

12 Note that under this procedure, a situation may develop in which a creditor may need to pay. For example, if $E = 20$, the debt to Sam is $10, and the debt to Harry is $100, under Clarence's procedure Sam needs to pay $35, and Harry receives $55.

21.52 Let φ be a solution concept to the bankruptcy problem. The dual solution of φ is the solution concept φ^* defined as follows:

$$\varphi_i^*(E;d) = d_i - \varphi_i(D - E, d), \quad \forall i \in N, \tag{21.220}$$

where $D := \sum_{i=1}^n d_i$ is the sum of the claims. Since $D - E$ is the sum that the debtor cannot pay the creditors, φ^* divides the loss between the players in the same way that φ divides the profits.

(a) Prove that φ^* is a solution concept.
(b) Prove that the Rabbi Nathan solution is self-dual, i.e., satisfies $\varphi^* = \varphi$.
(c) Find the dual solution to proportional division defined in Exercise 21.50.
(d) Find the dual solution to the solution proposed by Clarence in Exercise 21.49.

21.53 Let $[E; d_1, d_2, \ldots, d_n]$ be a bankruptcy problem, where $d_1 \leq d_2 \leq \cdots \leq d_n$. Denote $D := \sum_{i=1}^n d_i$, and for every $i \in N$, denote $D^i := \sum_{j=1}^i d_j$. In particular, $D = D^n$. Show that the Rabbi Nathan solution to the problem $[E; d]$ is given by the following function φ:

$$\varphi(E;d) := \begin{cases} \left(\frac{E}{n}, \frac{E}{n}, \ldots, \frac{E}{n}\right), & \text{if } E \leq n\frac{D^1}{2}, \\ \left(\frac{d_1}{2}, \ldots, \frac{d_i}{2}, \frac{E-D^i}{n-i}, \ldots, \frac{E-D^i}{n-i}\right), & \text{if } 1 \leq i < n \text{ and } \frac{D^i}{2} + (n-i)\frac{d_i}{2} \\ & \quad < E \leq \frac{D^i}{2} + (n-i-1)\frac{d_{i+1}}{2}, \\ d - \varphi(D - E; d), & \text{if } \frac{D}{2} < E \leq D. \end{cases} \tag{21.221}$$

Remark: For the case $\frac{D}{2} < E \leq D$, use Exercise 21.52.

21.54 Consider the following situation. A corporation has regular shareholders, and preferred shareholders. If the corporation goes bankrupt, every shareholder is supposed to get the value of the shares he holds. During the division of the assets of the bankrupt corporation, preferred shareholders take precedence: they first receive the value of the shares they hold, and only afterwards do the regular shareholders receive what is left of the money.

Formally, a *corporate bankruptcy problem* is given by:

- E: the total worth of the assets of the corporation.
- n: the number of preferred shareholders.
- m: the number of regular shareholders.
- $d_1, \ldots, d_n$: the values of the shares of the preferred shareholders.
- $d_{n+1}, \ldots, d_{n+m}$: the values of the shares of the regular shareholders.

A *solution concept* for the corporation bankruptcy problem is a function associating every corporate bankruptcy problem $[E; d_1, \ldots, d_n; d_{n+1}, \ldots, d_{n+m}]$ with a vector of nonnegative numbers $(x_1, \ldots, x_{n+m})$ satisfying:

- $\sum_{i=1}^{n+m} x_i = E$.

- If $d_1 + \cdots + d_n \le E$, then $x_{n+1} + \cdots + x_{n+m} = 0$.
- If $d_1 + \cdots + d_n \ge E$, then $x_i = d_i$ for every $1 \le i \le n$.

A solution concept for the corporate bankruptcy problem is *consistent with the "contested garment" solution* if for every corporate bankruptcy problem $[E; d_1, \ldots, d_n; d_{n+1}, \ldots, d_{n+m}]$, and every pair of players i and j, if i and j hold the same class of shares, then

$$\varphi_i(E; d_1, \ldots, d_n; d_{n+1}, \ldots, d_{n+m}) = f_1(x; d_i, d_j), \qquad (21.222)$$

where

$$x = \varphi_i(E; d_1, \ldots, d_n; d_{n+1}, \ldots, d_{n+m}) + \varphi_j(E; d_1, \ldots, d_n; d_{n+1}, \ldots, d_{n+m}), \qquad (21.223)$$

and f_1 is the first coordinate of the function defined in Equation (21.166) on page 882.

(a) Construct a system of containers implementing a solution to the corporate bankruptcy problem that is consistent with the "contested garment" solution.
(b) Prove that there exists at most one solution concept to the corporate bankruptcy problem that is consistent with the "contested garment" solution.

21.55 Let $[E; d_1, d_2, \ldots, d_n]$ be a bankruptcy problem satisfying $\sum_{i=1}^{n} d_i > E$. Prove that the game $(N; v)$ defined by

$$v(S) := \max \left\{ E - \sum_{i \notin S} d_i, 0 \right\} \qquad (21.224)$$

is convex.

21.56 Prove that if one associates a bankruptcy problem $[E; d_1, d_2, \ldots, d_n]$ with the coalitional game $(N; w)$ where $w(S) = E - \sum_{i \in S^c} d_i$, and if $\tilde{x}$ is the Shapley value of this game, then the Hart–Mas-Colell reduced game $(S; w_S^{\tilde{x}})$ is the coalitional game corresponding to the bankruptcy problem $[\tilde{x}(S); (d_i)_{i \in S}]$.

For the definition of the Hart–Mas-Colell reduced game, see Definition 19.33 on page 816.

21.57 Prove that the Rabbi Nathan solution is consistent according to Definition 21.67 (page 891).

Chapter summary

In this chapter we present a model of social choice, which studies how a group of individuals makes a collective choice from among a set of alternatives. The model assumes that each individual in the group holds a preference relation over a given set of alternatives, and the problem is how to aggregate these preferences to one preference relation that is supposed to represent the *preference of the group*. A function that maps each vector of preference relations to a single preference relation is called a *social welfare function*. The main result on this topic is Arrow's Impossibility Theorem, which states that every social welfare function that satisfies two properties, unanimity and independence of irrelevant alternatives, is dictatorial.

This impossibility result is then extended to *social choice functions*. A social choice function assigns to every vector of preference relations of all individuals in the group a single alternative, interpreted as the alternative that is most preferred by the group.

A social choice function is said to be *nonmanipulable* if no individual can manipulate the group's choice and obtain a better outcome by reporting a preference relation that is different from his true preference relation. Using the impossibility result for social choice functions we prove the Gibbard–Satterthwaite Theorem, which states that any nonmanipulable social choice function that satisfies the property of unanimity is dictatorial.

Groups of decision makers are often called upon to choose between several possible alternatives: citizens are called upon to choose between political candidates on election day; union members select committees; family members need to choose which television program they will watch together. In any such example, each individual has his or her own preference ordering with respect to the different alternatives, and all the individuals together need to come to a collective decision that serves as the entire group's "most preferred" alternative. How are such decisions arrived at? In a dictatorship, the choice is made by the "dictator" (the national leader or the head of the family). In democratic countries, the choice is usually made by some variation of majority vote. The following example, Example 22.1, shows one way to generalize majority vote to cases in which there are more than two alternatives. Example 22.2 reveals that problems may arise in such generalizations. The following example, due to Borda [1784],[1] points to difficulties in using majority vote for collective decisions.

Example 22.1   A committee composed of 21 people needs to select one individual from among three candidates named *A*, *B*, and *C*. The committee members' preferences are given in the following table:

No. of committee members	First choice	Second choice	Third choice
1	A	B	C
7	A	C	B
7	B	C	A
6	C	B	A

In words, one committee member ranks the candidates in the order *A* first, *B* second, and *C* third; seven committee members share the preference ordering *A* first, *C* second, and *B* third; another seven share the ordering *B* first, *C* second, and *A* third; and six members rank the candidates by the order *C* first, *B* second, and *A* third. Which candidate will be chosen? The answer, obviously, depends on which voting system is used.

Since we are used to the idea of selecting candidates by majority vote, it seems natural to check whether there is a candidate who would defeat every other candidate by majority vote in a head-to-head competition. Such a candidate is called a "Condorcet winner," and if one exists, it seems reasonable to choose him as the collective choice of the committee. In our example, candidate *C* is a Condorcet winner, since he would defeat *A* by a vote of 13 to 8 if the two of them were the sole candidates, and similarly would win by 13 votes to 8 votes against *B*.   ◄

One problem with this "voting method" is that there might not always be a Condorcet winner, as can be seen in Example 22.2, which is due to Condorcet [1785].[2] In this case, the above voting method will not tell us who to choose.

Example 22.2   A 60-member committee needs to select one individual from candidates *A*, *B*, and *C*. The committee members' preferences are given in the following table:

No. of committee members	First choice	Second choice	Third choice
23	A	B	C
2	B	A	C
17	B	C	A
10	C	A	B
8	C	B	A

In head-to-head pairwise competition, *A* defeats *B* by 33 to 27, *B* trounces *C* by 42 to 18, and *C* wins against *A* by 35 to 25. In other words, there is no Condorcet winner: the preference ordering given by pairwise majority voting is not transitive. This leads to several implications. First of all, the order in which voting between candidates is conducted can affect the result – that is, if we first pit two candidates against each other and then have the winner between them compete against the third candidate, the order in which this is done may be crucial. If *A* and *B* compete head-to-head with the winner going up against *C*, then *C* will be selected. But if we first have *A* and *C* compete against each other with the winner squaring off against *B*, then *B* ends up being selected. And if *B*

---

1 Jean-Charles Chevalier de Borda (1733–99) was a French mathematician, physicist, social scientist, and sailor.
2 Marie Jean Antoine Nicolas Caritat (Marquis de Condorcet, 1743–94) was a French philosopher and mathematician who wrote about political science.

competes against C with the winner between them pitted against A, then A is the ultimate selection. The order of voting is absolutely critical.

Another consequence of the fact that the preference relation is not transitive is that in any voting method that generalizes majority vote between two candidates to a greater number of candidates, the results may depend on the presence or absence of a candidate who is not even the winner! For example, suppose that a certain voting method, which for two candidates chooses the winner by majority vote, leads to the selection of A. If B were to decline to participate, A and C would instead compete directly against each other – and then C would win by majority vote. In other words, B's presence as a candidate can affect the results, even though B does not win when he competes. A similar phenomenon would exist if the voting method were to select B or C.

The condition that the presence or absence of a candidate that is not selected by the procedure should not affect the results of a voting method is called the "independence of irrelevant alternatives." The above example shows that it is not true that every voting system which, in the presence of two candidates, chooses one of them using majority vote satisfies independence of irrelevant alternatives. This fact forms the basis of the results developed in this chapter. ◄

Another problem with pairwise majority voting is that even when a Condorcet winner exists, it is not always clear that he is the candidate who should be selected (see Exercise 22.5). We can check whether or not several well-known voting methods select the Condorcet winner when such a candidate exists. One popular method is to have each committee member vote for his or her most-preferred candidate, with the candidate receiving the most votes winning.[3] If this method were to be adopted in Example 22.1, then A would receive 8 votes, B would get 7 votes, and C only 6 votes, leading to the selection of candidate A and not the Condorcet winner C.

Another method chooses the winning candidate in a two-round process:[4] in round one, every committee member votes for his or her most-preferred candidate. The two candidates who received the greatest number of votes in round one go on to compete against each other in round two, with the candidate garnering the most votes in round two ultimately selected as the winner. In Example 22.1, this method would lead to candidates A and B proceeding to a head-to-head competition in round two, where B would defeat A by 13 votes to 8; once again the Condorcet winner, candidate C, fails to be selected.

Election results, therefore, are extremely sensitive to which voting method is adopted, and as we have seen, two very popular voting methods by-pass the Condorcet winner, when such a candidate exists, and may well end up selecting another candidate.

In addition, the two methods discussed above can be subject to manipulation, in the sense that committee members have incentives to misrepresent their preferences in order to change the results. To see that, note that in Example 22.1, under the voting system in which each committee member votes for only one candidate, and the candidate with the greatest number of votes is chosen, if the committee members who prefer C to B and B to A vote for B instead of C, then B, whom they prefer to A, will win instead of A. In

---

3 This is a method used by many committees, including committees selecting candidates for public service positions in Britain.

4 This is the method used to elect the President of France.

the same example with a two-round voting method, if the committee members who rank A over C and C over B vote for C instead of A in the first round, then C and B will be the candidates competing in the second round, with C, whom they prefer to B, ultimately winning. The subject of voting manipulation will be discussed again later in this chapter.

In all the examples so far, the main question was choosing one alternative (one candidate) from a set of alternatives (candidates). We will return to this question later in the chapter, but we will first consider a more general issue. Suppose that every individual in a given population has a preference ordering (or ranking) over a set of alternatives, and society in general seeks to derive, out of all the individual rankings, a single ranking representing society's collective preferences among the alternatives: society's first choice among the alternatives, society's second choice, and so forth. In other words, the question before us is how to "aggregate" all the individual preference rankings into one preference ranking that can be interpreted as that of society's.

For example, suppose several teachers are asked to rank the students in a class by academic achievement. Each teacher ranks the students based on their performance in the subject that he or she teaches, and it is quite reasonable that different teachers will produce different rankings. The teachers may want to find a way to aggregate their rankings into one collective ranking listing the students in order from the "best" student to the "weakest" student.

We will show that, surprisingly, there is no rule producing an aggregate preference ordering that satisfies three very natural-sounding democratic conditions. One of those conditions is that there should be no dictator. If we dispense with this condition, then the only rule that satisfies the other two conditions is dictatorship.

After that we will explore situations in which there is no need to rank all of the possible choices, because it is only necessary to select society's top choice. There are many examples of such situations: selecting a committee chairman, electing a president, the board of directors of a corporation choosing among different investment opportunities, army officers selecting a military course of action, and, in our above example, picking the best student in the class in the collective opinion of the teachers. We will see that in this case as well, there is no selection rule that satisfies three natural democratic conditions, and that the only rule that satisfies two of the conditions is dictatorship.

22.1 Social welfare functions

Let A be a nonempty finite set of *alternatives*, and $N = \{1, 2, \ldots, n\}$ be a finite set of *individuals* ("voters" or "decision makers"). In Chapter 2, which deals with utility theory, we defined a preference relation over the set A as a subset of $A \times A$, and assumed that the preference relations of the players over the set of outcomes are complete, reflexive, and transitive. In this chapter we will consider preference relations that are complete and transitive but not necessarily reflexive. For simplicity, we will include these properties as part of the definition: a preference relation will from here on be a complete, reflexive, and transitive binary relation, and a strict preference relation will be a complete, irreflexive, and transitive binary relation.

Definition 22.3 *A preference relation* $\succsim_{P_i}$ *of player i over a set A is a binary relation*[5] *satisfying the following properties:*

- *For every pair of elements* $a, b \in A$, *either* $a \succsim_{P_i} b$ *or* $b \succsim_{P_i} a$ *(the relation is* complete*).*
- $a \succsim_{P_i} a$ *(the relation is* reflexive*).*
- *If* $a \succsim_{P_i} b$ *and* $b \succsim_{P_i} c$ *then* $a \succsim_{P_i} c$ *(the relation is* transitive*).*

A strict preference relation $\succ_{P_i}$ *of player i over A is a binary relation satisfying the following properties:*

- *For every pair of distinct elements* $a, b \in A$, *either* $a \succ_{P_i} b$ *or* $b \succ_{P_i} a$.
- $a \not\succ_{P_i} a$ *(the relation is* irreflexive*).*
- *If* $a \succ_{P_i} b$ *and* $b \succ_{P_i} c$ *then* $a \succ_{P_i} c$ *(the relation is* transitive*).*

When P^* is a preference relation, if $a \succsim_{P^*} b$ and $b \succsim_{P^*} a$ then we will say that a and b are *equivalent* under the preference relation P^*, and denote this by $a \approx_{P^*} b$. As the following example shows, it is possible for $a \approx_{P^*} b$ even though $a \neq b$.

If the set of alternatives $A = \{-m, -m+1, \cdots, m\}$ is a finite set of natural numbers, then the relation $\geq$ is a preference relation, and the relation $>$ is a strict preference relation. The relation $\succsim_{P_i}$ defined by $a \succsim_{P_i} b$ if and only if $|a| \geq |b|$ is also a preference relation. Note that $k \approx_{P_i} -k$. The lexicographic relation $\succsim_L$ defined as follows is also a preference relation: the set A is the following set of pairs of positive integers, $A = \{(n, m) : 1 \leq n \leq N, 1 \leq m \leq M, n \in \mathbb{N}, m \in \mathbb{N}\}$, and the relation $\succsim_L$ is defined by $(n, m) \succsim_L (\hat{n}, \hat{m})$ if and only if $n > \hat{n}$, or $n = \hat{n}$ and $m \geq \hat{m}$.

Denote by $\mathcal{P}^*(A)$ the set of all preference relations over A and by $\mathcal{P}(A)$ the set of all strict preference relations over A.

Definition 22.4 *A strict preference profile is a list* $P^N = (P_i)_{i \in N}$ *of strict preferences, one per individual. The collection of all strict preference profiles is the Cartesian product*

$$(\mathcal{P}(A))^N = \mathcal{P}(A) \times \mathcal{P}(A) \times \cdots \times \mathcal{P}(A). \tag{22.1}$$

A strict preference profile describes how each individual in society ranks all the alternatives. The problem before us is how to "aggregate" all the preferences in a strict preference profile into one preference relation, "the social preference relation."

Definition 22.5 *A social welfare function is a function F that maps each strict preference profile* $P^N = (P_i)_{i \in N} \in (\mathcal{P}(A))^N$ *to a preference relation in* $\mathcal{P}^*(A)$ *(which is denoted by* $F(P^N)$*).*

In other words, a social welfare function summarizes the opinions of everyone in society: given the strict preference relations $P^N = (P_i)_{i \in N}$ of all the individuals, society as a collective ranks the alternatives in A by way of the preference relation $F(P^N)$.

---

5 In the chapter on utility theory (Chapter 2) we studied a preference relation of an individual i and denoted it by $\succsim_i$. In this chapter we may want an individual i to have different preference relations P_i, $\hat{P}_i$, and so on. We will therefore label a relation $\succsim$ not by the name of the individual but by his preference relation, i.e., $\succsim_{P_i}$, $\succsim_{\hat{P}_i}$, and so on.

If society ranks a above b, that is, if $a \succsim_{F(P^N)} b$, we will say that society (weakly) prefers a to b.

Note that we are assuming that every individual has a strict preference relation, meaning that no one is indifferent between any pair of alternatives. But the social preference relation, on the other hand, may exhibit indifference. The following example clarifies why we choose this definition. Recall that for every finite set X we denote the number of elements in X by $|X|$.

Example 22.6 **Simple majority rule, $|A| = 2$** Suppose there are only two alternatives $A = \{a, b\}$. For each strict preference profile P^N we will denote the number of individuals who prefer a to b by:

$$m(P^N) = \left|\{i \in N : a >_{P_i} b\}\right|. \tag{22.2}$$

The simple majority rule is the social welfare function F defined by:

- If $m(P^N) > \frac{n}{2}$ then society as a whole prefers a to b: $a >_{F(P^N)} b$.
- If $m(P^N) < \frac{n}{2}$ then society as a whole prefers b to a: $b >_{F(P^N)} a$.
- If $m(P^N) = \frac{n}{2}$ then society as a whole is indifferent between a and b: $a \approx_{F(P^N)} b$.

◄

If we do not permit society to be indifferent between alternatives, then, for this to be a social welfare function, it would need to rank a versus b even when $m(P^N) = \frac{n}{2}$. To avoid a situation in which arbitrary rankings are assigned, we accept indifference in the social preference, even when there is no indifference at the individual level.

Despite this, the theorems presented in this chapter obtain even when the preferences of the individuals are not necessarily strict preferences, but weakening the assumption of strict preference may require using different proofs.

A dictatorship is a simple social welfare function: if the dictator prefers a to b, society must prefer a to b.

Definition 22.7 *A social welfare function F is* dictatorial *if there is an individual $i \in N$ such that $F(P^N) = P_i$ for every profile of strict preferences P^N. In other words, for every pair of alternatives $a, b \in A$, and every strict preference profile P^N*

$$a >_{P_i} b \implies a >_{F(P^N)} b. \tag{22.3}$$

In this case, individual i is called a dictator.

The simple majority rule (see Example 22.6) is not a dictatorial social welfare function, because every individual in society may find himself part of the minority, in which case social preference between a and b will be contrary to his preference.

The approach we adopt for studying social welfare functions is the "normative" (or "axiomatic") approach. This means we ask which "reasonable" properties we want the social welfare function to satisfy, and which mathematical conclusions we can draw regarding functions satisfying those properties.

A reasonable property one may want a social welfare function to satisfy is that if all individuals in society prefer alternative a to alternative b, then society also prefers a to b.

Definition 22.8 *A social welfare function F satisfies the property of* unanimity *if F satisfies the following condition: for every two alternatives $a, b \in A$, and every strict preference profile $P^N = (P_i)_{i \in N}$, if $a >_{P_i} b$ for every individual $i \in N$, then $a >_{F(P^N)} b$.*

A second property one might wish a social welfare function to satisfy is that the way society determines whether alternative a is preferable to alternative b depends solely on the way the individuals compare a to b.

Definition 22.9 *A social welfare function F satisfies the* independence of irrelevant alternatives (IIA) *property if for every pair of alternatives $a, b \in A$, and every pair of strict preference profiles P^N and Q^N*

$$a >_{P_i} b \iff a >_{Q_i} b, \quad \forall i \in N, \tag{22.4}$$

implies that

$$a \gtrsim_{F(P^N)} b \iff a \gtrsim_{F(Q^N)} b. \tag{22.5}$$

In other words, if every individual answers identically in both P^N and in Q^N to the question "which do you prefer between a and b?" then the social preference between a and b should be identical according to both $F(P^N)$ and $F(Q^N)$.

In the example presented above of the teachers ranking the pupils in a class, if the weighted rankings of all the teachers indicate that Ann is ranked higher than Dan, and then Tanya's grades are changed (because she retook an exam), this should have no effect on (i.e., be irrelevant to) the relative ranking of Ann and Dan: Ann should still be ranked higher than Dan.

A dictatorial social welfare function satisfies the properties of unanimity and independence of irrelevant alternatives (prove this). Similarly, when $|A| = 2$, the simple majority rule (Example 22.6) satisfies the properties of unanimity and independence of irrelevant alternatives (prove this). Can the simple majority rule be extended to any number of alternatives to yield a social welfare function that satisfies unanimity and independence of irrelevant alternatives? As the following surprising theorem shows, the answer to this question is negative.

Theorem 22.10 (Arrow [1951]) *If $|A| \geq 3$, then every social welfare function satisfying the properties of unanimity and independence of irrelevant alternatives is dictatorial.*

An equivalent formulation of the theorem is given by considering nondictatorship to be a desired property.

Definition 22.11 *A social welfare function F satisfies the property of* nondictatorship *if it is not dictatorial.*

Theorem 22.12 *If $|A| \geq 3$, there does not exist a social welfare function satisfying the properties of unanimity, independence of irrelevant alternatives, and nondictatorship.*

Theorem 22.12 is called Arrow's Impossibility Theorem. The significance of the theorem is that when we seek a social welfare function defined over the set of all preference profiles, if dictatorship is not something we desire, we must give up either unanimity or independence of irrelevant alternatives, or restrict the domain of preference profiles over which the function is defined.

Example 22.13 **Three individuals, three alternatives** Suppose there are three individuals $N = \{1, 2, 3\}$, and three alternatives $A = \{a, b, c\}$. The social welfare function F is defined as follows:

- To determine society's most-preferred alternative, first check if there is an alternative that is ranked highest by at least two individuals. If such an alternative exists, this is society's most-preferred alternative.
- If no such alternative exists, check if there is one alternative that is ranked highest or second-highest by all three individuals. If such an alternative exists, this is society's most-preferred alternative.
- If the above two checks fail to determine a most-preferred alternative for society, society is indifferent between the three alternatives.
- After the most-preferred alternative is chosen using the above rules, we use majority vote to determine the ranking of the other two alternatives.

The following table depicts several strict preference profiles, along with the social preference relation corresponding to each preference profile according to the social welfare function F:

	Individual 1	Individual 2	Individual 3	Society
1	$c >_{P_1} b >_{P_1} a$	$c >_{P_2} b >_{P_2} a$	$c >_{P_1} b >_{P_3} a$	$c >_{F(P^N)} b >_{F(P^N)} a$
2	$c >_{P_1} b >_{P_1} a$	$c >_{P_2} b >_{P_2} a$	$b >_{P_3} c >_{P_3} a$	$c >_{F(P^N)} b >_{F(P^N)} a$
3	$c >_{P_1} b >_{P_1} a$	$a >_{P_2} b >_{P_2} c$	$b >_{P_3} c >_{P_3} a$	$b >_{F(P^N)} c >_{F(P^N)} a$
4	$c >_{P_1} b >_{P_1} a$	$b >_{P_2} a >_{P_2} c$	$a >_{P_3} c >_{P_3} b$	$c \approx_{F(P^N)} b \approx_{F(P^N)} a$
5	$c >_{P_1} b >_{P_1} a$	$b >_{P_2} a >_{P_2} c$	$c >_{P_3} a >_{P_3} b$	$c >_{F(P^N)} b >_{F(P^N)} a$

This social welfare function is not dictatorial, because if two individuals share the same strict preference relation, that preference relation is also society's preference relation (check that this is true). It satisfies the unanimity property: if all the individuals prefer a to b, then either a is society's most-preferred alternative (if at least two individuals rank a highest), or c is ranked first by society and a is ranked second (if at most one individual ranks a highest according to his preference relation). In either case, society prefers a to b.

Theorem 22.10 then implies that this social welfare function cannot satisfy the independence of irrelevant alternatives property. Indeed, if we compare preference profiles 4 and 5 above, we see that in both of them $b >_{P_1} a$, $b >_{P_2} a$, $a >_{P_3} b$, but in the fourth profile $b \approx_{F(P^N)} a$, while in the fifth profile $b >_{F(P^N)} a$. ◀

In proving Theorem 22.10 we will make use of several definitions and denotations:

Definition 22.14 *A* coalition *is a set of individuals* $S \subseteq N$.

Definition 22.15 *Let F be a social welfare function, and let $a, b \in A$ be two different alternatives. A coalition $S \subseteq N$ is called* decisive *for a over b (relative to F) if for every $P^N \in (\mathcal{P}(A))^N$ satisfying:*

1. $a >_{P_i} b$ for every $i \in S$,
2. $b >_{P_j} a$ for every $j \notin S$,

one has $a >_{F(P^N)} b$. The coalition S is called decisive *(relative to F) if there exists a pair of alternatives for which it is decisive.*

In words, a set of individuals S is decisive for a over b if when every member of S prefers a to b, and all the other individuals prefer b to a, society prefers a to b.

For example, it is possible for the President, the Secretary of the Treasury, and the Chairman of the Federal Reserve to be a decisive coalition for matters pertaining to economic policy; when issues of national defense require a decision, the President, the Secretary of Defense, and the National Security Adviser may be a decisive coalition.

Before we turn our attention to the characteristics of decisive coalitions, we will check whether there always exists at least one decisive coalition. The definition of the unanimity property leads to the following theorem (Exercise 22.11).

Theorem 22.16 *Let F be a social welfare function satisfying the unanimity property. For every $a, b \in A$, the coalition N is decisive for a over b and the empty coalition $\emptyset$ is not decisive for a over b.*

The next theorem shows that when a social welfare function satisfies the property of independence of irrelevant alternatives, it is easy to check whether a particular coalition is decisive for a given pair of alternatives.

Theorem 22.17 *Let F be a social welfare function satisfying the independence of irrelevant alternatives property, and let $a, b \in A$ be two alternatives. A coalition $S \subseteq N$ is decisive for a over b, if and only if there exists a strict preference profile P^N satisfying:*

(a1) $a >_{P_i} b$ for all $i \in S$,
(a2) $b >_{P_j} a$ for all $j \notin S$,
(a3) and $a >_{F(P^N)} b$.

It follows that if a coalition S is not decisive for a over b, and if a strict preference profile P^N satisfies:

(b1) $a >_{P_i} b$ for all $i \in S$,
(b2) $b >_{P_j} a$ for all $j \notin S$,

then $b \succsim_{F(P^N)} a$.

In other words, the theorem states that if the function F satisfies the independence of irrelevant alternatives property, then the condition "for all $P^N \in (\mathcal{P}(A))^N \cdots$" in Definition 22.15 can be replaced by the condition "there exists $P^N \in (\mathcal{P}(A))^N \cdots$."

Proof: Start with the first direction: suppose that S is decisive for a over b. Let P^N be a strict preference profile satisfying (a1) and (a2) (give an example of such a preference profile). Since the coalition S is decisive for a over b, (a3) is satisfied, and P^N therefore satisfies (a1)–(a3), as required.

For the other direction, we need to show that if there exists a strict preference profile P^N satisfying the three conditions, then S is decisive for a over b. In other words, we need to show that every strict preference profile Q^N that satisfies the first two conditions also satisfies the third condition. But that follows from the fact that F satisfies the independence of irrelevant alternatives property.

The second part of the statement follows from the first part.   □

The next theorem states that if a coalition is decisive for a^* over b^*, then it is decisive for all pairs of alternatives.

Theorem 22.18 *Suppose that* $|A| \geq 3$ *and that F satisfies the unanimity and independence of irrelevant alternatives properties. If coalition V is decisive for* a^* *over* b^*, *then V is decisive for any pair of alternatives in A.*

Proof: Let a and b be a pair of alternatives.

Part 1: If V is decisive for a over b then V is decisive for a over c, for any alternative $c \in A\backslash\{a\}$.

If $c = b$ the claim follows by assumption. Otherwise $c \in A\backslash\{a, b\}$. Consider the following strict preference profile P^N:

$$\begin{cases} a >_{P_i} b >_{P_i} c & i \in V, \\ b >_{P_i} c >_{P_i} a & i \notin V. \end{cases} \tag{22.6}$$

All the other alternatives in A are ordered by each individual arbitrarily.

As V is decisive for a over b, it follows that $a >_{F(P^N)} b$. Since F satisfies the unanimity property, $b >_{F(P^N)} c$. Since $F(P^N)$ is a transitive ordering relation, we deduce that $a >_{F(P^N)} c$. Theorem 22.17 then implies that V is decisive for a over c.

Part 2: If V is decisive for a over b then V is decisive for b over c, for any $c \in A\backslash\{a, b\}$.

Let $c \in A\backslash\{a, b\}$. Consider the following strict preference profile P^N:

$$\begin{cases} b >_{P_i} a >_{P_i} c & i \in V, \\ c >_{P_i} b >_{P_i} a & i \notin V. \end{cases} \tag{22.7}$$

All the other alternatives in A are ordered by each individual arbitrarily.

From Part 1 it follows that V is decisive for a over c, and therefore $a >_{F(P^N)} c$. Since F satisfies the unanimity property, $b >_{F(P^N)} a$. Since $F(P^N)$ is a transitive ordering relation, we deduce that $b >_{F(P^N)} c$. Theorem 22.17 then implies that V is decisive for b over c.

Part 3: The first two parts are sufficient for proving Theorem 22.18.

Let $a \neq b$ be any pair of alternatives in A. We will prove that V is decisive for a over b. Recall that V is decisive for a^* over b^*.

- If $a = a^*$, from Part 1 and the fact that V is decisive for a^* over b^*, we deduce that V is decisive for a over b.
- If $a \neq a^*$ and $b \neq a^*$, from Part 1 and the fact that V is decisive for a^* over b^*, one has that V is decisive for a^* over a. That in turn implies from Part 2 that V is decisive for a over b.
- If $a \neq a^*$ and $b = a^*$, then there exists an alternative $c \in A\backslash\{a, b\}$ since A contains at least three alternatives (it is possible for $c = b^*$). From Part 1, and the fact that V is decisive for a^* over b^*, one has that V is decisive for b over c. From Part 2, this then implies that V is decisive for c over a. Finally, Part 2 implies that V is decisive for a over b.

This concludes the proof of Theorem 22.18. $\qquad\qquad\qquad\qquad\qquad\qquad\qquad$ $\square$

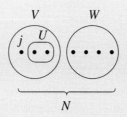

Figure 22.1 The notations of the proof of Claim 22.19

We next prove Theorem 22.10.

Proof of Theorem 22.10 (Arrow's Theorem): Let F be a social welfare function satisfying the properties of unanimity and independence of irrelevant alternatives. We show that there exists a decisive coalition containing a single individual, who is a dictator.

Claim 22.19 *There exists a decisive coalition V containing a single individual.*

Proof: Let V be a nonempty decisive coalition containing a minimal number of individuals. Since by Theorem 22.16 the coalition N is decisive and the empty coalition $\emptyset$ is not decisive, there must exist such a coalition V. If V contains a single individual, there is nothing more to prove. Suppose that V contains at least two individuals; we will show that this leads to a contradiction.

Let $j \in V$. Denote $U = V \setminus \{j\}$ and $W = N \setminus V$ (see Figure 22.1). Since V contains at least two individuals, the coalition U is nonempty. Since by definition, V contains a minimal number of individuals among the nonempty decisive coalitions, the coalition U is nondecisive, and the coalition $\{j\}$ is nondecisive.

Since $|A| \geq 3$, we can choose three distinct alternatives a, b, c. Consider the strict preference profile $P^N = (P_i)_{i \in N}$ defined as follows:

$$\begin{cases} a >_{P_i} b >_{P_i} c & i = j, \\ c >_{P_i} a >_{P_i} b & i \in U, \\ b >_{P_i} c >_{P_i} a & i \in W. \end{cases} \tag{22.8}$$

The other alternatives in A are ordered by each individual arbitrarily.

Since V is decisive, it is decisive for any pair of alternatives (Theorem 22.18). In particular, it is decisive for a over b. Since $a >_{P_i} b$, for every individual $i \in V = U \cup \{j\}$ and $b >_{P_i} a$ for every individual $i \in N \setminus V = W$, one has $a >_{F(P^N)} b$. Since U is not decisive, it is not decisive for c over b. Since $c >_{P_i} b$ for every individual $i \in U$ and $b >_{P_i} c$ for every individual $i \in N \setminus U = W \cup \{j\}$, Theorem 22.17 implies that $b \gtrsim_{F(P^N)} c$. Since $F(P^N)$ is a transitive ordering relation, we deduce that $a >_{F(P^N)} c$.

Note that $a >_{P_i} c$ for $i = j$, and $c >_{P_i} a$ for all $i \neq j$. By Theorem 22.17 we conclude that $\{j\}$ is a decisive coalition for a over c, and it is therefore a decisive coalition, contradicting the assumption that $\{j\}$ is not a decisive coalition. This contradiction establishes that $|V| = 1$. □

Let $V = \{j\}$ be a decisive coalition containing a single individual. We next prove that j is a dictator.

Claim 22.20 *Individual j is a dictator, i.e., $F(P^N) = P_j$ for every $P^N = (P_i)_{i \in N} \in (\mathcal{P}(A))^N$.*

Proof: Let P^N be a strict preference profile, and let $a, b \in A$ be two different alternatives such that $a >_{P_j} b$. We wish to show that $a >_{F(P^N)} b$.

Since A contains at least three alternatives, there exists an alternative $c \in A \setminus \{a, b\}$. Consider the following strict preference profile Q^N:

$$\begin{cases} a >_{Q_i} c >_{Q_i} b & i = j, \\ c >_{Q_i} a >_{Q_i} b & i \neq j, a >_{P_i} b, \\ c >_{Q_i} b >_{Q_i} a & i \neq j, b >_{P_i} a. \end{cases} \tag{22.9}$$

The other alternatives in A are ordered by each individual arbitrarily. Since $V = \{j\}$ is decisive for any two alternatives, it is in particular decisive for a over c, and therefore $a >_{F(Q^N)} c$. Since F satisfies the unanimity property, it follows that $c >_{F(Q^N)} b$. Since $F(Q^N)$ is a transitive ordering relation, we deduce that $a >_{F(Q^N)} b$.

Now, individual j prefers a over b, both according to P_j, and according to Q_j, and every individual $i \neq j$ prefers a over b according to P_i if and only if he prefers a over b according to Q_i. Since F satisfies the independence of irrelevant alternatives property, and since $a >_{F(Q^N)} b$, we deduce that $a >_{F(P^N)} b$, as required. □

We have proved that there exists a decisive coalition containing a single individual, and that this individual is a dictator. The proof of Theorem 22.10 is complete. □

One might imagine that the conclusion of the theorem holds because we asked for too much: we want a social welfare function to rank all the alternatives. The next section, however, shows that a similar negative result holds even if all we ask is for society to choose its most-preferred alternative.

22.2　Social choice functions

In many cases, society is not required to rank all possible alternatives, because it suffices to choose only one alternative. Examples of such situations include the election of a president, congressman, or committee chairman. An additional example is the selection by policymakers of the "best possible" political or economic policy, from a range of alternative policies. In this section, we study the question of associating every strict preference profile with one alternative that is most preferred by society, and striving to ensure that the process of choosing the most-preferred alternative satisfies desirable properties without being dictatorial.

Definition 22.21 *A social choice function is a function $G : (\mathcal{P}(A))^n \to A$.*

A social choice function associates every strict preference profile with one alternative, which is called society's "most-preferred alternative." By this definition, society cannot choose two different alternatives as most preferred, and it is not possible to choose the most-preferred alternative by tossing a coin.

It is reasonable to require that a social choice function be monotonic; if P^N and Q^N are two preference profiles in which, for each individual i, the ranking of a in Q^i is not lower that its ranking in P^i, and if $G(P^N) = a$, then $G(Q^N) = a$ as well.

Definition 22.22 *A social choice function G is called* monotonic *if for every pair of strict preference profiles P^N and Q^N satisfying*

$$a >_{P_i} c \implies a >_{Q_i} c, \quad \forall c \neq a, \forall i \in N, \tag{22.10}$$

if $G(P^N) = a$, then $G(Q^N) = a$.

Dictatorship is a simple social choice function:

Definition 22.23 *A social choice function G is* dictatorial *if there is an individual i such that for every strict preference profile P^N, $G(P^N)$ is the preferred alternative of individual i. Such an individual i is called a* dictator.

A dictatorial social choice function is monotonic (prove this).

Example 22.24 **Simple majority rule, $|A| = 2$** Denote $A = \{a, b\}$. When n is larger than 1 and odd, the social choice function defined by majority rule is monotonic and nondictatorial (prove this).

When n is even, the social choice function defined by majority rule, where alternative a is chosen in case of a tied vote, is monotonic and nondictatorial. ◀

Example 22.25 Order the alternatives according to: $A = \{1, 2, \ldots, K\}$, where K is the number of alternatives. From among the alternatives that at least one individual most prefers, choose the one of minimal index:

$$F(P^N) = \min \{k \in A : \text{ there exists } i \in N \text{ such that } k >_{P_i} b \text{ for all } b \in A \setminus \{k\}\}. \tag{22.11}$$

This social choice function is neither dictatorial nor monotonic (Exercise 22.19). ◀

As for social welfare functions, it is reasonable to require that social choice functions satisfy the property that if every individual prefers a to every other alternative, then society as a whole should prefer alternative a.

Definition 22.26 *A social choice function G satisfies the property of* unanimity *if for every alternative $a \in A$, and every strict preference profile $P^N = (P_i)_{i \in N}$: if $a >_{P_i} b$ for every individual $i \in N$ and every alternative $b \neq a$, then $G(P^N) = a$.*

If G satisfies unanimity, the range of G is A: for every alternative $a \in A$, there exists a strict preference profile P^N satisfying $G(P^N) = a$ (give an example of such a profile).

Theorem 22.27 *If $|A| \geq 3$, all social choice functions satisfying the properties of unanimity and monotonicity are dictatorial.*

Before proving this theorem, we need several definitions and properties of monotonic social choice functions.

Let P and Q be two strict preference relations over a set of alternatives A, and let R be a subset of the set of alternatives A. Define a strict preference relation over A as follows: place the elements of R prior to the elements that are not in R; the strict preference relation

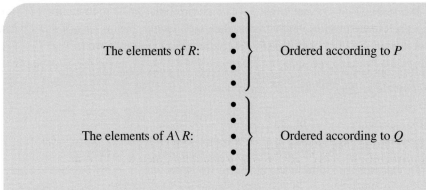

Figure 22.2 The preference relation $Z(P, Q; R)$

over the elements of R is given by P, and the strict preference relation over the elements that are not in R is given by Q (see Figure 22.2). This strict preference relation is denoted $Z(P, Q; R)$.

The formal definition is as follows:

Definition 22.28 *Let P and Q be strict preference relations, and let $R \subseteq A$ be a subset of alternatives. Denote by $Z(P, Q; R)$ the following strict preference relation:*

- *$Z(P, Q; R)$ is identical with P over R: if $a, b \in R$ then*

$$a >_{Z(P,Q;R)} b \iff a >_P b. \tag{22.12}$$

- *$Z(P, Q; R)$ is identical with Q over $A \backslash R$: if $a, b \notin R$ then*

$$a >_{Z(P,Q;R)} b \iff a >_Q b. \tag{22.13}$$

- *The alternatives in R are preferred to the alternatives not in R: if $a \in R$ and $b \notin R$, then $a >_{Z(P,Q;R)} b$.*

Example 22.29 Suppose that the set of alternatives is $A = \{a_1, a_2, a_3, a_4\}$, and $R = \{a_1, a_4\}$. Furthermore, suppose that two strict preference relations P and Q are given by

$$a_1 >_P a_2 >_P a_3 >_P a_4,$$
$$a_2 >_Q a_4 >_Q a_1 >_Q a_3. \tag{22.14}$$

The relation $Z(P, Q; R)$ is given by

$$a_1 >_{Z(P,Q;R)} a_4 >_{Z(P,Q;R)} a_2 >_{Z(P,Q;R)} a_3. \tag{22.15}$$

◀

The analogue to Definition 22.28 for strict preference relations is the following:

Definition 22.30 *Let P^N and Q^N be two strict preference profiles, and let $R \subseteq A$ be a subset of alternatives. Denote by $Z(P^N, Q^N; R)$ the strict preference profile in which the strict preference of individual i is $Z(P_i, Q_i; R)$, for each $i \in N$.*

Let $a \in R$ be an alternative in R, and suppose that $G(P^N) = a$. Compared to the strict preference profile P^N, in the strict preference relation $Z(P_i, Q_i; R)$ the ranking of the alternatives in R is improved relative to the alternatives not in R. If the social choice function is monotonic, one would expect that after this improvement, society chooses a. This property is expressed in the next theorem, whose proof is left as an exercise to the reader (Exercise 22.25).

Theorem 22.31 *Let G be a monotonic social choice function, let P^N and Q^N be two strict preference profiles, and let $R \subseteq A$. If $a \in R$, and $G(P^N) = a$, then $G(Z(P^N, Q^N; R)) = a$. Equivalently, if $G(Z(P^N, Q^N; R)) \neq a$ and $a \in R$, then $G(P^N) \neq a$.*

Theorem 22.32 *Let G be a monotonic social choice function satisfying the property of unanimity, let P^N be a strict preference profile, and let $a, b \in A$. If*

$$a >_{P_i} b, \quad \forall i \in N, \tag{22.16}$$

then $G(P^N) \neq b$.

In words, under the conditions of the theorem, if there is an alternative b that is ranked by all of the individuals below a, then alternative b is not chosen by society.

Proof: Define $Q^N := Z(P^N, P^N; \{a\})$. Under the preference profile Q^N, all individuals rank a highest. Since G satisfies unanimity, $G(Q^N) = a$. Suppose, by contradiction, that $G(P^N) = b$. Since all the individuals prefer a to b according to both P^N and Q^N, and since the preference relations of all the individuals over the set of alternatives $A \setminus \{a\}$ according to both P^N and Q^N are identical, it follows that for each individual i,

$$b >_{P_i} c \iff b >_{Q_i} c, \quad \forall c \neq b. \tag{22.17}$$

Since G is monotonic, we deduce that $G(Q^N) = b$, contradicting $G(Q^N) = a$. This contradiction shows that the original supposition was wrong, and therefore $G(P^N) \neq b$. □

Under the strict preference profile $Z(P^N, Q^N; R)$, every individual prefers every result in R to every result not in R. This leads to the following corollary of Theorem 22.32.

Corollary 22.33 *Let G be a monotonic social choice function satisfying unanimity, let P^N and Q^N be two strict profile preferences, and let $R \subseteq A$. If R is nonempty, then $G(Z(P^N, Q^N; R)) \in R$.*

Proof of Theorem 22.27: We will prove that a monotonic social choice function G satisfying the unanimity property is dictatorial. Towards this end, using the social choice function G we will construct a social welfare function F. We will show that if G is monotonic and satisfies the unanimity property then F satisfies unanimity and independence of irrelevant alternatives. Using Theorem 22.10 (page 907) we will then deduce that F is dictatorial. In conclusion, we will show that the dictator in the social welfare function F is also the dictator in the social choice function G.

Let $W^N \in (\mathcal{P}(A))^N$ be a strict preference profile. Fix this profile throughout the rest of the proof.

Step 1: Defining the function F.

For every strict preference profile P^N, define a binary relation $F(P^N)$ as follows. For every pair of distinct alternatives $a, b \in A$,

$$G(Z(P^N, W^N; \{a, b\})) = a \implies a >_{F(P^N)} b, \tag{22.18}$$

$$G(Z(P^N, W^N; \{a, b\})) = b \implies b >_{F(P^N)} a. \tag{22.19}$$

For this relation to be reflexive, define, in addition,

$$a \succsim_{F(P^N)} a, \quad \forall a \in A. \tag{22.20}$$

We will prove that F is a social welfare function, by showing that the binary relation $F(P^N)$ is complete and transitive.

By Corollary 22.33, $G(Z(P^N, W^N; \{a, b\})) \in \{a, b\}$. Equations (22.18) and (22.19) then imply that for every pair of distinct alternatives a, b in A, either $a >_{F(P^N)} b$, or $b >_{F(P^N)} a$, i.e., $F(P^N)$ is a complete preference relation over R. Note that the relation $F(P^N)$ expresses no indifference: either society strictly prefers a to b, or it strictly prefers b to a.

Step 2: $F(P^N)$ is a transitive relation.

Suppose by contradiction that for $a, b, c \in A$ one has $a >_{F(P^N)} b$, $b >_{F(P^N)} c$, but $c >_{F(P^N)} a$. It is not possible that $a = c$, since if $a = c$ one deduces that both $a >_{F(P^N)} b$ and $b >_{F(P^N)} a$, which is impossible. It follows that a, b, and c are distinct alternatives.

Since $a >_{F(P^N)} b$, one has $G(Z(P^N, W^N; \{a, b\})) = a$. Note that the following identity holds:

$$Z(P^N, W^N; \{a, b\}) = Z(Z(P^N, P^N; \{a, b, c\}), W^N; \{a, b\}). \tag{22.21}$$

To see this, over the complement of $\{a, b\}$ the preference relation is determined in both cases by W^N, while over $\{a, b\}$, the preference relation is determined in both cases by P^N.

Equation (22.21) and $a >_{F(P^N)} b$ imply that

$$G(Z(Z(P^N, P^N; \{a, b, c\})), W^N; \{a, b\}) = a. \tag{22.22}$$

In particular:

$$G(Z(Z(P^N, P^N; \{a, b, c\})), W^N; \{a, b\}) \neq b. \tag{22.23}$$

Theorem 22.31 implies that

$$G(Z(P^N, P^N; \{a, b, c\})) \neq b. \tag{22.24}$$

We have therefore shown that

$$a >_{F(P^N)} b \implies G(Z(P^N, P^N; \{a, b, c\})) \neq b. \tag{22.25}$$

Similarly, since $b >_{F(P^N)} c$, we deduce that

$$G(Z(P^N, P^N; \{a, b, c\})) \neq c, \tag{22.26}$$

and since $c >_{F(P^N)} a$, we get

$$G(Z(P^N, P^N; \{a, b, c\})) \neq a. \tag{22.27}$$

Equations (22.24), (22.26), and (22.27) imply that

$$G(Z(P^N, P^N; \{a, b, c\})) \notin \{a, b, c\}. \tag{22.28}$$

On the other hand, by Corollary 22.33, $G(Z(P^N, P^N; \{a, b, c\})) \in \{a, b, c\}$, contradicting Equation (22.28). We deduce that the assumption that the relation $F(P^N)$ is not transitive is false.

We have shown that $F(P^N)$ is a complete, reflexive and transitive relation, and therefore F is a social welfare function.

Step 3: The social welfare function F satisfies the unanimity property.
Let $a \neq b$ be two alternatives in A, and let P^N be a strict preference profile satisfying $a >_{P_i} b$ for every $i \in N$. This means that for every $i \in N$, the alternative a is most preferred under the strict preference relation $Z(P_i, W_i; \{a, b\})$. Theorem 22.32 and Corollary 22.33 imply that $G(Z(P^N, W^N; \{a, b\})) = a$, and by Equation (22.18) one has $a >_{F(P^N)} b$.

Step 4: The social welfare function F satisfies the independence of irrelevant alternatives property.
Let $a, b \in A$ be two distinct alternatives, and let P^N, Q^N be two strict preference profiles satisfying

$$a >_{P_i} b \iff a >_{Q_i} b, \quad \forall i \in N. \tag{22.29}$$

It follows that for every $i \in N$,

$$Z(P_i, W_i; \{a, b\}) = Z(Q_i, W_i; \{a, b\}). \tag{22.30}$$

To see this, in both strict preference relations, the alternatives $\{a, b\}$ are preferred to all the other alternatives; the strict preference relation over the alternatives that are not in $\{a, b\}$ is determined in both cases by W_i, and by Equation (22.29), the ranking between a and b is identical in both cases.

By the definition of F,

$$a >_{F(P^N)} b \iff a >_{F(Q^N)} b, \tag{22.31}$$

and therefore the function F satisfies the property of independence of irrelevant alternatives.

Step 5: Using Theorem 22.10 (page 907).
Since F is a social welfare function satisfying the properties of unanimity and independence of irrelevant alternatives, and since A contains at least three alternatives, we can apply Theorem 22.10. This enables us to deduce that F is dictatorial. In other words, there is an individual i such that

$$F(P^N) = P_i, \quad \forall P^N \in (\mathcal{P}(A))^N. \tag{22.32}$$

We will next show that i is also a dictator in the social choice function G.

Let P^N be a strict preference relation, and suppose that a is the alternative most preferred by individual i. To see that i is a dictator under G, we need to show that $G(P^N) = a$. Let $b \neq a$ be an alternative. Since a is the alternative preferred by individual i, one has $a >_{P_i} b$. Since i is a dictator under F, one also has $a >_{F(P^N)} b$. The definition of F implies that $G(Z(P^N, W^N; \{a, b\})) = a \neq b$, and Theorem 22.31 implies that $G(P^N) \neq b$. Since this is true for every alternative $b \neq a$, we deduce that $G(P^N) = a$. This establishes that G is a dictatorial social choice function, thus completing the proof of Theorem 22.27. □

Theorem 22.27 states that dictatorial social choice functions are the only monotonic social choice functions satisfying the property of unanimity. As the following example shows, there do exist monotonic social choice functions that are not dictatorial (but they do not satisfy the property of unanimity).

Example 22.34 The set of alternatives is $A = \{a, b, c\}$, and $N = \{1, 2\}$. Consider the social choice function F defined by

$$F(P^N) := \begin{cases} b & b >_{P_1} c, \\ c & c >_{P_1} b. \end{cases} \tag{22.33}$$

In words, the alternative that is chosen by society is the alternative preferred by Player 1 from the set $\{b, c\}$. This social choice function is not dictatorial since alternative a will not be chosen even if it is the preferred alternative of both players, and hence neither player is a dictator. This also shows that F does not satisfy the property of unanimity. ◄

This example leads to the introduction of the following concept. Denote the image of a social choice function G by range(G):

$$\text{range}(G) = \{a \in A : \text{ there exists } P^N \in (\mathcal{P}(A))^N \text{ for which } G(P^N) = a\}. \tag{22.34}$$

That is, range(G) is the set of alternatives that may be chosen by society, if society applies the social choice function G. If a social choice function G satisfies the unanimity property then range$(G) = A$.

Theorem 22.35, whose proof is left to the reader (Exercise 22.27), is the generalization of Theorem 22.27 to the case in which range$(G) \neq A$.

Theorem 22.35 *For any monotonic social choice function G satisfying $|\text{range}(G)| \geq 3$, there exists a player i such that for every strict preference profile P^N, the alternative $G(P^N)$ is player i's preferred alternative from among the alternatives in* range(G).

22.3 Non-manipulability

The model presented in the previous section is a model in which each individual is assumed to report (to, say, a governing body) his or her strict preference relation over the set of alternatives, with the social choice function then choosing an alternative that is declared to be society's most-preferred alternative. The model thus assumes implicitly that each individual reports his or her true preference relation. But why should an individual always report his or her true preference relation? Perhaps there might be cases in which by reporting a preference relation that is different from his true preference, an individual can cause society to choose an alternative that is more preferred by him than the alternative that would be chosen if he were to report his true preference relation. If this is possible, we say that the social choice function is manipulable.

Given a strict preference profile P^N, denote by $P_{-i} = (P_j)_{j \neq i}$ the strict preferences of all the individuals who are not individual i. In other words, (P_i, P_{-i}) is an alternative denotation for the profile P^N.

Definition 22.36 *A social choice function G is called* manipulable *if there exist a strict preference profile P^N, an individual $i \in N$, and a strict preference relation Q_i satisfying*

$$G(Q_i, P_{-i}) >_{P_i} G(P^N). \tag{22.35}$$

In words, a social choice function G is manipulable if there exists a strict preference profile such that there is an individual who can, by reporting a strict preference relation different from his true one, cause society to choose an alternative that is more preferred by him than the alternative that would be chosen if he were to report his true preference relation. If this is not possible, the social choice function is called *nonmanipulable*. If a social choice function is nonmanipulable, the situation in which every individual reports his or her true strict preference relation is a Nash equilibrium in the game in which the set of strategies of each individual is the set of strict preference relations $\mathcal{P}(A)$, and the outcome is the alternative chosen by society.

Remark 22.37 *Definition 22.36 touches on the possibility that a single individual may influence the alternative that is chosen by reporting a preference relation that differs from his true preference relation. As we saw in Example 22.1, social choice functions may also be manipulable by sets of individuals. We will not expand on this idea in this chapter.* ◆

A dictatorial social choice function is nonmanipulable. The dictator cannot gain by reporting a strict preference relation that is different from his true preference relation, because society's choice is always the most-preferred alternative that he reports. Neither can the other individuals gain by reporting false preference relations, because their reported preference relations have no effect on society's choice, in any event. The next example presents a social choice function that is manipulable by a single voter.

Example 22.38 **A manipulable social choice function** Lisa (individual 1), Mickey (individual 2), and Emily (individual 3) comprise the membership of a village social committee, charged with choosing the theme of the annual village social event. The committee makes its choice by majority vote. If each committee member votes for a different alternative, the deciding vote is the one cast by Lisa, the committee chairman. Three alternatives have been suggested: a bingo night (B), a dance party (D), or a village singalong (S).

Consider the following strict preference profile P^N in which P_1 is Lisa's preference relation, P_2 is Mickey's preference relation, and P_3 is Emily's preference relation:

$$P^N: \quad \begin{array}{l} B >_{P_1} D >_{P_1} S, \\ D >_{P_2} B >_{P_2} S, \\ S >_{P_3} D >_{P_3} B. \end{array} \tag{22.36}$$

If Lisa, Mickey, and Emily all report their true preference relations, the chosen alternative will be a bingo night. If, however, Emily changes her reported preference relation to

$$D >_{Q_3} S >_{Q_3} B, \tag{22.37}$$

the chosen alternative will be a dance party, which Emily prefers to bingo. We see that the social choice function in this example, in which the majority rule is applied, with the committee chairman granted the tie-breaking vote, is manipulable. ◄

Gibbard [1973] and Satterthwaite [1975] proved the following theorem:

Theorem 22.39 (Gibbard, Satterthwaite) *Let G be a nonmanipulable social choice function satisfying the unanimity property. If $|A| \geq 3$ then G is dictatorial.*

The practical implication of this theorem is that if we wish to apply a nondictatorial social choice function, there are necessarily situations in which one (or more) of the individuals has an incentive to report a preference relation that is different from his or her true preference relation.

Proof: By Theorem 22.27, it suffices to show that every nonmanipulable social choice function that satisfies the unanimity property is monotonic.

Let G be a nonmanipulable social choice function satisfying the unanimity property. Suppose that G is not monotonic, i.e., that there exist two distinct strict preference profiles P^N and Q^N, and two distinct alternatives a, b such that

$$a >_{P_i} c \quad \Longrightarrow \quad a >_{Q_i} c, \quad \forall c \neq a, \forall i \in N, \tag{22.38}$$

while

$$G(P^N) = a, \text{ and } G(Q^N) = b. \tag{22.39}$$

Since P^N and Q^N are distinct strict preference profiles there is at least one individual i for whom $P_i \neq Q_i$. From among all pairs of alternatives a, b and strict preference profiles P^N and Q^N with respect to which the above conditions hold, choose those for which the number of individuals i for which $P_i \neq Q_i$ is minimal.

For such P^N and Q^N, denote by I the set of individuals i for whom $P_i \neq Q_i$:

$$I = \{i \in N : P_i \neq Q_i\}. \tag{22.40}$$

By assumption, the set I contains at least one individual.

Let j be an individual in I. We claim that $G(P_j, Q_{-j}) = a$. Suppose by contradiction that $G(P_j, Q_{-j}) = c \neq a$ (c may be equal to b). The pair of alternatives a, c, along with the pair of strict preference profiles P^N and (P_j, Q_{-j}) satisfy the above conditions but the number of individuals whose strict preference relations differ in the two profiles is $|I| - 1$ (because the preferences of individual j in the profiles P^N and (P_j, Q_{-j}) are identical), which contradicts the minimality of I. This contradiction establishes that indeed $G(P_j, Q_{-j}) = a$.

In summary, we have deduced that $G(Q^N) = b$ and $G(P_j, Q_{-j}) = a$. Since G is nonmanipulable, when the preference profile is Q^N, individual j has no incentive to report P_j as his preference profile, and therefore

$$b = G(Q^N) >_{Q_j} G(P_j, Q_{-j}) = a. \tag{22.41}$$

Similarly, since G is nonmanipulable, when the preference profile is (P_j, Q_{-j}), individual j has no incentive to report Q_j as his preference profile, and therefore:

$$a = G(P_j, Q_{-j}) >_{P_j} G(Q^N) = b. \tag{22.42}$$

Equations (22.38) and (22.42) imply that

$$a >_{Q_j} b. \tag{22.43}$$

Equation (22.43) contradicts Equation (22.41). This contradiction establishes that G is monotonic. $\qquad\square$

22.4 Discussion

In this chapter, we have studied the question of how to aggregate the preferences of a group of individuals into a single "social preference." The approach we have adopted is the normative, or axiomatic, approach. In other words, to construct a choice function that associates every strict preference profile of individual preference relations with a social preference relation, we asked what properties such a function should satisfy. Surprisingly, this led us to conclude that if there are at least three alternatives, seemingly natural and reasonable properties cannot hold unless the choice function is dictatorial.

The most fundamental result in this section is Arrow's Impossibility Theorem (Theorem 22.10 on page 907), which states that when there are at least three alternatives that are to be ranked, the only social welfare function satisfying the properties of unanimity and independence of irrelevant alternatives is dictatorial. This implies that the only social choice function (which chooses one alternative, "the best alternative," based on the strict preference profiles of the individuals) satisfying monotonicity or nonmanipulability is again dictatorial.

These results form the foundations of an important branch of study (especially for the disciplines of economics and political science) called "social choice." One way to obtain positive results in this field is to limit the domain of the social welfare (or choice) functions. In other words, if one does not allow individuals to have every possible preference relation, and instead restricts preference relations to a smaller set than the set of all preference relations, it is in some cases possible to obtain positive results. For example, when studying political or economic preferences (from conservative to liberal) it is customary to assume that preferences are single-peaked, meaning that every individual has an "ideal point" along a scale of alternatives that he prefers, with his ranking of other alternatives decreasing the farther those alternatives are from his ideal point. If one assumes that preferences are single-peaked, it is possible to find social choice functions that are not dictatorial and satisfy monotonicity or nonmanipulability.

Another direction of inquiry in social choice theory involves "taking manipulation into account": constructing games whose sole equilibria are "desired outcomes." In other words, one studies implementations of social choice functions by appropriate game mechanisms, taking into account that each individual will do his best to have his preferred alternatives chosen (possibly by not reporting his true preferences). The interested reader is directed to Peleg [1984] for a detailed analysis of this subject.

22.5 Remarks

Example 22.1 was first presented by Borda [1784]. The interested reader may find three simple proofs of Theorem 22.10 in Geanakoplos [2005].

Both the Borda Method (Exercise 22.3) and the Condorcet Method (Exercise 22.4) were suggested as early as the thirteenth century by Ramon Llull. Approval voting (see Exercise 22.28) was used as the voting procedure of the Major Council of the Republic of

Venice in the Middle Ages. Exercise 22.5 is based on an example appearing in Balinski and Laraki [2007]. The authors thank Rida Laraki for kindly answering many questions during the composition of this chapter.

22.6 Exercises

22.1 For each of the following relations, determine whether it is complete, reflexive, irreflexive, or transitive, and use this to determine whether it is a preference relation or a strict preference relation.

(a) A is the set of all subsets of some set S, and $a \succsim b$ if and only if b is a subset of a.

(b) A is the set of all natural numbers, and $a \succsim b$ if and only if b is a divisor of a (i.e., $a = bq$ for some integer q).

(c) A is the set of all 26 letters in the Latin alphabet, and $\alpha \succsim \beta$ if and only if $\alpha\beta$ is a standard word in English (where α is the first letter of the word, and β the second letter of the word).

(d) A is the set of all natural numbers, and $a \succsim b$ if and only if $a \times b = 30$.

(e) A is the set of all human beings, past and present, and $b \succsim a$ if and only if a is a descendant of b (meaning a child, grandchild, great-grandchild, etc.).

(f) A is the set of people living in a particular neighborhood, and $a \succsim b$ if and only if a likes b.

22.2 Show that if P^* is a strict preference relation then $P := P^* \cup \{(a,a) : a \in A\}$ is a preference relation.

22.3 The Borda Method The French mathematician Borda proposed the following voting method. Every voter ranks the candidates, from most preferred to least preferred. A candidate receives k points (called Borda points) from a voter if that voter ranks the candidate higher than exactly k other candidates. The Borda ranking of a candidate is given by the total number of Borda points he receives from all the voters. The winning candidate (called the Borda winner) is then the candidate who has amassed the most Borda points.

(a) For every pair of candidates a and b, let $N_{a,b}$ be the number of voters ranking a ahead of b. Show that the Borda ranking of candidate a equals $\sum_{b \neq a} N_{a,b}$.

(b) Compute the Borda ranking, and the Borda winner, from among the three candidates A, B, and C in Example 22.2.

22.4 The Condorcet Method The French mathematician Condorcet proposed the following method for determining a social preference order based on the strict preferences of the individuals in society. A voter i with a strict preference order P_i grants k Condorcet points to a strict preference relation P if there are exactly k pairs of alternatives a, b satisfying $b >_P a$ and $b >_{P_i} a$. The number of Condorcet points amassed by the strict preference relation P is the total sum of the Condorcet points it receives from all the voters. The strict social preference order is the one that has amassed the greatest number of Condorcet points.

(a) Is the strict preference relation amassing the greatest number of Condorcet points unique? If yes, prove this claim. If no, present a counterexample.

(b) Show that if there exists a Condorcet winner, then every strict preference relation receiving the maximal number of Condorcet points ranks the Condorcet winner highest in its preference ordering.

(c) Find the number of Condorcet points that each strict preference relation receives in Examples 22.1 and 22.2, and determine the preference relation that the Condorcet Method chooses.

22.5 The Borda and Condorcet Methods The following example was presented by Condorcet, in a critique of the Borda Method. A committee composed of 81 members is to choose a winner from among three candidates, A, B, and C. The rankings of the committee members appear in the following table:

No. of voters	First candidate	Second candidate	Third candidate
30	A	B	C
1	A	C	B
29	B	A	C
10	B	C	A
10	C	A	B
1	C	B	A

(a) Is there a Condorcet winner? If yes, who is the Condorcet winner?

(b) What is the Borda ranking, and who is the Borda winner?

(c) Based on your answers above, what is Condorcet's critique of the Borda Method?

A counterclaim to Condorcet's critique might be given by analyzing the preference profile in the following way. A *Condorcet component* is a set of $3n$ individuals whose strict preference relations are as follows:

No. of voters	First candidate	Second candidate	Third candidate
n	a_1	a_2	a_3
n	a_3	a_1	a_2
n	a_2	a_3	a_1

The variables a_1, a_2, a_3 are three distinct alternatives (this example can be generalized to an arbitrary number of alternatives). In a certain sense, these voters "neutralize" each other, and they can therefore be removed from the list of voters.

(a) What are all the Condorcet components in this example?

(b) Remove all the individuals appearing in one of the Condorcet components. From among the remaining individuals, find another Condorcet component and remove all the individuals in that component. Repeat this process until there remain no Condorcet components. Is there a Condorcet winner according to the strict preference profile that remains at the end of this process? If so, which candidate is the Condorcet winner?

(c) Given the above two items, elucidate a counterclaim to Condorcet's critique of the Borda Method.

22.6 Show that there is at most one dictator in every social welfare function F: if i is a dictator in F, and j is also a dictator in F, then $i = j$.

22.7 A committee comprised of 15 members is called upon to rank three colors: red, blue, and yellow, from most preferred to least preferred. The committee members simultaneously announce their strict preference relations over the three colors. If red is the preferred color of at least five members of the committee, red is determined to be the prettiest color. Otherwise, if blue is the preferred color of at least five members of the committee, blue is determined to be the prettiest color. Otherwise, yellow is determined to be the prettiest color. Once the prettiest color is determined, the remaining two colors are then ranked by the simple majority rule.

(a) Is the social welfare function described here dictatorial? Justify your answer.

(b) Does the social welfare function described here satisfy the unanimity property? Justify your answer.

(c) Does the social welfare function described here satisfy the independence of irrelevant alternatives property? Justify your answers.

22.8 Repeat Exercise 22.7 for the following situation. There are two alternatives, $A = \{a, b\}$, and n voters. Let $k \in \{0, 1, 2, \ldots, n\}$ and let F_k be the following social welfare function: $a \succsim_{F_k(P^N)} b$ if and only if the number of individuals who prefer a over b is greater than or equal to k.

22.9 Let F be a social welfare function satisfying the independence of irrelevant alternatives property, and let a, b be two distinct alternatives. Let P^N and Q^N be two strict preference profiles satisfying

$$a >_{P_i} b \iff a >_{Q_i} b, \quad \forall i \in N. \tag{22.44}$$

Prove that $a \approx_{F(P^N)} b$ if and only if $a \approx_{F(Q^N)} b$.

22.10 Denote by $K = |A|$ the number of alternatives in A. For each alternative $a \in A$, denote by $j_a(P_i)$ the ranking of a in the strict preference relation P_i (for example, $j_a(P_i) = 1$ when alternative a is the most-preferred alternative according to P_i). Define a social welfare function as follows. For each alternative a, compute the sum $s_a = \sum_{i \in N} j_a(P_i)$. We say that alternative a is (weakly) preferred to alternative b if and only if $s_a \leq s_b$.

(a) Prove that this defines a social welfare function.

(b) Is this a dictatorial function? Does it satisfy the unanimity property? Does it satisfy the independence of irrelevant alternatives property? Justify your answers.

(c) What is the connection between this voting system and the Borda system appearing in Exercise 22.3?

22.11 Prove Theorem 22.16 (page 909): let F be a social welfare function satisfying the unanimity property. Then for every $a, b \in A$ the coalition N is decisive for a over b, and the empty coalition $\emptyset$ is not decisive for a over b.

22.12 A jury composed of seven members is called upon to find an accused individual either guilty or innocent. Debbie is the jury forewoman, with Bobby and Jack appointed vice-foremen. The jury includes four more jurors, in addition to Debbie, Bobby, and Jack. For each of the following cases, describe the set of all decisive coalitions for "guilty" over "innocent," and the set of all minimal decisive coalitions for this pair of alternatives.

(a) The accused is found guilty only if all the jurors unanimously agree that he is guilty.

(b) The accused is found guilty if a majority of jurors declare him to be guilty.

(c) The accused is found guilty if at least four jurors, including Debbie, declare him to be guilty.

(d) The accused is found guilty if at least four jurors, including Debbie, declare him to bc guilty, or if lcast fivc jurors, including Bobby and Jack, dcclarc him to be guilty.

(e) The accused is found guilty if at least four jurors declare him to be guilty, or if Debbie, Bobby, and Jack declare him to be guilty.

(f) The accused is found guilty if at least five jurors, including Debbie and at least one of her vice-foremen, declare him to be guilty.

22.13 Suppose that $|A| \geq 3$, and let F be a social welfare function satisfying the properties of unanimity and independence of irrelevant alternatives. What are all the decisive coalitions?

22.14 Show that the assumptions of Theorem 22.18 (page 910) are necessary for its conclusion: if we remove any one of the three assumptions of the theorem, the conclusion does not hold.

22.15 Sam wishes to prove Claim 22.20 (page 912) using the following strict preference profile, instead of the preference profile Q^N appearing in the proof of the claim on page 912. How can you help Sam complete his proof of the claim?

$$\begin{cases} a >_{Q_i} c >_{Q_i} b & i = j, \\ a >_{Q_i} b >_{Q_i} c & i \neq j, a >_{P_i} b, \\ b >_{Q_i} a >_{Q_i} c & i \neq j, b >_{P_i} a. \end{cases} \tag{22.45}$$

22.16 Ben wishes to prove Claim 22.20 (page 912) using the following strict preference profile, instead of the preference profile Q^N appearing in the proof of the claim on page 912. Why does the proof of the claim fail when using this preference relation?

$$\begin{cases} a >_{Q_i} c >_{Q_i} b & i = j, \\ a >_{Q_i} c >_{Q_i} b & i \neq j, a >_{P_i} b, \\ c >_{Q_i} b >_{Q_i} a & i \neq j, b >_{P_i} a. \end{cases} \tag{22.46}$$

22.17 A social welfare function F is called *monotonic* if for every alternative $a \in A$, and every pair of strict preference profiles P^N and Q^N satisfying

$$a >_{P_i} c \implies a >_{Q_i} c, \quad \forall c \neq a, \ \forall i \in N, \tag{22.47}$$

the following is also satisfied:

$$a >_{F(P)} c \implies a >_{F(Q)} c, \quad \forall c \neq a. \tag{22.48}$$

In words, if for each individual i the ranking of alternative a relative to the other alternatives is not lowered in moving from P_i to Q_i, then its ranking is not lowered in society's ranking, according to the social welfare function, when moving from profile P^N to profile Q^N.

Answer the following questions:

(a) Are the social welfare functions in Exercises 22.7 and 22.10 monotonic? Justify your answer.

(b) Does every monotonic social welfare function satisfy the unanimity property? Justify your answer.

(c) Does every monotonic social welfare function satisfy the independence of irrelevant alternatives property? Justify your answer.

(d) Is every social welfare function satisfying the independence of irrelevant alternatives property monotonic? Justify your answer.

22.18 Ron and Veronica need to choose a name for their newborn daughter. After giving the matter much thought, they have narrowed the list of possible names to four: Abigail, Iris, Irene, and Olga. They now must choose one name from this list. Each parent ranks the four names in order of preference. Given each of the following decision rules, determine whether it is a social choice function. If yes, determine whether it is monotonic, and whether it is manipulable. Justify your answers. (If a rule is monotonic, provide a direct proof that it satisfies the property of monotonicity. If a rule is manipulable, provide an example showing how it may be manipulated.)

(a) If both parents select a name as being the most preferred, that name is chosen. Otherwise, if there is only one name that both parents rank within their top two most-preferred names, that name is chosen. Otherwise, Abigail is the chosen name.

(b) If both parents select a name as being the most preferred, that name is chosen. Otherwise, if there is only one name that both parents rank within their top two most-preferred names, that name is chosen. Otherwise, the parents toss a coin to determine the name of their daughter, with Iris chosen if the coin shows heads, and Olga chosen if the coin shows tails.

(c) If Ron most prefers the name Irene, that name is chosen. Otherwise, the name that Veronica most prefers is chosen.

(d) As a first step, the name that each parent ranks last by preference is removed from the list under consideration. This leaves two or three names in contention. In the next step, the name that each parent ranks last by preference from among the two or three remaining names is removed from the list under consideration. This leaves zero, one, or two names. If two names remain, the process of removing the name that each parent least prefers from the list under consideration is repeated again. If only one name remains, that name is chosen. Otherwise, Olga is chosen as the child's name.

22.19 A committee comprised of 15 members is called upon to choose the prettiest color: red, blue, or yellow. The committee members simultaneously announce their strict preference relations among these three colors. If red is the most-preferred color of at least one committee member, red is declared the prettiest color. Otherwise, if blue is the most-preferred color of at least one committee member, blue is declared the prettiest color. Otherwise, yellow is declared the prettiest color.

(a) Is the social choice function described above dictatorial? Justify your answer.
(b) Is the social choice function described above monotonic? Justify your answer.
(c) Is the social choice function described above manipulable? Justify your answer.

22.20 The following electoral method is used to choose the mayor of Whoville: Every resident ranks the candidates from most preferred to least preferred, and places this ranked list in a ballot box. Each candidate receives a number of points equal to the number of residents who prefer him to all the other candidates. The candidate who thus amasses the greatest number of points wins the election. If two or more candidates are tied for first place in the number of points, the winner of the election is the candidate among them whose social security number is smallest. Assume there are at least three candidates.

(a) Show by example that this electoral method is not monotonic.
(b) Show by example that this electoral method is manipulable.

22.21 Repeat Exercise 22.20, under the following scenario. The following electoral method is used to choose the mayor of Sleepy Hollow: every resident ranks the candidates from most preferred to least preferred, and places this ranked list in a ballot box. Each candidate receives a number of points equal to the number of residents who rank him or her in the first two positions. The candidate who thus amasses the greatest number of points wins the election. If two or more candidates are tied for first place in the number of points, the winner of the election is the candidate among them whose social security number is smallest. Assume there are at least three candidates.

22.22 The following electoral method is used to choose the mayor of Hobbiton: every resident ranks the candidates from most preferred to least preferred, and places this ranked list in a ballot box. Each candidate receives a number of points equal to the number of residents who rank him or her least preferred. The candidate who thus amasses the greatest number of points is then removed from the list of candidates. If two or more candidates are tied for first place in the number of points, the candidate among them whose social security number is greatest is removed from the list of candidates. This candidate is then ignored in the strict preference relations submitted by the residents, and the process is repeated as often as is necessary, until only one candidate remains, who is declared the new mayor. Assume there are at least three candidates.

(a) Is it possible for the winner of the election to not be the most preferred candidate of any resident? Justify your answer.
(b) Is it possible for the winner of the election to be ranked least preferred by at least half of the residents? Justify your answer.
(c) Is the social choice function described here dictatorial? Justify your answer.
(d) Is it monotonic? Prove why if yes, or show by example that it is not monotonic.
(e) Is it manipulable? If yes, provide an example or otherwise prove that it is not.
(f) After the election of the mayor, using the above method, is completed, the local Elections Board checks which candidate would have won had they implemented instead the electoral method used in Whoville (see Exercise 22.20). Will the same candidate necessarily be chosen under both electoral methods? Justify your answer.

22.23 Repeat Exercise 22.20 for the following situation. The following electoral method is used to choose the mayor of Hogsmeade Village: every resident ranks the candidates from most preferred to least preferred, and places this ranked list in a ballot box. For each candidate a denote by $N_{a,k}$ the ratio of residents (using a number between 0 and 1) who ranked him or her in the top k positions. Further denote:

$$k_0 = \min \left\{ k \in \mathbb{N} \colon \text{there is a candidate } a \text{ such that } N_{a,k} > \frac{k}{k+1} \right\}. \qquad (22.49)$$

The winning candidate is the one whose value of N_{a,k_0} is maximal (if there are two or more such candidates, the winner is the candidate among them whose social security number is smallest).

Under this method, if there is a candidate who is ranked first by more than half of the population, he or she wins the election. Otherwise, if there are one or more candidates who are ranked first or second by more than two-thirds of the population, the winner of the election is the candidate who is ranked first or second by the greatest number of residents, and so on.

22.24 Let A be a set of alternatives, and let P^N be a strict preference profile. Alternative $a \in A$ is termed the *Condorcet winner* if for every alternative $b \neq a$, more than half of the individuals rank a above b. A social choice function G satisfies the *Condorcet criterion* if for every strict preference profile P^N for which there exists a Condorcet winner a, it chooses the Condorcet winner, i.e., $G(P^N) = a$ holds.

(a) Does a Condorcet winner a exist for every strict preference profile P^N? Justify your answer.
(b) Which of the social choice functions described in Exercises 22.19–22.23 satisfy the Condorcet criterion? Justify your answer.

22.25 Let G be a monotonic social choice function, let P^N and Q^N be two strict preference profiles, and let $R \subseteq A$. Show that if $a \in R$ and $G(P^N) = a$, then $G(Z(P^N, Q^N; R)) = a$ (for the definition of $Z(P^N, Q^N; R)$, see Definition 22.30 on page 914).

22.26 Let G be a monotonic social choice function, let $a \in \text{range}(G)$, and let P^N be a strict preference profile. Show that if

$$a >_{P_i} b, \quad \forall i \in N, \tag{22.50}$$

then $G(P^N) \neq b$.

22.27 In this exercise we prove Theorem 22.35 (page 918).

   (a) Prove that if G is a monotonic social choice function, then for any pair of strict preference relations P^N and Q^N satisfying

$$a >_{P_i} b \iff a >_{Q_i} b, \quad \forall a, b \in \text{range}(G), \forall i \in N, \tag{22.51}$$

   $G(P^N) = G(Q^N)$. In words, the claim states that the alternatives that are not in range(G) have no effect on the choice of G.

   (b) Show that if G is a monotonic social choice function satisfying $|\text{range}(G)| \geq 3$, then there is an individual i such that for every strict preference profile P^N the alternative $G(P^N)$ is the most prefered alternative from i's perspective, from among all the alternatives in range(G).

   Guidance: For the first part, choose a strict preference profile W^N, and denote $R = \text{range}(G)$. Show that $Z(P^N, W^N; R) = Z(Q^N, W^N; R)$, and use Theorem 22.31 to derive the claim. For the proof of the second part, use Exercise 22.26.

22.28 **Approval voting** In this question, we consider the case in which the individuals are called upon to choose candidates for a task, by specifying which candidates they most approve for the task. Let A be a nonempty set of alternatives. A binary relation P_i over A is called (at most) *two-leveled* if there exists a set $B(P_i) \subseteq A$ satisfying: (i) $b \approx_{P_i} c$ for every $b, c \in B(P_i)$, (ii) $b \approx_{P_i} c$ for every $b, c \in A \backslash B(P_i)$, (iii) $b >_{P_i} c$ for every $b \in B(P_i)$, and $c \in A \backslash B(P_i)$. In words, the individual is indifferent between all the alternatives in $B(P_i)$, he is indifferent between all the alternatives that are not in $B(P_i)$, and he prefers all the elements in $B(P_i)$ to all the elements that are not in $B(P_i)$. The interpretation that we give to such a preference relation is that the individual approves of all the alternatives in $B(P_i)$, and disapproves of all the alternatives not in $B(P_i)$. A two-leveled preference profile P^N is a profile of preference relations all of which are two-leveled.

   Consider a choice function H associating every two-leveled profile with a single alternative, which is declared to be society's most-preferred alternative. Such a choice function H is called *monotonic* if for every pair of two-leveled preference profiles P^N and Q^N, if $H(P^N) = a$, and if every individual i satisfies $B(Q_i) = B(P_i)$ or $B(Q_i) = B(P_i) \cup \{a\}$, then $H(Q^N) = a$. In other words, if alternative a is chosen under preference profile P^N, and if Q^N

is a preference profile that is identical to P^N except that some individuals have added a to the set of their approved alternatives, then a is also chosen under Q^N.

A choice function H is called *nonmanipulable* if for every two-leveled preference profile P^N, for every individual i, and for every two-leveled preference relation Q_i, it is the case that $H(P^N) \succsim_{P_i} H(Q_i, P_{-i})$.

Define a choice function H^* as follows: a winning alternative is one that is approved by the greatest number of individuals; in other words, a is a winning alternative if it maximizes the value of $|\{i \in N : a \in B(P_i)\}|$. If there are two or more alternatives receiving the greatest number of approval votes, the alternative whose serial number is lowest is chosen.

Is this choice function monotonic? Is it manipulable? Justify your answer.

22.29 This exercise is similar to Exercise 22.28, but we now assume that the individuals are called upon to agree on a set of approved alternatives (as opposed to one most-approved alternative). In other words, the function H associates each two-leveled preference profile P^N with a two-leveled preference profile $H(P^N)$. In this case, a choice function H is called *nonmanipulable* if for every two-leveled preference profile P^N, and every individual i, if $a \in B(P_i)$ and if $a \notin B(H(P^N))$, then $a \notin B(H(Q_i, P_{-i}))$ for every two-leveled preference relation Q_i.

Define a function H^* as follows: the set of approved alternatives, $H^*(P^N)$, is the set of alternatives that are approved by the greatest number of individuals according to P^N. Is this function manipulable? Justify your answer.

23 Stable matching

Chapter summary

In this chapter we present the subject of *stable matching*. Introduced in 1962 by David Gale and Lloyd Shapley, stable matching became the starting point of a rich literature on matching problems in two-sided markets (e.g., workers and employers, interns and hospitals, students and universities), and remains one of the most applied areas in game theory to date.

We present Gale and Shapley's basic model of matching *men* to *women*, the concept of stable matching, and an algorithm for finding it. It is proved that the set of stable matchings has a lattice structure based on the preferences of women and men. We then study several variations of the model: the case in which there are more men than women; the case in which bachelorhood is not the worst outcome; the case of many-to-one matchings (e.g., many students to one college); and matchings in a single-gender population. It is also shown that the Gale–Shapley algorithm is not immune to strategic manipulations.

The study of the subject of this chapter began at the end of the nineteenth century, with the introduction of residency requirements for recent medical school graduates. Fresh medical school graduates needed to find a hospital in which to pursue their medical internships. Over the years, the residents played an increasingly important role in the staffs of hospitals, and hospitals began competing with each other for the best medical school graduates. To get a jump on the competition, hospitals kept moving up the dates on which they granted medical students residency positions. By 1944, medical students beginning their third year of medical school (out of four years) were interviewed for residency positions. This state of affairs did not serve the interests of either students or hospitals, and as the situation only deteriorated further, medical schools and hospitals agreed in 1951 to adopt a formal system for matching graduating medical students with hospitals, beginning the following year. The system works as follows: after interviews are conducted, the fourth-year medical students rank the hospitals at which they were interviewed, while at the same time the hospitals rank the students that they interviewed. Each hospital also announces the maximum number of residents that it can hire. The data are collected by a special national resident matching program, which then inputs the data into an algorithm composed for the purpose of matching hospitals and residents. The algorithm takes into account the preferences of both the hospitals and the medical students with an attempt to arrive at a "best fit."

Participation in this central mechanism, on the part of both hospitals and medical students, is voluntary. The satisfaction that all parties derive from a good suggested "matching" between residents and hospitals is therefore a significant factor in determining the extent of participation in the matching system and its success.

It is not easy to arrive at matches that please everyone. For example, if Mark prefers Massachusetts General Hospital to Johns Hopkins Hospital, and Massachusetts General Hospital prefers Mark to Andrew, it would be unwise to send Mark to Johns Hopkins and Andrew to Massachusetts General. Such a matching will generate dissatisfaction for both Mark and Massachusetts General, and both of them will then have an incentive to disregard the matching program. If too many such cases multiply, the entire system could be abandoned (this actually happened in the United Kingdom, where the system matching house officer posts at British hospitals with medical students led to so many unsatisfactory matches that it fell into disuse).

The beauty of the algorithm used by the American national resident matching program is that it leads to matches in which no pair is dissatisfied: if Mark is matched with Johns Hopkins Hospital, then Massachusetts General Hospital must have been matched with residents whom it preferred to Mark, and Mark has no justified complaint, because his preferred hospital simply preferred others to him; no injustice was involved, nor any inefficiency in the algorithm.

The problem of matching elements from two different populations is not limited to the example of hospitals and potential residents. Two additional examples that may be adduced are matching workers and employers, and matching men and women in couples.

In 1962, David Gale and Lloyd Shapley published a paper defining the matching problem and the concept of "stable matching." In that paper, they also proved that stable matchings always exist, and spelled out an algorithm for computing stable matchings. Several years later, Alvin Roth connected the Gale–Shapley result to the algorithms used to match residents and hospitals in the United States, by showing that the algorithms used in the resident matching system created stable matchings according to Gale and Shapley's definition of the term.

The subject of matching raises many natural questions. What is the best definition of a stable placement of candidates for residency with open positions? Do such stable placements always exist? If so, how can they be found? Can a hospital (or a candidate for residency) obtain a more satisfactory placement by submitting a preference ordering over candidates that differs from the honest preference ordering?

In this chapter, we will first consider the simple case in which the number of residency candidates equals the number of hospitals, and each hospital is seeking only one resident. Such a situation better describes the matching of men and women in married couples, and we will therefore use the language of that metaphor in analyzing this problem. The matching situation we consider then consists of n men and n women. Each man orders the women in decreasing order, from the woman he most prefers to the woman he least prefers as a mate, and each woman similarly orders the men in decreasing order of preference. The goal is to match each man to one woman in such a way that no complaints will be registered: if Julius is matched to Cornelia and Mark is matched to Cleopatra, then Julius and Cleopatra should not leave their spouses for each other: either Julius prefers Cornelia to Cleopatra or Cleopatra prefers Mark to Julius (or both).

Later in the chapter we will study extensions of this basic model.

23.1) The model

We begin by recalling the definition of a preference relation. In words, a preference relation enables us to compare any two elements of a set, and state which of the two is more preferred.

Definition 23.1 *Let X be a set. A* preference relation[1] *over X is a binary relation $>$ satisfying the following properties:*

- *For every $x \neq y$, either $x > y$ or $y > x$ (the relation is* complete*; i.e., every pair of distinct elements can be compared).*
- *$x \not> x$ (the relation is* irreflexive*; i.e., x is not preferred to itself).*
- *If $x > y$, and $y > z$, then $x > z$ (the relation is* transitive*; i.e., if x is preferred to y, and y is preferred to z, then x is also preferred to z).*

Every complete, irreflexive, and transitive relation is *asymmetric*: if $x \neq y$, then $x > y$ if and only if $y \not> x$ (Exercise 23.1).

Note that a preference relation, as we have defined it, represents strict preferences; we are not allowing for the possibility of indifference. We are assuming this for the sake of simplifying the analysis. Some of the results presented in this chapter can be generalized to preference relations with indifference (see Exercise 23.35).

We are now ready for the formal definition of a matching problem.

Definition 23.2 *A* matching problem *is given by:*

- *A natural number n representing the number of men and the number of women in a population (thus, we assume that the number of women equals the number of men).*
- *Every woman has a preference relation over the set of men.*
- *Every man has a preference relation over the set of women.*

The set of women will be denoted by W, and an element in that set is denoted by w. The set of men will be denoted by M, and an element in that set is denoted by m. The fact that a woman w prefers a man m_1 to a man m_2 is denoted

$$w : m_1 > m_2. \tag{23.1}$$

For example, "Cleopatra prefers Julius to Mark" is denoted as:

$$\text{Cleopatra: Julius} > \text{Mark.}$$

Definition 23.3 *A* matching *is a bijection from the set of men to the set of women.*

Equivalently, a matching is a collection of n pairs $\{(w_1, m_1), (w_2, m_2), \ldots, (w_n, m_n)\}$ such that $\{m_1, m_2, \ldots, m_n\} = M$ and $\{w_1, w_2, \ldots, w_n\} = W$. If a pair (w, m) is included in a matching, then we say that the man m is matched to the woman w (or that the woman w is matched to the man m). We will henceforth denote matchings using the letters A, B, or C, etc.

---

1 The definition appearing here is of a complete and strict ordering relation (meaning that there is no possibility of indifference between any two elements). In other places in this book (Chapters 2 and 22) we have presented definitions of ordering relations that satisfy other properties.

Definition 23.4 *A man and a woman* object *to a matching, if they prefer each other to the mates to whom they are matched under the matching. A matching is* stable *if there is no pair consisting of a man and a woman who have an objection to the matching.*

The following definition is equivalent to that of a stable matching (Exercise 23.4).

Definition 23.5 *A matching A is* stable *if in every case that a man prefers another woman to the woman to whom he is matched under A, that woman prefers the man to whom she is matched to him.*

The definition may be similarly phrased by interchanging the roles of the men and the women: matching A is *stable* if in every case that a woman prefers another man to the man to whom she is matched under A, that man prefers the woman to whom he is matched to her.

Example 23.6 Consider the following example, where $n = 4$: the set of men is $\{$Adam, Ben, Charles, Dean$\}$, and the set of women is $\{$Anne, Bess, Carol, Donna$\}$. The preferences of these men and women are presented in Figure 23.1. The preferences of the women appear in the lower right-hand side of each cell (read vertically) and the preferences of the men appear in the upper left-hand side of each cell (read horizontally). For example, in the upper left cell of the table, corresponding to the pair Anne–Adam, the numbers 2 and 4 are listed: Adam is second on Anne's preference list, and Anne is fourth on Adam's preference list.

The matching depicted in Figure 23.1 by stars, and detailed again in Figure 23.2, is not stable. This is because Carol and Adam have an objection to the matching: Carol prefers Adam (number 2 on her list) to Charles (number 3 on her list), and Adam prefers Carol (number 2 on his list) to Anne (number 4 on his list).

	Anne	Bess	Carol	Donna
Adam	4 ★ 2	3 2	2 ♣ 2	1 4
Ben	2 ♣ 1	1 ★ 4	3 4	4 3
Charles	4 3	1 ♣ 1	3 ★ 3	2 2
Dean	1 4	4 3	3 1	2 ★ ♣ 1

Figure 23.1 The preference relations of the men and the women, along with two matchings (one denoted by ★, and the other by ♣)

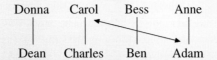

Figure 23.2 An unstable matching (denoted by ★ in Figure 23.1) and an objection to that matching

In contrast, the matching

$$(\text{Adam–Carol, Ben–Anne, Charles–Bess, Dean–Donna}),$$

depicted in Figure 23.1 by ♣, is stable. To see this, note that Anne, Bess, and Donna are all matched with the men who are number 1 on their lists, so that none of them will object to the matching with any man. Carol is matched with Adam, who is number 2 on her list, and therefore the only possible objection she may have is with Dean, who is number 1 on her list. But Dean prefers Donna (number 2 on his list) to Carol (number 3 on his list). This matching is thus stable, because no pair consisting of a man and a woman has an objection.   ◄

23.2 Existence of stable matching: the men's courtship algorithm

. . . .

The first theorem we prove states that there always exists a stable matching. The proof is attained by presenting an algorithm that leads to a stable matching. The algorithm is due to Gale and Shapley [1962].

Theorem 23.7 *To every matching problem there exists a stable matching.*

Proof: Step 1: Description of the algorithm.
Consider the following algorithm:

1. Stage 1(a): Every man goes to stand in front of the house of the woman he most prefers.
2. Stage 1(b): Every woman asks the man whom she most prefers from among the men standing in front of her house, if there are any, to wait, and dismisses all the other men.
3. Stage 2(a): Every man who was dismissed by a woman in the first stage goes to stand in front of the house of the woman he most prefers from among the women who have not previously dismissed him (i.e., the woman who is second on his list).
4. Stage 2(b): Every woman asks the man whom she most prefers from among the men standing in front of her house, if there are any (including the man whom she told to wait in the previous stage), to wait, and dismisses all the other men. In general:
5. Stage k(a): Every man who was dismissed by a woman in the previous stage goes to stand in front of the house of the woman he most prefers from among the women who have not previously dismissed him.
6. Stage k(b): Every woman asks the man whom she most prefers from among the men standing in front of her house, if there are any, to wait, and dismisses all the other men.
7. The algorithm terminates when there is one man standing in front of every woman's house.

It is possible, in principle, that a particular man will be dismissed by every woman. We will show that this cannot happen. The algorithm will always terminate, and every woman will have one man standing in front of her house. The algorithm therefore always terminates by finding a matching. We will further prove that the algorithm always terminates by finding a stable matching.

Before proceeding to the proof of the theorem, we note that the algorithm satisfies the following three properties that will later be needed. The reader can readily ascertain that the first and third properties are satisfied. The reader is further asked to show that the second property is also satisfied, in Exercise 23.2.

(1) The preferred women have been courted in the past. If, in stage k, Henry stands in front of the house of Anne, but prefers Catherine to Anne, then it must be the case that he previously courted Catherine by standing in front of her house, and was dismissed. In other words, the men go down their preference list along the course of the algorithm.

(2) The preferred men will come courting in the future. If, in stage k, Cleopatra asks Mark to wait, and in a later stage asks Julius to wait, then she prefers Julius to Mark. In other words, the women go up their preference list along the course of the algorithm.

(3) Once a woman is courted, she will always be courted. If, in stage k, Mark stands in front of Cleopatra's house, then from stage k onwards, there will always be at least one man courting Cleopatra by standing in front of her house.

Step 2: The algorithm terminates in a finite number of stages and produces a matching. We first show that there is a stage at which no man is dismissed. A man who is dismissed by a women never returns to court her again. This means that each woman dismisses at most $n - 1$ men. It follows that after at most $n(n - 1) = n^2 - n$ stages, there are no more rejections, and therefore after at most $n^2 - n + 1$ stages we arrive at a stage at which no woman dismisses any man.**2**

We next show that a man cannot be dismissed by all women. Assume by way of contradiction that there exists a man, let's call him Joe, who was dismissed by all the women. By the algorithm's construction, Joe must have paid a visit to the house of every woman. By the "once a woman is courted, she will always be courted" property, after Joe has courted every woman, every woman has a man standing in front of her house. Since the number of women equals the number of men, and Joe is not standing in front of any woman's house, there must be a woman who has no man in front of her house, a contradiction. Hence there cannot be a man who has been dismissed by every woman.

It follows that the algorithm terminates by producing a matching. Indeed, if at the end of any particular stage no man is sent home, it follows that in front of each woman's house there is one and only one man left standing, who is then her mate. A matching has been attained.

Step 3: The resulting matching is stable.
Suppose by contradiction that the resulting matching is unstable. Then there exist at least one man and one woman, let's call them Julius and Cleopatra, who prefer each other to the

---

2 In fact, the algorithm terminates after at most $(n - 1)^2 + 1$ stages (see Exercise 23.13).

mates to which they have been matched under the algorithm. Suppose that the algorithm has matched Julius to Cornelia, and Cleopatra to Mark.

Since Julius prefers Cleopatra to Cornelia, by "the preferred women were courted in the past" property, Julius must have courted Cleopatra before he courted Cornelia. Since Cleopatra has been matched by the algorithm to Mark, by "the preferred men will come courting in the future" property, she prefers Mark to Julius. This contradicts the assumption that Julius and Cleopatra have an objection to the matching.   □

Example 23.6 (*Continued*) We apply the matching algorithm to Example 23.6. The table in Figure 23.3 describes the run of the algorithm.

	Anne	Bess	Carol	Donna	Dismissed men
Stage 1(a)	Dean(1)	Ben(1), Charles(1)		Adam(1)	
Stage 1(b)	Dean(1)	Charles(1)		Adam(1)	Ben
Stage 2(a)	Dean(1), Ben(2)	Charles(1)		Adam(1)	
Stage 2(b)	Ben	Charles(1)		Adam(1)	Dean
Stage 3(a)	Ben(2)	Charles(1)		Adam(1), Dean(2)	
Stage 3(b)	Ben(2)	Charles(1)		Dean(2)	Adam
Stage 4(a)	Ben(2)	Charles(1)	Adam(2)	Dean(2)	

Figure 23.3 Men's courtship algorithm

Each stage of the run of the algorithm is described by two consecutive rows. In the row corresponding to part (a) we note the men who are standing in front of women's houses after the application of part (a) of that stage (prior to the dismissals of the women), and in the row corresponding to part (b) we note the men who are standing in front of women's houses after the application of part (b) of that stage (after the women have announced their dismissals). The number appearing by the name of each man represents the ranking of the woman in front of whose house he is standing, in his preference relation.

The algorithm ends with the matching:

$$(\text{Adam–Carol, Ben–Anne, Charles–Bess, Dean–Donna}),$$

which is the stable matching previously mentioned.   ◄

23.3) The women's courtship algorithm

In the algorithm presented in the previous section, the men courted the women, and the women kept the men waiting or dismissed them. We call the resulting matching a "*men's courtship matching*," and denote it by O^m. The roles of the men and women, however, may be reversed, with women taking the courting initiative, going to the mens' houses, with each man keeping only the most preferred woman from among those standing in front of his house and dismissing all the others. By the proof of Theorem 23.7, this algorithm also leads to a stable matching, which we call the "*women's courtship matching*," denoted by O^w.

Example 23.6 (*Continued*) We apply the women's courtship algorithm to Example 23.6 (see Figure 23.4).

	Adam	Ben	Charles	Dean	Dismissed women
Stage 1(a)		Anne(1)	Bess(1)	Carol(1), Donna(1)	
Stage 1(b)		Anne(1)	Bess(1)	Donna(1)	Carol
Stage 2(a)	Carol(2)	Anne(1)	Bess(1)	Donna(1)	

Figure 23.4 Women's courtship algorithm

The algorithm ends with the matching:

(Adam–Carol, Ben–Anne, Charles–Bess, Dean–Donna),

which is exactly the same matching that the men's courtship algorithm produced. Do the two different algorithms always lead to the same matching? The answer to that question is negative: as the next example shows, the men's courtship algorithm may lead to a different matching from the women's courtship algorithm, which indicates that there may be more than one stable matching. In addition, there may be stable matchings that are different from those attained by applying either the men's courtship or the women's courtship algorithms described above. ◄

Example 23.8 Consider the matching problem depicted in Figure 23.5, with three men and three women.

	Anne	Bess	Carol
Adam	1 ■ 3	2 ★ 2	3 ♣ 1
Ben	3 ♣ 1	1 ■ 3	2 ★ 2
Charles	2 ★ 2	3 ♣ 1	1 ■ 3

Figure 23.5 The preferences of the men and women in Example 23.8, and three stable matchings

The matching indicated by darkened squares is the men's courtship matching (attained by each man matched to the woman he most prefers), the matching indicated by clubs is the women's courtship matching (attained by each woman matched to the man she most prefers), and the matching indicated by stars is a third stable matching that differs from the previous two matchings (the reader is asked to ascertain that each of these three matchings is indeed stable). ◄

The number of possible matchings equals $n!$, the number of permutations of n elements. This number rapidly grows large as n grows. In principle the number of stable matchings could still be rather small. However, Gusfield and Irving [1989] show that matching problems may have a very large number of stable matchings. Using their method, one can construct a matching problem with 8 men and 8 women, with 268 stable matchings; a matching problem with 16 men and 16 women, with 195,472 stable matchings; and a matching problem with 32 men and 32 women, with 104,310,534,400 stable matchings.

23.4 Comparing matchings

So far we have found ways to attain two possible matchings: the men's courtship algorithm and the women's courtship algorithm. As shown in Example 23.8, there may be more stable matchings. Since these algorithms may lead to the creation of different pairs, if we compare two stable matchings there may be men and women who will prefer the application of one matching, and others who will prefer the application of the other matching.

Example 23.9 Consider a matching problem with four women and four men, with the preference relations depicted in Figure 23.6. This matching problem has four stable matchings (check that this is true):

$$A^1 : \text{Adam–Anne,}\quad \text{Ben–Bess,}\quad \text{Charles–Carol,}\quad \text{Dean–Donna}$$

$$A^2 : \text{Adam–Bess,}\quad \text{Ben–Anne,}\quad \text{Charles–Carol,}\quad \text{Dean–Donna}$$

$$A^3 : \text{Adam–Anne,}\quad \text{Ben–Bess,}\quad \text{Charles–Donna,}\quad \text{Dean–Carol}$$

$$A^4 : \text{Adam–Bess,}\quad \text{Ben–Anne,}\quad \text{Charles–Donna,}\quad \text{Dean–Carol}$$

	Anne	Bess	Carol	Donna
Adam	1	2	3	4
	2	1	3	3
Ben	2	1	3	4
	1	2	4	4
Charles	3	4	1	2
	3	3	2	1
Dean	3	4	2	1
	4	4	1	2

Figure 23.6 The preference relations of the men and women in Example 23.9

Matching A^1 is the men's courtship matching, and matching A^4 is the women's courtship matching. Matching A^1 is the best from the perspective of the men, because each man is matched with the woman ranked highest on his preference list, and matching A^4 is the best from the perspective of the women, because each woman is matched with the man ranked highest on her list. From among these four matchings, the men's courtship matching A^1 is the "worst" for the women, and the women's courtship matching A^4 is the "worst" for the men.

Comparing the matchings A^2 and A^3, Anne and Bess prefer A^2 to A^3 (because under A^2 each is matched with the man she ranks highest), while Donna and Carol prefer A^3 to A^2 (because under A^3 each is matched with the man she ranks highest). Similarly, Charles and Dean prefer A^2 to A^3, and Adam and Ben prefer A^3 to A^2. ◀

The last example raises several broad questions regarding the preferences of men and women over stable matchings. Is there a stable matching that is the worst for all the men, among all the stable matchings? Which matching algorithm is better for the men, the men's courtship algorithm or the women's courtship algorithm?

Definition 23.10 *Let A and B be two matchings. Denote* $A \succsim^m B$ *if every man who is matched under A and B to different women prefers the woman to whom he is matched under A to the woman to whom he is matched under B. Denote* $A \succsim^w B$ *if and only if every woman who is matched under A and B to different men prefers the man to whom she is matched under A to the man to whom she is matched under B.*

This is a definition of two ordering relations $\succsim^m$ and $\succsim^w$ over the set of matchings: $A \succsim^m B$ if and only if every man matched to two different women under matchings A and B prefers the woman to whom he is matched under A. Equivalently, no man prefers matching B to matching A. It follows that $A \succsim^m A$ for every stable matching, and therefore $\succsim^m$ (and similarly $\succsim^w$) is a reflexive relation. It can be ascertained that the relations $\succsim^m$ and $\succsim^w$ are also transitive relations (Exercise 23.18).

Despite the fact that these ordering relations are defined for all matchings, we will mostly be interested in using them to order stable matchings. As we will show, in stable matchings these orderings induce a special structure. First of all, note that even if we restrict attention to stable matchings, these orderings are not complete orderings; in Example 23.9 $A^2 \not\succsim^w A^3$ and $A^3 \not\succsim^w A^2$ and similarly $A^2 \not\succsim^m A^3$ and $A^3 \not\succsim^m A^2$.

The next theorem states that if one stable matching is better for the men than another stable matching, then it is worse for the women.

Theorem 23.11 *For every pair of stable matchings A and B, $A \succsim^m B$ if and only if $B \succsim^w A$.*

Proof: We will prove that if $A \succsim^m B$ then $B \succsim^w A$. The other direction of the statement of the theorem is then proved by reversing the roles of the women and the men.

Let A and B be two stable matchings, and suppose that $A \succsim^m B$. We need to show that $B \succsim^w A$, i.e., every woman who is matched to different men under A and under B prefers her mate under matching B to her mate under matching A. Let Lena be such a woman, and suppose that she is matched with Aaron under A, and with Benjamin under B. Suppose that under matching B, Aaron is matched with Mandy. Since $A \succsim^m B$, Aaron prefers the woman with whom he is matched under A, Lena, to the woman with whom he is matched under B, Mandy:

$$\text{Aaron: Lena} \succ \text{Mandy.}$$

Since B is a stable matching, Aaron and Lena do not have an objection under B. Since Aaron prefers Lena to Mandy, his mate under matching B, it follows that Lena prefers the man with whom she is matched under B, Benjamin, to Aaron, with whom she is matched under A, which is what we wanted to show.   □

The following theorem states that the phenomenon we saw in Example 23.9, in which the men's courtship matching O^m is the best stable matching from the perspective of all the men, and the worst from the perspective of all the women, and in which the women's courtship matching O^w is the best stable matching from the perspective of all the women, and the worst from the perspective of all the men, holds true for every matching problem.

Theorem 23.12 *For every stable matching A, one has* $O^m \succsim^m A \succsim^m O^w$ *and* $O^w \succsim^w A \succsim^w O^m$.

Proof: To prove the theorem, it suffices to prove that $O^m \succsim^m A$ holds for every stable matching A. To see this, note that by Theorem 23.11 this would imply that $A \succsim^w O^m$. By reversing the roles of the men and the women, we also get $O^w \succsim^w A$ and $A \succsim^m O^w$.

We will say that a woman w is *possible* for a man m if there exists a stable matching under which they are matched to each other.

Step 1: Any woman who dismissed a man under the men's courtship algorithm is not possible for him.

The proof will be by induction over the stages k in which the man is dismissed. Start with the first stage, $k = 1$. We will prove that if Adam is dismissed by Bess in the first stage of the men's courtship algorithm then Bess is not possible for Adam. To see this, suppose that Adam and Bill stand in front of Bess's house in the first stage and that Bess dismisses Adam in that first stage while telling Bill to stay. This means that Bess prefers Bill to Adam and that Bill prefers Bess to any other woman, because he went to her house in the first stage of the men's courtship algorithm. It follows that any matching A that matches Bess to Adam is unstable, because the pair (Bill, Bess) objects to it, since Bess prefers Bill to Adam and Bill prefers Bess to any other woman, and in particular to any women to whom he is matched under A. We deduce that Bess is not possible for Adam.

Let $k \geq 1$ and suppose by induction that every woman who dismisses a man in the first k stages of the algorithm is not possible for him. Suppose that Adam is dismissed by Bess in stage $k + 1$ of the algorithm. We will prove that she is not possible for him; in other words, every matching A in which Bess is matched to Adam is unstable. To see this, suppose that Adam and Ben stand in from of Bess's house in stage $k + 1$ of the algorithm and that Bess dismisses Adam while telling Ben to stay. Then Bess prefers Ben to Adam. Suppose that Ben's mate under the matching A is Abigail. If the matching A were stable, then since under A Abigail is matched to Ben, by the inductive hypothesis she could not have dismissed Ben in the first k stages of the algorithm. It follows that Ben did not go to Abigail's house before he went to Bess's house (which he does in stage $k + 1$), and therefore he prefers Bess to Abigail. Hence, the pair (Ben, Bess) objects to the matching A, and A is unstable. This completes the inductive stage.

Step 2: $O^m \succsim^m A$ for every stable matching A.

Suppose that under the men's courtship algorithm a particular man, Adam, is matched to Bess. We wish to show that for every stable matching A in which Adam is matched to a woman who is not Bess, say Betty, he prefers Bess to Betty. If he were to prefer Betty to

Bess then that means that under the men's courtship algorithm Adam visits Betty before he visits Bess and that Betty dismissed him (since he is matched to Bess under the men's courtship algorithm). But then by Step 1, Betty is not possible for him, contradicting the assumption that she is matched to him in a stable matching.   □

For two stable matchings A and B define a rule under which every woman chooses a mate: if the woman is matched to the same man under A and B, then she chooses that man. If she is matched to two different men under the two matchings, then she chooses the man whom she most prefers from among those two. Is the resulting outcome a matching, or can this lead to a situation in which two women choose the same man? If this process leads to a matching, is it stable? If the answer to these questions is affirmative, clearly this matching is at least as good for the women as the original two matchings.

Definition 23.13 *Let A and B be two matchings. Denote by $A \vee^w B$ the set of all n pairs $\{(m_1, w_1), (m_2, w_2), \ldots, (m_n, w_n)\}$ that satisfies $\{w_1, w_2, \ldots, w_n\} = W$ and for all $i = 1, 2, \ldots, n$, m_i is the one man whom woman w_i prefers from among the men to whom she is matched under A and B.*

Theorem 23.14 *If A and B are stable matchings, then $A \vee^w B$ is also a stable matching.*

Proof: The theorem is proved in two steps. We first prove that $A \vee^w B$ is a matching, and then that it is a stable matching. Denote $C := A \vee^w B$.

Step 1: C is a matching.
Suppose by contradiction that C is not a matching. In other words, suppose that after each woman chooses the man whom she most prefers among those matched to her under A and B, there is a man who is chosen by two women. For example, suppose that in C Adam is chosen by both Anne and Bess. It then follows that Adam is matched to one of them under A, and matched to the other one under B. Suppose in particular that under A Adam is matched to Anne and Elton is matched to Bess, and that under B Adam is matched to Bess and Dan is matched to Anne.

Matching A: Adam–Anne,   Elton–Bess

Matching B: Adam–Bess,   Dan–Anne.

(Note that Elton and Dan may be the same person.) Since both Anne and Bess choose Adam in C:

Anne: Adam $>$ Dan,

Bess: Adam $>$ Elton.

If

Adam : Anne $>$ Bess

then the pair (Adam, Anne) has an objection to matching B.
    If

Adam: Bess $>$ Anne

then the pair (Adam, Bess) has an objection to matching A, contradicting the fact that both A and B are stable matchings. This contradiction proves that C is a matching.

Step 2: C is a stable matching.

Suppose by contradiction that *C* is not stable. Then there is a pair, say Adam and Claire, who are not matched to each other under *C* and have an objection.

Suppose that under the matching *C*:

$$\text{Matching } C: \text{Adam–Bess,} \quad \text{Elton–Claire.}$$

Since Adam and Claire have an objection, it must be true that

$$\text{Claire: Adam} > \text{Elton,}$$

$$\text{Adam: Claire} > \text{Bess.}$$

Since under the matching *C* Claire is matched to Elton, she must be matched to him under either *A* or *B*. Suppose without loss of generality that she is matched to him under *A*, and suppose that she is matched to Frank under matching *B*. (Our claims still hold if Claire is also matched to Elton under matching *B*.)

$$\text{Matching } A: \text{Elton–Claire,} \qquad \text{Matching } B: \text{Frank–Claire.}$$

Claire prefers Adam to Elton, and Elton to Frank (since under matching *C* she chooses Elton and not Frank), and therefore she prefers Adam to Frank:

$$\text{Claire: Adam} > \text{Elton} > \text{Frank.}$$

We claim that Bess is not matched to Adam under matching *A*. Since matching *A* is a stable matching, Adam and Claire have no objection to it. Since Claire prefers Adam to Elton, Adam must prefer the woman to whom he is matched under matching *A* to Claire. Since Adam prefers Claire to Bess, it is impossible for Bess to be matched to Adam under *A*.

Finally, we show that Bess is not matched to Adam under matching *B*. Since *B* is a stable matching, Adam and Claire have no objection to it. Since Claire prefers Adam to Frank, Adam must prefer the woman to whom he is matched under *B* to Claire. Since Adam prefers Claire to Bess, it is impossible for Bess to be matched to Adam under *B*.

In other words, Bess is not matched to Adam under either *A* or *B*. If so, how could she be matched to Adam under the matching *C*? The contradiction establishes that *C* is a stable matching. □

Clearly, the matching $C := A \vee^w B$ is, for every woman, at least as good as *A*, and at least as good as *B*; that is, $C \succsim^w A$ and $C \succsim^w B$. By Theorem 23.11, the matching *C* is, for every man, worse than (or equally preferred to) both *A* and *B*; that is, $A \succsim^m C$ and $B \succsim^m C$.

Similarly, we can define, for every pair of matchings *A* and *B*, the collection of *n* pairs $D := A \vee^m B$, in which every man chooses the woman who is most preferred by him from among the women to whom he is matched under *A* and *B*. By reversing the roles of the men and the women in Theorem 23.14, we deduce that *D* is a stable matching, and that $D \succsim^m A$, $D \succsim^m B$, $A \succsim^w D$, and $B \succsim^w D$.

23.4.1 The lattice structure of the set of stable matchings

A partial ordering $\succsim$ is a reflexive and transitive binary relation.[3] In words, a partial ordering relation enables us to compare the members of some pairs of elements in a given set. A *partially ordered set* is a set with a partial ordering relation defined over it. An example of a partially ordered set is the pair $(X, \succsim)$, where X is the collection of all subsets of a set S, and for every two subsets U and V of S one has $U \succsim V$ if $U \supseteq V$. This is not a complete ordering when S contains at least two elements, because in this case there are two subsets of S that cannot be compared by this ordering (that is, two sets neither of which is a subset of the other).

Using the relation $\succsim$, we defined in Chapter 2 the concept of a *strict preference relation* $\succ$:

$$x \succ y \iff x \succsim y \text{ and } y \not\succsim x. \tag{23.2}$$

We also defined the *indifference* relation $\approx$:

$$x \approx y \iff x \succsim y \text{ and } y \succsim x. \tag{23.3}$$

Definition 23.15 *Let X be a finite set, let $\succsim$ be a partial ordering over X, and let $x_1, x_2 \in X$ be two elements in X. The element $y \in X$ is called the maximum of x_1 and x_2, and denoted $y = \max\{x_1, x_2\}$, if the following two conditions hold:*

1. $y \succsim x_1$ and $y \succsim x_2$.
2. *If $z \succsim x_1$ and $z \succsim x_2$, then $z \succsim y$.*

If X is the collection of subsets of a set S, and the relation $\succsim$ is the set inclusion relation, then the maximum of a pair of subsets of S is their union. The next example shows that there are partial orderings for which the maximum does not exist.

Example 23.16 Let $X = \{x_1, x_2, x_3, x_4\}$, and let the ordering relation be given by

$$x_1 \succ x_3, \quad x_2 \succ x_3, \quad x_1 \succ x_4, \quad x_2 \succ x_4. \tag{23.4}$$

The elements x_3 and x_4 have no maximum. Indeed, both x_1 and x_2 are greater than x_3 and greater than x_4, but one cannot compare them to each other, and therefore neither of them is a maximum for x_3 and x_4. The elements x_1 and x_2 also do not have a maximum, because there is no element greater than both of them. ◀

The minimum of a set is defined analogously to the definition of the maximum of a set.

Definition 23.17 *Let X be a finite set, $\succsim$ be a partial ordering relation over X, and let $x_1, x_2 \in X$ be two elements of X. An element $y \in X$ is a minimum of x_1 and x_2, denoted $y = \min\{x_1, x_2\}$, if the following conditions are satisfied:*

1. $x_1 \succsim y$ and $x_2 \succsim y$.
2. *If $x_1 \succsim z$ and $x_2 \succsim z$, then $y \succsim z$.*

---

3 We previously encountered, earlier in this chapter and in Chapter 2, the concept of a complete ordering in which all elements are comparable. In contrast, under a partial ordering it is possible for two elements to be incomparable.

Definition 23.18 *A* lattice *is a partially ordered set satisfying the property that any pair of elements in the set has a minimum and a maximum.*

For the partial ordering $\succsim^w$ over the set of stable matchings, the maximum of a pair of stable matchings A and B is the matching $A \vee^w B$; in other words, $\max\{A, B\} = A \vee^w B$, and the minimum of this pair of stable matchings is the matching $\min\{A, B\} = A \vee^m B$ (Exercise 23.20). Similarly, for the partial ordering $\succsim^m$ over a set of stable matchings, $\max\{A, B\} = A \vee^m B$ and $\min\{A, B\} = A \vee^w B$.

The above discussion leads to the following theorems.

Theorem 23.19 *Under the ordering relation $\succsim^w$, the set of stable matchings is a lattice.*

Similarly:

Theorem 23.20 *Under the ordering relation $\succsim^m$, the set of stable matchings is a lattice.*

Theorem 23.11 (page 940) states that in effect the lattices described by Theorems 23.19 and 23.20 are the same lattice: both are defined over the same set of elements (the set of stable matchings) and the maximum under the ordering relation $\succsim^w$ is the minimum under the ordering relation $\succsim^m$ (and vice versa).

23.5 Extensions

In this section we consider several extensions of the basic model that has been studied up to now.

23.5.1 When the number of men does not equal the number of women

We have so far dealt only with models in which the number of men equals the number of women. Suppose instead that n_m, the number of men, is greater than n_w, the number of women. The case in which the number of women is greater than the number of men is analyzed similarly. Since $n_m > n_w$, under every stable matching there must remain $n_m - n_w$ men who are not matched to a woman.

To fit this new situation, we need to change the definition of a matching. Recall that we denote by M the set of men, and by W the set of women.

Definition 23.21 *A* matching *is a function associating every man with an element of the set $W \cup \{single\}$, such that every woman is associated under this function with one man.*

We assume here that being single is considered by every man to be a worse outcome than being matched to any of the women.

Definition 23.22 *Suppose that a matching is given. A man m and a woman w* object *to the matching if the following conditions hold: (a) the man m is single, or is matched to a woman $\hat{w}$ and he prefers w to $\hat{w}$; and (b) the woman w prefers m to the man to whom she is matched under the matching.*

The Gale–Shapley algorithm that is presented in the previous sections is applicable to this case, and the proof of Theorem 23.7 goes through with minor modifications. In particular, the algorithm is guaranteed to terminate with a stable matching (Exercise 23.24). The next theorem, whose proof is left to the reader (Exercise 23.25), establishes that under all stable matchings, the set of singles is the same.

Theorem 23.23 *Suppose that the number of men is greater than the number of women. If a particular man is not matched to any woman under some stable matching, then he is not matched to a woman under any stable matching.*

23.5.2   Strategic considerations

In the men's courtship algorithm presented above, in every stage, every man goes to the house of the woman whom he ranks highest among all the women who have not previously dismissed him, and every woman asks the man she ranks highest from among the men standing in front of her house to stay, while dismissing all the rest. Does this algorithm leave any room for "strategic behavior"? In other words, is it possible that by pretending to have a preference relation that differs from her true preference relation, a woman can obtain a better match for herself than by being honest? The next example shows that this may indeed be possible.

Example 23.24   **An example of strategic behavior**   Consider an example with three men and three women whose preference relations are given by the tables shown in Figure 23.7, where 1, 2, and 3 denote placement within the preference list, with 1 representing highest preference.

	1	2	3
Hector:	Helena	Andromache	Lavinia
Aeneas:	Helena	Lavinia	Andromache
Paris:	Andromache	Helena	Lavinia

	1	2	3
Helena:	Paris	Hector	Aeneas
Andromache:	Hector	Paris	Aeneas
Lavinia:	Aeneas	Hector	Paris

Figure 23.7   The preferences of the men and the women

We trace the men's courtship algorithm (Figure 23.8).

	Helena	Andromache	Lavinia	Dismissed men
Stage 1(1a)	Aeneas(1), Hector(1)	Paris(1)		
Stage 1(b)	Hector(1)	Paris(1)		Aeneas
Stage 2(a)	Hector(1)	Paris(1)	Aeneas(2)	

Figure 23.8   Men's courtship algorithm

The resulting matching is

(Hector–Helena,   Aeneas–Lavinia,   Paris–Andromache).

Suppose, instead, that Helena were to act as if her preference relation is:

	1	2	3
Helena:	Paris	Aeneas	Hector

Then the men's courtship algorithm would look as shown in Figure 23.9.

	Helena	Andromache	Lavinia	Dismissed men
Stage 1(a)	Hector(1), Aeneas(1)	Paris(1)		
Stage 1(b)	Aeneas(1)	Paris(1)		Hector
Stage 2(a)	Aeneas(1)	Paris(1), Hector(2)		
Stage 2(b)	Aeneas(1)	Hector(2)		Paris
Stage 3(a)	Aeneas(1), Paris(2)	Hector(2)		
Stage 3(b)	Paris(2)	Hector(2)		Aeneas
Stage 4(a)	Paris(2)	Hector(2)	Aeneas(2)	

Figure 23.9 The men's courtship algorithm when Helena behaves strategically

The resulting matching is

(Hector–Andromache,   Aeneas–Lavinia,   Paris–Helena).

As can be seen, Helena has improved her situation by pretending that her preference relation is different from her true one: under this matching, she is matched to Paris, who is ranked first in her (true) preference relation, instead of to Hector, who is ranked second in her (true) preference relation. The matching that results from Helena's strategic behavior is a stable matching relative to the true preferences of the participants (check that this is true). This is no coincidence; in Exercise 23.29 we present conditions relating to a woman's strategic behavior that guarantee that the men's courtship algorithm terminates with a matching that is stable relative to the true preferences of all participants. ◄

The last example shows that a woman may sometimes obtain a more preferred mate under the men's courtship algorithm if she does not dismiss men according to her true preferences. It turns out that this is not possible for the men: under the men's courtship algorithm, a man cannot obtain a more preferred mate if he courts the women in an ordering that is different from his true preference ordering (Exercise 23.28). It follows in particular that when there are more men than women, a man who remains single at the end of the men's courtship algorithm will also remain single if he courts women under a different ordering than his true preference ordering.

23.5.3   The desire to remain single, or: getting married, but not at any price

In the model we have regarded so far, we assumed that every man prefers being with any woman to remaining single, and that every woman prefers being with any man to remaining single. How does our analysis change if some participants prefer the single life to being in a match that they dislike? We first need to define a model that enables this possibility.

Definition 23.25 A matching problem *is defined by:*

- *A set of men M and a set of women W.*
- *For every woman w, a preference relation over the set* $M \cup \{(w\text{-single})\}$.
- *For every man, a preference relation over the set* $W \cup \{(m\text{-single})\}$.

The elements "m-single" and "w-single" enable the participants to rank the single life in their list of preferences. For example, if

$$\text{Juliet: Romeo} > \text{Juliet-single,}$$

then Juliet prefers a match with Romeo to remaining single, but if

$$\text{Juliet: Juliet-single} > \text{Benvolio,}$$

then she prefers remaining single to a match with Benvolio.

The definition of a matching in this case is:

Definition 23.26 *A matching is a function associating every man $m \in M$ with an element of the set $W \cup \{(m\text{-single})\}$ and every woman $w \in W$ with an element of the set $M \cup \{(w\text{-single})\}$, such that if a man m is matched to a woman w, the woman w is matched to the man m.*

We also update the definitions of an objection and a stable matching. In contrast to Definition 23.4, where only pairs could object to a matching, in this model an objection to a matching can be raised by a single woman or a single man, in case one of them prefers remaining single to the person to whom he or she is matched under the matching. In addition, we also allow objections to be raised by pairs who are not necessarily matched under the matching, because one, or both of them, is single under the matching.

Definition 23.27 *Given a matching,*

1. *A man objects to the matching, if he is matched to a woman but prefers remaining single to the woman to whom he is matched.*
2. *A woman objects to the matching if she is matched to a man but prefers remaining single to the man to whom she is matched.*
3. *A man m and a woman w object to the matching if (a) the man prefers w to the woman to whom he is matched under the matching, or prefers w to remaining single, if he is not matched to any woman under the matching; and (b) the woman prefers m to the man to whom she is matched under the matching, or prefers m to remaining single, if she is not matched to any man under the matching.*

A matching is stable *if no man, no woman, and no pair of a man and a woman object to it.*

So far, we have changed our model by adding fictitious elements of the form $(w\text{-single})$ and $(m\text{-single})$; every woman w has a preference relation over the set $M \cup \{(w\text{-single})\}$ and every man m has a preference relation over the set $W \cup \{(m\text{-single})\}$. To generalize the Gale–Shapley algorithm to this model, expand the set of women and the set of men as follows:

- The set of men is $M' := M \cup \{(w\text{-single}) : w \in W\}$.
- The set of women is $W' := W \cup \{(m\text{-single}) : m \in M\}$.

We also expand the preference relation of every woman to a preference relation over M', and the preference relation of every man to a preference relation over W'. Define the preference relations of the fictitious elements, as follows:

- Every woman w prefers the element (w-single) to the element ($\hat{w}$-single), for every woman $\hat{w} \neq w$. The precise ordering under which the elements $\{(\hat{w}\text{-single}), \hat{w} \in W \backslash \{w\}\}$ are ordered is immaterial.
- Every man m prefers the element (m-single) to the element ($\hat{m}$-single), for every man $\hat{m} \neq m$. The precise ordering under which the elements $\{(\hat{m}\text{-single}), \hat{w} \in W \backslash \{w\}\}$ are ordered is immaterial.
- The element (w-single) prefers w to every other element in W'. The precise ordering under which the other elements are ordered in the preference relation of this element is immaterial.
- The element (m-single) prefers m to every other element in M'. The precise ordering under which the other elements are ordered in the preference relation of this element is immaterial.

In the men's courtship algorithm, every man courts the women in descending order according to his preference list. If m gets far enough down his list to reach the fictitious (m-single), then he will remain "at the door" of the element (m-single) when the algorithm terminates. Indeed, since the fictitious element (m-single) prefers m to all the other men, the man m will not be dismissed by (m-single). The algorithm terminates when at most one man stands in front of the house of each woman $w \in W$, i.e., when there can be no more dismissals.

Example 23.28   Consider a matching problem with the set of men $M = \{\text{Alan, Basil, Colin}\}$ and the set of women $W = \{\text{Rose, Sara}\}$. The preference relations of the men and women are depicted in the following tables, where 1, 2, and 3 denote placement within the preference list, with 1 representing highest preference.

	1	2	3
Alan:	Sara	Rose	Alan-single
Basil:	Rose	Basil-single	Sara
Colin:	Rose	Sara	Colin-single

	1	2	3	4
Rose:	Alan	Basil	Rose-single	Colin
Sara:	Basil	Colin	Sara-single	Alan

Two elements are now added to the set of men: (Rose-single) and (Sara-single), and similarly three elements are added to the set of women: (Alan-single), (Basil-single), and (Colin-single). One possible definition of a preference relation following the addition of the fictitious elements is:

	1	2	3	4	5
Alan:	Sara	Rose	Alan-single	Colin-single	Basil-single
Basil:	Rose	Basil-single	Sara	Colin-single	Alan-single
Colin:	Rose	Sara	Colin-single	Alan-single	Basil-single
Rose-single:	Rose	Sara	Colin-single	Alan-single	Basil-single
Sara-single:	Sara	Rose	Colin-single	Alan-single	Basil-single

	1	2	3	4	5
Rose:	Alan	Basil	Rose-single	Colin	Sara-single
Sara:	Basil	Colin	Sara-single	Alan	Sara-single
Alan-single:	Alan	Basil	Colin	Sara-single	Rose-single
Basil-single:	Basil	Alan	Colin	Sara-single	Rose-single
Colin-single:	Colin	Basil	Alan	Sara-single	Rose-single

The men's courtship matching and the women's courtship matching of the expanded problem is as follows (check that this is true):

Basil–(Basil-single), Alan–Rose, Colin–Sara,
(Rose-single)–(Alan-single), (Sara-single)–(Colin-single).

It follows that the only stable matching to the original problem is

(Basil–Basil-single, Alan–Rose, Colin–Sara).

◄

In Exercise 23.30, the reader is asked to spell out in detail the Gale–Shapley algorithm for this model and to prove that the algorithm always terminates after finding a stable matching.

23.5.4 Polygamous matching: placement of students in universities

We have so far assumed that every man is permitted to marry only one woman, and each woman is permitted to marry only one man. In some cases, however, such as matching medical residents and hospitals, universities and students, and corporations and employees, there is an asymmetry between the two sides of the market: hospitals, universities, and corporations are interested in more than one resident, student, or employee, while each resident, student, and employee generally chooses only one hospital, university, or employing corporation. A model that can accommodate such situations is as follows (for convenience, in the definition we have adopted terms used in student placement in universities).

Definition 23.29 *A polygamous matching problem is given by:*

- *A finite set of universities U and a finite set of students S.*
- *For each university $u \in U$ a quota $q_u \in \mathbb{N}$ that represents the maximal number of students it will accept.*
- *For each student $s \in S$, a preference relation over the set U.*
- *For each university $u \in U$, a preference relation over the set S.*

Definition 23.30 *A matching is a function assigning, to each university $u \in U$, a subset S containing between 0 and q_u students, such that each student in S is associated with at most one university. In other words, the sets of students associated to two different universities are disjoint sets.*

The concept of an objection is defined as follows:

Definition 23.31 *A university u and a student s object to a matching if both of the following conditions are met:*

- *The student s prefers university u to the university to which he is matched.*
- *University u is matched to fewer than q_u students, or it is matched with q_u students but prefers s to one of the students that are matched to it.*

A matching is stable *if there is no pair consisting of a university and a student who have an objection to it.*

To show that there always exists a stable matching, consider the following "student courtship" algorithm, under which students apply to universities and each university u asks the q_u students that it most prefers from among the students gathered at the university's gate to remain (instead of asking only one) and rejecting all the rest; if less than q_u students have applied, it asks all of them to remain. Every rejected student then goes to the university next down on his or her preference list. The proof that this algorithm always terminates after finding a stable matching is similar to the proof in the monogamous matching case (Exercise 23.31).

23.5.5 Unisexual matchings

We have so far matched men to women, thus assuming that pairs must be composed of at least one member of the two different sexes. But there are cases in which pairs need to be matched from a homogeneous population: students being paired for dormitory rooms, police officers paired in patrol cars, and so on. Interestingly, while heterosexual stable matchings are guaranteed always to exist, unisexual stable matchings may not exist, as the next example shows.

Example 23.32 **A unisexual population without a stable matching** Consider an example with four men, Alex, Benjamin, Chris, and Franklin, who are to be partitioned into two pairings. Each man has a preference relation over the other men given by the table shown in Figure 23.10.

	1	2	3
Alex:	Benjamin	Chris	Franklin
Benjamin:	Chris	Alex	Franklin
Chris:	Alex	Benjamin	Franklin
Franklin:	Alex	Chris	Benjamin

Figure 23.10 Preference relations in a single-sex example with no stable matching

We will now show that given these preference relations, there is no stable matching. Suppose, for example, that Franklin is paired with Alex, which then means that Benjamin is paired with Chris:

$$(\text{Franklin–Alex},\quad \text{Benjamin–Chris}).$$

Then Alex and Chris have an objection: Alex prefers Chris (number 2 on his list) to Franklin (number 3 on his list), and Chris prefers Alex (number 1 on his list) to Benjamin (number 2 on his list).

It can similarly be shown that there is no stable matching under which Franklin is paired with either Benjamin or Chris (Exercise 23.38). ◄

23.6 Remarks

The authors wish to thank Dov Samet for his assistance in the composition of this chapter. The introduction to this chapter is based on Roth [2005]. The reader interested in further study of the material in this chapter is directed to Roth and Sotomayor [1990] and Gusfield and Irving [1989], both of which contain a wealth of information on matching theory.

Exercise 23.17 is based on Dubins and Freedman [1981]. Exercises 23.27 and 23.28 are based on Gale and Sotomayor [1985].

23.7) Exercises

. . . .

23.1 Prove that every complete, irreflexive, and transitive relation is asymmetric: if $x \neq y$, then $x \succ y$ if and only if $y \nsucc x$.

23.2 Prove that the Gale–Shapley algorithm for finding a stable matching satisfies the following property: if Cleopatra asks Mark to stay in front of her house at stage k, and at a later stage she asks Julius to stay in front of her house, then she prefers Julius to Mark.

23.3 Consider the following system of preferences (recall that the preferences of the women appear in the lower right side of each cell (read vertically) and the preferences of the men appear on the upper left side (read horizontally)).

	Anne	Betty	Claire	Donna
Alfredo	1	2	3	4
	4	3	1	3
Ben	3	4	1	2
	3	1	3	4
Chris	2	4	1	3
	2	2	4	1
Dean	4	3	2	1
	1	4	2	2

Check whether the following matchings are stable. Justify your answers.

(Chris–Anne, Alfredo–Betty, Dean–Claire, Ben–Donna),
(Chris–Anne, Alfredo–Betty, Ben–Claire, Dean–Donna).

23.4 Prove that Definitions 23.4 and 23.5 on page 934 are equivalent.

23.5 In each of the following systems of preferences, find the stable matching that is obtained by the men's courtship algorithm, and the stable matching that is obtained by the women's courtship algorithm:

(a)

	1	2	3
Andre:	Anne	Barbara	Claire
Boris:	Barbara	Claire	Anne
Chris:	Claire	Anne	Barbara

	1	2	3
Anne:	Boris	Chris	Andre
Barbara:	Chris	Andre	Boris
Claire:	Chris	Boris	Andre

(b)

	1	2	3	4
Alex:	Ellen	Flora	Gail	Hillary
Bill:	Ellen	Hillary	Gail	Flora
Colin:	Flora	Ellen	Gail	Hillary
David:	Hillary	Flora	Gail	Ellen

	1	2	3	4
Ellen:	David	Colin	Alex	Bill
Flora:	Bill	David	Alex	Colin
Gail:	David	Alex	Bill	Colin
Hillary:	Colin	Bill	Alex	David

(c)

	1	2	3	4
Peter:	Olivia	Patty	Mary	Netty
Jacob:	Patty	Mary	Netty	Olivia
Kevin:	Mary	Netty	Olivia	Patty
Larry:	Patty	Olivia	Mary	Netty

	1	2	3	4
Mary:	Peter	Jacob	Kevin	Larry
Netty:	Peter	Jacob	Kevin	Larry
Olivia:	Jacob	Kevin	Peter	Larry
Patty:	Kevin	Peter	Jacob	Larry

(d)

	1	2	3	4
Ernest:	Felicia	Emma	Donna	Carol
Felix:	Emma	Donna	Carol	Felicia
George:	Donna	Carol	Felicia	Emma
Henry:	Emma	Felicia	Donna	Carol

	1	2	3	4
Carol:	Ernest	Felix	George	Henry
Donna:	Ernest	Felix	George	Henry
Emma:	George	Ernest	Felix	Henry
Felicia:	Felix	George	Ernest	Henry

(e)

	1	2	3	4
Peter:	Lisa	Melissa	Natasha	Octavia
Quentin:	Lisa	Melissa	Natasha	Octavia
Ron:	Melissa	Natasha	Lisa	Octavia
Sam:	Natasha	Lisa	Melissa	Octavia

	1	2	3	4
Lisa:	Ron	Sam	Peter	Quentin
Melissa:	Sam	Peter	Quentin	Ron
Natasha:	Peter	Quentin	Ron	Sam
Octavia:	Sam	Ron	Peter	Quentin

23.6 Suppose that the number of men equals the number of women.

(a) Prove that for every pair of matchings there exist preference relations for which these are two stable matchings.

(b) In this part we show that the claim in part (a) cannot be generalized to more than two matchings; that is, it is not true that for every three matchings there are preference relations for which these three matchings are stable. Suppose that the set of men is $M = \{X, Y, Z, W\}$ and the set of women is $\{x, y, z, w\}$. Prove that there are no preference relations to the set of men and the set of women for which the following three matchings are stable:

$$A_1 : \quad Y\text{–}w, Z\text{–}z, W\text{–}y, X\text{–}x, \qquad\qquad (23.5)$$

$$A_2 : \quad Z\text{–}w, W\text{–}z, Y\text{–}y, X\text{–}x, \qquad\qquad (23.6)$$

$$A_3 : \quad X\text{–}w, Z\text{–}z, Y\text{–}y, W\text{–}x. \qquad\qquad (23.7)$$

23.7 Gary is at the top of Gail's preference list, and Gail is at the top of Gary's preference list. Prove that in every stable matching Gary and Gail are matched to each other.

23.8 Dan is at the bottom of Donna's preference list, and Donna is at the bottom of Dan's preference list. Is it possible that there is a stable matching that matches Dan to Donna? Justify your answer.

23.9 Prove that if Romeo and Juliet are matched to each other under both the men's courtship and the women's courtship algorithms, then they are matched to each other under any stable matching.

23.10 Prove that if the result of the men's courtship algorithm yields the same result as the women's courtship algorithm, then this resulting matching is the unique stable matching.

23.11 Given a stable matching of n men and n women:

(a) Is it possible to find three pairs such that if the matching among them is changed, each man will be matched to a woman whom he prefers, and each woman will be matched to a man whom she prefers?

(b) Generalize this conclusion to a subset of k pairs, for every $4 \leq k \leq n$.

23.12 In Julius's list of preferences, Agrippina appears first, Messalina appears second, and Cleopatra appears third. Suppose there is a stable matching under which Julius is matched to Agrippina, and that there is a stable matching under which Julius is matched to Cleopatra. Is there necessarily a stable matching under which Julius is matched to Messalina? Either prove this statement or provide a counterexample.

23.13 In this exercise we consider a situation with n men and n women.

(a) Prove that if in stage t of the men's courtship algorithm, a particular man is dismissed for the $(n-1)$-th time, then the algorithm terminates at stage $(t+1)$.

(b) Prove that the men's courtship algorithm terminates after at most $(n-1)^2+1$ stages.

(c) Find preference relations under which the algorithm terminates after precisely $(n-1)^2+1$ stages (hence this is the lowest bound for the length of the algorithm).

23.14 Suppose that Fara is preferred by every man to all the other women. Prove that under every stable matching Fara is matched to the same man. Who is the lucky guy?

23.15 Suppose that the number of men equals the number of women, and that Vera is last on the preference list of every man. Prove that under every stable matching, Vera is matched to the same man.

23.16 Suppose that every man has the same preference relation over the set of women. Prove that there exists only one stable matching.

23.17 In this exercise, we present a family of algorithms, each of which produces the men's courtship matching, and contains the Gale–Shapley algorithm.

Consider the following algorithm for matching men and women. At the start of the algorithm, all the men leave the room, while all the women remain in the room. In every stage of the algorithm, one of the men who is outside the room enters, and goes directly to the woman whom he most prefers from among the women who have not previously dismissed him. If another man is already standing next to that woman, the woman asks the man whom she prefers from among those two who are now next to her to stay, and dismisses the other one, who then leaves the room. If, however, a man entering the room goes to a woman who is standing alone, she asks him to stay. The algorithm terminates when every woman has exactly one man standing next to her.

(a) Prove that this algorithm satisfies the three properties of the Gale–Shapley algorithm (specified on page 936).

(b) Prove that this algorithm terminates, and that it always yields a stable matching.

(c) Prove that the algorithm always produces the men's courtship matching O^m.

23.18 Prove that the preference relations on matchings $\succsim^m$ and $\succsim^w$ over the set of stable matchings are transitive relations.

23.19 Show that Theorem 23.11 on page 940 does not hold if the matchings A and B are not stable. In other words, find two matchings A and B satisfying $A \succsim^m B$ but $B \not\succsim^w A$.

23.20 Prove that when the partial ordering over the set of stable matchings is $\succsim^w$, then $\max\{A, B\} = A \vee^w B$ and $\min\{A, B\} = A \vee^m B$.

23.21 Show by example that if A and B are two matchings (not necessarily stable), then $A \vee^w B$ is not necessarily a matching.

23.22 Prove that when the partial ordering over the set of stable matchings is $\succsim^w$, the minimum of the stable matchings A and B is $A \vee^m B$.

23.23 In this exercise we generalize the definition of the maximum of two matchings to a definition of the maximum of any finite set with two or more matchings. Suppose that the number of women equals the number of men. Let $A_1, A_2, \ldots, A_K$ be stable matchings. Define a function B from the set of men to the set of women as follows. Under the function B, a man m is matched to the woman he most prefers from among the women to whom he is matched under the matchings $A_1, A_2, \ldots, A_K$.

(a) Prove that the function B is a matching.
(b) Prove that the function B is a stable matching.
(c) Prove that for each stable matching C, if $C \succsim^m A_k$ for every $k \in \{1, 2, \ldots, K\}$ then $C \succsim^m B$. Matching C is the maximum of $A_1, A_2, \ldots, A_K$ according to the preference relations of the men.

23.24 Suppose that the matching problem is to match n_m men to n_w women, where $n_w < n_m$.

(a) Describe in detail the generalization of the Gale–Shapley algorithm for this case. Prove that the algorithm terminates with a stable matching.
(b) What is the maximal number of stages in the men's courtship algorithm?
(c) Construct an example where $n_m > n_w$ such that the men's courtship algorithm runs through the maximal number of stages.

23.25 Prove Theorem 23.23 on page 946: when the number of men n_m is greater than the number of women n_w, if a particular man is not matched to any woman under some stable matching, then he is not matched to any woman under any stable matching.

23.26 In each of the following pairs of preference relation systems, find the men's courtship matching and the women's courtship matching:

(a)

	1	2	3
Oscar:	Kara	Lilly	Mary
Peter:	Kara	Lilly	Mary
Quinn:	Kara	Mary	Lilly
Ralph:	Lilly	Kara	Mary

	1	2	3	4
Kara:	Ralph	Quinn	Peter	Oscar
Lilly:	Ralph	Oscar	Quinn	Peter
Mary:	Oscar	Ralph	Peter	Quinn

(b) The notation ϕ signifies a preference for remaining single:

	1	2	3	4
Grant:	Gloria	Hanna	ϕ	Ida
Howard:	Hanna	Gloria	Ida	ϕ
Isaac:	Gloria	Ida	ϕ	Hanna
Jack:	Hanna	Gloria	ϕ	Ida

	1	2	3	4	5
Gloria:	Jack	Isaac	ϕ	Howard	Grant
Hanna:	Jack	Howard	Grant	ϕ	Isaac
Ida:	Isaac	Grant	ϕ	Howard	Jack

23.27 Let A be a matching (not necessarily stable), and let M_{A,O^m} be the set of men who prefer the women to whom they are matched under A to the women to whom they are matched under the men's courtship matching O^m.

(a) Prove that if A is a stable matching then $M_{A,O^m} = \varnothing$.

In this exercise we prove that if $M_{A,O^m} \neq \varnothing$, then there exists a pair (m, w) who object to the matching A, and $m \notin M_{A,O^m}$.

Denote by W_1 the set of the women who are matched to men in M_{A,O^m} under the matching A, and by W_2 the set of the women matched to men in M_{A,O^m} under O^m.

(b) Prove that if $W_1 \neq W_2$, then $W_1 \backslash W_2 \neq \varnothing$.
(c) Prove that if $W_1 \neq W_2$, every woman $w \in W_1 \backslash W_2$ objects to A along with the man to whom she is matched under O^m.
(d) From here to the end of the exercise, assume that $W_1 = W_2$. Prove that every woman in W_1 dismisses at least one man under the men's courtship algorithm (her match under the matching A).
(e) Consider the woman $w^* \in W_1$ who was the last woman approached by a man m^* from the set M_{A,O^m} under the men's courtship algorithm. Prove that when w^* receives an offer from m^*, there was another man at her doorstep, call him m', whom she dismissed in favor of m^*.
(f) Use the fact that w^* is the last woman to get an offer from a man in M_{A,O^m} to show that m' is not in M_{A,O^m}.
(g) Prove that the pair (m', w^*) object to the matching A.

23.28 Suppose we are given a matching problem G. Let O^m be the men's courtship matching of this problem. In this exercise we prove the claim on page 947: in the course of the Gale–Shapley algorithm, a man cannot obtain a better result by pretending to have a preference relation that is different from his true preference relation. We will, in fact, prove a stronger claim: even if a set of men all pretend to have preference relations that are different from their true preference relations, under any stable matching of the new problem that is different from O^m, one of these men does not gain; in other words, one of these men will be matched to the woman to whom he is matched under O^m or to a woman he prefers even less than the one he is matched to under O^m.

Let $\widehat{G}$ be the matching problem derived from G by changing the preference relations of some of the men: let $\widehat{M} \subseteq M$ be a set of men whom we term "dishonest," whose preference relations in matching problem $\widehat{G}$ differ from their preference relations in matching problem G.

Using Exercise 23.27, prove that there is no stable matching $\widehat{A}$ for matching problem $\widehat{G}$ satisfying the following properties: every man in $\widehat{M}$ prefers (according to his true preference relation) the woman to whom he is matched under $\widehat{A}$ to the woman to whom he is matched under O^m.

23.29 We saw in Example 23.24 that under the men's courtship algorithm a woman may be matched to a man whom she prefers to the man to whom she is matched under the men's courtship matching O^m by pretending that her preference relation is different from her true preference relation. In this exercise we present a condition that guarantees that a matching resulting from such strategic behavior on the part of a woman is a stable matching.

Suppose that under the men's courtship matching O^m Messalina is matched to Claudius. Consider the matching A that results from the men's courtship algorithm when Messalina pretends that her preference relation is different from her true preference relation.

(a) Prove that the matching A is a stable matching under the true preferences of the men and women if and only if the man to whom Messalina is matched under A is the man she most prefers from among the men that came to her door throughout the algorithm; that is, she does not regret any rejection she made.

(b) Conclude that if Messalina improved her result by this behavior then she necessarily makes at least one man worse off; i.e., there is at least one man who is matched under A to a woman whom he prefers less than the woman to whom he is matched under O^m.

23.30 Describe in detail the generalization of the Gale–Shapley algorithm for the case in which the single life is not universally considered the worst possible outcome (see Section 23.5.3 on page 947), and prove that the algorithm always terminates in finding a stable matching.

23.31 Describe in detail the generalization of the Gale–Shapley algorithm (the students' courtship algorithm) in the case in which each university has a quota for the maximal number of students that it can accept (see Section 23.5.4 on page 950), and prove that the algorithm always terminates in finding a stable matching. Describe the universities' courtship algorithm in this case. Which algorithm is more preferred by the students? Explain.

23.32 In this exercise, we work with polygamous matchings (see Section 23.5.4 on page 950).

(a) Prove that in the students' courtship algorithm, every student is matched to the university that is most preferred by him from among all the universities to which he is matched under all possible stable matchings.

(b) Given a stable matching, prove that every student who is not matched by any university under this matching is not matched to any university under any stable matching.

(c) Prove that if under one stable matching there is a university that does not fill its student quota, then that university does not fill its student quota under any stable matching.

23.33 In this exercise we generalize the model of polygamous matchings (see Section 23.5.4 on page 950).

Suppose that every university $u \in U$ is given a quota $q_u \geq 1$, a subset $S_u \subseteq S$ of the set of students, and a preference relation over the set S_u. The set S_u is interpreted as the set of students that university u is willing to accept: university u will not accept any student who is not in S_u, even if that means that it will not fill its quota of students. Suppose that each student $s \in S$ is given a subset $U_s \subseteq U$ of the set of universities, and a preference relation over U_s. The set U_s is interpreted as the set of universities that the student is willing to attend. If a student s is rejected by all the universities in S_u, then he prefers not attending any university.

(a) Generalize the definition of stable matching to this case.
(b) Generalize the Gale–Shapley algorithm to this case, and prove that it terminates after finding a stable matching.
(c) Prove that a student who is not accepted by any university under a particular stable matching will not be accepted into any university under any stable matching.

23.34 The following tables depict the preferences of three universities regarding a set of applicants, and the preferences of the applicants regarding the universities. Every university also has a specified quota for the number of students that it can accept. These preferences are strict preferences, i.e., there are no instances of indifference. Find a stable matching A between the universities and the applicants that is preferred by all the applicants to any other stable matching; i.e., for any stable matching B, an applicant who is matched to two different universities under A and B prefers the university to which he is matched under A to the university to which he is matched under B.

(a) The preferences of the universities (from left to right) and each university's quota of students (between the round brackets) are:
University X (4): $j\,b\,a\,k\,g\,d\,c\,e\,f\,h\,i$.
University Y (2): $d\,b\,h\,a\,j\,f\,k\,e\,c\,i\,g$.
University Z (3): $f\,c\,j\,b\,h\,d\,e\,g\,i\,k\,a$.

The preferences of the applicants (from left to right) are:

$a : ZYX$	$d : ZXY$	$g : XZY$	$j : XYZ$
$b : ZYX$	$e : ZXY$	$h : YXZ$	$k : XYZ$
$c : YZX$	$f : XZY$	$i : YXZ$	

(b) The preferences of the universities (from left to right) and each university's quota of students (between the round brackets) are:
University X (6): $a\,b\,c\,d\,e\,f\,g\,h\,i\,j\,k\,l\,m\,n$.
University Y (6): $n\,m\,l\,k\,j\,i\,h\,g\,f\,e\,d\,c\,b\,a$.
The preferences of the applicants: applicants $a, b, c, d, e, f, g, h, i, j$ prefer University X to University Y, and applicants k, l, m, n prefer University Y to University X.

23.35 In this exercise, we will assume a given matching problem in which the preference relations are weak preference relations, meaning that the preference relations may include indifference; a woman may be indifferent to being matched to any of several different men, and a man may be indifferent to being matched to any of several different women. For example, Yoko may be indifferent between John, Paul, George, and Ringo, and she may be indifferent between Tony and Allan, and she may prefer each of John, Paul, George, and Ringo to Tony and to Allan. That is,

$$\text{Yoko}: \text{Ringo} \approx \text{George} \approx \text{Paul} \approx \text{John} > \text{Allan} \approx \text{Tony}.$$

A man and a woman object to a matching if they both (strictly) prefer each other to the woman and man to whom they are respectively matched. A matching is stable if there are no men and women objecting to it.

(a) Given each man's weak preference relation, construct a strict preference relation by ordering the women to whom he is indifferent in an arbitrary way, while maintaining transitivity of preferences, and do the same with the preference relation of each woman. Prove that a stable matching under this constructed set of preference relations is also a stable matching in the original matching problem with weak preferences.

(b) Find at least two stable matchings for the following preference relations:

Tina: Albert > Boris > Chester ≈ David
Ursula: Chester ≈ Albert > Boris > David
Victoria: Chester ≈ David > Boris ≈ Albert

Albert: Tina ≈ Victoria > Ursula
Boris: Victoria > Ursula ≈ Tina
Chester: Tina > Victoria ≈ Ursula
David: Victoria ≈ Tina ≈ Ursula

23.36 As in Exercise 23.35, consider a matching problem in which the preference relations of the men and women may include instances of indifference. Given a stable matching to such a matching problem, is it always possible to replace the weak preference relations (i.e., with instances of indifference) with strict preference relations in such a way that the stable matching with respect to the weak preference relations is also a stable matching with respect to the strict preference relations? If your answer is yes, prove it; if your answer is no, provide a counterexample.

23.37 Theorem 23.23 is proved on page 946 under the assumption that all preference relations are strict. Show by example that the theorem does not hold if there may be instances of indifference in the preference relations of the men and the women.

23.38 Example 23.32 (page 951) has no stable matching. Complete the proof of this statement.

23.39 Suppose that a population of size $3n$ is partitioned into three subsets: n contractors, n carpenters, and n plumbers. Each person in this population has two preference relations: a preference relation over each one of the two subsets listed above to which he does not belong. For example, each contractor has a preference relation over the set of carpenters, and a preference relation over the set of plumbers, and so on. A matching A in this case is a partition of the population into n triples, each composed of a contractor, a carpenter, and a plumber. A trio composed of a contractor x, a carpenter y, and a plumber z has an objection to A if (a) the matching A does not contain the set $\{x, y, z\}$, and (b) every pair of workers within this trio who are not matched to each other under A prefer each other to the corresponding workers to whom they have been matched under A. In other words, x prefers y to the carpenter to whom he is matched under A (if he is matched to a carpenter other than y), x prefers z to the plumber to whom he is matched under A (if he is matched to a plumber other than z), y prefers x to the contractor to whom he is matched under A (if he is matched to a contractor other than x), and so on. A matching is stable if there is no trio composed of a contractor, a carpenter, and a plumber who object to it.

Does there always exist a stable matching in this model? If your answer is no, provide a counterexample. If your answer is yes, provide an algorithm for finding a stable matching, and prove that this algorithm always terminates in finding a stable matching.

23.40 Repeat Exercise 23.39, but this time assume that each member of the population has a preference relation over pairs of potential co-workers, i.e., every contractor has a preference relation over the set of pairs composed of a carpenter and a plumber, every carpenter has a preference relation over the set of pairs composed of a contractor and a plumber, and every plumber has a preference relation over the set of pairs composed of a contractor and a carpenter. A contractor x, carpenter y, and plumber z have an objection to a matching A if (a) A does not contain the set $\{x, y, z\}$, and (b) each member of the trio $\{x, y, z\}$ ranks the other two above the pair to which he is matched under A. A matching is stable if there is not a trio composed of a contractor, a carpenter, and a plumber who have an objection to it.

24 Appendices

Chapter summary

In this chapter we present some basic results from different areas of mathematics required for various proofs in the book. In Section 24.1 we state and prove several fixed point theorems. The main and best known is Brouwer's Fixed Point Theorem, which states that every continuous function from a compact and convex subset of a Euclidean space to itself has a fixed point. This theorem is used in Chapter 5 to prove the existence of a Nash equilibrium in mixed strategies. Using Brouwer's Fixed Point Theorem we prove Kakutani's Fixed Point Theorem, which states that every upper semi-continuous convex-valued correspondence from a compact and convex subset of a Euclidean space to itself has a fixed point. This result provides a shorter proof for the existence of a Nash equilibrium in mixed strategies in strategic-form games. We then prove the KKM Theorem, which is used to prove the nonemptiness of the bargaining set (Theorem 20.19, page 838). The main tool for proving both Brouwer's Fixed Point Theorem and the KKM Theorem is Sperner's Lemma, which is stated and proved first.

In Section 24.2 we prove the Separating Hyperplane Theorem, which states that for every convex set in a Euclidean space and a point not in the set there is a hyperplane separating the set and the point. This theorem is used in Chapter 14 to prove that every B-set is an approachable set.

Section 24.3 presents the formulation and the central result in linear programs, namely, the Duality Theorem of linear programming. This result is used to prove the Bondareva–Shapley Theorem that characterizes coalitional games with nonempty cores (Theorem 18.19, page 749) and to characterize balanced collections of coalitions (Theorem 21.25, page 864).

24.1 Fixed point theorems

In this section we formulate and prove three theorems: Brouwer's Fixed Point Theorem, Kakutani's Fixed Point Theorem, and the KKM Theorem. The reader interested in additional fixed point theorems used in game theory, and in a discussion of the connections between them, is directed to Border [1989].

We begin by presenting the statement and proof of Sperner's Lemma, which is a vital element in our proofs of fixed point theorems.

Figure 24.1 The extreme points of a circle and of a square

24.1.1 Sperner's Lemma

For $n \in \mathbb{N}$ denote the zero vector in $\mathbb{R}^n$ by $\vec{0}$. Recall that a set $X \subseteq \mathbb{R}^n$ is called *convex* if $\lambda x + (1 - \lambda)y \in X$ for all $x, y \in X$ and all $\lambda \in [0, 1]$.

Definition 24.1 *Let* $x^0, x^1, \ldots, x^k$ *be vectors in* $\mathbb{R}^n$. *The* convex hull *of* $x^0, x^1, \ldots, x^k$, *denoted* $\mathrm{conv}(x^0, x^1, \ldots, x^k)$, *is the smallest convex set (with respect to set inclusion) that contains* $x^0, x^1, \ldots, x^k$.

When $x = \sum_{l=0}^{k} \alpha^l x^l$ for nonnegative numbers $(\alpha^l)_{l=0}^k$ whose sum is 1, we say that x is a *convex combination* of the points $x^0, x^1, \ldots, x^k$. It follows (see Exercise 24.1) that

$$\mathrm{conv}(x^0, x^1, \ldots, x^k) = \left\{ x \in \mathbb{R}^n : x \text{ is a convex combination of } x^0, \ldots, x^k \right\}. \qquad (24.1)$$

Definition 24.2 *Let* $X \subseteq \mathbb{R}^n$ *be a convex set. A vector* $x \in X$ *is an* extreme point *of* X *if for every two distinct points* $y, z \in X$, *and for every* $\alpha \in (0, 1)$,

$$\alpha y + (1 - \alpha)z \neq x. \qquad (24.2)$$

In words, a point is an extreme point of a convex set if it cannot be expressed as a convex combination of two different points in that set. Equivalently, a point is an extreme point of a convex set if there is no open interval that both contains it and is contained in that set. If none of the vectors $x^0, x^1, \ldots, x^k$ is a convex combination of the other vectors, then the extreme points of the convex hull $\mathrm{conv}(x^0, x^1, \ldots, x^k)$ are $x^0, x^1, \ldots, x^k$ (Exercise 24.2). Figure 24.1 depicts the extreme points of a square (four points) and of a circle (all the boundary points of the circle) in $\mathbb{R}^2$.

Definition 24.3 *The vectors* $x^0, x^1, \ldots, x^k$ *in* $\mathbb{R}^n$ *are called* affine independent *if the only solution of the following system of equations with unknowns* $(\alpha^l)_{l=0}^k$ *in* $\mathbb{R}$:

$$\sum_{l=0}^{k} \alpha^l x^l = \vec{0}, \qquad (24.3)$$

$$\sum_{l=0}^{k} \alpha^l = 0, \qquad (24.4)$$

is given by $\alpha^0 = \alpha^1 = \cdots = \alpha^k = 0$. *If this condition is not satisfied, the vectors* $x^0, x^1, \ldots, x^k$ *in* $\mathbb{R}^n$ *are called* affine dependent.

We say that a vector $y \in \mathbb{R}^n$ *is affine independent of the vectors* $x^0, x^1, \ldots, x^k$ *if the vectors* $(x^0, x^1, \ldots, x^k, y)$ *are affine independent.*

It follows from the definition that every subset of a set of affine-independent vectors is also affine independent (why?), and every superset of a set of affine-dependent vectors is also affine dependent. In addition, affine dependence implies linear dependence, which means that linear independence implies affine independence. The following example shows that the converse does not hold. The example shows that the space $\mathbb{R}^n$ may contain $n + 1$ vectors that are affine independent. Since any $n + 1$ vectors in $\mathbb{R}^n$ are linearly dependent, it follows that affine independence does not imply linear independence. Thus, the concepts of linear independence and affine independence are not identical.

Example 24.4 For $n > 1$ denote by $e^l = (0, \ldots, 0, 1, 0, \ldots, 0)$ the l unit vector in $\mathbb{R}^n$; by this we mean the vector all of whose coordinates are 0 except for the l-th coordinate, which is equal to 1. The set $\{e^1, e^2, \ldots, e^n, \vec{0}\}$ is a set of $n + 1$ affine-independent vectors.
To see this, let $(\alpha^l)_{l=1}^{n+1}$ be a solution of the following system of equations:

$$\sum_{l=1}^{n} \alpha^l e^l + \alpha^{n+1} \vec{0} = \vec{0}, \tag{24.5}$$

$$\sum_{l=1}^{n+1} \alpha^l = 0. \tag{24.6}$$

For $l = 1, 2, \ldots, n$, the l-th coordinate on the left-hand side of Equation (24.5) equals α^l, and therefore $\alpha^l = 0$ for every $l = 1, 2, \ldots, n$. Equation (24.6) implies that $\alpha^{n+1} = 0$, and therefore the vectors $e^1, e^2, \ldots, e^n, \vec{0}$ are affine independent. ◀

Note that a set of vectors containing the vector $\vec{0}$ is necessarily linearly dependent. In contrast, as Example 24.4 shows, a set of vectors containing the vector $\vec{0}$ may be affine independent.

Example 24.5 Let $x^0, x^1, \ldots, x^k$ be affine-independent vectors. Denote their center of gravity by $y := \frac{1}{k+1} \sum_{l=0}^{k} x^l$. Then the set $\{x^1, \ldots, x^k, y\}$ is affine independent (note that x^0 is not in this set). To see this, let $(\alpha^l)_{l=1}^{k+1}$ be a solution of the following system of equations:

$$\sum_{l=1}^{k} \alpha^l x^l + \alpha^{k+1} y = \vec{0}, \tag{24.7}$$

$$\sum_{l=1}^{k+1} \alpha^l = 0. \tag{24.8}$$

Define

$$\beta^l := \begin{cases} \alpha^l + \frac{\alpha^{k+1}}{k+1} & \text{if } 1 \le l \le k, \\ \frac{\alpha^{k+1}}{k+1} & \text{if } l = 0. \end{cases} \tag{24.9}$$

Then $\sum_{l=0}^{k} \beta^l = \sum_{l=1}^{k+1} \alpha^l = 0$ (check that this true), and by Equation (24.7),

$$\sum_{l=0}^{k} \beta^l x^l = \frac{\alpha^{k+1}}{k+1} x^0 + \sum_{l=1}^{k} \left(\alpha^l + \frac{\alpha^{k+1}}{k+1} \right) x^l = \sum_{l=1}^{k} \alpha^l x^l + \alpha^{k+1} y = \vec{0}. \tag{24.10}$$

Since the vectors $x^0, x^1, \ldots, x^k$ are affine independent, $\beta^l = 0$ for all $l = 0, 1, \ldots, k$, and therefore $\alpha^l = 0$ for all $l = 1, 2, \ldots, k+1$. In other words, the vectors $x^1, \ldots, x^k, y$ are affine independent.   ◀

In Example 24.5, we can replace each of the vectors $x^1, \ldots, x^k$ (not necessarily x^0) with the center of weight y and the resulting set of vectors will still remain affine independent. In fact, we can replace each of the vectors $\{x^0, x^1, \ldots, x^k\}$ with any convex combination $z := \sum_{l=0}^{k} \gamma^l x^l$ in which all the weights $(\gamma^l)_{l=0}^{k}$ are positive (but not necessarily equal) and the resulting set of vectors will still remain affine independent (Exercise 24.6).

For every vector $x = (x_1, x_2, \ldots, x_n) \in \mathbb{R}^n$ denote $x_+ := (x_1, x_2, \ldots, x_n, 1) \in \mathbb{R}^{n+1}$. The definition of an affine independent set of vectors (Definition 24.3) implies that the set of vectors $\{x^1, x^2, \cdots, x^k\}$ is affine independent if and only if the set of vectors $\{x_+^1, x_+^2, \cdots, x_+^k\}$ is linearly independent.

Since every collection of $n + 2$ vectors in $\mathbb{R}^{n+1}$ is linearly dependent we obtain the following result.

Theorem 24.6 *Every subset of $\mathbb{R}^n$ containing $n + 2$ or more vectors is affine dependent.*

For $n = 1$ the space $\mathbb{R}^n$ is the real line, and vectors are real numbers. The theorem states that in that space every triple of real numbers is affine dependent. Any given three vectors in $\mathbb{R}^n$ are affine independent if and only if none of them is a convex combination of the other two (Exercise 24.10).

The following theorem shows how to find affine-independent vectors using linearly independent vectors. Its proof is left to the reader (Exercise 24.40).

Theorem 24.7 *Let $x^0, x^1, \ldots, x^k$ be affine-independent vectors in $\mathbb{R}^n$, and let y be a vector that is linearly independent of $\{x^0, x^1, \ldots, x^k\}$. Then the vectors $x^0, x^1, \ldots, x^k, y$ are affine independent.*

Definition 24.8 *A set $S \subseteq \mathbb{R}^n$ is called a k-dimensional simplex if it is the convex hull of $k + 1$ affine-independent vectors.*

If $x^0, x^1, \ldots, x^k$ are affine-independent vectors whose convex hull is the k-dimensional simplex S, then we write

$$S = \langle\langle x^0, x^1, \ldots, x^k \rangle\rangle := \text{conv}(x^0, x^1, \ldots, x^k). \tag{24.11}$$

A simplex is a compact and convex set. A zero-dimensional simplex is a set containing only one point. A one-dimensional simplex is a closed interval, and a two-dimensional simplex is a triangle.

The next theorem, whose proof is left to the reader (Exercise 24.7), states that every vector in a simplex can be uniquely represented as a convex combination of the extreme points of the simplex.

Theorem 24.9 *Let $x^0, x^1, \ldots, x^k$ be affine-independent vectors in $\mathbb{R}^n$. Let $y \in \langle\langle x^0, x^1, \ldots, x^k \rangle\rangle$. Then y has a unique representation as a convex combination of*

$x^0, x^1, \ldots, x^k$. *In other words, the following system of equations with unknowns* $(\alpha^l)_{l=0}^k$ *in* $\mathbb{R}$ *has a unique solution:*

$$\sum_{l=0}^k \alpha^l x^l = y, \tag{24.12}$$

$$\sum_{l=0}^k \alpha^l = 1, \tag{24.13}$$

$$\alpha^l \geq 0 \quad \forall l = 0, 1, \ldots, k. \tag{24.14}$$

If the system of Equations (24.13) and (24.14) has a solution (omitting Equation (24.14)) we say that y is an *affine combination* of $(x^l)_{l=0}^k$. It follows that if y is a convex combination of $(x^l)_{l=0}^k$, then it is an affine combination of those vectors (but the converse is not true).

Theorem 24.9 leads to the definition of a new coordinate system for vectors in the simplex $\langle\langle x^0, x^1, \ldots, x^k \rangle\rangle$: the coordinates of a point y in the simplex are the weights $(\alpha^l)_{l=0}^k$ satisfying Equations (24.12)–(24.14). Every point $y \in \mathbb{R}^n$ that is a linear combination of $x^0, x^1, \ldots, x^k$ but is not in their convex hull can also be represented by weights $(\alpha^l)_{l=0}^k$ satisfying Equations (24.12) and (24.13) but not Equation (24.14) (Exercise 24.9). This coordinate system is called the *barycentric coordinate system* (relative to the vectors $x^0, x^1, \ldots, x^k$).

The barycentric coordinates of a point in the simplex $\langle\langle x^0, x^1, \ldots, x^k \rangle\rangle$ can be given the following physical interpretation: if $(\alpha^l)_{l=0}^k$ are the barycentric coordinates of y (relative to the vectors $x^0, x^1, \ldots, x^k$), then if we place a weight α^l at each point x^l, the center of gravity of the resulting system is y.

Since every subset of a set of affine-independent vectors is itself a set of affine-independent vectors, we deduce the following theorem.

Theorem 24.10 *Let* $\langle\langle x^0, x^1, \ldots, x^k \rangle\rangle$ *be a k-dimensional simplex in* $\mathbb{R}^n$. *Then for every set* $\{x^{l_0}, x^{l_1}, \ldots, x^{l_t}\} \subseteq \{x^0, x^1, \ldots, x^k\}$, *the convex hull of* $x^{l_0}, x^{l_1}, \ldots, x^{l_t}$ *is a t-dimensional simplex in* $\mathbb{R}^n$.

The simplex $\langle\langle x^{l_0}, x^{l_1}, \ldots, x^{l_t} \rangle\rangle$ is called a *t-dimensional face* of S. The face of a simplex S, of any dimension, is a subsimplex of S, that is, a simplex contained in S. In particular, the simplex S is itself a face of S.

Definition 24.11 *Let* $S = \langle\langle x^0, x^1, \ldots, x^k \rangle\rangle$ *be a simplex in* $\mathbb{R}^n$. *The* boundary *of S is the union of all the* $(k-1)$-*dimensional subsimplices of S, i.e.,*[1]

---

1 For $l = 0$ and $l = k$, the simplices in the union are $\langle\langle x^1, x^2, \ldots, x^k \rangle\rangle$ and $\langle\langle x^0, x^1, \ldots, x^{k-1} \rangle\rangle$, respectively.

$$\bigcup_{l=0}^{k}\langle\langle x^0, x^1, \dots, x^{l-1}, x^{l+1}, \dots, x^k\rangle\rangle.$$

In other words, the boundary of S is the union of all the $(k-1)$ faces of S, and it contains all the points y in S whose barycentric coordinate representation contains at least one coordinate that is zero (Exercise 24.10).

Definition 24.12 *Let $S \subseteq \mathbb{R}^n$ be a k-dimensional simplex in $\mathbb{R}^n$. A simplicial partition of S is a collection $\mathcal{T} = \{T_1, T_2, \dots, T_M\}$ of simplices in $\mathbb{R}^n$ satisfying.[2]*

1. *$\bigcup_{m=1}^{M} T_m = S$: the union of all the simplices in $\mathcal{T}$ is the simplex S.*
2. *For every j, m, $0 \le j \le m \le M$, the intersection $T_j \cap T_m$ is either the empty set or a face both of T_j and of T_m.*
3. *If T is a simplex in the collection $\mathcal{T}$, then all of its faces are also elements of this collection.*
4. *If T is an l-dimensional simplex in $\mathcal{T}$, for $l < k$, then it is contained in an $l+1$-dimensional simplex in $\mathcal{T}$.*

Example 24.13   Let x^0, x^1, x^2 be three affine-independent vectors in $\mathbb{R}^2$. Figure 24.2 depicts three partitions of $\langle\langle x^0, x^1, x^2\rangle\rangle$.

In Partition A, the collection T_1, T_2 and all their faces is not a simplicial partition, because T_1 is not a simplex (T_1 is the convex hull of four points in $\mathbb{R}^2$, and in $\mathbb{R}^2$ any four points are affine dependent (see Theorem 24.6 on page 965)).

In Partition B, the collection of simplices T_1, T_2, T_3 and all their faces is not a simplicial partition, because the intersection $T_1 \cap T_2$ (as well as the intersection $T_1 \cap T_3$) is not a face of T_1.

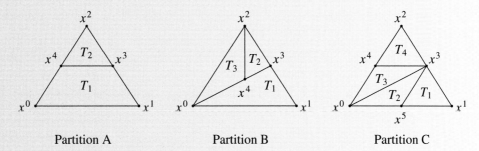

Partition A   Partition B   Partition C

Figure 24.2 Examples of partitions of a two-dimensional simplex

In Partition C, the collection of simplices T_1, T_2, T_3, T_4 and all their faces is a simplicial partition. In contrast, the collection $T_1, T_2, T_3, T_4, T_1 \cup T_2$ and all their faces is not a simplicial partition, because the intersection of T_1 and $T_1 \cup T_2$ is T_1, which is not a face of $T_1 \cup T_2$.   ◀

---

2 The fourth property follows from the other properties, and is therefore superfluous. We will not prove this fact here.

For every simplicial partition $\mathcal{T} = \{T_1, T_2, \ldots, T_M\}$, denote by $Y(\mathcal{T})$ the set of all the extreme points of the simplices $(T_m)_{m=1}^M$. In other words, every T_m is the convex hull of some of the points in $Y(\mathcal{T})$. For example, for Partition C in Figure 24.2,

$$Y(\mathcal{T}) = \{x^0, x^1, x^2, x^3, x^4, x^5\}. \tag{24.15}$$

The following theorem follows from Properties (1) and (4) in Definition 24.12 (Exercise 24.14).

Theorem 24.14 *Let S be a k-dimensional simplex in $\mathbb{R}^n$, and $\mathcal{T}$ be a simplicial partition of S. Then S equals the union of all the k-dimensional simplices in $\mathcal{T}$.*

For every simplex $S = \langle\langle x^0, x^1, \ldots, x^k\rangle\rangle$ in $\mathbb{R}^n$, denote by H_S the affine space spanned by the vectors in S,

$$H_S := \left\{ \sum_{l=0}^k \alpha^l x^l : \sum_{l=0}^k \alpha^l = 1 \right\} \subseteq \mathbb{R}^n. \tag{24.16}$$

The affine space H_S is a k-dimensional space, just like S.

Theorem 24.15 *Let $S = \langle\langle x^0, x^1, \ldots, x^k\rangle\rangle$ be a k-dimensional simplex in $\mathbb{R}^n$, let $\mathcal{T}$ be a simplicial partition of S, and let $T \in \mathcal{T}$ be a $(k-1)$-dimensional simplex. If T is in the boundary of S, then T is contained in a unique k-dimensional simplex in $\mathcal{T}$. If T is not in the boundary of S, then T is contained in two k-dimensional simplices in $\mathcal{T}$.*

Consider partition C in Figure 24.2 (Example 24.13). This is the partition containing T_1, T_2, T_3, T_4 and all their faces. The one-dimensional simplex $\langle\langle x^1, x^3\rangle\rangle$ is on the boundary of S and contained in a single two-dimensional simplex, T_1. In contrast, the one-dimensional simplex $\langle\langle x^3, x^5\rangle\rangle$ is not on the boundary of S and is contained in two two-dimensional simplices, T_1 and T_2.

Proof: Let $T = \langle\langle y^0, y^1, \ldots, y^{k-1}\rangle\rangle$ be a $(k-1)$-dimensional simplex in $\mathcal{T}$. By Property (4) in Definition 24.12, every $(k-1)$-dimensional simplex in $\mathcal{T}$ is contained in at least one k-dimensional simplex in $\mathcal{T}$, and by Property (2) it is a face of every such simplex.

Step 1: Preparations.
Let $\widehat{T} = \langle\langle y^0, y^1, \ldots, y^{k-1}, y\rangle\rangle$ and $\widehat{T}' = \langle\langle y^0, y^1, \ldots, y^{k-1}, y'\rangle\rangle$ be two k-dimensional simplices in $\mathcal{T}$ such that T is a face of both of them (the possibility that $\widehat{T} = \widehat{T}'$ is not ruled out). In particular, y and y' are not in T. Since $\widehat{T}$ and $\widehat{T}'$ are contained in S, it follows that $H_{\widehat{T}}$ and $H_{\widehat{T}'}$ are contained in H_S. These three spaces are all k-dimensional affine spaces, and therefore they coincide (Exercise 24.11),

$$H_{\widehat{T}} = H_{\widehat{T}'} = H_S. \tag{24.17}$$

It follows that the vector y' can be written as an affine combination of the vectors $y^0, y^1, \ldots, y^{k-1}, y$,

$$y' = \sum_{l=0}^{k-1} \alpha^l y^l + \beta y, \quad \sum_{l=0}^{k-1} \alpha^l + \beta = 1. \tag{24.18}$$

Since $y' \notin T$ it follows that $\beta \neq 0$. Indeed, if $\beta = 0$, then by Equation (24.18) we would deduce that y' is an affine combination of $(y^l)_{l=0}^k$, and then $H_{\widehat{T}'}$ would be a $(k-1)$-dimensional affine space, contradicting the fact that it is a k-dimensional affine space.

Step 2: If $\beta > 0$, then $\widehat{T} = \widehat{T}'$.
For every $\varepsilon \in (0, 1]$ the vector $z^\varepsilon := (1 - \varepsilon) \sum_{l=0}^{k-1} \frac{1}{k} y^l + \varepsilon y'$ is in $\widehat{T}'$ but not in T (since $y' \notin T$). For $\varepsilon > 0$ sufficiently small, the vector z^ε is also in $\widehat{T}$, since

$$z^\varepsilon = (1 - \varepsilon) \sum_{l=0}^{k-1} \frac{1}{k} y^l + \varepsilon y' = \sum_{l=0}^{k-1} \left((1 - \varepsilon) \frac{1}{k} + \varepsilon \alpha^l \right) y^l + \varepsilon \beta y, \tag{24.19}$$

and all the coefficients in the right-hand expression are positive for $\varepsilon > 0$ sufficiently small. It follows that the intersection $\widehat{T} \cap \widehat{T}'$ contains both T and z^ε for $\varepsilon > 0$ sufficiently small. Therefore $\widehat{T} \cap \widehat{T}'$ strictly contains T. On the other hand, by Property (2) this intersection is a face both of $\widehat{T}$ and of $\widehat{T}'$. But the only face of the simplex $\widehat{T}$ properly containing T is $\widehat{T}$ itself, and therefore $\widehat{T} \cap \widehat{T}' = \widehat{T}$. Similarly, $\widehat{T} \cap \widehat{T}' = \widehat{T}'$. We deduce from this that $\widehat{T} = \widehat{T}'$.

Step 3: If T is in the boundary of S, then it is contained in a unique k-dimensional simplex in $\mathcal{T}$.
We will show that if T is in the boundary of S then $\beta > 0$, and by Step 2 it then follows that T is contained in a unique k-dimensional simplex in $\mathcal{T}$. Recall that $x^0, x^1, \ldots, x^k$ are the extreme points of S. By assumption, the simplex T is in the boundary of S, which is equal to $\bigcup_{i=0}^k \langle\langle x^0, \ldots, x^{i-1}, x^{i+1}, \ldots, x^k \rangle\rangle$. Since every simplex is a convex set, T is in one of the $(k-1)$-dimensional faces of S. Suppose, without loss of generality, that $T \subseteq \langle\langle x^0, x^1, \ldots, x^{k-1} \rangle\rangle$. It follows that each of the vectors $(y^l)_{l=0}^{k-1}$ can be represented as a convex combination of $x^0, x^1, \ldots, x^{k-1}$,

$$y^l = \sum_{j=0}^{k-1} \alpha^{jl} x^j, \quad \sum_{j=0}^{k-1} \alpha^{jl} = 1, \quad l = 0, 1, \ldots, k-1. \tag{24.20}$$

Since the vectors y and y' are in S, they can be represented as convex combinations of the extreme points of S,

$$y = \sum_{j=0}^k \gamma^j x^j, \quad y' = \sum_{j=0}^k \gamma'^j x^j, \quad \sum_{j=0}^k \gamma^j = \sum_{j=0}^k \gamma'^j = 1, \tag{24.21}$$

where $\gamma^j, \gamma'^j \geq 0$ for every $j \in \{0, 1, \ldots, k\}$.

Since y and y' are not in T, the coefficients γ^k and γ'^k are in fact positive. Plugging in these representations of the vectors into Equation (24.18), we get

$$\sum_{j=0}^{k} \gamma'^j x^j = y' = \sum_{l=0}^{k-1} \alpha^l y^l + \beta y \tag{24.22}$$

$$= \sum_{l=0}^{k-1} \left(\alpha^l \sum_{j=0}^{k-1} \alpha^{jl} x^j \right) + \beta \sum_{j=0}^{k} \gamma^j x^j \tag{24.23}$$

$$= \sum_{j=0}^{k-1} \left(\sum_{l=0}^{k-1} \alpha^l \alpha^{jl} + \beta \gamma^j \right) x^j + \beta \gamma^k x^k. \tag{24.24}$$

Since every vector in a simplex can be represented in a unique way as a convex combination of extreme points of the simplex, we deduce that the coefficient of x^k in both representations must be identical: $\gamma'^k = \beta \gamma^k$. Since both γ'^k and γ^k are positive, the conclusion is that $\beta > 0$, which is what we wanted to show.

Step 4: If T is not in the boundary of S, then it is contained in at least two k-dimensional simplices in $\mathcal{T}$.

By Property (4) of simplicial partitions, T is contained in at least one k-dimensional simplex $\widehat{T}$ in $\mathcal{T}$. Suppose that such a simplex $\widehat{T}$ is given by $\widehat{T} = \langle\langle y^0, y^1, \ldots, y^{k-1}, y \rangle\rangle$. We will show that there exists an additional k-dimensional simplex $\widehat{T}' \neq \widehat{T}$ that contains T.

The simplex $\widehat{T}$ is the collection of all points that can be represented as a convex combination of its extreme points. For every $n \in \mathbb{N}$, the vector $z^n := \sum_{l=0}^{k-1} \frac{1 - \frac{1}{n}}{k} y^l - \frac{1}{n} y$ is not in $\widehat{T}$, since the coefficient of y is a negative number (Exercise 24.8). The sequence $(z^n)_{n \in \mathbb{N}}$ converges to $z^* = \sum_{l=0}^{k-1} \frac{1}{k} y^l \in T$, which lies in the relative interior[3] of T.

Since T is not in the boundary of S, the vector z^* is in the relative interior of S, and therefore there is $n_0 \in \mathbb{N}$ such that $z^n \in S$ for every $n \geq n_0$. Since S is the union of all the k-dimensional simplices in $\mathcal{T}$ (Theorem 24.14), and since there are a finite number of such simplices, there exists a subsequence $(n_j)_{j \in \mathbb{N}}$ such that $(z^{n_j})_{j \in \mathbb{N}}$ are all contained in the same k-dimensional simplex $\widehat{T}' \in \mathcal{T}$, which differs from $\widehat{T}$. Since the simplex is a closed set, $z^* \in \widehat{T}'$, and therefore $z^* \in \widehat{T} \cap \widehat{T}'$. Since the smallest simplex (with respect to set inclusion) in $\mathcal{T}$ that contains z^* is T (why?), the intersection $\widehat{T} \cap \widehat{T}'$, which is a face both of $\widehat{T}$ and of $\widehat{T}'$, equals T. It follows that T is contained also in $\widehat{T}'$, which is what we wanted to show.

Step 5: If T is not in the boundary of S, then it is contained in exactly two k-dimensional simplices in $\mathcal{T}$.

---

[3] A point x in a simplex T is in the *relative interior* of T if all its barycentric coordinates relative to T are positive.

Suppose by contradiction that there exists a third k-dimensional simplex $\widehat{T}'' = \langle\langle y^0, y^1, \ldots, y^{k-1}, y'' \rangle\rangle \in \mathcal{T}$ containing T, in addition to $\widehat{T}$ and $\widehat{T}'$. As we saw in the first part of the proof,

$$H_{\widehat{T}} = H_{\widehat{T}'} = H_{\widehat{T}''} = H_S. \tag{24.25}$$

Therefore in particular $y'' \in H_{\widehat{T}'}$ and $y' \in H_{\widehat{T}}$. Write $y'' = \sum_{l=0}^{k-1} \alpha''^l y^l + \beta' y'$, where $\sum_{l=0}^{k-1} \alpha''^l + \beta' = 1$. Recall that $y' = \sum_{l=0}^{k-1} \alpha^l y^l + \beta y$ (Equation (24.18)), and that $\beta < 0$ since $\widehat{T}' \neq \widehat{T}$ (step 2 of the proof). Similarly, since $\widehat{T}' \neq \widehat{T}''$ we deduce that $\beta' < 0$. Hence

$$y'' = \sum_{l=0}^{k-1} \alpha''^l y^l + \beta' y' \tag{24.26}$$

$$= \sum_{l=0}^{k-1} \alpha''^l y^l + \beta' \left(\sum_{l=0}^{k-1} \alpha^l y^l + \beta y \right) \tag{24.27}$$

$$= \sum_{l=0}^{k-1} (\alpha''^l + \beta''^l) y^l + \beta' \beta y. \tag{24.28}$$

Since $\beta < 0$ and $\beta' < 0$, it follows that $\beta' \beta > 0$, and therefore by the results of Step 2, $\widehat{T}'' = \widehat{T}$, contradicting the assumption that $\widehat{T}'' \neq \widehat{T}$. The contradiction proves that there are exactly two k-dimensional simplices in $\mathcal{T}$ containing T. □

Let $S = \langle\langle x^0, x^1, \ldots, x^k \rangle\rangle$ be a simplex in $\mathbb{R}^n$. By Theorem 24.9 (page 965), every vector $y \in S$ has a unique representation as a convex combination of $x^0, x^1, \ldots, x^k$,

$$\sum_{l=0}^{k} \alpha^l x^l = y, \tag{24.29}$$

where $(\alpha^l)_{l=0}^{k}$ are nonnegative numbers whose sum is 1 (the barycentric coordinates of y). Denote

$$\mathrm{supp}_S(y) = \{l \colon 0 \leq l \leq k, \quad \alpha^l > 0\}. \tag{24.30}$$

This set is called the *support* of y relative to S. This is the set of positive barycentric coordinates of y. Recall that if $\mathcal{T}$ is a simplicial partition of S, then $Y(\mathcal{T})$ is the set of all extreme points of the simplices in $\mathcal{T}$.

Definition 24.16 *Let $S = \langle\langle x^0, x^1, \ldots, x^k \rangle\rangle$ be a k-dimensional simplex in $\mathbb{R}^n$, for $n \geq k$, and let $\mathcal{T}$ be a simplicial partition of S. A coloring of $\mathcal{T}$ is a function $c : Y(\mathcal{T}) \to \{0, 1, \ldots, k\}$ associating every vertex y in $Y(\mathcal{T})$ with an index $c(y)$ in $\{0, 1, \ldots, k\}$ that is called the* color *of the vertex. A coloring c is called* proper *if for every $y \in Y(\mathcal{T})$ the color of y is one of the indices in the support of y (using its barycentric representation relative to S).*

Example 24.17   Three colorings of a simplicial partition of a two-dimensional simplex $S = \langle\langle x^0, x^1, x^2 \rangle\rangle$ in $\mathbb{R}^2$ are depicted in Figure 24.3. The color of each vertex is noted next to it. Colorings A and B in Figure 24.3 are proper colorings. Coloring C in Figure 24.3 is not proper, because one of the vertices in the simplicial partition, which is contained in the simplex $\langle\langle x^0, x^2 \rangle\rangle$ and is identified by an arrow, is colored by the color 1.

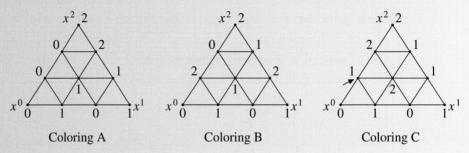

Coloring A   Coloring B   Coloring C

Figure 24.3 Examples of colorings

Definition 24.18 *Let $\mathcal{T}$ be a simplicial partition of a k-dimensional simplex S, and let c be a proper coloring of $\mathcal{T}$. The k-dimensional simplex $T \in \mathcal{T}$ is perfectly colored if its vertices are colored with $k + 1$ different colors $\{0, 1, \ldots, k\}$.*

Example 24.17   (*Continued*) Figure 24.4 depicts the colorings in Figure 24.3, with the two-dimensional perfectly colored simplices shaded in gray. In colorings A and B, which are proper colorings, the number of such simplices is indeed odd (1 in coloring A, and 5 in coloring B). When the coloring is not proper, the number of two-dimensional perfectly colored simplices may be even, as coloring C of the figure shows.

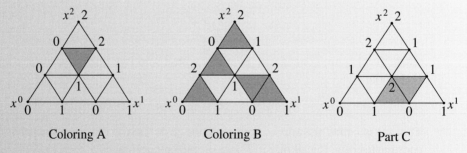

Coloring A   Coloring B   Part C

Figure 24.4 The perfectly colored simplices in Example 24.17

Theorem 24.19 (Sperner's Lemma) *Let S be a k-dimensional simplex in $\mathbb{R}^n$, for $n \geq k$, and let $\mathcal{T}$ be a simplicial partition of S. Let c be a proper coloring of $\mathcal{T}$. Then the number of perfectly colored k-dimensional simplices $T \in \mathcal{T}$ is odd.*

In particular, there is at least one perfectly colored k-dimensional simplex in $\mathcal{T}$.

Proof: The proof is conducted by induction on the dimension of the simplex, k.

Step 1: The case $k = 0$.
In this case, the simplex contains only one point, $S = \langle\langle x^0 \rangle\rangle$, and the only simplicial partition is the one containing the entire simplex, $\mathcal{T} = \{S\}$. In this case, $Y(\mathcal{T}) = \{x^0\}$. The only proper coloring associates the vertex x^0 with the color 0. It follows that the number of perfectly colored zero-dimensional simplices is 1, which is an odd number.

Step 2: Defining collections of simplices when $k > 0$.
Let $k > 0$. Suppose that the statement of the theorem is true for every $(k-1)$-dimensional simplex, and let $S = \langle\langle x^0, x^1, \ldots, x^k \rangle\rangle$ be a k-dimensional simplex. Let $\mathcal{T}$ be a simplicial partition of S and c a proper coloring of $\mathcal{T}$. We will make use of the following notation:

- $\mathcal{A}$ is the collection of all $(k-1)$-dimensional simplices in $\mathcal{T}$ contained in the boundary of S and colored by $\{0, 1, \ldots, k-1\}$.
- $\mathcal{B}$ is the collection of all the k-dimensional simplices in $\mathcal{T}$ (not necessarily in the boundary of S) whose vertices are colored by $\{0, 1, \ldots, k-1\}$. In other words, these are the simplices colored by $\{0, 1, \ldots, k-1\}$ satisfying the property that two of their vertices are colored by the same color.
- $\mathcal{C}$ is the collection of all the k-dimensional simplices in $\mathcal{T}$ whose vertices are colored by $\{0, 1, \ldots, k\}$.

In the example in Figure 24.5, $\mathcal{A}$ has three one-dimensional simplices, denoted by thick lines. $\mathcal{B}$ has four two-dimensional simplices, denoted by light shading. $\mathcal{C}$ has five two-dimensional simplices, denoted by darker shading.

Step 3: The number of simplices in $\mathcal{A}$ is odd.
First, we show that every simplex in $\mathcal{A}$ is contained in the face $\langle\langle x^0, x^1, \ldots, x^{k-1} \rangle\rangle$ of S. Recall that the boundary of the simplex $\langle\langle x^0, x^1, \ldots, x^k \rangle\rangle$ is the union of the $(k-1)$-dimensional faces,

$$\bigcup_{l=0}^{k} \langle\langle x^0, x^1, \ldots, x^{l-1}, x^{l+1}, \ldots, x^k \rangle\rangle.$$

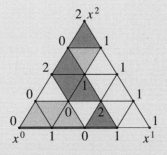

Figure 24.5 Collections of simplices $\mathcal{A}$, $\mathcal{B}$, and $\mathcal{C}$

It follows that if a vertex is colored by a color $l \in \{0, 1, \ldots, k-1\}$, then it cannot be on the face $\langle\langle x^0, x^1, \ldots, x^{l-1}, x^{l+1}, \ldots, x^k\rangle\rangle$, because the coloring is proper, and the index l is not in the support of any vector in this face of S. Since every simplex in $\mathcal{A}$ is colored by all the colors $0, 1, \ldots, k-1$, such a simplex cannot be in $\bigcup_{l=0}^{k-1} \langle\langle x^0, x^1, \ldots, x^{l-1}, x^{l+1}, \ldots, x^k\rangle\rangle$, and it must therefore be in the face $\langle\langle x^0, x^1, \ldots, x^{k-1}\rangle\rangle$ of S.

We therefore deduce that the simplices in $\mathcal{A}$ are exactly the $(k-1)$-dimensional simplices contained in the simplex $\langle\langle x^0, x^1, \ldots, x^{k-1}\rangle\rangle$ whose vertices are colored by $\{0, 1, \ldots, k-1\}$. By the induction hypothesis, the number of such simplices is odd.

Step 4: Completing the proof.
Define an undirected graph as follows:

- The set of vertices is $\mathcal{A} \cup \mathcal{B} \cup \mathcal{C}$; i.e., every simplex in the union $\mathcal{A} \cup \mathcal{B} \cup \mathcal{C}$ is a vertex of the graph.
- Let T_1 and T_2 be two different simplices in $\mathcal{A} \cup \mathcal{B} \cup \mathcal{C}$. Then there exists an edge connecting T_1 and T_2 if and only if the intersection $T_1 \cap T_2$ is a $(k-1)$-dimensional simplex whose vertices are colored by $\{0, 1, \ldots, k-1\}$.

The graph corresponding to the coloring in Figure 24.5 appears in Figure 24.6(a). In this figure, the one-dimensional simplices outlined with dark lines and the two-dimensional colored simplices are vertices of the graph. The lines connecting pairs of simplices denote the edges. Figure 24.6(b) illustrates the rule according to which the edges of the graph are determined. For example, the simplices T_1 and T_2 denoted in Figure 24.6(b) are two vertices of the graph: T_1 is in $\mathcal{C}$ and T_2 is in $\mathcal{B}$. Their intersection is a one-dimensional simplex that is colored by the colors 0 and 1, and therefore there is an edge connecting T_1 and T_2. The simplices T_3 and T_4, depicted in Figure 24.6(b), are also vertices in the graph: T_3 is in B and T_4 is in $\mathcal{A}$. Their intersection is the simplex T_4, which is a one-dimensional simplex colored by the colors 0 and 1, and hence there is an edge connecting T_3 and T_4. This explains all the edges in Figure 24.6(a).

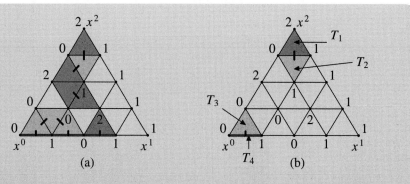

Figure 24.6 The collections $\mathcal{A}$ (dark lines), $\mathcal{B}$ (light triangles), and $\mathcal{C}$ (dark triangles) in Figure 24.5 and their associated graphs

Denote by R the number of edges in the graph. Using Theorem 24.15, we can count how many edges emanate from each vertex in the graph.

- There is only one edge emanating from each vertex in $\mathcal{A}$ to a vertex in $\mathcal{B}$ or $\mathcal{C}$. Indeed, by Theorem 24.15, every simplex $T = \langle\langle y^0, y^1, \ldots, y^{k-1}\rangle\rangle \in \mathcal{A}$ is contained in a single k-dimensional simplex $\hat{T} = \langle\langle y^0, y^1, \ldots, y^{k-1}, y^k\rangle\rangle$ in $\mathcal{T}$: if the color of vertex x^k is k, the simplex $\hat{T}$ is contained in $\mathcal{C}$. If not, $\hat{T}$ is in $\mathcal{B}$. In any case, $\hat{T} \cap T = T$, and since T is a $(k-1)$-dimensional simplex colored with $\{0, 1, \ldots, k-1\}$ there is an edge connecting T and $\hat{T}$.
- Two edges emanate from every vertex in $\mathcal{B}$. To see this, suppose that $T = \langle\langle x^0, x^1, \ldots, x^{k-1}, x^k\rangle\rangle \in \mathcal{B}$ and assume without loss of generality that the vertices x^{k-1} and x^k are colored in the same color. The only two $(k-1)$-dimensional subsimplices of T that are colored in the colors $\{0, 1, \ldots, k-1\}$ are $T_1 := \langle\langle x^0, x^1, \ldots, x^{k-2}, x^{k-1}\rangle\rangle$ and $T_2 := \langle\langle x^0, x^1, \ldots, x^{k-2}, x^k\rangle\rangle$. For $i = 1, 2$, consider the simplex T_i. Using Theorem 24.15 we deduce that there are two possibilities.
  - In this case, T_i is in $\mathcal{A}$ and there is an edge connecting T_i and T (because $T \cap T_i = T_i$).
  - T_i is not in the boundary of S. It is then contained in two k-dimensional simplices, one of which is T; denote the other by $\hat{T}_i$. If the simplex $\hat{T}_i$ is colored in the colors $\{0, 1, \ldots, k\}$, then $\hat{T}_i \in \mathcal{C}$. If not, $\hat{T}_i \in \mathcal{B}$. In both cases there is an edge connecting T and $\hat{T}_i$ (because $\hat{T}_i \cap T = T$).

We conclude that there are two edges emanating from T.

- There is only one edge emanating from every vertex in $\mathcal{C}$. To see this, suppose that $T = \langle\langle x^0, x^1, \ldots, x^{k-1}, x^k\rangle\rangle \in \mathcal{C}$. Since all the vertices are colored in different colors $\{0, 1, \ldots, k\}$, we will suppose without loss of generality that the subsimplex $T_1 = \langle\langle x^0, x^1, \ldots, x^{k-1}\rangle\rangle$ is colored with the colors $\{0, 1, \ldots, k-1\}$ (and this is the only $(k-1)$-dimensional subsimplex in T_1 colored in these colors). If T_1 is in the boundary of S, then it is an element of $\mathcal{A}$ and there is an edge connecting T and T_1 (because $T_1 \cap T = T_1$). If T_1 is not in the boundary of S, by Theorem 24.15 the simplex T_1 is contained in two k-dimensional simplices. One of those simplices is T. As in the previous case, the second k-dimensional simplex T_2 containing T_1 is either in $\mathcal{B}$ or in $\mathcal{C}$, and there is an edge connecting T_2 and T (because $T_2 \cap T = T_1$).

The sum total of edges emanating from all the vertices in the graph is twice the number of edges R, because every edge is counted twice. It follows that

$$2R = |\mathcal{A}| + 2|\mathcal{B}| + |\mathcal{C}|.$$

This implies that $|\mathcal{A}| + |\mathcal{C}|$ is an even number. Since the number of elements in $\mathcal{A}$ is odd (by Step 3), the number of elements in C must be odd. In other words, the number of perfectly colored k-dimensional simplices in $\mathcal{T}$ is odd. This establishes the statement for k-dimensional simplices, concluding the induction step and the proof of Sperner's Lemma.   □

Definition 24.20 *Let* $S = \langle\langle x^0, x^1, \ldots, x^k \rangle\rangle$ *be a simplex in* $\mathbb{R}^n$. *The diameter of S, denoted by* $\rho(S)$, *is defined as*[4]

$$\rho(S) = \max_{0 \le i < j \le k} ||x^i - x^j||. \tag{24.31}$$

The diameter of a simplex is also equal to the greatest (Euclidean) distance between two points in the simplex (not necessarily vertices; see Exercise 24.22).

Definition 24.21 *Let* $\mathcal{T} = \{T_1, T_2, \ldots, T_M\}$ *be a simplicial partition of a simplex S. The diameter of a simplicial partition* $\mathcal{T}$ *is denoted by* $\rho(\mathcal{T})$ *and defined by*

$$\rho(\mathcal{T}) = \max_{m=1,\ldots,M} \rho(T_m). \tag{24.32}$$

The diameter of $\mathcal{T}$ is the greatest (Euclidean) distance between two points located in the same simplex in $\mathcal{T}$. One simplicial partition of a simplex S is the partition that contains all faces of S. The next theorem enables us to deduce that every simplicial partition can be refined to a simplicial partition with an arbitrarily small diameter.

Theorem 24.22 *Let* $k \ge 1$ *and let* $\mathcal{T}$ *be a simplicial partition of a k-dimensional simplex* $S = \langle\langle x^0, x^1, \ldots, x^k \rangle\rangle$ *in* $\mathbb{R}^n$. *Then there exists a simplicial partition* $\mathcal{T}'$ *of S satisfying the following properties:*

(i) For every $T' \in \mathcal{T}'$ *there exists* $T \in \mathcal{T}$ *such that* $T' \subseteq T$.
(ii) $\rho(\mathcal{T}') \le \frac{k}{k+1}\rho(\mathcal{T})$.

For proving Theorem 24.22 we make use of the following two auxiliary theorems.

Theorem 24.23 *Let* $S = \langle\langle x^0, x^1, \ldots, x^k \rangle\rangle$ *be a k-dimensional simplex in* $\mathbb{R}^n$, *and denote* $y = \frac{1}{k+1}\sum_{l=0}^{k} x^l$. *Then the collection* $\mathcal{T}$ *containing the* $k+1$ *simplices* $\langle\langle x^0, x^1, \ldots, x^{l-1}, x^{l+1}, \ldots, x^k, y \rangle\rangle$, $l = 0, 1, \ldots, k$, *and all of their faces, is a simplicial partition of S.*

For a two-dimensional simplex $S = \langle\langle x^0, x^1, x^2 \rangle\rangle$, the collection $\mathcal{T}$ defined in Theorem 24.23 is depicted in Figure 24.7, and it is indeed a simplicial partition of S.

Proof: By Theorem 24.7 on page 965, for every $l = 0, 1, \ldots, k$, the vectors $x^0, x^1, \ldots, x^{l-1}, x^{l+1}, \ldots, x^k, y$ are affine-independent vectors (see Example 24.5), and $\mathcal{T}$ is therefore a collection of simplices. We now show that

$$S = \bigcup_{i=0}^{k} \langle\langle x^0, x^1, \ldots, x^{l-1}, x^{l+1}, \ldots, x^k, y \rangle\rangle. \tag{24.33}$$

Let $z \in S$. Since S is a simplex, there exist nonnegative numbers $\alpha^0, \alpha^1, \ldots, \alpha^k$ whose sum is 1 such that $z = \sum_{l=0}^{k} \alpha^l x^l$. Suppose that $\alpha^j = \min_{l=0,1,\ldots,k} \alpha^l$. We will show that the vector z is contained in the simplex $\langle\langle x^0, x^1, \ldots, x^{j-1}, x^{j+1}, \ldots, x^k, y \rangle\rangle$. Since α^j is minimal, we have $\alpha^j \le \frac{1}{k+1}$, or equivalently that $(k+1)\alpha^j \le 1$. Therefore,

---

4 Recall that $||x^i - x^j||$ is the Euclidean distance in $\mathbb{R}^n$ between the vectors x^i and x^j.

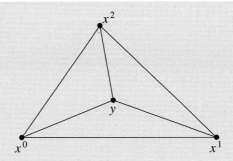

Figure 24.7 The collection $\mathcal{T}$ described in Theorem 24.23, for a two-dimensional simplex

$$z = \sum_{l=0}^{k} \alpha^l x^l = \alpha^j \sum_{l=0}^{k} x^l + \sum_{l \neq j} (\alpha^l - \alpha^j) x^l \tag{24.34}$$

$$= (k+1)\alpha^j \frac{1}{k+1} \sum_{l=0}^{k} x^l + \sum_{l \neq j} (\alpha^l - \alpha^j) x^l \tag{24.35}$$

$$= (k+1)\alpha^j y + \sum_{l \neq j} (\alpha^l - \alpha^j) x^l. \tag{24.36}$$

Since $\alpha^l - \alpha^j \geq 0$ for all $l \neq j$, and

$$(k+1)\alpha^j + \sum_{l \neq j} (\alpha^l - \alpha^j) = \sum_{l=0}^{k} \alpha^l = 1, \tag{24.37}$$

it follows that $z \in \langle\langle x^0, x^1, \ldots, x^{j-1}, x^{j+1}, \ldots, x^k, y \rangle\rangle$, which is what we wanted to show. We leave it to the reader to ascertain that any pair of simplices in $\mathcal{T}$ are either disjoint, or their intersection is also a simplex in $\mathcal{T}$ (Exercise 24.23). $\square$

Remark 24.24 *For the simplicial partition described in Theorem 24.23, we compute here an upper bound to the value of $\|x^j - y\|$, which we will need later. Let $j \in \{0, 1, \ldots, k\}$. By the triangle inequality,*

$$\|x^j - y\| = \left\| x^j - \frac{1}{k+1} \sum_{l=0}^{k} x^l \right\| = \left\| \frac{1}{k+1} \sum_{l \neq j} (x^j - x^l) \right\| \tag{24.38}$$

$$\leq \frac{1}{k+1} \sum_{l \neq j} \|x^j - x^l\| \leq \frac{k}{k+1} \max_{l \neq j} \|x^j - x^l\| = \frac{k}{k+1} \rho(S). \tag{24.39}$$

$\blacklozenge$

For every k-dimensional simplex $S = \langle\langle x^0, x^1, \ldots, x^k \rangle\rangle$ in $\mathbb{R}^n$ and every vector $y \in \mathbb{R}^n$ that is affine independent of the vectors $x^0, x^1, \ldots, x^k$, denote by $\langle\langle S, y \rangle\rangle$ the $(k+1)$-dimensional simplex whose extreme points are y and the extreme points of S,

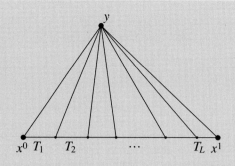

Figure 24.8 The collection $\widehat{T}$ described in Theorem 24.25, for the one-dimensional simplex $S = \langle\langle x^0, x^1 \rangle\rangle$

$$\langle\langle S, y \rangle\rangle := \langle\langle x^0, x^1, \dots, x^k, y \rangle\rangle. \tag{24.40}$$

Theorem 24.25 *Let $S = \langle\langle x^0, x^1, \dots, x^k \rangle\rangle$ be a k-dimensional simplex in $\mathbb{R}^n$, and let T be a simplicial partition of S. Let $y \in \mathbb{R}^n$ be a vector that is affine independent of the vectors $x^0, x^1, \dots, x^k$, and let $\widehat{S} = \langle\langle S, y \rangle\rangle$. Then the following collection of simplices $\widehat{T}$ is a simplicial partition of the simplex $\widehat{S}$,*

$$\widehat{T} := T \bigcup \{\langle\langle y \rangle\rangle\} \bigcup \{\langle\langle T, y \rangle\rangle : T \in T\}. \tag{24.41}$$

Figure 24.8 corresponds to the one-dimensional case of the theorem, i.e., when $S = \langle\langle x^0, x^1 \rangle\rangle$ is a one-dimensional simplex (the base of the triangle in the figure) and the partition T of S is composed of the points and intervals at the base of the triangle in the figure. The collection $\widehat{T}$ defined in Theorem 24.25 contains, in addition to the simplices in T, the triangles appearing in the figure, their sides, and the upper vertex.

Proof: We prove that the union of the simplices in the collection $\widehat{T}$ equals $\widehat{S}$. Ascertaining that the intersection of any two simplices in the collection $\widehat{T}$ is either the empty set, or is a simplex in $\widehat{T}$, is left to the reader (Exercise 24.24). Let z be a vector in $\widehat{S}$. Since $\widehat{S}$ is a simplex, there exist nonnegative numbers $(\alpha^i)_{i=0}^{k+1}$ whose sum is 1 such that $z = \sum_{i=0}^{k} \alpha^i x^i + \alpha^{k+1} y$. If $\alpha^{k+1} = 1$ then $z = y$, and therefore $z \in \langle\langle y \rangle\rangle$. Since $\langle\langle y \rangle\rangle$ is a simplex in $\widehat{T}$, the vector z is in the union of the simplices in $\widehat{T}$. If $\alpha^{k+1} < 1$, define $\widehat{z} := \sum_{i=0}^{k} \frac{\alpha^i}{1-\alpha^{k+1}} x^k$. Since the numbers $\{\frac{\alpha^i}{1-\alpha^{k+1}}\}_{i=0}^{k}$ are nonnegative numbers whose sum is 1, $\widehat{z} \in S$, and therefore it is contained in one of the simplices T in the simplicial partition T. Since $z = (1 - \alpha^{k+1})\widehat{z} + \alpha^{k+1} y$, it follows that $z \in \langle\langle T, y \rangle\rangle$, and therefore in this case the vector z is in the union of the simplices in $\widehat{T}$ as well. $\qquad\square$

The triangle inequality implies that the diameter of the partition $\widehat{T}$ constructed in Theorem 24.25 is

$$\rho(\widehat{T}) = \max\{\rho(T), \|x^0 - y\|, \|x^1 - y\|, \dots, \|x^k - y\|\}; \tag{24.42}$$

see Exercise 24.25.

Proof of Theorem 24.22: The proof is by induction on k.

Step 1: The case $k = 1$.

When $k = 1$ the simplex S is the interval $S = \langle\langle x^0, x^1 \rangle\rangle$ and the simplicial partition is given by a finite number of points in this interval; i.e., there exist points $z^1, z^2, \ldots, z^L$ such that

$$\mathcal{T} = \{\langle\langle x^0, z^1 \rangle\rangle, \langle\langle z^1, z^2 \rangle\rangle, \ldots, \langle\langle z^{L-1}, z^L \rangle\rangle, \langle\langle z^L, x^1 \rangle\rangle, \langle\langle x^0 \rangle\rangle, \langle\langle z^1 \rangle\rangle, \ldots, \langle\langle z^L \rangle\rangle, \langle\langle x^1 \rangle\rangle\}.$$
(24.43)

Define a new simplicial partition $\mathcal{T}'$ by partitioning each one of the one-dimensional simplices in $\mathcal{T}$ into two equal parts: for each $l \in \{1, \ldots, L+1\}$ let $y^l = \frac{1}{2} z^{l-1} + \frac{1}{2} z^l$ where $z^0 := x^0$ and $z^{L+1} := x^1$. The simplicial partition $\mathcal{T}'$ is therefore

$$\mathcal{T}' = \{\langle\langle x^0, y^1 \rangle\rangle, \langle\langle y^1, z^1 \rangle\rangle, \langle\langle z^1, y^2 \rangle\rangle, \langle\langle y^2, z^2 \rangle\rangle, \ldots, \langle\langle y^L, x^1 \rangle\rangle, \langle\langle x^0 \rangle\rangle,$$
$$\langle\langle y^1 \rangle\rangle, \langle\langle z^1 \rangle\rangle, \ldots, \langle\langle y^L \rangle\rangle, \langle\langle x^1 \rangle\rangle\}. \quad (24.44)$$

Then $\mathcal{T}'$ is a refinement of $\mathcal{T}$, and its diameter is half the diameter of $\mathcal{T}$.

Step 2: The case $k > 1$.

Suppose that the claim of the theorem holds for every $(k-1)$-dimensional simplex. We will prove that it then holds for every k-dimensional simplex. Let $\mathcal{T}$ be a simplicial partition of a k-dimensional simplex S. Let $\mathcal{T}_{k-1}$ be the collection of all the $(k-1)$-dimensional simplices in $\mathcal{T}$ and let $\mathcal{T}_k$ be the collection of all the k-dimensional simplices in $\mathcal{T}$. The construction of the desired simplicial partition $\mathcal{T}'$ of S is conducted in several steps:

- Using the induction hypothesis, we will prove that for every $(k-1)$-dimensional simplex $W \in \mathcal{T}_{k-1}$ there exists a simplicial partition $\mathcal{T}_W$ of W whose diameter is less than or equal to $\frac{k-1}{k} \rho(\mathcal{T})$. Figure 24.9 illustrates the simplex S in the case that $k = 2$ and the simplicial partition is $(\mathcal{T}_W)_{W \in \mathcal{T}_{k-1}}$.
- For every k-dimensional simplex $T \in \mathcal{T}$, denote by y_T its center of weight. These centers of weight are illustrated in Figure 24.10.

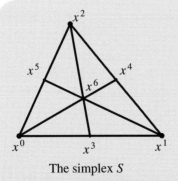
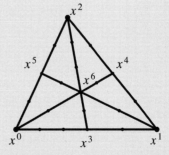

The simplex S The partitions $\mathcal{T}_W$ of the simplices in $\mathcal{T}_{k-1}$

Figure 24.9 The case $k = 2$ in the proof of Theorem 24.22: the simplex S and the partition $(\mathcal{T}_W)_{W \in \mathcal{T}_{k-1}}$

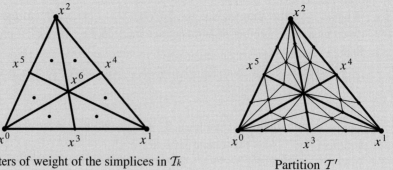

The centers of weight of the simplices in $\mathcal{T}_k$

Partition $\mathcal{T}'$

Figure 24.10 The case $k = 2$ in the proof of Theorem 24.22: centers of weight and the subdivision $\mathcal{T}'$

- Every simplex $T \in \mathcal{T}$ can be subdivided into the simplices $\langle\langle R, y_T \rangle\rangle$, for all the simplices $R \in \mathcal{T}_W$, for each face W of T. This partition is illustrated in Figure 24.10.
- Since $\cup_{T \in \mathcal{T}_k} T = S$, we obtain a refinement of the simplicial partition $\mathcal{T}$ of S.
- Finally, we prove that the diameter of this simplicial partition is less than or equal to $\frac{k}{k+1}\rho(\mathcal{T})$.

We next turn to the formal construction of the simplicial division that refines $\mathcal{T}$. For each $(k-1)$-dimensional simplex $W \in \mathcal{T}_{k-1}$, let $\widehat{\mathcal{T}}_W$ be the trivial partition containing all the faces of W. Since W is a simplex in the simplicial partition T one has $\rho(\widehat{\mathcal{T}}_W) \leq \rho(\mathcal{T})$. By the induction hypothesis there exists a simplicial partition $\mathcal{T}_W$ of W satisfying

$$\rho(\mathcal{T}_W) \leq \frac{k-1}{k}\rho(\widehat{\mathcal{T}}_W) \leq \frac{k-1}{k}\rho(\mathcal{T}). \tag{24.45}$$

For each k-dimensional simplex $T = \langle\langle y^0, y^1, \ldots, y^k \rangle\rangle \in \mathcal{T}_k$, let y_T be its center of weight:

$$y_T := \sum_{l=0}^{k} \frac{1}{k+1} y^l. \tag{24.46}$$

Let $\mathcal{T}'$ be the collection of all the simplices $\langle\langle R, y_T \rangle\rangle$ and their faces, where $T \in \mathcal{T}_k$, $W \in \mathcal{T}_{k-1}$ is a face of T and $R \in \mathcal{T}_W$. To conclude the proof, we need to show that the collection $\mathcal{T}'$ is a simplicial partition and that $\rho(\mathcal{T}') \leq \frac{k}{k+1}\rho(\mathcal{T})$. By construction, Properties (3) and (4) in the definition of simplicial partitions hold for the collection $\mathcal{T}'$. By Theorems 24.14 and 24.23 it follows that the union of the simplices in $\mathcal{T}'$ is S. We next show that the intersection of two simplices in $\mathcal{T}'$ is either empty or a face of both of them. Let R and $\widehat{R}$ be two simplices in $\mathcal{T}'$ whose intersection is nonempty.

- If R and $\widehat{R}$ are contained in the same k-dimensional simplex T in $\mathcal{T}$, Theorems 24.23 and 24.25 imply that R and $\widehat{R}$ are elements of a simplicial partition of T, and therefore in particular $R \cap \widehat{R}$ is a face of both R and $\widehat{R}$.

- Assume that R and $\widehat{R}$ are contained in two different k-dimensional simplices in $\mathcal{T}$, which we denote as T and $\widehat{T}$ respectively. Since $\mathcal{T}$ is a simplicial partition, the intersection $T \cap \widehat{T}$ is a face both of T and of $\widehat{T}$, and it is a simplex of a dimension smaller than k. Let W be a $(k-1)$-dimensional simplex in $\mathcal{T}$ containing $T \cap \widehat{T}$. Since $\mathcal{T}_W$ is a simplicial partition, it follows by construction that $R \cap \widehat{R}$ is an element in $\mathcal{T}_W$, and that this element is a face of both R and $\widehat{R}$.

By construction, and with the use of Equations (24.38) and (24.39), we deduce that the diameter of $\mathcal{T}'$ is given by

$$\rho(\mathcal{T}') = \max\{\max\{\rho(\mathcal{T}_W), W \in \mathcal{T}_{k-1}\}, \max\{||x^l - y||, 0 \le l \le k\}\} \tag{24.47}$$

$$\le \max\left\{ \frac{k-1}{k}\rho(\mathcal{T}), \frac{k}{k+1}\rho(\mathcal{T}) \right\} = \frac{k}{k+1}\rho(\mathcal{T}), \tag{24.48}$$

which is what we needed to show. This completes the proof of Theorem 24.22. □

By repeated use of Theorem 24.22 we obtain the following corollary.

Corollary 24.26 *For every simplex S, and every $\varepsilon > 0$, there exists a simplicial partition $\mathcal{T}_\varepsilon$ of S satisfying $\rho(\mathcal{T}_\varepsilon) \le \varepsilon$.*

24.1.2 Brouwer's Fixed Point Theorem

For every $i = 1, 2, \ldots, n$, the $(n-1)$-*dimensional standard simplex* is the simplex in $\mathbb{R}^n$ whose vertices are the unit vectors $e^1, e^2, \ldots, e^n$. This is the set $X(n) \subseteq \mathbb{R}^n$ defined as

$$X(n) := \left\{ x \in \mathbb{R}^n \colon \sum_{i=1}^n x_i = 1, \quad x_i \ge 0 \ \ \forall i \right\}. \tag{24.49}$$

The standard simplices $X(1)$, $X(2)$, and $X(3)$ are depicted in Figure 24.11.

When vectors in a simplex $S = \langle\langle x^0, x^1, \ldots, x^k \rangle\rangle$ are presented in barycentric coordinates, the simplex $X(k+1)$ is obtained. To see this, note that for each $l, 0 \le l \le k$,

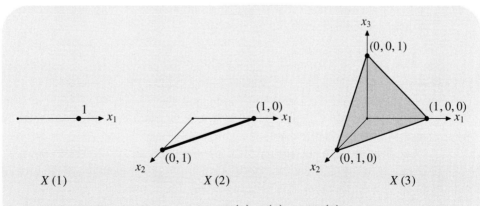

Figure 24.11 The standard simplices $X(1)$, $X(2)$, and $X(3)$

the barycentric coordinates of x^l are the unit vector e^l and every point in the simplex S can be uniquely presented as a convex combination of extreme points in the simplex (Theorem 24.9).

Brouwer's Fixed Point Theorem states that every continuous function from a convex and compact set X in $\mathbb{R}^n$ to itself has a fixed point. We first prove the theorem for the case in which the convex and compact set is $X(n)$. The statement of the theorem refers to a function defined on a standard simplex, but since every k-dimensional simplex S is equivalent to the standard simplex $X(k+1)$ when its points are represented in barycentric coordinates, the theorem holds for functions defined on any simplex.

Theorem 24.27 (Special case of Brouwer's Fixed Point Theorem) *Let $f : X(n) \rightarrow X(n)$ be a continuous function. Then there exists $x^* \in X(n)$ such that $f(x^*) = x^*$.*

In the proof of the theorem we will use the sup-norm in $\mathbb{R}^n$: for each vector $x \in \mathbb{R}^n$ denote

$$\|x\|_\infty := \max_{i=1,\ldots,n} |x_i|. \tag{24.50}$$

Proof: Since $y = \sum_{i=1}^n y_i e^i$ for every $y \in X(n)$ where $(e^i)_{i=1}^n$ are the unit vectors (see Example 24.4 on page 964), the support of y relative to the vertices of the simplex $X(n)$ is the collection of the indices i for which $y_i > 0$.

Step 1: For every $y \in X(n)$ there exists an index $i \in \text{supp}(y)$ satisfying $f_i(y) \leq y_i$.

Let $y \in X(n)$, and suppose by contradiction that the claim does not hold. Then:

- $f_i(y) > y_i$ for every index $i \in \text{supp}(y)$.
- $f_i(y) \geq 0 = y_i$ for every index $i \notin \text{supp}(y)$.

Sum together these equations for $i = 1, 2, \ldots, n$. Since $\text{supp}(y)$ contains at least one index, it follows that

$$1 = \sum_{i=1}^n f_i(y) > \sum_{i=1}^n y_i = 1. \tag{24.51}$$

This contradiction shows that the initial assumption was wrong, and therefore there exists an index $i \in \text{supp}(y)$ satisfying $f_i(y) \leq y_i$.

Step 2: Defining a coloring.

Recall that every continuous function defined on a compact space is uniformly continuous.[5]

Let $\varepsilon > 0$. Since f is uniformly continuous, there exists $\delta = \delta(\varepsilon) > 0$ such that if $\|x - y\|_\infty \leq \delta$, then $\|f(x) - f(y)\|_\infty \leq \varepsilon$. Note that δ may be chosen to be sufficiently small so as to be smaller than ε.

Let $\mathcal{T}_\varepsilon$ be a simplicial partition of $X(n)$ with diameter smaller than $\delta = \delta(\varepsilon)$. Color the simplicial partition $\mathcal{T}_\varepsilon$ with the colors $\{1, 2, \ldots, n\}$ corresponding to the vertices of $X(n)$,

---

[5] Let X be a subset of $\mathbb{R}^n$. A function $f : X \rightarrow \mathbb{R}^n$ is *uniformly continuous* if for every $\varepsilon > 0$ there exists $\delta > 0$ such that $\|f(x) - f(y)\|_\infty \leq \varepsilon$ for every $x, y \in X$ satisfying $\|x - y\|_\infty \leq \delta$.

which are $e^1, e^2, \ldots, e^n$, as follows. For every $y \in Y(\mathcal{T}_\varepsilon)$, let the color $c(y)$ be an index i satisfying $i \in \text{supp}(y)$ and $f_i(y) \leq y_i$ (recall that in Step 1 we showed that there exists at least one such index).

Since the color of every $y \in Y(\mathcal{T}_\varepsilon)$ is an index in $\text{supp}(y)$, this coloring satisfies the condition of Sperner's Lemma.

Step 3: Existence of a fixed point.

By Sperner's Lemma (Theorem 24.19 on page 972) there exists a simplex $\mathcal{T}_\varepsilon = \langle\langle x^1, x^2, \ldots, x^n \rangle\rangle \in \mathcal{T}_\varepsilon$, all of whose vertices are colored by $\{1, 2, \ldots, n\}$. Suppose without loss of generality that $c(x^i) = i$ for each $i = 1, 2, \ldots, n$, i.e., $f_i(x^i) \leq x_i^i$ (x_i^i is the i-th coordinate of x^i). Let x^ε be a vector in $\mathcal{T}_\varepsilon$. Since the diameter of $\mathcal{T}_\varepsilon$ is at most δ, it follows that $\|x^\varepsilon - x^i\|_\infty \leq \delta$ for each i, and since f is uniformly continuous, it follows that

$$f_i(x^\varepsilon) \leq f_i(x^i) + \varepsilon \leq x_i^i + \varepsilon \leq x_i^\varepsilon + \varepsilon + \delta \leq x_i^\varepsilon + 2\varepsilon, \quad \forall i = 1, 2, \ldots, n. \tag{24.52}$$

The last inequality holds because $\delta \leq \varepsilon$. This is true for every $\varepsilon > 0$, and therefore for every $\varepsilon > 0$ there exists a point $x^\varepsilon \in X(n)$ satisfying Equation (24.52), that is,

$$f_i(x^\varepsilon) \leq x_i^\varepsilon + 2\varepsilon, \quad \forall i = 1, 2, \ldots, n. \tag{24.53}$$

Since $X(n)$ is a compact set, there exists a sequence $(\varepsilon_k)_{k \in \mathbb{N}}$ converging to 0 such that the sequence $(x^{\varepsilon_k})_{k=1}^\infty$ converges to a limit in $X(n)$, denoted by x^*. Since f is continuous, by taking the limit in Equation (24.53) one has

$$f_i(x^*) \leq x_i^*, \quad \forall i = 1, 2, \ldots, n, \tag{24.54}$$

and therefore

$$1 = \sum_{i=1}^n f_i(x^*) \leq \sum_{i=1}^n x_i^* = 1. \tag{24.55}$$

If there existed i, $1 \leq i \leq n$, for which the inequality in Equation (24.54) were a strict inequality, the inequality in Equation (24.55) would also be a strict inequality, which is impossible, and therefore $f_i(x^*) = x_i^*$ for all $i = 1, 2, \ldots, n$; i.e., x^* is a fixed point of f. $\square$

Brouwer's Fixed Point Theorem (Theorem 24.27 on page 982) will now be generalized to a convex and compact set $X \subset \mathbb{R}^n$. We first show that for every point x that is not in a closed and convex set X there exists a unique point in X that is closest to it.

Recall that the distance of a point in $y \in \mathbb{R}^n$ from a set $X \subseteq \mathbb{R}^n$ is defined by

$$d(y, X) := \inf_{x \in X} d(y, x), \tag{24.56}$$

where $d(x, y) = \sqrt{\sum_{i=1}^n (x_i - y_i)^2}$ is the Euclidean distance between x and y.

Theorem 24.28 *Let $X \subset \mathbb{R}^n$ be a closed and convex set, and let $x \notin X$. Then there exists a unique point $y \in X$ such that $d(x, X) = d(x, y)$.*

Proof: Since the set X is closed and convex, there is at least one point $y \in X$ satisfying $d(x, X) = d(x, y)$. Suppose by contradiction that there are two such points y and $\hat{y}$. Since

X is a convex set, the point $\frac{y+\widehat{y}}{2}$ is contained in X. We will now show that $d(x, \frac{y+\widehat{y}}{2}) < d(x, y) = d(x, \widehat{y})$, in contradiction to the assumption that y and $\widehat{y}$ are points in X whose distance from x is minimal.

Define a function $D : \mathbb{R} \to \mathbb{R}$ by

$$D(\alpha) = d(x, \alpha y + (1 - \alpha)\widehat{y}) \tag{24.57}$$

$$= \sum_{i=1}^{n} (x_i - \alpha y_i - (1 - \alpha)\widehat{y}_i)^2 = \sum_{i=1}^{n} (x_i - \widehat{y}_i - \alpha(y_i - \widehat{y}_i))^2. \tag{24.58}$$

This is a nonnegative and nonconstant quadratic function of α. Since $d(x, y) = d(x, \widehat{y})$, one has $D(0) = D(1)$. The coefficient of α^2 in this function is positive, and therefore it has a unique minimum attained at the point $\alpha = \frac{1}{2}$. In other words, $d(x, \frac{y+\widehat{y}}{2}) < d(x, y)$, as we wanted to show. □

Let $X \subset \mathbb{R}^n$ be a closed and convex set. The following theorem, which is proved using the triangle inequality, states that the function associating each point in $\mathbb{R}^n$ with the point in X that is closest to it is a Lipschitz[6] function, and therefore, in particular, it is continuous (Exercise 24.27).

Theorem 24.29 *Let $X \subset \mathbb{R}^n$ be a closed and convex set. Define a function $g : \mathbb{R}^n \to X$ as follows: $g(x)$ is the closest point in X to x. Then $d(g(x), g(\widehat{x})) \leq d(x, \widehat{x})$ for every $x, \widehat{x} \in \mathbb{R}^n$.*

This last result is used to prove the following theorem.

Theorem 24.30 (Brouwer's Fixed Point Theorem) *Let $X \subseteq \mathbb{R}^n$ be a convex, compact, and nonempty set. Then every continuous function $f : X \to X$ has a fixed point.*

Proof: Since X is compact, there exists a simplex S sufficiently large to contain X. Define a function $h : S \to S$ by

$$h(x) := f(g(x)), \tag{24.59}$$

where g is the function associating every point x with the point in X that is closest to it. Note that the function g is well defined by Theorem 24.28 and that it satisfies $g(x) = x$ for every $x \in X$. By Theorem 24.29, the function g is continuous; hence h, as the composition of two continuous functions, is also continuous. By Theorem 24.27 the function h has a fixed point x^*; that is, $x^* = h(x^*)$. The range of h is the set X, and therefore $x^* \in X$. Since $g(x) = x$ for each $x \in X$, we have $x^* = h(x^*) = f(g(x^*)) = f(x^*)$, i.e., x^* is also a fixed point of f. □

24.1.3 Kakutani's Fixed Point Theorem

Brouwer's Fixed Point Theorem is generalized by Kakutani's Fixed Point Theorem, proved by Kakutani [1941], which we present in this section. This theorem does not deal with a function f, but rather with a correspondence, i.e., a set-valued function.

---

6 Let $X \subseteq \mathbb{R}^n$. A function $f : X \to \mathbb{R}$ is a *Lipschitz function* if there exists a nonnegative real number K satisfying $|f(x) - f(y)| \leq Kd(x, y)$ for every $x, y \in X$.

Definition 24.31 *Let* $X \subset \mathbb{R}^n$. *A* correspondence *(or a* set-valued function*) from X to X is a function F associating every* $x \in X$ *with a subset* $F(x)$ *of X. The* graph *of a correspondence F is the set* $\{(x, y) \in X \times X : y \in F(x)\}$, *which is a subset of* $X \times X$. *A correspondence F whose graph is closed is called an* upper semi-continuous *correspondence.*

Equivalently, a correspondence F is a function $F : X \to 2^X$, where 2^X is the power set of X, i.e., the set of all subsets of X. Note that if the graph of F is a closed set in $X \times X$, then in particular for each $x \in X$ the set $F(x)$ is a closed subset of X.

Theorem 24.32 (Kakutani [1941]) *Let* $X \subset \mathbb{R}^n$ *be a compact and convex set, and let F be an upper semi-continuous correspondence from X to X satisfying that for every* $x \in X$ *the set* $F(x)$ *is nonempty and convex. Then there exists a point* $x^* \in X$ *satisfying* $x^* \in F(x^*)$.

A point x^* satisfying $x^* \in F(x^*)$ is called a *fixed point* of the correspondence F.

Remark 24.33 *The Brouwer Fixed Point Theorem (Theorem 24.27) is a special case of Kakutani's Fixed Point Theorem: if* $f : X \to X$ *is a continuous function, then the correspondence F from X to X defined by* $F(x) = \{f(x)\}$ *for every* $x \in X$ *is an upper semi-continuous correspondence with nonempty and convex values. By Kakutani's Fixed Point Theorem it follows that this correspondence has a fixed point* x^*. *Every such fixed point is a fixed point of f (Exercise 24.28).* ◆

For every subset A of $\mathbb{R}^n$, and every $\varepsilon > 0$, denote the ε-*neighborhood* of A by $B(A, \varepsilon)$,

$$B(A, \varepsilon) := \{y \in \mathbb{R}^n : d(y, A) \leq \varepsilon\}. \tag{24.60}$$

If A is a convex set, then $B(A, \varepsilon)$ is also a convex set (Exercise 24.26). The following lemma states that for an upper semi-continuous correspondence F, if x is "close" to x^0 then $F(x)$ is also "close" to $F(X^0)$.

Lemma 24.34 *Let* $F : X \to X$ *be an upper semi-continuous correspondence. For each* $x^0 \in X$ *and each* $\varepsilon > 0$ *there exists* $\delta > 0$ *such that* $F(x) \subseteq B(F(x^0), \varepsilon)$ *for every* $x \in X$ *satisfying* $d(x, x^0) \leq \delta$.

Proof: Suppose by contradiction that the claim does not hold. Then there exists $x^0 \in X$, and $\varepsilon > 0$ such that for every $\delta > 0$ there is $x^\delta \in X$ satisfying $d(x^\delta, x^0) \leq \delta$, and there is $y^\delta \in F(x^\delta)$ such that $d(y^\delta, F(x^0)) > \varepsilon$. Since X is a compact set, by taking subsequences of (x^δ) and (y^δ), there exist sequences $(x^k)_{k \in \mathbb{N}}$ and $(y^k)_{k \in \mathbb{N}}$ satisfying (a) $\lim_{k \to \infty} x^k = x^0$; (b) $y^k \in F(x^k)$ for every $k \in \mathbb{N}$, and the limit $\widehat{y} := \lim_{k \to \infty} y^k$ exists; and (c) $d(y^k, F(x^0)) > \varepsilon$ for every $k \in \mathbb{N}$. By (a) and (b), and using the fact that the graph of F is a closed set, we deduce that $\widehat{y} \in F(x^0)$. But by (c), it follows that $d(\widehat{y}, F(x^0)) \geq \varepsilon$. These two conclusions contradict each other, with the contradiction showing that the original supposition does not hold; hence the statement of the theorem holds. $\square$

Proof of Kakutani's Fixed Point Theorem (Theorem 24.32): The idea behind the proof is to use the correspondence F to construct a sequence of continuous functions $(f^m)_{m \in \mathbb{N}}$ from X to X. By Brouwer's Fixed Point Theorem, for each $m \in \mathbb{N}$ the function f^m

so defined has a fixed point x^m. The functions $(f^m)_{m \in \mathbb{N}}$ will be defined in such a way that each accumulation point x^* of the sequence $(x^m)_{m \in \mathbb{N}}$ is a fixed point of the correspondence F.

Step 1: Defining sequences of continuous functions.

We first define, for every $m \in \mathbb{N}$, a continuous function $f^m : X \to X$. Let $m \in \mathbb{N}$. Since X is a compact set, it can be covered by a finite number of open balls K^m, each of which is of radius $\frac{1}{m}$. Denote the centers of these balls by $(x_k^m)_{k=1}^{K^m}$. Then for every $x \in X$ there exists $k \in \{1, 2, \ldots, K^m\}$ such that $d(x, x_k^m) < \frac{1}{m}$. For every $k \in \{1, 2, \ldots, K^m\}$ choose $y_k^m \in F(x_k^m)$. Denote the set of points whose distance from x_k^m is at least $\frac{1}{m}$ by C_k^m,

$$C_k^m := \left\{ x \in X : d(x, x_k^m) \geq \frac{1}{m} \right\}. \tag{24.61}$$

It follows that $d(x, x_k^m) < \frac{1}{m}$ if and only if $x \notin C_k^m$, and since C_k^m is closed, this can happen if and only if $d(x, C_k^m) > 0$. Define, for every $x \in X$ and for every $k \in \{1, 2, \ldots, K^m\}$,

$$\lambda_k^m(x) := \frac{d\left(x, C_k^m\right)}{\sum_{l=1}^{K^m} d\left(x, C_l^m\right)}. \tag{24.62}$$

The denominator in the definition of $\lambda_k^m(x)$ is a sum of nonnegative numbers, and hence is nonnegative. Since for every x there exists $k \in \{1, 2, \ldots, K^m\}$ such that $d(x, x_k^m) < \frac{1}{m}$, the denominator is positive. Since the distance function $x \mapsto d(x, C_k^m)$ is continuous, and the sum of a finite number of continuous functions is a continuous function, both the numerator and the denominator in the definition of λ_k^m are continuous functions. Since the ratio of two continuous functions where the denominator is positive is a continuous function, one deduces that λ_k^m is a continuous function. Note that

$$\sum_{k=1}^{K^m} \lambda_k^m(x) = 1, \quad \forall x \in X. \tag{24.63}$$

Define a function $f^m : X \to X$ as

$$f^m(x) := \sum_{k=1}^{K^m} \lambda_k^m(x) y_k^m. \tag{24.64}$$

In other words, $f^m(x)$ is a convex combination of the points $(y_k^m)_{k=1}^{K^m}$, with weights $(\lambda_k^m(x))_{k=1}^{K^m}$. Since the set X is convex, and since the points $(y_k^m)_{k=1}^{K^m}$ are in X, the range of f^m is contained in X.

Step 2: Using Brouwer's Fixed Point Theorem.

For every $m \in \mathbb{N}$, f^m is a continuous function, because it is a sum of a finite number of continuous functions. By Brouwer's Fixed Point Theorem (Theorem 24.30), this function has a fixed point: there exists $x^{*,m} \in X$ satisfying $x^{*,m} = f(x^{*,m})$.

The sequence of fixed points $(x^{*,m})_{m \in \mathbb{N}}$ is contained in the compact set X, and it therefore contains a convergent subsequence. Denote the subsequence by $(x^{*,m_l})_{l \in \mathbb{N}}$, and denote its limit by x^*.

Step 3: x^* is a fixed point of F.
The idea behind this is as follows. Since x^{*,m_l} is a fixed point of f^{m_l}, it follows that

$$x^{*,m_l} = f^{m_l}(x^{*,m_l}) = \sum_{k=1}^{K^{m_l}} \lambda_k^{m_l}(x^{*,m_l}) y_k^{m_l}. \tag{24.65}$$

The coefficient $\lambda_k^{m_l}(x^{*,m_l})$ is greater than 0 only if $x_k^{m_l}$ is close to x^{*,m_l}, which is close to x^*. Lemma 24.34 then implies that for every k such that $\lambda_k^{m_l}(x^{*,m_l}) > 0$, the point $y_k^{m_l}$ is close to $F(x^*)$. Since $F(x^*)$ is convex, we also deduce that x^{*,m_l}, as a convex combination of points close to $F(x^*)$, is also close to $F(x^*)$. By letting l go to infinity we conclude that $x^* \in F(x^*)$, since the graph of F is a closed set.

The formal proof is as follows. Let $\varepsilon > 0$, and let $\delta > 0$ be the number obtained by applying Lemma 24.34 for $x^0 = x^*$. Let L be sufficiently large such that for all $l \geq L$, (a) $\frac{1}{m_l} < \frac{\delta}{2}$, and (b) $d(x^*, x^{*,m_l}) < \frac{\delta}{2}$. Let $l \geq L$. For every k such that $\lambda_k^{m_l}(x^{*,m_l}) > 0$, one has $d(x_k^{m_l}, x^{*,m_l}) < \frac{1}{m_l} < \frac{\delta}{2}$. Therefore, by the triangle inequality, for each such k,

$$d\left(x^*, x_k^{m_l}\right) \leq d(x^*, x^{*,m_l}) + d\left(x^{*,m_l}, x_k^{m_l}\right) < \frac{\delta}{2} + \frac{\delta}{2} = \delta. \tag{24.66}$$

By Lemma 24.34, $y_k^{m_l} \in F(x_k^{m_l}) \in B(F(x^*), \varepsilon)$ for every such k; i.e., for every $k = 1, 2, \ldots, K^{m_l}$, either $\lambda_k^{m_l}(x^{*,m_l}) = 0$, or $y_k^{m_l} \in B(F(x^*), \varepsilon)$. By Equation (24.65), we then deduce that x^{*,m_l} is a convex combination of points located in the convex set $B(F(x^*), \varepsilon)$, and therefore $x^{*,m_l} \in B(F(x^*), \varepsilon)$. This holds for all $\varepsilon > 0$, and because $F(x^*)$ is a closed set, x^*, as the limit of the sequence $(x^{*,m_l})_{l \in \mathbb{N}}$, is also in $F(x^*)$. $\qquad\square$

Remark 24.35 *The properties of the set X that we used in the proof are: (a) convexity, (b) compactness, and (c) every continuous function $f : X \to X$ has a fixed point. Since Brouwer's Fixed Point Theorem holds also for compact and convex sets in infinite-dimensional spaces (see Schauder [1930] or Dunford and Schwartz [1988, Section V.10]), Kakutani's Fixed Point Theorem also holds in such spaces. Proofs of Kakutani's Fixed Point Theorem in infinite-dimensional spaces are given in Bohnenblust and Karlin [1950] and Glicksberg [1952].* $\qquad\blacklozenge$

24.1.4 The KKM Theorem

The next theorem we present here, known as the KKM Theorem, after the three researchers who first proved it, Knaster, Kuratowski, and Mazurkiewicz, is a central theorem in topology. It is equivalent to Brouwer's Fixed Point Theorem. A guided proof of the KKM Theorem, using Brouwer's Fixed Point Theorem, is given in Exercise 24.31, and a guided proof of Brouwer's Fixed Point Theorem, using the KKM Theorem, is given in Exercise 24.32. We present here a direct proof of the KKM Theorem, using Sperner's Lemma.

Theorem 24.36 (KKM) *Let $X^1, X^2, \ldots, X^n$ be compact subsets of $X(n)$ satisfying*

$$X^i \supseteq \{x \in X(n): x_i = 0\}, \quad i = 1, \ldots, n, \tag{24.67}$$

whose union is X(n),

$$\bigcup_{i=1}^{n} X^i = X(n).$$

(24.68)

Then their intersection is nonempty:

$$\bigcap_{i=1}^{n} X^i \neq \emptyset.$$

(24.69)

Proof: We first prove the theorem in the special case where the sets $(X^i)_{i=1}^{n}$ are relatively open sets[7] in $X(n)$. Suppose by contradiction that $\bigcap_{i=1}^{n} X^i = \emptyset$. In particular, for every $x \in X(n)$ there exists an index i satisfying $x \notin X^i$.

For every $k \in \mathbb{N}$, let $\mathcal{T}_k$ be a simplicial partition of $X(n)$ with diameter less than $\frac{1}{k}$. Define a coloring c of $\mathcal{T}_k$ as follows: for every vertex $y \in Y(\mathcal{T}_k)$, the color of y is one of the indices i such that $y \notin X^i$. Note that if $y_i = 0$, then $y \in X^i$ by Equation (24.67), and in particular the color of y is not i. It follows that if the color of y is i, then necessarily $y_i > 0$, i.e., the color of y is one of the indices in the support of y. In particular, the coloring c is proper. By Sperner's Lemma (Theorem 24.19), there exists a perfectly colored $(n - 1)$-dimensional simplex $T_k \in \mathcal{T}_k$. It follows that for every $i = 1, 2, \ldots, n$ there exists a vertex $x^{k,i}$ of T_k whose color is i, and it is therefore not in X^i.

Let $i \in \{1, 2, \ldots, n\}$, and consider the sequence $(x^{k,i})_{k \in \mathbb{N}}$. Since the set $X(n)$ is compact, the sequence has a subsequence converging to $x^{*,i}$. We next show that the following two claims regarding the limits $x^{*,1}, x^{*,2}, \ldots, x^{*,n}$ hold:

1. $x^{*,i} = x^{*,j}$ for all $i, j \in \{1, 2, \ldots, n\}$.
2. $x^{*,i} \notin X^i$ for all $i \in \{1, 2, \ldots, n\}$.

Claim (1) implies that there exists $x^{**} \in X(n)$ satisfying $x^{*,i} = x^{**}$ for all $i \in \{1, 2, \ldots, n\}$, and Claim (2) implies that $x^{**} \notin \bigcup_{i=1}^{n} X^i$. This will contradict the assumption that $\bigcup_{i=1}^{n} X^i = X(n)$ and lead to the conclusion that $\bigcap_{i=1}^{n} X^i \neq \emptyset$, thus completing the proof in the case there the sets $(X^i)_{i=1}^{n}$ are relatively open.

We start by proving Claim (1). Since $x^{k,i}$ is in T_k for every $i = 1, 2, \ldots, n$, and since the diameter of $\mathcal{T}_k$ is smaller than $\frac{1}{k}$, the distance between $x^{k,i}$ and $x^{k,j}$ is less than $\frac{1}{k}$ for every i, j. Taking the limit $k \to \infty$ yields $x^{*,i} = x^{*,j}$ for every i, j.

We next prove Claim (2). Since $x^{k,i} \notin X^i$ for every $k \in \mathbb{N}$, it follows that $x^{k,i} \in X(n) \setminus X^i$. Since the set X^i is relatively open in $X(n)$, its complement $X(n) \setminus X^i$ is relatively closed in $X(n)$, and therefore the limit $x^{*,i}$ is contained in it, i.e., $x^{*,i} \notin X^i$, which is what we needed to show.

Finally, we show that the statement of the theorem holds when the sets $(X^i)_{i=1}^{n}$ are closed sets. For every $\delta > 0$ let $X_0^{i,\delta}$ be the open δ-neighborhood of X^i,

$$X_0^{i,\delta} := \{y \in X(n) : d(X^i, y) < \delta\}.$$

(24.70)

---

7 A set $A \subseteq \mathbb{R}^n$ is called *relatively open* in a set $C \subseteq \mathbb{R}^n$ if it is the intersection of an open set U in $\mathbb{R}^n$ with C. A set $A \subseteq \mathbb{R}^n$ is called *relatively closed* in a set $C \subseteq \mathbb{R}^n$ if its complement in C, the set $C \setminus A$, is relatively open in C. If A is a relatively closed set in C, then for every sequence of points in A converging to y in C one has $y \in A$.

For every $i \in \{1, 2, \ldots, n\}$, the set $X^{i,\delta}$ is relatively open in $X(n)$, and contains X^i. In particular, $\cup_{i=1}^n X^{i,\delta} \supseteq \cup_{i=1}^n X^i = X(n)$. By the first part of the proof, the intersection $\cap_{i=1}^n X^{i,\delta}$ is nonempty: there exists a point x^δ satisfying $x^\delta \in X^{i,\delta}$ for every $i = \{1, 2, \ldots, n\}$. In particular, $d(X^i, x^\delta) < \delta$. Since $X(n)$ is a compact set, there is a subsequence of the sequence $(x^\delta)_{\delta > 0}$ converging to a limit denoted $\hat{x}$. By passing to the limit, one has $d(X^i, \hat{x}) = 0$, i.e., $\hat{x} \in X^i$, for every $i \in N$. Therefore, $\cap_{i=1}^n X^i \neq \emptyset$, which is what we wanted to prove.   □

24.2 The Separating Hyperplane Theorem

Recall that the inner product of two vectors in $\mathbb{R}^n$ is defined by

$$\langle x, y \rangle := \sum_{i=1}^n x_i y_i. \tag{24.71}$$

The relationship between the inner product of vectors and the distance between them is given by

$$d(x, y) = \sqrt{\langle x - y, x - y \rangle}. \tag{24.72}$$

Definition 24.37 *A hyperplane $H(\alpha, \beta)$ in $\mathbb{R}^n$ is defined by*

$$H(\alpha, \beta) := \{x \in \mathbb{R}^n : \langle \alpha, x \rangle = \beta\}, \tag{24.73}$$

where $\alpha \in \mathbb{R}^n$ and $\beta \in \mathbb{R}$.

Denote

$$H^+(\alpha, \beta) = \{x \in \mathbb{R}^n : \langle \alpha, x \rangle \geq \beta\} \tag{24.74}$$

and

$$H^-(\alpha, \beta) = \{x \in \mathbb{R}^n : \langle \alpha, x \rangle \leq \beta\}. \tag{24.75}$$

$H^+(\alpha, \beta)$ and $H^-(\alpha, \beta)$ are called the half-spaces defined by the hyperplane $H(\alpha, \beta)$ (see Figure 24.12).

The definition implies (see Exercise 24.33) that

$$H^+(\alpha, \beta) = H^-(-\alpha, -\beta) \text{ and } H^+(\alpha, \beta) \cap H^-(\alpha, \beta) = H(\alpha, \beta). \tag{24.76}$$

A hyperplane separates a set from a point if the set is contained in one of the half-spaces defined by the hyperplane, and the point is contained in the other half-space.

Definition 24.38 *Let $S \subseteq \mathbb{R}^n$ be a set, and $x \in \mathbb{R}^n$ be a vector. The hyperplane $H(\alpha, \beta)$ separates the vector x from the set S if:*

(i) $x \in H^+(\alpha, \beta)$ and $S \subseteq H^-(\alpha, \beta)$, or
(ii) $x \in H^-(\alpha, \beta)$ and $S \subseteq H^+(\alpha, \beta)$.

If the set S and the point x do not touch the separating hyperplane $H(\alpha, \beta)$, i.e., if:

- $x \in H^+(\alpha, \beta) \backslash H(\alpha, \beta)$ and $S \subseteq H^-(\alpha, \beta) \backslash H(\alpha, \beta)$, or

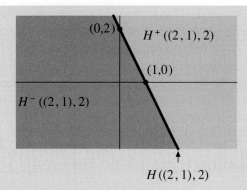

Figure 24.12 The hyperplane $H((2,1),2)$ in $\mathbb{R}^2$, which is the line $2x_1 + x_2 = 2$

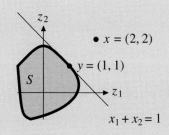

Figure 24.13 The line $x_1 + x_2 = 2$ is a hyperplane separating x from S

- $x \in H^-(\alpha, \beta) \backslash H(\alpha, \beta)$ and $S \subseteq H^+(\alpha, \beta) \backslash H(\alpha, \beta)$,

then we say that the separation of x and S is a *strict separation*.

Recall that if S is a closed set, then for every point $x \notin S$ there is at least one point $y \in S$ that is closest to x from among the points in S. If S is convex, the closest point is unique (Theorem 24.28 on page 983).

The following geometric claim, called the *Separating Hyperplane Theorem*, states that for every closed and convex set, and every point that is not in that set, there exists a hyperplane separating the point from the set. The theorem also shows how to construct such a separating hyperplane.

Theorem 24.39 (The Separating Hyperplane Theorem) *Let S be a closed and convex set, and let $x \notin S$. Let y be the closest point in S to x. Then the hyperplane $H(x - y, \langle x - y, y \rangle)$ separates x from S,*

$$S \subseteq H^-(x - y, \langle x - y, y \rangle), \tag{24.77}$$

$$x \in H^+(x - y, \langle x - y, y \rangle). \tag{24.78}$$

In addition, if the condition of the theorem is met, then there exists a hyperplane that strictly separates x from S (Exercise 24.42) (as in Figure 24.13).

Proof: *Step 1:* $x \in H^+(x - y, \langle x - y, y \rangle)$.
This statement is equivalent to the condition

$$\langle x - y, x \rangle \geq \langle x - y, y \rangle. \tag{24.79}$$

Since the inner product is bilinear, this condition is equivalent to the condition

$$\langle x - y, x - y \rangle \geq 0. \tag{24.80}$$

The left-hand side of this equation is equal to $\sum_{i=1}^{n}(x_i - y_i)^2$, a nonnegative number, and therefore Equation (24.80) indeed holds. Note that since $x \notin S$, it follows that $x \neq y$ and therefore $\langle x - y, x - y \rangle > 0$, that is, $x \in H^+(x - y, \langle x - y, y \rangle) \backslash H(x - y, \langle x - y, y \rangle)$.

Step 2: $S \subseteq H^-(x - y, \langle x - y, y \rangle)$.
We will show that $z \in H^-(x - y, \langle x - y, y \rangle)$ for every $z \in S$. This statement is equivalent to the condition

$$\langle x - y, z \rangle \leq \langle x - y, y \rangle, \quad \forall z \in S. \tag{24.81}$$

Since S is convex, $(1 - \lambda)y + \lambda z \in S$ for every $\lambda \in [0, 1]$. Since y is the closest point in S to x, it follows that

$$d(x, y) \leq d(x, (1 - \lambda)y + \lambda z), \quad \forall \lambda \in [0, 1]. \tag{24.82}$$

Since $d(x, y) = \sqrt{\langle x - y, x - y \rangle}$ for every pair of vectors $x, y \in \mathbb{R}^n$, it follows from Equation (24.82) that

$$\langle x - y, x - y \rangle \leq \langle x - (1 - \lambda)y - \lambda z, x - (1 - \lambda)y - \lambda z \rangle \tag{24.83}$$

$$= \langle (x - y) - \lambda(z - y), (x - y) - \lambda(z - y) \rangle \tag{24.84}$$

$$= \langle x - y, x - y \rangle - 2\lambda\langle x - y, z - y \rangle + \lambda^2\langle z - y, z - y \rangle. \tag{24.85}$$

Subtracting the term $\langle x - y, x - y \rangle$ yields, for all $\lambda \in [0, 1]$, the following:

$$0 \leq -2\lambda\langle x - y, z - y \rangle + \lambda^2\langle z - y, z - y \rangle. \tag{24.86}$$

This inequality holds for all $\lambda \in [0, 1]$, and in particular for $\lambda \in (0, 1]$, in which case we can divide by λ to obtain

$$0 \leq -2\langle x - y, z - y \rangle + \lambda\langle z - y, z - y \rangle. \tag{24.87}$$

Letting λ go to 0 yields the conclusion that $\langle x - y, z - y \rangle \leq 0$, which further implies that

$$\langle x - y, z \rangle \leq \langle x - y, y \rangle, \quad \forall z \in S, \tag{24.88}$$

which is what we wanted to show. $\square$

24.3 Linear programming

All the vectors appearing in this section are to be interpreted as row vectors. $y^\top$ is then the column vector corresponding to the row vector y. For $c, y \in \mathbb{R}^m$, the inner product $\langle c, y \rangle$ can be written as

$$\langle c, y \rangle = \sum_{i=1}^{m} c_i y_i = cy^\top. \tag{24.89}$$

The notation $y \geq c$ indicates inequality in every coordinate,

$$y_i \geq c_i, \quad i = 1, 2, \ldots, m, \tag{24.90}$$

and $y = c$ indicates equality in every coordinate, $y_i = c_i$ for all $i = 1, 2, \ldots, m$. Recall that for all $m \in \mathbb{N}$ we denote the zero vector in $\mathbb{R}^m$ by $\vec{0}$.

Definition 24.40 *Let* $c, y \in \mathbb{R}^m$, $b \in \mathbb{R}^n$, *and let A be an* $n \times m$ *matrix. The* (standard) *linear program in the unknowns* $y = (y_i)_{i=1}^m$ *defined by* A, b, c *is the following linear maximization program under linear constraints:*

> *Compute:* $Z_P := \max cy^\top,$
> *subject to:* $Ay^\top \leq b^\top,$
> $y \geq \vec{0}.$

The linear function $cy^\top$ is called the *objective function* of the program. The conditions $Ay^\top \leq b^\top$ and $y \geq \vec{0}$ are called *constraints*. Every vector y satisfying the constraints is called a *feasible vector*. The set of feasible vectors is called the *feasible region* of the linear program,

$$R_P := \{y \in \mathbb{R}^n : Ay^\top \leq b^\top, y \geq \vec{0}\}. \tag{24.91}$$

A feasible vector maximizing $cy^\top$ among all feasible vectors is called an *optimal solution*. This maximum, Z_P, is called the *value* of the linear program; it is the maximum of the objective function over the feasible region. When the feasible region is empty, define $Z_P := -\infty$. If the objective function $cy^\top$ is not bounded over R_P (which happens only if R_P is unbounded) define $Z_P := +\infty$. Since the objective function is linear, and the constraints are weak inequalities, if $Z_P < +\infty$ then the maximum is attained at one of the extreme points of R_P, whether R_P is bounded or not.

Definition 24.41 *Given the following linear program with unknowns* $y = (y_i)_{i=1}^m$:

> *Compute:* $Z_P := \max cy^\top,$
> *subject to:* $Ay^\top \leq b^\top,$ (24.92)
> $y \geq \vec{0};$

its dual program *is the following program with unknowns* $x = (x_j)_{j=1}^n$:

> *Compute:* $Z_D := \min xb^\top,$
> *subject to:* $xA \geq c,$ (24.93)
> $x \geq \vec{0}.$

The original program is called the primal program. *The number* Z_D *is called the* value *of the dual program.*

The conditions $xA \geq c$ and $x \geq \vec{0}$ are called the *constraints* of the dual program. Note that the primal program has m unknowns $y = (y_i)_{i=1}^m$, one for each column of A, i.e., one unknown for each constraint $xA \geq c$ of the dual program. The dual program has n unknowns $(x_j)_{j=1}^n$, one for each row of A, i.e., an unknown for each of the constraints $Ay^\top \leq b^\top$ of the primal program. If the feasible region of the dual program is empty, define $Z_D := +\infty$, and if the objective function $xb^\top$ is unbounded from below in R_D (this can only happen if R_D is unbounded) define $Z_D := -\infty$.

Example 24.42 Consider the primal program given by

$$\begin{aligned}
\text{Compute:} \quad & Z_P := \max\{6y_1 + 4y_2 + 6y_3\}, \\
\text{subject to:} \quad & 6y_1 + y_2 + y_3 \leq 3, \\
& y_1 + y_2 + 3y_3 \leq 4, \\
& y_1, y_2, y_3 \geq 0.
\end{aligned} \tag{24.94}$$

In this linear program

$$c = (6,4,6), \quad b = (3,4), \quad A = \begin{pmatrix} 6 & 1 & 1 \\ 1 & 1 & 3 \end{pmatrix}. \tag{24.95}$$

The dual program is

$$\begin{aligned}
\text{Compute:} \quad & Z_D := \min\{3x_1 + 4x_2\}, \\
\text{subject to:} \quad & 6x_1 + x_2 \geq 6, \\
& x_1 + x_2 \geq 4, \\
& x_1 + 3x_2 \geq 6, \\
& x_1, x_2 \geq 0.
\end{aligned} \tag{24.96}$$

◀

The constraints in a linear program may be given by equalities (and not necessarily only by inequalities). Every equality can be represented by two inequalities: a vector equality $Ay^\top = b^\top$ can be represented by the inequalities $Ay^\top \leq b^\top$ and $-Ay^\top \leq -b^\top$. It follows that a linear program with equalities can be rewritten as a system involving inequalities only.

Example 24.43 Consider the following linear program:

$$\begin{aligned}
\text{Compute:} \quad & Z_P := \max cy^\top, \\
\text{subject to:} \quad & Ay^\top = b^\top, \\
& y \geq \vec{0}.
\end{aligned} \tag{24.97}$$

This program can be rewritten as a system involving inequalities only:

$$\begin{aligned}
\text{Compute:} \quad & Z_P := \max cy^\top, \\
\text{subject to:} \quad & Ay^\top \leq b^\top, \\
& -Ay^\top \leq -b^\top, \\
& y \geq \vec{0}.
\end{aligned} \tag{24.98}$$

In this representation, the primal program has $2n$ constraints. The dual program must therefore have $2n$ unknowns, denoted (w, z), where $w = (w_j)_{j=1}^n$ and $z = (z_j)_{j=1}^n$. The dual program corresponding to this primal program is

$$\begin{aligned}
\text{Compute:} \quad & Z_D := \min(w - z)b^\top, \\
\text{subject to:} \quad & (w - z)A \geq c, \\
& w \geq \vec{0}, \\
& z \geq \vec{0}.
\end{aligned} \tag{24.99}$$

Set $x = w - z$. Since w and z are nonnegative, x is not constrained, and can take on any value, positive or negative. The dual program is then

$$\begin{array}{lll} \text{Compute:} & Z_D := \min xb^\top, \\ \text{subject to:} & xA \geq c. \end{array} \qquad (24.100)$$

In other words, for every feasible solution x of problem (24.100) there exists a feasible solution (w, z) of problem (24.99) satisfying $x = w - z$ (Exercise 24.47). ◄

As a corollary, we deduce the following theorem:

Theorem 24.44 *The dual program to the following primal program,*

$$\begin{array}{lll} \text{Compute:} & Z_P := \max cy^\top, \\ \text{subject to:} & Ay^\top = b^\top, \\ & y \geq 0, \end{array} \qquad (24.101)$$

is

$$\begin{array}{lll} \text{Compute:} & Z_D := \min xb^\top, \\ \text{subject to:} & xA \geq c. \end{array} \qquad (24.102)$$

The effect of equalities in the constraints of the primal problem can thus be summarized as follows: each variable in the dual problem that corresponds to a constraint with equality in the primal problem is unconstrained.

Example 24.42 *(Continued)* We solve both the primal and the dual program, starting with the primal program.

Since the numbers in the matrix A are nonnegative, and since the numbers in the vector c are positive, the maximum in the definition of Z_P is attained when the following equalities are satisfied:

$$6y_1 + y_2 + y_3 = 3, \qquad (24.103)$$

$$y_1 + y_2 + 3y_3 = 4. \qquad (24.104)$$

The solution to this system of equations is

$$y_1 = \tfrac{1}{5}(2y_3 - 1), \qquad (24.105)$$

$$y_2 = \tfrac{1}{5}(21 - 17y_3). \qquad (24.106)$$

The condition that $y_1, y_2, y_3 \geq 0$ implies that $\tfrac{1}{2} \leq y_3 \leq \tfrac{21}{17}$. The primal program is thus equivalent to

$$Z_P = \max\left\{ \tfrac{6}{5}(2y_3 - 1) + \tfrac{4}{5}(21 - 17y_3) + 6y_3 : \tfrac{1}{2} \leq y_3 \leq \tfrac{21}{17} \right\} \qquad (24.107)$$

$$= \max\left\{ \tfrac{78}{5} - \tfrac{26}{5}y_3 : \tfrac{1}{2} \leq y_3 \leq \tfrac{21}{17} \right\} = \tfrac{78}{5} - \tfrac{13}{5} = 13. \qquad (24.108)$$

The computation of the last maximum uses the fact that a linear function in y_3 with a negative slope attains its maximal value at the minimal value of y_3, which in this case is $y_3 = \tfrac{1}{2}$.

Next, we solve the dual program. The feasible region of the dual program is the shaded area in Figure 24.14. This is the intersection of the half-spaces corresponding to the inequalities defining the constraints of the dual program. As Figure 24.14 illustrates, the minimum of the function $3x_1 + 4x_2$ in the feasible region is attained at the point $(3, 1)$, and therefore $Z_D = 13$.

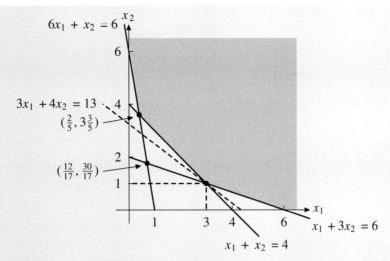

Figure 24.14 The feasible region and the solution of the dual program in Example 24.42

In Example 24.42 we computed $Z_P = Z_D$. This is not a coincidence, as the next two theorems show.

Theorem 24.45 (The Weak Duality Theorem) *Let Z_P and Z_D be, respectively, the values of the primal and the dual problems given in Definition 24.40. Then $Z_P \leq Z_D$.*

Proof: If R_P is empty, $Z_P = -\infty$, and if R_D is empty, $Z_D = +\infty$. In both cases, $Z_P \leq Z_D$ is satisfied. Suppose therefore that R_P and R_D are nonempty. Since every feasible vector x of the primal program and every feasible vector y of the dual program is nonnegative, one has

$$cy^\top \leq (xA)y^\top = x(Ay^\top) \leq xb^\top. \tag{24.109}$$

By taking the maximum on the left-hand side, and the minimum on the right-hand side, we conclude that $Z_P \leq Z_D$, which is what we wanted to show. □

The following theorem, for which we will not provide a proof, states that the inequality $Z_P \leq Z_D$ is actually an equality when Z_P is finite. A proof of the theorem can be found in many books on operations research, such as Vanderbei [2001].

Theorem 24.46 (The Strong Duality Theorem) *If Z_P is finite, then $Z_D = Z_P$.*

24.4 Remarks

The authors thank Nimrod Megiddo, David Schmeidler, and Rakesh Vohra for answering questions that arose during the composition of this chapter. The proof of Sperner's Lemma is from Kuhn [1968]. The proof of Brouwer's Fixed Point Theorem using Sperner's Lemma is a classical proof. The proof presented here is from Kuhn [1960].

24.5) Exercises

. . . .

24.1 Prove that for every set $\{x^0, x^1, \ldots, x^k\}$ of vectors in $\mathbb{R}^n$

$$\text{conv}(x^0, x^1, \ldots, x^k)$$

$$= \{x \in \mathbb{R}^n : x \text{ is a convex combination of } x^0, x^1, \ldots, x^k\}. \qquad (24.110)$$

The convex hull $\text{conv}(x^0, x^1, \ldots, x^k)$ is defined in Definition 24.1 (page 963).

24.2 Let $x^0, x^1, \ldots, x^k$ be vectors in $\mathbb{R}^n$, such that none of them is a convex combination of the other vectors. Prove that the extreme points of $\text{conv}(x^0, x^1, \ldots, x^k)$ are the vectors $x^0, x^1, \ldots, x^k$.

24.3 Let x^0, x^1, x^2 be three vectors in $\mathbb{R}^n$. Prove that these vectors are affine independent if and only if none of them is a convex combination of the other two.

24.4 For each of the following sets of vectors in $\mathbb{R}^4$, determine whether or not the vectors in the set are affine independent. Justify your answers.

(a) $x^0 = (1, 1, 0, 0)$, $x^1 = (0, 1, 1, 0)$, $x^2 = (0, 0, 1, 1)$, $x^3 = (1, 0, 0, -1)$, $x^4 = (1, 1, 1, 0)$.

(b) $x^0 = (1, 1, 0, 0)$, $x^1 = (0, 1, 1, 0)$, $x^2 = (0, 0, 1, 1)$, $x^3 = (1, 0, 0, -1)$, $x^4 = (1, 2, 1, 0)$.

(c) $x^0 = (1, 1, 0, 0)$, $x^1 = (0, 1, 1, 0)$, $x^2 = (0, 0, 1, 1)$, $x^3 = (1, 0, 0, -1)$, $x^4 = (1, 0, 0, 0)$.

24.5 Let $x^0, x^1, \ldots, x^k$ be affine-independent vectors in $\mathbb{R}^n$, and let y be a vector that is linearly independent of $\{x^0, x^1, \ldots, x^k\}$. Prove that $x^0, x^1, \ldots, x^k, y$ are affine-independent vectors.

24.6 Let $x^0, x^1, \ldots, x^k$ be affine-independent vectors in $\mathbb{R}^n$ and let $(\beta^l)_{l=0}^k$ be positive numbers summing to 1. Denote $y = \sum_{l=0}^k \beta^l x^l$. Prove that $x^1, \ldots, x^k, y$ are affine-independent vectors.

24.7 Prove that vectors $x^0, x^1, \ldots, x^k$ are affine independent in $\mathbb{R}^n$ if and only if every vector $y \in \text{conv}\{x^0, x^1, \ldots, x^k\}$ can be represented in a unique way as a convex combination of $x^0, x^1, \ldots, x^k$.

24.8 Let $S = \langle\langle x^0, x^1, \ldots, x^k \rangle\rangle$ be a simplex in $\mathbb{R}^n$ and let $y \in \mathbb{R}^n$. Prove that $y \in S$ if and only if all the solutions of the following system of equations in the variables $(\alpha^l)_{l=0}^k$ satisfy $\alpha^l \geq 0$ for all $l \in \{0, 1, \ldots, k\}$:

$$\sum_{l=0}^k \alpha^l x^l = y, \qquad (24.111)$$

$$\sum_{l=0}^k \alpha^l = 1. \qquad (24.112)$$

24.9 Let $x^0, x^1, \ldots, x^n$ be affine-independent vectors in $\mathbb{R}^n$. Prove that for every vector $y \in \mathbb{R}^n$ there exists a unique solution to the following system of equations in unknowns $(\alpha^l)_{l=0}^n$:

$$\sum_{l=0}^{n} \alpha^l x^l = y, \tag{24.113}$$

$$\sum_{l=0}^{n} \alpha^l = 1. \tag{24.114}$$

24.10 Prove that the boundary of a simplex S is the set of all the points y in S whose barycentric coordinate representation has at least one zero coordinate.

24.11 Prove that if H^1 and H^2 are two affine spaces of the same dimension k in $\mathbb{R}^n$ (that is, each one of them is spanned by a k-dimensional simplex; see page 968), and if $H^1 \subseteq H^2$, then $H^1 = H^2$.

24.12 For each of the following vectors $y^1 = (1, \frac{1}{2})$, $y^2 = (3, 0)$, $y^3 = (2, 2)$, and $y^4 = (\frac{3}{2}, \frac{1}{4})$, compute its barycentric coordinates relative to the three affine-independent vectors $x^0 = (0, 2)$, $x^1 = (1, 0)$, and $x^2 = (2, 0)$.

24.13 For each of the following partitions of a two-dimensional simplex, determine whether or not it is a simplicial partition. Justify your answer. In each case, the partition elements are the two-dimensional polytopes in it, their faces, and their vertices.

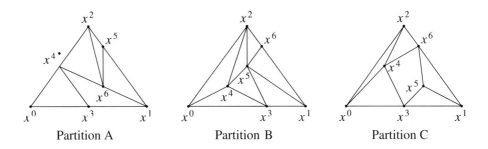

Partition A   Partition B   Partition C

24.14 Prove Theorem 24.14 (page 968): let S be a k-dimensional simplex in $\mathbb{R}^n$, and let $\mathcal{T}$ be a simplicial partition of it. Then S equals the union of all the k-dimensional simplices in $\mathcal{T}$.

24.15 Let S be a simplex, and let $\mathcal{T}$ be the collection of all the faces of S. Prove that $\mathcal{T}$ is a simplicial partition of S.

24.16 Let $T_1, T_2, \ldots, T_L$ be simplices whose union is a simplex S. Is the collection containing all the faces of $T_1, T_2, \ldots, T_L$ a simplicial partition of S? Either prove this claim, or find a counterexample.

24.17 Let $\mathcal{T}$ be a simplicial partition of a k-dimensional simplex $S = \langle\langle x^0, x^1, \ldots, x^k\rangle\rangle$. Define $\hat{S} := \langle\langle x^0, x^1, \ldots, x^{k-1}\rangle\rangle$ and $\hat{\mathcal{T}} := \{T \in \mathcal{T}: T \subseteq \hat{S}\}$. Prove that $\hat{\mathcal{T}}$ is a simplicial partition of $\hat{S}$.

24.18 How many proper colorings are there of the simplicial partition in Example 24.17 on page 972? Justify your answer. (For the definition of a proper coloring, see Definition 24.16 on page 971.)

24.19 Find a simplex, a simplicial partition of this simplex, and a nonproper coloring of the simplicial partition, for which the number of perfectly colored n-dimensional simplices is odd. In other words, show that in Sperner's Lemma (Theorem 24.19 on page 972) the properness of the coloring is a sufficient but not necessary condition for this number to be odd.

24.20 Let $\mathcal{T}$ be a simplicial partition of a k-dimensional simplex $S = \langle\langle x^0, x^1, \ldots, x^k\rangle\rangle$, and let $c : Y(\mathcal{T}) \to \{0, 1, \ldots, k\}$ be a proper coloring (see Definition 24.16 on page 971). Denote $\hat{S} := \langle\langle x^0, x^1, \ldots, x^{k-1}\rangle\rangle$ and $\hat{\mathcal{T}} := \{T \in \mathcal{T}: T \subseteq \hat{S}\}$. Prove that c restricted to $Y(\hat{\mathcal{T}})$ is a proper coloring of $\hat{\mathcal{T}}$.

24.21 Let $\mathcal{T}$ be the simplicial partition constructed in the proof of Theorem 24.22 (page 976). What is $Y(\mathcal{T})$?

24.22 Prove that the diameter $\rho(S)$ of a simplex S (see Definition 24.20 on page 975) equals the greatest (Euclidean) distance between two vectors in the simplex.

24.23 Complete the proof of Theorem 24.23 (page 976): show that the intersection of any two simplices in the simplicial partition $\mathcal{T}$ that is defined in the proof of the theorem is either empty or is contained in $\mathcal{T}$.

24.24 Complete the proof of Theorem 24.25 (page 978): show that the intersection of any two simplices in the simplicial partition $\hat{\mathcal{T}}$ that is defined in the proof of the theorem is either empty or is contained in $\hat{\mathcal{T}}$.

24.25 Prove that the diameter of the partition $\hat{\mathcal{T}}$ constructed in the proof of Theorem 24.25 (page 978) is

$$\rho(\hat{\mathcal{T}}) = \max\{\rho(\mathcal{T}), ||x^0 - y||, ||x^1 - y||, \ldots, ||x^k - y||\}. \qquad (24.115)$$

24.26 Prove that if $A \subseteq \mathbb{R}^n$ is a convex set, then the set $B(A, \varepsilon)$ (the ε-neighborhood of A; see Equation (24.60) on page 985) is also a convex set.

24.27 Prove Theorem 24.29 (page 984): let $X \subset \mathbb{R}^n$ be a closed and convex set. Define a function $g : \mathbb{R}^n \to X$ as follows: $g(x)$ is the closest point to x in X. Then $d(g(x), g(\hat{x})) \leq d(x, \hat{x})$ for all $x, \hat{x} \in \mathbb{R}^n$.

24.28 (a) Let $X \subseteq \mathbb{R}^n$. Prove that if $f : X \to X$ is a continuous function, then the correspondence $F : X \to X$ defined by $F(x) = \{f(x)\}$ for every $x \in X$ is upper semi-continuous.

(b) Use the result of the previous item to prove Brouwer's Fixed Point Theorem (Theorem 24.30, page 984) using Kakutani's Fixed Point Theorem (Theorem 24.32, page 985).

24.29 In this exercise, we prove a generalization of Brouwer's Fixed Point Theorem to compact sets that are not necessarily convex, but are homeomorphic to a convex set.

Two compact sets X and Y in $\mathbb{R}^n$ are called *homeomorphic* if there exists a continuous bijection $g : X \to Y$ satisfying the property that g^{-1} is also continuous.[8] Prove that if $X \subseteq \mathbb{R}^n$ is a compact set that is homeomorphic to a convex and compact set Y and if $f : X \to X$ is a continuous function, then f has a fixed point.

24.30 In this exercise, we prove a generalization of Nash's Theorem (Theorem 5.10 on page 150) using Kakutani's Fixed Point Theorem (Theorem 24.32 on page 985).

Let N be a nonempty, finite set of players. For each player $i \in N$, let X_i be a convex and compact subset of $\mathbb{R}^{d_i}$, where d_i is a natural number. Denote by $X = \times_{i \in N} X_i$ the Cartesian product of the sets $(X_i)_{i \in N}$. For every player $i \in N$, let $u_i : X \to \mathbb{R}$ be a function that is continuous and quasi-concave in x_i; that is, for every real number c and all $x_{-i} \in X_{-i}$, the set $\{x_i : u_i(x_i, x_{-i}) \geq c\}$ is convex.

Define a correspondence br from X to X as follows. For every $x \in X$ and for each $i \in N$,

$$\mathrm{br}_i(x) := \left\{ y_i \in X_i : u_i(y_i, x_{-i}) = \max_{z_i \in X_i} u_i(z_i, x_{-i}) \right\}, \quad \forall i \in N, \qquad (24.116)$$

and

$$\mathrm{br}(x) := \times_{i \in N} \mathrm{br}_i(x). \qquad (24.117)$$

(a) Prove that br is an upper semi-continuous correspondence with nonempty convex values. Using Kakutani's Fixed Point Theorem deduce that br has a fixed point.

(b) Prove that every fixed point of the correspondence br is a Nash equilibrium in the game $G = (N, (X_i)_{i \in N}, (u_i)_{i \in N})$. How is this a generalization of Nash's Theorem?

24.31 In this exercise, we prove the KKM Theorem (Theorem 24.36 on page 987) using Brouwer's Fixed Point Theorem (Theorem 24.30 on page 984). Suppose by contradiction that the conditions of the KKM Theorem hold yet its conclusion does not hold, i.e., $\bigcap_{i=1}^{n} X^i = \emptyset$.

(a) For each $\varepsilon > 0$ define

$$Y^{i,\varepsilon} = \{x \in X(n): d(x, X^i) \leq \varepsilon\}. \qquad (24.118)$$

Prove that $\bigcup_{i=1}^{n} Y^{i,\varepsilon} = X(n)$ for all $\varepsilon > 0$ and that there exists $\varepsilon_0 > 0$ such that $\bigcap_{i=1}^{n} Y^{i,\varepsilon_0} = \emptyset$.

---

8 The function g is called a *homeomorphism* between X and Y.

For $\varepsilon < \varepsilon_0$:

(b) Denote $Z^{i,\varepsilon} = X(n) \backslash Y^{i,\varepsilon}$ for every $i = 1, 2, \ldots, n$. Prove that $\sum_{i=1}^{n} d(x, Z^{i,\varepsilon}) \geq \varepsilon$ for every $x \in X(n)$.

(c) Prove that $\sum_{i=1}^{n} x_i d(x, Y^{i,\varepsilon}) = \sum_{\{i: \, x \notin Y^{i,\varepsilon}\}} x_i d(x, Y^{i,\varepsilon})$.

(d) Define a function $f^\varepsilon : X(n) \to X(n)$ as follows:

$$f_i^\varepsilon(x) = \begin{cases} x_i - x_i d(x, Y^{i,\varepsilon}) & \text{if } x \notin Y^{i,\varepsilon}, \\ x_i + \left(\sum_{j=1}^{n} x_j d(x, Y^{j,\varepsilon}) \right) \frac{d(x, Z^{i,\varepsilon})}{\sum_{j=1}^{n} d(x, Z^{j,\varepsilon})} & \text{if } x \in Y^{i,\varepsilon}. \end{cases} \tag{24.119}$$

Prove that the function f^ε is continuous and that its range is contained in $X(n)$. Deduce that f^ε has a fixed x^ε.

(e) Prove that $x^\varepsilon \in \bigcap_{i=1}^{n} Y^{i,\varepsilon}$.

(f) Let $(\varepsilon_k)_{k \in \mathbb{N}}$ be a sequence converging to 0 such that $x^* := \lim_{k \to \infty} x^{\varepsilon_k}$ exists. Prove that $x^* \in \bigcap_{i=1}^{n} X^i$, contradicting the assumption that $\bigcap_{i=1}^{n} X^i = \emptyset$.

24.32 Prove Brouwer's Fixed Point Theorem (Theorem 24.30 on page 984) using the KKM Theorem (Theorem 24.36 on page 987).
Hint: Define $X_i = \{x \in X(n) : f_i(x) \geq x_i\}$.

24.33 Prove that for every $\alpha \in \mathbb{R}^n$ and every $\beta \in \mathbb{R}$,

$$H^+(\alpha, \beta) = H^-(-\alpha, -\beta). \tag{24.120}$$

24.34 Prove that $x \in H^+(x - y, \langle x - y, y \rangle)$ for every pair of vectors $x, y \in \mathbb{R}^n$.

24.35 Let $x, y \in \mathbb{R}^m$ be two different vectors. Prove the following claims:

(a) $y \in H(y - x, \langle y - x, y \rangle)$.
(b) The hyperplane $H(y - x, \langle y - x, y \rangle)$ is perpendicular to $y - x$, i.e., $\langle y - x, y - z \rangle = 0$ for all $z \in H(y - x, \langle y - x, y \rangle)$.
(c) y is the point in $H(y - x, \langle y - x, y \rangle)$ that is closest to x, i.e., $\langle z - x, z - x \rangle > \langle y - x, y - x \rangle$ for all $z \in H(y - x, \langle y - x, y \rangle)$, $z \neq y$.

24.36 Let H be a hyperplane, let $x \notin H$ and let $y \in H$ be the point in H that is closest to x. Prove that $H = H(y - x, \langle y - x, y \rangle)$.

24.37 Let $H(\alpha, \beta)$ be a hyperplane and let $x \notin H(\alpha, \beta)$. Define

$$y := x + \frac{\beta - \langle \alpha, x \rangle}{\langle \alpha, \alpha \rangle} \alpha. \tag{24.121}$$

Prove the following claims:

(a) $y \in H(\alpha, \beta)$.
(b) $H(\alpha, \beta) = H(y - x, \langle y - x, y \rangle)$.

24.38 Let $H(\alpha, \beta)$ be a hyperplane separating a closed and convex set S from a vector $x \notin S$, and let $H(\hat{\alpha}, \hat{\beta})$ be a hyperplane separating a closed and convex set $\hat{S}$ from a vector $\hat{x} \notin \hat{S}$. Does the hyperplane $H(\alpha + \hat{\alpha}, \beta + \hat{\beta})$ separate the set $S + \hat{S} := \{y + \hat{y} : y \in S, \hat{y} \in \hat{S}\}$ and the vector $x + \hat{x}$? Either prove that this is true, or find a counterexample.

24.39 Let S be a closed set (not necessarily convex) and let $x \notin S$. Must there exist a hyperplane separating x from S? Either prove that this is true, or find a counter-example.

24.40 Each of the following items presents a closed and convex set S and a vector x. For each such pair, determine whether or not there is a hyperplane separating x from S, and if your answer is affirmative, find such a hyperplane. If your answer is negative, justify your answer.[9]

(a) $S = \{z \in \mathbb{R}^2 : (z_1)^2 + (z_2)^2 \le 1\}$, $x = (0, 0)$.
(b) $S = \{z \in \mathbb{R}^2 : (z_1)^2 + (z_2)^2 \le 1\}$, $x = (1, 1)$.
(c) $S = \{z \in \mathbb{R}^2 : (z_1)^2 + (z_2)^2 \le 1\}$, $x = (0, 1)$.
(d) $S = [(0, 0), (1, 1)] \cup [(0, 0), (-1, 1)]$, $x = (0, \frac{1}{2})$.
(e) $S = [(0, 0), (1, 1)] \cup [(0, 0), (-1, 1)]$, $x = (\frac{1}{2}, 1)$.
(f) $S = [(0, 0), (1, 1)] \cup [(0, 0), (-1, 1)]$, $x = (\frac{1}{4}, 2)$.
(g) $S = \{z \in \mathbb{R}^3 : (z_1)^2 + (z_2)^2 + (z_3)^2 = 1$, $x = (0, 0, 0)$.
(h) $S = \{z \in \mathbb{R}^3 : (z_1)^2 + (z_2)^2 + (z_3)^2 = 1$, $x = (0, 1, 1)$.

24.41 Each of the following items presents a closed and convex set S and a vector x. For each such pair, find the hyperplane separating x from S, as described in Theorem 24.39 (page 990).

(a) $S = \{z \in \mathbb{R}^3 : \max\{|z_1|, |z_2|, |z_3|\} \le 1\}$, $x = (2, 2, 2)$.
(b) $S = \{z \in \mathbb{R}^3 : \max\{|z_1|, |z_2|, |z_3|\} \le 1\}$, $x = (2, 3, 4)$.
(c) $S = \{z \in \mathbb{R}^3 : (z_1)^2 + (z_2)^2 + (z_3)^2 = 1\}$, $x = (2, 2, 2)$.
(d) $S = \{z \in \mathbb{R}^2 : z_1 \ge 0, z_1 + z_2 \le 1, z_2 \le z_1\}$, $x = (1, 2)$.
(e) $S = \{z \in \mathbb{R}^2 : z_1 \ge 0, z_1 + z_2 \le 1, z_2 \le z_1\}$, $x = (2, 3)$.

24.42 Let $S \subseteq \mathbb{R}^n$ be a closed and convex set, and let $x \notin S$. Find a hyperplane $H(\alpha, \beta)$ strictly separating x from S; i.e., x is in the interior of $H^+(\alpha, \beta)$, and S is in the interior $H^-(\alpha, \beta)$.

24.43 In this exercise, we provide a guided proof of Farkas' Lemma: let $v \in \mathbb{R}^n$ be a vector, and let T be an $n \times m$ matrix. Then the following two claims are equivalent.

(a) $\langle u, v \rangle = uv^\top \ge 0$ for every vector $u \in \mathbb{R}^n$ satisfying $uT \ge \vec{0}$.
(b) There exists a vector $w \in \mathbb{R}^m$, $w \ge \vec{0}$, satisfying $Tw^\top = v^\top$.

---

[9] For every $x, y \in \mathbb{R}^2$ denote the line segment connecting x and y by $[x, y]$, i.e., $[x, y] = \{z \in \mathbb{R}^2 : x = \lambda x + (1 - \lambda)y, 0 \le \lambda \le 1\}$.

Guidance: To prove that the first claim implies the second claim, define the set $A := \{Tw^\top : w \in \mathbb{R}^m, w \geq \vec{0}\} \subseteq \mathbb{R}^n$, and suppose by contradiction that $v \notin A$. Show that by the Separating Hyperplane Theorem there exists a hyperplane $H(\alpha, \beta)$ separating A from v, and that it is possible to assume without loss of generality that $\beta = 0$. Prove that $\alpha T \geq \vec{0}$, and derive a contradiction.

24.44 Prove the following theorem, which is a generalization of Theorem 24.39 (page 990).

Theorem 24.47 *Let X and Y be two closed and convex subsets of $\mathbb{R}^n$. If X and Y are disjoint sets, then there exists a hyperplane $H(\alpha, \beta)$ strictly separating X from Y, i.e.,*

$$\langle \alpha, x \rangle > \beta > \langle \alpha, y \rangle, \quad \forall x \in X, y \in Y. \tag{24.122}$$

Guidance: Denote by $d(X, Y)$ the distance between X and Y,

$$d(X, Y) := \min_{\{x \in X, y \in Y\}} d(x, y). \tag{24.123}$$

The minimum in the definition of $d(X, Y)$ is attained because X and Y are closed sets. Let $x \in X$ and $y \in Y$ be points that minimize the distance between the points in X and the points in Y,

$$d(X, Y) = d(x, y) > 0. \tag{24.124}$$

Write down the equation for the hyperplane separating the vector x from Y, as constructed in the proof of Theorem 24.39, and the equation for the hyperplane separating y from X, as constructed in the proof of Theorem 24.39. Using these two hyperplanes, construct a hyperplane strictly separating X from Y.

24.45 In this exercise we generalize Exercise 24.44, and show that any two disjoint convex sets can be separated.

(a) Let X be a convex set. For every $\varepsilon > 0$ denote by X_ε the set of all points whose distance from X^c, the complement of X, is at least ε:

$$X_\varepsilon := \{x \in X : d(x, X^c) \geq \varepsilon\}. \tag{24.125}$$

Prove that X_ε is a closed and convex set for every $\varepsilon > 0$.
Let X and Y be two disjoint convex sets.
(b) Prove that the sets X_ε and Y_ε are disjoint for every $\varepsilon > 0$.
(c) Deduce from Exercise 24.44 that for every $\varepsilon > 0$ there exists a hyperplane $H(\alpha_\varepsilon, \beta_\varepsilon)$ satisfying

$$\langle \alpha_\varepsilon, x \rangle > \beta_\varepsilon > \langle \alpha_\varepsilon, y \rangle, \quad \forall x \in X_\varepsilon, y \in Y_\varepsilon. \tag{24.126}$$

(d) Prove that if the hyperplane $H(\alpha_\varepsilon, \beta_\varepsilon)$ is the hyperplane constructed in the proof of Theorem 24.39 (page 990), then the sequence $(\alpha_\varepsilon, \beta_\varepsilon)$ has an accumulation point (α_*, β_*) when ε converges to 0.
(e) Prove that the hyperplane $H(\alpha_*, \beta_*)$ separates X from Y, i.e., $X \subseteq H^+(\alpha_*, \beta_*)$ and $Y \subseteq H^-(\alpha_*, \beta_*)$.

24.46 Find the dual program to each of the following linear programs:

(a)

Compute: $Z_P := \max\{2y_1 - 3y_2\}$,

subject to: $y_1 + 2y_2 \leq 1$,

$$-y_1 - 4y_2 \leq 4,$$
$$-6y_1 + 5y_2 \leq 7, \qquad (24.127)$$
$$y_1, y_2 \geq 0.$$

(b)

Compute: $Z_P := \max\{6y_1 + 2y_2 - 3y_3\}$,

subject to: $-2y_1 + 4y_2 \leq -3$,

$$5y_1 - 1y_3 \leq -6,$$
$$7y_1 + 2y_2 - 4y_3 \leq 17, \qquad (24.128)$$
$$y_1, y_2 \geq 0.$$

24.47 Prove that for every feasible solution x of problem (24.100) on page 994 there exists a feasible solution (w, z) of problem (24.99) satisfying $x = w - z$.

24.48 Express the dual program in Equation (24.93) (page 994) in the form of a primal program, as in Equation (24.92), and show that the dual program to this program is the primal program that appears in Equation (24.92).

24.49 Consider the following maximization problem:

Compute: $Z_P := \max cy^\top$,

subject to: $Ay^\top = b^\top$.   (24.129)

(a) Represent this problem as a standard linear program using Definition 24.40. Note that in this problem there is no constraint of the form $y \geq 0$.

(b) Show that the dual program is

Compute: $Z_D := \min xb^\top$,

subject to: $xA = c$.   (24.130)

24.50 Consider the following maximization problem:

Compute: $Z_P := \max cy^\top$,

subject to: $Ay^\top \leq b^\top$.   (24.131)

(a) Represent this problem as a standard linear program using Definition 24.40. Note that in this problem there is no constraint of the form $y \geq 0$.

(b) Show that the dual program is

Compute: $Z_D := \min xb^\top$,

subject to: $xA = c$,   (24.132)

$$x \geq \vec{0}.$$

REFERENCES

Akerlof G. A. (1970) The market for "lemons": quality uncertainty and the market mechanism. *Quarterly Journal of Economics*, **84**, 488–500.

Alon N., Brightwell G., Kierstead H. A., Kostochka A. V., and Winkler P. (2006) Dominating sets in *k*-majority tournaments. *Journal of Combinatorial Theory, Series B*, **96**, 374–87.

Altman E. and Solan E. (2009) Constrained games: the impact of the attitude to adversary's constraints. *IEEE Transactions on Automatic Control*, **54**, 2435–40.

Anscombe F. and Aumann R. J. (1963) A definition of subjective probability. *Annals of Mathematical Statistics*, **34**, 199–205.

Armbruster W. and Böge W. (1979) Bayesian game theory. In Moeschlin O. and Pallaschke D. (eds.), *Game Theory and Related Topics*. North-Holland, 17–28.

Arrow K. J. (1965) *Aspects of the Theory of Risk-Bearing*. Helsinki: Yrjö Jahnsson Foundation.

Aumann R. J. (1974) Subjectivity and correlation in randomized strategies. *Journal of Mathematical Economics*, **1**, 67–96.

Aumann R. J. (1976) Agreeing to disagree. *Annals of Statistics*, **4**, 1236–9.

Aumann R. J. (1987) Correlated equilibrium as an expression of Bayesian rationality. *Econometrica*, **55**, 1–18.

Aumann R. J. (1999) Interactive epistemology II: probability. *International Journal of Game Theory*, **28**, 301–14.

Aumann R. J. and Dréze J.-H. (1975) Cooperative games with coalition structures. *International Journal of Game Theory*, **4**, 217–37.

Aumann R. J. and Hart S. (1986) Bi-convexity and bi-martingales. *Israel Journal of Mathematics*, **54**, 159–80.

Aumann R. J. and Maschler M. (1964) The bargaining set for cooperative games. In Drescher M., Shapley, L. S., and Tucker A. W. (eds.), *Advances in Game Theory*, Annals of Mathematics Studies, **52**. Princeton University Press, 443–76.

Aumann R. J. and Maschler M. (1985) Game-theoretic analysis of a bankruptcy problem from the Talmud. *Journal of Economic Theory*, **36**, 195–213.

Aumann R. J. and Maschler M. (1995) *Repeated Games with Incomplete Information*. MIT Press.

Aumann R. J. and Shapley L. S. (1974) *Values of Non-Atomic Games*. Princeton University Press.

Aumann R. J. and Shapley L. S. (1994) Long-term competition: a game-theoretic analysis. In Megiddo N. (ed.), *Essays in Game Theory in Honor of Michael Maschler*. Springer, 1–15.

Avenhaus R., von Stengel B., and Zamir S. (2002) Inspection games. In Aumann R. J. and Hart S. (eds.), *Handbook of Game Theory with Economics Applications*, Vol. 3. North-Holland, 1947–87.

Balinski M. and Laraki R. (2007) A theory of measuring, electing and ranking. *Proceedings of the National Academy of Sciences of the USA*, **104**, 8720–25.

Banach S. (1922) Sur les opérations dans les ensembles abstraits et leur application aux équations intégrales. *Fundamenta Mathematicae*, **3**(1), 133–81.

Banks J. S. and Sobel J. (1987) Equilibrium selection in signaling games. *Econometrica*, **55**, 647–61.

Benoit J.-P. and Krishna V. (1985) Finitely repeated games. *Econometrica*, **53**, 905–22.

Bernheim B. D. (1984) Rationalizable strategic behavior. *Econometrica*, **52**, 1007–28.

Bernstein A., Mannor S., and Shimkin N. (2014) Opportunistic approachability and generalized no-regret problems. *Mathematics of Operations Research*, **39**, 949–1348.

Bewley T. and Kohlberg E. (1976) The asymptotic theory of stochastic games. *Mathematics of Operations Research*, **1**, 197–208.

Billingsley P. (1999) *Convergence of Probability Measures*. Wiley.

Biran D. and Tauman Y. (2007) The role of intelligence in a strategic conflict. Preprint.

Bird C. G. (1976) On cost allocation for a spanning tree: a game-theoretic approach. *Network*, **6**, 335–50.

Blackwell D. (1956) An analog of the Minimax Theorem for vector payoffs. *Pacific Journal of Mathematics*, **6**, 1–8.

Blackwell D. and Ferguson T. S. (1968) The big match. *The Annals of Mathematical Statistics*, **39**, 159–63.

Blume A. and Heidhues P. (2004) All equilibria of the Vickrey auction. *Journal of Economic Theory*, **114**, 170–177.

Bohnenblust H. F. and Karlin S. (1950) On a theorem of Ville. In *Contributions to the Theory of Games*, Annals of Mathematics Studies, **24**. Princeton University Press, 155–60.

Bollobás B. (1953) *Littlewood's Miscellany*. Cambridge University Press.

Bondareva O. (1963) Some applications of linear programming methods to the theory of cooperative games. *Problemy Kibernetiki*, **10**, 119–39 (in Russian).

Borda J. C. (1784) Mémoire sur les élections au scrutin. *Histoire de l'Académie Royale des Sciences*, Paris, 657–65.

Border K. C. (1989) *Fixed Point Theorems with Applications to Economics and Game Theory*. Cambridge University Press.

Bouton C. L. (1901) Nim, a game with a complete mathematical theory. *Annals of Mathematics*, **2**, 33–9.

Braess D. (1968) Über ein Paradoxon aus der Verkehrsplanung. *Unternehmensforschung*, **12**, 258–68. Translation from the original German by D. Braess, A. Nagurney, and T. Wakolbinger (2005) On a paradox of traffic planning. *Transportation Science*, **39**, 446–50.

Camerer C. and Weigelt K. (1988) Experimental tests of a sequential equilibrium reputation model. *Econometrica*, **56**, 1–36.

Cesa-Bianchi N. and Lugosi G. (2006) *Prediction, Learning and Games*. Cambridge University Press.

Cho I. K. and Kreps D. M. (1987) Signaling games and stable equilibria. *Quarterly Journal of Economics*, **102**, 179–221.

Claus A. and Kleitman D. J. (1973) Cost allocation for a spanning tree. *Network*, **3**, 289–304.

Condorcet, Marquis de (1785) *Essai sur L'Analyse à la Probabilité des Décisions Rendus à la Pluralité des Voix*. l'Imprimerie Royale.

Conway J. B. (1990) *A Course in Functional Analysis*. Springer.

Curiel I., Pederzoli G., and Tijs S. (1989) Sequencing games. *European Journal of Operations Research*, **40**, 344–51.

Dantzig G. B. (1963) *Linear Programming and Extensions*. Princeton University Press.

Davis M. and Maschler M. (1965) The kernel of cooperative games. *Naval Research Logistics Quarterly*, **12**, 223–59.

Davis M. and Maschler M. (1967) Existence of stable payoff configurations. In Shubik M. (ed.), *Essays in Mathematical Economics in Honor of Oskar Morgenstern*. Princeton University Press, 39–52.

Dawkins R. (1976) *The Selfish Gene*. Oxford University Press.

Derks J. J. M. (1992) A short proof of the inclusion of the core in the Weber set. *International Journal of Game Theory*, **21**, 149–50.

Diekmann A. (1985) Volunteer's Dilemma. *Journal of Conflict Resolution*, **29**, 605–10.

Dubey P. (1975) On the uniqueness of the Shapley value. *International Journal of Game Theory*, **4**, 131–9.

Dubins L. E. and Freedman D. A. (1981) Machiavelli and the Gale–Shapley algorithm. *American Mathematical Monthly*, **88**, 485–94.

Dunford N. and Schwartz J. T. (1988) *Linear Operators Part I: General Theory*. Wiley.

Engelbrecht-Wiggans R., Milgrom P. R., and Weber R. J. (1983) Competitive bidding and proprietary information. *Journal of Mathematical Economics*, **11**, 161–9.

Felsenthal D. S. and Machover M. (1998) *The Measurement of Voting Power: Theory and Practice, Problems and Paradoxes*. Edward Elgar.

Fibich G., Gavious A., and Sela A. (2004) Revenue equivalence in asymmetric auctions. *Journal of Economic Theory*, **115**, 309–21.

Filar J. A. and Vrieze K. (1997) *Competitive Markov Decision Processes*. Springer.

Fink A. M. (1964) Equilibrium in a stochastic n-person game. Journal of Science of the Hiroshima University, Series A-1 (Mathematics), **28**(1), 89–93.

Fisher I. (1891) Ph.D. Thesis, Yale University.

Flesch J., Thuijsman F., and Vrieze K. (1997) Cyclic Markov equilibria in stochastic games. *International Journal of Game Theory*, **26**, 303–314.

Ford L. K. and Fulkerson D. R. (1962) *Flows in Networks*. Princeton University Press.

Forges F. (1982) Infinitely repeated games of incomplete information: symmetric case with random signals. *International Journal of Game Theory*, **11**, 203–13.

Foster D. P. and Hart S. (2016) An integral approach to calibration. Preprint.

Foster D. P. and Vohra R. V. (1997) Calibrated learning and correlated equilibrium. *Games and Economics Behavior*, **21**, 40–55.

Fudenberg D. and Levine D. (1999) Conditional universal consistency. *Games and Economic Behavior*, **29**, 104–30.

Fudenberg D. and Maskin E. (1986) The folk theorem in repeated games with discounting or with incomplete information. *Econometrica*, **54**, 533–56.

Gaifman H. (1986) A theory of higher order probabilities. In Halpern J. Y. (ed.), *Theoretical Aspects of Reasoning about Knowledge: Proceedings of the 1986 Conference*. Kaufmann, 275–92.

Gale D. (1974) A curious Nim-type game. *American Mathematical Monthly*, **81**, 876–9.

Gale D. (1979) The game of Hex and the Brouwer fixed point theorem. *American Mathematical Monthly*, **86**, 818–27.

Gale D. and Shapley L. S. (1962) College admissions and the stability of marriage. *American Mathematical Monthly*, **69**, 9–15.

Gale D. and Sotomayor M. (1985) Some remarks on the stable matching problem. *Discrete Applied Mathematics*, **11**, 223–32.

Geanakoplos J. (1992) Common knowledge. In Aumann R. J. and Hart S. (eds.), *Handbook of Game Theory with Economics Applications*, Vol. 2. North-Holland, 1437–95.

Geanakoplos J. (2005) Three brief proofs of Arrow's impossibility theorem. *Economic Theory*, **26**, 211–15.

Geanakoplos J. and Polemarchakis H. M. (1982) We can't disagree forever. *Journal of Economic Theory*, **28**, 192–200.

Geanakoplos J. and Sebenius J. (1983) Don't bet on it: contingent agreements with asymmetric information. *Journal of the American Statistical Association*, **78**, 424–6.

Gibbard A. (1973) Manipulation of voting schemes: a general result. *Econometrica*, **41**, 587–601.

Gilboa I. and Zemel E. (1989) Nash and correlated equilibria: some complexity considerations. *Games and Economic Behavior*, **1**, 213–21.

Gillette D. (1957) Stochastic games with zero stop probabilities. *Contributions to the Theory of Games*, Annals of Studies, **39**. Princeton University Press, 179–88.

Gillies D. B. (1953) Some theorems on *n*-person games. Ph.D. Thesis, Princeton University.

Gillies D. B. (1959) Solutions to general non-zero-sum games. *Contributions to the Theory of Games*, Annals of Studies, **40**. Princeton University Press, 47–85.

Glazer J. and Ma A. (1989) Efficient allocation of a prize – King Solomon's dilemma. *Games and Economic Behavior*, **1**, 222–33.

Glicksberg I. L. (1952) A further generalization of the Kakutani fixed point theorem, with application to Nash equilibrium points. *Proceedings of the American Mathematical Society*, **3**, 170–4.

Gossner O. (1995) The folk theorem for finitely repeated games with mixed strategies. *International Journal of Game Theory*, **24**, 95–107.

Gossner O. and Tomala T. (2007) Secret correlation in repeated games with imperfect monitoring. *Mathematics of Operations Research*, **32**, 413–24.

Granot D. and Huberman G. (1981) Minimum cost spanning tree games. *Mathematical Programming*, **21**, 1–18.

Gusfield D. and Irving R. W. (1989) *The Stable Marriage Problem, Structure and Algorithm*. MIT Press.

Halpern J. Y. (1986) Reasoning about knowledge: an overview. In Halpern J. Y. (ed.), *Reasoning about Knowledge*. Morgan Kaufmann, 1–18.

Hannan J. (1957) Approximation to Bayes risk in repeated plays. *Contributions to the Theory of Games*, Annals of Studies, **39**. Princeton University Press, 97–139.

Harris C., Reny P., and Robson A. (1995) The existence of subgame-perfect equilibrium in continuous games with almost perfect information: a case of public randomization. *Econometrica*, **63**, 507–44.

Harsanyi J. C. (1967) Games with incomplete information played by "Bayesian" players. I. The basic model. *Management Science*, **14**, 159–82.

Harsanyi J. C. (1968a) Games with incomplete information played by "Bayesian" players. II. Bayesian equilibrium points. *Management Science*, **14**, 320–34.

Harsanyi J. C. (1968b) Games with incomplete information played by "Bayesian" players. III. The basic probability distribution of the game. *Management Science*, **14**, 486–502.

Harsanyi J. C. (1973) Games with randomly disturbed payoffs: a new rationale for mixed-strategy equilibrium points. *International Journal of Game Theory*, **2**, 1–23.

Hart S. (1985) Nonzero-sum two-person repeated games with incomplete information. *Mathematics of Operations Research*, **10**, 117–53.

Hart S. and Mas-Colell A. (1989) Potential, value and consistency. *Econometrica*, **57**, 589–614.

Hart S. and Mas-Colell A. (2000) A simple adaptive procedure leading to correlated equilibrium. *Econometrica*, **68**, 1127–50.

Heifetz A. and Samet D. (1998) Topology-free topology of beliefs. *Journal of Economic Theory*, **82**, 324–41.

Herz J. H. (1950) Idealist internationalism and the security dilemma. *World Politics*, **2**, 157–80.

Himmelberg C. J. (1975) Measurable relations. *Fundamenta Mathematicae*, **87**, 53–72.

Hofbauer J. and Sigmund K. (2003) *Evolutionary Games and Population Dynamics*. Cambridge University Press.

Holt C. (1980) Competitive bidding for contracts under alternative auction procedure. *Journal of Political Economics*, **88**, 433–45.

Hotelling H. (1929) Stability in competition. *Economic Journal*, **39**, 41–57.

Hou T. F. (1971) Approachability in a two-person game. *Annals of Mathematical Studies*, **42**, 735–44.

Huberman G. (1980) The nucleolus and essential coalitions. In Bensoussan A. and Lions J. (eds.), *Analysis and Optimization of Systems*, Lecture Notes in Control and Information Science, **28**. Springer, 416–22.

Isbell J. R. (1959) On the enumeration of majority games. *Mathematical Tables and Other Aids to Computation*, **13**, 21–8.

Jervis R. (1978) Cooperation under the security dilemma. *World Politics*, **30**, 167–214.

Kahan J. P. and Rapoport A. (1984) *Theories of Coalition Formation*. Erlbaum.

Kakutani S. (1941) A generalization of Brouwer's fixed point theorem. *Duke Mathematical Journal*, **8**, 457–9.

Kalai E. and Smorodinsky M. (1975) Other solutions to Nash's bargaining problem. *Econometrica*, **43**, 513–8.

Kalai E. and Zemel E. (1982a) Generalized network problems yielding totally balanced games. *Operations Research*, **30**, 998–1008.

Kalai E. and Zemel E. (1982b) Totally balanced games and games of flow. *Mathematics of Operations Research*, **7**, 476–9.

Kameda H. and Hosokawa Y. (2000) A paradox in distributed optimization of performance. Discussion Paper ISE-TR-00-164, Institute of Information Sciences and Electronics, University of Tsukuba.

Kaminski M. M. (2000) Hydraulic rationing. *Mathematical Social Sciences*, **40**, 131–55.

Kaplan T. R. and Zamir S. (2011) Multiple equilibria in asymmetric first-price auctions. Working Paper.

Kaplan T. R. and Zamir S. (2012) Asymmetric first-price auctions with uniform distributions: analytic solutions to the general case. *Economic Theory*, **50**, 269–302.

Kihlstrom R. E., Roth A. E., and Schmeidler D. (1981) Risk aversion and solutions to Nash's bargaining problem. In Moeschlin O. and Pallaschke D. (eds.), *Game Theory and Mathematical Economics*. North-Holland, 65–71.

Klemperer P. (2004) *Auctions: Theory and Practice (The Toulouse Lectures in Economics)*. Princeton University Press.

Knasker B., Kuratowski K., and Mazurkiewicz S. (1929) Ein Beweis des Fixpunktsatzes für *n*-dimensionale Simplexe. *Fundamenta Mathematicae*, **14**, 132–7.

Kohlberg E. and Mertens J. F. (1986) On the strategic stability of equilibria. *Econometrica*, **54**, 1003–37.

Kohlberg E. and Zamir S. (1974) Repeated games of incomplete information: the symmetric case. *Annals of Statistics*, **2**, 1040–41.

Kopelowitz A. (1967) Computation of the kernels of simple games and the nucleolus of *N*-person games. Research Memorandum.

Korevaar J. (2004) *Tauberian Theory: A Century of Developments*. Springer.

Kreps D. M. and Ramey G. (1987) Structural consistency, consistency, and sequential rationality. *Econometrica*, **55**, 1331–48.

Kreps D. M. and Wilson R. B. (1982) Sequential equilibria. *Econometrica*, **50**, 863–94.

Kripke S. (1963) Semantical analysis of model logic. *Zeitschrift für Mathematische Logik und Grundlagen der Mathematik*, **9**, 67–96.

Krishna V. (2002) *Auction Theory*. Academic Press.

Kuhn H. W. (1957) Extensive games and the problem of information. In Kuhn H. and Tucker A. W., *Contribution to the Theory of Games*, Annals of Studies, **28**. Princeton University Press, 193–216.

Kuhn H. W. (1960) Some combinatorial lemmas in topology. *IBM Journal of Research and Development*, **4**, 518–24.

Kuhn H. W. (1968) Simplicial approximation of fixed points. *Proceedings of the National Academy of Sciences of the USA*, **61**, 1238–42.

Kuratowski K. (1922) Une méthode délimination des nombres transfinis des raisonnements mathématiques. *Fundamenta Mathematicae*, **3**, 76–108.

Lebesgue H. (1905) Sur les fonctions représentables analytiquement. *Journal de Mathématiques Pures et Appliquées*, **1**, 139–216.

Lebrun B. (1999) First price auctions in the asymmetric *N* bidder case. *International Economic Review*, **40**, 125–42.

Lehrer E. (1989) Lower equilibrium payoffs in two-player repeated games with nonobservable actions. *International Journal of Game Theory*, **18**, 57–89.

Lehrer E. (1990) Nash equilibria of *n*-player repeated games with semi-standard information. *International Journal of Game Theory*, **19**, 191–217.

Lehrer E. (1992a) Correlated equilibria in two-player repeated games with nonobservable actions. *Mathematics of Operations Research*, **17**, 175–99.

Lehrer E. (1992b) On the equilibrium payoffs set of two player repeated games with imperfect monitoring. *International Journal of Game Theory*, **20**, 211–26.

Lehrer E. (2002) Approachability in infinitely dimensional spaces. *International Journal of Game Theory*, **31**, 255–70.

Lehrer E. and Solan E. (2006) Excludability and bounded computational capacity strategies. *Mathematics of Operations Research*, **31**, 637–48.

Lehrer E. and Solan E. (2007) A general internal regret-free strategy. Preprint.

Lehrer E. and Solan E. (2008) Approachability with bounded memory. *Games and Economic Behavior*, **66**, 995–1004.

Lehrer E., Solan E., and Viossat Y. (2010) Equilibrium payoffs in finite games. *Journal of Mathematical Economics*, **47**, 48–53.

Lensberg T. (1988) Stability and the Nash solution. *Journal of Economic Theory*, **45**, 330–41.

Lewis D. K. (1969) *Convention*. Harvard University Press.

Liggett T. M. and Lippman S. A. (1969) Stochastic games with perfect information and time average payoff. *SIAM Review*, **11**, 604–7.

Littlechild S. C. (1974) A simple expression for the nucleolus in a special case. *International Journal of Game Theory*, **3**, 21–9.

Luce R. D. and Raiffa H. (1957) *Games and Decisions: Introduction and Critical Survey*. Wiley.

Lugosi G., Mannor S., and Stoltz G. (2007) Strategies for prediction under imperfect monitoring. COLT2007, San Diego, California. In *Lecture Notes in Computer Sciences*, **4539**, 248–62.

Mailath G. J. and Samuelson L. (2006) *Repeated Games and Reputations: Long-Run Relationships*. Oxford University Press.

Marschak J. (1950) Rational behavior, uncertainty prospects, and measurable utility. *Econometrica*, **18**, 111–41.

Maschler M. (1966a) The inequalities that determine the bargaining set $M_1^{(i)}$. *Israel Journal of Mathematics*, **4**, 127–34.

Maschler M. (1966b) A price leadership method for solving the inspector's non-constant sum game. *Naval Research Logistics Quarterly*, **13**, 11–33.

Maschler M. (1967) The inspector's non-constant-sum game: its dependence on a system of detectors. *Naval Research Logistics Quarterly*, **14**, 275–90.

Maschler M. (1978) Playing an *n*-person game: an experiment. In Sauermann H. (ed.), *Beiträge zur Experimentellen Virtschaftsforschung*, Vol. VIII, Coalition-Forming Behavior. JCB Mohr, 231–328.

Maschler M. and Peleg B. (1966) A characterization, existence proof and dimension bounds for the kernel of a game. *Pacific Journal of Mathematics*, **18**, 289–328.

Maschler M., Peleg B., and Shapley L. S. (1979) Geometric properties of the kernel, nucleolus and related solution concepts. *Mathematics of Operations Research*, **4**, 303–38.

Maskin E. and Riley J. (2000) Asymmetric auctions. *Review of Economic Studies*, **67**, 413–38.

Maynard Smith J. (1982). *Evolution and the Theory of Games*. Cambridge University Press.

Maynard Smith J. and Price G. R. (1973) The logic of animal conflict. *Nature* (London), **2461**, 13–18.

McKelvey R. D. and Page T. (1986) Common knowledge, consensus, and aggregate information. *Econometrica*, **54**, 109–27.

Megiddo N. (1980) On repeated games with incomplete information played by non-Bayesian players. *International Journal of Game Theory*, **9**, 157–67.

Mertens J. F. and Neyman A. (1981) Stochastic games. *International Journal of Game Theory*, **10**, 53–66.

Mertens J. F. and Zamir S. (1985) Formulation of Bayesian analysis for games with incomplete information. *International Journal of Game Theory*, **14**, 1–29.

Milgrom P. R. (2004) *Putting Auction Theory to Work (Churchill Lectures in Economics)*. Cambridge University Press.

Milgrom P. R. and Roberts J. (1990) Rationalizability, learning, and equilibrium in games with strategic complementarities. *Econometrica*, **58**, 1255–77.

Milgrom P. R. and Weber R. J. (1982) A theory of auctions and competitve bidding. *Econometrica*, **50**, 1089–122.

Milgrom P. R. and Weber R. J. (1985) Distributional strategies for games with incomplete information. *Mathematics of Operations Research*, **10**, 619–32.

Milnor J. W. (1952) Reasonable outcomes for *n*-person games. Research Memorandum 916, The Rand Corporation, Santa Monica, CA.

Monderer D. and Samet D. (1989) Approximating common knowledge with common beliefs. *Games and Economic Behavior*, **1**, 170–90.

Mycielski J. (1992) Games with perfect information. In Aumann R. J. and Hart S. (eds.), *Handbook of Game Theory with Economic Applications*, Vol. 1. North-Holland, 41–70.

Myerson R. B. (1979) Incentive compatibility and the bargaining problem. *Econometrica*, **47**, 61–73.

Myerson R. B. (1981) Optimal auction design. *Mathematics of Operations Research*, **6**, 58–74.

Myerson R. and Weibull J. (2013) Settled equilibria. Preprint.

Nagel R. (1995) Unraveling in guessing games: an experimental study. *American Economic Review*, **85**, 1313–26.

Nash J. F. (1950a) The bargaining problem. *Econometrica*, **18**, 155–62.

Nash J. F. (1950b) Equilibrium points in *N*-person games. *Proceedings of the National Academy of Sciences of USA*, **36**, 48–9.

Nash J. F. (1951) Noncooperative games. *Annals of Mathematics*, **54**, 289–95.

Nash J. F. (1953) Two person cooperative games. *Econometrica*, **21**, 128–40.

Neyman A. (1985) Bounded complexity justifies cooperation in the finitely repeated prisoner's dilemma. *Economic Letters*, **19**, 227–39.

Neyman A. (1989) Uniqueness of the Shapley value. *Games and Economic Behavior*, **1**, 116–18.

Neyman A. and Sorin S. (1997) *Equilibria in Repeated Games with Incomplete Information: The Deterministic Symmetric Case*. Kluwer Academic Publishers, 129–31.

Neyman A. and Sorin S. (1998) Equilibria in repeated games with incomplete information: the general symmetric case. *International Journal of Game Theory*, **27**, 201–10.

Neyman A. and Sorin S. (2003) *Stochastic Games and Applications*. Kluwer Academic Publishers.

O'Neill, B. (1982) A problem of rights arbitration from the Talmud. *Mathematical Social Sciences*, **2**, 345–71.

Orshan G. (1993) The prenucleolus and the reduced game property: equal treatment replaces anonymity. *International Journal of Game Theory*, **22**, 241–8.

Parikh R. and Krasucki P. (1990) Communication, consensus and knowledge. *Journal of Economic Theory*, **52**, 178–89.

Pearce D. G. (1984) Rationalizable strategic behavior and the problem of perfection. *Econometrica*, **52**, 1029–50.

Peleg B. (1965) An inductive method for constructing minimal balanced collections of finite sets. *Naval Research Logistics Quarterly*, **12**, 155–62.

Peleg B. (1967) Existence theorem for the bargaining set $M_1(i)$. In Shubik M. (ed.), *Essays in Mathematical Economics in Honor of Oskar Morgenstern*. Princeton University Press, 53–6.

Peleg B. (1968) On weights of constant-sum majority games. *SIAM Journal on Applied Mathematics*, **16**, 527–32.

Peleg B. (1969) Equilibrium points for games with infinitely many players. *Journal of the London Mathematical Society*, **1**, 292–4.

Peleg B. (1984) *Game Theoretic Analysis of Voting in Committees*. Cambridge University Press.

Peleg B. and Sudhölter P. (2003) *Introduction to the Theory of Cooperative Games*. Kluwer Academic Publishers.

Perles M. A. and Maschler M. (1981) The super-additive solution for the nash bargaining game. *International Journal of Game Theory*, **10**, 163–93.

Piccione M. and Rubinstein A. (1997) On the interpretation of decision problems with imperfect recall. *Games and Economic Behavior*, **20**, 3–24.

Pigou A. C. (1920) *The Economics of Welfare* (1st edn). Macmillan and Co. London.

Pratt J. W. (1964) Risk aversion in the small and in the large. *Econometrica*, **32**, 122–36.

Reny P. J. and Zamir S. (2004) On the existence of pure strategy monotone equilibria in asymmetric first-price auctions. *Econometrica*, **72**, 1105–25.

Rosenthal R. W. (1981) Games of perfect information, predatory games and the chain-store paradox. *Journal of Economic Theory*, **25**, 92–100.

Roth A. E. (2005) Matching and allocation in medicine and health care. In *Building a Better Delivery System: A New Engineering/Health Care Partnership*. National Academy of Engineering and Institute of Medicine, National Academies Press, 237–9.

Roth A. E. and Sotomayor M. A. O. (1990) *Two-Sided Matching: A Study in Game-Theoretic Modeling and Analysis*, Econometric Society Monographs, **18**. Cambridge University Press.

Rothschild M. and Stiglitz J. E. (1970) Increasing risk: I. A definition. *Journal of Economic Theory*, **2**, 225–43.

Rubinstein A. (1979) Equilibrium in supergames with the overtaking criterion. *Journal of Economic Theory*, **21**, 1–9.

Rubinstein A. (1982) Perfect equilibrium in a bargaining model. *Econometrica*, **50**, 97–110.

Rubinstein A. (1989) The electronic mail game: a game with almost common knowledge. *American Economic Review*, **79**, 385–91.

Rudin W. (1966) *Real and Complex Analysis*. McGraw-Hill.

Rustichini, A. (1999) Minimizing regret: the general case. *Games and Economic Behavior*, **29**, 224–43.

Satterthwaite M. A. (1975) Strategy-proofness and Arrow's conditions: existence and correspondence theorems for voting procedures and social welfare functions. *Journal of Economic Theory*, **10**, 187–217.

Savage L. J. (1954) *The Foundations of Statistics*. Wiley.

Schauder J. (1930) Der Fixpunktsatz in Funktionalräaumen. *Studia Mathematica*, **2**, 171–80.

Schmeidler D. (1969) The nucleolus of a characteristic function game. *SIAM Journal on Applied Mathematics*, **17**, 1163–70.

Schmeidler D. (1972) Cores of exact games. *Journal of Mathematical Analysis and Applications*, **40**, 214–25.

Sebenius J. K. and Geanakoplos J. (1983) Don't bet on it: contingent agreements with asymmetric information. *Journal of the American Statistical Association*, **78**, 424–6.

Selten R. (1965) Spieltheoretische Behandlung eines Oligopolmodells mit Nachfrageträgheit. *Zeitschrift für die gesamte Staatswissenschaft*, **121**, 301–24 and 667–89.

Selten R. (1973) A simple model of imperfect competition, where four are few and six are many. *International Journal of Game Theory*, **2**, 141–201.

Selten R. (1975) Reexamination of the perfectness concept for equilibrium points in extensive games. *International Journal of Game Theory*, **4**, 25–55.

Selten R. (1978) The chainstore paradox. *Theory and Decision*, **9**, 127–59.

Selten R. and Schuster K. (1968) *Psychological Variables and Coalition Forming Behavior*. Proceedings of the Conference of the IEA (Smolenile), London, 221–46.

Shapley L. S. (1953a) A value for *n* person games. In Kuhn H. W. and Tucker A. W. (eds.), *Contributions to the Theory of Games*, Annals of Mathematics Studies, **28**, 307–19.

Shapley L. S. (1953b) Stochastic games. *Proceedings of the National Academy of Sciences*, **39**(10), 1095–100.

Shapley L. S. (1969) Utility comparison and the theory of games. In *La Decision Aggregation Ordres de Preference*. Editions du Centre National de la Recherche Scientifique, 251–63.

Shapley L. S. (1971) Cores of convex games. *International Journal of Game Theory*, **1**, 11–26.

Shapley L. S. (1994) *Notes for the Course Mathematics 147: Game Theory*. Department of Mathematics, UCLA.

Shapley L. S. and Shubik M. (1963) The core of an economy with nonconvex preferences. RM-3518, The Rand Corporation, Santa Monica, CA.

Shapley L. S. and Shubik M. (1966) Quasi-cores in a monetary economy with nonconvex preferences. *Econometrica*, **34**, 805–27.

Shapley L. S. and Shubik M. (1969) On market games. *Journal of Economic Theory*, **1**, 9–25.

Shiryaev A. N. (1995) *Probability*, 2nd edn. Springer.

Simon R. S. (2003) Games of incomplete information, ergodic theory, and the measurability of equilibria. *Israel Journal of Mathematics*, **138**, 73–92.

Simon R. S., Spież S., and Toruńczyk H. (1995) The existence of equilibria in certain games, separation for families of convex functions and a theorem of Borsuk–Ulam type. *Israel Journal of Mathematics*, **92**, 1–21.

Snijders C. (1995) Axiomatization of the nucleolus. *Mathematics of Operations Research*, **20**, 189–96.

Sobolev A. I. (1975) The characterization of optimality principles in cooperative games by functional operations. In Vorobiev N. N. (ed.), *Mathematical Methods in Social Sciences*, **6**. Vilnius Academy of Sciences of the Lithuanian SSR, 95–151 (in Russian).

Solan E. (1999) Three-player absorbing games. *Mathematics of Operations Research*, **24**, 669–698.

Solan E. and Vieille N. (2002) Quitting games – an example. *International Journal of Game Theory*, **31**, 365–381.

Solymosi T. (1999) On the bargaining set, kernel and core of superadditive games. *International Journal of Game Theory*, **28**, 229–40.

Sorin S. (1983) Some results on the existence of Nash equilibria for non-zero-sum games with incomplete information. *International Journal of Game Theory*, **12**, 193–205.

Sorin S. (1992) Repeated games with complete information. In Aumann R. J. and Hart S. (eds.), *Handbook of Game Theory with Economic Applications*, Vol. 1. North-Holland, 71–108.

Sorin S. (2002) *A First Course on Zero-Sum Repeated Games*. Mathématiques et Applications, **37**. Springer.

Sorin S. and Zamir S. (1985) A two-person game with lack of information on $1\frac{1}{2}$ sides. *Mathematics of Operations Research*, **10**, 17–23.

Spence A. M. (1974) *Market Signaling*. Harvard University Press.

Spinat X. (2002) A necessary and sufficient condition for approachability. *Mathematics of Operations Research*, **27**, 31–44.

Stearns R. E. (1968) Convergent transfer schemes for *N*-person games. *Transactions of the American Mathematical Society*, **134**, 449–59.

Sudhölter P. (1996) The modified nucleolus as canonical representation of weighted majority Games. *Mathematics of Operations Research*, **21**, 734–56.

Suslin M. (1917) Sur une définition des ensembles measurables B sans nombres transfinis. *C.R. Academie Science Paris Séries A*, **164**, 88–91.

Tamir A. (1991) On the core of network synthesis games. *Mathematical Programming*, **50**, 123–35.

Thompson F. B. (1952) Equivalence of games in extensive form. RM-759, The RAND Corporation, Santa Monica, CA. Reprinted in Kuhn H. (ed.), *Classics in Game Theory*, 1997. Princeton University Press, 36–45.

Tversky A. (1969) Intransitivity of preferences. *Psychological Review*, **76**, 31–48.

van Damme E. (1987) *Stability and Perfection of Nash Equilibria.* Springer.

van Zandt T. (2007) Interim Bayesian Nash equilibrium on universal type spaces for supermodular games. *Journal of Economic Theory*, **145**, 249–63.

van Zandt T. and Vives X. (2007) Monotone equilibria in Bayesian games of strategic complementarities. *Journal of Economic Theory*, **134**, 339–60.

Vanderbei R. J. (2001) *Linear Programming: Foundations and Extensions*, 2nd edn. International Series in Operations Research and Management Science, **37**. Springer.

Vassilakis S. and Zamir S. (1993) Common belief and common knowledge. *Journal of Mathematical Economics*, **22**, 495–505.

Vickery W. (1961) Counterspeculation, auctions and competitive sealed tenders. *Journal of Finance*, **16**, 8–37.

Vickery W. (1962) Auctions and bidding games. In Morgenstern O. and Tucker A. W. (eds.), *Recent Advances in Game Theory*, Princeton Conference Series, **29**. Princeton University Press, 15–27.

Vieille N. (1992) Weak approachability. *Mathematics of Operations Research*, **17**, 781–91.

Vieille N. (2000a) Two-player stochastic games I: A reduction. *Israel Journal of Mathematics*, **119**, 55–91.

Vieille N. (2000b) Two-player stochastic games II: The case of recursive games, *Israel Journal of Mathematics*, **119**, 93–126.

Vives X. (1990) Nash equilibrium with strategic complementarities. *Journal of Mathematical Economics*, **19**, 305–21.

von Neumann J. (1928) Zur Theorie der Gesellschaftsspiele. *Mathematische Annalen*, **100**, 295–320. English translation in Tucker A. W. and Luce R. D. (eds.), *Contribution to the Theory of Games*, Annals of Mathematics Studies, **40**, 1959, 295–320.

von Neumann J. and Morgenstern O. (1944) *Theory of Games and Economic Behavior*. Princeton University Press.

von Stengel B. and Forges F. (2008) Extensive form correlated equilibrium: definition and computation complexity. *Mathematics of Operations Research*, **33**, 1002–22.

Weber R. J. (1988) Probabilistic values for games. In Roth A. (ed.), *The Shapley Value: Essays in Honor of Lloyd Shapley*. Cambridge University Press, 101–19.

Wolfstetter E. (1996) Auctions: an introduction. *Journal of Economic Surveys*, **10**, 367–420.

Young H. P. (1985) Cost allocation in fair allocation. In Young H. P. (ed.), *Proceedings of Symposia in Applied Mathematics*, **33**. Providence, RI: American Mathematical Society, 69–94.

Zamir S. (1992) Repeated games of incomplete informatation: zero-sum. In Aumann R. J. and Hart S. (eds.), *Handbook of Game Theory with Economic Applications*, Vol. 1. North-Holland, 109–54.

Zeeman E. C. (1980) Population dynamics from game theory. In *Global Theory of Dynamical Systems*, Springer Lecture Notes in Mathematics, **819**. Springer.

Zorn M. (1935) A remark on methods in transfinite algebra. *Bulletin of the American Mathematical Society*, **41**, 667–70.

INDEX